Business
Plans
Handbook

Highlights

Business Plans Handbook, Volume 6 (BPH-6) is a collection of actual business plans compiled by entrepreneurs seeking funding for small businesses throughout North America. For those looking for examples of how to approach, structure, and compose their own business plans, *BPH-6* presents 24 sample plans, including plans for the following businesses:

- Airline
- Bed and Breakfast
- Caribbean Cafe
- Cookie Shop
- Health Plan Administrator
- Medical Equipment Manufacturer
- Paintball Sport Company

- Publisher
- Real Estate Investor
- Record Store
- Retail Art Furnishing Store
- Shave Ice Stand
- Software Developer
- Used Car Dealership

FEATURES AND BENEFITS

BPH-6 offers many features not provided by other business planning references including:

○ Twenty-four business plans, each of which represent an owner's successful attempt at clarifying (for themselves and others) the reasons that the business should exist or expand and why a lender should fund the enterprise.

○ Two fictional plans that are used by business counselors at a prominent small business development organization as examples for their clients. (You will find these in the Business Plan Template Appendix.)

○ An expanded directory section that includes: listings for venture capital and finance companies, which specialize in funding start-up and second-stage small business ventures, and a comprehensive listing of Service Corps of Retired Executives (SCORE) offices. In addition, the Appendix also contains updated listings of all Small Business Development Centers (SBDCs); associations of interest to entrepreneurs; Small Business Administration (SBA) Regional Offices; and consultants specializing in small business planning and advice. It is strongly advised that you consult supporting organizations while planning your business, as they can provide a wealth of useful information.

○ A Small Business Term Glossary to help you decipher the sometimes confusing terminology used by lenders and others in the financial and small business communities.

○ An expanded bibliography, arranged by subject, containing citations from over 1,500 small business reference publications and trade periodicals.

○ A Business Plan Template which serves as a model to help you construct your own business plan. This generic outline lists all the essential elements of a complete business plan and their components, including the Summary, Business History and Industry Outlook, Market Examination, Competition, Marketing, Administration and Management, Financial Information, and other key sections. Use this guide as a starting point for compiling your plan.

○ Extensive financial documentation required to solicit funding from small business lenders. *BPH-6* contains the most comprehensive financial data within the series to date. You will find examples of: Cash Flows, Balance Sheets, Income Projections, and other financial information included with the textual portions of the plan.

Business Plans Handbook

A COMPILATION
OF ACTUAL
BUSINESS PLANS
DEVELOPED BY
SMALL BUSINESSES
THROUGHOUT
NORTH
AMERICA

VOLUME

6

William H. Harmer
Terrance W. Peck,
Editors

GALE GROUP

Detroit
San Francisco
London
Boston
Woodbridge, CT

Editors: William Harmer and Terrance W. Peck

Contributing Editors: Rebecca Marlow-Ferguson, Brian Rabold, Amanda Quick, and Jennifer Zielinski

Technical Training Specialist: Gwen Turecki-Luczycka

Managing Editor: Erin Braun

Composition Manager: Mary Beth Trimper
Senior Buyer: Wendy Blurton

Artist: Gary Leach
Product Design Manager: Cynthia Baldwin

ISBN 0-7876-2077-7
ISSN 1084-4473

Printed in the United States of America

10 9 8 7 6 5 4 3 2

Contents

Appendixes

Introduction

Perhaps the most important aspect of business planning is simply *doing* it. More and more business owners are beginning to compile business plans even if they don't need a bank loan. Others discover the value of planning when they *must* provide a business plan for the bank. The sheer act of putting thoughts on paper seems to clarify priorities and provide focus. Sometimes business owners completely change strategies when compiling their plan, deciding on a different product mix or advertising scheme after finding that their assumptions were incorrect. This kind of healthy thinking and re-thinking via business planning is becoming the norm. The editors of *Business Plans Handbook, Volume 6 (BPH-6)* sincerely hope that this latest addition to the series is a helpful tool in the successful completion of your business plan, no matter what the reason for creating it.

This sixth volume, like each volume in the series, offers genuine business plans used by real people. *BPH-6* provides 24 business plans used by actual entrepreneurs to gain funding support for their new businesses. The business and personal names and addresses and general locations have been changed to protect the privacy of the plan authors.

NEW BUSINESS OPPORTUNITIES

As in other volumes in the series, *BPH-6* finds entrepreneurs engaged in a wide variety of creative endeavors. Examples in BPH-6 include a real estate renovation company's appeal to wealthy consumers and its strong evidence for growth; a detailed exploration of the development of a paintball sports outfit facility; a Christmas and wedding decoration manufacturer using scrolled inspirational verses; and the growth opportunities available for customers of an investor software company utilizing the latest technology. Varied companies in the health provider industry include a chiropractic clinic, a health insurer, and a medical devices designer and manufacturer. The continued popularity of take-out and dine-in establishments is reflected in three plans: a pizzeria franchise, a cookie and muffin shop, and a Caribbean Café. Other traditional businesses include a bridal salon, whose plan contains a thorough assessment of local competition; a records store, whose plan uses a specified customer profile as the target of its action steps; and a retail art furnishings store, whose plan outlines potential problems and how to successfully address them.

Comprehensive financial documentation has become increasingly important as today's entrepreneurs compete for the finite resources of business lenders. Our plans illustrate the financial data generally required of loan applicants, including Income Statements, Financial Projections, Cash Flows, and Balance Sheets.

ENHANCED APPENDIXES

In an effort to provide the most relevant and valuable information for our readers, we have updated the coverage of small business resources. For instance, you will find: a directory section, which includes listings of all of the Service Corps of Retired Executives (SCORE) offices; an informative glossary, which includes small business terms; and a bibliography, which includes reference titles essential to starting and operating a business venture in all 50 states. In addition we have updated the list of Small Business Development Centers (SBDCs); Small Business Administration Regional Offices; venture capital and finance companies, which specialize in funding start-up and second-stage small business enterprises; associations of interest to entrepreneurs; and consultants, specializing in small business advice and planning. For your reference, we have also reprinted the business plan template, which provides a comprehensive overview of the essential components of a business plan and two fictional plans used by small business counselors.

SERIES INFORMATION

If you already have the first five volumes of *BPH*, with this sixth volume, you will now have a collection of 155 real business plans (not including the one updated plan in the second volume, whose original appeared in the first, or the two fictional plans in the Business Plan Template Appendix section of the second, third, fourth, fifth, and sixth volumes); contact information for hundreds of organizations and agencies offering business expertise; a helpful business plan template; a foreword providing advice and instruction to entrepreneurs on how to begin their research; more than 1,500 citations to valuable small business development material; and a comprehensive glossary of terms to help the business planner navigate the sometimes confusing language of entrepreneurship.

ACKNOWLEDGEMENTS

The Editors wish to sincerely thank Palo Alto Software, makers of Business Plan Pro, the premier business planning software tool, for providing the use of several business plans in this volume (telephone: 800-229-7526; WWW: http://www.paloaltosoftware.com).

Thanks are also in order for the many contributors to *BPH-6*, whose business plans will serve as examples to future generations of entrepreneurs, as well as the users of the title who called with their helpful suggestions. Your help was greatly appreciated.

COMMENTS WELCOME

Your comments on *BPH-6* are appreciated. Please direct all correspondence, suggestions for future volumes of *BPH*, and other recommendations to the following:

Business Plans Handbook, Volume 6
The Gale Group
27500 Drake Rd.
Farmington Hills, MI 48331-3535

Phone: (248)699-4253
Fax: 800-339-3374
Toll-Free: 800-347-GALE

Airline Company

BUSINESS PLAN

PUDDLE JUMPERS AIRLINES, INC.

24265 Silver Way
Atlanta, GA 30301

This business plan for an airline company shows how to use competition both as a model for how to run a business and how not to run a business. Acknowledging that a competitor is not only competent but admirable allows the entrepreneur to point to a similar successful venture and concentrate on proving there is enough room in the market for both companies. Conservative business predictions and extensive experience by the owners indicate preparedness. This plan was compiled using Business Plan Pro, by Palo Alto Software.

- EXECUTIVE SUMMARY

- COMPANY SUMMARY

- SERVICES

- MARKET ANALYSIS SUMMARY

- STRATEGY AND IMPLEMENTATION SUMMARY

- MANAGEMENT SUMMARY

- FINANCIAL PLAN

EXECUTIVE SUMMARY

Puddle Jumpers Airlines, Inc. is a new consumer airline in its formative stages. It is being organized to take advantage of a specific gap in the short-haul domestic travel market. The gap exists in low cost service out of Atlanta, Georgia. The gap in the availability of low cost service in and out of the Atlanta hub coupled with the demand for passenger travel on selected routes from Atlanta indicates that a new entrant airline could be expected to capture a significant portion of current air travel business at that hub.

The management of Puddle Jumpers is experienced in airline start-ups. Previously management grew Private Jet Airlines from a single Boeing 727 to a fleet of of 16 MD-80 series aircraft. Revenues grew to $130 million in a 2-year period from 1992 through 1993.

Our research and projections indicate that air travel to and from Atlanta is sufficient to provide a new carrier with revenues of $110 million dollars in its first full year of operations, utilizing 6 aircraft and selected short-haul routes. These sales figures are based upon load factors of only 55% in year one. Second year revenues are expected to exceed $216 million dollars with additional aircraft and expanded routes. Load factors for year two are 62%. The Puddle Jumpers plan has the potential for a more rapid ramp-up than was the case with Private Jet due to the nature of the routes and the demand for travel currently in the targeted markets served. In short, the frequency of flights needed to serve Puddle Jumpers's target market exceeds the demand that dictated Private Jet's growth.

These sales levels will produce net profit of just over $1 million in the first operational year and $21.4 million dollars in flight year two. Profits in year one will be 1% of sales and will improve to 10% of sales with the economies gained in year two. The over-all operational long term profit target will be 16% of sales as net profit in years three, four, and five. The company's long term plan is part of the due diligence package. The first operational year is actually fiscal year two in this plan.

The first year of formative operations will burn cash until revenue can commence. This is due to the organizational and regulatory obligations of a new air carrier. Investment activity is needed to handle the expenses of this phase of the business.

Business Plan Highlights

	Sales	Gross	Net
FY1997	$0	$0	($278)
FY1998	$110,000	$95,700	$1,345
FY1999	$216,925	$188,725	$21,736

Objectives

The company has the following objectives:

1. To obtain required D.O.T. and F.A.A. certifications on or before March 1, 1997.
2. To commence revenue service on or before July 1, 1997.
3. To raise sufficient "seed" and "bridge" capital in a timely fashion to financially enable these objectives.
4. To commence operations with two McDonnell-Douglas MD-80 series aircraft in month one, four by end of month four, and six by end of month six.
5. To add one aircraft per month during year two for a total of 18 at year two end.

Puddle Jumpers Airlines, Inc. has a mission to provide safe, efficient, low-cost consumer air travel service. Our service will emphasize safety as its highest priority. We will operate the newest and best maintained aircraft available. We will never skimp on maintenance in any fashion whatsoever. We will strive to operate our flights on time. We will provide friendly and courteous "no frill" service.

Mission

The keys to success are:

Keys to Success

- Obtaining the required governmental approvals.
- Securing financing.
- Experienced management. (Already in place.)
- Marketing. Either dealing with channel problems and barriers to entry or solving problems with major advertising and promotion budgets. Targeted market share must be achieved even amidst expected competition.
- Product quality. Always with safety foremost.
- Services delivered on time, costs controlled, marketing budgets managed. There is a temptation to fix on growth at the expense of profits. Also, rapid growth will be curtailed in order to keep maintenance standards both strict and measurable.
- Cost control. The over-all cost per ASM (available seat mile) is pegged at 7.0 cents or less in 1996 dollars. This ASM factor places Puddle Jumpers in a grouping of the lowest four in the airline industry within the short-haul market. (Southern Air, the dominate carrier in the Atlanta market, averages 12.0 cents per ASM by comparison). The only three airlines with lower operating costs also operate older and less reliable equipment, and even then the lowest short-haul cost in the airline industry is currently FlyRight at 6.43 cents per ASM.

Puddle Jumpers Airlines is being formed in July 1996 as a South State Corporation. Its offices will be in Atlanta, Georgia. The founder of Puddle Jumpers is Kenneth D. Smith. Mr. Smith has extensive experience in consumer aviation. His bio as well as the backgrounds of all the members of Puddle Jumpers's management team follow.

COMPANY SUMMARY

Puddle Jumpers Airlines, Inc. will authorize 20,000,000 shares of common stock. One million shares are to be set aside as founder's stock to be divided among key management personnel. It is also expected that management stock options will be made available to key management personnel after operations commence. It is expected that founders stock plus option stock will not total more than 15% of authorized shares.

Company Ownership

Initial "seed" capital is to be attracted via a convertible debenture sold by Private Placement. This round of funding will have premium conversion privileges vs. later rounds and "bridge" capital. The company has plans to proceed to a public offering prior to initiating revenue service. The expected proceeds from Private Placement are expected to be $300,000 at "seed" stage, $3.5 million in "bridge" funding, and $10 million in IPO proceeds (projected at $6 per share). Management cannot assure that an IPO will be available at the time desired and at the price sought.

A sample of the offering proposed for "seed" investment is included with this plan.

In the second year of operations, Puddle Jumpers will expand revenue by adding flights to the most demanded and popular routes in current operation. This will serve to make our schedule the most convenient to these destinations, improving further our competitive advantage. The

Start-Up Summary

Start-Up Summary

Continued...

routes expected to be expanded first include Chicago, New York, and Atlanta. Second level expansions would include Philadelphia, Dallas, Washington D.C., Orlando, and Detroit.

Start-Up Expenses

Legal	$40,000
Stationery, etc.	$3,000
Business Plans	$3,000
Placement Memorandums	$3,000
Investment Banking Retainer	$25,000
Underwriting Consultant	$30,000
Offering Publicity	$60,000
Rent	$6,000
Government Compliance	$20,000
CEO Salary (6 mos.)	$48,000
Company Identity and Marketing	$40,000
Operating Expenses (1 year)	$40,000
Expensed equipment	$6,000
Other	$0
Total Start-up Expense	**$324,000**

START-UP ASSETS NEEDED

Cash Requirements	$0
Other Short-Term Assets	$0
Total Short-Term Assets	$0
Long-Term Assets	$0
Total Assets	$0
Total Start-Up Requirements	**$324,000**
Left to Finance	$0

START-UP FUNDING PLAN
Investment

Investor 1	$250,000
Investor 2	$100,000
Other	$0
Total Investment	$350,000

SHORT-TERM LIABILITIES

Unpaid Expenses	$0
Short-Term Loans	$0
Interest-Free Short-Term Loans	$0
Subtotal Short-Term Liabilities	$0
Long-Term Liabilities	$0
Total Liabilities	**$0**
Loss at Start-Up	($350,000)
Total Capital	$0
Total Capital and Liabilities	$0
Checkline	$0

Management plans to lease a small office in suburban Atlanta immediately upon closing "seed" funding.

The important business measurement ratios are presented here based upon projections for Puddle Jumpers.

Puddle Jumpers is in the business of providing low-cost, "discount" air travel to selected destinations from the Atlanta, Georgia hub. The service approach is "no frills" with emphasis on safe, courteous handling of domestic regional passenger travel.

All consumer surveys still indicate that the air travel customer's preference is for "low fares." However, he or she is not willing to compromise on issues of safety or on-time performance. Customers will, however, settle for lower levels of in-flight service in order to reduce the cost of travel.

Puddle Jumpers provides precisely the level of service today's air travel passenger demands.

The primary competition in the Atlanta market is Southern Air. Southern Air accounts for 86% of the air travel volume in this market. This is as high a single market dominance that exists in any U.S. market. Also, this results in the highest fares in the nation for travel in and out of Atlanta. None of the air travel is offered at discount fares in Atlanta.

Puddle Jumpers feels that we can obtain a significant portion of this business. Our costs will be lower than Southern Air (7 cents per ASM vs. 12 cents per ASM). Southern Air is already in financial difficulty due to "sins of the past." Our costs will be significantly lower than "major" carriers such as Mile High. This identifies a gap for only a "hub-based" short haul carrier in the Atlanta market.

Operation of a single type of aircraft will have significant cost, maintenance, and training expense reduction.

Our aircraft will operate out of this single hub with high utilization based on price advantage. We will have an over-all competitive advantage since we don't have aircraft or operations outside of our limited focus. Other airlines must maintain "system-wide" load factors and utilization, while Puddle Jumpers will operate profitably within our "niche" market. This will serve as a barrier to entry from other competitors once we are entrenched. It is unlikely that larger airlines will be able to compete with our low fares nor will they have the desire as they focus on more profitable "long-haul" routes with larger airplanes.

Puddle Jumpers will achieve its target of 7 cents or less per available seat mile by a combination of cost saving measures. Savings will come in the areas of labor costs and from operational economies. Puddle Jumpers will utilize its flight crews significantly more than its competition. Flight crew utilization will be 60% above industry average. Both pilots and flight attendants will be deployed an average of 85 hours per month vs. an industry average of 50-60 hours. The company will realize additional savings in the insurance and benefits areas by virtue of having fewer crew members.

Eliminating meal service in-flight will save approximately $3.00 per seat per flight. This will also increase airplane utilization due to no need for catering service while in port. It is Puddle Jumpers's goal to utilize its fleet an average of 11 hours per day, 7 days per week.

All aircraft will be configured to a single coach seating capacity of 165 seats. This will maximize revenue on short-haul flights. MD-80 series will be the only aircraft operated by the company. We will eliminate the need to cross-train employees. We will also reduce the requirements for parts inventories.

Our state-of-the-art reservations system will save time, allow us to employ fewer reservationists, and save training costs for new reservation personnel. The reservations system is discussed further in the "Technology" section of this plan.

Sales Literature

All company literature is yet to be developed. This includes basic corporate identity material as well as advertising executions. First year projections include an expense item for this necessary development work.

Sourcing

Aircraft will be obtained on a "dry lease" basis (without fuel) from one of several aircraft lessors at an approximate cost of $165,000 per month. Puddle Jumpers management has already been in contact with GE Capital Aviation Services. It is expected that GE Capital will have 80 MD-80 and/or MD-81 aircraft available for lease from Swiss Air over the next several years. Lease deposits, requirements, and terms are as follows.

Generally, first and last month's lease payments are required in advance. Lease is usually a five-year operating lease and most often qualifies as an expense item to the lessee. Terms of renewal are negotiable and no buy-out provision is included. There may or may not be an additional deposit required by the lessor as a maintenance reserve. Puddle Jumpers management feels that this will not be a requirement but is prepared to make such a deposit if it becomes required to obtain necessary aircraft for operations.

It is expected that up to 80 airplanes will be available over the next two years with an average of 120 days lead time required.

The advantages of utilizing McDonnell-Douglas MD-80 series aircraft, in addition to management's knowledge and prior successful experience with the same aircraft at Private Jet, are outlined in the "Technology" section of this plan.

Our reservations system will be obtained from CMS at a cost of $200,000 for the software license and approximately $1,000 each for 50 reservation stations (including modem and monitor). The advantages of this system are outlined in the "Technology" section of this plan.

Outsourcing of services are as follows:

Maintenance—All regular "A" and "B" maintenance will be performed by Puddle Jumpers personnel at our own leased facilities at each airport served. We will also have tools and parts inventory at each site. Puddle Jumpers management feels that it is both necessary and prudent in today's regulatory environment to perform this regular and routine maintenance "in-house." Periodic "C" and "D" overhauls and major maintenance will be outsourced to Widget Corp. in Lake City, Florida. Labor costs are budgeted at $32 per hour. It is common for many carriers in the aviation industry (including some quite large ones) to "sub-out" "C" and "D" scheduled maintenance. Thus, it is not viewed as a competitive or regulatory disadvantage to Puddle Jumpers to do likewise.

Ground Handling—Airplane parking services, baggage loading and unloading, and baggage and freight handling services will be outsourced at all airports other than the Atlanta hub where these services will be performed by Puddle Jumpers personnel.

Food Service—All condiments and beverages served on Puddle Jumpers flights will be purchased from in-flight food service providers.

All equipment and systems that will be utilized by Puddle Jumpers have been carefully and diligently evaluated. Management feels that it is an advantage to be starting an airline today vs. using many of the systems that burden even the largest domestic carriers with extra cost due to outmoded technology. The technological advantages to management's choices are outlined below:

Technology

Airplane advantages

The MD-80 series aircraft are both newer and more reliable that the DC-9s used by Penny Jet, for example. Many of Penny Jet's problems have been caused by using aircraft that often are more than 20 years old. Such aircraft, while they may be cheaply leased, are more expensive to maintain. Or, often are "maintained" on-the-fly with resulting service delays, customer dissatisfaction, and increased associated costs. It is the position of Puddle Jumpers management that the cheapest "over-all" operational costs are achieved by optimized "in air time." This becomes both a reliability and service standard for the operation of our airline. Puddle Jumpers's air travel customers will both feel safe flying Puddle Jumpers and will arrive at their destination on time.

In addition, the utilization of MD-80 series aircraft will avoid additional FAA compliance requirements mandated by the "Aging Fleet Program." These requirements apply to aircraft 20 years older or more. Since most aircraft to be used by Puddle Jumpers were built in the 1982 to 1985 time frame, they will not be subject to these mandates during the full initial five-year term of their respective leases. Many Penny Jet airplanes, by contrast, were built in the early 1970s.

Since these aircraft were built in the 1980s parts are still being manufactured and are readily available. Older aircraft often dictate that parts that are no longer manufactured are "cannibalized" from one aircraft to another or that old parts are "remanufactured" since new ones are nonexistent. The safety risks are evident. Puddle Jumpers will be able to maintain an inventory of new replacement parts.

Perhaps most importantly, the MD-80 series aircraft is already "Stage 3" noise compliant. New FAA guidelines mandate that 50% of an airline's fleet meet new noise emission standards by December 31, 1996. Another 25% must qualify by December 31, 1998, and the entire fleet must be in noise standards compliance by December 31, 2000. Several domestic air carriers are already protesting that they can't reasonably meet these standards but the FAA has demonstrated a past history of not bending on similar issues. Puddle Jumpers's fleet will not be effected by these requirements since it will comply as soon as it begins flying. There will be no cost to upgrade or retro-fit required. Again, this fits Puddle Jumpers's philosophy that the cheapest way to maintain aircraft is to adopt a "preventative" overview. All of the cost savings associated with the utilization of this superior aircraft are reflected in management's projections.

Finally, management is well acquainted with all facets of operation of the MD-80 from prior experience at Private Jet. Such experience was completely satisfactory.

Reservations advantages

The predominate reservations systems in the airline industry today, "Sabre" and "Apollo" are outmoded and obsolete. The major carriers are slow to change because of the huge capital requirement to "roll over" their entire reservations system at one time. Hence, they keep going with the old and outdated systems.

The CMS reservations system that Puddle Jumpers will use has three main advantages that all contribute to cost savings: 1) Speed, 2) Learning Curve, and 3) Integration. Since today's PCs operate so much faster than earlier versions, Puddle Jumpers's reservationists will be able to complete a typical reservation procedure up to 75% faster than industry averages. Most reservations will be completed in two minutes or less (as opposed to the frequent 8 to 10 minutes that almost everyone has experienced from time to time). The system simply searches and retrieves data much faster. The result is not only higher levels of customer satisfaction but also substantial savings in communications cost to Puddle Jumpers.

Training costs are also reduced exponentially. There is characteristically high turnover among airline reservationists. "Sabre" and "Apollo" take two weeks to learn and master. Puddle Jumpers's use of CMS will enable a basic computer literate employee to learn the system in only one day.

The CMS system also seamlessly integrates with other management information systems used by Puddle Jumpers. It is also designed to operate in a "ticketless" environment, something the other systems have difficulty accomplishing.

Operational advantages

Over-all operations will be seamless from area-to-area of Puddle Jumpers's management information systems as a whole. Most systems utilized by the major carriers today were put in place more than 20 years ago. Thus, there is a constant need for each operational area to "talk" or "re-transmit" essential data to one another. Not only will Puddle Jumpers's information systems operate "seamlessly" but they will also greatly enhance the ability to conform to all FAA compliance requirements. The biggest and toughest compliance issue facing carriers today is "record keeping." It is not enough to comply, but one must be able to prove compliance as well as have full and clearly defined and documented internal account-ability.

Future Products

Service will be one class with all aircraft configured for a seating capacity of 165. Travel will be ticketless. Reservations will be handled predominately by our own reservation system (even though we've budgeted travel agent commissions on 30% of sales). In-flight service will be on a pay-on-demand basis. Paid service will be for alcoholic beverages only. No meals will be served on these short-haul flights. A snack of soft drinks and peanuts will be included in the fare structure. Seating will be open with no reserved seats. No frequent flyer or travel incentives will be offered.

MARKET ANALYSIS SUMMARY

Atlanta, Georgia is the best place in the continental United States to start an airline. Puddle Jumpers's management decision to do just that is based upon extensive research compiled from the Department of Transportation O & D report data. This data provides a reliable source (based upon a compilation of actual airline arrivals and departures) of origination and destination demand by passenger, by day. The key measure of demand between any two given points in the grid is called "PDEW," that is "passengers departed each way." The PDEW compiles a total number of passengers on all carriers between two points, on average, each day. This total is irrespective of final destination.

The other key factors that resulted in the choice of Atlanta as a hub derive from management's experience and knowledge in commercial aviation. Principal to the decision is an airline industry insider's understanding of the problems that face Southern Air, the dominate carrier in the Atlanta market. Also, the lack of availability of a true "discount" fare option to the Atlanta traveler is pivotal.

Management is making the judgment that not only is the Atlanta market vulnerable to a new carrier, but also that the ability of Southern Air to retaliate will be limited. Further, the likelihood of a major carrier to respond is unlikely. The only real threat would be another new entry. So the opportunity may best be described as one ready and waiting for the first entrant who arrives with a well conceived plan, sufficient industry experience, and with the required capitalization.

The airline industry is dominated by the major carriers. It is an industry characterized by merger, acquisition, and consolidation. Like so many other industries it has quickly evolved into an industry that has room only for major players and smaller "specialty" or "niche" participants. There are two specialty segments that have characteristically been exploited by new entrants. One is the "price" niche and the other is the "route" niche. One focuses on charging less, the other on providing either the only service between two given points (the "commuter" or "feeder" concept) or else superior or more convenient or less costly service between two heavily traveled destinations.

Market Segmentation

In today's marketplace the "price" positioning, in and of itself, is no longer a sufficient concept on which to build an airline. Since deregulation the flying public has been inundated with low fares. Low fares have become an expectation, not a promise. Thus, the true market segment opportunities today have become a combination of service mix, price, and route selection. The more critical decision has become one of deciding on service mix and price in conjunction with length of route. The specialty carrier is now relegated to either "short-haul" or "long-haul" concentration. There is room for a long-haul carrier who efficiently serves limited routes with only the equipment designed to serve those routes and, conversely, there is room for a short-haul carrier to take advantage of similar economies available with new technology and the proper equipment. Puddle Jumpers feels that the likelihood of competition from major carriers is less likely in the short-haul segment.

Short-haul carriers also may operate efficiently out of a single hub. This enables consolidation of services and economies of down-sized scale. At the same time, the revenues available from short hauls are comparatively higher than long hauls on a per-passenger-mile basis.

Short haul revenues are simultaneously high enough to build a substantial business in the hundred million dollar multiple range.

Thus Puddle Jumpers may be said to target the short-haul, single hub, discount fare market segment. This is a new segment defined by the demands of today's traveler.

Potential Customers	Growth	1996	1997	1998	1999	2000	CAGR	**Market Analysis**
Atlanta-Atlanta	3%	245	252	260	268	276	3.03%	
Atlanta-Boston	3%	150	155	160	165	170	3.18%	
Atlanta-Dallas-Ft. Worth	3%	190	196	202	208	214	3.02%	
Atlanta-Chicago	3%	247	254	262	270	278	3.00%	
Atlanta-Ft. Lauderdale	3%	88	91	94	97	100	3.25%	
Atlanta-New York	3%	278	286	295	304	313	3.01%	
Atlanta-Detroit	3%	131	135	139	143	147	2.92%	
Atlanta-Orlando	3%	130	134	138	142	146	2.94%	
Atlanta-Philadelphia	3%	181	186	192	198	204	3.04%	

Market Analysis

Continued...

	Growth	1996	1997	1998	1999	2000	CAGR
Atlanta-Washington, D.C.	3%	52	54	56	58	60	3.64%
Other	0	0	0	0	0	0	0%
Total	**3.05%**	**1,692**	**1,743**	**1,798**	**1,853**	**1,908**	**3.05%**

Industry Analysis

The Federal Government deregulated the airline industry in 1978. Prior to that time the government virtually guaranteed the profitability of the airline industry, at the expense of the consumer. Routes were restricted. Fares were fixed. Costs got out of control. Today some of the major carriers still continue to operate at less than optimum efficiency. This has spawned the success of various "discount" carriers, most notably FlyRight, Penny Jet, and the new U2 planned by UAL.

The low cost carriers have proven that they can operate profitably, can garner market share, and have even spawned an increase in travel by luring those who would previously have traveled by bus, rail, or automobile or who would not have traveled at all.

In 1994, Penny Jet Airlines in Atlanta experienced considerable success and enjoyed rapid growth. It has forced TWA to abandon its mini hub in Atlanta and has grown to more than 40 aircraft in two years. Until recently, Atlanta was the most expensive major city in the U.S. to fly to or from. This was due, in part, to the near monopoly condition engendered by Mile High's dominance of the Atlanta market.

Penny Jet remains the economic success model for start-up airlines, although Puddle Jumpers management feels that it should not be the operational model. Penny Jet's current problems are the result of unbridled growth without commensurate control.

Many major airlines today are experiencing significant losses. The management of Puddle Jumpers feels that these losses can be traced directly to the high cost of labor, operational inefficiency, and poor management. Management further believes that the major carriers cannot profitably compete against start-up carriers with limited and specific market focus and lower over-all cost structures.

In retrospect, deregulation has succeeded in providing air travelers with better service but has not necessarily provided service at a lower price. In the recent times of financial trouble, many airlines have complained of an under supply of air travelers, when in fact there is an under supply of affordable seats. It is Puddle Jumpers's goal to provide these affordable seats while maintaining a profitable airline.

Industry Participants

The major air carriers in the U.S. are not the focus of this plan. They are not viewed as competition to a single hub, short-haul, low-cost entrant. The following three airlines are worthy of study. FlyRight as one to emulate. Penny Jet as one to improve upon. Southern Air as one to learn from and avoid similar pitfalls.

FlyRight Airlines is the model for operating a safe and successful discount carrier. Even though FlyRight has the lowest cost per ASM in the airline industry for short-haul carriers, they have never experienced a fatal crash in more than 25 years of operation.

Penny Jet remains the financial model for a start-up airline. The return to initial investors and early shareholders has been outstanding. However, operations have been marginal and growth was too fast.

Southern Air is the model for classically mismanaged labor cost within the airline industry. This plan focuses on a deeper discussion of Southern Air in the "Competition" section. Southern Air controls an 86% market share in Atlanta. Mile High is second with 2%.

Puddle Jumpers management has studied extensively the history of the above three airlines. All three have grown to substantial revenue size amidst the major airlines. None of the three existed in the not-too-distant past. Puddle Jumpers has taken the best parts of each growth story, heeded the alarms and cautions, and learned from the outright mistakes. The result is the plan for Puddle Jumpers Airlines, the airline for today's marketplace.

Distribution Patterns

Sales of airline tickets have historically been either direct from the airline itself or through various travel agents. Modern computer technology and communications capability are changing the mix dramatically. Travel agents once accounted for 80% of ticket sales. This channel of distribution has been one of very high cost to the airlines. Travel agent commissions at one time became the highest individual cost item to an airline. Perks and incentives amounted to coercion and bribery. The airlines found themselves held hostage. Not until Mile High boldly announced that commissions to travel agents would be held to 10% did the situation begin to change.

The physical cost of printing and distributing tickets is also substantial. Travel agents estimate that it costs them an average of $30 in total cost to originate an airline ticket. Many of them have begun to add their own service fees to the actual cost of a ticket.

Available technology has now afforded the opportunity both to sell one's own tickets and to eliminate the physical ticket altogether. The critical element for both strategies to be successful for an airline is simply to create the demand for travel on one's airline. If the airline makes it desirable for the consumer to want to fly it then it is just as easy to order tickets directly from the airline as it is from any other source. Puddle Jumpers will have fifty of its own reservations agents available via an 800 number (the service will be 24 hours from an available pool of 90 agents in total). In addition, we will have an Internet site where schedules are available and customers can book their own reservations and buy tickets via credit card.

Puddle Jumpers expects to sell as much as 90% of its air travel "direct" and "ticketless." Even so, we have budgeted 30% of sales as subject to agent's commission.

"Ticketless" travel has an additional advantage since Puddle Jumpers will not wait 30 days for collection of clearinghouse funds from other airlines on combined-carrier tickets. Also, it is not expected to be a competitive disadvantage for Puddle Jumpers's passengers to connect to other airlines. They will want to fly Puddle Jumpers to available destinations to save money even if they need to buy a paper ticket on another airline. Puddle Jumpers's flights will be listed in all available flight information systems.

Competition and Buying Patterns

The most critical factor for Puddle Jumpers or any new airline to overcome is the issue of brand awareness and name recognition. Customers prefer to fly with carriers they know and trust. There is little doubt that Puddle Jumpers will need to spend heavily and frequently to advertise and promote its product. The needed amounts are budgeted in this plan. The advantage is that local media can be utilized which is more cost effective on a per-impression basis. It can also be highly targeted. It has been proven in the past that market share can be achieved for a new airline.

Critical in today's environment is safety. Consumers will switch for lower costs, but not at the expense of a perception of a safety risk, or not at the expense of expected on-time performance. Puddle Jumpers's media executions will emphasize these two main themes.

In the Atlanta market, Puddle Jumpers expects to appeal to a mix of business oriented travelers and personal travelers. One issue is whether or not "frequent flier miles" are needed to compete and sell tickets. Management feels they are not. Industry estimates show that as many as 10% of occupied seats on domestic flights are currently "no revenue" as a result of redemption of premiums earned. It is also very expensive for an airline to administer its frequent flyer program. Puddle Jumpers feels that our cost advantage in Atlanta will outweigh the lack of "incentive" rewards. We expect that casual and personal travelers don't fly often enough for "points" to be significant. At the same time Puddle Jumpers will initiate a concerted sales effort directly to all major corporations in the Atlanta market. We hope to have business travel mandated by these corporations on a cost basis alone.

Main Competitors

The only significant competitor in the Atlanta market is Southern Air. At one time Wingspan and Appalachian Sky dominated the market. Wingspan went out and Appalachian Sky was acquired by Southern Air. Southern Air is highly vulnerable because of its high operating costs. ASM short-haul cost of 12 cents is currently the highest in the U.S. Southern Air commands 86% of the Atlanta air travel market. Mile High is a distant second with 2%.

As a result, Atlanta currently has the highest air travel costs in the country and 0% of air travel is at discount fares.

Southern Air's problems can be traced to two main factors. The first is the fact that their growth strategy has been by acquisition. It is apparent that management paid too much for many small regional carriers and also that the consolidation of these carriers has not produced the operational cost advantages that were anticipated. Secondly, and most important, has been out-of-control labor costs. Southern Air's stronghold is in the Northeast. The strongest labor unions are located in this part of the country and prior management has been completely ineffective in obtaining any concessions from these unions.

In spite of high costs, Southern Air has grown to become the nation's sixth largest carrier. However, recent press articles indicate a large measure of uncertainty in their future path. Berkshire Hathaway has asked Southern Air to buy back its 10% stake in the airline. Robert Wendt, Southern Air's new chairman has stated that Southern Air needs to become a carrier "of choice" not merely "of convenience." He said further that Southern Air must either buy another airline, be acquired itself, or form a partnership with another carrier. The question is who? No one in the industry wants Southern Air's high cost structure. And even if a new owner could obtain concessions, whose current routes are compatible with Southern Air? The management of Puddle Jumpers cannot identify a strategic suitor. Global or Columbia would be the most likely to acquire Southern Air from an economic standpoint but the routes don't match well.

Puddle Jumpers concludes that the Atlanta opportunity is likely to be free from imposing competition unless it comes from another start-up. If we are able to attack the market first with sufficient capitalization, we feel we will be difficult to overcome and should be able to build critical mass within two years.

Puddle Jumpers's market presence will be achieved by relying on the strategy of identifying and serving a specialized niche market well.

- Media executions will utilize local media, which is highly targeted and cost effective on a cost-per-impression basis.
- Air operations will be centralized and cost effective.
- Reservations will be centralized and cost effective.
- Marketing will be media generated to the leisure market and combined media/direct sales generated to corporate accounts.

Marketing is targeted locally. The advantage of a local and highly identifiable market is that media selections can be limited in scope. There is no need for a national media program to launch Puddle Jumpers. The most effective media is expected to be outdoor billboards. Private Jet relied heavily on a dozen well-placed billboards in and around Atlanta to build a $100 million plus business.

Other media will be local spot TV on highly visible programs such as local news and sports. Also, local radio. Newspapers and other print will not be used.

Marketing Strategy

Due to its low cost operating structure, Puddle Jumpers will be able to offer service at less than 50% of the competitive airfares to our selected destinations from our Atlanta hub. Projected fares are as follows:

Pricing Strategy

ROUTE	ADV	WALK	D.O.T.
Atlanta	$59.00	$89.00	$167.66
NY	$89.00	$129.00	$170.17
Dallas	$99.00	$159.00	$222.15
Boston	$99.00	$159.00	$185.25
Chicago	$89.00	$129.00	$184.99
Orlando	$79.00	$119.00	$141.69
Phil	$79.00	$119.00	$180.08
Detroit	$89.00	$129.00	$165,55
D.C.	$79.00	$109.00	$188.95
Ft. Lau	$79.00	$119.00	$148.70

The first column is for 14-day advance purchase. These fares are non-cancellable and non-refundable. The second column is for fares purchased inside of 14 days. The third column is current D.O.T. published average fare for all carriers.

Promotion will be primarily outdoor advertising, radio, and TV targeted at the Atlanta business and leisure traveler.

Promotion Strategy

In addition the company will employ a public relations firm for both consumer and financial purposes.

The combined amount budgeted for advertising, public relations, and reservations will be held under 15% of sales. Thus, the first year expenditure in these categories is expected to be $16.5 million. Past experience with Private Jet has demonstrated that this expenditure is sufficient to launch airline service in a single hub.

Sales Strategy

In addition to other marketing programs outlined the company will also market via the World Wide Web. We will establish our own web site with reservation, purchase, and payment capability.

Marketing Programs

In order to attract the Atlanta business traveler without the use of frequent flyer miles, the company will make direct sales contacts with the travel departments of Atlanta-based corporations and businesses. It is expected that our cost structure will be attractive to these businesses. Atlanta is now the third largest banking center in the U.S. and the Atlanta area economy in general is growing faster that the national average. We expect business travel to amount to at least 50% of our over-all revenue.

The sales personnel and salaries required to execute the direct sales strategy are included in these projections.

Sales Forecast

The company is forecasting annual sales in year one of flight operations at $110 million. Year two of flight operations will reach $216 million. Assumptions made for load factors are: 55% in year one, 62% in year two.

The year two numbers are based upon adding more flights and more airplanes to the routes already served. This will enable us to maximize profits within the market we have created without incurring the additional expense of opening new markets. It also allows for more controlled growth and eliminates the risks, early on, of the loss of control of operational procedures that can occur either with de-centralization or growth that is too rapid.

The basis of the sales projections illustrated in the chart below have been outlined in the "Market Analysis" section of this plan.

The company has also prepared five-year projections that are based upon expanded service to additional market areas. This five-year plan is a part of our due diligence package. Direct costs of sales are not included here but are instead reflected as a revenue discount in the projected P&L statement. These sales costs consist of travel agent commissions, credit card discounts, and federal excise taxes.

Sales Forecast

Sales	FY1996	FY1997	FY1998
Sales	$0	$110,000	$216,925
Other	$0	$0	$0
Total Sales	**$0**	**$110,000**	**$216,925**
Direct Cost of Sales			
Sales	$0	$0	$0
Other	$0	$0	$0
Subtotal Cost of Sales	**$0**	**$0**	**$0**

Milestones

The following table lists important program milestones, with dates and managers in charge, and budgets for each. The milestone schedule indicates our emphasis on planning for implementation.

Management expects that the current regulatory climate will loosen shortly. We expect it to be a long-term advantage to well operated airlines. We feel that 1996 is the ideal time both to invest and to start an airline.

The costs of adding airplanes are figured on the basis of first and last payment in advance plus one month's lease payment.

Business Plan Milestones

Milestone	Manager	Planned Date	Department	Budget	Actual Date	Actual Budget	Planned Date - Actual Date	Budget - Actual Budget
Seed Financing	KDS	7/1/96	Executive	$2,500	6/1/96	$2,500	30	$0
Incorporation	KDS	7/15/96	Executive	$2,500	7/15/96	$0	0	$2,500
Private Placement	KDS	7/15/96	Executive	$90,000	7/15/96	$0	0	$90,000
D.O.T. Filing	KDS	8/1/96	Executive	$10,000	8/1/96	$0	0	$10,000
F.A.A. Filing	KDS	10/1/97	Executive	$10,000	10/1/97	$0	0	$10,000
Hiring Key Executives	KDS	1/1/97	Executive	$0	1/1/97	$0	0	$0
I.P.O.	KDS	3/1/97	Executive	$0	3/1/97	$0	0	$0
Full Staffing	KDS	6/1/97	HR	$0	6/1/97	$0	0	$0
Lease 2 Airplanes	KDS	6/1/97	Executive	$960,000	6/1/97	$0	0	$960,000
Commence Revenue Service	KDS	7/1/97	Sales	$200,000	7/1/95	$0	731	$200,000
Lease 3rd Airplane	KDS	8/1/97	Executive	$480,000	8/1/95	$0	731	$480,000
Lease 4th Airplane	KDH	9/1/97	Executive	$480,000	9/1/97	$0	0	$480,000
Total				**$2,235,000**		**$2,500**	**1,492**	**$2,232,500**

MANAGEMENT SUMMARY

The management of Puddle Jumpers is highly experienced. There is no one on the management team who has not already performed his or her function for another airline. We are not in the business of training key people. We intend to hit the ground running with a highly qualified and experienced management team. Some of the individuals profiled are currently with other airline companies. They both know and respect Ken Smith and have expressed the desire to work for him and for Puddle Jumpers.

Ken Smith is both known and respected by the F.A.A. regional officers in Atlanta as well as at the Federal level in Washington. He enjoys similar status with key D.O.T. officers. The management of Puddle Jumpers is well versed in all governmental approval procedures, having traversed them in the past to a full approval and operational status. We feel that the resumes of the key people enclosed herein will only enhance our ability to obtain required approvals. It is expected to be a necessity from this point forward to have such a management team assembled in order to obtain the government charters from the D.O.T. and from the F.A.A.

The biographies of the management team follow.

Organizational Structure

The company will be organized into five major operational areas:

1. Flight Operations.
2. Maintenance.
3. Financial.
4. Marketing.
5. Customer Service.

Many of the specific positions and job descriptions are government mandated. Puddle Jumpers will fully comply with all such mandates.

Management Team

The following are the biographies and ages of the key members of Puddle Jumpers's management team:

KENNETH D. SMITH, President and CEO, 51

Ken Smith has 28 years of aviation experience beginning with his career in the U.S. Air Force, where he ultimately attained the rank of Captain. Ken was awarded the Distinguished Flying Cross, two Commendation Medals, and six Air Medals for his contributions as a pilot in the Vietnam War. When Ken left the Air Force in 1976 he was the Director of Flight Training Programs at the U.S. Air Force Academy in Colorado Springs. He has served as Chief Flight Instructor for Flight International Training School and as a pilot for Braniff Airlines. Ken then served as Executive Vice President and General Manager for Aerostar Airlines, leading a turn-around that enabled Aerostar to be acquired by Flight International in 1984.

Ken then became General Manager of Connie Jones Services, an air cargo airline which he expanded from five to twenty aircraft. He was then recruited by Widget Corporation where he became Vice President of Marketing for Widget's worldwide aircraft maintenance services.

Ken became President and CEO of Private Jet in January 1991. In less than two years Ken's leadership took Private Jet from a single aircraft to a fleet of 15 and revenue of more than $130 million dollars.

Ken then helped Eagle Airlines start-up and has also served as a consultant to the start-up of Nations Air.

JAMES B. JONES, EXECUTIVE VICE PRESIDENT, 49

Mr. Jones has 30 years of flying experience including distinguished military service. He has been chief pilot, Director of Operations, and General Manager of Air Nevada Airlines, a commuter carrier. He has also served as Director of Operations and Director of Training for Eagle Airlines.

GREER CLARK, VICE PRESIDENT, OPERATIONS, 56

Mr. Clark has taken early retirement from Mile High Airlines. He has since served as Chief Pilot for America International Airlines, and as Vice President, Operations for Private Jet and for Eagle Airlines. Currently, he is Manager, Flight Test for Penny Jet.

DON ADAMS, VICE PRESIDENT, MAINTENANCE, 47

Mr. Adams is an Aeronautical Engineer from Australia. He has served as Vice President of Ansett Airlines. He was Vice President of Technical Services for Intercredit Corporation, an aircraft leasing company. Currently, he is Vice President of Avitas, one of the world's leading aviation consulting companies. He is presently on loan to the National Transportation Safety Board investigating the Albatross Airlines B757 crash in Colombia.

BRUCE WING, VICE PRESIDENT, FINANCE, 50

Mr. Wing is a CPA who has been a Vice President with First Chicago Bank. He has previously served as CFO of United Express, the commuter division of Unified Airlines as well as CFO of Private Jet.

PAUL BERRY, DIRECTOR OF OPERATIONS, 57

Mr. Berry is a retired Air Force Colonel. Colonel Berry served as General Norman Schwarzkopf's Tanker Task Force Commander for Desert Storm. Mr. Berry is currently Director of Operations at America International Airlines.

TERRY MCADAMS, CHIEF PILOT, 57

Mr. McAdams served as a pilot with Eastern Airlines for more than 25 years. He later served as Chief Pilot for Private Jet and is the Chief Pilot for Penny Jet. Mr. McAdams is typed on the B-727, DC-9, and MD-80 aircraft.

SALVATORE DIANGELO, DIRECTOR OF MAINTENANCE, 41

Mr. Diangelo has been in aircraft maintenance in the military, at People's Express Airlines, and at Columbia Airlines. At Columbia Mr. Diangelo was responsible for preparing the maintenance budget for the entire fleet. He has also served as Director of Maintenance for Penny Jet.

CALVIN COBLE, DIRECTOR OF QUALITY ASSURANCE, 42

Mr. Coble served his apprenticeship in the military. He is qualified as a Class III Inspector, which requires both extensive training and recommendation from his peers at the FAA. Mr. Coble has served as Director of Quality Assurance at Shannon Aerospace, a large maintenance facility operated by Lufthansa and Swiss Air in Shannon, Ireland.

JIM BEND, DIRECTOR OF MARKETING, 49

Mr. Bend has over 15 years experience as Regional Sales Manager for Eastern Airlines. He received numerous awards for his sales performance while at Eastern. He has also served as Director of Sales at Private Jet.

JUDY LAND, DIRECTOR OF RESERVATIONS, 38

Ms. Land has more than 10 years experience as Reservations Manager at Eastern Airlines. She has also helped with design and implementation of the reservations system at Private Jet and at World Technologies. She has received numerous awards for her motivational training seminars.

MARY ANN BENNETT, DIRECTOR OF IN-FLIGHT SERVICES, 43

Ms. Bennett served as a flight attendant at Eastern Airlines and went on to open her own travel agency. She joined Private Jet as a supervisor of flight attendants and was later promoted to Director.

Personnel Plan

Personnel	FY1997	FY1998	FY1999
Chief Executive Officer	$96	$96	$108
Executive Vice President	$42	$84	$96
VP Operations	$36	$72	$84
VP Maintenance	$36	$72	$78
V.P. Finance	$30	$60	$66
Director of Operations	$20	$60	$66
Director of Maintenance	$20	$60	$66
Chief Pilot	$18	$72	$78
Director of Sales/Marketing	$10	$60	$66
Director of Quality Assurance	$8	$48	$56
Director of Reservations	$8	$48	$54
Director of In-Flight Services	$8	$48	$52
Flight Crews	$0	$4,221	$5,614
Reservations	$0	$860	$1,144
Maintenance	$0	$950	$1,264
Operations/Training/G&A	$0	$1,035	$1,376
Sales/Marketing	$0	$180	$240
Finance/Accounting	$0	$360	$480
Other	$0	$125	$150
Other	$0	$0	$0
Total Payroll	**$332**	**$8,511**	**$11,138**
Total Headcount	0	0	0
Payroll Burden	$83	$2,128	$2,785
Total Payroll Expenditures	**$415**	**$10,639**	**$13,923**

FINANCIAL PLAN

Adequate financing is essential for a start-up airline. Our strategy remains a "seed" to "bridge" to "IPO" progression. This has served as a successful model for airline starts in the past. Because of the amount of capital required to start an airline management feels it is restricted to this funding path. Once four to six airplanes are up and flying the company can continue to operate profitably for an indefinite period of time in the event additional capital becomes unavailable on attractive terms.

Important Assumptions

The financial plan depends on important assumptions, most of which are shown in the following table. They key underlying assumptions are:

- We assume a slow-growth economy, without major recession
- We assume that there are no unforeseen changes in technology to make products immediately obsolete.
- We assume access to equity capital and financing sufficient to maintain our financial plan.

In the airline business the most important measurements are cost per Available Seat Mile and the System Utilization Factor. If seat costs are kept below 7 cents and utilization is at 50% or better, the airline will operate profitably.

When we take out all operational costs for flying aircraft and include only fixed overhead and aircraft leases the company can break even on the first six airplanes by maintaining sales just over $2 million per month or approximately $24 million in year one. This is less than 25% of our expected sales forecast but it indicates that the company could survive without adding planes and routes for an indeterminate period with load factors of less than 15%.

Breakeven Analysis

Monthly Units Breakeven	2,107
Monthly Sales Breakeven	$2,107

Assumptions

Average Per-Unit Revenue	$1.00
Average Per-Unit Variable Cost	$0.13
Estimated Monthly Fixed Cost	$1,833

Our profits improve from approxmately 1% of sales in year one to 10% of sales in year two and are expected to peak at about 16% in year three and thereafter. In gross numbers, we will exceed $20 million in profit in the second operational year.

	FY1997	FY1998	FY1999
Sales	$0	$110,000	$216,925
Direct Cost of Sales	$0	$0	$0
Subtractions	$0	$14,300	$28,200
Total Cost of Sales	**$0**	**$14,300**	**$28,200**
Gross Margin	$0	$95,700	$188,725
Gross Margin %	0.00%	87.00%	87.00%
Operating Expenses			
Direct Operating Costs	$0	$68,280	$113,000
Fixed Operating Costs	$0	$14,073	$28,659
Other	$0	$0	$0
Payroll Expense	$332	$8,511	$11,138
Payroll Burden	$83	$2,128	$2,785
Depreciation	$0	$0	$0
Leased Equipment	$0	$0	$0
Rent and Utilities	$0	$701	$701
Other	$0	$0	$0
Rent	$0	$0	$0
Other	$0	$0	$0
Total Operating Expenses	**$415**	**$93,693**	**$156,283**
Profit Before Interest and Taxes	($415)	$2,007	$32,443
Interest Expense Short-term	$0	$0	$0
Interest Expense Long-term	$0	$0	$0
Taxes Incurred	($137)	$662	$10,706
Net Profit	($278)	$1,345	$21,736
Net Profit/Sales	0.00%	1.22%	10.02%

Key Financial Indicators

Breakeven Analysis

Projected Profit and Loss

Profit and Loss (Income Statement)

Projected Cash Flow | This business plan cash flows positively from the initial infusion of approximately $14 million and forward. It will continue to produce cash as long as sales targets are met. Borrowings may only be required if seasonal fluctuations occur or if expansion plans are further accelerated.

Pro-Forma Cash Flow

	FY1997	FY1998	FY1999
Net Profit	($278)	$1,345	$21,736
PLUS			
Depreciation	$0	$0	$0
Change in Accounts Payable	$0	$0	$0
Current Borrowing (repayment)	$0	$0	$0
Increase (decrease) Other Liabilities	$0	$0	$0
Long-term Borrowing (repayment)	$0	$0	$0
Capital Input	$13,850	$0	$0
Subtotal	**$13,572**	**$1,345**	**$21,736**
LESS			
Change in Other ST Assets	$0	$0	$0
Capital Expenditure	$0	$0	$0
Dividends	$0	$0	$0
Subtotal	**$0**	**$0**	**$0**
Net Cash Flow	$13,572	$1,345	$21,736
Cash Balance	$13,572	$14,917	$36,653

Cash Analysis

Cash Analysis	Cash Flow	Cash Balance
Jul	$243	$243
Aug	$93	$337
Sep	$493	$830
Oct	$993	$1,823
Nov	$1,993	$3,817
Dec	($7)	$3,810
Jan	($23)	$3,787
Feb	($28)	$3,760
Mar	$9,964	$13,724
Apr	($41)	$13,683
May	($55)	$13,627
Jun	($55)	$13,572

Projected Balance Sheet | The projected balance sheet illustrates the growth of the net worth of the business and may also be utilized to estimate future stock values based upon industry multiples.

Pro-Forma Balance Sheet

Assets	Starting Balances			
Short-term Assets		FY1997	FY1998	FY1999
Cash	$0	$13,572	$14,917	$36,653
Other Short-term Assets	$0	$0	$0	$0
Total Short-term Assets	$0	$13,572	$14,917	$36,653
LONG-TERM ASSETS				
Capital Assets	$0	$0	$0	$0
Accum. Depreciation	$0	$0	$0	$0
Total Long-term Assets	$0	$0	$0	$0
Total Assets	$0	$13,572	$14,917	$36,653

Starting Balances

Liabilities and Capital		FY1997	FY1998	FY1999
Accounts Payable	$0	$0	$0	$0
Short-term Notes	$0	$0	$0	$0
Other Short-term Liab.	$0	$0	$0	$0
Subtotal Short-term Liab.	$0	$0	$0	$0
Long-term Liabilities	$0	$0	$0	$0
Total Liabilities	$0	$0	$0	$0
Paid in Capital	$350	$14,200	$14,200	$14,200
Retained Earnings	($350)	($350)	($628)	$717
Earnings	$0	($278)	$1,345	$21,736
Total Capital	$0	$13,572	$14,917	$36,653
Total Liab. and Capital	$0	$13,572	$14,917	$36,653
Net Worth	$0	$13,572	$14,917	$36,653

The important business measurement ratios are based upon projections for Puddle Jumpers.   **Business Ratios**

Ratio Analysis

Profitability Ratios	FY1997	FY1998	FY1999	RMA
Gross Margin	0%	87%	87%	0
Net Profit Margin	0%	1.22%	10.02%	0
Return on Assets	-2.05%	9.02%	59.30%	0
Return on Equity	-2.05%	9.02%	59.30%	0
Activity Ratios				
AR Turnover	0	0	0	0
Collection Days	0	0	0	0
Inventory Turnover	0	0	0	0
Accts Payable Turnover	0	0	0	0
Total Asset Turnover	0	7.37	5.92	0
Debt Ratios				
Debt to Net Worth	0	0	0	0
Short-term Liab. to Liab.	0	0	0	0
Liquidity Ratios				
Current Ratio	0	0	0	0
Quick Ratio	0	0	0	0
Net Working Capital	$13,572	$14,917	$36,653	0
Interest Coverage	0	0	0	0
Additional Ratios				
Assets to Sales	n.a.	0.14	0.17	0
Debt/Assets	0%	0%	0%	0
Current Debt/Total Assets	0%	0%	0%	0
Acid Test	0	0	0	0
Asset Turnover	0	7.37	5.92	0
Sales/Net Worth	0	7.37	5.92	0
Dividend Payout	$0	0	0	0

Art Glass Studio

BUSINESS PLAN

PHYLLIS FARMINGTON, ART GLASS

76532 Rugby Court
Dayton, OH 45429

When selling art or any unique product, the market becomes somewhat unpredictable. Understanding this to be true, this business plan lists many ideas for reaching potential buyers. As exposure increases, so do sales, and this artist enumerates several ways she plans to come in contact with consumers. She also explains a policy that avoids any conflict between her own sales and the sales of her goods by retailers, both important parts of maintaining a healthy business climate.

- HISTORY AND DESCRIPTION OF BUSINESS

- PRODUCT AND SERVICE

- LOCATION

- TARGET MARKET

- PRICING POLICY

- MARKET STRATEGY

- SHARE OF MARKET

- PROMOTION AND ADVERTISING

- EVALUATING RESULTS OF ADVERTISING

- START-UP COSTS

- BALANCE SHEET

- SALES FORECAST FOR FIRST YEAR

- EMPLOYMENT HISTORY

**HISTORY AND
DESCRIPTION OF
BUSINESS**

Phyllis Farmington, Art Glass, is a company that designs and produces handcrafted jewelry, as well as decorative bowls and plates. The business is operated by artist Phyllis Farmington. Ms. Farmington has been working with glass for the past year, and has began to display and sell her work as of December 1991. These pieces may be seen at numerous art galleries in the Dayton, Ohio area.

**PRODUCT AND
SERVICE**

To create her product, Ms. Farmington works with glass manufactured by the Watershed Glass Works. These glasses are designed to be compatible with one another when they are fired in a kiln. The wide range of colors available make it possible to create an almost unlimited range of designs and patterns. Some of these glasses have metallic and iridescent effects, and are available in both transparent and opaque type. Designs are created by layering different pieces of hand-cut glass on top of a piece of base glass. Next, the piece is fired at temperatures up to 1600 degrees. This causes the glass to soften and partially melt, or "fuse" together. The glass is then slowly cooled to room temperature. Often these pieces are fired a second time after having been painted with glazes of gold, silver, or platinum. These glazes are bonded to the glass and become permanent and long wearing.

Working in this manner, the artist produces earrings, pendants, pins, and bolo ties. Metal jewelry parts are attached to the pieces with epoxy and are placed onto decorative cards, which are then hand-signed. The owner offers these jewelry items individually, and also in matched sets.

In manufacturing her bowls and plates, Ms. Farmington utilizes molds made of fired ceramic. She slumps glass into these molds, and after the glass is cooled, it takes on the shape and form of the mold. Some of these plates are very simple in shape and take their designs from the patterns already found in the glass. Others are decorated in intricate patterns designed by the artist.

Ms. Farmington's work is functional, unique, and beautiful. She designs her pieces with a contemporary flair, using bold colors and striking patterns. Her work is influenced by international folk arts, and elements of African, Slavic, and Middle Eastern art grace her creations. Ms. Farmington brings her unique perspective to her designs and maintains very high standards of quality.

Whether worn with casual clothing or evening wear, her jewelry is eye-catching and each is designed to be a conversation piece. With proper care, these pieces of wearable art will give years of enjoyment.

Her decorative plates and bowls are attractive and useful. Whether displayed in the home or in an office, they create a focal point and enhance the environment. These vessels are beautiful, yet durable. The colors in the glass are derived from metallic sources and, as a result, do not fade over the years. They may be displayed in areas where there is bright sunlight, with no danger of colors being affected, as in the case of a watercolor or oil painting. In fact, these vessels are at their best when seen with light flooding through them, and the interplay of colors that result are a delightful characteristic of art glass.

The owner can custom design work to suit a client's needs. She can design jewelry to match a costume, create a work of art to be used in the home, or custom design art glass for display in an office setting. She offers free delivery, and will do price quotes at no cost to the client. Ms. Farmington believes in having "something for everyone." She strives to maintain a balance of artistic integrity as well as pleasing her clients. Whether a client purchases fun, affordable jewelry, or one of her more expensive fine art vessels, she maintains the same quality of excellence that her clients deserve.

LOCATION

Phyllis Farmington operates her business out of a building that is owned by her husband, fellow glass artist Mark Farmington. The building is located on Dayton's northwest side. The building is 3200 square feet in size, and has a parking lot adjacent. It is situated in a location that is zoned for commercial use, three quarters of a mile from an active shopping area.

The building has previously been used as a production shop only, but Ms. Farmington, together with her husband, are renovating the property for the purpose of expanding into retail sales. The back area which was formerly used as a storage area, is being developed as the main production area. The Farmingtons have recently partitioned off this previously unheated space and installed a heater. Although this work area needs further development, it is now possible to utilize this space as a production area. This leaves the more attractive front half of the building free for use as a retail display area. Ms. Farmington will be able to use this as a location of special sales throughout the year.

This location does not put the owner in a good position to reach her target market. However, she will continue to retail her work out of galleries and gift shops to reach these customers. The location is excellent for manufacturing and storage purposes, and the owner is able to have access to equipment and tools previously purchased by her husband. This eliminates the necessity of purchasing such items as a glass kiln. The owner also is able to utilize her husband's computer and software and share office space with him.

One strong advantage of this location is that the owner will be able to help build her customer base by tapping into her husband's already established clients. Mr. Farmington was the artist selected to do the art glass restoration at a local historical landmark, which was designed and built in 1910 by Frank Lloyd Wright. This restoration received a Presidential Award for excellence in 1989, being judged as the finest restoration of a historical building for that year, on a national level.

Mr. Farmington uses his contacts to help promote his wife's business, and recently Ms. Farmington was able to make a $300.00 sale from one of these contacts. Her association with her husband's business helps to open doors for her when doing promotional presentations as many people in the area are familiar with her husband's work, and it creates a point of interest that she can use to promote her own company. The owner will also use her husband's contacts to build her mailing list.

This location does not have a sign that extends away from the building. However, there is a sign that will be completed in the near future and put into place. It is made of stained glass, is two-sided, and lights up at night. This sign will be an eye-catching display, not only promoting the location of the business, but as an example of what can be done in the medium of glass.

TARGET MARKET

Ms. Farmington has two target markets for her artwork. For her jewelry, she will be marketing primarily to middle income women ages 18 to 40. The main way for her to reach her target market will be through sales of her product at various retail outlets. She also will sell a certain percentage of work out of her location, but realizes that this will require advertising and promotion over a period of time.

Ms. Farmington received a very positive response at a local gallery from the college students who shop there. Her jewelry especially appeals to young persons who are trendy and enjoy artistic things but would not be able to afford an expensive piece. These persons would be more likely to purchase at a gift shop rather than a high priced gallery. The owner will be placing work in areas where colleges are located in order to reach this market.

The owner will be placing her work in gift shops that sell to persons purchasing gifts for holidays and other special occasions. Recently, the owner visited a nearby floral and gift shop, and felt that it would be an excellent place to show and sell her work. Such shops that sell flowers and gifts have a high traffic and are very busy during holiday seasons. Shoppers can purchase flowers, gifts, and cards, all in one location. When Ms. Farmington stopped in to this shop close to Valentine's Day, it was so busy that she was unable to speak to anyone. At the counter she observed a woman who was asking the sales clerk if they carried any unusual glass bowls. The clerk responded that all they had was what was on the shelves, but that they would be carrying new merchandise shortly for the spring season. Ms. Farmington was able to obtain a card with the buyer's name and will be contacting them.

Ms. Farmington will be targeting another segment of the population for her more expensive items. These will be persons with a higher income level who purchase fine art for their home or office. These persons also purchase items as gifts for others for special occasions such as holidays or anniversaries. She will be targeting professional persons with an income level of $40,000 and up. According to American Demographics for 1990, there are approximately 166,000 persons in the surrounding area who fall into this income bracket. The age range is from 35 to 65, and they tend to be homeowners, single, with no children, or married, with no children.

The activities that this segment of the population enjoys are art and cultural events, home furnishing and decoration, physical fitness, camping, avid reading, shopping by catalog, computers, and VCR viewing and recording.

Ms. Farmington will reach this segment of the population in various ways. Her work will be placed in gift shops and galleries and upscale boutiques frequented by this segment of the population. She will be contacting buyers and designers at furniture showrooms that feature unusual hard-to-find decorative ware. Recently, she has contacted the buyers from a local store who have expressed an interest in her work. This store specializes in unique decorative ware, and sells to an upper income clientele. Upscale clothing stores are also very suitable for Ms. Farmington's jewelry. Recently she has met with the manager and buyer of such a boutique in Cincinnati. Ms. Farmington will be designing a line of jewelry for this shop as well as a select line of giftware in her more expensive price range. This store is very active in the summer season, selling to tourists who purchase designer clothes as well as decor for their summer cottages. The owner has also spoken to the buyer of a glass shop in Cincinnati. She was told that this shop purchases giftware in April to sell during the summer season. This shop also has an upscale clientele.

Catalog sales are another area that the owner will be working in. In the near future, she will be sending letters and photographs to potential buyers. She will offer to work with these buyers in the same manner that has been previously mentioned, designing gift items to appeal to the catalog's customers.

PRICING POLICY

The owner's pricing policy is based upon her operating expenses and what she feels the market will bear. She has priced all of her products in the following manner. First, the owner needs to know what the bottom line production cost is on each item. She takes into account the cost of her materials, other variables, her fixed operating expenses, the time involved, and the hourly wage that she needs to receive to meet her personal expenses.

She then sets a suggested retail price, which is what she feels the item would sell for in a retail outlet. This is also the price the artist would sell the item for in her shop. If the item is sold on a consignment basis, the store's commission is subtracted from this retail price. If she sells the item on a wholesale basis, the price for which the item is sold to the store would be determined by that store's markup policy.

In doing her pricing research, the frequent complaint was heard from buyers that artists often undercut the retail outlets where their works are being sold. This creates a conflict of interest, and may result in the store's refusal to accept further work from that artist. For example, an artist may sell a piece for $100.00 to a store which then marks it up to $250.00. If the artist sells the piece for $100.00, eventually people will buy directly from the artist to get a discount. As soon as the retail outlet sees what is happening, they feels as if the artist is in competition with them. The owner does not want this situation to happen, as she will be very dependent on her retail outlets to help her to reach her target market. By selling the item out of her studio for the same price as the retail outlet, this problem will be avoided.

The owner has prepared a price list for all of the products that she offers. On the list she has included the production cost of each item and the suggested retail price. By being aware of what her production costs are on each item, she will be able to price her products with confidence, knowing that she will be able to meet her expenses and make a reasonable profit.

She will be able to determine how many units of a given item need to be sold on a monthly and yearly basis to meet her expenses. She will use this tool when planning her marketing strategy and to help her meet sales goals.

The terms of sale for the first year will be cash or check only. If a client commissions a piece of custom work, she will require a 50% deposit to start the work, with the remainder to be paid upon completion.

The owner has several sources of competition in the area: The Glass Palace, artists and hobbyists who do art and craft shows, and Gemstone Studio.

MARKET STRATEGY

The Glass Palace: This competitor is a large, well-stocked store that sells supplies to art glass hobbyists as well as gift items. They are also the main source of Ms. Farmington's retail supplies. They are located close to Westerland Mall. This competitor's staff is very knowledgeable and helpful, and they are located in an accessible high traffic area. Ms. Farmington will compete with this business on the quality and uniqueness of her giftware. The items that the Glass Palace sells are well made, but mostly made from patterns and kits. These items are pretty and attractive, but usually not very artistic. Ms. Farmington will only market and sell her original designs. Although her location is out of the way, she will work hard to promote her business and make her target market aware of where they can find her. If a client shows an interest in stained glass, the owner will turn the customer over to her husband, and he can answer questions and design and create leaded glasswork to their specifications. Also, Mr. Farmington specializes in repair work of antique glass which the Glass Palace does not do.

Hobbyists Who Do Art Fairs: Art fairs are very popular in Ohio, and many glass artists participate in these events. Ms. Farmington has seen much stained glass, and some fused glass jewelry at these shows. The prices are usually low, and the quality of these products range from mediocre to high. Some of the participants are artists, while others are hobbyists who do this work as a sideline. Ms. Farmington gets the impression that these exhibitors carefully keep an eye on one another so that they can produce similar work in the same price range. At a recent show the owner attended, she visited 5 art glass displays.

The work of each booth was almost identical, right down to the types of glass and the colors that were used. Also, fused glass is seldom found at these shows. Ms. Farmington does not want to appeal to a person who wants the best price on a piece of work, but the discriminating person who will pay a little more for a conversation piece. She carefully watches her competitors so that she can do work that is deliberately different than theirs.

Gemstone Studio: This competitor is located in Springfield, Ohio. It is a small studio that sells supplies to the glass trade, as well as fused glass jewelry. Their staff is knowledgeable and helpful, and the quality of their work is high. They also sell jewelry out of retail stores in the area. Most of these pieces are very heavy in weight and tend to be rendered in dark colors. The edges of the glass are covered with metal solder, which contributes to the weight, and adds a very heavy look to the pieces. Ms. Farmington's pieces are lighter in weight and more wearable. She offers a wide variety of colors and styles. Her earrings are light in weight and comfortable to wear, and there is no solder used in these designs.

SHARE OF MARKET

Ms. Farmington's strong points are her unique sense of style, her attention to quality, her high degree of professionalism, and her natural born sales ability. She will capture a relatively small share of the market, but it will be those persons who are very discriminating and will appreciate her work. Her enthusiasm and dedication, as well as her excellent customer servicing, will help her to hold those clients once she has them. Nowhere else will they be able to find what she has to offer, because her unique personality and personal vision is such an integral part of her work.

PROMOTION AND ADVERTISING

The owner will promote and advertise her business utilizing the following methods:

- Gallery presentations and sales.
- Specially designed promotional materials.
- Customer mailing list.
- Art show participation.
- Articles and photos submitted to trade publications.

The owner will use a combination of these techniques to promote her business and increase sales. There will be a series of seasonal shows and sales throughout the year on location. A Christmas Open House will be held at the beginning of December. This will be a festive event with live music and refreshments. A sale will go into effect at that time and continue through December 25. Similar sales will be held Valentine's Day and Easter. These sales will feature items with seasonal themes.

In this manner, customers will be able to shop in a festive atmosphere, avoid crowded shopping malls, and meet and chat with the artist. Gift certificates will also be offered for sale.

In the summer, two weeks before the Fourth of July holiday, Ms. Farmington will hold a mini art fair onsite. She will feature her work as well as the work of other local artists. This fair will be held inside as well as outside. This event will also be promoted by way of the mailing list.

The owner will promote these events with the use of flyers, ads, word of mouth, signs at the studio, and by direct mail. Promotional materials will be sent to all persons she is beginning to sell work to. She will continue to compile this list with information taken from company sales receipts. Ms. Farmington will be able to utilize her husband's computer for these promotional activities. The mailing list will be kept on the computer and it also will be used to print labels. A local community magazine will be utilized for advertising. This publication lists all cultural events in the Dayton area. Ms. Farmington feels this is an excellent way to reach her target market.

Ms. Farmington is using the services of a professional photographer to take photos of her work. These will be used in her promotional materials. She has designed a folder that will have photos of her work as well as a brief biography. This folder will be given to buyers when Ms. Farmington does presentations. On the folder is a space where she can attach her business card. This folder can also be given to persons who have purchased a piece of work from a gallery, in which case the gallery can attach their business card. This will promote the gallery and artist at the same time. This piece of literature is designed to create an image of quality and elegance. When the owner does a presentation at a gallery she will also utilize photographs and slides to show samples of her work.

Ms. Farmington will have business cards and stationery printed using her distinctive signature as her logo. These will be color coordinated and will match her promotional folder. In speaking with buyers and gallery owners, Ms. Farmington has heard the frequent complaint that artists are often poor business persons and present themselves in an unprofessional manner. By being prepared with promotional materials and carefully cultivating a dynamic and professional demeanor, she will create a positive image with the people who are in a position to promote her business.

The owner will be participating in art shows that have high standards of quality and that attract the target market that she wishes to sell to. In speaking with other artists who participate in the events she has learned important information. There is no guarantee that you will make a profit.

Some of these events are not appropriate for the type of product that the owner is selling. She has decided to be very selective in this area, and to see shows as a promotional opportunity rather than a direct sales opportunity. She will enter events where she has to chance to compete for awards. Any prizes or awards will be excellent publicity for her business. She also will use this as an opportunity to directly meet and talk with her target market. Promotional materials can be distributed, and if a person purchases a piece from her or shows a strong interest, they will be added to her mailing list.

Recently, the owner submitted slides and an application for a national art glass competition. Those artists selected to be semi-finalists are to be notified in early spring. Ms. Farmington is awaiting news on this competition. Also, she has recently sent a photo and letter to the *Dayton Observer*, suggesting that she be featured. There is a feature in the paper every Sunday in the Home section which highlights unusual home furnishings and gift items available locally. Publicity received from these events will be used to promote her business. Even if she is not immediately successful in these ventures, she will remain persistent in her efforts to increase her visibility.

The owner will be sending photos, slides, and articles to trade publications in order to promote her work. These publications welcome submissions of this sort and frequently feature work of emerging artists. Her photographs and slides are of very high quality and designed for publication. Ms. Farmington has good writing ability and is confident that this will be a successful method of promotion. This will increase her visibility to her target market and will be a good tool to use when designing future promotional materials.

Computer files will record labor, materials, expenses for each advertising method, as well as the amount of sales generated. This information will be analyzed to measure the effectiveness of each advertising strategy.

EVALUATING RESULTS OF ADVERTISING

START-UP COSTS

SUPPLIES

1 case Bullseye Glass\Shipping (approximately 20 sheets of glass in assorted colors. Includes $80.00 shipping)	$800.00
Jewelry parts from Rings 'n' Things	125.00

PROMOTIONAL MATERIALS

500 business cards speckled grey fiber paper with gold thermographic lettering. Print Masters-Wasau Grey fiber paper	34.00
500 sheets and 500 envelopes of matching stationery-black logo	100.00
100 promotional folders grey 80 1b. paper with typeset	50.00
TOTAL	**$1,109.00**

BALANCE SHEET

AS OF MARCH 6, 1992

ASSETS		LIABILITIES	
CASH IN BANK	0.0	ACCOUNTS PAYABLE	0.0
ACCOUNTS RECEIVABLE	40.00	OWNERS NET WORTH	1,365.00
INVENTORY		(Assets minus	1,365.00
		liabilities)	
Davis Gallery	400.00		
Founders' Place	125.00		
E.M. Art Glass	500.00		
Raw materials on hand	300.00		
TOTAL ASSETS	**$1,365.00**		

SALES FORECAST FOR FIRST YEAR

This section shows projected sales goals for the coming year, how many units the owner sells to pay her operating expenses, loan principal and interest, and income taxes.

The owner has selected four products that show a wide price range in order to give a realistic projection. She has also estimated how many would be sold retail, wholesale, and on a consignment basis. Also included are services rendered, which represents income from a seasonal part-time job for the Photography House in Dayton. The owner provides art services for this studio on a subcontract basis over the holiday season.

There are periods of highs and lows in this business. As the owner is selling mainly to a giftware market, sales revolve around periods when her target market purchases these items. Highs also are caused by the sales that the owner will be having at her location.

U.C. stands for unit contribution and represents the net profit of each item after the production costs have been subtracted from the selling price.

The owner has based these figures upon what she feels she can realistically sell in one year, and also by what she needs to make to meet her minimum operating and personal expenses. She then used the sales projection as a basis for her estimated cash flow, which follows.

(How many to sell to break even on fixed expenses.)
C=Consignment R=Retail W=Wholesale

Product	Monthly	Yearly	Total Cash	U.C.
Spectrum Bowl-W	6	70	$2,100.00	$1,468.00
Spectrum Bowl-C	8	95	3,420.00	2,563.00
Spectrum Bowl-R	4	40	24,000.00	2,039.00
Phoenix Plate-W		5	1,355.00	631.00
Phoenix Plate-C		4	1,200.00	640.00
Glass Pin-C	10	115	2,084.00	1,093.00
Glass Pin-R	17	200	4,700.00	2,976.00
Earrings-R	9	100	1,350.00	773.00
SUBTOTAL			18,609.00	12,183.00
SERVICES RENDERED			1,219.33	1,219.00
TOTALS			**$19,828.33**	**$13,402.00**

SALES FORECAST FOR FIRST YEAR

...continued

	April	May	June	July	Aug	Sep	Oct
Beg. Cash		$317.00	$353.71	$460.34	$728.48	$928.16	$2,105.19
CASH IN							
Retail	$100.00	$150.00	$275.00	$500.00	$550.00	$600.00	$800.00
Wholesale	$100.00	$200.00	$250.00		$300.00	$735.00	$532.00
Consign.	$117.00	$175.00	$275.00	$495.00	$600.00	$705.00	$950.00
Services						$119.33	$300.00
Loan	$1,109.00						
Total	**$1,426.00**	**$842.00**	**$1,153.71**	**$1,455.34**	**$2,178.48**	**$3,087.49**	**$4,687.19**
CASH OUT							
Inventory	$925.00				$600.00		
Off. Supp.	$134.00	$25.00	$25.00	$25.00	$25.00	$25.00	$25.00
Adv. Promo.	$50.00		$175.00				$200.00
Taxes				$132.86			$676.47
Car		$40.00	$40.00	$40.00	$40.00	$40.00	$40.00
Rent/Util.		$200.00	$200.00	$200.00	$200.00	$200.00	$200.00
Misc.		$25.00	$25.00	$25.00	$25.00	$25.00	$25.00
Principal		$87.44	$88.31	$89.20	$90.09	$90.99	$91.90
Interest		$11.09	$10.22	$9.33	$8.44	$7.54	$6.63
Total C.O.	**$1,109.00**	**$388.53**	**$563.53**	**$521.39**	**$988.53**	**$388.53**	**$1,265.00**
Gross	$317.00	$453.47	$590.18	$933.95	$1,189.95	$2,698.96	$3,422.19
Withdrawal	$0.00	$99.76	$129.84	$205.47	$261.79	$593.77	$752.88
End Cash	$317.00	$353.71	$460.34	$728.48	$928.16	$2,105.19	$2,669.31
Net	$158.50	$136.47	$236.47	$473.61	$461.47	$1,770.80	$1,317.00

Nov	Dec	Jan	Feb	March	April	Totals
$2,669.31	$4,275.01	$4,669.45	$2,785.33	$3,121.40	$3,161.24	$25,574.62
$1,200.00	$1,100.00	$500.00	$900.00	$700.00	$800.00	$8,175.00
	$300.00			$300.00	$400.00	$3,117.00
$1,200.00	$1,000.00	$125.00	$705.00	$420.00	$550.00	$7,317.00
$800.00						$1,219.33
						$1,109.00
$5,869.31	**$6,375.01**	**$5,594.45**	**$4,390.33**	**$4,541.40**	**$4,911.24**	**$20,937.33**
						$1,525.00
$25.00	$25.00	$25.00	$25.00	$25.00	$25.00	$434.00
	$175.00			$100.00		$700.00
		$1,459.99			$262.36	$2,531.67
$40.00	$40.00	$40.00	$40.00	$40.00	$40.00	$480.00
$200.00	$200.00	$200.00	$200.00	$200.00	$200.00	$2,400.00
$25.00	$25.00	$25.00	$25.00	$25.00	$25.00	$300.00
$92.82	$93.75	$94.68	$95.63	$96.59	$97.55	$1,108.95
$5.71	$4.78	$3.85	$2.90	$1.94	$0.98	$73.41
$388.53	**$388.53**	**$2,023.52**	**$388.53**	**$488.53**	**$650.89**	**$9,553.03**
$5,480.78	$5,986.48	$3,570.94	$4,001.80	$4,052.87	$4,260.36	$11,1384.30
$1,205.77	$1,317.02	$785.61	$880.40	$891.63	$916.06	$8,040.00
$4,275.01	$4,669.45	$2,785.33	$3,121.40	$3,161.24	$3,344.30	
$2,811.47	$1,711.47	($1,098.51)	$1,216.47	$931.47	$1,099.11	

EMPLOYMENT HISTORY

Phyllis Farmington

March 1991 to present, Dayton Art Glass, Dayton, Ohio

Working as an assistant to my husband while developing my own business. Duties include sales, client contact work, and assisting in the design of stained glass windows.

Sept. 1988 to March 1991, Photography House, Dayton, Ohio

Photo retouch artist and manager of in-house Art Department. In control of supplies and inventory, final inspection of all outgoing work, quality control, and training of new Art Department personnel. Retained by Photography House on a freelance, subcontract basis as an artist and trainer.

Sept. 1987 to Sept. 1988, CBI Photo Lab, Dayton, Ohio

Photo retouch artist and manager of in-house Art Department. Control of supplies and inventory, inspection, and quality control.

June 1985 to Sept. 1987, Wellington Studio, Chicago, Illinois

Assisted my mother in a family owned and operated photography studio. Duties included sales, public relations, pricing of goods and services, photography, and general office work. Also, hired and trained new photographers and scheduled photography sessions.

Bed and Breakfast Company

FINANCIAL PLAN AND MARKETING STRATEGY   FANTASY BED AND BREAKFAST

510 Old Town Rd.
Petoskey, MI 49770

A strong and complete vision for the renovation of an existing bed and breakfast is described in this plan with special attention given to area competitors. An outline for an aggressive marketing campaign, thorough market analysis, and detailed financial projections show proof of the entrepreneur's competence and dedication, aiding in the apparent feasibility of the idea.

- EXECUTIVE SUMMARY

- COMPANY DESCRIPTION

- MARKETING

- OPERATIONS PLAN

- FINANCIALS

EXECUTIVE SUMMARY

At the heart of our company is a commitment to providing a quality bed and breakfast experience to all visitors in the Vermont area. With the availability of ski resorts in the winter, color tours in the fall and a spectacular season of fun and sun in the summer, Vermont is a year-round tourist destination for thousands of travelers and sightseers. Fantasy is to capitalize on that tourist traffic and focus on providing a popular stop for those exploring the region. This plan serves to illustrate the profit potential that can be obtained through the renovation of an existing structure that serves a specialty clientele. If done with flair and a sense of style, it is our belief that we can turn Fantasy into a reality.

COMPANY DESCRIPTION

Fantasy Bed and Breakfast is aiming to be one of the most exclusive and upscale establishments of its kind in the New England area. Located in the sprawling countryside near Marlboro, Vermont, Fantasy will take a solid hospitality approach to the bed and breakfast industry and carve out a specialty niche in the marketplace. The charm of Fantasy will come from its unique perspective in selling romance and escapism to a popular demographic pool of urban professionals in the New England area. The specifics of this plan are illustrated below.

Building Description

The structure selected for Fantasy is both prominent and visually striking. The building chosen for the project is a large, three level A-frame style structure that is fully coded and architecturally sound. This building was used one time as an antique store in the area and already comes fully equipped with plenty of New England charm. Each room selected is open, with no divisions made at the present time. The interior is currently done completely in knotty pine with open, split-level staircases. The top level has eight skylights with plenty of natural interior lighting. The building is built against a hill, so the second level has a complimentary walkout section in the back of the house.

Floor Planning

Lower Level: Includes front desk and lobby, a separate large country kitchen, one house-keeper suite with bathroom, and one generic guest suite which is fully handicapped accessible (in keeping with A.D.A. requirements). This level can also support a main storage room in addition to the water-heater / furnace room section.

Second Level: Includes six period theme-style guest suites (one of which is the multi-purpose generic suite), and three with their own private hot tubs located in separate courtyards.

Third Level: This floor serves as the dining room, lounge, and game room with juice bar. No alcohol will be served from the bar area to avoid concerns about liquor license liability; however, wine will be served with meals in the dining room and will be available for separate purchase in the gift shop section of the front lobby.

Lodging and Room Amenities

This bed and breakfast will specialize in unique theme-oriented rooms catering to specific parameters of decor and splendor. Architecturally, the building is capable of more than seven guest rooms in addition to the living space required by the operators; however, it is felt that in order to achieve the ambiance necessary for a premium experience, the rooms should be of a certain size and living capacity.

This bed and breakfast will be a true getaway. A place to escape hectic lifestyles of nearby commercial centers, and a place where fantasies and dreams can come true. Each of the following seven rooms will have a theme which is a trip back in time through a specific era, and comes complete with matching costumes and music. Each room will have a private bathroom area and modern hot tub amenities. Each room is also designed for a simulated gas operated fireplace, which will give each a distinctive look and a perceived value-added interior.

The rooms of Fantasy are as follows:

1. Great Northern Room:

Interior—Log cabin interior with knotty pine style wallboards, hardwood floors, field (gas) fireplace, and oak mantel.

Furniture—Handcrafted split-log bed, with split-log style window rods and bent vine settee. Amish quilt for bed along with matching scarves on window rods.

Wildlife pictures on walls and decor which further enhance the log cabin theme and setting.

Optional coordinating costumes—Lumberjack and flannel style, wilderness look.

2. Victorian Romance / Southern Plantation Room:

Interior—Soft colored walls with flowered border and hardwood floors with large central spiral style rugs. Colonial style mantel.

Furniture—Large cherrywood sleigh bed with matching dressers. Lace curtains and dry roses decorating window rods. Victorian style furniture with antique wash basin and stand.

Optional coordinating costumes—Southern plantation style. Antebellum dresses and formal menswear.

3. Nile Room:

Interior—Smooth stone wall facade with matching hieroglyphic style drawings. Lengthy curtains complementing an ancient Egyptian style look.

Furniture—Ornate gold and jeweled bed with veiled windows, fainting style couch, and Egyptian statues and wall hangings.

Optional coordinating costumes—Anthony and Cleopatra style costuming.

4. Seven Veils Room:

Interior—Standard walls with specific Middle Eastern color scheme. Sheer draped windows and matching sashes.

Furniture—Over-stuffed futon style mattress floorbed with a dozen large pillows and sheer veils surrounding bedroom area. Large Persian carpets and other Persian oriented furnishings.

Optional coordinating costumes—Aladdin and princess, King and harem girl, etc.

5. Renaissance Room:

Interior—Walls given a dark stone facade in order to simulate English castle style walls. Upon these walls hang decorative tapestries, coat-of-arms, and ornate candelabras.

Furniture—Centerpiece of room is a large covered bed made of oak and accentuated with sheer drapes. Over the large stone mantel would be crossed swords or maces. A full-length mirror and oak chest for guest storage would not be out of place. Rose petals would be spread on the bed in keeping with the customs of the time.

Optional coordinating costumes—Knight and Lady-in-waiting would be the predominant theme.

6. This room will be left generic so that it can be tailored for specific use.

7. This room will be left generic so that it can be tailored for specific use.

Fine Dining

Dining at Fantasy will be an experience, not simply an amenity. The kitchen will be supervised by an experienced chef who has already formed a working relationship with the owner and will consult on specific menu ideas and item preparation. Specialty menu items will include: wildflower pound cake, baked blueberries, brandied apple tarts, shrimp Creole, artichoke quiche, three cheese baked eggs, and other traditional fare. These menu items do not include any theme-oriented fare prepared specifically for a particular guest suite.

General Information

Fantasy will have a total guest capacity of seven rooms, double occupancy. Each room will have a private bathroom with indoor or outdoor Jacuzzi. The lower level room will be wheelchair accessible and smoking will be allowed in courtyard rooms only. No children or pets will be allowed under normal circumstances. The full breakfast will be included as part of the lodging cost; however, other meals will need to be purchased separately. Fantasy will be open year round and all major credit cards will be accepted.

Local Attractions

All of these attractions are located within a ten-mile radius of Fantasy:

Antique Shops	Canoe Rentals	Local Taverns
Beaches	Fishing	Mountain Climbing
Bike Rental	Golf	Restaurants
Bike Trails	Horseback Riding	Shopping
Boat Rentals	Hunting	Skiing

Note: Reciprocal agreements will be in place with most of these local attractions to cross advertise and feature package deals and specials. Please see marketing section for further details about reciprocal licensing agreements.

Pricing

Room rates for Fantasy:
    $150.00 per night (Mon. through Thurs.)
    $220.00 per night (Fri. through Sun.)
    Holidays and special events priced separately.

Additional Revenue

Additional revenues from such sales as the gift shop section, homemade jams and jellies, crafts, and specialty wines are included in these estimates as additional revenue.

Average Occupancy

For purposes of this business plan, an average room rate of five rooms (booked per night) will be used unless otherwise noted.

MARKETING

Service

Service and ambiance at Fantasy will set us apart from the competition. We need to be a destination, not simply a place to stay. Solid marketing will help us accomplish that goal. Our customer expects quality service and will judge our service with a fairly high level of expectation. The bed and breakfast industry in general is fueled by word of mouth, and repeat business is the lifeblood of any business in the hospitality sector. We intend to live up to that reputation and have developed several creative-marketing ideas to enhance a successful start-up. Networking and referrals will be the key but, initially, there simply will be aggressive marketing. The owner has experience and knowledge in marketing and the ideas outlined below are not only feasible, they can be accomplished with comparatively little effort using resources already at her disposal:

Initial Marketing Campaign

1. Local media will be invited to cover the grand opening and opening will be a media event.

2. Pre-made press releases and sample stories will be provided to local media outlets.

3. Selected celebrities will be given free stays on a limited basis to help generate word-of-mouth.

4. Cross advertising will be performed with other local attractions to enhance regional awareness.

5. Traditional mass mailings will be made through local mailing distributors.

6. Traditional cable (better value than television) and radio spots will be purchased in limited numbers.

7. Heavy Internet presence will be prepared and site selected by various search engines.

8. Telemarketing campaign to advertising agencies in the region will be performed prior to opening.

9. Selected travel-writers and travel agents will be given free stays on a limited basis to aid referrals.

10. Bookings will be aided by connecting with tourist and convention bureau, brochure distribution programs.

11. A specific market plan will be developed for the Bed and Breakfast channel.

12. An affiliation with the Professional Association of Innkeepers will be promoted.

13. The Bed and Breakfast Premium online confirmation system will be used to secure reservations.

14. The Directory of Holiday Accommodations will list our establishment.

15. A listing will be obtained with the Vermont Bed and Breakfast locator service.

Customer Profile

The ideal customer that Fantasy is targeting will be upscale urban professionals who scour the countryside on weekend antique excursions and are looking for various destination places in the New England area. It is a proven market that has existed since the turn of the century and is expected to accelerate well into the next century and beyond. The trend is for the blossoming in the industry to continue at an unprecedented level of expansion. With this in mind, we would like to address some of the key trends in the industry.

Key Strengths

Fantasy sells romance, a rather hot commodity in today's marketplace. With a strong location and an experienced owner, a bed and breakfast can truly be a profitable and enjoyable venture. Fantasy sells an excellent service, one that is highly desired yet hard to obtain. This bed and breakfast will be developed in an area that has strong ties to the bed and breakfast industry and one that is located in a market that is currently experiencing a growth rate in excess of 30%. For these reasons, Fantasy is expected to become profitable within its first year of business.

Economics

According to American Business Information (ABI), an industry tracking firm based in Omaha, growth in the bed and breakfast industry is up 33.1% nationwide. ABI actually tracks growth of the industry through national yellow page advertisements placed on an annual basis. ABI estimates that the average annual occupancy rate for all bed and breakfasts is 65% with an average annual booking increase of 3-5%. A 1998 survey found that while bed and breakfasts with less than four rooms were not profitable, overall, establishments with four or more rooms were at a break-even point in regards to profitability. This same survey also found that, in the industry, seven rooms is roughly the national average for building capacity, if the larger (20 plus rooms) inns were not counted. With an average of seven rooms, and if an establishment was not found to be absentee-owner (this factor decreases profitability considerably), the average profit estimate nationwide was found to be 8% per annum.

Tax Treatment

This establishment would fall under IRS section 280A and possibly section 262. It is prudent to note that depreciation can only be taken for rooms rented and not those shared with the guests.

Competition and Area Comparison

There are only four direct competitors in the immediate district:

Peep-Willow Farm
3 guest rooms
No private bath
$35-55 per night
Not a premium establishment and not considered a direct competitor.

Wright Masion Inn
6 guest rooms
4 with private baths
$115-190 per night
A premium competitor without the amenities of Fantasy.

Post & Bean Bed and Breakfast
6 guest rooms
2 with private baths
$55-85 per night
Not a premium establishment but favorable pricing.

Squires Inn Bed and Breakfast
5 guest rooms
5 private baths
$70-80 per night
Solid competitor and favorable pricing.

Even though there is limited competition in the area (which also goes to show that the area is destination driven), none of these competitors are truly direct because they lack a thematic orientation. Several competitors can compete on price alone; however, the customer who will consider the Squires Inn is not our target customer. Our customer wants an experience, not simply a place to stay, which is the key difference separating Fantasy from the competition.

Strategy

The strategy of Fantasy is to position itself as a unique experience among the competition in the area and a cut above anything the competition might have to offer. This exclusivity and charm will be promoted as a stand-alone principle that will appeal to our target demographic. This will ensure that our average annual occupancy rate is obtained quickly and increased incrementally over time.

OPERATIONS PLAN

Personnel

This will not be an absentee-owner operation. The owner plans to be directly involved in all key aspects of decision making and day-to-day operations of Fantasy. There will be no off-site control of the operation which would tend to minimize profits (as noted previously) and minimize service. With that in mind, however, there will be a small need for peripheral personnel to help maintain the facility. Since the owner plans to perform most of the meal service operation herself, with assistance from a well-known chef and a minimal kitchen staff, costs will be controlled in this phase of operation, which has the largest variable cost control environment. In addition, the owner will also be able to directly supervise the front desk functions and night auditor functions to a limited degree. In addition to herself, the owner plans to hire a full-time room cleaning person, a full-time kitchen assistant, and one to two part-time maintenance / handyman type positions. The total personnel requirement will be less than five employees at all time.

Credit Policies

All major credit cards will be accepted and merchant agreements are already in place.

Legal Environment

Zoning approval from the township is easily obtainable and the climate is favorable for economic development in the region. This specific piece of property has already been zoned commercial (prior use: antique store) so there are no zoning problems anticipated. Other licensing is also readily obtainable and there are no perceived regulatory obstacles that would tend to inhibit development.

Exclusive Licensing

An agreement has been formed to make Leelanau Cellars Winery the exclusive wine merchant of Fantasy. This agreement will allow for a reduced price on all wines obtained and will most likely lead to a reciprocal marketing agreement with the company.

Management

Linda Mark will be the owner and operator of Fantasy Bed and Breakfast. Her experience includes small business management and accounting oversight for other small businesses. In addition, her direct hospitality management experience comes from over seven years as a director for a twenty person adult foster care facility involving large-scale oversight in a heavily regulated environment. Linda currently co-owns and operates an entertainment company which generates revenues in excess of thirty thousand dollars a month. A separate detailed financial statement will be presented in the attachments section.

FINANCIALS

Startup Expenses and Capital Outlay Projection

Purchase of house and property (secured):	$140,000
Rewiring and coding	8,000
Plumbing rework	10,000
Carpentry	20,000
Subtotal (sec.)	$178,000

Remodeling:

Great Northern Room	$8,500
Victorian Romance Room	9,500
Nile Room	8,500
Seven Veils Room	7,500
Renaissance Room	10,000
2 Multi-purpose suites	8,000
Kitchen	5,000
Kitchen equipment	9,000
Laundry (twin commercial W & D)	5,000
Misc. carpet, tile and vinyl	20,000
Subtotal (unsec.)	$91,000

Furniture & Fixtures

Dinette sets	$8,000
Pool table	2,500
Electric dart / pinball	6,000
Game room furniture & TV	3,000
Specialty lighting	2,000
Sound system	3,000
Suite hot tubs	21,000
Suite televisions	4,000
Suite phones	1,000
Suite room misc.	5,000
Subtotal (unsec.)	$55,000

Office & Misc.

Reservation tracking computer	$3,000
Landscaping & plowing	9,000
Linen / towels / bedding	5,000
Utensils	1,000
Glasses	2,000
Dishes	2,000
Office fax / copy / etc.	2,000

Parking lot expansion	12,000
Decking	4,000
Other misc.	6,000
Subtotal (unsec.)	$46,000
Total secured outlay	178,000
Total unsecured outlay	192,000
Total capital reserve	30,000
Total loan request (all sources)	$400,000

Pro Forma Balance Sheet

Assets		Liabilities	
Current Assets		Current Liabilities	
Cash	$30,000	Accounts payable	$0
Petty cash	$1,400	Notes payable	$8,000
Accounts receivable	$0	Interest payable	$0
Food Inventory	$2,300	Taxes payable	$0
Short-term investment	$500	Sales tax	$0
Long-term investment	$1,500	Payroll accrual	$0
Fixed assets		Long-term notes	$400,000
Land	$10,000	**Total liabilities**	$408,000
Buildings	$168,000	**NET WORTH (owner equity)**	
Improvements	$91,000	Proprietorship equity	$5,700
Equipment	$35,000	Partnership equity	$0
Fixtures	$20,000	Capital stock	$0
Automobile	$8,000	Surplus paid (earnings)	$0
Other assets	$46,000	Total net worth	$5,700
Total assets **Total net worth**	$413,700	**Total liabilities &**	$413,700

Profit and Loss Projection 12 Months

Expenses	Jan	Feb	Mar	Apr	May	Jun	Jul	Aug
Mortgage	850	850	850	850	850	850	850	850
Utilities	300	300	300	300	300	300	300	300
Phone	200	200	200	200	200	200	200	200
Advertising	150	150	150	150	150	150	150	150
Insurance	300	300	300	300	300	300	300	300
Leasing	0	0	0	0	0	0	0	0
Payroll	1,500	1,500	1,500	1,500	1,500	1,500	1,500	1,500
Dep. Exp.	0	0	0	0	0	0	0	0
Operation	250	250	250	250	250	250	250	250
Advertising	400	400	400	400	400	400	400	400
Food	1,600	1,600	1,600	1,600	1,600	1,600	1,600	1,600
Loan pay	3,500	3,500	3,500	3,500	3,500	3,500	3,500	3,500
Subscript	50	50	50	50	50	50	50	50
Fees	100	100	100	100	100	100	100	100
Misc.	100	100	100	100	100	100	100	100
TOTAL	9,300	9,300	9,300	9,300	9,300	9,300	9,300	9,300
Revenue								
Lodging	25,900	25,900	25,900	25,900	25,900	25,900	25,900	25,900
Dining	2,200	2,200	2,200	2,200	2,200	2,200	2,200	2,200
Misc.	100	100	100	100	100	100	100	100
Total Rev.	28,200	28,200	28,200	28,200	28,200	28,200	28,200	28,200

Profit

Note: These figures are based on a five room per night average at $185.00 per night. A break-even analysis shows that a two room per night average would suffice.

Sep	Oct	Nov	Dec	Total Exp.
850	850	850	850	10,200
300	300	300	300	3,600
200	200	200	200	2,400
150	150	150	150	1,800
300	300	300	300	3,600
0	0	0	0	0
1,500	1,500	1,500	1,500	18,000
0	0	0	0	0
250	250	250	250	3,000
400	400	400	400	4,800
1,600	1,600	1,600	1,600	19,200
3,500	3,500	3,500	3,500	42,000
50	50	50	50	600
100	100	100	100	1,200
100	100	100	100	1,200
9,300	9,300	9,300	9,300	111,600
25,900	25,900	25,900	25,900	310,800
2,200	2,200	2,200	2,200	26,400
100	100	100	100	1,200
28,200	28,200	28,200	28,200	338,400

Gross Pre-tax Profit   226,800
(rev - exp)

Bridal Salon

BUSINESS PLAN

MEGAN'S BRIDAL BOUTIQUE

4596 S. Huppard Dr.
Green Bay, WI 54303

This business plan for the establishment of a bridal boutique does an excellent job of assessing area competition. The detailed analysis of both the strengths and weaknesses of rival businesses effectively illustrates the need for a high quality and reasonably priced bridal salon in the region. It is also apparent that this entrepreneur is aware of fashion trends and receptive to customers' needs.

- GENERAL BUSINESS DESCRIPTION

- INVENTORY DESCRIPTION, ANALYSIS, AND STRATEGY

- PROMOTION PLAN

- FUTURE PLANS

- RESUME

- START-UP EXPENSES

- PROJECTED STATEMENT OF SALES AND EXPENSES

**GENERAL
BUSINESS
DESCRIPTION**

Megan's Bridal Boutique will be a full-service bridal salon and dress shop catering to the Wisconsin customer who is searching for reasonable quality products at affordable prices.

The inventory will consist of wedding gowns, bridesmaid dresses, headpieces, crinolines, jewelry, shoes, party dresses, more casual dresses, and tuxedo rentals.

I will run the business myself full-time and hire sales assistance as well as a bridal alterations specialist. The store has the potential of employing up to six full-time employees, estimating a minimum of three to start. The hours will be 10:00 a.m. to 5:00 p.m. Monday through Saturday, with evening appointments available for brides and their parties. All daily bookkeeping will be done by me. An accountant will take care of the necessary month-end work.

Megan's Bridal Boutique will be located on Hubbard Drive. I'm currently negotiating a lease on a very nice property of 1725 square feet. The rent on the space is only $435 per month plus approximately $250 per month for utilities. This is a good price, compared to other less desirable locations I've looked into. I plan to invest $5,000 in building renovations to meet the special needs of a bridal salon. The renovations will be free-standing and can be taken with me to another location if need be.

Megan's Bridal Boutique will open in mid to late October.

**INVENTORY
DESCRIPTION,
ANALYSIS, AND
STRATEGY**

Line: Bridal

Description: This line will consist of re-orderable wedding gowns, re-orderable headpieces, dyeable satin shoes, crinolines, re-orderable bridesmaid gowns, and jewelry. Megan's Bridal Boutique will carry 60 wedding gown samples featuring three manufacturer's lines (20 pieces at $200 wholesale, 20 at $300, 20 at $400, for a total start-up cost of $18,000). Three brands of bridesmaid gowns will also be carried with 12 samples per brand offered (36 pieces at $100 wholesale for a total start-up cost of $3,600). One headpiece line will be made available with 15 samples in the store (at a median price of $50 per piece wholesale for a start-up cost of $750). These items will be special order only items. A full range of sizes of basic dyeable shoes, in three heel heights, will be available in the store for off-the-rack purchase (30 pair of each style at $12 each wholesale for a start-up cost of $1,080). A catalog of other styles will complete the offering. Megan's Bridal Boutique will also carry full-length crinolines of all sizes, for purchase only (20 pieces at $15 each wholesale for a start-up cost of $300). Crinolines will be available free of charge for use in the dressing rooms for clients purchasing wedding or bridesmaid gowns or needing them for in-store alterations. In addition, a line of off-the-shelf jewelry will be carried and special order jewelry catalogs will be available (30 pair of earrings and 30 necklaces at $15 each wholesale for a start-up cost of $900).

Position of Marketplace: The items in the bridal line will consist of basic styles in the low to mid-price range appealing to the Wisconsin client. Megan's Bridal Boutique will develop a reputation for dependable service, fair pricing, and reliability.

Client Demographics: Some women will travel all over the state, or farther, to shop for their wedding gowns. The majority of Megan's Bridal Boutique's clients will be limited to the areas surrounding Green Bay. Nine out of 10 women eventually marry although, in general, they are waiting later in life to marry for the first time. Remarriages account for half the weddings taking place nationally. Sixty percent of couples currently living together will eventually get married. What all this means is, although one would think the economy, general trends, and changes in society would have a great impact on marriages, there has been only a 1.5% change in marriage rates over the past 27 years. Where the economy does have a big impact on weddings seems to be generally limited to reception and honeymoon expenses, with a lesser effect on the dollar amount spent on wedding gowns and accessories themselves (*Vows,* June/July 1996 issue). According to a recent published study, eight marriages took place per 1000 residents per year. Based on the surrounding area of eastern Wisconsin, Megan's Bridal Boutique will draw from, one can count on 1,888 weddings per year. Each of these couples will spend, on the average, $852.00 for a wedding dress, $167.00 on a headpiece, and $50.00 for shoes. Estimating four attendants per wedding, spending $175 each on dresses and shoes, an additional $1,321,600 can be added. Added together, there are $3,339,872 dollars to be captured in this line alone, per year, in eastern Wisconsin.

Pricing Strategy: To meet the needs of the eastern Wisconsin client, all of Megan's Bridal Boutique's offerings will be in the low to mid price range. Specifically:

Wedding Gowns: $350.00-$800.00
Headpieces: $25.00-$40.00
Bridesmaid Dresses: $100.00-$150.00

Cost: $24,630 start-up inventory cost.

Competition

I have broken down the competition, product line by product line, following each line's inventory description. The overall competition for the bridal line can be broken down into two: local shops (Mary Ann's) and regional shops. I feel the threat created by Mary Ann's can be easily overcome through good service, great selection, and affordable pricing. The competition created by the out-of-town shops will be harder to address. Details of how I will deal with each follow the competition descriptions.

1. Local Competition

Mary Ann's Bridal Salon
Oshkosh, Wisconsin

Weaknesses: Mary Ann's Bridal Salon is a very poorly run retail outlet featuring old and outdated stock off the rack. Most merchandise is sold "as is." This shop experiences almost no repeat business and is generally thought of as the last place to go for bridal and prom needs.

Strengths: Mary Ann's has been in business for 40 years (although there have been three different owners). Old warehoused stock originally priced at $500.00 to $1000.00 is bought from other shops and sold at attractive prices of $350.00 to $500.00.

Overcoming Local Competition

Service: Megan's Bridal Boutique will be a cleaner, more attractively designed store offering a variety of guaranteed services at reasonable prices, or in some cases, free services. For example, Mary Ann's charges $8.00 to dye shoes purchased in the store and $15.00 to dye shoes purchased elsewhere. A dye job takes about five minutes. I will dye my shoes for free and charge $5.00 to dye shoes purchased elsewhere.

Although Mary Ann's provides skilled seamstresses for the alterations, pricing is set by the owner on a per dress basis. A client may be told at the time of purchase her alterations will cost $25.00, only to discover upon picking up the dress that the charge is $50.00. Worse yet, many clients are never told there is a charge at all. Megan's Bridal Boutique will have a published list of charges provided at the time a purchase decision is being made. There will be no surprises, and the client will know exactly how much to budget for her total expenses.

Mary Ann's also has a problem getting special orders in the store in a timely manner. All special orders are delivered COD and often the cash is not available, resulting in returns and re-orders. Many suppliers will not deliver until prior problems are reconciled, again resulting in delays. I have found most suppliers have liberal terms and are very willing to work with new accounts. It is only after payment problems occur, and are not resolved, that these shipping problems take place. Megan's Bridal Boutique will be able to get special orders in the store and to the client in a more timely manner by establishing and maintaining good terms with all suppliers.

Pricing: Mary Ann's's pricing has always been high. The idea on management's part has been to price everything high, then offer a "special deal." Megan's Bridal Boutique's pricing will be more modest and clients will know they can find value everyday. I will accomplish this by working with the lower-priced suppliers while maintaining healthy profit margins. The question of course is, why doesn't Mary Ann's do this already? The following scenario will provide an explanation: Mary Ann's used to buy shoes from Supplier A for $12, marking them up to $25. After numerous payment problems, Supplier A refused to deal further with Mary Ann's. Next, Mary Ann's found Supplier B who wholesaled the same shoe for $15. Mary Ann's maintained the selling price of $25 resulting in profit erosion. After the same payment problems occurred with Supplier B, Mary Ann's moved onto Supplier C which charged $17 for the same shoe. This time the cost was passed onto the customer. The shoes are now priced at $33 plus $8 for dyeing. Of course sales have dropped off significantly. This is just one specific example. The same type of thing has happened with dozens of other suppliers covering all lines offered by Mary Ann's. I have already established contact with the "Supplier A" types and will be offering these lower priced, good quality lines.

Stock: Mary Ann's's stock is old and outdated. In fact, I am asked several times per week if Mary Ann's is a used clothing store (these inquiries were made to me while I was an employee there). Megan's Bridal Boutique's stock will be fresh and new. As stock ages, it will be discounted. If still not sold, it will be taken off the rack and stored, until sidewalk sales, and then the price will be drastically slashed. Anything left after that will be donated to charity or destroyed.

2. Regional Competition

Appleton Bridals
Appleton, Wisconsin

Weaknesses: Poor management makes shopping at Appleton Bridals a difficult experience. Customers are treated as a bother instead of as an opportunity. Because of the location, most area people assume the prices are considerably higher in general. Actually, their pricing structure is about the same as other shops in the area and they carry the same lines.

Strengths: Location. Appleton Bridals can draw very easily from Green Bay and Oshkosh because of the proximity. Clients from all over eastern Wisconsin will travel to this shop based on the location alone. The town of Appleton has an excellent reputation for being a place to shop for variety and most people will expect Appleton Bridals to be a well run establishment with good selection, but with higher prices. Megan's Bridal Boutique's reputation for good prices and excellent service, as well as a regional advertising plan, will draw many clients away from this shop.

White Bird Bridal
Manitowoc, Wisconsin

Weaknesses: Poor sales techniques, lackluster stock, and ugly displays explain why people will travel all over Wisconsin to shop for their bridal needs instead of spending their money at White Bird. The general atmosphere in this shop would be fine for a discount store or a warehouse, but not for a shop which sells women's clothing for special occasions. The pricing structure is similar to other bridal shops and offers no real advantage for clients.

Strengths: The Apple Blossom is also a flower shop specializing in bridal arrangements. The advantage to this is increased traffic, but it also adds to the junky atmosphere. The Apple Blossom also spends a considerable amount of money on TV advertising during the prom season.

> CJ's Bridal Shop
> Fond du Lac, Wisconsin

Weaknesses: This store is very difficult to shop in due to the way the dresses are literally packed into one place. I found it hard to pull even one dress out to examine and the poor lighting made it even more difficult to see what I had my hands on. The prices were average and the displays nonexistent. It was a chore to even get around the place.

Strengths: They carried almost every line available and the sales staff was quite helpful. Although they do no advertising in this area, many potential clients from eastern Wisconsin will delay their purchasing decision until they have made the trip down to Fond du Lac, not only for wedding dresses, but even more so for prom dresses.

> Sarah's Bridals
> Cheboygan, Wisconsin

Weaknesses: Sarah's owner recently moved to this smaller facility from a large and beautiful location. She is suffering from burnout and has cut back considerably on her inventory. She no longer has the commitment or interest in her business she once had.

Strengths: This is a well-run attractive shop with standard pricing and good service.

Other Shops to Be Explored:

> I Do Bridals, Green Bay, Wisconsin
> Bridal Fashions, Milwaukee, Wisconsin
> Bridals on the Bay, Milwaukee, Wisconsin

Meeting the Regional Competition

Advertising: Most of my ad dollars will be spent on small awareness-generating, space ads in nonlocal newspapers. Money will also be spent on listings in the surrounding areas, including Milwaukee's Yellow Pages and phone guides. Some radio ads will be placed during the grand opening weeks. In addition, different promotions will take place throughout the year.

Line: Party Dresses and Other Dresses

Description: A variety of party and less formal dresses will be offered. These dresses will appeal to the client who wants to go all out for that special occasion such as the prom, New Year's Eve, cruises, plus off-the-rack dresses for work or formal occasions will be available. The dresses will be strictly off-the-rack ranging in sizes 3-24 with the emphasis on sizes 10-18.

Position in Marketplace: Green Bay offers little to the public in the way of dresses. The few women's shops currently open in town offer only a handful of casual dress styles to choose from. The majority of dress purchases made by women in Green Bay are made out of town, usually during day, or weekend-long shopping trips. Those who do not plan ahead, and find themselves in need of a lastminute outfit, are simply out of luck. Megan's Bridal Boutique will be filling a need in the community by offering a wide selection of dresses at a good price. No longer will having to "dress up" automatically mean an out-of-town shopping trip. By keeping Green Bay women in town for their dress purchases, other monies often spent on these trips will also remain in Green Bay. In addition, regional shoppers will be brought in spending their money not only at Megan's Bridal Boutique, but in other area retail establishments and restaurants as well.

Client Demographics: Women, age 16-50, will travel regionally to shop for these types of dresses. The party dresses will appeal to the younger age of this market segment in general, other lines appealing of the mid to upper age range. There will be considerable crossover depending on the type of event the client is planning.

Pricing Strategy: Prices will be in the low to mid range to appeal to the Wisconsin client who does not want to spend a lot on a dress she may wear only a few times at the most. These dresses will range in price from $75.00-$150.00.

Cost: Start-up cost for this line will be $12,000.00 (200 dresses at $60 per dress).

Competition: There are no other dress shops in the immediate area. Several retail outlets in Green Bay offer a few dresses to choose from, and only a very limited selection is available.

Weaknesses: Very limited selection available. A person dress shopping in Green Bay can see all there is to see in five minutes at local dress shops since they carry only a handful of dresses which are of low quality or overpriced (respectively).

Strengths: There are basically no competitor strengths in this category.

Line: Tuxedos

Description: One full-service line will be offered which will include a variety of tuxedos (tails, double-breasted, shawl, and notch collar, as well as the popular Western style), shirts, shoes, ties, cumberbuns, and vests. Clients will be able to customize their choices with a wide variety of color-coordinating accessories. Tuxedos offer the opportunity to bring in thousands of dollars worth of business per month, while taking up only a few square feet of selling space.

Client Demographics: The majority of clients for this line will not be the actual decision makers. The decision makers will be the party dates and brides who will pick out the tuxedos she wants to accessorize her outfit. The draw will be limited to Green Bay and the immediate area.

Pricing Strategy: Prices will be at industry suggested retail pricing of $65.00 to $95.00 for the complete outfit.

Cost: The cost to carry this line will be limited to try-on jackets at $1,000 for a selection of 10.

Competition:

Smith's Apparel
Green Bay, Wisconsin

Weaknesses: Smith's only edge over the competition in this case is purely by taking advantage of the opportunity to sell to someone who is already in a decision-making state of mind. While the client is making the wedding gown purchase, she is ripe for additional sales such as tuxedos.

Once enough trust has been established for her to spend several hundred dollars on a gown, the hardest part of the sale is already complete and add-ons will be relatively easy. In addition, the floor space and initial investment needed to carry tuxedos is so small, it would be foolish not to carry the line.

Strengths: This store will be tough to compete with for several reasons. For one, it's a store carrying men's clothing and, in general, men will feel more comfortable walking into this shop than a dress shop. The reputation and prices are also very good.

Almost every month the business will feature a special event or some type of sale. Window and store front displays will promote the event, as well as a few small local space ads and more frequent non-local space ads. For a real big event, radio will be used to strengthen the promotion. Listed below is an event calendar for the first year. Each promotion will be evaluated and the following year's plan will be based on the successes of prior events. Each year several new ideas will be tried as well. **PROMOTION PLAN**

Month	Event
October	Grand Opening Host First BPW Meeting of the year
November	Fall Dress Promotion Host Business After Hours Party
December	Early Bird 1998 Promotion New Year's Dress Sale
January	Post Christmas Engagement Promotion Early Tux Registration Promotion
February	Early Tux Registration Promotion
March	Early Tux Registration Promotion Prom Tux Sale
April	Prom Tux Sale Prom Dress Sale (First Week of the Month)
May, June, July	No special promotions needed for these three busy Bridal months, just awareness advertising
August	Summer Sidewalk Sales
September	Homecoming Dress Promotion

In general, the product line, offerings, service, and pricing strategy will remain the same for the first two years, with the following expectations: **FUTURE PLANS**

- After a year of doing business, some samples will be old and no longer re-orderable. These items will be significantly discounted and sold off the rack as is.
- All lines will be expanded to offer more choices, and slow moving stock will be moved from the re-orderable section to the sale rack.
- The stock will be honed to increase profitability. Research will be conducted to determine what is selling best, most profitable price points, etc.

Client surveys will be conducted. After a wedding, brides will be contacted and asked about the quality of the service, product, and selection. This information will be used to improve the shop and help me determine where to increase my efforts.

At the end of the third year, I plan to purchase my own building and expand the business to offer a larger selection. At this time, the number of employees will be at least six full-time.

RESUME

Megan Martin

HIGHLIGHTS OF QUALIFICATIONS

- Nine years experience in multiple-media marketing.
- Five years management experience in Chicago firms, running each product line as an independent entity. Additional two years in management at manufacturing facility.
- Extremely well organized and self motivating.
- Committed to producing results above and beyond what is expected, through good management of resources and sound decision-making abilities.
- Works very well with people and is generally liked by clients and co-workers alike.
- Two years experience as executive administrator to the president at Chicago Paper Company, wearing many hats including human resources manager, collections manager, and public relations coordinator.

RELEVANT EXPERIENCE

Marketing
- Set sales records for 75% of product lines which fell within responsibility at Burton Engineering.
- Developed new markets for multiple product lines.
- Proven successful at new product research and development.
- Product manager for one company's flagship line, increasing sales by 25% while reducing expenses by 30% over two years.
- Coordinated all marketing and logistic efforts for 110 educational seminars per year (Burton).
- Originated and implemented new marketing strategies which bolstered sales of aging product line.
- Designed, coordinated, produced, and distributed the company's four 64-page catalogs per year at Burton.
- Successfully sold and distributed $6,000.00 worth of technical training programs through direct mail marketing techniques.

Management
- Five years of success in marketing management.
- Two years management in manufacturing environment.
- Completely implemented new 401K program with 94% sign-up rate.
- Developed, implemented, and continue to manage collections program for multi-million dollar manufacturing facility.
- Run anti-union campaign.
- Created, implemented, and continue to manage review system for production employees.
- Proven success as skilled, multi-faceted, and valuable employee (increased salary from $13,520 to $41,100 in two years).

- Developed and implemented effective cost-cutting measures which streamlined operations and improved productivity.
- Represented the organization at company-sponsored conferences throughout the United States and acted as the Italian liaison.
- Coordinated and supervised multiple interdepartmental products.
- Responsible for marketing department's strategic planning and implementation including all facets of annual budget management.
- Developed ideas for creating new business throughout the company.
- Prioritized work projects within the department: designed and implemented follow-up procedures which resulted in more efficient and profitable workflow.
- Interviewed and hired top-notch marketing and administrative staff.
- Currently responsible for all aspects of hiring at every level at Chicago Paper Company.

EMPLOYMENT HISTORY

1995-Current	Executive Administrator and Human Resources Manager	Chicago Paper Company Green Bay, Wisconsin
1994-1995*	Retail Salesperson	Mary Ann's Bridal Salon Oshkosh, Wisconsin
1993-1994*	Owner	Greystone Antiques Lighting Restoration Milwaukee, Wisconsin
1992-1993	Manager	Polk Publishing Detroit, Wisconsin
1985-1992	Sr. Marketing Manager Marketing Division	Burton Engineering Toledo, Ohio
	Marketing Administrator Conferencing Division	
	Assistant Marketing Administrator Membership Division	

Concurrent

RELEVANT EDUCATION

Bachelor of Science, Business Administration and Marketing
Chicago University—1983

Daytimer Time Management Techniques Seminar—1992

Dale Carnegie Sales Course—1993

Franklin Management Program—1994

Successful Negotiations-Wisconsin State University—1995

Successful Supervisor Techniques-Fred Pryor Seminars—1997

OTHER

Public Relations Director
Green Bay Business and Professional Women's Club

Past Member
Green Bay Public Library Millage Committee

Member
Green Bay Chamber of Commerce Ambassadors Club

**START-UP
EXPENSES**

STOCK

Bridesmaid dress samples	$ 3,600
Cocktail dresses	12,000
Crinolines	300
Headpieces samples	750
Jewelry	900
Shoes	1,080
Tuxedo Try-On Jackets	1,000
Wedding Dress Samples	18,000
Misc.	1000
Total Starting Stock/Samples $38,630	

OFFICE

Adding Machine	70
Calculator	10
Chairs (2-Used)	85
Computer (3,000 Value-Personal)	0
Copier (Used)	500
Desk (Used)	100
Filing Cabinet (4 Drawer-Used)	50
Misc. Supplies	500
Total Office Set-Up	**1,315**

SHOP

Business Cards	35
Cash Drawer Start-Up	300
Bags	400
Chairs and Settee	2,500
Coffee Maker/Supplies	70
Credit Card Terminal	250
Crinolines for Alterations	120
Dye Set-Up	300
Filing Cabinet (2-Drawer)	100
Forms/Contracts	300
Hangers	125
Iron	100
Mannequins (4)	350
Misc.	300

Rolodex	25
Sewing Machine	
(500 Value-Personal)	0
Shelving/Racks	600
Signage	300
Sissors	25
Stationery	250
Steamer	150
Stereo	360
Telephones (2, one w/machine)	200
Telephone Installation	120
Vacuum (200 Value-Personal)	0
Window Display Fixtures	500
Decorating and Construction	5,000
Contingencies	3,000
First Month Rent/Deposit	870
Total Shop Set-Up	16,650
Working Capital	5,000
Total Start-Up Cost	**$61,595**

August 4, 1997

Mr. Victor Case
Executive Vice-President
Wisconsin BIDCO, Inc.
P.O. Box 170
Milwaukee, WI 00000

Dear Mr. Case:

Attached, please find the information we discussed in our meeting last week, specifically the cash flow analysis, statement of income and expenses for three years, personal financial statement, and balance sheet for my proposed business, Megan's Bridal Boutique.

I am requesting a loan in the amount of $65,000.00 to cover start-up inventory, office and shop expenses, and $5,000.00 working capital for my shop. The business will be wholly owned by me as an individual proprietorship and I plan to run it myself, with the help of one full-time assistant, who will also do the alterations. When the shop is fully established (approximately 3-5 years), it could employ up to six full-time employees at various skill levels.

I have access to $5,000.00 cash and my mother is willing to give me property, valued at approximately $35,000.00 to use as collateral. I also have $3,700.00 in equipment.

I would like to discuss this proposal further with you, prior to your board meeting next week. I can be reached at 616-628-1234. As we discussed, this project must remain confidential as I would have to leave Chicago Paper Company to pursue my dream of owning my own business. I wouldn't want to jeopardize the wonderful relationship I have with my boss if this project fails to get off the ground.

Thank you for your time and consideration in this matter.

Sincerely,
Megan Martin

Asset Equipment | Packard Bell Pack-Mate 3500 CD   Est. Value: $3,000.00
Computer and Deskjet 682C
Hewlett Packard Printer

Kenmore Sewing Machine $500.00

Hoover Elite Vacuum Cleaner $200.00

This page left intentionally blank to accommodate tabular material following.

**Cash Flow/
Requirement
Analysis**

1997 Start-Up	Oct	Nov	Dec	Jan	Feb	March	April
Beginning Cash	5,000	5,892	9,624	6,196	7,048	9,900	10,752
Cash Inflows							
Collection of A/R		2,640	5,280	7,260	7,260	7,260	7,920
Other Income/Sales	8,000	8,000	6,000	8,000	8,000	8,000	10,000
Total Cash Inflow	8,000	10,640	11,280	15,260	15,260	15,260	17,920
Cash Outflows							
Accts. Payable	0.0	0.0	8,000	8,000	6,000	8,000	8,000
Past Due: Accts. Payable							
Operating Expenses	5,319	5,119	4,919	4,619	4,619	4,619	5,119
Taxes	589	589	589	589	589	589	589
Other Expenses							
Total Cash Outflow	5,908	5,708	13,508	13,208	11,208	13,208	13,708
Cash Position	7,092	10,824	7,396	8,248	11,100	11,952	14,964
Short-Term Loan							
Long-Term Loan	1,200	1,200	1,200	1,200	1,200	1,200	1,200
Ending Cash	**5,892**	**9,624**	**6,196**	**7,048**	**9,900**	**10,752**	**13,764**

May	June	July	Aug	Sep
13,764	18,236	21,368	25,160	28,952
8,580	9,240	9,900	9,900	9,900
10,000	10,000	10,000	10,000	8,000
18,580	19,240	19,900	19,900	17,900
8,000	10,000	10,000	10,000	10,000
4,319	4,319	4,319	4,319	4,819
589	589	589	589	589
12,908	14,908	14,908	14,908	15,408
19,436	22,568	26,360	30,152	31,444
1,200	1,200	1,200	1,200	1,200
18,236	**21,368**	**25,160**	**28,952**	**30,244**

**Statement of
Income and
Expense—Year One**

	Oct	Nov	Dec	Jan	Feb
Net Sales	16,000	16,000	12,000	16,000	16,000
Cost of Goods Sold	*50% of net sales*	*50% of net sales*	*50% of net sales*	*50% of net sales*	*50% of net sales*
Gross Margin	8,000	8,000	6,000	8,000	8,000
Expenses					
Salaries	3,000	3,000	3,000	3,000	3,000
Advertising Expenses	800	800	600	300	300
Business Insurance	59	59	59	59	59
Telephone	170	170	170	170	170
Membership/ Subscriptions	200	0	0	0	0
Rent/Utilities	700	700	700	700	700
Accountant	140	140	140	140	140
Travel, Entertainment, Gifts	100	100	100	100	100
Misc. Expenses	100	100	100	100	100
Donations	50	50	50	50	50
Total Operating Expenses	5,319	5,119	4,919	4,619	4,619
Net Operating Profit	2,681	2,881	1,081	3,381	3,381

(Before Taxes and Loan Payment)

March	April	May	June	July	Aug	Sep	1st Year End
16,000	20,000	20,000	20,000	20,000	20,000	16,000	208,000
50% of net sales	*50% of net sales*	*50% of net sales*	*50% of net sales*	*50% of net sales*	*50% of net sales*	*50% of net sales*	
8,000	10,000	10,000	10,000	10,000	10,000	8,000	104,000
3,000	3,000	3,000	3,000	3,000	3,000	3,000	36,000
300	300	0	0	0	0	300	3,700
59	59	59	59	59	59	59	708
170	170	170	170	170	170	170	2,040
0	0	0	0	0	0	200	400
700	700	700	700	700	700	700	8,400
140	140	140	140	140	140	140	1,680
100	600	100	100	100	100	100	1,700
100	100	100	100	100	100	100	1,200
50	50	50	50	50	50	50	600
4,619	5,119	4,319	4,319	4,319	4,319	4,819	56,428
3,381	4,881	5,681	5,681	5,681	5,122	3,266	47,098

Statement of Income and Expenses—Year Two

	Oct	Nov	Dec	Jan	Feb
Net Sales	18,400	18,400	13,800	18,400	18,400
Cost of Goods Sold	*50% of net sales*	*50% of net sales*	*50% of net sales*	*50% of net sales*	*50% of net sales*
Gross Margin	9,200	9,200	6,900	9,200	9,200
Expenses					
Salaries	4,000	4,000	4,000	4,000	4,000
Advertising Expenses	800	800	600	300	300
Business Insurance	59	59	59	59	59
Telephone	170	170	170	170	170
Membership/ Subscriptions	200	0	0	0	0
Rent/Utilities	700	700	700	700	700
Accountant	140	140	140	140	140
Travel, Entertainment, Gifts	200	200	200	200	200
Misc. Expenses	100	100	100	100	100
Donations	100	100	100	100	100
Total Operating Expenses	6,469	6,269	6,069	5,769	5,769
Net Operating Profit (Before Taxes and Loan Payment)	2,731	2,931	831	3,431	3,431

March	April	May	June	July	Aug	Sep	1st Year End
18,400	23,000	23,000	23,000	23,000	23,000	18,400	239,200
50% of net sales	*50% of net sales*	*50% of net sales*	*50% of net sales*	*50% of net sales*	*50% of net sales*	*50% of net sales*	
9,200	11,500	11,500	11,500	11,500	11,500	9,200	119,600
4,000	4,000	4,000	4,000	4,000	4,000	4,000	48,000
300	300	0	0	0	0	300	3,700
59	59	59	59	59	59	59	708
170	170	170	170	170	170	170	2,040
0	0	0	0	0	0	0	200
700	700	700	700	700	700	700	8,400
140	140	140	140	140	140	140	1,680
200	700	200	200	200	200	200	2,900
100	100	100	100	100	100	100	1,200
100	100	100	100	100	100	100	1,200
5,769	6,269	5,469	5,469	5,469	5,469	5,769	70,028
3,431	5,231	6,031	6,031	6,031	6,031	3,431	49,572

Statement of Income and Expenses—Year Three

	Oct	Nov	Dec	Jan	Feb
Net Sales	21,160	21,160	15,870	21,160	21,160
Cost of Goods Sold	*50% of net sales*	*50% of net sales*	*50% of net sales*	*50% of net sales*	*50% of net sales*
Gross Margin	10,580	10,580	7,935	10,580	10,580
Expenses					
Salaries	5,000	5,000	5,000	5,000	5,000
Advertising Expenses	800	800	600	300	300
Business Insurance	70	70	70	70	70
Telephone	200	200	200	200	200
Membership/ Subscriptions	200	0	0	0	0
Rent/Utilities	700	700	700	700	700
Accountant	140	140	140	140	140
Travel, Entertainment, Gifts	200	200	200	200	200
Misc. Expenses	150	150	150	150	150
Donations	150	150	150	150	150
Total Operating Expenses	7,610	7,410	7,210	6,910	6,910
Net Operating Profit (Before Taxes and Loan Payment)	2,970	3,170	725	3,670	3,670

March	April	May	June	July	Aug	Sep	1st Year End
21,160	26,450	26,450	26,450	26,450	26,450	21,160	275,080
50% of net sales	*50% of net sales*	*50% of net sales*	*50% of net sales*	*50% of net sales*	*50% of net sales*	*50% of net sales*	
10,580	13,225	13,225	13,225	12,335	13,225	10,580	136,650
5,000	5,000	5,000	5,000	5,000	5,000	5,000	60,000
300	300	0	0	0	0	300	3,700
70	70	70	70	70	70	70	840
200	200	200	200	200	200	200	2,400
0	0	0	0	0	0	0	200
700	700	700	700	700	700	700	8,400
140	140	140	140	140	140	140	1,680
200	800	200	200	200	200	200	3,000
150	150	150	150	150	150	150	1,800
150	150	150	150	150	150	150	1,800
6,910	7,510	6,610	6,610	6,610	6,610	6,910	83,820
3,670	5,715	6,615	6,615	5,725	6,615	3,670	52,830

Caribbean Cafe

BUSINESS PLAN

CALYPSO CAFE

1002 Pelican St.
Fort Wayne, IN 47711

This business plan for an ethnic restaurant is highlighted by an exhaustive financial analysis, complete with monthly projections. The fine attention to number specifics indicates an understanding of all the details that go into running a business. Furthermore, stressing the owner's personal financial investment underscores his commitment to success.

INTRODUCTION

This business plan is for Calypso Cafe, owned and operated by Josh Benson. It will be a multicultural restaurant which will serve clients desiring Jamaican and American foods. Calypso Cafe seeks to meet the needs of the varied and growing ethnicity of the greater Fort Wayne area by being the first to offer authentic Jamaican foods. Food from this restaurant will be prepared primarily from fresh food products.

This restaurant will seek to create a Caribbean atmosphere. International music and culture will be incorporated into the restaurant through paintings, murals, and West Indian reggae music.

The restaurant's location is in the south central district of Fort Wayne. The restaurant's size of 1200 square feet will consist of the cooking area with refrigerator and freezer, counter eating area, dining area, waiting area for takeout food, and restroom.

Planned financing for the restaurant is initially directed toward personal savings and the Micro-Loan Program, with later reinvestment of earnings. Calypso Cafe needs $15,000 to begin business. Plans are to borrow $10,000 from the Micro-Loan Program and $5,000 of the owner's savings. The money will be used to buy and lease equipment, pay rent, pay employees, pay product vendors, and meet various other expenses. Planned schedule for repayment of this loan is in the amount of $1,000 per month including interest. The management expects to repay all of the loan within two years of the loan date.

There will be three full-time employees and the owner: a cashier, two cooks, and the owner/manager. Management plans to adopt a "just in time inventory system" to avoid unnecessary refrigeration and excess stock. To effectively and efficiently manage the inventory, there will be an independent buyer for the restaurant.

SELF-ANALYSIS

The owner's previous experience in restaurant management has led to his desire of wanting to own and manage a restaurant. Currently, he operates his own catering service, J&A Catering and Entertainment Corporation. He services special events and plans to incorporate this business into the new restaurant, Calypso Cafe. His work with Burger Boy Restaurant in Fort Wayne, Indiana, was so successful and profitable that he was introduced to the idea of owning his own restaurant. His higher scores of evaluation and good standing with Burger Boy earned him an opportunity to create some menus for the restaurant. He has worked for Burger Boy from 1992-1996. His responsibilities include line cook and kitchen management. His goal is to own and operate a restaurant where he can utilize his professional skills and proven experience.

Josh Benson's experience and skills in restaurant business go back as far as 1981. From 1991-1992, he served as a cook at Burger King Restaurant in Fort Wayne, Indiana. From 1990-1991, he worked as a cook for Popeye's, Fort Wayne, Indiana. In 1990, Josh held two jobs as a waiter at Cyprus Inn and My Place Restaurant in Fort Wayne, Indiana. In 1989, he was the manager and social director for Bella's Resort in Kingston Harbor, Jamaica. At Bella's he was responsible for managing the bar and planning special events for the guests of the resort. Josh has also experienced an extraordinary activity during his years of professional service. From 1986 to 1988, while working at Blue Waters Resort in Kingston Harbor, he overcame Hurricane Gilbert by using his leadership skills and positive sense of direction to manage tourists during the disaster. He was able to take charge of the situation and control panic. From 1981-1985, while working as a fine dining waiter at Wonder Island Hotel in Kingston Harbor, Jamaica, Josh also attended school. After graduating from high school in 1981, he got his Certificate in Catering from Kingston Harbor Catering School.

Josh's strengths include the ability to work long hours, use creative problem-solving skills, lead with a positive sense of direction, and give constructive criticism when necessary. His weakness is the tendency for impatience. He is willing to take risks such as when he relocated to the United States.

Josh has also had other areas of interest before his career pursuit. He was awarded high honors for best performance in the Jamaican Combined Cadet Force for two consecutive years, while he was serving as a Corporal. He also played in the town band. While in high school, Josh was very involved with the track team.

Josh is a family oriented individual. He is married and has children. He has lived in the Fort Wayne area for six years.

In pursuit of his dream to become a successful entrepreneur, Josh is prepared to take a calculated risk. He has strong confidence in himself as a businessman and is determined to set clear, attainable, and challenging goals.

Josh Benson

RESUME

OBJECTIVE

Seeking to use my professional experience and proven skills in cooking. I desire a position which offers opportunity for personal and professional growth.

EXPERIENCE

Present: Cook at Falcon's Restaurant, Fort Wayne, IN

1992-1996: Line Cook and Kitchen Manager at Burger Boy Restaurant, Fort Wayne, IN

1991-1992: Cook at Burger King Restaurant, Fort Wayne, IN

1990-1991: Cook at Popeye's, Fort Wayne, IN

1990: Waiter at Cyprus Inn, Fort Wayne, IN

1990: Waiter at My Place Restaurant, Fort Wayne, IN

1989: Bartender for the Bella's Resort in Kingston Harbor, Jamaica—Responsible for management of the bar, social direction of visitors, and planning of special events

1986-1988: Waiter in fine dining at Blue Waters Resort, Kingston Harbor, Jamaica— Overcame Hurricane Gilbert and managed tourists during the disaster, entertained during Staff Concert Night

1981-1985: Waiter in fine dining at the Wonder Island Hotel, Kingston Harbor, Jamaica

EDUCATION

1983: Certificate in Catering from Kingston Harbor Catering School

1981: Diploma from Kingston Harbor High School

ADDITIONAL INFORMATION

High Honors: Jamaican Combined Cadet Force—Corporal, played in the Town Band, winning an award for best performance in 1984 and 1985, track team in 1978.

PERSONAL

Married, have resided in Fort Wayne for 6 years, good health, commended for being a very congenial person

MARKET SURVEY

The city of Fort Wayne is one of the largest in Indiana, with a population of approximately 175,000. The proposed business location for Calypso Cafe has a population concentration of approximately 76,000 that may be served by this restaurant. The average area income is $25,129 per household. The median effective buying income per household is $27,744. The effective buying power by group is 53% with households of $18,000 and over. The target age group is 18 to 64. The median age of population is 31 with ages 18 to 24 being 13.8%, age 25 to 24 being 15%, age 35-44 being 15.6%, and ages 45 and older being 27.9%.

Young people are more prone to assimilation. They are more aware of changes that occur in their society as compared to the elderly. Youth prefer to get firsthand experience of something new, most especially when changes are taking place within their surroundings.

A major part of this market survey has been conducted using data for social events such as Jamaican Reggae festivals, African-American festivals, and other cultural events. It has been proven that the majority of people at these events relate their fun in terms of what kind of food and music they enjoy. These events create memories to be shared with friends and family, the significant connection of people, music, and food unique to a culture. Through Josh's recognition by others, for the food he has prepared and served at such gatherings, and by the request of many community members to open a Jamaican restaurant, he has been inspired to pursue this dream.

Josh has already established a market audience for the proposed restaurant. Recently, there have been many people who have come to him inquiring about such a restaurant in the vicinity. He has discovered that an increasing number of people go to a restaurant not necessarily because they are hungry, but because of the desire to experience a new or particular taste.

Josh is confident that this restaurant will be successful to generate big sales and profit. The nearest competition for this kind of restaurant is in Chicago, keeping competition for Jamaican cuisine at a minimum. The proposed business district for this restaurant has already been established and is growing fast. With the opening of a large sports arena nearby, business is growing in Fort Wayne's inner city and surrounding area. The percentage change for the population in 1980-1990 was 1.6%, resulting in an approximated population of 76,000, and a projected requirement for fast food restaurants in the area to average about 15%. Therefore, it is possible to meet the projected sale of $200,000.

MARKETING PLAN

The indirect competition and advantages of Calypso Cafe over other fast food restaurants in the area are as follows:

McDonald's Restaurant serves a good breakfast and is famous for its Egg McMuffin and coffee. They do not use seasoning in their food. They use a regular broiler to cook their burgers and lard grease to fry. This type of cooking is undesirable to many customers and a big disadvantage to their business.

Burger King offers their customers high quality service and a family oriented atmosphere. Food is expensive and generally unhealthy.

Pizza Hut is an alternative food restaurant. It does not offer breakfast and has a limited menu.

Kentucky Fried Chicken does too much deep frying. This is not healthy for customers. Also, a long wait in line is commonplace.

Calypso Cafe is planned to provide meals that will take the customer on a culinary adventure. It is evident that natural food is more nutritious and healthy for the body, and Calypso Cafe plans to provide this healthy menu. The restaurant will prepare mostly fresh food products, using only a minor and unavoidable portion of frozen food products.

The Calypso Cafe menu has been created quite differently from the customary American menu. Though food items may be similar to American foods, the special spices, ingredients, and methods of preparation will provide a unique flavor unmatched by any other. The menu has been created by the finest Jamaican cook. He sincerely hopes that customers will enjoy the entrees.

The marketing plan for this restaurant is designed to incorporate the customer as a share benefactor in the profitability of this business. The goal and profitability of this restaurant will be attained through the guarantee of customer satisfaction. There is provision for additional menu items. Customer suggestions and evaluations will be considered.

Calypso Cafe expects to build an enormously successful restaurant through emphasis on product and service. Quality work produces more than just a steady income, it leads to an endless stream of referrals, more business, and higher profits.

New competitors pose a threat to related and existing businesses, however Calypso Cafe policies will constitute a strategy that will be oriented toward creating the highest quality image possible—fresh, high quality food products, provided with outstanding service.

The impact of social and economic concerns in the community play a vital role in the success of a business. In turn, Calypso Cafe will strive to contribute to the community through charities, participation in anti-drug programs, and employment of area residents.

Advertising media for Calypso Cafe will be via radio, newspaper, telephone directory, direct mail coupons, and customer referrals.

Menu

DAILY

All burgers served with cheddar cheese...

Jamaica Bacon Burger	$4.50
with fries	
Jamaica Turkey Burger	$5.00
with fries	
Jamaica Ham Burger	$4.95
with fries	
Jamaica Chicken Burger	$4.50
with fries	
Jamaica Garden Burger	$4.75
with fries	
Jamaica Mushroom Burger	$4.25
with fries	
Jamaica Seasoned Chicken	$4.85
Breast Sandwich with fries	
Jamaica Jerk Chicken	$5.00
Breast Sandwich with fries	

JAMAICA SOUP OF THE DAY

Monday - Vegetable beef   Cup $1.00
Tuesday - Vegetable chicken   Bowl $1.50
Wednesday - Vegetable seafood
Thursday - Vegetable pork
Friday - Vegetable shrimp
Saturday - Jamaka Manaswat

BREAKFAST

All omelettes and eggs served with Jamaica style hashbrowns....
All omelettes are health smart and cooked with secret Jamaican seasonings....

Jamaica ham omelette	$4.25
Jamaica Chicken omelette	$4.00
Jamaica seafood omelette	$6.00
Jamaica steak omelette	$5.00
Jamaica vegetable omelette	$3.75

KID'S MENU

Corn Dog with fries	$1.50
Hamburger with fries	$1.75
Cheeseburger with fries	$2.00
Chicken Nuggets with fries	$2.25

BEVERAGES

Coffee or Tea	$1.00
Jamaican Blue Mountain Coffee	$2.00
Soda - Coke, Diet Coke, Cherry Coke, Sprite, Orange	$1.00

2 eggs cooked to order with wheat or rye toast served with sausage and bacon
$3.00

DAILY DINNER SPECIALS

Monday
Jamaica Curried Chicken $6.95

Tuesday
Jamaica Jerk Chicken $7.50

Wednesday
Jamaica Jerk Baby Back Ribs $8.00

Thursday
Jamaica Fish Dinner $9.85

Friday
Jamaica Jerk Pork $8.50

Saturday
Jamaica Curried Goat $9.00

All dinners served with Jamaica fried dumplings
and seasoned rice or mixed vegetables....

SALADS

Jamaica Chicken Salad $3.25

Jamaica Sea Breeze Beef Salad $4.00

DAILY DINNER SPECIALS

LOCATION SITE ANALYSIS

The restaurant will be located in one of the popular zoning business areas of south central Fort Wayne. There is direct access from the expressway. Also, there is easy access from other smaller connecting streets. There are three fast-food restaurants and a donut shop within the two block radius of the proposed business site. This area was chosen as it is a successful business area. Through its history, the district has expended and attracted new businesses.

PROPOSED PROFIT

Josh will set goals that are consistent with his interests, values, and talents. His belief in the ability to achieve his goals is needed to succeed.

The desired profit by the end of the year, decided before opening, is $3,480. Through continuous planning, profits are to be increased every year by 30 to 50 percent after the first year. While expecting to make money, the main motivation is not wealth, but to do something extremely well. Recognizing that money is an important factor in running a business, Josh has decided not to use profits as a route to wealth, but as an indicator of the success of the business.

On the average, U.S. companies make about 5% net income. Calypso Cafe must make enough profit to provide continuous growth through reinvestment. There must be a profit after all normal business expenses have been accounted for, including fair wages for the owner.

SOURCE OF FINANCING

Calypso Cafe will be financed initially through combined savings of the owner, his friends and family, public offering, the Micro-Loan program (Small Business Administration), commercial banks, trade credit, and credit extended by equipment vendors.

The owner's drawing account is not expected to be active until the restaurant is fully established or after three years of successful operation. Earnings will be reinvested and the owner will be an employee when collecting his wages. This step ensures that debts incurred by the restaurant are paid for within the shortest possible time to help other businesses on the waiting list to secure loans.

Before the bank failures of the 1980s, capital funds were readily available to small business people and prospective entrepreneurs. The Clinton administration's economic reform and small business incentives has made more money available today than at any time in recent history. This is due mostly from consumer savings in liquid investments. The SBA received a new influx of funds, however, the demands are high because of the growing economy. Small business owners appreciate the efforts of the Urban League to offer opportunities and programs for small business loans. With respect to this, Josh Benson has high hopes that his business operations will commence in the shortest possible time.

TYPE OF OWNERSHIP

Calypso Cafe will be a sole proprietor ownership so that it can be content with the limited start-up capital. The owner's plan for instantaneous growth of this business is to reinvest earnings. Reinvestment will be the backbone of this business after start-up. Reinvestment will also ensure a smooth transition of its incorporation in the future. In the initial stages, this business can not exist independent of its owner. However, the most important legal aspect of the sole proprietor type of ownership is its unlimited liability stature. Personal assets of the business owner can be seized to settle claims against the business. The owner in this case takes over all the operation aspects of the business and makes decisions as he pleases. The characteristics of a small business establishment make it more comfortable and compelling to organize in this manner. Josh Benson intends for the attorney of the business to act as a consultant on business decisions that are legally connected, since the attorney presumably has the expertise necessary to handle the legal records of the business.

The management of employees in the service industry involves several interrelated personnel activities: recruitment, selection, training, compensation, and supervision. The goals of this process are to obtain, develop, and retrain employees.

Calypso Cafe will employ between two or three people in the future. Recruitment of retail personnel will be done through sources of potential employees from educational institution, employment agencies, employee recommendations, and from within the business when it expands.

Compensation would include direct monetary payments and as the business progressed, some indirect payments will be paid to full-time employees. Because this is a small business, personnel will be paid a comfortable wage and possible bonuses. Total compensation would be fair to both the employees and the business. In the event of a difficult situation, the business banker, lawyer, insurance agent, and accountant would be consulted.

The manager would be responsible for organizing money, pricing, handling produce, equipment, and people resources. The manager will also arrange the organizational environment so that employees can achieve their own goals by directing their efforts toward business objectives.

Employees will be responsible to give friendly, courteous, helpful, and honest service at all times. The Calypso Cafe image will be built around the special services offered.

HUMAN RESOURCE MANAGEMENT

Since the Calypso Cafe will be in its introductory stages, purchases will be paid for in cash and check only. In the future, Visa, Mastercard, Discover, and American Express will be accepted. In the future, charge accounts will also apply to contract agreements for food services at organized functions.

Credit policy requires the establishment of the major policy variables within which accounts receivable will be managed. These variables include deciding to whom credit should be extended, the length of time allowed for payment of invoices, and whether discounts will be offered for prompt payment. It is also possible to use accounts receivable as collateral for a short-term loan. It is even possible, under an arrangement known as factoring, to sell accounts receivable as a discount to a commercial bank or a commercial factor. This type of arrangement relieves the business of needing to make additional credit policy decisions. Once the policy factoring is established, the factor will dictate credit terms.

The final working capital policy issue deals with the establishment of an account payable payment policy. Suppliers commonly offer discounts on accounts payable to induce prompt payment by customer. There are two major concerns in establishing a business' payment policy. The first concern is cost and availability of money. The cost of missing the discount can be translated easily into an approximate annual percentage rate of interest: the shorter the lending period, the higher the cost of missed discounts. Once the discount is missed, payments should be delayed until the latest allowable payment date. As a general rule, a business should not make an early payment after the discount is missed, or if there is no discount. The second major concern involves establishing an accounts payable payment policy and its impact on the business' credit rating. Calypso Cafe will pay their payable promptly and take discounts even though the discounts are not particularly attractive strictly on a cost basis. This is done because a record of prompt payment enhances the credit reputation of the business' future access to and cost of external financing.

CREDIT POLICY

Attaining dreams requires new behavior, and new behavior involves taking risks. Lenders need assurance that a person is committed to their dream. The owner of Calypso Cafe will be

RISK MANAGEMENT

risking some of his personal money and assets, reputation, and time. There is total commitment to this dream. From the perspective of a lender or investor, financing a new business always carries more risk than lending to or investing in an established enterprise. Many uncertainties vanish as the business establishes a track record. Most businesses take three years to generate enough ongoing income for a living wage. During those three years, personal living expenses, as well as equity capital for the business must come from the owner. Calypso Cafe has planned to reserve business earnings to eliminate hardship, including guarding against property damages, liabilities to employees and customers, and in the event of the owner's death. To prevent bad debts, cash only will be used for purchases. The store will have hidden cameras to protect employees, clients, and the property. The manager and other employees will be trained to spot criminals, and verification will be made on all payments made with checks.

Management must also consider the risk that the business must assume in its business affairs. Economic theory and common sense both argue that a dollar of risky profit is less valuable than a dollar of certain profit. The two general categories of risk management must contend with business risk and financial risk, business risk being risk imposed by the business and economic environment. Financial risk is risk imposed by the manner in which the firm is financed. There are no set rules of regulation that will guarantee success.

FINANCIAL INFORMATION

The following personal information is relevant as of October 31, 1996.

ASSETS

Bank Accounts
    Checking $ 500
    Savings   5,000
Automobile   16,000
Real Estate   78,000

Total assets   99,500

LIABILITIES

Payable
    Charge   300
Mortgage payable   75,000
Account (auto)   9,145

Total liabilities   84,445

    NET WORTH $15,055

Bank: Fort Wayne Teachers' Credit Union

Lawyer: Pending

Accountant: Pending

Start-Up Costs

#	ITEM	COST	HAVE IT?
	RENT/MO	$ 800	-
8	TABLES	312	No
32	CHAIRS	960	No
1	LARGE FREEZER	1,450	No
1	LARGE COOLER	1,400	No
1	FRENCH FRYER/WARMER	175	No
1	HEAVY DUTY SCALE	49	No
1	SANDWICH WORKTOP UNDER COUNTER UNIT	1,195	No
1	GRILL	1,000	No
1	LARGE FRYER	1,000	No
2	FOOD WARMERS	250	Yes
1 case	FOOD WARMER CARTRIDGES	20	Yes
6	LARGE TONGS	36	Yes
5	LARGE SPOONS	85	Yes
6	SOUP SERVERS	31	Yes
5	KITCHEN KNIVES	100	No
5	SPATULAS	30	Yes
2	CUTTING BOARDS	35	No
4	BXS (100/BX) PLASTIC PLATES	25	Yes
4	BXS (100/BX) PLASTIC KNIVES	25	Yes
4	BXS (100/BX) PLASTIC FORKS	25	Yes
4	BXS (100/BX) PLASTIC SPOONS	25	Yes
1	BX (500/BX) DRINKING CUPS	10	No
1	BX (250/BX) HOT/COLD CUPS	10	No
10	SALT SHAKERS	50	No
10	PEPPER SHAKERS	50	No
10	SUGAR HOLDERS	75	No
2	LARGE COFFEE MACHINES	100	No
12	WHITE BIB APRONS	35	No
30	4 GL PLASTIC CONTAINER W/LID	226	Yes
2	GARBAGE CANS	60	No

TOTAL DOLLARS $ 9,644

Opening Day Balance Sheet as of 10/31/96

ASSETS

CURRENT ASSETS

Paid Equipment	$4,538.00
Prepaid Expenses	2,400.00
Supplies	35.00
Total Current Assets	**6,973.00**

FIXED ASSETS

Furniture & Fixtures	4,122.00
Food Prep Equipment	3,905.00
Total Fixed Assets	**8,027.00**

OTHER ASSETS

Total Other Assets	0.00
Total Assets	**15,000.00**

CURRENT LIABILITIES

Current Liabilities	0.00

LONG TERM LIABILITIES

Notes payable—Noncurrent	10,000.00
Total Long Term Liability	10,000.00
Total Liabilities	**10,000.00**

EQUITY

Owner's Contribution	5,000.00
Current Earnings	0.00
Total Equity	**5,000.00**

TOTAL LIABILITY & EQUITY	**$15,000.00**

ASSETS

CURRENT ASSETS

Regular Checking Account	$5,348.00
Payroll Checking Account	1,596.08
Special Account	62.50-
Cash on Hand	300.00
Prepaid Expenses	1,600.00
Petty Cash	65.00
Supplies	35.00
Total Current Assets	**8,881.58**

FIXED ASSETS

Furniture & Fixtures	4,122.00
Food Prep Equipment	4,405.00
Total Fixed Assets	**8,527.00**

OTHER ASSETS

Total Other Assets	0.00
Total Assets	**17,408.58**

LIABILITES & EQUITY

CURRENT LIABILITIES

Total Current Liabilities	0.00

LONG TERM LIABILITIES

Notes Payable—Noncurrent	9,000.00
Total Long Term Liability	9,000.00
Total Liabilities	**9,000.00**

EQUITY

Owner's Contribution	5,000.00
Current Earnings	3,408.58
Total Equity	8,408.00
Total Liabilities & Equity	**$17,408.58**

**Projected Balance
Sheet as of 12/31/97**

ASSETS

CURRENT ASSETS

Regular Checking Account	$14,817.80
Payroll Checking Account	2,145.12
Special Account	972.50-
Petty Cash	90.00
Cash on Hand	630.00
Inventory	1,500.00-
Prepaid Expenses	4,400.00
Supplies	35.00
Total Current Assets	**19,645.42**

FIXED ASSETS

Furniture & Fixtures	6,183.00
Food Prep Equipment	8,505.00
Trucks & Automobiles	8,000.00
Accum Deprec-Furn & Fix	883.00-
Accum Deprec-Food Prp Eqt	1,215.00-
Accum Deprec-Trucks/Autos	1,600.00-
Total Fixed Assets	**18,990.00**

OTHER ASSETS

Total Other Assets	0.00
Total Assets	**38,635.42**

LIABILITIES & EQUITY

CURRENT LIABILITIES

Current Prt—Long Term Dbt	1,300.00
Credit Card Payable,	1,400.00
Total Current Liabilities	**2,700.00**

LONG TERM LIABILITIES

Notes Payable—Noncurrent	11,100.00
Total Long Term Liability	11,100.00
Total Liabilities	**13,800.00**

EQUITY

Owner's Contribution	5,000.00
Beginning Capital	8,880.46
Current Earnings	10,954.96
Total Equity	24,835.42
Total Liability & Equity	**$38,635.42**

ASSETS

CURRENT ASSETS

Regular Checking Account	$42,698.87
Payroll Checking Account	4,298.08
Special Account	1,667.50-
Petty Cash	90.00
Cash on Hand	515.00
Inventory	500.00
Prepaid Expenses	2,800.00
Supplies	35.00
Total Current Assets	**49,269.45**

FIXED ASSETS

Furniture & Fixtures	6,183.00
Food Prep Equipment	8,505.00
Trucks & Automobiles	8,000.00
Accum Deprec-Furn & Fix	1,766.00-
Accum Deprec-Food Prp Eqt	2,430.00-
Accum Deprec-Trucks/Autos	3,200.00-
Total Fixed Assets	**15,292.00**

OTHER ASSETS

Total Other Assets	0.00
Total Assets	**64,561.45**

CURRENT LIABILITIES

Current Prt—Long Term Debt	1,300.00
Credit Card Payable	700.00
Total Current Liabilities	**2,000.00**

LONG TERM LIABILITIES

Notes Payable—Noncurrent	7,500.00
Total Long Term Liability	7,500.00
Total Liabilities	**9,500.00**

EQUITY

Owner's Contribution	5,000.00
Beginning Capital	19,835.42
Current Earnings	30,226.03
Total Equity	55,061.41
Total Liability & Equity	**$64,561.43**

**First Month
Operation Income
Statement for the
Month Ending
11/30/96**

CURRENT PERIOD RATIO: NET REVENUE
YTD RATIO: NET REVENUE

	THIS MONTH	RATIO	11 MONTHS	RATIO
INCOME				
Sales #1	15,000.00	100.0	15,178.00	100.0
Net Income	15,000.00	100.0	15,178.00	100.0
COST OF GOODS SOLD				
Cost of Goods Sold #1	1,150.00	7.7	1,150.00	7.0
Total Cost of Goods Sold	1,150.00	7.7	1,150.00	7.0
Gross Profit	**13,850.00**	**92.3**	**14,028.00**	**92.0**
EXPENSES				
Accounting	750.00	5.0	750.00	5.0
Insurance	300.00	2.0	300.00	2.0
Legal	100.00	0.7	100.00	0.0
Maintenance & Repairs	220.00	1.5	280.00	2.0
Office Supplies	80.00	0.5	80.00	0.0
Advertising & Promotion	500.00	3.3	500.00	3.0
Bank Charges	80.00	0.5	80.00	0.0
Interest	250.00	1.7	250.00	1.0
Licenses	150.00	1.0	150.00	1.0
Postage	20.00	0.1	20.00	0.0
Rent-Office	800.00	5.3	800.00	5.0
Telephone	150.00	1.0	150.00	1.0
Disposables	0.00	0.0	118.00	0.0
Utilities	265.00	1.8	265.00	1.0
Dues & Subscriptions	150.00	1.0	150.00	1.0
Employee Meals	62.50	0.4	62.50	0.0
Entertainment	45.00	0.3	45.00	0.0
Cash Over & Short	15.00	0.1	15.00	0.0
Sales Taxes	900.00	6.0	900.00	5.0
Wages Expense	3,923.36	26.2	3,923.36	25.0
Federal Withholding	744.00	5.0	744.00	5.0
State Withholding	228.16	1.5	228.16	1.5
City Withholding	64.48	0.4	64.48	0.0
FICA	307.52	2.1	307.52	2.0
Medicare	71.92	0.5	71.92	0.0
FUTA	39.68	0.3	39.68	0.0
SUTA	24.80	0.2	24.80	0.0
Other Expense	200.00	1.3	200.00	1.0
Total Expenses	10,441.42	69.6	10,619.42	70.0
Net Operation Income	3,408.58	22.7	3,408.58	22.0
Net Income	**3,408.58**	**22.7**	**3,408.58**	**22.0**

CURRENT PERIOD RATIO: NET REVENUE
YTD RATIO: NET REVENUE

	THIS MONTH	RATIO	12 MONTHS	RATIO
INCOME				
Sales #1	18,600.00	100.0	33,778.00	100.0
Net Income	18,600.00	100.0	33,778.00	100.0
COST OF GOODS SOLD				
Cost of Goods Sold #1	2,080.00	11.2	3,230.00	9.0
Total Cost of Goods Sold	2,080.00	11.2	3,230.00	9.0
Gross Profit	16,520.00	88.8	30,548.00	90.0
EXPENSES				
Accounting	750.00	4.0	1,500.00	4.0
Insurance	0.0	0.0	300.00	0.0
Legal	100.00	0.5	200.00	0.0
Maintenance & Repairs	0.0	0.0	280.00	0.0
Office Supplies	0.0	0.0	80.00	0.0
Advertising & Promotion	200.00	1.1	700.00	2.0
Bank Charges	80.00	0.4	160.00	0.0
Interest	250.00	1.3	500.00	1.0
Licenses	100.00	0.5	250.00	0.0
Postage	15.00	0.1	35.00	0.0
Rent-Office	800.00	4.3	1,600.00	4.0
Telephone	0.0	0.0	150.00	0.0
Disposables	0.0	0.0	118.00	0.0
Utilities	0.0	0.0	265.00	0.0
Dues & Subscriptions	50.00	0.3	200.00	0.0
Employee Meals	70.00	0.4	132.5	0.0
Entertainment	50.00	0.3	95.00	0.0
Cash Over & Short	5	0.0	20.00	0.0
Sales Taxes	1,116	6.0	2,016.00	6.0
Wages Expense	3,923.36	21.1	7,846.72	23.0
Federal Withholding	744.00	4.0	1,488.00	4.0
State Withholding	228.16	1.2	456.32	1.0
City Withholding	64.48	0.3	128.96	0.0
FICA	307.52	1.7	615.04	1.0
Medicare	71.92	0.4	143.84	0.0
FUTA	39.68	0.2	79.36	0.0
SUTA	24.8	0.1	49.6	0.0
Income Taxes	1,808.20	9.7	1,808.20	5.0
Other Expenses	250.00	1.3	450.00	1.0
Total Expenses	11,048.12	59.4	21,667.54	64.0
Net Operating Income	5,471.88	29.4	8,880.46	26.0
Net Income	**5,471.88**	**29.4**	**8,880.46**	**26.0**

Projected Income Statement for the Month Ending 12/31/97

YTD RATIO: NET REVENUE	12 MONTHS	RATIO
INCOME		
Sales #1	130,000.00	100.0
Net Income	130,000.00	100.0
COST OF GOODS SOLD		
Cost of Goods Sold #1	17,060.00	13.1
Total Cost of Goods Sold	17,060.00	13.1
Gross Profit	112,940.00	86.9
EXPENSES		
Auto Expenses	960.00	0.7
Accounting	9,000.00	6.9
Insurance	1,200.00	0.9
Legal	1,200.00	0.9
Maintenance & Repairs	220.00	0.2
Office Supplies	190.00	0.1
Advertising & Promotion	2,000.00	1.5
Bank Charges	360.00	0.3
Interest	3,000.00	2.3
Licenses	600.00	0.5
Postage	240.00	0.2
Deprec Exp-Furn & Fix	883.00	0.7
Deprec Exp-Food Prep Eqpt	1,215.00	0.9
Deprec Exp-Trucks/Autos	1,600.00	1.2
Rent-Office	9,600.00	7.4
Telephone	800.00	0.6
Disposables	1,200.00	0.9
Dues & Subscriptions	240.00	0.2
Travel	1,400.00	1.1
Employee Meals	840.00	0.6
Entertainment	350.00	0.3
Cash Over & Short	40.00	0.0
Wages Expense	47,080.32	36.2
Federal Withholding	8,928.00	6.9
State Withholding	2,737.92	2.1
City Withholding	773.76	0.6
FICA	3,690.24	2.8
Medicare	863.04	0.7
FUTA	476.16	0.4
SUTA	297.6	0.2
Total Expenses	101,985.04	78.5
Net Operating Income	**10,954.96**	**8.4**

YTD RATIO: NET REVENUE	12 MONTHS	RATIO
INCOME		
Sales #1	152,000.00	100.0
Net Income	152,000.00	100.0
COST OF GOODS SOLD		
Cost of Goods Sold #1	15,000.00	9.9
Total Cost of Goods Sold	15,000.00	9.9
Gross Profit	137,000.00	90.1
EXPENSES		
Auto Expenses	700.00	0.5
Accounting	9,000.00	5.9
Insurance	1,200.00	0.8
Legal	1,200.00	0.8
Maintenance & Repairs	96.00	0.1
Office Supplies	80.00	0.1
Advertising & Promotion	200.00	0.1
Bank Charges	960.00	0.6
Interest	2,500.00	1.6
Licenses	600.00	0.4
Postage	120.00	0.1
Deprec Exp-Furn & Fix	883.00	0.6
Deprec Exp-Food Prep Eqpt	1,215.00	0.8
Deprec Exp-Trucks/Autos	1,600.00	1.1
Rent-Office	9,600.00	6.3
Telephone	754.00	0.5
Disposables	1,008.93	0.7
Dues & Subscriptions	100.00	0.1
Travel	600.00	0.4
Employee Meals	695.00	0.5
Entertainment	200.00	0.1
Cash Over & Short	5.00-	0.0
Sales Taxes	7,800.00	5.1
Wages Expense	47,080.32	31.0
Federal Withholding	8,928.00	5.9
State Withholding	2,737.92	1.8
City Withholding	773.76	0.5
FICA	3,690.24	2.4
Medicare	863.04	0.6
FUTA	476.16	0.3
SUTA	297.60	0.2
Income Taxes	· 820.00	0.5
Total Expenses	106,773.97	70.2
Net Income	30,226.03	19.9

Projected Income Statement for the Month Ending 12/31/98

SUMMARY

Calypso Cafe is a planned multicultural restaurant. It will be one of a kind in the area with no direct competition. The owner, Josh Benson, has well established, practical experience in this business.

The market survey and strategy promise strong success of this business venture. The restaurant's menu reflects diversity and its operational intent.

Food from this restaurant will be prepared mainly with fresh food products. The restaurant's location is in a strategic area that will attract sales from targeted customers and shoppers in the area.

The form of ownership for this restaurant will be a sole proprietorship. The owner will be in charge of all business operations, including public relations. Initially, the owner will have three employees and an independent buyer working with him.

The owner plans to finance this restaurant through family savings and the Micro-Loan Program. He also plans to suspend the owner's drawing account in order to repay the loan amount including any associated interest within two years of the loan date. Further financing is intended to come from reinvestment of earnings.

The owner is confident that the restaurant will be a successful business venture with prospects of future franchises.

Chiropractic Office

FINANCIAL PLAN AND MARKETING STRATEGY

COLE'S CHIROPRACTIC

1450 East Wells Street
Madison, WI 53705

This plan is balanced and economical, avoiding verbosity by dedicating only as much time as necessary for each section. Competence in Chiropractic Science is displayed and a brief description of the business operations is given, making the proposal focused and streamlined. Emphasized are the expenditures and startup costs, justifying the loan amount requested.

- PURPOSE

- CHIROPRACTIC

- LOCATION

- MARKET

- PROMOTION PLAN

- PATIENT MANAGEMENT

- PROGRAM OF CARE

- DURATION OF CARE

- FEE SCHEDULE 1994

- FEE SCHEDULE 1998

- PRE-OPERATING EXPENSES

- MONTHLY OPERATING EXPENSES

CHIROPRACTIC OFFICE
BUSINESS PLAN

PURPOSE

We are seeking to lease a Continental X-ray Vertical TV Imaging System with a TM-30 R/F generator, approximate value $70,000, for use in the to be established Cole's Chiropractic Clinic.

The following prospectus will provide information concerning the profession of chiropractic, office description, specific expenditures, practice and marketing plans, and supporting documents. We expect to be open during June 1994 at 1450 East Wells Street, Madison, Wisconsin.

CHIROPRACTIC

Chiropractic is a profession that has been rapidly developing since its discovery in 1895 by D.D. Palmer. Today, there are approximately 40,000 doctors of chiropractic in the United States. Chiropractors are primary health care providers, licensed in all 50 states, and are participants in most major medical insurances.

Chiropractic is defined as the philosophy, science, and art of things natural, with the objective of locating, analyzing, and correcting the vertebral subluxation complex. The subluxation is the improper positioning of a vertebra from the ideal spinal model which causes interference of a nerve impulse from the brain to the body and back. According to *Gray's Anatomy* we know that the central nervous system controls and regulates the entire body. If we have an interference of a nerve to a particular part of the body, this part has lost the necessary communication to function properly. The rest of the body is also adversely affected since no one part affected can not effect the whole body.

Doctors of chiropractic are the only professionals who are trained to locate, analyze, and correct the vertebral subluxation complex. Chiropractors adjust the vertebral subluxation complex by introducing a specific force in the direction that would thereby restore the biomechanical integrity, thus restoring the nerve impulse.

LOCATION

Cole's Chiropractic Clinic will be located at 1450 East Wells St. This office is centrally located in Madison, and allows for easy access both entering and exiting the parking area.

The office space is 1050 square feet, consisting of the following: 1 Reception Room, 1 Secretary Office, 1 X-ray Department, 1 Darkroom, 1 Restroom, 2 Adjusting Rooms, and 1 private office.

MARKET

Cole's Chiropractic Clinic will primarily serve a population of over 51,000 in a ten-mile radius.

There are only 20 doctors of chiropractic in this ten-mile radius. The equipment that we will use in our office is the latest in chiropractic technology. The Videofluoroscopy X-ray unit in our office will be the only one within 150 miles of Madison. This machine is capable of recording motion, with a significant reduction of radiation exposure to the patient. We will offer other doctors of chiropractic use of this equipment for a small fee so their patients can also benefit.

PROMOTION PLAN

Grand Opening: Personal invitations to family and friends. Invitations to residence and commercial establishments within 1 mile.

Advertisement: Newspaper and other publications press releases. Yellow pages in phone book. Large business sign in front of office.

Public Relations: Continuous series of public health awareness seminars. Participation in local civic groups.

Patient Education: Quarterly newsletter, *Health Tracks: Chiropractic a New Beginning,* Office lending library.

Patient Relations: Systematic patient follow-up procedure. Special occasion and thank-you for referral mailings.

Day 1 - Initial office visit
    Consultation
    Terms of acceptance
    Case History
    Comprehensive Examination
    X-rays
    Videofluoroscopy / Cineradiography
    Patient Education

Day 2 - Extended office visit
    Report of findings
    Recommended program
    Instrumentation
    Spinal Examination and Adjustment
    Scheduling of next appointment

Future Office Visits
    Instrumentation
    Spinal Examination and Adjustment if necessary

PATIENT MANAGEMENT

Initial Care: (Acute) 3 visits per week

Reconstructive Care: (Subacute) 2 visits per week; (Chronic) 1 - 2 visits per month

Maintenance Care: 1 - 2 visits per month

PROGRAM OF CARE

Initial Care: 3 - 6 weeks

Reconstructive Care: 4 - 8 weeks

DURATION OF CARE

**FEE SCHEDULE
1994**

Initial Care:

Examination	$ 35.00
Office Visit / Adjustments	25.00
X-rays: Cervical	20.00 / per view
Lumbar / Pelvic	30.00 / pervie
Cineradiography	75.00 / per region

Reconstructive Care

Office Visit / Adjustments	$ 25.00

**FEE SCHEDULE
1998**

Initial Care:

Examination	$ 45-100
Office Visit / Adjustments	32.00
X-rays: Cervical	30.00./per view
Lumbar / Pelvic	40.00/per view
Cineradiography	100.00/per region

Reconstructive Care

Office Visit / Adjustment	$ 32.00

**PRE-OPERATING
EXPENSES**

DEPOSITS:

Lease (building)	$ 1,000.00
Insurances	250.00
Lease (X-ray)	5,000.00

OFFICE SUPPLIES:

Bookkeeping	250.00
Letterhead	100.00
Filing Cabinet	150.00
Business Cards	30.00
Patient Folders	50.00
Telephones (2)	100.00
Computer Paper	25.00
Miscellaneous	200.00

PATIENT EDUCATION:

Health Tracks	50.00

OFFICE EQUIPMENT:

Reception Room Chairs	700.00
Secretarial Chair	150.00
Adding Machine	30.00
Answering Machine	100.00
Computer	1,800.00
Office desk	300.00
Executive Chair	150.00

CHIROPRACTIC EQUIPMENT:

Automatic Processor	3,600.00
X-ray Film	200.00
Hylo (Zenith 230)	7,150.00
X-ray view box	100.00
Precision Adjustor	**
DT-25 Graph system	**

REMODELING:	Room Divider, Carpeting,	
	Paint, etc.	2,000.00
	Electrical Wiring	500.00
	Miscellaneous	500.00
TOTAL		$ 10,250.00
TOTAL PRE-OPERATING EXPENSES		$ 24,485.00

** Note: This equipment has been purchased.

Precision Adjustor	$ 1,800.00
DT-25 Graph System	2,200.00

MONTHLY OPERATING EXPENSES

OFFICE:

Lease (Building)	$1,000.00	
Lease (X-ray)	1,050.00	
Acct.	133.00	
Telephone	40.00	
Advertising	100.00	
Utilities	100.00	
Office Manager	900.00	
Equipment loan payment ($ 25,000 / 10 years)	300.00	
Office Supplies	75.00	
Insurances (Malpractice, Fire, Theft)	100.00	
TOTAL MONTHLY OFFICE EXPENSES	$ 3,798.00	

PERSONAL:

Rent	375.00	
Student Loan	600.00	**
Utilities	100.00	
Telephone	40.00	
Transportation (Insurance, Gas, Maint.)	150.00	
Food	200.00	
Clothing	100.00	
Retirement	200.00	
Miscellaneous	200.00	
TOTAL PERSONAL EXPENSES	$ 1,965.00	

BUSINESS:

Monthly	$ 3,665.00	
6 Months	21,990.00	
12 Months	43,980.00	
PERSONAL:		
June, July, August	1,365.00	*
Sept thru March	1,965.00	**
April, May	2,565.00	***
6 Months	9,990.00	
12 Months	22,980.00	
COMBINED:	(Business + Personal)	
June, July, August	$15,090.00	
6 Months	31,980.00	
12 Months	66,960.00	

  * These months no student loan payments are due
 ** Dr. Jill Cole begins repayment of student loans in Sept. 1994
*** Dr. Roger Cole begins repayment of student loans in March 1995

AWARDS AND HONORS

Received by Roger Cole

- Selected to be in *Who's Who Among Students in American Colleges* as a Student at Sherman College.
- Selected to the National Deans List.
- President of Student Government.
- Administrative Council Representative.
- Strategic Planning Committee Member.

Received by Roger Cole

Christmas Ornament Company

BUSINESS PLAN   SCRIPTURES FOR YOU, INC.

P.O. Box 1300
Bay City, MI 48707

This business plan serves as an excellent model for long-term and large-scale expansion for a small, self-owned business, as well as how spirituality and business practices can be successfully combined. The exposure to and knowledge gained from tradeshows complement the ultimate ambitions of the entrepreneurs and past success so as to create an optimistic forecast. The plan is also strengthened by the assessment of the competition.

- MISSION STATEMENT

- OVERVIEW

- DESCRIPTION OF BUSINESS

- 1997 BUSINESS PLAN

- BUSINESS SUMMARY FOR 1996

- FINANCIAL INFORMATION

- INTRODUCTION TO PROJECTIONS

- THE APPENDIX

CHRISTMAS ORNAMENT COMPANY
BUSINESS PLAN

MISSION STATEMENT

The mission of Scriptures For You, Inc. is to create and provide quality products which reinforce Christian values.

OVERVIEW

Scriptures For You, Inc. is a manufacturing company founded by Martha Smith in December of 1990. Struggling with commercialism during the Christmas season, Albert (Martha's husband) knew a change was needed in the way Christmas has been celebrated. He expressed his concerns and directed them towards the Christmas tree. In wanting to keep the tradition of the tree, Martha developed a scroll type ornament on which various Bible verses were written. Today the company has two patented products. The first patent was issued on February 14, 1996 and the second patent is expected soon.

Scriptures For You, Inc. is a sub chapter "S" corporation with authorized stock of 60,000 shares, of which Albert and Martha Smith own 51%. There are currently 18 shareholders. A meeting was held on November 7, 1996 to introduce the company to the Bay City community and to look for potential investors. Stock was offered to raise capital to finance the 1997 Marketing/Business Plan. According to company by-laws, this stock has to be offered first to current shareholders.

DESCRIPTION OF BUSINESS

Scriptures For You, Inc. was founded in 1990 and incorporated in 1995. Currently a line of ornaments is being manufactured and a variety of quality products are being developed. In addition to scrolls for Christmas trees, scrolls are being added to new floral arrangements. The wedding scroll will be displayed in an attractive wedding card/box which can be converted into a frame for a favorite wedding photo.

Our vision is to offer our scrolls in a variety of languages, exporting them to different countries. By the end of 1998 we would like to open our first all-year "Holiday Heaven" store here in the Bay City area with the possibilities of branches around the country. The scrolls would be sold along with specialized products geared towards the Christian perspective of the holidays. By 1999 we will have our own mail-order catalog with products tested in "Holiday Heaven."

We are currently a sub chapter "S" corporation with 18 shareholders. Martha Smith is the president of the corporation with Albert Smith the secretary/treasurer. The board of seven directors controls the corporation. Our mission is to create and provide quality products which reinforce Christian values.

1997 BUSINESS PLAN

Market Analysis

The present and overall goal of Scriptures For You, Inc., is to create and offer products which reinforce Christian values. The scroll products have great potential to be directed to different markets depending on the way they are used. Our current marketing methods consist of using all-year Christmas stores, gift, craft, floral and hospital gift shops, Christian bookstores, direct marketing, mail-order catalogs, speciality magazines, distributors, and sale representatives.

Our products are new and unique to the market and made with the quality one expects when purchasing an American-made product. After extensive marketing research it has been found there are no other products like ours on the market, thereby giving us the opportunity to obtain two patents and an unlimited market. As far as product development is concerned, specialized scrolls are currently being added to our line, including scrolls for the Girl Scouts of America and DeColores scrolls pending approval from the companies who have requested them. We would also like to have available for sale our new product: the Wedding Scroll/Card.

Bronner's Christmas Wonderland became our first customer in 1993, selling our scrolls for $4.95 each. Bronner's has consistently reordered from us over the past four years, selling 3,765 scrolls. As in the past, we continue to add new accounts to our database.

The marketing knowledge gained this year has helped open the door to many different ways of marketing our product and has helped provide an understanding of the time of year that different sellers do their buying. In January, the all-year round Christmas stores and major chain stores do their Christmas shopping for the next Christmas season. Gift stores begin to look for new products around March and Christian bookstores start looking around June and July. By the end of August most of the Christmas buying is over.

In 1997 our goal is to continue with an aggressive marketing campaign including a television advertising campaign. The profit margin is higher when we direct market the product ourselves. Therefore, it is our decision to apply our energies to the area of direct marketing, including being set up on the Internet as of January 1997. Professional photographs for brochures will be mailed out to different targeted markets during their buying season. Pathways, located here in Bay City, has the capability to assist us in our mailing at a very reasonable cost. Using Sprint's "Friday Free Phone Calling" program, we will be contacting stores all over the United States in order to expand our customer base.

At this time we are working with The Works and John MacDonald as our sales representatives. The Works is homebased in Philadelphia, Pennsylvania and provides us with 45 road representatives. John MacDonald has 6 representatives and displays our products in two of their permanent showrooms. One of the showrooms is in Plymouth, Michigan and the other one is in Fort Wayne, Indiana.

Exporting our products to different countries will become a reality after attending a seminar in Chicago, with Brazil being the first to receive our Portuguese scrolls. This seminar will last for 6 months with a goal to ultimately set us up in an international trade show. In May of 1997 we would like to attend the Spanish trade show held in Miami. We will continue to gather pertinent information for trade shows to be held in 1998.

In 1998 we are planning to open our first "Holiday Heaven" store in the Bay City area. In keeping with the overall goal, this store will specialize in merchandise geared for all holidays, but from a Christian perspective. In 1999 we would like to begin the year with a comprehensive mail-order catalog of products tested in our "Holiday Heaven" store. A long range marketing goal is that of establishing a chain of "Holiday Heaven" stores throughout the country.

Funds are needed to accomplish our goals outlined in the 1997 marketing plan. Ten thousand shares of stock are currently being offered. Six months of aggressive marketing will enable us to achieve our sales projections. In turn, this will benefit our Bay City community by adding new jobs and patronizing local businesses.

Management

Martha Smith, president of Scriptures For You, Inc. has experience and strength in the areas of product development, marketing, and sales. As a manager of Tupperware Home Parties for 10 years she was responsible for training and motivating dealers. Also, she worked for the U.S. Navy in graphic arts and has taken advanced courses in the area of art/graphics. Her salesmanship and creativity, in addition to her willingness to persevere and educate herself in all areas of the company, make her an asset to Scriptures For You, Inc.

When production meets the projected goals Albert Smith is to take on the responsibilities of bookkeeper/production manager. Albert has kept the books for the past three years and is familiar with the work required to meet the demands of the business. Albert has over fifteen years experience in the accounting field and is now working at CEI Instruments and Costco, where he is gaining production and retailing experience.

The corporation's lawyer is Walter Warner. At this time Albert Smith handles our tax and other financial reports. The Board of Directors, which meets regularly, contributes in great part to the growth of the corporation through their advice and counsel.

Production

In 1994, Scriptures For You, Inc. ran a prototype assembly line after receiving an order for 10,000 scrolls from Martindales, a distributor in South Bend, Indiana. Management was able to accurately determine the cost of materials and labor required for production of scrolls at that time.

A production line is planned consisting of eight people with the ability to produce approximately 2,000 units per week. A supervisor for each line would be responsible for production and product quality. All necessary training and skill development are learned on the job. The work hours are to be flexible based upon each employee's family needs. This coming year, as the orders come in, production lines are to be set up to meet the demand.

In May of this past year we hired two employees to produce our scrolls. They work approximately 40 hours per week in the window at the Heavenly Roads bookstore. We subcontract out the actual burning of the scroll. We currently have on hand 1,925 completed scrolls with enough raw materials to produce an additional 1,250.

We have created a way to increase the value of our irregular scrolls by adding holly leaves to them or by incorporating them into floral arrangements. This not only minimizes the number of irregulars but also maximizes our profit.

As much as possible, Scriptures For You, Inc. purchases our raw materials from local suppliers. Our new floral line will be coming from a cooperative arrangement with two of our local florists.

BUSINESS SUMMARY FOR 1996

The past three years have been spent building a solid foundation for Scriptures For You, Inc. In 1992 the scroll was developed, being made ready for market in March of 1993. Bronner's of Frankenmuth, Michigan became our first customer. In 1994 a production line was organized making 10,000 magnet scrolls for Martindales. The year 1996 has been spent in the area of marketing and capital formation. For next year, 1997, it is anticipated that work will continue in all three of these areas: product development, production, and marketing.

Reviewing the year's marketing milestones, 1996 began with raising capital in January so we could attend two major trade shows. In the beginning of February we went to Atlanta. It was there we got a taste of the national market. We were approached by several representatives. President Smith gained much knowledge in marketing strategies. After returning from the trade show, scrolls were mailed to some of the key accounts on the Christian market to increase product visibility.

In March we went to the Nashville Gift Show. Storeowners were encouraged to place their orders early by offering them 90 day billing from date of shipment. At the end of April the investors were contacted and our first meeting was scheduled for May 7 to review the outcome and possibilities from the trade shows. We signed on with The Works. Small Wonders agreed to pick up our line in their Christmas catalog. John MacDonald wanted to put the scrolls in their permanent showroom in Plymouth, Michigan and in Fort Wayne, Indiana. Monthly meetings with the Board of Directors and lots of paperwork became a reality.

The rest of the year saw continued development of the corporation. In the middle of May we hired our first employee. A scroll stand is being developed to encourage stores to pick up scrolls as a year-round product. We came up with a new way to package the scroll for stores who take their merchandise out of the original package. We applied for our UPC Code and by the end of June had company by-laws. In August, a craft magazine featured our scrolls in their catalog through which we have received 39 inquiries to date.

By September we were working on professional photographs for 1997 brochures. A new sticker was designed for our magnet line and we are currently preparing a Portuguese translation of the product and its packaging. Prototypes for the Girl Scouts of America and a DeColores scroll have been developed. We have also been looking at the possibility of adding a floral line which two of the floral shops located here in Bay City, are collaborating with us. As of October we acquired a computer, fax, and small Xerox machine. On November 7, the company was formally introduced to the Bay City community. Stock was offered to raise capital to finance the 1997 Marketing/Business Plan.

It was with commitment and creativity that the scroll was perfected as it is today. The experience gained working with a production line in 1994 has prepared us for a smooth transition to mass production when the opportunity presents itself. The marketing knowledge obtained this past year has opened the door to the many different ways our products could be marketed. Most importantly, Scriptures For You, Inc. plans to offer ever expanding lines of products which reinforce Christian values.

December 5, 1996

FINANCIAL INFORMATION

To the Shareholders of
Scriptures For You, Inc.
Bay City, MI 00000

I have prepared the following balance sheet, dated September 30, 1996, and statement of income and expense for the nine months ended September 30, 1996 for Scriptures For You, Inc., using the accrual method of accounting and following generally accepted accounting principles.

These statements have been prepared from the corporate books and records only and have not been independently verified by any other entity.

Very truly yours,
Albert Smith
Secretary/Treasurer
Scriptures For You, Inc.

Balance Sheet as of September 30, 1996

ASSETS

Current Assets

Inventory	$6,225
Accounts Receivable - Trade	5,074
Less: Allowance for Doubtful Accounts	(507)
Accounts Receivable - Shareholders	3,864
Incorporation Fees	75
Licensing Agreement	8,100
Covenant not to compete	5,000
Goodwill	17,175
Accumulated Amortization	(2,034)
	$43,002

Fixed Assets

Machinery and Equipment	1,900
Accumulated Depreciation	(190)
Net Assets	1,710
TOTAL ASSETS	**$44,712**

LIABILITIES AND CAPITAL

Current Liabilities

Bank Overdraft	529
Accounts Payable - Trade	4,159
Accounts Payable - Other	1,212
Total Liabilities	**5,900**

Capital Accounts

Common Stock	34,832
($1 par; 60,000 shares authorized 34,832 issued)	
Additional paid in capital	13,900
Accumulated adjustments account	(9,920)
Total capital	**38,812**
TOTAL LIABILITIES AND CAPITAL	**$44,712**

Statement for Income and Expense

For the nine months ended September 30, 1996

SALES	**$7,056**	
Cost of Goods Sold		
Materials	$1,889	
Labor	2,688	
Commission	414	
Royalty	363	
Total Cost of Goods Sold	5,354	
GROSS PROFIT	**$1,702**	**24%**
OPERATING EXPENSES		
Trade Shows	$4,375	
Advertising and Promotions	1,114	
Insurance	113	
Supplies	598	
Legal and Accounting	480	
Telephone	830	
Repairs and Maintenance	404	

Bad Debt Expense	405
Depreciation Expense	190
Amortization Expense	2,034
Office	904
Miscellaneous Expense	181
Total Operating Expenses	**11,628**

Net Loss from Operations   **(9,926)**

Miscellaneous Income   **6**

NET LOSS   **$ (9,920)**

Accounts Receivable as of 9/30/96	**$5,074**	**Accounts Receivable Aging as of 9/30/96**
0 - 30 days	3,732	
30 - 60 days	1,220	
60 - 90 days	122	
	$5,074	

INTRODUCTION TO PROJECTIONS

The current marketing plan is an aggressive approach to increase sales, and the following projections are a reflection of what management believes will happen with the implementation of this plan.

The goal of management is to triple ornament sales in each of the next 3 years. There is a realistic premise for these projections given the many potential sales outlets and combination product sales now being pursued.

The breakeven analysis computed is for the operation in full operation as shown in the 1998 projected income statement. That analysis shows that sales would have to be at 4,070 units per month or 48,840 units per year to break even. Management believes that can be obtained in 1999. The projected shortfall for 1998 will have to be addressed through cuts in projected expenses, additional capital from shareholders, or possibly a short-term loan.

The 1997 projection shows the immediate effect of the projected marketing plan. This loss will not be offset until later years of profitability, beginning with 1999.

We show here the full amount of the projected cost of the 1997 marketing plan, however, we will only spend on marketing those amounts we receive in new capital.

The hierarchy of implementation of the marketing plan is as follows:

1) Training our sales representatives
2) Producing brochures for direct mailings and trade shows
3) Telemarketing
4) Magazine advertising
5) CBA show
6) Wedding card prototype
7) TV advertising campaign

Projected Income Statement 1997 - 1999

	1997	1998	1999
Sales	$34,538	$103,613	$310,840
Cost of Goods Sold	21,274	63,824	191,478
Gross Profit	**13,264**	**39,789**	**119,362**
Operating Expenses			
Rent	0	9,600	9,600
Electric	0	1,200	1,200
Heat	0	1,500	1,500
Telephone	1,620	1,800	1,800
Office Supply & Expense	1,320	1,800	1,800
Salary Management	6,000	16,800	16,800
Salary - Other	0	6,720	6,720
Payroll Taxes	266	4,300	4,300
Insurance	384	420	420
Promotional Advertising	40,000	1,800	1,800
Vehicle Expense	0	5,400	5,400
Legal & Accounting	750	1,200	1,200
Product Development	0	1,800	1,800
Miscellaneous	0	1,800	1,800
Total Operating Expenses	**50,340**	**56,142**	**56,140**
	$ (37,076)	**$ (16,351)**	**$63,222**

1 Month Projected Income Statement

*Based on projected production and sales of 8,000 scrolls per month:

	With Rep	Without Rep
Sales ($2.50)	20,000	20,000
Cost of Goods Sold: ($1.86 per unit)	14,880	10,880
Gross Profit	**5,120**	**9,120**
Projected Overhead Costs	4,656	4,656
NET PROFIT	**$464**	**$4,464**

Our sale price of $2.50 per scroll covers our direct cost of $1.86 per unit plus our projected overhead costs of 60 cents per scroll computed as follows:

Projected overhead costs	$4,656
Projected monthly production	**8,000 = .58 cents**

	With Rep	Without Rep
Direct cost per scroll	$1.86	$1.36
Overhead cost per scroll	0.58	0.58
Total Cost of scroll	**$2.44**	**$1.94**
Sale Price	2.50	2.50
Projected profit per scroll	**$0.06**	**$0.56**

Rent	$800	**Projected Overhead Costs for 1 Month**
Electric	100	
Heat	100	
Phone	150	
Office Supply & Expense	150	
Management	1,400	
Office/Bookkeeper	560	
Payroll Taxes	361	
Insurance	35	
(Product Liability $500,000)		
(Property Liability $100,000)		
Promotional Advertising	150	
Vehicle	450	
Product Development	150	
Miscellaneous	150	
Legal	100	
	$4,656	

Martha Smith	President, Scriptures For You, Inc. Owner, Heavenly Roads Bookstore	**Board of Directors**
Albert Smith	Secretary/Treasurer, Scriptures For You, Inc. Accounting/Retailing/Manager	
Miller A. Fisher	President, PJC Corporation Other Board Positions: CEI Instruments Cincinnati Fabrications	
William Fines	Registered Architect, The Architect Forum Artist/Designer	
Mary Smolinski	Retailing	
Flora Lopez	Director/Crisis Pregnancy Center Team Manager/Avon	
Sharon Metcalf	Human Relations/Buyer	
Margaret Abbott	Office Manager, City of Bay City	

Scroll cost per unit:	With a Rep	Without a Rep	**Scroll Production Costs**
Material	$0.49	$0.49	
Labor	0.74	0.74	
Waste Factor	0.03	0.03	
Commission	0.5	0.0	
Royalty	0.1	0.1	
Total cost per unit	**$1.86**	**$1.36**	

Cookie Shop

BUSINESS PLAN

GRANDMA MILLER'S COOKIES & MUFFINS

216 Hawke Rd.
Muskegon, MI 49440

This plan for the purchase of an existing small business does a nice job of illustrating, in specifics, how the business will be improved. Dynamic ideas for increasing community involvement and exposure are clearly stated. The low overhead cost of operation and the creative ability of the entrepreneur are stressed as the keys to a successful venture, and both are displayed in the plan's content.

- BUSINESS PLAN

- STRATEGY

- SUPPLIER

- SALES

- COMPETITION

- DAY-TO-DAY CHALLENGES AND OPPORTUNITIES

- LAYOUT

- MISCELLANEOUS

- MENU

- RESUME

BUSINESS PLAN

Background

Grandma Miller's Cookies & Muffins was established about eight and a half years ago, and the current owner, Hannah Welles, has owned it for about two and a half years, selling it for health reasons. Hannah has an excellent rapport with her customers and is very knowledgeable about the area. Currently, the business shows a modest profit. Although the markup on the cookies is very good (i.e., sugar cookie dough sells for $1.85/lb., and the retail price of the finished cookies is $6.59/lb), the overall cost of goods sold is about 50 percent due to the serving of light lunches, muffins, soda, and juices (see menu).

As pointed out by an accountant, any sales over the current volume, 50 percent, is profit. As a result, sales could be doubled within the first twelve to eighteen months.

STRATEGY

The first of two steps to increase sales would be to become an active member of the Muskegon Chamber of Commerce (membership is over 400). Through past Grand Rapids Chamber membership and previous employment in Muskegon, I have made many business contacts in the area: Electronics Midwest, Rogers H. Theatre, H&G Sales, and Paper Towne Goods.

The business climate in Muskegon is very good. There are very few empty stores and there is strong merchant cooperation (on the Saturday before Halloween the stores offered treats and I help hand out over 1,000 cookies). The cookie shop is open three Sundays a year during the January Ice Fair, Summer Art in the Streets, and the September Fall Festival.

The second step would be implementing a strong advertising campaign. I plan to begin six months of advertising in the local paper, the *Town Tattler* (circulation about 21,000), announcing the new ownership and inviting people in to meet the new Grandma Miller, and some monthly specials. Both the *Tattler* and *Sentryman* newspapers do public relations articles on new businesses and ownership changes. I will change the name to Grandma Miller's Cookie Pantry and use a pantry as a focus for advertising, flyers, and business cards in the shop.

After becoming familiar with the day-to-day operations, I plan to employ one person (a relative) one day a week to learn the business in case of an extended absence. This will also allow me to visit the various industrial and office complexes to market cookie and muffin trays for business meeting and promotions. My contacts will be mostly with companies' seminar/group meeting planners.

My marketing strategies include but are not limited to:

- Cookie, muffin, and chocolate tie-ins to all major holidays, such as heart-shaped cookies for Valentine's Day and Sweetest Day, muffin birthday "cakes," cookies for Santa, and cookie exchanges.
- "Sweet Sixteen Special" offered every sixteenth of the month. Customers have to come into the shop to find out what the special is for that day. Can also use the day to offer free samples of new ideas.
- Promote the first full week of February, which is National Muffin Week.
- Offer a welcome wagon type of promotion to new residents of the Muskegon area, using published real estate closings.
- Develop a special recipe for a "morning cookie" not to be offered in the shop, but only for business breakfast meetings.

- Promote one day a week as D-Day (Dipit Day), for dipping customers' cookies in chocolate.
- Find the right combination of food and nonfood items for a bereavement basket, which is becoming a fast-growing segment of the basket industry. I would also like to expand the gift basket business already in use in the shop. (I attended a gift basket convention and seminar in Louisville, Kentucky, in 1993, and would like to attend one this spring.)

SUPPLIER

On November 10, 1994, I visited Grandma Miller's dough supplier, in Holland, Michigan. She had originally started Grandma Miller's Cookies in three locations: Lansing, Grand Rapids, and Muskegon. After a death in the family of the initial cookie dough supplier, Ceceila offered the opportunity to buy the dough business. She subsequently sold the Grandma Miller's stores and moved to Holland and is currently involved with retail and wholesale business under the name of Jolene's Cookies. Cecelia has indicated her willingness to help with new ideas and products.

SALES

My future plans for the business are to maximize sales potential, which may take several years. I anticipate the expansion of the gift basket market, a build-up of wholesale accounts, including the introduction of party planning. I believe both previous owners looked into franchising, but I do not see that as an option in the short run.

COMPETITION

Area competition is very small for the cookie and muffin business. The lunch business in downtown Muskegon consists mainly of Karen's Cafi across the street, which serves the quiche/croissant, sandwich, and dessert trade. One block away is Penny's Deli, which serves deli sandwiches, salads, and beverages. The Boothe Bar takes care of the hamburger crowd. There are few other eateries in town. Limited seating at Grandma Miller's (eight inside and two outside during the summer) has encouraged customers to phone in their orders and pick them up along with a drink and dessert. Two blocks away a coffeehouse has opened and stays open until 11:00 p.m. Although it serves some of the same muffins and cookies as Grandma Miller's, and the coffee bean prices are comparable, the coffeehouse attracts a different crowd than Grandma Miller's.

DAY-TO-DAY CHALLENGES AND OPPORTUNITIES

The most difficult function is following the fine line of quantity overbaking and not having enough cookies later in the day. Despite a sophisticated cash register that totals an hourly sales figure, and detailed recording by Hannah, there is no set pattern of daily activity. One Tuesday could be a sellout and the next Tuesday there could be several bags of day-old cookies, which sell quickly the next day. Hannah has developed some recipes for bar cookies—using crumbled cookies as a base and adding a fruit topping and a "drizzle." These could be sold in the store or packaged for a catering truck.

I have dropped in the shop at various times during the day and observed a very busy opening (at 8:00 a.m.) with people getting their coffee and muffins before going to work. The business slows down until lunchtime and varies throughout the afternoon. This allows for a build-up of the business, so that the ovens are used more than 10 percent of the day. (Using convection ovens, a batch of cookies can be baked in 15 minutes.)

LAYOUT

The store still looks good after almost nine years. The custom-made counters and cabinets are made of oak, with glass fronts, and good quality wallpaper makes for a neat appearance.

Besides bringing in a pantry, I want to use an oak trim along the ceiling to give an overall cozy appearance. New wallpaper with matching material for curtains and for the liners of the cookie baskets will freshen up the sales area for a long time. I would like to put in a new floor covering and paint the back work area.

MISCELLANEOUS

Since this is going to be a one-person operation, I plan to add business interruption insurance to the overall business insurance package. I also plan to add a disability package to my personal health insurance.

Attached is a current resume of my educational background and a work history. However, it does not reflect my creative talents, which I have used in an antique and collectible business and in extensive family party planning. I have taken a floral design class and mold my own chocolates. I hope to expand my business, Your Organizing Friend, through Grandma Miller's Cookie Pantry.

Although my professional team is not complete, I have an attorney who is handling the closing and other aspects of the purchase and lease negotiations. I also have a CPA consultant, but he is a relative and won't be handling the actual accounting functions.

Hannah's interest in Grandma Miller's is waning, and I feel that it is the right time and niche for me to devote my full-time and creative energies to the business.

MENU

Grandma Miller's Cookie Pantry

An Adventure in Richness Filled with Memories of Home

Grandma Miller's Cookie Pantry Offers...

Gourmet Cookies	**Muffins**
Sugar	Banana Chocolate Chip
Oat Bran Chocolate Chip (no cholesterol)	Cranberry Nut
Oatmeal & Golden Raisin	Cherry Yogurt
Peanut Butter Crunchie	Blueberry
Chocolate Chocolate Chip/	Apple Cinnamon
White Chocolate Chunks	
Chocolate Chunk	Orange Blossom
Chocolate Chip	Carrot Cake
Chocolate Chip Pecan	Almond Poppyseed
Crispie Chewie	Lemon Poppyseed
Macadamia Nut/White Chocolate Chunks	Zucchini Raisin
Cookie of the Month	Pumpkin
	Peach Granola
	Corn
Cookie Shipping	Low-Fat Fruit Bran
(includes gift wrapping and postage)	Five-Grain
	Mini Muffins (dozen only)
2-pound cookie heart	

Fresh-brewed flavored coffee by the cup/or buy by the pound

Light Lunches	Other Menu Items
Sandwiches or Croissants	Variety of Beverages

Soup of the Day   Sticky Buns
Chili (in season)   Bagels
Chicken & Tuna Salads

SPECIALITIES
Molded Chocolates, Cookie & Muffin Trays, Gift Baskets

Donna Crawford

Business professional with proven effectiveness in sales, personnel, and consumer relations. Skilled in coordinating resources, people, and ideas to produce maximum results. Analytical, creative, and capable of working with minimal supervision. Interest and demonstrated ability in public relations, events planning, and fundraising.

PROFESSIONAL EXPERIENCE

Sales: 10 years in real estate sales

- *Residential:* Marketed new and used homes and condominiums with effective advertising; researched financing to guide buyers through to closing.
- *Commercial:* Sold small businesses using financial analysis and research; negotiated details between buyer and seller, their attorneys, accountants, and landlords; marketed office space at the Center Point Building.

Personnel: Six years in civil service and at a private personnel agency

- Administered tests, conducted interviews, implemented special programs.
- Restructured and organized manual office systems to more efficiently meet the demands of a municipal agency.

Project Management: One year as a field representative with Floral Worldwide Delivery Group (FWDG) and long-term association with the Muskegon Historical Society.

- Traveled nationally to audit FWDG's members' floral orders for quality to insure association standards, supported audits with written and photographic evaluations.
- Wrote monthly newsletter for historical society, prepared press releases.
- Planned fundraising events with proceeds ranging from $500 to $85,000, generated publicity for activities.
- Developed theme events for various individuals and organizations.

Self-Employment: 15 years in family antique business

- Set up displays at various locations in Michigan. Sales included sharing information regarding antiques, their history, and use.

EDUCATION

MichiganTechnological University
B.S., business administration; Major: marketing

Continuing Education
Courses in management, special events marketing, travel tourism and convention planning, and introductory computer course

PROFESSIONAL AFFILIATIONS/SOCIETIES

Muskegon Chamber of Commerce; Zeeland Historical Society; Community Assistance Services, Inc. (group homes), board of directors.

Food Manufacturer

BUSINESS PLAN

CLARENCE PRATT ENTERPRISES, INC.

14001 Western Hwy.
Salt Lake City, UT 84101

This plan for an established minority-owned food manufacturer seeks to expand the distribution of its products within the U.S. military, to build brand equity in retail distribution, to expand the company's product line, and to continue a promotional program. Action steps include featuring company products on the founder's talk show, directing donations to nonprofit youth groups, and donation and promotion programs with the U.S. Defense and Commissary Agency.

- EXECUTIVE SUMMARY

- INTRODUCTION

- PROPOSED TRANSACTION

- SUMMARY FINANCIAL INFORMATION

- KEY INVESTMENT CONSIDERATIONS

- MARKETING

- OPERATIONS

- SUMMARY FINANCIAL PROJECTIONS

**EXECUTIVE
SUMMARY**

Clarence Pratt Enterprises, Inc. is a minority-owned Utah Corporation founded and owned by Clarence Pratt, a graduate of the University of Vermont. The company was incorporated May 24, 1994. To date Clarence Pratt Enterprises, Inc. has developed a line of products marketed under the Clarence Pratt's Original™ brand that are in distribution in the military resale market through the Defense Commissary Agency and in retail distribution in Lindstrom's, Abner Stevens, and Fosters Food and Drug Centers. The company's military distribution is accomplished through a contract allowing access to the market for the company's approved products.

**Progress to Date
and Recent
Accomplishments**

The company has quality product formulas, contracted co-packing arrangements, an established network of authorized military distributors, brokerage representation in the military resale market, regional retail, and arrangements with Save-Mart in place.

The company holds a Resale Order Agreement (ROA) with the Defense Commissary Agency that provides access to the market for the company's products. The commissary market averages $5.4 billion in grocery sales annually. There are 300 stores systemwide.

The company, with its ROA, has approved distribution of three products nationwide, four products worldwide, and sixteen products regionally.

The company has established distribution of five products in the Utah Region of Abner Stevens.

The company has established distribution in Fosters Food and Drug Centers Utah division, with product approved for systemwide distribution into 159 stores.

The company has an established retail distributor in the Gulf Coast region of Florida, with four products.

The company is in the final stages of approved distribution in Save-Mart.

**Clarence Pratt's
Original Products**

Barbecue Sauce
Spicy Barbecue Sauce
Honey Mustard
Teriyaki Glaze
Roasted Garlic Marinade
Sweet & Sour Sauce
Salsa
Disposable Aluminum Baking Pans
Bean Coffees
Spices
Potato Shells
Fresh Pasta
FastBind
Doodle Stick
Pasta Sauce Mixes
Chocolate Truffles

The company has established distribution in the Utah Division of Lindstrom's with five products.

Major food manufacturers and corporate co-promotion partners, such as The Shaker Foods company and Foods America, support and participate in the company's cause-marketing programs because they feel it is the right thing to do. Shaker Foods provides advisory consultation and Foods America offers ongoing promotional support of the company's products in military distribution. These relationships are rewarding for both parties.

Foods America is developing a fat-free bacon product, which they will manufacture, market, and distribute under the Clarence Pratt's Original™ label. This type of relationship is consistent with the company's programs. Other companies are suggesting similar types of programs.

A number of high-level industry and commissary marketing executives have expressed a desire to join the company.

Mr. Edward Maas is a national spokesperson for the youth at risk program associated with the company's marketing program.

Proposed Transaction

The company is currently seeking to fund further development of its existing military distribution to market the company's products and build brand equity in retail distribution, expand the company's product line with higher margin products, and carry on an advertising and promotion program to drive and stimulate product sales.

The company projects sales levels in year one of $2,968,389, year two sales of $6,508,268, year three sales of $8,421,342, year four sales of $8,972,021, and year five sales of $9,421,639.

Marketing Strategy

The company has a three-faceted marketing strategy. A national strategy, a retail strategy, and a military resale strategy, based on cause-marketing.

The company's national strategy encompasses "The Clarence Pratt Show™" a topical 30-minute talk show.

The company's retail strategy is to direct a donation of 3% of gross sales to nonprofit groups working to stem the gang problem through interfacing with the stores, the community, and the consumer, who can make a difference.

The company's military strategy encompasses the donation program, as well as promotion periods established by DeCA headquarters.

The company's cause related marketing program centers around the donation of 3% of the company's gross revenues to nonprofit organizations that are helping to fight gang problems in markets where the products are sold. For retail distribution, youth at risk boards are being formed to help determine the recipients of the donations. In the military, the Armed Services YMCA's national and branch offices are our youth at risk boards.

Clarence Pratt, president of the company, also hosts a solution-based television program, "The Clarence Pratt Show™" that promotes the products and establishes strong name recognition and production positioning in markets where the show airs.

The company's innovative cause-marketing program and solution-based television and radio programs position it to garner and secure considerable support, including:

- Retailers foregoing slotting fees
- Retailers foregoing initial free distribution of products

- Retailers either reducing allowances or allowance periods
- Marketing programs and in-store mandatory promotions not required

Television and radio stations offer opportunities to air public service announcements relative to the company's products and youth at risk programs, the cause-marketing program, and charitable donation aspects of the program. The FCC also requires stations to air and support minority and youth-based programs through airing of specific information about specific organizations and or programs that impact the community they are licensed to serve.

Growth Opportunities

Government regulations provide that government entities and companies that do business with the U.S. government are required to purchase and do business with minority-owned companies. This meets this requirement.

The company will vigorously participate in all bidding and "RFP" (Request for Proposal) opportunities to increase and diversify the company's sales activity. These opportunities will come through the Armed Services Support Center (DPSC). This organization is responsible for all troop and support provisioning, worldwide.

Federal acquisition requirements provide for contracts set aside for minority-owned small business and minority preference contracts. Minority preference contracts provide for 10% price advantage over non-minority bidders.

The company has the opportunity through its military broker to penetrate other areas of the military resale marketplace, including the exchanges of all the services.

Key Investment Considerations

The company's strategy of contracting product manufacturing, allows it to operate with smaller staff levels than would be required if the company did its own manufacturing. As the company is able to penetrate additional markets, the costs of operation will increase at a substantially lower rate than revenues will increase.

The company has the ability to increase its margins through negotiation with additional manufacturers and suppliers of products.

Clarence Pratt, president and founder of the company, has consistently demonstrated his ability to implement his vision. Mr. Pratt's unique abilities to attract and develop experienced and skilled management support, secure contacts and contracts, and market his products and company is a great asset to the fast growth of the company. The company's current market penetration is the result of Mr. Pratt's efforts.

Due to the nature of the commissary market and the entry requirements, the company and Mr. Pratt, because of his unique abilities, are constantly presented with new opportunities relating to products and companies wishing access to the commissary market. Each opportunity is evaluated on its merits and its compatibility with the current operations of the company.

The company has filed an application for the 8(a) program which, when approved, will provide a basis for increasing sales, with lower costs, and provide minority preferences for potential contracts with many areas of government purchasing.

The company is pursuing Friendly Inns of America International Corporation for institutional distribution of its products. Friendly Inns of America Corporation is developing a "Market Place" concept to increase its utilization of small businesses in its purchasing. This program will also allow small businesses to purchase goods at the same price that Friendly Inns of America International does.

The company is also working with Friendly Inns of America International as a potential sub-contractor for responses to "requests for proposals" from the government. For example, the company is pursuing a "Prime Vendor" contract for Guam.

Clarence Pratt Enterprises, Inc. is a minority-owned for profit Utah corporation, founded by Clarence Pratt. Incorporated in May 1994 to engage in the private labeling of food and food-related products, the company markets 40 products under the Clarence Pratt's Original™ brand.

INTRODUCTION

The company has established distribution as follows: seven products in the Defense Commissary Agency (DeCA), five products in Lindstrom's (Utah Division), seven products in Fosters Food and Drug Centers, six products in Abner Stevens (Utah Division), four products in Top Savings (Gulf Coast of Florida), and sixteen products authorized for Save-Mart.

The company has established contracted manufacturing arrangements for production of the company's products. The company has established worldwide brokerage representation to all elements of the military resale market through R.J. Steele Company of Daytona Beach, Florida. The company has established brokerage representation at Save-Mart and regionally in retail to coincide with its retail distribution.

The company, through its founder, Clarence Pratt, has established significant relationships in its distribution channels. This has created additional opportunities for the company to expand its distribution, increase sales of its products, and through funding implement strategies to achieve projected sales and profitability levels. Mr. Pratt has also developed relationships in several arenas important for the company, including political, government, business, media, and community.

Mr. Pratt hosts "The Clarence Pratt Show™," a weekly 30-minute talk show focusing on solutions to the issues that affect all communities across America. While this show has been on the air longer than the company has been in existence, the affect it has on the company's products and the potential for relationships that benefit the company is significant.

The company was publicly launched on May 27, 1994 with a widely attended press conference and announcement in the Mayor of Provo's office. Attending were representatives of the Governor of the State of Utah, the Attorney General of the State of Utah, and many other dignitaries.

The company's pourable (liquid) food products are based on family recipes of Mr. Pratt. The company contracts for manufacturing as there is an abundance of manufacturing capacity available, the capital costs are significantly less than instituting the company's own manufacturing, and the company has more flexibility with new product development.

The company's central marketing program is cause-related to youth at risk. The company donates 3% of its gross sales (which translates to 50% of the profits from the sale of the products) to nonprofit groups working with youth at risk. This 3% is factored into the pricing of the company's products and is calculated in addition to gross margins on the products. The company has aligned itself with the national Armed Services Youth of Faith Association for distribution of the donation from the company's military commissary distribution. The company's youth at risk program has in part been the reason major manufacturers, such as Foods America and The Shaker Foods company, have supported the company's military distribution through participating in advertising support, or through co-promotions (see Marketing). The company's youth at risk program is also presented to retail grocery chains, as a cause-marketing program, and has, in effect, persuaded retailers to participate by waiving traditional slotting fees and merchandising programs.

This ability to impact this important issue from a positive perspective positions the company distinctly apart from its competitors. Through inclusion of retailers and other participants into the program, the consumer motivation to purchase the company's products is enhanced and translated to these participants. This is true of the company's products and "The Clarence Pratt Show™," which helps television and radio stations meet their programming mandates and is a motivator for them to participate.

The company is minority-owned, which accords the company certain benefits in relation to sales activities with the U.S. government, including potential set aside contracts and minority preferences in purchasing. The company's thrust in this area is directed at the Armed Services Support Center, in Pittsburgh, which is responsible for purchasing all manner of materials, food, and food-related products for provisioning of active duty personnel.

The benefits of cause-marketing and the company's youth at risk program come from the passion of the founder, Clarence Pratt, to make a difference. Knowing that literally no neighborhood in America is exempt from gangs, knowing that solutions come from positive efforts, Mr. Pratt has taken the youth of America as a goal, and through Clarence Pratt's Original™ products and "The Clarence Pratt Show™," he is building a strong foundation for profitability and positive change.

This cause translates directly to benefits for the company. Retailers have waived slotting fees; corporations like Foods America and The Shaker Foods company have taken an active part in helping to establish the company's business. The company's products are advertised in "The Clarence Pratt Show™." The company's promotional activities are enhanced through the youth at risk program with co-demos and co-promotions with complimentary products, thus reducing the cost to the company and through donated assistance in promotions, i.e., Foods America meats for sampling.

Likely to Switch

Total Population	66%
Influentials	78%
Household Income $50,000+	82%

The effect of the company's cause-marketing on the consumer is positive. The company's product labels carry the following statement: "3% of gross sales (which translates to 50% of the profits from the sale of the products) are donated to nonprofit groups working with youth at risk." In 1994, Seehaver Worldwide, Inc., a preeminent research company and Keye/Wilson Communications completed which is commonly called the Keye/Wilson Study of the power of cause-marketing on consumers' buying habits.

The foremost guiding findings that emerged from the study were that "consumers believe that business has a responsibility to help improve social ills" and "consumers respond positively with increased brand equity and sales to companies that practice cause-marketing sincerely." Key to the results of the study is the effect of what Keye/Wilson calls "Influentials." These are people who by their nature, income, education, and circumstance affect others.

The company has advantages in its products and distribution. Having access to the military commissary market and the contacts to expand products in distribution in this market is an important aspect to securing new business, new revenue streams, and avenues of profitability. This market averages $5.4 billion in sales annually, ranking it as one of the largest grocery chains in America. The company is also moving to tap the very large Armed Services Support Center market. This agency is responsible for purchasing all materials, food, and food-related products for support of active duty personnel, worldwide. The company is also moving to tap the military base exchange marketplace, with products for this distribution channel.

The company anticipates, through funding, significant growth in its retail distribution within its current distribution channels—i.e., Lindstrom's, Abner Stevens, Fosters Food and Drug Centers, Top Savings, and Save-Mart—increases in its military distribution, and in penetration of other market segments.

From the beginning, Mr. Pratt has successfully sought the advice and help of others to develop Clarence Pratt Enterprises, sell his products, and further his ideas to help youth at risk. For example, Senators Alan Bennett and Robert Thatch were instrumental in making introductions to appropriate persons in the military commissaries (administered by the Defense Commissary Agency, DeCA). In addition, past Representatives Smathers and Hanusik supported the company's entree into the commissary market. Senators Thatch and Bennett are members of the New Challenges Honorary Advisory Board.

With its youth at risk program and through Mr. Pratt's efforts, the company has developed significant co-promotion and advertising support from major food manufacturers, such as Shaker Foods and Foods America, a regional Venture Cola bottling company, and Mountain Bank U.S.

PROPOSED TRANSACTION

Clarence Pratt Enterprises, Inc. has developed high quality products, which together with its innovative marketing program have resulted in the products' rapid sale into military commissary, military exchange, and retail grocery outlets.

To enable the company to develop these profitable distribution channel relationships, along with its favorable manufacturing, brokerage, and distributor agreements in successfully exploiting the company's market opportunity, CPS is currently seeking $1,000,000 of equity funding.

The funds will be used primarily to provide working capital and to implement programs to drive sales of the company's products in its established lines of distribution. See the attached financial statements (additional detail is available upon request) and the Summary Financial Information section, which follows.

Common Stock Investment

Voting Rights—The stock will be Class A voting stock and will be entitled to one vote for each share of stock.

Distribution Rights—The stock will be co-equal with existing shares held by Mr. Pratt.

Exit Strategy—It is anticipated that the company will do an initial public offering of its stock within the first five years. The company also believes that it will receive attractive buyout offers due to its ability to penetrate retail and especially government markets on behalf of the acquirer. (The company has and expects to continue to receive numerous requests for help in obtaining distribution of other companies' products—especially in government organizations.)

SUMMARY FINANCIAL INFORMATION

The company's founder and president has demonstrated ability to obtain distribution in military and retail markets for the company's products. Clarence Pratt has also negotiated favorable manufacturing and distribution contracts and developed substantial financing and marketing support from retail grocery chains, manufacturers in the food industry, and politicians and government. Clarence Pratt Enterprises, Inc. is demonstrating that it is the company for the next millennium.

The proposed financing is to accomplish the following:

(1) Marketing and advertising to increase and drive sales in established commissary and retail grocery markets. Increased volume in sales through commissaries and retail grocery chains.

(2) Increase gross margins on the company's products through reducing costs of production of the company's pourable products.

(3) Open distribution in military exchange markets, including Army, Air Force, Navy, Marine Corps, and Coast Guard.

(4) Develop vendor status in institutional markets, including the Defense Personnel Support Center, the government agency responsible for purchasing of all materials for support of active duty personnel and their dependents. Other distribution channels include food service suppliers, such as Food Monarch and Friendly Inns of America, etc., and federal and state prisons.

(5) Open new retail market areas, through placement of "The Clarence Pratt Show™" in new markets (see Marketing).

(6) Bring to market new products and product lines with higher gross margins and introduce these products to the company's established lines of distribution.

(7) Position the company to take advantage of marketing opportunities for current products and to take advantage of new product procurement.

(8) Develop infrastructure and supplement management team to bring the company through breakeven to profitability.

The company enjoys several competitive advantages that are either unique to the company or unique to its markets.

(1) "The Clarence Pratt Show™." This 30-minute television program focuses on bringing solutions to the issues that affects all of our communities. The program is entertaining and insightful and presents the solutions in a positive perspective. Clarence Pratt hosts the program. The program meets the mandates that stations have for community-based programming and offers advantages to the stations to air the program. Television stations regularly are judged as to whether to keep their broadcast licenses by the programming they air. "The Clarence Pratt Show™" meets the litmus test in several areas surveyed by the Federal Communications Commission. Thus the advantage to television stations is that they can air a high production value program, with no production costs to them, share the advertising availabilities in the program with the company, and therefore generate advertising revenue with no out of pocket costs for programming.

Year	1	2	3	4	5
Total Revenue	$2,968,389	$6,508,268	$8,421,342	$8,972,021	$9,421,639
Gross Margin - %	17.7%	18.8%	19.3%	19.3%	19.3%
G & A Expenses	$749,221	$978,281	$1,055,435	$1,110,229	$1,160,636
Earnings Before Int. + Tax	-222,448	$245,936	$569,003	$620,414	$662,064

(2) A significant portion of the company's distribution is in a "protected" market, the Defense Commissary Agency. This vital market is not widely known and many medium sized and large companies do not market their products in this channel. The commissaries account for approximately $5.4 billion in sales per year, ranking it as the ninth largest grocery chain in America.

Unlike retail grocery, entry into the military commissary market is based on approval of a company's product(s), program, and pricing structure. The goal and mission of the commissaries are to provide their patrons (active duty personnel and their dependents, reservists, and National Guard personnel, and retirees) with quality products at the lowest possible price. Shelf pricing generally must be between 25% and 40% less than the same product on retail grocery shelves to be considered for placement in distribution.

Distribution in this channel requires selling product(s) into the system at DeCA headquarters in Arlington, obtaining authorized military distributors to serve the bases, and obtaining authorized military brokerage to serve the bases. Companies who desire can field a direct sales force to supplant the military broker. However, with the exception of perishable products, authorized military distributors, who are independent businesses, not affiliated or aligned with the Defense Commissary Agency, must deliver all products to the base. The number of distributors has recently decreased through acquisitions and mergers, in effect, lessening the opportunities for new products, or new entrants into the market to obtain distribution, even though they may have products authorized by DeCA headquarters.

(3) With the company's ability to utilize contracted manufacturing and with the company's ability to be a conduit for other company's products into the DeCA system, the company has the advantage of flexibility in its products offered. Uniquely positioned in the military, the company can offer other companies products under the company's contract. This is accomplished under the most favorable possible terms negotiated with each company.

(4) The company's youth at risk program and its donation of 3% of gross sales to nonprofit groups working with youth at risk, position the company to request and receive accommodations from retailers in foregoing traditional slotting fees and participation in mandatory marketing programs. This significantly reduces the cost of entry for the company.

The consumer can react positively to the company's marketing program of its donation to youth at risk. When price and quality are equal, consumers will choose the product that is identified with a cause that they care about, according to the definitive study of cause-related marketing conducted by Keye Wilson Communications and Seehaver Starch Worldwide, a preeminent market research firm. (See Marketing.)

The company's competitive advantages, management team, cause-marketing program, and established distribution position it very well to obtain significant profitability through the proposed funding.

KEY INVESTMENT CONSIDERATIONS

The company in its operating history has not shown a profit, as its funds and efforts have been directed at building the product lines and completing development of manufacturing, logistics, transportation, and distribution strategies. There are numerous factors contributing to the operating strength, stability, and exceptional potential growth of Clarence Pratt Enterprises, Inc.

The company's contract with the Defense Commissary Agency (DeCA) provides for the company's access to the commissary market. Only contract holders are authorized to distribute and sell products into the commissary system. The commissary, while like a grocery store, is primarily an important benefit to armed services personnel, their dependents, and retirees, as they can buy food at significantly reduced cost. The contract is not product specific. Products are approved separately. The company can therefore include new Clarence Pratt's Original™

products and/or new products of other companies under its contract. This flexibility will provide for excellent future growth of the product lines of the company, both its own brand and others, as entry into the commissary system is not easy, or profit-driven, and harbors pitfalls for most companies, including brokerage, distributors, and the system of doing business with the military.

The grocery market is large, stable, and showing recurring long-term growth. In 1994 the grocery market was estimated at over $71.6 billion dollars in sales. At the end of the fifth year of operations in this plan, the company projects penetrating less and .03% of this market. Thus, the growth potential in this distribution channel is favorable.

The company principal, Clarence Pratt, has the ability to develop relationships with key individuals and groups that result in numerous and potentially profitable business opportunities for the company in both established lines of distribution and potential lines of distribution.

The company's food products are attractively packaged and manufactured to the highest quality standards. The products are also competitively priced and the company has developed strategies for lowering the costs of production, while not diminishing quality, in order to expand the company's profit margins.

Minority ownership of the company, that meets the federal guidelines, permits the company to participate in various small business and small disadvantaged business programs in various areas of the government market. These include, but are not limited to, the Defense Personnel Support Center (troop provisioning), the General Service Administration (operation of government-owned facilities), and the Department of Justice (federal prisons).

Privately and publicly held corporations often are required to do business with small business and small disadvantaged businesses. As there are relatively few minority-owned companies operating successfully in the food industry, especially in the military resale markets, the opportunity for increasing product lines, sales, and profitability is inherently excellent.

The company's central cause-related community-based marketing program and its donation of 3% of its gross sales to nonprofit groups fighting the gang problem, is a significant marketing strategy. Not only has the company garnered support due to the program from the retail marketplace, food industry and food-industry related companies, such as The Shaker Oats Company, Foods Midwest America, and Venture Cola, have provided marketing and advertising support to the company's products. This support reduces the cost of doing business in the company's distribution channels.

Current management has developed the company's product, infrastructure, and business relationships to get the company to this point. It is anticipated that additional management personnel will be hired and utilized to further the company's strategy of meeting its distribution and product sales goals.

The market conditions under which the company operates, and has operated, have been favorable and it is anticipated to remain so. The company, with funding, will increase it sales and take full advantage of the distribution channels and products established, through increased marketing efforts.

The company's products have been well accepted by the consuming public. The consumer needs to be further educated as to the cause-marketing program of the company. While the Keye Seehaver Study shows the positive bottom line effects of cause-marketing, the consumer must be informed to make the right choice. With funding, the prospects for mid-term and long-term growth are excellent.

Distribution Growth	Products	Year
Save-Mart	16	12/97
Foster's Food and Drug	7	9/97
Top Savings Gulf Coast	4	6/97
Lindstrom Utah	5	6/97
Abner Stevens Utah	5	4/97
Eastern Con. U.S.		2/96
Con. U.S. Mandated		7/95
Midwest DeCA		5/95
Southwest DeCA		2/95
Company Incorporate		5/94

MARKETING

Market Analysis

The company's two primary distribution channels—retail grocery and military resale—are similar in that they both resell the company's products, however, the similarity does not continue with the business systems used by these two distinct groups. It is important to understand the system as it relates to marketing to judge the merits of the programs and funding allocations in this business plan.

The most significant difference between the two is that retail is profit-driven and the commissary segment of the military resale system is not, while the Exchange segment of the military resale system, is only marginally profit-driven.

Retail generates revenue from consumer sales and from manufacturers in the form of slotting fees, price allowances, promotional programs, mandatory marketing programs, discounts, incentive programs, and free distribution of product. Thus, entry into this channel is traditionally beyond the financial capability of most small businesses, on other than a limited basis or on a local distribution basis only. The company, with its advantageous youth at risk program, can enter retail without these costly programs.

The commissary sells products to the consumer at the cost it buys the products from the manufacturer, plus a 5% surcharge to cover overhead. DeCA operates from appropriated funds and the revenue generated from the surcharge. DeCA's mission is to provide the patron, active military, dependents, and retirees with the highest quality and lowest cost products. It is not profit-driven. With active competition from discount stores, Save-Mart, and other retail giants, DeCA's growth is certain through its legislated status.

The buying habits of the commissary shopper are beneficial to the company. The commissary shopper often only shops once per month, unless they live on base or within close proximity. It is not uncommon for a customer to drive hundreds of miles to shop at a commissary. Often, rather than buying one of a product, the consumer will buy a month's supply or more at one time.

The commissary market has stabilized and the patronage of the system by authorized consumers is expected to increase. The commissary system has undergone rapid changes, including category management and performance based operation, since its inception only six years ago. At that time the individual commissaries of the U.S. Army, U.S. Navy, U.S. Marine Corps, and the U.S. Air Force were combined into one operation. The same type of consolidation is occurring with the exchanges. The U.S. Army and U.S. Air Force consolidated some years ago.

Total Authorized Commissary and Exchange Patrons

Active Duty	1,692,609
Dependents	2,347,116
Retirees	1,748,320
Total Authorized	**5,788,045**

The fact that the company has obtained distribution in several retail chains without paying slotting fees, or participating in free products programs or mandatory marketing programs, has been to the advantage of lower costs of entry into these distribution channels.

Marketing of the company's products is essential to the continued success in these channels. The company's cause-marketing program is best suited to independent marketing of the Clarence Pratt's Original™ brand, rather than as one of the many participants in store marketing programs. The company does participate in in-store couponing and demo programs.

Retail Program Participation	Yes	No
Slotting Fees		X
Price Allowances	X	
Store Marketing		X
Free Distribution		X

There are important differences in the makeup of the consumer base of the company's two main channels of distribution that require two approaches.

The consumer base for retail distribution is literally everyone within the local trading area of a grocery store. The consumer base for the military is limited. However, sales from the total authorized commissary and exchange shoppers exceed their small numbers.

The commissaries, with a total of approximately 300 stores worldwide, typically rank as the ninth largest grocery chain in America, with approximately $5.4 billion in annual sales. The number one grocery chain, typically either McSweeney's or Stores U.S.A., have 2,000 plus stores producing $22 billion in sales. Each commissary sells approximately 38.8% more per stores that the leading chains.

One factor that can account for this difference is that within the military resale consumer base are two different elements. First the active duty and dependents either live on base or within close proximity. If the base is located within a populated area, as most are, then they have a choice whether to buy their groceries down the street at the local store or go to the commissary. Retirees on the other hand, will drive many miles to shop at the closest store and will likely purchase more products per shopping trip than they do when they shop at a grocery store.

Product Marketing Strategy

Product formulations, production, distribution, and sales into distribution channels are only part of the process of the success of the company. Once the products are on the shelf, marketing will drive sales to reach projected sales levels.

The company has a three-faceted marketing strategy: a national strategy, a retail strategy, and a military resale strategy, with the national strategy having positive impact on the other two.

National Strategy: "The Clarence Pratt Show™"

This weekly 30-minute, fast-paced, entertaining and informative talk show, is the company's national marketing vehicle. The show has been on the air in the Intermountain market for seven years. It is growing in popularity and this plan calls for expansion of the airing of the program into other markets. Clarence Pratt hosts the program. Clarence Pratt's Original™ products are showcased in the shows. There are cooking segments, using Clarence Pratt's Original™ products in the shows, as well.

This program can have more marketing impact, more impact on product sales, and opening new distribution than any other potential national program, including a national media blitz campaign.

The Clarence Pratt Show™, like the food products, began as an effort to bring about positive change in America's communities. The show has grown and evolved into one of sufficient prominence to become regional and even national in scope. The program serves several needs that make this happen.

First, the television stations of America must show that their programming meets the need and necessity of their broadcast areas, to either obtain or keep their broadcast licenses. Therefore, meeting the Federal Communications Commission's regulations and requirements are important. Stations must ascertain the issues of importance to stations and broadcast programming to meet these needs. Stations must air programming for children and stations must air programming for their minority communities. These are mandated requirements. The Clarence Pratt Show™ meets these requirements.

The show is offered on a barter basis to the stations. This means that the stations receive the show, via satellite, with half the commercial time taken, and half available to them to sell, with no cost for the production of the program to the station. This is important, as other than local news operations, stations have a difficult time producing local programming of note. Most have weekend shows, hosted by either reporters or weekend news anchors, talking about various charity events in their communities. The Clarence Pratt Show™ offers a viable alternative, with shows on topics that can bring positive change to the station's audiences and solutions to the issues. The show adds to the effectiveness and impact of the company's cause-marketing program.

Solutions to the issues that affect our community are presented on the program. The show topics shown below are representative and are the most recent 13 program series produced (11/97).

Show Topics

Youth Support Programs
- Successful methods of turning youth from gangs.

Chamber of Commerce
- Resources for vital information and business assistance.

Teen Pregnancy
- Successful solutions, focusing on prevention and education.

National Academy Group
- Solutions in schools to bridging the gap between academia and work reality.

Mayors
- Solutions to local issues through the Mayor's office.

City Councils
- The most power rests here. Solutions to gangs, youth problems, community involvement from this perspective.

What Are Our Differences?
- Through the talents of "Boys to Females," a performing female impersonator group, solutions to understanding and accepting differences, while recognizing that we're really all the same.

Republicans and Democrats
- The philosophical differences between the two and how are solutions presented through the party system.

TV—Who Does It Serve?
- Does TV meet our information needs or are we mesmerized by the sensationalism of the news and hypnotized by the entertainment programming? What is TV's role?

U.S. Women Business Owners Organization
- The fastest growing segment of small business—someone has developed solutions to the glass ceiling.

Children's Justice System
- Revolving door? Successful solutions for youth continually going in and out of the system, with no redirection to the positive.

Community Affairs
- Solutions from county government, local charities, and media.

The benefits to the company from "The Clarence Pratt Show™" are significant, and include:

- Significant host recognition transferring to product image
- Builds brand awareness
- Develops commitment to cause-marketing program
- Advertises the products in use
- Advertises the youth at risk program
- Develops broad based community support for the products and program
- Generates revenue
- More effective and less costly than regional/national media campaign

Retail Strategy

The strategy is to direct 3% of the gross sales of the products to nonprofit groups working with youth at risk, in an effort to stem the rising tide of gangs in America. The company uses a cause-related marketing strategy, for two reasons.

The company was founded with one barbecue sauce developed from an old family recipe by Clarence Pratt. The idea came from a need to fund the television show, then called "New Challenges," and on public broadcast television. With the intensely competitive donation solicitation market often barring media applicants, and with having to compete with community groups that the show served for funding, Clarence Pratt thought there had to be a better way. Thus, the barbecue sauce was born.

Grocery stores are members of their communities. They are affected by the rapidly rising gang problem in America, with shootings in their parking lots, rapid rising in pilferage, and shoplifting. They would like to do something about it and consumers would like to do something about it. Clarence Pratt's Original™ products and the grocery store can provide them a way.

The company positions itself, both to store and consumer, as a method to help the youth of the community. While unique, this strategy is effective when it is sincere.

In 1994, Keye/Wilson Communications and Seehaver Worldwide, Inc., a preeminent research firm issued the "Keye Seehaver Study" of the effects of cause-marketing on consumer buying habits. Their foremost finding was that "'consumers believe that business has a responsibility to help improve social ills," and that consumers respond positively with purchases from companies that practice cause-marketing sincerely.

Likely to Switch

Total Population	62%
Influentials	77%
Household Income $50,000+	78%

Given that quality of the product and price are equal, the graphic below illustrates the Keye Seehaver finding for how likely consumers are to switch brands, they will also switch stores to meet their need. This is important for stores in their decision to take Clarence Pratt's Original™ products.

The 3% donation, which is detailed on product labels, all marketing and advertising materials, all publicity, and all information used or sent by the company, is what allows the consumer to participate and is central to the marketing strategy.

The declaration on the product labels reads:

3% of the price (which translates to approximately 50% of the profits from the sale of these products) is donated to military youth and nonprofit groups helping youth at risk" in your community.

The retail strategy also includes traditional marketing methods used in innovative ways. Because of the donation from the sale of product, television and radio stations have run public service announcements emphasizing the youth at risk aspects of the program. The program is ideal for interfacing with local community groups much in the same manner as the company has done with the Armed Services YMCA program (see Military Strategy).

Other elements of the retail strategy are:

- Product Demonstrations
- Co-Promotions
- In-store Couponing
- Store Circulars
- Electronic Media

The donation is accomplished through local boards comprised of community, business, government, and education leadership. The boards determine which group(s) receive the allocated donation by their effectiveness in doing the job. There is no grant or application procedure, although direct solicitation is not discouraged.

"The Clarence Pratt Show™" affects the retail strategy in that the celebrity status of the host—the transference of image to the products and the community-based nature of both the products and the television show—reinforces product marketing and influences retail grocery chains to take Clarence Pratt's Original™ products, when they might not otherwise have.

The cause-marketing strategy and the 3% donation are also effective in the military. The company has aligned itself with the national Armed Services YMCA program as both the recipient and determinator of which of the many deserving Armed Services YMCA programs receive donations from the company.

Military Strategy

Due to the distinctly different nature of the commissary shopper, the company's strategy is to direct its marketing efforts at the authorized patron, and in locations and through means that reach them specifically. The strategy is to utilize a mix of traditional with innovative uses of media.

Elements of the military strategy are:

- Product Demonstrations
- Co-Promotions
- In-store Couponing
- Base Newspaper Advertising
- DeCA Specific Promotional

Definition of Retail and Military Elements

Product Demonstrations

Product demonstrations are serving sample portions of the products in the store to the consumer. Often a 25-cent coupon that is only immediately redeemable is used. The military allows for and the company participates in setting minimum case purchases for demos. The company currently has a 5 case per product minimum for demos.

Co-Promotions

Through relationships developed by Clarence Pratt with major corporations, the company undertakes co-promotions with other manufacturers. For example, Foods America is a co-promoter of the company's products and annually participates in a holiday promotion with Clarence Pratt's Original™ Disposable Baking Pans in the military. The company is talking with other corporations to develop a cross-couponing program.

In-store Couponing

The company uses 25-cent-off discount coupons affixed to the bottles or shelf (in pads) to help drive sales.

Store Circulars

The company, in retail, participates with 25-cent coupons in the stores' shoppers guides and/or direct-mail newspaper inserts.

Electronic Media

The company uses radio advertising to promote its products in retail. Radio is also used to reinforce store-specific promotions and promote the company's products through its youth at risk program.

Base Newspaper Advertising

There are approximately 120 newspaper publications that are targeted at readers around specific military bases of all services. These papers report on the local military community and happenings on or in the base community. The readership is very high among authorized commissary and exchange patrons. There is a prohibition regarding advertising prices of products offered in the commissaries and exchanges in any public media. The company has advertised its youth at risk program and the product image and will continue to do so.

DeCA Specific Promotional

DeCA headquarters establishes two-week promotional periods, most of which are theme-related and that carry specific pricing promotional requirements. The company participates in these programs, where they are beneficial to the company. The company participates in the holiday promotional period, which is a 60-day promotion. DeCA promotes primarily based on price. The pricing structure of the system includes VPR (Variable Promotional Pricing), when required or used by a manufacturer the regular price is lowered during the promotional period. There is usually a functional minimum of 15% reduction for a 30-day period required to participate. The company also uses coupons to drive sales during promotional periods.

The plan calls for expending the following budgets in advertising, promotion, and demonstrations. It should be noted that "The Clarence Pratt Show™" is included in the budgets for advertising.

Market Budget Elements	Year 1
Advertising	$355,000
Promotion	$341,520
Demonstrations	$147,397
Total	$828,917

Market Budget Elements	Years 2-5
Year Two	$1,190,782
Year Three	$1,248,598
Year Four	$1,313,217
Year Five	$1,394,892

Demonstrations and Promotions

Year	Demos	Promotions
2	$200,000	$390,000
3	$250,000	$400,000
4	$300,000	$410,000
5	$375,000	$425,000

Demos are included for both retail and military distribution, as found in previous sections.

Advertising—Television and Radio

Year	Radio	Television
2	$90,000	$80,000
3	$100,000	$80,000
4	$100,000	$80,000
5	$100,000	$80,000

Television Show and Base Newspapers

Year	Television Show	Base Newspapers
2	$200,000	$50,000
3	$325,000	$50,000
4	$375,000	$50,000
5	$375,000	$50,000

The budget for promotions will be expended on an as-needed basis that is determined by the events and retail distribution channels. The same is true of co-promotions.

Co-promotions and promotional events especially tailored to the distribution channel, incorporating the youth at risk program and coordinated with the company's brokers, are the main thrust of the promotional program. Initial entries into new markets include press conferences announcing the products and youth at risk program.

Conclusion

The company has established products in established distribution channels. Funding is needed to support the marketing programs as previously outlined for the company to drive sales to projected levels.

There are a number of positive factors relating to the company's position that are not reflected in the analysis in the marketing section. The most important in this regard is the company's attractiveness to other companies as an outlet for access to military distribution with products they wish to put into the military resale system.

The marketing analysis is based upon what is currently in-house. As the company and its founder Clarence Pratt attract significant opportunities on a regular basis, it is pertinent to assume that the profit potential possibilities through marketing new products, whether private, labeled, or not, and/or services, and accessing new less costly lines of distribution, i.e., the Armed Services Support Center, will play integral roles in developing the company's positive financial picture.

The attractiveness of the company's youth at risk program generates interest from companies wishing to co-promote their products and/or become involved in solving the gang problem. The food products and the television show, as the major marketing thrust of the company is unique in the industry and positions the company to control its destiny.

OPERATIONS

The company produces its products in three ways. The company's pourable food products are produced under contract, using the company's formulas and quality control mechanisms. The company purchases private label Clarence Pratt's Original™ products from manufacturers, as in the case of Clarence Pratt's Original™ Disposable Baking Pans. And third, the company puts other companys' products under its contract with the Defense Commissary Agency, or under its representation to the military resale market for exchanges.

The company currently negotiates the most favorable terms possible for the purchase of the products. This is usually 30 days and sometimes longer, if the company's creditor is willing to allow for the cash flow cycle in the military. With funding, the company anticipates to seek out and secure other sources of contract manufacturing of the company's products. The logistical and bottom line benefit of shipping the products only the shortest distance possible will accrue to the bottom line.

While the company maintains an account with a reputable commercial warehouse to store products, orders to either distributors or customers are produced to order and drop shipped.

The following are the resources and or sources of products marketed by the company:

Clarence Pratt's Original™ Products
    Private Label Food Manufacturer
    GB Great Foods, Portland, Maine
    Remarkable Foods, Grand Rapids, Minnesota
    Sun Burst, Boise, Idaho
    Private Label Disposable Baking Pans
    FoilRite
    Private Label Pastas and Sauce Mixes
    Natalina's Premiere Pasta
    Spices
    Natalina's Premiere Pasts

Products Marketed by Clarence Pratt Enterprises, Inc.
Fast Bind
Fast Bind Enterprises, Phoenix, Arizona
Yummy Bite Dog Biscuits
Joan's Products, Kansas City, Missouri
Cookware
Greg's Marketing Group/Direct Europe, Orlando, Florida
Crank Case Aid
A1 Quality of Redding, California

The Defense Commissary Agency requires manufacturers to participate in their distribution system. This means that a company has to have a business relationship with independent distributor(s), authorized by the system, and representation by authorized military brokerage or a direct sales force, to meet the distribution sold into the Marketing Business Unit in Arlington, Virginia. The company has established relationships with some of the top military distribution companies, including the following and the territories they serve:

Distribution and Brokerage

Southeastern U.S. and Central America
Top Savings Military, Savannah, Georgia

Northeast Atlantic Region
Byrd Lowrey, Emmittsburg, Massachusetts

Central Atlantic Region and Europe
Armed Forces Distributors of Virginia, Norfolk, Virginia

Central States and Midwest
Orrion Tackett, Springfield, Illinois
Hayden Aaron Sales, Lubbock, Texas
G&A Distributors, Norman, Oklahoma
C&D Distribution, Kansas City, Kansas
Byrd Lowrey Denver, Colorado

Southwest Desert Wholesale, Socorro, New Mexico
Southwest, Northwest and Pacific Rim
Wagner Military Distribution

The company is represented by the following brokerage firms, and the territories they serve:

Military Resale Market World Wide
Sisson company, Daytona Beach, Florida

Retail Grocery
Young Brokerage, Provo, Utah
Moscow, Idaho, Tempe, Arizona, and Socorro, New Mexico

Save-Mart, Sam's Clubs
HCS, Hope, Arizona

Wherever possible, the company utilizes minimum order quantities for a freight discount. The company has negotiated discount tariffs with Greene Freight and Continental U.S. Transport, to transport products nationwide.

Transportation

Product and Cash Flow System

To date, the company has put into place all of the ingredients for a successful operation, with the exception of the funding. Accomplishments include the following:

- Established channels of distribution through which: (1) its products have been mandated to be carried and sold, and (2) favorable shelving space has been obtained. The company has existing agreements with both military and retail grocery chains that alone would enable it to attain the sales projections represented in the accompanying financial projections.
- The company's youth program has been embraced by its customers as providing a benefit over and above the profit potential represented by the company's products.
- A business concept that enables the company to operate with a small organization with minimal fixed costs.
- Profitable contracts with reputable manufacturers that provide significant contribution towards the company's profitability.

Management

The management of the company has more than 75 years of combined experience in developing contacts; selling products; staffing, organizing and developing start-up organizations; and accounting and management information systems. Mr. Clarence Pratt, a minority executive, has particular expertise in generating and utilizing support for his causes and companies.

A major advantage of the company derives from the fact that it contract manufactures its products. As a result, the organization initially will be very small, consisting of a president, an operations manager, a part-time financial manager, two administrative people, a retail sales vice president, and in a year, a military resale markets sales vice president. Mr. Pratt will continue to develop relationships with various military and retail organizations. The sales vice presidents will also be responsible for expanding sales. Mr. Perkins will come on board full-time when warranted.

Clarence Pratt, Jr., President, is the founder and developer of Clarence Pratt's Original™ products. He has a B.A. in Business Administration from the University of California at Berkeley. With 25 years of experience in advertising, marketing, and developing products and programs, Mr. Pratt has a proven ability to develop and organize sales programs that work. His entertainment and television production experience has helped him in impressing others with the benefit and opportunity that his products and companies offer. In addition, his remarkable vision has enabled him to identify opportunities presented by others' products and ideas, such that others have repeatedly requested his assistance in developing their opportunities. Mr. Pratt serves on numerous boards and committees and is able to use his contacts to put together coalitions that develop solutions. He has also formed numerous partnerships with other companies that have resulted in support of his products.

Russ O'Leary, Vice President of Operations, studied political science and philosophy at the University of the South. Mr. O'Leary has 25 years of experience in distribution management and planning, marketing, and advertising. He has had profit and loss responsibility serving as a branch manager, where he increased sales and related distribution by over 50% in one year. He also served as director of traffic of a common carrier, where he increased sales and distribution by 700% over a 7-year period. This distribution experience has served him well in assisting to put CPE supply agreements in place. His experience in media has helped him to develop an understanding of product positioning. As Mr. Pratt's partner, he has participated in the development of the program since its inception, including developing the business concept and preparing the business plan, designing and developing product labels, co-producing PSA's and other company videos. He has also assisted in developing and setting up the distribution network for the company's products. In conjunction with Mr. Pratt, he prepared the pricing model used to set competitive prices and helped negotiate with manufacturers.

Gregory S. Perkins, Chief Financial Officer. An M.B.A. and a CPA with a B.A. in physics, Mr. Perkins has 25 years of experience in all aspects of financial operations, including 7 years living and working overseas. During 15 years with Intercontinental Corporation, he was CFO of a foreign subsidiary, and as an operations consultant, he developed and sold to senior operating and staff managements over $42 million of profit and controls improvements. As an investment banker he developed $300 million in debt and equity funding for small and medium-size companies. As Executive Vice President and CFO, working with a company suffering significant losses and a severe cash shortage, he cut expenditures and controlled cash outlays to attain profitability. He has developed strategic plans for dozens of different companies in diverse industries and has developed and implemented management information systems, budgeting procedures, and internal controls. He has implemented cash management systems, developed and maintained banking, auditing, and legal relationships. He has extensive experience in contract negotiation and administration.

The following information is an overview of our financial projections.

SUMMARY FINANCIAL PROJECTIONS

	Yr. 1	Yr. 2	Yr. 3	Yr. 4	Yr. 5
Sales Military	2,041,393	3,480,779	4,063,328	4,392,346	4,719,208
Sales Exchanges	182,917	257,306	289,440	345,544	415,674
Sales Retail	744,078	2,770,182	4,068,574	4,234,131	4,286,757
Total Sales	**2,968,389**	**6,508,268**	**8,421,342**	**8,972,021**	**9,421,639**
Cost of Goods Sold	2,441,616	5,284,050	6,796,904	7,241,378	7,598,939
Gross Margin	526,773	1,224,218	1,624,428	1,730,643	1,822,700
General & Admin. Expenses	676,847	1,349,813	1,458,775	1,513,569	1,563,976
Earnings Before Interest & Taxes	-150,074	-125,595	165,663	217,074	258,724
Net Income	-104,194	-87,541	101,374	135,591	161,815

Hair Salon

BUSINESS PLAN

EPIPHANY SALON

9504 Winding Row Ave.
Green Bay, WI 54303

This business plan for a hair salon supports its commitment to a dynamic, cutting-edge, hair care establishment by using an energetic and lively format. The aggressive scheme of expansion and watertight description of all aspects of the business contribute to the innovative and elite image being conveyed by the business. This plan is testament to the value of extensive forethought, as it outlines the business direction for the next 15 years.

- VISION/MISSION

- COMPANY OVERVIEW

- PRODUCT STRATEGY

- MARKET ANALYSIS

- FINANCIALS

VISION/MISSION

Present Situation

This business plan is written to end in the year 2015 for the purpose of retirement for myself, Rhonda Walters. Said shares from the business will be sold at an assessed market value. In that year, it is the responsibility of the acting president to write a continued plan for the good of the cosmetology industry and community.

The name of the corporation is Epiphany Salon. The theme is urban, industrial, techno, chic. The first question that rises for most is, "What does it mean?" If you asked that question, know that you probably are a baby boomer and haven't been watching MTV or ESPN, where mass symbols and visualization play an important part in marketing. We refer to it as being, "hip and cool" and that is what Epiphany is, "a hip and cool service and product center for cosmetology including an educational center for Green Bay's urban youth committed to excellence. Green Bay's population is doubling by the year 2000, putting the target market of Generation X at 61,282. The educational center will be an elite school of cosmetology, servicing to a class of 10 every 6 months. This will serve 2 purposes:

1. Basic training for the industry focusing on feeding Epiphany the Salon and Epiphany Male Room.
2. Service the price conscious economy in the Green Bay Area.

Epiphany Male Room is the only salon to have professional salon services for men in a male environment. Epiphany the Salon offers a full line of Bettiva products noted for their commitment to the environment. As a concept salon for Bettiva, Epiphany is allowed to carry products other Bettiva salons do not. The front of the salon is committed to being a strong retail center, inviting shoppers to interact. The target is 35% retail sales to service dollar sales. Epiphany is the only area salon to be online and fully automated. Epiphany will have the most aggressive marketing campaign of any other area salon.

Epiphany is in its infant stage, however, it carries goodwill from a previous business in respect of retail sales. Both Barbara, the president of Ephiphany Salon, and I have strong backgrounds in business and retail management. A school will complete the 4 major areas of business in 1998. To summarize, the areas of business will include a full service women's salon, a men's salon, a retail center, and an educational center. The target market will be the young professional and the area tourist. The school will be marketed to the price conscious in the clinic and will be an elite school for basic training in cosmetology.

The challenges for the industry are the same challenges for Epiphany. These are recruitment, retention, and productivity. Being a native of the Green Bay Area, where I received my cosmetology license in 1977, I know the area businesses and the people who work at them. As a teacher, I have aided in licensing over 120 cosmetologists at the Vocational Training Center. Presently, there is a mixture of veteran and new talent.

Retention is a problem for salons that lack structure and management. Both Barbara and I have owned and operated successful businesses. Productivity is assessed through employee evaluation by way of salon management software. Client retention, retail dollar to service dollar sales, and goals are all part of the productivity picture. Veteran stylists and technicians are attracted to employers who offer flexible hours and adding to their education by becoming instructors. The Epiphany Male Room will supply a guaranteed hourly rate for new talent, thus keeping payroll predictable for management purposes.

Productivity will be monitored through automation. It is realistic to believe that each department can operate at 80% productivity for top-end projections.

Financing is 20% personal investment from the president and vice president of the corporation, 50% from financial institute, and 30% from investors. A total of $163,880 is needed to safely grow the business, keeping interests secure and the business healthy. Ten percent or $20,100 will be put into savings for security.

Vision and Mission

Epiphany Salon's vision is to create a harmonious, productive, and profitable salon environment, supplying the community with a retail center, a Bettiva share-school of cosmetology, and separate men's and women's salons.

The mission statement is very clean in the approach: Having fun doing business by sharing the passion of cosmetology combining technology, art, and science.

Future planning includes, expansion of retail department with virtual shopping which will be an online shopping center. The school will conduct advanced evening classes, maximizing productivity. Ownership of the present building is planned, expanding an additional 3,000 square feet for school and salon. Presently there are apartments in the upper level. These would add to revenue.

Epiphany Salon, Inc. was founded in 1997 and is presently in its start-up stage. Epiphany Salon can best be described as currently being in the business of cosmetology, education, and wellness. In recent times our key strengths have been customer service, retailing, and education, teaching the most recent technological aspects of cosmetology and business management. The corporation brings together talent with a retail manager and an educator in cosmetology and business who each have more than 20 years experience in the industry. Refer to resumes for background and references.

To profile the issues of the president and vice president, it is the responsibility of management to increase profitability, improve productivity, motivate and inspire associates, create promotional calendars, increase client retention by way of maintaining the policies and procedures, conducting evaluations, and controlling the numbers. Annual board meetings will set the fiscal year with goals, review of policies, and share worth. An advisory board will enhance objectivity and provide guidelines to corporate directors.

Corporate directors will also be employees of the corporation. Barbara will head the skin department, including cosmetic and retail sales. I will be the acting manager of the hair department and work as a technician. After the school opens I will transfer my clientele to other technicians managing the operations of the school.

Growing professional cosmetologists is the focus of the mission. Cosmetology holds a poor professional image. It is an industry that Hollywood loves to exploit, portraying it as an industry that requires little training. Entry-level cosmetology positions require strong technical skills, strong communication skills, and strong sales. In addition to these skills, cosmetologists need to be trained in personal financial management and estate planning. Maslow's hierarchy theory states that after survival, when basic needs are being met, one can go on to higher levels. Our commitment is to have fun doing what we love and be profitable at the same time, while growing the business long term and committing to the personal development of our people. This will help improve the image of the industry. This will attract the best cosmetologists in our area. It is our vision of harmony for the community.

The mission statement also states that this is achieved by combining technology, art, and science. Epiphany Salon will use automation to retain clients. It takes 3 times the amount of effort to attract a new client versus the effort required to retain a happy client. Professional Salon software makes direct marketing a breeze. Presently, 10% of all salons are automated. Locally, 3 salons are automated and none use the technology to market and track clients. Automation is key to growing and maintaining our target market.

Goals and Objectives

It is the goal of Epiphany Salon to provide the community with an institution of cosmetology that targets all socioeconomic standings and is a model for the industry nationally. This models the Bettiva Institute's objective, placing an emphasis on personal as well as environmental wellness. It is this objective that ties together the school, the retail center, and salons.

The Ten Commitments of Excellence

1. Commitment to well-being.
We believe well-being is the cornerstone of personal and professional growth. Without personal and professional well-being our mission cannot be achieved.

2. Commitment to the team objective.
We believe in total commitment to the team. The team objective is a guide for us to follow in our service to our clients, support of each other, and team growth.

3. Commitment to goal attainment.
We believe every individual should have personal and economic goals. Students and staff work within a framework of daily evaluation in order to identify and achieve their long-term objectives.

4. Commitment to our time management system.
We believe our time management system should be utilized in all clinic activities to provide maximum efficiency and effectiveness for our clients. We commit to managing our time and setting specific goals within that time.

5. Commitment to excellence in all we do.
With our philosophy we become team members, working for ourselves and each other. We have high expectations in terms of conduct, and know that each of us is a reflection of the team.

6. Commitment to incredible, outstanding, unbelievable client service.
We believe in extending such incredible service to all clients that they feel like honored guests in our establishment. We constantly anticipate, meet, and exceed our clients' expectations.

7. Commitment to retailing through client experience.
We believe that each team member is also a salesperson. Retailing is a vital prerequisite to client experience and ultimately leads to professional success.

8. Commitment to value-added service.
Value-added means doing and giving more than is expected. We believe each of us needs to go above and beyond the call of duty. The school and salon will benefit in direct proportion to the value-added service provided by each team member.

9. Commitment to innovation.
We believe our strength lies in our passion to implement new ideas and embrace change. We realize that innovation involves risking failure, but we choose to risk failure in our pursuit of success rather than fail passively.

10. Commitment to personal property.
Commitment to respecting all equipment and belongings of others (as well as to Epiphany Salon). Stealing from others is stealing from oneself.

Through strong commitment, strong marketing, and a solid financial plan, Epiphany will service the community and be recognized as a business leader. We feel very confident that the goals can be reached.

Legal Business Description

The legal name of the company is Epiphany Salon Inc. However, there are departments within the corporation: Epiphany the Salon, Epiphany Male Room, and Epiphany Educational Center. The legal form of the business is Subchapter S Corporation. Refer to article papers submitted to the state, June 26, 1997. The business location is in downtown Green Bay, Wisconsin.

Management Team

Our management team consists of people that have mastered their technical skills and have a desire to share that knowledge with new talent enetering the industry. Career experience expands over three decades. Refer to resumes of myself and Barbara. Portfolio also available for viewing.

Flowchart for team members is available for in-house management. Other charts will explain roles and responsibilities along with compensation of each position available at Epiphany. This includes the roles and responsibilities of Barbara, the president, and me, the vice president. This does not presently include the school staff and its management team.

The outside management team consists of Wally Smart, accountant and Jim Johnson, corporate lawyer. Our outside management advisors provide tremendous support for management decisions and creativity.

By January 1998 an advisory board, including two highly qualified business and industry professionals, will assist our management team in making appropiate decisions and taking the most effective action; however, they will not be responsible for management decisions.

Staffing

Epiphany team recognizes that additional staff is required to properly support our growth. Presently, there are thirteen people on staff. We are currently interviewing for new staff. As a teacher of cosmetology, I have seven years of former students that hold cosmetology positions in the community. Growth opportunities improve employee retention within our industry. Epiphany recognizes the need for growth of the individual.

As executive officers of Epiphany Salon, it is our responsibility to improve the image of our industry through solid business management. This is achieved through increasing profitability for the business, its officers, and staff. It means improving productivity for each department. Motivating and inspiring management, technicians, and associate staff with leadership will improve the image, as well as having fun sharing the passion for cosmetology combining technology, art, and science.

To grow a healthy business is to continually assess the needs of the people who hold the same vision. This vision creates a harmonious, productive, and profitable salon environment. It is our responsibility to be committed to this process.

Responsibilities:

Barbara, President
- Retail center. Oversee the operations of the retail area. This includes inventory, stocking, and displays.
- Oversee receptionist duties and scheduling.
- Oversee the Male Room operations.
- Participate with salon managers. Managers should report to Barbara for needs.

- Handle payroll operations.
- Participate with interviewing.
- Act as salon manager until department can support a head.
- Develop color specialization.

Rhonda, Vice President

- Educational director for Epiphany Salon Education Center.
- Marketing planner.
- Staff meetings.
- Oversee goals and evaluations.
- Co-associate program. Participate with Artistic Director.
- Develop Epiphany fashion newsletter.
- Develop epiphany.com web page and future shopping center.
- Salon technology and training.
- Participate with interviewing.
- Number cruncher.

Education and Experience:

Refer to resumes and portfolios.

Compensation:

It is the responsibility of the officers to provide themselves with a comfortable wage. However, these wages will not take away from the business. The business then, is paid first with a formulation of 15% from the gross. This ensures a healthy business growth. Also in this formulation is reward for long-term employment with shares given and retirement plans for its staff members. A financial advisor will help with the education needed for benefit of all. Growth is a process. We are committed to this process.

Role: Artistic Director

As the artistic director you hold a strong leadership position within the company as well as within the community. By carrying out the company's vision and mission on a daily basis, you will ensure a harmonious, productive, creative, and profitable salon environment. You will instill the importance of our mission of having fun doing business by sharing the passion of cosmetology combining technology, art, and science with the technicians and co-associates who in turn will share this with their clientele.

Responsibilities:

- Co-associates program. Be able to determine at what point a stylist should work with a co-associate based on 75% productivity over a three-month period. This program must be rewarding to each party. It must be financially beneficial to the stylist and it must be educationally rewarding to the co-associate. The educational process for the co-associate must be measurable with a competency based closure.
- Monitor the orientation of the co-associate program and evaluate the progress.
- Self-direction and education will be a must, keeping up with the latest trends. The staff will look to you as the fashion leader.
- There will be a Spring/Summer Collection and a Fall/Winter Collection. It will be your expertise to communicate these collections to the staff and community.
- Active involvement in recruiting and interviewing potential staff.
- Coordinate training and development between departments.
- Attend department head meetings on a quarterly basis.
- Participate in staff meetings on a quarterly basis.

Education and Experience:

An endorsed high school diploma. Five years experience in the field of cosmetology. Attendance at an advanced academy of education committing to updates on a national level annually. Minimum overall service sales of 25% in chemical services. Public speaking skills are needed to communicate trends to the community, department managers, technicians, and co-associates.

Compensation:

This is an optioned position, whichever produces the most revenue for the director. Once this option is made, it holds in place for one year before review.

Option 1:
- Salary based at $9.25 hourly for this full-time position. This is also a stipend position paid bi-annually based on 80 hours per year with staff and co-associate training and development. The pay for the stipend is derived from average weekly pay over a 6-month period.
- Bonus program. Productivity bonus of 2% for each department hitting 100% of service goal or 1% bonus for 80% reach of goal.
- Individual retail sales commissioned at 10%.
- Paid vacation. One week paid after 2 years service. Two weeks paid after 5 years service.
- Health insurance, 50/50 pay after 90 days.

Option 2:
- 45% commission with benefit package and stipend. 10% retail commission.

Option 3:
- Self-employed at 62% commission. No benefits. Stipend for 80 hours education. 10% retail commission. Productivity bonus.

Role: Receptionist

A salon receptionist is a viable position to a successful and harmonious salon. You, as the receptionist, give the first impression and the last impression to everyone who passed through the front door. All clients and customers come first and it is your responsibility to create a balance of all daily duties. It is also your role to facilitate the vision of having fun doing business by sharing the passion of cosmetology combining technology, art, and science and to communicate that vision to the clientele.

Educational Requirements: Endorsed high school diploma with a background in basic computer skills. Related customer service experience is also necessary.

Compensation Base: An annual salary of $12,000 is a base for this full-time position. Performance is to be rewarded. Meeting retail sales goals by 100% results in a 2% bonus. Meeting retail sales goals by 80% results in an 1% bonus. Payment of bonuses will be given through quarterly evaluations. Paid vacations are given with years of service. One week paid after two years and two weeks paid after five years of service.

Health insurance is to be self-funded. Group rates are available.

Part-time employees are given a flat rate hourly plan at $6.00 per hour.

Responsibilities:
- Customer service. Greet all clients and customers within the first 10 seconds with a smile. Make them feel welcomed and comfortable. Offer a beverage, reading

material, and take their coat. Direct them to a dressing area if appropriate.
- All new clients are given a menu and tour of the facilities. If you are unable to do so, find an associate who is available, introducing them to the client by name.
- Handle all phone calls politely and professionally using your name when answering the call.
- Booking appointments. Taking client's name, phone number, and type of service. Repeat the time, day, and date of appointment to client. Resource information for available times to book appointments of each technician.
- Confirming appointments. Appointments for the following day are to be confirmed by the end of the shift.
- Communicate product knowledge to clients with confidence. Have knowledge of all services offered and their prices.
- Check in clients. Clients are to be checked in after being greeted. Check-in includes gathering data for client file. All data for that day is to be entered before the end of your shift.
- As a receptionist, you will be responsible for handling all financial transactions of clients. You will have a complete understanding of the POS terminal as well as the credit card terminal and their functions.
- Gift certificates will be issued, monitored, and filed by the receptionist on duty.
- Proper maintenance of change in the cash drawer is expected.
- New inventory shipments will be promptly checked into stock.
- The answering machine is to be attended to every morning and the calls returned immediately.
- It is the receptionist's duty to close out the POS terminal and credit card terminal at the end of the day or shift.
- Maintenance of the reception area, waiting area, and display units are also responsibilities.
- Inform technicians when their clients have arrived or canceled.
- Dayrunners will be given with data cards each morning.

Role: The Male Room Manager

The main responsibility of the Male Room Manager is to encourage, inspire, motivate, and retain staff and clientele. This is achieved through relaying the vision and mission of Epiphany, creating a salon environment that is harmonious, productive, and profitable. Having fun doing business by sharing the passion of cosmetology combining technology, art, and science is the mission of Epiphany. The manager who models this vision and provides support in its mission will be a strong leader. It will be your responsibility to be this leader.

The manager will help guide and find solutions for the staff if problems should arise. Being a leader in the company, you will ensure customer service to its fullest potential, thereby maintaining client retention and achieving retail goals.

Responsibilities:
- Active involvement in recruiting and interviewing potential staff.
- Orientation of new staff, job description, policy, and procedures of Epiphany Salon.
- Making sure that clients are getting the best customer service.
- Ensure all staff is supplied with business cards.
- Handle customer complaints and suggestions in a pleasant, efficient, and professional manner.
- Attend department head meetings on a quarterly basis.
- Participate in presenting staff meetings on a quarterly basis.
- Evaluate Male Room staff quarterly. This includes reviewing client retention and productivity in service and sales.

- Coordinate training and development of Male Room staff with Artistic Director.

Manager will be responsible for receptionist duties, until the Male Room is productive enough to support the investment of a receptionist. This includes nightly drawer closings.

Education and Experience: An endorsed high school diploma with a minimum of 5 years experience in the field of cosmetology. Advanced education in communication and technical skills are required and reviewed on an individual basis.

Compensation: This is a optioned position to be chosen at time of employment. It is to be most financially beneficial to the manager.

Option 1:
- Hourly base of $9.00. Annually bringing the position to $17,280.00. This is based on full-time employment. Also included is a bonus for productivity. Paid quarterly a 2% bonus for 100% service goal or a 1% bonus based on an 80% service goal.
- Retail commission of 10%.
- Paid vacation. One week after 2 years service and two weeks after 5 years service.
- Health insurance. 50/50 pay after 90 days.

Option 2:
- 50% commission with the above incentives. Whichever is the greater revenue producer for the manager.

Role: Technician

As a technician it is your role to communicate and listen to the clients you service and ensure complete satisfaction by focusing on their needs. In turn, you will be implementing the vision of Epiphany Salon. Your clientele will feel the harmonious, productive, and creative environment of the salon.

The mission to build this environment must be one which is having fun doing business by sharing the passion for cosmetology combining technology, art, and science. Placing the clients' needs first, to be creative, productive, and profitable is a balancing act. An act that creates harmony and a sense of well being. It is your personal responsibility to commit to this process.

Responsibilities:
- Focusing on clients' needs first. This cannot be stressed enough. Listening to verbal and nonverbal cues is imperative to client retention.
- Continually furthering your education. It will be expected that you attend one seminar annually. Within 3 years of employment, you will attend an advanced academy. Education is key to profitability.
- Be involved within the community. Participate with one local event each year. Also be a part of one charity event.
- Communicate product knowledge and service knowledge to the clients you service.
- Incorporate stress-relieving treatments and finishing touches with each client.
- Encourage and educate clients on new trends focusing on the total look.
- Encourage client referrals. Develop strong business building skills and do DTA's (downtime activities).
- Identify professional goals annually.
- Participate with daily cleaning following the golden rules.
- Enhance the image of the industry maintaining a professional relationship with the clientele.
- Actively participate with the team.

Education and Experience:

Hold a current cosmetology license. Be a high school graduate. Have a background with servicing people.

Compensation:

Option 1: Full-time. Guaranteed $7.50 per hour. Above $701.00 weekly, 45% commission. Sliding scale wage. Above $850 weekly results in 50% commission. 10% commission on retail. Paid vacation one week after 2 years of service and two weeks after 5 years of service. Health insurance, self funded. After 2 years of service, 20% paid by company. After 5 years of service, 50/50.

Option 2: Full-time. Subcontractor starting at 55% up to $699, weekly. 60% after $700, weekly. Retail 10% commission.

Option 3: Part-time. 50% commission.

Role: Nail Technician

A nail technician is a vital link to the operations of all departments. It is your part as a team to communicate the company's vision and mission to the clients you service, taking a holistic approach to nail care. It is your responsibility to educate the clientele you serve. Harmony created by being productive, profitable, and creative is the vision of Epiphany. It is your mission to have fun doing business by sharing the passion for cosmetology combining technology, art, and science. Communication is key. Education is key. Self-marketing is key. It is your responsibility to be committed to the process.

Responsibilities:
- Placing the clients' needs first. This cannot be stressed enough. Listening to verbal and nonverbal cues is imperative to client retention.
- Continually furthering your education. It will be expected that you attend one seminar annually. Education is key to profitability.
- Be involved with the community. Participate with one local event each year. Also play a part as a team to one charity event a year.
- Communicate product knowledge and service knowledge to the clients you serve.
- Incorporate stress-relieving treatments and finishing touches with each client.
- Encourage and educate clients on new trends focusing on the total look.
- Encourage client referrals. Develop strong business building skills and do DTA's (downtime activities).
- Identify professional goals annually.
- Maintain a sanitary and organized work area. Follow the golden rules with other team members.
- Enhance the image of the industry maintaining a professional relationship with the clientele.
- Participate with the team.
- Follow up with the clients you service.
- Pre-book return visits with clients.

Education and Experience:

A current nail technician's license in the state of Wisconsin. A high school diploma. A background in servicing people.

Compensation:

Option 1: Employee based. Hourly at $7.50. Paid vacation 1 week after 2 years of service. 2

weeks after 5 years of service. Health insurance. Self-funded first two years. 20% paid after two years. 30% after five years.

Option 2: Subcontractor. 65% commission. No benefits. Own supplies.

PRODUCT STRATEGY

Current Product

Proprietary information is available to investors upon signature of a Non-Disclosure Agreement.

What sets Epiphany Salon, Inc. apart from the competition is the separation of the Male Room and Epiphany the Salon. The separation allows for direct target markets in service and product. The school feeds the two departments. Epiphany Education Center also is the only private school in the Green Bay Area. Epiphany Salon, Inc. is to be the most technologically advanced cosmetology establishment in Wisconsin. I believe with the funding changes with vocational education, you will see more advanced academies forming. Locally, our vocational school has facilitated two such trade academies. Epiphany could be their third. These are industry-driven.

Bettiva is a product well-known in Wisconsin. It is used by many salons. This is not a threat, however, it is support for the school and for retail. We have the largest inventory of any salon. Our goal is to produce 35% in retail. This is a conservative number. Offering a singular note to product lines provides manageable inventory control. Bettiva also compliments our technological position, having a website that provides advertising and referrals. Presently, we are having a web site designed for Epiphany Salon, Inc. Here retailing will expand along with consultation services.

For their education center, Bettiva offers 40% discounts on all professional sizes. This complements clinic pricing, keeping overhead down. At the Vocational Training Center, I used Bettiva and the clinic retailed an average of 32%. The average salon retails 25%. Automation is key for inventory control.

The services offered include:

- The Male Room—Hair cuts, color, hand, and nail treatments and American Crew products. This is a product line designed for men. The price point is average. $16 haircuts.
- Epiphany the Salon—Hair design, colorization, chemical reconstruction, scalp massage and reconstruction, natural and alternative nail treatments, makeup (lessons and application, facials, waxing), and full body massage. Stress-relieving treatments completed the wellness services.
- Epiphany Education Center—1500-hour cosmetology course, a 300-hour nail technician course, a 500-hour skin care course, an instructors' course. The future will expand into full body/massage day spa course. Of course, there will be a clinic of cosmetology offered to the public. These are discounted services performed by senior students. Retail will also enhance the operation.

High end salons are addressing the consumer that is spending less and still wanting quality service. Epiphany Salon, Inc. has designed the business to meet this current trend. Today's consumers want money, time, and stress levels under control. We provide this.

MARKET ANALYSIS

Market Definition

According to the *Occupational Outlook Quarterly*, published by the U.S. Department of Labor, it shows cosmetology as a steadily growing occupation in the U.S. through 2005. However, the Department of Labor also shows Nail Technicians as one of the 11 fastest growing occupations in the U.S. and cosmetologists as number 37 in the top 100 occupations. This is because Baby Boomers are youth oriented and will be the driving force for our industry for the next 20 years. Generation X is the target we are going after but the Baby Boomers will be paying the way. Wellness, relaxation, and nurturing the soul will supersede "beauty services."

Cosmetology is as large an industry as the tobacco industry. Big businesses are recognizing the billions of dollars consumers spend each year in our industry and they are buying up the major manufacturers. Redken was bought by Cosimar, Matrix by Proctor and Gamble to use as two examples.

Locally, consumers demand pampering treatments while on vacation. Today's stress-relieving treatments replace the 1980s party scene and corporate rewards are given with "Day of Beauty" packages.

The overall market demands quality service at a fair price.

Future Opportunities

As our client base builds in the local market, targeting marketing to the tourism trade will bring new opportunities. Bettiva already offers products on airlines. This could be carried through with lodging businesses. Still another opportunity involves providing custom packages for special groups. "Sweet Sixteen" parties, stress-relieving treatments that travel to corporations or participate with the American Cancer Society program "Look Good, Feel Good," teaching cancer victims how to address hair loss.

Customer Profile

I believe I have already covered this. It depends on how the target is and how Epiphany Salon, Inc. is able to hit each segment of the market. This is unique. Automation plays an important role in tracking clients, finding out which marketing areas are returning an investment, who the client is, and what their spending habits are. This is a continuous process.

Competition

The three top salons in Green Bay are Wonders, the Green Bay Spa & Salon, and Minerva's. They all target only Baby Boomers and are high end quality salons all competing for the same clients. None target male clients. One has layered pricing for new talent and only one has a strong management system in place that allow their staff to grow. That one is Wonders and they do a terrific job for the industry. They are a Redken Salon.

The Vocational Training Center markets to high school students. We will be marketing to adult students.

Risk

Barbara or I could die before the business has established its systems.

Planned financing may not be met in the timeframe we would like. This would postpone the school.

Addressing risks is part of our regular planning. The better the plan, the less the risk, but they need to be addressed continually.

The marketing plans are presently in the development stages. Bettiva is playing an important role in this area of business. Strategy can be defined as the science of planning and directing large-scale operations, specifically of maneuvering forces into the most advantageous position prior to taking action. It is this area of business I enjoy the most. It is creative and easily measured. More time is needed for proper planning. We have already budgeted this area to 3% of total revenue.

On July 16, 1997, Bettiva will be mapping out a 12-month promotional grid. In the next two weeks the logo should be complete and ready for copy. The storefront design will soon be finalized. Press releases will be sent out August 1. Direct marketing will introduce the new service and product menus. Recruitment for the school will be done quarterly. Employees will involve themselves in the community.

All of this will be developed, mapped out, and evaluated.

Measurable results include:

- increased sales
- increased marketshare
- improved image
- increased knowledge of business
- identified competitive advantage
- created improved climate for future sales

When completed, it will be the best for the industry in this area and it will safely grow the business 10% annually. Although in the past, I have experienced up to 30% in a year. 10% is conservative and steady.

"With high-tech there must be high touch," says John Nesbitt, *Mega Trends 2000*. Our society is stressed out and salons are convenient retreats. A relaxing environment, with customer service providing preventative services and products at a good price is key to salon success in the new century. Many women enjoy a relaxing facial for skin maintenance benefits, however, with an average household income of $26,949.00, it is a luxury. Now market the same service, networking a facial with a purchase of $50.00 in cosmetics, and you have an affordable value-added service. Marketing is key. Know the clients, their habits, likes, and dislikes. To do this, the salon must be automated.

The educational center will provide the community with the only private school in the Green Bay Area. Vocational Training Center caters to high school students. They have enrolled adult students in the past, however, they have publicly agreed to discontinue this in the event a private school would provide such services. These services of education include: 1500-hour basic cosmetology license, 300-hour nail technician license, 500-hour skin care license, and 500-hour instructor license.

FINANCIALS

Profit and Loss Projections for the First 12 Months

	80% Productivity Rate		70% Productivity Rate		50% Productivity Rate	
Gross Services	1,155,481.60	74.07%	1,011,046.40	74.07%	722,176.00	74.07%
Gross Retail	404,418.56	25.93%	353,866.24	25.93%	252,761.60	25.93%
Gross Revenue	**1,559,900.16**	**100.00%**	**1,364,912.64**	**100.00%**	**974,937.60**	**100.00%**
Cost of Sales						
Stylist Compensation	618,182.66	39.63%	540,909.82	39.63%	386,364.16	39.63%
Product COS	202,209.28	12.96%	176,933.12	12.96%	126,380.80	12.96%
Total Cost of Sales	**820,391.94**	**52.59%**	**717,842.94**	**52.59%**	**512,744.96**	**52.59%**
Gross Margin	739,508.22	47.41%	647,069.70	47.41%	462,192.64	47.41%
OPERATING EXPENSES						
Rent	40,200.00	13.00%	40,200.00	13.00%	40,200.00	13.00%
Supplies	77,995.01	5.00%	68,245.63	5.00%	48,746.88	5.00%
Advertising	46,797.00	3.00%	40,947.38	3.00%	29,248.13	3.00%
Depreciation	46,797.00	3.00%	40,947.38	3.00%	29,248.13	3.00%
Laundry	15,599.00	1.00%	13,649.13	1.00%	9,749.38	1.00%
Cleaning	15,599.00	1.00%	13,649.13	1.00%	9,749.38	1.00%
Light Power	15,599.00	1.00%	13,649.13	1.00%	9,749.38	1.00%
Repairs	23,396.50	1.50%	20,473.69	1.50%	14,624.06	1.50%
Insurance	11,699.25	0.75%	10,236.84	0.75%	7,312.03	0.75%
Telephone	11,699.25	0.75%	10,236.84	0.75%	7,312.03	0.75%
Misc.	23,396.50	1.50%	20,473.69	1.50%	14,624.06	1.50%
Legal & Accounting	15,599.00	1.00%	13,649.13	1.00%	9,749.38	1.00%
Total Operating Expenses	**344,380.53**	**32.50%**	**306,357.97**	**32.50%**	**230,312.83**	**32.50%**
Net Operating Income\(Loss)	395,127.69	25.33%	340,711.73	24.96%	231,879.81	23.78%
OTHER EXPENSES						
Interest Expense	11,514.74	0.74%	11,514.74	0.84%	11,514.74	1.18%
Net Income\(Loss)	**383,612.95**	**24.59%**	**329,196.99**	**24.12%**	**220,365.07**	**22.60%**

Amortization Schedule

CLS
Declining Balance
Run Date: 7/02/97
Note Payable - Commercial Lender

Principal: 130,880.00   Annual Interest Rate: 9.500
Term: 60 Payments   Payments per Year: 12

Pmt. No.	Check No.	Date Paid	Payment Amount	Interest Expense	Principal Reduction	Payoff Amount
						130,880.00
1	.....	....	2,748.72	1,036.13	1,712.59	129,167.41
2	.....	....	2,748.72	1,022.58	1,726.14	127,441.27
3	.....	....	2,748.72	1,008.91	1,739.81	125,701.46
4	.....	....	2,748.72	995.14	1,753.58	123,947.88
5	.....	....	2,748.72	981.25	1,767.47	122,180.41
6	.....	....	2,748.72	967.26	1,781.46	120,398.95
7	.....	....	2,748.72	953.16	1,795.56	118,603.39
8	.....	....	2,748.72	938.94	1,809.78	116,793.61
9	.....	....	2,748.72	924.62	1,824.10	114,969.51
10	.....	....	2,748.72	910.18	1,838.54	113,130.97
11	.....	....	2,748.72	895.62	1,853.10	111,277.87
12	.....	....	2,748.72	880.95	1,867.77	109,410.10
Subtotal			**32,984.64**	**11,514.74**	**21,469.90**	**109,410.10**
13	.....	....	2,748.72	866.16	1,822.56	107,527.54
14	.....	....	2,748.72	851.26	1,897.46	105,630.08
15	.....	....	2,748.72	836.24	1,912.48	103,717.60
16	.....	....	2,748.72	821.10	1,927.62	101,789.98
17	.....	....	2,748.72	805.84	1,942.88	99,847.10
18	.....	....	2,748.72	790.46	1,958.26	97,888.84
19	.....	....	2,748.72	774.95	1,973.77	95,915.07
20	.....	....	2,748.72	759.33	1,989.39	93,925.68
21	.....	....	2,748.72	743.58	2,005.14	91,920.54
22	.....	....	2,748.72	727.70	2,021.02	89,899.52
23	.....	....	2,748.72	711.70	2,037.02	87,862.50
24	.....	....	2,748.72	695.58	2,053.14	85,809.36
Subtotal			**32,984.64**	**9,383.90**	**23,600.74**	**85,809.36**
25	.....	....	2,748.72	679.32	2,069.40	83,739.96
26	.....	....	2,748.72	662.94	2,085.78	81,654.18
27	.....	....	2,748.72	646.43	2,102.29	79,551.89
28	.....	....	2,748.72	629.79	2,118.93	77,432.96
29	.....	....	2,748.72	613.01	2,135.71	75,297.25
30	.....	....	2,748.72	596.10	2,152.62	73,144.63
31	.....	....	2,748.72	579.06	2,169.66	70,974.97
32	.....	....	2,748.72	561.89	2,186.83	68,788.14
33	.....	....	2,748.72	544.57	2,204.15	66,583.99
34	.....	....	2,748.72	527.12	2,221.60	64,362.39
35	.....	....	2,748.72	509.54	2,239.18	62,123.21
36	.....	....	2,748.72	491.81	2,256.91	59,866.30
Subtotal			**32,984.64**	**7,041.58**	**25,943.06**	**59,866.30**
37	.....	....	2,748.72	473.94	2,274.78	57,591.52
38	.....	....	2,748.72	455.93	2,292.79	55,298.73
39	.....	....	2,748.72	437.78	2,310.94	52,987.79

Amortization Schedule

continued

Pmt. No.	Check No.	Date Paid	Payment Amount	Interest Expense	Principal Reduction	Payoff Amount
40	.....	....	2,748.72	419.49	2,329.23	50,658.56
41	.....	....	2,748.72	401.05	2,347.67	48,310.89
42	.....	....	2,748.72	382.46	2,366.26	45,944.63
43	.....	....	2,748.72	363.73	2,384.99	43,559.64
44	.....	....	2,748.72	344.85	2,403.87	41,155.77
45	.....	....	2,748.72	325.82	2,422.90	38,732.87
46	.....	....	2,748.72	306.64	2,442.08	36,290.79
47	.....	....	2,748.72	287.30	2,461.42	33,829.37
48	.....	....	2,748.72	267.82	2,480.90	31,348.47
Subtotal			**32,984.64**	**4,466.81**	**28,517.83**	**31,348.47**
49	.....	.....	2,748.72	248.18	2,500.54	28,847.93
50	.....	.....	2,748.72	228.38	2,520.34	26,327.59
51	.....	.....	2,748.72	208.43	2,540.29	23,787.30
52	.....	.....	2,748.72	188.32	2,560.40	21,226.90
53	.....	.....	2,748.72	168.05	2,580.67	18,646.23
54	.....	.....	2,748.72	147.62	2,601.10	16,045.13
55	.....	.....	2,748.72	127.02	2,621.70	13,423.43
56	.....	.....	2,748.72	106.27	2,642.45	10,780.98
57	.....	.....	2,748.72	85.35	2,663.37	8,117.61
58	.....	.....	2,748.72	64.26	2,684.46	5,433.15
59	.....	.....	2,748.72	43.01	2,705.71	2,727.44
60	.....	.....	2,749.03	21.59	2,727.44	0.00
Subtotal			**32,984.95**	**1,636.48**	**31,348.47**	**0.00**
Total			**164,923.51**	**34,043.51**	**130,880.00**	**0.00**

Purchase of business	$60,000.00	
Male Room equipment and inventory	16,500.00	
School equipment	42,000.00	
Plumbing	2,000.00	
Interior needs	1,000.00	
Retail displays	14,000.00	
Storefront and artwork	5,000.00	
Advertising	3,000.00	
	143,500.00	
6 months rent in savings	20,100.00	
	163,600.00	
20% personal investment	32,720.00	
To be financed	130,880.00	
25% private investor(s)	32,720.00	
Financial Institute	$98,160.00	

How $65,440.00 will be spent:

[School equipment $42,000 is already figured in, however, classroom and junior clinic are not.]

Structural needs	$7,000.00
Classroom equipment	18,000.00
$10,000 Bond for school	1,500.00
State license	300.00
Text, mannequin, classroom supplies	3,000.00
Printing costs	3,000.00
Office equipment	3,000.00
Computer software	2,590.00
Hardware in clinic	1,825.00
Retail inventory	1,000.00
Phone expenses	925.00
Misc.	1,963.00
	44,103.00
Cash on hand	21,337.00
	$65,440.00

How this will be paid back

Refer to amortization for loan repayment. 5-year return on investment.

Refer to financial statements following.

Refer to projected income based on salon productivity. In reality, a salon should base maximum productivity at 80%. This is realistic in theory and application. It should be noted that rent is a fixed number annually based at $40,200.00 or $3,350.00 monthly. These projections do not include the nail department or the skin department. This sheet is the male room, the salon and the retail center.

Projected income for the educational center encompasses tuition		$73,000.00
by 10 students each 6 months		73,000.00
		73,000.00
Retail sales at 20%		14,600.00
Clinic operation	first year	20,000.00
		$180,600.00
Operating expenses	12% inventory and supplies	21,672.00
Payroll		$25,000.00
Taxes		
M&R		
Insurance		
Special services		
Depreciation		
Office supplies		
Advertising		
Utilities		
Dues		
Bank Chg.		
Travel		

This means running the company at an 80% productivity rate.

Salon hours are:	Monday	Thursday
	Tuesday	Friday
	Wednesday	Saturday

Total productive hours	62 per week
With 16 stations =	992 revenue productive hours
x Aver. service $28. per hour is	$27,776.00
x .8 productivity	$22,220.80 revenue producing $
x 4 weeks (month)	$88,883.20 revenue producing monthly $
x 12 months	1,066,598.40 revenue producing annual

Retail at 35% of service sales is	$373,309.44 annually
+ 12 months	$31,109.12
+ 4 weeks	$7,777.28
+ 6 days	$1,296.21 daily retail

Service annual dollars	$1,066,598.40
Retail annual dollars	$373,309.44

$1,439,907.84   maximum productivity

The questions that need to be answered are

What would the salon look like at a 70% productivity rate within its departments?
What does the salon look like at a 50% productivity rate within its department?

Figures for the school need to be separate, however, for the business plan they need to be totaled for financing proposes.

The Nail Salon Operating at 80% Productivity

This means running the company at an 80% productivity rate.

Salon hours are:	Monday	Thursday
	Tuesday	Friday
	Wednesday	Saturday

Total productive hours	62 per week
With 3 stations	186 revenue producing hours
x average service $20 per hr.	$3,720.00
x .8 productivity	$2,976.00
x 4 weeks (month)	$11,904.00
x 12 months	$142,848.00

Retail at 35% of service sale is

	$49,996.00 annually
divided by 12 months	$4,166.33
divided by 4 weeks	$1,041.58
divided by 6 days	$173.60 daily retail

Service annual dollars	**$142,848.00**
Retail annual dollars	**$49,996.00**
	$192,844.00

ASSETS

CURRENT ASSETS
CASH ON HAND $150.00
CHECKING - CB NORTH   1,386.28
A/R - EMPLOYEE   422.50
INVENTORY   10,916.15
PREPAID EXPENSE   1,626.00

   TOTAL CURRENT ASSETS $14,500.93

FIXED ASSETS
FIXTURES & EQUIPMENT   50,000.00
DECORATION   1,215.90
UNIFORMS   360.40
ACCUMULATED DEPRECIATION   (12,630.90)

TOTAL FIXED ASSETS   38,945.40

TOTAL ASSETS $53,446.33

LIABILITIES & NET WORTH

CURRENT LIABILITIES
ACCRUED TAXES $2,490.06
N/P - CB NORTH   60,072.00

TOTAL CURRENT LIABILITIES   62,562.06

EQUITY
RETAINED EARNINGS   (16,170.23)
COMMON STOCK ($1 PAR)   500.00
STOCKHOLDER CONTRIBUTIONS   14,228.20
CURRENT EARNINGS   (7,673.70)

   TOTAL EQUITY   (9,115.73)

   TOTAL LIABILITIES & NET WORTH $53,446.33

**Balance Sheet
Subsidiary
Schedule
May 31, 1997**

	Current	Balance
INVENTORY		
INVENTORY - PRODUCT	$(323.24)	$4,701.37
INVENTORY - SUPPLIES	(155.41)	6,214.78
TOTAL	**$(478.65)**	**$10,916.15**
PREPAID EXPENSE		
PREPAID RENT	$1,626.00	$1,626.00
TOTAL	**$1,626.00**	**$1,626.00**
ACCRUED TAXES		
SALES TAX & STATE W/H	$331.19	$2,214.09
FED W/H & FICA	39.01	230.59
MESC	33.10	28.35
FUTA	9.46	17.03
TOTAL	**$412.76**	**$2,490.06**

Statement of Income for the Five Months Ended May 31, 1997

	Current Actual	Percent	Year to Date Actual	Percent
INCOME				
PRODUCT SALES	$4,910.36	27.4	$23,350.79	31.2
SERVICE SALES	12,728.00	71.0	50,138.83	67.0
SALES TAX	292.77	1.6	1,389.88	1.9
* TOTAL INCOME	17,931.13	100.0	74,879.50	100.0
COST OF SALES				
PRODUCT	2,455.18	13.7	12,545.71	16.8
CONTRACTOR	7,421.37	41.4	31,923.64	42.6
SALES TAX	286.77	1.6	1,359.88	1.8
* TOTAL COST OF SALES	10,613.32	56.7	45,829.23	61.2
* GROSS MARGIN	7,767.81	43.3	29,050.27	38.8
EXPENSES				
OFFICERS SALARY	200.00	1.1	200.00	0.3
PAYROLL	982.29	5.5	4,940.54	6.6
PAYROLL TAXES	133.00	0.7	578.31	0.8
LICENSE & TAXES			62.00	0.1
RENT	1,626.00	9.1	10,888.00	14.5
MAINT. & REPAIR	25.00	0.1	245.17	0.3
INSURANCE			554.13	0.7
SPECIAL SERVICES	200.00	1.1	1,200.00	1.6
DEPRECIATION	1,052.58	5.9	5,262.90	7.0
SUPPLIES	1,434.49	8.0	5,887.21	7.9
OFFICE SUPPLIES			61.73	0.1
ADVERTISING & PROMOTIONS	506.99	2.8	1,258.75	1.7
UTILITIES & PHONE	1,050.60	5.9	4,850.54	6.5
DUES & SUBSCRIPTIONS	200.00	1.1	214.95	0.3
BANK CHARGES	67.37	0.4	400.17	0.5
TRAVEL & ENTERTAINMENT	39.77	0.2	119.57	0.2
* TOTAL EXPENSES	7,518.09	41.9	36,723.97	49.0
* NET OPERATING PFT/(LOSS)	249.72	1.4	(7,673.70)	(10.2)
* NET PROFIT/(LOSS)	$249.72	1.4	(7,673.70)	(10.2)

Statement of Income - Subsidiary Schedule - for the Five Months Ended May 31, 1997

	Current Actual	Percent	Year to Date Actual	Percent
TRAVEL & ENTERTAINMENT				
MEALS & ENTERTAINMENT	$39.77	0.2	$119.57	0.2
* TOTAL	$39.77	0.2	$119.57	0.2

**Statement of Cash
Flows for the Five
Months Ended
May 31, 1997**

INCREASE (DECREASE) IN CASH AND CASH EQUIVALENTS

	Current	Year to Date
CASH FLOWS FROM OPERATING ACTIVITIES		
NET INCOME (LOSS)	$249.72	$(7673.70)
ADJ TO RECONCILE TO NET CASH		
DEPRECIATION AND AMORTIZATION	1,052.58	5,262.90
CHANGES IN ASSETS/LIABILITIES:		
ACCOUNTS RECEIVABLE		(422.50)
INVENTORY	478.65	1,866.92
PREPAID EXPENSES	(1,626.00)	(1,626.00)
PAYROLL TAXES PAYABLE	81.57	42.87
OTHER TAXES PAYABLE	331.19	1,569.45
TOTAL ADJUSTMENTS	**317.99**	**6,693.64**
NET CASH FROM OPERATIONS	567.71	(980.06)
CASH FLOWS FROM FINANCING ACTIVITIES		
NOTES PAYABLE - STOCKHOLDER	(1,267.63)	490.51
NET CASH PROVIDED BY FINANCING	(1,267.63)	490.51
CHANGE IN CASH & EQUIVALENTS	(699.92)	(489.55)
BEGINNING CASH & EQUIVALENTS	2,236.20	2,025.83
ENDING CASH & EQUIVALENTS	**$1,536.28**	**$1,536.28**

This page left intentionally blank to accommodate tabular matter following.

Profit and Loss Projections Based on Productivity Rates

	80% Productivity Rate		70% Productivity Rate		50% Productivity Rate	
Gross Services	1,468,953.60	74.07%	1,285,334.40	74.07%	918,096.00	74.07%
Gross Retail	514,133.76	25.93%	449,867.04	25.93%	321,333.60	25.93%
Gross Revenue	**1,983,087.36**	**100.00%**	**1,735,201.44**	**100.00%**	**1,239,429.60**	**100.00%**
COST OF SALES						
Stylist Compensation	932,785.54	47.04%	626,187.34	47.04%	582,990.96	47.04%
Product COS	282,773.57	14.26%	247,426.87	14.26%	176,733.48	14.26%
Total Cost of Sales	**1,215,559.10**	**61.30%**	**1,063,614.22**	**61.30%**	**759,724.44**	**61.30%**
Gross Margin	767,528.26	38.70%	671,587.22	38.70%	479,705.16	38.70%
OPERATING EXPENSES						
Rent	40,200.00	2.74%	40,200.00	3.13%	40,200.00	4.38%
Supplies	158,646.99	8.00%	138,416.12	8.00%	99,154.37	8.00%
Advertising	59,492.62	3.00%	52,056.04	3.00%	37,182.89	3.00%
Depreciation	59,492.62	3.00%	52,056.04	3.00%	37,182.89	3.00%
Laundry	19,830.87	1.00%	17,352.01	1.00%	12,394.30	1.00%
Cleaning	19,830.87	1.00%	17,352.01	1.00%	12,394.30	1.00%
Light Power	19,830.87	1.00%	17,352.01	1.00%	12,394.30	1.00%
Repairs	29,746.31	1.50%	26,028.02	1.50%	18,591.44	1.50%
Insurance	14,873.16	0.75%	13,014.01	0.75%	9,295.72	0.75%
Telephone	14,873.16	0.75%	13,014.01	0.75%	9,295.72	0.75%
Miscellaneous	29,746.31	1.50%	26,028.02	1.50%	18,591.44	1.50%
Legal & Accounting	19,810.87	1.00%	17,352.01	1.00%	12,394.30	1.00%
Total Operating Expenses	**486,394.66**	**25.24%**	**430,620.32**	**25.63%**	**319,071.66**	**26.88%**
Net Operating Income\						
(Loss)	281,133.60	14.18%	240,966.90	13.89%	160,633.50	12.96%
OTHER EXPENSES						
Interest Expense	11,514.74	0.58%	11,514.74	0.66%	11,514.74	0.93%
Officers Salary	156,663.90	7.90%	137,080.91	7.90%	97,914.94	7.90%
Corporate Income Taxes	22,590.99	1.14%	18,474.25	2.06%	10,240.76	0.83%
Net Income\(Loss)	**90,363.97**	**4.56%**	**73,897.00**	**4.26%**	**40,963.06**	**3.30%**

40% Productivity Rate		30% Productivity Rate		20% Productivity Rate	
734,476.80	74.07%	550,857.60	74.07%	367,238.40	74.07%
257,066.88	25.93%	192,800.16	25.93%	128,533.44	25.93%
991,543.68	**100.00%**	**743,657.76**	**100.00%**	**495,771.84**	**100.00%**
466,392.77	47.04%	349,794.58	47.04%	233,196.38	47.04%
141,386.78	14.26%	106,040.09	14.26%	70,693.39	14.26%
607,779.55	**61.30%**	**455,834.66**	**61.30%**	**303,889.78**	**61.30%**
383,764.13	38.70%	287,823.10	38.70%	191,882.05	38.70%
40,200.00	5.47%	40,200.00	7.30%	40,200.00	10.95%
79,323.49	8.00%	59,492.62	8.00%	39,661.75	8.00%
29,746.31	3.00%	22,309.73	3.00%	14,873.16	3.00%
29,746.31	3.00%	22,309.73	3.00%	14,873.16	3.00%
9,915.44	1.00%	7,436.58	1.00%	4,957.72	1.00%
9,915.44	1.00%	7,436.58	1.00%	4,957.72	1.00%
9,915.44	1.00%	7,436.58	1.00%	4,957.72	1.00%
14,873.16	1.50%	11,154.87	1.50%	7,436.58	1.50%
7,436.58	0.75%	5,577.43	0.75%	3,718.29	0.75%
7,436.58	0.75%	5,577.43	0.75%	3,718.29	0.75%
14,873.16	1.50%	11,154.87	1.50%	7,436.58	1.50%
9,915.44	1.00%	7,436.58	1.00%	4,957.72	1.00%
263,297.33	**27.97%**	**207,523.00**	**29.80%**	**151,748.66**	**33.45%**
120,466.80	12.15%	80,300.10	10.80%	40,133.40	6.10%
11,514.74	1.16%	11,514.74	1.55%	11,514.74	2.32%
78,331.95	7.90%	58,748.96	7.90%	39,165.98	7.90%
6,124.02	0.62%	2,007.28	0.27%	0.0	0.00%
24,496.09	**2.47%**	**8,029.12**	**1.08%**	**(10,547.32)**	**-2.13%**

Gross Revenue Breakdown Based on Productivity Rates

	80% Productivity Rate	**70% Productivity Rate**	**50% Productivity Rate**
Salon	1,066,590.40	933,273.60	666,624.00
Male Room	152,372.20	133,324.80	95,232.00
Facial Department	107,136.00	93,744.00	66,960.00
Nail Department	142,846.00	124,992.00	89,280.00
Gross Service Revenue	**1,468,953.60**	**1,285,334.40**	**918,096.00**

40% Productivity Rate	30% Productivity Rate	20% Productivity Rate
533,299.20	399,974.40	266,649.60
76,185.60	57,139.20	38,092.80
53,568.00	40,176.00	26,784.00
71,424.00	53,568.00	35,712.00
734,476.80	**550,857.60**	**367,238.40**

Cash Flow Analysis Based on Productivity Rates

	80% Productivity Rate	70% Productivity Rate	50% Productivity Rate
Beginning Cash Balance	$23,000	$23,000	$23,000
Net Income/(Loss) After	90,364	73,697	40,963
Adjust to Reconcile Cash			
Depreciation	59,493	52,056	37,183
Changes in Assets/Liabilities			
Fixed Assets	(75,000)	(75,000)	(75,000)
Payables	(20,000)	(20,000)	(20,000)
Cash Flows from Financing Activities			
Loan Proceeds	98,000	98,000	98,000
Debt Reduction	(16,000)	(16,000)	(16,000)
Stockholder Dist.	0	0	0
Net Cash Increase/Decrease	136,857	112,953	65,146
Ending Cash & Equivalent	**$159,857**	**$135,953**	**$88,146**

40% Productivity Rate	30% Productivity Rate	20% Productivity Rate
$23,000	$23,000	$23,000
24,496	8,029	(10,547)
29,746	22,310	14,873
(75,000)	(75,000)	(75,000)
(20,000)	(20,000)	(20,000)
98,000	98,000	98,000
(16,000)	(16,000)	(16,000)
0	0	0
41,242	17,339	(8,674)
$64,242	**$40,339**	**$14,326**

Health Insurance Company

BUSINESS PLAN   SOUTHEAST HEALTH PLANS, INC.

1117 Perimeter Center W., Ste. 500 E.
Atlanta, GA 30338

This plan's emphasis lies in implementation. Extensive attention is given in concrete terms as to how the goals will be reached, and abstractions are avoided. Marketing, pricing, and sales strategies are all presented and extensive financial figures accompany the plan, giving these sections credibility and support. This plan was compiled using Business Plan Pro, by Palo Alto Software.

- EXECUTIVE SUMMARY

- COMPANY SUMMARY

- SERVICES

- MARKET ANALYSIS SUMMARY

- STRATEGY AND IMPLEMENTATION SUMMARY

- MANAGEMENT SUMMARY

- FINANCIAL PLAN

EXECUTIVE SUMMARY

Southeast Health Plans, Inc. is a service company that will provide health plan administrative services to self-insured employers. The company will concentrate on employers with 50 to 500 employees. Many of these employers have current HMO, PPO, or major national insurance carrier health plans. While the majority of employers with 500 or more employees have at least some element of self-insurance incorporated into their health care programs, our target market is often ignored by the major national insurance companies. While more than 80% of companies with 500 or more employees are self-insured, the management of Southeast Health Plans has identified that less than 25% of Atlanta area companies with 50 to 500 employees have self-insured plans.

The market for self-insured and administrative services consist of those companies that are currently self-insured and companies that have other types of health plans that will be encouraged to shift to self-insurance. One factor in the transition to self-insurance is the availability of quality administrative and consultative services. Southeast Health Plans, Inc. is led by experienced management and has formed a strategic alliance with Blair Mill Administrator, a wholly owned subsidiary of Blue Cross/Blue Shield of Pennsylvania, for the purpose of providing first class benefits management services to its target market.

Southeast Health Plans, Inc. will achieve revenue of more than $5 million in five years with a net profit after tax of $1.6 million. The company will turn profitable in year three with after-tax earnings of $560,000. As a marketing organization and service provider, margins will be extremely high with gross margins above 80% (less only sales incentive costs) and approaching 50% after all operating expenses, once market penetration has reached maturity.

The key to success for Southeast Plans, Inc. will be the ability to attract the initial capital in order to successfully market its services in the metro Atlanta area and in northern Georgia. Adequate professional sales staffing is essential. The company must then expand a successful formula throughout Southeastern markets. Cost control, particularly with regard to sales and marketing programs, will enable controlled expansion that is fully funded by internal cash flow.

Business Plan Highlights

	Sales	Gross	Net
1997	$288,599	$231,599	($354,444)
1998	$1,399,223	$1,198,223	($85,302)
1999	$3,067,966	$2,640,466	$561,223

Objectives

The objectives for the company are:

1. To initiate co-operative marketing, utilizing Blair Mill advertising executions with media in the Atlanta metro market.
2. To hire sales staff both currently identified and unidentified to implement sales lead follow-up strategy.
3. To have at least 4,800 cumulative employees under management by the end of 1997.
4. To approach breakeven by the end of year two (1998) holding total loss for the second year under $100,000 while increasing market share.
5. To shift to earnings in year three (1999) and to accelerate gross margin contributions by building market maturity on top of infrastructure.
6. To expand regionally with both media and sales personnel to penetrate new markets while consolidating service capability.

7. To constantly achieve cost benefit through an expanding provider network while not compromising patient care.

8. To have more than 98,000 cumulative employees under management by the end of year five.

Mission

Southeast Health Plans, Inc. is dedicated to providing small and mid-size employers with a comprehensive benefits administration program that will enable employers to control health benefits costs while allowing employees within the plan to have access to quality health care. By combining self-insurance with stop-loss programs and efficient plan administration Southeast will provide to its clientele, both employers and employees, the best of health care with the minimum of restrictions and the broadest individual choice of providers. Southeast will deliver a balance of quality care and freedom of choice at a fair price.

Keys to Success

The keys to success in this business are:

1. **Marketing.** Southeast Health Plans will have the ability to sell both directly to employers and through independent insurance brokers and agents. It will be necessary to establish name recognition among more established programs. It is essential that media budgets be controlled and that closing ratios of at least 5% of leads per year be maintained.

2. **Product quality.** The services provided by Blair Mill Administrators are already state-of-the art among small-employer providers. The value added experience of the Southeast Health Plans, Inc. management team and their provider networks will ensure customer satisfaction. It is a necessity that clients maintain satisfaction both with service and plan cost to minimize client erosion and to combat competition. Renewals should exceed 85% of established clients.

3. **Controlled growth.** Growth needs to be aggressive with rapid expansion to new geographic markets but also must focus on profitability. Each established market must mature as new markets develop so that growth can be internally funded. Cash flow management is essential. Both market expansion and media effectiveness must be constantly tested, and then reviewed or refined as required.

COMPANY SUMMARY

Southeast Health Plans, Inc. is a service company founded by experienced medical insurance industry executives to both serve and capitalize upon the growing number of small and midsize companies that seek to control health benefits costs and manage risk by self-insurance.

The utilization of Blair Mill's existing services, products and infrastructure enables Southeast to provide necessary service without incurring the costs of establishing proprietary programs. In addition, Blair Mill's existing provider networks enable Southeast to serve employers with multiple locations or a wide-spread workforce.

Southeast targets those employers who have from 50 to 500 employees. Services include all-encompassing benefit management programs. Blair Mill Administrators will be utilized to provide benefits management services including:

- A full array of managed care services
- Patient care management
- Local, regional, and national provider networks
- Tailored administrative services
- Flexible plan design
- Underwriting and actuarial services

- Comprehensive information management and data reporting
- Thorough stop-loss insurance administration.

Company Ownership

Southeast Health Plans, Inc. is a privately held Georgia corporation. It is owned by its founders and managing partners: James J. Peters, Thomas R. Cormier, and L. Richard Schumacher, M.D.

The company has been established with the founders' own capital. The founders have negotiated an exclusive strategic alliance with Blair Mill Administrators for certain markets in the state of Georgia.

The founders are now seeking to extend outside ownership interest for the first time in order to raise the funds required to execute the expansion plans of the business.

Start-Up Summary

Start-Up Plan
Start-Up Expenses

Legal	$0
Consultants	$12,500
Offering Expenses	$15,000
Other	$0
Total Start-Up Expense	**$27,500**

Start-Up Assets Needed

Cash Requirements	$256,000
Other Short-term Assets	$0
Total Short-term Assets	$256,000
Long-term Assets	$0
Total Assets	$256,000
Total Start-Up Requirements	**$283,500**
Left to finance	$0

Start-Up Funding Plan
INVESTMENT

Private Placement 1996	$300,000
Other	$0
Other	$0
Total investment	$300,000

Short-term Liabilities

Unpaid Expenses	$0
Short-term Loans	$0
Interest-free Short-term Loans	$0
Subtotal Short-term Liabilities	$0
Long-term Liabilities	$0
Total Liabilities	$0
Loss at Start-Up	($44,000)
Total Capital	$256,000
Total Capital and Liabilities	$256,000
Checkline	$0

Start-Up Chart

Expenses	$27,500
Assets	$256,000
Investment	$300,000

Southeast Health Plans, Inc. currently occupies office space at 1117 Perimeter Center West, Suite 500 East, Atlanta, GA. 30338.

Company Locations and Facilities

The current offices provide sufficient space to launch business in the Atlanta and north Georgia market. More space will be required as the Atlanta market matures and central services are provided to other geographic markets. In addition, local sales offices will be required in other markets.

Increases in rental costs are included in the plan's pro forma as they are expected to be incurred.

As health care in the United States has been changing rapidly over the past two decades, so has the way health care has been provided and how it is billed and paid. Large insurance companies and private physicians have given way to HMOs and Managed Care Plans and the TPA (Third Party Administrator) has been prospering. A TPA (like Blair Mill) exists to administer all the health care functions for a company that would have been handled by an insurance company. HMOs primarily contract for services based upon price, then re-sell those services to groups. Often, service and choice are less than satisfactory. But, most importantly, cost-effective concerns predominate. Employers are seeking to provide health care for employees at an affordable cost. A backlash has been the increase in self-insured programs administered by TPAs.

SERVICES

In short, a business now demands much more in the way of service and analysis than traditional support institutions have been providing to their clients. The claims processor is a case in point. Merely processing claims does nothing to help a business analyze and control its health benefits plan and to control the costs associated with the plan. And there has not traditionally been a measure for the "quality" of health care service.

Southeast has compiled, through its own proprietary systems and an alliance of external providers, a service mix that includes Network Administration Services, Network Contracting Services, Policy Formation and Quality Assurance, and Marketing Services.

Health benefits are a fact of life for any business. The small and mid-size business is concerned with cost control and administration, just as in any other department of their business operations, except they are ill-equipped in personnel, know-how, and in systems, to administer health care internally.

Thus a full array of TPA self-insured services would include:

- Claims experience analysis and cost projections
- Plan design consulting
- Comprehensive plan analysis
- Provider network analysis
- Plan documentation
- Stop-loss brokerage and administration
- Prescription drug programs
- Vision benefits administration

- Dental benefits administration
- COBRA administration
- Short-term disability administration
- Worker's compensation services
- Custom tailored services

Competitive Comparison

Health plans for businesses and their employees comprise a multi-billion dollar industry that is highly competitive. Well known national insurance companies like Monolith, Beta, Chariot Healthcare, and the regional Blue Cross and Blue Shield companies seek the employer's dollar. A plenitude of HMOs, both regional and national, also compete. Many companies are already self-insured. Some of these companies use TPAs for outside claims processing while others use insurers or attempt to self-administer. Certain claims processors are also gravitating toward benefits management services.

Southeast Health Plans believes that a niche exists that is both too small for concentrated coverage by large national companies and that is not well served with broad enough quality services by other TPAs. Most TPAs are still evolving toward the service mix that small and mid-size companies are demanding. By providing those quality services now, at a fair price, Southeast believes a competitive sales advantage exists that will permit attainment of the market shares sought.

Sales Literature

Much of the sales materials and literature prepared by Blair Mill will be utilized by Southeast. Advertising executions are included in a supplement to this plan. Direct mail pieces are being developed. A Blair Mill portfolio and videotape provides a professional presentation to prospective clients.

Sourcing

The Strategic Alliance with Blair Mill Administrators of Philadelphia, Pennsylvania, provides the principal source of health plan administrative services. Southeast will earn revenue both from enrollment sales as well as from cost advantages in the delivery of health care services.

From a product perspective, this relationship is analogous to the role of a regional dealer that sells services and brand name products within a licensed and protected geographic area. The dealer brings competence and value-added expertise to the enterprise while the source brings the credibility of brand name recognition and a substantial existing client base. This serves to reduce the risk normally associated with an early stage, unrecognized health services provider.

On the health care provider side, the sourcing of health care services is already in place from a variety of provider organizations. Southeast management has had working relationships with Georgia Baptist Health Care System, Meridian Medical Group, Emory Health System, Columbia/HCA, Northside Hospitals, Scottish Rite Medical Centers, and other independent health care organizations.

The management of Southeast Health Plans remains in ongoing negotiations with physician groups and hospitals to obtain the optimum mix of quality service and price for its clients. The health care providers are receptive both from the standpoint of pricing and freedom to control care. Both consumer and provider benefit from a cost/benefit mix that they find preferable to the insured HMO or Managed Care models. It is not anticipated that service sourcing will be a problem for Southeast Health Plans. Rather, the key to success will be marketing to employers coupled with provider cost negotiation. Quality of care will not be compromised.

Future services will include establishing both a geographic network of clients and health care providers throughout the southeast. As Southeast Health Plans grows and expands it will begin to look less like a TPA and more like a Health Plan. As critical mass of clientele and medical providers is achieved, cost benefit is attained and administrative functions and services are consolidated in economies of scale. At that point of critical mass, when approximately 50,000 cumulative employees are under managed care, the option exists for Southeast to develop its own proprietary heath plan. Many administrative services and functions that will be outsourced by Southeast can be developed as internal company centers.

At that point options exist to finance the shift to a health plan company. Mezzanine or venture funding will be obtainable for a company with $5 million in revenue and $1.6 million in earnings (and no debt). After ramp-up to a $10 to $20 million dollar company, an IPO is a potential. Also, the company would be an attractive target for acquisition.

Future Products

The initial target market is the Atlanta metro and north Georgia market. The agreement with Blair Mill encompasses the following zip codes: all three digits beginning with 300-303, 305-307, and 311.

This includes all of metro Atlanta and surrounding counties in north Georgia. At present Southeast Health Plans holds the only strategic marketing alliance with Blair Mill in the entire southeastern United States. Both sides recognize and desire an expanded agreement after phase one goals and objectives are attained.

The critical data to establish potential customer base and market share is to sort employers within the region by number of employees, regardless of whether they are currently with an HMO, an outside insurance carrier, are self-insured, or have no insurance. All are potential clients of Southeast Health Plans. The curve to attainment of critical mass is one of education, media, contact, and sales closure.

MARKET ANALYSIS SUMMARY

Within the targeted zip codes defined by the agreement with Blair Mill, the management of Southeast Health Plans has identified 1,801 employers with 50 to 500 employees. Of these, 1,289 are known to have an identifiable insurance carrier, 446 are known to be self-insured, and 66 are known to have no insurance.

Southeast has a clearly defined and identifiable market niche that enables highly targeted and efficient marketing of its services.

Market Segmentation

Market Analysis

Potential Customers	Growth	1997	1998	1999	2000	2001	CAGR
Self-Insured	10%	446	491	540	594	653	10.00%
No Insurance	0%	66	66	66	66	66	0.00%
Carrier Identified	0%	1,289	1,289	1,289	1,289	1,289	0.00%
Other	0%	0	0	0	0	0	0.00%
Total	**2.76%**	**1,801**	**1,846**	**1,895**	**1,949**	**2,008**	**2.76%**

Together the national insurance carriers, HMOs, and PPOs account for 72% of the current market for employer-based health plan services. The majority of HMOs and PPOs have their own marketing and sales programs which include company employed sales forces. National insurance companies may have company sales people or may utilize independent insurance agents. Both have strong media programs.

Industry Analysis

Neither, however, provide the mix of services that Southeast Health Plans can provide. Nor can they provide the quality/cost ratio or the ancillary consultative and custom services of Southeast combined with Blair Mill. Thus, Southeast feels that this entire employer universe of 1,801 companies is vulnerable to penetration.

Industry Participants

Insurance carriers provide economic protection only. Such protection is at a high cost. Deductibles are increasing and the employer's ability to handle the cost burden of medical insurance coverage is diminishing. Compromises must be made in the extent of coverage, the size of the deductible, the medical services included, or often the employee is required to cover an ever-increasing percentage of the cost of his own plan as a payroll deduction. These are all unattractive options both for the employer and the individual client. The spiraling cost of health care is the culprit.

HMOs have gained substantial and significant market share over the past two decades. Their cumulative share of covered insured employees now exceeds the national commercial insurance carriers by a wide margin. However, these plans have been ruled primarily by cost containment strictures. Freedom of choice is severely limited—there is a perception that the quality of care is at an all-time low. Liability issues are beginning to surface based on compromised or neglected care due to cost parameters. Many service costs are not adequately covered under these plans and the provider base of physicians are extremely dissatisfied with compensation allowances. Many physicians complain that the freedom of decision is diminishing constantly from time and cost constraints that are imposed upon them. The ultimate client, the individual patient, is equally dissatisfied. Thus, the employer becomes dissatisfied as well.

The market niche for the quality TPA is ripe for picking. However, services must be of high quality. Many small TPAs are promising high levels of service but often don't deliver as promised because of the expense of building the internal resources required to compete effectively. Southeast Health Plans, by virtue of its alliance with Blair Mill Administrators, already has the necessary resources in place.

Distribution Patterns

HMOs and Managed Care Companies are experienced and effective direct marketers. They employ media marketing and company sales forces to good effect. The primary problem they face is increasing dissatisfaction with their product. They will not be able to provide the multi-regional, customizable services that an increasing number of employers will demand. In addition, self-insurance is contrary to the buy-and-resell philosophy of these providers.

Many national insurance companies market through company sales forces and independent brokers and agents. Herein lies a potential barrier to entry into the small company market for an emerging TPA. Often the company has a pre-existing relationship with an insurance agent that may encompass a broader range of insurance services than health care. The company is, in fact, buying a "package" of varied insurance coverages that are necessary to business operation and also happen to include health care coverage. The task here is one of general education about the potential of self-insurance programs. If the insurance agent doesn't provide this alternative, he stands to eventually lose the health insurance coverage. But his current "franchise" with his client can be a barrier.

It is the intention of Southeast Health Plans both to market directly and to work through independent agents to reach their existing clients. A competitive agent compensation program is in place to accomplish this objective. It is the intention of the company to both work with independent agents who recognize the mutual value of co-operation or to sell in head-to-head competition with those who don't.

Ultimately, product, service, and price will prevail. All sales forecasts of the company recognize the timeline of market penetration, and have realistic, if not conservative, market share goals.

Buying patterns vary by the size of the employer and according to the internal organization.

Competition and Buying Patterns

The company with 50 to 100 employers may have health care handled by the owner or a key executive. Often it is the responsibility of the personnel administrator as an individual (if that function is internal to the company). Also, the personnel administration may be outsourced, but benefits may not. Sometimes an independent benefits brokerage firm handles all recommendations.

Larger companies from 200 to 500 employees may have personnel departments of several people. They might also employ a broker or a consultant.

Thus, it is imperative that Southeast have flexible programs and sales and marketing efforts that are targeted to a diverse set of potential buying patterns.

It is worthy to note that customer buying patterns for health plan coverage tend to revolve around annual renewal dates. That's when competition intensifies from traditional providers. Southeast will have an extremely significant marketing advantage since an employer may retain Southeast for its proprietary service mix at any time. Southeast can initiate service for a client by helping him analyze and administer his current plan. Often, such an engagement will progress to full service and to administration of self-insurance.

With provider services already in place, the launching of sales and marketing strategies and implementation is the next task of Southeast Health Plans. Executions include print media in targeted general business publications, direct mail programs, and sales contact follow-up.

STRATEGY AND IMPLEMENTATION SUMMARY

In addition contacts and seminars directed at independent agents and benefit brokerage firms will be launched. Additional sales materials will be produced that are targeted specifically toward these intermediary "customers."

Print media utilized will be the weekly *Atlanta Business Chronicle*.

Marketing Strategy

An extensive direct mail lead generation campaign will also be employed, targeted at employers, brokers, and consultants.

Both will be followed by direct sales contact by Southeast's professional sales executives.

Pricing for administrative services provided by Blair Mill is billed on a cost-per-employee basis.

Pricing Strategy

Actual medical costs within self-insured programs will vary as a combination function of negotiated provider service costs coupled with the level of stop-loss (deductible) coverage.

Revenues to Southeast Health Plans, Inc. are determined by sales commission formulas and also by cost advantages for medical services negotiated by Southeast contracted care providers. Thus, if Southeast provides medical service to the plan at a cost below the expected cost for the same service, differential revenue accrues to Southeast.

In both cases there is a time lag to realization of revenue. Sales commissions are paid 30 to 60 days in arrears based upon collection from customers. Service cost revenues are based upon actual services utilized and are also paid 30 to 60 days in arrears. All revenue projections included in this plan are based upon these delayed collection premises while all expenses are treated as cash when incurred (even if paid on 30 day terms). Thus, all cash flow analyses will err on the conservative side.

According to the terms of the existing agreement with Blair Mill, Southeast Health Plans will earn 25% of medical facility cost savings (as incurred) in years one and two and 17% in year three.

All services revenues generated by Southeast for new clients produced for Blair Mill will be paid as sales commissions according to the formula contained in the agreement.

The sales commissions are as follows:

- 11.2% of all fees in the first year of the sale.
- 2% of all fees in the second and third years.
- 5% of all fees in the fourth year and in each renewal year thereafter.
- Blair Mill administrative service costs average about $15 per month per employee covered.
- In addition, commissions on new stop-loss policies will average 15% in year one.

Sales Strategy

The sales strategy for Southeast Health Plans is based upon concentrated targeted direct marketing with sales call follow-up. Closing ratios are estimated at only 5% of prospects to yield cumulative covered plan employees projected in the sales forecasts. Thus, higher closing ratios are potentially possible and would accelerate growth and revenue beyond the forecasts.

All forecasts are based upon per employee estimates. Dollar charges are based upon "A," "B," and "C" size markets and the prevailing costs for medical care for those markets respectively. Back-up market data is too extensive to include in this plan.

Note: An "A" market is defined as metro Atlanta. A "B" market is a population center over one million. A "C" market is any market below one million in population.

Monthly sales forecasts for the first year are included in the appendices.

Note: A total of 23 employer groups have already become active through Blair Mill as of November 1, 1996. Revenues based upon health care cost savings will show up in the beginning of 1997. Initial monthly revenues are based upon these employer groups, which represent approximately 1,500 employees (already 31% of the first year goal of 4,800 covered employees).

On an average annual basis, the revenue projections for health care savings revenue to Southeast are based upon $7.40 per employee for 1997. This number is for "A" markets. "B" markets are estimated at $5.66, and "C" markets at $3.71 per employee. Rationale: Atlanta is over-bedded and under-utilized, while in smaller markets the reverse is true.

Additional selling and retention fees are added to the above estimates to obtain total revenue numbers. In "A" markets, for example, this is set at $1.75 for new employees and at $0.75 for renewal/retention fees.

Our sales forecasts are based upon the premises previously presented. Management feels these forecasts are highly attainable.

Sales	1997	1998	1999
Sales	$288,599	$1,399,223	$3,067,966
Other	$0	$0	$0
Total Sales	**$288,599**	**$1,399,223**	**$3,067,966**
Direct Cost of Sales			
Sales	$57,000	$201,000	$427,500
Other	$0	$0	$0
Subtotal Cost of Sales	**$57,000**	**$201,000**	**$427,500**

Total Sales by Month in Year 1

Jan	$11,101
Feb	$11,102
Mar	$12,017
Apr	$13,845
May	$15,674
Jun	$18,415
Jul	$22,985
Aug	$27,554
Sep	$32,123
Oct	$36,692
Nov	$41,261
Dec	$45,830

In addition to the primary strategic alliance with Blair Mill, Southeast Health Plans, Inc. has already formed alliances on the health care provider network side which will provide cost advantages and thereby guaranteed revenue via Blair Mill on billed medical services.

The initial agreement with Columbia Health Care Systems will provide coverage to a substantial portion of metro Atlanta. In addition, a second agreement is forthcoming with Independent Health Care Providers, which includes DeKalb Medical Center, Scottish Rite Hospitals, and Northside Hospital System. Comprehensive availability for Atlanta metro will then be in place. Fifty-two percent of available hospital beds will then be included. Cost savings are reflected in revenue projections on a per covered employee basis.

Milestones already achieved:

- Founder "seed" funding of $200K to develop and research plan, secure strategic alliances, and establish initial infrastructure.
- Strategic alliances in place with Blair Mill and with Columbia Health Systems.
- 23 employer groups and 1,500 employees already under managed care contracts.
- 52% of Atlanta metro area available hospital beds under contract at acceptable cost discounts.

Upcoming milestones:

- Obtain $300K capital to staff and launch full sales and marketing executions.
- Present Blair Mill products and services to 50 of the largest employers in our target market by March 1, 1997.

- To reach stated first year goal of 4,800 covered plan employees by January 1, 1998.
- To reach first year revenue goal of $288K by December 31, 1997.
- To attain breakeven cash flow by the end of year two.

MANAGEMENT SUMMARY

The founding management of Southeast Health Plans has an accumulated 75 plus years of industry related experience. All are well versed in industry fundamentals, educated in the evolution of the health care services industry, and share a vision for the successful positioning of Southeast Health Plans, Inc. within the industry.

Organizational Structure

The three founders will manage the company's growth jointly as managing partners.

All staff and sales and marketing personnel will report to them through a sales manager (heavy in industry experience) who has also been identified.

Future branch offices will each have a general manager.

Management Team

James J. Peters, Managing Partner

Mr. Peters has more than 25 years experience in sales and marketing management in employee benefits, securities, and real estate.

He has managed the marketing and sale of pension investment services for MegaLife in their Western region and for CNA and Oceanic Mutual nationally.

Mr. Peters joined the MegaLife HealthCare Network of Georgia as Regional Director for managed care sales in 1992. He built the marketing, sales, and service organizations for the Georgia network. Under his leadership, the network added 40,000 new, fully insured members over three years.

Mr. Peters holds a B.A. from the University of Notre Dame and an M.A. from the University of Oregon.

Thomas R. Cormier, Managing Partner

Mr. Cormier has more than 25 years of experience in the field of Employee Benefits. He began his career with Chariot Life and Casualty as a group insurance underwriter. As Project Team Leader in the Group Actuarial Department he developed procedures for the coordination of operations among departments within the Group Insurance Division.

He then spent 15 years with MegaLife in the sale and servicing of large group accounts, support for regional sales staff, and budget administration.

Most recently, he was responsible for integration of capitated services with fee-for-service contracts, and the installation of risk pool arrangements for MegaLife networks. He also was responsible for interfacing with corporate MIS.

Mr. Cormier holds a B.A. from the University of Notre Dame.

L. Richard Schumacher, M.D., Managing Partner

Dr. Schumacher is a specialist in internal medicine with 25 years in practice who has been in leadership positions in managed care organizations since 1983. He has more than eight years experience in two major national insurance companies serving as Regional Medical Director and then as Vice President of Medical Affairs for Monolith in the Southeast. He later became CEO of MegaLife's Georgia HMO. He has established himself as a well respected advisor/consultant within the managed care industry.

Dr. Schumacher holds a B.A. from Amherst College and a Doctor of Medicine from the University of Pennsylvania School of Medicine.

Jeffrey E. Farmer, Sales Manager
Mr. Farmer is a sales management professional with a consistently outstanding record of production achievement in employee benefits and managed care sales. He worked first for U.S. Healthcare in their Boston office and was subsequently recruited by Patrick Henry.

He later joined MegaLife Group Benefits in their Tampa regional office and graduated from the MegaLife Group Benefits Training Program. With MegaLife Health Care, Mr. Farmer led all MegaLife sales representatives in 1995 with more than $12 million in managed health care sales.

Mr. Farmer has a current extensive and active client base. He has completed all Health Insurance of America (HIAA) courses with honors. He is a member of the National Association of Health Underwriters, and the Atlanta Association of Health Underwriters.

Mr. Farmer holds a B.A. from Boston College.

Two current gaps exist within the management team:

Management Team Gaps

1) a Chief Financial Officer
2) a Business Development (Capitalization) Specialist.

Both functions will be performed on a consultative basis in the first year of operations (1997). The CFO position can later be filled on a full-time basis, and capitalization will be handled by Investment Banking Relationships.

The interim positions will be staffed by:

John Fraier, Interim CFO
Mr. Fraier's last position was VP of Finance and Treasurer for Vacation Inn Worldwide headquartered in Atlanta.

Mr. Fraier holds a B.A. in Finance from the College of Wooster in Ohio and an M.B.A. in Finance from Emory University in Atlanta.

Mr. Fraier is Senior Partner of Leprechaun Capital in suburban Atlanta.

Timothy Dineen, Interim VP Corporate Development
Mr. Dineen is Principal and Founder of Leprechaun Capital. He is experienced in raising capital for both public and private companies in an advisory capacity.

Mr. Dineen holds a B.A. from the University of Notre Dame.

We have created a Personnel Plan for Southeast Health Plans, Inc., where specific needs, compensation, and timing are indicated for each position. Future branch office staffing needs are lumped together as one line item.

Personnel Plan

Personnel Plan

Personnel	1997	1998	1999
James J. Peters	$60,000	$60,000	$66,000
Thomas R. Cormier	$60,000	$60,000	$66,000
L. Richard Schumacher	$60,000	$60,000	$66,000
Jeffrey E. Farmer	$64,992	$66,000	$66,000
Sales Executive	$42,000	$45,000	$48,000
Sales Executive	$42,000	$45,000	$48,000
Sales Executive	$10,500	$45,000	$48,000
Account Service Exec.	$36,000	$38,000	$40,000
Administrative Asst.	$30,000	$30,000	$32,000
Administrative Asst.	$6,000	$24,000	$25,000
VP Corp. Dev.	$18,000	$24,000	$30,000
CFO	$12,000	$60,000	$66,000
Branch Sales	$0	$200,000	$380,000
Other	$0	$0	$0
Other	$0	$0	$0
Total Payroll	**$441,492**	**$757,000**	**$981,000**
Total Headcount	0	0	0
Payroll Burden	$97,128	$166,540	$215,820
Total Payroll Expenditures	**$538,620**	**$923,540**	**$1,196,820**

Other Management Considerations

An advisory board of prominent managed health care professionals is already being assembled. These individuals are available for consultative assignment as well as Strategic Planning for Southeast Health Plans, Inc. The preliminary advisory board includes:

Dr. Nancy W. Ashbach, M.D., M.B.A.

Dr. Ashbach is a former CEO of MegaLife of Colorado and Utah with responsibility for HMO, POS, and PPO products. Her areas of expertise include outcomes management, reference standard benefits, and doctor/plan relationships.

Dr. Leslie Moldauer, M.D.

Dr. Moldauer is a psychiatrist who was formerly the National Director of Mental Health and Chemical Dependency Services at MegaLife Health Care Management Corporation. Her special interest is in the integration of mental health and chemical dependency programs into health plans as a whole.

Dr. Tighe E. Shomer, M.D.

Dr. Schomer has been Medical Director for a national managed care company with more than 200,000 HMO members and 1,250,000 PPO members. He has been a partner and director in a medical software and hardware company. He also advises Fortune 500 clients on issues pertaining to managed care, particularly preventative care and quality improvement.

FINANCIAL PLAN

Initial capitalization (after $300,000 founders' seed funding) is pegged at $1 million (with cash streaming in from April through September). This capitalization is intended to grow a company with retained equity in excess of $3.35 million in year five.

The company will be debt free at that point (barring any interim management decisions to accelerate growth further). The company will also have significant IPO potential in the future and/or be an acquisition candidate in an industry that traditionally undergoes consolidation.

It was necessary to outline the financial assumptions upon which this plan is based in order to address any that seemed unreasonable.

General Assumptions	1997	1998	1999
Short-term Interest Rate %	8%	8%	8%
Long-term Interest Rate %	8%	8%	8%
Payment Days Estimator	30	30	30
Collection Days Estimator	30	30	30
Inventory Turnover Estimator	1	1	1
Tax Rate %	33%	33%	33%
Expenses in Cash %	100%	100%	100%
Sales on Credit %	100%	100%	100%
Personnel Burden %	22%	22%	22%

Key financial indicators are increasing sales volume coupled with maintenance and improvement of margins. Ongoing cost control is paramount to success.

Benchmark Comparison

	1997	1998	1999
Sales	1.0	4.25	10.5
Gross	1.0	1.0	1.0
OpEx	1.0	1.75	2.25
AR Est.	0.0	0.0	0.0
Turns Est.	0.0	0.0	0.0

Breakeven, based upon fixed initial market overheads, will be attained prior to the end of year two.

Cost control and market maturation will then accelerate profitability which increases disproportionately as market development costs are offset with a critical mass of baseline business in each new market.

Breakeven Analysis

Monthly Units Breakeven	73,259
Monthly Sales Breakeven	$73,259

Assumptions

Average Per-Unit Revenue	$1.00
Average Per-Unit Variable Cost	$0.20
Estimated Monthly Fixed Cost	$58,608

Projected Profit and Loss

Southeast Health Plans, Inc. projects over-all profitability in year three. Profits after tax will exceed $560K in year three and $1.6 million in year five (shown in long-term plan in the appendix).

Profit and Loss (Income Statement)	1997	1998	1999
Sales	$288,599	$1,399,223	$3,067,966
Direct Cost of Sales	$57,000	$201,000	$427,500
Other	$0	$0	$0
Total Cost of Sales	**$57,000**	**$201,000**	**$427,500**
Gross Margin	$231,599	$1,198,223	$2,640,466
Gross Margin %	80.25%	85.63%	86.07%
Operating expenses			
SALES AND MARKETING EXPENSES			
Sales and Marketing Payroll	$0	$0	$0
Advertising/Promotion	$90,000	$180,000	$300,000
Travel	$24,000	$48,000	$66,000
Miscellaneous	$30,000	$60,000	$90,000
Other	$0	$0	$0
Payroll Expense	$441,492	$757,000	$981,000
Payroll Burden	$97,128	$166,540	$215,820
Depreciation	$0	$0	$0
Leased Equipment	$0	$0	$0
Telephone/Utilities	$12,000	$24,000	$30,000
Insurance	$0	$0	$0
Rent	$30,000	$90,000	$120,000
Other	$0	$0	$0
Other	$0	$0	$0
Contract/Consultants	$36,000	$0	$0
Total Operating Expenses	**$760,620**	**$1,325,540**	**$1,802,820**
Profit Before Interest and Taxes	($529,021)	($127,317)	$837,646
Interest Expense Short-term	$0	$0	$0
Interest Expense Long-term	$0	$0	$0
Taxes Incurred	($174,577)	($42,015)	$276,423
Net Profit	($354,444)	($85,302)	$561,223
Net Profit/Sales	-122.82%	-6.10%	18.29%

Projected Cash Flow

Cash flow is the most critical indicator of business success. At no point does our business model run out of cash. Significant margin for error is included. Initial and second round investment is procured prior to need and allowing for potential time lag to close.

All future growth is based upon a debt-free internally funded model. Attainment of targeted sales revenues will ensure the accumulation of required cash to execute expansion plans as presented.

Plans can always be curtailed or postponed in the event of future sales shortfalls.

	1997	1998	1999
Net Profit	($354,444)	($85,302)	$561,223
PLUS			
Depreciation	$0	$0	$0
Change in Accounts Payable	$0	$0	$0
Current Borrowing (repayment)	$0	$0	$0
Increase (decrease) Other Liabilities	$0	$0	$0
Long-term Borrowing (repayment)	$0	$0	$0
Capital Input	$1,000,000	$0	$0
Subtotal	**$645,556**	**($85,302)**	**$561,223**
LESS	1997	1998	1999
Change in Other ST Assets	$0	$0	$0
Capital Expenditure	$0	$0	$0
Dividends	$0	$0	$0
Subtotal	**$0**	**$0**	**$0**
Net Cash Flow	$645,556	($85,302)	$561,223
Cash Balance	$901,556	$816,253	$1,377,476

Pro-Forma Cash Flow

Cash Analysis	Cash Flow	Cash Balance
Jan	($33,906)	$222,094
Feb	($33,906)	$188,188
Mar	($34,298)	$153,890
Apr	$165,922	$319,812
May	$67,148	$386,960
Jun	$167,979	$554,939
Jul	$69,031	$623,970
Aug	$172,092	$796,062
Sep	$175,153	$971,215
Oct	($26,281)	$944,934
Nov	($23,220)	$921,714
Dec	($20,159)	$901,556

We project our net worth to be over $1.3 million after our fourth year.

Pro-Forma Balance Sheet

Assets	Starting Balances			
Short-term Assets		**1997**	**1998**	**1999**
Cash	$256,000	$901,556	$816,253	$1,377,476
Other Short-term Assets	$0	$0	$0	$0
Total Short-term Assets	$256,000	$901,556	$816,253	$1,377,476
Long-term Assets				

Projected Balance Sheet

Capital Assets	$0	$0	$0	$0
Accumulated Depreciation	$0	$0	$0	$0
Total Long-term Assets	$0	$0	$0	$0
Total Assets	**$256,000**	**$901,556**	**$816,253**	**$1,377,476**
Liabilities and Capital				
Accounts Payable	$0	$0	$0	$0
Short-term Notes	$0	$0	$0	$0
Other Short-term Liabilities	$0	$0	$0	$0
Subtotal Short-term Liabilities	**$0**	**$0**	**$0**	**$0**
Long-term Liabilities	$0	$0	$0	$0
Total Liabilities	**$0**	**$0**	**$0**	**$0**
Paid in Capital	$300,000	$1,300,000	$1,300,000	$1,300,000
Retained Earnings	($44,000)	($44,000)	($398,444)	($483,747)
Earnings	$0	($354,444)	($85,302)	$561,223
Total Capital	**$256,000**	**$901,556**	**$816,253**	**$1,377,476**
Total Liabilities and Capital	$256,000	$901,556	$816,253	$1,377,476
Net Worth	$256,000	$901,556	$816,253	$1,377,476

Our business ratios are only partially relevant as long as the business is able to remain debt free.

Ratio Analysis

Profitability Ratios	1997	1998	1999	RMA
Gross Margin	80.25%	85.63%	86.07%	0
Net Profit Margin	-122.82%	-6.10%	18.29%	0
Return on Assets	-39.31%	-10.45%	40.74%	0
Return on Equity	-39.31%	-10.45%	40.74%	0

Business Ratios

Activity Ratios				
AR Turnover	0	0	0	0
Collection Days	0	0	0	0
Inventory Turnover	0	0	0	0
Accts Payable Turnover	0	0	0	0
Total Asset Turnover	0.32	1.71	2.23	0

Debt Ratios				
Debt to Net Worth	0	0	0	0
Short-term Liab. to Liab.	0	0	0	0

Liquidity Ratios	1997	1998	1999	RMA
Current Ratio	0	0	0	0
Quick Ratio	0	0	0	0
Net Working Capital	$901,556	$816,253	$1,377,476	0
Interest Coverage	0	0	0	0

Additional Ratios				
Assets to Sales	3.12	0.58	0.45	0

Debt/Assets	0%	0%	0%	0
Current Debt/Total Assets	0%	0%	0%	0
Acid Test	0	0	0	0
Asset Turnover	0.32	1.71	2.23	0
Sales/Net Worth	0.32	1.71	2.23	0

Our long-term sales forecast illustrates that the company will, in fact, be a marketing company with excellent cash flow and profitability by year five which will open a myriad of strategic potentials.

Not the least of these potentials is growth via becoming a full-service health plan. Premiums would then flow directly to Southeast Health Plans, Inc. All that would be necessary is to capitalize government mandated reserve requirements. This could be done partially, if not wholly, with debt, thereby enhancing cash flows, investment incomes, and shareholder value.

The successful establishment of a marketing company creates the platform for all other strategic options.

Investor Trading Software Company

BUSINESS PLAN   INVESTOR TRENDS, INC.

40324 Woodward Ave.
Detroit, Michigan 48202

This business plan for a software company is unique in its concise display of keys to success. Pairing easily identifiable and relevant focal points with equally salient objectives gives a clear representation of the company's goals and a strong impression of direction. The plan also does a nice job of selling its product by differentiating it from the competition.

- EXECUTIVE SUMMARY

- INDUSTRY ANALYSIS

- MANAGEMENT SUMMARY

- FINANCIALS

EXECUTIVE SUMMARY

Investor Trends, Inc. is designed specifically for Wall Street professionals and other investors to take advantage of the lucrative day trading activities trend currently sweeping the country. Investor Trends is located in Detroit, Michigan and designs and assembles its product from one central location. Investor Trends is a firm specializing only in software design and its current profits come solely from sales of its one line of software.

Investor Trends, Inc. wishes to expand the software product line to include software meant for other Wall Street functions and commodity trading, including forecasting trends and analysis of all commodities currently offered on the market. This plan is designed to seek expansion capital to help us with our new line of software.

Objectives

Specifically, our objectives are as follows:

- To design and develop the Investor Trends commodity software in an expeditious fashion using designers already on board the company.

- To then market the Investor Trends software to professional investors in the Detroit area and then worldwide.

- To grow sales from our current $75,000 per month revenue to more than $200,000 by the end of fiscal year 2000.

- To promote the company and position it to be the predominant source of Wall Street investor software for the next millennium.

Mission

Our mission is to develop software solutions for the busy investor. We have located a need in the financial industries sector. Investors need reliable software they can count on to do their job properly. Investor Trends is the type of software they are seeking. They want to push the envelope in regards to investing and they have a lot riding on their results. We have identified a niche market and seek to capitalize on it. When we generate an excellent return for our investors, we not only help build a future for them, but a future for ourselves as well. We want our company to be a true leader in the niche market we have identified and we feel strongly that we are on the right path to success.

Keys to Success

1) Product sophistication: It is very important to let consumers know that your product is sophisticated enough for their use, but yet easy enough for them to operate. This certainly reassures the buyer of our products that they are working with a quality software product.

2) Product enhancement: Does it have a lot of features that make it a value-added product? If given the choice, customers will almost always opt for the product with the most features in a quantitative sense.

3) Future updating and customer support must be available.

4) Pricing must be reasonable for the standard of business or personal software that is being offered. The days of $495.00 retail pricing on software are long over.

5) Name recognition is a key factor and growing stronger every day.

6) Compatibility with all systems. We are currently working on several Mac applications to go hand-in-hand with our line of PC compatible software.

7) Product debugging. A software product that needs a lot of patching will anger customers in the long run. Revenue considerations cannot exceed solid beta testing parameters.

Company Summary

Investor Trends, Inc. was originally formed under the company name B & B software in 1991. Specializing predominantly in educational software, the company changed focus during 1994 and 1995 in order to capitalize on the huge growth of day trading activity that started to flood the Wall Street investment community. As this market was tapped and software was developed, the company experienced a huge downturn as its product was essentially retooled for the marketplace. B & B software changed names in late 1995 to Investor Trends, Inc. and its software line has flourished ever since. Investor Trends recognizes that the current trading activities may be a trend, although we do believe this is now an entrenched part of financial investing strategies for quite a few investors. With this in mind, we seek new lines to ensure the steady growth and survival of our company. By 1998, we maintained the same incorporation and same level of senior executives for three consecutive years. Under this stable new management, growth and opportunity has been outstanding. The company is poised for additional growth and our history proves that we can manage tough times and emerge as a leader of our particular industry.

Company Ownership

Investor Trends Inc. is a privately held corporation located in Detroit, Michigan. Jason Majors is currently the majority stockholder while John Abraham and Helen Martinez (the corporate board) are significant minority stockholders. Exact percentages are not available for public release.

Start-Up Costs

Start-up Expenses	$0
Legal	$0
Stationery, etc.	$0
Brochures	$0
Consultants	$0
Insurance	$0
Rent	$0
Research and development	$0
Expensed equipment	$0
Other	$0
Total Start-up Expense	**$0**
Start-up Assets Needed	
Cash requirements	$0
Start-up inventory	$0
Other Short-term Assets	$0
Total Short-term Assets	$0
Long-term Assets	$0
Total Assets	$0
Total Start-up Requirements	$0
Left to finance:	$0

Start-Up Costs

Continued...

Start-up Funding Plan

Investment	
Investor 1	$0
Investor 2	$0
Other	$0
Total investment	$0
Short-term borrowing	
Unpaid expenses	$0
Short-term loans	$0
Interest-free short-term lo	$0
Subtotal Short-term Borrow	$0
Long-term Borrowing	$0
Total Borrowing	$0
Loss at start-up	$0
Total Equity	$0
Total Debt and Equity	$0
Checkline	$0

Company Locations and Facilities

Our headquarters and production facilities operate out of the same general location in Detroit, Michigan. We have approximately 9,000 square foot of developed space with an option to access another 6,000 square feet for future expansion if the need warrants it. Once we have reached this artificial ceiling of 15,000 square feet, the only option would then be to move the facility and operate out of a completely different structure. No employees will need to be added for the foreseeable future until the new product line is developed. Once that occurs, then expansion to the full capacity of the building is anticipated.

The split between office area is currently 6,000 square feet administrative and office space, and 3,000 square feet for software production and packaging. Shipping is currently handled by an independent vendor through a small shipping dock at the rear of the facility.

Services

Investor Trends allows day trading investors to monitor their stock transactions throughout the day and track exactly how much profit and loss is occurring at any given moment during the trading day. While conducting this function, this software also keeps track of commissions generated by the trades and factors them in to the ongoing profit and loss experienced by the investor. This allows the trader to know exactly what his given performance is at that moment. This is precisely what this kind of trader is looking to do with their software. Day trading is a rather unusual type of trading in stocks and bonds where investors invest for quick short-term gains throughout the trading day. At the close of each trading session, the investor considers the day's activities as his income for the day. Needless to say, this is an extremely high-stress way to invest and similar to that of an air traffic controller: exact tracking and monitoring is crucial to their success. Failing to receive a key piece of information can lead to enormous losses and so timing is critical. Also, if the market takes an unexpected downturn, traders need to be aware of that trend so that they can quickly leverage their way out of a bad situation and prevent it from turning worse.

Service Description

Investor Trends is completely supported by both an online technical support staff and one reachable by phone or fax. Because of the relative simplicity of both installing and running the program, support services are minimal. They are expected to grow in volume and cost with the addition of new software; however, this should be offset by the 1-900 number in connection with future support services. The support staff hopes to be self-funding within six months of the new software being introduced to the market.

Competitive Comparison

Our software is exclusive to the market. There is no current competition for our product; however, it has been learned that one new software company on the West Coast is in the design and testing stages for a similar product. Goldstein Software operates day trading software, but their product is not similar because it concentrates on anticipating trends and forecasting as opposed to record keeping. Operating primarily under the notion that the market has pivot points, Goldstein guesses that level II pivot calculations will help locate the market's daily equilibrium point. Moving away from ADX, MOVA, and trend lines, his software specializes in a segment of the industry that has more to do with sophisticated prediction than actual tracking, hence, his software does not appear to be in direct competition with our own.

Sales Literature

Sales literature and sales tool development are always being refined here at Investor Trends, Inc. Copies of planned company advertisements and sales literature (including web site design) will be attached in an appendix at the conclusion of this plan.

Sourcing

Our net cost per sale is approximately $43.39 per unit before taxes and our wholesale price per unit is $89.95 with a retail sales price of $159.95. This means that we have a net margin of $46.56 per unit sold. Selling approximately 16,000 units in 1997 at $89.95 (last year's figures are available) produces a total gross income of approximately $1,439,200 on a sales volume of less than 1400 unit sales per month. Considering that Investor Trends Software uses CompUSA and Best Buy as exclusive distributors, this is considered to be a healthy sales per month volume. Our volume could grow by sourcing other vendor distributors, but then we would lose the advantageous pricing structure currently in place.

Technology

Our current technology is patented and trademarked; however, the commodity trading program is still in the design phase and will not be patented until it moves into the testing phase. Future technological applications and software are still in the preliminary idea phase and are not suitable for disclosure at the present time.

Future Services

Our future development plan is for Investor Trends, Inc. to continue to offer cutting edge software technology for the financial sector. Looking to expand our software base in the realm of financial software, we are looking not only at taking over several other nondirect software competitors, but also to a strategic merger with another strong software developer and expansion into a noticeable marketshare position.

INDUSTRY ANALYSIS

Trending for the software industry as a whole is up dramatically. Software trends in general continue to climb at a rate exceeding most other computer industries. The software Information Industry Association estimates that the software industry has 200,000 employees and is worth an estimated 70 billion dollars in the U.S. alone. The room for growth in this industry is phenomenal and is only limited by the lack of saleable product. That is one reason this plan hinges on future expenditures in research and development. Once the products are developed, our existing distribution network will access to the consumer. Our software placement focuses on the larger computer superstores of 20,000 square feet or more, which means that customers will be exposed to our product once they are developed. In addition, online sales of software

are now accounting for a prestigious 20% of annual growth, and that number is expected to rise with the continued expansion and development of the Internet.

Distribution Patterns

The main channel of distribution for our software is through the supplier CompUSA. They provide all of our distribution resources and also provide us with itemized accounting for units sold, units in transit, units in store, etc. This exclusive software arrangement may be changing as our need for expansion grows, but we fully expect CompUSA to remain as one of our active partners in the continuing development of our distribution system.

Competitive and Buying Patterns

Industry consolidation as a whole has brought tremendous change to the market. With the mergers of AOL, Sun Microsystems, and Netscape, the industry has been completely realigned. Microsoft is no longer the exclusive and sole dominant player in the computer industry. The mergers are helpful in generating large enough companies to be able to take on the large-scale monopolies in the industry, but there are still not enough of them in sufficient quantities to break the stranglehold on competition. With this in mind, Investor Trends, Inc., has explored merger possibilities with other software firms in the region. Several offers are pending, but none are conclusive.

Strategy and Implementation Summary

Our marketing strategy is threefold:

1. Concentrate on Internet and web sales.

2. Expand our strategic magazine ad presence.

3. Continue our computing trade and Wall Street trade specific marketing.

All of these factors will help us to develop our brand name for the rollout of future products, which is critical to the success of the business.

Marketing Strategy

Daily traders tend to be individuals primarily and brokerage operators secondarily. Since they are most frequently responsible for all of the results of their trades, they look for products that work, and they cannot afford major mistakes. They use our software because it helps them by tracking so many more parameters than the user could accomplish by using standard mathematical programs or programs not specifically designed for this function.

Pricing Strategy

Presently, our pricing strategy is to maintain the current $159.95 retail and net wholesale costs of $89.95. We plan to lower the price dramatically when our expected competition develops later during the fiscal year. We will then increase our volume as compared to our competition's introductory pricing structure and then beat that pricing at every turn. This will expand our marketshare and keep our competition from gaining a strong foothold in the market.

Promotion Strategy

In order to successfully promote the software, we need to appeal to the average Investor Trends. We can usually reach them in one of two ways: through his contact with the computer industry and through his contact with the brokerage industry. Both of these groups have separate trade publications which appeal to this target demographic. When targeting the demographic, we need to appeal to trade newspapers and magazines, which is the thrust of our strategy. A lesser focus is pure Internet sales because although web traffic to our site is strong and increasing, the impressive 20% of Internet sales has leveled off and remains fairly constant considering the medium. With this in mind, our advertising for fiscal year 1999 will increase from 12 to 14% in all categories.

Sales of our current product are strong. Product development will lead to a renewed sales effort once the product is positioned. When true competition enters the market, we will not only aggressively pursue a new pricing strategy, but we will also adopt a new way of distribution. Instead of simply dealing with one major distributor for all of our software products, we will expand into new distributor agreements.

Sales Strategy

Total Sales by Month in Year 1	1997	1998	1999
Sales	$890,344	$2,000,000	$2,500,000
Direct Cost of Sales	$96,967	$200,000	$300,000

Sales Forecast

Our company currently searches for new hires from recruiting colleges all around the country. Bright people are attracted to the software industry, not only for its challenges but because they are from a generation raised on the sort of technology that their parents only dreamt of. Even so, the current labor market is very tight and the technology sector is experiencing shortages like any other industry. This trend is expected to continue into the foreseeable future as demographics show an aging population starting to retire and not enough young people having the experience and sheer numbers to fill the gap. Wages are expected to rise and it will continue to be difficult for all of industry to find the talent that it needs. We plan on needing 20 or more programmers for the upcoming months and we are unwilling to hire temporary help to fill those gaps. Not only have most of the temporary people we've hired been underqualified, but it is difficult to turn some of the more talented temporary workers into full-time staffers. We will continue to seek qualified applicants in traditional ways and use creative approaches to solve this staffing challenge.

MANAGEMENT SUMMARY

Investor Trends, Inc. is a top down company with all of the senior managers having a direct hand in operations or in research and development. Besides the board and executive positions, there are five key departments which control 90% of the business activity of the company. Those departments and their individual slogans are:

Organizational Structure

A) Research and development - The cornerstone of the company.
B) Human resources - Managing our most important asset.
C) Sales and marketing - Promoting our products and our prospects.
D) Internet & web design - Designing the tools of tomorrow.
E) Finance and accounting - Counting our successes and adding our achievements.

Jason Majors: President and CEO of Investor Trends, Inc. Majors has had over twenty years of management experience with Rockford Marketing and as a senior marketing specialist at Philadelphia FilmWorks. His experience with graphical file interfacing in the computing department at Philadelphia FilmWorks led to his direct involvement with the computer industry. After leaving Philadelphia FilmWorks and while pursuing day trading activities as an active member of the investment community, Jason recognized that the market was lacking software which would aid the trader in following their transaction. Planning at first to just develop a simple aid for his own personal use, he developed the software in 1994 in conjunction with John Abraham. Together, they realized that a product had been developed for the market that would have universal appeal to all traders. Purchasing B & B Software for

Management Team

$250,000 in 1995 led to a resurgence of the company under his direction. The change of focus has proven successful and is happening in a market that has literally untapped potential. Jason has an MBA from Yale, a bachelor of science degree from the University of Michigan, is 42 years old, married, with three children.

John Abraham: Vice President and Director of Technology. Previously director of MIS for Lear and also an information specialist for Boeing. John is a recognized member of the computing industry, having developed multiple software products for production and distribution. John has special knowledge and experience with multitasking of various programs and will keep Investor Trends, Inc. at the forefront of financial software technology. John has a bachelor's degree in computer science and mathematics from Columbia University and is 40 years old.

Helen Martinez: Vice President and CFO. Previously an account executive for General Motors, Helen has a great deal of actual and applied experience with financial systems and accounting software. One of Helen's projects under development is a financial management tool for commodities trading which is discussed elsewhere in this plan. Helen has an MBA from the University of Chicago, is 45 years old, married, with three children.

Management Team Gaps

There are no senior management gaps at Investor Trends, Inc. We do have several positions which need to be filled, including that of Human Resources Director and a handful of lower level HTML programmer positions which have proven to be very difficult positions to fill.

Personnel Plan

Our personnel plan calls for increasing total employee head count by 15%, to a total 85 persons, within the next 12 months. This additional increase in personnel is expected to be filled more quickly once the Human Resources Director position is placed. Most of the new positions are in web design and management and our most pressing need is for HTML experience. Details are included in the personnel plan on file in our departmental office.

FINANCIALS

The primary financial need for Investor Trends, Inc. is for expansion capital to fund new product development. We want to finance a long-term loan of $154,000 to help pay for salaries of our research and development team, in addition to funds to help with expanding our product line and to help with our initial product rollout costs.

This loan would be paid back from current profits generated by our Investor Trends software and backed by corporate assets of approximately $350,000 in a strategic reserve fund and liquid investment funds. Most of our building space and equipment is leased, so all loans would be strictly on a promissory note basis.

Important Assumptions

This financial plan depends on important assumptions, most of which are shown below.

1. We assume a slow-growth economy, without a major recession.
2. We assume that there will be no technological changes which would make our products immediately obsolete.
3. We assume access to equity capital and financing which would be sufficient to maintain our plan.
4. We assume a continuation of strong interest in day trading activities.
5. We assume our commodities package can be fully tested and designed within the specified time.

General Assumptions

	1997	1998	1999
Short-Term Interest Rate	10%	10%	10%
Long-Term Interest Rate	8%	8%	8%
Payment days estimator	30	30	30
Collection days estimator	45	45	45
Inventory Turnover estimator	6	6	6
Tax Rate Percent	25%	25%	25%
Expenses in cash %	10%	10%	10%
Sales on credit	75%	75%	75%
Personnel Burden %	15%	15%	15%

Note: Ratios in assumptions are used as estimators and may therefore have different values than ratios calculated in the ratios section.

Breakeven Analysis

Our breakeven analysis shows that our plan is viable as long as we maintain approximately 400 units per month in sales or more. Currently, our sales forecast shows a minimum 50% increase for the next fiscal year. These ratios are subject to change without notice.

Breakeven Analysis	
Monthly Units Breakeven	430
Monthly Sales Breakeven	$38,638
Assumptions	
Average Unit Sale	$89.95
Average Per-Unit Cost	$43.39
Fixed Cost	$20,000

Projected Profit and Loss

We expect gross revenues to approach 2 million dollars in the year 2000 and 2.5 million in 2001. Our net income should grow correspondingly.

	1997	1998	1999
Sales	$890,344	$2,000	$2,500,000
Direct Cost of Sales	$96,967	$200,000	$300,000
Other	$0	$0	$0
Total Cost of Sales	**$96,967**	**$200,000**	**$300,000**
Gross margin	$793,377	$1,800,000	$2,200,000
Gross margin percent	89.11%	90%	88%
OPERATING EXPENSES			
Advertising/Promotion	$14,753	$20,000	$30,000
Travel	$12,000	$15,000	$20,000
Miscellaneous	$2,400	$3,000	$3,000
Other	$900	$1,000	$2,000
Payroll expense	$330,000	$0	$0
Leased Equipment	$2,250	$3,000	$4,000
Utilities	$9,600	$11,000	$12,000
Insurance	$4,800	$5,000	$6,000
Rent	$72,000	$100,000	$120,000
Depreciation	$18,000	$20,000	$25,000
Payroll Burden	$49,500	$0	$0
Other	$5,400	$7,000	$9,000
Contract/Consultants	$6,000	$8,000	$9,000
Other	$2,400	$4,000	$5,000

Projected Profit and Loss
Continued...

	1997	1998	1999
Total Operating Expenses	**$530,003**	**$197,000**	**$245,000**
Profit Before Interest and Taxes	$263,374	$1,603,000	$1,955,000
Interest Expense ST	$2,292	$5,000	$5,000
Interest Expense LT	$0	$0	$0
Taxes Incurred	$65,271	$399,500	$487,500
Net Profit	$195,812	$1,198,500	$1,462,500
Net Profit/Sales	**21.99%**	**59.93%**	**58.50%**

Projected Cash Flow

	1997	1998	1999
Net Profit	**$195,812**	**$1,198,500**	**$1,462,500**
PLUS			
Depreciation	$18,000	$20,000	$25,000
Change in Accounts Payable	$16,792	$10,146	$10,042
Current Borrowing (repayment)	$50,000	$0	$0
Increase (decrease) Other Liabilitie	$0	$0	$0
Long-term Borrowing (repayment)	$0	$0	$0
Capital Input	$0	$0	$0
Subtotal	**$280,604**	**$1,228,646**	**$1,497,542**
LESS			
Change in Accounts Receivable	$102,059	$127,198	$57,314
Change in Inventory	$13,964	$14,838	$14,401
Change in Other ST Assets	$0	$0	$0
Capital Expenditure	$0	$0	$0
Dividends	$0	$0	$0
Subtotal	**$116,023**	**$142,036**	**$71,715**
Net Cash Flow	$164,581	$1,086,610	$1,425,827
Cash Balance	**$164,581**	**$1,251,191**	**$2,677,018**

Projected Balance Sheet

	1997	1998	1999
SHORT-TERM ASSETS			
Cash	$164,581	$1,251,191	$2,677,018
Accounts receivable	$102,059	$229,257	$286,571
Inventory	$13,964	$28,802	$43,202
Other Short-term Assets	$0	$0	$0
Total Short-term Assets	$280,604	$1,509,250	$3,006,792
LONG-TERM ASSETS			
Capital Assets	$0	$0	$0
Accumulated Depreciation	$18,000	$38,000	$63,000
Total Long-term Assets	($18,000)	($38,000)	($63,000)
Total Assets	**$262,604**	**$1,471,250**	**$2,943,792**
DEBT AND EQUITY			
Accounts Payable	$16,792	$26,938	$36,981
Short-term Notes	$50,000	$50,000	$50,000
Other ST Liabilities	$0	$0	$0
Subtotal Short-term Liabilities	$66,792	$76,938	$86,981
Long-term Liabilities	$0	$0	$0
Total Liabilities	$66,792	$76,938	$86,981

	1997	1998	1999	
Paid in Capital	$0	$0	$0	**Projected Balance Sheet**
Retained Earnings	$0	$195,812	$1,394,312	
Earnings	$195,812	$1,198,500	$1,462,500	*Continued...*
Total Equity	$195,812	$1,394,312	$2,856,812	
Total Debt and Equity	$262,604	$1,471,205	$2,943,792	
Net Worth	**$195,812**	**$1,394,312**	**$2,856,812**	

PROFITABILITY RATIOS	1997	1998	1999	
Gross margin	89.11%	90.00%	88.00%	**Projected Business Ratios**
Net profit margin	21.99%	59.93%	58.50%	
Return on Assets	74.57%	81.46%	49.68%	
Return on Equity	100.00%	85.96%	51.19%	
ACTIVITY RATIOS				
AR Turnover	6.54	6.54	6.54	
Collection days	28	40	50	
Inventory Turnover	13.89	9.35	8.33	
Accts payable turnover	13.26	13.26	13.26	
Total asset turnover	3.39	1.36	0.85	
DEBT RATIOS				
Debt to net Worth	0.34	0.06	0.03	
Short-term Debt to Liab.	1.00	1.00	1.00	
LIQUIDITY RATIOS				
Current Ratio	4.20	19.62	34.57	
Quick Ratio	3.99	19.24	34.07	
Net Working Capital	$213,812	$1,432,312	$2,919,812	
Interest Coverage	114.93	320.6	391.00	
ADDITIONAL RATIOS				
Assets to sales	0.29	0.74	1.18	
Debt/Assets	25%	5%	3%	
Current debt/Total Assets	25%	5%	3%	
Acid Test	2.46	16.26	30.78	
Asset Turnover	3.39	1.36	0.85	
Sales/Net Worth	4.55	1.43	0.88	

Medical Equipment Producer

BUSINESS PLAN   MEDQUIP, INC.

45000 Miller Blvd.
Greensboro, NC 27530

This plan illustrates how to inform prospective lenders about products that are highly specialized and technical. Avoiding both over-simplification and cryptic industry-specific terms, the plan elucidates the products' functions and benefits, leaving the reader neither overwhelmed nor skeptical about what the company is producing, and thereby strengthening reader interest. This plan was compiled using Business Plan Pro, by Palo Alto Software.

- EXECUTIVE SUMMARY

- COMPANY SUMMARY

- PRODUCTS AND SERVICES

- MARKET ANALYSIS SUMMARY

- STRATEGY AND IMPLEMENTATION SUMMARY

- MANAGEMENT SUMMARY

- FINANCIAL PLAN

**EXECUTIVE
SUMMARY**

Medquip, Inc. is a medical device development company that intends to design, patent, and market medical devices related to endoscopic surgical niche markets. Three devices have already been designed with the participation of leading physicians and surgeons in gastroenterology. Seven patents are initially incorporated.

The company projects $20 million in sales in year three with a net profit of approximately $7.5 million.

The company expects to have $50 million in revenue by year five.

Patent applications on its first three market entries have already been accomplished using a top patent law firm.

The market segments are clearly defined and all are subject to a high growth trend. One market is projected to exceed $200 million in the next three years. That is the endoscopic variceal ligation market. One of the founders of Medquip participated in the design of the current market leader in that field and has improved upon the product significantly.

Another market addresses a well-defined and unanswered need in endoscopic surgery: the clearing of fundal pools of blood and tissue during surgical procedures. A new and innovative design has been created to answer the needs of surgeons.

This market should begin at $20 million but could expand to several hundred million as soon as approvals are obtained for many varied surgical procedures. Medquip intends to license this technology to a larger company.

The following chart of the highlights of the business plan indicate modest profits in year one and two in the $200k range. The company is profitable in year one only if a proposed licensing agreement can be closed.

The company becomes mature in year three with gross margins of 65%, producing $7.5 million in net earnings.

Objectives

The principal objectives of Medquip, Inc. are as follows:

1. To achieve a 10% market penetration in the endoscopic variceal ligation market by the year 2000.
2. To achieve $20 million in revenue by the year 2000.
3. To raise $1 million in private seed capital in the first half of 1998.
4. To win low interest loans and grants from the government of Puerto Rico, totalling $1.2 million in 1998.
5. To license its technology for the obliteration/suction/irrigation market for $1 million dollars in 1998.

Mission

The mission of Medquip, Inc. is to design, develop, and market new patented technologies in the medical device field. The technologies will fill market niches that each account for a minimum of $20 million dollars in potential sales. Each technology will fill a current need in medical procedure by improving upon an existing technology or device, or by designing a device to serve a need that is clearly defined and acknowledged by medical professionals. Each product shall be priced to appeal to a managed-care market that stresses lowest cost of total treatment parameters.

The keys to success for Medquip, Inc. are as follows:

1. Initial capitalization obtained.
2. All patent applications filed.
3. The ability to generate early revenue from non-regulated markets in Europe.
4. Licensing at least one technology and application to a major medical device corporation.
5. Getting low interest loans and/or grants to fully fund product development and prototype manufacture.
6. Recruiting top-notch CEO prior to second round financing and market roll-out.
7. Successful 510k approval from FDA to market Visi-Band in the U.S.
8. Successful implementation of sales and marketing plan to U.S. managed care market to obtain a minimum 10% market share in the second full year to generate $20 million in revenue.
9. Increased product development and continued market share gains to produce a $50 million revenue company by year five.

Medquip, Inc. will develop and market endoscopic medical devices through multiple distribution channels both foreign and domestic. The company is currently developing its patent-applied technologies to final product and approval stage. It is also seeking to establish its corporate identity in the medical products field. Growth strategy calls for one joint venture license as well as the following objectives:

1. Complete the patent process.
2. Establish corporate identity, brand names, trademarks.
3. Establish a medical advisory board.
4. Build staff, infrastructure, and retain consultants for trial and compliance issues.
5. Conduct animal trials.
6. Prepare for FDA clinical trials.
7. Continue R&D and product development.
8. Explore options for second-round financing (venture capital, corporate alliance, licensing, public offering) to maximize value to shareholders.

Note: Management believes that accelerated FDA approval process will be available on the band ligation device since it involves only modifications on an existing, approved device. There is past precedent in 510k approvals (in an average of 3 months) in documented cases.

Medquip, Inc. is a South State "C" corporation.

Its founding shareholders are:

Eric Smith (2,545,000 shares)
Timothy Jones (500,000 shares)

At the date of this plan, two additional shareholders are of record:

Arthur C. Clark (50,000 shares)
Genesis Corp. (14,000 shares)

Start-Up Summary

The key elements in the Start-Up plan for Medquip, Inc. are:

1. The legal expense for filing all patent applications.
2. The establishment of corporate identity.
3. The location and place of doing business.
4. Funding of additional capital raising alternatives.
5. Salary for the two key managers and founders.
6. Formulation of strategic plan. Costs of raising capital through private placement.

The initial two investors raised $128,000 for these purposes. This funding came in early 1998 and these tasks have either been completed successfully or are in the final process of completion.

These are treated purely as start-up expenses by this plan. The $128,000 is treated as cash-on-hand as of the start of this plan on January 1, 1998. The remainder of the start-up capital required as well as capital required for the continuation of operations in the first six months will be provided by selling the shares in the private placement. The capital obtained from these sales is expected to total an additional $850,000, and the plan calls for this cash to be infused in May and June 1998.

START-UP EXPENSES

Legal	$50,000
Stationery, etc.	$2,000
Brochures	$0
Consultants	$3,000
Insurance	$3,000
Rent	$9,300
Research and development	$0
Expensed equipment	$0
Custom Cad Software	$5,700
Logo Design	$975
Management Salaries	$56,000
Total Start-up Expense	$129,975

START-UP ASSETS NEEDED

Cash Requirements	$128,000
Start-up inventory	$0
Other Short-term Assets	$0
Total Short-term Assets	$128,000
Long-term Assets	$0
Total Assets	$128,000
Total Start-up Requirements:	$257,975
Left to finance:	$129,975

START-UP FUNDING PLAN

INVESTMENT

Investor 1	$100,000
Investor 2	$28,000
Other	$0
Other	$0
Total investment	$128,000

SHORT-TERM LIABILITIES

Unpaid Expenses	$0
Short-term Loans	$0
Interest-free Short-term Loans	$0
Subtotal Short-term Liabilities	$0
Long-term Liabilities	$0
Total Liabilities	$0
Loss at Start-up	$0
Total Capital	$128,000
Total Capital and Liabilities	$128,000
Checkline	$0

Medquip, Inc. business offices are in Greensboro, North Carolina. These offices are leased month-to-month on a temporary basis.

This business plan calls for the establishment of corporate offices, R&D facilities, and prototype and small-run manufacturing facilities.

These facilities are to be located in Puerto Rico with 10,000 square feet initially expandable to 30,000 square feet. Rental costs in Puerto Rico range from $1.75 to $4.00 per square foot.

Currently, available space in Puerto Rico may also be used on a joint-venture basis to be negotiated.

Company Locations and Facilities

Medquip, Inc. will initially market three distinct products.

1. The Visi-Band, a disposable device that is used in endoscopic variceal ligation procedures.
2. The Visi-Gator, a partially disposable device that is used to remove blood clots during various endoscopic surgical procedures.
3. The Visi-Lyser, a suction/irrigation device for laproscopic procedures.

The technology used in these products is the subject of seven patents in the application process. These three product areas may be more generally defined as follows:

Endoscopy Devices—used for esophageal variceal ligation, hemorrhoidal ligation.

- The Visi-Band: Consisting of ligating bands with greater stretchability and grip (Super-Elastic bands incorporated into a multi-band dispensing device).

Endoscopy Devices—used for lysis (tissue dissolving).

- The Visi-Gator: Consisting of a rotary cutting tool to clear fundal pools of blood in the stomach.

Endoscopy Devices—used for suction/irrigation and tissue removal.

- The Visi-Lyser: Consisting of a suction/irrigation tool to remove tissue effectively.

PRODUCTS AND SERVICES

A detailed and technical description of the Medquip, Inc. initial product line follows:

Multiple Ligating Band Dispenser: The Visi-Band. Application is endoscopic variceal ligation, which is a rapidly growing surgical procedure quickly replacing schlerotherapy for the removal of polyps in both upper and lower gastro-intestinal exploration.

Product and Service Description

Scope: This innovation applies to the internal technology of ligating bands independent of the dispenser or delivery system. Visi-Band is a pre-loaded delivery device for applying multiple ligating bands remotely from the distal tip of an endoscope. (The leading current product in this category is the Speedband made by Boston Scientific).

Clinical Advantages: A perceived clinical advantage of these bands is ligation of a greater range of tissue sizes with a single band. These ligating bands stretch easily over the largest tissue to be ligated and yet will grip securely even the tiniest tissue to be removed. These bands can have an inner diameter near zero so that even tiny varices are gripped firmly.

Current State of the Art Technology: Market-leading bands today are molded of homogeneous rubber materials. Material properties of elasticity have limited the stretch of conventional ligating bands to a range of about seven-fold. A typical market-leading band for esophageal variceal ligation has an inner diameter of 1.8mm. This band can stretch to a maximum inner diameter of 12.4mm to ligate a varix. This maximum size roughly corresponds to the endoscope diameter. A varix of 1.8mm would not be ligated because the band would be loose around the tissue.

Medquip Technology: The Super-Elastic Band innovation effectively engineers the band material stresses in a way that increases the apparent stretchability of the band many times. We have created bands with proximate zero inner diameters, which can be stretched at least as large as conventional bands with large inner diameters. Bands created with this technology can also hold their elasticity for longer periods of time. The basis of our technology is an internal compressive pre-stress at the band inner diameter. This can be achieved in at least five practical ways covered in our patent documentation. The true zero inner diameter band is a result of the compressive forces creating small scale creasing or wrinkling which fill the band interior. Bands made to date exhibit an effective elasticity of 20 times and more versus the seven times stretch in the market-leading band.

Medquip ligation devices should have an unprecedented and superior range of application to meet ligation requirements. Super-Elastic Bands can mean fewer special sized devices to manufacture, purchase, specify, and stock. This fits well in a managed-care environment through lower costs with inherent clinical advantages. Medquip and the health care system could benefit from higher volumes of a smaller number of different products.

Further Clinical Advantages:

- Visi-Band is designed for multiple band ligations with a single scope insertion.

- Visi-Band delivers maximum visibility with zero "tunnel vision" during insertion and exploration, a limitation of all competitors.

- Visi-Band delivers maximum mobility by being nearly flush with the distal end of the endoscope during insertion and exploration.

- Visi-Band should be significantly faster to install to the endoscope by having many fewer assembly parts and steps than the competition.

- Visi-Band is smaller in diameter than Speedband for patient acceptance and comfort.

- Visi-Band patient entry is smoother and protected at all times from misfires by a smooth, transparent outer shield.

- Visi-Band can ligate smaller varices with the super-elastic bands as described above.

- Visi-Band can be supplied in a single configuration with multiple bands, seven or eight, at a cost similar to the competition's three or six band unit.

Note: Today's multiple ligating band dispensers release bands off a tube at the distal endoscope end with typically two filaments for each band. This tube is at least as long as the endoscope diameter and creates severe "tunnel vision" because the bands typically cover the outside surface of the clear plastic tube. This added length also reduces the mobility of the distal tip. Each filament must be precisely assembled and triggered for each band. Bands exposed on the outside of the tube are prone to misfire as evidenced by a clear shield with instruction to remove just prior to insertion into the patient. A conically tapered dispenser is typical and necessary to help bands roll off the distal end. This taper increases the diameter of the ligating unit. Installation is a complex, multiple step process often involving a separate ligating unit, handle unit, a trip wire, scope fastener, and irrigation catheter. Actuating a competitive unit can cause the distal tip to move from the tension of the trip wire.

Medquip Technology: The Medquip Visi-Band multiple band ligator is planned to have two components, the ligating unit and handle. The Ligating Unit comprises a clear tubular base with bands stretched around the distal end, a clear sleeve outside of and concentric with the base, and a trip tube which passes through the biopsy channel of the scope. The ligating unit mounts in a retracted position around and substantially flush with the distal tip of the endoscope. The ligating unit is placed on the distal tip of the scope by pushing the trip tube through the biopsy channel. The handle is then snapped on the free end of the trip tube. The unit is extended distally prior to ligation, and the sleeve is moved axially to load then deliver a single band at a time. No individual filaments are required for each band so manufacturing cost is low. The unit is "digitally" actuated by repeated axial motion of the sleeve rather than small incremental displacements. The tip of the scope should not move because a compressive force in the tube cancels the tension in the trip wire internal to the trip tube.

Summary of advantages over currently available products:

1. Better visibility due to side-mounting of band dispensing device.
2. Smaller band, more stretch, enabling banding of smaller varices.
3. Internal loading of bands, enabling protection (bands are not dislodged).
4. Capable of carrying more bands (8 vs. 6).
5. Significant reduction in manufacturing and assembly costs.

Lysis (tissue dissolving) Rotary Cutting/Suction Tool: The Visi-Gator. Applications include the removal of blood clot and stray tissue during suction irrigation in laparoscopic surgery, examination of bleeding ulcers in the stomach, hemotoma, clot in the fallopian tube, or cerebral aneurysm. Current solutions employ crude tubes that incorporate a few holes for anti-clogging combined with drug treatments that are largely ineffective.

Scope: An uncleared fundal pool of retained blood in the stomach precludes complete visualization of the stomach in 5.6% of cases of acute upper gastrointestinal bleeding. According to an October 1997 article in *Gastrointestinal Endoscopy:* "In conclusion, the results of this study provide evidence that the inability to clear a fundal pool of blood at the time of emergent upper endoscopy for acute UGI bleeding is associated with substantial morbidity and mortality and ... Aggressive mechanical and/or pharmacological measures to clear the fundus of blood are warranted in patients undergoing urgent endoscopy for acute UGI bleeding."

Clinical Advantages: The Visi-Gator tool may be inserted from the outside into the biopsy channel of the endoscope as needed. The scope does not need to be withdrawn to install and use the Visi-Gator.

Current State of the Art Technology: Lavage with suction is frequently ineffective due to clot integrity and clogging of suction channels. High-pressure water jets penetrate beyond the clot, potentially penetrating and damaging soft tissues.

Medquip Technology: Visi-Gator is a thin, ultra-flexible, spring-like device that is introduced through the biopsy channel to the distal end of the endoscope. High-speed rotations of one or more of many concentric spiral elements both drive rotating lysing filaments and positively pump solids and liquids out. Centripetal force expands and stiffens the filaments from a stored position during insertion to a generally planar and circular path. Vacuum may also be applied. A hollow central channel may also be provided for irrigation, access, or other therapy.

Further Clinical Advantages:

- Visi-Gator clot dissolving aggressiveness varies from mild to intense and is proportional to the adjustable input speed control.

- Visi-Gator actively draws fluid and solids up through the biopsy channel with a positive pumping action.

- Visi-Gator continues to dissolve solids even as they pass through the biopsy channel.

- Visi-Gator will tend to be non-clogging and self-cleaning.

- Visi-Gator does not rub high-speed surfaces against the biopsy channel and cause high rates of wear.

- Visi-Gator provides a central channel for clear water irrigation, additional suction or other therapy.

- Visi-Gator motor driver is envisioned to be reusable. The fluid path and lysis head is likely to be disposable.

- Visi-Gator dissolving action and lysing head is transparent. One can see through the scope real time in the zone of clot lysis continuously as the lysing progresses.

- Visi-Gator appears to be capable of rapid clot lysis yet is gentle to tissue.

- Visi-Gator tip is soft and pliant to flex over any non-clot tissues.

- Visi-Gator lysis zone is generally a defined planar disc perpendicular to the axis of the distal end of the scope.

- Visi-Gator allows lysis not to penetrate beyond the disc boundaries.

Suction Irrigation Device for General Laparoscopic Surgery: (incorporated into Visi-Gator): The Visi-Lyser.

Scope: Visi-Lyser suction irrigation device includes a self contained, stand-alone suction/irrigation device to aid the surgeon during laparoscopic surgical procedures.

Clinical Advantages: Lysis of the clot or tissue at the entry point, which will tend to be clog resistant. A likely disposable fluid path and reusable power head.

Current State of the Art Technology: Conventional suction irrigation devices are prone to clog when presented with a clot during surgery.

Medquip Technology: Similar to the Visi-Gator tool with the lysing filaments contained within a perforated suction tube.

Note: The Visi-Lyser is designed to work with the Visi-Gator in laproscopic procedures but may also be used by itself in distinct procedures.

One embodiment inserts into the working channel of an endoscope as an accessory. A flexible spiral spring-like element rotates at several thousand RPM inside of a close spiral spring tube of opposite hand wind. A tiny motor on the outside proximal end of the endoscope spins the spiral element. Liquid or solid material inside the spiral element windings is drawn from distal to proximal positions by the interaction of the rotating and stationary spiral geometry. Suction is preferably applied at the proximal end of the spiral element before the motor. At the distal end of the spiral element, a generally spherical ball tip covers the spiral end to protect soft tissues from the spiral screwing into tissue and causing trauma. Projecting from the tip is a single or multiple of filaments, which spin at the high speed of the spiral element. The filaments lyse the unwanted clot or soft tissue fragments, depending on speed of rotation, diameter, material, and construction details. The filaments may optionally be extended or retracted from the outside to lyse differing diameters or body cavity sections. Rotation speed of the motor is a direct way to control aggressiveness of lysis dynamically from the outside. A flexible tube may be placed at the center of the rotating spiral element to carry water or saline to flush the cavity being lysed. A single or multiple of apertures near the distal end of the water tube may spray a jet sideways to clear potential clogs. The water center tube is preferentially not rotating.

In a second embodiment, designed for suction irrigation of a surgical site, the rotating filaments and spiral are placed in a tube with small apertures. The filaments rotating inside serve to lyse clot and tissue which would normally clog the apertures. A rotating jet of water inside could also serve to clear any clogs. The spiral element could also be present inside.

Advantages over currently available products: no products currently available.

Note: A variety of medical journal articles and research studies are available that cover both potential product areas.

Patent searches and filings are under way with Sidley and Austin. Opinion is that as many as seven distinct patents may be available and obtainable on the three devices cumulatively. Mr. Smith has assigned these patents (as obtained) and any future issued patents in the medical device arena to Medquip, Inc.

Competitive Comparison

The leading product currently available in the endoscopic variceal ligation market is the Speedband made by Boston Scientific. Other product entries are from C.R. Bard and Wilson-Cook. The Speedband from the Microvasive division of Boston Scientific is far and away the market leader with an estimated 60% market share. The Six Shooter from Wilson-Cook has a 20% market share. Rapid-Fire made by C.R. Bard has a 10% market share. All of the devices are disposable (single patient use).

Eric Smith, a founder of Medquip and the developer of Medquip's patented technologies had significant participation in the design of the Speedband. He is aware of both its strengths and shortcomings. The Visi-Band is a much improved product in a rapidly growing market application. Many of the product advantages were highlighted in the previous section of this plan. To summarize the key advantages:

- Band itself enables smaller varices to be banded.
- Smaller hole plus more stretch in band.
- Device has better field of view.

- Device has better mobility.
- Bands are fired internally vs. externally.
- Significant cost reductions in manufacturing.

The Visi-Gator and the Visi-Lyser represent an entirely new application with no current competition. Their use can potentially range from stomach procedures to heart procedures and a variety of other surgical procedures. Together they solve the well documented and acknowledged problem of lack of visibility in endoscopic procedures where blood clots are involved. The Visi-Lyser also allows an improved and more efficient means of removing fundal pools of clotted blood and tissue.

Sales Literature

Sales literature for Medquip, Inc. remains to be developed.

Sourcing

Primary raw materials needed for Medquip products are as follows:

1. Molded plastic parts.
2. The tooling and molds (capital expenditure).
3. Band material (polymer).
4. Small electric motor.

All of these components are easily sourced and multiple suppliers have been identified. In addition, injection molders have been identified to manufacture the molded components for Medquip products. There are multiple potential sources.

A potential source for additional research and design help and compliance is Valnet in Puerto Rico.

Medquip will perform final assembly and distribution from its own facility in Puerto Rico or utilizing contract manufacturing depending on the extent of financial support from the government of Puerto Rico.

Technology

Sidley and Austin is the patent attorney for Medquip, Inc. Seven patents have been authored and filed. All patents take into account both offensive and defensive postures in their claims. Opinion of legal counsel is strong and firm that all of Medquip's patent applications are enforceable and defensible.

The principal areas (general descriptions) of the patents applied for are as follows:

1. The ligating band itself.
2. The moveable dispenser.
3. The dispenser itself.
4. Two additional alternative dispensers.
5. The tissue dissolving device.
6. The transporting catheter.
7. The dispenser control device.

Care has been taken to take into account all potential claims of the inventions as well as to protect them from possible competition from other technologies (including inferior ones).

All patent application documents are available for examination by potential investors. The first document is entitled "A ligating structure having greater stretchability, greater shelf life, and greater ligating characteristics and method of manufacture." It lists more than 40 independent claims.

Also available is the assignment of all patents in the medical device field (above listed and future developed) by Eric Smith to Medquip, Inc. The first four patents listed above relate to the Visi-Band. The last two relate to the Visi-Gator.

Trademark application has been filed on the name Medquip. Trademark applications are in process on the names Visi-Band, Visi-Gator, and Visi-Lyser. No conflicts or other use of these names has been found in an initial search.

Plans for future development by Medquip include additional ideas and technologies to be created by Eric Smith as vice president of R&D for Medquip. In addition Medquip may seek to acquire technologies developed by others once it attains sufficient capitalization to do so. It is the objective of Medquip to both innovate and market its products. Once an industry reputation has been achieved and marketing channels open, expansion into other medical device areas becomes potentially rewarding.

A recent article in *Red Herring* indicates the bio-tech field in general is a current hotbed of activity and most of the companies involved are early-stage development companies.

Future Products and Services

The two key factors influencing discussion of Medquip Inc.'s market are the medical procedures and product usage statistics and the customer or chain of distribution considerations.

In both cases the trends are upwards in favor of Medquip. Banding is growing rapidly, replacing schlerotherapy, and managed care stresses lowest cost of total treatment. The following sections explain how both offer great market potential to Medquip.

MARKET ANALYSIS SUMMARY

The potential customers of Medquip, Inc. are both domestic and foreign.

Domestic customers include managed care groups, hospital buying groups, physician groups, independent physicians, and other (catalogues), and medical supply houses. The market is dominated by managed care groups. More than 50% of all purchases of medical devices are made by these groups and that is forecast to reach 75% by the year 2000.

Our research indicates that the approximate total number of these buying groups is increasing. But initial concentration may be more defined by targeting the largest 50 customers in each segment. This data is clearly definable and available.

The foreign market includes many of the above segments but also includes key distributors. For example, only four distributors are required to penetrate the European, Middle Eastern, African, Central and South American, and Japanese markets. These distributors have already been identified.

Market Segmentation

Market Analysis

Potential Customers	Growth	1998	1999	2000	2001	2002	CAGR
Managed Care	25%	300	375	469	586	733	25.02%
Hospital Groups	10%	200	220	242	266	293	10.02%
Physician Groups	10%	400	440	484	532	585	9.97%
Independent Practices	0%	200	200	200	200	200	0.00%
Foreign Markets	50%	100	150	225	338	507	50.06%
Other	0%	10	10	10	10	10	0.00%
Total	17.77%	1,210	1,395	1,630	1,932	2,328	17.77%

Industry Analysis

The health care industry in the United States has been dominated by managed care and hospital buying groups. Lowest total cost treatment has been the evolution of the pricing model. Medquip is ideally positioned to capitalize on this trend. There has been a rapid trend to endoscopic variceal ligation from the previous norm of schlerotherapy for the following reasons:

1. Fewer post-op complications.
2. Better control of bleeding.
3. Lower risk of re-bleeding.
4. Reduction of over-all treatment cost.
5. Positioned ideally for managed care.
6. Current research studies available.

The growth of banding has been as high as 30% per quarter according to IMI.

The top 25 to 50 customers in each market category may account for as much as 70% of the potential business, making it easy to target customers with a multi-channel tiered strategy.

The foreign markets may be penetrated initially with as few as four key distributors.

Industry Participants

The major companies in the endoscopic device field directly competitive with Medquip proposed products are Microvasive (Boston Scientific), Bard, and Wilson-Cook.

No manufacturer has a product competitive with the Visi-Gator, although a company like Richter and Sklar could be a likely joint venture partner or licensee.

Managed care providers such as Humana, Kaiser, Blue Cross, etc. are easily identified.

Hospital groups are also easily identified as are physician groups.

However, buying methods are diverse, and there is significant overlap of decision making between these segments. That is why it is imperative that Medquip have an experienced CEO and an experienced Sales and Marketing Manager to effectively attack these channels.

Distribution Patterns

Distribution patterns in the health care industry are such that the large buying groups dictate what products are used for certain procedures throughout their sphere of influence. Thus, our products could be mandated or forced out for thousands of patients due to their health plan or hospital group. Others recommend several alternatives that require physician education and intervention, similar to pharmaceuticals.

Distributors are key for foreign markets.

Competition and Buying Patterns

Large companies with established brand names and distribution patterns have a distinct advantage in the medical device arena. But new small companies are succeeding on a regular basis dependent on their technology and its over-all cost-of-treatment advantages. Product cost in and of itself is not paramount but education and training are. The product must deliver performance as promised in order to do a procedure more effectively with the fewest complications.

Time saving and effectiveness are the key economic parameters.

Medquip will succeed based upon the capability of its products. They are already competitively priced in addition to being more effective. After initial market resistance to any new product, Medquip's products can grow to dominate a market segment ... in this case distinct surgical applications.

Variceal ligation is a huge and growing market.

The market for the band dispenser is a currently existing one with accurate, up-to-date data from IMI. This clearly defined market represents one of the fastest growing segments in the medical device industry. The reason is that doctors are transitioning rapidly from the old and traditional sclerotherapy surgical protocol to banding procedures.

The entire endoscopic market is a $1 billion annual market. Nationally, upper GI endoscopy accounts for more than 1.2 million procedures per year according to MDI. The trend from endoscopic sclerotherapy (ES) to endoscopic variceal ligation (EVL) has been rapid.

In dollars the Endoscopy-miscellaneous supplies category has been growing by 30% per quarter. The most recent quarter ending June 1997 was $18.8 million (IMI). The market segment exceeds $70 million in annual sales. This growth can be pegged almost exclusively to the market share gained by EVL at the expense of ES. Best estimates indicate that the percent of EVL procedures to total procedures is still in the 30% to 40% range. Thus, the potential market for EVL could be as high as $180 million.

Main Competitors

The most important competitor to be considered is Microvasive (Boston Scientific). Its strengths are its reputation, current market position, and its entrenched loyalty among physicians using its products. Its weakness is that it is not particularly innovative, normally depending on other companies to develop and perfect its technologies. This makes it vulnerable to a new, improved entry.

Eric Smith did significant design work for the company that perfected the Speedband for Microvasive. He is well aware of the performance gaps in the product.

STRATEGY AND IMPLEMENTATION SUMMARY

Medquip, Inc. will pursue specific, definable, market segments with a multi-tiered, multi-channel approach. We will leverage our technologies with a licensing agreement in one key area and a direct sales and distribution strategy in the other using established distributors.

We will look to foreign markets first with established distributors for initial revenue.

Domestic revenue will follow.

Large groups and plans will be targeted first.

Marketing Strategy

Marketing will follow from industry and trade and physician awareness campaigns to specific executions directed at specific customer segments. The top tier of 20 to 30 customers in each segment will be attacked first. Only a few sales hits in these top tiers will enable achievement of targeted forecasts. Medquip will achieve its initial sales goals from direct and distributed sales of the Visi-Band. This product is targeted first since it is an existing, well-defined market and 510k approval is anticipated.

Worldwide sales through distributors will provide needed cash flow.

Pricing Strategy

Pricing for the Visi-Band is $250 per unit. Terms are 2% 10 days net 30. All collections in this plan for cash flow purposes are based on an average 45-day collection span.

A 30% discount will be offered to distributors. Quantity discounts are not included but remain possible in negotiations with major buying groups. Our 80% gross margin is also for factoring receivables if that should become viable or necessary.

The Visi-Gator is priced in two components:

1. The motorized unit is $1,000.00.
2. The cutting/irrigation/suction component is $200 (disposable).

Note: These are suggested retails. They represent ten times our estimated cost of manufacture. However, the strategy is to license these products for a 10% royalty. Pricing would be negotiated with the licensee.

Promotion Strategy

Public relations, industry media, will help in over-all industry awareness plans. Feature articles and product reviews will help launch awareness. Direct mail to buying groups and ads in trade publications will help with buyer impressions. Finally, all will be integrated with physician materials and training videotapes once approval has been obtained to increase point-of-surgery usage.

Medquip has already worked closely with physicians to design its products. The importance of working with physicians is well known. As an outgrowth of our Physician Advisory Board, Medquip will actively recruit allied physicians with sponsored events and seminars. Every major market area will be targeted. An annual event will also be sponsored.

Sales Strategy

Medquip's sales strategy is to open foreign markets on a limited basis at the end of 1998. To fully exploit them in 1999 along with initial penetration of the U.S. market with the Visi-Band (assuming 510k approval). Then to grow both markets in 2000 up to a 10% penetration.

Additionally, the strategy is to license the Visi-Gator to a major company such as R&S due to its increased regulatory requirements and initial marketing costs due to the fact that it is a new segment entry. The objective for the license is a $500,000 fee, $500,000 in advance royalties and a 10% royalty level per unit. Royalty projections are included in 1999 and 2000 sales forecasts.

Sales Forecast

Our sales forecast includes small unit sales into the international market. The product is the Visi-Band. Unit sales are at $250 U.S. Product cost of direct sales is 20% while product cost through distributors is 50%. We fully expect to have $16.5 million in sales by the turn of the century.

It is important to note that $500k license fee and $500k advance royalties are the target figures for a license on the Visi-Gator. If these figures are not attainable or turn out to be a lesser number (but still acceptable to the Medquip board) then they should not be considered for cash flow purposes.

Investment money sought for Medquip will still be based on a sales forecast that does not include a successful license sale.

Sales Forecast

Sales	1998	1999	2000
Visi-Band (direct)	$47,500	$1,000,000	$4,000,000
Visi-Band (distributor)	$105,000	$2,000,000	$12,500,000
Other	$0	$0	$0
Total Sales	**$152,500**	**$3,000,000**	**$16,500,000**

Direct Cost of Sales			
Visi-Band (direct)	$9,500	$200,000	$500,000
Visi-Band (distributor)	$52,500	$1,000,000	$6,250,000
Other	$0	$0	$0
Subtotal Cost of Sales	**$62,000**	**$1,200,000**	**$6,750,000**

Sales Programs

Sales programs include direct wholesale sales to international distributors. Sales materials, video training tapes, and support materials will be produced. Physician materials will be included. Direct sales will be by personal contact, direct mail, public relations, and media directed at key industry segments.

In addition, electronic marketing will be deployed whenever it fits with the buying patterns of a key group. A web site and electronic commerce site will be utilized to cultivate direct sales to key industry groups.

Milestones

The following are the key milestones for the first year of operations.

1. All patents will be applied for by the May 1 date. The total legal fees are expected to be less than the $50k allocated.
2. Start-up capital was successfully raised.
3. The business plan has been completed.
4. The government of Puerto Rico has been presented on April 8, 1998.
5. All other first-year milestones are currently on target, time wise and budget wise.

Business Plan Milestones

Milestone	Manager	Planned Date	Department	Budget	Actual Date	Actual Budget	Planned Date - Actual Date	Budget - Actual Budget
Patent Applications Complete	Mears	5/1/98	R&D	$50,000	4/8/98	$20,000	23	$30,000
Start-up Investment	Dineen	1/1/98	Finance	$0	2/1/98	$0	(31)	$0
Business Plan	Dineen	4/7/98	Finance	$3,000	4/7/98	$3,000	0	$0
Private Placement	Dineen	6/1/98	Finance	$0	6/1/98	$0	0	$0
Puerto Rico Funding	Dineen	6/1/98	Finance	$0	4/8/98	$0	54	$0
Corporate Identity	Dineen	4/1/98	Finance	$975	4/1/98	$975	0	$0
CEO hire	Dineen	6/1/98	G&A	$50,000	4/8/98	$0	54	$50,000
Engineering Personnel	Mears	6/1/98	R&D	$0	1/1/95	$0	1,247	$0
Puerto Rico Operation	Mears	6/1/98	R&D	$1,000,000	4/8/98	$0	54	$1,000,000
Initial Sales	CEO	10/1/98	Marketing	$0	10/1/98	$0	0	$0
Totals				**$1,103,975**		**$23,975**	**1,401**	**$1,080,000**

The founders of Medquip, Inc. are Eric Smith and Timothy Jones. Eric will serve the company as Vice-President of Research & Development. Tim will serve as Vice-President of Corporate Development. Their biographies follow in the Management Team section.

Several key people are actively being sought. These are summarized in Management Team Gaps.

MANAGEMENT SUMMARY

Medquip, Inc. will have a CEO to be recruited (see Management Team Gaps) who will have Eric Smith reporting to him as well as Timothy Jones and a VP of Sales and Marketing (see Management Team Gaps).

Eric will handle responsiblilty for R&D, design, compliance, and initial manufacturing and sourcing. Tim will handle strategic growth plans, capitalization, and serve as CFO initially.

Reporting to Eric will be additional design engineers and compliance documentation personnel. Some of these tasks can also be handled by outside consultants early on. The ramp-up of essential personnel and tasks are included in the Personnel Plan that follows.

Organizational Structure

Eric Smith (40)
B.S., Mechanical Engineering, MIT, 1980

Eric Smith began his training in mechanical engineering at MIT and has a broad background in leading edge medical, semiconductor, biotechnology, and cleanroom product design and management. Creatively integrating technologies from diverse fields and transforming these elements into world class product solutions is his specialty. He has spent the past two years developing two medical devices, a full visibility ligating band dispenser and a revolutionary tissue dissolving lysis technology. Recent accomplishments include innovations for the Boston Scientific Speedband multiple ligating band dispenser. He was also responsible for the mechanism design of the Boston Scientific Corp. Alliance esophageal balloon inflation device through their supplier, ACT Medical Corp. Both devices have rapidly attained significantly greater than a 50% world market share for Boston Scientific Corp. Smith pioneered the application of high-energy particle beams to titanium hip and knee implants to increase their life by a factor of ten and for this work received an Industrial Research and Development IR100 award for one of the 100 best technology products. He initiated the development of a peritoneal dialysis system for Millipore Corporation, which incorporated ultra pure water and sterile connection technologies. Earlier research and development on the first Nitinol blood clot filter at Harvard Medical School was in cooperation with Dr. Morris Simon. Mr. Smith also was a founder of ABS, Inc., in 1995, a bio remediation products company currently manufacturing and cross licensing technology sold worldwide.

Ten United States Patents have been issued to Smith to date. Several more have also been granted internationally. A total of sixty-four subsequent United States patents granted to corporations including CDA, Meditech, Price McLain, Application Materials, Stockton, Soyano, and others cite these ten patents granted to Smith, a strong indication of the strategic significance of his diverse body of work. A number of biotechnology patent applications are currently being prosecuted in the United States and in several other countries. Patents issued to Smith include a medical X-ray system, cleanroom laminar airflow systems, chemical and thermal transfer processes, and robotic mechanisms for semiconductor and medical particle accelerators used worldwide by leading corporations such as Innovel, CDA, Soyano, Techola. A detailed list is below.

Management Team

Mr. Smith has led new product developments for the past 17 years as Director of Engineering and Technology and various Research and Development positions. He led the systems design team for a $3 million production particle accelerator with a $50 million product development budget as Mechanical Systems Manager for Varian Associates, a large multinational technology corporation. He has managed an international staff of engineers and successfully transferred leading edge technology from Far East joint venture partners. His responsibilities have also included manufacturing management for a supplier of critical production equipment to CDA, Innovel, and Rogers Optical CD. Systems plagued by months of installation, rework, and errors performed flawlessly the first time and every time at Intel wafer fabrication cleanrooms after Smith re-designed the product and assumed full manufacturing responsibility.

An invited speaker at a worldwide technical conference in Kyoto, Japan, publications include a recent cover story for *Cleanrooms* magazine, and numerous technical articles related to high purity manufacturing, robotics, heat transfer, and mechanism designs.

United States patent numbers and titles currently issued to Eric Smith as inventor:

5040484 Apparatus for retaining wafers [Semiconductor].
4997606 Methods and apparatus for fabricating a high purity thermally-conductive polymer.
4927438 Horizontal laminar air flow work station [Semiconductor and medical applications].
4899059 Disk scanning apparatus for batch ion implanters.
4836733 Wafer transfer system [Robot].
4832781 Methods and apparatus for thermal transfer with a semiconductor wafer in a vacuum.
4817556 Apparatus for retaining wafers.
4580058 Scanning treatment apparatus [Application: human hip and knee implants].
4531821 Item transporting [medical X-ray].

Timothy Jones (50)
B.B.A., Marketing, University of Notre Dame, 1970
M.B.A., Finance, Executive Program, Loyola University, 1972

Mr. Jones has more than 27 years of business management experience. He is the founder of Trinity Capital in Norcross, Georgia. He has successfully assisted early stage companies in capital formation, strategic planning, and business growth. His background includes management positions with two Fortune 500 companies, Lever Brothers Company, and the LCR Division of Squibb, Inc. Mr. Jones has previously been an executive in three start-up ventures and one turn-around.

His experience includes working with two investment banking firms, one that focused on privately held companies and the other on early stage publicly traded companies in development stage.

Additionally, the management team of Medquip, Inc. includes a physician advisory board which is already being assembled.

The Board of Directors is currently open.

Management Team Gaps

An experienced CEO is actively being sought. Timothy Jones is presently conducting the search. The desired profile is for a CEO experienced in the medical device arena, ideally who was part of a previous start-up venture that grew to exceed a minimum of $20 million in sales and had a successful exit strategy.

The CEO will help to identify and bring in a VP of Sales and Marketing.

Eric Smith is actively searching for design engineers and consultants. Several have been identified and are available.

Personnel Plan

Our Personnel Plan chronicles the growth of the organization to 31 employees in the first three years. The third year could require a few additional people besides those indicated, especially if sales are at $20 million.

Production assembly people are grouped together at approximately $15k per person. Payroll costs and benefits are pegged at 22% although they could be lower in Puerto Rico.

Personnel Plan

Production	1998	1999	2000
Production Manager	$20,000	$60,000	$64,000
Assembly Workers	$24,000	$72,000	$90,000
Other	$0	$0	$0
Other	$0	$0	$0
Other	$0	$0	$0
Subtotal	$44,000	$132,000	$154,000

Sales and Marketing Personnel			
VP Sales & Marketing	$30,000	$90,000	$94,000
Sales Manager	$20,000	$60,000	$66,000
Field Sales Mgr.	$0		$56,000
Marketing/Product Mgr.	$0		$66,000
Sales Reps (3)	$0		$144,000
Sales Administrator	$8,000	$24,000	$26,500
Other	$0	$0	$0
Subtotal	$58,000	$174,000	$452,500

General and Administrative Personnel			
CEO	$70,000	$120,000	$130,000
VP Corp Development	$78,000	$84,000	$90,000
CFO	$0	$84,000	$90,000
Executive Assistant	$16,800	$30,000	$32,000
Executive Secretary	$0		$24,000
Controller	$25,200	$45,000	$48,000
Administrative Staff (4)	$0		$88,000
Other	$0	$0	$0
Subtotal	$190,000	$363,000	$502,000

Other Personnel			
VP Research & Development	$96,000	$100,000	$108,000
Design Engineer	$42,000	$84,000	$88,000
Compliance Specialist	$24,000	$50,000	$52,000
Junior Engineer	$16,000	$48,000	$50,000
Research Engineers (2)	$0		$140,000
Other	$0	$0	$0
Subtotal	$178,000	$282,000	$438,000

Personnel Plan

Continued...

Total Headcount	0	0	0
Total Payroll	$470,000	$951,000	$1,546,500
Payroll Burden	$103,400	$209,220	$340,230
Total Payroll Expenditures	**$573,400**	**$1,160,220**	**$1,886,730**

FINANCIAL PLAN

The value of the patents and the size of their potential markets enables several back-up plans of action if this plan doesn't work as indicated. Venture funds are available early on and historically investments of $3 to $5 million are common for similar companies.

Even after successfully completing the start and seed stage as indicated, second round venture or mezzanine funding is potentially available in the $5 million range.

However, cash flow achievement within the parameters of the indicated plan plus further funding on the senior debt side will lead to the best value for shareholders. Then, strategy can dictate the best valuation for ramp-up and roll-out.

There is a safety net within cash flow if year one investment is obtained on schedule.

Important Assumptions

Several of the assumptions could be considerably less if the business is located in Puerto Rico. The personnel burden could go from 22% to 12%. The short term interest rate could go from 10% to 5% or less. The tax rate could go from 25% to less than 10%. So, all of the bottom line projections in this plan could improve appreciably.

However, the plan is still based on the following assumptions as if it were a U.S. based North Carolina operation.

General Assumptions	**1998**	**1999**	**2000**
Short-term Interest Rate %	10.00%	10.00%	10.00%
Long-term Interest Rate %	9.00%	9.00%	9.00%
Payment Days Estimator	30	30	30
Collection Days Estimator	45	45	45
Inventory Turnover Estimator	6	6	6
Tax Rate %	25.00%	25.00%	25.00%
Expenses in Cash %	10.00%	10.00%	10.00%
Sales on Credit %	75.00%	75.00%	75.00%
Personnel Burden %	22.00%	22.00%	22.00%

Key Financial Indicators

All of our benchmarks being attained will allow expansion strategies of merger, acquisition, roll-up or IPO.

Breakeven Analysis

Medquip, Inc. has calculated a breakeven maintenance point for sales once full management staffing and facility costs are reached. Included are payroll and rent considerations. Monthly payroll is calculated to be $41,000 for 6 key people. Monthly rent for administrative and initial manufacturing needs is pegged at $7,500. Debt service of $8,333 is also included in order to obtain a safe, conservative, breakeven number. This is based on $1 million in debt at 10% interest. (Debt from the Puerto Rican program may be at less than half that interest rate and may include additional grant money at no interest or repayment).

The sales price of $175.00 per unit is based on company sales through distributors to be achieved primarily in the foreign market. Actual product retail is $250.00 U.S. dollars. The distributors average margin is 30%.

The manufacturing cost of $20.00 per unit includes all materials and labor for assembly.

The breakeven unit target of 367 units per month or $64,166 can sustain Medquip, Inc. in operation in late 1998 and throughout 1999 even if expansion and capitalization plans are late in materializing.

It is anticipated that direct sales can produce these numbers and more in Europe, Middle Eastern and African markets since those markets are not as dominated by managed care; there is more direct purchasing, and 367 units per month accounts for less than 2% of projected procedures. A distributor has been identified for those markets as well as a distributor for Latin and South America, and a distributor for Japan. No Japanese sales are included, however, since regulatory barriers are more pronounced there.

The breakeven analysis is restricted to this late 1998 and early 1999 time frame since the early ramp-up phase in business development is characteristic of most cash-flow shortages that represent exposure to early stage investors.

Breakeven Analysis

Monthly Units Breakeven	367
Monthly Sales Breakeven	$64,166

Assumptions

Average Per-Unit Revenue	$175
Average Per-Unit Variable Cost	$20
Estimated Monthly Fixed Cost	$56,833

Projected Profit and Loss

The profit in each of the first two years of operation is expected to exceed $200k. However that includes $1 million in revenue in the first year from the sale of a license. If that does not occur, then over $800k will be burned in year one. That must come from investment infusion.

The third year number of $7.5 million in profit reflects the performance of a mature company.

Over-all gross margins of 65% are excellent.

Profit and Loss (Income Statement)

	1998	1999	2000
Sales	$152,500	$3,000,000	$16,500,000
Direct Cost of Sales	$62,000	$1,200,000	$6,750,000
Production	$44,000	$132,000	$154,000
Other	$0	$0	$0
Total Cost of Sales	**$106,000**	**$1,332,000**	**$6,904,000**
Gross Margin	$46,500	$1,668,000	$9,596,000
Gross Margin %	30.49%	55.60%	58.16%
OPERATING EXPENSES			
Sales and Marketing Expenses			
Sales and Marketing Payroll	$58,000	$174,000	$452,500
Advertising/Promotion	$16,000	$150,000	$700,000
Travel	$13,000	$66,000	$88,000
Miscellaneous	$6,000	$15,000	$24,000
Other	$0	$0	$0
Total Sales and Marketing Expenses	**$93,000**	**$405,000**	**$1,264,500**
Sales and Marketing %	60.98%	13.50%	7.66%
GENERAL AND ADMINISTRATIVE EXPENSES			
General and Administrative Payroll	$190,000	$363,000	$502,000
Payroll Expense	$0	$0	$0
Payroll Burden	$103,400	$209,220	$340,230
Depreciation	$41,665	$100,000	$100,000
Leased Equipment	$0	$0	$0
Utilities	$5,000	$0	$0
Insurance	$39,000	$60,000	$75,000
Rent	$58,950	$90,000	$120,000
Legal Expenses	$46,013	$36,000	$36,000
Other	$0	$0	$0
Total General and Administrative Expenses	**$484,028**	**$858,220**	**$1,173,230**
General and Administrative %	317.40%	28.61%	7.11%
Other Expenses			
Other Payroll	$178,000	$282,000	$438,000
Contract/Consultants	$15,000	$30,000	$60,000
Other			

We began the year with $128,000 in cash from initial sales of shares to investors at $2.00 per share. This provided our start-up capital. The private placement to 13 or fewer investors is expected to bring in another $450,000 in May and $400,000 in June. We are targeting an additional $400,000 in equity investment from Puerto Rico and $800,000 in long-term loans. Thus, our cash flow will be sufficient in year one even if we can't conclude a licensing agreement. Capital expenditures in plant and equipment will total $1 million. Second round financing will include venture, mezzanine, or IPO options. If sales and profits hit targets then further investment needs will be limited to higher value options to roll-up a national level and worldwide company.

Projected Cash Flow

	1998	1999	2000
Net Profit	($569,646)	$15,585	$4,941,203
PLUS			
Depreciation	$41,665	$100,000	$100,000
Change in Accounts Payable	$53,552	$255,591	$1,098,192
Current Borrowing (repayment)	$0	$0	$0
Increase (decrease) Other Liabilities	$0	$0	$0
Long-term Borrowing (repayment)	$800,000	$0	$0
Capital Input	$1,250,000	$0	$0
Subtotal	$1,575,571	$371,176	$6,139,394
LESS			
Change in Accounts Receivable	$69,375	$1,295,379	$6,141,393
Change in Inventory	$80,000	$925,283	$4,205,283
Change in Other ST Assets	$0	$0	$0
Capital Expenditure	$1,000,000	$0	$0
Dividends	$0	$0	$0
Subtotal	$1,149,375	$2,220,662	$10,346,676
Net Cash Flow	$426,196	($1,849,486)	($4,207,282)
Cash Balance	$554,196	($1,295,290)	($5,502,572)

Pro-Forma Cash Flow

The highlights of the balance sheets are a cash position of $1.1 million and a net worth of $9.3 million at the end of year three. (Accomplished with an investment of less than 2.5 million).

Projected Balance Sheet

Pro-Forma Balance Sheet

Assets

	Starting Balances			
Short-term Assets		**1998**	**1999**	**2000**
Cash	$128,000	$554,196	($1,295,290)	($5,502,572)
Accounts Receivable	$0	$69,375	$1,364,754	$7,506,148
Inventory	$0	$80,000	$1,005,283	$5,210,566
Other Short-term Assets	$0	$0	$0	$0
Total Short-term Assets	$128,000	$703,571	$1,074,747	$7,214,141
LONG-TERM ASSETS				
Capital Assets	$0	$1,000,000	$1,000,000	$1,000,000
Accum. Depreciation	$0	$41,665	$141,665	$241,665
Total Long-term Assets	$0	$958,335	$858,335	$758,335
Total Assets	**$128,000**	**$1,661,906**	**$1,933,082**	**$7,972,476**
Liabilities and Capital				
Accounts Payable	$0	$53,552	$309,143	$1,407,335
Short-term Notes	$0	$0	$0	$0
Other Short-term Liab.	$0	$0	$0 $0	
Subtotal Short-term Liab.	$0	$53,552	$309,143	$1,407,335
Long-term Liabilities	$0	$800,000	$800,000	$800,000
Total Liabilities	$0	$853,552	$1,109,143	$2,207,335
Paid in Capital	$128,000	$1,378,000	$1,378,000	$1,378,000
Retained Earnings	$0	$0	($569,646)	($554,061)
Earnings	$0	($569,646)	$15,585	$4,941,203
Total Capital	$128,000	$808,354	$823,939	$5,765,142
Total Liab. and Capital	$128,000	$1,661,906	$1,933,082	$7,972,476
Net Worth	$128,000	$808,354	$823,939	$5,765,142

The ratios are misstated in year one due to the $1 million projected licensing revenue. However, by year three the return on equity of more than 80% should be very attractive to early investors. All ratios are in good shape for traditional borrowing to fund further growth.

Profitability Ratios	1998	1999	2000	RMA
Gross Margin	30.49%	55.60%	58.16%	0
Net Profit Margin	-373.54%	0.52%	29.95%	0
Return on Assets	-34.28%	0.81%	61.98%	0
Return on Equity	-70.47%	1.89%	85.71%	0
Activity Ratios				
AR Turnover	1.65	1.65	1.65	0
Collection Days	111	116	131	0
Inventory Turnover	2.65	2.45	2.22	0
Accts Payable Turnover	5.09	5.09	5.09	0
Total Asset Turnover	0.09	1.55	2.07	0
Debt Ratios				
Debt to Net Worth	1.06	1.35	0.38	0
Short-term Liab. to Liab.	0.06	0.28	0.64	0
Liquidity Ratios				
Current Ratio	13.14	3.48	5.13	0
Quick Ratio	11.64	0.22	1.42	0
Net Working Capital	$650,019	$765,604	$5,806,807	0
Interest Coverage	-20.1	1.29	92.5	0
Additional Ratios				
Assets to Sales	10.9	0.64	0.48	0
Debt/Assets	51%	57%	28%	0
Current Debt/Total Assets	3%	16%	18%	0
Acid Test	10.35	-4.19	-3.91	0
Asset Turnover	0.09	1.55	2.07	0
Sales/Net Worth	0.19	3.64	2.86	0

Paintball Sport Company

BUSINESS PLAN

PAINTBALL SPORT PALACE

18940 Barrister Ave.
Akron, OH 44309

This plan's lengthy exploration of the business development leaves little question about the direction of the endeavor. All aspects of the necessary tasks to get the business started are covered and the entrepreneur's absence of salary emphasizes his commitment to profitability. The hardboiled approach of the plan echoes the businesslike manner with which the company will likely be run.

- EXECUTIVE SUMMARY

- COMPANY OVERVIEW

- SERVICES PROVIDED

- MARKETING AND SALES

- DEVELOPMENT

- OPERATIONS

- MANAGEMENT

- SUMMARY OF FINANCIALS

- OFFERING

- APPENDICES

PAINTBALL SPORT COMPANY
BUSINESS PLAN

EXECUTIVE SUMMARY

The mission of Paintball Sport Palace is to provide playing locations and equipment rental service to paintball players in the area who are currently involved in the sport or who wish to become involved in action pursuit games. The purpose of this presentation is to seek start-up financing for capital investment in both equipment and location procurement.

COMPANY OVERVIEW

History and Current Status—Paintball Sport Palace is a new company in the start-up phase of development. Incorporated in Ohio, it seeks to be located in Summit County so as to be close to a major population center. Because the company is still in the preliminary phases, the availability of capital investment is a primary consideration.

Markets and Products—The products used and the overall market strategy will closely follow that of other successful paintball field operations throughout the United States. Products used will be industry standard, allowing for endorsement revenue for product placement and an incentive for paintball equipment companies to sponsor contests and events which will help draw in players from throughout the region. All products will be viewed from a cost-benefit perspective, and will take into account factors such as safety, reliability, and price. The market targeted for development will be primarily young adults 16-25 years of age, and the secondary market will be older adults 26-46 years of age.

Objectives—The objective of Paintball Sport Palace is to develop an indoor and outdoor play field while generating revenue through field rental and admission. Additionally, revenue will be developed from rental of paintball equipment, expendable supplies, and food concessions. These four revenue streams should make the initial investment profitable within its first year of operation and allow for a steadily increasing pool of income on a yearly basis, as the sport of paintball grows nationwide.

SERVICES PROVIDED

Description—Paintball is both a sport and a game. It is already a hundred million dollar business nationwide, with revenue, which continues to grow on an annual basis. Similar to bowling in some organizational aspects, a paintball service company provides rental space for players and equipment in a structured environment. League play is not only possible, but strongly encouraged and a necessary component of building a profitable local business. Scores are kept and posted, and tournaments can be held in order to stimulate player activity and generate free publicity. The largest fields in the country have hundreds, and even thousands, of players who participate in tournament style events and compete for prizes sponsored by savvy equipment manufacturers. Other opportunities for revenue generation include selling constantly in-demand supplies: paintballs, CO_2 propellant refills, and assorted other forms of necessary and expendable equipment. Concessions are another source of steady and significant revenue which, if properly managed, can lead to a sizeable profit margin.

Location Considerations—For a paintball service company to be successful, it is absolutely imperative to offer both indoor and outdoor playing fields. This is especially true in a state like Ohio, which has a variable climate. Bookings and reservations are made far in advance. Not taking this factor into consideration will be highly detrimental to the success of the business. Many other fields have had trouble retaining clientele without some sort of indoor facility to operate. This would normally mean that a location would be very expensive property to lease; however, this principle consideration is mitigated by the fact that a paintball playing field does not have to concern itself with aesthetics. Playing locations are not decided on appearance, rather, the lack of aesthetics is just as appealing to most players, and a gruff atmosphere can enhance the "feel" of the game for many players. Therefore, a large amount of capital that would ordinarily be spent improving the appearance of the facility can be saved and expended elsewhere.

Market Analysis Nationwide—The market for paintball nationwide is outstanding. Fields throughout the United States are reporting record growth, and the need for fields is increasing, not decreasing. As more seasoned players develop and move to various parts of the country, the overall number of participants continues to grow. Likewise, the longer the games are played and the longer people are exposed to the sport, the more that paintball becomes legitimized and the more that national advertising will be expended in the promotion of paintball.

Market Analysis Statewide—The market statewide is encouraging. Several fields have opened while two others have shut down. The primary reason for the shutdown of the two fields in the southern part of the state did not have to do with a lack of business, but instead had to do with local zoning requirements and the fact that these businesses were not being run in a professional manner. The closest known competitor in the western part of the state is located in the Cincinnati area and, while it is fairly well known, it is not heavily advertised and players from this area only travel to this particular field infrequently.

Market Analysis Locally—The market locally consists of one competitor. Located in the southwest quadrant of the city, this competitor is chiefly an indoor arena. There is no room for expansion nor for any large-scale redesign of the playing field, which is an essential element of field design. Even though it is a small facility, with erratic hours, during the hours that it is open it does terrific business in booking events and maintaining repeat clientele. The business is owned by two current police officers that also rent out the field to the city to use as a police training ground for close quarter encounter situations. This is the largest competitor in town for paintball dollars and, even though they are currently operating successfully, they have not tapped even a portion of the market due to their minimal advertising and lack of space. Since this business is not the owner's primary source of income, the competition from this facility is thought to be manageable, and even helpful, in developing paintball players locally.

Overall Marketing Strategy—The target market for paintball is young and even middle-aged, predominantly male adults. The younger players might have had experience in laser tag, or similar virtual-reality type games, and are looking for simple strategy games with a lot of action. Older players tend to be interested in more complex and challenging games where patience is more of a premium. These players would be the weekend outdoorsmen (or sports enthusiasts) types and they would typically involve either a group of close friends or work associates, while the younger players tend to come in smaller groups of more immediate friends. Both groups depend heavily on interaction with their peers, and utilizing this peer pressure as a positive marketing tool is essential. There are many females who also participate in paintball games but, usually, they are drawn as either part of a corporate work outing or from some similar situation. Paintball is a demanding sport and though some degree of basic physical fitness will add to the enjoyment of the game, it is not essential to be completely fit in order to play. Older players, and those with physical limitations, need to be reminded of the demands of the game and encouraged to play appropriately to their level of skill. This is also true of the sedentary weekend warrior type of person who is drawn to the game. Since young and middle-aged males tend to be the target demographic audience, advertising will be geared to attract these types of players.

Sales Strategy—Marketing will be targeted to a younger audience initially. Even though corporate bookings and older players will eventually become a large part of the target audience, initially, the best chance for positive cash flow comes from an appeal to younger players who will grow into repeat customers and truly provide a financial base upon which to build. Normal

MARKETING AND SALES

media channels, which target all young adults, best reach these customers. Radio advertising seems especially effective when trying to reach this market and various radio stations with a rock or hard rock format would seem ideally suited for advertising. Also, there are plenty of local establishments that cater to young people where co-op advertising deals can be made. The laser tag game arena, for instance, would provide an excellent place to recruit members. There are also local paintball supply shops that can provide a steady source of interested customers willing to play the game and a complete co-op arrangement can be made. Once this target market has been reached, and moderate success achieved, the next target of advertising revenue will be middle-aged players. These players can be reached primarily through corporate advertising as a team-building exercise and through an appeal to the competitive and sportslike nature of the game. Many local paintball fields have had great success in recruiting corporate membership by offering specialized recruiting discount packages. Once again, if the field is packaged correctly as a paintball destination and not merely as a paintball field, then the local corporate sponsors will feel comfortable bringing their employees to engage in team-building activities.

DEVELOPMENT

Current Status—A site has been pre-selected for development of the paintball field. It is located in the southeast section of the city and is the site of an abandoned multiscreen drive-in theater. It is in a demographically popular part of town and very close to the shopping malls and main thoroughfares of the city. There is plenty of room for outdoor playing and there are several centralized buildings that would provide an indoor playing arena as well. The facility is not currently being used and is a liability and non-performing asset for the current owners, a regional theater chain which would like to divest itself from the property.

Development Plans—The plan to develop Paintball Sport Palace into something more than a simple playing field is essential to the overall concept. The business should strive to make it a paintball destination within the local community. There is a certain atmosphere that needs to be created in order for this to happen. The type of atmosphere necessary to be successful depends on developing a theme for the play field. The theme can be post-industrial or military or something similar. The theme is very important to making the paintball field a destination instead of simply as a place to play. The more successful the theme, the more likely that repeat players will come back and use the field on a permanent basis. Several themes have been discussed and a military theme adopted for the field itself.

Development Timetable—An aggressive strategy of growth requires us to adopt the following timetable:

Winter 1997—Lease of primary land site in southeast section of the city.
January 1997—Bid specifications prepared for contract construction services.
February 1997—Bids awarded for March and April above ground construction.
March 1997—Above surface rehabilitation of standing buildings for indoor portion of play field.
April 1997—Above surface rehabilitation of outdoor playing field surfaces and construction.
May 1997—Equipment set-up and distribution center established.
May 15, 1997—Initial advertising blitz.
June 1, 1997—Grand opening of Paintball Sport Palace.

Development Risks—Financial risks associated with the project are specified below. Development risks are minimal and mainly concern liability and other operating risks. The risks associated with liability are as follows:

    a. Players have to be given a certain amount of latitude in regards to movement and even though the field and boundaries are well marked and defined, some players may wander from the play area and may try to shoot paintballs at unspecified targets. This would not be a problem in some locations; however, this location is close to a main thoroughfare. Fencing would eliminate this problem, yet that would be an expensive solution to a relatively small security problem.

b. There are problems associated with booking very large events that are mainly logistical in nature. Equipment, which must be provided, may be limited and cause difficulties with supply. Affiliating with a local paintball supply store could alleviate this problem, but it may be a less than ideal solution if not enough equipment is available.

c. The indoor portion of the arena may require more extensive renovation than originally anticipated because a site survey of the property has indicated that interior walls of the main arena structure may have to be braced and/or removed.

A Note on Safety and Liability—There are several safety issues worth considering. Although paintball is recognized as a completely safe sport, and few permanent injuries happen, there are occasionally injuries due to physical exertion and these cannot be mitigated. Further, there is a potential injury problem stemming from the misuse of equipment which can cause more serious injury. These issues are addressed in a safety briefing given to each player at the start of the game. Also, each player is required to sign a liability waiver upon entering the play area. Violators are banned for the day and, if the offense is serious enough, they may be banned from future play. A general liability insurance policy is obtainable for this type of sport and readily available if policies and procedures are properly followed.

OPERATIONS

Scope of Operations

Personnel—The number of weekend personnel will remain fairly static and will only increase significantly if there is a large event taking place. Approximately 10 workers per day will be needed to run the entire field. The breakdown of personnel needed is as follows:

1 onsite manager for the entire operation
4 rotating counter people and equipment lessors
2 food concession personnel
3 referees and safety inspectors

Field Leasing Cost—The cost of leasing the field for the season will be approximately $6000.00 for the duration of the year, plus utilities and a nominal year-end cleanup fee for any areas that need to be restored to their original state.

Equipment—The following is a list of some of the equipment (pricing obtained at discount rates) and projected quantities that will be needed to start-up operations:

50 Stingray Paintball Guns—semi-auto, durable, carbon fiber @ $94.95 ea. = $4,747.50
20 Tracer Paintball Pump Guns—pump action, easy to operate @ 94.95 ea. = 1,899.00
20,000 Paintballs—water soluble, 2500 per case, various colors @ 89.95 ea. = 719.60
2 N2 Compressed Air System plus C1 CO2 Nitro refillable tanks @ 329.95 ea. = 659.90
100 CO2 Portable Canisters—refillable and for use with weapons @ 39.95 ea. = 3,995.00
100 VL 2000 Paintball Loaders—reusable and holding 200 balls @ 9.95 ea. = 995.00
10 VL 2000 Electronic Loaders—primarily for resale on site @ 54.95 ea. = 549.50
70 Goggle and Visor Combinations—with fully protective visor @ 54.95 ea. = 3,846.50
100 Barrel squeegees—for use with gun, reusable and durable @ 9.95 ea. = 995.00
100 Barrel Plugs—reusable and brightly colored for locating @ 4.95 ea. = 495.00
10 Vent Grips—forward barrel hold, primarily for resale on site @ 24.95 ea. = 249.50

10 Head Wraps—for further head protection, optional equipment @ 9.95 ea. = 99.50
Misc. Equipment—lens bags, ordinance, smoke, trip flares, etc. @ various = 1,000.00

TOTAL EQUIPMENT COST = $20,251.00

Ongoing Operations—The cost of ongoing operations is estimated to be as follows:

In the off-season, amortized costs are expected to hover in the $1000.00 range per month, as the business is somewhat seasonal in nature. As soon as warm weather breaks (and even this is not completely necessary), income will be expected to rise in tandem with an increase in the use of the outdoor playing field.

MANAGEMENT

Company Organization—The company will have one primary owner holding an initial 51% of the outstanding shares of the facility. All stock will be preferred and par value of the stock is expected to be $1.00 per share. All other investors in the project will be silent partners concerning day-to-day operations of the facility; however, this shall not preclude investors from offering input as to the financial decisions affecting the company, according to their respective share holdings.

Management Team—Onsite management will consist of one weekend management coordinator and nine support personnel. Initial management will be performed by the owner and turned over to an assistant manager once the facility reaches suitable profitability. All personnel can be adjusted according to bookings obtained and these figures project personnel costs at Paintball Sport Palace's anticipated peak operating capacity.

About Gerald Summers—Gerald Summers has had previous experience in a number of small business settings including ownership of a local automated carwash and a local area laundromat located on Main Street. Gerald Summers graduated with honors from the University of Indiana with a degree in business. He has helped develop several large multi-investor projects and is currently a participant in a restaurant site location team. Previously, Gerald has worked in the insurance industry as a commercial lines underwriter. He lives in the Cleveland area with his wife and two children.

Management Compensation—Initially, management will not be compensated until the business can obtain a suitable level of profitability. Once that occurs and all reinvestment has been made, the current shareholders will be offered a chance to redeem their holdings at a level exceeding the par value of the stock. If that option is not exercised and no stock can be bought back from any of the current shareholders, then compensation will be divided pro-rata according to shareholder equity in the business. The owner is not expected to draw a salary for the duration of the operation of the business, instead choosing to take the pro-rata portion of anticipated profits. Not only does this help to insure that the business will reach and maintain profitability, but it will also insure that unnecessary cash flow is not diverted from the business at a critical time during the operation of the facility.

SUMMARY OF FINANCIALS

Financial Assumptions—All accounting will be done through an accredited accounting firm using standard accounting practices. All financial reporting and audits that become necessary during the operation of the business will use the actual method of accounting and be backed up with suitable documentation. All specific financial assumptions have been spelled out in the sections listed above.

Financial Forecasts—This business is projected to become profitable during its first year of business and continue moderate growth following its first full year of operation. As income streams are enhanced, the net profitability is forecasted to rise at a rate approximately 1.5% times greater than at current projections.

Capital Requirements—It has been determined that the initial capital offering will be for 30,000 shares. This offering is believed to represent the minimum capital outlay necessary to get the business up and running and generating revenue. No other capital outlay is necessary at this time; however, a capital reserve pool of $20,000 is available through owner contribution, if it becomes imperative, to add additional capital prior to start-up.

Financial Risks—There are risks associated with any business endeavor. We have tried to minimize risks associated with the development of this project. Even so, there are some considerations worth noting:

> Capital development is still in the preliminary phase; however, $10,000 has been pledged for capital investment by a past investor in previous projects.

> The owner's track record with this kind of business has not been established because this is a relatively new type of business to impact the market; yet, the owner of Paintball Sport Palace has a record for developing businesses similar in size and scope to the one being proposed.

> The investment made by shareholders will initially have minimal equity necessary to secure the business except for a large inventory of equipment that will depreciate in value quickly because of the heavy anticipated use of the equipment.

Investment Requirements—The initial private offering will be based on the expected par value of $1.00 per share. One hundred thousand shares will be available immediately with 51% held in reserve for management ownership. Thirty thousand shares will be offered in exchange for investment capital at its par value rate. Ten thousand shares have already been pledged and tentatively purchased by an investor at the shares expected par value. The shares purchased will convey genuine ownership and voting rights within the organizational structure and will entitle the shareholder to a dividend of profits based on ownership of the business. The shares may be redeemed at par value at any time for any shareholder willing to divest themselves of ownership; however, share redemption will be at the initiative of the shareholder and will not be forced upon them.

OFFERING

A. All shareholders retain rights to the company, which are fully transferrable and assignable according to their individual disposition of shares.
B. Shares will be distributed on a first-come, first-serve basis and, even though total share distribution is expected to be set at 30,000 shares, nothing in this offering will prohibit the sale of up to 49,000 shares or more of the stock if it becomes necessary for capital outlay purposes.
C. Ownership of shares conveys specific legal rights and remedies. Proper legal representation should be obtained if necessary.
D. This is a private offering and the number of investors shall be limited to 35 shareholders or less to avoid any conflicts with the securities laws of the United States. The predominant state law authority for all disputes arising among shareholders will be Ohio State law.

Valuation of Business—The business will be valued according to the aggregate amount of all building acquisitions, cash on hand, accounts receivable, furniture / fixtures purchases, and all capital outlays divided by the par value of the stock. The total valuation of the company shall be obtained with the oversight of an accredited accounting firm and at the request of any shareholder of the business at any time.

APPENDICES

Income Projection Sheet

Appendix A

REVENUE	Jan	Feb	Mar	Apr	May	Jun	Jul	Aug
Total sales	2,000	2,000	2,000	4,400	6,800	9,900	9,900	9,900
Cost of sales	300	300	300	300	300	300	300	300
Gross profit	1,700	1,700	1,700	4,100	6,500	9,600	9,600	9,600
EXPENSES								
Salaries	0	0	0	0	0	0	0	0
Payroll	1,000	1,000	1,000	1,000	1,500	3,000	3,000	3,000
Accounting	100	100	100	100	100	100	100	100
Legal	80	80	80	80	80	80	80	80
Insurance	200	200	200	200	200	200	200	200
Advertising	(300)	(300)	(300)	(300)	(300)	(300)	(300)	(300)
Automobile	0	0	0	0	0	0	0	0
Office misc.	50	50	50	50	50	50	50	50
General miscellaneous	200	200	200	200	200	200	200	200
FIXED EXP								
Rent	500	500	500	500	500	500	500	500
Utilities	100	100	100	100	100	100	100	100
Permits	50	50	50	50	50	50	50	50
Loan repay	100	100	100	100	100	100	100	100
Phone	50	50	50	50	50	50	50	50
Fax/comp.	30	30	30	30	30	30	30	30
Postage	20	20	20	20	20	20	20	20
General miscellaneous	50	50	50	50	50	50	50	50
All Expenses	2,530	2,530	2,530	2,530	3,030	4,530	4,530	4,530
Net Profit before taxes	-830	-830	-830	1,570	3,470	5,070	5,070	5,070

TOTAL 1ST YEAR REVENUE = $58,700

TOTAL 1ST YEAR EXPENSES = $38,360

TOTAL OF ALL 1ST YEAR REVENUE MINUS EXPENSES = $20,340

Sep	Oct	Nov	Dec
7,000	4,400	2,000	2,000
300	300	300	300
6,700	4,100	1,700	1,700
0	0	0	0
2,000	1,500	1,000	1,000
100	100	100	100
80	80	80	80
200	200	200	200
(300)	(300)	(300)	(300)
0	0	0	0
50	50	50	50
200	200	200	200
500	500	500	500
100	100	100	100
50	50	50	50
100	100	100	100
50	50	50	50
30	30	30	30
20	20	20	20
50	50	50	50
3,530	3,030	2,530	2,530
3,170	1,070	-830	-830

Six-Month Cash Flow Projection

APPENDIX B
SEASONALLY ADJUSTED

	May	Jun	Jul	Aug	Sep	Oct
Cash on hand	$30,000	$0	$0	$0	$0	$0
Cash receipts	6,800	9,900	9,900	9,900	7,000	4,400
Total cash available	**36,800**	**9,900**	**9,900**	**9,900**	**7,000**	**4,400**
Cash paid out/fixed expenses	3,890	3,930	3,930	3,930	2,930	2,430
Cash paid out/capital purchases	22,000	500	500	500	500	500
Total cash paid out for all expenses	**25,890**	**4,430**	**4,430**	**4,430**	**3,430**	**2,930**
Cash position/end of season	**$10,910**	**$5,470**	**$5,470**	**$5,470**	**$3,570**	**$1,470**

TOTAL CASH AVAILABLE = $77,900
TOTAL CASH PAID OUT = $45,540
CASH POSITION = $32,360

APPENDIX C

As of 3/2/97

Balance Sheet (for Start-Up)

Assets		**Liabilities**	
Current Assets		Current Liabilities	
Cash	$1,000	Accounts payable	$0
Petty cash	$100	Notes payable	$0
Accounts receivable	$0	Interest payable	$0
Inventory	$0	Taxes payable	$0
Short-term investments	$3,500	Sales tax	$0
Long-term investments	$16,500	Payroll accrual	$0
Fixed assets		Long-term notes	$0
Land	$0	**Total liabilities**	$0
Buildings	$0	**NET WORTH (owner equity)**	
Improvements	$0	Proprietorship equity	$21,100
Equipment	$0	Partnership equity	$0
Fixtures	$0	Capital stock	$0
Automobile	$0	Surplus paid (earnings)	$0
Other assets	$0	Total net worth	$0
Total assets	$21,100	**Total liabilities & Total net worth**	$21,100

Pizzeria

BUSINESS PLAN

PIZZA TO GO, INC.

3215 Sturges St.
Pittsburgh, PA 15233

This plan relies on a proven name and business philosophy to propose the creation of a franchise takeout pizza store. The company does an excellent job of establishing the typical area these franchises are started in, then showing the proposed location to be identical. Ideas for capital cost reduction, as well as the proven success of the other franchises, solidifies this proposal's viability.

PIZZERIA BUSINESS PLAN

INTRODUCTION

Pizza to Go, Inc. is a Pennsylvania corporation, having been incorporated in September of 1996, primarily for the purpose of selling pizza, salads, submarine sandwiches, and various other food products, as a licensed franchisee under the franchise name of "Mama's Pizza." The company presently maintains an office in Pittsburgh, Pennsylvania. The president and principal shareholder of the company is Robert Warren.

STRATEGIC PLAN

The company intends to open, over the course of the next three years, several franchised retail pizza establishments in the greater Pittsburgh, Pennsylvania area, with its first store scheduled to open in January of 1997. The company's primary thrust will be to locate each of its stores in newly developing, high density, residential areas, with little pre-existing competition. The company also will maintain high quality control standards, strictly adhering to the Mama's Pizza "formula," which has, to date, proven successful (Mama's Pizza has previously been voted the number 1 best tasting pizza in Pennsylvania). The company also will utilize mid-level pricing.

STRATEGIC PLAN

The name of the franchisor is Mama's Pizza Franchising, Inc., a Pennsylvania corporation formed in 1996 for the purpose of offering and selling Mama's Pizza franchises, and servicing, supporting, and administering all functions inherent in operating the franchise system. William A. Becker is the president, treasurer, director, and 50% shareholder of Mama's Pizza Franchising, Inc.

The names of Mama's Pizza predecessors are William A. Becker, Inc. and the Becker Group, Inc., both Pennsylvania corporations. William A. Becker, Inc. and Mama's Pizza Franchising, Inc. maintain their principal business address in Pittsburgh, Pennsylvania. Since its inception in 1990, William A. Becker, Inc. has been engaged in the ownership and operation of Mama's Pizza stores that specialize in the sale of pizza and other food products in the metropolitan Pittsburgh area. Over the last three years William A. Becker, Inc. has owned and operated two Mama's Pizza stores, located in nearby suburbs. There are presently eight additional franchised Mama's Pizza establishments in the metropolitan Pittsburgh area. Negotiations are pending for additional stores. Another company store is expected to open in January of 1997.

THE FRANCHISE AGREEMENT

On November 12, 1996 the company did execute with Mama's Pizza Franchising, Inc. the Franchisor's standard franchise agreement with numerous amendments, deletions, and additions. Under the agreement, the company has a protected territory defined as a five-mile radius from each of its stores. Under the agreement, no other Mama's Pizza franchise or company store can be opened within this five-mile radius protected area. Furthermore, the company has negotiated and the agreement provides that the company has a 30-day right of first refusal anywhere within Washington and Westmoreland counties. This right of first refusal will allow the company, if it chooses, to "lock-in" these counties, thereby becoming and remaining the sole Mama's Pizza franchisee in such counties.

Finally, under the agreement, the company is required to pay an ongoing franchise royalty equal to 3% of gross revenues during the first year of operations and 4% thereafter. An industry wide review of franchise fees and royalties reveals that the Mama's Pizza royalty is substantially less than those found with competing pizza franchises.

The company is seeking financing for the express purpose of providing cash funding to allow (1) the acquisition of various machinery, equipment, and supplies and (2) the construction of its first retail pizza establishment.

PURPOSE OF
FINANCING

(1) **The Equipment:** Schedule A, is a pro-forma list of the equipment and supplies anticipated to be required for the operation of the company's first pizza store, together with a projected aggregate cost of such items. It is important to note that the company has decided to acquire wherever possible used equipment and supplies, recognizing that quality used equipment is readily available in the marketplace at substantial savings. The purchase of high quality, well maintained used equipment will allow the company to reduce its capital outlays to approximately 30% of what would otherwise be expected as a result of purchasing new equipment. This will obviously preserve working capital, reduce ongoing interest costs, and increase net profitability.

(2) **The Build-Out:** Schedule B is a list of the items associated with the "Build-out," which is capable of being financed together with their anticipated cost.

The total cash financing sought for both the equipment and the "Build-out" is $90,000.

THE INITIAL STORE

The company's initial store will consist of 1,600 square feet of retail space. Indeed, the company has executed a five-year lease with a five-year renewal option at an annual rent of $12.00 per square foot. This results in a monthly rent charge of $1,600, plus common area charges which are anticipated to approximate $300 monthly. The initial store will be located in a plaza consisting of 7 retail establishments. The plaza includes two other retail food establishments an Outback Steak House which can be described as an "anchor" and Bagel Factory. Neither the Outback Steak House nor Bagel Factory are considered to be direct competitors. Each of their product lines are substantially different and their markets are likewise different. The company is a takeout retail pizza franchise, while both Outback Steak House and Bagel Factory are essentially sit-down restaurants with different product lines. The remaining retail outlets in the plaza include Delta Florist, Century Cellunet, Airway Oxygen, and Benjamin Moore.

THE COMPETITION

The company has examined in detail the geographic area consisting of a two-mile radius from the initial store to determine the extent of competition. It is apparent that little competition exists. The nearest retail pizza establishment west of the initial store is located in a town which is approximately five miles further west. In this town one will find a wide array of pizza establishments, including Little Caesars, Dominos, Pizza Hut, and Hungry Howies. The nearest competing business is approximately one quarter mile to the east and is a nonfranchised, independent pizza establishment known as Jack's Pizza. Approximately two miles to the east are Little Caesars and Papa Mario's. Approximately one and one half miles to the south is a Whatta Pizza. There are no competing pizza establishments within three miles to the north of the initial store.

MARKETING PLAN

The company's marketing thrust will be twofold. First, the company will be participating in and benefiting from the franchise wide marketing fund. Under the "agreement," each franchisee pays to the franchisor a marketing fee equal to $.10 per pizza box purchased. This amount is then forwarded to the franchisor by the box manufacturer and utilized for the benefit of the franchise. The advertising is not store specific and is geared toward promoting the franchise name and the franchise's product line as a whole. Second, under the "agreement," the company is obligated to expend 1% of its gross revenues on local advertising. However, the company fully expects to exceed the 1% requirement. Indeed, the company's marketing thrust will consist of fliers, discount coupons, and inserts as well as direct mail promotions.

With respect to packaging, it is important to understand that as a franchisee, the company will be licensed to utilize each and every one of the Mama's Pizza trademarks. Indeed, the "agreement" specifically requires that each of the franchisees strictly adheres to trademark packaging. This is common industry practice.

Editor's note: this plan also includes a Schedule C reflecting the probable pricing structure of each of the company's proposed products. This pricing is mid-tier and represents, in the opinion of the company, good value, when compared to the quality of the company's product line.

PRO-FORMA FINANCIAL STATEMENTS

Schedule C is a pro-forma income statement, before depreciation charges, reflecting the company's anticipated cash flow generated by the initial store during the calendar year ending December 31, 1997.

SCHEDULE A

DESCRIPTION	COST
MIDDLYBY MARSHALL	
350 DOUBLE OVENS	15,000
ACME SHEETER	1,600
VCM MIXER	3,000
3 DOOR PIZZA PREP TABLE	1,800
3 DOOR SALAD PREP TABLE	1,500
THREE COMPARTMENT SINK	675
TWO HAND SINKS (125ea.)	250
FREEZER	400
THREE 8' SS TABLES (275ea.)	825
ONE 6' SS TABLE	125
SMALLWARES	6,000
EXTERIOR SIGNS	4,000
INTERIOR SIGNS	600
UNDERCOUNTER COOLER	900
PROOFER	1,100
PHONE SYSTEM	2,600
CAR TOP SIGNS	850
FAX MACHINE &	
CASH REGISTER	600
PIZZA BAGS	265
8' X 12' WALK-IN COOLER	
(INSTALLED)	5,300
TOTAL	47,390
TAX	2,843
DELIVERY AND SET-UP	750
TOTAL	**$50,983**

DESCRIPTION	COST
FLOORING	$3,680
CEALING	840
WALLS	4,100
COUNTERS & CABINETS	2,000
HVAC	1,000
MAKEUP AIR	5,000
HOOD FOR MAKEUP AIR	2,000
ELECTRICAL	2,600
PLUMBING	4,400
MISC. LABOR & RELATED SERVICES	7,200
MISC. EXTRAS	1,200
TOTAL	**$34,020**

SCHEDULE C		**Jan**	**Feb**	**Mar**	**April**	**May**
Pro-Forma Income	INCOME					
Statement	Sales-Food	36,000	37,080	38,192	39,338	40,518
	Sales-Pop & Bottles	1,800	1,854	1,910	1,967	2,026
	Sales-Deliv.	2,600	2,678	2,758	2,841	2,926
Net Income Before						
Depreciation &	**Total Gross Income**	40,400	41,612	42,860	44,146	45,471
Taxes	COST OF GOODS SOLD					
	Purchases	10,100	10,403	10,715	11,037	11,368
First Year-3% Per	Delivery Expense	1,620	1,669	1,719	1,770	1,823
Month Growth	Operating Supplies	121	124	128	132	136
	Total C.O.G. Sold	11,841	12,196	12,562	12,939	13,327
	Gross Profit	28,559	29,416	30,298	31,207	32,144
	EXPENSES					
	Franchise Fee	1,212	1,248	1,286	1,324	1,364
	Insurance	350	350	350	350	350
	Maintenance & Repair	400	400	400	400	400
	Office Supplies	40	42	43	44	45
	Advertising	3,500	2,000	1,000	1,000	1,000
	Bank Charges	40	42	43	44	45
	Laundry	121	125	129	132	136
	Rent - Office	1,900	1,900	1,900	1,900	1,900
	Equipment Lease	1,500	1,500	1,500	1,500	1,500
	Rubbish Removal	40	40	40	40	40
	Telephone	300	300	300	300	300
	Utilities	525	541	557	574	591
	Sales Tax	2,160	2,225	2,292	2,360	2,431
	Wages	9,898	10,195	10,501	10,816	11,140
	Total Expenses	21,987	20,907	20,340	20,785	21,244
	Net Operating Income	6,572	8,509	9,959	10,422	10,900
	Cumulative Net Operating Income		15,081	25,040	35,462	46,361

June	July	Aug	Sept	Oct	Nov	Dec
41,734	42,986	44,275	45,604	46,972	48,381	49,832
2,087	2,149	2,214	2,280	2,349	2,419	2,492
3,014	3,105	3,198	3,294	3,392	3,494	3,599
46,835	48,240	49,687	51,178	52,713	54,294	55,923
11,709	12,060	12,422	12,794	13,178	13,574	13,981
1,878	1,934	1,992	2,052	2,114	2,177	2,243
140	144	149	153	158	162	167
13,727	14,139	14,563	15,000	15,450	15,913	16,391
33,108	34,101	35,124	36,178	37,263	38,381	39,533
1,405	1,447	1,491	1,535	1,581	1,629	1,678
350	350	350	350	350	350	350
400	400	400	400	400	400	400
47	48	50	51	53	54	56
1,000	1,000	1,000	1,024	1,054	1,086	1,118
47	48	50	51	53	54	56
141	145	149	154	158	163	168
1,900	1,900	1,900	1,900	1,900	1,900	1,900
1,500	1,500	1,500	1,500	1,500	1,500	1,500
40	40	40	40	40	40	40
300	300	300	300	300	300	300
609	627	646	665	685	706	727
2,504	2,579	2,657	2,736	2,818	2,903	2,990
11,474	11,819	12,173	12,538	12,915	13,302	13,701
21,717	22,203	22,705	23,245	23,807	24,387	24,984
11,391	11,898	12,419	12,933	13,456	13,994	14,549
57,753	69,650	82,070	95,003	108,459	122,453	137,001

Cash Flow

	01/31	02/07	02/14	02/21	02/28
BEGINNING BALANCE					
Checking	14,154	12,337	14,534	13,216	15,111
SALES					
Food	0	2,900	3,335	3,835	4,411
Pop	0	100	110	121	133
Deliveries	0	200	220	242	266
Total	0	3,200	3,665	4,198	4,810
COSTS					
Drivers	30	102	117	134	154
Food	0	598	992	1,099	1,259
Total	30	700	1,109	1,234	1,413
Subtotal	14,124	14,837	17,090	16,180	18,507
EXPENSE					
Franchise Fee				217	
Insurance					
Maintenance & Repair					
Office Supplies			50		
Advertising			590	460	
Bank Charges					
Laundry			34	34	34
Rent - Office	0				1,975
Equipment Lease	0	0	0	0	0
Rubbish Removal		129		128	
Telephone	354				354
Utilities	79				350
Wages - Gross	1,354		3,000		3,000
Taxes	0	174	200	230	265
Total Expenses	1,787	303	3,874	1,069	5,978
Ending Balance	12,337	14,534	13,216	15,111	12,530
Labor					38.2%

03/07	03/14	03/21	03/28	04/07	04/14	04/21	04/28
12,530	14,799	15,286	19,479	17,342	23,030	24,685	29,903
5,072	5,833	6,708	7,714	8,871	8,871	8,871	8,871
146	161	177	195	214	214	214	214
293	322	354	390	429	429	429	429
5,511	6,316	7,239	8,299	9,514	9,514	9,514	9,514
176	202	232	266	304	304	304	304
1,443	1,653	1,895	2,172	2,490	2,854	2,854	2,854
1,619	1,856	2,126	2,437	2,794	3,159	3,159	3,159
16,422	19,260	20,399	25,341	24,063	29,386	31,040	36,259
270	0	355	0	466	0	571	0
336	0		336	0	0	0	336
50			50	0	0	0	50
500	590						
34	34	34	34	34	34	34	34
			1,975	0	0	0	1,975
0	0	0	1,149	0	0	0	1,149
128		128					
			354	0	0	0	354
			500	0	0	0	500
	3,000		3,137	0	4,135	0	4,412
304	350	402	463	532	532	532	532
1,623	3,974	919	7,998	1,032	4,701	1,137	9,343
14,799	15,286	19,479	17,342	23,030	24,685	29,903	26,916
	29.1%		23.1%		23.2%		23.2%

Publisher

BUSINESS PLAN

THE GROUP PUBLISHING

3245 Rawlins Blvd.
Memphis, TN 38101

This plan for a publishing company demonstrates the entrepreneurs' commitment to what they feel is the most important aspect of their business: marketing. Distribution, pricing, exposure, and networking are all covered in the plan's body, reassuring the lender that they have confronted the biggest threats to success. This plan was compiled using Business Plan Pro, by Palo Alto Software.

- EXECUTIVE SUMMARY

- COMPANY SUMMARY

- PRODUCTS

- MARKET ANALYSIS SUMMARY

- STRATEGY AND IMPLEMENTATION SUMMARY

- MANAGEMENT SUMMARY

- FINANCIAL PLAN

EXECUTIVE SUMMARY

The Group Publishing, Inc. is the publisher of *Artists in Business* magazine. The magazine, which has already printed an initial issue in July/August 1996, is directed at artists at all levels of business throughout the United States. The management of The Group Publishing is targeting a total combined circulation of 206,000 in year one, increasing to 310,000 by the end of year three. The magazine will be published bi-monthly with increased press runs throughout the first three years. Sample distribution, organizational sales, and direct mail to targeted lists of artists will be utilized to build subscriptions.

In addition, The Group Publishing will market books via direct marketing and through established artist distribution channels. The direct marketing of The Group Publishing books will be implemented through its magazine readership base.

Publishing is a high profit and high margin business. The key to success is successful marketing. The Group has a highly focused multi-dimensional sales and marketing plan to build its total circulation base quickly. The same channels and methods were utilized to establish a circulation of 500,000 in the first year for the *Visionary Artist* periodical.

Successful execution of The Group's plan will produce sales revenues of $3.1 million in year one, $4.8 million in year two, and $6.4 million in year three. Net profit will reach $2.4 million in year three. Margins are in excess of 38% after tax.

Objectives

The initial objectives of The Group are as follows:

1. To raise seed capital of $150,000 to ensure publication by February 1997 and to establish a cash reserve to market subscriptions.
2. To have 90,000 subscribers by the end of year one through direct sampling and marketing.
3. To have an additional 50,000 subscribers by the end of year one through organizational sales.
4. To have 10,000 more two-year subscriptions sold.
5. To publish two 36-page issues initially with press runs of 50,000 promotional copies each.
6. To go to 48 pages by issue number three and increase press runs to 75,000 promotional copies.
7. Increase to 100,000 promotional copies in issues five and six.
8. Increase average ad page cost from $1,819 to $2,618 by the end of the first year.
9. To sell an average of 17.5 ad pages per issue throughout year one.

Mission

Artists in Business magazine is for the artist who is a worker at any level. The magazine has a commitment to be a platform to profile artists who are representing artistic vision in the marketplace and who can both encourage and provide role models to other men and women. The Group Publishing, through its magazine, books, and editorial content, will be a vessel to inform artists about artistic principles in everyday business and will encourage interaction among artists as business people. Our mission is to promote the concept of "community" in the workplace.

The keys to success are:

Attaining targeted circulation levels.
Controlling costs while spending the maximum on subscription marketing in year one.
Carefully monitoring response rates of all media executions.
Follow-on marketing of two to four book titles in the first year.
Attaining targeted advertising sales revenues.
Having quality editorial content in each issue.
Making all production and distribution dates in a timely fashion for each issue.

The Group Publishing, Inc. began as a joint concept between two avocational artists, Red Brushwielder, an advertising executive, and Thallos Green, a former insurance executive and owner of the "Artists in Business" name. Mr. Green will promote *Artists in Business* as a radio program for syndication (a separate business entity).

Mr. Green is licensing the "Artists in Business" name to The Group Publishing, Inc. for the sum of $1 (one dollar). Mr. Green will also receive one page of advertising at no charge in each and every issue of the magazine and one page of editorial in each issue (as the founder of the magazine). It is expected that the radio show produced by Mr. Green will be a powerful promotional vehicle for the magazine.

The Group Publishing, Inc. will have exclusive rights to *Artists in Business* for all print media, electronic media (Internet home page, CD-ROM, interactive publications, etc.), catalogue business, and possible seminars and workshops devoted to the artistic business person.

Red Brushwielder is the founder of The Group Publishing, Inc. a newly formed Southwest "C" corporation. He currently owns all its stock.

Equity investment in the company is now being made available to outside investors for the first time. The purpose of this investment is to raise the needed "seed" capital to launch the magazine. An initial Private Placement offering to raise from $150K to $375K is in progress. The minimum amount of the offering would be sufficient to publish the first new issue in 1997. Money raised in excess of the minimum will enable full-scale sampling and marketing of subscriptions. It is possible that no further investment may be needed. However, it cannot be assured that additional capital will not be required in the future or that sufficient capital will be available to continue publication.

The Group Publishing, Inc. has current offices in downtown Memphis, Tennessee. The office is fully equipped and functional. It is not anticipated that expanded facilities will be needed for the first few years of the plan. All business, management and editorial functions will be performed there. All printing, mailing, warehousing, and fulfillment is outsourced.

The Group Publishing will publish *Artists in Business* magazine. The magazine is high gloss, 48 pages, contemporary in look and appeal. Quality art content is the constant goal. The magazine will be entertaining, newsworthy, and thought-provoking. It will appeal to a broad artist readership. No magazine like it is available today.

The Group Publishing will also publish softcover and hardcover books. Certain titles will be published in softcover "trade" size. Others (called "booklets" in this plan) will be similar to "paperback" size. Contemporary arts themes will prevail, particularly those that deal with the demands placed on both business and family life by today's business climate.

MARKET ANALYSIS SUMMARY

The target market is broadly based and is defined as the artist business person at all levels in any organization.

Market segments are defined by organizational affiliation.

Media strategy and execution may vary by segment.

STRATEGY AND IMPLEMENTATION SUMMARY

Our strategy is based on serving a clearly defined niche market well. By having an identifiable market with available lists and related memberships, the management of The Group believes we can exceed publishing industry standards for conversion of potential subscribers. Committed artists are a passionate and loyal clientele. A thirst exists for the published periodical product that *Artists in Business* will provide. The initial issue, published in late summer of 1996 met with rave reviews at booksellers and distributors conventions and was profiled on Arts News radio. The task is to reach and inform the target market. The strategy is to combine sampling, direct mail, and group membership solicitation to build circulation through both subscriptions and newsstand distribution. Multi-channel distribution principles will be employed. Each has a differing margin structure but the combination will maximize the potential reach of the magazine.

Marketing Strategy

New subscriptions are both sample and media based. Sampling will be done to both known art organization members and to artist mailing lists. Several of these databases are already available to The Group. *Artists in Business* has access to a list of 100,000 artist business leaders. All will be sampled with the magazine.

Sample runs will be: 50,000 issues on the first and second runs, 75,000 issues on the second and third runs, and 100,000 issues on the fifth and sixth issues of 1997. All cost associated with these sampling programs are included in the advertising and promotion budgets for those months. A total of $362,000 will be spent on direct-mailed sampling geared to subscription.

In alternate months, print media will be used. Arts publications will be employed. *New Brush* magazine, *Colours* magazine, and *Artistic License Today* will have the early insertions. As subscription base grows, secular media will be used later in the year. *Inc.* magazine and *Business Week* are likely choices.

Finally, sales to arts supply and retail bookstores through magazine distributors will also be accomplished. Key distributors have already expressed interest in the publication.

All sales projections through this multi-channel approach will reflect the different pricing and margin considerations pertinent to each.

Pricing Strategy

The *Artists in Business* magazine will sell for $3.95 per single issue on the newsstand. A one-year subscription is $16.95. A two-year subscription is $29.95. "Trade" soft-cover books will sell for $14.95. Paperback size "booklets" will sell for $7.95. Future hardcover books will sell for $19.95 to $22.95. No hardcover sales are projected in this 3-year plan.

Promotion Strategy

In addition to advertising, direct mail, and media executions, public relations exposure will benefit magazine circulation significantly. Red Brushwielder has already appeared and been interviewed on arts news radio programs four times. Tapes of these interviews are available. In one instance more than 1,800 calls were received requesting subscription information from a single program.

Red Brushwielder has also been asked to tape programs for a Memphis radio station on the subject of artists in the workplace.

Promotion strategy for sales through organizations to their memberships includes a split of the first year's subscription revenue with the selling organization.

Distribution Strategy

Distribution of magazines and books through retail channels are projected at retail less 60%.

Subscriptions through organizations are projected at list less 50%.

All direct sales are booked at full revenue. Cost of product is deducted for 6 issues per year. Fulfillment costs are expensed.

Direct sales of books are billed to credit cards and drop shipped. The magazine is an ideal vehicle to promote these sales.

Future sales are planned directly over the Internet from the AIB web site.

Strategic Alliances

The strategic alliance with Thallos Green and his AIB radio broadcasts holds great potential. Thallos plans to syndicate the broadcasts on arts news radio stations across the U.S.

Sales Strategy

Our combined sales strategy of sampling, direct mail, and organizations will result in the following first-year sales goals:

- 90,000 one-year subscriptions.
- 50,000 one-year subscriptions through organizations.
- 10,000 two-year subscriptions.

Four book titles are factored in the second half of the year. Two are "trade" and two are "booklets." Sales goals are modest.

The following sections illustrate annual revenue over the next three years of $3.1, $4.8, and $6.4 million respectively.

Sales Forecast

We have forecasted our sales by product, by month, over the first year of sales development. Years two and three are cumulative totals only. All sales project the relevant unit cost and margin differences to reflect discounts, commissions, and revenue splits.

Discount on ad revenue is 15% agency commission and 20% sales commission for a total of 35%.

All product costs for subscriptions are based on $.40 per issue, 6 issues for one year, 12 issues for two years.

The only cost not included is an author's royalty on book sales, expected to be 15%. These royalty costs are incurred on the P & L statement as an expense item.

Sales Forecast

Continued...

Unit Sales	1997	1998	1999
Mag Subscript Sales 1 Yr	90,000	120,000	150,000
Mag Subscript Sales 2 Yr	10,000	20,000	30,000
Mag Subscript Sales Whsl	50,000	50,000	50,000
Newsstand Sales Whsl	56,500	72,000	80,000
Ad Revenue Pages	118	150	150
Book Sales—Direct	27,500	50,000	80,000
Book Sales—Whsl	5,000	20,000	30,000
Booklet Sales—Direct	14,500	30,000	50,000
Booklet Sales—Whsl	0	15,000	20,000
Other	0	0	0
Total Unit Sales	**253,618**	**377,150**	**490,150**
Unit Prices			
Mag Subscript Sales 1 Yr	$16.95	$16.95	$16.95
Mag Subscript Sales 2 Yr	$29.95	$29.95	$29.95
Mag Subscript Sales Whsl	$8.50	$8.50	$8.50
Newsstand Sales Whsl	$0.99	$0.99	$0.99
Ad Revenue Pages	$2,252.29	$3,365.00	$3,976.00
Book Sales—Direct	$14.95	$14.95	$14.95
Book Sales—Whsl	$5.98	$5.98	$5.98
Booklet Sales—Direct	$7.95	$7.95	$7.95
Booklet Sales—Whsl	$0.00	$3.18	$3.18
Other	$0.00	$0.00	$0.00
SALES			
Mag Subscript Sales 1 Yr	$1,525,500	$2,034,000	$2,542,500
Mag Subscript Sales 2 Yr	$299,500	$599,000	$898,500
Mag Subscript Sales Whsl	$425,000	$425,000	$425,000
Newsstand Sales Whsl	$55,935	$71,280	$79,200
Ad Revenue Pages	$265,770	$504,750	$596,400
Book Sales—Direct	$411,125	$747,500	$1,196,000
Book Sales—Whsl	$29,900	$119,600	$179,400
Booklet Sales—Direct	$115,275	$238,500	$397,500
Booklet Sales—Whsl	$0	$47,700	$63,600
Other	$0	$0	$0
Total Sales	**$3,128,005**	**$4,787,330**	**$6,378,100**
Direct Unit Costs			
Mag Subscript Sales 1 Yr	$2.40	$2.40	$2.40
Mag Subscript Sales 2 Yr	$4.80	$4.80	$4.80
Mag Subscript Sales Whsl	$2.40	$2.40	$2.40
Newsstand Sales Whsl	$0.40	$0.40	$0.40
Ad Revenue Pages	$788.02	$1,178.00	$1,392.00
Book Sales—Direct	$2.99	$2.99	$2.99
Book Sales—Whsl	$2.99	$2.99	$2.99
Booklet Sales—Direct	$1.59	$1.59	$1.59
Booklet Sales—Whsl	$0.00	$1.59	$1.59
Other	$0.00	$0.00	$0.00

Direct Cost of Sales	1997	1998	1999
Mag Subscript Sales 1 Yr	$216,000	$288,000	$360,000
Mag Subscript Sales 2 Yr	$48,000	$96,000	$144,000
Mag Subscript Sales Whsl	$120,000	$120,000	$120,000
Newsstand Sales Whsl	$22,600	$28,800	$32,000
Ad Revenue Pages	$92,986	$176,700	$208,800
Book Sales—Direct	$82,225	$149,500	$239,200
Book Sales—Whsl	$14,950	$59,800	$89,700
Booklet Sales—Direct	$23,055	$47,700	$79,500
Booklet Sales—Whsl	$0	$23,850	$31,800
Other	$0	$0	$0
Subtotal Direct Cost of Sales	**$619,816**	**$990,350**	**$1,305,000**

Total Sales by Month in Year 1

	Sales
Jan	$21,250
Feb	142,485
Mar	169,875
Apr	257,180
May	229,450
Jun	299,279
Jul	274,770
Aug	346,879
Sep	300,700
Oct	390,361
Nov	304,675
Dec	391,101

Milestones

Important milestones are:

    Raising "seed" capital.
    Publishing magazine by February.
    Launching subscription marketing programs.
    Achieving subscription goals.

MANAGEMENT SUMMARY

With production and fulfillment services outsourced, The Group Publishing, Inc. has a need for general management, editorial, artistic, sales and marketing, and financial expertise.

Management Team

Red Brushwielder (44), President & CEO, Publisher & Editor

Mr. Brushwielder founded and successfully grew an advertising agency over a thirteen-year period. He is accomplished in both publishing and direct marketing. One of his largest clients over the years has been Payne's Gray Publishers, Inc. a NASDAQ public company and art book publisher.

Mr. Brushwielder has a total of 20 years experience in advertising and publishing. His advertising clients have included UltraCharge, Ripken Brothers Piano Company, Magnolia Software, Venetian Department Stores, and CDI Payroll Services. Red Brushwielder attended the University of South Carolina.

Ochre & Sienna Burnt, Executive Editors

Ochre (50) and Sienna (48) are the founders of Painting Restoration, which has the mission of restoring old family portraits. They are accomplished authors, with the titles *Restoring the Early Portrait* and *Demolishing Portrait Forgeries* to their credit. Ochre served in the U.S. Navy, serving three deployments in Vietnam as a helicopter pilot.

Ochre holds a B.A. in Economics from the University of Connecticut, an M.B.A. from California Lutheran College, and a Master's of Art Education from the University of North Carolina at Charlotte. Sienna holds a B.S. in Education from the University of Connecticut.

John Crimson (50), Interim Chief Financial Officer

Mr. Crimson was last VP and Treasurer for Holiday Inn Worldwide. He previously was President of a $30 million dollar credit union. John has a B.A. in Finance from the College of Wooster in Ohio and an M.B.A. in Finance from Emory University.

Timothy Clark (48), VP of Corporate Development

Mr. Clark has successfully raised capital for both public and private companies and has written and executed strategic growth plans as both an executive and as a consultant. He has previously been in executive positions with three growth stage companies and also was part of a turn-around team that successfully righted a failed venture-backed start-up. In his early career he held sales and marketing management positions with Lever Brothers Company and the LCR Division of Squibb, Inc., both in Chicago and New York. He is skilled in Strategic Planning and Capital Formation. Mr. Clark holds a B.A. in Marketing from the University of Notre Dame.

Management Team Gaps

An art director is needed. Also a freelance artist. Ad sales manager and circulation manager are factored in as needed.

Personnel Plan

Salaries for key people have been figured according to a hierarchical scale.

	1997	1998	1999
Production			
Other	$0	$0	$0
Subtotal	$0	$0	$0
Sales and Marketing Personnel			
Ad Sales Mgr.	$36,000	$40,000	$44,000
Subscription Mgr.	$15,000	$30,000	$33,000
Name or title	$0	$0	$0
Other	$0	$0	$0
Subtotal	$51,000	$70,000	$77,000
General and Administrative Personnel			
Red Brushwielder, CEO	$60,000	$66,000	$72,000
Ochre & Sienna Burnt, Executive Editors	$52,800	$60,000	$66,000
John Crimson, CFO	$12,000	$52,000	$60,000
Executive Assistant	$18,000	$22,000	$24,000
Timothy Clark, VP Corporate Dev.	$18,000	$36,000	$48,000
Other	$0	$0	$0
Subtotal	**$160,800**	**$236,000**	**$270,000**

	1997	1998	1999
Other Personnel			
Art Director	$52,800	$60,000	$66,000
Freelance Artist	$6,000	$6,000	$6,000
Bookkeeper	$5,400	$0	$0
Other	$0	$0	$0
Subtotal	**$64,200**	**$66,000**	**$72,000**
Total Headcount	0	0	0
Total Payroll	$276,000	$372,000	$419,000
Payroll Burden	$55,200	$74,400	$83,800
Total Payroll Expenditures	**$331,200**	**$446,400**	**$502,800**

FINANCIAL PLAN

After initial capitalization, growth can be financed largely through internal cash flow provided subscription targets are met. In the event of a sales shortfall, marketing can be cut back temporarily to preserve cash. Or, more likely, additional investment may be sought to re-accelerate productive campaigns if growth demands more funding.

The company created by this plan will generate cash as soon as subscription base reaches critical mass.

Important Assumptions

The key element of our assumptions is six inventory turns per year. This reflects the issues of the magazine as well as ad revenue. Ad space is treated as an inventory item.

Subscriptions are paid in advance. Only 10% of receivables are collected in 30 days, primarily from wholesale accounts. These are notoriously slow payers, so care must be taken not to let these collections run past 60 days. This will be more significant if book sales become a higher-than-expected percentage of revenue.

General Assumptions

	1997	1998	1999
Short-term Interest Rate %	8.00%	8.00%	8.00%
Long-term Interest Rate %	8.00%	8.00%	8.00%
Payment Days Estimator	30	30	30
Collection Days Estimator	30	30	30
Inventory Turnover Estimator	6.00	6.00	6.00
Tax Rate %	33.00%	33.00%	33.00%
Expenses in Cash %	30.00%	30.00%	30.00%
Sales on Credit %	10.00%	10.00%	10.00%
Personnel Burden %	20.00%	20.00%	20.00%

Key Financial Indicators

We expect varying changes in critical profit variables. We expect margins and expenses to be consistently controlled and net profit to increase nicely. Furthermore, we predict inventory turns will slow down somewhat in the third year due to the burden of higher inventories for increasing book sales.

Breakeven Analysis

This breakeven analysis is applicable to the early 1997 time frame only. Key fixed costs are pegged at $40K per month. This represents the "burn" rate prior to major acceleration of marketing plans. Thus, if subscriptions didn't flow in as planned, this represents the point at which the company could continue to survive without increasing marketing. In that event, management could "buy" time to raise additional capital.

Average unit cost per magazine is $.40 and average unit revenue is $2.82 (a weighted average of subscriptions over one and two years and newsstand sales). Thus, the company could survive on a breakeven basis as soon as 16,529 magazines are sold per month.

Breakeven Analysis

Monthly Units Breakeven	16,529
Monthly Sales Breakeven	$46,612

Assumptions

Average Per-Unit Revenue	$2.82
Average Per-Unit Variable Cost	$0.40
Estimated Monthly Fixed Cost	$40,000

Projected Profit and Loss

We expect net income to hit $1 million in year one and $2.4 million in year three. Margin will improve from 32% to 38% of sales as subscriptions mature and marketing costs decrease.

Income Statement

	1997	1998	1999
Sales	$3,128,005	$4,787,330	$6,378,100
Direct Cost of Sales	$619,816	$990,350	$1,305,000
Production payroll	$0	$0	$0
Other	$0	$0	$0
Total Cost of Sales	**$619,816**	**$990,350**	**$1,305,000**
Gross Margin	$2,508,189	$3,796,980	$5,073,100
Gross Margin %	80.18%	79.31%	79.54%
OPERATING EXPENSES			
Sales and Marketing Expenses			
Sales and Marketing Payroll	$51,000	$70,000	$77,000
Advertising/Promotion	$386,176	$72,000	$90,000
Author's Royalties—15%	$83,446	$173,000	$276,000
Travel	$7,500	$9,000	$11,000
Entertainment & Meals	$2,400	$3,000	$3,600
Miscellaneous	$12,000	$15,000	$18,000
Other	$0	$0	$0
Total Sales and Marketing Expenses	**$542,522**	**$342,000**	**$475,600**
Sales and Marketing %	17.34%	7.14%	7.46%
GENERAL AND ADMINISTRATIVE EXPENSES			
General and Administrative Payroll	$160,800	$236,000	$270,000
Payroll Burden	$55,200	$74,400	$83,800
Depreciation	$0	$0	$0
Leased Equipment	$10,200	$12,500	$14,000
Telephone	$7,200	$7,500	$7,800
Utilities	$9,000	$10,000	$10,500
Postage	$138,200	$279,000	$465,000
Insurance	$12,000	$12,000	$14,000
Rent	$30,000	$30,000	$36,000
Other	$0	$0	$0
Total General and Admin Expenses	**$422,600**	**$661,400**	**$901,100**
General and Administrative %	13.51%	13.82%	14.13%

OTHER EXPENSES	1997	1998	1999
Other Payroll	$64,200	$66,000	$72,000
Contract/Consultants	$0	$0	$0
Total Other Expenses	**$64,200**	**$66,000**	**$72,000**
Other %	2.05%	1.38%	1.13%
Total Operating Expenses	**$1,029,322**	**$1,069,400**	**$1,448,700**
Profit Before Interest and Taxes	$1,478,867	$2,727,580	$3,624,400
Interest Expense Short-term	$0	$0	$0
Interest Expense Long-term	$0	$0	$0
Taxes Incurred	$488,026	$900,101	$1,196,052
Net Profit	$990,841	$1,827,479	$2,428,348
Net Profit/Sales	31.68%	38.17%	38.07%

Projected Cash Flow

If we assume an initial $150K capital infusion, at no point does the company run out of cash. At the end of year three a cash balance of $5.3 million has been created.

Cash flow in year one is critical. Note that early contributions on a monthly basis are minimal and only gain momentum in the second half of the year. If shortfalls occur early on more capital may be required.

Pro-Forma Cash Flow

	1997	1998	1999
Net Profit	$990,841	$1,827,479	$2,428,348
PLUS			
Depreciation	$0	$0	$0
Change in Accounts Payable	$144,445	$32,377	$69,875
Current Borrowing (repayment)	$0	$0	$0
Increase (decrease) Other Liabilities	$0	$0	$0
Long-term Borrowing (repayment)	$0	$0	$0
Capital Input	$150,000	$0	$0
Subtotal	$1,285,286	$1,859,855	$2,498,223
LESS			
Change in Accounts Receivable	$39,110	$20,747	$19,890
Change in Inventory	$163,374	$97,667	$82,937
Change in Other ST Assets	$0	$0	$0
Capital Expenditure	$0	$0	$0
Dividends	$0	$0	$0
Subtotal	$202,484	$118,414	$102,827
Net Cash Flow	$1,082,801	$1,741,441	$2,395,396
Cash Balance	$1,149,801	$2,891,243	$5,286,639

Projected Balance Sheet

At the end of year three the company has a net worth of $5.5 million dollars. It might be an attractive IPO candidate or an attractive acquisition.

Pro-Forma Balance Sheet

ASSETS	Starting Balances			
Short-term Assets		**1997**	**1998**	**1999**
Cash	$67,000	$1,149,801	$2,891,243	$5,286,639
Accounts Receivable	$0	$39,110	$59,857	$79,747
Inventory	$0	$163,374	$261,041	$343,978
Other Short-term Assets	$0	$0	$0	$0
Total Short-term Assets	$67,000	$1,352,286	$3,212,141	$5,710,364
LONG-TERM ASSETS				
Capital Assets	$0	$0	$0	$0
Accumulated Depreciation	$0	$0	$0	$0
Total Long-term Assets	$0	$0	$0	$0
Total Assets	$67,000	$1,352,286	$3,212,141	$5,710,364
Liabilities and Capital				
Accounts Payable	$0	$144,445	$176,821	$246,696
Short-term Notes	$0	$0	$0	$0
Other Short-term Liabilities	$0	$0	$0	$0
Subtotal Short-term Liabilities	$0	$144,445	$176,821	$246,696
Long-term Liabilities	$0	$0	$0	$0
Total Liabilities	$0	$144,445	$176,821	$246,696
Paid in Capital	$150,000	$300,000	$300,000	$300,000
Retained Earnings	($83,000)	($83,000)	$907,841	$2,735,319
Earnings	$0	$990,841	$1,827,479	$2,428,348
Total Capital	$67,000	$1,207,841	$3,035,319	$5,463,667
Total Liabilities and Capital	$67,000	$1,352,286	$3,212,141	$5,710,364
Net Worth	$67,000	$1,207,841	$3,035,319	$5,463,667

Business Ratios

Our business ratios are limited in value since the company projects no debt. This will also be an advantage if debt capital is desired later without dilution to shareholders.

Ratio Analysis

Profitability Ratios	**1997**	**1998**	**1999**	**RMA**
Gross Margin	80.18%	79.31%	79.54%	0
Net Profit Margin	31.68%	38.17%	38.07%	0
Return on Assets	73.27%	56.89%	42.53%	0
Return on Equity	82.03%	60.21%	44.45%	0
Activity Ratios				
AR Turnover	8	8	8	0
Collection Days	23	38	40	0
Inventory Turnover	7.59	4.67	4.31	0
Accts Payable Turnover	6.39	6.39	6.39	0
Total Asset Turnover	2.31	1.49	1.12	0

Debt Ratios	1997	1998	1999	RMA
Debt to Net Worth	0.12	0.06	0.05	0
Short-term Liab. to Liab.	1	1	1	0
Liquidity Ratios				
Current Ratio	9.36	18.17	23.15	0
Quick Ratio	8.23	16.69	21.75	0
Net Working Capital	$1,207,841	$3,035,319	$5,463,667	0
Interest Coverage	0	0	0	0
Additional Ratios				
Assets to Sales	0.43	0.67	0.9	0
Debt/Assets	11%	6%	4%	0
Current Debt/Total Assets	11%	6%	4%	0
Acid Test	7.96	16.35	21.43	0
Asset Turnover	2.31	1.49	1.12	0
Sales/Net Worth	2.59	1.58	1.17	0

Real Estate Investment Company

BUSINESS PLAN

WOLFE PARTNERS

45001 Washington Blvd.
Jefferson City, MO 65101

This business plan emphasizes the entrepreneur's experience, knowledge, and savvy, as well as the symbiotic philosophy of the business. The requirements for successful real estate investing are clearly explored and a concise response to each concern gives the plan its authority. Notice how the cautious short-term goals are tempered with the ambitious outlook.

- BUSINESS GOALS

- DEVELOPING KNOWLEDGE OF MARKETPLACE

- BUSINESS OPERATIONS

- TIMELINE

BUSINESS GOALS

Mission

Wolfe Partners has been a family-owned business for more than 10 years. Its principle, Ron Wolfe, is a licensed builder in the state of Missouri and has been working in the construction industry for more than 25 years. Wolfe Partners, L.L.C. is now being established to make the business a full-time venture and to include real property investing, primarily single-family homes, into our strategy. Mr. Wolfe also has over 20 years experience in corporate operations, ranging from a Mechanical Engineer, upon college graduation, to his most recent position as an executive in a Fortune 100 information technology company, managing a $13 million business unit with 120 employees.

Our mission is to create investment income through the purchasing and reselling of distressed homes. A targeted 100% profitability will be generated by performing cosmetic or functional improvements to single-family homes. These renovations will significantly increase the value of the property and make it available for sale to a focused customer marketplace.

Short-Term Goals

The first year of Wolfe Partners will be spent expanding our building opportunities. The company will strive to create and maintain an image and reputation in the industry as an honest, cooperative, and creative enterprise, characterized by ethics, fair play, and win-win results. Our operations will be noted for our high technology processes that will utilize state-of-the-art information and management systems. In order to ensure success, Wolfe Partners will focus on the development of strong partnerships with key real property professionals, i.e., sales brokers/agents, financial institutions, law firms, building trade contractors, real estate service firms, and others.

During this period we will purchase, renovate, and sell approximately one home per month for a total of nine units in 1999. Also during this period one home will be selected, based on its financial performance quality, as a rental unit to be held. This will be the beginning of our long-term investment strategy around rental income properties, and the developing of our expertise in property management.

Long-Term Goals

During the year 2000, Wolfe Partners will become a full-time enterprise. During 2000 and each year thereafter, 2 homes per month will be purchased and renovated. This will allow for one house per month to be kept in the rental income property portfolio, while the second unit is sold to continue the cash income stream. Holding to this strategy over a seven-year period will yield a portfolio of 85 investment units each returning an average $2,000 positive cashflow per year for a total annual income of $170,000, and annual asset appreciation of 5%. Also during this seven-year period, more than 80 homes would have been sold for an average $15,000 profit each for a total of more than $1.3 million cash income. At an average investment of $10,000 per unit, a 100% to 150% profit margin is expected.

Ownership & Employees

Wolfe Partners, L.L.C. is intended to be a highly leveraged organization with only one employee, that being the principle and sole owner, Ron Wolfe. All tasks to be performed on behalf of the enterprise, that cannot be done by the employee, will be hired contract services.

Target Neighborhoods

Wolfe Partners will operate in the southeast corridor of Mixci County. This area will include the communities of Birmingham, Jones, Royal, and Rickston. This area was chosen because of its significant population of homes in our target price range of $80,000 to $100,000 and because of the recent popularity of this area by our target customer base of young, first-time, or first-upgrade homebuyers. Also, we have significant familiarity with those neighborhoods after living in the area for more than 16 years.

Selecting Properties

Wolfe Partners has developed a strategy around the purchase of homes in the $80,000 to $100,000 price range. This price represents homes on the lower end of home values in the targeted neighborhoods. A price differential of at least $30,000 between our purchase price and typical sales prices is necessary for each purchase. This will allow us to absorb a renovation and acquisition expense of approximately $10,000 to $15,000 and still net $15,000 to $20,000 profit from each deal.

In order to appeal to the widest audience of homebuyers, these homes will be at least 3 bedrooms, located on side streets close to schools, and inclusive of certain amenities which are desired by young, professional families.

Locating Flexible/Desperate Sellers

The target neighborhoods are also well populated with sellers that are significantly motivated to be creative in the sale of their property. This "distressed" seller situation can be created for several reasons. The owner may be having trouble selling the property, or may be forced to move quickly to satisfy some pressing personal issue. We will attempt to locate sellers that fit one or more of the following profiles: divorce, estate sales, unemployment, property in disrepair, job transfer, property management problems, absentee ownership, investor washout, tenant problems, retirement, or any other emotional dissatisfaction with the property. It is anticipated that these homeowners will be willing to negotiate on price, terms, or possibly both.

Working with Real Estate Professionals

To be successful in real estate investing, a strong partnership must be built with many service providers that have an intimate knowledge of the neighborhoods we have selected. This list of business contacts includes but is not limited to real estate brokers/agents, chamber of commerce, local investment clubs, financial institutions, utility company repair personnel, title insurance companies, local government personnel, and others.

BUSINESS OPERATIONS

Target Customer

According to recent demographic studies, more than 30% of the U.S. population will be in the age group of 25-44 by the year 2000. In addition, work force studies indicate that the number of trained professionals for most industry categories is inadequate to meet business growth demands and attrition rates. Therefore not only is there a large population of homebuyers in this age bracket, but their long-term employability, and thus their ability to make house payments, is quite favorable. With these trends in mind, our target customer is a young, professional, dual-income family. These buyers will have good credit and income potential, but may not have significant cash reserves. Our approach to these buyers, therefore, will be to get them into our houses with creative solutions to their cash shortage problems.

Establishing a Buyer Profile

Several strategies will be employed to publicize the name of Wolfe Partners and its attempt to be a frequent buyer of distressed real estate. A professional public relations firm was hired to develop a corporate image and identity system which will be incorporated into every correspondence for the business, including business cards, stationery, flyers, postcards, signage, and all other advertising. Once a reputation has been built for the business, it is anticipated that much of the purchase volume will be a result of word-of-mouth advertising. It will be important to these types of transactions to have cash on hand to move quickly when opportunities present themselves.

To endear the business to the real estate broker community, a commitment was made to work with specific firms to conduct all transactions for their areas. In exchange for that commitment, a real estate investor account has been established and preferential commission rates negotiated with these firms.

Communication Plan

To announce the newly established operations of Wolfe Partners, and to further our penetration into the real estate investment process, we will advertise our approach through several media. This includes newspaper advertisements for buying and selling homes, personal contact with real estate agents and building trade contractors, flyers placed on vehicles in parking lots and in mailboxes of homes needing improvement, and by driving through neighborhoods to talk to residents. We will also begin networking with people at businesses and functions involved in real estate investing, for example, county courthouses, bank real estate foreclosure offices, investment clubs, neighborhood association meetings, etc. The following communication plan outlines how Wolfe Partners will begin to inform the community of our business process.

Buying Properties

Working with Home Sellers

A significant amount of time and vehicle mileage can be spent in the pursuit of good home deals. In order to minimize this expense, a rigorous process has been developed to qualify properties for their investment potential, and sellers for their flexibility and compatibility. The process includes two components: a telephone screening script and a property analysis form.

It will be imperative during this process that we establish a rapport with the seller to create comfort with one another, a win-win environment, and an opportunity to drive to closure on the business transaction. The property analysis form is used throughout the process by first recording any information that is contained in the advertisement, so as not to waste the seller's time, except to clarify understanding. During the following phone screening, the form is used to record additional data that is pertinent to our investment strategy. Then, in the event a visit to the property is warranted, the form would be completed during the property inspection.

Communication Item/Description	Location	Frequency and Media	Audience	Origination Date	Delivery Date
Buyer Flyers	Lower income neighborhood Apartment complex	Monthly Mail	Buyers looking to move up First time buyer	4/1/99	4/15/99
Seller Flyers	All homes in subdivision Direct to home	Monthly Mail	Elderly homeowners Homes long time on market	3/1/99	3/15/99
Buyer postcard	Office parking lots Coffee shops Laundromats	Quarterly Personal drop	Young professionals	5/1/99	5/1/99
Sellers postcard	Shopping centers Direct to homes	Quarterly Personal drop	Anxious sellers	4/1/99	4/1/99
Businesscard	Hardware store Building supply store	Weekly	Contractors Do-it-yourselfers Fixup owners	3/1/99	3/15/99
Real Estate Advertisement	City news	Sunday newspaper	Home buyers Home sellers	6/1/99	7/1/99
Real Estate business intent phone call	Real estate agent	Telephone	Continuous	3/1/99	Ongoing

The telephone screening script was developed to provide a consistent way to build this rapport, in a nonoffensive manner, to obtain the information needed to make our buying decisions. The phone screening is intended to be very conversational and informal. The conversation includes questions about the following topics:

> May I ask your name? Could you please tell me about your home?
> What is size, square footage, lot size, garage?
> How many rooms, what configuration, bathroom layouts?
> What special features or amenities, appliances?
> What is existing financing, mortgage type, terms, interest, payments, assumability?
> Are you current on all payments to banks, contractors, taxes (liens)?
> Are you willing to assist in the financing?
> How much cash is needed at close? Can the down payment be spread out?
> What is the asking price? How long on the market?
> How long have you been there? Why are you selling?
> What do you like most/least about the property?
> Are there any renters in the neighborhood and what are they paying for rent?

It is anticipated that in order to find a home that meets our investment criterion, we will have to call on approximately 25 advertised listings. Of these, only approximately 5 will justify a property visit, yielding 2 or 3 offers, and 1 purchase.

Performing Appraisals

A database is currently under construction to capture and report the sale price of all homes in our targeted neighborhoods for the past 12 months. The data for this appraisal tool is available from 3 sources and is being used to build a profile of potential market value and budget for renovation investments. The data sources include: property sold listing books available through real estate brokers that subscribe to the MLS (Multi Listing Service). This listing is created monthly and is only available to licensed real estate professionals (or people they choose to share it with). The second source is available on the Internet, online at the *Detroit News* web site of Sunday's "Real Estate Sold in Your Area" section of the newspaper. The listing from each Sunday paper is downloaded and scanned into our computer into the appropriate city section of our database. The third source of homes sold in the area is the county courthouse and/or Mixci County Legal News paper, under "property ownership transfers." This database is a critical tool in our efforts to properly estimate the value of a home and determine the up side and down side potential of our transactions.

Financial Analysis

Each property to be purchased will go through an extensive financial analysis in a spreadsheet that has been created for this purpose. This analysis will provide the decisionmaking data to determine the appraisal value, appropriate purchase price, detailed estimates of potential renovation, acquisition costs, and potential sale price as well as anticipated profitability.

Creative Financing Techniques

One of the most difficult and critical components of our purchase strategy is the elimination or minimizing of the down payment required to obtain the property. Quite often, the down payment represents a significant portion of the out-of-pocket investment, which is used to calculate the overall rate of return of the transaction. That is, the less money invested to turn the property, the higher the rate of return on the purchase. Several strategies will be employed to take advantage of money that is available from traditional, as well as slightly more obscure sources of funding.

The following sources represent opportunities to purchase property with lower initial costs:

- The seller—quite often a seller will finance some portion if not all of the purchase transactions, especially if the interest rate is attractive and the term is short
- Equity in other homes or vacant land can be used as down payments or collateral for future payments
- Land contracts or private mortgages on other properties can be discounted and sold for cash; Wolfe Partners professional skills and services could be used as "sweat equity"
- Real estate brokers will sometimes take their commissions on a note or as an account receivable
- Investors could be used when larger amounts or quick cash is needed
- Tenants of rental properties could be enticed to convert their lease to a lease with option and apply some money down at the time of lease creation
- Existing loans on the property can sometimes be cashed out or leveraged
- Conventional institutional lenders

Banks and savings and loan institutions will typically be considered as a last resort. This is due to their high closing costs and long delays in processing mortgages. When a seller is not in a hurry to close, and the property will carry the added costs, conventional mortgages might be an option, especially in the current low interest market.

The investment strategy for Wolfe Partners includes a renovation for every property purchased. Obviously, homes that can be purchased well below market value with very little repair required are optimum investments, but difficult to find. It is anticipated that every home will require at least cosmetic improvements to bring the home up to maximum value and allow it to be sold quickly. | **Renovation Process**

To perform these renovations, Wolfe Partners will enlist the help of building trade contractors to perform each of the tasks needed. Wolfe Partners will act as the general contractor and manage each rehab according to rigorous project management and timeline processes. Once we reach our goal of two houses per month, the volume of work should keep a consistent crew of quality contractors busy nearly full-time. Each project is expected to be completed over a 4-6 week period, depending on the complexity of the renovation.

During the last several years, extensive research into home resale value and consumer buying habits has yielded six specific cosmetic home improvements that significantly increase the desirability of a home. These tasks can become more difficult and costly in homes of severe disrepair, but the costs are usually more than accounted for in a lower purchase price. The six tasks and corresponding estimated costs for a typical 1,200-1,400 square-foot home are:

Kitchen cabinet and counter tops—cosmetic improvements are usually adequate but on occasion a complete replacement is necessary	$1,000-$3,000
All vinyl and carpeted floors will be replaced or overlaid	$1,500-$2,000
Bathroom fixtures (including vanities) will be replaced	$1,000
Entire interior of home will be repainted	$1,000
Vinyl siding will be applied to any house that is lacking in curb appeal	$3,000-$4,000
Landscaping (seasonal) to improve lawn, trim shrubbery, plant flowers	$500
Misc. "polishing"	$500

Again, each house will be evaluated on its own merits but the renovation costs are expected to range from $8,500-$12,000. Any property purchased at $25,000-$30,000 below the market value of the neighborhood, will provide sufficient differential to achieve our 100% return on investment in a 2-3 month period.

The Wolfe Partners renovation process model assumes that the above 6 tasks represent the entire work to be done on the property. This assumption will be validated prior to purchase, due to a thorough inspection of the home to ensure mechanical and structural integrity. On occasion, however, a home will be available that represents a larger purchase—resale differential opportunity, but requires structural or other major remodeling expenses. These could be homes that are in terrible disrepair, natural disaster damage, or simply a small ranch home that is surrounded by larger colonial style homes in an affluent neighborhood. These cases do not meet our typical investment strategy, but could be considered, depending on the money needed and the longer time that the money will be tied up during the completion of the project.

Selling Properties

Once the homes have been renovated, they will be placed back on the market through the traditional real estate sales process, with our chosen broker partner. The terms that will be offered to prospective buyers, however, will be equally as creative as our purchase techniques. Since our target market is young professionals that have good earning potential but probably not much of a down payment, we expect to offer assistance with portions of their closing costs, and/or down payment, in order to make it easier for them to get into the home. The actual sale price of the home could be negotiated up as well if the buyer wanted to add some amenity to the home to suit their lifestyle, for example, central air, garage, appliances, furniture, or any other capital expenditure that they wanted to roll into the loan. The sales contract itself could be structured any way that works best for the buyer, as long as we can obtain our initial cash investment back out of the property at close.

Cash Out

It is expected that with the current low interest rates, most buyers will choose conventional bank financing to purchase the home. This works out well for all parties and provides us the money to immediately reinvest in another property.

Wrap Around Financing

In the event we were able to obtain favorable financing at the time the property was purchased, and the buyer has enough down payment to return our initial cash investment, a wrap around financing plan may be possible. In this scenario, Wolfe Partners would have assumed an FHA, VA, private mortgage, or contract for deed (land contract) for the majority of the original purchase price. We could then write a private mortgage or contract for deed for the new equity basis above the old loan, for the buyer. The buyer makes payments to Wolfe Partners for a mortgage on the full market price (minus down payment), and we in turn make payments on the underlying loan. The underlying financing amortizes faster than the wrap around financing, creating an increasing equity position with each payment. When the underlying loan is paid in full, the entire monthly payment from the wrap financing is profit on the equity.

Lease with Option

If a buyer is a good credit risk, but just does not have enough cash or the desire to buy, we could sell the property to them on a lease with option contract. In this arrangement, we and the buyer would agree upon a sale price, usually 10%-15% higher than current market, at a date 2-3 years in the future. The buyer would put some money down as earnest money to ensure the contract will be met. They will also get a credit of some portion of the monthly rent, which is accumulated with the earnest money to be used as the purchase down payment at the end of the contract period. This situation also works out well for the seller if we don't have much cash invested in the property or don't need it right away. We will usually get a much higher quality renter that will take better care of the property, invest their own money in improvements, be more diligent in their monthly payments to avoid forfeit of the contract, as well as gain the tax benefits of rental properties during the option period.

Rental Properties

As previously mentioned, careful attention will be made during the purchase process to locate properties that could be entered into our long-term investment portfolio of rental homes. To meet our standards for inclusion in the rental portfolio the property must pass three performance measures. First, we must be able to buy and prepare the home with very little cash outlay. Second, the home must be located in a desirable area that will ensure better than average appreciation, which we define as twice the inflation rate. Thirdly, and most importantly, the loan structure, maintenance costs, operational expenses and income stream must be favorable to net a positive cash flow of at least $2,000 per year. Since our intention is to hold these houses in our portfolio for 7-8 years, the combination of appreciation and cash flow will yield an estimated 20% return on our investment over this period. In addition, all properties in the portfolio will be managed by a professional property management firm, which is included in the operational expense.

Building Speculation Homes

During the course of normal property buy/fixup/sell processes, it is expected that Wolfe Partners will occasionally obtain ownership of vacant land that is traded as part of a transaction or split off from a larger parcel. As a secondary source of income, and an opportunity to add diversity to our enterprise, we will use our expertise as a licensed builder to develop a piece of property from the ground up. Since these ventures are very capital intensive and time consuming, it is anticipated that we would only build approximately one house per year. Since the property will probably be held free and clear, and the construction crews would be the same contract labor companies that provide us with good rates on renovations, it is expected that a $150,000 property could be completed for under $100,000 and net a $50,000 profit on each deal.

Managing the Business

As a hybrid home construction and real estate investing firm with a high technology flair, Wolfe Partners will be managed much differently than traditional construction or small investment companies. Utilizing our significant expertise in information systems, financial controls, and project management, Wolfe Partners will be a very tightly managed enterprise. In addition to the individual property financial analysis process mentioned earlier, a corporate financial control and reporting system has been developed for the business as a whole. Meticulous recordkeeping and continuous transaction monitoring will be accompanied each month by a profit and loss statement that would be used to track the performance of the company for all parties involved.

Quarterly revenue and expense outlooks will be performed and, each month, actual results will be compared to the outlooks to monitor performance and make adjustments as necessary in daily operations to achieve the desired corporate profit attainment. A sample of the profit and loss statement is contained on the following page.

Timeline

Wolfe Partners, L.L.C. was officially formed on March 5, 1999. The month of March has been, and will continue to be, a period of organization and preparation with our first "official" home purchase expected in April. Following the timeline identified throughout this document, we would expect to purchase another home in May and turn the first home during the later half of May or early June. Another home would be purchased in June and one each month thereafter through the end of 1999, at which time we will ramp up to our fully operational level of 2 houses per month.

FINANCIAL INFORMATION

Wolfe Partners, L.L.C. - Financial Information
Monthly Profit & Loss Statement
U.S. Dollars

Prepared by:	Ron Wolfe
Date:	12/25/98
Report Sector:	Consolidated
Rate Tables:	Personal Income
Report Time:	04:49 pm
Report Basis:	Calendar Year 1999
Reporting Period:	Month 1 thru 12

	Jan-Act	Feb-Act	Mar-Out	Apr-Out	May-Out
Revenues:					
Home sales	0	0	0	0	0
Rental Income	0	0	0	0	0
Interest Income	0	0	0	0	0
Other Revenue	0	0	0	0	0
Total Revenue	0	0	0	0	0
Direct Expenses:					
Salaries/OT	0	0	0	0	0
Contract Labor	0	0	0	0	0
Bonus/Incentive	0	0	0	0	0
Fringe/Vac/Hol/Sick	0	0	0	0	0
Employee Related	0	0	0	0	0
Travel	0	0	0	0	0
Hardware Costs—Expensed	0	0	0	0	0
Hardware—Deprec/Amort	0	0	0	0	0
Hardware Maintenance	0	0	0	0	0
Software Costs—Expensed	0	0	0	0	0
Software—Deprec/Amort	0	0	0	0	0
Software Maintenance	0	0	0	0	0
Property Maintenance	0	0	0	0	0
Gain/Loss on Assets	0	0	0	0	0
Property—Depreciation	0	0	0	0	0
Tools	0	0	0	0	0
Computer and Office Supplies	0	0	0	0	0
Advertising/ Communications Costs	0	0	0	0	0
Building Materials	0	0	0	0	0
Insurance	0	0	0	0	0
Utilities	0	0	0	0	0
Property Management	0	0	0	0	0
Home Furnishings	0	0	0	0	0
Professional Services Fees	0	0	0	0	0
Munincipal Services	0	0	0	0	0
Real Estate Commissions	0	0	0	0	0
Office Space Related Expense	0	0	0	0	0
Loans Payable Principle	0	0	0	0	0
Real Estate Taxes	0	0	0	0	0
Total Direct Expense	**0**	**0**	**0**	**0**	**0**
DEBIT	0	0	0	0	0
Memo Information					
Interest Paid	0	0	0	0	0
Income Taxes Paid	0	0	0	0	0
Net Profit	0	0	0	0	0
Net Profit Margin %	**0**	**0**	**0**	**0**	**0**

Jun-Out	Jul-Out	Aug-Out	Sep-Out	Oct-Out	Nov-Out	Dec-Out	Total	Pct %
0	0	0	0	0	0	0	0	0.0
0	0	0	0	0	0	0	0	0.0
0	0	0	0	0	0	0	0	0.0
0	0	0	0	0	0	0	0	0.0
0	0	0	0	0	0	0	0	0.0
0	0	0	0	0	0	0	0	0.0
0	0	0	0	0	0	0	0	0.0
0	0	0	0	0	0	0	0	0.0
0	0	0	0	0	0	0	0	0.0
0	0	0	0	0	0	0	0	0.0
0	0	0	0	0	0	0	0	0.0
0	0	0	0	0	0	0	0	0.0
0	0	0	0	0	0	0	0	0.0
0	0	0	0	0	0	0	0	0.0
0	0	0	0	0	0	0	0	0.0
0	0	0	0	0	0	0	0	0.0
0	0	0	0	0	0	0	0	0.0
0	0	0	0	0	0	0	0	0.0
0	0	0	0	0	0	0	0	0.0
0	0	0	0	0	0	0	0	0.0
0	0	0	0	0	0	0	0	0.0
0	0	0	0	0	0	0	0	0.0
0	0	0	0	0	0	0	0	0.0
0	0	0	0	0	0	0	0	0.0
0	0	0	0	0	0	0	0	0.0
0	0	0	0	0	0	0	0	0.0
0	0	0	0	0	0	0	0	0.0
0	0	0	0	0	0	0	0	0.0
0	0	0	0	0	0	0	0	0.0
0	0	0	0	0	0	0	0	0.0
0	0	0	0	0	0	0	0	0.0
0	**0**	**0**	**0**	**0**	**0**	**0**	**0**	**0.0**
0	0	0	0	0	0	0	0	0.0
0	0	0	0	0	0	0	0	0.0
0	0	0	0	0	0	0	0	0.0
0	0	0	0	0	0	0	0	0.0
0	**0**	**0**	**0**	**0**	**0**	**0**	**0**	**0.0**

Real Estate Renovation Company

BUSINESS PLAN · ABC CORPORATION

14034 W. Circle Dr.
Sacramento, CA 95831

This corporation admits the narrowness of this niche market but persuasively counters with the enormous payoffs possible and the absence of competition as well as a highly specific target group. The idea of real estate renovation is given a twist to appeal to wealthy consumers, and ample evidence convincingly illustrates the growth of demand. Optimism accompanies each section of the plan and helps convey a confidence necessary to succeed in such a risky endeavor.

- EXECUTIVE SUMMARY

- THE BUSINESS

- MARKET ANALYSIS

- MARKETING

- MARKETING STRATEGY

- MARKET EXPOSURE AND RISKS

- FINANCIAL CONSIDERATIONS

- CONCLUSION

EXECUTIVE SUMMARY

Introduction

ABC Corporation is formed to help meet the growing demand for unique homes in the Sacramento area of northern California.

ABC Corporation is initially focusing on the renovation of one unique estate, which is detailed in this document. Other land development opportunities can be addressed in the future which will provide additional profit with reduced expenses.

ABC Corporation has reached an agreement with a building renovator (a builder and architect that has been recognized by receiving numerous awards for quality renovation projects) to partner in the development of this estate. In addition to the builder, ABC Corporation has secured the services of an experienced real estate professional to assist in the marketing assessment and the marketing of the property.

This building renovation will conform to the guidelines established by the local city government for zoning and setback restrictions.

ABC Corporation will negotiate the purchase of the property. The oversight of the renovation will be the responsibility of ABC Corporation with the builder's participation in the profit being based on his ability to deliver the project on time and within budget. The marketing of the estate will be done by the real estate professional that will be paid based on a consulting fee.

Due to the size of this renovation project, ABC Corporation has decided to limit the scope of the initial project to this one renovation project only.

The profit from this initial project will help provide the basis for funding other land development projects and be the initial start-up capital necessary for this business.

Due to the high and increasing demand for unique homes in the 2 to 5 million dollar price range, ABC Corporation will be able to renovate this estate at a low cost, thus providing the opportunity to result in substantial profit.

Please note that this project will be completed within 18 months and will sell for over $4,500,000, generating a profit of $1,000,000.

Mission Statement

ABC Corporation can be characterized as a developer of unique homes, catering to the discriminating buyer who needs a home that makes a statement. ABC Corporation was developed to provide rapid access to the type of unique home that is expected by the person buying a home in the over 3 million dollar price range.

Before the end of this project, ABC Corporation will be recognized as a highly visible company in the estate renovation market. We will be known for developing a unique quality product. We will have renovated a unique historical home in the most exclusive area in metropolitan Sacramento. Our revenues will exceed $4.5 million. ABC Corporation will actively seek to promote expansion into other additional renovation opportunities within this market from the profit that we have obtained from this project.

The ABC Corporation's mission is to provide unique, practical, and quality homes on a timely basis, utilizing state-of-the-art renovation techniques and practices. We believe that our first responsibility is to our customers. Our strong financial position will enable us to establish an attractive option in the geographic market we serve. In carrying out our day-to-day business we strive to:

- Follow the philosophy that our customers are entitled to select a unique quality that is available in a reasonable amount of time.
- Treat our partners with fairness and consideration.
- Be considered an asset in our community.

Through long-term commitment to this mission statement, we will be recognized as an organization that is responsive to our customers.

The concept of renovating unique estates is a stable financial model in the Sacramento metropolitan market which is experiencing a rapid growth in the demand for houses in the over 3 million dollar market. This is truly a niche market as there have traditionally been houses built on speculation for people in the 1.5 million dollar range and below, however, there is a very limited quantity of homes available in the over 3 million dollar price range. This demand is producing a rapid escalation in the price of homes in this category.

Unique Features

ABC Corporation has formed a partnership with two key people that bring a relationship with the building trade, experience in renovating other historical estates, and success in marketing the completed product.

The concept that "new is better" may work for home buyers in lower price ranges, but our research shows that homes in the over 2 million dollar range built in the early 1900s (this home was built in 1924) are consistently valued at higher prices per square foot.

The ABC Corporation's marketing objective is to promote and support the fact that people can purchase truly unique homes that make a statement about their way of life.

Marketing Objectives

People have a right to demand a truly unique home that is not just a large box with so many square feet of floor space. It is appropriate for buyers to expect to have this type of unique quality home available in a reasonable period of time.

Marketing Strategy

Our target market focuses on the top 600 executives in metropolitan Sacramento. These executives that have rapidly moved up their organization have achieved new status through the consolidation of the High-Tech suppliers, or have been relocated to Sacramento by global High-Tech corporations establishing a North American headquarters in California. Since all of the executives in this target market will have recently moved into new positions, their expectations will be to quickly acquire a unique home that is commensurate with their new social status.

Our houses will be seen as desirable and unique by the prospective homebuyer.

Positioning

The recognition that our builder has received for spectacular renovations, coupled with the historical significance and exclusive appeal of the adjacent golf course, make this a very unique and highly desired estate.

In terms of market segmentation advantages, our house will appeal to the thirty people that we anticipate entering this market looking for a unique home.

The "selling basis" for our home is a high customer demand for unique homes. Once in the door, the customer will sell himself on his need for this unique spectacular estate.

Pricing

The price for our home will be based on the market midpoint price per square foot of houses built in the same period and in the same geographic location.

The price in the financial model will be conservatively forecasted with no escalation for property values over the period required to complete the project.

We feel that our house is reasonably priced within the ability of our target customer's ability to pay and receive superior value for the dollars spent.

Expected Accomplishments

In order for ABC Corporation to attain its vision in the manner described in our mission statement, the following primary goals need to be achieved:

- Purchase the house at or below the price forecasted in the financial model.
- Complete the renovation of the home at or below the price forecasted in the financial model.
- Complete the renovation of the home on or before the deadline in the project plan.
- Complete the renovation with a home that is recognized for its spectacular quality.
- Secure a contract with purchaser at or before the completion of the renovation.
- To utilize the customer of this house as a reference for the next potential customer.

To utilize the recognition of the quality of this home to develop a demand for other homes of similar quality and uniqueness.

Corporate

By the end of the project plan, ABC Corporation will have achieved each of the named goals and will be moving forward toward the next renovation opportunity.

Products

Upon completion of the Seeley Estate, ABC Corporation will have identified the next renovation project. We expect to market our own unique renovation projects for the Sacramento market.

Market

ABC Corporation forecasts completing and selling our first renovation project within budget and on time, resulting in achieving our initial financial goals. We will have received recognition for renovating a historically unique estate with a spectacular style. We will identify further potential renovation efforts and develop the plan to continue to generate additional revenues through additional renovations.

Sales

ABC Corporation projects completing the renovation of this unique home and selling it for total revenue of 4.5 million dollars.

- First-year total sales will be zero (annually).
- Second-year total sales will exceed $4.5 million (annualized).

Required Capital

According to the opportunities and requirements for ABC Corporation, described in this business plan, and based on what we feel are sound business assumptions, our initial total capital requirements total $3,040,000. This amount will enable us to purchase the estate and place required deposit down on the initial startup costs.

Problem Statement

In today's market, there are an insufficient number of unique estates in the Sacramento market for the number of prospective buyers. The increasing number of people in the three million dollar home and above home market are feeling constrained by the limited amount of land available for development and their time to locate a new home. These people need someone with the vision necessary to renovate or develop the limited amount of available land. These people need someone with knowledge of the marketplace and the building trades that can quickly provide them with truly unique homes of distinction.

Currently, prospective homebuyers have two choices when looking for a new home. They can engage a builder to build a new home that can be built in twelve to eighteen months. They can knock down an existing home and replace it with a new home in eighteen months. Most of these prospective buyers have just relocated or are people that have just gained new stature that requires them to quickly move into a unique estate designed for entertaining.

ABC Corporation will provide a rapid solution to the expanding market demand for readily available unique estates. The market knowledge of the realtor and trade network and renovation experience of the builder assure that prospective buyers will be able to move into truly unique estates in significantly less time than they can today.

Description of the Business

ABC Corporation is a business that provides prospective estate buyers with rapid access to their new homes. The renovation of this estate will be accomplished through a partnership between ABC Corporation and Harris Partners. ABC Corporation will provide the funding for acquiring the estate and the renovation. ABC Corporation and Bill Jones, the realtor, will also provide the contacts for acquiring the property and selling the property. Harris Partners will provide the expertise and capacity for performing the renovation. Harris Partners has the experience and the staff necessary to assure the prospective buyer that they will be able to move into a unique estate in a short period of time.

This unique renovation would be targeted at the top 600 executives, entrepreneurs, and professional athletes in the Sacramento metropolitan area. The sale price of this estate would provide over a 20% return on our investment and be within the income of our typical customer, someone receiving a total annual income of over one million dollars.

History of the Business

Company

ABC Corporation was founded in 1998 to meet the demand for truly unique estates in the Sacramento metropolitan market and to take advantage of the knowledge that Harris Partners has gained in the renovation business and the market knowledge of the owner and the realtor.

It is the intention of ABC Corporation to continue to grow core business after the completion of this project by locating, renovating, and selling additional estates. Since these other projects would not take place until the completion of this project, and we cannot accurately forecast the purchase prices or the cost of renovations for specific homes yet to be identified. Projections for future projects are not be included in this plan.

ABC Corporation can best be described as a business specialized in the renovation of historically significant, unique homes. Our key strengths are derived from the partnerships that we have built with Harris Partners and Bill Jones, to provide experience in locating and renovating this prime property. The team is a strong and experienced management group, and has a proven track record in marketing.

Management

The core management team is in place; however, we are in the process of reviewing the project plan in order to select the appropriate skilled trade people for this project.

Services

Our renovation partner, Harris Partners, has been tested and recognized by receiving many awards for the quality of their work.

Market Environment

The market demand, which has been growing for the past 10 years, continues to undergo rapid growth with an increasing number of new executive positions being created through corporate consolidation, relocation, and promotion. We are now poised to take advantage of this opportunity and expect to have an offer for purchase on the home before we have completed the renovation.

Pricing and Profitability

Current prices on homes in the above three million dollar price range are increasing very rapidly in the Sacramento marketplace. However, to insure profitability, we are basing the forecasted sales price on the current market price which will provide us some flexibility to negotiate a quick sale.

Customers

Our customers are the top 600 executives, privates business owners, and professional athletes in the Sacramento metropolitan area.

Founder of the Business

David L. Seeley, President

Mr. David L. Seeley founded the company in August of 1998 and has been president of the company since that time. Mr. Seeley has had extensive involvement in various business enterprises since starting his career in 1976 in the building material business with ARBCO Inc. and Sand Hill Road Partners where he worked on architectural specifications and with local building code officials in Sacramento, CA. Mr. Seeley was owner of his own computer resale business where he employed a total of over 90 employees. In addition, Mr. Seeley has been a manager for High-Tech Energy Systems for over the last nine years where he has been responsible for an organization with over 210 employees and $80,000,000 in annual revenue. Mr. Seeley has also been in significant leadership roles for two other corporations where he has held profit and loss responsibility. Mr. Seeley has been project manager for several large multi-million dollar projects and is very experienced with project management tools and processes. Mr. Seeley is an alumnus of Oakhurst College with majors in business administration and history. Mr. Seeley attended graduate school at California State University—Davis and has attended at least one graduate level class per quarter for the last three years. Mr. Seeley is also on the Board of Directors of a private school and is the advertising coordinator for his church.

Real Estate Marketing Partner
Bill Jones, Marketing Agent
Real Estate Professional Partners

Bill Jones has 24 years of experience in the real estate business in the state of California. Mr. Jones has a real estate brokers license with the state of California and is an accredited buyer representative, a certified residential brokerage manager, a certified residential specialist, and a graduate of the Realtors Institute. Mr. Jones has managed sales offices for twelve years, overseeing as many as 90 sales people and managing a budget in excess of three million dollars. He has received recognition for multi-million dollar production for every year since 1975. He graduated from San Francisco College with majors in history and mathematics and also received a master's degree in history from the University of Wisconsin.

Building and Architectural Partner
John Harris, President
Harris Partners—San Ramon, California

John Harris has over 18 years of experience in building and architecture. He is a licensed architect and builder in the state of California and is on the National Council of Architectural Registration Board. Mr. Harris is a member of the American Institute of Architects, the California Society of Architects, and the American Institute of Architects Design Build Committee. He is also a member of the National Building Officials Code Association, Northwestern California Building Officials Association, the National Association of Home Builders, the National Association of Home Builders Remodelers Council, and the Building Industry Association of California. He has received the National Association of Home Builders Merit Award for Residential Design and Construction and the National Association of Home Builders Grand Builder Award for Residential Design and Construction. In addition to his extensive background and awards he has a bachelor degree in architecture from Montana State University.

To attain the primary goal of profitably purchasing this unique home, ABC Corporation will carry out the following objectives:

- Purchase the house at the lowest price possible.
- Use the cost of updating the existing structure to negotiate a lower purchase price.
- Use the marketing information to help reduce the purchase price of the house.

To attain the primary goal of completing the renovation under or within budget, ABC Corporation will carry out the following objectives:

- Use the earned value method of project management (where expenses are tracked according to percent accomplishment of task as well as by dollars spent).
- Evaluate the impact on expenses and the sale price of any proposed scope changes in the renovation effort.

To attain the primary goal of completing the project on deadline, ABC Corporation will carry out the following objectives:

- Utilize computerized project management tools to insure that each task is being completed on time.
- Utilize project management tools to balance the staff's load so that everyone's time can be optimized.
- Reward the members of the team financially to complete the project at or before the deadline.

To attain the primary goal of obtaining recognition for the spectacular quality of the renovation of this home, ABC Corporation will carry out the following objectives:

- Develop a high quality marketing brochure.
- Have an article created describing this project and history of the home. This article will be placed in local newspapers and in historical building publication *Historical Homes.*
- Advertise the home in local and national publications.

To attain the primary goals of securing a sales contract prior to the completion of the project, ABC Corporation will carry out the following objectives:

- Begin advertising the home before the construction is completed.
- Have the public relations communication pieces done before the house is completed.

To attain the primary goals of developing a strong reference and developing the demand for future homes, ABC Corporation will carry out the following objectives:

- Work closely with the buyer before the completion of the project to insure that their expectations are exceeded.
- Insure that this home is appointed with features that are truly unique in this market.

Regulatory & Licensing

The legal form of ABC Corporation is a California corporation, located in Danville, California.

ABC Corporation will offer a unique home that conforms to all local, state, and national building codes and zoning ordinances. ABC Corporation is being formed to renovate this historical home and then continue with other projects as they are identified.

Objectives

Revenue projections for this project, with external funding, are expected to be $4.5 million based on the renovation of this one home. Our objective at this time is to renovate this estate and, while we are completing this project, to identify another project to propel the company into a prominent market position by establishing ourselves as the renovator of unique historical homes.

This renovation is forecasted to provide a net profit of $1,000,000.

MARKET ANALYSIS

Market Research

ABC Corporation's market is growing rapidly. Sacramento (the county of the target market) is the second largest contributor to the Republican Party in the country. Nearby San Francisco is one of eleven cities in the United States that has four major athletic teams. It is the only city in the country that is undergoing dramatic creation of high level executive positions within one industry (due to the fact that the High-Tech industry is consolidating the smaller suppliers and is spinning off large pieces of the PC OEM business). In addition to these facts, the stock market is producing more wealth for people all over the world. All of these factors contribute to the rapid increase in the demand for spectacular homes.

The market trends show that the number of homes sold in the over two million dollar range has almost doubled (with the exception of 1997). Already through July of 1998 there have been twice as many homes in the over two million dollar range sold than all of last year. The market trend also shows that the price per square foot of the houses sold has increased by approximately 22% from 1993 to 1998. The current average price for all houses in this market segment has already gone up another 32% per square foot. All of these increases have occurred while the average number of days the house is on the market for 1997 is only two more than in 1993 (and less than any other year between 1993 and 1997).

ABC Corporation's target market includes all adults that are making over one million dollars per year. The following chart is based on the research that we have done through Calvin's Sacramento Business, Internet websites for all of the corporations that we could locate in the Sacramento area, and our personal knowledge of the professional athletes and business professionals. There are currently approximately 600 people in this target market. The following chart shows the breakdown of this population by profession.

Target Market

Business Owners	208
Brokers	65
Athletes	58
Lawyers	58
Suppliers	43
Health Care	43
Non-Tech	41
High-Tech	37
Engineers	36
Franchises	22

Distribution of People by Industry

ABC Corporation's sole service is to provide spectacular homes to people in a quantifiable market. At least 600 people in metropolitan Sacramento make over one million dollars per year.

Customer Profile

National Real Estate publishes that the average American moves once every 6.9 years. That means that at any time 14.5% of this target market will be looking for a new home. That translates into 87 people looking for homes in this market at any time. With the current trend of increasing income it will not be unreasonable for the number of potential buyers to increase to 100 within a very short period of time.

The existing competition in this market are other properties that cost over two million dollars.

Competition

There are currently only 17 other homes on the market that are priced at over two million dollars. Other homes in this price range consist of new homes, renovated homes, and homes needing renovation. There is not a wide selection between the homes that are available. There are no other homes available that border a country club, have a swimming pool, tennis court, over 12,500 square feet of space, and are historically significant.

A key factor in the development of this particular home is that it is unique, and is probably the only property available that has a tennis court, while bordering the prestigious Blackhawk Country Club. The home is being renovated by Harris Partners, who is recognized as being the leader in renovations of historic homes in the area.

The major competitors' objectives are:

- **New Homes:** To build a new home that is unique from other homes and to offer the prospective homebuyer the opportunity to create their own home. The reality is that due to zoning restrictions and the lack of large parcels of available land it is very difficult to create a unique design for the home.

- **Renovations:** To utilize the historical significance of the home to create a unique dwelling. The challenge with renovations is that many times the existing structure does not provide the basis for developing a home that conforms to today's living and entertaining requirements.
- **Homes Requiring Renovation:** This competitive situation poses two problems. One is the same as that listed under renovations; the other is that many prospective buyers have difficulty visualizing the potential that the home possesses.

Our home is positioned to provide the prospective homebuyer with the most unique spectacular home that they can buy. ABC Corporation will also address our clients' need to rapidly move into a home that fits their general lifestyle needs.

MARKETING

Functional Description

ABC Corporation will offer a unique estate that offers a broad spectrum of appeal for people interested in entertaining and enjoying the things in life that their success has earned. The specific needs that this home addresses are:

Ability to Entertain: This home provides all of the facilities necessary to entertain any guest. The home will have a kitchen capable of serving large numbers of guests. There will be a home theater and entertainment center capable of providing any state of the art movies and interactive video experiences to individuals or large groups of people. There is a large wet bar and dance floor to respond to the need to provide dancing and drinks for large groups. There will be a complete exercise room, sauna, and whirlpool to provide top physical conditioning.

Provide Access to All Major Recreational Activities: The grounds contain a large outdoor swimming pool for pool parties or for using swimming as a means of conditioning. There is a tennis court, which will be resurfaced for ability to play competitive matches or tune up your game. The home is located on the middle of the third fairway of the Blackhawk Country Club, enabling you to practice your chip shots or drive over to the club house for a round of golf. The reflecting pond, gardens, and sprinkler systems will all be redesigned or cosmetically enhanced to provide pleasant surroundings when walking through the grounds.

Provide Showers and Changing Facilities for Recreational Activities: The home currently has separate showers and changing rooms for men and women to use when accessing the pool, tennis courts, or golf course.

Easy Access for Physically Limited Persons: The home will be retrofitted with an elevator that will travel from the basement to the third floor. This will enable any guest to have access to the entire home. It will also allow for the owner of the home to have elderly parents stay with them in the home and be able to freely move about the home.

State of the Art Security, Communications, and HVAC: This home will have a state-of-the-art security system to provide safety and peace of mind for the owner. The home will also have an intercom, stereo, and be wired for network communications in order to provide the owner with the best communications available. The home will have the heating and electrical systems updated. The home will have air conditioning and central vacuuming installed. These systems will provide the homeowner with a comfortable environment and one that requires little maintenance.

Updated Bathrooms and Bedrooms: To provide the homeowner with bedrooms and bathrooms to enjoy a standard expected by people of this level. To provide the elegance expected by houseguests.

Open Entranceway and Driveway: To provide the spectacular entrance to the home that is expected in a home that is in this market segment.

It is the intention of ABC Corporation to use this project to further establish the reputation of Harris Partners and develop the reputation of ABC Corporation as the developer of truly unique homes.

Related Products

ABC Corporation's marketing strategy is to aggressively promote the fact that our home—the Seeley Estate—is the most unique and spectacular home in the Sacramento area.

MARKETING STRATEGY

The key to marketing is education and awareness. ABC Corporation will support an educational effort, which will contact all of the local newspapers and major home publications to provide awareness to the current local residents and prospective new residents. ABC Corporation also will support opportunities to market the home through membership in Blackhawk Country Club.

Our advertising and promotion strategy is to position ABC Corporation as the leading developer of unique homes in the Sacramento market.

Sales Promotions

The ABC Corporation marketing strategy incorporates plans to educate and recruit potential homeowners through several proven channels:

- Newspaper advertising will target specific local buyers.
- Direct contact will address a highly focused segment of the high-income population.
- Referral networking with other real estate agencies will provide a source of prescreened prospects.

In the building area, ABC Corporation has entered into preliminary agreements with the leading renovator of historically significant estates and the top real estate agent in Sacramento to renovate and then market this unique estate. ABC Corporation will focus on the following publicity strategies:

Publicity & Public Relations

- The majority of advertising for this home will be paid for by the consulting fees of the real estate company that has been engaged by ABC Corporation; in addressing all broad advertising issues, this will be relatively unchallenged.
- Local newspapers will help promote the general awareness of ABC Corporation and this project.
- National promotion through home magazines dealing with quality of lifestyle issues is innovative and largely untapped in this market.

ABC Corporation should be viewed as the premier renovator of unique homes. It is the fulfillment of success to be able to live a lifestyle in keeping with your achievements.

Market Perception

As such, our target market focuses on people that are earning over one million dollars per year, but will be best received by people that have a large equity position to invest in the home.

Objectives & Strategies

ABC Corporation's marketing strategy is to promote the fact that ABC Corporation is a developer that provides the quality of life we all expect to enjoy, and that this quality of life is attainable.

Positioning

Our home will be seen as desirable and unique by the prospective homebuyer.

The exclusiveness of our home and the quality of the workmanship will offer an advantage whereby the prospective homebuyer arrives at a highly satisfied position in his mind.

In terms of market segmentation advantages, our home will appeal to a wide variety of interests within this economic segment.

The "selling basis" for our home is awareness and education. Once in the door, the prospective homebuyer will sell himself on his need for a home that provides this quality of life.

Unique Selling Advantage

Margin Structure

Factoring in all carrying costs, expenses for the property, salaries of the workers, material costs, advertising, and the fact that the home should sell prior to completion (based on the current market average of houses selling within six months and the fact that the renovation will be completed within 12 months) the project will result in a margin of approximately 20%.

During the twelve months that it will take to complete the construction, the real estate values should increase, thus, the profit margin should improve.

Selling Tactics

Advertising and Promotion

ABC Corporation recognizes the key to success requires extensive promotion of our home. This must be done aggressively and consistently. To accomplish our sales goals, we will employ an extremely capable real estate agent supported by the top real estate agency in the area with public relations capabilities. Direct advertising will be concentrated on a local and regional basis, with national advertising contracted on a cooperative basis through some of the existing contacts that exist with national magazines.

Objectives

Our objectives are to:

- Position ABC Corporation as the leading supplier of unique homes in this market and increase the company's awareness and name recognition in the community.
- Develop, through continued analysis of market research, significant information to create immediate marketing plans and budgets.
- Create advertising programs supporting prosperous lifestyles.

Media Objectives

Our media objectives are to:

- Select primary print media advertising with specific market demographics penetration.
- Schedule adequate frequency of ads to impact targeted market with image and quality messages.
- Take advantage of special high-interest inserts or special publications when possible.
- Get the most out of our promotional budget; our media coverage will focus on the over one million dollar income bracket.

The best way to reach our potential customers is to develop an advertising campaign promoting our basic premise—"The Seeley Estate is the most spectacular and unique home available."

To maintain the ABC Corporation image, the delivery and tone of our statements will be informational.

- Ads will convey the "look and feel" of a unique, spectacular home.
- The prospective homebuyer is typically unaware of how difficult it is to find a truly unique home with historical significance.

Ideally, after becoming familiar with this project, the prospective homebuyer will feel compelled in turning to ABC Corporation as their only first choice to find a truly unique home.

To eliminate the biggest obstacle to immediate action, our advertisements must create the impression of exclusivity and create the desire to call for an appointment to see the home.

Because homebuying is such a personal issue, it is important to develop a promotional campaign that is consistent and easy to understand.

In addition to newspaper advertising, we will utilize regional advertising in some of the national home publications. We will gain considerable name recognition through the media. Homebuying is not an impulse decision, so the primary thrust of the advertising will be to inform our prospective homebuyers.

Our publicity efforts are intended to accomplish the following:

- Position ABC Corporation as the leading provider of unique and spectacular homes.
- Increase ABC Corporation's reputation and name recognition in the community that we serve.

ABC Corporation will focus on the following publicity strategies:

- Develop a public relations effort, with ongoing contact between key historical building and real estate interest editors. Present consistent update programs for the target media, keeping editors aware of new construction completion.
- Develop a minimum of four articles edited by our builder and real estate agent, to be placed in newspapers within the next 12 months.
- Produce a complete company background on ABC Corporation to be used as a public relations tool for all grand opening announcements in print media.

Brochure

We currently plan to produce a 2-page, 4-color brochure, which will be available at real estate offices and in the home to serve as an informational piece for potential homebuyers.

The price for our home is determined by the average price per square foot of all the houses that are on the market at the time the house is listed. The cost model is based on the house selling at $4.5 million, which is twenty dollars per foot less than the current average.

We feel that this is a conservative price and that we actually should be able to get a higher price per square foot due to the rapidly increasing property values in this area.

Advertising Campaign

Public Relations

Publicity Strategy

Channels of Distribution

Pricing

MARKET EXPOSURE AND RISKS

Description

The risks that ABC Corporation faces are:

- Adverse changes in the market demand for exclusive real estate. While we do not anticipate a drop in the real estate market, changes in the marketplace do occur due to changes in interest or a downturn in the High-Tech industry.
- Unanticipated repair costs to the home necessitated by unforeseen damage to the property. Even with the extensive background and experience that our builder has, he may discover some items requiring renovation that were not part of the original budget. Even if this does occur, we are operating with sufficient profit margins and conservative assumptions on the purchase price of property, the cost of the renovation, and the sale price of the finished product, that we will still be able to obtain a reasonable profit.

Contingency Plans

We elected to be conservative in our projections; to reflect only the sales price for the finished property that is below the current average market price per square foot. In addition we are setting the purchase price of the house in the cost model at the highest possible purchase price. We are also setting the cost of renovations at the highest possible point. The builder's actual experience in performing similar renovations indicates that we should be able to increase the profit margin by approximately 30%.

With respect to the security of the market demand, the house is an asset that can be secured for at least 80% of its value. This base level of revenues is sufficient to cover all of the expenses for this project and still provide us with a breakeven. We also know from experience that, even in an economic downturn, that high-income earners will still pay for homes that provide them with the ability to fulfill their lifestyle. Furthermore, this projection does not take into account any income that we anticipate as we identify future renovation projects and the additional income potential that may be derived from them.

FINANCIAL CONSIDERATIONS

Use of Capital

Capital Required $3,610,000

Detail	1st Quarter	2nd Quarter	3rd Quarter	4th Quarter	Total
	$3,040,000	$270,000	$160,000	$140,000	$3,610,000
Property Aquisition	$1,500,000				
Property Improvements	$1,430,000	$270,000	$160,000	$140,000	$2,000,000
Fees/Interest	TBD				
Legal Fees	$10,000				$10,000
Real Estate Fees	$100,000				$100,000
Total	**$3,040,000**	**$270,000**	**$160,000**	**$140,000**	**$3,610,000**

Forecasted Balance Sheet (Year End)

Balance Sheet

Assets	Year One
Current Assets	
Cash & equivalents	$110,000
Property & investments	
Property	$1,500,000
Property investments	$2,000,000
Total Property & Investments	$3,500,000
Total Assets	**$3,610,000**

Forecasted Statement of Income (Year End)

Income Statement

	Year One	Year Two	Total
Net Revenues	$0	$0	$4,500,000
Expenses			
Property Acquisition	$1,500,000		
Property Improvement	$2,000,000		
Fees and Interest	TBD		
Legal Fees	$10,000		
Real Estate Fees	$100,000		
Total Expenses	$1,500,000		$2,110,000
Income from Operations			$2,390,000
Other Income Interest			
Income from Operations Before taxes		($1,500,000)	$2,390,000
Provisions for Income Taxes			$150,000
Net Income		**($1,500,000)**	**$2,240,000**

Forecasted Cash Flow (Year End)

Income Statement

	Year One	Year One
Proceeds from Loans	$3,610,000	$0
Cash Used in Start-up Activities	$3,040,000	
Purchase of Property	$1,500,000	$0
Property Improvements	$2,000,000	$0
Legal Fees	$10,000	$0
Real Estate Fees	$100,000	$0
Interest	TBD	TBD
Net Income from Operations		$4,500,000
Net Increase in Cash		
Cash at Beginning of Year		
Cash at Year End		

CONCLUSION

We have highlighted the most obvious concerns and opportunities relating to the development of the Seeley Estate as focused in this business plan. Other development projects not mentioned here can be addressed in the future. Revenues have not been projected or financially determined for any future additional development projects.

Please be reminded that all the financials and calculations have been based on a sale price that is twenty (20) dollars per square foot below the current industry average. We also have based all costs on the most conservative expenses available. Traditionally, experience has proven that we can easily expect to improve the profit margin by another 10%.

Should there be a major downturn in the market or an increase in some of the projected costs, neither of these occurrences should affect our ability to generate a profit on this project and provide security through assets at all times. We believe that all of our estimates are conservative enough to provide a profit even in the most extreme conditions.

The future holds well for ABC Corporation, where the unique quality of our renovations will be recognized in the marketplace and we will be able to grow through the reputation gained on this project.

This renovation can be achieved during the next eighteen months. It will be noted that once the project is completed, it will generate a conservative net profit for Harris Partners.

Accomplishments

The development of this estate is expected to conservatively generate a 20% profit in less than 18 months (probably in 12 months if we meet our target of selling the house before it is completed). Depending on the changes in scope that the prospective makes, and our ability to control the cost of the project, we should be able to increase the profit by up to an additional 15%.

The chart below provides an overview of the expected breakdown in real estate, forecasted hard costs, controllable costs, and sales price.

Distribution of Building Costs

Real Estate Costs	$1,500,000
Hard Improvement Costs	$1,450,000
Manageable Improvement Costs	$555,000

Objectives

The growth of the company will focus on obtaining a 20% profit on the first renovation project, then use this profit to fund other development projects.

Market Segments

The current market that the ABC Corporation will address is currently fragmented among new building, renovations, and knockdowns. The other two options are limited by the parcels of land to develop and the restrictions placed on rebuilding.

This distribution is based on all of the homes that are currently on the market and have sold year to date in the over two million dollar price range.

Distribution of Houses in This Price Range

New Construction	14
Renovations	7
Knock-Downs	2

The price per square foot for renovations is much higher than the price for new housing. In order to maintain a conservative estimate of the sales price, our project has been priced at the price per square foot for which the new homes are selling.

This price per square foot is based on all of the homes that are currently on the market and have sold year to date in the over two million dollar price range.

New Housing	$350.00
Renovations	$488.00

Price per Square Foot of Houses

The ABC Corporation's target market includes anyone that makes over one million dollars per year. The following chart, according to our research shows by profession how this market segment is broken down by profession within the Sacramento metropolitan area. High-Tech suppliers are the companies that sell products to the computer industry. Franchises are the owners of the four pizza companies in the area and major owners of the other franchises. Non high-tech represents the executives of other major companies located in Sacramento (i.e. XtraSys, Blackrock Systems, Barrek Homes).

Brokers are real estate, insurance , and stock brokers. Business owners indicate owners of small businesses and independently wealthy people.

Target Market

ABC Corporation's sole service is to develop a unique estate that can be marketed to a quantifiable market. There are currently only about 20 homes in this price range on the market to supply a market demand for over 85 families.

The number of families entering this market will be increasing which will make it easy to sell this estate for the premium price that it deserves.

Customer Profile

ABC Corporation should be able to sell the estate before the development has been completed.

The average number of days that homes over two million dollars were on the market in 1997 was 127 days. The chart below shows the trend of the average number of days to sell homes over two million dollars during the last five years.

1993	123
1994	206
1995	184
1996	190
1997	127

Sales Targets

Average Number of Days to Sell Homes

Rates are generally set by the average price per square foot of the homes being sold in the marketplace.

Pricing

We will utilize a variety of media to promote ABC Corporation.

Newspapers	50%
Magazines	25%
Brochures	18%
Newsletters	7%

Advertising

Distribution of Advertising Budget

Newspaper advertising will be the primary source of advertising on a consistent basis, augmented with magazines, newsletters, and print material.

Sales Promotions

Record Store

BUSINESS PLAN

HIDDEN TREASURE RECORDS L.C.

7145 Schilling Park Ave.
Northbrook, IL 60062

Identifying target customers is important for any business, and in this plan the entrepreneur actually creates a realistic hypothetical character sketch. The potential patron is clearly illustrated, providing evidence of the businessman's knowledge of his selected buyers. Entering into a niche market, the plan does an excellent job of illustrating the existence of demand and stating the desires of buyers, as well as how the business will fill the independent record label sales void in the area.

- PLAN SUMMARY

- PROBLEM STATEMENT

- BUSINESS DESCRIPTION

- RESUME

- MARKETING PLAN

- PROFIT AND LOSS FORECAST

- CAPITAL SPENDING PLAN

- FUTURE TRENDS

- RISK ANALYSIS

- PERSONAL GOAL STATEMENT

PLAN SUMMARY

This plan discusses opening a record store catering to the import and independent music buyer. It supports a loan request for $50,000.

Continuing changes in the dynamics of downtown Northbrook have resulted in a large growth within recent years in the number of people of all ages who enjoy shopping here. Primarily though, there is a high percentage of young people who come to Northbrook that like to purchase music, movies, clothes, coffee, antiques, and gifts. There is currently no store in Northbrook that adequately caters to this group's needs for a record store with a fairly priced, wide selection of imported and independent music. I propose to open Hidden Treasure Records to fill this gap. My goal is simple: to sell a wide selection of competitively priced music products to the alternative music connoisseur, and to provide a comfortable atmosphere for customers to listen to certain artists before purchasing their work.

My qualifications include over four years experience as a music buyer and assistant manager at both Atomic Records (previously in Northbrook) and Record Exchange in Bloomington, Illinois. During my tenure at Record Exchange, as the buyer for alternative import and independent music, I more than doubled sales from this department in less than two years. I achieved this by getting to know the market very well, catering to my customers' needs and pricing accordingly.

The funds I wish to borrow will be allocated to procure my initial inventory as well as equipment, fixtures, lease arrangements, advertising, and working capital as indicated in this proposal. I hope to open my store by May 1, 1997. I am committed both to serving the alternative music buying customers of Northbrook and beyond, and meeting my personal financial and career goals.

—March 1997

**PROBLEM
STATEMENT**

Many music consumers enjoy purchasing for collectability along with their passion for the music. I am one of these people. Many people have a hard time finding the things they want at existing chain and mall record stores. One major reason for this is that many record stores do not take the time to teach their employees to research the specialized nature of the market. These customers are also looking for convenience of location and fair market prices. Also, these people enjoy talking to someone who is knowledgeable, interested in the same types of music they want, and in what the store carries in general. In many cases, people will come from many miles away because there are few stores offering the same specific goods.

**BUSINESS
DESCRIPTION**

Hidden Treasure Records will be a retail music shop designed to serve the increasing number of consumers interested in import and independent music products. The store will buy music and accessories from a variety of distributors that provide good quality and dependable service along with fair return policies. Hidden Treasure Records will resell them "as is" to our target market. Hidden Treasure Records will specialize in new records and compact discs that are current, and some that are hard to find at existing music stores. The store will only carry a limited amount of used records and compact discs. We will carry accessories like stickers and blank audio cassettes.

Hidden Treasure Records will advertise occasionally in the regional weekly and monthly publications. These newspapers will be widely distributed, and cover an expansive and diverse reading audience. Hidden Treasure will advertise sale items, as well as promote specialized items, so as to broaden our customer base. We will rely heavily on walk-in and drive-by traffic as opposed to relying on advertising. Hidden Treasure Records will schedule occasional in-store appearances, along with promotions and giveaways as marketing devices.

Hidden Treasure Records will offer a relaxed atmosphere with personalized attention, and listening stations for compact discs along with a record player behind the counter so potential customers can listen before purchasing. Our store will be decorated in a simple, comfortable style, with chairs to sit in while reading a magazine or listening to a compact disc. Hidden Treasure's future employees will be knowledgeable about music in general, but even more so about the specific nature of what we carry. Hidden Treasure Records will be located in approximately 1,000-1,500 square feet in the downtown Northbrook district. The store will maintain regular hours of Monday through Saturday from 10:00 a.m. to 8:00 p.m., with the possibility of staying open later Thursday, Friday, Saturday night, and Sunday from 11:00 a.m. to 6:00 p.m. This location and these hours will be convenient to our customer base. Hidden Treasure Records will offer the opportunity for customers to special-order specific items if they are not in stock. Our store will also have a fax machine available to send and receive orders. We will also have a personal computer to offer goods through the Internet and, more specifically, the Hidden Treasure Records official web site where everything we have in stock will be posted and available for purchase by mail order. We expect it will take a little longer to generate sales through this method, as it will take longer to set up than the general store. Hidden Treasure Records will offer mail order service via UPS throughout the United States, and the world, for both computer and non-computer generated sales.

John Webster

EXPERIENCE

Owner, Hidden Treasure Records L.C., Northbrook, IL (1997)

- Started mail order business with intent to expand onto the Internet and start a retail store.

Assistant Manager, Atomic Records, Northbrook, IL (1994-1997)

Assistant Manager of independently owned record store with modest sales and absentee owner.

- Conceived and carried out promotional in store appearances which resulted in higher sales goals for that day.

- Developed inventory list for web site which resulted in higher sales.

- Created advertisements that were placed in a record collector's magazine, which increased mail-order sales for a continued period of time.

- Responsible for condensing distribution contacts which made for better working relationships and created economics of scale, providing a higher profit margin. Processed orders on a regular basis.

- Developed basic accounting skills by completing daily sales reports, and was responsible for balancing books on a daily basis. Deposited money daily.

Import/Independent Music Buyer, Record Exchange, Bloomington, IL (1992-1994)

Worked for chain retail record store with high-volume sales. Developed a comprehensive knowledge of import and independent music as buyer.

RESUME

- Implemented efficient inventory plan for import and independent section which help bminimize returns and maximize consistent sales.

- Increased sales in this department from 6% to 14% within two years. Maintained effective working relationships with many distributors.

- Processed orders and developed strong customer base, resulting in higher sales.

Assistant Manager, Record Exchange, Bloomington, IL (1993)
Managed high volume sales store when other managers were absent.

- Responsible for completing daily sales reports, opening and closing store, and making regular bank deposits.

- Delegated responsibility to sales staff and achieved high volume sales skills through marketing devices such as key product placement.

EDUCATION

Bachelor of Arts degree, Business Administration, University of Illinois, 1994

MARKETING PLAN

Typical Target Customer

Mike is 21 years of age with some college education. He is a cultured student, but works too, so he has plenty of money for entertainment: particularly music, books, movies, and shows. Mike is an intelligent, open minded, and unique individual, not your ordinary Top 40 radio music purchaser. Primarily, Mike spends most of his free time listening to music and reading magazines to keep updated on the music he enjoys. Although music is a hobby for Mike, it is something he takes very seriously. He collects rarities not only for listening pleasure, but also for their collectability and will search everywhere to find exactly what he wants. Mike likes going to shows frequently, and the best way for him to find out about them is to pick up the local alternative newspaper or visit a record store that posts fliers for upcoming music events. Mike also likes to give his business to independently owned stores whenever possible due to the comfortable, personalized shopping experience. Occasionally, Mike logs on to a friend's or the school's computer to search the Internet for other specialty shops carrying the items he is interested in.

Reaching the Target Customer

—Advertising in weekly newspapers
—Create mailing list for upcoming in-store appearances and periodic sales
—Enter notices in computer networks
—Place announcements in weekly newspapers
—Possible free promotion in form of an article in the local daily paper

Marketing Budget

Pre-Opening Promotion

— Flyer-full page and quarter page to scatter throughout key metro areas	$150
— Advertisement in weekly newspapers	$250-$500ea
— Grand Opening publicity from the Chicago Chamber of Commerce	$195
TOTAL	**$900-1,300**

Monthly Advertising

— Regular newsletters to mailing list detailing new release listening
   parties, sale items, and upcoming in-store appearances $50
— Advertising in weekly newspapers every other month or less $175
TOTAL   **$225 and up**

Competition

The northern Chicago area has four active record stores that will compete with Hidden Treasure Records.

1. Atomic Records: Although not located in Northbrook, its inventory competes most directly with Hidden Treasure's. Recently, it has suffered from high employee turnover. Atomic also has high prices, and its quantity of current releases has been lacking, primarily because of a decrease in business due to its relocation. Hidden Treasure will differ from Atomic by being in a highly visible location, offering a wider selection at lower prices, and having a friendly staff and atmosphere.

2. Cool Beats: This record store has been a Northbrook staple for a number of years. It offers a wide selection of fairly priced items. It also contains listening stations for people to sit down and sample the music before purchasing. The main difference between Cool Beats and Hidden Treasure is that they do not specialize in the same product lines. Also, their interior space is limited. Cool Beats has recently moved from Schilling Park Avenue to First Street. This would make Hidden Treasure the sole record store on Schilling Park.

3. Surrounded by Sound: This is also a very popular store in the northern Chicago area. Its basic problem is that it lacks a proficient sales staff. It also has a crowded, unorganized interior. Hidden Treasure will take particular pride in its customer friendly environment and knowledgeable staff. Hidden Treasure Records also plans to be very competitive with prices on items that are also carried by Surrounded by Sound. They, however, also cater to a different music consumer than Hidden Treasure—they do not carry the off-the-wall, hard-to-find, trendsetting products that Hidden Treasure will specialize in.

4. Underground Records: This is a very convenient store for the one-stop shopper. They carry all types of music, along with having a Ticketmaster machine. Underground Records also has a computerized special ordering system, which is very helpful. A major fault of Underground Records is that they have high prices. One major benefit for Hidden Treasure is that they are not located in the downtown Northbrook area. Also, Hidden Treasure will offer much greater personalized service, and have an efficient special ordering system of its own that should satisfy the customer with the most particular of tastes.

PROFIT AND LOSS FORECAST

Profit and Loss Forecast-Year One

	May	June	July	Aug	Sep	Oct	Nov
Sales Revenue	11,620	13,280	18,260	17,430	19,920	17,430	19,920
Less COS 65%	-7,553	-8,632	-11,869	-11,330	-12,948	-11,330	-12,948
Gross profit 35%	4,067	4,648	6,391	6,100	6,972	6,100	6,972
Fixed Expenses:							
Wages	1,667	1,667	1,667	1,667	1,667	1,667	1,667
Payroll Tax	235	235	235	235	235	235	235
Rent/Lease	1,800	1,800	1,800	1,800	1,800	1,800	1,800
Marketing & Advertising	250	250	250	250	250	250	250
Insurance	35	35	35	35	35	35	35
Accounting	0	0	0	0	0	0	0
Int. Expense							
Depreciation							
Utilities	100	100	100	100	100	100	100
Telephone	300	300	300	300	300	300	300
Supplies	66	66	66	66	66	66	66
Freight	60	60	60	60	60	60	60
Misc.	100	100	100	100	100	100	100
Less: Total Fixed Exp	4,613	4,613	4,613	4,613	4,613	4,613	4,613
Profit/(Loss)	**-546**	**35**	**1,778**	**1,487**	**2,359**	**1,487**	**2,359**

Dec	Jan	Feb	March	April	Year Total	As a %
23,240	11,620	13,280	16,600	17,430	200,030	100%
-15,106	-7,553	-8,632	-10,790	-11330	-130,021	65%
8,134	4,067	4,648	5,810	6,100	70,009	35%
1,667	1,667	1,667	1,667	1,667	20,004	10%
235	235	235	235	235	2,820	1.41%
1,800	1,800	1,800	1,800	1,800	21,600	10.80%
250	250	250	250	250	3,000	1.50%
35	35	35	35	35	420	0.21%
0	0	0	0	0	0	0%
100	100	100	100	100	1,200	0.60%
300	300	300	300	300	3,600	1.80%
66	66	66	66	66	792	0.40%
60	60	60	60	60	720	0.36%
100	100	100	100	100	1,200	0.60%
4,613	4,613	4,613	4,613	4,613	55,356	27.67%
3,521	-546	35	1,197	1,487	14,653	7.32%

Profit and Loss Forecast-Year Two

	May	June	July	Aug	Sep	Oct	Nov
Sales Revenue	22,166	21,203	20,239	19,275	20,239	19,275	21,203
Less COS 65%	-14,407	-13,782	-13,155	-12,530	-13,155	-12,530	-13,782
Gross profit 35%	7,759	7,421	7,084	6,745	7,084	6,745	7,421
Fixed Expenses:							
Wages	2,364	2,364	2,364	2,364	2,364	2,364	2,364
Payroll Tax	331	331	331	331	331	331	331
Rent/Lease	1,800	1,800	1,800	1,800	1,800	1,800	1,800
Marketing & Advertising	205	205	205	205	205	205	205
Insurance	36	36	36	36	36	36	36
Accounting	0	0	0	0	0	0	0
Int. Expense							
Depreciation							
Utilities	103	103	103	103	103	103	103
Telephone	308	308	308	308	308	308	308
Supplies	62	62	62	62	62	62	62
Freight	77	77	77	77	77	77	77
Misc.	103	103	103	103	103	103	103
Less: Total Fixed Exp	5,389	5,389	5,389	5,389	5,389	5,389	5,389
Profit/(Loss)	**2,370**	**2,032**	**1,695**	**1,356**	**1,695**	**1,356**	**2,032**

Inflation 2.8% added to each figure from year 1.

Dec	Jan	Feb	March	April	Year Total	As a %
25,057	13,493	14,455	15,420	19,275	231,300	100%
-16,287	-8,769	-9,395	-10,023	-12,530	-150,345	65%
8,770	4,724	5,060	5,397	6,745	80,955	35%
2,364	2,364	2,364	2,364	2,364	28,368	12.26%
331	331	331	331	331	3,972	1.72%
1,800	1,800	1,800	1,800	1,800	21,600	9.34%
205	205	205	205	205	2,460	1.06%
36	36	36	36	36	432	0.19%
0	0	0	0	0	0	0%
103	103	103	103	103	1236	0.53%
308	308	308	308	308	3,696	1.60%
62	62	62	62	62	744	0.32%
77	77	77	77	77	924	0.40%
103	103	103	103	103	1,236	0.53%
5,389	5,389	5,389	5,389	5,389	64,668	27.96%
3,381	**-665**	**-329**	**8**	**1,356**	**16,287**	**7.04%**

**Profit and Loss
Forecast-Year Three**

	May	June	July	Aug	Sept	Oct	Nov
Sales Revenue	25,122	24,030	22,937	21,845	22,937	21,845	24,030
Less COS 65%	-16,330	-15,620	-14,909	-14,199	-14,909	-14,199	-15,620
Gross profit 35%	8,792	8,410	8,028	7,646	8,028	7,646	8,410
Fixed Expenses:							
Wages	2,848	2,848	2,848	2,848	2,848	2,848	2,848
Payroll Tax	399	399	399	399	399	399	399
Rent/Lease	1,950	1,950	1,950	1,950	1,950	1,950	1,950
Marketing & Advertising	180	180	180	180	180	180	180
Insurance	37	37	37	37	37	37	37
Accounting	0	0	0	0	0	0	0
Int. Expense							
Depreciation							
Utilities	106	106	106	106	106	106	106
Telephone	334	334	334	334	334	334	334
Supplies	63	63	63	63	63	63	63
Freight	93	93	93	93	93	93	93
Misc.	106	106	106	106	106	106	106
Less: Total Fixed Exp	6,116	6,116	6,116	6,116	6,116	6,116	6,116
Profit/(Loss)	**2,676**	**2,294**	**1,912**	**1,530**	**1,912**	**1,530**	**2,294**

Inflation 2.8% added to each figure from year 2.

Dec	Jan	Feb	March	April	Year Total	As a %
28,398	15,291	16,384	17,476	21,845	262,140	100%
-18,458	-9,540	-10,649	-11,359	-14,199	-170,391	65%
9,940	5,351	5,735	6,117	7,646	91,749	35%
2,848	2,848	2,848	2,848	2,848	34,176	13.04%
399	399	399	399	399	4,788	1.83%
1,950	1,950	1,950	1,950	1,950	23,400	8.93%
180	180	180	180	180	2,160	0.08%
37	37	37	37	37	444	0.02%
0	0	0	0	0	0	0%
106	106	106	106	106	1,272	0.49%
334	334	334	334	334	4,008	1.53%
63	63	63	63	63	756	0.29%
93	93	93	93	93	1116	0.42%
106	106	106	106	106	1,272	0.49%
6,116	6,116	6,116	6,116	6,116	73,392	28%
3,924	-765	-381	1	1,530	18,357	7%

CAPITAL SPENDING PLAN

This is a list of all the necessary expenses for opening and operating Hidden Treasure Records L.C.

Inventory	$20,000
Computer and Printer	3,200
Outside Sign	3,000
Fixtures and Counter	3,500
Alarm System	1,000
Advertising	1,200
Stereo System	1,000
Interior Lighting	500
Phone System	350
Cash Register	250
Listening Stations	1,500
City Permits and Fees	250
Supplies	2,500
Working Capital	11,750
TOTAL CAPITAL	**$50,000**

Other capital items, such as furniture and the fax machine, have already been paid for.

FUTURE TRENDS

There are two conflicting trends affecting my business. First, more consumers are purchasing through the Internet. However, there is still a percentage of the population without access to this technology. They prefer to personally visit stores and shop. Hidden Treasure Records L.C. will accommodate both types of consumers by having a retail store and a web site.

Second, large media and bookstores carry a wide selection of music. As a result, Hidden Treasure Records will concentrate heavily on the latest trends in music and the more obscure items not likely to be found in the larger stores.

RISK ANALYSIS

Like every new business, Hidden Treasure Records L.C. faces risks. I believe I can overcome each risk with the actions discussed below, and Hidden Treasure can thrive for many years.

Here are the major risks I anticipate and how I plan to deal with them:

1. **Thin Capitalization**

   The primary risk we face is thin capitalization. This meaning our inventory may have to turn over more than the average record store. This will be compensated by the specialized nature of new products. This creates a sense of urgency to purchase goods before they go out of print and become unavailable to our consumer. A second problem with thin capitalization lies with sales volume projections. If these are not met for the first year, the small working capital reserves may be inadequate. On the positive side, we believe our sales projects are very conservative and we will have little trouble meeting and exceeding them. Also, we have had several potential customers express an interest in specifically shopping at our store. In addition, by starting with relatively modest capital, our loan payments will be smaller.

2. **Slow Times**

   A secondary risk is slow times. The proposed site experiences very slow times during the first few months of the year. Having worked in the area before, I am aware of this and will set aside money from profitable months to cushion against such down time. Also by keeping overhead low, primarilyin the number of employees, I should be able to reduce the effect of slow times.

3. Competition

There is a slight risk with competition, two records stores within downtown Northbrook. However, most of what Hidden Treasure will carry is unavailable at these other shops. Proper pre-opening promotion and regular advertising, along with a helpful, knowledgeable, and friendly staff will attract our target customers. A similar store, Replay Records, thrived at this location for six years, confirming a large existing market.

4. Owner's Ability

I have never operated an independent business before, however, I have managed a similar store with an absentee owner. I can see no insurmountable problems resulting from being on my own. I already have an accountant, lawyer, and the advice of a retired family member who built a million dollar business. I have taken steps toward my goal by filing Hidden Treasure Records L.C. as a business, opening accounts with distributors, and achieving profits through a small customer base.

In short, I believe that I have addressed the major risks facing my business and have demonstrated that those risks are manageable.

PERSONAL GOAL STATEMENT

I want to accomplish a number of goals by starting Hidden Treasure Records. I want to prove that I can operate a successful and worthwhile business by drawing on my educational background and experience. I feel that choosing and selling alternative music at a fair price will be an honest service to my customers and the community in general. I want to spend my time working with customers and people in the music industry who share my values.

Finally, I want the chance to make a better living than I can make by working for others, along with the responsibility and freedom to be my own boss.

Retail Art Furnishings Business

BUSINESS PLAN   WOOD DESIGNS GALLERY

75711 Cherokee Dr.
Springfield, MA 01101

Considering most businesses take longer to hit full stride than expected, this plan is a fine example of how to illustrate awareness of this fact. The entrepreneurs outline various recourses for possible problems, proving they are realistic and prepared for the unexpected. Note the clearly stated per day sales breakdown necessary to break even, establishing a readable gauge of success.

OUR MISSION

A huge market exists in the in retail art furnishings business serving affluent customers who appreciate fine art and Native American design. People whose incomes fall in the $80,000 to $150,000 range often aspire to own high quality decorative art, but they are not necessarily interested in owning an art collection that is usually priced beyond their means. It is very hard for consumers in this particular market segment to locate a broad selection of truly accessible art that is appealing to them. High priced furniture stores and interior decorators do a fine job of providing this type of art, but it is usually not available in the retail setting and placed directly in front of the customer. This is the problem that the Wood Designs Gallery proposes to solve.

COMPANY OVERVIEW

The solution to the consumer retail problem posed above is simply this: to sell fine quality serialized and commercially produced artwork for consumers in the $200-1,200 dollar range. Wood Designs Gallery's competitive advantage will lie in the fact that it will have a huge selection of framed, ready-to-hang artwork available for the discriminating consumer. As a sideline to ensure variety and a component draw, Wood Designs Gallery will also sell approved Native American art and sculptures. We have a source for high quality Native American art produced by a certified Native American artist who will sell us art and sculptures at a very low wholesale price. Wood Designs Gallery also plans to offer its art to interior decorators at slightly reduced prices. This should ensure a steady flow of interior design specialists to our location. This would be convenient for them and allow them to have more selection and variety than what they would find in larger, wholesale outlets. Another niche sideline would be for sales of local artists who wish to produce exclusive pieces for sale in our store. They would provide art for a fraction of what they could normally be purchased, and any artist who developed a reputation would have several pieces of his work set aside as promotional pieces for the store.

SERVICES, LOCATION AND TIMING

Wood Designs Gallery will be located in the Timberland Mall shopping center, in the heart of Springfield, Massachusetts. Farber and Associates, the mall's landlord and developer, have approved the site selection. The space approved is premium space and the rental cost will be just under $4,000 per month. The timing for the project is critical and if initial financing is made available, Wood Designs Gallery will open this fall in time for the expected rush of holiday shoppers.

Project Timeline:

> May—Obtain initial financing and secure all funds for development.
> June—Refurbish site of current store and install shelving for sculptures. Obtain registers and charge authorizations.
> July—Procure initial inventories and have it in place for opening day.
> August—Make sure store has positive initial publicity.
> September—Grand opening sale.

MARKET STRATEGY

The market goal of Wood Designs Gallery is to become known as the leading source of decorative art for households and the decorative trade in the area. The market appeal will come from creating the appearance of fine quality art available exclusively through us and through the presentation of the art and the expertise of the staff. Within three years from the start of the business, Wood Designs Gallery wishes to become widely known as a leading source of home and office decorative furnishings. Within five years, the goal will be to become a clearinghouse for local artists and a one-stop store for interior decorators. This appeal will come from our unique approach to the business and by providing decorative items in a greater variety than any other single store in Massachusetts. The same comparable merchandise can currently be found in furniture stores and framing studios, but there is little or no expert advice available in such stores. Customers find themselves entirely on their own and usually have to make many visits to find exactly what they are looking for. Customers at Wood Designs Gallery will be assisted so that they have a sense of competence and sophistication associated with their selections. Repeat business will come in the form of customers needing additional pieces for their homes and interior decorators who need a local source for their furnishings. There are over 120 interior decorators in the area and each one will be heavily marketed. Bringing one interior decorator back time and time again will make our market strategy much stronger and far more successful.

Market Background

There is an extensive market background for Wood Designs Gallery to draw inspiration from. Decorative wall hangings are commonly sold in furniture stores and art galleries. The nature of the latter varies from traditional galleries carrying "fine art" to retail establishments stocked with cheap prints. Fine art is outside our scope because of the inherent investment value placed with the art itself. Galleries that sell this kind of fine art earn 30-50% of the sale price in commission. Shops selling prints and mass-produced "original" art are generally a special kind of furniture store. Their product is distributed through wholesalers and generally marked up about 100%. Such galleries often posture themselves as being more artistic than they really are and try to appear as fine art galleries. Yet, most of these stores only handle a few paintings and prints, which they classify as accessories. When professional decorators purchase paintings and prints for their clients, wholesalers who specialize in the accessory end of the furniture business supply these products. Wholesalers tend to be clustered in larger cities, so decorators from our area have trouble getting to them on a consistent basis.

Serving the Customer

Our customer needs a wide selection of traditional wall decorations with a few exotic pieces to round out their upper- middle-class lifestyle. Customers who are affluent, but not wealthy, generally do not wish to take the time and expense of hiring a decorator for something so simple, but they want something better than can be found in a print shop. Even though the furniture stores carry the appropriate merchandise, the selection is too limited to be useful. This means that retail customers are also hard put to find a wide selection to choose from without going to a major trade center. Information from the last census put over 47,000 people fitting our customer profile within a thirty-mile radius of Timberland Mall. While there is a newer mall being built in the next county, Timberland Mall has recently undergone a multi-million dollar expansion and renovation and is located close to our target customers. Both of these malls are premium locations, but Timberland has a proven track record to support their estimates of daily traffic. Mall management has informed us that we can expect mall traffic in excess of 5,000 people during non-peak days and 20,000 people during peak shopping periods.

The Competition

Located within thirty miles of Timberland Mall are two major shopping malls, a small downtown shopping zone, and several strip malls. There are ten major furniture stores offering a variety of furnishings, twelve small art galleries, and three combination art/frame shops. The availability, price, and quality characteristics of these businesses are summarized in the following chart:

Type	Number	# in Stock	Range/Quality
Furniture Stores	10	25	50-350/Excellent
Furniture Depts.	5	22	40-200/Good
Art Galleries	12	200+	35-200/Fair
Combinations	3	75+	55-300/Fair

Our analysis indicates that none of these competitors provide a substantial challenge for what we are intending to do. Only the furniture stores offer comparable products, but not in large enough quantities to meet demand. The art galleries typically deal in the lower-end merchandise, usually with a contemporary theme. Their market is the young household or apartment. This is also true of the frame shops and all of the other combination galleries. Finally, none of these stores offer any meaningful advice or help to their clients, something the market is sadly lacking.

Business Categories

Wood Designs Gallery will operate three distinct lines of business:

A. Retail

The bulk of our business will be retail. We will sell product purchased through wholesalers to the general public. This business is expected to gross approximately $10,000 per month at the onset and grow to about $30,000 per month over three years, after which time it is expected to level off.

B. Interior Decorators

Interior decorators will account for our second line of business. These decorators will be offered goods at a professional discount of 35% off list price. They can then either save their own clients money or keep the difference. Early expectations for this portion of the market are modest. Sales are planned to increase from nothing to about $3,000 per month over three years and perhaps 5,000 per month after five years. Some of the items offered to the decorators will be of a finer quality than those sold directly to the retail market, so the margin for some of these items will be smaller initially.

C. Local Artists

Local artists are a good draw for the store. Many people like to own art that comes from someone they know or someone who lives in the same city that they do. Total sales of approximately $1,000 per month have been allotted to this segment with a sales commission rate of 33%. Several artists have agreed to have their work exhibited with Wood Designs Gallery. Periodic showings of original work are also planned to increase exposure for the store.

ADVERTISING

The retail customer will be contacted through direct mail advertising and localized insertions in the *Springfield Press*. General advertising will be restricted to the small segment of the population in our target market. The professional decorator market will be targeted through direct mailings and possibly some follow-up phone calling by staff during non-peak hours. A special event will be held for the decorating trade at some point and will likely coincide with an artists showing. Wood Designs Gallery will also work to attract bigger name artists with large followings and will dovetail efforts with companies such as Northwest Galleries to provide serialized lithographs and auction quality art whenever possible.

Pricing

The following pricing and breakeven analysis is based on the core retail business alone, because the other lines are more high risk and we wish to show that the core business is viable.

Two major factors go into the pricing guidelines: quality and size. Sizes are quoted, but exclude the width of the frame. A 24" x 36" sofa piece provides the benchmark for pricing. Decorators will normally carry such pieces in the $250-800 price range with the smaller pieces being commensurately less expensive. The price range per size is shown below:

24" x 36"	$250-800
20" x 24"	$125-275
18" x 20"	$100-225
9" x 12"	$50-125

It is generally assumed that more of the smaller articles will be sold (based on prior experience) and the mixture of sales is expected to be along the lines of the chart shown below:

24" x 36"	15%
20" x 24"	25%
18" x 20"	20%
9" x 12"	40%

The largest percentages of sales are expected to be with the smallest pieces. That is due to the fact that customers tend to purchase them individually or in groupings and they also tend to be the items most likely to be an impulse buy. Overall, the average sale is expected to be in the neighborhood of $175 at the retail list rate. This amount could vary greatly if a large, artist commissioned sale took place.

Profit Margin

The usual retail mark-up for art sold in furniture stores is 100%, or twice the total wholesale cost of the item. This factor is mitigated by the fact that as much as 30% of a typical retailer's business is done at discounted sale prices in order to accelerate the impulse buying factor. The average discount for this 30% of business is 20%. Therefore, the average discount on all sales is calculated as 70% at list (100 x .70 = 70) and 30% at 20% off list (80 x .30 = 24) giving us an average sale made at 94% of list or an across-the-board 6% discount. If the cost is 50% of list, the cost ratio is 50/94 or 53.2% giving us a gross margin percent of 46.8%. This profit margin of 46.8% is considered to be fairly standard in the industry and a good indicator of where our expectations are placed.

Our Breakeven Point

Since the only expected variable cost is the wholesale cost of the product, the contribution margin is also 46.8%. With this in mind, we need to take a look at our estimated fixed costs on a monthly basis:

Rent	$3,947
Utilities	350
Depreciation	364
Insurance	150
Advertising	1,500
Interest	750
Salaries	6,402
Total	**$13,463**

This means that our breakeven volume is as follows: our fixed cost of $13,463 divided by our margin of .468 gives us a breakeven of $28,767 and assuming the average sale will be $175 or more, we need to make roughly 165 sales per month to equal $28,875. This translates into roughly 5.5 sales per day, which should be considered as reasonable for a busy, high volume mall location.

OPERATIONS

The merchandising advantage of Wood Designs Gallery comes from our wholesale distributors. We have several preliminary agreements signed with wholesale distributors in the area. Northwest Galleries will be our main supplier in the Massachusetts area. They are well known in the wholesale art industry and they have a wide selection of prints, seriographs, lithographs, and animated cells. Many are hand-signed and numbered and some art may sell for much higher than the average list price if the artist is considered a hot commodity. The initial agreements involve paying cash at full wholesale prices. After six months of successful business, however, credit will be extended on a limited basis. Discounts may also be available based on volume.

Fixed Costs

Timberland Mall rental rates are in the neighborhood of $25-40 per square foot. This is the total aggregate cost and there are no fees except for a 10% mall take of any business in excess of $400,000 per year. For adequate display space, Wood Designs Gallery will require approximately 1,500 square feet of space. Timberland Mall has space available at a prime location for $3,947 per month. There is a free one-month preparation period and a deposit of the first month's rent required for the move.

Leasehold Improvements

The only significant improvement to be made involves signage and track lighting. Parker Electric has bid the cost of hanging display lights at $1,800. Signage has been quoted as $2,300 by Acme Signs. Other improvements are estimated to cost less than $2,500 and involve minor touchups to paint and facade replacement. The display of wall hangings will require that some of the space be broken up into bays to increase the available wall area. This can be done with removable partitioning and a preliminary floor plan indicates that it can be accomplished with relative ease. Counters, registers, and partitioning should cost less than $6,500. The total cost of all improvements will be $13,100. This cost will be depreciated over the life of the anticipated three-year lease. The monthly depreciation cost will therefore be $364 over the three-year period. Miscellaneous costs include incorporation and banking fees, deposits, permits, licenses, and grand opening costs. All of these are anticipated to amount to $5,300 and are expensed in the financial projection section.

Terms of Sale

Sales will be paid with cash, check, or credit card. The professional interior decorators will be offered sixty days to pay, based upon prior credit approval. This is expected to be the only way to get their business, as they have to wait until their customers pay them. A check approval service has already been found to handle check collections and a credit account will be set up to handle Visa, MasterCard, American Express, etc.

Inventory Levels

Since we are selling variety as the cornerstone of our business, a large inventory will have to be maintained to back up our promise. Initial stock will include approximately 450 pieces at a total cost of $40,000. About one third of these will be on display in the showroom while the remainder will be kept in back. We can open with $25,000 and build to $40,000 within three months of opening. Fast sellers can be replaced overnight if that becomes a necessity.

BUSINESS ORGANIZATION

Wood Designs Gallery will be incorporated as a subchapter S corporation. The business will be owned and operated by Neal and Melanie Armstrong.

Neal Armstrong is currently an employee of IBM and works as a risk manager for the company. Neal will continue to work at IBM and provide a stable income for the household in addition to working part-time and on weekends at the store. Neal will handle the books and finances of Wood Designs Gallery and provide a quarterly revision to this plan. Neal graduated from University of Massachusetts in 1975 and served proudly as a lieutenant in the U.S. Army from 1968-69 in Vietnam.

Melanie Armstrong is currently the customer service manager in the furnishings department of ABC Furniture at Fullerton Mall. Melanie plans to quit her present position and run Wood Designs Gallery full-time. She has twelve years of experience in the furniture industry and has worked extensively in the interior decorating trade since graduating from college in 1976. She has a lifelong interest in traditional and contemporary art and has spent a great deal of time learning about Native American art and lifestyle. Melanie graduated from Boston University with a degree in marketing and was a merit scholar finalist her senior year.

Employees

Wood Designs Gallery will employ two additional staff members to help with inside sales. One person can be a relatively unskilled clerk, but one must have some prior experience with home furnishings and/or art. While Melanie is working, only the clerk will be required to assist. The pay for these positions will range from $8.00 to $10.00 per hour and will be either full- or part-time. Assuming benefits at a rate of 15% per employee, the total cost for payroll and benefits with a manager, sales consultant, and clerk will be $6,402. Melanie will not take a salary the first six months of operation. This will reduce payroll to $3,987 during the first six months of operation.

Contingency Plans

In the event that the business has a slower start-up than anticipated, expenses may be reduced as follows:

1. Melanie may work up to two years without a salary, as the main source of household income will still be available.
2. The sales consultant position can be eliminated, producing savings of over $2,000 per month.
3. Inventory can be reduced by $20,000 overall and that will save in both inventory expenses and the interest expense of $300 per month.
4. All new interior decorating business can be shifted to a cash basis to improve cash flow.
5. Licensing agreements could be implemented with several artists to bring in their entire line at significant cost savings.

These quantified savings can reduce operating expenses by a total of $5,107 per month and this would in turn reduce the monthly breakeven volume in the core business by $10,912 to $17,855. This would entail a significant reduction in sales and would mean that the store would have to sell just over 100 items per month. That reduces the sales volume to a mere 3.3 sales per day, obtainable by virtually any standard within the industry.

FINANCIAL ASSUMPTIONS

The following financial projections are based on sales forecasts in the three distinct areas of activity mentioned previously. The core business is the retail sale of commercially produced artwork to consumers. Sales to decorators and sales of original work by local artists are forecast separately. Each forecast is stated in terms of an equivalent "average" unit, that is, the hypothetical unit that represents a weighted average of the sizes and qualities sold. Implicit in the use of an average unit is the assumption that the size mix of product within each line will remain constant over time. It is a simple matter to change that assumption or to forecast each size individually. The use of an average unit makes the buildup of revenue and cost considerably easier to follow.

Averages:

	Price	Cost	Margin
Retail	$165	$88	46.8%
Decorator	$195	$150	23.1%
Originals	$500	$333	33.3%

The retail price reflects an average discount of 6% from list while the decorator figure represents a 35% discount. All projections are presented by month for the first year and by quarter for the following year.

Profitability

Sales the first year are expected to be approximately $250,000. These sales are expected to grow to $422,000 in the second year. At $500,000 in sales, the business will generate profits of approximately $58,000 for a return on sales of 11.6%. Wood Designs Gallery is expected to lose money at a decreasing rate during the first year of operation while it builds a customer base. Profitability will improve until the end of the third year, when it will level off along with the expected sales volume.

Loan Request

The business can open with less than $22,000 in borrowed funds. At that point, the debt to equity ratio will be 48% debt to 52% equity. The loan request will be used to set up the business and enable it to operate the first full year. Since the projected cash flow turns positive after nine months, bank borrowing will peak in the ninth month at just under $62,000. Subsequent to that time, the loan will be steadily reduced by operating cash flows until it is entirely repaid during the second quarter of the third year.

This page left intentionally blank to accommodate tabular matter following.

APPENDIX

Unit Sales and Revenue - First Year by Month

MONTHS		1	2	3	4	5	6
Retail Trade Units		100	60	70	80	90	100
Avg Price	$165 (Discounted)						
Revenue		$16,500	9,900	11,550	13,200	14,850	16,500
Cost	0.532	$8,778	5,267	6,145	7,022	7,900	8,778
G.M.		$7,722	4,633	5,405	6,178	6,950	7,722
Decorator Trade Units		0	1	2	2	3	4
Avg Price	$195 (Discounted)						
Revenue		0	195	390	390	585	780
Cost	0.769	0	150	300	300	450	600
G.M.		0	45	90	90	135	180
Local Artists Units		2	3	4	4	4	5
Avg Price	$500 (Discounted)						
Revenue		$1,000	1,500	2,000	2,000	2,000	2,500
Cost	0.667	$667	1,001	1,334	1,334	1,334	1,668
G.M.		$333	500	666	666	666	833

7	8	9	10	11	12	TOTAL
110	120	130	140	150	150	1,300
18,150	19,800	21,450	23,100	24,750	24,750	$214,500
9,656	10,534	11,411	12,289	13,167	13,167	$114,114
8,494	9,266	10,039	10,811	11,583	11,583	$100,386
5	5	7	9	10	11	59
975	975	1,365	1,755	1,950	2,145	$11,505
750	750	1,050	1,350	1,500	1,650	$8,847
225	225	315	405	450	495	$2,658
5	5	6	6	6	6	56
2,500	2,500	3,000	3,000	3,000	3,000	$28,000
1,668	1,668	2,001	2,001	2,001	2,001	$18,676
833	833	999	999	999	999	$9,324

Balance Sheet - First Year by Month

MONTHS	Opening	1	2	3	4	5
ASSETS						
Cash	$5,000	$5,000	$5,000	$5,000	$5,000	$5,000
Accounts Receivable	$0	$0	$0	$195	$390	$390
Inventory	$25,000	$30,000	$35,000	$40,000	$40,000	$40,000
Current Assets	$30,000	$35,000	$40,000	$45,195	$45,390	$45,390
Deposits	$3,500	$3,500	$3,500	$3,500	$3,500	$3,500
FIXED ASSETS						
Gross	$13,100	$13,100	$13,100	$13,100	$13,100	$13,100
Accum Depr	$0	($364)	($728)	($1,092)	($1,456)	($1,820)
Net	$13,100	$12,736	$12,372	$12,008	$11,644	$11,280
Total Assets	$46,600	$51,236	$55,872	$60,703	$60,534	$60,170
LIABILITIES						
Accounts Payable	$0	$0	$0	$0	$2,885	$3,228
Current Liabilities	$0	$0	$0	$0	$2,885	$3,228
Debt	$21,600	$33,189	$43,520	$53,213	$54,323	$56,998
Equity	$25,000	$18,047	$12,352	$7,490	$3,326	($56)
Total L & E	$46,600	$51,236	$55,872	$60,703	$60,534	$60,170

6	7	8	9	10	11	12
$5,000	$5,000	$5,000	$5,000	$5,000	$5,000	$5,000
$585	$780	$975	$975	$1,365	$1,755	$1,950
$40,000	$40,000	$40,000	$40,000	$40,000	$40,000	$40,000
$45,585	$45,780	$45,975	$45,975	$46,365	$46,755	$46,950
$3,500	$3,500	$3,500	$3,500	$3,500	$3,500	$3,500
$13,100	$13,100	$13,100	$13,100	$13,100	$13,100	$13,100
($2,184)	($2,548)	($2,912)	($3,276)	($3,640)	($4,004)	($4,368)
$10,916	$10,552	$10,188	$9,824	$9,460	$9,096	$8,732
$60,001	$59,832	$59,663	$59,299	$59,325	$59,351	$59,182
$5,523	$6,037	$8,634	$9,641	$15,640	$16,668	$16,818
$5,523	$6,037	$8,634	$9,641	$15,640	$16,668	$16,818
$56,948	$60,306	$60,838	$61,747	$57,162	$56,691	$56,858
($2,469)	($6,511)	($9,809)	($12,089)	($13,477)	($14,008)	($14,493)
$60,001	$59,832	$59,663	$59,299	$59,325	$59,351	$59,182

Income Statement - First Year by Month

MONTHS	1	2	3	4	5	6	7
ASSETS							
Revenue	$17,500	$11,595	$13,940	$15,590	$17,435	$19,780	$21,625
Cost	$9,445	$6,417	$7,779	$8,656	$9,684	$11,045	$12,073
Gross Margin	$8,055	$5,178	$6,161	$6,934	$7,751	$8,735	$9,552
Expenses							
Rent	$3,947	$3,947	$3,947	$3,947	$3,947	$3,947	$3,947
Salaries	$3,987	$3,987	$3,987	$3,987	$3,987	$3,947	$6,402
Advertising	$1,500	$1,500	$1,500	$1,500	$1,500	$1,500	$1,500
Util/Insur	$500	$500	$500	$500	$500	$500	$500
Depreciation	$364	$364	$364	$364	$364	$364	$364
Start Up Exp	$4,300						
Total	$14,598	$10,298	$10,298	$10,298	$10,298	$10,298	$12,713
EBIT	($6,543)	($5,120)	($4,137)	($3,364)	($2,547)	($1,563)	($3,161)
Interest	$410	$575	$725	$800	$835	$850	$880
PBT	($6,953)	($5,695)	($4,862)	($4,164)	($3,382)	($2,413)	($4,041)
Tax	$0	$0	$0	$0	$0	$0	$0
PAT	($6,953)	($5,695)	($4,862)	($4,164)	($3,382)	($2,413)	($4,041)

Dividend

8	9	10	11	12	TOTAL
$23,275	$25,815	$27,855	$29,700	$29,895	$254,005
$12,951	$14,462	$15,640	$16,668	$16,818	$141,637
$10,324	$11,353	$12,215	$13,032	$13,077	$112,368
$3,947	$3,947	$3,947	$3,947	$3,947	$47,364
$6,402	$6,402	$6,402	$6,402	$6,402	$62,334
$1,500	$1,500	$1,500	$1,500	$1,500	$18,000
$500	$500	$500	$500	$500	$6,000
$364	$364	$364	$364	$364	$4,368
					$4,300
$12,713	$12,713	$12,713	$12,713	$12,713	$142,366
($2,389)	($1,360)	($498)	$319	$364	($29,998)
$910	$920	$890	$850	$850,	$9,495
($3,299)	($2,280)	($1,388)	($531)	($486)	($39,493)
$0	$0	$0	$0	$0	$0
($3,299)	($2,280)	($1,388)	($531)	($486)	($39,493)
					$0

Cash Flow Statement - First Year by Month

MONTHS	1	2	3	4	5	6
Cash from Operating Activities						
PAT	($6,953)	($5,695)	($4,862)	($4,164)	($3,382)	($2,413)
Depreciation	$364	$364	$364	$364	$364	$364
Decr/(Incr) in A/R	$0	$0	($195)	($195)	$0	($195)
Decr/(Incr) in Inv	($5,000)	($5,000)	($5,000)	$0	$0	$0
Incr/(Decr) in A/P	$0	$0	$0	$2,885	$343	$2,295
Cash from Ops	($11,589)	($10,331)	($9,693)	($1,110)	($2,675)	$50
Cash from Investing Activities						
Decr(Incr) in Fixed Assets	$0	$0	$0	$0	$0	$0
Cash from Financing Activities						
Incr/(Decr) in Debt	$11,589	$10,331	$9,693	$1,110	$2,675	($50)
Dividend	$0	$0	$0	$0	$0	$0
Case from Fin	$11,589	$10,331	$9,693	$1,110	$2,675	$50
Net Cash Flow	$0	($0)	$0	$0	($0)	$0
Beginning Cash Balance	$5,000	$5,000	$5,000	$5,000	$5,000	$5,000
Net Cash Flow	$0	($0)	$0	$0	($0)	$0
Ending Cash Balance	$5,000	$5,000	$5,000	$5,000	$5,000	$5,000

7	8	9	10	11	12	TOTAL
($4,041)	($3,299)	($2,280)	($1,388)	($531)	($486)	($39,493)
$364	$364	$364	$364	$364	$364	$4,368
($195)	($195)	$0	($390)	($390)	($195)	($1,950)
$0	$0	$0	$0	$0	$0	($15,000)
$514	$2,597	$1,007	$5,998	$1,028	$150	$16,818
($3,358)	($532)	($909)	$4,585	$471	($167)	($35,258)
						$0
$0	$0	$0	$0	$0	$0	$0
						$0
$3,358	$532	$909	($4,585)	($471)	$167	$35,258
$0	$0	$0	$0	$0	$0	$0
$3,358	$532	$909	($4,585)	($471)	$167	$35,258
$0	$0	($0)	$0	($0)	$0	$0
$5,000	$5,000	$5,000	$5,000	$5,000	$5,000	
$0	$0	$0	($0)	($0)	$0	
$5,000	$5,000	$5,000	$5,000	$5,000	$5,000	

Unit Sales and Revenue - Second Year by Quarter

QUARTERS		1	2	3	4	TOTAL
Retail Trade Units		475	500	550	600	2,125
Avg Price	165 (discounted)					
Revenue		78,375	82,500	90,750	99,000	$350,625
Cost	0.532	41,695.50	43,890	48,279	52,668	$186,533
G.M.		36,679.50	38,610	42,471	46,332	$164.093
Decorator Trade Units		33	35	38	40	146
Avg Price	195 (discounted)					
Revenue		6,435	6,825	7,410	7,800	$28470
Cost	0.769	4,948.52	5,248.43	5,698.29	5,998.20	$21893
G.M.		1,486.48	1,576.58	11,711.71	1,801.80	$6577
Local Artists Units		20	21	22	23	86
Avg Price	500 (discounted)					
Revenue		10,000	10,500	11,000	11,500	$43,000
Cost	0.667	6,670	7,003.50	7,337	7,670.50	$28,681
G.M.		3,330	3,496.50	3,663	3,829.50	$14,319

Balance Sheet - Second Year by Quarter

QUARTERS	1	2	3	4
ASSETS				
Cash	$5,000	$5,000	$5,000	$5,000
Accts Receivable	$2,145	$2,145	$2,275	$2,470
Inventory	$40,000	$40,000	$40,000	$40,000
Current Assets	**$47,145**	**$47,145**	**$47,275**	**$47,470**
Deposits	$3,500	$3,500	$3,500	$3,500
FIXED ASSETS				
Gross	$13,100	$13,100	$13,100	$13,100
Accum Depr	($5,460)	($6,552)	($7,644)	($8,736)
Net	**$7,640**	**$6,548**	**$5,456**	**$4,364**
Total Assets	$58,285	$57,193	$56,231	$55,334
LIABILITIES				
Accts Payable	$17,771	$18,714	$20,438	$22,112
Current Liabs	**$17,771**	**$18,714**	**$20,438**	**$22,112**
Debt	$54,150	$48,871	$38,428	$23,423
Equity	($13,636)	($10,392)	($2,636)	$9,799
Total L & E	**$58,285**	**$57,193**	**$56,231**	**$55,334**

Cash Flow Statement - Second Year by Quarter

QUARTERS	1	2	3	4	Total
Cash from Operating Activities					
PAT	$857	$3,244	$7,757	$12,434	$24,292
Depreciation	$1,092	$1,092	$1,092	$1,092	$4,368
Decr/(Incr) in A/R	($195)	$0	($130)	($195)	($520)
Decr/(Incr) in Inv	$0	$0	$0	$0	$0
Incr/(Decr) in A/P	$954	$943	$1,724	$1,674	$5,295
Cash from Ops	$2,708	$5,279	$10,443	$15,005	$33,435
Cash from Investing Activities					
Decr/(Incr) in Fixed Assets	$0	$0	$0	$0	$0
Cash from Financing Activities					
Incr/(Decr) in Debt	($2,708)	($5,279)	($10,443)	($15,005)	($33,435)
Dividend	$0	$0	$0	$0	$0
Cash From Fin	($2,708)	($5,279)	($10,443)	($15,005)	($33,435)
Net Cash Flow	$0	$0	$0	$0	$0
Beginning Cash Balance	$5,000	$5,000	$5,000	$5,000	$20,000
Net Cash Flow	$0	$0	$0	$0	$0
Ending Cash Balance	$5,000	$5,000	$5,000	$5,000	$20,000

Income Statement - Second Year by Quarter

QUARTERS	1	2	3	4	TOTAL
Revenue	$94,810	$99,825	$109,160	$118,300	$422,095
Cost	$53,314	$56,142	$61,314	$66,337	$237,107
Gross Margin	$41,496	$43,683	$47,846	$51,963	$184,988
Expenses					
Rent	$11,841	$11,841	$11,841	$11,841	$47,364
Salaries	$19,206	$19,206	$19,206	$19,206	$76,824
Advertising	$4,500	$4,500	$4,500	$4,500	$18,000
Util/Insur	$1,500	$1,500	$1,500	$1,500	$6,000
Depreciation	$1,092	$1,092	$1,092	$1,092	$4,368
Total	$38,139	$38,139	$38,139	$38,139	$152,556
EBIT	$3,357	$5,544	$9,707	$13,824	$32,432
Interest	$2,500	$2,300	$1,950	$1,390	$8,140
PBT	$857	$3,244	$7,757	$12,434	$24,292
Tax	$0	$0	$0	$0	$0
PAT	$857	$3,244	$7,757	$12,434	$24,292
Dividend					$0

Shave Ice Business

BUSINESS PLAN   ICE DREAMS

12700 Maria St.
El Centro, CA 92244

This plan does an excellent job of touting the location of the proposed small business as a key to success. High exposure due to automotive and pedestrian traffic, a climate-suited product, and a business shaped to the neighborhood's preferences assure prospective lenders that this venture will have every opportunity to succeed. This plan was compiled using Business Plan Pro, by Palo Alto Software.

- EXECUTIVE SUMMARY

- COMPANY SUMMARY

- PRODUCTS

- MARKET ANALYSIS SUMMARY

- STRATEGY AND IMPLEMENTATION SUMMARY

- MANAGEMENT SUMMARY

- FINANCIAL PLAN

SHAVE ICE BUSINESS
BUSINESS PLAN

EXECUTIVE SUMMARY

Ice Dreams will sell shave ice as its primary product in addition to soft drinks and frosty Latin drinks called licuados. Shave ice is the hottest new dessert since frozen yogurt. Shave ice is heating up rapidly and shows no sign of cooling (Crystal Fresh, Inc., 1995).

Shave ice has been around for many years, beginning in Asia, then becoming popular in Hawaii. People would shave ice by hand, creating a cold, flaky snow. Then they'd top it with fruit juices to create a refreshing treat. Something this good couldn't remain a secret. In recent years, the taste for shave ice has spread all over the world.

Shave ice is much different than a sno-cone in that it is made by a small counter-top machine that shaves ice rather than grinding it like a sno-cone machine, which results in ice so fine that it rivals real snow. The snow is then placed in a bowl or cup and filled with high quality tropical fruit flavors. Because the snow is so soft the syrup is held within its tender texture versus settling to the bottom like traditional sno-cones. Since the syrup is absorbed into the snow, it must be eaten with a spoon instead of a straw.

Because shave ice is so tender and made with the thickest, best-tasting tropical fruit flavors, it is a preferred treat of adults and children of all ages and ethnic backgrounds.

A drive-through business will be built on privately owned commercial property on Highway 86 (Adams Avenue) in El Centro, California. Other products which will be incorporated into the business including beverages (soft drinks and licuados).

Business Objectives

Our business objectives are:

1. To construct a drive-through building (12' x 20') on existing privately owned commercial property (50' x 120').
2. To produce a net profit of at least $50,000 by the third year of operation.
3. To sell 20 different tropical and Mexican flavored syrups.
4. To sell other products such as soft drinks and licuados.

Mission

Ice Dreams will produce and sell shave ice with 20 different flavored syrups, soft drinks, and licuados to consumers in El Centro, California. Retail customers will be in the low- to mid-range income bracket, and will span in age from children to adults.

Keys to Success

The keys to success are that:

1. This will be the first business of its kind in the city of El Centro, California.
2. This business will be located on a major city highway, next to several housing developments, the city pool, near schools and parks, and along a major restaurant and motel strip.
3. Product quality will include a large variety of tropical and Mexican flavored syrups.
4. Business has the potential for expansion into other Imperial County communities.
5. The city of El Centro experiences warm to hot weather approximately seven months of the year.
6. Two-way traffic on Highway 86 averages 48,300 vehicles on a daily basis.

Ice Dreams will be known for selling shave ice with 20 different tropical and Mexican flavored syrups to children and adults in El Centro, California. Other products will include soft drinks and licuados.

Ice Dreams will be owned by Ofelia R. Arellano as a sole proprietorship.

Start-up costs will be approximately $52,010, which will include facility construction, including sidewalks, parking, inventory, mandatory city permits, and other expenses associated with opening this business. The start-up costs will be financed through a loan. Detailed information follows regarding permit requirements, equipment, construction costs, and land improvements required to open this new business.

Start-Up Expenses

Consultants	$100
Insurance	$1,200
Other	$34,710
Total Start-up Expense	$36,010

START-UP ASSETS NEEDED
Start-up

Cash Requirements	$10,000
Start-up inventory	$1,325
Other Short-term Assets	$675
Total Short-term Assets	$12,000
Long-term Assets	$4,000
Total Assets	$16,000
Total Start-up Requirements	**$52,010**
Left to Finance	$0

START-UP FUNDING PLAN
Investment

Investor 1	$0
Other	$10,000
Total investment	$10,000

SHORT-TERM LIABILITIES

Unpaid Expenses	$0
Short-term Loans	$42,010
Interest-free Short-term Loans	$0
Subtotal Short-term Liabilities	$42,010
Long-term Liabilities	$0
Total Liabilities	$42,010

Loss at Start-up	($36,010)
Total Capital	($26,010)
Total Capital and Liabilities	$16,000
Checkline	$0

Company Locations and Facilities	Ice Dreams will be located on Highway 86 in El Centro, California, which experiences a high volume of traffic on a daily basis. According to a study by Cal Trans (*Traffic Volumes*, 1995), approximately 48,300 vehicles pass through this location on a daily basis, making it an ideal location for business. The majority of traffic enters and exits via Imperial Avenue and Fourth Avenue traveling through Highway 86.

A 240-square-foot drive-through facility will be built on privately owned commercial property, which will also include parking facilities, landscaping, and a small sitting area. Other major businesses located on Highway 86 include Carl's Jr., Roberto's Restaurant, La Fonda Restaurant, Raging Bull Restaurant, China Restaurant, Donut Shop, Steak House, Big John gas station, Recreation Center, and several motels.

The appendices provide additional information on the company facilities, a tentative plot plan, and highlights of the traffic study conducted by Cal Trans.

PRODUCTS

Main products to be sold through the Ice Dreams business will be shave ice topped with tropical and Mexican flavored syrups in three main sizes: small, medium, and large. Other products will include three soft drinks (Sprite, Coke, and Diet Coke), and licuados.

Product Description

One major product will be sold through Ice Dreams: shave ice topped with tropical and Mexican flavored syrups. Twenty different tropical and Mexican flavored syrups will be sold and include the following:

> Wild Watermelon, Pina Colada, Pink Lemonade, Guava Grape, Cherry Jubilee, Root Beer, Kiwi, Strawberry, Blue Bubble Gum, Orange Mango, Raspberry Red, Luscious Lime, Bodacious Banana, Tamarindo, Jamaica, Hortacha, Melon, Papaya, Manzana, and Limon.

Other products will include soft drinks in three flavors: Coke, Diet Coke, and Sprite, and licuados in three flavors (strawberry, banana, and mango).

Competitive Comparison

No other business in El Centro specifically caters to the shave ice market on a large scale. It is anticipated that prices will be competitive with other businesses that sell shave ice on a smaller basis.

Sales Literature

Sales literature to be distributed to the general community will include fliers, advertisement in the local newspaper (*Imperial Valley Press*), and other print media.

Sourcing

Ice Dreams will purchase products from Crystal Fresh, Inc. which manufactures and distributes high-quality syrups and ice shavers. All equipment and supplies are available through a regional distributor. Mexican flavored syrups will be purchased in Mexicali, Baja California, Mexico.

Future Products

It is anticipated that 10-15 additional syrups will be added, such as Spearmint, Black Cherry, Cinnamon, Blueberry, Peach, Red Apple, Tutti Frutti, Coconut, Cola, Green Apple, Tangerine, and Vanilla. Also, future products to be sold will include ice cream in vanilla and chocolate flavors.

El Centro is geographically situated at the junction of major east-west and north-south transportation routes. El Centro is also referred to as the "center of opportunity" with benefits created by the North American Free Trade Agreement (NAFTA) becoming one of southern California's most promising new commercial/industrial areas.

El Centro is accessible via Interstate 8, State Highway 111, and State Highway 86, where Ice Dreams will be located.

Shave ice is an ideal business for El Centro given the potential market segment, location, and climate. Utilizing averaged priced units ($1.25) for shave ice and other products to be sold, the shave ice business has the potential market of $104,446 gross sales by the third year of operation.

MARKET ANALYSIS SUMMARY

According to *Advertising Age* (September 1995), premium ice cream and frozen yogurt products are losing market share to mid-priced and other frozen dessert products. *Information Resources* reported that frozen ice products comprised a third of the $2.4 billion ice cream category for the year ending May 21, 1995, generating $717.7 million, up 9.3% from the previous year.

Based on this information, it is anticipated that the frozen dessert market can be divided into two customer segments. The first segment prefers premium ice cream and frozen yogurt products. The other segment obviously includes those that prefer frozen ice products. Shave ice products are ideal for today's health-conscious consumers. They boast no fat, no cholesterol, and are relatively low in calories.

Ice Dreams will target all segments of El Centro's population: children, teenagers, and adults. The Hispanic population will be of special interest since it comprises 65% of El Centro's total population. This population will be targeted with Mexican flavored syrups and licuados.

Market Segmentation

Ice Dreams will target the low- to mid-income consumers who want to have a high quality dessert for moderate prices. Ice Dream's shave ice meets the quality required by these customers since it will also cater to the large Latino population in El Centro with its Mexican flavored syrups.

Target Market Segment Strategy

One of the best-known shave ice businesses is Sno Biz Shave Ice under the parent company of Crystal Fresh, Inc. Dealerships such as Sno Biz have demonstrated the success and feasibility of selling shave ice. The Sno Biz dealership has been in existence for the last 11 years with over 3,000 individual dealerships throughout the United States. Sno Biz syrup products are also sold in Wal Marts throughout the country. While no Sno Biz dealership currently exists in California, Sno Biz products are sold at the San Diego Zoo, Lion Country Safari, and the San Diego Military base with great success. The potential success for selling shave ice is attributed to the following:

Industry Analysis

1. Compared to other food service products, Ice Dreams will be a relatively simple business to operate.
2. Shave ice is similar to a Mexican favorite called raspado, but because it is softer and tastier, it is preferred over raspados.
3. Shave ice has a low food cost and is easy to prepare, which keeps speed-of-service at optimum levels to keep up with high-traffic volumes.
4. Ice Dreams will be easy to maintain and clean.

5. Shave ice is a product that has yielded a considerable profit in terms of cost to produce at $0.16.

6. Shave ice is an ideal product for the health-conscious consumer.

Market research conducted in El Centro did surface one raspado (sno-cone) business on a small scale called "Snow Shack" located on State Street. Snow Shack consists of a small trailer that accommodates only one employee. Sno-cones are sold in cups at prices ranging from $1.00 (small), $1.25 (medium) to $1.50 (large).

Sno-cones were also found to be sold at Garcia's Food Market and Wal-Mart. Each sold sno-cones in one regular size at $1.00 each.

Research conducted in Bullhead City, Arizona noted that the Sno Biz dealership only sells shave ice as their primary product. Shave ice units sold for $1.25 (small), $1.75 (medium) to $2.25 (large) per unit. In interviewing the current owner, he indicated that during his first year in business he was selling 200 units per day.

Research in San Diego, California revealed that shave ice is sold along with other products. Several businesses in Mission Bay sold shave ice with prices ranging from $1.79 (small), $1.99 (medium) and $2.39 (large). In terms of licuados, prices were $2.79 (regular) and $3.15 (large).

Research conducted in Honolulu, Hawaii, showed that in some locations, shave ice sold as high as $5.00 for a regular size. However, the majority of sno-cones were sold by the flavor and not necessarily by the size. For example, one flavor was $1.79, two flavors were $2.29, and three flavors sold for $2.79.

Industry Participants

The shave ice industry in El Centro, California currently has no key players since no other business of this type currently exists in the Imperial Valley.

Competition and Buying Patterns

The shave ice business will be new to El Centro. Competitors in this type of business primarily sell raspados or sno-cones and do not focus on the shave ice market. One major competitor is the "Snow Shack" located on State Street. Snow Shack sells sno-cones through a small, one-person trailer with limited choices of syrups. Other competitors sell sno-cones through Garcia's Market and the Wal-Mart store which also have limited syrup selections and do not necessarily focus on the sno-cone or shave ice industry as their primary product.

The keys to success will definitely focus on selling shave ice and not sno-cones made with coarse ice and selling high quality syrups. Prices will also be competitive with those of the competition.

Main Competitors

Main competitors include the Snow Shack, Garcia's Market, and Wal-Mart. The following are strengths and weaknesses of each.

Snow Shack

Strengths: The main strength of Snow Shack is that it is the only business in El Centro that caters to the sno-cone market. It also has very reasonable prices.

Weaknesses: The primary weakness of Snow Shack is that it does not sell shave ice but rather sno-cones made from very coarse ice. Syrups are also not of good quality.

Garcia's Market

Strengths: The main strength of sno-cones sold by Garcia's Market is their low price of $1.00 and the convenience to the shopper in buying sno-cones while doing their shopping.

Weaknesses: The main weakness of sno-cones sold by Garcia's Market is that they do not sell quality syrups and prefer to sell the more inexpensive brand with lower quality taste.

Wal-Mart

Strengths: Main strength of sno-cones sold by Wal-Mart is the convenience to the shopper and low price.

Weaknesses: Wal Mart's weakness, like Garcia's Market, is that they do not sell quality syrups. Also, the sno-cone business is not their primary focus or product.

Ice Dreams is planning for slow growth by expanding flavors available from 20 to 30 in year two of operation. Also, an additional product to be sold in year two will include ice cream in flavors of vanilla and chocolate.

STRATEGY AND IMPLEMENTATION SUMMARY

Ice Dream's overall marketing strategy will be to create an image of offering the highest quality shave ice in Imperial County. The business will be located in a high traffic area of El Centro. Customers will be reached through advertisements such as fliers, newspaper ads, and through its grand opening ceremonies.

Marketing Strategy

A special marketing program will also be incorporated by offering special coupon prices for nearby restaurants, motels, city pool, the donut shop, and the gas station to customers who purchase any product at Ice Dreams.

Distribution of shave ice will be through the business facility only. It is anticipated that in the future, a small portable ice shaver will be purchased such that the product could be sold on site at various fundraising functions through churches, schools, etc.

Positioning Statement

Shave ice will be offered at the following prices:

Pricing Strategy

Small $1.00
Medium $1.25
Large $1.50

Soft Drinks
Regular $0.79
Large $0.99

Licuados
Regular $1.35

Products will be sold on a cash basis only.

Promotion Strategy	Ice Dreams will promote shave ice to customers by:

1. Flier distribution to consumers' homes within a five-mile radius.
2. Newspaper advertisements will be purchased during the first three months of business until a clientele is built.
3. Ice Dreams will offer discounts to recreational groups such as children/adult baseball and football teams who play in nearby facilities.
4. Promoting products for an introductory price at its Grand Opening.
5. Ice Dreams will "adopt a school" and provide shave ice to individuals who are selected for having excellent attendance, good grades, and good citizenship. Other incentives will include sponsoring a good attendance program by purchasing a bike and raffling it to students with the best attendance. This will be a promotional strategy to encourage business.

Marketing Programs

Major marketing will be conducted through newspaper advertisements and local flier distribution during the first three months of operation. Total costs will be approximately $500.

Sales Strategy

Sales strategy will be directly linked to marketing programs since all sales will be through the business facility only.

Sales Forecast

Consumer sales will start in January 1997 (or sooner if construction is completed before targeted date) with its grand opening anticipated by then. As indicated, primary sales will occur during the peak warm weather months.

Sales	1997	1998	1999
Sales	$52,217	$77,383.00	$104,446.00
Other	$0	$0	$0
Total Sales	**$52,217**	**$77,383**	**$104,446**
Direct Cost of Sales			
Sales	$12,114	$17,772	$24,227
Other	$0	$0	$0
Subtotal Cost of Sales	**$12,114**	**$17,772**	**$24,227**

MANAGEMENT SUMMARY

Ice Dreams will hire an employee to assist with the business. Ice Dreams will require minimum daily supervision after it has been established since all three products are fairly easy to make.

Organizational Structure

Ofelia R. Arellano, the owner, will have one individual assisting her with the business. Long-range plans will include a second employee to assist with the weekend hours.

Management Team

Ofelia R. Arellano is the most important member of the management team. Dr. Arellano is a graduate of the University of California, Santa Barbara with several advanced degrees (Masters and Doctorate in Psychology). She has spent the last six years working as an administrator overseeing a budget of approximately $800,000. Ofelia will oversee the business primarily during the weekend hours and her husband, Frank Arellano, will oversee the business during weekdays along with one employee.

Business expertise include:

Budget Control
  History Based Budgeting
  Object-Code Budgeting
  Program Budgeting
  Planned Programming Budgeting Systems

Personnel Management
  Management by Goals and Objectives

Strategic Planning
  Long-Range Planning
  Total Quality Management
  Operational Planning

Public Relations
  Advertising for Educational Purposes
  Marketing Research
  Consulting

Community Leadership
  Advisory Boards
  Business and Educational Partnerships

City Planning and Development
  Board of Director, San Ysidro Planning and Development Group

Business Needs Assessment and Consultation
  Board of Directors, San Ysidro Chamber of Commerce

Frank Arellano will serve as a consultant on a volunteer basis. Mr. Arellano spent over 35 years in the retail business, handling marketing and inventory for a major food chain. He is familiar with all aspects of business management and operations having owned and operated his own grocery store in El Centro. Mr. Arellano will also assist in the building design, landscaping layout, and business marketing. Mr. Arellano will supervise the business during the weekdays, which means managing one employee.

With such a small staff, payroll expenditures will only total $13,200 for the first year.

Personnel Plan

Personnel	1997	1998	1999
Assistant	$10,800	$11,232	$11,681
Other	$0	$0	$0
Other	$0	$0	$0
Total Payroll	**$10,800**	**$11,232**	**$11,681**
Total Headcount	0	0	0
Payroll Burden	$2,484	$2,583	$2,687
Total Payroll Expenditures	**$13,284**	**$13,815**	**$14,368**

FINANCIAL PLAN

We want to finance growth mainly through cash flow. We recognize that this means we will have to grow slowly. The most important indicator in our case is that minimal inventory will have to be stored for these products.

Important Assumptions

Monthly sales are the largest indicator for this business. There are some seasonal variations, with the months of March through September being the highest sales months.

General Assumptions

	1997	1998	1999
Short-term Interest Rate %	13.50%	13.50%	13.50%
Long-term Interest Rate %	0.00%	0.00%	0.00%
Payment Days Estimator	30	30	30
Inventory Turnover Estimator	12	12	12
Tax Rate %	30.00%	30.00%	30.00%
Expenses in Cash %	0.00%	0.00%	0.00%
Sales on Credit %	0.00%	0.00%	0.00%
Personnel Burden %	23.00%	23.00%	23.00%

Breakeven Analysis

The operation will require sales of approximately $2,900 to break even during the first year of operation.

Breakeven Analysis

Monthly Units Breakeven	2,500
Monthly Sales Breakeven	$2,900

Assumptions

Average Per-Unit Revenue	$1.16
Average Per-Unit Variable Cost	$0.36
Estimated Monthly Fixed Cost	$2,000

Projected Profit and Loss

We expect a profit of $6,740 in year one, $19,212 in year two, and $32,886 in year three of operation.

	1997	1998	1999
Sales	$52,217	$77,383	$104,446
Direct Cost of Sales	$12,114	$17,772	$24,227
Other	$0	$0	$0
Total Cost of Sales	**$12,114**	**$17,772**	**$24,227**
Gross Margin	$40,103	$59,611	$80,219
Gross Margin %	76.80%	77.03%	76.80%
OPERATING EXPENSES			
Advertising/Promotion	$600	$624	$649
Travel	$450	$468	$487
Miscellaneous	$0	$0	$0
Other	$360	$374	$389
Payroll Expense	$10,800	$11,232	$11,681
Payroll Burden	$2,484	$2,583	$2,687
Depreciation	$2,196	$2,284	$2,375
Leased Equipment	$0	$0	$0

	1997	**1998**	**1999**
Utilities	$1,720	$1,789	$1,861
Insurance	$1,200	$1,248	$1,298
Rent	$0	$0	$0
Other	$0	$0	$0
Contract/Consultants	$0	$0	$0
Total Operating Expenses	**$19,810**	**$20,602**	**$21,427**
Profit Before Interest and Taxes	$20,293	$39,009	$58,792
Interest Expense Short-term	$5,672	$5,672	$5,672
Interest Expense Long-term	$0	$0	$0
Taxes Incurred	$4,386	$10,001	$15,936
Net Profit	$10,235	$23,336	$37,184
Net Profit/Sales	**19.60%**	**30.16%**	**35.60%**

Projected cash flow is estimated as follows for the next three years:

1997 - $31,715
1998 - $63,931
1999 - $109,900

	1997	**1998**	**1999**
Net Profit	$10,235	$23,336	$37,184
PLUS			
Depreciation	$2,196	$2,284	$2,375
Change in Accounts Payable	$1,266	$365	$374
Current Borrowing (repayment)	$3	$0	$0
Increase (decrease) Other Liabilities	$0	$0	$0
Long-term Borrowing (repayment)	$10,500	$10,500	$10,500
Capital Input	$0	$0	$0
Subtotal	**$24,200**	**$36,485**	**$50,433**
LESS	1997	1998	1999
Change in Inventory	($1,013)	$146	$166
Change in Other Short-term Assets	$0	$0	$0
Capital Expenditure	$0	$0	$0
Dividends	$0	$0	$0
Subtotal	**($1,013)**	**$146**	**$166**
Net Cash Flow	$25,213	$36,339	$50,267
Cash Balance	$35,213	$71,553	$121,820

The balance sheet shows a slow but steady upward growth in net worth after initial start-up as follows:

1997: ($19,272)
1998:   ($61)
1999: $32,825

Projected Cash Flow

Pro-Forma Cash Flow

Projected Balance Sheet

Pro-Forma Balance Sheet

ASSETS	Starting Balances	1997	1998	1999
Short-term Assets				
Cash	$10,000	$35,213	$71,553	$121,820
Inventory	$1,325	$312	$458	$624
Other Short-term Assets	$675	$675	$675	$675
Total Short-term Assets	$12,000	$36,200	$72,685	$123,119
Long-term Assets				
Capital Assets	$4,000	$4,000	$4,000	$4,000
Accumulated Depreciation	$0	$2,196	$4,480	$6,855
Total Long-term Assets	$4,000	$1,804	($480)	($2,855)
Total Assets	**$16,000**	**$38,004**	**$72,205**	**$120,264**
LIABILITIES AND CAPITAL				
Accounts Payable	$0	$1,266	$1,632	$2,005
Short-term Notes	$42,010	$42,013	$42,013	$42,013
Other Short-term Liabilities	$0	$0	$0	$0
Subtotal Short-term Liabilities	$42,010	$43,279	$43,645	$44,018
Long-term Liabilities	$0	$10,500	$21,000	$31,500
Total Liabilities	$42,010	$53,779	$64,645	$75,518
Paid in Capital	$10,000	$10,000	$10,000	$10,000
Retained Earnings	($36,010)	($36,010)	($25,775)	($2,439)
Earnings	$0	$10,235	$23,336	$37,184
Total Capital	**($26,010)**	**($15,775)**	**$7,561**	**$44,745**
Total Liabilities and Capital	$16,000	$38,004	$72,205	$120,264
Net Worth	($26,010)	($15,775)	$7,561	$44,745

Business Ratios

Ratio Analysis

Standard business ratios show a plan for balanced healthy growth.

PROFITABILITY RATIOS	1997	1998	1999	RMA
Gross Margin	76.80%	77.03%	76.80%	0
Net Profit Margin	19.60%	30.16%	35.60%	0
Return on Assets	26.93%	32.32%	30.92%	0
Return on Equity	0.00%	308.64%	83.10%	0
ACTIVITY RATIOS				
AR Turnover	0	0	0	0
Collection Days	0	0	0	0
Inventory Turnover	14.8	46.18	44.79	0
Accts Payable Turnover	14.72	15.05	15.6	0
Total Asset Turnover	1.37	1.07	0.87	0
DEBT RATIOS				
Debt to Net Worth	0	8.55	1.69	0
Short-term Liab. to Liab.	0.8	0.68	0.58	0
LIQUIDITY RATIOS				
Current Ratio	0.84	1.67	2.8	0
Quick Ratio	0.83	1.65	2.78	0
Net Working Capital	($7,079)	$29,041	$79,100	0
Interest Coverage	3.58	6.88	10.37	0

ADDITIONAL RATIOS	1997	1998	1999	RMA
Assets to Sales	0.73	0.93	1.15	0
Debt/Assets	142%	90%	63%	0
Current Debt/Total Assets	114%	60%	37%	0
Acid Test	0.83	1.65	2.78	0
Asset Turnover	1.37	1.07	0.87	0
Sales/Net Worth	0	10.23	2.33	0

Small Producer

BUSINESS PLAN

SALVADOR SAUCES, INC.

7243 Franklin St.
Perrysburg, OH 43551

This business plan is a fine example of a small producer looking to expand aggressively. The course of action is superbly detailed and the owners' expectations are clearly stated, leaving no mystery about their vision. The ethnic authenticity of the product is demonstrated and then touted as the key to the business's success. This plan was compiled using Business Plan Pro, by Palo Alto Software.

- EXECUTIVE SUMMARY

- COMPANY SUMMARY

- PRODUCTS

- MARKET ANALYSIS SUMMARY

- STRATEGY AND IMPLEMENTATION SUMMARY

- MANAGEMENT SUMMARY

- FINANCIAL PLAN

**EXECUTIVE
SUMMARY**

By focusing on its heritage and the strength it brings into the products, their quality, and uniqueness, Salvador Sauces will increase its sales to more than $2 million by the year 2000, while improving the gross margin on sales cash management and working capital.

This business plan leads the way. It renews our vision and strategic focus on the quality and value we put in our products and the market segment originally targeted. Our vision has been broadened by the success we have found in the marketplace, to the extent of adding new products and current plans on additional items and services. It has given us a step-by-step plan to meet and exceed our goals for increased sales, gross margin, and profitability.

This plan includes this summary, chapters on the company, products and services, market focus, action plans and forecasts, management team, and financial plan.

Business Plan Highlights

	Sales	Gross	Net
1996	$168,602	$103,685	$67,818
1997	$217,320	$130,392	$49,920
1998	$312,052	$187,231	$59,911

Objectives

1. Increase sales to more than $1 million over the next three years.
2. Move gross margin to above 55% over the current product line and maintain that level.
3. Add products and services to meet market demand, again at 55% margin or above.
4. Sell $2 million of salsa and related Hispanic food items and service by 2000.
5. Improve inventory turnover, reduce the cost of goods sold while maintaining the high quality of the products.
6. To provide jobs to the Hispanic community that are rewarding and fulfilling.

Mission

Salvador Sauces was built on offering the highest quality and value in its authentic hot salsa, filled with the history of the Hispanic community. Time-honored family recipes have been passed down through generations, rich with ethnic heritage. Knowledgeable consumers were looking for authentic products, filled with the best ingredients. The consumer was crying out for a change. They wanted real down-home Hispanic salsa.

Salvador Sauces answered this call, first with its hot salsa, then adding mild and extra hot salsa, followed by yellow and blue corn chips. Constantly striving to supply what the consumer is asking for, we continually review what is available in the marketplace, and what is not. Improving on what is available and providing new products and services to the areas of need will assure our success in a market driven by consumer demand.

Keys to Success

1. Delivering high quality products that set themselves apart from the others in taste and value.
2. Providing service, support, and a better than average margin to our dealers.
3. Increase gross margin to over 55%.
4. Bring new products into the mix to increase sales volume.

Salvador Sauces is in its third year of operation, increasing sales five-fold in its second year, and is on track to repeat this in its third year. It has a good reputation, excellent people, an increasing position in the local market, and opportunities to reach out into other states. Starting with a few outlets for our products, we now have over 40, with two large grocery chains in the approval process of carrying our full line of products, and a large distributor intending to sell over $100,000 worth of our products annually.

Salvador Sauces is a privately held C Corporation owned in total by its co-founders, Ricardo and Pat Torres.

Salvador Sauces has been hindered only by the lack of working capital it had in its initial stages of setup and operation. Sales are growing steadily, with the cost of goods sold consistently decreasing. But to make significant headway in this area, additional capital is needed to purchase ingredients and processing in larger volumes, thereby reducing the costs of goods sold in excess of 32% overall.

Past Performance	1993	1994	1995
Sales	$0	$4,224	$21,050
Gross Margin	$0	$2,451	$14,160
Gross % (calculated)	0.00%	58.03%	67.27%
Operating Expenses	$0	$12,028	$20,719
Collection period (days)	0	10	15
Inventory turnover	0	6	5

BALANCE SHEET

Short-term Assets

Cash	$0	$0	$126
Accounts receivable	$0	$0	$0
Inventory	$0	$0	$3,492
Other Short-term Assets	$0	$0	$0
Total Short-term Assets	$0	$0	$3,618
Long-term Assets			
Capital Assets	$0	$0	$23,368
Accumulated Depreciation	$0	$0	$9,792
Total Long-term Assets	$0	$0	$13,576
Total Assets	$0	$0	$17,194

CAPITAL AND LIABILITIES

Accounts Payable	$0	$0	$0
Short-term Notes	$0	$0	$16,207
Other ST Liabilities	$0	$0	$0
Subtotal Short-term Liabilities	$0	$0	$16,207
Long-term Liabilities	$0	$0	$0
Total Liabilities	$0	$0	$16,207
Paid in Capital	$0	$0	$25,000
Retained Earnings	$0	$0	($9,755)
Earnings	$0	$0	($14,258)
Total Capital	$0	$0	$987
Total Capital and Liabilities	$0	$0	$17,194

OTHER INPUTS	1993	1994	1995
Payment days	0	0	0
Sales on credit	$0	$0	$0
Receivables turnover	0	0	0

Company Locations and Facilities

Currently we have one location in suburban Perrysburg, Ohio. It includes the production area, offices, and warehouse area. We are currently looking into plans to increase the size of the warehouse by adding a location, and providing a storefront to enhance the current business sales practices, while providing a high quality, ethnic outlet for Hispanic foods.

PRODUCTS

Salvador Sauces sells its authentic Hispanic salsa and chips to an ever-growing clientele. Originally geared toward the local Hispanic community, the market has expanded to include a much larger geographical area, in addition to a very broad consumer response.

We are selling quality and product-uniqueness in a market segment filled with competition. Our approach is to take our product image up-market because of our rich heritage and uncompromising view of product quality. This focus has enabled us to view the voids in the market and add product to our line that will fill it. We have researched and reviewed other ethnic food item organizations, tracking their successes and positioning ourselves similarly.

Salvador Sauces is building a reputation for high quality and strong value in a product filled with authentic Hispanic flavor. We service our dealers just as if they were a part of the family and that is our unique approach to marketing our products. You are not just a dealer, not just a consumer, you are special to us—you are family. We go to great lengths to provide our dealers with high quality products and the ability to make a good margin on them. In addition, we make ourselves available for on-site demonstrations of the product at no charge. We hope to continue offering this service, but at a minimal cost to lower our expenses in the future.

Product Description

We currently offer two basic product lines:

- Our original product, Salsa, was available only in a hot flavor. Because of consumer demand, we have added extra hot and mild flavors.
- Chips, both yellow corn and blue corn.

Competitive Comparison

To differentiate ourselves from all of the others, we stress quality and authenticity of the ingredients, and the heritage of the family recipe.

We sell more than a jar with salsa in it. We sell high quality ingredients, carefully put together in a masterful blend that can't be matched in taste or true Hispanic authenticity.

These are simple products that must be presented in a way that encourage the consumer to give us a chance. Once they try our product, we will have a long-term relationship with them.

As in similar food items, we can charge a premium for what we supply. The market has shown it will buy our product over more readily known names because of the richness and authentic taste of our salsa.

Sales Literature

We are currently working on a new line of brochures and sales materials to assist our marketing and that of our dealers. Our newly designed labels show the direction we are taking in this area.

Our costs are a part of the margin squeeze. As our orders go up, we need to increase our production in a way that also increases our margin. We have found a local supplier that can reduce our costs by handling much larger batches of salsa than we are currently able, yet maintain our high quality. This will reduce our costs over 32% per jar in the production of our salsa.

We need to continue to find additional opportunities that will afford us lower costs of production while maintaining the quality that has put us on the map. Our outsourcing for the corn chips has shown we can contract for a high quality product that we will be able to put our name on, and meet our goals for gross-profit margin.

We are currently researching the addition of an authentic Hispanic sauce, as well as other Hispanic food items to offer our current clients and to build increased interest in Salvador Sauces, Inc.

We are now looking into additional products, sauce, and other Hispanic food items, as well as other ways of marketing the overall line.

We are also looking into creation of a small storefront, and eventually a lunch counter or small restaurant setting.

We have been selling at the rate of $2,500 per month to local restaurants, small grocery stores and distributors of Hispanic food stuffs. Salvador Sauces is currently awaiting approval for a large grocery chain to carry our products and has received a commitment from a large distributor to sell from $100,000 to $150,000 of products per year. There are several other large grocery chains that have been approached and are in various stages of interest in carrying the Salvador Sauces line of product.

The Hispanic food industry is in a boom period. While there are many items from various vendors available, Salvador Sauces has approached the market as a specialty retailer: a provider of authentic high quality Hispanic salsa and chips.

We have made significant inroads with several area restaurants and a small grocer, each providing us with a market presence. We are now looking at developing our own storefront as an adjunct to our current marketing. There is a need for a specialty retailer catering specifically to the Hispanic client and to the individuals that appreciate authentic Hispanic cuisine.

In addition to the above, we are also looking at packaging our products for other groups to use for fundraising events, gift baskets for corporate promotions, and the possibility of a house restaurant to further advertise and promote the products.

Potential Customers	Growth	1996	1997	1998	1999	2000	CAGR
Grocery Stores	75%	53	93	163	285	499	75.17%
Distributors	100%	5	10	20	40	80	100.00%
Restaurants	45%	18	26	38	55	80	45.20%
Other	12%	10	11	12	13	15	10.67%
Total	**67.32%**	**86**	**140**	**233**	**393**	**674**	**67.32%**

We are initially focusing on the Hispanic community. They will be able to appreciate more readily the authenticity of the product. The market will observe the products they choose and they will indirectly become promoters of our products.

Market Growth

The market analysis shows us a broad range of prospective clients, covering more than one ethnic group or body. The largest of these groups of customers is that of the mainstream American, which is projected to grow at 12% per year. The fasting growing segment is Hispanic, which is projected to grow at 22% per year.

Industry Analysis

The Hispanic food industry is relatively new, and its popularity is ever on the increase. The authentic taste is not common in this industry, which gives Salvador Sauces a leg up on the competition.

In an industry currently in a steady upward growth curve, Salvador Sauces is poised to capitalize on the consumer's desire for authentic, high quality, Hispanic cuisine.

While a troubling economy can affect many areas, food items are generally not as affected, with specialty items seeming to always find favor in the marketplace.

Industry Participants

While there are currently several vendors in this market selling competitive products, the commonality of those products provides an opening in the marketplace for the vibrant packaging and positioning of Salvador Sauces salsa and chips. We stand out on the shelf, we stand out in the restaurant, and we will stand out in the mind of the consumer.

Distribution Patterns

While current brand names carry more weight in the marketplace, because of our unique marketing approach using local restaurants, and displaying and demonstrating our wares in local grocery stores, we are able to build consumer awareness at a margin of the cost of television and radio advertising.

In going to food fairs and neighborhood festivals, we build consumer awareness and generate demand at the same time. While at these events we are also able to directly research the market and hear firsthand what the consumer is seeking.

Competition and Buying Patterns

There are many suppliers of salsa and similar products currently available on the shelves at the local grocer. However, there is still a lot of room for new products and new companies.

By positioning ourselves at the higher end of the market, we expose ourselves to consumers trying to get out of the rut, who continue to use a product that they have long forgotten why they buy. By not trying to compete head-on, we are selling our product consistently and increasingly. With entrance into some of the larger grocery chains we will broaden our audience considerably.

Main Competitors

Although Salvador Sauces is staking out the high end of this market, we cannot fail to be compared with some of the current leaders in this arena. Adios, Juarez, and Mrs. Brown's are just a few of the participants in this segment. Most have been on the shelf for so long they are taken for granted by the consumer. Our fresh approach to authentic taste and texture makes us different.

STRATEGY AND IMPLEMENTATION SUMMARY

Our strategy is based on serving niche markets well. The world is full of consumers who can't get what they perceive to be high quality or authentic. We are capitalizing on the family heritage in our product line.

We are building a marketing infrastructure that will provide what appears to be a seamless approach to our products, covering multiple avenues of utilizing grocery stores and major distributors. Each location will accent the other, providing for continuous exposure of Salvador Sauces name.

Marketing Strategy

We are focusing on the consumer first through grocery exposure, and then impacting them through restaurants and other food places.

Pricing Strategy

We are able to price our products competitively. Even though we are subject to some impulse buying, we can provide a product to be resold at a generous mark-up for our dealers, while still providing a satisfactory experience for the consumer. At a retail range of $2.79 to $3.05 per jar of salsa, we cover the mid to upper price range of the salsa market, while providing a 33% margin for the dealers.

Promotion Strategy

The long-range goal is to gain enough visibility to leverage the product into other distribution sites within our region, then to move on to other geographical regions as inquiries and distribution requests come in.

Although our current contacts in the grocery chains are for local consumption, they all move out of this region in their normal distribution. It is our goal to move with them.

Marketing Programs

To this means we have been continually reworking our packaging for better corporate identity, providing a more attractive package, a very important ingredient in the food industry. An example is the recent addition of bar-coding and nutritional information to our label.

Sales Strategy

The keys to our continuing success are in the areas we are adding to our current distribution channels. This will remain our main focus for the next five years. Sales calls on the following enterprises have resulted in Salvador Sauces Salsa being stocked and sold by them.

Roosevelt Supermarkets
Kazmaiers
LaPeria (Toledo)
LaMexicana (Toledo)
Gift Baskets (Perrysburg)
Barney's (Perrysburg)
E & L Meats (Detroit)
La Colmena (Detroit)
Gerrards (Rossford)
Wolfert's (Toledo)
CGA (Delta)
Ottawa Market (Toledo)
Schorlings (Toledo)
Char's Best Market (Toledo)
Luna Bakery and Grocery (Detroit)
La Bottelia (Detroit)
D & D's Carryout (Pemberville)
Grumpy's (Toledo)
Pauken Wine and Liquor (Maumee)

K.O.A. Campground (Stoney Ridge)
Mad Anthony's (Waterville)
Brinkman's Country Corner (Findlay)
Connie Mac's (Toledo)
El Aguila Bakery (Fremont)
Elmore Super Value (Elmore)
Stephenson's Farm Market (Toledo)
Falls Crestview Market (Toledo)
Moser's Farm Market (Perrysburg)
Bassets CGA (Oak Harbor)
Dels (Woodville)
South Point Carryout (Toledo)
Markada (Ann Arbor)
Partners in Wine II (Ann Arbor)
Vernor Foods (Detroit)
Brownings (Whitehouse)
Stephen's Restaurant (Perrysburg)
Kirwen's (Gibsonburg)

Sales Forecast

We currently forecast our sales to grow at the rate of 514% for the next 12 months because of written commitments we have received from distributors intending to take on our product line in larger volumes in the future.

This growth will continue, but at a lower rate of 45% for the next year, and by 45% the following year. We anticipate the growth rate to flatten out to a consistent 12% within five years, but to remain steady. Should the market on Hispanic food items continue at its current pace, we will keep pace with it. Our forecast does assume a downturn in the product within a three-year period, and the lower figures of 12% are a reflection of that forecast. We would be happy if it didn't falter.

Sales	1996	1997	1998
Sales	$168,602	$217,320	$312,052
Other	$0	$0	$0
Total Sales	**$168,602**	**$217,320**	**$312,052**
Direct Cost of Sales			
Sales	$64,917	$86,928	$124,821
Other	$0	$0	$0
Subtotal Cost of Sales	**$64,917**	**$86,928**	**$124,821**

Sales Programs

Dealer sales—thorough and persistent effort to generate sales through major names including:

Big Chain, Inc.
Grocerytown, Inc.
Buster's
Tenochtitlan Foods, Inc.
CGA (various)
Roosevelt's
Stephenson's

To this means, we are currently interviewing distributors to assist us with the marketing and distribution of our salsa. Again, the hiring of a distributor, and a modest performance increase on their efforts for Salvador Sauces would make our sales projections conservative. Key to the sale and distribution of our products through this channel is the constant care and feeding of the buyers for each of the organizations. Sales calls on a regular basis, along with samples of new product, will keep the doors open to us.

We do have some opportunity for building strategic alliances with several local restaurants some of which are listed below:

Milestones

Connie Mac's
La Perla
Zingerman's

Approached properly, they will not only serve our products in their restaurants, but also sell for carry-out.

We have assembled a list of important program milestones, with dates and budgets for each. The milestone schedule indicates our emphasis on planning and for having a sure method of implementation when the time comes for each action.

Milestone	Manager	Planned Date	Department	Budget	Actual Date	Actual Budget	Planned Date - Actual Date	Budget - Actual Budget
SBA Loan	Patricia	11/1/96	Finance	$1,500	1/1/97	$0	(61)	$1,500
Hirzel Contract	Ricardo	6/15/97	Finance	$9,600	6/16/97	$0	(1)	$9,600
1st Employee	Patricia	12/1/96	Admin./Mgmt	$9,600	11/1/96	$0	30	$9,600
Store Front/Warehouse	Ricardo	3/1/97	Sales	$12,000	3/1/97	$0	0	$12,000
2nd Employee	Ricardo	5/1/97	Production	$24,000	5/1/97	$0	0	$24,000
New Product Development	Pat/Ric	12/1/97	Marketing	$350	12/1/97	$0	0	$350
Marketing Development	Ricardo	3/1/97	Marketing	$500	3/1/97	$0	0	$500
3rd Employee - Administration	Pat	3/1/98	Admin.	$18,500	3/1/98	$0	0	$18,500
4th Employee - Warehouse/Deliver	Ricardo	6/1/98	Warehouse	$24,500	6/1/98	$0	0	$24,500
Other	ABC	1/1/98	Department	$0	1/1/98	$0	0	$0
Totals				**$100,550**		**$0**	(32)	**$100,550**

MANAGEMENT SUMMARY

Salvador Sauces was founded by Ricardo and Patricia Torres and has operated without the burden of any payroll or salary expense to this point.

Patricia Torres—President

Patricia is currently responsible for the preparation of salsa and maintaining the various inventories of raw materials; purchasing of food ingredients; assistance with packaging and shipping. In addition, she maintains the company records and is in direct communication with the accountant and other advisors.

Richardo Torres—Vice President

Richardo assists with the preparation and production of salsa; maintains the inventory of the finished products; is responsible for packing and shipping; assists with recordkeeping and cost containment. Richardo also shares in the marketing and promotion of the product.

Current plans are to bring Patricia on board in a paid capacity on or about August 1, and we have forecast the proper expenses to do so. As orders are processed and goals met, Ricardo will take charge of the logistics and become a full-time paid employee as well. We are currently forecasting this to transpire in the first quarter of 1997. We plan on hiring additional personnel as the need for them arises, and as we have the ability to pay them.

Organizational Structure

Salvador Sauces planned organization calls for sales and marketing, product development, finance and administration. Actual production falls under the finance and administrative area. We are currently using outside consultants to assist in these areas.

Management Team

The management team is currently comprised of Ricardo and Patricia Torres, the founders of Salvador Sauces, Inc. In addition, they have a board of advisors with over 78 years of administrative, financial, and sales management experience to assist them with management decisions on daily operations, and the long-range planning necessary for continued, consistent growth.

The team is currently composed of the following professionals:

Mr. Lupe T. Hinojosa
(419)868-8055
Branch Manager
Mariner Financial Services, Inc.
Money Management, Insurance and Financial Advice
5640 Southwyck Blvd., Suite 101
Toledo, Ohio 43614

Mr. Jack L. Karsten
(419)893-8248
President
IHN Consulting Services, Inc.
Administrative, Marketing and Strategic Planning
P.O. Box 746
Maumee, Ohio 43537-0746

Mr. Douglas Holthues
(419)476-4677
C.P.A.
Holthues & Sheperd
Bookkeeping, Financial Reporting and Tax Planning
4415 Lewis Avenue
Toledo, Ohio 43612

Mike Hood
Attorney at Law
Legal Advice and Assistance

The gaps in the management team are currently being addressed through the use of outside consultants as shown above, and will continue to be until the cash flow allows for the hiring of employees to fill those capacities. The identifiable gaps are in administration, finance management, and marketing.

Management Team Gaps

The current personnel plan calls for Patricia to become a paid employee on or about August 1. Although she has been working for Salvador Sauces since its inception two years ago, she has not drawn a salary or been reimbursed for expenses. We are then planning on Ricardo taking a paid position with Salvador Sauces by early 1997, or the successful approval of a Link Deposit Loan; whichever comes first.

Personnel Plan

Personnel Plan	1996	1997	1998
Payroll	$9,600	$43,500	$72,800

We have forecast a very rapid growth for Salvador Sauces this year. Although this may seem ambitious based on historic sales, this rate of growth is due to the large orders we have received to date from several distributors, letters of commitment from Big Chain and Buster's, and the increasing number of orders from current clients.

FINANCIAL PLAN

The financial plan depends on the following assumptions:

Important Assumptions

- We assume a slow-growth economy, without major recession.
- We assume, of course, that there are no unforeseen changes in the consumer market to make products immediately obsolete or out of favor (or not increasing in popularity).
- We assume access to equity capital and financing sufficient to maintain our financial plan as shown in the tables, addendum, and additional documentation.

General Assumptions	1996	1997	1998
Short-term Interest Rate %	1.00%	1.00%	1.00%
Long-term Interest Rate %	0.00%	0.00%	0.00%
Payment Days Estimator	30	30	30
Collection Days Estimator	30	30	30
Inventory Turnover Estimator	5	5	5
Tax Rate %	1.00%	1.00%	1.00%
Expenses in Cash %	10.00%	10.00%	10.00%
Sales on Credit %	15.00%	15.00%	15.00%
Personnel Burden %	10.00%	10.00%	10.00%

Key Financial Indicators

The most important factor in our case is the ability to procure financing to go to the next level. The size of the orders currently being asked of us are well beyond our current production capability, but well within the production capability of a local processor. *Note: purchasing from this supplier will also reduce our per unit production costs in excess of 30%. An additional alternative would be to purchase the production equipment necessary, and not be subject to the local manufacturer's production scheduling.

We must maintain gross margins of at least 55% and hold marketing costs to no more than 20% of sales to provide the income to reduce our debt, and equip us to sustain the growth we anticipate. We will meet and exceed all of these conditions through buying at increased volumes. Then we'll pass the savings on to our customers through increases in the margins at which they retail the product.

Benchmark Comparison

	1993	1994	1995	1996	1997	1998
Sales	0.0	0.25	1.0	7.5	10.0	14.5
Gross	0.0	1.0	1.1	1.0	1.0	1.0
OpEx	0.0	0.75	1.0	1.75	3.75	6.0
AR Est.	0.0	0.75	1.0	1.9	1.9	1.0
Turns Est.	0.0	1.75	1.0	$1.0	$1.0	1.0

Breakeven Analysis

Our breakeven analysis shows that Salvador Sauces has a good balance of fixed costs and sufficient sales to remain healthy. The breakeven point is close to 1,426 jars (119 cases) of salsa a month, while our sales forecast for the next year calls for almost 10,000 jars (833 cases) of salsa a month, on average.

We have just recently contracted with another jar supplier that will reduce our costs by 18% per jar of salsa with the next supply order. This will further reduce the breakeven point, and add to our goal of increasing the margin on our salsa.

Breakeven Analysis

Monthly Units Breakeven	1,426
Monthly Sales Breakeven	$2,852

Assumptions

Average Per-Unit Revenue	$2.00
Average Per-Unit Variable Cost	$1.40
Estimated Monthly Fixed Cost	$856

Projected Profit and Loss

We expect to close out this year with over $100,000 in sales, and to increase our sales to more than $400,000 per year by the turn of the century, with net earnings averaging in excess of 10%.

Profit and Loss (Income Statement)	1996	1997	1998
Sales	$168,602	$217,320	$312,052
Direct Cost of Sales	$64,917	$86,928	$124,821
Other	$0	$0	$0
Total Cost of Sales	**$64,917**	**$86,928**	**$124,821**
Gross Margin	$103,685	$130,392	$187,231
Gross Margin %	61.50%	60.00%	60.00%

OPERATING EXPENSES	**1996**	**1997**	**1998**
Advertising/Promotion	$466	$750	$1,250
Travel	$916	$1,250	$3,500
Miscellaneous	$637	$1,000	$1,850
Other	$792	$700	$900
Payroll Expense	$9,600	$43,500	$72,800
Depreciation	$5,520	$5,520	$8,950
Leased Equipment	$465	$1,000	$1,000
Utilities	$3,850	$3,900	$4,500
Insurance	$1,044	$2,010	$2,650
Rent	$3,500	$12,000	$16,500
Other	$4,290	$4,225	$6,275
Other	$0	$0	$0
Other	$3,953	$4,015	$6,500
Total Operating Expenses	**$35,033**	**$79,870**	**$126,675**
Profit Before Interest and Taxes	$68,652	$50,522	$60,556
Interest Expense Short-term	$149	$98	$40
Interest Expense Long-term	$0	$0	$0
Taxes Incurred	$685	$504	$605
Net Profit	$67,818	$49,920	$59,911
Net Profit/Sales	40.22%	22.97%	19.20%

We expect to manage cash flow over the next three years with the assistance of a Small Business Administration supported loan of $165,000. This financing assistance is required to provide the working capital to meet the current needs while providing a solid foundation to build the growth of the organization. After a six-month period, we anticipate requesting an open line of credit of between $50,000 and $100,000 to further the company's ability to meet and exceed sales projections, gross margin, and return on investment.

Projected Cash Flow

Pro-Forma Cash Flow	**1996**	**1997**	**1998**
Net Profit	$67,818	$49,920	$59,911
PLUS			
Depreciation	$5,520	$5,520	$8,950
Change in Accounts Payable	$7,402	$2,699	$4,539
Current Borrowing (repayment)	($3,650)	($5,555)	($6,000)
Increase (decrease) Other Liabilities	$0	$0	$0
Long-term Borrowing (repayment)	($7,100)	($17,042)	($17,042)
Capital Input	$0	$0	$0
Subtotal	**$69,990**	**$35,542**	**$50,358**
LESS			
Change in Accounts Receivable	$2,435	$704	$1,368
Change in Inventory	$11,225	$4,990	$8,590
Change in Other ST Assets	$0	$0	$0
Capital Expenditure	$0	$0	$0
Dividends	$45,000	$0	$0
Subtotal	**$58,660**	**$5,694**	**$9,959**
Net Cash Flow	$11,330	$29,849	$40,399
Cash Balance	$11,456	$41,305	$81,704

Projected Balance Sheet

We expect a healthy growth in net worth through the end of the plan period.

Pro-Forma Balance Sheet

Assets	Starting Balances	1996	1997	1998
Short-term Assets				
Cash	$126	$11,456	$41,305	$81,704
Accounts Receivable	$0	$2,435	$3,139	$4,507
Inventory	$3,492	$14,717	$19,707	$28,297
Other Short-term Assets	$0	$0	$0	$0
Total Short-term Assets	$3,618	$28,608	$64,151	$114,508
Long-term Assets				
Capital Assets	$23,368	$23,368	$23,368	$23,368
Accumulated				
Depreciation	$9,792	$15,312	$20,832	$29,782
Total Long-term Assets	$13,576	$8,056	$2,536	($6,414)
Total Assets	**$17,194**	**$36,664**	**$66,687**	**$108,094**
LIABILITIES AND CAPITAL				
Accounts Payable	$0	$7,402	$10,102	$14,640
Short-term Notes	$16,207	$12,557	$7,002	$1,002
Other Short-term Liab.	$0	$0	$0	$0
Subtotal Short-term				
Liabilities	$16,207	$19,959	$17,104	$15,642
Long-term Liabilities	$0	($7,100)	($24,142)	($41,184)
Total Liabilities	**$16,207**	**$12,859**	**($7,038)**	**($25,542)**
Paid in Capital	$25,000	$25,000	$25,000	$25,000
Retained Earnings	($9,755)	($69,013)	($1,195)	$48,725
Earnings	($14,258)	$67,818	$49,920	$59,911
Total Capital	**$987**	**$23,805**	**$73,725**	**$133,636**
Total Liabilities/Capital	$17,194	$36,664	$66,687	$108,094
Net Worth	$987	$23,805	$73,725	$133,636

Business Ratios

Ratio Analysis

Our standard business ratios show a plan for well balanced, healthy growth.

Profitability Ratios	1996	1997	1998	RMA
Gross Margin	61.50%	60.00%	60.00%	0
Net Profit Margin	40.22%	22.97%	19.20%	0
Return on Assets	184.97%	74.86%	55.42%	0
Return on Equity	284.89%	67.71%	44.83%	0
Activity Ratios				
AR Turnover	10.39	10.39	10.39	0
Collection Days	18	31	30	0
Inventory Turnover	7.13	5.05	5.2	0
Accts Payable Turnover	10.99	10.99	10.99	0
Total Asset Turnover	4.6	3.26	2.89	0
Debt Ratios				
Debt to Net Worth	0.54	-0.1	-0.19	0
Short-term Liab. to Liab.	1.55	0	0	0

Liquidity Ratios	1996	1997	1998	RMA
Current Ratio	1.43	3.75	7.32	0
Quick Ratio	0.7	2.6	5.51	0
Net Working Capital	$8,649	$47,047	$98,866	0
Interest Coverage	459.89	516.61	1513.14	0

Additional Ratios				
Assets to Sales	0.22	0.31	0.35	0
Debt/Assets	35%	-11%	-24%	0
Current Debt/Total Assets	54%	26%	14%	0
Acid Test	0.57	2.41	5.22	0
Asset Turnover	4.6	3.26	2.89	0
Sales/Net Worth	7.08	2.95	2.34	0

Sports Bar

BUSINESS PLAN

TAKE FIVE SPORTS BAR & GRILL

16777 W. Barnes St.
Americus, GA 31709

This business plan serves as a good model for a restaurant looking to franchise. The existing company's profitability is described in full detail and the demand for similar restaurants is communicated well. Note, too, the focused objectives and keys to success. The narrowed focus assures the company won't be spread too thin to achieve their goals. This plan was compiled using Business Plan Pro, by Palo Alto Software.

- EXECUTIVE SUMMARY

- COMPANY SUMMARY

- MARKET SUMMARY

- MARKETING STRATEGY

- MANAGEMENT SUMMARY

- FINANCIAL PLAN

EXECUTIVE SUMMARY

Take Five Sports Bar & Grill has established a successful presence in the food and beverage service industry. The flagship location in suburban Americus (Medlock Bridge) will gross in excess of $2 million in sales in its first year of operation, ending July 1996. First year operations will produce a net profit of $433,000. This will be generated from an investment of $625,000 in initial capital. Since 10 months of operations have already been completed, the confidence level for final first year numbers is extremely high. The first 10 months of start-up costs, sales revenues, and operating expenses are actual.

Expansion plans are already underway. Owner funding and internally generated cash flow will enable additional stores to open. Sales projections for the next four years are based upon current planned store openings. Site surveys have been completed and prime locations have been targeted for store expansion.

The sales figures and projections presented here are based upon an additional four store locations at the most premium sites available in the Americus Metro market area as well as a prime resort location in Destin, Florida.

This plan will result in sales revenues growing to $25 million by FY2000 and generating net income in excess of $5.6 million.

Management has recognized the rapid growth potential made possible by the quick success and fast return-on-investment from the first location. Payback of total invested capital on the first location will be realized in less than 18 months of operation. Cash flow becomes positive from operations immediately and profits are substantial in the first year.

Objectives

Take Five has the objective of opening additional stores in Americus Metro at Ashford-Dunwoody, Lawrenceville, Buckhead, and East Cobb. Additionally, a store will be opened on the beach at Destin, Florida, a year-round resort destination.

The management of Take Five has demonstrated its concept, execution, marketability, and controls, and feels confident of its ability to successfully replicate the quick ramp-up of the Medlock Bridge location to additional venues.

The following objectives have been established:

- Have all five stores operational by 1998 with a sequential time-line of openings.
- Maintain tight control of costs and operations by hiring quality management at each location and utilizing automated computer control.
- Keep food cost under 32% of revenue.
- Keep beverage cost under 21% of revenue.
- Select only locations that meet all the parameters of success.
- Grow each location to the $3 to $5 million annual sales level.

Mission

Take Five Sports Bar & Grill strives to be the premier sports theme restaurant in the Southeast Region. Our goal is to be a step ahead of the competition. We want our customers to have more fun during their leisure time. We provide more televisions with more sporting events than anywhere else in the region. We provide state-of-the-art table-top audio control at each table so the customer can listen to the selected program of his or her choice without interference from background noise. We combine menu selection, atmosphere, ambiance, and service to create a sense of "place" in order to reach our goal of over-all value in a dining/entertainment experience.

The keys to success in achieving our goals are:

- Product quality. Not only great food but great service.
- Managing finances to enable new locations to open at targeted intervals.
- Controlling costs at all times without exception.
- Instituting management controls to insure replicability of operations over multiple locations. This applies equally to product control and to financial control.

The key elements of Take Five's restaurant store concept are as follows:

- Sports based themes—The company will focus on themes that have mass appeal.
- Distinctive design features—All stores will be characterized by spectacular visual design and layout. Each store will display a collection of authentic sports memorabilia.
- High profile locations—The company selects its store locations based on key demographic indicators, including traffic counts, average income, number of households, hotels, and offices within a certain radius.
- Celebrity events—The company stores will be distinguished by the promotional activities of sports celebrities and by media coverage of appearances and special events.
- Retail merchandising—Each store will include an integrated retail store offering premium quality merchandise displaying the company's logo design. In addition, sports memorabilia will be sold.
- Quality food—Each Take Five store will serve freshly prepared, high quality, popular cuisine that is targeted to appeal to a variety of tastes and budgets with an emphasis on reasonably and moderately priced signature items of particular appeal to a local market.
- Quality service—In order to maintain its unique image the company provides attentive and friendly service with a high ratio of service personnel to customers and also invests in the training and supervision of its employees.

Take Five Sports Bar & Grill is a privately held Georgia company. Joseph A. Smith is the principal owner. It is Mr. Smith's intention to offer limited outside ownership in Take Five on an equity, debt, or combination basis in order to facilitate a more rapid expansion of the Take Five concept.

Mr. Smith holds an M.B.A. in Finance from the University of Georgia. He has held executive level positions in finance with Global Electric and Vacation Inn Worldwide. He is previously experienced in the restaurant industry, having opened Smith's Italian Restaurant in 1993, which still operates successfully under his ownership.

Take Five Sports Bar & Grill was founded in 1995 by Joseph Smith to capitalize on the ever growing market demand for high end technology enhanced sports theme restaurants. Take Five has promoted its brand through the operation of its existing location at Medlock Bridge Road and State Bridge Road in Americus, Georgia. The flagship location provides a unique dining and entertainment experience in a high-energy environment. Customer acceptance has been proven. Regular and repeat customers cross many age demographics and families are frequent diners.

Take Five has promoted heavily with tie-ins to Atlanta professional teams and celebrities. Take Five Sports Bar & Grill is the radio home for the live Monday Night WWHK Americus Horsecats coaches show. This show is broadcast during the hour preceding the telecast of "Monday Night Football." In addition, Take Five hosts the Americus Backboards sports talk show on ABC 750 AM featuring local basketball celebrities. The local baseball team often celebrates victories at Take Five.

Past Performance	FY1993	FY1994	FY1995
Sales	$0	$0	$634,900
Gross Margin	$0	$0	$394,000
Gross % (calculated)	0%	0%	62.06%
Operating Expenses	$0	$0	$301,000
Collection period (days)	0	0	0
Inventory turnover	0	0	20

BALANCE SHEET

Short-term Assets	FY1993	FY1994	FY1995
Cash	$0	$0	$67,136
Accounts receivable	$0	$0	$0
Inventory	$0	$0	$15,297
Other Short-term Assets	$0	$0	$17,310
Total Short-term Assets	$0	$0	$99,643

Long-term Assets			
Capital Assets	$0	$0	$475,495
Accumulated Depreciation	$0	$0	$29,713
Total Long-term Assets	$0	$0	$445,782
Total Assets	$0	$0	$545,425

CAPITAL AND LIABILITIES

	FY1993	FY1994	FY1995
Accounts Payable	$0	$0	$20,040
Short-tem Notes	$0	$0	$0
Other ST Liabilites	$0	$0	$40,826
Subtotal Short-term Liabilities	$0	$0	$60,866
Long-term Liabilities	$0	$0	$0
Total Liabilites	$0	$0	$60,866
Paid in Capital	$0	$0	$625,000
Retianed Earnings	$0	$0	($218,401)
Earnings	$0	$0	$77,960
Total Capital	$0	$0	$484,559
Total Capital and Liabilities	$0	$0	$545,425

Other Inputs	FY1993	FY1994	FY1995
Payment days	0	0	0
Sales on credit	$0	$0	$0
Receivables turnover	0.00	0.00	0.00

Company Locations and Facilities

The company units will range in size from 6,000 to 9,000 square feet and will seat from 225 to 400 persons. Each Take Five Sports Bar & Grill will feature authentic sports memorabilia such as game jerseys to signed tennis racquets. Each store will be equipped with state-of-the-art audio and video systems to enable the customer to enjoy the game of their choice. Every restaurant will be built to existing specifications, clean looking, open, and pleasing to the customer.

Unit locations are as follows:

- Medlock Bridge—This unit is located at one of the busiest intersections in North Fulton County. It is surrounded by four major country clubs, upper middle class neighborhoods, office complexes, and shopping. It encompasses 6,000 square feet of space and has been open since August 1995.
- Ashford-Dunwoody—This unit will open in late summer 1996. Size will be 7,200 square feet. The location is one and one half miles north of Perimeter Mall. Within a three-mile radius there is 20 million square feet of professional office space. Also, an abundance of upscale apartment complexes adjoins the unit. Major chain hotels are located nearby. Perimeter Mall is one of the regional upscale shopping destinations.
- Lawrenceville (New Market)—This site will occupy 6,500 square feet and is scheduled to open in the spring of 1997. It will be built as a free-standing building on a more than 2-acre parcel at the intersection of Route 120 and Route 316. Adjacent to the property is an 18-screen movie theater opened by AMC in March 1996. This is the largest theater AMC has built in the Americus area. New Market Mall has as master anchors Bullseye, Tool Box, and Edwards, among others. The demographics are very favorable with no competition from other sports bar restaurants.
- Peachtree and Piedmont (Buckhead)—This unit will be in the heart of Buckhead, which is Americus's most comprehensive business and entertainment center. In addition to retail space being constructed at this sight the unit will be adjacent to a 200-room America's Suite Hotel. Buckhead is one of the nation's largest and fastest-growing mixed use urban areas. It includes a dynamic combination of concentrated offices, retail, hotel, shopping, restaurant/entertainment, and residential development.

Take Five Sports Bar & Grill also maintains a corporate business office at 7155 Main Street, Americus, Georgia 31709.

MARKET SUMMARY

Potential Customers	Growth	1995	1996	1997	1998	1999	CAGR
Medlock Bridge	10%	20,000	22,000	24,200	26,620	29,282	10.00%
Ashford-Dunwoody	6%	40,000	42,400	44,944	47,641	50,499	6.00%
Lawrenceville	8%	30,000	32,400	34,992	37,791	40,814	8.00%
Buckhead	5%	80,000	84,000	88,200	92,610	97,241	5.00%
Other	0%	0	0	0	0	0	0.00%
Total	**6.39%**	**170,000**	**180,800**	**192,336**	**204,662**	**217,836**	**6.39%**

Target Market Segment Strategy

Our strategy is based on serving our niche markets well. The sports enthusiast, the business entertainer and traveler, the local night crowd, as well as families dining out all can enjoy the Take Five experience.

What begins as a customized version of a standard product, tailored to the needs of a local clientele, can become a niche product that will fill similar needs in similar markets across the Southeast.

We are building our infrastructure so that we can replicate the product, the experience, and the environment across broader geographic lines. Concentration will be on maintaining quality and establishing a strong identity in each local market. The identity becomes the source of "critical mass" upon which expansion efforts are based. Not only does it add marketing muscle, but it also becomes the framework for further expansion using both company-owned and franchised store locations. Franchises will first be marketed in late 1997 or early 1998.

MARKETING STRATEGY

A combination of local media and event marketing will be utilized at each location. Radio is most effective, followed by local print media. As soon as a concentration of stores is established in a market, then broader media will be employed.

The strategy of live broadcasting and pro sports tie-ins has been most effective in generating free publicity for the flagship location which has been more effective than any advertising that could have been purchased.

Pricing Strategy

All menu items are moderately priced. An average customer ticket is between $10 and $20 including food and drink. Tickets are considerably larger for game day visitors. Our average customer spends more than the industry average for moderately priced establishments. We tend to believe that this is due to our creating an atmosphere that encourages longer stays and more spending but still allows adequate table turns due to extended hours of appeal.

Promotion Strategy

We promote sports, sports, and more sports. The universal appeal of sports and sports marketing has never been higher. A high growth area such as Americus has an annual influx of new residents from many other parts of the country. This trend is true in the Sunbelt in general.

Many new residents and many existing ones are fans of teams in other markets. Take Five is a place for all. Each patron can watch his or her game of interest. The enabling technology is the benchmark for Take Five.

Advertising budgets and sports event promotion is an on-going process of management geared to promote the brand name and keep Take Five at the forefront of sports theme establishments in each local marketing area.

In addition, funds are budgeted to launch franchise sales activity and lead generation. These funds amount to 20% of projected franchise sales.

Marketing Programs

Take Five will create an "identity" oriented marketing strategy with executions particularly in local media. Radio spots, print ads, and in-store promotions are designed for transplantation to other markets. A portion of the ad and promo budget is set aside to develop these programs.

Sales Strategy

The sales strategy is to build and open new locations on schedule in order to increase revenue. Each individual location will continue to build its local customer base over the first three years of operation. The goal is $3 to $5 million in annual sales per unit. A unit will be considered mature once it has passed the $3.5 million mark in annual sales.

Sales Forecast

We anticipate a rapid sales ramp-up for our first location in only its first twelve months of operation. The two million dollar sales volume represents somewhat less than 50% of the revenue potential of the location.

Sales	**FY1996**	**FY1997**	**FY1998**
Food	$1,026,242	$4,411,500	$7,497,000
Drinks	$998,276	$4,238,500	$7,203,000
Retail	$18,126	$48,000	$84,000
Franchise Fees	$0	$500,000	$1,300,000
Other	$0	$0	$0
Total Sales	$2,042,644	$9,198,000	$16,084,000

Direct Cost of sales	**FY1996**	**FY1997**	**FY1998**
Food	$349,013	$1,449,910	$2,548,980
Drinks	$219,561	$932,470	$1,584,660
Retail	$9,064	$24,000	$42,000
Franchise Fees	$0	$125,000	$260,000
Other	$0	$0	$0
Subtotal Cost of Sales	$577,638	$2,531,380	$4,435,640

Our milestone schedule indicates our emphasis on planning for implementation.　　　**Milestones**

Business Plan Milestones

Milestone	Manager	Planned Date	Dept.	Budget	Actual Date	Actual Budget	Planned Date - Actual Date	Budget - Actual Budget
Open Medlock Bridge	JDP	8/1/95	Exec	$625,000	1/1/95	$0	212	$625,000
Open Ashford-Dunwoody	JDP	8/1/96	Exec	$700,000	1/1/95	$0	578	$700,000
Open Lawrenceville	JDP	2/1/97	Exec	$1,000,000	2/1/95	$0	731	$1,000,000
Open Buckhead	JDP	6/1/97	Exec	$700,000	1/1/95	$0	882	$700,000
Open Destin, Fla.	JDP	3/1/98	Exec	$1,500,000	1/1/95	$0	1,155	$1,500,000
Open East Cobb	JDP	6/1/98	Exec	$600,000	1/15/95	$0	1,233	$600,000
Private Placement	LC	9/1/96	Finance	$82,500	1/1/95	$0	609	$82,500
Sample	ABC	1/1/98	Department	$0	1/1/98	$0	0	$0
Sample	ABC	1/1/98	Department	$0	1/1/98	$0	0	$0
Other	ABC	1/1/98	Department	$0	1/1/98	$0	0	$0
Totals				$5,207,500		$0	5,400	$5,207,500

MANAGEMENT SUMMARY

At the present time Joseph Smith runs all operations for Take Five Sports Bar & Grill. Other key personnel are the management at each location. Candidates have already been identified for the first additional Americus area location. There is not expected to be any shortage of qualified and available staff and management from local labor pools in each market area.

Organizational Structure

Future organizational structure will include a director of store operations when store locations exceed five and/or the Florida store opens. This will provide a supervisory level between the executive level and the store management level.

A full-time accountant has already been added. Also, a sales/marketing director has been added to oversee the expansion effort both to support the growth of existing business and to execute the franchise expansion strategy. Their salaries are included in the projections.

Operations of individual stores will be the responsibility of the general manager.

Management Team

Joseph Smith

Personal Data:

> Born 11/19/53, Philadelphia, Pennsylvania
> Married 17 years—two children ages 10 and 13
> Excellent health
> U.S. Air Force—1971 to 1975, Vietnam veteran, Communication Surveillance, Top Security Clearance

Education:

> LaSalle University, M.B.A., Finance; B.S., Finance

Professional Experience:

- RCA/GE—1978-1988: Finance, Strategic Planning, Corporate Development
- Scientific Americus—1988-1990: VP Finance, Electronic Systems Group
- Vacation Inn Worldwide—1990-1993: Strategic Planning and Corporate Development, reporting to the CFO
- Resigned in 1993 to open and operate Smith's Italian Restaurant

Management Team Gaps

Specific opportunities exist in the store operations supervisory area (not needed initially) and in franchise sales development (not needed initially).

It is expected that these people can be recruited when needed in the Americus market. Americus is now home to more than 40 franchise company headquarters.

Store managers are readily available when needed. Food service managers are plentiful.

Personnel	FY1996	FY1997	FY1998	**Personnel Plan**
Total Payroll	$484,800	$2,800,000	$4,850,000	
Name or title	$0	$0	$0	
Name or title	$0	$0	$0	
Other	$0	$0	$0	
Other	$0	$0	$0	
Total Payroll	**$484,800**	**$2,800,000**	**$4,850,000**	
Total Headcount	0	0	0	
Payroll Burden	$58,176	$336,000	$582,000	
Total Payroll Expenditures	**$542,976**	**$3,136,000**	**$5,432,000**	

The over-all financial plan for growth allows for use of the significant cash flow generated by operations.

FINANCIAL PLAN

Equity/debt infusion of $1.5 to $2 million allows for more rapid expansion of store starts than could be accomplished from cash flow alone. Outside investment capital also allows a buffer of excess cash so that the expansion plan can be revised on short notice. Every opportunity will be seized to accelerate expansion past the critical dates in this plan if cash flow from new stores exceeds projections.

It is management's intent to build equity in the brand name and in its franchise. Other models exist in the recent past of successful IPOs on similar concepts.

The financial plan depends on the following key assumptions:

Important Assumptions

- We assume a slow-growth economy, without major recession.
- We assume access to equity capital and financing sufficient to maintain our financial plan as shown in the tables.
- We assume the continued popularity of sports in America and the growing demand for sports theme venues.

General Assumptions	FY1996	FY1997	FY1998
Short-term Interest Rate %	8.50%	8.50%	8.50%
Long-term Interest Rate %	0.00%	0.00%	0.00%
Payment Days Estimator	7	7	7
Inventory Turnover Estimator	52	52	52
Tax Rate %	33.00%	33.00%	33.00%
Expenses in Cash %	80.00%	80.00%	80.00%
Personnel Burden %	12.00%	12.00%	12.00%

The most important indicator in our case is inventory turnover. In the restaurant business turnover exceeds 50, with product being purchased and sold often within the week.

Key Financial Indicators

Food costs must be kept below 32%. Beverage costs must be kept below 21%. Above all, controls must be instituted and maintained over multiple store locations.

Take Five now uses state-of-the-art restaurant management control and inventory systems. All systems are computer-based that allow for accurate off-premises control of all aspects of food and beverage service business. The systems used are point-of-sale from HSI and inventory and recipe management from VIP. Also, both are PC-based and have become industry standards.

Management's background in corporate finance indicates understanding of the importance of these control systems.

Breakeven Analysis

The breakeven analysis is based upon fixed costs at the Medlock Bridge location. This location exceeded required volume to break even in only its second month of operation.

At $15 per average ticket, the breakeven volume at Medlock Bridge is attained in less than one full seating per day. The industry average is between 3 and 4 turns of seating capacity.

Breakeven Analysis

Monthly Units Breakeven	91,892
Monthly Sales Breakeven	$91,892

Assumptions

Average Per-Unit Revenue	$1.00
Average Per-Unit Variable Cost	$0.26
Estimated Monthly Fixed Cost	$68,000

Projected Profit and Loss

We project rapid expansion of sales and profits. Net profits remain above 16% of sales even in the most aggressive expansion period.

Profit and Loss (Income Statement)	FY1996	FY1997	FY1998
Sales	$2,042,644	$9,198,000	$16,084,000
Direct Cost of Sales	$577,638	$2,531,380	$4,435,640
Other	$0	$0	$0
Total Cost of Sales	**$577,638**	**$2,531,380**	**$4,435,640**
Gross Margin	$1,465,006	$6,666,620	$11,648,360
Gross Margin %	71.72%	72.48%	72.42%
OPERATING EXPENSES			
Advertising/Promotion	$33,500	$458,000	$800,000
Travel	$0	$18,000	$24,000
Miscellaneous	$36,000	$36,000	$36,000
Other	$0	$0	$0
Payroll Expense	$484,800	$2,800,000	$4,850,000
Payroll Burden	$58,176	$336,000	$582,000
Depreciation	$69,996	$280,000	$320,000
Leased Equipment	$0	$0	$0
Utilities	$28,800	$150,000	$180,000
Insurance	$36,000	$96,000	$125,000
Rent	$52,800	$197,000	$460,000
Total Operating Expenses	**$800,072**	**$4,371,000**	**$7,377,000**
Profit Before Interest and Taxes	$664,934	$2,295,620	$4,271,360
Interest Expense Short-term	$0	$0	$0
Interest Expense Long-term	$0	$0	$0
Taxes Incurred	$219,428	$757,555	$1,409,549
Net Profit	$445,506	$1,538,065	$2,861,811
Net Profit/Sales	21.81%	16.72%	17.79%

We expect to manage cash flow with an additional investment totaling $1.5 to $2 million. All additional requirements can be met from internally generated funds. With investment coming in during late 1996 and mid 1997 there is no point at which future cash flow appears to be in danger.

Projected Cash Flow

Pro-Forma Cash Flow

	FY1996	FY1997	FY1998
Net Profit	$445,506	$1,538,065	$2,861,811
PLUS			
Depreciation	$69,996	$280,000	$320,000
Change in Accounts Payable	($15,566)	$15,713	$14,012
Current Borrowing (repayment)	$0	$0	$0
Increase (decrease) Other Liabilities	$0	$0	$0
Long-term Borrowing (repayment)	$0	$0	$0
Capital Input	$625,000	$960,000	$1,250,000
Subtotal	**$1,124,936**	**$2,793,778**	**$4,445,823**
LESS			
Change in Inventory	$2,127	$58,594	$57,110
Change in Other ST Assets	$0	$0	$0
Capital Expenditure	$600,000	$700,000	$1,700,000
Dividends	$0	$0	$0
Subtotal	$602,127	$758,594	$1,757,110
Net Cash Flow	$522,809	$2,035,184	$2,688,713
Cash Balance	$589,945	$2,625,129	$5,313,842

We expect a healthy growth in net worth, from approximately $1 million at present to more than $8 million by the end of the third year of operations.

Projected Balance Sheet

Pro-Forma Balance Sheet

ASSETS	Starting Balances			
Short-term Assets		FY1996	FY1997	FY1998
Cash	$67,136	$589,945	$2,625,129	$5,313,842
Inventory	$15,197	$17,324	$75,918	$133,029
Other Short-term Assets	$17,310	$17,310	$17,310	$17,310
Total Short-term Assets	$99,643	$624,579	$2,718,357	$5,464,180
LONG-TERM ASSETS				
Capital Assets	$475,495	$1,075,495	$1,775,495	$3,475,495
Accumulated Depreciation	$29,713	$99,709	$379,709	$699,709
Total Long-term Assets	$445,782	$975,786	$1,395,786	$2,775,786
Total Assets	$545,425	$1,600,365	$4,114,143	$8,239,966
LIABILITIES AND CAPITAL				
Accounts Payable	$20,040	$4,474	$20,187	$34,199
Short-term Notes	$0	$0	$0	$0
Other Short-term Liab.	$40,826	$40,826	$40,826	$40,826
Subtotal Short-term Liab.	$60,866	$45,300	$61,013	$75,025
Long-term Liabilities	$0	$0	$0	$0
Total Liabilities	$60,866	$45,300	$61,013	$75,025

Projected Balance Sheet

Continued...

Paid in Capital	$625,000	$1,250,000	$2,210,000	$3,460,000
Retained Earnings	($218,401)	($140,441)	$305,065	$1,843,130
Earnings	$77,960	$445,506	$1,538,065	$2,861,811
Total Capital	$484,559	$1,555,065	$4,053,130	$8,164,941
Total Liab. and Capital	$545,425	$1,600,365	$4,114,143	$8,239,966
Net Worth	$484,559	$1,555,065	$4,053,130	$8,164,941

Business Ratios

Our business ratios are future estimates based upon current assumptions.

Ratio Analysis

Profitability Ratios	FY1996	FY1997	FY1998	RMA
Gross Margin	71.72%	72.48%	72.42%	0
Net Profit Margin	21.81%	16.72%	17.79%	0
Return on Assets	27.84%	37.38%	34.73%	0
Return on Equity	28.65%	37.95%	35.05%	0

Activity Ratios	FY1996	FY1997	FY1998	RMA
AR Turnover	0	0	0	0
Collection Days	0	0	0	0
Inventory Turnover	35.52	54.3	42.46	0
Accts Payable Turnover	37.31	37.31	37.31	0
Total Asset Turnover	1.28	2.24	1.95	0

Debt Ratios	FY1996	FY1997	FY1998	RMA
Debt to Net Worth	0.03	0.02	0.01	0
Short-term Liab. to Liab.	1	1	1	0

Liquidity Ratios	FY1996	FY1997	FY1998	RMA
Current Ratio	13.79	44.55	72.83	0
Quick Ratio	13.41	43.31	71.06	0
Net Working Capital	$579,279	$2,657,344	$5,389,155	0
Interest Coverage	0	0	0	0

Additional Ratios	FY1996	FY1997	FY1998	RMA
Assets to Sales	0.78	0.45	0.51	0
Debt/Assets	3%	1%	1%	0
Current Debt/Total Assets	3%	1%	1%	0
Acid Test	13.41	43.31	71.06	0
Asset Turnover	1.28	2.24	1.95	0
Sales/Net Worth	1.31	2.27	1.97	0

Used Car Business

BUSINESS PLAN

BUDGET CARS

145 Water Street
Alpena, MI 49707

This business plan addresses all relevant concerns by presenting a comprehensive account of a month-by-month marketing strategy coupled with an extensive report on all aspects of the needs of a successful used car center. The care and detail of the financial figures assures a well-thought and carefully considered proposition. Note the effort to make the lender comfortable and familiar with the staff.

- SUMMARY

- PRODUCTS AND SERVICES

- INDUSTRY DESCRIPTION

- MARKET DEFINITION

- MARKETING PLAN

- OPERATIONS

- COMPANY STRUCTURE

- FINANCIAL PLAN

- LOCATION

- RESUMES AND PERSONALITY PROFILES

SUMMARY

A. Description of the business

1. Mission—The mission of Budget Cars will be to buy and sell a desirable mix of quality used cars, trucks, and vans, and to create a friendly atmosphere where Budget Cars will be known for being your family used car center.

2. Legal Status/Location—The legal status of Budget Cars is a subchapter "S" corporation. The location is in Alpena, Michigan.

B. Products and Services—The products that Budget Cars will offer are quality used cars, trucks, and vans at below market value. The services that will be offered are in-house financing provided by area banks with approved credit and a full automotive detail center that will recondition all units for sale.

C. Market and Sales Strategy

Due to several different factors (season changes, market changes, opening date, etc.), our advertising strategies are going to vary accordingly. We are going to be consistent with our advertising in the "Out and About" section that runs every other week in the *Alpena Journal* and at least one ad once a month in the *Daily Herald.*

January 15, 1997—Our goal is to open the doors and start our advertising in the "Out and About" section of the *Alpena Journal*, $40.00 each run, reaching 5,000 homes, and an ad in the *Daily Herald.*

February—First week, buy the front page of the *Daily Herald,* $525.00, reaching 17,000 homes and continue with every other week in the *Alpena Journal.* Also concentrate on 3 spots a week in the classifieds, about $27.00 per week.

March—This month we'll continue our "Out and About" section, 3 spots a week in the classifieds, and at least one ad in the *Daily Herald* to keep in contact with the out county.

April—"Grand Opening" will be held this month. With the snow gone and everyone ready for a cookout, we'll have our "Family Festive." Included in this will be a tent, grilling hot dogs, contacting acquaintances with "Victorian" cars, and asking them to bring them to the lot for display. Also, the "Out and About" section and the ads in the classifieds will be run along with an ad in the *Daily Herald.*

May, June, and July—We'll start with a little radio advertising, maybe sponsoring a morning weather program and continuing with our "Out and About" section and an ad in the *Daily Herald.* As for the classifieds, we'll determine at that time if they are worth using.

August, September, and October—Still keeping with radio, sponsor a local high school sport and continue the "Out and About" section and an ad in the *Daily Herald.*

November—We'll go with the "Out and About" section and the ad in the *Daily Herald* and determine if it's time to advertise in the classifieds.

December—Have a coloring contest for the kids, with prizes that tie in with the holidays, advertising in the *Alpena Journal* and the *Daily Herald.*

Budgeting $575.00 a month, a total of $6,900.00 a year, this should be a realistic dollar amount and provide us with plenty of exposure.

D. Management Team and Responsibilities—The management team members are Ben Heath, Margerie Heath, and Peter James, with Ben ultimately being the leader. Margerie's responsibilities will include F&I, bookkeeping, answering and routing phone calls and payroll. Peter will be maintaining and operating the automotive detail center. Ben will be responsible for the buying and selling of automobiles and overseeing all operations.

The number one responsibility of our management team is to create a friendly atmosphere where our customers come first. They will always be courteously acknowledged with a friendly smile and a handshake.

E. Objectives of the Management Team

1. Our main objective is to buy and sell 180 quality used vehicles in the first year of operation, with an increase per year of 60 vehicles, ultimately reaching an average of 300 cars per year.
2. We project $171,000.00 in gross profit for the first year, making that a $950.00 per unit gross after marketing sales expense is deducted, increasing accordingly with the number of units sold per year to reach our $315,000.00 gross profit by the fourth year.

F. Financial Considerations

1. Profit Projections—Budget Cars will have a net profit in the first year of operations.
2. Balance Sheet Projections—We are projecting an increase of net worth of the business by $39,154.05.

A. Initial Products and Services—When we first open in January 1997, if the weather is typically like most northern Michigan winters, there will be snow on the ground. Purposely the inventory will be minimal and focus on 4x4 trucks, utility units, and a family budget row of used cars that will satisfy the second car needs.

B. Need for the Product and Service—With the prices of new vehicles reaching an average of $20,000.00 plus, and continually raising each year, the used car, truck, and van market has become stronger. That's why Budget Cars is opening their doors in January 1997 to take a share of the market which is wide open in this area.

C. Major Suppliers—A majority of the vehicles that Budget Cars will offer will come from auctions and new car dealerships. The auctions will be our major suppliers of late model vehicles and the new car dealerships will be an access to the vehicles we can offer between $3,000.00 - $7,500.00. Other vehicles will come from trade-ins and private purchase units.

PRODUCTS AND SERVICES

A. Background of the Industry—Immediately following World War II, there were roughly nine buyers for every new car produced. Sales personnel merely had to find out who could afford a new car. "Afford" was defined as paying cash. This condition existed until the early 1950s when supply began to discover that some new terms were creeping into the retail salesperson's vocabulary. Words like "overallowance," "discount," "deal," and "terms." The emphasis, however, was still not on product but on price. In addition, the asking price was no longer final. There was also, if you could haggle a little, a taking price. It was possible to bargain with the dealer for the first time.

During the 1960s, other new merchandising techniques were introduced. "Sticker price," "fleet price," "hard sell," "50 over invoice," "high-powered advertising," and "free" accessories were but a few new innovations. The buyer was becoming better educated, better able to buy—thanks to 24- and 36-month payments—but still confused and fearful of price. "Good

INDUSTRY DESCRIPTION

deals" became "bad deals" after talking to friends and neighbors. Caution became the watchword when buying a car.

The advent of the 1970s brought more confusion to buyers with new procedures like leasing, 48-month payments, credit unions, rebates, and consumer advocates. However, in defense of the consumer, books on "How to Buy a Car," "Invoice Prices U.S. Cars," and "Used Car Buyers Guide," were published and sold by the millions.

During the 1970s automobile salespeople became conditioned to the notion that customers were interested in only one thing—the very lowest price. The automobile showroom atmosphere didn't change very much from the 1970s to the 1980s. Most retail salespeople saw the business of selling automobile as an "us against them" hard-sell game. Those who sold popular Japanese products became arrogant and insensitive to their customers and those of us who sold American vehicles continued with the approach that price, and price alone, sells vehicles.

As the 1980s came to a close, however, the winds of change began to impact the retail automobile marketplace. Today, in the mid 1990s, the business of retailing automobiles is quite different than it has ever been in the past.

In today's marketplace, 5 out of every 6 cars sold in the United States are used.

B. Trade Association Assistance—Federal Register offers assistance with compliance guidelines for used car rules and (NADA) National Auto Dealers Association offers assistance.

C. Industry Trends—Vehicle sales seems to be a trend with our Michigan seasons. While the sun is shining and the temperatures are warm, outdoor family activities become more popular, encouraging camping, vacations, and sight seeing. These activities increase the demand for minivans, station wagons, and sport utility vehicles. As the kids head back to school and the weather turns cold, road conditions deteriorate. This creates demand for a more rugged, durable unit such as light duty trucks and vans. The extra security of four-wheel drive is also more popular during this season.

D. Number and Kind of Businesses in the Area in the Industry—There are four new car dealerships in Alpena that offer a line of used vehicles. There are also three used car lots in town offering a very limited selection of units.

E. Major Influences on the Industry

1. Government Regulations—An important regulation of the government is to obtain and maintain a class "B" license. The Federal Trade Commission also publishes rules and regulations for operating a used car lot. The used car rule has four basic components. (1) Prepare and display a Buyers Guide on each used vehicle offered to the consumer. (2) To include a special disclosure in the contract of sale. (3) To identify the final warranty terms in the contract of sale. (4) To give the purchaser a copy of the Buyers Guide that includes the final warranty terms.

2. Business Cycle—Ups and downs go with any industry, but with the sale of used vehicles there seems to be more of a plateau. When the economy is good, sales are great. When the economy is sluggish, used cars are still in demand because of their price factor.

A. Who Is the Customer?

1. Customer Profile—Budget Cars will be focusing on three customer profiles. One being a first-time buyer, age 16-25, next being the middle-class family looking for a second car, and third, age 50 and over low-income adults.

2. Buying Decision Determinants—After presenting to the customer quality used vehicles that have been safety checked, backed with a warranty and a competitive low price, the main determinant that we believe will bring the customer to the close is working one on one with the owners and their honesty and reputations.

3. Customer Awareness of Product/Service—Our advertising campaign will ensure that the customer knows who and where we are. Our up close and personal interview process will be a thorough, detailed, step-by-step explanation of our product and commitment to our customers' needs.

B. Market Size

1. Geographic—Our primary source of customer base will come from the local and surrounding counties. Starting from our location in Alpena, all of the counties are within a thirty-mile radius.

2. Population—The total population of our targeted customer base is 93,945 people. Using Alpena as a comparison, according to the Census taken in 1990, the total population of Alpena County was 21,265. The number of 18- to 25-year-olds was 1,547, the number of people 25-54 was 8,344, leaving a total of 6,273 over the age of 55. The percentage of population that was over the age of 18 at that time was 76%.

3. Sales—A statistic taken in 1990 determined the number of vehicles available per occupied housing unit in Alpena County. Of 8,580 housing units, 777 had no means of motorized transportation, 3,132 owned one vehicle, 3,346 housing units owned two vehicles, and 1,325 had three or more. In order for Budget Cars to reach its projected first-year goal of 15 units per month, only 2.4% of the Alpena market needs to be cornered. Any units sold to customers within the rest of the targeted counties will be additional business.

C. Market Growth—An estimated population increase throughout our targeted counties can only mean more people with a need for transportation. There was a population increase from 21,265 to 27,912 in Alpena County by 1995.

D. Competition

1. Who's the Competition in Alpena?
  a. New and Used Car Dealerships
    1. Jenson's Sales and Service
      Dodge, Chrysler, Jeep, Eagle, and used vehicles
    2. Alpena Ford Mercury
      Ford, Mercury and used vehicles
    3. Boji Buick Pontiac Oldsmobile GMC
      Buick, Pontiac, Oldsmobile, GMC Trucks, and used vehicles
    4. Miller Chevrolet Cadillac Geo
      Chevrolet, Cadillac, Geo, and used vehicles
  b. Used Vehicle Dealers Only
    1. Car Trade Center
    2. Thunderbird Auto
    3. Jake's Auto Parts

2. Strengths and Weaknesses of the Competition—Jenson's Sales and Service is selling new and used cars on a more relaxed approach. Alpena Ford Mercury is aggressive in both new and used vehicle sales, with the majority of their used cars being higher priced program cars. Boji's is focused on new car sales. Miller offers new and used vehicles but are not very aggressive. There are three older used car lots in town that maintain a "B" license. Selling cars is not their main source of income. Very little, if any, priority is given to car sales.

E. Pricing—Budget Cars is in a better position than our larger competitors because the overhead is much lower. All deals will be conducted between the owner and customer with no commission paid salesperson taking a cut from the profit made on the deal. The clean-up and reconditioning of all vehicles will be completed in-house. This way we will be able to beat the larger dealers' prices every time and still make enough profit to maintain business expenses and build capital for future expansion. Our main goal will be to sell more for less and be known as "Your Family Used Car Center."

MARKETING PLAN

A. Marketing Overview—Budget Cars plans to focus on young first-time auto buyers, familes with second car needs, and low-income adults aged 50 and over. To capture this market we plan to advertise with the local newspaper and radio. But, more importantly, is the support and participation that we will show in community activities.

B. Marketing Objectives—Budget Cars's main marketing objective is to focus on the customers' wants and needs and, at the same time, maintain a marketable selection of vehicles at all times. This will allow us to effectively influence and persuade them to buy.

C. Marketing Strategy

1. Advertising—Our main advertising strategy is to let our potential customer know that we are aware of their wants and needs and have quality inventory and prices. To prove it, we will let them know that if we don't have what they're looking for, we'll get it.

2. Marketing Budget—From the time that Budget Cars takes possession, until the point of sale, the marketing budget will average $300.00 per unit. This includes the driver's expense, a safety check, repair work, if needed, reconditioning, and all forms and documents used to track market trends.

OPERATIONS

A. Facility Requirements—The ideal facility for Budget Cars is a highly visible location with a lot large enough to hold 30 units and enough space for customer parking. Also, we will need a building large enough to house a reconditioning center and a sales floor with several private offices.

B. Equipment Requirements

1. Reconditioning Department—The equipment needed for this area will be a rug doctor, shop vacuum, stripping wheel, six-foot ladder, hose and nozzle, buffer, heat gun, miscellaneous small tools, and a plow vehicle for snow removal.

2. Office and Sales Department—The equipment needed for this area will be two desks, nine chairs, one computer and printer, one fax machine, two phones, copy machine, two calculators, and a coffee machine.

C. Labor Requirements—Budget Cars will have two salaried owners as their main operators. Ben will be manning the sales and Peter will take care of the reconditioning department. Margerie, a full-time employee, will be handling the office duties.

A. Legal Status—Budget Cars will be a subchapter "S" corporation.

B. Business Advisors

    1. Accountant—William P. Johnson of William P. Johnson Company PC CPAs, Alpena, Michigan, will be Budget Cars' accountant.

    2. Insurance—Cheryl Booker and Robert Ordowski of The Floyd Agency, Alpena, Michigan, will be Budget Cars' insurance agents.

    3. Consultant—Phillip J. West of Alpena Community College, Alpena, Michigan, has been a consultant for Budget Cars.

COMPANY STRUCTURE

A. Start-Up Costs—The start-up cost for Budget Cars will be $9,994.00. This figure includes office supplies, $377.00; marketing and reconditioning, $4,215.00; accounting and legal, $1,350.00; rental security deposit, $1,100.00; insurances, $1,575.00; gas expenses, $300.00; car phone and pager, $100.00; Chamber of Commerce dues, $177.00; and improvements to location, $800.00.

B. Sources/Uses of Funds—Personal funds, a $25,000.00 ten-year loan and $150,000.00 of floor plan will be used to operate the business.

C. Summary of Financial Projections

    1. Cash Flow Projections—Budget Cars foresees no cash flow projection problems.

    2. Profit/Loss Projections/Breakeven Analysis—The Company expects to have a gross profit the first year of $60,237.00.

    3. Balance Sheet Projections—Budget Cars projects an increase of net worth the first year to be $39,154.05.

FINANCIAL PLAN

A. Business Location—Budget Cars will be located in Alpena, Michigan.

B. Location Costs—The lease of the building will be $600.00 per month for two years.

C. Licenses, Permits and other Regulations—Budget Cars will need a class "B" dealership license, a sales tax I.D. number, and a city permit for the opening.

D. Insurance Needs—Budget Cars will need Fleet Insurance, Workman's Compensation, Renters' Insurance, and will be carrying health insurance for the shareholders.

LOCATION

This chart is a projection of our monthly cash flow after expenses. These figures have been meticulously researched and should be very close to the actual amounts. A start-up cost of $9,994.00 has not been included with these calculations.

Income Statement

Projected Yearly Gross Profit

This chart shows the average gross profit per unit and the profit potential with volume. Budget Cars has established goals in gross profit and volume for the next four years.

Projected Yearly Gross Profit (with sales marketing expenses deducted)

Average # of Units Per Month	Average Profit Per Unit					
	900	950	1000	1050	1100	1150
15	162,000	171,000	180,000	189,000	198,000	207,000
17	183,600	193,800	204,000	214,200	224,400	234,600
18	194,400	205,200	216,000	226,800	237,600	248,400
20	216,000	228,000	240,000	252,000	264,000	276,000
23	248,400	262,200	276,000	289,800	303,600	317,400
25	270,000	285,000	300,000	315,000	330,000	345,000

Projected Monthly Material Expenses

This chart shows the materials required monthly for the clean-up and reconditioning of 15 safety-checked units.

Projected Monthly Material Expenses Based on 15 Units

AMOUNT REQ.	ITEM DESCRIPTION	PRICE EACH	TOTAL
2 Gallons	Tire Dressing	25.00/Gal.	50.00
2 Gallons	Interior Cleaner	10.50/Gal	21.00
2 Gallons	Mag Wheel Cleaner	15.50/Gal	31.00
1 Gallon	Window Cleaner	9.00/Gal	9.00
1/4 Gallon	Miracle Wax	24.00/Gal	6.00
1/4 Gallon	Rubbing Compound	16.00/Gal	4.00
1/2 Gallon	Bug Remover	10.50/Gal	5.25
4 Each	Buffing Pads	4.50/each	18.00
3 Each	Stripping Pads	8.50/each	25.50
6 Each	Interior Paint	4.50/each	27.00
6 Each	Semi Gloss Paint	3.00/each	18.00
1/4 Gallon	Interior Deodorant	21.00/Gal	5.25
3 Gallons	Wash Soap	12.50/Gal	37.50
1 Each	Chamois	20.00/each	20.00
2 Gallons	Mineral Spirits	5.00/Gal	10.00
1/4 Package	Razor Blades	12.00/each	3.00
1 Case	Paper Towels	18.00/Case	18.00
5 Each	Wax Applicator	2.00/each	10.00
1/2 Roll	Polishing (Cheese) Cloth	30.00/Roll	15.00
6 Each	Touch up Paint	4.00/each	24.00
TOTAL			**357.50**

(These figures are included in the Sales Marketing Expense.)

This list includes the necessary steps to take when acquiring a Class "B" Dealers License.

Class "B" Licensing Requirements
Original Application
Assumed Name and/or Corporate Filing
Fingerprint Cards
Sketch or Photo of Business Location
Zoning Approval
Sheriff or Police Signature
Repair Facility or Service Agreement
Sales Tax License
Secretary of State Branch Designation
Fleet Insurance
2 Dealer Plates (Minimum)
$10,000 Vehicle Dealer Surety Bond

Class "B" Licensing Requirements

This chart shows the number of vehicles per housing unit in Alpena County. We only need 2.4% of this market to reach our first-year gross profit goal.

Number of Vehicles Available per Household

Townships	Occupied Housing Units	None	One	Two	Three or More
Ashland	245	8	89	99	49
Botten	544	24	158	248	114
Cathro	199	0	40	92	67
Grass Island	244	25	73	107	39
Herron	316	20	140	112	44
Hubbard Lake	763	40	241	333	149
Lachine	2,896	492	1,256	888	260
Leer	1,092	33	350	505	204
Long Rapids	449	43	162	172	72
Metz	108	2	43	31	32
Ossineke	470	34	166	198	72
Polaski	521	36	163	208	114
Posen	257	3	98	122	34
Presque Isle	200	7	63	91	39
Sprat	276	10	90	140	36
Alpena County	**8,580**	**777**	**3,132**	**3,346**	**1,325**

Source: United States 1990 Census (April 1, 1990) summary tape file 3A. Tables compiled by the Alpena County Planning Department for Alpena County Planning Department for Alpena County municipalities.

Resumes and personality profiles of Budget Cars's management team.

RESUMES AND PERSONALITY PROFILES

BEN HEATH

CAREER GOAL

To own and operate a successful used-car dealership that I can devote all my energy and enthusiasm to.

WORK EXPERIENCE

Pine Country Ford, August 1986 - October 1990/July 1996 - Present (Sales Manager / Consultant)

*Create and maintain a diverse customer base *Conduct telephone interviews with potential customers *Maintain a thorough knowledge of all current inventory *Determine which inventory is marketable and contact buyers that may be interested *Persuade buyers into a one-on-one meeting *Recognize and satisfy customers' wants and needs *Assist customers in determining which vehicle and financing terms best fit their needs *Be the connecting link between the buyer and dealer while settling on a price which satisfies all parties involved

Alpena Ford Mercury, January 1991-June 1996 (Sales Consultant / Sales Manager)

*Oversee all sales operations to include showroom, display lot, and reconditioning shop *Appraise trade-in vehicles and offer a fair price that will encourage a sale and create a marketable trade-in *Order new vehicles from factory for retail and dealership inventory *Create a positive, enthusiastic atmosphere for the subordinate sales consultants that will promote increasing sales and high moral *Devise and carry out marketing plans to include advertising & promotions that will ensure growth and sales *Recognize customer needs and limitations through brief descriptions provided by sales consultants *Request and accept dealer trades that will satisfy a multitude of parties involved *Interact with the public on a constant daily basis in a positive, friendly, honest manner *Create and maintain a consistent marketable lot that will stimulate sales and growth through consumer tracking, market trends, and analyzing area economic status

United States Marines, March 1982 - July 1986 (Medical Administration Specialist)

*Decipher doctor-prepared patient charts and type them for future reference *Monitor, maintain, file, and organize patient records to ensure quality care *Operate all office equipment to include multi-line telephone, computer, printer, copy machine, facsimile machine

EDUCATIONAL BACKGROUND

University of Miami, Miami, Florida - December 1989, Used Vehicle Management

Ford Division Increasing Sales through Prospecting Course - April 1987

Ford Division Compact and Full-Size Light Truck Selling Course - March 1987

Ford Division National Walk Around Course (First place in competition) - February 1987

Roger Bolt Advance Sales Course - October 1986

Roger Bolt Professional Sales Course - November 1986

Alpena Community College, Alpena, Michigan - September 1981-June 1982, Business Management

*Psychology *Public Speaking

Central High School, New York, New York - September 1981-June 1982

*Algebra *Geometry *Accounting *English *Government *Economics *History *Social Studies

SPECIAL QUALIFICATIONS

*Ford Division Legend Leaders 300/500 Leadership Recognition Award 1995 *Top 10%
Customer Satisfaction Diplomat Society Honors 1991, 1992, 1993, and 1994 *Ford Division
Recognition for being the Top Salesperson for Alpena Ford 1990, 1991, 1992, 1993, promoted
to Sales Manager in 1994 *Ford Division Recognition for being the Top Salesperson for Pine
Country Ford 1986, 1987, promoted to Sales Manager in 1988 and in 1989 won Ford Division
Professional Sales Managers Award, Top 10%

OUTSIDE INTERESTS

*Sunday School Teaching *Camping *Horseback Riding *Participating in outdoor activities
with family *Gardening *Handy work around the house

REFERENCES AVAILABLE UPON REQUEST

Summary of Predictive Index Results

Name: Ben Heath
Survey Date: June 12, 1996
Report Date: June 24, 1996

Ben is an engaging, stimulating communicator, poised and capable of projecting enthusiasm
and warmth, and of motivating other people.

He has a strong sense of urgency, initiative, and competitive drive to get things done, with
emphasis on working with people in the process. He understands people well and uses that
understanding effectively in influencing and persuading others to act.

Impatient for results, and particularly impatient with details and routines, Ben is a confident
and venturesome "doer" and decision-maker who will delegate details and can also delegate
responsibility and authority when necessary. Ben is a self-starter who is skillful at training and
developing others. He applies pressure for results, but in doing so, his style is more "selling"
than "telling."

At ease and self-assured with groups or in making new contacts, Ben is gregarious and
extroverted, has an invigorating impact on people, and is always "selling" in a general sense.
He learns and reacts quickly and works at a faster-than-average pace. Able to adapt quickly
to change and variety in his work, he will become impatient and less effective if required to
work primarily with repetitive routines and details.

In general terms, Ben is an ambitious and driving person who is motivated by opportunity for
advancement to levels of responsibility where he can use his skills as team builder, motivator,
and mover.

MANAGEMENT STRATEGIES

To maximize his effectiveness, productivity, and job satisfaction, consider providing Ben with
the following:

* Opportunities for involvement and interaction with people
* Some independence and flexibility in his activities

* Freedom from repetitive routine and details in work which provide variety and change of pace
* Opportunities to learn and advance at a fairly fast pace
* Recognition and reward for communications and leadership skills demonstrated
* Social and status recognition as rewards for achievement.

Prepared by: John Harper
Copyright © 1994 by Profiles, Inc. All rights reserved.

PETER JAMES

OCCUPATIONAL GOAL

Seeking employment with a professional establishment that provides a challenging stimulating work atmosphere to individuals who demonstrate a positive self-starting attitude.

WORK EXPERIENCE

* Alpena Ford Mercury, 1/17/95-Present Employer (Automotive Appearance Enhancement Technician) *Clean and detail engine compartments. *Strip excess finishes and imperfections with low RPM power wheel. *Repair minor scratches and discolorations of surface paints. *Rustproof over spray removal. *Paint Protection application. *Apply new finishes. *Perform interior cleaning and minor repair. *Apply dye to carpets and upholstery. *Operate industrial debris extractor. *Apply after market and OEM accessories.

* American Waste Systems, 1/14/94-11/9/94 (Route Coordinator) *Maintain continuity of 10 collection routes by filling in and training new drivers for routes with short callings. *Organize route changes for maximum efficiency and make changes in computer automated route sheets. *Complete route audits and analysis.

* Jackson's Disposal Service Inc., 1/6/91-1/13/94 (Collection Route Driver) *Operate manual and automatic transmission heavy trucks *Operate Clark Pneumatic Forklift. *Operate industrial recycling equipment such as cardboard baler, paper shredder, and glass crusher. *Operate FCC licensed two-way radios. *Operate front end loaders.

* Holiday Inn of Alpena, 7/11/90-10/12/90 (Night Auditor) *Investigate cashier discrepancies *Credit card collection. *Complete computer automated audits. *Computer interfacing. *Accounts Payable/Receivable. *Word processing. *Facsimile sending & receiving *Modem communication. *Automated telephone switchboard operation.

* United States Marines, 8/9/84-2/23/90 (Food Service Shift Leader, 4/1/89-2/20/90) (Shift Supervisor 3/10/88-4/1/89) (Night Auditor 1/1/86-3/10/88) (Desk Clerk 10/15/84-1/1/86) *Operate Wang Mainframe Computer. *Operate NCR cash register. *Utilize manual and computerized telephone switchboards. *Prepare City Ledger Accounts. *Accounts Payable/Receivable. *Bank deposits. *Assign Duties. *Prepare schedules. *Train personnel on computer. *Complete employee performance reports. *Meal preparation and stock ordering. *Calculate amount of food required for each day's consumption.

EDUCATIONAL BACKGROUND

- ASB Leadership School, June 7, 1989-July 6, 1989 *People/Resource Management

- Alpena Community College, August 28, 1988-June 1, 1989 *Mathematics *Music

- Community College of the Marines, October 15, 1984-February 23, 1990 *Hotel/
  Restaurant Management

- Alpena High School, September 1, 1982-June 1, 1984 [Diploma 3.5 GPA] *Accounting
  *Algebra *Art *Geometry *English *Drafting *Physics

SPECIAL QUALIFICATIONS

*Own and operate Acer 7100 personal computer with Microsoft Windows/Works & MS DOS.
Also Installed Drivers for a Canon BJC 4000 Ink Jet Printer that is used with this computer.
*Clean driving record with a commercial Class B endorsement. *Own & operate various
Multi-Track sound recorders and mixers. *Perform extensive automobile repair & Car Stereo
installations.

OUTSIDE INTERESTS

*Playing Guitar *Sound Recording *Operating my personal computer *Electronics *Auto-
mobiles *Home remodeling

REFERENCES AVAILABLE UPON REQUEST

Summary of Predictive Index Results

Name: Peter James
Survey Date: September 11, 1996
Report Date: September 11, 1996

Peter is an intense, results-oriented, self-starter, whose drive and sense of urgency are
tempered and disciplined by his concern for the accuracy and quality of his work. His approach
to anything he does, or is responsible for, will be carefully thought-out, based on thorough
analysis and detailed knowledge of all pertinent facts.

Strongly technically oriented, he has confidence in his professional knowledge and ability to
get things done quickly and correctly. With experience, he will develop a high level of
expertise in his work and will be very aware of mistakes made either by himself or anybody
doing work under his supervision. Peter takes his work and responsibilities very seriously and
expects others to do the same.

In social matters, Peter is reserved and private, with little interest in small talk. His interest and
his energy will be focused primarily on his work and, in general, he is more comfortable and
open in the work environment than he is in purely social situations. In expressing himself in
his work environment he is factual, direct, and authoritative.

Imaginative and venturesome, Peter is a creative person, capable of developing new ideas,
systems, plans, or technology, or of analyzing and improving old ones. He relies primarily on
his own knowledge and thinking, with little reference to others, relying as much as possible

on himself alone to get things done. He will find it difficult to delegate, feeling strongly that if he is to be sure that something is done right, he must do it himself.

When, as a supervisor, it may be necessary for Peter to delegate details, he will follow up very closely and will be quick to spot and correct mistakes. His primary concern is to get things done right and quickly, and in accomplishing that goal he will be demanding of himself and others. While he may be perceived by other people as a rather aloof person, he will earn their respect for his knowledge of his work and the soundness of his decisions.

MANAGEMENT STRATEGIES

To maximize his effectiveness, productivity, and job satisfaction, consider providing Peter with the following:

- Opportunities to broaden the technical knowledge of his work with learning experience in increasingly responsible positions
- As much autonomy as possible in expressing his ideas and putting them into action
- Recognition for tangible results obtained, rather than for political or selling skills

Prepared by: John Harper
Copyright © 1994 by Profiles, Inc. All rights reserved.

MARGERIE HEATH

CAREER GOAL

To contribute the skills and abilities needed in the successful formation and continued operation of a profitable business.

WORK EXPERIENCE

Henderson Real Estate, June 1996-Present - Smith Realty, May 1987-June 1989 [Receptionist/Sales Agent]

*Receive and route phone calls *Arrange and store of documents *Prepare legal documents and business forms with word processor *Greet customers *Build and maintain a customer base *Identify the needs of customer requests *Present a list of available options *Conduct tours of properties of their interests *Acting as Liaison between Seller and Buyer to reach a result which is suitable to all parties

Hidden Valley Resort, June 1984-May 1996 - Duchess Inn, July 1987-January 1989 (Waitress/Hostess/Bartender/Supervision)

*Provide people a with warm, friendly atmosphere *Take orders and relay them to the kitchen staff utilizing a data processor *Fulfill orders and beverage requests in a quick and orderly manner *Monitor dining area and recognizing patrons' needs *Prepare guest check on computer *Process payment and provide correct change to guest *Recognize personnel shortages and take necessary action *Delegate responsibilities to co-workers *Train new personnel *Credit card collection *Prepare bank deposits

EDUCATIONAL BACKGROUND

Michigan State University, September 1984-February 1987 *Business Administration/ Psychology

Northern High School, September 1980-June 1984 *Business *Accounting *Algebra *Geometry *Pre-Calculus *English *Typing

SPECIAL QUALIFICATIONS

*Maintain a valid real estate license *Teach Sunday School Courses *Full-time parent *Outgoing *6 year Cheerleader *Awarded for top monthly sales October 1995 *Caring *Enthusiastic

OUTSIDE INTERESTS

*Camping *Riding bike *Participating in outdoor sports of all kinds *Cooking *Playing cards *Gardening

REFERENCES AVAILABLE UPON REQUEST

Summary of Predictive Index Results

Name: Margerie Heath
Survey Date: July 10, 1996
Report Date: July 10, 1996

Margerie is a patient, stable, and cooperative person who will do her work as instructed and will depend on management and professional training to provide the necessary guidelines. She has the patience and tolerance required for routine work and can be relied on to do such work consistently and in a relaxed manner.

She will focus on the details of her work and will handle them with somewhat better-than-average accuracy. In work involving repeated contact with people, Margerie will be pleasant and agreeable, helpful and cooperative. She derives satisfaction from being of service to others, works comfortably under close supervision, and likes to feel part of a secure team.

Fairly easygoing, Margerie works at a steady, relatively unhurried pace and is comfortable doing the same things in the same way repeatedly. In the event of change in her work and responsibility, she needs to be given time to learn the new work thoroughly, which is best done with some opportunity for practice. Once having learned, she retains well.

In social terms, Margerie is unassuming, friendly and pleasant in general contact. She is a patient and willing listener, particularly with people she knows well and with whom she feels at ease.

Dependably consistent and steady in her work habits, Margerie will need close support and encouragement from supervision when she is required to work under pressure or in changing conditions.

MANAGEMENT STRATEGIES

To maximize her effectiveness, productivity, and job satisfaction, consider providing Margerie with the following:

- Thorough, careful training in all detailed aspects and routines of her job

- Opportunity for repetitive practice doing what she has been trained to do

- A stable, familiar work environment and organization, with assurance of security provided by helpful, supportive management

- Expressions of recognition for long service, cooperation and work well done

- Assurances of stability, security, and continuity of relations with familiar coworkers

Prepared by: John Harper

Appendix A - Business Plan Template

Business Plan Template

USING THIS TEMPLATE

A business plan carefully spells out a company's projected course of action over a period of time, usually the first two to three years after the start-up. In addition, banks, lenders, and other investors examine the information and financial documentation before deciding whether or not to finance a new business venture. Therefore, a business plan is an essential tool in obtaining financing and should describe the business itself in detail as well as all important factors influencing the company, including the market, industry, competition, operations and management policies, problem solving strategies, financial resources and needs, and other vital information. The plan enables the business owner to anticipate costs, plan for difficulties, and take advantage of opportunities, as well as design and implement strategies that keep the company running as smoothly as possible.

This template has been provided as a model to help you construct your own business plan. Please keep in mind that there is no single acceptable format for a business plan, and that this template is in no way comprehensive, but serves as an example.

The business plans provided in this section are fictional and have been used by small business agencies as models for clients to use in compiling their own business plans.

GENERIC BUSINESS PLAN

Main headings included below are topics that should be covered in a comprehensive business plan. They include:

Business Summary

Purpose
Provides a brief overview of your business, succinctly highlighting the main ideas of your plan.

Includes
- Name and Type of Business
- Description of Product/Service
- Business History and Development
- Location
- Market
- Competition
- Management
- Financial Information
- Business Strengths and Weaknesses
- Business Growth

Table of Contents

Purpose

Organized in an Outline Format, the Table of Contents illustrates the selection and arrangement of information contained in your plan.

Includes

- Topic Headings and Subheadings
- Page Number References

Business History and Industry Outlook

Purpose

Examines the conception and subsequent development of your business within an industry specific context.

Includes

- Start-up Information
- Owner/Key Personnel Experience
- Location
- Development Problems and Solutions
- Investment/Funding Information
- Future Plans and Goals
- Market Trends and Statistics
- Major Competitors
- Product/Service Advantages
- National, Regional, and Local Economic Impact

Product/Service

Purpose

Introduces, defines, and details the product and/or service that inspired the information of your business.

Includes

- Unique Features
- Niche Served
- Market Comparison
- Stage of Product/Service Development
- Production
- Facilities, Equipment, and Labor
- Financial Requirements
- Product/Service Life Cycle
- Future Growth

Market Examination

Purpose

Assessment of product/service applications in relation to consumer buying cycles.

Includes

- Target Market
- Consumer Buying Habits
- Product/Service Applications
- Consumer Reactions
- Market Factors and Trends
- Penetration of the Market
- Market Share
- Research and Studies
- Cost
- Sales Volume and Goals

Competition

Purpose

Analysis of Competitors in the Marketplace.

Includes

- Competitor Information
- Product/Service Comparison
- Market Niche
- Product/Service Strengths and Weaknesses
- Future Product/Service Development

Marketing

Purpose

Identifies promotion and sales strategies for your product/service.

Includes

- Product/Service Sales Appeal
- Special and Unique Features
- Identification of Customers
- Sales and Marketing Staff
- Sales Cycles
- Type of Advertising/Promotion
- Pricing
- Competition
- Customer Services

Operations

Purpose

Traces product/service development from production/inception to the market environment.

Includes

- Cost Effective Production Methods
- Facility
- Location
- Equipment
- Labor
- Future Expansion

Administration and Management

Purpose

Offers a statement of your management philosophy with an in-depth focus on processes and procedures.

Includes

- Management Philosophy
- Structure of Organization
- Reporting System
- Methods of Communication
- Employee Skills and Training
- Employee Needs and Compensation
- Work Environment
- Management Policies and Procedures
- Roles and Responsibilities

Key Personnel

Purpose

Describes the unique backgrounds of principle employees involved in business.

Includes

- Owner(s)/Employee Education and Experience
- Positions and Roles
- Benefits and Salary
- Duties and Responsibilities
- Objectives and Goals

Potential Problems and Solutions

Purpose

Discussion of problem solving strategies that change issues into opportunities.

Includes

- Risks
- Litigation
- Future Competition
- Economic Impact
- Problem Solving Skills

Financial Information

Purpose

Secures needed funding and assistance through worksheets and projections detailing financial plans, methods of repayment, and future growth opportunities.

Includes

- Financial Statements
- Bank Loans
- Methods of Repayment
- Tax Returns
- Start-up Costs
- Projected Income (3 years)
- Projected Cash Flow (3 Years)
- Projected Balance Statements (3 years)

Appendices

Purpose

Supporting documents used to enhance your business proposal.

Includes

- Photographs of product, equipment, facilities, etc.
- Copyright/Trademark Documents
- Legal Agreements
- Marketing Materials
- Research and or Studies
- Operation Schedules
- Organizational Charts
- Job Descriptions
- Resumes
- Additional Financial Documentation

Food Distributor

FICTIONAL BUSINESS PLAN

COMMERCIAL FOODS, INC.

3003 Avondale Ave.
Knoxville, TN 37920

October 31, 1992

This plan demonstrates how a partnership can have a positive impact on a new business. It demonstrates how two individuals can carve a niche in the specialty foods market by offering gourmet foods to upscale restaurants and fine hotels. This plan is fictional and has not been used to gain funding from a bank or other lending institution.

- STATEMENT OF PURPOSE

- DESCRIPTION OF THE BUSINESS

- MANAGEMENT

- PERSONNEL

- LOCATION

- PRODUCTS AND SERVICES

- THE MARKET

- COMPETITION

- SUMMARY

- INCOME STATEMENT

- FINANCIAL STATEMENTS

FOOD DISTRIBUTOR
BUSINESS PLAN

STATEMENT OF PURPOSE

Commercial Food, Inc. seeks a loan of $75,000 to establish a new business. This sum together with $5,000 equity investment by the principals will be used as follows:

Merchandise inventory	$25,000
Office fixture/equipment	12,000
Warehouse equipment	14,000
One delivery truck	10,000
Working capital	39,000
Total	**$100,000**

DESCRIPTION OF THE BUSINESS

Commercial Foods, Inc. will be a distributor of specialty food service products to hotels and upscale restaurants in the geographical area in a 50 mile radius of Knoxville. Richard Roberts will direct the sales effort and John Williams will manage the warehouse operation and the office. One delivery truck will be used initially with a second truck added in the third year.

We expect to begin operation of the business within 30 days after securing the requested financing.

MANAGEMENT

A. Richard Roberts is a native of Memphis, Tennessee. He is a graduate of Memphis State University with a Bachelor's degree from the School of Business. After graduation, he worked for a major manufacturer of specialty food service products as a detail sales person for five years and for the past three years, he has served as a product sales manager for this firm.

B. John Williams is a native of Nashville, Tennessee. He holds a B.S. Degree in Food Technology from the University of Tennessee. His career includes five years as a product development chemist in gourmet food products and five years as operations manager for a food service distributor.

Both men are healthy and energetic. Their backgrounds complement each other which will ensure the success of Commercial Foods, Inc. They will set policies together and personnel decisions will be made jointly. Initial salaries for the owners will be $1,000 per month for the first few years. The spouses of both principals are successful in the business world and earn enough to support the families.

They have engaged the services of Foster Jones, CPA, and William Hale, Attorney to assist them in an advisory capacity.

PERSONNEL

The firm will employ one delivery truck driver at a wage of $8.00 per hour. One office worker will be employed at $7.50 per hour. One part-time employee will be used in the office at $5.00 per hour. The driver will load and unload his own trucks. Mr. Williams will assist in the warehouse operation as needed to assist one stock person at $7.00 per hour. An additional delivery truck and driver will be added the third year.

LOCATION

The firm will lease a 20,000 square foot building at 3003 Avondale Ave., in Knoxville, which contains warehouse and office areas equipped with two-door truck docks. The annual rental is $9,000. The building was previously used as a food service warehouse and very little modification to the building will be required.

The firm will offer specialty food service products such as soup bases, dessert mixes, sauce bases, pastry mixes, spices, and flavors, normally used by upscale restaurants and nice hotels. We are going after a niche in the market with high quality gourmet products. There is much less competition in this market than in standard run of the mill food service products. Through their work experiences, the principals have contacts with supply sources and with local chefs.

PRODUCTS AND SERVICES

We know from our market survey that there are over 200 hotels and upscale restaurants in the area we plan to serve. Customers will be attracted by a direct sales approach. We will offer samples of our products and product application data on use of our products in the finished prepared foods. We will cultivate the chefs in these establishments. The technical background of John Williams will be especially useful here.

THE MARKET

We find that we will be only distributor in the area offering a full line of gourmet food service products. Other foodservice distributors offer only a few such items in conjunction with their standard product line. Our survey shows that many of the chefs are ordering products from Atlanta and Memphis because of lack of adequate local supply.

COMPETITION

Commercial Foods, Inc. will be established as a foodservice distributor of specialty food in Knoxville. The principals, with excellent experience in the industry are seeking a $75,000 loan to establish the business. The principals are investing $25,000 as equity capital.

SUMMARY

The business will be set up as an "S" Corporation with each principal owning 50% of the common stock in the corporation.

Attached is a three year pro forma income statement we believe to be conservative. Also attached are personal financial statements of the principals and a projected cash flow statement for the first year.

	1st Year	2nd Year	3rd Year
Gross Sales	300,000	400,000	500,000
Less Allowances	1,000	1,000	2,000
Net Sales	299,000	399,000	498,000
Cost of Goods Sold	179,400	239,400	298,800
Gross Margin	119,600	159,600	199,200
Operating Expenses			
Utilities	1,200	1,500	1,700
Salaries	76,000	79,000	102,000
Payroll Taxes/Benefits	9,100	9,500	13,200
Advertising	3,000	4,500	5,000
Office Supplies	1,500	2,000	2,500
Insurance	1,200	1,500	1,800
Maintenance	1,000	1,500	2,000
Outside Services	3,000	3,000	3,000
Whse Supplies/Trucks	6,000	7,000	10,000
Telephone	900	1,000	1,200
Rent	9,000	9,500	9,900
Depreciation	2,500	2,000	3,000
Total Expenses	114,400	122,000	155,300
Other Expenses			
Bank Loan Payment	15,000	15,000	15,000
Bank Loan Interest	6,000	5,000	4,000
Total Expenses	**120,400**	**142,000**	**174,300**
Net Profit (Loss)	**(800)**	**17,600**	**24,900**

PRO FORMA INCOME STATEMENT

FINANCIAL STATEMENT I

Assets		Liabilities	
Cash	15,000		
1991 Olds	11,000	Unpaid Balance	8,000
Residence	140,000	Mortgage	105,000
Mutual Funds	12,000	Credit Cards	500
Furniture	5,000	Note Payable	4,000
Merck Stock	10,000		
	182,200		117,500
Net Worth			**64,700**
	182,200		**182,200**

FINANCIAL STATEMENT II

Assets		Liabilities	
Cash	5,000		
1992 Buick Auto	15,000	Unpaid Balance	12,000
Residence	120,000	Mortgage	100,000
U.S. Treasury Bonds	5,000	Credit Cards	500
Home Furniture	4,000	Note Payable	2,500
AT&T Stock	3,000		
	147,000		115,000
Net Worth			**32,000**
	147,000		**147,000**

Hardware Store

FICTIONAL BUSINESS PLAN

OSHKOSH HARDWARE, INC.

123 Main St.
Oshkosh, WI 54901

June 1994

The following plan outlines how a small hardware store can survive competition from large discount chains by offering products and providing expert advice in the use of any product it sells. This plan is fictional and has not been used to gain funding from a bank or other lending institution.

- EXECUTIVE SUMMARY

- THE BUSINESS

- THE MARKET

- SALES

- MANAGEMENT

- GOALS IMPLEMENTATION

- FINANCE

- JOB DESCRIPTION-GENERAL MANAGER

- QUARTERLY FORECASTED BALANCE SHEETS

- QUARTERLY FORECASTED STATEMENTS OF EARNINGS AND RETAINED EARNINGS

- QUARTERLY FORECASTED STATEMENTS OF CHANGES IN FINANCIAL POSITION

- FINANCIAL RATIO ANALYSIS

- DETAILS FOR QUARTERLY STATEMENTS OF EARNINGS

EXECUTIVE SUMMARY

Oshkosh Hardware, Inc. is a new corporation which is going to establish a retail hardware store in a strip mall in Oshkosh, Wisconsin. The store will sell hardware of all kinds, quality tools, paint and housewares. The business will make revenue and a profit by servicing its customers not only with needed hardware but also with expert advice in the use of any product it sells.

Oshkosh Hardware, Inc. will be operated by its sole shareholder, James Smith. The company will have a total of four employees. It will sell its products in the local market. Customers will buy our products because we will provide free advice on the use of all of our products and will also furnish a full refund warranty.

Oshkosh Hardware, Inc. will sell its products in the Oshkosh store staffed by three sales representatives. No additional employees will be needed to achieve its short and long range goals. The primary short range goal is to open the store by October 1, 1994. In order to achieve this goal a lease must be signed by July 1, 1994 and the complete inventory ordered by August 1, 1994.

Mr. James Smith will invest $30,000 in the business. In addition the company will have to borrow $150,000 during the first year to cover the investment in inventory, accounts receivable, and furniture and equipment. The company will be profitable after six months of operation and should be able to start repayment of the loan in the second year.

THE BUSINESS

The business will sell hardware of all kinds, quality tools, paint, and housewares. We will purchase our products from three large wholesale buying groups.

In general our customers are homeowners who do their own repair and maintenance, hobbyists, and housewives. Our business is unique in that we will have a complete line of all hardware items and will be able to get special orders by overnight delivery. The business makes revenue and profits by servicing our customers not only with needed hardware but also with expert advice in the use of any product we sell. Our major costs for bringing our products to market are cost of merchandise of 36%, salaries of $45,000, and occupancy costs of $60,000.

Oshkosh Hardware, Inc.'s retail outlet will be located at 1524 Frontage Road, which is in a newly developed retail center of Oshkosh. Our location helps facilitate accessibility from all parts of town and reduces our delivery costs. The store will occupy 7500 square feet of space. The major equipment involved in our business is counters and shelving, a computer, a paint mixing machine, and a truck.

THE MARKET

Oshkosh Hardware, Inc. will operate in the local market. There are 15,000 potential customers in this market area. We have three competitors who control approximately 98% of the market at present. We feel we can capture 25% of the market within the next four years. Our major reason for believing this is that our staff is technically competent to advise our customers in the correct use of all products we sell.

After a careful market analysis we have determined that approximately 60% of our customers are men and 40% are women. The percentage of customers that fall into the following age categories are:

Under 16:	0%
17-21:	5%
22-30:	30%
31-40:	30%

41-50:	20%
51-60:	10%
61-70:	5%
Over 70:	0%

The reasons our customers prefer our products is our complete knowledge of their use and our full refund warranty.

We get our information about what products our customers want by talking to existing customers. There seems to be an increasing demand for our product. The demand for our product is increasing in size based on the change in population characteristics.

SALES

At Oshkosh Hardware, Inc. we will employ 3 sales people and will not need any additional personnel to achieve our sales goals. These salespeople will need several years experience in home repair and power tool usage. We expect to attract 30% of our customers from newspaper ads, 5% of our customers from local directories, 5% of our customers from the yellow pages, 10% of our customers from family and friends and 50% of our customers from current customers. The most cost effect source will be current customers. In general our industry is growing.

MANAGEMENT

We would evaluate the quality of our management staff as being excellent. Our manager is experienced and very motivated to achieve the various sales and quality assurance objectives we have set. We will use a management information system which produces key inventory, quality assurance and sales data on a weekly basis. All data is compared to previously established goals for that week and deviations are the primary focus of the management staff.

GOALS IMPLEMENTATION

The short term goals of our business are:

1. Open the store by October 1, 1994
2. Reach our breakeven point in two months
3. Have sales of $100,000 in the first six months

In order to achieve our first short term goal we must:

1. Sign the lease by July 1, 1994
2. Order a complete inventory by August 1, 1994

In order to achieve our second short term goal we must:

1. Advertise extensively in Sept. and Oct.
2. Keep expenses to a minimum

In order to achieve our third short term goal we must:

1. Promote power tool sales for the Christmas season
2. Keep good customer traffic in Jan. and Feb.

The long term goals for our business are:

1. Obtain sales volume of $600,000 in three years
2. Become the largest hardware dealer in the city
3. Open a second store in Fond du Lac

The most important thing we must do in order to achieve the long term goals for our business is to develop a highly profitable business with excellent cash flow.

FINANCE

Oshkosh Hardware, Inc. Faces some potential threats or risks to our business. They are discount house competition. We believe we can avoid or compensate for this by providing quality products complimented by quality advice on the use of every product we sell. The financial projections we have prepared are located at the end of this document.

JOB DESCRIPTION: GENERAL MANAGER

The General Manager of the business of the corporation will be the president of the corporation. He will be responsible for the complete operation of the retail hardware store which is owned by the corporation. A detailed description of his duties and responsibilities is as follows:

Train and supervise the three sales people. Develop programs to motivate and compensate these employees. Coordinate advertising and sales promotion effects to achieve sales totals as outlined in budget. Oversee purchasing function and inventory control procedures to insure adequate merchandise at all times at a reasonable cost.

Sales Finance

Prepare monthly and annual budgets. Secure adequate line of credit from local banks. Supervise office personnel to insure timely preparation of records, statements, all government reports, control of receivables and payables and monthly financial statements.

Administration

Perform duties as required in the areas of personnel, building leasing and maintenance, licenses and permits and public relations.

QUARTERLY FORECASTED BALANCE SHEETS

	Beg Bal	1st Qtr	2nd Qtr	3rd Qtr	4th Qtr
Assets					
Cash	30,000	418	(463)	(3,574)	4,781
Accounts Receivable	0	20,000	13,333	33,333	33,333
Inventory	0	48,000	32,000	80,000	80,000
Other Current Assets	0	0	0	0	0
Total Current Assets	30,000	68,418	44,870	109,759	118,114
Land	0	0	0	0	0
Building & Improvements	0	0	0	0	0
Furniture & Equipment	0	75,000	75,000	75,000	75,000
Total Fixed Assets	0	75,000	75,000	75,000	75,000
Less Accum. Depreciation	0	1,875	3,750	5,625	7,500
Net Fixed Assets	0	73,125	71,250	69,375	67,500
Intangible Assets	0	0	0	0	0
Less Amortization	0	0	0	0	0
Net Intangible Assets	0	0	0	0	0
Other Assets	0	0	0	0	0
Total Assets	**30,000**	**141,543**	**116,120**	**179,134**	**185,614**

	Beg Bal	1st Qtr	2nd Qtr	3rd Qtr	4th Qtr
Liabilities and Shareholders' Equity					
Short-Term Debt	0	0	0	0	0
Accounts Payable	0	12,721	10,543	17,077	17,077
Dividends Payable	0	0	0	0	0
Income Taxes Payable	0	(1,031)	(2,867)	(2,355)	(1,843)
Accured Compensation	0	1,867	1,867	1,867	1,867
Other Current Liabilities	0	0	0	0	0
Total Current Liabilities	0	13,557	9,543	16,589	17,101
Long-Term Debt	0	110,000	110,000	160,000	160,000
Other Non-Current Liabilities	0	0	0	0	0
Total Liabilities	0	123,557	119,543	176,589	177,101
Common Stock	30,000	30,000	30,000	30,000	30,000
Retained Earnings	0	(12,014)	(33,423)	(27,455)	(21,487)
Shareholders' Equity	30,000	17,986	(3,423)	2,545	8,513
Total Liabilities & Shareholders' Equity	30,000	141,543	116,120	179,134	185,614

QUARTERLY FORECASTED STATEMENTS OF EARNINGS AND RETAINED EARNINGS

	Beg Actual	1st Qtr	2nd Qtr	3rd Qtr	4th Qtr	Total
Total Sales	0	60,000	40,000	100,000	100,000	300,000
Goods/Services	0	21,600	14,400	36,000	36,000	108,000
Gross Profit	0	38,400	25,600	64,000	64,000	192,000
Operating Expenses	0	47,645	45,045	52,845	52,845	198,380
Fixed Expenses						
Interest	0	1,925	1,925	2,800	2,800	9,450
Depreciation	0	1,875	1,875	1,875	1,875	7,500
Amortization	0	0	0	0	0	0
Total Fixed Expenses	0	3,800	3,800	4,675	4,675	16,950
Operating Profit (Loss)	0	(13,045)	(23,245)	6,480	6,480	(23,330)

	Beg Actual	1st Qtr	2nd Qtr	3rd Qtr	4th Qtr	Total
Other Income (Expense)	0	0	0	0	0	0
Interest Income	0	0	0	0	0	0
Earnings (Loss) Before Taxes	0	(13,045)	(23,245)	6,480	6,480	(23,330)
Income Taxes	0	(1,031)	(1,836)	512	512	(1,843)
Net Earnings	0	(12,014)	(21,409)	5,968	5,968	(21,487)
Retained Earnings, Beginning	0	0	(12,014)	(33,423)	(27,455)	0
Less Dividends	0	0	0	0	0	0
Retained Earnings, Ending	0	(12,014)	(33,423)	(27,455)	(21,487)	(21,487)

QUARTERLY FORECASTED STATEMENTS OF CHANGES IN FINANCIAL POSITION

	Beg Bal	1st Qtr	2nd Qtr	3rd Qtr	4th Qtr	Total
Sources (Uses) of Cash						
Net Earnings (Loss)	0	(12,014)	(21,409)	5,968	5,968	(21,487)
Depreciation & Amortization	0	1,875	1,875	1,875	1,875	7,500
Cash Provided by Operations	0	(10,139)	(19,534)	7,834	7,834	(13,987)
Dividends	0	0	0	0	0	0
Cash Provided by (Used For) Changes in						
Accounts Receivable	0	(20,000)	6,667	(20,000)	0	(33,333)
Inventory	0	(48,000)	16,000	(48,000)	0	(80,000)
Other Current Assets	0	0	0	0	0	0
Accounts Payable	0	12,	721	(2,178)	6,534 0	17,077
Income Taxes	0	(1,031)	(1,836)	512	512	(1,843)
Accrued Compensation	0	1,867	0	0	0	1,867
Dividends Payable	0	0	0	0	0	0
Other Current Liabilities	0	0	0	0	0	0

	Beg Bal	1st Qtr	2nd Qtr	3rd Qtr	4th Qtr	Total
Other Assests	0	0	0	0	0	0
Net Cash Provided by (Used For)						
Operating Activities	0	(54,443)	18,653	(60,954)	512	(96,233)
Investment Transactions						
Furniture & Equipment	0	(75,000)	0	0	0	(75,000)
Land	0	0	0	0	0	0
Building & Improvements	0	0	0	0	0	0
Intangible Assets	0	0	0	0	0	0
Net Cash From Investment Transactions	0	(75,000)	0	0	0	(75,000)
Financing Transactions						
Short-Term Debt	0	0	0	0	0	0
Long-Term Debt	0	110,000	0	50,000	0	160,000
Other Non-Current Liabilities	0	0	0	0	0	0
Sale of Common Stock	30,000	0	0	0	0·	0
Net Cash from Financing Transactions	30,000	110,000	0	50,000	0	160,000
Net Increase (Decrease) in Cash	30,000	(29,582)	(881)	(3,111)	8,355	(25,219)
Cash, Beginning of Period	0	30,000	418	(463)	(3,574)	30,000
Cash, End of Period	30,000	418	(463)	(3,574)	4,781	4,781

FINANCIAL RATIO ANALYSIS		**Beg Act**	**1st Qtr**	**2nd Qtr**	**3rd Qtr**	**4th Qtr**
Overall Performance						
Return on Equity		0.00	(66.80)	625.45	234.50	70.10
Return on Total Assets		0.00	(8.49)	(18.44)	3.33	3.22
Operating Return		0.00	(9.22)	(20.02)	3.62	3.49
Profitability Measures						
Gross Profit Percent		0.00	64.00	64.00	64.00	64.00
Profit Margin (AIT)		0.00	(20.02)	(53.52)	5.97	5.97
Operating Income per Share		0.00	0.00	0.00	0.00	0.00
Earnings per Share		0.00	0.00	0.00	0.00	0.00
Test of Investment Utilization						
Asset Turnover		0.00	0.42	0.34	0.56	0.54
Equity Turnover		0.00	3.34	(11.69)	39.29	11.75
Fixed Asset Turnover		0.00	0.82	0.56	1.44	1.48
Average Collection Period		0.00	30.00	30.00	30.00	30.00
Days Inventory		0.00	200.00	200.00	200.00	200.00
Inventory Turnover		0.00	0.45	0.45	0.45	0.45
Working Capital Turns		0.00	1.09	1.13	1.07	0.99
Test of Financial Condition						
Current Ratio		0.00	5.05	4.70	6.62	6.91
Quick Ratio		0.00	1.51	1.35	1.79	2.23
Working Capital Ratio		1.00	0.43	0.33	0.57	0.60
Dividend Payout		0.00	0.00	0.00	0.00	0.00
Financial Leverage						
Total Assets		1.00	7.87	(33.92)	70.39	21.80

	Beg Act	1st Qtr	2nd Qtr	3rd Qtr	4th Qtr
Debt/Equity	0.00	6.87	(34.92)	69.39	20.80
Debt to Total Assets	0.00	0.87	1.03	0.99	0.95

Year-End Equity History

Shares Outstanding	0	0	0	0	0
Market Price per Share (@20x's earnings)	0.00	0.00	0.00	0.00	0.00
Book Value per Share	0.00	0.00	0.00	0.00	0.00

Altman Analysis Ratio

1.2x (1)	1.20	0.47	0.37	0.62	0.65
1.4x (2)	0.00	(0.12)	(0.40)	(0.21)	(0.16)
3.3x (3)	0.00	(0.35)	(0.72)	0.07	0.07
0.6x (4)	0.00	0.00	0.00	0.00	0.00
1.0x (5)	0.00	0.42	0.34	0.56	0.54

Z Value	1.20	.042	(.041)	1.04	1.10

DETAILS FOR QUARTERLY STATEMENTS OF EARNINGS

	Beg Act	1st Qtr	2nd Qtr	3rd Qtr	4th Qtr	Total	%Sales	Fixed
Sales								
Dollars Sales Forecasted								
Product 1	0	60,000	40,000	100,000	100,000	300,000		
Product 2	0	0	0	0	0	0		
Product 3	0	0	0	0	0	0		
Product 4	0	0	0	0	0	0		
Product 5	0	0	0	0	0	0		
Product 6	0	0	0	0	0	0		
Total Sales	0	60,000	40,000	100,000	100,000	300,000		

DETAILS FOR QUARTERLY STATEMENTS OF EARNINGS
...continued

	Beg Act	1st Qtr	2nd Qtr	3rd Qtr	4th Qtr	Total	%Sales	Fixed
Cost of Sales								
Dollar Cost Forecasted								
Product 1	0	21,600	14,400	36,000	36,000	108,000	36.00%	0
Product 2	0	0	0	0	0	0	0.00%	0
Product 3	0	0	0	0	0	0	0.00%	0
Product 4	0	0	0	0	0	0	0.00%	0
Product 5	0	0	0	0	0	0	0.00%	0
Product 6	0	0	0	0	0	0	0.00%	0
Total Cost of Sales	0	21,600	14,400	36,000	36,000	108,000		
Operating Expenses								
Payroll	0	12,000	12,000	12,000	12,000	48,000	0.00%	12,000
Paroll Taxes	0	950	950	950	950	3,800	0.00%	950
Advertising	0	4,800	3,200	8,000	8,000	24,000	8.00%	0
Automobile Expenses	0	0	0	0	0		0.00%	0
Bad Debts	0	0	0	0	0	0	0.00%	0
Commissions	0	3,000	2,000	5,000	5,000	15,000	5.00%	0
Computer Rental	0	1,200	1,200	1,200	1,200	4,800	0.00%	1,200
Computer Supplies	0	220	220	220	220	880	0.00%	220
Computer Maintenance	0	100	100	100	100	400	0.00%	100
Dealer Training	0	1,000	1,000	1,000	1,000	4,000	0.00%	1,000
Electricity	0	3,000	3,000	3,000	3,000	12,000	0.00%	3,000
Employment Ads and Fees	0	0	0	0	0	0	0.00%	0
Entertainment: Business	0	1,500	1,500	1,500	1,500	6,000	0.00%	1,500
General Insurance	0	800	800	800	800	32,000	0.00%	800
Health & W/C Insurance	0	0	0	0	0	0	.00%	0
Interest: LT Debt	0	2,500	2,500	2,500	2,500	10,000	0.00%	2,500
Legal & Accounting	0	1,500	1,500	1,500	1,500	6,000	0.00%	1,500
Maintenance & Repairs	0	460	460	460	460	1,840	0.00%	460

	Beg Act	1st Qtr	2nd Qtr	3rd Qtr	4th Qtr	Total	%Sales	Fixed
Office Supplies	0	270	270	270	270	1,080	0.00%	270
Postage	0	85	85	85	85	340	0.00%	85
Prof. Development	0	0	0	0	0	0	0.00%	0
Professional Fees	0	1,000	1,000	1,000	1,000	4,000	0.00%	1,000
Rent	0	8,000	8,000	8,000	8,000	32,000	0.00%	8,000
Shows & Conferences	0	0	0	0	0	0	0.00%	0
Subscriptions & Dues	0	285	285	285	285	1,140	0.00%	285
Telephone	0	1,225	1,225	1,225	1,225	4,900	0.00%	1,225
Temporary Employees	0	0	0	0	0	0	0.00%	0
Travel Expenses	0	750	750	750	750	3,000	0.00%	750
Utilities	0	3,000	3,000	3,000	3,000	12,000	0.00%	3,000
Research & Devlpmnt.	0	0	0	0	0	0	0.00%	0
Royalties	0	0	0	0	0	0	0.00%	0
Other 1	0	0	0	0	0	0	0.00%	0
Other 2	0	0	0	0	0	0	0.00%	0
Other 3	0	0	0	0	0	0	0.00%	0
Total Operating Expenses	0	47,645	45,045	52,845	52,845	198,380		
Percent of Sales	0.00	79.41	112.61	52.85	52.85	66.13		

DETAILS FOR QUARTERLY STATEMENT OF EARNINGS
...continued

BUSINESS PLAN TEMPLATE

Appendix - B
Organizations, Agencies and Consultants

Organizations, Agencies, & Consultants

A listing of Associations and Consultants of interest to entrepreneurs, followed by the 10 Small Business Administration Regional Offices, Small Business Development Centers, Service Corps of Retired Executives offices, and Venture Capital & Finance companies.

ASSOCIATIONS

This section contains a listing of associations and other agencies of interest to the small business owner. Entries are listed alphabetically by organization name.

American Association for Consumer Benefits
PO Box 100279
Fort Worth, Texas 76185
Phone: (800)872-8896
Free: (800)872-8896
Fax: (817)377-5633
E-mail: info@aacb.org

American Association of Family Businesses
PO Box 547217
Surfside, Florida 33154
Phone: (305)864-1184
Fax: (305)864-1187

American Federation of Small Business
American Small Businesses Association
206 E. College St.
Grapevine, Texas 76051-5364

American Society of Independent Business
c/o Keith Wood
777 Main St., Ste. 1600
Fort Worth, Texas 76102
Phone: (817)870-1880

American Women's Economic Development Corporation
71 Vanderbilt Ave., 3rd Fl.
New York, New York 10169
Phone: (212)692-9100
Fax: (212)692-9296

Association for Enterprise Opportunity
70 E Lake St., Ste. 1120
Chicago, Illinois 60601

Phone: (312)357-0177
Fax: (312)357-0180
E-mail: aeochicago@ad.com

Association of Small Business Development Centers
3108 Columbia Pike No. 300
Arlington, Virginia 22204-4304
Phone: (703)448-6124
Fax: (703)448-6125
E-mail: jjohns1012@aol.com

BEST Employers Association
2515 McCabe Way
Irvine, California 92614
Phone: (714)756-1000
Free: (800)854-7417
Fax: (714)553-1232
E-mail: bestplans@bestplans.com

Business Market Association
4131 N. Central Expy., Ste. 720
Dallas, Texas 75204

Coalition of Americans to Save the Economy
1100 Connecticut Ave. NW, Ste. 1200
Washington, District of Columbia 20036-4101
Phone: (202)293-1414
Fax: (202)293-1702

Employers of America
520 S. Pierce, Ste. 224
Mason City, Iowa 50401
Phone: (515)424-3187
Free: (800)728-3187
Fax: (515)424-1673
E-mail: employer@employerhelp.org

Family Firm Institute
221 N. Beacon St.
Boston, Massachusetts 02135-1943
Phone: (617)789-4200
Fax: (617)789-4220
E-mail: ffi221@msn.com

International Association of Business
701 Highlander Blvd., Ste. 110
Arlington, Texas 76015-4325
Phone: (817)465-2922
Fax: (817)467-5940

International Association for Business Organizations
PO Box 30149
Baltimore, Maryland 21270
Phone: (410)581-1373

International Council for Small Business
c/o Jefferson Smurfit Center for Entrepreneurial Studies
St. Louis University
3674 Lindell Blvd.
St. Louis, Missouri 63108
Phone: (314)977-3628
Fax: (314)977-3627
E-mail: icsb@slu.edu

National Alliance for Fair Competition
3 Bethesda Metro Center, Ste. 1100
Bethesda, Maryland 20814
Phone: (410)235-7116
Fax: (410)235-7116

National Association for Business Organizations
PO Box 30149
Baltimore, Maryland 21270
Phone: (410)581-1373

National Association of Private Enterprise
PO Box 5
Georgetown, Texas 78627-0005
Phone: (512)863-2699
Free: (800)223-6273
Fax: (512)868-8037
E-mail: info@nape.org

National Association for the Self-Employed
PO Box 612067

Dallas, Texas 75261-2067
Free: (800)232-NASE
Fax: (800)551-4446

National Association of Small
Business Investment Companies
666 11th St. NW, No. 750
Washington, District of Columbia
20001
Phone: (202)628-5055
Fax: (202)628-5080
E-mail: nasbic@nasbic.org

National Business Association
PO Box 700728
Dallas, Texas 75370
Phone: (214)458-0900
Free: (800)456-0440
Fax: (214)960-9149
E-mail: nbal2@airmail.net

National Business Owners Association
1033 N. Fairfax St., Ste. 402
Alexandria, Virginia 22314
Phone: (202)737-6501
Free: (888)713-NBOA
Fax: (703)838-0149
E-mail: mikenboa@erols.com

National Center for Fair Competition
8421 Frost Way
Annandale, Virginia 22003
Phone: (703)280-4622
Fax: (703)280-0942
E-mail: kentonp1@aol.com

National Council for Industrial
Innovation
National Federation of Independent
Business
53 Century Blvd., Ste. 205
Nashville, Tennessee 37214
Phone: (615)872-5800
Fax: (615)872-5353

National Small Business Benefits
Association
2244 N. Grand Ave. E.
Springfield, Illinois 62702
Phone: (217)753-2558
Fax: (217)753-2558

National Small Business United
1156 15th St. NW, Ste. 1100
Washington, District of Columbia
20005

Phone: (202)293-8830
Free: (800)345-6728
Fax: (202)872-8543
E-mail: nsbu@nsbu.org

Network of Small Businesses
5420 Mayfield Rd., Ste. 205
Lyndhurst, Ohio 44124
Phone: (216)442-5600
Fax: (216)449-3227

Research Institute for Small and
Emerging Business
722 12th St. NW
Washington, District of Columbia
20005
Phone: (202)628-8382
Fax: (202)628-8392
E-mail: rise@bellatlantic.net

Score Association
c/o Service Corps of Retired
Executives Association
409 3rd St. SW, 4th Fl.
Washington, District of Columbia
20024
Phone: (202)205-6762
Free: (800)634-0245
Fax: (202)205-7636

Small Business Assistance Center
554 Main St.
PO Box 15014
Worcester, Massachusetts 01615-
0014
Phone: (508)756-3513
Fax: (508)770-0528

Small Business Legislative Council
1156 15th St. NW, Ste. 510
Washington, District of Columbia
20005
Phone: (202)639-8500
Fax: (202)296-5333

Small Business Network
PO Box 30149
Baltimore, Maryland 21270
Phone: (410)581-1373
E-mail: natibb@ix.netcom.com

Small Business Service Bureau
554 Main St.
PO Box 15014
Worcester, Massachusetts 01615-
0014

Phone: (508)756-3513
Fax: (508)770-0528

Small Business Support Center
Association
c/o James S. Ryan
8811 Westheimer Rd., No. 210
Houston, Texas 77063-3617

Support Services Alliance
PO Box 130
Schoharie, New York 12157-0130
Phone: (518)295-7966
Free: (800)322-3920
Fax: (518)295-8556
E-mail: ssainfo@telenet.net

CONSULTANTS

*This section contains a listing of consult-
ants specializing in small business
development. It is arranged alphabetically
by country, then by state or province, then
by city, then by firm name.*

CANADA

Alberta

Varsity Consulting Group
Faculty of Business
University of Alberta
Edmonton, Alberta T6G 2R6
Phone: (403)492-2994
Fax: (403)492-5400
Web: http://www.bus.ualberta.ca/vcg

Viro Hospital Consulting
42 Commonwealth Bldg., 9912-106
St. NW
Edmonton, Alberta T5K 1C5
Phone: (403)425-3871
Fax: (403)425-3871
E-mail: rpb@freenet.edmonton.ab.ca

British Columbia

SRI Strategic Resources Inc.
4330 Kingsway, Ste. 1600
Burnaby, British Columbia V5H 4G7
Phone: (604)435-0627
Fax: (604)435-2782

E-mail: inquiry@sri.bc.ca
Web: http://www.sri.com

DeBoda & DeBoda
1523 Milford Ave.
Coquitlam, British Columbia
V3J 2V9
Phone: (604)936-4527
Fax: (604)936-4527
E-mail: deboda@iutcugate.bc.ca
Web: http://
www.ourworld.compuserve.com/
homepages/dcboda

The Sage Group Ltd.
980 - 355 Burrard St.
744 W. Haistings, Ste. 410
Vancouver, British Columbia
V6C 1A5
Phone: (604)669-9269
Fax: (604)669-6622

Ontario

The Cynton Company
17 Massey St.
Brampton, Ontario L6S 2V6
Phone: (905)792-7769
Fax: (905)792-8116
E-mail: cynton@netcom.ca
Web: http://www.netcom.ca/~cynton

Begley & Associates
RR 6
Cambridge, Ontario N1R 5S7
Phone: (519)740-3629
Fax: (519)740-3629
E-mail: begley@in.on.ca
Web: http://www.in.on.ca/~begley/
index.htm

Tikkanen-Bradley
RR No. 1
Consecon, Ontario K0K 1T0
Phone: (613)669-0583
E-mail: consult@mortimer.com
Web: http://204.191.209/consult/

Task Enterprises
Box 69, RR 2 Hamilton
Flamborough, Ontario L8N 2Z7
Phone: (905)659-0153
Fax: (905)659-0861

HST Group Ltd.
430 Gilmour St.
Ottawa, Ontario K2P 0R8

Phone: (613)236-7303
Fax: (613)236-9893

Harrison Associates
BCE Place
181 Bay Street, Ste. 3740
PO Box 798
Toronto, Ontario M5J 2T3
Phone: (416)364-5441
Fax: (416)364-2875

Ken Wyman & Associates Inc.
64B Shuter St., Ste. 200
Toronto, Ontario M5B 1B1
Phone: (416)362-2926
Fax: (416)362-3039
E-mail: kenwyman@compuserve.com

JPL Business Consultants
82705 Metter Rd.
Wellandport, Ontario L0R 2J0
Phone: (905)386-7450
Fax: (905)386-7450
E-mail:plamarch@freenet.npiec.on.ca

Quebec

The Zimmar Consulting Partnership Inc.
Westmount
PO Box 98
Montreal, Quebec H3Z 2T1
Phone: (514)484-1459
Fax: (514)484-3063

UNITED STATES

Alabama

Business Planning Inc.
300 Office Park Dr.
Birmingham, Alabama 35223-2474
Phone: (205)870-7090
Fax: (205)870-7103

Tradebank of Eastern Alabama
546 Broad St., Ste. 3
Gadsden, Alabama 35901
Phone: (205)547-8700
Fax: (205)547-8718
E-mail: mansion@webex.com
Web: http://www.webex.com/~tea

Alaska

AK Business Development Center
3335 Arctic Blvd., Ste. 203

Anchorage, Alaska 99503
Phone: (907)562-0335
Fax: (907)562-6988
Web: http://www.customcpu.com/
commercial/abdc

Business Matters
PO Box 287
Fairbanks, Alaska 99707
Phone: (907)452-5650

Arizona

Carefree Direct Marketing Corp.
8001 E. Serene St.
PO Box 3737
Carefree, Arizona 85377-3737
Phone: (602)488-4227
Fax: (602)488-2841

Trans Energy Corporation
1739 W. 7th Ave.
Mesa, Arizona 85202
Phone: (602)921-0433
Fax: (602)967-6601
E-mail: aha@getnet.com

CMAS
5125 N. 16th St.
Phoenix, Arizona 85016
Phone: (602)395-1001
Fax: (602)604-8180

Harvey C. Skoog
PO Box 26439
Prescott Valley, Arizona 86312
Phone: (520)772-1714
Fax: (520)772-2814

LMC Services
8711 E. Pinnacle Peak Rd., No. 340
Scottsdale, Arizona 85255-3555
Phone: (602)585-7177
Fax: (602)585-5880
E-mail: louws@earthlink.com

Gary L. McLeod
PO Box 230
Sonoita, Arizona 85637
Fax: (602)455-5661

Van Cleve Associates
6932 E. 2nd St.
Tucson, Arizona 85710
Phone: (602)296-2587
Fax: (602)296-2587

California

Acumen Group, Inc.
Phone: (650)949-9349
Fax: (650)949-4845
E-mail: acumen-g@ix.netcom.com
Web: http://pw2.netcom.com/~janed/
acumen.html

Thomas E. Church & Associates, Inc.
PO Box 2439
Aptos, California 95001
Phone: (408)662-7950
Fax: (408)662-7955
E-mail: church@ix.netcom.com

Keck & Company Business Consultants
410 Walsh Rd.
Atherton, California 94027
Phone: (650)854-9588
Fax: (650)854-7240
Web: http://www.keckco.com

Ben W. Laverty III, Ph.D., REA, CEI
4909 Stockdale Hwy., Ste. 132
Bakersfield, California 93309
Phone: (805)283-8300
Fax: (805)283-8313
E-mail: cstc@cstcsafety.com
Web: http://www.csfcsafety.com/cstc

Lindquist Consultants-Venture Planning
225 Arlington Ave.
Berkeley, California 94707
Phone: (510)524-6685
Fax: (510)527-6604

Larson Associates
PO Box 9005
Brea, California 92822
Phone: (714)529-4121
Fax: (714)572-3606

Kremer Management Consulting
PO Box 500
Carmel, California 93921
Phone: (408)626-8311
Fax: (408)624-2663
E-mail: ddkremer@aol.com

W & J Partnership
18876 Edwin Markham Dr.
PO Box 1108
Castro Valley, California 94552
Phone: (510)583-7751
Fax: (510)583-7645

E-mail:
warmorgan@wjpartnership.com
Web: http://www.wjpartnership.com

JB Associates
21118 Gardena Dr.
Cupertino, California 95014
Phone: (408)257-0214
Fax: (408)257-0216
E-mail: semarang@sirius.com

House Agricultural Consultants
PO Box 1615
Davis, California 95617-1615
Phone: (916)753-3361
Fax: (916)753-0464
E-mail: infoag@houseag.com
Web: http://www.houseag.com/

Technical Management Consultants
3624 Westfall Dr.
Encino, California 91436-4154
Phone: (818)784-0626
Fax: (818)501-5575
E-mail: tmcrs@aol.com

RAINWATER-GISH & Associates,
Business Finance & Development
317 Third St., Ste. 3
Eureka, California 95501
Phone: (707)443-0030
Fax: (707)443-5683

Ted Butteriss Management &
Technology
451 Pebble Beach Pl.
Fullerton, California 92835
Phone: (714)441-2280
Fax: (714)441-2281
E-mail:
Global_Tradelinks@compuserve.com
Web: http://www.consultapc.org/
Butter2.htm

Strategic Business Group
800 Cienaga Dr.
Fullerton, California 92835-1248
Phone: (714)449-1040
Fax: (714)525-1631

Burnes Consulting
20537 Wolf Creek Rd.
Grass Valley, California 95949
Phone: (916)346-8188
Fax: (916)346-7704
Free: (800)949-9021
E-mail: ktalk94@aol.com

Pioneer Business Consultants
9042 Garfield Ave., Ste. 312
Huntington Beach, California 92646
Phone: (714)964-7600

Beblie, Brandt & Jacobs, Inc.
16 Technology, Ste. 164
Irvine, California 92618
Phone: (714)450-8790
Fax: (714)450-8799
E-mail: darcy@bbjinc.com
Web: http://198.147.90.26

Fluor Daniel Consulting
3353 Michelson Dr.
Irvine, California 92698
Phone: (714)975-2000
E-mail:
sales.consulting@fluordaniel.com
Web: http://
www.fluordanielconsulting.com

MCS Associates
18300 Von Karman, Ste. 1000
Irvine, California 92612
Phone: (949)263-8700
Fax: (949)553-0168
E-mail: mcs@earthlink.net

The Laresis Companies
PO Box 3284
La Jolla, California 92038
Phone: (619)452-2720
Fax: (619)452-8744

RCL & Co.
PO Box 1143
La Jolla, California 92038
Phone: (619)454-8883
Fax: (619)454-8880

Comprehensive Business Services
3201 Lucas Cir.
Lafayette, California 94549
Phone: (510)283-8272

The Ribble Group
27601 Forbes Rd., Ste. 52
Laguna Niguel, California 92677
Phone: (714)582-1085
Fax: (714)582-6420
E-mail: ribble@deltanet.com

Norris Bernstein, CMC
9309 Marina Pacifica Dr. N
Long Beach, California 90803
Phone: (562)493-5458

Fax: (562)493-5459
E-mail: norris@ctecomputer.com

Horizon Consulting Services
1315 Garthwick Dr.
Los Altos, California 94024
Phone: (415)967-0906
Fax: (415)967-0906

Brincko Associates, Inc.
1801 Ave. of the Stars, Ste. 1054
Los Angeles, California 90067
Phone: (310)553-4523
Fax: (310)553-6782

F.J. Schroeder & Associates
1926 Westholme Ave.
Los Angeles, California 90025
Phone: (310)470-2655
Fax: (310)470-6378
E-mail: fjsacons@aol.com
Web: http://www.mcninet.com/
GlobalLook/Fjschroe.html

Western Management Associates
8351 Vicksburg Ave.
Los Angeles, California 90045-3924
Phone: (310)645-1091
Fax: (310)645-1092
E-mail: CFOForRent@aol.com
Web: http://www.expert-market.com/
cfoforrent

Darrell Sell and Associates
Los Gatos, California 95030
Phone: (408)354-7794
E-mail: darrell@netcom.com

Leslie J. Zambo
3355 Michael Dr.
Marina, California 93933
Phone: (408)384-7086
Fax: (408)647-4199
E-mail:
104776.1552@compuserve.com

Marketing Services Management
PO Box 1377
Martinez, California 94553
Phone: (510)370-8527
Fax: (510)370-8527
E-mail: markserve@biotechnet.com

William M. Shine Consulting Service
PO Box 127
Moraga, California 94556-0127
Phone: (510)376-6516

Palo Alto Management Group, Inc.
2672 Bayshore Pkwy., Ste. 701
Mountain View, California 94043
Phone: (415)968-4374
Fax: (415)968-4245
E-mail: mburwen@pamg.com

The Market Connection
4020 Birch St., Ste. 203
Newport Beach, California 92660
Phone: (714)731-6273
Fax: (714)833-0253

Muller Associates
PO Box 7264
Newport Beach, California 92658
Phone: (714)646-1169
Fax: (714)646-1169

International Health Resources
PO Box 329
North San Juan, California 95960-0329
Phone: (530)292-1266
Fax: (530)292-1243
Web: http://
www.futureofhealthcare.com

NEXUS - Consultants to Management
PO Box 1531
Novato, California 94948
Phone: (415)897-4400
Fax: (415)898-2252
E-mail: jimnexus@aol.com

Adelphi Communications Incorporated
PO Box 28831
Oakland, California 94604-8831
Phone: (510)430-7444
Fax: (510)530-3411
Web: http://www.adelphi.com

Intelequest Corp.
722 Gailen Ave.
Palo Alto, California 94303
Phone: (415)968-3443
Fax: (415)493-6954
E-mail: frits@iqix.com

McLaughlin & Associates
66 San Marino Cir.
Rancho Mirage, California 92270
Phone: (760)321-2932
Fax: (760)328-2474
E-mail: jackmcla@aol.com

Carrera Consulting Group
2110 21st St., Ste. 400
Sacramento, California 95818
Phone: (916)456-3300
Fax: (916)456-3306
E-mail:
central@carreraconsulting.com
Web: http://
www.carreraconsulting.com

Bay Area Tax Consultants and
Bayhill Financial Consultants
1150 Bayhill Dr., Ste. 1150
San Bruno, California 94066-3004
Phone: (415)952-8786
Fax: (415)588-4524
E-mail: baytax@compuserve.com
Web: http://www.baytax.com/

California Business Incubation Network
101 W. Broadway, No. 480
San Diego, California 92101
Phone: (619)237-0559
Fax: (619)237-0521

G.R. Gordetsky Consultants Inc.
11414 Windy Summit Pl.
San Diego, California 92127
Phone: (619)487-4939
Fax: (619)487-5587
E-mail: gordet@pacbell.net

Freeman, Sullivan & Co.
131 Steuart St., Ste. 500
San Francisco, California 94105
Phone: (415)777-0707
Fax: (415)777-2420
Free: (800)777-0737
Web: http://www.fsc-research.com

Ideas Unlimited
2151 California St., Ste. 7
San Francisco, California 94115
Phone: (415)931-0641
Fax: (415)931-0880

Russell Miller Inc.
300 Montgomery St., Ste. 900
San Francisco, California 94104
Phone: (415)956-7474
Fax: (415)398-0620
E-mail: rmi@pacbell.net
Web: http://www.rmisf.com

PKF Consulting
425 California St., Ste. 1650

San Francisco, California 94104
Phone: (415)421-5378
Fax: (415)956-7708
E-mail: callahan@pkfe.com
Web: http://www.cquest.com/
pkfb.html

Welling & Woodard, Inc.
1067 Broadway
San Francisco, California 94133
Phone: (415)776-4500
Fax: (415)776-5067

ORDIS, Inc.
6815 Trinidad Dr.
San Jose, California 95120-2056
Phone: (408)268-3321
Fax: (408)268-3582
Free: (800)446-7347
E-mail: ordis@aol.com
Web: http://www.ordis.com

Stanford Resources, Inc.
20 Great Oaks Blvd., Ste. 200
San Jose, California 95119
Phone: (408)360-8400
Fax: (408)360-8410
E-mail: stanres@ix.netcom.com
Web: http://
www.stanfordresources.com

Technology Properties Ltd., Inc.
4010 Moore Park, St. 215
San Jose, California 95117
Phone: (408)243-9898
Fax: (408)296-6637

Helfert Associates
1777 Borel Pl., Ste. 508
San Mateo, California 94402-3514
Phone: (415)377-0540
Fax: (415)377-0472

Mykytyn Consulting Group, Inc.
185 N. Redwood Dr., Ste. 200
San Rafael, California 94903
Phone: (415)491-1770
Fax: (415)491-1251
E-mail: info@mcgi.com
Web: http://www.mcgi.com

Omega Management Systems, Inc.
3 Mount Darwin Court
San Rafael, California 94903-1109
Phone: (415)499-1300
Fax: (415)492-9490
E-mail: omegamgt@ix.netcom.com

The Information Group, Inc.
4675 Stevens Creek Blvd., Ste. 100
Santa Clara, California 95051
Phone: (408)985-7877
Fax: (408)985-2945
E-mail: dvincent@tig-usa.com
Web: http://www.tig-usa.com

Cast Management Consultants
1620 26th St., Ste. 2040N
Santa Monica, California 90404
Phone: (310)828-7511
Fax: (310)453-6831

Cuma Consulting Management
Box 724
Santa Rosa, California 95402
Phone: (707)785-2477
Fax: (707)785-2478

The E-Myth Academy
131B Stony Cir., Ste. 2000
Santa Rosa, California 95401
Phone: (707)569-3600
Fax: (707)569-5700
Free: (800)221-0266
E-mail: emyth1@aol.com

Reilly, Connors & Ray
1743 Canyon Rd.
Spring Valley, California 91977
Phone: (619)698-4808
Fax: (619)460-3892
E-mail: davidray@adnc.com

Management Consultants
Sunnyvale, California 94087-4700
Phone: (408)773-0321

RJR Associates
1639 Lewiston Dr.
Sunnyvale, California 94087
Phone: (408)737-7720
Fax: (408)737-7720
E-mail: bobroy@netcom
Web: http://www.rjroy.mcni.com

Schwafel Associates
333 Cobalt Way, Ste. 107
Sunnyvale, California 94086
Phone: (408)720-0649
Fax: (408)720-1949
E-mail:
102065.234@compuserve.com
Web: http://www.patca.org/patca

Out of Your Mind...and Into the
Marketplace
13381 White Sands Dr.
Tustin, California 92780-4565
Phone: (714)544-0248
Fax: (714)730-1414
Free: (800)419-1513
E-mail: lpinson@aol.com
Web: http://www.business-plan.com

Independent Research Services
PO Box 2426
Van Nuys, California 91404-2426
Phone: (818)993-3622

Ingman Company Inc.
7949 Woodley Ave., Ste. 120
Van Nuys, California 91406-1232
Phone: (818)375-5027
Fax: (818)894-5001

Innovative Technology Associates
3639 E. Harbor Blvd., Ste. 203E
Ventura, California 93001
Phone: (805)650-9353

Ridge Consultants, Inc.
100 Pringle Ave., Ste. 580
Walnut Creek, California 94596
Phone: (925)274-1990
Fax: (510)274-1956
E-mail: info@ridgecon.com
Web: http://www.ridgecon.com

Bell Springs Publishing
PO Box 1240
Willits, California 95490
Phone: (707)459-6372
E-mail: bellsprings@sabernet

Hutchinson Consulting and
Appraisals
23245 Sylvan St., Ste. 103
Woodland Hills, California 91367
Phone: (818)888-8175
Fax: (818)888-8220
Free: (800)977-7548
E-mail: hcac.@sprintmall.com

J.H. Robinson & Associates
20695 Deodar Dr., Ste. 100
PO Box 351
Yorba Linda, California 92686-0351
Phone: (714)970-1279

Colorado

Sam Boyer & Associates
4255 S. Buckley Rd., No. 136
Aurora, Colorado 80013
Fax: (303)766-8740
Free: (800)785-0485
E-mail: samboyer@samboyer.com
Web: http://www.samboyer.com/

GVNW, Inc./Management
2270 La Montana Way
PO Box 25969
Colorado Springs, Colorado 80936
Phone: (719)594-5800
Fax: (719)599-0968

M-Squared, Inc.
755 San Gabriel Pl.
Colorado Springs, Colorado 80906
Phone: (719)576-2554
Fax: (719)576-2554

Western Capital Holdings, Inc.
7500 E. Arapahoe Rd., Ste. 395
Englewood, Colorado 80112
Phone: (303)290-8482
Fax: (303)770-1945

Thornton Financial FNIC
1024 Centre Ave., Bldg. E
Fort Collins, Colorado 80526-1849
Phone: (970)221-2089
Fax: (970)484-5206

TenEyck Associates
1760 Cherryville Rd.
Greenwood Village, Colorado 80121-1503
Phone: (303)758-6129
Fax: (303)761-8286

Associated Enterprises Ltd.
13050 W. Ceder Dr., Unit 11
Lakewood, Colorado 80228
Phone: (303)988-6695
Fax: (303)988-6739
E-mail: ael1@classic.msn.com

The Vincent Company Inc.
200 Union Blvd., Ste. 210
Lakewood, Colorado 80228
Phone: (303)989-7271
Fax: (303)989-7570
Free: (800)274-0733
E-mail: vincent@vincentco.com
Web: http://www.vincentco.com

Johnson & West Management
Consultants, Inc.
7612 S. Logan Dr.
Littleton, Colorado 80122
Phone: (303)730-2810
Fax: (303)730-3219

Connecticut

Stratman Group Inc.
40 Tower Ln.
Avon, Connecticut 06001-4222
Phone: (860)677-2898
Fax: (860)677-8210
Free: (800)551-0499

Cowherd Consulting Group, Inc.
106 Stephen Mather Rd.
Darien, Connecticut 06820
Phone: (203)655-2150
Fax: (203)655-6427

Greenwich Associates
8 Greenwich Office Park
Greenwich, Connecticut 06831-5149
Phone: (203)629-1200
Fax: (203)629-1229
E-mail: lisa@greenwich.com
Web: http://www.greenwich.com

Franchise Builders
185 Pine St., Ste. 818
Manchester, Connecticut 06040
Phone: (860)647-7542
Fax: (860)646-6544
E-mail: watchisle@.aol.com

JC Ventures, Inc.
4 Arnold St.
Old Greenwich, Connecticut 06870-1203
Phone: (203)698-1990
Fax: (203)698-2638
Free: (800)698-1997

Charles L. Hornung Associates
52 Ned's Mountain Rd.
Ridgefield, Connecticut 06877
Phone: (203)431-0297

Manus
100 Prospect St., S. Tower
Stamford, Connecticut 06901
Phone: (203)326-3880
Fax: (203)326-3890
Free: (800)445-0942

E-mail: manus1@aol.com
Web: http://www.RightManus.com

Sternbach Associates International
16 Tamarac Rd.
Westport, Connecticut 06880
Phone: (203)227-2059
Fax: (203)454-7341

Delaware

Focus Marketing
61-7 Habor Dr.
Claymont, Delaware 19703
Phone: (302)793-3064

Daedalus Ventures, Ltd.
PO Box 1474
Hockessin, Delaware 19707
Phone: (302)239-6758
Fax: (302)239-9991
E-mail: daedalus@mail.del.net

The Formula Group
PO Box 866
Hockessin, Delaware 19707
Phone: (302)456-0952
Fax: (302)456-1354
E-mail: formula@netaxs.com

Selden Enterprises Inc.
2502 Silverside Rd., Ste. 1
Wilmington, Delaware 19810-3740
Phone: (302)529-7113
Fax: (302)529-7442
E-mail: seldenl@juno.com
Web: http://www.wld.com/id/w26209001750

District of Columbia

Bruce W. McGee and Associates
7826 Eastern Ave. NW, Ste. 30
Washington, District of Columbia 20012
Phone: (202)726-7272
Fax: (202)726-2946

McManis Associates, Inc.
1900 K St. NW, Ste. 700
Washington, District of Columbia 20006
Phone: (202)466-7680
Fax: (202)872-1898

Florida

Whalen & Associates, Inc.
4255 Northwest 26 Ct.
Boca Raton, Florida 33434
Phone: (561)241-5950
Fax: (561)241-7414
E-mail: drwhalen@ix.netcom.com

Eric Sands Consulting Services
6193 Rock Island Rd., Ste. 412
Fort Lauderdale, Florida 33319
Phone: (954)721-4767
Fax: (954)720-2815

Host Media Corp.
3948 S. Third St., Ste. 191
Jacksonville Beach, Florida 32250
Phone: (904)285-3239
Fax: (904)285-5618
E-mail:
msconsulting@compuserve.com

William V. Hall
1925 Brickell, Ste. D-701
Miami, Florida 33129
Phone: (305)856-9622
Fax: (305)856-4113
E-mail:
williamvhall@compuserve.com

F.A. McGee, Inc.
800 Claughton Island Dr., Ste. 401
Miami, Florida 33131
Phone: (305)377-9123

Taxplan, Inc.
Mirasol International Center
2699 Collins Ave.
Miami Beach, Florida 33140
Phone: (305)538-3303

T.C. Brown & Associates
8415 Excalibur Cir., Apt. B1
Naples, Florida 34108
Phone: (941)594-1949
Fax: (941)594-0611
E-mail: tcater@naples.net.com

RLA International Consulting
713 Lagoon Dr.
North Palm Beach, Florida 33408
Phone: (407)626-4258
Fax: (407)626-5772

Comprehensive Franchising, Inc.
2465 Ridgecrest Ave.

Orange Park, Florida 32065
Phone: (904)272-6567
Fax: (904)272-6750
Free: (800)321-6567
E-mail: theimp@cris.com
Web: http://www.franchise411.com

Hunter G. Jackson Jr. - Consulting
Environmental Physicist
PO Box 618272
Orlando, Florida 32861-8272
Phone: (407)295-4188

F. Newton Parks
210 El Brillo Way
Palm Beach, Florida 33480
Phone: (561)833-1727
Fax: (561)833-4541

Avery Business Development Services
2506 St. Michel Ct.
Ponte Vedra Beach, Florida 32082
Phone: (904)285-6033
Fax: (904)285-6033

Strategic Business Planning Company
PO Box 821006
South Florida, Florida 33082-1006
Phone: (954)704-9100
Fax: (954)438-7333
E-mail: info@bizplan.com
Web: http://www.bizplan.com

Dufresne Consulting Group, Inc.
10014 N. Dale Mabry, Ste. 101
Tampa, Florida 33618-4426
Phone: (813)264-4775
Fax: (813)931-5845

Agrippa Enterprises, Inc.
PO Box 175
Venice, Florida 34284-0175
Phone: (941)355-7876
E-mail: webservices@agrippa.com
Web: http://www.agrippa.com

Center for Simplified Strategic
Planning, Inc.
PO Box 3324
Vero Beach, Florida 32964-3324
Phone: (561)231-3636
Fax: (561)231-1099

Georgia

Marketing Spectrum Inc.
115 Perimeter Pl., Ste. 440

Atlanta, Georgia 30346
Phone: (770)395-7244
Fax: (770)393-4071

Business Ventures Corporation
6030 Dawson Blvd., Ste. E
Norcross, Georgia 30093
Phone: (770)729-8000
Fax: (770)729-8028

Informed Decisions Inc.
PO Box 219
Sautee Nacoochee, Georgia 30571
Fax: (706)878-1802
Free: (800)982-0676

Tom C. Davis & Associates, P.C.
3189 Perimeter Rd.
Valdosta, Georgia 31602
Phone: (912)247-9801
Fax: (912)244-7704
E-mail: mail@tcdcpa.com
Web: http://www.tcdcpa.com/

Illinois

TWD and Associates
431 S. Patton
Arlington Heights, Illinois 60005
Phone: (847)398-6410
Fax: (847)255-5095
E-mail: tdoo@aol.com

Management Planning Associates, Inc.
2275 Half Day Rd., Ste. 350
Bannockburn, Illinois 60015-1277
Phone: (847)945-2421
Fax: (847)945-2425

Phil Faris Associates
86 Old Mill Ct.
Barrington, Illinois 60010
Phone: (847)382-4888
Fax: (847)382-4890
E-mail: pfaris@meginsnet.net

Seven Continents Technology
787 Stonebridge
Buffalo Grove, Illinois 60089
Phone: (708)577-9653
Fax: (708)870-1220

Grubb & Blue, Inc.
2404 Windsor Pl.
Champaign, Illinois 61820
Phone: (217)366-0052
Fax: (217)356-0117

ACE Accounting Service, Inc.
3128 N. Bernard St.
Chicago, Illinois 60618
Phone: (773)463-7854
Fax: (773)463-7854

AON Consulting
123 N. Wacker Dr.
Chicago, Illinois 60606
Phone: (312)701-4800
Fax: (312)701-4855
Free: (800)438-6487
Web: http://aonconsulting.com/

FMS Consultants
5801 N. Sheridan Rd., Ste. 3D
Chicago, Illinois 60660
Phone: (773)561-7362
Fax: (773)561-6274

Kingsbury International, Ltd.
1258 N. LaSalle St.
Chicago, Illinois 60610
Phone: (312)787-6756
Fax: (312)787-3136
E-mail: jetlag@mcs.com

MacDougall & Blake, Inc.
1414 N. Wells St., Ste. 311
Chicago, Illinois 60610-1306
Phone: (312)587-3330
Fax: (312)587-3699
E-mail: jblake@compuserve.com

James C. Osburn Ltd.
2701 W. Howard St.
Chicago, Illinois 60645
Phone: (773)262-4428
Fax: (773)262-6755

Tarifero & Tazewell Inc.
211 S. Clark
PO Box 2130
Chicago, Illinois 60690
Phone: (312)665-9714
Fax: (312)665-9716

William J. Igoe
3949 Earlston Rd.
Downers Grove, Illinois 60515
Phone: (630)960-1418

Human Energy Design Systems
620 Roosevelt Dr.
Edwardsville, Illinois 62025
Phone: (618)692-0258
Fax: (618)692-0819

BioLabs, Inc.
15 Sheffield Ct.
Lincolnshire, Illinois 60069
Phone: (847)945-2767

Clyde R. Goodheart
15 Sheffield Ct.
Lincolnshire, Illinois 60069
Phone: (847)945-2767

China Business Consultants Group
931 Dakota Cir.
Naperville, Illinois 60563
Phone: (630)778-7992
Fax: (630)778-7915
E-mail: cbcq@aol.com

Center for Workforce Effectiveness
500 Skokie Blvd., Ste. 222
Northbrook, Illinois 60062
Phone: (847)559-8777
Fax: (847)559-8778
E-mail: office@cwelink.com
Web: http://www.cwelink.com

Smith Associates
1320 White Mountain Dr.
Northbrook, Illinois 60062
Phone: (847)480-7200
Fax: (847)480-9828

Francorp, Inc.
20200 Governors Dr.
Olympia Fields, Illinois 60461
Phone: (708)481-2900
Fax: (708)481-5885
Free: (800)372-6244
E-mail: francorp@aol.com
Web: http://www.francorpinc.com

Camber Business Strategy
Consultants
PO Box 986
Palatine, Illinois 60078-0986
Phone: (847)705-0101
Fax: (847)705-0101

Partec Enterprise Group
5202 Keith Dr.
Richton Park, Illinois 60471
Phone: (708)503-4047
Fax: (708)503-9468

McGladrey & Pullen, LLP
1699 E. Woodfield Rd., Ste. 300
Schaumburg, Illinois 60173

Phone: (847)517-7070
Fax: (847)517-7095
Free: (800)365-8353
Web: http://www.mcgladrey.com

A.D. Star Consulting
320 Euclid
Winnetka, Illinois 60093
Phone: (847)446-7827
Fax: (847)446-7827
E-mail: startwo@worldnet.att.net

Indiana

Modular Consultants Inc.
3109 Crabtree Ln.
Elkhart, Indiana 46514
Phone: (219)264-5761
Fax: (219)264-5761
E-mail: sasabo5313@aol.com

Midwest Marketing Research
PO Box 1077
Goshen, Indiana 46527
Phone: (219)533-0548
Fax: (219)533-0540
E-mail: 103365.654@compuserve

Ketchum Consulting Group
8021 Knue Rd., Ste. 112
Indianapolis, Indiana 46250
Phone: (317)845-5411
Fax: (317)842-9941

MDI Management Consulting
1519 Park Dr.
Munster, Indiana 46321
Phone: (219)838-7909
Fax: (219)838-7909

Iowa

McCord Consulting Group, Inc.
4533 Pine View Dr. NE
PO Box 11024
Cedar Rapids, Iowa 52410
Phone: (319)378-0077
Fax: (319)378-1577
E-mail: sam.mccord@usa.net

Management Solutions, L.C.
3815 Lincoln Place Dr.
Des Moines, Iowa 50312
Phone: (515)277-6408
Fax: (515)277-3506

E-mail:
102602.1561@compuserve.com

Grandview Marketing
15 Red Bridge Dr.
Sioux City, Iowa 51104
Phone: (712)239-3122
Fax: (712)258-7578
E-mail: eandrews@pionet.net

Kansas

Assessments in Action
513A N. Mur-Len
Olathe, Kansas 66062
Phone: (913)764-6270
Fax: (913)764-6495
Free: (888)548-1504
E-mail: solution@assessments-in-action.com
Web: http://www.assessments-in-action.com

Maine

Edgemont Enterprises
PO Box 8354
Portland, Maine 04104
Phone: (207)871-8964
Fax: (207)871-8964

Pan Atlantic Consultants
148 Middle St.
Portland, Maine 04101
Phone: (207)871-8622
Fax: (207)772-4842
E-mail: panatl@worldnet.att.net

Maryland

Clemons & Associates, Inc.
5024-R Campbell Blvd.
Baltimore, Maryland 21236
Phone: (410)931-8100
Fax: (410)931-8111
E-mail: Clemonsc@msn.com.
Web: http://www.clemonsmgmt.com/clemons

Grant Thornton
2 Hopkins Plaza
Baltimore, Maryland 21201
Phone: (410)685-4000
Fax: (410)837-0587

Imperial Group, Limited
305 Washington Ave., Ste. 204
Baltimore, Maryland 21204-6009
Phone: (410)337-8500
Fax: (410)337-7641

Burdeshaw Associates, Ltd.
4701 Sangamore Rd.
Bethesda, Maryland 20816-2508
Phone: (301)229-5800
Fax: (301)229-5045
E-mail: sklement@mindspring.com

Michael E. Cohen
5225 Pooks Hill Rd., Ste. 1119 S
Bethesda, Maryland 20814
Phone: (301)530-5738
Fax: (301)530-2988

World Development Group, Inc.
5272 River Rd., Ste. 650
Bethesda, Maryland 20816-1405
Phone: (301)652-1818
Fax: (301)652-1250
E-mail: wdg@has.com

Swartz Consulting
PO Box 4301
Crofton, Maryland 21114-4301
Phone: (301)262-6728

Software Solutions International Inc.
9633 Duffer Way
Gaithersburg, Maryland 20886
Phone: (301)977-3743
Fax: (301)330-4136

Strategies, Inc.
8 Park Center Ct., Ste. 200
Owings Mills, Maryland 21117
Phone: (410)363-6669
Fax: (410)363-1231

Hammer Marketing Resources
179 Inverness Rd.
Severna Park, Maryland 21146
Phone: (410)544-9191
Fax: (410)544-9189
E-mail: bhammer@gohammer.com
Web: http://www.gohammer.com

Andrew Sussman & Associates
13731 Kretsinger
Smithsburg, Maryland 21783
Phone: (301)824-2943
Fax: (301)824-2943

Massachusetts

Geibel Marketing and Public
Relations
PO Box 611
Belmont, Massachusetts 02478-0005
Phone: (617)484-8285
Fax: (617)489-3567
E-mail: jgeibel@geibelpr.com
Web: http://www.geibelpr.com

Bain
2 Copley Pl.
Boston, Massachusetts 02117-0897
Phone: (617)572-2000
Fax: (617)572-2427
Web: http://www.rec.bain.com

Mehr & Company
62 Kinnaird St.
Cambridge, Massachusetts 02139
Phone: (617)876-3311
Fax: (617)876-3023

Monitor Company, Inc.
25 First St.
Cambridge, Massachusetts 02141
Phone: (617)252-2000
Fax: (617)252-2100

Data and Strategies Group, Inc.
Three Speen St.
Framingham, Massachusetts 01701
Phone: (508)820-2500
Fax: (508)820-1626
E-mail: dsginc@dsggroup.com
Web: http://www.dsggroup.com

Information & Research Associates
PO Box 3121
Framingham, Massachusetts 01701
Phone: (508)788-0784

Easton Consultants Inc.
252 Pond St.
Hopkinton, Massachusetts 01748
Phone: (508)435-4882
Fax: (508)435-3971
Web: http://www.easton-ma.com

Jeffrey D. Marshall
102 Mitchell Rd.
Ipswich, Massachusetts 01938-1219
Phone: (508)356-1113
Fax: (508)356-2989

Consulting Resources Corporation
6 Northbrook Park
Lexington, Massachusetts 02420
Phone: (781)863-1222
Fax: (781)863-1441
E-mail: conresco@world.std.com

The Planning Technologies Group, Inc.
92 Hayden Ave.
Lexington, Massachusetts 02173
Phone: (781)861-0999
Fax: (781)861-1099
E-mail: ptg@plantcc.com

VMB Associates, Inc.
115 Ashland St.
Melrose, Massachusetts 02176
Phone: (781)665-0623

The Co. Doctor
14 Pudding Stone Ln.
Mendon, Massachusetts 01756
Phone: (508)478-1747
Fax: (508)478-0520

The Enterprise Group
73 Parker Rd.
Needham, Massachusetts 02194
Phone: (617)444-6631
Fax: (617)433-9991
E-mail: lsacco@world.std.com
Web: http://www.enterprise-group.com

PSMJ Resources, Inc.
10 Midland Ave.
Newton, Massachusetts 02158
Phone: (617)965-0055
Fax: (617)965-5152
Free: (800)537-7765
E-mail: psmj@tiac.net
Web: http://www.psmj.com

IEEE Consultants' Network
255 Bear Hill Rd.
Waltham, Massachusetts 02154-1017
Phone: (617)890-5294
Fax: (617)890-5290

Kalba International, Inc.
1601 Trapelo Rd.
Waltham, Massachusetts 02154
Phone: (781)259-9589
Fax: (781)466-8440
E-mail: mail17495@pop.net

Business Planning and Consulting
Services
20 Beechwood Terr.
Wellesley, Massachusetts 02181
Phone: (617)237-9151
Fax: (617)237-9151

Interim Management Associates
21 Avon Rd.
Wellesley, Massachusetts 02181
Phone: (781)237-0024

Michigan

Walter Frederick Consulting
1719 South Blvd.
Ann Arbor, Michigan 48104
Phone: (313)662-4336
Fax: (313)769-7505

Fox Enterprises
6220 W. Freeland Rd.
Freeland, Michigan 48623
Phone: (517)695-9170
Fax: (517)695-9174
E-mail: foxjw@concentric.net
Web: http://www.cris.com/~foxjw

G.G.W. and Associates
1213 Hampton
Jackson, Michigan 49203
Phone: (517)782-2255
Fax: (517)782-2255

Altamar Group Ltd.
6810 S. Cedar, Ste. 2-B
Lansing, Michigan 48911
Phone: (517)694-0910
Fax: (517)694-1377
Free: (800)443-2627

Sheffieck Consultants, Inc.
23610 Greening Dr.
Novi, Michigan 48375-3130
Phone: (248)347-3545
Fax: (248)347-3530
E-mail: cfsheff@concentric.net

Rehmann, Robson PC
5800 Gratiot
PO Box 2025
Saginaw, Michigan 48605
Phone: (517)799-9580
Fax: (517)799-0227
Web: http://www.rrpc.com

Francis & Company
17200 W. Ten Mile Rd., Ste. 207
Southfield, Michigan 48075
Phone: (248)559-7600
Fax: (248)559-5249

Private Ventures, Inc.
16000 W. Nine Mile Rd., Ste. 504
Southfield, Michigan 48075
Phone: (248)569-1977
Fax: (248)569-1838
Free: (800)448-7614
E-mail: pventuresi@aol.com

JGK Associates
14464 Kerner Dr.
Sterling Heights, Michigan 48313
Phone: (810)247-9055

Minnesota

Health Fitness Corporation
3500 W 80th St., Ste. 130
Bloomington, Minnesota 55431
Phone: (612)831-6830
Fax: (612)831-7264

Consatech Inc.
PO Box 1047
Burnsville, Minnesota 55337
Phone: (612)953-1088
Fax: (612)435-2966

Robert F. Knotek
14960 Ironwood Ct.
Eden Prairie, Minnesota 55346
Phone: (612)949-2875

DRI Consulting
7715 Stonewood Ct.
Edina, Minnesota 55439
Phone: (612)941-9656
Fax: (612)941-2693
E-mail: dric@dric.com
Web: http://www.dric.com

Kinnon Lilligren Associates Incorporated
6211 Oakgreen Ave. S
Denmark Township
Hastings, Minnesota 55033-9153
Phone: (612)436-6530
Fax: (612)436-6530

Markin Consulting
12072 87th Pl. N
Maple Grove, Minnesota 55369
Phone: (612)493-3568

Fax: (612)493-5744
E-mail:
markin@markinconsulting.com
Web: http://
www.markinconsulting.com

Minnesota Cooperation Office for
Small Business & Job Creation, Inc.
5001 W. 80th St., Ste. 825
Minneapolis, Minnesota 55437
Phone: (612)830-1230
Fax: (612)830-1232
E-mail: mncoop@msn.com
Web: http://www.mnco.org

Enterprise Consulting, Inc.
PO Box 1111
Minnetonka, Minnesota 55345
Phone: (612)949-5909
Fax: (612)906-3965

Amdahl International
724 1st Ave. SW
Rochester, Minnesota 55902
Phone: (507)252-0402
Fax: (507)252-0402
E-mail: amdahl@best-service.com
Web: http://www.wp.com/amdahl_int

Power Systems Research
1365 Corporate Center Curve, 2nd Fl.
St. Paul, Minnesota 55121
Phone: (612)905-8400
Fax: (612)454-0760
Free: 888625-8612
E-mail: Barb@Powersys.com
Web: http://www.powersys.com

Small Business Success
PO Box 21097
St. Paul, Minnesota 55121-0097
Phone: (612)454-2500
Fax: (612)456-9138

Missouri

Business Planning and Development
Corp.
4030 Charlotte St.
Kansas City, Missouri 64110
Phone: (816)753-0495
E-mail: humph@bpdev.demon.co.uk
Web: http://www.bpdev.demon.co.uk

CFO Service
10336 Donoho

St. Louis, Missouri 63131
Phone: (314)750-2940
E-mail: jskae@cfoservice.com
Web: http://www.cfoservice.com

Nebraska

International Management Consulting
Group, Inc.
1309 Harlan Dr., Ste. 205
Bellevue, Nebraska 68005
Phone: (402)291-4545
Fax: (402)291-4343
Free: (800)665-IMCG
E-mail: imcg@neonramp.com
Web: http://www.mgtconsulting.com

Heartland Management Consulting
Group
1904 Barrington Pkwy.
Papillion, Nebraska 68046
Phone: (402)339-1319
Fax: (402)339-1319

Nevada

The DuBois Group
865 Tahoe Blvd., Ste. 108
Incline Village, Nevada 89451
Phone: (702)832-0550
Fax: (702)832-0556
Free: (800)375-2935

New Hampshire

Wolff Consultants
10 Buck Rd.
PO Box 1003
Hanover, New Hampshire 03755
Phone: (603)643-6015

BPT Consulting Associates Ltd
12 Parmenter Rd. , Ste. B-6
Londonderry, New Hampshire 03053
Phone: (603)437-8484
Fax: (603)434-5388
Free: (888)278-0030
E-mail: bptcons@tiac.net
Web: http://www.bptconsulting.com

New Jersey

ConMar International, Ltd.
283 Dayton-Jamesburg Rd.
PO Box 437

Dayton, New Jersey 08810
Phone: (908)274-1100
Fax: (908)274-1199

Kumar Associates, Inc.
260 Columbia Ave.
Fort Lee, New Jersey 07024
Phone: (201)224-9480
Fax: (201)585-2343

John Hall & Company, Inc.
PO Box 187
Glen Ridge, New Jersey 07028
Phone: (201)680-4449
Fax: (201)680-4581
E-mail: jhcompany@aol.com

Strategic Management Group
PO Box 402
Maplewood, New Jersey 07040
Phone: (973)378-2470

Vanguard Communications Corp.
100 American Rd.
Morris Plains, New Jersey 07950
Phone: (201)605-8000
Fax: (201)605-8329
Web: http://www.vanguard.net/

KLW New Products
156 Cedar Dr.
Old Tappan, New Jersey 07675
Phone: (201)358-1300
Fax: (201)664-2594
E-mail: lrlarsen@usa.net
Web: http://
www.klwnewproducts.com

PA Consulting Group
315 A Enterprise Dr.
Plainsboro, New Jersey 08536
Phone: (609)936-8300
Fax: (609)936-8811
Web: http://www.pa-consulting.com

Aurora Marketing Management, Inc.
212 Carnegie Ctr., Ste. 206
Princeton, New Jersey 08540-6233
Phone: (609)520-8863

Smart Business Supersite
88 Orchard Rd., CN-5219
Princeton, New Jersey 08543
Phone: (908)321-1924
Fax: (908)321-5156
E-mail: irv@smartbiz.com
Web: http://www.smartbiz.com

Tracelin Associates
1171 Main St., Ste. 6K
Rahway, New Jersey 07065
Phone: (732)381-3288

Schkeeper Inc.
130-6 Bodman Pl.
Red Bank, New Jersey 07701
Phone: (732)219-1965
Fax: (732)530-3703

Henry Branch Associates
2502 Harmon Cove Tower
Secaucus, New Jersey 07094
Phone: (201)866-2008
Fax: (201)601-0101
E-mail: HDPW18A@prodigy.com
Web: http://www.mcninet.com/
globallook/hbranch.html

Robert Gibbons & Co., Inc.
46 Knoll Rd.
Tenafly, New Jersey 07670-1050
Phone: (201)871-3933
Fax: (201)871-2173
E-mail: crisisbob@aol.com

PMC Management Consultants, Inc.
11 Thistle Ln.
PO Box 332
Three Bridges, New Jersey 08887-
0332
Phone: (908)788-1014
Fax: (908)806-7287
E-mail: int@pmc-management.com
Web: http://www.wwpmc-
management.com

R.W. Bankart & Associates
20 Valley Ave., Ste. D-2
Westwood, New Jersey 07675-3607
Phone: (201)664-7672

New Mexico

Vondle & Associates, Inc.
4926 Calle de Tierra, NE
Albuquerque, New Mexico 87111
Phone: (505)292-8961
Fax: (505)296-2790
E-mail: vondle@aol.com

InfoNewMexico
2207 Black Hills Road, NE
Rio Rancho, New Mexico 87124

Phone: (505)891-2462
Fax: (505)896-8971

New York

Powers Research and Training
Institute
PO Box 78
Bayville, New York 11709
Phone: (516)628-2250
Fax: (516)628-2252
E-mail:
73313.1315@compuserve.com
Web: http://
www.coachfederation.org/crs/
67.nancy.powers.htm

Consortium House
139 Wittenberg Rd.
Bearsville, New York 12409
Phone: (914)679-8867
Fax: (914)679-9248
E-mail: eugenegs@aol.com
Web: http://www.chpub.com

Progressive Finance Corporation
(PFC)
3549 Tiemann Ave.
Bronx, New York 10469
Phone: (718)405-9029
Fax: (718)405-1170
Free: (800)225-8381

Wave Hill Associates
2621 Palisade Ave., Ste. 15-C
Riverdale
Bronx, New York 10463
Phone: (718)549-7368
Fax: (718)601-9670

Overton Financial
7 Allen Rd.
Cortlandt Manor, New York 10566
Phone: (914)737-4649
Fax: (914)737-4696

Samani International Enterprises,
Marions Panyaught Consultancy
2028 Parsons
Flushing, New York 11357-3436
Phone: (917)287-8087
Fax: (800)873-8939
E-mail: vjp2@compuserve.com
Web: http://www.dorsai.org/~vjp2

Marketing Resources Group
71-58 Austin St.
Forest Hills, New York 11375
Phone: (718)261-8882

North Star Enterprises
670 N. Terrace Ave.
Mount Vernon, New York 10552
Phone: (914)668-9433

E.N. Rysso & Associates
21 Jordan Rd.
New Hartford, New York 13413-
2311
Phone: (315)732-2206
Fax: (315)732-2206

Boice Dunham Group
437 Madison Ave.
New York, New York 10022
Phone: (212)752-5550
Fax: (212)752-7055

Elizabeth Capen
27 E. 95th St.
New York, New York 10128
Phone: (212)427-7654

Haver Analytics
60 E. 42nd St., Ste. 2424
New York, New York 10017
Phone: (212)986-9300
Fax: (212)986-5857
E-mail: data@haver.com
Web: http://www.haver.com

The Jordan, Edmiston Group, Inc.
150 E 52nd Ave., 18th Fl.
New York, New York 10022
Phone: (212)754-0710
Fax: (212)754-0337

KPMG Peat Marwick - Management
Consultants
345 Park Ave.
New York, New York 10154
Phone: (212)909-5000
Fax: (212)738-9819
Web: http://www.kpmg.com

Mahoney Cohen Consulting Corp.
111 W. 40th St., 12th Fl.
New York, New York 10018
Phone: (212)490-8000
Fax: (212)790-5913

Management Practice, Inc.
342 Madison Ave.

Ste. 1230
New York, New York 10173-1230
Phone: (212)867-7948
Fax: (212)972-5188
Web: http://www.mpiweb.com

Moseley Associates, Inc.
342 Madison Ave., Ste. 1414
New York, New York 10016
Phone: (212)213-6673
Fax: (212)687-1520

Practice Development Counsel
60 Sutton Pl. S
New York, New York 10022
Phone: (212)593-1549
Fax: (212)980-7940
E-mail: phaserot@counsel.com

Unique Value International, Inc.
575 Madison Ave., 10th Fl.
New York, New York 10022-1304
Phone: (212)605-0590
Fax: (212)605-0589

The Van Tulleken Company Limited
126 E. 56th St.
New York, New York 10022
Phone: (212)355-1390
Fax: (212)755-3061
E-mail: newyork@vantelleken.com

Vencon Management, Incorporated
301 W. 53rd St.
New York, New York 10019
Phone: (212)581-8787
Fax: (212)397-4126

R.A. Walsh Consultants
429 E. 52nd St.
New York, New York 10022
Phone: (212)688-6047
Fax: (212)535-4075

Werner International Inc.
55 East 52nd, 29th floor
New York, New York 10055
Phone: (212)909-1260
Fax: (212)909-1273
E-mail: maryorourke@rgh.com
Web: http://www.inforesint.com

Zimmerman Business Consulting,
Inc.
44 E. 92nd St., Ste. 5-B
New York, New York 10128

Phone: (212)860-3107
Fax: (212)860-7730
E-mail: ljzzbcl@aol.com

Stromberg Consulting
2500 Westchester Ave.
Purchase, New York 10577
Phone: (914)251-1515
Fax: (914)251-1562
E-mail:
strategy@stromberg_consulting.com
Web: http://
www.stromberg_consulting.com

ComputerEase Co.
9 Hachaliah Brown Dr.
Somers, New York 10589
Phone: (914)277-5317
Fax: (914)277-5317
E-mail: crawfordc@juno.com

Innovation Management Consulting,
Inc.
209 Dewitt Rd.
Syracuse, New York 13214-2006
Phone: (315)425-5144
Fax: (315)445-8989
E-mail: missonneb@axess.net

M. Clifford Agress
891 Fulton St.
Valley Stream, New York 11580
Phone: (516)825-8955
Fax: (516)825-8955

Destiny Kinal Marketing Consultancy
105 Chemung St.
Waverly, New York 14892
Phone: (607)565-8317
Fax: (607)565-4083

Management Insight
96 Arlington Rd.
Williamsville, New York 14221
Phone: (716)631-3319
Fax: (716)631-0203
Free: (800)643-3319

Navitar Consulting, Inc.
5350 Main St., Ste. 7
Williamsville, New York 14221-5338
Phone: (716)634-2553
Fax: (716)634-2554
E-mail: navitar@localnet.com
Web: http://www.fbdi.com

North Carolina

Best Practices, LLC
6320 Quadrangle Dr., Ste. 120
Chapel Hill, North Carolina 27514
Phone: (919)403-0251
Web: http://www.best-in-class.com

Norelli & Company
Nations Bank Corporation Center
100 N. Tyron St., Ste. 5160
Charlotte, North Carolina 28202-4000
Phone: (704)376-5484
Fax: (704)376-5485
E-mail: consult@norelli.com
Web: http://www.norelli.com

North Dakota

Center for Innovation
4300 Dartmouth Dr.
Grand Forks, North Dakota 58202
Phone: (701)777-3132
Fax: (701)777-2339
Web: http://www.und.nodak.edu/
dept/cibd/welcome.htm

Ohio

Transportation Technology Services
208 Harmon Rd.
Aurora, Ohio 44202
Phone: (330)562-3596

Delta Planning, Inc.
PO Box 22618
Beachwood, Ohio 44122
Phone: (216)752-6578
Fax: (216)752-6579
Free: (800)672-0762
E-mail: DeltaP@worldnet.att.net

Empro Systems, Inc.
4777 Red Bank Expy., Ste. 1
Cincinnati, Ohio 45227-1542
Phone: (513)271-2042
Fax: (513)271-2042

Alliance Management International,
Ltd.
1440 Windrow Ln.
Cleveland, Ohio 44147-3200
Phone: (440)838-1922
Fax: (440)838-0979
E-mail: bgruss@amiltd.com
Web: http://www.amiltd.com

Bozell Kamstra Public Relations
1301 E. 9th St., Ste. 3400
Cleveland, Ohio 44114
Phone: (216)623-1511
Fax: (216)623-1501
E-mail:
jfeniger@cleveland.bozellkamstra.com
Web: http://www.bozellkamstra.com

Cory Dillon Associates
111 Schreyer Pl. E
Columbus, Ohio 43214
Phone: (614)262-8211
Fax: (614)262-3806

Holcomb Gallagher Adams
300 Marconi, Ste. 303
Columbus, Ohio 43215
Phone: (614)221-3343
Fax: (614)221-3367
E-mail: riadams@acme.freenet.oh.us

Ransom & Assoc.
106 E. Pacemont Rd.
Columbus, Ohio 43202-1225
Phone: (614)267-7100
Fax: (614)267-7199
E-mail: wjrnetworkWalk.com

Young & Associates
PO Box 711
Kent, Ohio 44240
Phone: (330)678-0524
Fax: (330)678-6219
Free: (800)525-9775
Web: http://www.younginc.com

Robert A. Westman & Associates
8981 Inversary Dr. SE
Warren, Ohio 44484-2551
Phone: (330)856-4149
Fax: (330)856-2564

Oklahoma

Innovative Resources Inc.
4900 Richmond Sq., Ste. 100
Oklahoma City, Oklahoma 73118
Phone: (405)840-0033
Fax: (405)843-8359
E-mail: ipartners@juno.com

Oregon

INTERCON - The International
Converting Institute

5200 Badger Rd.
Crooked River Ranch, Oregon 97760
Phone: (541)548-1447
Fax: (541)548-1618
E-mail: intercon@transport.com

Talbott ARM
HC 60, Box 5620
Lakeview, Oregon 97630
Phone: (541)635-8587
Fax: (503)947-3482

Management Technology Associates,
Ltd.
1618 SW 1st Ave., Ste. 315
Portland, Oregon 97201
Phone: (503)224-5220
Fax: (503)224-6704

Pennsylvania

Elayne Howard & Associates, Inc.
3501 Masons Mill Rd., Ste. 501
Huntingdon Valley, Pennsylvania
19006-3509
Phone: (215)657-9550

GRA, Incorporated
115 West Ave., Ste. 201
Jenkintown, Pennsylvania 19046
Phone: (215)884-7500
Fax: (215)884-1385
E-mail: gramail@gra-inc.com
Web: http://www.gra-inc.com

Mifflin County Industrial
Development Corporation
Mifflin County Industrial Plaza
6395 SR 103 N
Bldg. 50
Lewistown, Pennsylvania 17044
Phone: (717)242-0393
Fax: (717)242-1842
E-mail: mcide@acsworld.net

Autech Products
1289 Revere Rd.
Morrisville, Pennsylvania 19067
Phone: (215)493-3759
Fax: (215)493-9791

Advantage Associates
434 Avon Dr.
Pittsburgh, Pennsylvania 15228
Phone: (412)343-1558
Fax: (412)362-1684
E-mail: ecocba1@aol.com

Regis J. Sheehan & Associates
291 Foxcroft Rd.
Pittsburgh, Pennsylvania 15220
Phone: (412)279-1207

James W. Davidson Co., Inc.
23 Forest View Rd.
Wallingford, Pennsylvania 19086
Phone: (610)566-1462

Puerto Rico

Diego Chevere & Co.
Ste. 301, Metro Parque 7
Metro Office Park
Caparra Heights, Puerto Rico 00920
Phone: (787)782-9595
Fax: (787)782-9532

Manuel L. Porrata and Associates
898 Munoz Rivera Ave., Ste. 201
Rio Piedras, Puerto Rico 00927
Phone: (809)765-2140
Fax: (809)754-3285

South Carolina

Aquafood Business Associates
PO Box 16190
Charleston, South Carolina 29412
Phone: (803)795-9506
Fax: (803)795-9477

Strategic Innovations International
12 Executive Court
Lake Wylie, South Carolina 29710
Phone: (803)831-1225
Fax: (803)831-1177
E-mail: stratinnov@aol.com
Web: http://
www.strategicinnovations.com

Minus Stage
Box 4436
Rock Hill, South Carolina 29731
Phone: (803)328-0705
Fax: (803)329-9948

Tennessee

Daniel Petchers & Associates
8820 Fernwood CV
Germantown, Tennessee 38138
Phone: (901)755-9896

Business Choices
1114 Forest Harbor, Ste. 300

Hendersonville, Tennessee 37075-9646
Phone: (615)822-8692
Fax: (615)822-8692
Free: (800)737-8382
E-mail: bz-ch@juno.com

RCFA Healthcare Management Services, LLC
9648 Kingston Pike, Ste. 8
Knoxville, Tennessee 37922
Phone: (423)531-0176
Fax: (423)531-0722
Free: (800)635-4040
Web: http://www.rcfa.com

Growth Consultants of America
3917 Trimble Rd.
PO Box 158382
Nashville, Tennessee 37215
Phone: (615)383-0550
Fax: (615)269-8940
E-mail: 70244.451@compuserve.com

Texas

Integrated Cost Management Systems, Inc.
2261 Brookhollow Plz. Dr., Ste. 104
Arlington, Texas 76006
Phone: (817)633-2873
Fax: (817)633-3781
Free: (800)955-2233
E-mail: abm@icms.net
Web: http://www.icms.net

Lori Williams
1000 Leslie Ct.
Arlington, Texas 76012
Phone: (817)459-3934
Fax: (817)459-3934

Erisa Adminstrative Services Inc.
12325 Haymeadow Dr., Bldg. 4
Austin, Texas 78750-1847
Phone: (512)250-9020
Fax: (512)250-9487
Web: http://www.cserisa.com

R. Miller Hicks & Company
1011 W. 11th St.
Austin, Texas 78703
Phone: (512)477-7000
Fax: (512)477-9697
E-mail: millerhicks@rmhicks.com

Pragmatic Tactics, Inc.
3303 Westchester Ave.
College Station, Texas 77845
Phone: (409)696-5294
Fax: (409)696-4994
Free: (800)570-5294
E-mail: ptactics@aol.com
Web: http://www.ptatics.com

Perot Systems
12377 Merit Dr., Ste. 1100
Dallas, Texas 75251
Phone: (972)383-5600
Free: (800)688-4333
E-mail: corp.comm@ps.net
Web: http://www.ps.net

High Technology Associates - Division of Global Technologies, Inc.
1775 St. James Pl., Ste. 105
Houston, Texas 77056
Phone: (713)963-9300
Fax: (713)963-8341
E-mail: hta@infohwy.com

MasterCOM
103 Thunder Rd.
Kerrville, Texas 78028
Phone: (830)895-7990
Fax: (830)443-3428
E-mail: jmstubblefield@mastertraining.com
Web: http://www.mastertraining.com

PROTEC
4607 Linden Pl.
Pearland, Texas 77584
Phone: (281)997-9872
Fax: (281)997-9895
E-mail: p.oman@ix.netcom.com

Business Strategy Development Consultants
PO Box 690365
San Antonio, Texas 78269
Phone: (210)696-8000
Fax: (210)696-8000
Free: (800)927-BSDC

Tom Welch, CPC
6900 San Pedro Ave., Ste. 147
San Antonio, Texas 78216-6207
Phone: (210)737-7022
Fax: (210)737-7022
E-mail: bplan@iamerica.net
Web: http://www.moneywords.com

Virginia

Elliott B. Jaffa
2530-B S. Walter Reed Dr.
Arlington, Virginia 22206
Phone: (703)931-0040

Koach Enterprises - USA
5529 N. 18th St.
Arlington, Virginia 22205
Phone: (703)241-8361
Fax: (703)241-8623

Federal Market Development
5650 Chapel Run Ct.
Centreville, Virginia 22020-3601
Phone: (703)502-8930
Fax: (703)502-8929
Free: (800)821-5003

Barringer, Huff & Stuart
2107 Graves Mills Rd., Ste. C
Forest, Virginia 24551
Phone: (804)316-9356
Fax: (804)316-9357

AMX International, Inc.
1420 Spring Hill Rd. , Ste. 600
McLean, Virginia 22102-3006
Phone: (703)690-4100
Fax: (703)643-1279
E-mail: amxmail@amxi.com
Web: http://www.amxi.com

Performance Support Systems
11835 Canon Blvd., Ste. C-101
Newport News, Virginia 23606
Phone: (757)873-3700
Fax: (757)873-3288
Free: (800)488-6463
E-mail: sales@2020insight.net
Web: http://www.2020insight.net

Charles Scott Pugh (Investor)
4101 Pittaway Dr.
Richmond, Virginia 23235-1022
Phone: (804)560-0979
Fax: (804)560-4670

John C. Randall and Associates, Inc.
PO Box 15127
Richmond, Virginia 23227
Phone: (804)746-4450
Fax: (804)747-7426

McLeod & Co.
410 1st St.

Roanoke, Virginia 24011
Phone: (540)342-6911
Fax: (540)344-6367
Web: http://www.mcleodco.com/

The Small Business Counselor
12423 Hedges Run Dr., Ste. 153
Woodbridge, Virginia 22192
Phone: (703)490-6755
Fax: (703)490-1356

Washington

Burlington Consultants
10900 NE 8th St., Ste. 900
Bellevue, Washington 98004
Phone: (425)688-3060
Fax: (425)454-4383
E-mail:
mmckennirey@burlingtonconsultants.com
Web: http://
www.burlingtonconsultants.com

Perry L. Smith Consulting
800 Bellevue Way NE, Ste. 400
Bellevue, Washington 98004-4208
Phone: (425)462-2072
Fax: (425)462-5638

Independent Automotive Training
Services
PO Box 308
Kirkland, Washington 98083
Phone: (425)822-5715
E-mail: ltunney@autosvccon.com
Web: http://www.autosvccon.com

Kahle Associate, Inc.
6203 204th Dr. NE
Redmond, Washington 98053
Phone: (425)836-8763
Fax: (425)868-3770
E-mail:
randykahle@kahleassociates.com
Web: http://www.kahleassociates.com

Dan Collin
2515 E. McGraw St.
Seattle, Washington 98112
Phone: (206)325-3762
E-mail: d.collin@worldnet.att.net
Web: http://home.att.net/~d.collin

ECG Management Consultants, Inc.
1111 3rd Ave., Ste. 2700
Seattle, Washington 98101-3201

Phone: (206)689-2200
Fax: (206)689-2209
E-mail: ecg@ecgmc.com
Web: http://www.ecgmc.com

Northwest Trade Adjustment
Assistance Center
900 4th Ave., Ste. 2430
Seattle, Washington 98164-1003
Phone: (206)622-2730
Fax: (206)622-1105
E-mail: nwtaac@sprynet.com

Business Planning Consultants
S. 3510 Ridgeview Dr.
Spokane, Washington 99206
Phone: (509)928-0332
Fax: (509)921-0842
E-mail: bpci@nextdim.com

Wisconsin

White & Associates, Inc.
5349 Somerset Ln. S
Greenfield, Wisconsin 53221
Phone: (414)281-7373
Fax: (414)281-7006
E-mail: wnaconsult@aol.com

SMALL BUSINESS ADMINISTRATION REGIONAL OFFICES

This section contains a listing of Small Business Administration offices arranged numerically by region. Service areas are provided. Contact the appropriate office for a referral to the nearest field office.

Region 1

U.S. Small Business Administration
10 Causeway St., Rm. 812
Boston, Massachusetts 02222
Phone: (617)565-8415
Fax: (617)565-8420
Serves Connecticut, Maine,

Massachusetts, New Hampshire, Rhode Island, and Vermont.

Region 2

U.S. Small Business Administration
26 Federal Plz., Rm. 3108
New York, New York 10278
Phone: (212)264-1450
Fax: (212)264-0038
Serves New Jersey, New York, Puerto Rico, and the Virgin Islands.

Region 3

U.S. Small Business Administration
475 Allendale Rd., Ste. 201
King of Prussia, Pennsylvania 19406
Phone: (610)962-3710
Fax: (610)962-3743
Serves Delaware, the District of Columbia, Maryland, Pennsylvania, Virginia, and West Virginia.

Region 4

U.S. Small Business Administration
1375 Peachtree St. NE, Rm. 500
Atlanta, Georgia 30367-8102
Phone: (404)347-4999
Fax: (404)347-2355
Serves Alabama, Florida, Georgia, Kentucky, Mississippi, North Carolina, South Carolina, and Tennessee.

Region 5

U.S. Small Business Administration
Gateway IV Bldg., Ste. 1975 South
300 S. Riverside Plz.
Chicago, Illinois 60606-6611
Phone: (312)353-8089
Fax: (312)353-3426
Serves Illinois, Indiana, Michigan, Minnesota, Ohio, and Wisconsin.

Region 6

U.S. Small Business Administration
8625 King George Dr., Bldg. C
Dallas, Texas 75235-3391

Phone: (214)767-7611
Fax: (214)767-7870
Serves Arkansas, Louisiana, New
Mexico, Oklahoma, and Texas.

Region 7

U.S. Small Business Administration
Lucas Place, Ste. 307
323 W. 8th St.
Kansas City, Missouri 64105
Phone: (816)374-6380
Fax: (816)374-6339
Serves Iowa, Kansas, Missouri, and
Nebraska.

Region 8

U.S. Small Business Administration
633 17th St., 7th Fl.
Denver, Colorado 80202
Phone: (303)294-7186
Fax: (303)294-7153
Serves Colorado, Montana, North
Dakota, South Dakota, Utah, and
Wyoming.

Region 9

U.S. Small Business Administration
71 Stevenson St., 20th Fl.
San Francisco, California 94105
Phone: (415)744-6404
Serves American Samoa, Arizona,
California, Guam, Hawaii, Nevada,
and the Trust Territory of the Pacific
Islands.

Region 10

U.S. Small Business Administration
1200 6th Ave., Ste. 1805
Seattle, Washington 98101-1128
Phone: (206)553-5676
Fax: (206)553-4155
Serves Alaska, Idaho, Oregon, and
Washington.

SMALL BUSINESS DEVELOPMENT CENTERS

*This section contains a listing of all Small
Business Development Centers organized
alphabetically by state/U.S. territory
name, then by city, then by agency name.*

Alabama

Auburn University
SBDC
108 College of Business
Auburn, Alabama 36849-5243
Phone: (334)844-4220
Fax: (334)844-4268
Devron Veasley, Director
E-mail:
veasley@businness.auburn.edu

Alabama Small Business
Development Center
1717 11th Ave. S., Suite 419
Birmingham, Alabama 35294-4410
Phone: (205)934-4410
Fax: (205)934-7645
Ernie Gauld, Associate State Director
E-mail: Ernieg@asbdc.uab.edu

Alabama Small Business Procurement
System
University Of Alabama at
Birmingham
SBDC
1717 11th Ave. S., Ste. 419
Birmingham, Alabama 35294-4410
Phone: (205)934-7260
Fax: (205)934-7645
Charles Hobson, Procurement
Director
E-mail:
charlesh@asbdc.asbdc.uab.edu

University of Alabama at
Birmingham
Alabama Small Business
Development Consortium
SBDC
1717 11th Ave. S., Ste. 419
Birmingham, Alabama 35294-4410
Phone: (205)934-7260
Fax: (205)934-7645
John Sandefur, State Dir.
E-mail: sandefur@uab.edu

University of Alabama at
Birmingham
SBDC
E-mail: sbdc@uab.edu
1601 11th Ave. S.
Birmingham, Alabama 35294-2180
Phone: (205)934-6760
Fax: (205)934-0538
Brenda Walker, Director

University of North Alabama
Small Business Development Center
Box 5248, Keller Hall
Florence, Alabama 35632-0001
Phone: (256)765-4629
Fax: (256)765-4813
Dr. Kerry Gatlin, Director
E-mail: clong@unanov.una.edu

Alabama A & M University
University of Alabama at Huntsville
NE Alabama Regional Small
Business Development Center
SBDC
P.O. Box 168
225 Church St., N.W.
Huntsville. Alabama 35804-0168
Phone: (256)535-2061
Fax: (256)535-2050
David Taylor, Director
E-mail: dtaylor@hsv.chamber.org

Jacksonville State University
Small Business Development Center
E-mail: sbdc@jsucc.jsu.edu
114 Merrill Hall
700 Pelham Rd. N.
Jacksonville, Alabama 36265
Phone: (256)782-5271
Fax: (256)782-5179
Pat W. Shaddix, Director

Univeristy of West Alabama
SBDC
Station 35
Livingston, Alabama 35470
Phone: (205)652-3665
Fax: (205)652-3516
Paul Garner, Director
E-mail:
livpwg01@uwamail.westal.edu

University of South Alabama
Small Business Development Center
College of Business, Rm. 8

Mobile, Alabama 36688
Phone: (334)460-6004
Fax: (334)460-6246
Thomas Tucker, Director
E-mail:
btbrown@jaguar1.usouthal.edu

Alabama State University
SBDC
915 S. Jackson St.
Montgomery, Alabama 36195
Phone: (334)229-4138
Fax: (334)265-9144
Lorenzo G. Patrick, Director
E-mail: lpatrick@asunet.alasu.edu

Troy State University
Small Business Development Center
Bibb Graves, Rm. 102
Troy, Alabama 36082-0001
Phone: (334)670-3771
Fax: (334)670-3636
Janet W. Kervin, Dir.
E-mail: jkervin@trojan.troyst.edu

Alabama International Trade Center
University of Alabama
SBDC
E-mail: aitc@aitc.cba.ua.edu
Bidgood Hall, Rm. 201
PO Box 870396
Tuscaloosa, Alabama 35487-0396
Phone: (205)348-7621
Fax: (205)348-6974
Brian Davis, Dir.

University of Alabama
Alabama International Trade Center
Small Business Devlopment Center
Bidgood Hall, Rm. 250
Box 870397
Tuscaloosa, Alabama 35487-0396
Phone: (205)348-7011
Fax: (205)348-9644
Paavo Hanninen, Dir.
E-mail: phanninen@ualvm.ua.edu

Alaska

University of Alaska
Small Business Development Center
Rural Outreach Program
430 West Seventh Ave., Suite 110
Anchorage, Alaska 99501-3550
Phone: (907)274-7232

Fax: (907)274-9524
Mr. Bill Bear, Director

University of Alaska (Anchorage)
Small Business Development Center
E-mail: anerw@uaa.alaska.edu
430 West seventh Ave., Suite 110
Anchorage, Alaska 99501-3550
Phone: (907)274-7232
Fax: (907)274-9524
Ms. Jean Wall, Director

University of Alaska (Fairbanks)
Small Business Development Center
510 Second Ave., Ste. 101
Fairbanks, Alaska 99701
Phone: (907)474-6700
Fax: (907)474-1139
Billie Ray Allen, Dir.
E-mail: fnwra@aurora.alaska.edu

University of Alaska (Juneau)
Small Business Development Center
612 W. Willoughby Ave., Ste. A
Juneau, Alaska 99801
Phone: (907)463-1732
Fax: (907)463-3929
Norma Strickland, Acting Dir.

Kenai Peninsula Small Business
Development Center
PO Box 3029
Kenai, Alaska 99611-3029
Phone: (907)283-3335
Fax: (907)283-3913
Mark Gregory, Dir.

University of Alaska (Matanuska-Susitna)
Small Business Development Center
201 N. Lucile St., Ste. 2-A
Wasilla Alaska 99654
Phone: (907)373-7232
Fax: (907)373-7234
Timothy J. Sullivan, Dir.

Arizona

Mohave Community College
SBDC
Bullhead City Center
3400 Hwy 95
Bullhead City, Arizona 86442
Phone: (520)758-3926

Central Arizona College
Pinal County Small Business
Development Center
8470 N. Overfield Rd.
Coolidge, Arizona 85228
Phone: (520)426-4341
Fax: (520)426-4363
Carol Giordano, Director
E-mail: carolg@cac.cc.az.us

Coconino County Community
College
Small Business Development Center
3000 N. 4th St., Ste. 17
Flagstaff, Arizona 86003-8000
Phone: (520)526-5072
Free: (800)350-7122
Fax: (520)526-8693
Mike Lainoff, Director
E-mail: mlainoff@coco.cc.az.us

Northland Pioneer College
Small Business Development Center
E-mail: npcsbdc@cybertrails.com
PO Box 610
Holbrook, Arizona 86025
Phone: (520)537-6172
Free: (800)266-7232
Fax: (520)524-6171
Mike Engle, Director

Mohave Community College
Small Business Development Center
1971 Jagerson Ave.
Kingman, Arizona 86401
Phone: (520)757-0895
Fax: (520)757-0836
Kathy McGehee, Director
E-mail: katmcg@et.mohave.cc.az.us

Mohave Community College
SBDC
Lake Havasu Center
1971 W. Acoma Blvd.
Lake Havasu, Arizona 86403

Yavapai College
Small Business Development Center
Elks Building
117 E. Gurley St., Ste. 206
Prescott, Arizona 86301
Phone: (520)778-3088
Free: (800)922-6787
Fax: (520)778-3109
Richard Senopole, Director
E-mail: pdc_rich@uavapai.cc.az.us

Cochise College
Small Business Development Center
E-mail: sbdc@cochise.cc.az.us
901 N. Colombo, Rm. 308/309
Sierra Vista, Arizona 85635
Phone: (520)515-5478
Free: (800)966-7943
Fax: (520)515-5437
Shelia Devoe Heidman, Dir.

Arizona Small Business Development
Center Network
E-mail: york@maricopa.bitnet
2411 W. 14th St., Ste. 132
Tempe, Arizona 85281
Phone (602)731-8720
Fax: (602)731-8729
Michael York, State Director

Maricopa Community Colleges
Arizona Small Business Development
Center Network
2411 W. 14th St., Ste. 132
Tempe, Arizona 85281
Phone (602)230-7308
Fax: (520)230-7989
Michael York, State Director
Sonny Quinonez, Dir.
E-mail: york@maricopa.edu

Eastern Arizona College
Small Business Development Center
622 College Ave.
Thatcher, Arizona 85552-0769
Phone: (520)428-8590
Fax: (520)428-8462
Greg Roers, Dir.

Eastern Arizona College/Thatcher
SBDC
622 College Ave.
Thatcher, Arizona 85552-0769
Phone: (520)428-8590
Free: (800)322-5780
Fax: (520)428-8591
Frank Granberg, Director
E-mail: granberg@eac.cc.az.us

Pima Community College
Small Business Development and
Training Center
4905-A E. Broadway Blvd., Ste. 101
Tucson, Arizona 85709-1260
Phone: (520)206-4906
Fax: (520)206-4585

Linda Andrews, Director
E-mail: landrews@pimacc.pima.edu

Arizona Western College
Small Business Development Center
Century Plz., No. 152
281 W. 24th St.
Yuma, Arizona 85364
Phone: (520)341-1650
Fax: (520)726-2636
Hank Pinto, Director
E-mail: aw_lundin@awc.cc

Arkansas

Henderson State University
Small Business Development Center
1100 Henderson St.
PO Box 7624
Arkadelphia, Arkansas 71999-0001
Phone: (870)230-5224
Fax: (870)230-5236
Jeff Doose, Director
E-mail: dooseja@oaks.hsu.edu

Genesis Technology Incubator
SBDC Satellite Office
University of Arkansas - Engineering
Research Center
Fayetteville, Arkansas 72701-1201
Phone: (501)575-7473
Fax: (501)575-7446
Bob Penquite, Business Consultant

University of Arkansas at Fayetteville
Small Business Development Center
College of Business - BA 106
Fayetteville, Arkansas 72701
Phone: (501)575-5148
Fax: (501)575-4013
Ms. Jimmie Wilkins, Director

University of Arkansas at Little Rock,
Regional Office (Fort Smith)
Small Business Development Center
1109 S. 16th St.
PO Box 2067
Ft. Smith, Arkansas 72901
Phone: (501)785-1376
Fax: (501)785-1964
Byron Branch, Business Specialist

West Arkansas Regional Office
Small Business Development Center
1109 S. 16th St.

P.O. Box 2067
Ft. Smith, Arkansas 72901-2067
Phone: (501)785-1376
Fax: (501)785-1964
Vonelle Vanzant, Business Specialist
E-mail: rxevans2@ualr.edu

University of Arkansas at Little Rock,
Regional Office (Harrison)
Small Business Development Center
818 Hwy. 62-65-412 N
PO Box 190
Harrison, Arkansas 72601
Phone: (870)741-8009
Fax: (870)741-1905
Bob Penquite, Business Specialist
E-mail: rdpenquite@ualr.edu

University of Arkansas at Little Rock,
Regional Office (Hot Springs)
Small Business Development Center
835 Central Ave., Box 402-D
Hot Springs, Arkansas 71901
Phone: (501)624-5448
Fax: (501)624-6632
Richard Evans, Business Specialist
E-mail: rxevans2@ualr.edu

Arkansas State University
Small Business Development Center
College of Business
PO Box 2650
Jonesboro, Arkansas 72467
Phone: (870)972-3517
Fax: (870)972-3868
Herb Lawrence, Director
E-mail:
hlawrence@cherokee.astate.edu

University of Arkansas at Little Rock
SBDC
Little Rock Techonology Center
Bldg.
100 S. Main St., Ste. 401
Little Rock, Arkansas 72201
Phone: (501)324-9043
Fax: (501)324-9049
Janet Nye, State Dir.

University of Arkansas at Little Rock,
Regional Office (Magnolia)
Small Business Development Center
600 Bessie
PO Box 767
Magnolia, Arkansas 71753-3056

Phone: (870)234-4030
Fax: (870)234-6610
Mr. Lairie Kincaid, Business
Specialist

University of Arkansas at Little Rock,
Regional Office (Pine Bluff)
Small Business Development Center
The Enterprise Center III
400 Main, Ste. 117
Pine Bluff, Arkansas 71601
Phone: (870)536-0654
Fax: (870)536-7713
Russell Barker, Business Specialist
E-mail: rlbarker@ualr.edu

University of Arkansas at Little Rock,
Regional Office (Stuttgart)
Small Business Development Center
301 S. Grand, Ste. 101
PO Box 289
Stuttgart, Arkansas 72160
Phone: (870)673-8707
Fax: (870)673-8707
Larry Lefler, Business Specialist
E-mail: lelefler@ualr.edu

West Memphis Regional Office
Mid-South Community College
SBDC
2000 W. Broadway
P.O. Box 2067
West Memphis, Arkansas 72303-
2067
Phone: (870)733-6767
Fax: (870)733-6890
Ronny Brothers, Business Consultant
E-mail: rlbrothers@ualr.edu

California

Central Coast Small Business
Development Center
E-mail: sbdc@cabrillo.cc.ca.us
6500 Soquel Dr.
Aptos, California 95003
Phone: (408)479-6136
Fax: (408)479-6166
Teresa Thomae, Dir.

Sierra College Small Business
Development Center
E-mail:
smallbuz@sierra.campus.mci.net
560 Wall St., Ste. J

Auburn, California 95603
Phone: (530)885-5488
Fax: (530)823-2831
Mary Wollesen, Director

Weill Institute Small Business
Development Center
E-mail: weill@lightspeed.net
1706 Chester Ave., Ste. 200
Bakersfield, California 93301
Phone: (805)322-5881
Fax: (805)322-5663
Jeffrey Johnson, Director

Butte College
Small Business Development Center
260 Cohasset Rd., Ste. A
Chico, California 95926
Phone: (530)895-9017
Fax: (530)895-9099
Sophie Konuwa, Director
E-mail: konuwaso@butte.cc.ca.us

Southwestern College
Small Business Development and
International Trade Center
900 Otay Lakes Rd., Bldg. 1600
Chula Vista, California 91910
Phone: (619)482-6391
Fax: (619)482-6402
Mary Wylie, Director
E-mail: mwylie@sbditc.org

Contra Costa SBDC
2425 Bisso Ln., Ste. 200
Concord, California 94520
Phone: (925)646-5377
Fax: (925)646-5299
Maurice Williams, Director

North Coast Small Business
Development Center
207 Price Mall, Ste. 500
Crescent City, California 95531
Phone: (707)464-2168
Fax: (707)465-6008
Fran Clark, Director
E-mail: fransbdc@northcoast.com

Imperial Valley Satellite SBDC
Town & Country Shopping Center
E-mail: ivsbdc@quix.net
1240 State St.
301 N. Imperial Ave., Ste. B
El Centro, California 92243

Phone: (760)312-9800
Fax: (760)312-9838
Debbie Trujillo, Manager

Export SBDC/El Monte Outreach
Center
E-mail: info@exportsbdc.org
10501 Valley Blvd., Ste. 106
El Monte, California 91731
Phone: (626)459-4111
Fax: (626)443-0463
Charles Blythe, Manager

Export Small Business Development
Center of Southern California
E-mail: info@exportsbdc.org
222 N Sepulveda, Ste. 1690
El Segundo, California 90245
Phone: (310)606-0166
Fax: (310)606-0155
Gladys Moreau, Director

North Coast
Small Business Development Center
520 E St.
Eureka, California 95501
Phone: (707)445-9720
Fax: (707)445-9652
Ms. Fran Clark, Director
E-mail: fransbdc@northcoast.com

West Company Coast Office
Fort Bragg SBDC
306 Redwood Ave.
Fort Bragg, California 95437
Phone: (707)964-7571
Fax: (707)964-7571

Central California
Small Business Development Center
E-mail: sbdc@abrillo.cc.ca.us
3419 W. Shaw Ave., Ste. 102
Fresno, California 93711
Phone: (209)275-1223
Free: (800)974-0664
Fax: (209)275-1499
Dennis Winans, Director

Gavilan College Small Business
Development Center
E-mail: l.nolan@gilroy.com
7436 Monterey St.
Gilroy, California 95020
Phone: (408)847-0373
Fax: (408)847-0393
Peter Graff, Director

Pasadena Small Business
Development Center
SBDC
330 N Brand, Ste. 190
Glendale, California 91203
Phone: (818)552-3254
Fax: (818)398-3059
David Ryal, Manager

Accelerate Technology Assistance
Small Business Development Center
4199 Campus Dr.
University Towers, Ste. 240
Irvine, California 92715
Phone: (714)509-2990
Fax: (714)509-2997
Tiffany Haugen, Dir.

Amador SBDC
1500 N. Hwy. 49
P.O. Box 1077
Jackson, California 95642
Phone: (209)223-0351
Fax: (209)223-2261
Ron Mittelbrunn, Manager

Greater San Diego Chamber of
Commerce
Small Business Development Center
E-mail: sbdc@smallbiz.org
4275 Executive Sq., Ste. 920
La Jolla, California 92037
Phone: (619)453-9388
Fax: (619)450-1997
Hal Lefkowitz, Director

Lakeport Small Business
Development Center
SBDC
PO Box 1566
Lakeport, California 95453
Phone: (707)263-0330
Fax: (707)263-8516

Yuba College SBDC
PO Box 1566
15145 Lakeshore Dr.
PO Box 4550
Lakeport, California 95453
Phone: (707)263-0330
Fax: (707)263-8516
George McQueen, Dir.

East Los Angeles SBDC
5161 East Pomona Blvd., Ste. 212
Los Angeles, California 90022

Phone: (213)262-9797
Fax: (213)262-2704

South Central LA
SBDC
E-mail: sbdcla@ibm.net
3650 Martin Luther King Blvd., Ste.
246
Los Angeles, California 90008
Phone: (213)290-2832
Fax: (213)290-7190
Cope Norcross, Manager

Alpine Chamber of Commerce &
Visitor Authority
SBDC
P.O. Box 265
3 Webster St.
Markleeville, California 96120
Phone: (530)694-2475
Fax: (530)694-2478

Yuba College Small Business
Development Center
SBDC
429 10th St.
PO Box 262
Marysville, California 95901
Phone: (530)749-0152
Fax: (530)749-0155
Jim Bengson, Interim Director

Valley Sierra SBDC
Merced Satellite
1632 N St.
Merced, California 95340
Phone: (209)725-3800
Fax: (209)383-4959
Nick Starianoudakis, Satellite Mgr.

Valley Sierra Small Business
Development Center
1012 11th St., Ste. 400
Modesto, California 95354
Phone: (209)521-6177
Fax: (209)521-9373
Kelly Bearden, Director
E-mail: bearden@scedco.org

Napa Valley College Small Business
Development Center
1556 First St., Ste. 103
Napa, California 94559
Phone: (707)253-3210
Fax: (707)253-3068
Chuck Eason, Director
E-mail: charles.eason@usa.net

Inland Empire Business Incubator
SBDC
155 S. Memorial Dr.
Norton Air Force Base, California
92509
Phone: (909)382-0065
Fax: (909)382-8543
John O'Brein, Incubator Manager

East Bay Small Business
Development Center
E-mail: sbdc@peralta.cc.ca.us
519 17th. St., Ste. 210
Oakland, California 94612
Phone: (510)893-4114
Fax: (510)893-5532
Mr. Faneem Hameed, Director

International Trade Office
SBDC
3282 E. Guasti Rd., Ste. 100
Ontario, California 91761
Phone: (909)390-8071
Fax: (909)390-8077
John Hernandez, Trade Manager

Coachella Valley SBDC
Palm Springs Satellite Center
501 S. Palm Canyon Dr., Ste. 222
Palm Springs, California 92264
Phone: (760)864-1311
Fax: (760)864-1319
Brad Mix, Business Consultant

Pico Rivera SBDC
9058 E. Washington Blvd.
Pico Rivera, California 90660
Phone: (310)942-9965
Fax: (310)942-9745
Beverly Taylor, Satellite Mgr.

Eastern Los Angeles County Small
Business Development Center
375 S. Main St., Ste. 101
Pomona, California 91766
Phone: (909)629-2247
Fax: (909)629-8310
Toni Valdez, Director

Pomona SBDC
375 S. Main St., Ste. 101
Pomona, California 91766
Phone: (909)629-2247
Fax: (909)629-8310
Paul Hischar, Satellite Manager

Cascade Small Business Development Center
737 Auditorium Dr., Ste. A
Redding, California 96001
Phone: (530)225-2770
Fax: (530)225-2769
Carole Enmark, Director
E-mail: cenmark@awwwsome.com

Inland Empire Small Business Development Center
E-mail: sbdc@winriverside.org
1157 Spruce St.
Riverside, California 92507
Phone: (909)781-2345
Free: (800)750-2353
Fax: (909)781-2353
Michael Stull, Director

California Trade and Commerce Agency
California SBDC
801 K St., Ste. 1700
Sacramento, California 95814
Phone: (916)324-5068
Free: (800)303-6600
Fax: (916)322-5084
Kim Neri, State Director

Greater Sacramento SBDC
1410 Ethan Way
Sacramento, California 95825
Phone: (916)563-3210
Fax: (916)563-3266
Cynthia Steimle, Director
E-mail:
steimlc@mail.do.losrios.cc.ca.us

Calaveras SBDC
P.O. Box 431
3 N. Main St.
San Andreas, California 95249
Phone: (209)754-1834
Fax: (209)754-4107

San Francisco SBDC
E-mail: sfsbdc@ziplink.net
711 Van Ness, Ste. 305
San Francisco, California 94102
Phone: (415)561-1890
Fax: (415)561-1894
Tim Sprinkles, Director

Orange County Small Business Development Center
901 E. Santa Ana Blvd., Ste. 101
Santa Ana, California 92701

Phone: (714)647-1172
Fax: (714)835-9008
Gregory Kishel, Director
E-mail: gkishel@pacbell.net

Southwest Los Angeles County Westside Satellite
SBDC
3233 Donald Douglas Loop S., Ste. C
Santa Monica, California 90405
Phone: (310)398-8883
Fax: (310)398-3024
Ken Davis, Administrative Assistant

Redwood Empire Small Business Development Center
520 Mendocino Ave., Ste. 210
Santa Rosa, California 95401
Phone: (707)524-1770
Fax: (707)524-1772
Chrus Facas, Director
E-mail:
chris_facas@garfield.santarosa.edu

San Joaquin Delta College Small Business Development Center
445 N. San Joaquin St., 2nd Fl.
Stockton, California 95202
Phone: (209)943-5089
Fax: (209)943-8325
Gillian Murphy, Director
E-mail: gmurphy@sjdccd.cc.ca.us

Solano County SBDC
424 Executive Court N., Ste C
Suison, California 94585
Phone: (707)864-3382
Fax: (707)864-8025
Beth Pratt, Director
E-mail: epratt@solano.cc.ca.us

Silicon Valley SBDC
298 S. Sunnyvale Ave., Ste. 204
Sunnyvale, California 94086
Phone: (408)736-0680
Fax: (408)736-0679
Eliza Minor, Director
E-mail: rebecca@siliconvalley-sbdc.org

Southwest Los Angeles County Small Business Development Center
2377 Crenshaw Blvd., Ste. 120
Torrance, California 90501
Phone: (310)787-6466
Fax: (310)782-8607
Susan Hunter, Director

West Company SBDC
367 N. State St., Ste. 201
Ukiah, California 95482
Phone: (707)468-3553
Fax: (707)468-3555
Sheilah Rogers, Director

North Los Angeles Small Business Development Center
E-mail: vnsbdc@aol.com
4717 Van Nuys Blvd., Ste. 201
Van Nuys, California 91403-2100
Phone: (818)907-9922
Fax: (818)907-9890
Wilma Berglund, Director

Export SBDC Satellite Center
E-mail: esbdc@primenet.com
5700 Ralston St., Ste. 310
Ventura, California 93003
Phone: (805)644-6191
Fax: (805)658-2252
Heather Wicka, Manager

Gold Coast SBDC
E-mail: gcsbdc@aol.com
5700 Ralston St., Ste. 310
Ventura, California 93003
Phone: (805)658-2688
Fax: (805)658-2252
Joe Huggins, Manager/Business Consultant

High Desert SBDC
Victorville Satellite Center
15490 Civic Dr., Ste. 102
Victorville, California 92392
Phone: (760)951-1592
Fax: (760)951-8929
Janice Moore, Manager/Business Consultant

Central California /Visalia Satellite SBDC
E-mail: wendim@csufresno.edu
430 W. Caldwell Ave., Ste. D
Visalia, California 93277
Phone: (209)625-3051
Fax: (209)625-3053
Randy Mason, Manager

Colorado

Adams State College
Small Business Development Center
School of Business, Rm. 105
Alamosa, Colorado 81102

Phone: (719)589-7372
Fax: (719)589-7603
Mary Hoffman, Director
E-mail: mchoffma@adams.edu

Community College of Aurora
Small Business Development Center
E-mail: asbdc@henge.com
9905 E. Colfax Ave.
Aurora, Colorado 80010-2119
Phone: (303)341-4849
Fax: (303)361-2953
Randy Johnson, Director

Boulder Chamber of Commerce
Small Business Development Center
Boulder Chamber of Commerce
2440 Pearl St.
Boulder, Colorado 80302
Phone: (303)442-1475
Fax: (303)938-8837
Marilynn Force, Director
E-mail:
marilyn@chamber.boulder.co.us

Pueblo Community College (Canon
City)
Small Business Development Center
E-mail: canonsbdc@attmail.com
3080 Main St.
Canon City, Colorado 81212
Phone: (719)275-5335
Fax: (719)269-7334
Elwin Boody, Director

Douglas County SBDC
Castle Rock Chamber of Commerce
420 Jerry St.
PO Box 282
Castle Rock, Colorado 80104
Phone: (303)814-0936
Fax: (303)688-2688
Dennie Kamlet

University of Colorado at Colorado
Springs
Small Business Development Center
Colorado Springs Chamber of
Commerce
E-mail: sbdc@uccs.edu
CITTI Bldg.
1420 Austin Bluff Pkwy.
Colorado Springs, Colorado 80933
Phone: (719)592-1894
Fax: (719)533-0545
Iris Clark, Director

Colorado Northwestern Community
College
Small Business Development Center
E-mail: cnwcc@attmail.com
50 College Dr.
Craig, Colorado 81625
Phone: (970)824-7078
Fax: (970)824-1134
Ken Farmer, Director

Delta Montrose Vocational School
Small Business Development Center
E-mail: dmvs@attmail.com
1765 US Hwy. 50
Delta, Colorado 81416
Phone: (970)874-8772
Free: (888)234-7232
Fax: (970)874-8796
Bob Marshall, Director

Community College of Denver
Greater Denver Chamber of
Commerce
Small Business Development Center
E-mail: ccd@attmail.com
1445 Market St.
1445 Market St.
Denver, Colorado 80202
Phone: (303)620-8076
Fax: (303)534-3200
Tamela Lee, Director

Office of Business Development
Colorado SBDC
1625 Broadway, Ste. 1710
Denver, Colorado 80202
Phone: (303)892-3809
Free: (800)333-7798
Fax: (303)892-3848
Lee Ortiz, State Dir.
E-mail: cec.ortiz@state.co.us

Fort Lewis College
Small Business Development Center
136-G Hesperus Hall
1000 Rim Dr.
Durango, Colorado 81301-3999
Phone: (970)247-7009
Fax: (970)247-7623
Jim Reser, Director
E-mail: reser-j@fortlewis.edu

Front Range Community College (Ft.
Collins)
Small Business Development Center
E-mail: ftcsbdc@attmail.com
125 S. Howes, Ste. 105

Key Tower Bldg.
Ft. Collins, Colorado 80526
Phone: (970)498-9295
Fax: (970)221-2811
Frank Pryor, Director

Morgan Community College (Ft.
Morgan)
Small Business Development Center
E-mail: comcc@attmail.com
300 Main St.
Ft. Morgan, Colorado 80701
Phone: (970)867-3351
Fax: (970)867-3352
Dan Simon, Director

Colorado Mountain College
(Glenwood Springs)
Small Business Development Center
E-mail: lwiltse@coloradomtn.edu
215 9th St.
Glenwood Springs, Colorado 81601
Phone: (970)928-0120
Free: (800)621-1647
Fax: (970)947-8385
Alisa Zimmerman, Director

Red Rocks Community College
Small Business Development Center
E-mail: sbdcrrcc@rmii.com
1726 Cole Blvd., Bldg. 22, Ste. 310
Golden, Colorado 80401
Phone: (303)277-1840
Fax: (303)277-1899
Jayne Reiter, Director

Mesa State College
Small Business Development Center
E-mail: mesastate@attmail.com
304 W. Main St.
Grand Junction, Colorado 81505-
1606
Phone: (970)243-5242
Fax: (970)241-0771
Julie Morey, Director

Aims Community College
Greeley/Weld Chamber of Commerce
Small Business Development Center
Aims Community College
E-mail: aimcc@attmail.com
902 7th Ave.
Greeley, Colorado 80631
Phone: (970)352-3661
Fax: (970)352-3572
Ron Anderson, Director

Red Rocks Community College Small
Business Development Center
777 S. Wadsworth Blvd., Ste. 254
Bldg. 4
Lakewood, Colorado 80226
Phone: (303)987-0710
Fax: (303)987-1331
Jayne Reiter, Acting Dir.

Lamar Community College
Small Business Development Center
E-mail: lcc@attmail.com
2400 S. Main
Lamar, Colorado 81052
Phone: (719)336-8141
Fax: (719)336-2448
Dan Minor, Director

Small Business Development Center
Arapahoe Community College
South Metro Chamber of Commerce
7901 S. Park Plz., Ste. 110
Littleton, Colorado 80120
Phone: (303)795-5855
Fax: (303)795-7520
Selma Kristel, Dir.

Pueblo Community College Small
Business Development Center
900 W. Orman Ave.
Pueblo, Colorado 81004
Phone: (719)549-3224
Fax: (719)549-3139
Rita Friberg, Director
E-mail: friberg@pcc.cccoes.edu

Morgan Community College
(Stratton)
Small Business Development Center
PO Box 28
Stratton, Colorado 80836
Phone: (719)348-5596
Fax: (719)348-5887
Roni Carr, Dir.

Trinidad State Junior College
Small Business Development Center
E-mail: tsjc@attmail.com
136 W. Main St.
Davis Bldg.
Trinidad, Colorado 81082
Phone: (719)846-5644
Fax: (719)846-4550
Dennis O'Connor, Director

Front Range Community College
(Westminster)

Small Business Development Center
E-mail: fr_henry@cccs.ccoes.edu
3645 W. 112th Ave.
Westminster, Colorado 80030
Phone: (303)460-1032
Fax: (303)469-7143
Joe Pariseau, Director

Connecticut

Bridgeport Regional Business
Council
Small Business Development Center
E-mail:
Bridgeport@ct.sbdc.uconn.edu
10 Middle St., 14th Fl.
Bridgeport, Connecticut 06604-4229
Phone: (203)330-4813
Fax: (203)366-0105
Juan Scott, Regional Director

Quinebaug Valley Community
Technical College
Small Business Development Center
E-mail:
Danielson@ct.sbdc.uconn.edu
742 Upper Maple St.
Danielson, Connecticut 06239-1440
Phone: (860)774-1133
Fax: (860)774-6737
Roger Doty, Director

University of Connecticut (Groton)
Small Business Development Center
E-mail: Groton@ct.sbdc.uconn.edu
Administration Bldg., Rm. 300
1084 Shennecossett Rd.
Groton, Connecticut 06340-6097
Phone: (860)405-9002
Fax: (860)405-9041
Louise Kahler, Regional Director

Middlesex County Chamber of
Commerce
SBDC
E-mail:
Middletown@ct.sbdc.uconn.edu
393 Main St.
Middletown, Connecticut 06457
Phone: (860)344-2158
Fax: (860)346-1043
John Serignese, Counselor

Greater New Haven Chamber of
Commerce
Small Business Development Center
E-mail:

NewHaven@ct.sbdc.uconn.edu
900 Chapel St., 10th Floor
New Haven, Connecticut 06510-2009
Phone: (203)782-4390
Fax: (203)782-4329
Pete Rivera, Regional Director

Southwestern Area Commerce and
Industry Association (SACIA)
Small Business Development Center
E-mail: Stamford@ct.sbdc.uconn.edu
1 Landmark Sq., Ste. 230
Stamford, Connecticut 06901
Phone: (203)359-3220
Fax: (203)967-8294
Harvey Blomberg, Regional Director

University of Connecticut
School of Business Administration
Connecticut SBDC
E-mail:
statedirector@ct.sbdc.uconn.edu
2 Bourn Place, U-94
Storrs, Connecticut 06269-5094
Phone: (860)486-4135
Fax: (860)486-1576
Dennis Gruel, State Director
E-mail:
EMLstatedirecor@ct.sbdc.uconn.edu

Naugatuck Valley Development
Center
Small Business Development Center
E-mail:
Waterbury@ct.sbdc.uconn.edu
100 Grand St., 3rd Fl.
Waterbury, Connecticut 06702
Phone: (203)757-8937
Fax: (203)756-9077
Ilene Oppenheim, Regional Director

University of Connecticut (Greater
Hartford Campus)
Small Business Development Center
E-mail:
WestHartford@ct.sbdc.uconn.edu
1800 Asylum Ave.
West Hartford, Connecticut 06117-
2659
Phone: (860)570-9109
Fax: (860)570-9107
Ben Chepovsky, Regional Director

Eastern Connecticut State University
Small Business Development Center
E-mail:
Williamantic@ct.sbdc.uconn.edu

83 Windham St.
Williamantic, Connecticut 06226-2295
Phone: (860)465-5349
Fax: (860)465-5143
Richard Cheney, Counselor

Delaware

Delaware State University
Small Business Resource &
Information Center
SBDC
146 S Governor's Ave.
Dover, Delaware 19904
Phone: (302)678-1555
Fax: (302)739-2333
Jim Crisfield, Director

Delaware Technical and Community
College
SBDC
Industrial Training Bldg.
PO Box 610
Georgetown, Delaware 19947
Phone: (302)856-1555
Fax: (302)856-5779
William F. Pfaff, Director

University of Delaware
Delaware SBDC
Purnell Hall, Ste. 005
Newark, Delaware 19716-2711
Phone: (302)831-1555
Fax: (302)831-1423
Clinton Tymes, State Dir.

Small Business Resource &
Information Center
SBDC
1318 N. Market St.
Wilmington, Delaware 19801
Phone: (302)571-1555
Fax: (302)571-5222
Barbara Necarsulmer, Director

District of Columbia

Central Region Sub-Center
Howard University Center for Urban
Progress
SBDC
14th and U St., NW
2nd Floor
Frank Reeves Municipal Center

Washington, District of Columbia
20001
Phone: (202)939-3018
Fax: (202)673-4557
Jose Hernandez, Director

District of Columbia Small Business
Development Center
Economic Development Office of the
Mayor
441 4th St., NW
Ste 1140 N
Washington, District of Columbia
20001
Phone: (202)727-6365
Fax: (202)727-6703

Friendship House/Southern
University
SBDC
Southwest Region Sub-Center
921 Pennsylvania Ave., SE
Washington, District of Columbia
20003
Phone: (202)547-7944
Fax: (202)546-3080
Elise Ashby, Acting Director

George Washington University
East of the River Community
Development Corp.
SBDC
3101 MLK Jr. Ave., SE, 3rd Fl.
Washington, District of Columbia
20032
Phone: (202)561-4975
Howard Johnson, Accounting
Specialist

Howard University
SBDC
Satellite Location
2600 6th St., NW, Rm. 128
Washington, District of Columbia
20059
Phone: (202)806-1550
Fax: (202)806-1777
Edith McCloud, Director

Howard University
George Washington Small Business
Legal Clinic
SBDC
2000 G St., NW, Ste. 200

Washington, District of Columbia
20052
Phone: (202)994-7463
Fax: (202)994-4946
Susan Jones, Director

Howard University
Office of Latino Affairs
SBDC
2000 14th St., NW, 2nd Fl.
Washington, District of Columbia
20009
Phone: (202)939-3018
Fax: (202)994-4946
Jose Hernandez, Gov. Procurement
Specialist

Marshall Heights Community
Development Organization
SBDC
3917 Minnesota Ave., NE
Washington, District of Columbia
20019
Phone: (202)396-1200
Terry Strong, Financing Specialist

Washington District Office
Business Information Center
SBDC
1110 Vermont Ave., NW, 9th Fl.
Washington, District of Columbia
20005
Phone: (202)737-0120
Fax: (202)737-0476
Johnetta Hardy, Marketing Specialist

Florida

Central Florida Development Council
Small Business Development Center
600 N. Broadway, Ste. 300
Bartow, Florida 33830
Phone: (941)534-4370
Fax: (941)533-1247
Marcela Stanislaus, Vice President

Florida Atlantic University (Boca
Raton)
Small Business Development Center
777 Glades Rd.
Bldg. T9
PO Box 3091
Boca Raton, Florida 33431
Phone: (561)362-5620
Fax: (561)362-5623
Nancy Young, Director

UCF Brevard Campus
Small Business Development Center
1519 Clearlake Rd.
Cocoa, Florida 32922
Phone: (407)951-1060

Dania Small Business Development
Center
46 SW 1st Ave.
Dania, Florida 33304-3607
Phone: (954)987-0100
Fax: (954)987-0106
William Healy, Regional Mgr.

Daytona Beach Community College
Florida Regional SBDC
Daytona Beach Community College
1200 W. International Speedway
Blvd.
Daytona Beach, Florida 32114
Phone: (904)225-8131
Fax: (904)258-3846
Laurene A. Burgwin, Director
E-mail: lburgwin@bellsouth.net

Florida Atlantic University
Commercial Campus
Small Business Development Center
1515 W. Commercial Blvd., Rm. 11
Ft. Lauderdale, Florida 33309
Phone: (954)771-6520
Fax: (954)351-4120
Marty Zients, Manager

Minority Business Development
Center
SBDC
5950 West Oakland Park Blvd., Ste.
307
Ft. Lauderdale, Florida 33313
Phone: (954)485-5333
Fax: (954)485-2514

Edison Community College
Small Business Development Center
8099 College Pky. SW
Ft. Myers, Florida 33919
Phone: (941)489-9200
Fax: (941)489-9051
Dan Regelski, Management
Consultant

Florida Gulf Coast University
Small Business Development Center
Small Business Development Center
17595 S. Tamiami Trail, Ste. 200
Midway Ctr.

Ft. Myers, Florida 33908-4500
Phone: (941)590-7316
Fax: (941)590-1010
Dan Regleski, Management
Consultant

Indian River Community College
Small Business Development Center
3209 Virginia Ave., Rm. 114
Ft. Pierce, Florida 34981-5599
Phone: (561)462-4756
Fax: (561)462-4796
Marsha Thompson, Director

Okaloosa-Walton Community
College
SBDC
1170 Martin Luther King, Jr. Blvd.
Ft. Walton Beach, Florida 32547
Phone: (904)863-6543
Fax: (904)863-6564
Walton Craft, Manager

University of North Florida
(Gainesville)
Small Business Development Center
505 NW 2nd Ave., Ste. D
PO Box 2518
Gainesville, Florida 32602-2518
Phone: (352)377-5621
Fax: (352)377-0288
Bill Stensgaard, Regional Manager
E-mail: lsheehy@ugcdc.org

University of North Florida
(Jacksonville)
Small Business Development Center
E-mail: smallbiz@unf.edu
College of Business
Bldg. 11, Rm. 2163
4567 St. John's Bluff Rd. S
Jacksonville, Florida 32216
Phone: (904)646-2476
Fax: (904)646-2567
Lowell Salter, Director

Gulf Coast Community College
SBDC
2500 Minnesota Ave.
Lynn Haven, Florida 32444
Phone: (904)271-1108
Fax: (904)271-1109
Doug Davis, Director

Brevard Community College
(Melbourne)
Small Business Development Center

3865 N. Wickham Rd., CM 207
Melbourne, Florida 32935
Phone: (407)632-1111
Fax: (407)634-3721
Victoria Peak, Manager

Florida International University
Small Business Development Center
Trailer M01 - Tamiami Campus
CEAS-2620
Miami, Florida 33199
Phone: (305)348-2272
Fax: (305)348-2965
Marvin Nesbit, Regional Director

Florida International University
(North Miami Campus)
Small Business Development Center
Academic Bldg. No. 1, Rm. 350
NE 151 and Biscayne Blvd.
Miami, Florida 33181
Phone: (305)919-5790
Fax: (305)919-5792
Royland Jarrett, Regional Manager

Miami Dade Community College
Small Business Development Center
6300 NW 7th Ave.
Miami, Florida 33150
Phone: (305)237-1906
Fax: (305)237-1908
Frederic Bonneau, Manager

Ocala Small Business Development
Center
E-mail: sbdcoca@mercury.net
110 E. Silver Springs Blvd.
PO Box 1210
Ocala, Florida 34470-6613
Phone: (352)622-8763
Fax: (352)351-1031
Philip Geist, Area Director

University of Central Florida
Small Business Development Center
College of Business Administration,
Ste. 309
PO Box 161530
Orlando, Florida 32816-1530
Phone: (407)823-5554
Fax: (407)823-3073
Al Polfer, Director

Palm Beach Gardens
Florida Atlantic University
SBDC
Northrop Center

3970 RCA Blvd., Ste. 7323
Palm Beach Gardens, Florida 33410
Phone: (407)691-8550
Fax: (407)692-8502
Steve Windhaus, Regional Mgr.

Procurement Technical Assistance
Program
University of West Florida
Small Business Development Center
19 W. Garden St., Ste. 302
UFW Downtown Center
Pensacola, Florida 32501
Phone: (904)470-4980
Fax: (904)470-4987
Larry A. Strain, Director

University of West Florida
Florida SBDC Network
E-mail: fsbdc@uwf.edu
19 West Garden St., Ste. 300
Pensacola, Florida 32501
Phone: (850)595-6060
Fax: (850)595-6070
Jerry Cartwright, State Dir.

Seminole Community College
SBDC
100 Weldon Blvd., Bldg R
Sanford, Florida 32773
Phone: (407)328-4722
Fax: (407)330-4489
Wayne Hardy, Regional Manager

Florida Agricultural and Mechanical
University
Small Business Development Center
1157 E. Tennessee St.
Tallahassee, Florida 32308
Phone: (904)599-3407
Fax: (904)561-2049
Patricia McGowan, Director

University of South Florida—CBA
SBDC Special Services
4202 E. Fowler Ave., BSN 3403
College of Business Administration
Tampa, Florida 33620
Phone: (813)974-4371
Fax: (813)974-5020
Dick Hardesty, Program Manager
E-mail:
SBDC@smtc_fla.enterprise.state.fl.us

University of South Florida (Tampa)
Small Business Development Center
1111 N. Westshore Dr., Annex B, Ste.

101-B
4202 E. Fowler Ave., BSN 3403
Tampa, Florida 33607
Phone: (813)554-2341
Free: (800)733-7232
Fax: (813)554-2356
Irene Hurst, Interim Director

Georgia

University of Georgia
Small Business Development Center
Southwest Georgia District
E-mail: sbdcalb@uga.cc.uga.edu
230 S. Jackson St., Ste. 333
Albany, Georgia 31701-2885
Phone: (912)430-4303
Fax: (912)430-3933
Sue Ford, Assistant State Director
E-mail: sford@sbdc.uga.edu

NE Georgia District
SBDC
University of Georgia
1180 E. Broad St.
Athens, Georgia 30602-5412
Phone: (706)542-7436
Fax: (706)542-6823
Gayle Rosenthal, Mgr.

NW Georgia District
University of Georgia
SBDC
1180 E. Broad St.
Athens, Georgia 30602-5412
Phone: (706)542-6756
Fax: (706)542-6776

University of Georgia
Chicopee Complex
Georgia SBDC
E-mail: sbdcath@uga.cc.uga.edu
University of Georgia
1180 E. Broad St.
Athens, Georgia 30602-5412
Phone: (706)542-6762
Fax: (706)542-6776
Hank Logan, State Dir.
E-mail: hlogan@uga.cc.uga.edu

Georgia State University
Small Business Development Center
E-mail: sbdjlq@langate.gsu.edu
University Plz.
Box 874
Atlanta, Georgia 30303-3083

Phone: (404)651-3550
Fax: (404)651-1035
Mr. Lee Quarterman, Area Director

Morris Brown College
Small Business Development Center
643 Martin Luther King, Jr., Dr. NW
Atlanta, Georgia 30314
Phone: (404)220-0205
Fax: (404)688-5985
Ray Johnson, Center Mgr.

Augusta Small Business Development
Center
Small Business Development Center
E-mail: sbdcaug@uga.cc.uga.edu
1054 Claussen Rd., Ste. 301
Augusta, Georgia 30907-3215
Phone: (706)737-1790
Fax: (706)731-7937
Jeff Sanford, Area Director
E-mail: jsanford@sbdc.uga.edu

Brunswick Small Business
Development Center
Small Business Development Center
E-mail: sbdcbrun@uga.cc.uga.edu
1107 Fountain Lake Dr.
Brunswick, Georgia 31525-3039
Phone: (912)264-7343
Fax: (912)262-3095
David Lewis, Area Director
E-mail: dlewis@sbdc.uga.edu

Carrollton Small Business
Development Center
SBDC
E-mail: wlankfor@sbf.bus.westga.edu
Cobb Hall
Carrollton, Georgia 30118-4130

Columbus Small Business
Development Center
Small Business Development Center
University of Georgia
E-mail: sbdccolu@uga.cc.uga.edu
1030 First Ave.
928 45th St.
Columbus, Georgia 31901-2402
Phone: (706)649-7433
Fax: (706)649-1928
Jerry Copeland, Area Director
E-mail: copyeland@sbdc.uga.edu

DeKalb Chamber of Commerce
Decatur Small Business Development
Center

E-mail: sbdcdec@uga.cc.uga.edu
750 Commerce Dr., Ste. 201
Decatur, Georgia 30030-2622
Phone: (404)373-6930
Fax: (404)687-9684
Eric Bonaparte, Area Director
E-mail: bonapart@sbdc.uga.edu

Gainesville Small Business
Development Center
E-mail: sbdcgain@uga.cc.uga.edu
500 Jesse Jewel Pkwy., Ste. 304
Gainesville, Georgia 30501-3773
Phone: (770)531-5681
Fax: (770)531-5684
Ron Simmons, Area Director
E-mail: resimmons@sbdc.uga.edu

Kennesaw State University
Small Business Development Center
E-mail: sbdcmar@uga.cc.uga.edu
1000 Chastain Rd.
Kennesaw, Georgia 30144-5591
Phone: (770)423-6450
Fax: (770)423-6564
Carlotta Roberts, Area Director
E-mail:
carobert@ksumail.kennesaw.edu

LaGrange Small Business
Development Center
SBDC
601 Broad St.
LaGrange, Georgia 30240-2955
Phone: (706)812-7353
Fax: (706)845-0391

Southeast Georgia District (Macon)
Small Business Development Center
E-mail: sbdcmac@uga.cc.uga.edu
401 Cherry St., Ste. 701
PO Box 13212
Macon, Georgia 31208-3212
Phone: (912)751-6592
Fax: (912)751-6607
Wendell Perkins, Area Director
E-mail: wperkins@sbdc.uga.edu

Clayton State College & State
University
Small Business Development Center
E-mail: sbdcmorr@uga.cc.uga.edu
PO Box 285
Morrow, Georgia 30260
Phone: (770)961-3440
Fax: (770)961-3428

Bernie Meincke, Area Director
E-mail: meincke@ce.clayton.edu

Norcross Small Business
Development Center
University of Georgia
SBDC
E-mail: sbdclaw@uga.cc.edu
Oakbrook Plaza
1770 Indian Trail Rd., Ste. 410
Norcross, Georgia 30093
Phone: (770)806-2124
Fax: (770)806-2129
Robert Andoh, Area Director
Robert Andoh, Center Mgr.
E-mail: randoh@sbdc.uga.edu

Floyd College
Small Business Development Center
E-mail: sbdcrome@uga.cc.uga.edu
PO Box 1864
Rome, Georgia 30162-1864
Phone: (706)295-6326
Fax: (706)295-6732
Drew Tonsmeire, Area Director
E-mail:
drew_tonsmeire@mail.fc.peachnet.edu

Savannah Small Business
Development Center
Small Business Development Center
E-mail: sbdcsav@uga.cc.uga.edu
111 E Liberty St., Ste. 200
Savannah, Georgia 31401-4410
Phone: (912)651-3200
Fax: (912)651-3209
Lynn Vos, Area Director
E-mail: sbdcsav@uga.cc.uga.edu

Statesboro Small Business
Development Center
Small Business Development Center
E-mail: sbdcstat@uga.cc.uga.edu
Landrum Center
PO Box 8156
Statesboro, Georgia 30460-8156
Phone: (912)681-5194
Fax: (912)681-0648
Mark Davis, Area Director
E-mail:
jmdavis@gsvms2.cc.gasou.edu

Valdosta Small Business
Development Center
Valdosta State University
SBDC

E-mail: sbdcval@uga.cc.uga.edu
College of Business Administration
Thaxton Hall
Valdosta, Georgia 31698-0065
Phone: (912)245-3738
Fax: (912)245-3741
Suzanne Barnett, Area Director
E-mail:
sbarnett@grits.valdosta.peachnet.edu

Warner Robins SBDC
University of Georgia
SBDC
E-mail: sbdccwr@uga.cc.uga.edu
400 Corder Rd., Ste.B
Warner Robins, Georgia 31088
Phone: (912)329-4825
Fax: (912)329-4827
David Mills, Asst. Dir. for
Development Research

Guam

Pacific Islands SBDC Network
University of Guam
UOG Station
303 University Dr.
Mangilao, Guam 96923
Phone: (671)735-2590
Fax: (671)734-2002
Dr. Sephen L. Marder, Director
E-mail: smarder@uog9.uog.edu

Hawaii

Kona Circuit Rider
SBDC
200 West Kawili St.
Hilo, Hawaii 96720-4091
Phone: (808)933-3515
Fax: (808)933-3683
Rebecca Winters, Center Director
E-mail: winters@interpac.net

University of Hawaii at Hilo
Hawaii County
SBDC
200 W Kawili St.
Hilo, Hawaii 96720-4091
Phone: (808)969-1814
Fax: (808)969-7669
Rebecca Winters, Center Director
E-mail: winters@interpac.net

University of Hawaii at West Oahu
Honolulu County

SBDC
1111 Bishop St., Ste. 204
Honolulu, Hawaii 96813
Phone: (808)522-8131
Fax: (808)522-8135
Laura Noda, Center Director
E-mail: lnoda@aloha.net

Maui Community College
Small Business Development Center
Maui Research and Technology
Center
590 Lipoa Pkwy., Ste. 128
Kihei, Hawaii 96753-6900
Phone: (808)875-2400
Fax: (808)875-2452
David B. Fisher, Center Director
E-mail: dfisher@maui.com

Kauai Community College
Small Business Development Center
3-1901 Kaumualii Hwy.
Lihue, Hawaii 96766-9591
Phone: (808)246-1748
Fax: (808)246-5102
Randy Gingas, Center Director
E-mail: randyg@aloha.net

Leeward Satellite
SBDC
94-229 Waifahu Depot Rd, Ste 402
Waipahu, Hawaii 96797
Phone: (808)671-8837
Fax: (808)671-0476
Michael Keltos, Consultant

Idaho

Boise State University
Small Business Development Center
1910 University Dr.
Boise, Idaho 83725
Phone: (208)426-3875
Free: (800)225-3815
Fax: (208)426-3877
Robert Shepard, Regional Director

Boise State University
College of Business
Idaho SBDC
1910 University Dr.
Boise, Idaho 83725
Phone: (208)385-1640
Free: (800)225-3815
Fax: (208)385-3877
James Hogge, State Director

Idaho State University (Idaho Falls)
Small Business Development Center
2300 N. Yellowstone
Idaho Falls, Idaho 83401
Phone: (208)523-1087
Free: (800)658-3829
Fax: (208)523-1049
Betty Capps, Regional Director
E-mail: cappmary@fs.isu.edu

Lewis-Clark State College
Small Business Development Center
500 8th Ave.
Lewiston, Idaho 83501
Phone: (208)799-2465
Free: (800)933-5272
Fax: (208)799-2878
Helen Le Boeuf-Binninger, Regional
Director
E-mail: hleboeuf@lcsc.edu

Idaho Small Business Development
Center
305 E. Park St., Ste. 405
PO Box 1901
McCall, Idaho 83638
Phone: (208)634-2883
Larry Smith, Associate Business
Consultant

Idaho Small Business Development
Center
2407 Caldwell Blvd
Nampa, Idaho 83651
Phone: (208)467-5707
Ben Dicus, Associate Business
Consultant
E-mail: bdicus@bsu.idbsu.edu

Idaho State University (Pocatello)
Small Business Development Center
1651 Alvin Ricken Dr.
Pocatello, Idaho 83201
Phone: (208)232-4921
Free: (800)232-4921
Fax: (208)233-0268
Paul Cox, Regional Director
E-mail: coxpaul@isu.edu

North Idaho College
SBDC
525 W. Clearwater Loop
Post Falls, Idaho 83854
Phone: (208)769-3444
Fax: (208)769-3223
John Lynn, Regional Director
E-mail: jalynn@nic.edu

College of Southern Idaho
Small Business Development Center
315 Falls Ave.
PO Box 1238
Twin Falls, Idaho 83303-1238
Phone: (208)733-9554
Fax: (208)733-9316
Cindy Bond, Regional Director
E-mail:
cbond@evergreen2.csi.cc.id.us

Illinois

Waubonsee Community College
(Aurora Campus)
Small Business Development Center
5 E. Galena Blvd.
Aurora, Illinois 60506-4178
Phone: (630)801-7900
Fax: (630)892-4668
Mike O'Kelley, Director

Southern Illinois University at
Carbondale
Small Business Development Center
150 E. Pleasant Hill Rd.
Carbondale, Illinois 62901-6702
Phone: (618)536-2424
Fax: (618)453-5040
Dennis Cody, Director

John A. Logan College
Small Business Development Center
700 Logan College Rd.
Carterville, Illinois 62918-9802
Phone: (618)985-3741
Fax: (618)985-2248
Richard Fyke, Dir.

Kaskaskia College
Small Business Development Center
27210 College Rd.
Centralia, Illinois 62801-7878
Phone: (618)532-2049
Fax: (618)532-4983
Richard McCullum, Director

University of Illinois at Urbana-
Champaign
International Trade Center
Small Business Development Center
428 Commerce W.
1206 S. 6th St.
Champaign, Illinois 61820-6980
Phone: (217)244-1585
Fax: (217)333-7410
Tess Morrison, Dir.

Apparel Industry Board
SBDC
350 N Orleans, Ste 1047
Chicago, Illinois 60654
Phone: (312)836-1041
Nancy Berman

Asian American Alliance
SBDC
6246 N Pulaski Rd., Ste 101
Chicago, Illinois 60646
Phone: (773)202-0600
Fax: (773)202-1007
Mr. Joon H. Lee, Director

Back of the Yards Neighborhood
Council
Small Business Development Center
1751 W. 47th St.
Chicago, Illinois 60609-3889
Phone: (773)523-4419
Fax: (773)254-3525
Bill Przybylski, Director

Chicago Small Business Development
Center
DCCA / James R. Thompson Center
100 W. Randolph, Ste. 3-400
Chicago, Illinois 60601-3219
Phone: (312)814-6111
Fax: (312)814-2807
Carson A. Gallagher, Director

Eighteenth Street Development Corp.
Small Business Development Center
1839 S. Carpenter
Chicago, Illinois 60608-3347
Phone: (312)733-2270
Fax: (312)733-7315
Maria Munoz, Director

Greater North Pulaski Development
Corp.
Small Business Development Center
4054 W. North Ave.
Chicago, Illinois 60639-5223
Phone: (773)384-2262
Fax: (773)384-3850
Paul Petersen, Director

Industrial Council of Northwest
Chicago
Small Business Development Center
2023 W. Carroll
Chicago, Illinois 60612-1601
Phone: (312)421-3941

Fax: (312)421-1871
Melvin Eiland, Director

Latin American Chamber of
Commerce
Small Business Development Center
2539 N Kedzie, Ste.11
Chicago, Illinois 60647-2655
Phone: (773)252-5211
Fax: (773)252-7065
Mr. Arturo Venecia, Director

Midwest Chicago Business
Association
SBDC
3709 W Chicago Ave.
Chicago, Illinois 60651
Phone: (773)826-4055
Fax: (773)826-7375
Sonja Davis

North Business and Industrial Council
(NORBIC)
SBDC
2500 W. Bradley Pl.
Chicago, Illinois 60618-4798
Phone: (773)588-5855
Fax: (773)588-0734
Tom Kamykowski, Director

Richard J. Daley College
Small Business Development Center
7500 S. Pulaski Rd., Bldg. 200
Chicago, Illinois 60652-1299
Phone: (773)838-0319
Fax: (773)838-0303
Jim Charney, Dir.

University of Illinois at Chicago
SBDC
CUB 601 S Morgan
2231 UH M/C 075
Chicago, Illinois 60607
Phone: (773)996-4057
Fax: (773)996-4567

Women's Business Development
Center
Small Business Development Center
8 S. Michigan, Ste. 400
Chicago, Illinois 60603-3302
Phone: (312)853-3477
Fax: (312)853-0145
Joyce Wade, Director

McHenry County College
Small Business Development Center

8900 U.S. Hwy. 14
Crystal Lake, Illinois 60012-2761
Phone: (815)455-6098
Fax: (815)455-9319
Susan Whitfield, Director

Danville Area Community College
Small Business Development Center
28 W. North St.
Danville, Illinois 61832-5729
Phone: (217)442-7232
Fax: (217)442-6228
Ed Adrain, Director

University of Illinois Extension
SBDC
Ste. 1105
2525 E. Federal Dr.
Decatur, Illinois 62526-1573
Phone: (217)875-8284
Fax: (217)875-8288
William Wilkinson, Director

Sauk Valley Community College
Small Business Development Center
173 Illinois, Rte. 2
Dixon, Illinois 61021-9110
Phone: (815)288-5511
Fax: (815)288-5958
John Nelson, Director

Black Hawk College
Small Business Development Center
301 42nd Ave.
East Moline, Illinois 61244-4038
Phone: (309)755-2200
Fax: (309)755-9847
Donna Scalf, Director

East St. Louis Small Business
Development Center
State Office Building
10 Collinsville
East St. Louis, Illinois 62201-2955
Phone: (618)583-2270
Fax: (618)583-2274
Robert Ahart, Director

Southern Illinois University at
Edwardsville
Small Business Development Center
Campus Box 1107
Campus Box 1107
Edwardsville, Illinois 62026-0001
Phone: (618)692-2929
Fax: (618)692-2647
Alan Hauff, Director

Elgin Community College
Small Business Development Center
1700 Spartan Dr.
Elgin, Illinois 60123-7193
Phone: (847)888-7488
Fax: (847)931-3911
Craig Fowler, Director

Evanston Business and Technology
Center
Small Business Development Center
1840 Oak Ave.
Evanston, Illinois 60201-3670
Phone: (847)866-1817
Fax: (847)866-1808
Rick Holbrook, Director

College of DuPage
Small Business Development Center
425 22nd St.
Glen Ellyn, Illinois 61832
Phone: (630)942-2771
Fax: (630)942-3789
David Gay, Director

Lewis and Clark Community College
SBDC
5800 Godfrey Rd.
Godfrey, Illinois 62035
Phone: (618)466-3411
Fax: (618)466-0810
Bob Duane, Director

College of Lake County
Small Business Development Center
19351 W. Washington St.
Grayslake, Illinois 60030-1198
Phone: (847)543-2033
Fax: (847)223-9371
Linda Jorn, Director

Southeastern Illinois College
Small Business Development Center
303 S. Commercial St.
Harrisburg, Illinois 62946-2125
Phone: (618)252-5001
Fax: (618)252-0210
Becky Williams, Director

Rend Lake College
Small Business Development Center
Rte. 1
Ina, Illinois 62846-9801
Phone: (618)437-5321
Fax: (618)437-5677
Lisa Payne, Director

Joliet Junior College
Small Business Development Center
Renaissance Center, Rm. 312
214 N. Ottawa St.
Joliet, Illinois 60431-4097
Phone: (815)727-6544
Fax: (815)722-1895
Denise Mikulski, Director

Kankakee Community College
Small Business Development Center
River Rd., Box 888
Kankakee, Illinois 60901-7878
Phone: (815)933-0376
Fax: (815)933-0217
Kelly Berry, Director

Western Illinois University
Small Business Development Center
214 Seal Hall
Macomb, Illinois 61455-1390
Phone: (309)298-2211
Fax: (309)298-2520
Dan Voorhis, Director

Maple City Business and Technology
Center
Small Business Development Center
620 S. Main St.
Monmouth, Illinois 61462-2688
Phone: (309)734-4664
Fax: (309)734-8579
Carol Cook, Director

Illinois Valley Community College
Small Business Development Center
815 N. Orlando Smith Ave., Bldg. 11
Oglesby, Illinois 61348-9692
Phone: (815)223-1740
Fax: (815)224-3033
Boyd Palmer, Director

Illinois Eastern Community College
Small Business Development Center
401 E. Main St.
Olney, Illinois 62450-2119
Phone: (618)395-3011
Fax: (618)395-1922
Debbie Chilson, Director

Moraine Valley Community College
Small Business Development Center
10900 S. 88th Ave.
Palos Hills, Illinois 60465-0937
Phone: (708)974-5469
Fax: (708)974-0078
Hilary Gereg, Director

Bradley University
Small Business Development Center
141 N. Jobst Hall, 1st Fl.
Peoria, Illinois 61625-0001
Phone: (309)677-3075
Fax: (309)677-3386
Roger Luman, Director

Illinois Central College
Procurement Technical Assistance
Center
Small Business Development Center
124 SW Adams St., Ste. 300
Peoria, Illinois 61602-1388
Phone: (309)676-7500
Fax: (309)676-7534
Susan Gorman, Dir.

John Wood Community College
Procurement Technical Assistance
Center
Small Business Development Center
301 Oak St.
Quincy, Illinois 62301-2500
Phone: (217)228-5511
Fax: (217)228-5501
Edward Van Leer, Dir.

Triton College Small Business
Development Center
SBDC
2000 5th Ave.
River Grove, Illinois 60171
Phone: (708)456-0300
Fax: (708)583-3118
Lon Bancroft

Rock Valley College
Small Business Development Center
1220 Rock St.
Rockford, Illinois 61110-1437
Phone: (815)968-4087
Fax: (815)968-4157
Shirley DeBenedetto, Director

Department of Commerce &
Community Affairs
Illinois SBDC
620 East Adams St., Third Fl.
Springfield, Illinois 62701
Phone: (217)524-5856
Fax: (217)524-0171
Jeff Mitchell, State Director

Illinois Easter Seal Society
SBDC
2715 S 4th St.

Springfield, Illinois 62703
Phone: (217)525-0398
Fax: (217)525-0442
Tom Berkshire

Lincoln Land Community College
Small Business Development Center
100 N. 11th St.
Springfield, Illinois 62703-1002
Phone: (217)789-1017
Fax: (217)789-9838
Freida Schreck, Director

Shawnee Community College
Small Business Development Center
Shawnee College Rd.
Ullin, Illinois 62992
Phone: (618)634-9618
Fax: (618)634-9028
Donald Denny, Director

Governors State University
Small Business Development Center
College of Business, Rm. C-3305
University Park, Illinois 60466-0975
Phone: (708)534-4929
Fax: (708)534-8457
Christine Cochrane, Director

Indiana

Batesville Office of Economic
Development
SBDC
132 S. Main
Batesville, Indiana 47006
Phone: (812)933-6110

Bedford Chamber of Commerce
SBDC
1116 W. 16th St.
Bedford, Indiana 47421
Phone: (812)275-4493

Bloomfield Chamber of Commerce
SBDC
c/o Harrah Realty Co.
23 S. Washington St.
Bloomfield, Indiana 47424
Phone: (812)275-4493

Bloomington Area Regional Small
Business Development Center
216 W Allen St.
Bloomington, Indiana 47403
Phone: (812)339-8937

Fax: (812)335-7352
David Miller, Director

Clay Count Chamber of Commerce
SBDC
12 N. Walnut St.
Brazil, Indiana 47834
Phone: (812)448-8457

Brookville Chamber of Commerce
SBDC
PO Box 211
Brookville, Indiana 47012
Phone: (317)647-3177

Clinton Chamber of Commerce
SBDC
292 N. 9th St.
Clinton, Indiana 47842
Phone: (812)832-3844

Columbia City Chamber of
Commerce
SBDC
112 N. Main St.
Columbia City, Indiana 46725
Phone: (219)248-8131

Columbus Regional Small Business
Development Center
4920 N. Warren Dr.
Columbus, Indiana 47203
Phone: (812)372-6480
Free: (800)282-7232
Fax: (812)372-0228
Jack Hess, Director
E-mail: jackhess@hsonline.net

Connerville SBDC
504 Central
Connersville, Indiana 47331
Phone: (317)825-8328

Harrison County
Development Center
SBDC
The Harrison Center
405 N. Capitol, Ste. 308
Corydon, Indiana 47112
Phone: (812)738-8811

Montgomery County Chamber of
Commerce
SBDC
211 S. Washington St.
Crawfordsville, Indiana 47933
Phone: (317)654-5507

Decatur Chamber of Commerce
SBDC
125 E. Monroe St.
Decatur, Indiana 46733
Phone: (219)724-2604

City of Delphi Community
Development
SBDC
201 S. Union
Delphi, Indiana 46923
Phone: (317)564-6692

Southwestern Indiana Regional Small
Business Development Center
100 NW 2nd St., Ste. 200
Evansville, Indiana 47708
Phone: (812)425-7232
Fax: (812)421-5883
Kate Northrup, Director
E-mail: northrup@mevcc.org

Northeast Indiana Regional Small
Business Development Center
E-mail: sbdc@mailfwi.com
1830 Wayne Trace
Fort Wayne, Indiana 46803
Phone: (219)426-0040
Fax: (219)424-0024
Nick Adams, Director

Clinton County Chamber of
Commerce
SBDC
207 S. Main St.
Frankfort, Indiana 46041
Phone: (317)654-5507

Northlake Small Business
Development Center
487 Broadway, Ste. 201
Gary, Indiana 46402
Phone: (219)882-2000

Greencastle Partnership Center
SBDC
2 S. Jackson St.
Greencastle, Indiana 46135
Phone: (317)653-4517

Greensburg Area Chamber of
Commerce
SBDC
125 W. Main St.
Greensburg, Indiana 47240
Phone: (812)663-2832

Hammond Development Corp.
SBDC
649 Conkey St.
Hammond, Indiana 46324
Phone: (219)853-6399

Blackford County Economic
Development
SBDC
PO Box 43
Hartford, Indiana 47001-0043
Phone: (317)348-4944

Indiana SBDC Network
E-mail: sthrash@in.net
One North Capitol, Ste. 420
Indianapolis, Indiana 46204
Phone: (317)264-6871
Fax: (317)264-3102
Stephen Thrash, Exec. Dir.
E-mail: sthrash@in.net

Indianapolis Regional Small Business
Development Center
342 N. Senate Ave.
Indianapolis, Indiana 46204-1708
Phone: (317)261-3030
Fax: (317)261-3053
Glenn Dunlap, Director
E-mail: gdunlap@speanet.iupui.edu

Clark County Hoosier Falls
Private Industry Council Workforce
1613 E. 8th St.
Jeffersonville, Indiana 47130
Phone: (812)282-0456

Southern Indiana Regional Small
Business Development Center
1613 E. 8th St.
Jeffersonville, Indiana 47130
Phone: (812)288-6451
Fax: (812)284-8314
Patricia Stroud, Dir.

Kendallville Chamber of Commerce
SBDC
228 S. Main St.
Kendallville, Indiana 46755
Phone: (219)347-1554

Kokomo-Howard County Regional
Small Business Development Center
E-mail: sbdc5@holli.com
106 N. Washington
Kokomo, Indiana 46901

Phone: (765)457-7922
Fax: (765)452-4564
Kim Moyers, Director

LaPorte Small Business Development
Center
414 Lincolnway
La Porte, Indiana 46350
Phone: (219)326-7232

Greater Lafayette Regional Area
Small Business Development Center
122 N. 3rd
Lafayette, Indiana 47901-0311
Phone: (765)742-2394
Fax: (765)742-6276
Susan Davis, Director
E-mail: susan@glpi.wintek.com

Union County Chamber of Commerce
SBDC
102 N. Main St., No. 6
Liberty, Indiana 47353-1039
Phone: (317)458-5976

Linton/Stockton Chamber of
Commerce
SBDC
PO Box 208
Linton, Indiana 47441
Phone: (812)847-4846

Southeastern Indiana Regional Small
Business Development Center
E-mail: seinsbdc@seidata.com
975 Industrial Dr.
Madison, Indiana 47250
Phone: (812)265-3127
Fax: (812)265-5544
Connie Combs, Director

Crawford County
Private Industry Council Workforce
SBDC
Box 224 D, R.R. 1
Marengo, Indiana 47140
Phone: (812)365-2174

Greater Martinsville Chamber of
Commerce
SBDC
210 N. Marion St.
Martinsville, Indiana 46151
Phone: (317)342-8110

Lake County Public Library
Small Business Development Center

1919 W. 81st. Ave.
Merrillville, Indiana 46410-5382
Phone: (219)756-7232

First Citizens Bank
SBDC
515 N. Franklin Sq.
Michigan City, Indiana 46360
Phone: (219)874-9245

Mitchell Chamber of Commerce
SBDC
1st National Bank
Main Street
Mitchell, Indiana 47446
Phone: (812)849-4441

Mt. Vernon Chamber of Commerce
SBDC
405 E. 4th St.
Mt. Vernon, Indiana 47620
Phone: (812)838-3639

East Central Indiana Regional Small
Business Development Center
401 S. High St.
PO Box 842
Muncie, Indiana 47305
Phone: (765)284-8144
Fax: (765)751-9151
Barbara Armstrong, Director

Brown County Chamber of
Commerce
SBDC
PO Box 164
Nashville, Indiana 47448
Phone: (812)988-6647

Southern Indiana Small Business
Development Center
Private Industry Council Workforce
4100 Charleston Rd.
New Albany, Indiana 47150
Phone: (812)945-0266
Fax: (812)948-4664
Gretchen Mahaffey, Director
E-mail: gretchen@aye.net

Henry County Economic
Development Corp.
SBDC
1325 Broad St., Ste. B
New Castle, Indiana 47362
Phone: (317)529-4635

Jennings County Chamber of
Commerce
SBDC
PO Box 340
North Vernon, Indiana 47265
Phone: (812)346-2339

Orange County
Private Industry Council Workforce
SBDC
326 B. N. Gospel
Paoli, Indiana 47454-1412
Phone: (812)723-4206

Northwest Indiana Regional Small
Business Development Center
Small Business Development Center
6100 Southport Rd.
Portage, Indiana 46368
Phone: (219)762-1696
Fax: (219)763-2653
Mark McLaughlin, Director

Jay County Development Corp.
SBDC
121 W. Main St., Ste. A
Portland, Indiana 47371
Phone: (219)726-9311

Richmond-Wayne County Small
Business Development Center
33 S. 7th St., Ste. 200
Richmond, Indiana 47374
Phone: (765)962-2887
Fax: (765)966-0882
Cliff Fry, Director
E-mail: cliff@infocom.com

Rochester and Lake Manitou
Chamber of Commerce
Fulton Economic Development
Center
SBDC
617 Main St.
Rochester, Indiana 46975
Phone: (219)223-6773

Rushville Chamber of Commerce
SBDC
PO Box 156
Rushville, Indiana 46173
Phone: (317)932-2222

St. Mary of the Woods College
SBDC
St. Mary-of-the-Woods, Indiana

47876
Phone: (812)535-5151

Washington County
Private Industry Council Workforce
SBDC
Hilltop Plaza
Salem, Indiana 47167
Phone: (812)883-2283

Scott County
Private Industry Council Workforce
SBDC
752 Lakeshore Dr.
Scottsburg, Indiana 47170
Phone: (812)752-3886

Seymour Chamber of Commerce
SBDC
PO Box 43
Seymour, Indiana 47274
Phone: (812)522-3681

Minority Business Development
Project Future
SBDC
401 Col
South Bend, Indiana 46634
Phone: (219)234-0051

South Bend Regional Small Business
Development Center
300 N. Michigan
South Bend, Indiana 46601
Phone: (219)282-4350
Fax: (219)236-1056
Carolyn Anderson, Director

Economic Development Office
SBDC
46 E. Market St.
Spencer, Indiana 47460
Phone: (812)829-3245

Sullivan Chamber of Commerce
SBDC
10 S. Crt. St.
Sullivan, Indiana 47882
Phone: (812)268-4836

Tell City Chamber of Commerce
SBDC
Regional Federal Bldg.
645 Main St.
Tell City, Indiana 47586
Phone: (812)547-2385
Fax: (812)547-8378

Terre Haute Area Small Business
Development Center
Indiana State University
School of Business, Rm. 510
Terre Haute, Indiana 47809
Phone: (812)237-7676
Fax: (812)237-7675
Orville Alexander, Director

Tipton County Economic
Development Corp.
SBDC
136 E. Jefferson
Tipton, Indiana 46072
Phone: (317)675-7300

Porter County
SBDC
911 Wall St.
Valparaiso, Indiana 46383
Phone: (219)477-5256

Vevay/Switzerland Country
Foundation
SBDC
PO Box 193
Vevay, Indiana 47043
Phone: (812)427-2533

Vincennes University
SBDC
PO Box 887
Vincennes, Indiana 47591
Phone: (812)885-5749

Wabash Area Chamber of Commerce
Wabash Economic Development
Corp.
SBDC
67 S. Wabash
Wabash, Indiana 46992
Phone: (219)563-1168

Washington Daviess County
SBDC
1 Train Depot St.
Washington, Indiana 47501
Phone: (812)254-5262
Fax: (812)254-2550
Mark Brochin, Dir.

Purdue University
SBDC
Business & Industrial Development
Center
1220 Potter Dr.

West Lafayette, Indiana 47906
Phone: (317)494-5858

Randolph County Economic
Development Foundation
SBDC
111 S. Main St.
Winchester, Indiana 47394
Phone: (317)584-3266

Iowa

Iowa SBDC
137 Lynn Ave.
Ames, Iowa 50014
Phone: (515)292-6351
Free: (800)373-7232
Fax: (515)292-0020
Ronald Manning, State Director

Iowa State University
Small Business Development Center
ISU Branch Office
Bldg. 1, Ste. 615
2501 N. Loop Dr.
Ames, Iowa 50010-8283
Phone: (515)296-7828
Free: (800)373-7232
Fax: (515)296-6714
Steve Carter, Director
E-mail: stc@iastate.edu

DMACC Small Business
Development Center
E-mail: 76756.136@compuserve.com
Circle West Incubator
PO Box 204
Audubon, Iowa 50025
Phone: (712)563-2623
Fax: (712)563-2301
Lori Webb, Director

Iowa Western Community College
Small Business Development Center
E-mail: 76756.155@compuserve.com
2700 College Rd., Box 4C
Council Bluffs, Iowa 51502
Phone: (712)325-3260
Fax: (712)325-3408
Ronald Helms, Director

Southwestern Community College
Small Business Development Center
E-mail:
103063.3634@compuserve.com
1501 W. Townline Rd.
Creston, Iowa 50801

Phone: (515)782-4161
Fax: (515)782-3312
Robin Beech Travis, Director

Eastern Iowa Community College
Eastern Iowa Small Business
Development Center
E-mail: 76756.143@compuserve.com
314 W. 2nd St.
Davenport, Iowa 52801
Phone: (319)336-3440
Fax: (319)336-3494
Jon Ryan, Director

Drake University
Small Business Development Center
E-mail: 76756.141@compuserve.com
2507 University Ave.
Drake Business Center
Des Moines, Iowa 50311-4505
Phone: (515)271-2655
Fax: (515)271-1899
Benjamin Swartz, Director

Northeast Iowa Small Business
Development Center
E-mail: 76756.161@compuserve.com
770 Town Clock Plz.
Dubuque, Iowa 52001
Phone: (319)588-3350
Fax: (319)557-1591
Charles Tonn, Director

Iowa Central Community College
SBDC
E-mail: 76756-146@compuserve.com
900 Central Ave., Ste. 4
Ft. Dodge, Iowa 50501
Phone: (515)576-5090
Free: (800)362-2793
Fax: (515)576-0826
Todd Madson, Director

University of Iowa
Small Business Development Center
108 Papajohn Business
Administration Bldg., Ste. S-160
Iowa City, Iowa 52242-1000
Phone: (319)335-3742
Free: (800)253-7232
Fax: (319)353-2445
Paul Heath, Director
E-mail: paul-heath@uiowa.edu

Kirkwood Community College
Small Business Development Center
E-mail:

104702.2376@compuserve.com
2901 10th Ave.
Marion, Iowa 52302
Phone: (319)377-8256
Fax: (319)377-5667
Steve Sprague, Director

North Iowa Area Community College
Small Business Development Center
500 College Dr.
Mason City, Iowa 50401
Phone: (515)422-4342
Fax: (515)422-4129
Richard Petersen, Director

Indian Hills Community College
Small Business Development Center
E-mail: 76756.145@compuserve.com
525 Grandview Ave.
Ottumwa, Iowa 52501
Phone: (515)683-5127
Fax: (515)683-5263
Bryan Ziegler, Director

Western Iowa Tech Community
College
Small Business Development Center
E-mail: 76756.171@compuserve.com
4647 Stone Ave.
PO Box 5199
Sioux City, Iowa 51102-5199
Phone: (712)274-6418
Free: (800)352-4649
Fax: (712)274-6429
Dennis Bogenrief, Director

Iowa Lakes Community College
(Spencer)
Small Business Development Center
E-mail: sbdcjb@rconnect.com
1900 N. Grand Ave., Ste. 8
Hwy. 71 N
Spencer, Iowa 51301
Phone: (712)262-4213
Fax: (712)262-4047
John Beneke, Director

University of Northern Iowa
Small Business Development Center
200 E 4th St.
Waterloo, Iowa 50703
Phone: (319)273-2696
Free: (888)237-8124
Fax: (319)236-8240
Lyle Bowlin, Director
E-mail: lyle.bowlin@uni.edu

Southeastern Community College
Small Business Development Center
E-mail: 76756.164@compuserve.com
Drawer F
West Burlington, Iowa 52655
Phone: (319)752-2731
Free: (800)828-7322
Fax: (319)752-3407
Deb Dalziel, Director

Kansas

Bendictine College
SBDC
1020 N. 2nd St.
Atchison, Kansas 66002
Phone: (913)367-5340
Fax: (913)367-6102
Don Laney, Dir.

Butler County Community College
Small Business Development Center
600 Walnut
Augusta, Kansas 67010
Phone: (316)775-1124
Fax: (316)775-1370
Dorinda Rolle, Dir.

Neosho County Community College
SBDC
1000 S. Allen
Chanute, Kansas 66720
Phone: (316)431-2820
Fax: (316)431-0082
Duane Clum, Dir.

Coffeyville Community College
SBDC
11th and Willow Sts.
Coffeyville, Kansas 67337-5064
Phone: (316)251-7700
Fax: (316)252-7098
Charles Shaver, Dir.

Colby Community College
Small Business Development Center
1255 S. Range
Colby, Kansas 67701
Phone: (913)462-3984
Fax: (913)462-8315
Robert Selby, Dir.

Cloud County Community College
SBDC
2221 Campus Dr.
PO Box 1002
Concordia, Kansas 66901

Phone: (913)243-1435
Fax: (913)243-1459
Tony Foster, Dir.

Dodge City Community College
Small Business Development Center
2501 N. 14th Ave.
Dodge City, Kansas 67801
Phone: (316)227-9247
Fax: (316)227-9200
Wayne E. Shiplet, Dir.

Emporia State University
Small Business Development Center
130 Cremer Hall
Emporia, Kansas 66801
Phone: (316)342-7162
Fax: (316)341-5418
Lisa Brumbaugh, Regional Director
E-mail:
brumbaul@esumail.emporia.edu

Ft. Scott Community College
SBDC
2108 S. Horton
Ft. Scott, Kansas 66701
Phone: (316)223-2700
Fax: (316)223-6530
Steve Pammenter, Dir.

Garden City Community College
SBDC
E-mail: sbdc@gcnet.com
801 Campus Dr.
Garden City, Kansas 67846
Phone: (316)276-9632
Fax: (316)276-9630
Bill Sander, Regional Director

Ft. Hays State University
Small Business Development Center
E-mail: sbdc@fhsuvm.fhsu.edu
109 W. 10th St.
Hays, Kansas 67601
Phone: (785)628-6786
Fax: (785)628-0533
Susan Bittel, Regional Director

Hutchinson Community College
Small Business Development Center
815 N. Walnut, Ste. 225
Hutchinson, Kansas 67501
Phone: (316)665-4950
Free: (800)289-3501
Fax: (316)665-8354
Clark Jacobs, Dir.

Independence Community College
SBDC
Arco Bldg.
11th and Main St.
Independence, Kansas 67301
Phone: (316)332-1420
Fax: (316)331-5344
Preston Haddan, Dir.

Allen County Community College
SBDC
1801 N. Cottonwood
Iola, Kansas 66749
Phone: (316)365-5116
Fax: (316)365-3284
Susan Thompson , Dir.

University of Kansas
Small Business Development Center
E-mail: kusbdc@idir.net
734 Vermont St., Ste. 104
Lawrence, Kansas 66044
Phone: (785)843-8844
Fax: (785)865-4400
Ms. Randee Brady, Regional Director

Seward County Community College
Small Business Development Center
1801 N. Kansas
PO Box 1137
Liberal, Kansas 67901
Phone: (316)629-2650
Fax: (316)629-2689
Dale Reed, Dir.

Kansas State University (Manhattan)
Small Business Development Center
College of Business Administration
2323 Anderson Ave., Ste. 100
Manhattan, Kansas 66502-2947
Phone: (785)532-5529
Fax: (785)532-5827
Fred Rice, Regional Director
E-mail:
fhrsbdc@business.cba.ksu.edu

Ottawa University
SBDC
College Ave., Box 70
Ottawa, Kansas 66067
Phone: (913)242-5200
Fax: (913)242-7429
Lori Kravets, Dir.

Johnson County Community College
Small Business Development Center
CEC Bldg., Rm. 223

Overland Park, Kansas 66210-1299
Phone: (913)469-3878
Fax: (913)469-4415
Kathy Nadlman, Regional Director
E-mail: knadlman@johnco.cc.ks.us

Labette Community College
SBDC
200 S. 14th
Parsons, Kansas 67357
Phone: (316)421-6700
Fax: (316)421-0921
Mark Turnbull, Dir.

Pittsburg State University
Small Business Development Center
Shirk Hall
1501 S. Joplin
Pittsburg, Kansas 66762
Phone: (316)235-4920
Fax: (316)235-4919
Kathryn Richard, Regional Director
E-mail: krichard@pittstate.edu

Pratt Community College
Small Business Development Center
Hwy. 61
Pratt, Kansas 67124
Phone: (316)672-5641
Fax: (316)672-5288
Pat Gordon, Dir.

Salina Area Chamber of Commerce
Small Business Development Center
PO Box 586
Salina, Kansas 67402
Phone: (785)827-9301
Fax: (785)827-9758
Jerry Gaines, Regional Director

Kansas SBDC
E-mail: ksbdc@cjnetworks.com
214 SW 6th St., Ste. 205
Topeka, Kansas 66603-3261
Phone: (785)296-6514
Fax: (785)291-3261
Debbie Bishop, State Dir.

Washburn University of Topeka
SBDC
School of Business
1010 Henderson Learning Center
Topeka, Kansas 66621
Phone: (785)231-1010
Fax: (785)231-1063
Dan Kingman, Regional Director
E-mail: zzsbdc@acc.wuacc.edu

Wichita State University
Kansas SBDC
1845 Fairmont
Wichita, Kansas 67260
Phone: (316)978-3193
Fax: (316)978-3647
Lori Usher, Regional Director
E-mail: usher@wsuhub.uc.twsu.edu

Kentucky

Morehead State University College of
Business
Boyd-Greenup County Chamber of
Commerce
SBDC
1401 Winchester Ave., Ste. 305
207 15th St.
Ashland, Kentucky 41101
Phone: (606)329-8011
Fax: (606)324-4570
Kimberly A. Jenkins, Director

Western Kentucky University
Bowling Green Small Business
Development Center
2355 Nashville Rd.
Bowling Green, Kentucky 42101
Phone: (502)745-1905
Fax: (502)745-1931
Richard S. Horn, Director

University of Kentucky
(Elizabethtown)
Small Business Development Center
133 W. Dixie Ave.
Elizabethtown, Kentucky 42701
Phone: (502)765-6737
Fax: (502)769-5095
Lou Ann Allen, Director

Northern Kentucky University
SBDC
BEP Center 463
Highland Heights, Kentucky 41099-
0506
Phone: (606)572-6524
Fax: (606)572-6177
Sutton Landry, Director

Murray State University
(Hopkinsville)
Small Business Development Center
300 Hammond Dr.
Hopkinsville, Kentucky 42240
Phone: (502)889-8666

Fax: (502)886-3211
Michael Cartner, Director

Southwest Community College
Small Business Development Center
Lexington Central Library, 4th Fl.
140 E. Main St.
Lexington, Kentucky 40507-1376
Phone: (606)257-7666
Fax: (606)257-1751
Marge Berge, Program Coordinator
David Stevens, Dir.

University of Kentucky
Center for Entrepreneurship
Kentucky SBDC
225 Gatton Business and Economics
Bldg.
Lexington, Kentucky 40506-0034
Phone: (606)257-7668
Fax: (606)323-1907
Janet S. Holloway, State Director

Bellarmine College
Small Business Development Center
School of Business
600 W. Main St., Ste. 219
Louisville, Kentucky 40202
Phone: (502)574-4770
Fax: (502)574-4771
Thomas G. Daley, Director

University of Louisville
Center for Entrepreneurship and
Technology
Small Business Development Centers
Burhans Hall, Shelby Campus, Rm.
122
Louisville, Kentucky 40292
Phone: (502)852-7854
Fax: (502)852-8573
Lou Dickie, Director

Southeast Community College
SBDC
1300 Chichester Ave.
Middlesboro, Kentucky 40965-2265
Phone: (606)242-2145
Fax: (606)242-4514
Kathleen Moats, Director

Morehead State University
Small Business Development Center
CB 309
UPO 2479
Morehead, Kentucky 40351
Phone: (606)783-2895

Fax: (606)783-5020
Wilson Grier, District Director

Murray State University
West Kentucky Small Business
Development Center
College of Business and Public
Affairs
PO Box 9
Murray, Kentucky 42071
Phone: (502)762-2856
Fax: (502)762-3049
Rosemary Miller, Director

Murray State University
Owensboro Small Business
Development Center
3860 U.S. Hwy. 60 W
Owensboro, Kentucky 42301
Phone: (502)926-8085
Fax: (502)684-0714
Mickey Johnson, District Director

Moorehead State University
Pikeville Small Business
Development Center
Route 7
110 Village St.
Pikeville, Kentucky 41501
Phone: (606)432-5848
Fax: (606)432-8924
Michael Morley, Director

Eastern Kentucky University
South Central Small Business
Development Center
The Center for Rural Development,
Ste. 260
2292 S. Hwy. 27
Somerset, Kentucky 42501
Phone: (606)677-6120
Fax: (606)677-6083
Donald R. Snyder, Director

Louisiana

Alexandria SBDC
Hibernia National Bank Bldg., Ste.
510
934 3rd St.
Alexandria, Louisiana 71301
Phone: (318)484-2123
Fax: (318)484-2126
Kathey Hunter, Consultant

Southern University
Capital Small Business Development
Center
9613 Interline Ave.
Baton Rouge, Louisiana 70809
Phone: (504)922-0998
Fax: (504)922-0999
Gregory Spann, Director

Southeastern Louisiana University
Small Business Development Center
College of Business Administration
Box 522, SLU Sta.
Hammond, Louisiana 70402
Phone: (504)549-3831
Fax: (504)549-2127
William Joubert, Director

University of Southwestern Louisiana
Acadiana Small Business
Development Center
College of Business Administration
Box 43732
Lafayette, Louisiana 70504
Phone: (318)262-5344
Fax: (318)262-5296
Kim Spence, Director

McNeese State University
Small Business Development Center
College of Business Administration
Lake Charles, Louisiana 70609
Phone: (318)475-5529
Fax: (318)475-5012
Paul Arnold, Director

Louisiana Electronic Assistance
Program
SBDC
NE Louisiana, College of Business
Administration
Monroe, Louisiana 71209
Phone: (318)342-1215
Fax: (318)342-1209
Dr. Jerry Wall, Director

Northeast Louisiana University
Small Business Development Center
College of Business Administration,
Rm. 2-57
Monroe, Louisiana 71209
Phone: (318)342-1224
Fax: (318)342-1209
Dr. Paul Dunn, Director

Northwestern State University
Small Business Development Center

College of Business Administration
Natchitoches, Louisiana 71497
Phone: (318)357-5611
Fax: (318)357-6810
Mary Lynn Wilkerson, Director

Louisiana International Trade Center
SBDC
World Trade Center, Ste. 2926
2 Canal St.
New Orleans, Louisiana 70130
Phone: (504)568-8222
Fax: (504)568-8228
Ruperto Chavarri, Director

Loyola University
Small Business Development Center
College of Business Administration
Box 134
New Orleans, Louisiana 70118
Phone: (504)865-3474
Fax: (504)865-3496
Ronald Schroeder, Director

Southern University at New Orleans
Small Business Development Center
College of Business Administration
New Orleans, Louisiana 70126
Phone: (504)286-5308
Fax: (504)286-5131
Jon Johnson, Director

University of New Orleans
Small Business Development Center
1600 Canal St., Ste. 620
New Orleans, Louisiana 70112
Phone: (504)539-9292
Fax: (504)539-9205
Norma Grace, Director

Louisiana Tech University
Small Business Development Center
College of Business Administration
Box 10318, Tech Sta.
Ruston, Louisiana 71271-0046
Phone: (318)257-3537
Fax: (318)257-4253
Tracey Jeffers, Director

Louisiana State University at
Shreveport
Small Business Development Center
College of Business Administration
1 University Dr.
Shreveport, Louisiana 71115
Phone: (318)797-5144
Fax: (318)797-5208

Peggy Connor, Director
E-mail: pconnor@pilot.lsus.edu

Nicholls State University
Small Business Development Center
College of Business Administration
PO Box 2015
Thibodaux, Louisiana 70310
Phone: (504)448-4242
Fax: (504)448-4922
Weston Hull, Director

Maine

Androscoggin Valley Council of
Governments
Small Business Development Center
125 Manley Rd.
Auburn, Maine 04210
Phone: (207)783-9186
Fax: (207)783-5211
Jane Mickeriz, Counselor

Coastal Enterprises Inc.
SBDC
Weston Bldg.
7 N. Chestnut St.
Augusta, Maine 04330
Phone: (207)621-0245
Fax: (207)622-9739
W. Bradshaw Swanson, Counselor

Eastern Maine Development Corp.
Small Business Development Center
1 Cumberland Pl., Ste. 300
PO Box 2579
Bangor, Maine 04402-2579
Phone: (207)942-6389
Free: (800)339-6389
Fax: (207)942-3548
Ron Loyd, Sub-Center Director

Belfast Satellite
Waldo County Development Corp.
SBDC
67 Church St.
Belfast, Maine 04915
Phone: (207)942-6389
Free: (800)339-6389
Fax: (207)942-3548

Brunswick Satellite
Midcoast Council for Business
Development
SBDC
8 Lincoln St.
Brunswick, Maine 04011

Phone: (207)882-4340
Fax: (207)882-4456

Northern Maine Development
Commission
Small Business Development Center
2 S. Main St.
PO Box 779
Caribou, Maine 04736
Phone: (207)498-8736
Free: (800)427-8736
Fax: (207)498-3108
Rodney Thompson, Sub-Center
Director

East Millinocket Satellite
Katahdin Regional Development
Corp.
SBDC
58 Main St.
East Millinocket, Maine 04430
Phone: (207)746-5338
Fax: (207)746-9535

East Wilton Satellite
Robinhood Plaza
Rte. 2 & 4
East Wilton, Maine 04234
Phone: (207)783-9186
Fax: (207)783-5211

Fort Kent Satellite
SBDC
Aroostook County Registry of Deeds
Elm and Hall Sts.
Fort Kent, Maine 04743
Phone: (207)498-8736
Free: (800)427-8736
Fax: (207)493-3108

Houlton Satellite
SBDC
Superior Court House
Court St.
Houlton, Maine 04730
Phone: (207)498-8736
Free: (800)427-8736
Fax: (207)498-3108

Lewiston Satellite
Business Information Center (BIC)
SBDC
Bates Mill Complex
35 Canal St.
Lewiston, Maine 04240
Phone: (207)783-9186
Fax: (207)783-5211

Machias Satellite
Sunrise County Economic Council
(Calais Area)
SBDC
Washington County Economic
Planning Commission
63 Main St.
PO Box 679
Machias, Maine 04654
Phone: (207)454-2430
Fax: (207)255-0983

University of Southern Maine
Maine SBDC
E-mail: msbdc@portland.maine.edu
96 Falmouth St.
P.O. Box 9300
Portland, Maine 04104-9300
Phone: (207)780-4949
Fax: (207)780-4810
John Entwistle, Sub-Center Director

Rockland Satellite
SBDC
Key Bank of Maine
331 Main St.
Key Bank of Maine
Rockland, Maine 04841
Phone: (207)882-4340
Fax: (207)882-4456

Rumford Satellite
River Valley Growth Council
Hotel Harris Bldg.
23 Hartford St.
Rumford, Maine 04276
Phone: (207)783-9186
Fax: (207)783-5211

Saco Satellite
Biddeford-Saco Chamber of
Commerce and Industry
SBDC
110 Main St.
Saco, Maine 04072
Phone: (207)282-1567
Fax: (207)282-3149
Frederick Aiello, Counselor

Southern Maine Regional Planning
Commission
Small Business Development Center
255 Main St.
PO Box Q
Sanford, Maine 04073
Phone: (207)324-0316

Fax: (207)324-2958
Joseph Vitko, Sub-Center Director

Skowhegan Satellite
SBDC
Norridgewock Ave.
Skowhegan Cooperative Extension
Service
Skowhegan, Maine 04976
Phone: (207)621-0245
Fax: (207)622-9739

South Paris Satellite
SBDC
166 Main St.
South Paris, Maine 04281
Phone: (207)783-9186
Fax: (207)783-5211

Waterville Satellite
Thomas College
SBDC
Administrative Bldg. - Library
180 W. River Rd.
Waterville, Maine 04901
Phone: (207)621-0245
Fax: (207)622-9739

Coastal Enterprises, Inc. (Wiscasset)
Small Business Development Center
Water St.
PO Box 268
Wiscasset, Maine 04578
Phone: (207)882-4340
Fax: (207)882-4456
James Burbank Jr., Dir.

York Satellite
York Chamber of Commerce
SBDC
449 Rte. 1
York, Maine 03909
Phone: (207)363-4422
Fax: (207)324-2958

Maryland

Anne Arundel, Office of Economic
Development
SBDC
2666 Riva Rd., Ste. 200
Annapolis, Maryland 21401
Phone: (410)224-4205
Fax: (410)222-7415
Mike Fish, Consultant

Central Maryland
SBDC
University of Baltimore
Towson State University
Small Business Resource Center
3 W Baltimore St.
Baltimore, Maryland 21201-5779
Phone: (410)659-1930
Fax: (410)659-1939
Sonia Stockton, Executive Director

Department of Business & Economic
Development
SBDC
217 E Redwood St.
Baltimore, Maryland 21202-3316
Phone: (410)333-6901

Hartford County Economic
Development Office
SBDC
220 S. Main St.
Bel Air, Maryland 21014
Phone: (410)893-3837
Fax: (410)879-8043
Maurice Brown, Consultant

Maryland Small Business
Development Center
7100 Baltimore Ave., Ste. 401
College Park, Maryland 20740
Phone: (301)403-8300
Fax: (301)403-8303
Renee Sprow, State Director
E-mail: jgraham@mbs.umd.edu

University of Maryland
SBDC
Dingman Center for Entrepreneurship
College of Business and Management
College Park, Maryland 20742-1815
Phone: (301)405-2144
Fax: (301)314-9152

Howard County Economic
Development Office
SBDC
6751 Gateway Dr., Ste. 500
Columbia, Maryland 21044
Phone: (410)313-6552
Fax: (410)313-6556
Ellin Dize, Consultant

Western Maryland Small Business
Development Center
Western Region, Inc.
3 Commerce Dr.

Cumberland, Maryland 21502
Phone: (301)724-6716
Free: (800)457-7232
Fax: (301)777-7504
Sam LaManna, Executive Director

Cecil County Chamber of Commerce
SBDC
135 E. Main St.
Elkton, Maryland 21921
Phone: (410)392-0597
Fax: (410)392-6225
Maurice Brown, Consultant

Frederick Community College
SBDC
7932 Opossumtown Pike
Frederick, Maryland 21702
Phone: (301)846-2683
Fax: (301)846-2689
Mary Ann Garst, Program Dir.

Arundel Center N.
SBDC
101 Crain Hwy., NW, Rm. 110B
Glen Burnie, Maryland 21061
Phone: (410)766-1910
Fax: (410)766-1911
Mike Fish, Consultant

Community College at Saint Mary's
County
SBDC
PO Box 98, Great Mills Rd.
Great Mills, Maryland 20634
Phone: (301)868-6679
Fax: (301)868-7392
James Shepherd
E-mail: Business Analyst

Hagerstown Junior College
SBDC
Technology Innovation Center
11404 Robinwood Dr.
Hagerstown, Maryland 21740
Phone: (301)797-0327
Fax: (301)777-7504
Tonya Fleming Brockett, Dir.

Landover SBDC
7950 New Hampshire Ave., 2nd Fl.
Langley Park, Maryland 20783
Phone: (301)445-7324
Fax: (301)883-6479
Avon Evans, Consultant

Charles County Community College
Southern Maryland SBDC
SBDC
Mitchell Rd.
P.O. Box 910
LaPlata, Maryland 20646-0910
Phone: (301)934-7583
Free: (800)762-7232
Fax: (301)934-7681
Betsy Cooksey, Executive Director

Garrett Community College
SBDC
Mosser Rd.
McHenry, Maryland 21541
Phone: (301)387-6666
Fax: (301)387-3096
Sandy Major, Business Analyst

Montgomery County Office of
Economic Development
SBDC
101 Monroe St., 15th Floor
Rockville, Maryland 20850
Phone: (301)217-2345
Fax: (301)217-2045
Linda Miller, Director

Salisbury State University
Eastern Shore Region Small Business
Development Center
Power Professional Bldg., Ste. 170
Salisbury, Maryland 21801
Phone: (410)546-4325
Free: (800)999-7232
Fax: (410)548-5389
Marty Green, Executive Director

Maryland Small Business
Development Center
Center for Business and Industry
SBDC
9200 Basil Ct., Ste. 200
Springdale, Maryland 20774
Phone: (301)386-5600
James McGinnis

Baltimore County Chamber of
Commerce
SBDC
102 W. Pennsylvania Ave., Ste. 402
Towson, Maryland 21204
Phone: (410)832-5866
Fax: (410)821-9901
John Casper, Consultant

Prince George's County Minority
Business Opportunities Commission
Suburban Washington Region Small
Business Development Center
1400 McCormick Dr., Ste. 282
Upper Marlboro, Maryland 20774
Phone: (301)883-6491
Fax: (301)883-6479
Avon Evans, Acting Executive Dir.

Carrol County Economic
Development Office
SBDC
125 N. Court St., Rm. 101
Westminster, Maryland 21157
Phone: (410)857-8166
Fax: (410)848-0003
Michael Fish, Consultant

Eastern Region - Upper Shore SBDC
Chesapeake College
PO Box 8
Wye Mills, Maryland 21679
Phone: (410)822-5400
Free: (800)762SBDC
Fax: (410)827-5286
Patricia Ann Marie Schaller,
Consultant

Massachusetts

International Trade Center
University of Massachusetts Amherst
SBDC
205 School of Management
Amherst, Massachusetts 01003-4935
Phone: (413)545-6301
Fax: (413)545-1273
Georgeanna Parhen, Acting State
Director

University of Massachusetts
Massachusetts SBDC
205 School of Management
Amherst, Massachusetts 01003-4935
Phone: (413)545-6301
Fax: (413)545-1273
John Ciccarelli, State Director
Laura Howard
E-mail: jciccarelli@umassp.edu

Massachusetts Export Center
World Trade Center, Ste. 315
Boston, Massachusetts 02210
Phone: (617)478-4133
Free: (800)478-4133

Fax: (617)478-4135
Paula Murphy, Director

University of Massachusetts (Boston)
Minority Business Assistance Center
SBDC
University of Massachusetts (Boston)
College of Management, 5th Fl.
Boston, Massachusetts 02125-3393
Phone: (617)287-7750
Fax: (617)287-7725
Hank Turner, Director

Boston College
Capital Formation Service Statewide
SBDC
142 Beacon St.
Coordinating Site
Chestnut Hill, Massachusetts 02167
Phone: (617)552-4091
Fax: (617)552-2730
Don Reilley, Director

Metropolitan Boston Regional Office
Boston College SBDC
Boston College
142 Beacon St.
96 College Rd.
Chestnut Hill, Massachusetts 02167
Phone: (617)552-4091
Fax: (617)552-2730
Dr. Jack McKiernan, Regional
Director

University of Massachusetts
Southeastern Region SBDC
University of Massachusetts-
Dartmouth
200 Pocasset St.
PO Box 2785
Fall River, Massachusetts 02722
Phone: (508)673-9783
Fax: (508)674-1929
Clyde Mitchell, Regional Director

Salem State College
SBDC
Salem State College
197 Essex St.
Salem, Massachusetts 01970
Phone: (781)741-6343
Fax: (781)741-6345
Frederick Young, Director

University of Massachusetts
Western Region Small Business
Development Center

University of Massachusetts-Amherst
101 State St., Ste. 424
Springfield, Massachusetts 01103
Phone: (413)737-6712
Fax: (413)737-2312
Dianne Fuller Doherty, Director

Clark University
Central Region Small Business
Development Center
Dana Commons
950 Main St.
Worcester, Massachusetts 01610
Phone: (508)793-7615
Fax: (508)793-8890
Laurence March, Director

Michigan

Lenawee County Chamber of
Commerce
SBDC
202 N. Main St., Ste. A
Adrian, Michigan 49221-2713
Phone: (517)266-1488
Fax: (517)263-6065
Sally Pinchock, Director
E-mail:
spin@orchard.washtenaw.cc.mi.us

Albion Economic Development
Center
SBDC
940 Auston Ave.
PO Box 725
Albion, Michigan 49224
Phone: (517)629-3926
Fax: (517)629-3929
Peggy Sindt, Director

Allegan County Economic
Department Alliance
SBDC
E-mail: aceda@accn.org
Allegan Intermediate School Bldg.
2891 M-222 E
P.O. Box 277
Allegan, Michigan 49010-8042
Phone: (616)673-8442
Fax: (616)650-8042
Chuck Birr, Director

Ottawa County Economic
Development Office, Inc.
Small Business Development Center
6676 Lake Michigan Dr.

PO Box 539
Allendale, Michigan 49401-0539
Phone: (616)892-4120
Fax: (616)895-6670
Ken Rizzio, Director
E-mail: krizzio@altelco.net

Gratiot Area Chamber of Commerce
SBDC
110 W. Superior St.
P.O. Box 516
Alma, Michigan 48801-0516
Phone: (517)463-5525
Fax: (517)463-6588
Sherri O. Graham, Director

Alpena Community College
SBDC
666 Johnson St.
Alpena, Michigan 49707
Phone: (517)356-9021
Fax: (517)354-0698
Carl Bourdelais, Regional Director
E-mail: bourdelc@alpena.cc.mi.us

Ann Arbor Center for Independent
Living
SBDC
2568 Packard Rd.
Ann Arbor, Michigan 48104-6831
Phone: (734)971-0277
Fax: (734)971-0826
Edward Wollmann, Director
E-mail: edwoll@provide.net

Michigan Manufacturing Technology
Center
SBDC
2901 Hubbard Rd.
PO Box 1485
Ann Arbor, Michigan 48106-1485
Phone: (734)769-4110
Fax: (734)769-4064
William Loomis, Director
E-mail: wrl@iti.org

Michigan State University Extension
Center
SBDC
L'Anse, Michigan 49946
Phone: (906)524-6300

Huron County Economic
Development Corp.
Small Business Development Center
Huron County Bldg., Rm. 303
250 E. Huron Ave.

Bad Axe, Michigan 48413
Phone: (517)269-6431
Fax: (517)269-7221
Carl Osentoski, Director
E-mail: cjo@avci.net

Battle Creek Area Chamber of
Commerce
SBDC
E-mail: bizstore@net-link.net
4 Riverwalk Centre, Lower Level
34 W. Jackson, Ste. A
Battle Creek, Michigan 49017
Phone: (616)962-8996
Fax: (616)962-3692
Kevin R. Wells, Director

Bay Area Chamber of Commerce
SBDC
901 Saginaw
Bay City, Michigan 48708
Phone: (517)893-4567
Fax: (517)893-7016
Deb Wieland, Director

Lake Michigan College
Corporation and Community
Development Department
Small Business Development Center
2755 E. Napier
Benton Harbor, Michigan 49022-
1899
Phone: (616)927-8179
Fax: (616)927-8103
Milton E. Richter, Director
E-mail: richter@raptor.lmc.cc.mi.us

Ferris State University
Small Business Development Center
330 Oak St.
West 025
Big Rapids, Michigan 49307-2031
Phone: (616)592-2082
Fax: (616)592-3539
Lora Swenson, Director
E-mail: yc26@ferris.bitnet

Mecosta County Development
Corporation
SBDC
246 S State St., Ste B
Big Rapids, Michigan 49307
Phone: (616)592-3403
Fax: (616)796-1625
Brenda Flory, Director

Northern Lakes Economic Alliance
SBDC
1048 East Main St.
P.O. Box 8
Boyne City, Michigan 49712-0008
Phone: (616)582-6482
Fax: (616)582-3213
Thomas Johnson, Dir.

Livingston County Small Business
Development Center
E-mail: livibusi@bizserve.com
131 S. Hyne
Brighton, Michigan 48116
Phone: (810)227-3556
Fax: (810)227-3080
Dennis Whitney, Director

Buchanan Chamber of Commerce
SBDC
119 Main St.
Buchanan, Michigan 49107
Phone: (616)695-3291
Fax: (616)695-4250
Joni Tumbleson, Director

Tuscola County Economic
Development Corp.
Small Business Development Center
194 N. State St., Ste. 200
Caro, Michigan 48723
Phone: (517)673-2849
Fax: (517)673-2517
James McLoskey, Director

Branch County Economic Growth
Alliance
SBDC
E-mail: bcega@orion.branch-
co.lib.mi.us
20 Division St.
Coldwater, Michigan 49036
Phone: (517)369-2239
Fax: (517)279-8936
Harry Adamson, Director

University of Detroit-Mercy
Small Business Development Center
Commerce and Finance Bldg., Rm.
105
4001 W. McNichols
PO Box 19900
Detroit, Michigan 48219-0900
Phone: (313)993-1115
Fax: (313)993-1052
Dr. Ram Kesavan, Director

Wayne State University
Michigan SBDC
E-mail:
stateoffice@misbdc.wayne.edu
2727 Second Ave., Ste. 107
Detroit, Michigan 48201
Phone: (313)964-1798
Fax: (313)964-3648
Ronald R. Hall, State Director
E-mail: ron@misbdc.wayne.edu

Southwestern Michigan College
SBDC
58900 Cherry Grove Rd.
Dowagiac, Michigan 49047
Phone: (616)782-1277
Fax: (616)782-1382
Clyde Remmo, Director

First Step, Inc.
Small Business Development Center
E-mail: cuppad@up.net
2415 14th Ave., S.
Escanaba, Michigan 49829
Phone: (906)786-9234
Fax: (906)786-4442
David Gillis, Regional Director

Community Capital Development
Corp.
SBDC
E-mail: ccdc@bizserve.com
Walter Ruether Center
711 N. Saginaw, Ste. 102
Flint, Michigan 48503
Phone: (810)239-5847
Fax: (810)239-5575
Kim D. Yarber, Regional Director

Macomb Community College
Center For Continuing Education
SBDC
32101 Caroline
Fraser, Michigan 48026
Phone: (810)296-3516
Fax: (810)293-0427
Dr. Donald Amboyer, Director
E-mail: ambo01@macomb.cc.mi.us

North Central Michigan College
SBDC
800 Livingston Blvd.
Gaylord, Michigan 49735
Phone: (517)731-0071

Association of Commerce and
Industry

SBDC
E-mail: acisbdc@hotmail.com
1 S. Harbor Ave.
PO Box 509
Grand Haven, Michigan 49417
Phone: (616)846-3153
Fax: (616)842-0379
Karen K. Benson, Director

Grand Valley State University
SBDC
Eberhard Center, Ste. 718S
301 W. Fulton St.
Grand Rapids, Michigan 49504
Phone: (616)771-6693
Fax: (616)458-3872
Carol R. Lopucki, Regional Director
E-mail: lopuckie@gvsu.edu

The Right Place Program
SBDC
820 Monroe NW, Ste. 350
Grand Rapids, Michigan 49503-1423
Phone: (616)771-0571
Fax: (616)458-3768
Raymond P. DeWinkle, Director
E-mail: dewinkler@rightplace.org

Oceana County Economic
Development Corp.
SBDC
100 State St.
PO Box 168
Hart, Michigan 49420-0168
Phone: (616)873-7141
Fax: (616)873-5914
Charles Persenaire, Director

Hastings Industrial Incubator
SBDC
E-mail: edohast.im4u.net
1035 E. State St.
Hastings, Michigan 49058
Phone: (616)948-2305
Fax: (616)948-2947
Joe Rahn, Director

Dickinson County Chamber of
Commerce
SBDC
Iron Mountain, Michigan 49801
Phone: (906)774-2002

Gogebic County Economic
Development Center
Gogebic County Community College
SBDC

4946 Jackson Rd.
Ironwood, Michigan 49938
Phone: (906)932-4321
Fax: (906)932-2129
Jerry Murphy, Director

Greater Gratiot Development, Inc.
Small Business Center
136 S. Main
Ithaca, Michigan 48847
Phone: (517)875-2083
Fax: (517)875-2990
Don Schurr, Director
E-mail: don.scurr@gratiot.com

Jackson Small Business Development
Center
SBDC
E-mail: jbdc@jacksonmi.com
414 N. Jackson St.
Jackson, Michigan 49201
Phone: (517)787-0442
Fax: (517)787-3960
Duane Miller, Director

Kalamazoo College
Small Business Development Center
E-mail: sbdc@kzoo.edu
Stryker Center for Management
Studies
1327 Academy St.
Kalamazoo, Michigan 49006-3200
Phone: (616)337-7350
Fax: (616)337-7415
Carl R. Shook, Regional Director

Lansing Community College
Small Business Development Center
Continental Bldg.
333 N. Washington Sq.
PO Box 40010
Lansing, Michigan 48901-7210
Phone: (517)483-1921
Fax: (517)483-9803
Mr. Deleski Smith, Regional Director
E-mail: ds1921@lois.lansing.cc.mi.us

Lapeer Development Corp.
Small Business Development Center
E-mail: ldc@tir.com
449 McCormick Dr.
Lapeer, Michigan 48446
Phone: (810)667-0080
Fax: (810)667-3541
Matthew Hufnagel, Director

Economic Development Center
Office
SBDC
Manistique, Michigan 49854
Phone: (906)341-5126

Marquette Area Chamber of
Commerce
SBDC
Marquette, Michigan 49855
Phone: (906)226-6591

Menominee Area Chamber of
Commerce
SBDC
Menominee, Michigan 49858
Phone: (906)8632679

Midland Chamber of Commerce
SBDC
E-mail: chamber@macc.org
300 Rodd St.
Midland, Michigan 48640
Phone: (517)839-9522
Fax: (517)835-3701
Ms. Christine Greve, Director

Monroe County Industrial
Development Corporation
SBDC
E-mail: mcidc@ic.net
111 Conant Ave.
Monroe, Michigan 48161
Phone: (313)243-5947
Fax: (313)242-0009
Mr. Randy Thelan, Director

Macomb County Business Assistance
Network
Small Business Development Center
E-mail: bacmac@bizserve.com
115 S. Groesbeck Hwy.
Mt. Clemens, Michigan 48043
Phone: (810)469-5118
Fax: (810)469-6787
Donald L. Morandi, Regional
Director

Central Michigan University
Small Business Development Center
E-mail:
34ntjen@cmuvm.csv.cmich.edu
256 Applied Business Studies
Complex
Mt. Pleasant, Michigan 48859
Phone: (517)774-3270

Fax: (517)774-2372
Charles Fitzpatrick, Regional Director

Michigan State University Extension
Center
SBDC
Munising, Michigan 49862
Phone: (906)387-2530

Muskegon Economic Growth
Alliance
Small Business Development Center
230 Terrace Plz.
PO Box 1087
Muskegon, Michigan 49443-1087
Phone: (616)724-3180
Fax: (616)728-7251
Eddie Garner, Director

Harbor County Chamber of
Commerce
SBDC
530 S Whittaker St., Ste. F
New Buffalo, Michigan 49117
Phone: (616)469-5409
Fax: (616)469-2257
Peggy King, Office Manager

Greater Niles Economic Development
Fund
SBDC
1105 N. Front St.
Niles, Michigan 49120
Phone: (616)683-1833
Fax: (616)683-7515
Sharon Witt, Director

Ontonagon County Economic
Development Center-Courthouse
SBDC
725 Greenland Rd.
Ontonagon, Michigan 49953
Phone: (906)884-4188
Fax: (906)884-2916
Dorothy Bussiere, Director

Alpena Community College
Huron Shores Campus
SBDC
5800 Skeel Ave.
Oscoda, Michigan 48750
Phone: (517)739-1445
Fax: (517)739-1161
Dave Wentworth, Director

Pontiac Economic Development
Center
SBDC
8 N Saginaw Ave.
Pontiac, Michigan 48342
Phone: (248)857-5603
Fax: (248)857-5713
Mattie Lasseigne, Executive Director

St. Clair County Community Small
Business Development Center
800 Military St., Ste. 320
Port Huron, Michigan 48060-5015
Phone: (810)982-9511
Fax: (810)982-9531
Todd Brian, Director

Kirtland Community College
SBDC
10775 N. St. Helen Rd.
Roscommon, Michigan 48653
Phone: (517)275-5121
Fax: (517)275-8745
John Loiacano, Director
E-mail: loiacanj@k2.kirtland.cc.mi.us

Saginaw County Chamber of
Commerce
SBDC
E-mail: jroe@voyager.net
901 S. Washington Ave.
Saginaw, Michigan 48601
Phone: (517)752-7161
Fax: (517)752-9055
James Bockelman, Director

Saginaw Future, Inc.
Small Business Development Center
301 E. Genesee, 3rd Fl.
Saginaw, Michigan 48607
Phone: (517)754-8222
Fax: (517)754-1715
Steven Black, Director

Women's Christian Association of
Berrien County
SBDC
508 Pleasant St.
St. Joseph, Michigan 49058
Phone: (616)983-4453
Fax: (616)983-4564
Suzanne Thursby, Director

Washtenaw Community College
SBDC
E-mail:
dstotz@orchard.washtenaw.cc.mi.us

740 Woodland
Saline, Michigan 48176
Phone: (734)944-1016
Fax: (734)944-0165
Richard King, Regional Director

Eastern U.P. Planning &
Development Corporation
SBDC
PO Box 520
Sault Ste. Marie, Michigan 49783
Phone: (906)635-1581
Fax: (906)632-4255
Roy Mayry, Director

West Shore Community College
Small Business Development Center
Business and Industrial Development
Institute
3000 N. Stiles Rd.
PO Box 277
Scottville, Michigan 49454-0277
Phone: (616)845-6211
Fax: (616)845-0207
Mark Bergstrom, Director
E-mail: bergtr@westshore.cc.mi.us

South Haven Chamber of Commerce
SBDC
E-mail: cofc@southhavenmi.com
300 Broadway
South Haven, Michigan 49090
Phone: (616)637-5171
Fax: (616)639-1570
Larry King, Director

Lawrence Technological University
Division of Continuing Education
SBDC
21000 W. Ten Mile Rd.
Southfield, Michigan 48076-1058
Phone: (248)204-4053
Fax: (248)204-4016
Daniel Belknap, Regional Director
E-mail: belknap@bizserve.com

Downriver Small Business
Development Center
15100 Northline Rd.
Southgate, Michigan 48195
Phone: (313)281-0700
Fax: (313)281-3418
Paula Boase, Director
E-mail: pboase@bizserve.com

Arenac County Extension Service
SBDC
E-mail: arenac@msue.msu.edu
County Bldg.
P.O. Box 745
Standish, Michigan 48658
Phone: (517)846-4111
Ken Kernstock, Director

Michigan State University Extension
Center
SBDC
Stephenson, Michigan 49887
Phone: (906)753-2209

Sterling Heights Area Chamber of
Commerce
Small Business Development Center
E-mail: suscc.com
12900 Hall Rd., Ste. 110
Sterling Heights, Michigan 48313
Phone: (810)731-5400
Fax: (810)731-3521
Lillian Adams, Director

Northwest Michigan Council of
Governments
Small Business Development Center
2194 Dendrinos Dr.
PO Box 506
Traverse City, Michigan 49685-0506
Phone: (616)929-5000
Fax: (616)929-5017
Richard J. Beldin, Director
E-mail: dbeldin@nwm.cog.mi.us

Northwestern Michigan College
Small Business Development Center
Center for Business and Industry
1701 E. Front St.
Traverse City, Michigan 49686
Phone: (616)922-1720
Fax: (616)922-1722
Cheryl Throop, Director
E-mail: cthroop@nmc.edu

Traverse Bay Economic Development
Corp.
Small Business Development Center
E-mail: chamber@gtii.com
202 E. Grandview Pkwy.
PO Box 387
Traverse City, Michigan 49684-0387
Phone: (616)946-1596
Fax: (616)946-2565
Matthew Meadors, Regional Director

Traverse City Area Chamber of
Commerce
Small Business Development Center
202 E. Grandview Pkwy.
PO Box 387
Traverse City, Michigan 49684
Phone: (616)947-5075
Fax: (616)946-2565
Matthew Meadors, Dir.

Oakland Count Small Business
Development Center
Walsh College/OCC
SOC Bldg.
4555 Corporate Dr., Ste. 201
PO Box 7085
Troy, Michigan 48098
Phone: (810)641-0088
Fax: (810)267-3809
Daniel V. Belknap, Dir.

Saginaw Valley State University
Small Business Development Center
Business & Industrial Development
Institute
7400 Bay Rd.
Wickes 387
University Center, Michigan 48710-
0001
Phone: (517)790-4388
Fax: (517)790-4983
Charles B. Curtiss Jr., Interim
Regional Director

Macomb Community College
SBDC
14500 12 Mile Rd.
Warren, Michigan 48093
Phone: (810)445-7348
Fax: (810)445-7316
Geary Maiurini, Dir.

Warren - Centerline - Sterling Heights
Chamber of Commerce
Small Business Development Center
30500 Van Dyke, Ste. 118
Warren, Michigan 48093
Phone: (810)751-3939
Fax: (810)751-3995
Janet Masi, Director
E-mail:
janetmorris@chambercom.com

Michigan State University Extension
Center
SBDC

205 S Eighth St.
West Branch, Michigan 48661
Phone: (517)345-0692
Fax: (517)345-1284
Bonnie Wichtner-Zoia, Director

Minnesota

Northwest Technical College
SBDC
905 Grant Ave., SE
Bemidji, Minnesota 56601
Phone: (218)755-4286
Fax: (218)755-4289
Susan Kozojed, Director

Normandale Community College
(Bloomington)
Small Business Development Center
9700 France Ave. S
Bloomington, Minnesota 55431
Phone: (612)832-6221
Fax: (612)832-6352
Scott Harding, Director

Central Lakes College
Small Business Development Center
501 W. College Dr.
Brainerd, Minnesota 56401
Phone: (218)825-2028
Fax: (218)825-2053
Pamela Thomsen, Director

University of Minnesota at Duluth
Small Business Development Center
School of Business and Economics,
Rm. 150
10 University Dr.
Duluth, Minnesota 55812-2496
Phone: (218)726-8758
Fax: (218)726-6192
Lee Jensen, Director
E-mail: ljensen@d.umn.edu

Itasca Development Corp.
Grand Rapids Small Business
Development Center
E-mail: idsbdc@uslink.net
19 NE 3rd St.
Grand Rapids, Minnesota 55744
Phone: (218)327-2241
Fax: (218)327-2242
John Damjanovich, Director

Hibbing Community College
Small Business Development Center
1515 E. 25th St.

Hibbing, Minnesota 55746
Phone: (218)262-6703
Fax: (218)262-6717
Jim Antilla, Director
E-mail: j.antilla@hi.cc.mn.us

Rainy River Community College
Small Business Development Center
1501 Hwy. 71
International Falls, Minnesota 56649
Phone: (218)285-2255
Fax: (218)285-2239
Tom West, Director

Region Nine Development
Commission
SBDC
410 Jackson St.
PO Box 3367
Mankato, Minnesota 56002-3367
Phone: (507)389-8863
Fax: (507)387-7105
Jill Miller, Director
E-mail: jillm@rndc.mankato.mn.us

Southwest State University
Small Business Development Center
Science and Technical Resource
Center, Ste. 105
1501 State St.
Marshall, Minnesota 56258
Phone: (507)537-7386
Fax: (507)537-6094
Jack Hawk, Director
E-mail:
hawk@ssu.southwest.msus.edu

Minneapolis Small Business
Development Center
SBDC
610-C Butler Square
100 N Sixth St.
Minneapolis, Minnesota 55403
Phone: (612)370-2343
Fax: (612)370-2303
Michael J. Lyons, SBDC Project
Officer
E-mail: michael.lyons@sba.gov

Minnesota Project Innovation
Small Business Development Center
111 3rd Ave. S., Ste. 100
Minneapolis, Minnesota 55401
Phone: (612)338-3280
Fax: (612)338-3483
Pat Dillon, Director
E-mail: pdillon@mpi.org

University of St. Thomas
SBDC
1000 LaSalle Ave.
Mail Stop 25H 225
Minneapolis, Minnesota 55403
Phone: (612)962-4500
Fax: (612)962-4810
Gregg Schneider, Director
E-mail: gwschneider@stthomas.edu

Moorhead State University
Small Business Development Center
1104 7th Ave. S.
MSU Box 303
Moorhead, Minnesota 56563
Phone: (218)236-2289
Fax: (218)236-2280
Len Sliwoski, Director

Owatonna Incubator, Inc.
SBDC
560 Dunnell Dr., Ste. 203
PO Box 505
Owatonna, Minnesota 55060
Phone: (507)451-0517
Fax: (507)455-2788
Ken Henrickson, Director

Pine Technical College
Small Business Development Center
1100 4th St.
Pine City, Minnesota 55063
Phone: (320)629-7340
Fax: (320)629-7603
John Sparling, Director

Hennepin Technical College
SBDC
1820 N. Xenium Lane
Plymouth, Minnesota 55441
Phone: (612)550-7218
Fax: (612)550-7272
Danelle Wolf, Dir.

Pottery Business and Tech. Center
Small Business Development Center
2000 Pottery Pl. Dr., Ste. 339
Red Wing, Minnesota 55066
Phone: (612)388-4079
Fax: (612)385-2251
Marv Bollum, Dir.

Rochester Community and Tech.
College
Small Business Development Center
Riverland Hall
851 30th Ave. SE

Rochester, Minnesota 55904
Phone: (507)285-7425
Fax: (507)285-7110
Michelle Pyfferoen, Director
E-mail: mpyffero@ucrpo.roch.edu

Dakota County Technical College
SBDC
1300 145th St. E.
Rosemount, Minnesota 55068
Phone: (612)423-8262
Fax: (612)423-8761
Tom Trutna, Director

Dakota County Technical College
Small Business Development Center
1300 E. 145th St.
Rosemount, Minnesota 55068
Phone: (612)423-8262
Fax: (612)322-5156
Tom Trutna, Director

Southeast Minnesota Development
Corp.
SBDC
111 W. Jessie St.
PO Box 684
Rushford, Minnesota 55971
Phone: (507)864-7557
Fax: (507)864-2091
Terry Erickson, Director

St. Cloud State University
Small Business Development Center
720 4th Ave. S.
St. Cloud, Minnesota 56301-3761
Phone: (320)255-4842
Fax: (320)255-4957
Dawn Jensen-Ragnier, Director

Department of Trade and Economic
Development
Minnesota SBDC
500 Metro Sq.
121 7th Pl. E.
St. Paul, Minnesota 55101-2146
Phone: (612)297-5770
Fax: (612)296-1290
Mary Kruger, State Director
E-mail: mary.krugerstationte.mn.us

North Shore Business Enterprise
Center
SBDC
5 Fairgrounds Rd
PO Box 248
Two Harbors, Minnesota 55616

Phone: (218)834-3494
Fax: (218)834-5074
Allen Jackson, Director
E-mail: ajackso2@d.umn.edu

Minnesota Technology, Inc.
Small Business Development Center
Olcott Plaza Bldg., Ste. 140
820 N. 9th St.
Virginia, Minnesota 55792
Phone: (218)741-4251
Fax: (218)741-4249
John Freeland, Dir.

Wadena Chamber of Commerce
SBDC
222 2nd St., SE
Wadena, Minnesota 56482
Phone: (218)631-1502
Fax: (218)631-2396
Paul Kinn, Dir.

Century College
SBDC
3300 Century Ave., N., Ste. 200-D
White Bear Lake, Minnesota 55110-
1894
Phone: (612)773-1794
Fax: (612)779-5802
Ernie Brodtmann, Dir.

Mississippi

Northeast Mississippi Community
College
SBDC
Holiday Hall, 2nd Fl.
Cunningham Blvd.
Booneville, Mississippi 38829
Phone: (601)720-7448
Fax: (601)720-7464
Kenny Holt, Director
E-mail: kholt@necc.cc.ms.us

Delta State University
Small Business Development Center
E-mail: sbdc@dsu.deltast.edu
PO Box 3235 DSU
1417 College St.
Cleveland, Mississippi 38733
Phone: (601)846-4236
Fax: (601)846-4235
David Holman, Director
E-mail: dmhend@dsu.deltast.edu

East Central Community College
SBDC
275 Broad St.
PO Box 129
Decatur, Mississippi 39327
Phone: (601)635-2111
Fax: (601)635-4031
Ronald Westbrook, Director
E-mail: rwestbrook@eccc.cc.ms.us

Jones County Junior College
SBDC
E-mail: crc@jcjc.cc.ms.us
900 Court St.
Ellisville, Mississippi 39437
Phone: (601)477-4165
Fax: (601)477-4166
Gary Suddith, Director

Mississippi Gulf Coast Community
College
SBDC
Jackson County Campus
PO Box 100
2300 Hwy 90
Gautier, Mississippi 39553
Phone: (601)497-7723
Fax: (601)497-7788
Janice Mabry, Director

Mississippi Delta Community College
Small Business Development Center
E-mail: mdccsbdc@tecinfo.com
1656 E Union
PO Box 5607
Greenville, Mississippi 38704-5607
Phone: (601)378-8183
Fax: (601)378-5349
Chuck Herring, Director

Mississippi Contract Procurement
Center
SBDC
3015 12th St.
PO Box 610
Gulfport, Mississippi 39502-0610
Phone: (601)864-2961
Fax: (601)864-2969
C. W. "Skip" Ryland, Exec. Dir.

Pearl River Community College
Small Business Development Center
5448 U.S. Hwy. 49 S.
Hattiesburg, Mississippi 39401
Phone: (601)544-9133
Fax: (601)544-9149
Heidi McDuffie, Director

Mississippi Valley State University
Affiliate SBDC
14000 Hwy 82 W
Itta Bena, Mississippi 38941
Phone: (601)254-3601
Fax: (601)254-3600
Dr. Jim Breyley, Director

Jackson State University
Small Business Development Center
Jackson Enterprise Center, Ste. A-1
931 Hwy. 80 W
Unit 43
Jackson, Mississippi 39204
Phone: (601)968-2795
Fax: (601)968-2796
Henry Thomas, Director
E-mail: hthomas@ccaix.jsums.edu

University of Southern Mississippi
Small Business Development Center
136 Beach Park Pl.
Long Beach, Mississippi 39560
Phone: (601)865-4578
Fax: (601)865-4581
Lucy Betcher, Director
E-mail: lbetcher@medea.yp.usm.edu

Alcorn State University
SBDC
1000 ASU Dr.
PO Box 90
Lorman, Mississippi 39096-9402
Phone: (601)877-6684
Fax: (601)877-3900
Sharon Witty, Director
E-mail: sawitty@lorman.alcorn.edu

Meridian Community College
Small Business Development Center
910 Hwy. 19 N
Meridian, Mississippi 39307
Phone: (601)482-7445
Fax: (601)482-5803
Mac Hodges, Director
E-mail: mhodges@mcc.cc.ms.us

Mississippi State University
Small Business Development Center
1 Research Bldg., Ste 201
PO Drawer 5288
Mississippi State, Mississippi 39762
Phone: (601)325-8684
Fax: (601)325-4016
Sonny Fisher, Director
E-mail: sfisher@cobilan.msstate.edu

Copiah-Lincoln Community College
Small Business Development Center
11 County Line Circle
Natchez, Mississippi 39120
Phone: (601)445-5254
Fax: (601)446-1221
Bob D. Russ, Director
E-mail: robertr@natl.colin.cc.ms.us

Hinds Community College
Small Business Development Center
International Trade Center
E-mail: hccsbdc@netdoor.com
1500 Raymond Lake Rd., 2nd Fl.
PO Box 1170
Raymond, Mississippi 39154
Phone: (601)857-3536
Fax: (601)857-3474
Ms. Leigh Kirtley, Program Director

Holmes Community College
SBDC
413 W. Ridgeland Ave.
Ridgeland, Mississippi 39157
Phone: (601)853-0827
Fax: (601)853-0844
John Deddens, Director

Northwest Mississippi Community
College
SBDC
DeSoto Ctr., rm. 208
5197 W.E. Ross Pkwy.
Southaven, Mississippi 38671
Phone: (601)280-1421
Fax: (601)342-7648
Jody Dunning, Director

Southwest Mississippi Community
College
SBDC
E-mail: sbdc@bears.smcc.cc.ms.us
College Dr.
Summit, Mississippi 39666
Phone: (601)276-3890
Fax: (601)276-3883
Kathryn "Sissy" Whittington,
Director

Itawamba Community College
Small Business Development Center
2176 S Eason Blvd.
Tupelo, Mississippi 38801
Phone: (601)680-8515
Fax: (601)680-8547
Rex Hollingsworth, Director

E-mail:
rbhollingsworth@icc.cc.ms.us

University of Mississippi
SBDC
E-mail: msbdc@olemiss.edu
Old Chemistry Bldg., Ste. 216
University, Mississippi 38677
Phone: (601)232-5001
Free: (800)725-7232
Fax: (601)232-5650
Walter D. Gurley Jr., Director
E-mail:
wgurly@sunset.backbone.olemiss.edu

University of Mississippi
Mississippi SBDC
E-mail: sbdc@olemiss.edu
N.C.P.A., Rm. 1082
University, Mississippi 38677
Phone: (601)234-2120
Fax: (601)232-1220
Michael Vanderlip, Director

Missouri

Camden County
SBDC Extension Center
113 Kansas
PO Box 1405
Camdenton, Missouri 65020
Phone: (573)882-0344
Fax: (573)884-4297
Jackie Rasmussen, B&I Spec.

Missouri PAC - Southeastern
Missouri State University
SBDC
222 N. Pacific
Cape Girardeau, Missouri 63701
Phone: (573)290-5965
Fax: (573)651-5005
George Williams, Dir.

Southeast Missouri State University
Small Business Development Center
E-mail: sbdc-cg@ext.missouri.edu
222 N Pacific
MS 5925
Cape Girardeau, Missouri 63701
Phone: (573)290-5965
Fax: (573)651-5005
Frank "Buz" Sutherland, Director
E-mail: SBDC-
CG@EXT.MISSOURI.EDU

Chillicothe City Hall
SBDC
715 Washington St.
Chillicothe, Missouri 64601-2229
Phone: (816)646-6920
Fax: (816)646-6811
Brian Olson, Director

East Central Missouri/St. Louis
County
Extension Center
121 S. Meramac, Ste. 501
Clayton, Missouri 63105
Phone: (314)889-2911
Fax: (314)854-6147
Carole Leriche-Price, B&I Specialist

Boone County Extension Center
SBDC
1012 N. Hwy UU
Columbia, Missouri 65203
Phone: (573)445-9792
Fax: (573)445-9807
Mr. Casey Venters, B&I Specialist

MO PAC-Central Region
University of Missouri-Columbia
SBDC
E-mail: mopcol@ext.missouri.edu
University Pl., Ste. 1800
1205 University Ave.
Columbia, Missouri 65211
Phone: (573)882-3597
Fax: (573)884-4297
Morris Hudson, Dir.

University Extension Small Business
Development Center
Business & Industrial Specialists
SBDC
821 Clark Hall
Columbia, Missouri 65211
Phone: (573)882-4142
Fax: (573)882-2595
Dr. Tom Henderson, Director

University of Missouri
Missouri SBDC System
E-mail: sbdc-mso@ext.missouri.edu
300 University Place
Columbia, Missouri 65211
Phone: (573)882-0344
Fax: (573)884-4297
Max E. Summers, State Director
E-mail: summersm@missouri.edu

University of Missouri—Columbia
Small Business Development Center
E-mail: sbdc-c@ext.missouri.edu
University Pl., Ste. 1800
1205 University Ave.
Columbia, Missouri 65211
Phone: (573)882-9931
Fax: (573)882-6156
Frank Siebert, Director
E-mail: SBDC-
C@EXT.MISSOURI.EDU

Mineral Area College
SBDC
PO Box 1000
Flat River, Missouri 63601
Phone: (573)431-4593
Eugene Cherry, Director

Hannibal Satellite Center
Hannibal, Missouri 63401
Phone: (816)385-6550
Fax: (816)385-6568

Jefferson County
Courthouse, Annex No. 203
Extension Center
Courthouse, Annex 203
725 Maple St.
PO Box 497
Hillsboro, Missouri 63050
Phone: (573)789-5391
Fax: (573)789-5059

Cape Girardeau County
SBDC Extension Center
815 Hwy. 25S
PO Box 408
Jackson, Missouri 63755
Phone: (573)243-3581
Fax: (573)243-1606
Richard Sparks, B&I Specialist

Cole County Extension Center
SBDC
2436 Tanner Bridge Rd.
Jefferson City, Missouri 65101
Phone: (573)634-2824
Fax: (573)634-5463
Mr. Chris Bouchard, B&I Specialist

Missouri Southern State College
Small Business Development Center
E-mail: sbdc-j@ext.missouri.edu
Matthews Hall, Ste. 107
3950 Newman Rd.
Joplin, Missouri 64801-1595

Phone: (417)625-9313
Fax: (417)625-9782
Jim Krudwig, Director

Rockhurst College
Small Business Development Center
1100 Rockhurst Rd.
VanAckeren Hall, Rm. 205
Kansas City, Missouri 64110-2599
Phone: (816)501-4572
Fax: (816)501-4646
Rhonda Gerke, Director

Truman State University
Small Business Development Center
E-mail: sbdc-k@ext.missouri.edu
200 E Patterson
Kirksville, Missouri 63501-4419
Phone: (816)785-4307
Fax: (816)785-4181
Glen Giboney, Director
E-mail: SBDC-
K@EXT.MISSOURI.EDU

Thomas Hill Enterprise Center
SBDC
1409 N. Prospect Dr.
PO Box 246
Macon, Missouri 63552
Phone: (816)385-6550
Fax: (816)562-3071
Jane Vanderham, Dir.

Northwest Missouri State University
Small Business Development Center
423 N. Market St.
Maryville, Missouri 64468-1614
Phone: (816)562-1701
Fax: (816)582-3071
Brad Anderson, Director

Audrain County Extension Center
SBDC
Courthouse, 4th Fl.
101 Jefferson
Mexico, Missouri 65265
Phone: (573)581-3231
Fax: (573)581-2766
Virgil Woolridge, B&I Specialist

Randolph County
Extension Center
417 E. Urbandale
Moberly, Missouri 65270
Phone: (816)263-3534
Fax: (816)263-1874
Ray Marshall, B&I Specialist

Mineral Area College
SBDC
E-mail: sbdc-fr@ext.missouri.edu
PO Box 1000
Park Hills, Missouri 63601-1000
Phone: (573)431-4593
Fax: (573)431-2144
Eugene Cherry, Dir.
E-mail: SBDC-
FR@EXT.MISSOURI.EDU

Telecommunications Community
Resource Center
Longhead Learning Center
Small Business Development Center
1121 Victory Ln.
3019 Fair St.
Poplar Bluff, Missouri 63901
Phone: (573)840-9450
Fax: (573)840-9456
Judy Moss, Dir.
E-mail: SBDC-
PB@EXT.MISSOURI.EDU

Washington County SBDC
102 N. Missouri
Potosi, Missouri 63664
Phone: (573)438-2671
Fax: (573)438-2079
LaDonna McCuan, B&I Specialist

Phelps County
SBDC Extension Center
Courthouse
200 N. Main
PO Box 725
Rolla, Missouri 65401
Phone: (573)364-3147
Fax: (573)364-0436
Paul Cretin, B&I Specialist

University of Missouri at Rolla
SBDC
E-mail: sbdc-rt@ext.missouri.edu
223 Engineering Management Bldg.
Rolla, Missouri 65401-0249
Phone: (314)341-4561
Fax: (314)341-2071
Robert Laney, Director
E-mail:
MOPROLLA@EXT.MISSOURI.EDU

University of Missouri (Rolla)
Center for Technology Transfer and
Economic Development
SBDC

University of Missouri—Rolla
Nagogami Ter., Bldg. 1, Rm. 104
Rolla, Missouri 65401-0249
Phone: (573)341-4559
Fax: (573)341-4922
Fred Goss, Director
E-mail: SBDC-
RT@EXT.MISSOURI.EDU

Missouri PAC - Eastern Region
SBDC
E-mail:
MOPSTL@EXT.MISSOURI.EDU
3830 Washington Ave.
St. Louis, Missouri 63108
Phone: (314)534-4413
Fax: (314)534-3237
Ken Konchel, Dir.
E-mail:
MOPSTL@EXT.MISSOURI.EDU

St. Louis County
Extension Center
207 Marillac, UMSL
8001 Natural Bridge Rd.
St. Louis, Missouri 63121
Phone: (314)553-5944
John Henschke, Specialist

St. Louis University
Small Business State University
SBDC
E-mail: sbdc-stl@ext.missouri.edu
3750 Lindell Blvd.
St. Louis, Missouri 63108-3412
Phone: (314)977-7232
Fax: (314)977-7241
Viginia Campbell, Director

St. Louis / St. Charles County
Economic Council
SBDC Extension Center
260 Brown Rd.
St. Peters, Missouri 63376
Phone: (314)970-3000
Fax: (314)274-3310
Tim Wathen, B&I Specialist

Pettis County
Extension Center
1012A Thompson Blvd.
Sedalia, Missouri 65301
Phone: (816)827-0591
Fax: (816)827-4888
Betty Lorton, B&I Specialist

Southwest Missouri State University
Center for Business Research
Small Business Development Center
901 S. National
Box 88
Springfield, Missouri 65804-0089
Phone: (417)836-5685
Fax: (417)836-6337
Jane Peterson, Director

Franklin County
SBDC Extension Center
414 E. Main
PO Box 71
Union, Missouri 63084
Phone: (573)583-5141
Fax: (573)583-5145
Rebecca How, B&I Specialist

Central Missouri State University
SBDC
Grinstead, No. 75
Warrensburg, Missouri 64093-5037
Phone: (816)543-4402
Fax: (816)747-1653
Cindy Tanck, Coordinator

Technology Development Center
Central Missouri State University
SBDC
Grinstead, No. 9
Warrensburg, Missouri 64093-5037
Phone: (816)543-4402
Fax: (816)543-8159
Wes Savage, Assistant Director

Howell County
SBDC Extension Center
217 S. Aid Ave.
West Plains, Missouri 65775
Phone: (417)256-2391
Fax: (417)256-8569
Mick Gilliam, B&I Specialist

Montana

Big Sky Economic Development
Authority
Small Business Development Center
2722 3rd Ave., Ste. W300
115 N. Broadway, 2nd Fl.
Billings, Montana 59101-1931
Phone: (406)256-6875
Fax: (406)256-6877
Tom McKerlick, Director
E-mail: mckerlick@mt-tradeport.org

Gallatin Development Corporation
Bozeman Small Business
Development Center
Gallatin Development Corp.
222 E. Main St., Ste. 102
Bozeman, Montana 59715
Phone: (406)587-3113
Fax: (406)587-9565
Michele DuBose, Director
E-mail: mdubose@bozeman.org

Southwest Montana Service Center
Butte Small Business Development
Center
Headwaters RC&D
305 W. Mercury, Ste. 211
Butte, Montana 59701
Phone: (406)782-7333
Fax: (406)782-9675
John Donovan, Director
E-mail: connietd@in-tech.com

SouthEastern Montana Development
Corporation
SBDC
E-mail: semdc@mcn.net
6200 Main St.
PO Box 1935
Colstrip, Montana 59323
Phone: (406)748-2990
Kent Wood, Director

High Plains Development Authority
Great Falls SBDC
710 1st. Ave. N.
P.O. Box 2568
Great Falls, Montana 59403
Phone: (406)454-1934
Fax: (406)454-2995
Suzanne David, Director
E-mail: suzie@mt.net

BearPaw Development Corporation
Havre Small Business Development
Center
Bear Paw Development Corp.
PO Box 170
Havre, Montana 59501
Phone: (406)265-9226
Fax: (406)265-5602
Randy Hanson, Director
E-mail: rhanson@bearpaw.org

Gateway Economic Development
SBDC
225 Cruse Ave.

Helena, Montana 59604
Phone: (406)447-1534
Fax: (406)444-1532
Ron Chevalier, Director
E-mail: ronsbdc@mt.net

Montana Department of Commerce
Montana SBDC
1424 9th Ave.
PO Box 200505
Helena, Montana 59620
Phone: (406)444-4780
Fax: (406)444-1872
Ralph Kloser, State Director
E-mail: rkloser@state.mt.gov

Kalispell Small Business
Development Center
Northwest Montana Service Center
Flathead Valley Community College
218 Main St.
PO Box 8300
Kalispell, Montana 59904-1300
Phone: (406)758-5412
Fax: (406)257-7283
George Bonham, Director
E-mail: gbonham@digisys.net

Montana Community Development
Corporation
Missoula Small Business
Development Center
Missoula Business Incubator
127 N. Higgins, 3rd Fl.
Missoula, Montana 59802
Phone: (406)728-9234
Fax: (406)721-4584
Bret George, Director
E-mail: bgeorge@montana.com

Sidney Small Business Development
Center
Eastern Plains RC&D
123 W. Main
Sidney, Montana 59270
Phone: (406)482-5024
Fax: (406)482-5306
Dwayne Heintz, Contact

Missouri Valley Development
Corporation
SBDC
220 3rd Ave. S, D
Wolf Point, Montana 59201
Phone: (406)653-2246
Fax: (406)653-1844

Laura McPherson, Director
E-mail: laursbdc@midrivers.com

Nebraska

Chadron State College
SBDC
Administration Bldg.
1000 Main St.
Chadron, Nebraska 69337
Phone: (308)432-6282
Fax: (308)432-6430
Cliff Hanson, Director
E-mail: mchanson@cscl.csc.edu

University of Nebraska at Kearney
SBDC
Welch Hall
19th St. and College Dr.
Kearney, Nebraska 68849-3035
Phone: (308)865-8344
Fax: (308)865-8153
Susan Jensen, Director
E-mail: jensens@platte.unk.edu

University of Nebraska at Lincoln
SBDC
E-mail: nbdclincol@aol.com
1135 M St., No. 200
11th and Cornhusker Hwy.
Lincoln, Nebraska 68508
Phone: (402)472-3358
Fax: (402)472-0328
Cliff Mosteller, Director

Mid-Plains Community College
SBDC
416 N. Jeffers, Rm. 26
North Platte, Nebraska 69101
Phone: (308)635-7513
Fax: (308)534-5117
Dean Kurth, Director
E-mail:
mdkurth@ziggy.mpcc.cc.ne.us

Nebraska Small Business
Development Center
Omaha Business and Technology
Center
Procurement Technological
Assistance Center
2505 N. 24 St., Ste. 103
Omaha, Nebraska 68110
Phone: (402)595-3511
Fax: (402)595-3832

Jerry Dalton, Manager
E-mail: gd92036@navix.net

University of Nebraska at Omaha
Peter Kiewit Conference Center
SBDC
1313 Farnam-on-the-Mall, Ste. 132
Omaha, Nebraska 68182-0248
Phone: (402)595-2381
Fax: (402)595-2385
Nate Brei, Director
E-mail:
nate@nbdcoffice.unomaha.edu

University of Nebraska at Omaha
Nebraska Business Development
Center
College of Business Administration,
Rm. 407
60th & Dodge Sts.
CBA Rm. 407
Omaha, Nebraska 68182-0248
Phone: (402)554-2521
Fax: (402)554-3473
Robert Bernier, State Director
E-mail: rberniew@unomaha.edu

Peru State College
SBDC
T.J. Majors Hall, Rm. 248
Peru, Nebraska 68421
Phone: (402)872-2274
Fax: (402)872-2422
Jerry Breazile, Director
E-mail: breazile@pscosf.peru.edu

Scottsbluff Small Business
Development Center
SBDC
Nebraska Public Power Bldg.
1620 Broadway, Ste. 201
Scottsbluff, Nebraska 69361
Phone: (308)635-7513
Fax: (308)635-6596
Ingrid Battershell, Director
E-mail: ibatters@unomaha.edu

Wayne State College
SBDC
Gardner Hall
1111 Main St.
Wayne, Nebraska 68787
Phone: (402)375-7575
Fax: (402)375-7574
Loren Kucera, Director
E-mail: lkucera@wsgate.wsc.edu

Nevada

Carson City Chamber of Commerce
Small Business Development Center
1900 S. Carson St., Ste. 100
Carson City, Nevada 89702
Phone: (702)882-1565
Fax: (702)882-4179
Larry Osborne, Executive Director

Great Basin College
Small Business Development Center
1500 College Pkwy.
Elko, Nevada 89801
Phone: (702)753-2205
Fax: (702)753-2242
John Pryor, Director

Incline Village Chamber of
Commerce
SBDC
969 Tahoe Blvd.
Incline Village, Nevada 89451
Phone: (702)831-4440
Fax: (702)832-1605
Sheri Woods, Exec. Dir.

Las Vegas SBDC
SBDC
3270 Howard Hughes Pkwy., Ste. 130
Las Vegas, Nevada 89109
Phone: (702)734-7575
Fax: (702)734-7633
Sharolyn Craft, Director

University of Nevada at Las Vegas
Small Business Development Center
4505 Maryland Pkwy.
Box 456011
Las Vegas, Nevada 89154-6011
Phone: (702)895-0852
Fax: (702)895-4095
Nancy Buist, Business Development
Specialist

North Las Vegas Small Business
Development Center
19 W. Brooks Ave., Ste. B
North Las Vegas, Nevada 89030
Phone: (702)399-6300
Fax: (702)399-6301
Janis Stevenson, Business
Development Specialist

Business Environmental Program
Nevada Small Business Development
Center

Sierra Pacific Power Company
6100 Neil Rd., Ste. 400
Reno, Nevada 89511
Phone: (702)689-6688
Fax: (702)689-6689

University of Nevada at Reno
Small Business Development Center
E-mail: nsbdc@scs.unr.edu
College of Business Administration
Business Bdlg., Rm. 411
Reno, Nevada 89557-0100
Phone: (702)784-1717
Fax: (702)784-4337
Sam Males, State Director

Tri-County Development Authority
Small Business Development Center
50 W. 4th St.
PO Box 820
Winnemucca, Nevada 89446
Phone: (702)623-5777
Fax: (702)623-5999
Teri Williams, Director

New Hampshire

University of New Hampshire
Small Business Development Center
108 McConnell Hall
15 College Rd.
Durham, New Hampshire 03824-
3593
Phone: (603)862-2200
Fax: (603)862-4876
Mary Collins, State Director
E-mail: mec@christa.unh.edu

Keene State College
Small Business Development Center
Keene State College
Keene, New Hampshire 03431-2101
Phone: (603)358-2602
Fax: (603)358-2612
Gary Cloutier, Regional Manager
E-mail: gc@cchrista.unh.edu

Littleton Small Business
Development Center
120 Main St.
Littleton, New Hampshire 03561
Phone: (603)444-1053
Fax: (603)444-5463
Liz Ward, Regional Manager
E-mail: eaward@christa.unh.edu

Manchester Small Business
Development Center
1000 Elm St., 12th Fl.
Manchester, New Hampshire 03101
Phone: (603)624-2000
Fax: (603)647-4410
Bob Ebberson, Regional Manager
E-mail: rte@christa.unh.edu

Office of Economic Initiatives
SBDC
E-mail: ahj@hopper.unh.edu
1000 Elm St., 12th Fl.
Manchester, New Hampshire 03101
Phone: (603)624-2000
Fax: (603)647-2410
Amy Jennings, Director
E-mail: ahj@hooper.unh.edu

New Hampshire Small Business
Development Center
c/o Center for Economic
Development
1 Indian Head Plz., Ste. 510
Nashua, New Hampshire 03060
Phone: (603)886-1233
Fax: (603)598-1164
Judy Orfao, Acting Regional
Manager
E-mail: bwilburn@sbdc-bw.mv.com

Plymouth State College
Small Business Development Center
Outreach Center, MSC24A
Plymouth, New Hampshire 03264-
1595
Phone: (603)535-2523
Fax: (603)535-2850
Janice Kitchen, Regional Manager
E-mail: janice.kitchen@plymouth.edu

SBDC
Chamber of Commerce
18 S. Main St., Ste. 3A
Rochester, New Hampshire 03867
Phone: (603)330-1929
Fax: (603)330-1948
Jeanine DiMario, Regional Manager

New Jersey

Greater Atlantic City Chamber of
Commerce
Small Business Development Center
1125 Atlantic Ave.
Atlantic City, New Jersey 08401

Phone: (609)345-5600
Fax: (609)345-1666
William R. McGinley, Regional
Director

Rutgers University At Camden
Small Business Development Center
227 Penn St., 3rd Fl., Rm. 334
Camden, New Jersey 08102
Phone: (609)225-6221
Fax: (609)225-6621
Patricia Peacock, Regional Director
E-mail:
ppeacock@camden.rutgers.edu

Brookdale Community College
Small Business Development Center
E-mail: sbdcbrookdale@infl-pos.com
765 Newman Springs Rd.
Lincroft, New Jersey 07738
Phone: (732)842-8685
Fax: (732)842-0203
Larry Novick, Regional Co-Director
E-mail: lnovick@brookdale.cc.nj.us

Middlesex County Office of
Economic Development
Middleses County Small Business
Development Center
1 JFK Square
New Brunswick, New Jersey 08901
Phone: (732)745-5836
Fax: (732)745-5911
Carlos M. Maldonado, Regional
Director
E-mail:
carlos@andromeda.rutgers.edu

Rutgers Graduate School of
Management
New Jersey SBDC
Graduate School of Management
49 Bleeker St.
Newark, New Jersey 07102
Phone: (973)353-1927
Fax: (973)353-1110
Brenda B. Hopper, State Director
Leroy A. Johnson, Dir.
E-mail:
bhooper@andromeda.rutgers.edu

Bergen County Community College
SBDC
400 Paramus Rd., Rm. A328
3rd Floor
Paramus, New Jersey 07652-1595

Phone: (201)447-7841
Fax: (201)447-9405
Melody Irvin, Director
E-mail: vdelia@pilot.njin.net

Paterson Small Business
Development Center
SBDC
131 Ellison St.
Paterson, New Jersey 07505
Phone: (973)754-8695
Fax: (973)754-9153
Joseph M. Bair, Regional Director
E-mail: jbair@andromeda.rutgers.edu

Mercer County Community College
Small Business Development Center
West Windsor Campus
1200 Old Trenton Rd.
PO Box B
Trenton, New Jersey 08690
Phone: (609)586-4800
Fax: (609)890-6338
Herb Spiegel, Regional Director
E-mail: hss@mccc.edu

Trenton Business & Technology
Center
SBDC
E-mail: tbto@mccc.edu
36 S Broad St.
Trenton, New Jersey 08608
Phone: (609)396-8801
Fax: (609)396-8603
Joe Kielec, Manager

Urban Center
Mercer County Community College
SBDC
36 S Broad St.
Trenton, New Jersey 08608
Phone: (609)396-7246
Fax: (609)396-8603
Mari Galvez de Cerdas, Assistant
Regional Director
E-mail: galvez@mccc.edu

Kean College
Small Business Development Center
East Campus, Rm. 242
Union, New Jersey 07083
Phone: (908)527-2946
Fax: (908)527-2960
Mira Kostak, Regional Director
E-mail: mkostak@turbo.kean.edu

Warren County Community College
Small Business Development Center
475 Rte 57 W
Rte. 57 W.
Washington, New Jersey 07882-9605
Phone: (908)689-9620
Fax: (908)689-2247
James Smith, Regional Director
E-mail: jhsmith@nac.net

New Mexico

New Mexico State University at
Alamogordo
Small Business Development Center
2230 Lawrence Blvd.
Alamogordo, New Mexico 88310
Phone: (505)434-5272
Fax: (505)434-1432
Dwight Harp, Director

Albuquerque Technical-Vocational
Institute
Small Business Development Center
525 Buena Vista SE
Albuquerque, New Mexico 87106
Phone: (505)272-7980
Fax: (505)272-7969
Ray Garcia, Director

South Valley SBDC
SBDC
700 4th St. SW, Ste. A
Albuquerque, New Mexico 87102
Phone: (505)248-0132
Fax: (505)248-0127
Steven Becerra, Director

New Mexico State University at
Carlsbad
Small Business Development Center
1500 University Dr., Rm. 254
PO Box 1090
Carlsbad, New Mexico 88220
Phone: (505)234-9435
Fax: (505)885-1515
Larry Coalson, Director

Clovis Community College
Small Business Development Center
417 Schepps Blvd.
Clovis, New Mexico 88101
Phone: (505)769-4136
Fax: (505)769-4190
Sandra Taylor-Smith, Director

Northern New Mexico Community
College
Small Business Development Center
921 Paseo De Onate
Espanola, New Mexico 87532
Phone: (505)747-2236
Fax: (505)757-2234
Ralph Prather, Director

San Juan College
Small Business Development Center
4601 College Blvd.
Farmington, New Mexico 87402
Phone: (505)599-0528
Fax: (505)599-0385
Cal Tingey, Director

University of New Mexico at Gallup
Small Business Development Center
103 W. Hwy. 66
PO Box 1395
Gallup, New Mexico 87301
Phone: (505)722-2220
Fax: (505)863-6006
Elsie Sanchez, Director

New Mexico State University at
Grants
Small Business Development Center
709 E. Roosevelt Ave.
Grants, New Mexico 87020
Phone: (505)287-8221
Fax: (505)287-2125
Clemente Sanchez, Director

New Mexico Junior College
Small Business Development Center
5317 Lovington Hwy.
Hobbs, New Mexico 88240
Phone: (505)392-5614
Fax: (505)392-2594
Don Leach, Director

Dona Ana Branch Community
College
Small Business Development Center
3400 S. Espina St.
Dept. 3DA, Box 30001
Las Cruces, New Mexico 88033-0001
Phone: (505)527-7601
Fax: (505)527-7515
Terry Sullivan, Director

Luna Vocational-Technical Institute
Small Business Development Center
Camp Luna Site
Hot Springs BLVD

PO Box 1510
Las Vegas, New Mexico 87701
Phone: (505)454-2595
Fax: (505)454-2518
Don Bustos, Director

University of New Mexico at Los
Alamos
Small Business Development Center
901 18th St., No. 11800
PO Box 715
Los Alamos, New Mexico 87544
Phone: (505)662-0001
Fax: (505)662-0099
Kevin Holsapple, Director

University of New Mexico at
Valencia
Small Business Development Center
280 La Entrada
Los Lunas, New Mexico 87031
Phone: (505)925-8980
Fax: (505)925-8981
David Ashley, Director
E-mail: dashley@unm.edu

Eastern New Mexico University at
Roswell
Small Business Development Center
57 University Ave.
PO Box 6000
Roswell, New Mexico 88201-6000
Phone: (505)624-7133
Fax: (505)624-7132
Eugene D. Simmons, Director

Santa Fe Community College
New Mexico SBDC
6401 Richards Ave.
Santa Fe, New Mexico 87502
Phone: (505)438-1343
Free: (800)281-SBDC
Fax: (505)428-1469
Roy Miller, State Director
Monica Montoya, Dir.
E-mail: rmiller@santa=fe.cc.nm.us

Western New Mexico University
Small Business Development Center
PO Box 2672
Silver City, New Mexico 88062
Phone: (505)538-6320
Fax: (505)538-6341
Harry Paxton, Assistant Director

Mesa Technical College
Small Business Development Center

911 S. 10th St.
PO Box 1143
Tucumcari, New Mexico 88401
Phone: (505)461-4413
Fax: (505)461-1901
Carl Rainey, Director

New York

State University of New York at
Albany
Small Business Development Center
Draper Hall, Rm. 107
135 Western Ave.
Albany, New York 12222
Phone: (518)442-5577
Fax: (518)442-5582
Peter George III, Director

State University of New York (Suny)
New York SBDC
E-mail: kingjl@cc.sunycentral.edu
Suny Plaza, S-523
Albany, New York 12246
Phone: (518)443-5398
Free: (800)732-SBDC
Fax: (518)465-4992
James L. King, State Director
E-mail: kingj1@cc.sunycentral.edu

Binghamton University
Small Business Development Center
E-mail: sbdcbu@spectra.net
PO Box 6000
Binghamton, New York 13902-6000
Phone: (607)777-4024
Fax: (607)777-4029
Joanne Bauman, Director
E-mail: sbdcbu@spectra.net

State University of New York
Small Business Development Center
74 N. Main St.
Brockport, New York 14420
Phone: (716)637-6660
Fax: (716)637-2102
Wilfred Bordeau, Director

Bronx Community College
Small Business Development Center
McCracken Hall, Rm. 14
W. 181st St. & University Ave.
Bronx, New York 10453
Phone: (718)563-3570
Fax: (718)563-3572
Eugene Williams, Director

Bronx Outreach Center
Con Edison
SBDC
Con Edison
560 Cortlandt Ave.
Bronx, New York 10451
Phone: (718)563-9204
David Bradley

Downtown Brooklyn Outreach Center
Kingsborough Community College
SBDC
395 Flatbush Ave., Extension Rm.
413
Brooklyn, New York 11201
Phone: (718)260-9783
Fax: (718)260-9797
Stuart Harker, Associate Director

Kingsborough Community College
Small Business Development Center
2001 Oriental Blvd., Bldg. T4, Rm.
4204
Manhattan Beach
Brooklyn, New York 11235
Phone: (718)368-4619
Fax: (718)368-4629
Edward O'Brien, Dir.

State University of New York at
Buffalo
Small Business Development Center
Bacon Hall 117
1300 Elmwood Ave.
Buffalo, New York 14222
Phone: (716)878-4030
Fax: (716)878-4067
Susan McCartney, Director

Canton Outreach Center (SUNY)
Jefferson Community College
SBDC
SUNY Canton
SUNY Canton
Canton, New York 13617
Phone: (315)386-7312
Fax: (315)386-7945

Cobleskill Outreach Center
SBDC
SUNY Cobleskill
Warner Hall, Rm. 218
Cobleskill, New York 12043
Phone: (518)234-5528
Fax: (518)234-5272
Peter Desmond, Business Advisor

Corning Community College
Small Business Development Center
24 Denison Pkwy. W
Corning, New York 14830
Phone: (607)962-9461
Free: (800)358-7171
Fax: (607)936-6642
Bonnie Gestwicki, Director

Mercy College Outreach Center
SBDC
555 Broadway
Dobbs Ferry, New York 10522-1189
Phone: (914)674-7485
Fax: (914)693-4996
Tom Milton, Coordinator

State University of New York at
Farmingdale
Small Business Development Center
Campus Commons Bldg.
2350 Route 110
Farmingdale, New York 11735
Phone: (516)420-2765
Fax: (516)293-5343
Joseph Schwartz, Director

Marist College Outreach Center
Kingston SBDC
Fishkill Extension Center
2600 Rte. 9, Unit 90
Fishkill, New York 12524-2001
Phone: (914)897-2607
Fax: (914)897-4653

Geneseo Outreach Center
SBDC
South Hall, No. 111
1 College Circle
Geneseo, New York 14454-1485
Phone: (716)245-5429
Fax: (716)245-5430
Charles VanArsdale, Director

Geneva Outreach Center
SBDC
122 N. Genesee St.
Geneva, New York 14456
Phone: (315)781-1253
Sandy Bordeau, Administrative
Director

Hempstead Outreach Center
SBDC
269 Fulton Ave.
Hempstead, New York 11550
Phone: (516)564-8672

Fax: (516)481-4938
Lloyd Clarke, Assistant Director

York College/City University of New
York
Small Business Development Center
Science Bldg., Rm. 107
94-50 159th St.
Jamaica, New York 11451
Phone: (718)262-2880
Fax: (718)262-2881
James A. Heyliger

Jamestown Community College
Small Business Development Center
525 Falconer St.
PO Box 20
Jamestown, New York 14702-0020
Phone: (716)665-5754
Free: (800)522-7232
Fax: (716)665-6733
Irene Dobies, Director

Kingston Small Business
Development Center
1 Development Ct.
Kingston, New York 12401
Phone: (914)339-0025
Fax: (914)339-1631
Patricia La Susa, Director

OCC-IBIG
SBDC
115 South St.
Middletown, New York 10940
Phone: (914)341-4771
Fax: (914)341-4921

Baruch College
SBDC
360 Park Ave. S., Rm. 1101
New York, New York 10010
Phone: (212)802-6620
Fax: (212)802-6613
Cheryl Fenton, Director

East Harlem Outreach Center
SBDC
145 E. 116th St., 3rd Fl.
New York, New York 10029
Phone: (212)346-1900
Fax: (212)534-4576
Anthony Sanchez, Coordinator

Harlem Outreach Center
SBDC
163 W. 125th St., Rm. 1307

New York, New York 10027
Phone: (212)346-1900
Fax: (212)534-4576
Anthony Sanchez, Coordinator

Mid-Town Outreach Ctr.
Baruch College
SBDC
360 Park Ave. S. Rm. 1101
New York, New York 10010
Phone: (212)802-6620
Fax: (212)802-6613
Barrie Phillip, Coordinator

Pace University
Small Business Development Center
1 Pace Plz., Rm. W483
New York, New York 10038
Phone: (212)346-1900
Fax: (212)346-1613
Ira Davidson, Director

KNEC Office
SBDC
62 Grand St.
Newburgh, New York 12550
Phone: (914)569-1680
Fax: (914)569-1630

Niagara Falls Satellite Office
SBDC
Carborundum Center
345 3rd St.
Niagara Falls, New York 14303-1117
Phone: (716)285-4793
Fax: (716)285-4797

SUNY at Oswego
Operation Oswego County
SBDC
44 W. Bridge St.
Oswego, New York 13126
Phone: (315)343-1545
Fax: (315)343-1546

Clinton Community College
SBDC
Lake Shore Rd., Rte. 9 S.
136 Clinton Point Dr.
Plattsburgh, New York 12901
Phone: (518)562-4260
Fax: (518)563-9759
Merry Gwynn, Coordinator

Business Center Development
Building
SBDC

3 Neptune Rd.
Poughkeepsie, New York 12601
Phone: (914)463-3714
Fax: (914)462-7215

Suffolk County Community College
Riverhead Outreach Center
SBDC
Orient Bldg., Rm. 132
Riverhead, New York 11901
Phone: (516)369-1409
Fax: (516)369-1507
Al Falkowski, Contact

SUNY at Brockport
SBDC
Temple Bldg.
14 Franklin St., Ste. 200
Rochester, New York 14604
Phone: (716)232-7310
Fax: (716)637-2182

Niagara County Community College
at Sanborn
Small Business Development Center
3111 Saunders Settlement Rd.
Sanborn, New York 14132
Phone: (716)693-1910
Fax: (716)731-3595
Richard Gorko, Director

Long Island University at
Southhampton
SBDC
Southampton Outreach Center
Abney Peak, Montauk Hwy.
Southampton, New York 11968
Phone: (516)287-0059
Fax: (516)287-8287
George Tulmany, Business Advisor

College of Staten Island
SBDC
Bldg 1A, Rm. 211
2800 Victory Blvd.
Staten Island, New York 10314-9806
Phone: (718)982-2560
Fax: (718)982-2323
Dr. Ronald Sheppard, Acting Director

SUNY at Stony Brook
SBDC
Harriman Hall, Rm. 109
Stony Brook, New York 11794-3775
Phone: (516)632-9070
Fax: (516)632-7176
Judith McEvoy, Director

Rockland Community College
Small Business Development Center
145 College Rd.
Suffern, New York 10901-3620
Phone: (914)356-0370
Fax: (914)356-0381
Thomas J. Morley, Director

Onondaga Community College
Small Business Development Center
Excell Bldg., Rm. 108
4969 Onondaga Rd.
Syracuse, New York 13215-1944
Phone: (315)498-6070
Fax: (315)492-3704
Robert Varney, Director

Manufacturing Field Office
SBDC
Rensselaer Technology Park
385 Jordan Rd.
Troy, New York 12180-7602
Phone: (518)286-1014
Fax: (518)286-1006
Bill Brigham, Acting Director

State University Institute of
Technology
Small Business Development Center
PO Box 3050
Utica, New York 13504-3050
Phone: (315)792-7546
Fax: (315)792-7554
David Mallen, Director

SUNY Institute of Technology at
Utica/Rome
SBDC
P.O. Box 3050
Utica, New York 13504-3050
Phone: (315)792-7546
Fax: (315)792-7554
David Mallen, Director

Jefferson Community College
Small Business Development Center
Coffeen St.
Watertown, New York 13601
Phone: (315)782-9262
Fax: (315)782-0901
John F. Tanner, Director

SBDC Outreach Small Business
Resource Center
222 Bloomingdale Rd., 3rd Fl.
White Plains, New York 10605-1500
Phone: (914)644-4116

Fax: (914)644-2184
Marie Circosta, Coordinator

North Carolina

WCU Sub-Center at Asheville
SBDC
Wachovia Bank Bldg.
Hamwood St.
PO Box 2510
Asheville, North Carolina 28802
Phone: (828)251-6025
Fax: (828)251-6025
Sandra Trivett, Assistant Director

Appalachian State University
Northwest Region
Small Business and Technology
Development Center
Walker College of Business
2125 Raley Hall
Boone, North Carolina 28608
Phone: (828)262-2492
Fax: (828)262-2027
Bill Parrish, Director

University of North Carolina at
Chapel Hill
Central Carolina Regional Small
Business Development Center
608 Airport Rd., Ste. B
Chapel Hill, North Carolina 27514
Phone: (919)962-0389
Fax: (919)962-3291
Ron Iliwitic, Director

University of North Carolina at
Charlotte
Small Business and Technology
Development Center (Southern
Piedmont Region)
The Ben Craig Center
8701 Mallard Creek Rd.
Charlotte, North Carolina 28262
Phone: (704)548-1090
Fax: (704)548-9050
George McAllister, Director

Western Carolina University Western
Region
Small Business and Technology
Development Center
Center for Improving Mountain
Living
Bird Bldg.
Cullowhee, North Carolina 28723

Phone: (828)227-7494
Fax: (828)227-7422
Allan Steinburg, Director

Elizabeth City State University
Small Business and Technology
Development Center (Northeastern
Region)
1704 Weeksville Rd.
PO Box 874
Elizabeth City, North Carolina 27909
Phone: (252)335-3247
Fax: (252)335-3648
Mr. Wauna Dooms, Director

Fayetteville State University
Cape Fear Small Business and
Technology Development Center
Continuing Education Center
PO Box 1334
Fayetteville, North Carolina 28302
Phone: (910)486-1727
Fax: (910)486-1949
Dr. Sid Gautam, Director

North Carolina A&T State University
Northern Piedmont Small Business
and Technology Development Center
(Eastern Region)
C. H. Moore Agricultural Research
Center
1601 E. Market St.
PO Box D-22
Greensboro, North Carolina 27411
Phone: (336)334-7005
Fax: (336)334-7073
Cynthia Clemons, Director

East Carolina University Eastern
Region
Small Business and Technology
Development Center
Willis Bldg.
300 E 1st St.
Greenville, North Carolina 27858-
4353
Phone: (252)328-6157
Fax: (252)328-6992
Walter Fitts, Director

ASU Sub Center at Hickory
SBTDC
514 Hwy. 321 NW, Ste. A
Hickory, North Carolina 28601-4738
Phone: (828)345-1110

Fax: (828)326-9117
Mr. Blair Abee, Assistant Director

Pembroke State University
SBDC
PO Box 1510
Pembroke, North Carolina 28372-
1510
Phone: (910)521-6611
Fax: (910)521-6550
Ms. Cammie Flurry, Assistant
Director

North Carolina SBTDC
SBDC
333 Fayette St. Mall, Ste. 1150
Raleigh, North Carolina 27601
Phone: (919)715-7272
Fax: (919)715-7777
Scott R. Daugherty, Executive
Director

North Carolina State University
Capital Region
SBTDC
MCI Small Business Resource Center
800 1/2 S. Salisbury St.
Raleigh, North Carolina 27601
Phone: (919)715-0520
Fax: (919)715-0518
Mike Seibert, Director

North Carolina Wesleyan College
SBTDC
3400 N. Wesleyan Blvd.
Rocky Mount, North Carolina 27804
Phone: (252)985-5130
Fax: (252)977-3701
Mr. Chris Johnson

University of North Carolina at
Wilmington
Southeastern Region
SBTDC
601 S. College Rd.
Wilmington, North Carolina 28403
Phone: (910)395-3744
Fax: (910)350-3014
Dr. Warren Guiko, Acting Dir.

University of North Carolina at
Wilmington
Small Business and Technology
Development Center (Southeast
Region)
601 S. College Rd.
Cameron Hall, Rm. 131

Wilmington, North Carolina 28403
Phone: (910)962-3744
Fax: (910)962-3014
Dr. Warren Gulko, Director

Winston-Salem State University
Northwestern Piedmont Region Small
Business Center
PO Box 19486
Winston Salem, North Carolina
27110
Phone: (336)750-2030
Fax: (336)750-2031
Dr. Tony Johnson, Director

North Dakota

Bismarck Regional Small Business
Development Center
400 E Broadway, Ste. 416
Bismarck, North Dakota 58502
Phone: (701)323-8583
Fax: (701)250-4799
Jan M. Peterson, Regional Director

Devils Lake Outreach Center
SBDC
417 5th St.
Devils Lake, North Dakota 58301
Free: (800)445-7232
Gordon Synder, Regional Director

Dickinson Regional Small Business
Development Center
Small Business Development Center
314 3rd Ave. W
Drawer L
Dickinson, North Dakota 58602
Phone: (701)227-2096
Fax: (701)225-5116
Bryan Vendsel, Regional Director

Fargo Regional SBDC
SBDC
657 Second Ave. N, Rm. 219
PO Box 1309
Fargo, North Dakota 58108-1309
Phone: (701)237-0986
Free: (800)698-5726
Fax: (701)237-9734
Jon Grinager, Regional Director

Procurement Assistance Center
Fargo Regional Small Business
Development Center
657 2nd Ave. N, Rm. 219
PO Box 1309

Fargo, North Dakota 58107-1309
Phone: (701)237-9678
Fax: (701)237-9734
Jon Grinager, Regional Manager

Grafton Outreach Center
Red River Regional Planning Council
SBDC
PO Box 633
Grafton, North Dakota 58237
Free: (800)445-7232
Gordon Snyder, Regional Director

Grand Forks Regional Small Business
Development Center
202 N. 3rd St., Ste. 200
The Hemmp Center
Grand Forks, North Dakota 58203
Phone: (701)772-8502
Fax: (701)772-9238
Gordon Snyder, Regional Director

University of North Dakota
North Dakota SBDC
118 Gamble Hall
University Station, Box 7308
Grand Forks, North Dakota 58202-7308
Phone: (701)777-3700
Fax: (701)777-3225
Walter "Wally" Kearns, State
Director

Jamestown Outreach Center
North Dakota Small Business
Development Center
210 10th St. SE
PO Box 1530
Jamestown, North Dakota 58402
Phone: (701)252-9243
Fax: (701)251-2488
Jon Grinager, Regional Director

Minot Regional Small Business
Development Center
SBDC
900 N. Broadway, Ste. 300
Minot, North Dakota 58703
Phone: (701)852-8861
Fax: (701)858-3831
Brian Argabright, Regional Director

Williston Outreach Center
SBDC
Tri-County Economic Development
PO Box 2047
Williston, North Dakota 58801

Free: (800)445-7232
Bryan Vendsel, Regional Director

Ohio

Akron Regional Development Board
Small Business Development Center
1 Cascade Plz., 8th Fl.
Akron, Ohio 44308-1192
Phone: (330)379-3170
Fax: (330)379-3164
Charles Smith, Director
E-mail: smith@ardb.org

Western Reserve Business Center for
Women
The University of Akron
SBDC
Polsky Bldg M-185V
Akron, Ohio 44325-6002
Phone: (330)972-5592
Fax: (330)9725573
Karen Franks, Director
E-mail: dkf@uakron.edu

Women's Entrepreneurial Growth
Organization
Small Business Development Center
The University of Akron
Buckingham Bldg., Rm. 55
PO Box 544
Akron, Ohio 44309
Phone: (330)972-5179
Fax: (330)972-5513
Dr. Penny Marquette, Exec. Dir.

Women's Network
SBDC
1540 West Market St., Ste. 100
Akron, Ohio 44313
Phone: (330)864-5636
Fax: (330)884-6526
Marlene Miller, Dir.

Enterprise Development Corp.
SBDC
900 E. State St.
Athens, Ohio 45701
Phone: (614)592-1188
Fax: (614)593-8283
Karen Patton, Dir.

Southeastern Ohio
Small Business Development Center
Ohio University
Enterprise & Technical Bldg., Rm.
155

20 East Circle Dr.
Athens, Ohio 45701
Phone: (740)593-1797
Fax: (740)593-1795
Debra McBride, Director
E-mail: 99428@seorf.ohiou.edu

Bowling Green State University
Training Center
Wood County SBDC
WSOS Community Action
Commission, Inc.
40 College Park
PO Box 539
Bowling Green, Ohio 43403
Phone: (419)372-9536
Fax: (419)372-8667
Pat Fligor, Director
E-mail: fligor@bgnet.bgsu.edu

Geauga County SBDC
Kent State University/Geauga
Campus
14111 Claridon-Troy Rd.
Burton, Ohio 44021
Phone: (440)834-4187
Fax: (440)834-8846
Jayne Kracker, Director
E-mail: jkracker@geauga.kent.edu

Kent State University/Stark Campus
SBDC
6000 Frank Ave., NW
Canton, Ohio 44720
Phone: (330)499-9600
Fax: (330)494-6121
Annette Chunko, Coordinator
E-mail: achunko@stark.kent.edu

Women's Business Development
Center
SBDC
2400 Cleveland Ae., NW
Canton, Ohio 44709
Phone: (330)453-3867
Fax: (330)773-2992

Wright State University—Lake
Campus
Small Business Development Center
West Central Office
7600 State Rte. 703
Celina, Ohio 45882
Phone: (419)586-0355
Free: (800)237-1477
Fax: (419)586-0358

Dr. Tom Knapke, Director
E-mail: tknapke@lake.wright.edu

Clermont County Chamber of
Commerce
Clermont County Area SBDC
E-mail: ccclink@aol.com
4440 Glen Este-Withamsville Rd.
Cincinnati, Ohio 45245
Phone: (513)753-7141
Fax: (513)753-7146
Russ Cone, Director

Hamilton County Development
Company
SBDC
1776 Mentor Ave.
Cincinnati, Ohio 45212-3597
Phone: (513)632-8292
Fax: (513)351-0610
Danielle K. Remmy, Director
E-mail: dremmy@hcdc.com

University of Cincinnati
SBDC
1275 Section Rd.
Cincinnati, Ohio 45237-2615
Phone: (513)556-2072
Fax: (513)556-2074
Bill Fioretti, Director
E-mail: bill.fioretti@uc.edu

Greater Cleveland Growth
Association
Small Business Development Center
200 Tower City Center
50 Public Sq.
Cleveland, Ohio 44113-2291
Phone: (216)696-1294
Fax: (216)621-4617
Maria Coyne, Director
E-mail: mcoyne@clevegrowth.com

Northern Ohio Manufacturing
SBDC
Prospect Park Bldg.
4600 Prospect Ave.
Cleveland, Ohio 44103-4314
Phone: (216)432-5300
Fax: (216)361-2900
Gretchen Faro, Dir.

Central Ohio Manufacturing
SBDC
1250 Arthur E. Adams Dr.
Columbus, Ohio 43221

Phone: (614)688-5136
Fax: (614)688-5001

Department of Development
Ohio SBDC
77 S. High St., 28th Fl.
Columbus, Ohio 43215-6108
Phone: (614)466-2711
Fax: (614)466-0829
Holly I. Schick, State Director

Greater Columbus Area Chamber of
Commerce
Central Ohio SBDC
37 N. High St.
Columbus, Ohio 43215-3065
Phone: (614)225-6910
Fax: (614)469-8250
Ms. Leslie Weilbacher, Director
E-mail:
leslie_weilbacher@columbus.org

Dayton Area Chamber of Commerce
Small Business Development Center
Chamber Plz.
5th & Main Sts.
Dayton, Ohio 45402-2400
Phone: (937)226-1444
Fax: (937)226-8254
Harry Bumgarner, Director
E-mail: harryb@dacc.org

Wright State University/Dayton
Satellite
SBDC
Center for Small Business Assistance
College of Business
Rike Hall, Rm. 120
Dayton, Ohio 45433
Phone: (937)775-3503
Fax: (937)775-3545
Dr. Mike Bodey, Director
E-mail: mbodey@wright.edu

Maumee Valley Planning
Organization
Northwest SBDC
SBDC
E-mail: nwsbdc@bright.net
197-2-B1 Park Island Ave.
Defiance, Ohio 43512
Phone: (419)782-6270
Fax: (419)782-6273
Don Wright, Director

Northwest Technical College
Small Business Development Center

1935 E. 2nd St., Ste. D
Defiance, Ohio 43512
Phone: (419)784-3777
Fax: (419)782-4649
Don Wright, Dir.

Columbiana County/Salem SBDC
Kent State University/Salem Campus
400 E Fourth St.
East Liverpool, Ohio 43920
Phone: (330)385-3805
Fax: (330)385-6348
Doris Davis, Director
E-mail: ddavis@e14.kenteliv.kent.edu

Terra Community College
North Central Small Business
Development Center
North Central Fremont Office
2830 Napolean Rd.
Fremont, Ohio 43420-9967
Phone: (419)334-8400
Free: (800)825-2431
Fax: (419)334-9414
Bill Auxter, Director
E-mail: bauxter@terra.cc.oh.us

Greater Hamilton Chamber of
Commerce
Greater Hamilton Small Business
Development Center
201 Dayton St.
Hamilton, Ohio 45011
Phone: (513)844-8100
Fax: (513)844-1999
Marilyn J. Collmer, Director
E-mail: marilyn@hamilton-ohio.com

Enterprise Center
Small Business Development Center
129 E. Main St.
PO Box 756
Hillsboro, Ohio 45133
Phone: (937)393-9599
Fax: (937)393-8159
Bill Grunkemeyer, Interim Dir.

Southern State Community College
SBDC
100 Hobart Dr.
Hillsboro, Ohio 45133
Phone: (937)393-3431
Free: (800)628-7722
Fax: (937)393-9370
Roderick Daniels, Director
E-mail: rdaniels@dalco.net

Ashtabula Small Business
Development Center
Growth Partnership for Ashtabula
County
36 W. Walnut St.
Jefferson, Ohio 44047
Phone: (440)576-9134
Fax: (440)576-5003
Stephanie Ward, Director
E-mail: stephward@yahoo.com

Kent - Portage Small Business
Development Center
SBDC
Kent State University
Kent State University
College of Business Administration,
Rm. 300A
Summit and Terrace
Kent, Ohio 44242
Phone: (330)672-2772
Fax: (330)672-9338
Linda Yost, Director
E-mail: lyost@bsa3.kent.edu

EMTEC/Southern Area
Manufacturing
SBDC
3155 Research Park, Ste. 206
Kettering, Ohio 45420
Phone: (513)258-6180
Fax: (513)258-8189
Harry Bumgarner, Dir.

Lake County Small Business
Development Center
SBDC
E-mail: lcedc@ds2.ncweb.com
Lakeland Community College
7750 Clocktower Dr.
Kirtland, Ohio 44094
Phone: (440)951-1290
Fax: (440)951-7336
Cathy Haworth, Director

Lima Technical College
West Central Small Business
Development Center
West Central Office
545 W. Market St., Ste. 305
Lima, Ohio 45801-4717
Phone: (419)228-5320
Fax: (419)229-5424
Gerald J. Biedenharn, Director
E-mail: biedenhj@worcnet.gen.oh.us

Lorain County Chamber of
Commerce
SBDC
6100 S. Boadway
Lorain, Ohio 44053
Phone: (440)233-6500
Fax: (440)246-4050
Dennis Jones, Director
E-mail: djones@lorcham.org

Mid-Ohio Small Business
Development Center
Mansfield - Richland Businesss
Incubator
E-mail: mosbdc@richnet.net
246 E. 5th St., Ste 200
PO Box 1208
Mansfield, Ohio 44901
Phone: (419)521-2655
Free: (800)366-7232
Fax: (419)522-6811
Barbara Harmony, Director

Marietta College
SBDC
213 Fourth St., 2nd Fl.
Marietta, Ohio 45750
Phone: (740)376-4832
Free: (800)789-7232
Fax: (740)376-4832
Pamela Lankford, Director
E-mail: lankforp@mcnet.marietta.edu

Marion Area Chamber of Commerce
Heart of Ohio SBDC
206 S. Prospect St.
Marion, Ohio 43302
Phone: (740)387-0188
Fax: (740)387-7722
Catherine Gaines, Director

Mid-Miami Valley SBDC
36 City Centre Plaza
Middletown, Ohio 45042
Phone: (513)422-4551
Fax: (513)422-6831
Dave Daugherty, Director
E-mail: david75bsu@aol.com

Tuscarawas SBDC
Kent State University
300 University Dr., NE
New Philadelphia, Ohio 44663-9447
Phone: (330)339-3391
Fax: (330)339-2637

Patricia Cowanitz, Director
E-mail: pcowan@tusc.kent.edu

Miami University
Small Business Development Center
Department of Decision Sciences
336 Upham Hall
Oxford, Ohio 45056
Phone: (513)529-4841
Fax: (513)529-1469
Dr. Michael Broida, Dir.

Upper Valley Joint Vocational School
Small Business Development Center
8811 Career Dr.
N. Country Rd., 26A
Piqua, Ohio 45356
Phone: (937)778-8419
Free: (800)589-6963
Fax: (937)778-9237
Stephen Michaels, Co-Director

Enterprise Development Corporation
SBDC
E-mail: edc2@eurekanet.com
9030 Hocking Hills Dr.
The Plains, Ohio 45780
Phone: (740)797-9646
Free: (800)822-6096
Fax: (614)797-9659
Jackie LeBerth, Coordinator

Ohio Valley Minority Business
Association
SBDC
1208 Waller St.
P.O. Box 847
Portsmouth, Ohio 45662
Phone: (614)353-8395
Fax: (614)353-3695
Clemmy Womack, Dir.

Department of Development
CIC of Belmont County
Small Business Development Center
100 E. Main St.
St. Clairsville, Ohio 43950
Phone: (614)695-9678
Fax: (614)695-1536
Mike Campbell, Dir.

Kent State University/Salem Campus
Columbiana SBDC
2491 State Rte. 45 S.
Salem, Ohio 44460
Phone: (330)332-0361
Free: (800)385-5150

Fax: (330)332-9256
Doris Davis, Director

Lawrence County Chamber of
Commerce
Southeast Small Business
Development Center
E-mail: sesbdc@zoomnet.net
216 Collins Ave.
PO Box 488
South Point, Ohio 45680
Phone: (740)377-4550
Free: (800)408-1334
Fax: (740)377-2091
Amber Wilson, Director

Springfield Small Business
Development Center
300 E. Auburn Ave.
Springfield, Ohio 45505
Phone: (937)322-7821
Fax: (937)322-7874
William Ray, Director
E-mail: billray@smbusdev.org

Jefferson County Small Business
Development Center
E-mail: chamber@clover.net
Greater Steubenville Chamber of
Commerce
630 Market St.
PO Box 278
Steubenville, Ohio 43952
Phone: (740)282-6226
Fax: (740)282-6285
Tim McFadden, Director

Toledo Small Business Development
Center
Toledo Chamber of Commerce
300 Madison Ave., Ste. 200
Toledo, Ohio 43604-1575
Phone: (419)243-8191
Fax: (419)241-8302
Wendy Gramza, Director
E-mail:
wgramza@toledochamber.com

Youngstown/Warren SBDC Satellite
Youngstown/Warren Regional Center
E-mail: ccsbdc@cc.ysu.edu
Region Chamber of Commerce
180 E. Market St., Ste. 225
Warren, Ohio 44482
Phone: (330)746-3350
Fax: (330)392-6040
Jim Rowlands, Counselor

Youngstown State University
SBDC
Cushwa Center for Industrial
Development
1 University Plaza
Youngstown, Ohio 44555
Phone: (330)746-3350
Fax: (330)746-3324
Patricia Veisz, Director
E-mail: pkveisz@cc.ysu.edu

Zanesville Area Chamber of
Commerce
Mid-East Small Business
Development Center
205 N. 5th St.
Zanesville, Ohio 43701
Phone: (740)452-4868
Fax: (740)454-2963
Bonnie J. Winnett, Director
E-mail: bwinnett@cyberzane.net

Oklahoma

East Central University
Small Business Development Center
E-mail: osbdcecu@chickasaw.com
1036 E. 10th St.
Ada, Oklahoma 74820
Phone: (580)436-3190
Fax: (580)436-3190
Frank Vater, Director
E-mail: osbdcecu@chickasaw.com

Northwestern Oklahoma State
University
Small Business Development Center
709 Oklahoma Blvd.
Alva, Oklahoma 73717
Phone: (580)327-8608
Fax: (580)327-0560
Guy Forell, Director
E-mail: gvfore@ranger2.nwalva.edu

Southeastern Oklahoma State
University
Oklahoma SBDC
517 University
Station A, Box 2584
Durant, Oklahoma 74701
Phone: (580)924-0277
Free: (800)522-6154
Fax: (580)920-7471
Dr. Grady Pennington, State Director
Claire Livingston, Business

Development Specialist
E-mail: gpennington@sosu.edu

Phillips University
Small Business Development Center
100 S. University Ave.
Enid, Oklahoma 73701
Phone: (580)242-7989
Fax: (580)237-1607
Bill Gregory, Coordinator
E-mail: b9finger@enid.com

Langston University Center
Small Business Development Center
Minority Assistance Center
Hwy. 33 E.
Langston, Oklahoma 73050
Phone: (405)466-3256
Fax: (405)466-2909
Robert Allen, Dir.

AmQuest Bank, N.A.
Small Business Development Center
American National Bank Bldg.
601 SW D Ave., Ste. 209
Lawton, Oklahoma 73501
Phone: (580)248-4946
Fax: (580)248-4946
James C. Elliot, Business
Development Specialist

Northeastern Oklahoma A&M
Miami Satellite
SBDC
Dyer Hall, Rm. 307
215 I St., NE
Miami, Oklahoma 74354
Phone: (918)540-0575
Fax: (918)540-0575
Hugh Simon, Business Development
Specialist

Rose State College
SBDC
Procurement Speciality Center
6420 Southeast 15th St.
Midwest City, Oklahoma 73110
Phone: (405)733-7348
Fax: (405)733-7495
Judy Robbins, Director
Michael Cure, Bus. Dev. Specialist
E-mail: jrobbins@ms.rose.cc.ok.us

University of Central Oklahoma
SBDC
115 Park Ave.
PO Box 1439

Oklahoma City, Oklahoma 73101-1439
Phone: (405)232-1968
Fax: (405)232-1967
Susan Urbach, Director
E-mail: surbach@aix1.ucok.edu

Carl Albert College
Small Business Development Center
1507 S. McKenna
Poteau, Oklahoma 74953
Phone: (918)647-4019
Fax: (918)647-1218
Dean Qualls, Director
E-mail: kqualls@casc.cc.ok.us

Northeastern Oklahoma State University
Small Business Development Center
E-mail: meigs@cherokee.nsuok.edu
Oklahoma Small Business Development Center
Tahlequah, Oklahoma 74464
Phone: (918)458-0802
Fax: (918)458-2105
Danielle Coursey, Business Development Specialist

Tulsa SBDC
Small Business Development Center
State Office Bldg.
616 S. Boston, Ste. 100
Tulsa, Oklahoma 74119
Phone: (918)583-2600
Fax: (918)599-6173
Jeff Horvath, Director
John Maloy, Dir.
E-mail: jeffhorvath@tulsachamber.com

Southwestern Oklahoma State University
Small Business Development Center
E-mail: sbdcswsu@brightok.net
100 Campus Dr.
Weatherford, Oklahoma 73096
Phone: (580)774-1040
Fax: (580)774-7091
Chuck Felz, Director

Oregon

Linn-Benton Community College
Small Business Development Center
6500 S.W. Pacific Blvd.
Albany, Oregon 97321

Phone: (541)917-4923
Fax: (541)917-4445
Dennis Sargent, Director
E-mail: sargend@peak.org

Southern Oregon State College/Ashland
Small Business Development Center
Regional Services Institute
Ashland, Oregon 97520
Phone: (541)482-5838
Fax: (541)482-1115
Liz Shelby, Dir.

Central Oregon Community College
Small Business Development Center
2600 NW College Way
Bend, Oregon 97701
Phone: (541)383-7290
Fax: (541)383-3445
Bob Newhart, Director
E-mail: robert_newhart@cocc.edu

Southwestern Oregon Community College
Small Business Development Center
2110 Newmark Ave.
Coos Bay, Oregon 97420
Phone: (541)888-7100
Fax: (541)888-7113
Jon Richards, Director
E-mail: jrichards@class.orednet.org

Columbia Gorge Community College SBDC
400 E. Scenic Dr., Ste. 257
The Dalles, Oregon 97058
Phone: (541)298-3118
Fax: (503)298-3119
Mr. Bob Cole, Director
E-mail: bcole@cgcc.cc.or.us

Lane Community College
Oregon SBDC
44 W. Broadway, Ste. 501
Eugene, Oregon 97401-3021
Phone: (541)726-2250
Fax: (541)345-6006
Dr. Edward Cutler, State Director
E-mail: cutlers@lanecc.edu

Lane Community College SBDC
1059 Williamette St.
Eugene, Oregon 97401
Phone: (541)726-2255
Fax: (541)686-0096

Jane Scheidecker, Director
E-mail: scheideckerj@lanecc.edu

Rogue Community College
Small Business Development Center
214 SW 4th St.
Grants Pass, Oregon 97526
Phone: (541)471-3515
Fax: (541)471-3589
Paul Mallonee, Director
E-mail: pmallonee@rogue.cc.or.us

Mount Hood Community College
Small Business Development Center
323 NE Roberts St.
Gresham, Oregon 97030
Phone: (503)667-7658
Fax: (503)666-1140
Don King, Director
E-mail: donking@teleport.com

Oregon Institute of Technology
Small Business Development Center
3201 Campus Dr. S. 314
Klamath Falls, Oregon 97601
Phone: (541)885-1760
Fax: (541)885-1855
Jamie Albert, Director
E-mail: albertj@oit.edu

Eastern Oregon State College
Small Business Development Center
Regional Services Institute
1410 L Ave.
La Grande, Oregon 97850
Phone: (541)962-3391
Free: (800)452-8639
Fax: (541)962-3369
Steve Turner, Director
E-mail: sturner@eou.edu

Oregon Coast Community College
Small Business Development Center
4157 NW Hwy. 101, Ste. 123
PO Box 419
Lincoln City, Oregon 97367
Phone: (541)994-4166
Fax: (541)996-4958
Guy Faust, Director
E-mail: guyfaust@hotmail.com

Southern Oregon State University/Medford
Small Business Development Center
Regional Services Institute
332 W. 6th St.
Medford, Oregon 97501

Phone: (541)772-3478
Fax: (541)734-4813
Liz Shelby, Director
E-mail: shelby@wpo.sosc.osshe.edu

Clackamas Community College
Small Business Development Center
7616 SE Harmony Rd.
Milwaukee, Oregon 97222
Phone: (503)656-4447
Fax: (503)652-0389
Jan Stennick, Director
E-mail: jans@clackamas.cc.or.us

Treasure Valley Community College
Small Business Development Center
650 College Blvd.
Ontario, Oregon 97914
Phone: (541)889-6493
Fax: (541)881-2743
Kathy Simko, Director
E-mail:
simko@mailman.tvcc.cc.or.us

Treasure Valley Community College
SBDC
650 College Blvd.
Ontario, Oregon 97914
Phone: (541)889-6493

Blue Mountain Community College
Small Business Development Center
37 SE Dorion
Pendleton, Oregon 97801
Phone: (541)276-6233
Fax: (541)276-6819
John Fletcher, Director
E-mail: jfletcher@bmcc.cc.or.us

Portland Community College
Small Business Development Center
2701 N.W. Vaughn St., No. 499
Portland, Oregon 97210
Phone: (503)978-5080
Fax: (503)222-2570
Tom Niland, Director
E-mail: tniland@pcc.edu

Portland Community College
Small Business International Trade
Program
121 SW Salmon St., Ste. 300
Portland, Oregon 97204
Phone: (503)274-7482
Fax: (503)228-6350
Tom Niland, Director
E-mail: tniland@pcc.edu

Umpqua Community College
Small Business Development Center
744 SE Rose
Roseburg, Oregon 97470
Phone: (541)672-2535
Fax: (541)672-3679
Terry Swagerty, Director
E-mail: swagert@rosenet.net

Chemeketa Community College
Small Business Development Center
365 Ferry St. SE
Salem, Oregon 97301
Phone: (503)399-5088
Fax: (503)581-6017
Ms. Jimmie Wilkins, Director
E-mail: jimmiew@chemek.cc.or.us

Clatsop Community College
Small Business Development Center
1761 N. Holladay Dr.
Seaside, Oregon 97138
Phone: (503)738-3347
Fax: (503)738-7843
Jim Entler, Interim Director
E-mail: jentler@teleport.com

Tillamook Bay Community College
Small Business Development Center
401 B Main St.
Tillamook, Oregon 97141
Phone: (503)842-2551
Fax: (503)842-2555
Kathy Wilkes, Director
E-mail: kwilkes@tbcc.cc.or.us

Pennsylvania

Lehigh University
Small Business Development Center
Rauch Business Ctr., No. 37
621 Taylor St.
Bethlehem, Pennsylvania 18015
Phone: (610)758-3980
Fax: (610)758-5205
Dr. Sandra Holsonback, Director

Clarion University of Pennsylvania
Small Business Development Center
Dana Still Bldg., Rm. 102
Clarion, Pennsylvania 16214
Phone: (814)226-2060
Fax: (814)226-2636
Dr. Woodrow Yeaney, Director

Bucks County SBDC Outreach Center
2 E. Court St.
Doylestown, Pennsylvania 18901
Phone: (215)230-7150
Bruce Love, Dir.

Gannon University
Small Business Development Center
AJ Palumbo Academic Center
U. Square
Erie, Pennsylvania 16541
Phone: (814)871-7714
Fax: (814)871-7383
Ernie Post, Director

Kutztown University
Small Business Development Center
2986 N. 2nd St.
Harrisburg, Pennsylvania 17110
Phone: (717)720-4230
Fax: (717)720-4262
Ernie Post, Director

Indiana University of Pennsylvania
SBDC
208 Eberly College of Business
Indiana, Pennsylvania 15705-1071
Phone: (412)357-7915
Fax: (412)357-5985
Dr. Tony Palamone, Director

St. Vincent College
Small Business Development Center
Alfred Hall, 4th Fl.
300 Fraser Purchase Rd.
Latrobe, Pennsylvania 15650
Phone: (412)537-4572
Fax: (412)537-0919
Jack Fabean, Director

Bucknell University
Small Business Development Center
Product Development Specialty
Center
E-mail: sbdc@coral.bucknell.edu
126 Dana Engineering Bldg., 1st Fl.
Lewisburg, Pennsylvania 17837
Phone: (717)524-1249
Fax: (717)524-1768
John Politis, Director

Lock Haven University
SBDC
105 Court House Annex
Lock Haven, Pennsylvania 17745
Phone: (717)893-2589

Fax: (717)893-2588
Dawn Datt, Director

St. Francis College
Small Business Development Center
Business Resource Center
Loretto, Pennsylvania 15940
Phone: (814)472-3200
Fax: (814)472-3202
Edward Huttenhower, Director

LaSalle University
Small Business Development Center
1900 W. Olney Ave.
Box 365
Philadelphia, Pennsylvania 19141
Phone: (215)951-1416
Fax: (215)951-1597
Andrew Lamas, Dir.

Temple University
Small Business Development Center
1510 Cecil B. Moore Ave., 2nd Floor
Philadelphia, Pennsylvania 19121
Phone: (215)204-7282
Fax: (215)204-4554
Gerald Perkins, Director

University Of Pennsylvania
Pennsylvania SBDC
E-mail:
ghiggins@sec1.wharton.upenn.edu
The Wharton School
423 Vance Hall
3733 Spruce St.
Philadelphia, Pennsylvania 19104-6374
Phone: (215)898-1219
Fax: (215)573-2135
Gregory L. Higgins Jr., State Director
Paul Morin, Dir.
E-mail:
ghiggins@sec1.wharton.upenn.edu

Duquesne University
Small Business Development Center
E-mail: duqsbdc@duq.edu
Rockwell Hall, Rm. 10, Concourse
600 Forbes Ave.
Pittsburgh, Pennsylvania 15282
Phone: (412)396-6233
Fax: (412)396-5884
Dr. Mary T. McKinney, Director

University of Pittsburgh
Small Business Development Center
E-mail: sbdc@pitt.edu

The Joseph M. Katz Graduate School
of Business
208 Bellefield Hall
315 S. Bellefield Ave.
Pittsburgh, Pennsylvania 15213
Phone: (412)648-1544
Fax: (412)648-1636
Ann Dugan, Director

University of Scranton
Small Business Development Center
St. Thomas Hall, Rm. 588
Scranton, Pennsylvania 18510-4639
Phone: (717)941-7588
Free: (800)829-7232
Fax: (717)941-4053
Elaine M. Tweedy, Director

Pennsylvania State University
SBDC
117 Technology Center
University Park, Pennsylvania 16827
Phone: (814)865-0427
Fax: (814)865-5909
Donna Holmes, Director

West Chester University
SBDC
319 Anderson Hall
211 Carter Dr.
West Chester, Pennsylvania 19383
Phone: (610)436-2162
Fax: (610)436-2577
Bob Scanlon, Director

Wilkes University
Small Business Development Center
E-mail: sbdc@wilkes1.wilkes.edu
Hollenback Hall
192 S. Franklin St.
Wilkes Barre, Pennsylvania 18766-0001
Phone: (717)831-4340
Free: (800)572-4444
Fax: (717)824-2245
Ruth Hughes, Director

Puerto Rico

Arecibo Regional Center
Inter American University Arecibo
Campus
SBDC
PO Box 4050
Arecibo, Puerto Rico 00614
Phone: (787)878-5475

Fax: (787)880-1624
Wanda Vega Rosado, Regional
Director
E-mail: wanvega@ns.inter.edu

Fajardo Regional Center
Inter American University Fajardo
Campus
SBDC
PO Box 70003
Fajardo, Puerto Rico 00738
Phone: (787)863-2390
Fax: (787)860-3470
Joy C. Vilardi de Camacho, Regional
Director
E-mail: jvilardi@ns.inter.edu

Puerto Rico Small Business
Development Center
Edificio Union Plaza, Ste. 701
416 Ponce de Leon Ave.
Hato Rey, Puerto Rico 00918
Phone: (787)763-6811
Fax: (787)763-4629
Carmen Marti, Executive Director
E-mail: cmarti@ns.inter.edu

San Juan Regional Center
Union Plaza Bldg, Ste. 701
416 Ponce de Leon Ave.
Hato Rey, Puerto Rico 00918
Phone: (787)763-5108
Fax: (787)763-4629
Dr. Mario Sverdlik, Regional Director
E-mail: msverdik@ns.inter.edu

Ponce Regional Center
Inter American University Ponce
Campus
SBDC
Carr. 1, Km. 123.2
Mercedita, Puerto Rico 00715
Phone: (787)284-1912
Fax: (787)841-0103
Carlos Maldonado, Regional Director
E-mail: carmaldo@ns.inter.edu

San German Regional Center
Inter American University San
German Campus
SBDC
PO Box 5100
San German, Puerto Rico 00683
Phone: (787)264-1912
Fax: (787)892-6350
Luis E. Valderrama, Regional

Director
E-mail: lvalderr@ns.inter.edu

Rhode Island

Northern Rhode Island Chamber of
Commerce
SBDC
6 Blackstone Valley Pl., Ste. 105
Lincoln, Rhode Island 02865-1105
Phone: (401)334-1000
Fax: (401)334-1009
Shelia Hoogeboom, Case Manager

E. Bay Small Business Development
Center
Newport County Chamber of
Commerce
45 Valley Rd.
Middletown, Rhode Island 02842-
6377
Phone: (401)849-6900
Fax: (401)849-5848
Samuel Carr, Case Manager

Fishing Community Program Office
SBDC
PO Box 178
Narragansett, Rhode Island 02882
Phone: (401)783-2466
Angela Caporelli, Program Mgr.

South County SBDC
QP/D Industrial Park
35 Belver Ave., Rm. 212
North Kingstown, Rhode Island
02852-7556
Phone: (401)294-1227
Fax: (401)294-6897
Elizabeth Kroll, Case Manager

Bryant College
Small Business Development Center
Greater Providence Chamber of
Commerce
30 Exchange Terrace, 4th Fl.
Providence, Rhode Island 02903-
1793
Phone: (401)831-1330
Fax: (401)274-5410
Erwin Robinson, Program Manager

Enterprise Community Rhode Island
SBDC/BIC
550 Broad St.
Providence, Rhode Island 02905-
1445

Phone: (401)272-1083
Fax: (401)272-1186
Jaime Aguayo, Program Manager

Rhode Island Department of
Transportation
RIDOT/SBDC
Supportive Services Program
2 Capitol Hill, Rm. 106
Providence, Rhode Island 02903-
1111
Phone: (401)277-4576
Fax: (401)277-6168
O.J. Silas, Progam Manager

Bryant College
Rhode Island SBDC
1150 Douglas Pike
Smithfield, Rhode Island 02917-1284
Phone: (401)232-6111
Fax: (401)232-6933
Richard Brussard, State Dir.
Michael Franklin, Financial Mgr.
E-mail: djobling@bryant.edu

Bryant College
Export Assistance Center
SBDC
1150 Douglas Pike
Smithfield, Rhode Island 02917
Phone: (401)232-6407
Fax: (401)232-6416
Raymond Fogarty, Dir.

Entrepreneurship Training Program
Bryant College
SBDC
1150 Douglas Pike
Smithfield, Rhode Island 02917-1284
Phone: (401)232-6115
Fax: (401)232-6933
Cheryl Faria, Assistant Director

Export Assistance Center
SBDC
1150 Douglas Pike
Smithfield, Rhode Island 02917-1284
Phone: (401)232-6407
Fax: (401)232-6416
Raymond Fogarty, Director

NYNEX Telecommunications Center
Bryant College Koffler Technology
Center
1150 Douglas Pke.
Smithfield, Rhode Island 02917-1284
Phone: (401)232-0220

Fax: (401)232-0242
Kate Dolan, Managing Director

Bristol County Chamber of
Commerce
SBDC
P.O. Box 250
Warren, Rhode Island 02885-0250
Phone: (401)245-0750
Fax: (401)245-0110
Samuel Carr, Case Manager

Central Rhode Island Chamber of
Commerce
SBDC
3288 Post Rd.
Warwick, Rhode Island 02886-7151
Phone: (401)732-1100
Fax: (401)732-1107
Mr. Thomas J. Moakley, Case
Manager

South Carolina

University of South Carolina at Aiken
Aiken Small Business Development
Center
E-mail: billie@aiken.sc.edu
School of Business
171 University Pkwy., Ste. 100
Box 9
Aiken, South Carolina 29801
Phone: (803)641-3646
Fax: (803)641-3647
Jackie Moore, Area Manager

University of South Carolina at
Beaufort
Small Business Development Center
800 Carteret St.
Beaufort, South Carolina 29902
Phone: (803)521-4143
Fax: (803)521-4142
Martin Goodman, Area Manager
E-mail: goodman@hargray.com

Clemson University
Small Business Development Center
College of Business and Public
Affairs
425 Sirrine Hall
Box 341392
Clemson, South Carolina 29634-1392
Phone: (864)656-3227
Fax: (864)656-4869
Becky Hobart, Regional Director

Jill Burroughs, Area Mgr.
E-mail: Hobart@clemson.edu

University of South Carolina
College of Business Administration
South Carolina SBDC
Hipp Bldg.
1710 College St.
Columbia, South Carolina 29208
Phone: (803)777-4907
Fax: (803)777-4403
John Lenti, State Director
E-mail: lenti@darla.badm.sc.edu

University of South Carolina
Small Business Development Center
College of Business Administration
Hipp Bldg
1710 College St.
Columbia, South Carolina 29208
Phone: (803)777-5118
Fax: (803)777-4403
James Brazell, Director
Shawn Mewborn, Area Mgr.
E-mail: brazell@darla.badm.sc.edu

Coastal Carolina College
Conway Small Business Development
Center
School of Business Administration
Wall Bldg., Ste. 111
PO Box 261954
Conway, South Carolina 29528-6054
Phone: (803)349-2170
Fax: (803)349-2455
Nancy Robinson, Area Manager
E-mail: robinson@coastal.edu

Florence-Darlington Technical
College
Small Business Development Center
PO Box 100548
Florence, South Carolina 29501-0548
Phone: (803)661-8256
Fax: (803)661-8041
David Raines, Area Manager
E-mail: raines@A1.flo.tec.sc.us

Greenville Manufacturing Field
Office
SBCD
53 E. Antrim Dr.
Greenville, South Carolina 29607
Phone: (803)271-3005

Greenville Small Business
Development Center

SBDC
University Center
216 S. Pleasantburg Dr., Rm. 140
Greenville, South Carolina 29607
Phone: (864)250-8894
Fax: (864)250-8897
Susan Dunlap, Area Manager
E-mail: sdunlap@clemson.edu

Spartanburg Small Business
Development Center
University Center, Rm. 140
216 S Pleasantburg Dr.
Greenville, South Carolina 29607
Phone: (864)250-8894
Fax: (864)250-8897
David Tinsley, Area Manager
E-mail: dtinsle@clemson.edu

Upper Savannah Council of
Government
Small Business Development Center
Exchange Bldg.
222 Phoenix St., Ste. 200
PO Box 1366
Greenwood, South Carolina 29648
Phone: (864)941-8071
Fax: (864)941-8090
George Long, Area Manager
E-mail: Glong@emeraldis.com

University of South Carolina at Hilton
Head
Small Business Development Center
1 College Center Dr.
10 Office Park Rd.
Hilton Head, South Carolina 29928-
7535
Phone: (803)785-3995
Fax: (803)785-3995
Pat Cameron, Consultant
E-mail: cameron@hargray.com

Williamsburg Enterprise Community
SBDC
128 Mill St.
PO Box 428
Kingstree, South Carolina 29556
Phone: (803)354-9070
Fax: (803)354-3252
Nicole Singleton, Area Manager
E-mail: nsinglet@webplanets.com

Charleston SBDC
5900 Core Dr., Ste. 104
North Charleston, South Carolina
29406

Phone: (803)740-6160
Fax: (803)740-1607
Bill R. Pointer, Area Manager
E-mail: pointer@infoave.net

South Carolina State University
Small Business Development Center
School of Business
Algernon Belcher Hall
300 College St.
Campus Box 7176
Orangeburg, South Carolina 29117
Phone: (803)536-8445
Fax: (803)536-8066
John Gadson, Regional Director
Mr. Francis Heape, Area Mgr.
E-mail: Jgadson@scsu.edu

Winthrop University
Winthrop Regional Small Business
Development Center
School of Business Administration
118 Thurmond Bldg.
Rock Hill, South Carolina 29733
Phone: (803)323-2283
Fax: (803)323-4281
Nate Barber, Regional Director
Dianne Hockett, Area Mgr.
E-mail: barbern@winthrop.edu

Spartanburg Chamber of Commerce
Small Business Development Center
105 Pine St.
PO Box 1636
Spartanburg, South Carolina 29304
Phone: (803)594-5080
Fax: (803)594-5055
John Keagle, Area Mgr.

University of South Carolina - Sumter
SBDC
200 Miller Rd.
Sumter, South Carolina 29150-2498
Phone: (803)775-6341
Fax: (803)775-2180
Lee Eron, Consultant
E-mail:
Leron@uscsumter.uscsu.sc.edu

South Dakota

Northeast Region Small Business
Development Center
2201 6th Ave., SE
Box 1985
Aberdeen, South Dakota 57402

Phone: (605)626-2565
Fax: (605)626-2975
Kelly Weaver, Regional Director
E-mail: kweaver@midco.net

Sinte Gleska University
SBDC
PO Box 8
Mission, South Dakota 57555
Phone: (605)856-4039
Fax: (605)856-2011
Shawn Bordeaux, Regional Director
E-mail: shawnb@rosebud.sinte.edu

Pierre Small Business Development
Center
105 S. Euclid, Ste. C
Pierre, South Dakota 57501
Phone: (605)773-5941
Fax: (605)773-5942
Greg Sund, Dir.

Western Region Small Business
Development Center
444 N. Mount Rushmore Rd., Rm.
208
Rapid City, South Dakota 57701
Phone: (605)394-5311
Fax: (605)394-6140
Valerie S. Simpson, Regional
Director
E-mail: vsimpson@silver.sdsmt.edu

Sioux Falls Region
SBDC
405 S. 3rd Ave., Ste. 101
Sioux Falls, South Dakota 57104
Phone: (605)367-5757
Fax: (605)367-5755
Wade Bruin, Regional Director
E-mail: wdruin@aol.com

University of South Dakota
South Dakota SBDC
SBDC
E-mail: sbdc@sundance.usd.edu
School of Business
414 E. Clark
Vermillion, South Dakota 57069-
2390
Phone: (605)677-5287
Fax: (605)677-5427
Steve Tracy Jr., Acting State Director
E-mail: stracy@usd.edu

Watertown Small Business
Development Center
E-mail: sbdc@icontrol.net
124 1st. Ave., N.W.
PO Box 1207
Watertown, South Dakota 57201
Phone: (605)882-5115
Fax: (605)882-5049
Belinda Engelhart, Regional Director

Yankton Small Business
Development Center
SBDC
E-mail: distiii@willinet.net
321 W Third
PO Box 687
Yankton, South Dakota 57078
Phone: (605)665-4408
Fax: (605)665-0303
Troy Grovenburg, Regional Director

Tennessee

Chattanooga State Technical
Community College
SBDC
100 Cherokee Blvd., No. 202
Chattanooga, Tennessee 37405-3878
Phone: (423)752-1774
Fax: (423)752-1925
Donna Marsh, Small Business
Specialist

Southeast Tennessee Development
District
Small Business Development Center
25 Cherokee Blvd.
PO Box 4757
Chattanooga, Tennessee 37405-0757
Phone: (423)266-5781
Fax: (423)267-7705
Sherri E. Bishop, Business Specialist

Austin Peay State University
Small Business Development Center
College of Business
Clarksville, Tennessee 37044
Phone: (615)648-7764
Fax: (615)648-5985
John Volker, Dir.

Cleveland State Community College
Small Business Development Center
Adkisson Dr.
PO Box 3570
Cleveland, Tennessee 37320-3570

Phone: (423)478-6247
Fax: (423)478-6251
Don Green, Director

Small Business Development Center
(Columbia)
Maury County Chamber of
Commerce Bldg.
106 W. 6th St.
PO Box 8069
Columbia, Tennessee 38402-8069
Phone: (615)898-2745
Fax: (615)893-7089
Eugene Osekowsky, Business
Specialist

Tennessee Technological University
SBDC
College of Business Administration
PO Box 5023
Cookeville, Tennessee 38505
Phone: (931)372-3648
Fax: (931)372-6249
Dorothy Vadem, Business Specialist

Dyersburg State Community College
Small Business Development Center
Office of Extension Services
1510 Lake Rd.
Dyersburg, Tennessee 38024-2450
Phone: (901)286-3201
Fax: (901)286-3271
Bob Wylie, Senior Business Specialist

Four Lakes Regional Industrial
Development Authority
SBDC
PO Box 63
Hartsville, Tennessee 37074-0063
Phone: (615)374-3521
Fax: (615)374-4608
Dorothy Vadem, Small Business
Specialist

Jackson State Community College
Small Business Development Center
McWherter Center, Rm. 213
2046 N. Parkway St.
Jackson, Tennessee 38305-3797
Phone: (901)424-5389
Fax: (901)425-2641
David L. Brown, Business Counselor

Lambuth University
SBDC
705 Lambuth Blvd.
Jackson, Tennessee 38301

Phone: (901)425-3326
Fax: (901)425-3327
Phillip Ramsey, SB Specialist

East Tennessee State University
College of Business
SBDC
College of Business
P.O. Box 70698
Johnson City, Tennessee 37614-0625
Phone: (423)439-5630
Fax: (423)439-7080
Bob Justice, Director

Knoxville Area Chamber Partnership
International Trade Center
SBDC
Historic City Hall
601 W. Summit Hill Dr.
Knoxville, Tennessee 37915-2572
Phone: (423)632-2990
Fax: (423)521-6367
Richard Vogler, IT Specialist

Pellissippi State Technical
Community College
Small Business Development Center
601 W. Summit Hill Dr.
601 W. Summit Hill Dr.
Knoxville, Tennessee 37902-2011
Phone: (423)632-2980
Fax: (423)971-4439
Teri Brahams, Director

University of Memphis
International Trade Center
SBDC
320 S. Dudley St.
Memphis, Tennessee 38152-0001
Phone: (901)678-4174
Fax: (901)678-4072
Gene Odom, International Trade
Specialist

University of Memphis
Tennessee SBDC
320 S. Dudley St.
Building 1
Memphis, Tennessee 38104-3206
Phone: (901)678-2500
Fax: (901)678-4072
Dr. Kenneth J. Burns, State Director

University of Memphis
Tennessee Small Business
Development Center
Technology & Energy Services

Memphis, Tennessee 38152-0001
Phone: (901)678-4057
Fax: (901)678-4072
Dr. Paul Jennings, Director

Walters State Community College
Tennessee Small Business
Development Center
500 S. Davy Crockett Pky.
Morristown, Tennessee 37813
Phone: (423)585-2675
Fax: (423)585-2679
Jack Tucker, Dir.
E-mail: jtucker@wscc.cc.tn.us

Middle Tennessee State University
Small Business Development Center
Rutherford County Chamber of
Commerce Bldg.
501 Memorial Blvd.
PO Box 487
Murfreesboro, Tennessee 37129-0001
Phone: (615)898-2745
Fax: (615)893-7089
Patrick Geho, Director

Tennessee State University
Small Business Development Center
College of Business
330 10th Ave. N.
Nashville, Tennessee 37203-3401
Phone: (615)963-7179
Fax: (615)963-7160
Billy E. Lowe, Director

Tennesse Small Business
Development Center
SBDC
1020 Commerce Park Dr.
Technology 2020 Office
Oak Ridge, Tennessee 37830-8026
Phone: (423)483-2668
Fax: (423)220-2030
Dan Collier, Business Specialist

Texas

Abilene Christian University
Small Business Development Center
College of Business Administration
648 E. Hwy. 80
Abilene, Texas 79601
Phone: (915)670-0300
Fax: (915)670-0311
Judy Wilhelm, Director

Sul Ross State University
SBDC
PO Box C-47, Rm. 319
Alpine, Texas 79832
Phone: (915)837-8694
Fax: (915)837-8104
Michael Levine, Director

Alvin Community College
Small Business Development Center
3110 Mustang Rd.
Alvin, Texas 77511-4898
Phone: (713)388-4686
Fax: (713)388-4903
Gina Mattei, Dir.

West Texas A&M University
Small Business Development Center
T. Boone Pickens School of Business
1800 S. Washington, Ste. 209
Amarillo, Texas 79102
Phone: (806)372-5151
Fax: (806)372-5261
Don Taylor, Director

Trinity Valley Community College
Small Business Development Center
500 S. Prairieville
Athens, Texas 75751
Phone: (903)675-7403
Free: (800)335-7232
Fax: (903)675-5199
Judy Loden, Director

Lower Colorado River Authority
Small Business Development Center
Jack Miller Bldg.
Mail Stop M104
3700 Lake Austin Blvd.
PO Box 220
Austin, Texas 78767
Phone: (512)473-3510
Fax: (512)473-3285
Larry Lucero, Director

Lee College
Small Business Development Center
Rundell Hall
PO Box 818
Baytown, Texas 77522-0818
Phone: (281)425-6309
Fax: (713)425-6307
Tommy Hathaway, Director

Lamar University
Small Business Development Center
855 E Florida Ave., Ste. 101

Beaumont, Texas 77705
Phone: (409)880-2367
Fax: (409)880-2201
Gene Arnold, Director

Bonham Satellite
Small Business Development Center
SBDC
Sam Rayburn Library, Bldg. 2
1201 E. 9th St.
Bonham, Texas 75418
Phone: (903)583-7565
Fax: (903)583-6706
Darroll Martin, Coordinator

Blinn College
Small Business Development Center
902 College Ave.
Brenham, Texas 77833
Phone: (409)830-4137
Fax: (409)830-4135
Phillis Nelson, Director

Brazos Valley Small Business
Development Center
Small Business Development Center
4001 E. 29th St., Ste. 175
PO Box 3695
Bryan, Texas 77805-3695
Phone: (409)260-5222
Fax: (409)260-5229
Jim Pillans, Director

Greater Corpus Christi Business
Alliance
Small Business Development Center
1201 N. Shoreline
Corpus Christi, Texas 78403
Phone: (512)881-1857
Fax: (512)882-4256
Rudy Ortiz, Director

Navarro Small Business Development
Center
120 N. 12th St.
Corsicana, Texas 75110
Phone: (903)874-0658
Free: (800)320-7232
Fax: (903)874-4187
Leon Allard, Director

Dallas County Community College
North Texas SBDC
Bill J. Priest Institute for Economic
Development
1402 Corinth St.
Dallas, Texas 75215

Phone: (214)860-5835
Free: (800)350-7232
Fax: (214)860-5813
Elizabeth (Liz) Klimback, Regional
Director

International Assistance Center
SBDC
World Trade Center, Ste. 150
2050 Stemmons Fwy.
PO Box 58299
Dallas, Texas 75258
Phone: (214)747-1300
Free: (800)337-7232
Fax: (214)748-5774
Beth Huddleston, Director

Bill J. Priest Institute for Economic
Development
North Texas-Dallas Small Business
Development Center
1402 Corinth St.
Dallas, Texas 75215
Phone: (214)860-5842
Free: (800)348-7232
Fax: (214)860-5881
Pamela Speraw, Dir.

Technology Assistance Center
SBDC
1402 Corinth St.
Dallas, Texas 75215
Phone: (800)355-7232
Fax: (214)860-5881
Pamela Speraw, Dir.

Texas Center for Government
Contracting and Technology
Assistance
Small Business Development Center
1402 Corinth St.
Dallas, Texas 75215
Phone: (214)860-5841
Free: (800)348-7232
Fax: (214)860-5881
Gerald Chandler, Director

Grayson County College
Small Business Development Center
6101 Grayson Dr.
Denison, Texas 75020
Phone: (903)463-8787
Free: (800)316-7232
Fax: (903)463-5437
Karen Stidham, Director

Denton Satellite Small Business
Development Center
PO Drawer P
Denton, Texas 76201
Phone: (254)380-1849
Fax: (254)382-0040
Carolyn Birkhead, Coordinator

Best Southwest
SBDC
214 S, Main, Ste. 102A
Duncanville, Texas 75116
Phone: (214)709-5878
Free: (800)317-7232
Fax: (214)709-6089
Herb Kamm, Director

Best Southwest Small Business
Development Center
214 S. Main, Ste. 102A
Duncanville, Texas 75116
Phone: (972)709-5878
Free: (800)317-7232
Fax: (972)709-6089
Neil Small, Director

University of Texas—Pan American
Small Business Development Center
1201 W. University Dr., Rm. BA-124
Center for Entrepreneurship &
Economic Development
Edinburg, Texas 78539-2999
Phone: (956)316-2610
Fax: (956)316-2612
Pedro Salazar, Director

El Paso Community College
Small Business Development Center
103 Montana Ave., Ste. 202
El Paso, Texas 79902-3929
Phone: (915)831-4410
Fax: (915)831-4625
Roque R. Segura, Director

Small Business Development Center
for Enterprise Excellence
SBDC
7300 Jack Newell Blvd., S.
Fort Worth, Texas 76118
Phone: (817)272-5930
Fax: (817)272-5952
Jo An Weddle, Director

Tarrant County Junior College
Small Business Development Center
Mary Owen Center, Rm. 163
1500 Houston St.

Ft. Worth, Texas 76102
Phone: (817)871-6028
Fax: (817)871-0031
David Edmonds, Director

North Central Texas College
Small Business Development Center
1525 W. California
Gainesville, Texas 76240
Phone: (254)668-4220
Free: (800)351-7232
Fax: (254)668-6049
Cathy Keeler, Director

Galveston College
Small Business Development Center
4015 Avenue Q
Galveston, Texas 77550
Phone: (409)740-7380
Fax: (409)740-7381
Georgette Peterson, Director

Western Bank and Trust Satellite
SBDC
PO Box 461545
Garland, Texas 75046
Phone: (214)860-5850
Fax: (214)860-5857
Al Salgado, Dir.

Grand Prairie Satellite
SBDC
Chamber of Commerce
900 Conover Dr.
Grand Prairie, Texas 75053
Phone: (214)860-5850
Fax: (214)860-5857
Al Salgado, Dir.

Houston Community College System
Small Business Development Center
10405 Stancliff, Ste. 100
Houston, Texas 77099
Phone: (281)933-7932
Fax: (281)568-3690
Joe Harper, Director

Houston International Trade Center
Small Business Development Center
1100 Louisiana, Ste. 500
Houston, Texas 77002
Phone: (713)752-8404
Fax: (713)756-1515
Mr. Carlos Lopez, Director

North Harris Montgomery County
College District

Small Business Development Center
250 N. Sam Houston Pkwy. E.
Houston, Texas 77060
Phone: (281)260-3174
Fax: (281)260-3162
Kay Hamilton, Director

University of Houston
Texas Information Procurement
Service
Small Business Development Center
1100 Louisiana, Ste. 500
Houston, Texas 77002
Phone: (713)752-8477
Free: (800)252-7232
Fax: (713)756-1515
Jacqueline Taylor, Director

University of Houston
Texas Manufacturing Assistance
Center (Gulf Coast)
1100 Louisiana, Ste. 500
Houston, Texas 77002
Phone: (713)752-8440
Fax: (713)756-1500
Roy Serpa, Regional Director

University of Houston
Southeastern Texas SBDC
1100 Louisiana, Ste. 500
Houston, Texas 77002
Phone: (713)752-8444
Fax: (713)756-1500
J.E. "Ted" Cadou, Reg. Dir.
Dr. Elizabeth J. Gatewood, Exec. Dir.

Sam Houston State University
Small Business Development Center
843 S. Sam Houston Ave.
PO Box 2058
Huntsville, Texas 77341-2058
Phone: (409)294-3737
Fax: (409)294-3612
Bob Barragan, Director

Kingsville Chamber of Commerce
Small Business Development Center
635 E. King
Kingsville, Texas 78363
Phone: (512)595-5088
Fax: (512)592-0866
Rudy Ortiz, Director

Brazosport College
Small Business Development Center
500 College Dr.
Lake Jackson, Texas 77566

Phone: (409)266-3380
Fax: (409)265-3482
Patricia Leyendecker, Director

Laredo Development Foundation
Small Business Development Center
Division of Business Administration
616 Leal St.
Laredo, Texas 78041
Phone: (210)722-0563
Fax: (210)722-6247
David Puig, Director

Kilgore College
SBDC
Triple Creek Shopping Plaza
110 Triple Creek Dr., Ste. 70
Longview, Texas 75601
Phone: (903)757-5857
Free: (800)338-7232
Fax: (903)753-7920
Brad Bunt, Director

Texas Tech University
Northwestern Texas SBDC
E-mail: odbea@ttacs.ttu.edu
Spectrum Plaza
2579 S. Loop 289, Ste. 114
Lubbock, Texas 79423
Phone: (806)745-3973
Fax: (806)745-6207
Craig Bean, Regional Director
Steve Anderson, Dir.

Angelina Community College
Small Business Development Center
Hwy. 59 S.
PO Box 1768
Lufkin, Texas 75902-1768
Phone: (409)639-1887
Fax: (409)639-3863
Brian McClain, Director

Midlothian SBDC
330 N. 8th St., Ste. 203
Midlothian, Texas 76065-0609
Phone: (214)775-4336
Fax: (214)775-4337

Northeast Texarkana
Small Business Development Center
PO Box 1307
Mt. Pleasant, Texas 75455
Phone: (903)572-1911
Free: (800)357-7232
Fax: (903)572-0598
Bob Wall, Director

University of Texas—Permian Basin
Small Business Development Center
College of Management
4901 E. University Blvd.
Odessa, Texas 79762
Phone: (915)552-2455
Fax: (915)552-2433
Karl Painter III, Director

Paris Junior College
Small Business Development Center
2400 Clarksville St.
Paris, Texas 75460
Phone: (903)784-1802
Fax: (903)784-1801
Pat Bell, Director

Courtyard Center for Professional and
Economic Development
Small Business Development Center
4800 Preston Park Blvd., Ste. A126
Box 15
Plano, Texas 75093
Phone: (972)985-3770
Fax: (972)985-3775
Chris Jones, Director

Angelo State University
Small Business Development Center
2610 West Ave. N.
Campus Box 10910
San Angelo, Texas 76909
Phone: (915)942-2098
Fax: (915)942-2096
Patti Warrington, Director

University of Texas (Downtown San
Antonio)
South Texas Border SBDC
E-mail: rmckinley@utsa.edu
1222 N. Main, Ste. 450
San Antonio, Texas 78212
Phone: (210)458-2450
Fax: (210)458-2464
Robert McKinley, Regional Director
Morrison Woods, Dir.
E-mail: mckinley@utsa.edu

University of Texas at San Antonio
International Trade Center
SBDC
1222 N. Main, Ste. 450
San Antonio, Texas 78212
Phone: (210)458-2470
Fax: (210)458-2464
Sara Jackson, Director

University of Texas at San Antonio
Technology Center
Small Business Development Center
Technology Center
1222 N. Main St., Ste. 450
San Antonio, Texas 78212
Phone: (210)458-2458
Fax: (210)458-2464
Judith Ingalls, Director

Tarleton State University
Small Business Development Center
College of Business Administration
Box T-0650
Stephenville, Texas 76402
Phone: (817)968-9330
Fax: (817)968-9329
Rusty Freed, Director

College of the Mainland
Small Business Development Center
1200 Amburn Rd.
Texas City, Texas 77591
Phone: (409)938-1211
Free: (800)246-7232
Fax: (409)938-7578
Elizabeth Boudreau, Director

Tyler Junior College
Small Business Development Center
1530 South SW Loop 323, Ste. 100
Tyler, Texas 75701
Phone: (903)510-2975
Fax: (903)510-2978
Frank Viso, Director

Middle Rio Grande Development
Council
Small Business Development Center
209 N. Getty St.
Uvalde, Texas 78801
Phone: (210)278-2527
Fax: (210)278-2929
Mario Riojas, Director

University of Houston—Victoria
Small Business Development Center
700 Main Center, Ste. 102
Victoria, Texas 77901
Phone: (512)575-8944
Fax: (512)575-8852
Carole Parks, Director
E-mail: parks@jade.vic.uh.edu

McLennan Community College
Small Business Development Center
401 Franklin

Waco, Texas 76701
Phone: (254)714-0077
Free: (800)349-7232
Fax: (254)714-1668
Lu Billings, Director

LCRA
SBDC
PO Box 148
Wharton, Texas 77488
Phone: (409)532-1007
Fax: (409)532-0056
Allen Maffett, Director

Wharton County Junior College
SBDC
911 Boling Hwy
Administration Bldg, Rm. 102
Wharton, Texas 77488-0080
Phone: (409)532-0604
Fax: (409)532-2410
Mr. Lynn Polson, Director

Midwestern State University
Small Business Development Center
3410 Taft Blvd.
3410 Taft Blvd.
Wichita Falls, Texas 76308
Phone: (817)689-4373
Fax: (817)689-4374
Tim Thomas, Director

Utah

Blanding/Moab/Monticello Center
SBDC
639 W 100 South
College of Eastern Utah
Blanding, Utah 84511
Phone: (801)678-2201

Southern Utah University
Small Business Development Center
351 W. Center
Cedar City, Utah 84720
Phone: (435)586-5400
Fax: (435)586-5493
Derek Snow, Regional Director
E-mail: snow@suu.edu

Snow College
Small Business Development Center
345 West 100 North
Ephraim, Utah 84627
Phone: (435)283-7472
Fax: (435)283-6913

Russell Johnson, Regional Director
E-mail: russ.johnson@snow.edu

Utah State University
Small Business Development Center
East Campus Bldg., Rm. 24
Logan, Utah 84322-8330
Phone: (435)797-2277
Fax: (435)797-3317
Franklin C. Prante, Regional Director
E-mail: fprante@ext.usu.edu

Weber State University
Small Business Development Center
School of Business and Economics
Ogden, Utah 84408-3815
Phone: (801)626-7232
Fax: (801)626-7423
Bruce Davis, Regional Director
E-mail: brdavis@weber.edu

Utah Valley State College
Utah Small Business Development
Center
800 West 1200 South
Orem, Utah 84058
Phone: (801)222-8230
Fax: (801)225-1229
Chuck Cozzens, Regional Director
E-mail: cozzench@uvsc.edu

South Eastern Utah AOG
Small Business Development Center
Price Center
Price Center
PO Box 1106
Price, Utah 84501
Phone: (435)637-5444
Fax: (435)637-7336
Dennis Rigby, Regional Director
E-mail:
drigby@seuaognet.seuaog.dst.ut.us

Dixie College
Small Business Development Center
225 South 700 East
St. George, Utah 84770-3876
Phone: (435)652-7751
Fax: (435)652-7870
Jill Ellis, Regional Director
E-mail: ellisj@dixie.edu

Salt Lake Community College
SBDC
1623 S. State St.
Salt Lake City, Utah 84115
Phone: (801)957-3480

Fax: (801)957-3489
Mike Finnerty, State Director
E-mail: finnermi@slcc.edu

Salt Lake Community College
South City Center
SBDC
1623 S. State St.
Salt Lake City, Utah 84115
Phone: (801)957-3480
Fax: (801)957-3489
Pamela Hunt, Regional Director
E-mail: huntpa@slcc.edu

Salt Lake Community College
Sandy SBDC
8811 South 700 East
Sandy, Utah 84070
Phone: (801)255-5878
Fax: (801)255-6393
Barry Bartlett, Regional Director
E-mail: bartleba@slcc.edu

Utah State University Extension
Office
SBDC
1680 W Hwy 40
Vernal, Utah 84078
Phone: (435)789-6100
Fax: (435)789-3916
Mark Holmes, Regional Director
E-mail: markh@ext.usu.edu

Vermont

Brattleboro Development Credit
Corp.
SBDC
E-mail: bdcc@sover.net
72 Cotton Mill Hill
PO Box 1177
Brattleboro, Vermont 05301-1177
Phone: (802)257-7731
Fax: (802)257-0294
William McGrath, Executive Vice
President

Greater Burlington Industrial Corp.
Northwestern Vermont Small
Business Development Center
E-mail: gbic@vermont.org
PO Box 786
Burlington, Vermont 05402-0786
Phone: (802)658-9228
Fax: (802)860-1899
Thomas D. Schroeder, Specialist

Addison County Economic
Development Corp.
SBDC
E-mail: acedc@sover.net
RD4, Box 1309A
Middlebury, Vermont 05753
Phone: (802)388-7953
Fax: (802)388-0119
James B. Stewart, Executive Director

Central Vermont Economic
Development Center
SBDC
E-mail: cvedc@plainfield.bypass.com
PO Box 1439
Montpelier, Vermont 05601-1439
Phone: (802)223-4654
Fax: (802)223-4655
Richard Angney, Executive Director

Lamoille Economic Development
Corp.
SBDC
E-mail: ledc@together.net
Sunset Dr.
P.O. Box 455
Morrisville, Vermont 05661-0455
Phone: (802)888-5640
Fax: (802)888-7612
John Sullivan, Executive Director

Bennington County Industrial Corp.
SBDC
PO Box 357
North Bennington, Vermont 05257-
0357
Phone: (802)442-8975
Fax: (802)442-1101
Lance Matteson, Executive Director
E-mail: lance@bcic.org

Lake Champlain Islands Chamber of
Commerce
SBDC
E-mail: ilandfun@together.net
PO Box 213
North Hero, Vermont 05474-0213
Phone: (802)372-5683
Fax: (802)372-3205
Barbara Mooney, Executive Director

Vermont Technical College
Small Business Development Center
PO Box 422
Randolph Center, Vermont 05060-
0422

Phone: (802)728-9101
Free: (800)464-7232
Fax: (802)728-3026
Donald L. Kelpinski, State Director
E-mail: dkelpins@vtc.vsc.edu

Rutland Economic Development
Corp.
Southwestern Vermont Small
Business Development Center
256 N. Main St.
Rutland, Vermont 05701-0039
Phone: (802)773-9147
Fax: (802)773-2772
Wendy Wilton, SBDC Specialist
E-mail: wwilton@vtc.vsc.edu

Franklin County Industrial
Development Corp.
SBDC
E-mail: fcidc@together.net
PO Box 1099
St. Albans, Vermont 05478-1099
Phone: (802)524-2194
Fax: (802)524-6793
Timothy J. Soule, Executive Director

Northeastern Vermont Development
Association
Northeastern Vermont Small Business
Development Center
E-mail: nvda@plainfield.bypass.com
44 Main St.
PO Box 630
St. Johnsbury, Vermont 05819-0630
Phone: (802)748-1014
Fax: (802)748-1223
Charles E. Carter, Executive Director
Joseph P. Wynne, SBDC Specialist

Springfield Regional Development
Corp.
Southeastern Vermont Small Business
Development Center
E-mail: srdc@sover.net
PO Box 58
Springfield, Vermont 05156-0058
Phone: (802)885-2071
Fax: (802)885-3027
Steve Casabona, Specialist

Green Mountain Economic
Development Corporation
Central Vermont SBDC
E-mail: gmedc@aol.com
PO Box 246

White River Jct., Vermont 05001-
0246
Phone: (802)295-3710
Fax: (802)295-3779
Jim Saudade, SBDC Specialist
Peter Markou, Executive Dir.

Virgin Islands

University of the Virgin Islands
Small Business Development Center
Sunshine Mall
No.1 Estate Cane, Ste. 104
Frederiksted, Virgin Islands 00840
Phone: (809)692-5270
Fax: (809)692-5629
Chester Williams, State Dir.

University of the Virgin Islands
SBDC
United Shopping Plaza
Ste. 5, Sion Farm
St. Croix, Virgin Islands 00820-4487
Phone: (809)778-8270
Fax: (809)778-7629
Ian Hodge, Director

University of the Virgin Islands
(Charlotte Amalie)
Small Business Development Center
8000 Nisky Center, Ste. 202
St. Thomas, Virgin Islands 00802-
5804
Phone: (809)776-3206
Fax: (809)775-3756
Chester Williams, Director

Virginia

Virginia Highlands SBDC
Rte. 372, off route 140
PO Box 828
Abingdon, Virginia 24212
Phone: (540)676-5615
Fax: (540)628-7576
Jim Tilley, Director
E-mail:
vhtillj%vccscent.bitnet@vtbit.cc.va.edu

Alexandria Small Business
Development Center
Alexandria Graduate Education
Center
1775-B Duke St.
Alexandria, Virginia 22314
Phone: (703)299-9146

Fax: (703)299-0295
Bill Reagan, Director
E-mail: bill@agec.dup.gwu.edu

South Fairfax Business Resource
Center of the Northern VA SBDC
Network
6911 Richmond Hwy, Ste. 290
Alexandria, Virginia 22306
Phone: (703)768-1440
Fax: (703)768-0547
Gwendolyn Reape

Arlington Small Business
Development Center
George Mason University, Arlington
Campus
4001 N. Fairfax Dr., Ste. 400
Arlington, Virginia 22001
Phone: (703)993-8129
Fax: (703)993-8130
Paul Hall, Director

Arlington Small Business
Develpment Center
4001 N Fairfax Dr., Ste. 450
GMU Arlington Campus
Arlington, Virginia 22001
Phone: (703)993-8129
Paul Hall, Director

Virginia Eastern Shore Corp.
SBDC
36076 Lankford Hwy.
PO Box 395
Belle Haven, Virginia 23306
Phone: (757)442-7179
Fax: (757)442-7181
Susan Tyler, Business Analyst

Mountain Empire Community
College
Southwest Small Business
Development Center
Drawer 700, Rte. 23, S.
Big Stone Gap, Virginia 24219
Phone: (540)523-6529
Fax: (540)523-8139
Tim Blankenbecler, Director
E-mail: meblant@me.cc.va.us

Central Virginia Small Business
Development Center
918 Emmet St., N., Ste. 200
Charlottesville, Virginia 22903-4878
Phone: (804)295-8198
Fax: (804)295-7066

Robert A. Hamilton Jr., Director
E-mail:
hamilton@sbdc.acs.virginia.edu

Hampton Roads Chamber of
Commerce
SBDC
400 Volvo Pkwy.
P.O. Box 1776
Chesapeake, Virginia 23320
Phone: (757)664-2590
Fax: (757)548-1835
William J. Holoran Jr., Dir.

George Mason University
Northern Virginia Small Business
Development Center
4031 University Dr., Ste. 200
Fairfax, Virginia 22030-3409
Phone: (703)277-7700
Fax: (703)277-7722
Julie Janoski, Director
E-mail: jjanoski@gmu.edu

Northern Virginia Small Business
Development Center
4301 University Dr., Ste. 200
Fairfax, Virginia 22030
Phone: (703)277-7700
Fax: (703)227-7722
Jody Keenan

Longwood College (Farmville)
Small Business Development Center
515 Main St.
Farmville, Virginia 23909
Phone: (804)395-2086
Fax: (804)395-2359
Gerald L. Hughes Jr., Director
E-mail: jhughes@longwood.lwc.edu

Rappahannock Region Small
Business Development Center
1301 College Ave.
Seacobeck Hall, Rm. 102
Fredericksburg, Virginia 22401
Phone: (540)654-1060
Fax: (540)654-1070
Jeffrey R. Sneddon, Director
E-mail: jsneddon@mwcgw.mwc.edu

Hampton Roads Inc.
Small Business Development Center
525 Butler Farm Rd., Ste. 102
Hampton, Virginia 23666
Phone: (757)825-2957
Fax: (757)825-2960

William J. Holloran Jr., Director
E-mail: bhollara@chespo.hrccva.com

James Madison University
Small Business Development Center
James Madison University College of
Business
Zane Showker Hall, Rm. 527
PO Box MSC 0206
Harrisonburg, Virginia 22807
Phone: (540)568-3227
Fax: (540)568-3106
Karen Wigginton, Director
E-mail: vancesn@jmu.edu

Lynchburg Regional Small Business
Development Center
E-mail: lrsbdc@aol.com
147 Mill Ridge Rd.
Lynchburg, Virginia 24502-4341
Phone: (804)582-6170
Free: (800)876-7232
Fax: (804)582-6169
Barry Lyons, Director

Flory Small Business Development
Center
10311 Sudley Manor Dr.
Manassas, Virginia 20109-2962
Phone: (703)335-2500
Fax: (703)335-1700
Linda Decker, Director
E-mail: florysbdc@aol.com

SBDC Satellite Office of Longwood
P.O. Box 709
115 Broad St.
Martinsville, Virginia 24114
Phone: (540)632-4462
Fax: (540)632-5059
Ken Copeland, Director

Lord Fairfax Community College
SBDC
173 Skirmisher Ln.
PO Box 47
Middletown, Virginia 22645
Phone: (540)869-6649
Fax: (540)868-7002
Robert Crosen, Dir.

Small Business Development Center
of Hampton Roads, Inc. (Norfolk)
420 Bank St.
PO Box 327
Norfolk, Virginia 23501
Phone: (757)664-2528

Fax: (757)622-5563
Warren Snyder, Dir.

Tri-Cities Small Business
Development Center of the Capital
Area SBDC
E-mail: kgbus@sprynet.com
325 Washington St.
Petersburg, Virginia 23804
Phone: (804)643-7232
Kathryn Culbertson, Director

New River Valley
Radford University
SBDC
600-H Norwood St.
PO Box 3726
Radford, Virginia 24141
Phone: (540)831-6056
Fax: (540)831-6057
David O. Shanks, Director
E-mail: dshanks@runet.edu

Southwest Virginia Community
College
Southwest Small Business
Development Center
PO Box SVCC, Rte. 19
Richlands, Virginia 24641
Phone: (540)964-7345
Fax: (540)964-5788
Jim Boyd, Director
E-mail: jim_boyd@sw.cc.va.us

Department of Business Assistance
Virginia SBDC
SBDC
901 E. Byrd St., Ste. 1400
Richmond, Virginia 23219
Phone: (804)371-8253
Fax: (804)225-3384
Bob Wilburn, State Director
E-mail: rwilburn@dba.state.va.us

Department of Economic
Development
SBDC
901 E Byrd St.
Richmond, Virginia 23219-4069
Phone: (804)371-8106

Greater Richmond Small Business
Development Center
E-mail: pwinter@richmond.infi.net
1 N. 5th St., Ste. 510
Richmond, Virginia 23219
Phone: (804)648-7838

Free: (800)646-SBDC
Fax: (804)648-7849
Taylor Cousins, Executive Director

Regional Chamber Small Business
Development Center
Western Virginia SBDC
Mez. Level
212 S. Jefferson St.
Roanoke, Virginia 24011
Phone: (540)983-0717
Fax: (540)983-0723
Doug Murray, Director
E-mail: djmr@roanoke.infi.net

South Boston Small Business
Development Center of Longwood
515 Broad St.
PO Box 1116
South Boston, Virginia 24592
Phone: (804)575-0044
Fax: (804)572-1762
Vincent Decker, Director

Loudoun County Small Business
Development Center
Satellite Office of Northern Virginia
207 E. Holly Ave., Ste. 214
Sterling, Virginia 20164
Phone: (703)430-7222
Fax: (703)430-7258
Ted London, Director
E-mail: tedlongon@aol.com

Northern Virginia Small Business
Development Center
Loudoun Information
SBDC
207 Holly Ave., Ste. 214
Sterling, Virginia 20146
Phone: (703)430-7222
Ted London, Director

Warsaw Small Business Development
Center
Satellite Office of Rappahannock
E-mail: sbdcwarsaw@sylvaninfo.net
5559 W. Richmond Rd.
PO Box 490
Warsaw, Virginia 22572
Phone: (804)333-0286
Free: (800)524-8915
Fax: (804)333-0187
John Clickener, Director

Lord Fairfax Small Business
Development Center
Lord Fairfax Community College
E-mail: lfstevp@lf.cc.va.us
156 Dowell J Circle
Winchester, Virginia 22602
Phone: (540)722-7580
Fax: (540)722-7582
Pamela Stevens, Coordinator

Wytheville Community College
Wytheville Small Business
Development Center
1000 E. Main St.
Wytheville, Virginia 24382
Phone: (540)223-4798
Free: (800)468-1195
Fax: (540)223-4778
Rob Edwards, Director
E-mail: redwards@naxs.com

Washington

Aberdeen/Grays Harbor College
SBDC
1620 Edward P. Smith Dr.
Aberdeen, Washington 98520
Phone: (360)538-4021

Bellevue Small Business
Development Center

Bellevue Community College
3000 Landerholm Circle SE
Bellevue, Washington 98007-6484
Phone: (206)643-2888
Fax: (206)649-3113
Bill Huenefeld, Business
Development Specialist

Western Washington University
Small Business Development Center
College of Business and Economics
308 Parks Hall
Bellingham, Washington 98225-9073
Phone: (360)650-3899
Fax: (360)650-4844
Mr. Lynn Trzynka, Business
Development Specialist

Whatcom Community College
SBDC
237 W Kellogg Rd.
Bellingham, Washington 98226
Phone: (360)676-2170

Centralia Community College
Small Business Development Center
600 W. Locust St.
Centralia, Washington 98036
Phone: (360)736-9391
Fax: (360)753-3404
Don Hayes, Business Development
Specialist

Columbia Basin College—TRIDEC
Small Business Development Center
901 N. Colorado
Kennewick, Washington 99336
Phone: (509)735-6222
Fax: (509)735-6609
Blake Escudier, Business Dev.
Specialist

Edmonds Community College
Small Business Development Center
6600 196th St., SW
Lynnwood, Washington 98036
Phone: (206)640-1435
Fax: (206)640-1532
Jack Wicks, Business Development
Specialist

Big Bend Community College
Small Business Development Center
7662 Chanute St.
Moses Lake, Washington 98837-3299
Phone: (509)762-6306
Fax: (509)762-6329
Ed Baroch, Business Dev. Specialist

Skagit Valley College
Small Business Development Center
2405 College Way
Mount Vernon, Washington 98273
Phone: (360)428-1282
Fax: (360)336-6116
Peter Stroosma, Business
Development Specialist

Wenatchee Valley College
SBDC
PO Box 741
Okanogan, Washington 98840
Phone: (509)826-5107
Fax: (509)826-1812
John Rayburn, Business Dev.
Specialist

South Puget Sound Community
College
Small Business Development Center
721 Columbia St. SW

Olympia, Washington 98501
Phone: (360)753-5616
Fax: (360)586-5493
Douglas Hammel, Business
Development Specialist

Clallam County Economic
Development Center
SBDC
102 E Front St.
PO Box 1085
Port Angeles, Washington 98362
Phone: (360)457-7793

Washington State University
(Pullman)
Small Business Development Center
501 Johnson Tower
PO Box 644851
Pullman, Washington 99164-4851
Phone: (509)335-1576
Fax: (509)335-0949
Carol Riesenberg, Acting State
Director

North Seattle Community College
Small Business Development Center
Small Business Development Center
US Export Assistance Center
2001 6th Ave., Ste. 650
Seattle, Washington 98121
Phone: (206)553-5615
Fax: (206)553-7253
Ann Tamura, IT Specialist

Seattle Small Business Development
Center
180 Nickerson, Ste. 207
Seattle, Washington 98109
Phone: (206)464-5450
Fax: (206)464-6357
Bill Jacobs, Business Development
Specialist

South Seattle Community College
Small Business Development Center
Duwamish Industrial Education
Center
6770 E. Marginal Way S
Seattle, Washington 98108-3405
Phone: (206)764-5375
Fax: (206)764-5838
Ruth Ann Halford, Business
Development Specialist

Washington State University
(Spokane)
Small Business Development Center
665 North Riverpoint Blvd.
Spokane, Washington 99202
Phone: (509)358-7894
Fax: (509)358-7896
Richard Thorpe, Business Dev.
Specialist

Tacoma Small Business Development
Center
950 Pacific Ave., Ste. 300
PO Box 1933
Tacoma, Washington 98401-1933
Phone: (206)272-7232
Fax: (206)597-7305
Neil Delisanti, Business Development
Specialist

Columbia River Economic
Development Council
Small Business Development Center
217 S.E. 136th Ave., Ste. 105
Vancouver, Washington 98660
Phone: (360)260-6372
Fax: (360)260-6369
Janet Harte, Business Dev. Specialist

Port of Walla Walla SBDC
500 Tausick Way
Rte. 4, Box 174
Walla Walla, Washington 99362
Phone: (509)527-4681
Fax: (509)525-3101
Rich Monacelli, Business Dev.
Specialist

Quest Small Business Development
Center
37 S. Wenatchee Ave., Ste. C
Industrial Bldg. 2, Ste. D.
Wenatchee, Washington 98801-2443
Phone: (509)662-8016
Fax: (509)663-0455
Rich Reim, Business Dev. Specialist

Yakima Valley College
Small Business Development Center
PO Box 1647
Yakima, Washington 98907
Phone: (509)454-3608
Fax: (509)454-4155
Audrey Rice, Business Dev.
Specialist

West Virginia

College of West Virginia
SBDC
E-mail: sbdc@cwv.edu
306 S Kenawha St.
PO Box AG
Beckley, West Virginia 25802
Phone: (304)255-4022
Free: (800)766-4556
Fax: (304)252-9584
Deanna Corder, Financial Analyst

West Virginia Development Office
West Virginia SBDC
950 Kanawha Blvd. E., 2nd Floor
Charleston, West Virginia 25301
Phone: (304)558-2960
Free: (888)WVA-SBDC
Fax: (304)348-0127
Dr. Hazel Kroesser-Palmer, State-
Director
E-mail: palmeh@mail.wvnet.edu

Elkins Satellite
SBDC
10 Eleventh St., Ste. 1
Elkins, West Virginia 26241
Phone: (304)637-7205
Fax: (304)637-4902
James Martin, Business Analyst
E-mail: jrjm@access.mountain.net

Fairmont State College
Small Business Development Center
1000 Technology Dr., Ste. 1120
Fairmont, West Virginia 26554
Phone: (304)367-2712
Fax: (304)367-2717
Jack Kirby, Program Manager
E-mail: jrkl@fscvax.wvnet.edu

Marshall University
Small Business Development Center
2000 7th Ave.
Huntington, West Virginia 25703-
1527
Phone: (304)696-6246
Fax: (304)696-6277
Edna McClain, Program Manager
E-mail: emcclain@marshall.edu

West Virginia University
Small Business Development Center
439 B & E Bldg.
PO Box 6025

Morgantown, West Virginia 26506-6025
Phone: (304)293-5839
Fax: (304)293-8905
Sharon Stratton, Business
Development Specialist
E-mail: strahon@wvubel.be.wvu.edu

Southern West Virginia Community
College
SBDC
PO Box 2900
Mount Gay, West Virginia 25637
Phone: (304)792-7098
Fax: (304)792-7056
Larry Salyers, Program Manager
E-mail: larrys@southern.wvnet.edu

West Virginia Institute of Technology
SBDC
912 E Main St.
Oak Hill, West Virginia 25901
Phone: (304)465-1434
Fax: (304)465-8680
James Epling, Program Manager
E-mail: jeepli@wvit.wvnet.edu

West Virginia University
(Parkersburg)
Small Business Development Center
Rte. 5, Box 167-A
Parkersburg, West Virginia 26101
Phone: (304)424-8277
Fax: (304)424-8266
Greg Hill, Program Manager
E-mail: ghill@alpha.wvup.wvnet.edu

Shepherd College
Small Business Development Center
Gardiner Hall
120 N. Princess St.
Shepherdstown, West Virginia 25443
Phone: (304)876-5261
Fax: (304)876-5467
Fred Baer, Program Manager
E-mail: fbaer@shepherd.wvnet.edu

West Virginia Northern Community
College
Small Business Development Center
1701 Market St.
College Sq.
Wheeling, West Virginia 26003
Phone: (304)233-5900
Fax: (304)232-0965
Ron Trevellini, Program Manager
E-mail: rtrevellini@nccvax.wvnet.edu

Wisconsin

University of Wisconsin—Eau Claire
Small Business Development Center
Schneider Hall, Rm. 113
PO Box 4004
Eau Claire, Wisconsin 54702-4004
Phone: (715)836-5811
Fax: (715)836-5263
Kevin Jones, Director

University of Wisconsin—Green Bay
Small Business Development Center
Wood Hall, Rm. 460
2420 Nicolet Dr.
Green Bay, Wisconsin 54311-7001
Phone: (920)465-2089
Fax: (920)465-2552
Jan Thornton, Director
E-mail: thorntoj@uwgb.edu

University of Wisconsin—Parkside
Small Business Development Center
Tallent Hall, Rm. 284
900 Wood Rd.
PO Box 2000
Kenosha, Wisconsin 53141-2000
Phone: (414)595-2620
Fax: (414)595-2513
Patricia Deutsch, Director
E-mail: pduetsch@vm.uwp.edu

University of Wisconsin—La Crosse
Small Business Development Center
North Hall, Rm. 120
1701 Farwell St.
La Crosse, Wisconsin 54601
Phone: (608)785-8782
Fax: (608)785-6919
Jan Gallagher, Director
E-mail: jgallagh@uwlax.edu

University of Wisconsin
Wisconsin SBDC
432 N. Lake St., Rm. 423
Madison, Wisconsin 53706
Phone: (608)263-7794
Fax: (608)262-3878
Erica Kauten, State Director
E-mail: kauten@admin.uwex.edu

University of Wisconsin—Madison
Small Business Development Center
975 University Ave., Rm. 3260
Grainger Hall
Madison, Wisconsin 53706
Phone: (608)263-2221

Fax: (608)263-0818
Neil Lerner, Director
E-mail: jtg@mi.bus.wisc.edu

University of Wisconsin—Milwaukee
Small Business Development Center
161 W. Wisconsin Ave., Ste. 6000
Milwaukee, Wisconsin 53204
Phone: (414)227-3240
Fax: (414)227-3142
Lucy Holifield, Director

University of Wisconsin—Oshkosh
Small Business Development Center
800 Algoma Blvd.
201 Clow Faculty
Oshkosh, Wisconsin 54901
Phone: (920)424-1453
Fax: (920)424-7413
John Mozingo, Director
E-mail:
mozingo@vaxa.cis.uwash.edu

University of Wisconsin at Platteville
SBDC
133 Warner Hall
1 University Plaza
Platteville, Wisconsin 53818
Phone: (608)342-1038
Fax: (608)342-1454
Karen Steindorf, Director

University of Wisconsin Parkside
SBDC
4701 Washington Ave., Ste. 215
Racine, Wisconsin 53406
Phone: (414)638-1713
Fax: (414)638-0250
Joan Larson, Coordinator

University of Wisconsin—Stevens
Point
Small Business Development Center
Old Main Bldg., Rm. 103
2100 Main St.
Stevens Point, Wisconsin 54481
Phone: (715)346-3838
Fax: (715)346-4045
Vicki Lobermeier, Director
E-mail: mstover@uwspmail.uwsp.edu

University of Wisconsin—Superior
Small Business Development Center
1800 Grand Ave.
Superior, Wisconsin 54880-2898
Phone: (715)394-8351
Fax: (715)394-8454

Loren Erickson, Director
E-mail: nhensrud@wpo.uwsuper.edu

University of Wisconsin—
Whitewater
Small Business Development Center
2000 Carlson Bldg.
800 W Main St.
Whitewater, Wisconsin 53190
Phone: (414)472-3217
Fax: (414)472-4863
Carla Lenk, Director
E-mail: lenkc@uwwvax.uww.edu

University of Wisconsin at
Whitewater
Wisconsin Innovation Service Center
SBDC
E-mail: malewicd@uwwvax.uww.edu
416 McCutchen Hall
Whitewater, Wisconsin 53190
Phone: (414)472-1365
Fax: (414)472-1600
Debra Malewicki, Dir.
E-mail: malewicd@uwwvax.uww.edu

Wisconsin Innovation Service Center/
Technology
SBDC
University of Wisconsin at
Whitewater
402 McCutchan Hall
Whitewater, Wisconsin 53190
Phone: (414)472-3217
Fax: (414)472-1600
Debra Malewicki, Director

Wyoming

Casper Small Business Development
Center
Region III
E-mail: sbdc@trib.com
111 W. 2nd St., Ste. 502
Casper, Wyoming 82601
Phone: (307)234-6683
Free: (800)348-5207
Fax: (307)577-7014
Leonard Holler, Regional Director

Cheyenne SBDC
Region IV
E-mail: sewsbdc@wyoming.com
1400 E. College Dr.
Cheyenne, Wyoming 82007-3298
Phone: (307)632-6141

Free: (800)348-5208
Fax: (307)632-6061
Arlene Soto, Regional Director

Region 5 Small Business
Development Center
E-mail: sbdc@vcn.com
222 S Gillette Ave., Ste. 313
Gillette, Wyoming 82716
Phone: (307)682-5232
Free: (888)956-6060
Fax: (307)686-7268
Judith Semple, Regional Director

Wyoming Small Business
Development Center
State Office
University of Wyoming
PO Box 3922
Laramie, Wyoming 82071-3922
Phone: (307)766-3505
Free: (800)348-5194
Fax: (307)766-3406
Diane Wolverton, State Director
E-mail: ddw@uwyo.edu

Northwest Community College
Small Business Development Center
Region II
E-mail: nwwsbdc@wave.park.wy.us
146 South Bent St.
John Dewitt Student Center
Powell, Wyoming 82435
Phone: (307)754-2139
Free: (800)383-0371
Fax: (307)754-0368
Dwane Heintz, Regional Director

Rock Springs Small Business
Development Center
Region I
PO Box 1168
Rock Springs, Wyoming 82902
Phone: (307)352-6894
Free: (800)348-5205
Fax: (307)352-6876
Bill Ellis, Regional Director
E-mail: bellis@uwyo.edu

SERVICE CORPS OF RETIRED EXECUTIVES (SCORE) OFFICES

This section contains a listing of all SCORE offices organized alphabetically by state/U.S. territory name, then by city, then by agency name.

Alabama

SCORE Office (Northeast Alabama)
c/o Chamber of Commerce
1330 Quintard Ave.
Anniston, Alabama 36202
Phone: (256)237-3536

SCORE Office (North Alabama)
1601 11th Ave. S
Birmingham, Alabama 35294-4552
Phone: (205)934-6868
Fax: (205)934-0538

SCORE Office (Baldwin County)
c/o Eastern Shore Chamber of
Commerce
29750 Larry Dee Cawyer Dr.
Daphne, Alabama 36526
Phone: (334)928-5838

SCORE Office (Shoals)
Florence, Alabama 35630
Phone: (256)760-9067

SCORE Office (Mobile)
c/o Mobile Area Chamber of
Commerce
600 S Court St.
Mobile, Alabama 36104
Phone: (334)240-6868
Fax: (334)240-6869

SCORE Office (Alabama Capitol
City)
c/o Montgomery Area Chamber of
Commerce
41 Commerce St.
PO Box 79
Montgomery, Alabama 36101-1114
Phone: (334)270-5637
Fax: (334)265-4745

SCORE Office (East Alabama)
E-mail: score636@hotmail.com

601 Ave. A
Opelika, Alabama 36801
Phone: (334)745-4861

SCORE Office (Tuscaloosa)
2200 University Blvd.
Tuscaloosa, Alabama 35402
Phone: (205)758-7588

Alaska

SCORE Office (Anchorage)
c/o SBA/67
222 W. 8th Ave.
Anchorage, Alaska 99513-7559
Phone: (907)271-4022
Fax: (907)271-4545

Arizona

SCORE Office (Lake Havasu)
10 S. Acoma Blvd.
Lake Havasu City, Arizona 86403
Phone: (520)453-5951

SCORE Office (East Valley)
Federal Bldg., Rm. 104
26 N. MacDonald St.
Mesa, Arizona 85201
Phone: (602)379-3100
Fax: (602)379-3143

SCORE Office (Phoenix)
2828 N. Central Ave., Ste. 800
Central & One Thomas
Phoenix, Arizona 85004
Phone: (602)640-2329
Fax: (602)640-2360

SCORE Office (Prescott Arizona)
1228 Willow Creek Rd., Ste. 2
Prescott, Arizona 86301
Phone: (520)778-7438
Fax: (520)778-0812

SCORE Office (Tucson)
E-mail: score@azstarnet.com
110 E. Pennington St.
Tucson, Arizona 85702
Phone: (520)670-5008
Fax: (520)670-5011

Arkansas

SCORE Office (South Central)
201 N. Jackson Ave.
El Dorado, Arkansas 71730-5803

Phone: (870)863-6113
Fax: (870)863-6115

SCORE Office (Ozark)
Fayetteville, Arkansas 72701
Phone: (501)442-7619

SCORE Office (Northwest Arkansas)
Glenn Haven Dr., No. 4
Ft. Smith, Arkansas 72901
Phone: (501)783-3556

SCORE Office (Garland County)
Grand & Ouachita
PO Box 6012
Hot Springs Village, Arkansas 71902
Phone: (501)321-1700

SCORE Office (Little Rock)
U.S. Small Business Administration
2120 Riverfront Dr., Rm. 100
Little Rock, Arkansas 72202-1747
Phone: (501)324-5893
Fax: (501)324-5199

SCORE Office (Southeast Arkansas)
121 W. 6th
Pine Bluff, Arkansas 71601
Phone: (870)535-7189
Fax: (870)535-1643

California

SCORE Office (Golden Empire)
1706 Chester Ave., 200
Bakersfield, California 93301
Phone: (805)322-5881
Fax: (805)322-5663

SCORE Office (Greater Chico Area)
1324 Mangrove St., Ste. 114
Chico, California 95926
Phone: (916)342-8932
Fax: (916)342-8932

SCORE Office (Concord)
2151-A Salvio St., Ste. B
Concord, California 94520
Phone: (510)685-1181
Fax: (510)685-5623

SCORE Office (Covina)
935 W. Badillo St.
Covina, California 91723
Phone: (818)967-4191
Fax: (818)966-9660

SCORE Office (Rancho Cucamonga)
8280 Utica, Ste. 160
Cucamonga, California 91730
Phone: (909)987-1012
Fax: (909)987-5917

SCORE Office (Culver City)
PO Box 707
Culver City, California 90232-0707
Phone: (310)287-3850
Fax: (310)287-1350

SCORE Office (Danville)
380 Diablo Rd., Ste. 103
Danville, California 94526
Phone: (510)837-4400

SCORE Office (Downey)
11131 Brookshire Ave.
Downey, California 90241
Phone: (310)923-2191
Fax: (310)864-0461

SCORE Office (El Cajon)
109 Rea Ave.
El Cajon, California 92020
Phone: (619)444-1327
Fax: (619)440-6164

SCORE Office (El Centro)
1100 Main St.
El Centro, California 92243
Phone: (619)352-3681
Fax: (619)352-3246

SCORE Office (Escondido)
720 N. Broadway
Escondido, California 92025
Phone: (619)745-2125
Fax: (619)745-1183

SCORE Office (Fairfield)
1111 Webster St.
Fairfield, California 94533
Phone: (707)425-4625
Fax: (707)425-0826

SCORE Office (Fontana)
17009 Valley Blvd., Ste. B
Fontana, California 92335
Phone: (909)822-4433
Fax: (909)822-6238

SCORE Office (Foster City)
1125 E. Hillsdale Blvd.
Foster City, California 94404
Phone: (415)573-7600
Fax: (415)573-5201

SCORE Office (Fremont)
2201 Walnut Ave., Ste. 110
Fremont, California 94538
Phone: (510)795-2244
Fax: (510)795-2240

SCORE Office (Central California)
2719 N. Air Fresno Dr., Ste. 200
Fresno, California 93727-1547
Phone: (559)487-5605
Fax: (559)487-5636

SCORE Office (Gardena)
1204 W. Gardena Blvd.
Gardena, California 90247
Phone: (310)532-9905
Fax: (310)515-4893

SCORE Office (Lompoc)
c/o Lompoc Chamber of Commerce
330 N. Brand Blvd., Ste. 190
Glendale, California 91203-2304
Phone: (818)552-3206
Fax: (818)552-3323

SCORE Office (Los Angeles)
330 N. Brand Blvd., Rm. 190
Glendale, California 91203-2304
Phone: (818)552-3206
Fax: (818)552-3323

SCORE Office (Glendora)
131 E. Foothill Blvd.
Glendora, California 91740
Phone: (818)963-4128
Fax: (818)914-4822

SCORE Office (Grover Beach)
177 S. 8th St.
Grover Beach, California 93433
Phone: (805)489-9091
Fax: (805)489-9091

SCORE Office (Hawthorne)
12477 Hawthorne Blvd.
Hawthorne, California 90250
Phone: (310)676-1163
Fax: (310)676-7661

SCORE Office (Hayward)
22300 Foothill Blvd., Ste. 303
Hayward, California 94541
Phone: (510)537-2424

SCORE Office (Hemet)
1700 E. Florida Ave.
Hemet, California 92544-4679

Phone: (909)652-4390
Fax: (909)929-8543

SCORE Office (Hesperia)
16367 Main St.
PO Box 403656
Hesperia, California 92340
Phone: (619)244-2135

SCORE Office (Holloster)
c/o Holloster Small Business
Development Center
321 San Felipe Rd., No. 11
Hollister, California 95023

SCORE Office (Hollywood)
7018 Hollywood Blvd.
Hollywood, California 90028
Phone: (213)469-8311
Fax: (213)469-2805

SCORE Office (Indio)
82503 Hwy. 111
PO Drawer TTT
Indio, California 92202
Phone: (619)347-0676

SCORE Office (Inglewood)
330 Queen St.
Inglewood, California 90301
Phone: (818)552-3206

SCORE Office (La Puente)
218 N. Grendanda St. D.
La Puente, California 91744
Phone: (818)330-3216
Fax: (818)330-9524

SCORE Office (La Verne)
2078 Bonita Ave.
La Verne, California 91750
Phone: (909)593-5265
Fax: (714)929-8475

SCORE Office (Lake Elsinore)
132 W. Graham Ave.
Lake Elsinore, California 92530
Phone: (909)674-2577

SCORE Office (Lakeport)
PO Box 295
Lakeport, California 95453
Phone: (707)263-5092

SCORE Office (Lakewood)
5445 E. Del Amo Blvd., Ste. 2
Lakewood, California 90714
Phone: (213)920-7737

SCORE Office (Antelope Valley)
c/o Bruce Finlayson, Chair
747 E. Ave. K-7
Lancaster, California 93535
Phone: (805)948-4518

SCORE Office (Long Beach)
1 World Trade Center
Long Beach, California 90831

SCORE Office (Los Alamitos)
901 W. Civic Center Dr., Ste. 160
Los Alamitos, California 90720

SCORE Office (Los Altos)
c/o Los Altos Chamber of Commerce
321 University Ave.
Los Altos, California 94022
Phone: (415)948-1455

SCORE Office (Manhattan Beach)
PO Box 3007
Manhattan Beach, California 90266
Phone: (310)545-5313
Fax: (310)545-7203

SCORE Office (Merced)
1632 N. St.
Merced, California 95340
Phone: (209)725-3800
Fax: (209)383-4959

SCORE Office (Milpitas)
75 S. Milpitas Blvd., Ste. 205
Milpitas, California 95035
Phone: (408)262-2613
Fax: (408)262-2823

SCORE Office (Yosemite)
c/o SCEDCO
1012 11th St., Ste. 300
Modesto, California 95354
Phone: (209)521-9333

SCORE Office (Montclair)
5220 Benito Ave.
Montclair, California 91763

SCORE Office (Monterey)
Montery Penninsula Chamber of
Commerce
380 Alvarado
Monterey, California 93940-1770
Phone: (408)649-1770

SCORE Office (Moreno Valley)
25480 Alessandro
Moreno Valley, California 92553

SCORE Office (Morgan Hill)
Morgan Hill Chamber of Commerce
25 W. 1st St.
PO Box 786
Morgan Hill, California 95038
Phone: (408)779-9444
Fax: (408)778-1786

SCORE Office (Morro Bay)
Morro Bay Chamber of Commerce
880 Main St.
Morro Bay, California 93442
Phone: (805)772-4467

SCORE Office (Mountain View)
580 Castro St.
Mountain View, California 94041
Phone: (415)968-8378
Fax: (415)968-5668

SCORE Office (Napa)
1556 1st St.
Napa, California 94559
Phone: (707)226-7455
Fax: (707)226-1171

SCORE Office (North Hollywood)
5019 Lankershim Blvd.
North Hollywood, California 91601
Phone: (818)552-3206

SCORE Office (Northridge)
8801 Reseda Blvd.
Northridge, California 91324
Phone: (818)349-5676

SCORE Office (Novato)
807 De Long Ave.
Novato, California 94945
Phone: (415)897-1164
Fax: (415)898-9097

SCORE Office (East Bay)
519 17th St.
Oakland, California 94612
Phone: (510)273-6611
Fax: (510)273-6015

SCORE Office (Oceanside)
928 N. Coast Hwy.
Oceanside, California 92054
Phone: (619)722-1534

SCORE Office (Ontario)
121 West B. St.
Ontario, California 91762
Fax: (714)984-6439

SCORE Office (Oxnard)
c/o Oxnard Chamber of Commerce
PO Box 867
Oxnard, California 93032
Phone: (805)385-8860
Fax: (805)487-1763

SCORE Office (Pacifica)
450 Dundee Way, Ste. 2
Pacifica, California 94044
Phone: (415)355-4122

SCORE Office (Palm Desert)
72990 Hwy. 111
Palm Desert, California 92260
Phone: (619)346-6111
Fax: (619)346-3463

SCORE Office (Palm Springs)
650 E. Tahquitz Canyon Way Ste. D
Palm Springs, California 92262-6706
Phone: (760)320-6682
Fax: (760)323-9426

SCORE Office (Lakeside)
c/o Paul Heindel
2150 Low Tree
Palmdale, California 93551
Phone: (805)948-4518
Fax: (805)949-1212

SCORE Office (Palo Alto)
Thoits/Love, Hershaberger, Inc.
325 Forest Ave.
Palo Alto, California 94301
Phone: (415)324-3121
Fax: (415)324-1215

SCORE Office (Pasadena)
117 E. Colorado Blvd., Ste. 100
Pasadena, California 91105
Phone: (818)795-3355
Fax: (818)795-5663

SCORE Office (Paso Robles)
c/o Paso Robles Chamber of
Commerce
1225 Park St.
Paso Robles, California 93446-2234
Phone: (805)238-0506
Fax: (805)238-0527

SCORE Office (Petaluma)
799 Baywood Dr., Ste. 3
Petaluma, California 94954
Phone: (707)762-2785
Fax: (707)762-4721

SCORE Office (Pico Rivera)
9122 E. Washington Blvd.
Pico Rivera, California 90660

SCORE Office (Pittsburg)
2700 E. Leland Rd.
Pittsburg, California 94565
Phone: (510)439-2181
Fax: (510)427-1599

SCORE Office (Pleasanton)
777 Peters Ave.
Pleasanton, California 94566
Phone: (510)846-9697

SCORE Office (Monterey Park)
485 N. Garey
Pomona, California 91769

SCORE Office (Pomona)
c/o Pomona Chamber of Commerce
485 N. Garey Ave.
Pomona, California 91766
Phone: (909)622-1256

SCORE Office (Antelope Valley)
E-mail: avscore@ptw.com
4511 West Ave. M-4
Quartz Hill, California 93536
Phone: (805)272-0087

SCORE Office (Shasta)
c/o Cascade SBDC,
737 Auditorium Dr.
Redding, California 96099
Phone: (916)225-2770

SCORE Office (Redwood City)
1675 Broadway
Redwood City, California 94063
Phone: (415)364-1722
Fax: (415)364-1729

SCORE Office (Richmond)
3925 MacDonald Ave.
Richmond, California 94805

SCORE Office (Ridgecrest)
c/o Ridgecrest Chamber of
Commerce
PO Box 771
Ridgecrest, California 93555
Phone: (619)375-8331
Fax: (619)375-0365

SCORE Office (Riverside)
3685 Main St., Ste. 350
Riverside, California 92501
Phone: (909)683-7100

SCORE Office (Sacramento)
E-mail: sacchapter@directcon.net
9845 Horn Rd., 260-B
Sacramento, California 95827
Phone: (916)361-2322
Fax: (916)361-2164

SCORE Office (Salinas)
C/o. Salinas Chamber of Commerce
PO Box 1170
Salinas, California 93902
Phone: (408)424-7611
Fax: (408)424-8639

SCORE Office (Inland Empire)
777 E. Rialto Ave.
Purchasing
San Bernardino, California 92415-
0760
Phone: (909)386-8278

SCORE Office (San Carlos)
San Carlos Chamber of Commerce
PO Box 1086
San Carlos, California 94070
Phone: (415)593-1068
Fax: (415)593-9108

SCORE Office (Encinitas)
550 W. C St., Ste. 550
San Diego, California 92101-3540
Phone: (619)557-7272
Fax: (619)557-5894

SCORE Office (San Diego)
550 West C. St., Ste. 550
San Diego, California 92101-3540
Phone: (619)557-7272
Fax: (619)557-5894

SCORE Office (Menlo Park)
1100 Merrill St.
San Francisco, California 94105
Phone: (415)325-2818
Fax: (415)325-0920

SCORE Office (San Francisco)
455 Market St., 6th Fl.
San Francisco, California 94105
Phone: (415)744-6827
Fax: (415)744-6812

SCORE Office (San Gabriel)
401 W. Las Tunas Dr.
San Gabriel, California 91776
Phone: (818)576-2525
Fax: (818)289-2901

SCORE Office (San Jose)
Small Business Institute
Deanza College
208 S. 1st St., Ste. 137
San Jose, California 95113
Phone: (408)288-8479
Fax: (408)535-5541

SCORE Office (Santa Clara County)
280 S. 1st St., Rm. 137
San Jose, California 95113
Phone: (408)288-8479
Fax: (408)535-5541

SCORE Office (San Luis Obispo)
3566 S. Hiquera, No. 104
San Luis Obispo, California 93401
Phone: (805)547-0779

SCORE Office (San Mateo)
1021 S. El Camino, 2nd Fl.
San Mateo, California 94402
Phone: (415)341-5679

SCORE Office (San Pedro)
390 W. 7th St.
San Pedro, California 90731
Phone: (310)832-7272

SCORE Office (Orange County)
200 W. Santa Anna Blvd., Ste. 700
Santa Ana, California 92701
Phone: (714)550-7369
Fax: (714)550-0191

SCORE Office (Santa Barbara)
3227 State St.
Santa Barbara, California 93130
Phone: (805)563-0084

SCORE Office (Central Coast)
509 W. Morrison Ave.
Santa Maria, California 93454
Phone: (805)347-7755

SCORE Office (Santa Maria)
Santa Maria Chamber of Commerce
614 S. Broadway
Santa Maria, California 93454-5111
Phone: (805)925-2403
Fax: (805)928-7559

SCORE Office (Santa Monica)
501 Colorado, Ste. 150
Santa Monica, California 90401
Phone: (310)393-9825
Fax: (310)394-1868

SCORE Office (Santa Rosa)
777 Sonoma Ave., Rm. 115E
Santa Rosa, California 95404
Phone: (707)571-8342
Fax: (707)541-0331

SCORE Office (Scotts Valley)
c/o Scotts Valley Chamber of
Commerce
4 Camp Evers Ln.
Scotts Valley, California 95066
Phone: (408)438-1010
Fax: (408)438-6544

SCORE Office (Simi Valley)
c/o Simi Valley Chamber of
Commerce
40 W. Cochran St., Ste. 100
Simi Valley, California 93065
Phone: (805)526-3900
Fax: (805)526-6234

SCORE Office (Sonoma)
453 1st St. E
Sonoma, California 95476
Phone: (707)996-1033

SCORE Office (Los Banos)
222 S. Shepard St.
Sonora, California 95370
Phone: (209)532-4212

SCORE Office (Tuolumne County)
222 S. Shepherd St.
Sonora, California 95370
Phone: (209)532-4212

SCORE Office (South San Francisco)
445 Market St., Ste. 6th Fl.
South San Francisco, California
94105
Phone: (415)744-6827
Fax: (415)744-6812

SCORE Office (Stockton)
401 N. San Joaquin St., Rm. 215
Stockton, California 95202
Phone: (209)946-6293

SCORE Office (Taft)
314 4th St.
Taft, California 93268
Phone: (805)765-2165
Fax: (805)765-6639

SCORE Office (Conejo Valley)
c/o Conejo Valley Chamber of
Commerce

625 W. Hillcrest Dr.
Thousand Oaks, California 91360
Phone: (805)499-1993
Fax: (805)498-7264

SCORE Office (Torrance)
Torrance Chamber of Commerce
3400 Torrance Blvd., Ste. 100
Torrance, California 90503
Phone: (310)540-5858
Fax: (310)540-7662

SCORE Office (Truckee)
PO Box 2757
Truckee, California 96160
Phone: (916)587-2757
Fax: (916)587-2439

SCORE Office (Visalia)
C/o Tulare County E.D.C.
113 S. M St,
Tulare, California 93274
Phone: (209)627-0766
Fax: (209)627-8149

SCORE Office (Upland)
C/o Upland Chamber of Commerce
433 N. 2nd Ave.
Upland, California 91786
Phone: (909)931-4108

SCORE Office (Vallejo)
2 Florida St.
Vallejo, California 94590
Phone: (707)644-5551
Fax: (707)644-5590

SCORE Office (Van Nuys)
14540 Victory Blvd.
Van Nuys, California 91411
Phone: (818)989-0300
Fax: (818)989-3836

SCORE Office (Ventura)
5700 Ralston St., Ste. 310
Ventura, California 93001
Phone: (805)658-2688
Fax: (805)658-2252

SCORE Office (Vista)
201 E. Washington St.
Vista, California 92084
Phone: (619)726-1122
Fax: (619)226-8654

SCORE Office (Watsonville)
PO Box 1748
Watsonville, California 95077

Phone: (408)724-3849
Fax: (408)728-5300

SCORE Office (West Covina)
C/o West Covina Chamber of
Commerce
811 S. Sunset Ave.
West Covina, California 91790
Phone: (818)338-8496
Fax: (818)960-0511

SCORE Office (Westlake)
C/o Westlake Chamber of Commerce
30893 Thousand Oaks Blvd.
Westlake Village, California 91362
Phone: (805)496-5630
Fax: (818)991-1754

Colorado

SCORE Office (Colorado Springs)
2 N. Cascade Ave., Ste. 110
Colorado Springs, Colorado 80903
Phone: (719)636-3074

SCORE Office (Denver)
US Custom's House, 4th Fl.
721 19th St.
Denver, Colorado 80201-0660
Phone: (303)844-3985
Fax: (303)844-6490

SCORE Office (Tri-River)
1102 Grand Ave.
Glenwood Springs, Colorado 81601
Phone: (970)945-6589

SCORE Office (Grand Junction)
c/o Larry R. Poage
304 W. Main St.
Grand Junction, Colorado 81501
Phone: (970)243-5242

SCORE Office (Gunnison)
c/o Russ Gregg
608 N. 11th
Gunnison, Colorado 81230
Phone: (303)641-4422

SCORE Office (Montrose)
1214 Peppertree Dr.
Montrose, Colorado 81401
Phone: (970)249-6080

SCORE Office (Pagosa Springs)
c/o Will Cotton
PO Box 4381

Pagosa Springs, Colorado 81157
Phone: (970)731-4890

SCORE Office (Rifle)
0854 W. Battlement Pky., Apt. C106
Parachute, Colorado 81635
Phone: (970)285-9390

SCORE Office (Pueblo)
c/o Chamber of Commerce
302 N. Santa Fe
Pueblo, Colorado 81003
Phone: (719)542-1704
Fax: (719)542-1624

SCORE Office (Ridgway)
c/o Ken Hanson
143 Poplar Pl.
Ridgway, Colorado 81432

SCORE Office (Silverton)
c/o EF Homann
PO Box 480
Silverton, Colorado 81433
Phone: (303)387-5430

SCORE Office (Minturn)
PO Box 2066
Vail, Colorado 81658
Phone: (970)476-1224

Connecticut

SCORE Office (Greater Bridgeport)
230 Park Ave.
Bridgeport, Connecticut06601-0999
Phone: (203)576-4369
Fax: (203)576-4388

SCORE Office (Bristol)
10 Main St. 1st. Fl.
Bristol, Connecticut 06010
Phone: (203)584-4718
Fax: (203)584-4722

SCORE Office (Greater Danbury)
246 Federal Rd.
Unit LL2, Ste. 7
Brookfield, Connecticut 06804
Phone: (203)775-1151

SCORE Office (Greater Danbury)
100 Mill Plain Rd.
Danbury, Connecticut 06811
Phone: (203)791-3804

SCORE Office (Eastern Connecticut)
University of Connecticut
Administration Bldg., Rm. 313
PO 625
61 Main St. (Chapter 579)
Groton, Connecticut 06475
Phone: (203)388-9508

SCORE Office (Greater Hartford County)
330 Main St.
Hartford, Connecticut 06106
Phone: (860)548-1749
Fax: (860)240-4659

SCORE Office (Manchester)
c/o Manchester Chamber of Commerce
20 Hartford Rd.
Manchester, Connecticut 06040
Phone: (203)646-2223
Fax: (203)646-5871

SCORE Office (New Britain)
185 Main St.,Ste. 431
New Britain, Connecticut 06051
Phone: (203)827-4492
Fax: (203)827-4480

SCORE Office (New Haven)
25 Science Pk., Bldg. 25, Rm. 366
New Haven, Connecticut 06511
Phone: (203)865-7645

SCORE Office (Fairfield County)
24 Beldon Ave., 5th Fl.
Norwalk, Connecticut 06850
Phone: (203)847-7348
Fax: (203)849-9308

SCORE Office (Old Saybrook)
Old Saybrook Chamber of Commerce
146 Main St.
Old Saybrook, Connecticut 06475
Phone: (860)388-9508

SCORE Office (Simsbury)
Simsbury Chamber of Commerce
Box 244
Simsbury, Connecticut 06070
Phone: (203)651-7307
Fax: (203)651-1933

SCORE Office (Torrington)
Northwest Chamber of Commerce
23 North Rd.
Torrington, Connecticut 06791
Phone: (203)482-6586

Delaware

SCORE Office (Dover)
Dover Chamber of Commerce
Treadway Towers
P.O. Box 576
Dover, Delaware 19903
Phone: (302)678-0892
Fax: (302)678-0189

SCORE Office (Lewes)
PO Box 1
Lewes, Delaware 19958
Phone: (302)645-8073
Fax: (302)645-8412

SCORE Office (Milford)
Milford Chamber of Commerce
204 NE Front St.
Milford, Delaware 19963
Phone: (302)422-3301

SCORE Office (Wilmington)
824 Market St., Ste. 610
Wilmington, Delaware 19801
Phone: (302)573-6652
Fax: (302)573-6092

District of Columbia

SCORE Office (George Mason University)
409 3rd St. SW, 4th Fl.
Washington, District of Columbia 20024
Free: (800)634-0245

SCORE Office (Washington DC)
1110 Vermont Ave. NW, 9th Fl.
Washington, District of Columbia 20043
Phone: (202)606-4000
Fax: (202)606-4225

Florida

SCORE Office (Desota County Chamber of Commerce)
16 South Velucia Ave.
Arcadia, Florida 34266
Phone: (941)494-4033

SCORE Office (Suncoast/Pinellas)
Airport Business Ctr.
4707 - 140th Ave. N, No. 311
Clearwater, Florida 34622
Phone: (813)532-6800
Fax: (813)532-6800

SCORE Office (DeLand)
DeLand Chamber of Commerce
336 N. Woodland Blvd.
DeLand, Florida 32720
Phone: (904)734-4331
Fax: (904)734-4333

SCORE Office (South Palm Beach)
1050 S. Federal Hwy., Ste. 132
Delray Beach, Florida 33483
Phone: (561)278-7752
Fax: (561)278-0288

SCORE Office (Ft. Lauderdale)
Federal Bldg., Ste. 123
299 E. Broward Blvd.
Ft. Lauderdale, Florida 33301
Phone: (954)356-7263
Fax: (954)356-7145

SCORE Office (Southwest Florida)
The Renaissance
8695 College Pky., Ste. 345 & 346
Ft. Myers, Florida 33919
Phone: (941)489-2935
Fax: (941)489-1170

SCORE Office (Treasure Coast)
Professional Center, Ste. 2
3220 S. US No. 1
Ft. Pierce, Florida 34982
Phone: (561)489-0548

SCORE Office (Gainesville)
101 SE 2nd Pl., Ste. 104
Gainesville, Florida 32601
Phone: (904)375-8278

SCORE Office (Hialeah Dade Chamber)
c/o Serry Stein
59 W. 5th St.
Hialeah, Florida 33010
Phone: (305)887-1515
Fax: (305)887-2453

SCORE Office (Daytona Beach)
E-mail: score87@dbeach.com
921 Nova Rd., Ste. A
Holly Hills, Florida 32117
Phone: (904)255-6889
Fax: (904)255-0229

SCORE Office (South Broward)
3475 Sheridian St., Ste. 203
Hollywood, Florida 33021
Phone: (305)966-8415

SCORE Office (Citrus County)
5 Poplar Ct.
Homosassa, Florida 34446
Phone: (352)382-1037

SCORE Office (Jacksonville)
7825 Baymeadows Way, Ste. 100-B
Jacksonville, Florida 32256
Phone: (904)443-1911
Fax: (904)443-1980

SCORE Office (Jacksonville Satellite)
c/o Jacksonville Chamber of
Commerce
3 Independent Dr.
Jacksonville, Florida 32256
Phone: (904)366-6600
Fax: (904)632-0617

SCORE Office (Central Florida)
5410 S. Florida Ave., No. 3
Lakeland, Florida 33801
Phone: (941)687-5783
Fax: (941)687-6225

SCORE Office (Lakeland)
Lakeland Public Library
100 Lake Morton Dr.
Lakeland, Florida 33801
Phone: (941)686-2168

SCORE Office (St. Petersburg)
800 W. Bay Dr., Ste. 505
Largo, Florida 33712
Phone: (813)585-4571

SCORE Office (Leesburg)
Lake Sumter Community College
9501 US Hwy. 441
Leesburg, Florida 34788-8751
Phone: (352)365-3556
Fax: (352)365-3501

SCORE Office (BCC/Space Coast)
Melbourn Professional Complex
1600 Sarno, Ste. 205
Melbourne, Florida 32935
Phone: (407)254-2288
Fax: (407)254-2288

SCORE Office (Cocoa)
1600 Farno Rd., Unit 205
Melbourne, Florida 32935
Phone: (407)254-2288

SCORE Office (Melbourne)
Melbourne Professional Complex
1600 Sarno, Ste. 205

Melbourne, Florida 32935
Phone: (407)254-2288
Fax: (407)245-2288

SCORE Office (Merritt Island)
1600 Sarno Rd., Ste. 205
Melbourne, Florida 32935
Phone: (407)254-2288
Fax: (407)254-2288

SCORE Office (Dade)
49 NW 5th St.
Miami, Florida 33128
Phone: (305)371-6889
Fax: (305)374-1882

SCORE Office (Naples of Collier)
E-mail: score@naples.net
Barnett Bank
3285 Tamiami Trl. E
PO Box 413002
Naples, Florida 34112
Phone: (941)417-1280
Fax: (941)417-1281

SCORE Office (Pasco County)
6014 US Hwy. 19, Ste. 302
New Port Richey, Florida 34652
Phone: (813)842-4638

SCORE Office (Southeast Volusia)
Chamber of Commerce
115 Canal St.
New Smyrna Beach, Florida 32168
Phone: (904)428-2449
Fax: (904)423-3512

SCORE Office (Ocala)
110 E. Silver Springs Blvd.
Ocala, Florida 34470
Phone: (352)629-5959

Clay County SCORE Office
Clay County Chamber of Commerce
1734 Kingsdey Ave.
PO Box 1441
Orange Park, Florida 32073
Phone: (904)264-2651
Fax: (904)269-0363

SCORE Office (Orlando)
80 N. Hughey Ave.
Rm. 445 Federal Bldg.
Orlando, Florida 32801
Phone: (407)648-6425
Fax: (407)648-6425

SCORE Office (Emerald Coast)
19 W. Garden St., No. 325
Pensacola, Florida 32501
Phone: (904)444-2060
Fax: (904)444-2070

SCORE Office (Charlotte County)
Punta Gorda Professional Center
201 W. Marion Ave., Ste. 211
Punta Gorda, Florida 33950
Phone: (941)575-1818

SCORE Office (St. Augustine)
c/o St. Augustine Chamber of
Commerce
1 Riberia St.
St. Augustine, Florida 32084
Phone: (904)829-5681
Fax: (904)829-6477

SCORE Office (Bradenton)
2801 Fruitville, Ste. 280
Sarasota, Florida 34237
Phone: (813)955-1029

SCORE Office (Manasota)
2801 Fruitville Rd., Ste. 280
Sarasota, Florida 34237
Phone: (941)955-1029
Fax: (941)955-5581

SCORE Office (Tallahassee)
c/o Leon County Library
200 W. Park Ave.
Tallahassee, Florida 32302
Phone: (850)487-2665

SCORE Office (Hillsborough)
4732 Dale Mabry Hwy. N, Ste. 400
Tampa, Florida 33614-6509
Phone: (813)870-0125

SCORE Office (Lake Sumter)
First Union National Bank
122 E. Main St.
Tavares, Florida 32778-3810
Phone: (352)365-3556

SCORE Office (Titusville)
2000 S. Washington Ave.
Titusville, Florida 32780
Phone: (407)267-3036
Fax: (407)264-0127

SCORE Office (Venice)
257 N. Tamiami Trl.
Venice, Florida 34285

Phone: (941)488-2236
Fax: (941)484-5903

SCORE Office (Palm Beach)
500 Australian Ave. S, Ste. 100
West Palm Beach, Florida 33401
Phone: (561)833-1672
Fax: (561)833-1712

SCORE Office (Wildwood)
Sumter County Small Business
Services
103 N. Webster St.
Wildwood, Florida 34785

Georgia

SCORE Office (Atlanta)
1720 Peachtree Rd. NW, 6th Fl.
Atlanta, Georgia 30309
Phone: (404)347-2442
Fax: (404)347-1227

SCORE Office (Augusta)
3126 Oxford Rd.
Augusta, Georgia 30909
Phone: (706)869-9100

SCORE Office (Columbus)
School Bldg.
P.O. Box 40
Columbus, Georgia 31901
Phone: (706)327-3654

SCORE Office (Dalton-Whitfield)
305 S. Thorton Ave.
Dalton, Georgia 30720
Phone: (706)279-3383

SCORE Office (Gainesville)
Chamber of Commerce
PO Box 374
Gainesville, Georgia 30503
Phone: (770)532-6206
Fax: (770)535-8419

SCORE Office (Macon)
711 Grand Bdlg.
Macon, Georgia 31201
Phone: (912)751-6160

SCORE Office (Brunswick)
4 Glen Ave.
St. Simons Island, Georgia 31520
Phone: (912)265-0620
Fax: (912)265-0629

SCORE Office (Savannah)
111 E. Liberty St., Ste. 103
Savannah, Georgia 31401
Phone: (912)652-4335
Fax: (912)652-4184

Guam

SCORE Office (Guam)
Pacific News Bldg., Rm. 103
238 Archbishop Flores St.
Agana, Guam 96910-5100
Phone: (671)472-7308

Hawaii

SCORE Office (Hawaii, Inc.)
E-mail: hnlscore@juno.com
1111 Bishop St., Ste. 204
PO Box 50207
Honolulu, Hawaii 96813
Phone: (808)522-8132
Fax: (808)522-8135

SCORE Office (Kahului)
SCORE of Maine Inc.
c/o Chamber of Commerce
250 Alamaha, Unit N16A
Kahului, Hawaii 96732
Phone: (808)871-7711

SCORE Office (Maui, Inc.)
590 E. Lipoa Pkwy., Ste. 227
Kihei, Hawaii 96753
Phone: (808)875-2380

Idaho

SCORE Office (Treasure Valley)
1020 Main St., No. 290
Boise, Idaho 83702
Phone: (208)334-1696
Fax: (208)334-9353

SCORE Office (Eastern Idaho)
2300 N. Yellowstone, Ste. 119
Idaho Falls, Idaho 83401
Phone: (208)523-1022
Fax: (208)528-7127

Illinois

SCORE Office (Fox Valley)
40 W. Downer Pl.
PO Box 277
Aurora, Illinois 60506

Phone: (630)897-9214
Fax: (630)897-7002

SCORE Office (Greater Belvidere)
Greater Belvidere Chamber of
Commerce
419 S. State St.
Belvidere, Illinois 61008
Phone: (815)544-4357
Fax: (815)547-7654

SCORE Office (Bensenville)
Greater O'Hare Association
1050 Busse Hwy. Suite 100
Bensenville, Illinois 60106
Phone: (708)350-2944
Fax: (708)350-2979

SCORE Office (Central Illinois)
402 N. Hershey Rd.
Bloomington, Illinois 61704
Phone: (309)644-0549
Fax: (309)663-8270

SCORE Office (Southern Illinois)
150 E. Pleasant Hill Rd.
Box 1
Carbondale, Illinois 62901
Phone: (618)453-6654
Fax: (618)453-5040

SCORE Office (Chicago)
Northwest Atrium Center
500 W. Madison St., No. 1250
Chicago, Illinois 60661
Phone: (312)353-7724
Fax: (312)886-5688

SCORE Office (Chicago—Oliver
Harvey College)
Oliver Harvey College
Pullman Bldg.
1000 E. 11th St., 7th Fl.
Chicago, Illinois 60628
Fax: (312)468-8086

SCORE Office (Danville)
Danville Area Chamber of Commerce
28 W. N. Street
Danville, Illinois 61832
Phone: (217)442-7232
Fax: (217)442-6228

SCORE Office (Decatur)
Millikin University
1184 W. Main St.
Decatur, Illinois 62522

Phone: (217)424-6297
Fax: (217)424-3993

SCORE Office (Downers Grove)
Downers Grove Chamber of
Commerce
925 Curtis
Downers Grove, Illinois 60515
Phone: (708)968-4050
Fax: (708)968-8368

SCORE Office (Elgin)
Elgin Area Chamber of Commerce
24 E. Chicago, 3rd Fl.
PO Box 648
Elgin, Illinois 60120
Phone: (847)741-5660
Fax: (847)741-5677

SCORE Office (Freeport Area)
Freeport Area Chamber of Commerce
26 S. Galena Ave.
Freeport, Illinois 61032
Phone: (815)233-1350
Fax: (815)235-4038

SCORE Office (Galesburg)
Galesburg Area Chamber of
Commerce
292 E. Simmons St.
PO Box 749
Galesburg, Illinois 61401
Phone: (309)343-1194
Fax: (309)343-1195

SCORE Office (Glen Ellyn)
Glen Ellyn Chamber of Commerce
500 Pennsylvania
Glen Ellyn, Illinois 60137
Phone: (708)469-0907
Fax: (708)469-0426

SCORE Office (Greater Alton)
Alden Hall
5800 Godfrey Rd.
Godfrey, Illinois 62035-2466
Phone: (618)467-2280
Fax: (618)466-8289

SCORE Office (Grayslake)
College of Lake County
19351 W. Washington St.
Grayslake, Illinois 60030
Phone: (708)223-3633
Fax: (708)223-9371

SCORE Office (Harrisburg)
Ec. Devel. Services Center
303 S. Commercial
Harrisburg, Illinois 62946-1528
Phone: (618)252-8528
Fax: (618)252-0210

SCORE Office (Joliet)
Joliet Region Chamber of Commerce
100 N. Chicago
Joliet, Illinois 60432
Phone: (815)727-5371
Fax: (815)727-5374

SCORE Office (Kankakee)
Kankakee Small Business
Development Center
101 S. Schuyler Ave.
Kankakee, Illinois 60901
Phone: (815)933-0376
Fax: (815)933-0380

SCORE Office (Macomb)
Western Illinois University
216 Seal Hall, Rm. 214
Macomb, Illinois 61455
Phone: (309)298-1128
Fax: (309)298-2520

SCORE Office (Matteson)
Prairie State College
210 Lincoln Mall
Matteson, Illinois 60443
Phone: (708)709-3750
Fax: (708)503-9322

SCORE Office (Mattoon)
Mattoon Association of Commerce
1701 Wabash Ave.
Mattoon, Illinois 61938
Phone: (217)235-5661
Fax: (217)234-6544

SCORE Office (Quad Cities)
E-mail: qscore@oconline.com
c/o Chamber of Commerce
622 19th St.
Moline, Illinois 61265
Phone: (309)797-0082
Fax: (309)757-5435

SCORE Office (Naperville)
Naperville Area Chamber of
Commerce
131 W. Jefferson Ave.
Naperville, Illinois 60540

Phone: (708)355-4141
Fax: (708)355-8355

SCORE Office (Northbrook)
Northbrook Chamber of Commerce
2002 Walters Ave.
Northbrook, Illinois 60062
Phone: (847)498-5555
Fax: (847)498-5510

SCORE Office (Palos Hills)
Moraine Valley Community College
10900 S. 88th Ave.
Palos Hills, Illinois 60465
Phone: (847)974-5468
Fax: (847)974-0078

SCORE Office (Peoria)
c/o Peoria Chamber of Commerce
124 SW Adams, Ste. 300
Peoria, Illinois 61602
Phone: (309)676-0755
Fax: (309)676-7534

SCORE Office (Prospect Heights)
Harper College, Northeast Center
1375 Wolf Rd.
Prospect Heights, Illinois 60070
Phone: (847)537-8660
Fax: (847)537-7138

SCORE Office (Quincy Tri-State)
c/o Quincy Chamber of Commerce
300 Civic Center Plz., Ste. 245
Quincy, Illinois 62301
Phone: (217)222-8093
Fax: (217)222-3033

SCORE Office (River Grove)
Triton College
2000 5th Ave.
River Grove, Illinois 60171
Phone: (708)456-0300
Fax: (708)583-3121

SCORE Office (Northern Illinois)
515 N. Court St.
Rockford, Illinois 61103
Phone: (815)962-0122
Fax: (815)962-0122

SCORE Office (St. Charles)
St. Charles Chamber of Commerce
103 N. 1st Ave.
St. Charles, Illinois 60174-1982
Phone: (847)584-8384
Fax: (847)584-6065

SCORE Office (Springfield)
511 W. Capitol Ave., Ste. 302
Springfield, Illinois 62704
Phone: (217)492-4416
Fax: (217)492-4867

SCORE Office (Sycamore)
Greater Sycamore Chamber of
Commerce
112 Somunak St.
Sycamore, Illinois 60178
Phone: (815)895-3456
Fax: (815)895-0125

SCORE Office (University)
Governors State University
Hwy. 50 & Stuenkel Rd. Ste. C3305
University Park, Illinois 60466
Phone: (708)534-5000
Fax: (708)534-8457

Indiana

SCORE Office (Anderson)
c/o Anderson Chamber of Commerce
205 W. 11th St.
Anderson, Indiana 46015
Phone: (317)642-0264

SCORE Office (Bloomington)
E-mail: wtfische@indiana.edu
c/o Bloomington Chamber of
Commerce
Star Center
216 W. Allen
Bloomington, Indiana 47403
Phone: (812)335-7334

SCORE Office (South East Indiana)
c/o Chamber of Commerce
500 Franklin St.
Box 29
Columbus, Indiana 47201
Phone: (812)379-4457

SCORE Office (Corydon)
310 N. Elm St.
Corydon, Indiana 47112
Phone: (812)738-2137
Fax: (812)738-6438

SCORE Office (Crown Point)
Old Courthouse Sq. Ste. 206
P.O. Box 43
Crown Point, Indiana 46307
Phone: (219)663-1800

SCORE Office (Elkhart)
418 S. Main St.
Elkhart, Indiana 46515
Phone: (219)293-1531
Fax: (219)294-1859

SCORE Office (Evansville)
1100 W. Lloyd Expy., Ste. 105
Evansville, Indiana 47708
Phone: (812)426-6144

SCORE Office (Ft. Wayne)
1300 S. Harrison St.
Ft. Wayne, Indiana 46802
Phone: (219)422-2601

SCORE Office (Gary)
973 W. 6th Ave., Rm. 326
Gary, Indiana 46402
Phone: (219)882-3918

SCORE Office (Hammond)
7034 Indianapolis Blvd.
Hammond, Indiana 46324
Phone: (219)931-1000
Fax: (219)845-9548

SCORE Office (Indianapolis)
429 N. Pennsylvania St., Ste. 100
Indianapolis, Indiana 46204-1873
Phone: (317)226-7264
Fax: (317)226-7259

SCORE Office (Jasper)
PO Box 307
Jasper, Indiana 47547-0307
Phone: (812)482-6866

SCORE Office (Kokomo/Howard
Counties)
106 N. Washington St.
Kokomo, Indiana 46901
Phone: (765)457-5301
Fax: (765)452-4564

SCORE Office (Logansport)
Logansport County Chamber of
Commerce
300 E. Broadway, Ste. 103
Logansport, Indiana 46947
Phone: (219)753-6388

SCORE Office (Madison)
301 E. Main St.
Madison, Indiana 47250
Phone: (812)265-3135
Fax: (812)265-2923

SCORE Office (Marengo)
c/o Marengo Chamber of Commerce
Rt. 1 Box 224D
Marengo, Indiana 47140
Fax: (812)365-2793

SCORE Office (Marion/Grant
Counties)
215 S. Adams
Marion, Indiana 46952
Phone: (765)664-5107

SCORE Office (Merrillville)
255 W. 80th Pl.
Merrillville, Indiana 46410
Phone: (219)769-8180
Fax: (219)736-6223

SCORE Office (Michigan City)
200 E. Michigan Blvd.
Michigan City, Indiana 46360
Phone: (219)874-6221
Fax: (219)873-1204

SCORE Office (South Central
Indiana)
4100 Charleston Rd.
New Albany, Indiana 47150-9538
Phone: (812)945-0066

SCORE Office (Rensselaer)
104 W. Washington
Rensselaer, Indiana 47978

SCORE Office (Salem)
c/o Salem Chamber of Commerce
210 N. Main St.
Salem, Indiana 47167
Phone: (812)883-4303
Fax: (812)883-1467

SCORE Office (South Bend)
300 N. Michigan St.
South Bend, Indiana 46601
Phone: (219)282-4350

SCORE Office (Valparaiso)
150 Lincolnway
Valparaiso, Indiana 46383
Phone: (219)462-1105
Fax: (219)469-5710

SCORE Office (Vincennes)
Vincennes Chamber of Commerce
27 N. 3rd
P.O. Box 553
Vincennes, Indiana 47591

Phone: (812)882-6440
Fax: (812)882-6441

SCORE Office (Wabash)
PO Box 371
Wabash, Indiana 46992
Phone: (219)563-1168
Fax: (219)563-6920

Iowa

SCORE Office (Burlington)
Federal Bldg.
300 N. Main St.
Burlington, Iowa 52601
Phone: (319)752-2967

SCORE Office (Cedar Rapids)
Lattner Building, Ste. 200
215-4th Avenue, SE, No. 200
Cedar Rapids, Iowa 52401-1806
Phone: (319)362-6405
Fax: (319)362-7861

SCORE Office (Illowa)
333 4th Ave. S
Clinton, Iowa 52732
Phone: (319)242-5702

SCORE Office (Council Bluffs)
Chamber of Commerce
7 N. 6th St.
Council Bluffs, Iowa 51502
Phone: (712)325-1000

SCORE Office (Northeast Iowa)
3404 285th St.
Cresco, Iowa 52136
Phone: (319)547-3377

SCORE Office (Des Moines)
Federal Bldg., Rm. 749
210 Walnut St.
Des Moines, Iowa 50309-2186
Phone: (515)284-4760

SCORE Office (Ft. Dodge)
Federal Bldg., Rm. 436
205 S. 8th St.
Ft. Dodge, Iowa 50501
Phone: (515)955-2622

SCORE Office (Independence)
Independence Area Chamber of
Commerce
110 1st. St. East
Independence, Iowa 50644

Phone: (319)334-7178
Fax: (319)334-7179

SCORE Office (Iowa City)
210 Federal Bdlg.
PO Box 1853
Iowa City, Iowa 52240-1853
Phone: (319)338-1662

SCORE Office (Keokuk)
c/o Keokuk Area Chamber of
Commerce
401 Main St.
Pierce Bldg., No. 1
Keokuk, Iowa 52632
Phone: (319)524-5055

SCORE Office (Central Iowa)
Fisher Community College
709 S. Center
Marshalltown, Iowa 50158
Phone: (515)753-6645

SCORE Office (River City)
15 West State St.
Mason City, Iowa 50401
Phone: (515)423-5724

SCORE Office (South Central)
SBDC, Indian Hills Community
College
525 Grandview Ave.
Ottumwa, Iowa 52501
Phone: (515)683-5127
Fax: (515)683-5263

SCORE Office (Dubuque)
c/o Northeast Iowa Community
College
10250 Sundown Road
Peosta, Iowa 52068
Phone: (319)556-5110

SCORE Office (Southwest Iowa)
Chamber of Commerce
614 W. Sheridan
Shenandoah, Iowa 51601
Phone: (712)246-3260

SCORE Office (Sioux City)
Federal Bldg.
320 6th St.
Sioux City, Iowa 51101
Phone: (712)277-2324
Fax: (712)277-2325

SCORE Office (Iowa Lakes)
c/o SAABI
122 W. 5th St.
Spencer, Iowa 51301
Phone: (712)262-3059

SCORE Office (Vista)
Storm Lake Chamber of Commerce
119 W. 6th St.
Storm Lake, Iowa 50588
Phone: (712)732-3780

SCORE Office (Waterloo)
Chamber of Commerce
215 E. 4th
Waterloo, Iowa 50703
Phone: (319)233-8431

Kansas

SCORE Office (Southwest Kansas)
Dodge City Chamber of Commerce
501 W. Spruce
Dodge City, Kansas 67801
Phone: (316)227-3119

SCORE Office (Emporia)
Chamber of Commerce
811 Homewood
Emporia, Kansas 66801
Phone: (316)342-1600

SCORE Office (Golden Belt)
Chamber of Commerce
1307 Williams
Great Bend, Kansas 67530
Phone: (316)792-2401

SCORE Office (Hays)
c/o Empire Bank
PO Box 400
Hays, Kansas 67601
Phone: (913)625-6595

SCORE Office (Hutchinson)
One E. 9th St.
Hutchinson, Kansas 67501
Phone: (316)665-8468
Fax: (316)665-7619

SCORE Office (Southeast Kansas)
404 Westminster Pl.
PO Box 886
Independence, Kansas 67301
Phone: (316)331-4741

SCORE Office (McPherson)
Chamber of Commerce
306 N. Main
PO box 616
McPherson, Kansas 67460
Phone: (316)241-3303

SCORE Office (Salina)
c/o Four Rivers Development Inc.
120 Ash St.
Salina, Kansas 67401
Phone: (785)243-4290
Fax: (785)243-1833

SCORE Office (Topeka)
1700 College
Topeka, Kansas 66621
Phone: (785)231-1010

SCORE Office (Wichita)
SBA/100 E. English, Ste. 510
Wichita, Kansas 67202
Phone: (316)269-6273
Fax: (316)269-6499

SCORE Office (Ark Valley)
205 E. 9th St.
Winfield, Kansas 67156
Phone: (316)221-1617

Kentucky

SCORE Office (Ashland)
PO Box 830
Ashland, Kentucky 41105
Phone: (606)329-8011
Fax: (606)325-4607

SCORE Office (Bowling Green)
Bowling Green-Warren Chamber of
Commerce
812 State St.
P.O. Box 51
Bowling Green, Kentucky 42101
Phone: (502)781-3200
Fax: (502)843-0458

SCORE Office (Tri-Lakes)
508 Barbee Way
Danville, Kentucky 40422-1548
Phone: (606)231-9902

SCORE Office (Glasgow)
301 W. Main St.
Glasgow, Kentucky 42141
Phone: (502)651-3161
Fax: (502)651-3122

SCORE Office (Hazard)
B & I Technical Center
100 Airport Gardens Rd.
Hazard, Kentucky 41701
Phone: (606)439-5856
Fax: (606)439-1808

SCORE Office (Lexington)
E-mail:
scorelex@uky.campus.mci.net
410 W. Vine St., Ste. 290, Civic C
Lexington, Kentucky 40507
Phone: (606)231-9902
Fax: (606)253-3190

SCORE Office (Louisville)
188 Federal Office Bldg.
600 Dr. Martin L. King Jr. Pl.
Louisville, Kentucky 40202
Phone: (502)582-5976

SCORE Office (Madisonville)
257 N. Main
Madisonville, Kentucky 42431
Phone: (502)825-1399
Fax: (502)825-1396

SCORE Office (Paducah)
Federal Office Bldg.
501 Broadway, Rm. B-36
Paducah, Kentucky 42001
Phone: (502)442-5685

Louisiana

SCORE Office (Central Louisiana)
802 3rd St.
Alexandria, Louisiana 71309
Phone: (318)442-6671

SCORE Office (Baton Rouge)
564 Laurel St.
PO Box 3217
Baton Rouge, Louisiana 70801
Phone: (504)381-7130
Fax: (504)336-4306

SCORE Office (NorthShore)
2 W. Thomas
Hammond, Louisiana 70401
Phone: (504)345-4457
Fax: (504)345-4749

SCORE Office (Lafayette)
E-mail: score302@aol.com
804 St. Mary Blvd.
Lafayette, Louisiana 70505-1307

Phone: (318)233-2705
Fax: (318)234-8671

SCORE Office (Lake Charles)
120 W. Pujo St.
Lake Charles, Louisiana 70601
Phone: (318)433-3632

SCORE Office (New Orleans)
365 Canal St., Ste. 3100
New Orleans, Louisiana 70130
Phone: (504)589-2356
Fax: (504)589-2339

SCORE Office (Shreveport)
400 Edwards St.
Shreveport, Louisiana 71101
Phone: (318)677-2536
Fax: (318)677-2541

Maine

SCORE Office (Augusta)
40 Western Ave.
Augusta, Maine 04330
Phone: (207)622-8509

SCORE Office (Bangor)
Husson College
Peabody Hall, Rm. 229
One College Cir.
Bangor, Maine 04401
Phone: (207)941-9707

SCORE Office (Central & Northern
Arroostock)
111 High St.
Caribou, Maine 04736
Phone: (207)492-8010
Fax: (207)492-8010

SCORE Office (Penquis)
Chamber of Commerce
South St.
Dover Foxcroft, Maine 04426
Phone: (207)564-7021

SCORE Office (Maine Coastal)
E-mail: score@arcadia.net
Mill Mall
Box 1105
Ellsworth, Maine 04605-1105
Phone: (207)667-5800

SCORE Office (Lewiston-Auburn)
BIC of Maine-Bates Mill Complex
35 Canal St.

Lewiston, Maine 04240-7764
Phone: (207)782-3708
Fax: (207)783-7745

SCORE Office (Portland)
66 Pearl St., Rm. 210
Portland, Maine 04101
Phone: (207)772-1147

SCORE Office (Western Mountains)
c/o Bangor Savings Bank
108 Congress St.
Rumford, Maine 04276
Phone: (207)364-8122

SCORE Office (Oxford Hills)
166 Main St.
South Paris, Maine 04281
Phone: (207)743-0499

Maryland

SCORE Office (Southern Maryland)
E-mail: score390@aol.com
2525 Riva Rd., Ste. 110
Annapolis, Maryland 21401
Phone: (410)266-9553
Fax: (410)573-0981

SCORE Office (Baltimore)
The City Crescent Bldg., 6th Fl.
10 S. Howard St.
Baltimore, Maryland 21201
Phone: (410)962-2233
Fax: (410)962-1805

SCORE Office (Bel Air)
Bel Air Chamber of Commerce
108 S. Bond St.
Bel Air, Maryland 21014
Phone: (410)838-2020
Fax: (410)893-4715

SCORE Office (Bethesda)
7910 Woodmont Ave., Ste. 1204
Bethesda, Maryland 20814
Phone: (301)652-4900
Fax: (301)657-1973

SCORE Office (Bowie)
6670 Race Track Rd.
Bowie, Maryland 20715
Phone: (301)262-0920
Fax: (301)262-0921

SCORE Office (Dorchester County)
c/o Chamber of Commerce
203 Sunburst Hwy.

Cambridge, Maryland 21613
Phone: (410)228-3575

SCORE Office (Upper Shore)
c/o Talbout County Chamber of
Commerce
210 Marlboro Ave.
Easton, Maryland 21601
Phone: (410)822-4606
Fax: (410)822-7922

SCORE Office (Frederick County)
43A S. Market St.
Frederick, Maryland 21701
Phone: (301)662-8723
Fax: (301)846-4427

SCORE Office (Gaithersburg)
9 Park Ave.
Gaithersburg, Maryland 20877
Phone: (301)840-1400
Fax: (301)963-3918

SCORE Office (Glen Burnie)
Glen Burnie Chamber of Commerce
103 Crain Hwy. SE
Glen Burnie, Maryland 21061
Phone: (410)766-8282
Fax: (410)766-9722

SCORE Office (Hagerstown)
111 W. Washington St.
Hagerstown, Maryland 21740
Phone: (301)739-2015
Fax: (301)739-1278

SCORE Office (Laurel)
7901 Sandy Spring Rd. Ste. 501
Laurel, Maryland 20707
Phone: (301)725-4000
Fax: (301)725-0776

SCORE Office (Salisbury)
c/o Chamber of Commerce
300 E. Main St.
Salisbury, Maryland 21801
Phone: (410)749-0185
Fax: (410)860-9925

Massachusetts

SCORE Office (Boston)
E-mail: boston-score-
20@worldnet.att.net
10 Causeway St., Rm. 265
Boston, Massachusetts 02222-1093
Phone: (617)565-5591
Fax: (617)565-5597

SCORE Office (Bristol/Plymouth
County)
Greenville Chamber of Commerce
53 N. 6th St., Federal Bldg.
Bristol, Massachusetts 02740
Phone: (508)994-5093

SCORE Office (SE Massachusetts)
60 School St.
Brockton, Massachusetts 02401
Phone: (508)587-2673
Fax: (508)587-1340

SCORE Office (North Adams)
Northern Berkshire Development
Corp.
820 N. State Rd.
Cheshire, Massachusetts 01225
Phone: (413)743-5100

SCORE Office (Clinton Satellite)
c/o Clinton Chamber of Commerce
1 Green St.
Clinton, Massachusetts 01510
Fax: (508)368-7689

SCORE Office (NE Massachusetts)
Danvers Savings Bank
1 Conant St.
Danvers, Massachusetts 01923
Phone: (978)777-2200

SCORE Office (Bristol/Plymouth
Counties)
Fall River Area Chamber of
Commerce and Industry
200 Pocasset St.
PO Box 1871
Fall River, Massachusetts 02722-
1871
Phone: (508)676-8226

SCORE Office (Greenfield)
PO Box 898
Greenfield, Massachusetts 01302
Phone: (413)773-5463
Fax: (413)773-7008

SCORE Office (Haverhill)
Haverhill Chamber
87 Winter St.
Haverhill, Massachusetts 01830
Phone: (508)373-5663
Fax: (508)373-8060

SCORE Office (Hudson Satellite)
c/o Hudson Chamber of Commerce
PO Box 578

Hudson, Massachusetts 01749
Phone: (508)568-0360
Fax: (508)568-0360

SCORE Office (Cape Cod)
Independence Pk., Ste. 5B
270 Communications Way
Hyannis, Massachusetts 02601
Phone: (508)775-4884
Fax: (508)790-2540

SCORE Office (Lawrence)
264 Essex St.
Lawrence, Massachusetts 01840
Phone: (508)686-0900
Fax: (508)794-9953

SCORE Office (Leominster Satellite)
c/o Leominster Chamber of
Commerce
110 Erdman Way
Leominster, Massachusetts 01453
Phone: (508)840-4300
Fax: (508)840-4896

SCORE Office (Newburyport)
29 State St.
Newburyport, Massachusetts 01950
Phone: (617)462-6680

SCORE Office (Pittsfield)
Central Berkshire Chamber
66 West St.
Pittsfield, Massachusetts 01201
Phone: (413)499-2485

SCORE Office (Haverhill-Salem)
32 Derby Sq.
Salem, Massachusetts 01970
Phone: (508)745-0330
Fax: (508)745-3855

SCORE Office (Springfield)
1350 Main St.
Federal Bldg.
Springfield, Massachusetts 01103
Phone: (413)785-0314

SCORE Office (Carver)
12 Taunton Green, Ste. 201
Taunton, Massachusetts 02780
Phone: (508)824-4068
Fax: (508)824-4069

SCORE Office (Worcester)
33 Waldo St.
Worcester, Massachusetts 01608

Phone: (508)753-2929
Fax: (508)754-8560

Michigan

SCORE Office (Allegan)
c/o Allegan Chamber of Commerce
PO Box 338
Allegan, Michigan 49010
Phone: (616)673-2479

SCORE Office (Ann Arbor)
425 S. Main St., Ste. 103
Ann Arbor
Michigan
48104
Phone: (313)665-4433

SCORE Office (Battle Creek)
c/o Battle Creek Chamber of
Commerce
34 W. Jackson Ste. 4A
Battle Creek
Michigan
49017-3505
Phone: (616)962-4076
Fax: (616)962-6309

SCORE Office (Cadillac)
c/o Cadillac Chamber of Commerce
222 Lake St.
Cadillac, Michigan 49601
Phone: (616)775-9776
Fax: (616)775-1440

SCORE Office (Detroit)
477 Michigan Ave., Rm. 515
Detroit, Michigan 48226
Phone: (313)226-7947
Fax: (313)226-3448

SCORE Office (Flint)
Mott Community College
708 Root Rd., Rm. 308
Flint, Michigan 48503
Phone: (810)233-6846

SCORE Office (Grand Rapids)
E-mail: scoreone@iserv.net
Grand Rapids Chamber of Commerce
111 Pearl St. NW
Grand Rapids, Michigan 49503-2831
Phone: (616)771-0305
Fax: (616)771-0328

SCORE Office (Holland)
c/o Holland Chamber of Commerce
480 State St.

Holland, Michigan 49423
Phone: (616)396-9472

SCORE Office (Jackson)
Jackson Chamber of Commerce
209 East Washington
PO Box 80
Jackson, Michigan 49204
Phone: (517)782-8221
Fax: (517)782-0061

SCORE Office (Kalamazoo)
E-mail: score@nucleus.net
c/o Kalamazoo Chamber of
Commerce
345 W. Michigan Ave.
Kalamazoo, Michigan 49007
Phone: (616)381-5382
Fax: (616)343-0430

SCORE Office (Lansing)
117 E. Allegan
PO Box 14030
Lansing, Michigan 48901
Phone: (517)487-6340
Fax: (517)484-6910

SCORE Office (Livonia)
Livonia Chamber of Commerce
15401 Farmington Rd.
Livonia, Michigan 48154
Phone: (313)427-2122
Fax: (313)427-6055

SCORE Office (Madison Heights)
26345 John R
Madison Heights, Michigan 48071
Phone: (810)542-5010
Fax: (810)542-6821

SCORE Office (Monroe)
Monroe Chamber of Commerce
111 E. 1st
Monroe, Michigan 48161
Phone: (313)242-3366
Fax: (313)242-7253

SCORE Office (Mt. Clemens)
Macomb County Chamber of
Commerce
58 S/B Gratiot
Mt. Clemens, Michigan 48043
Phone: (810)463-1528
Fax: (810)463-6541

SCORE Office (Muskegon)
c/o Muskegon Chamber of Commerce
PO Box 1087

230 Terrace Plz.
Muskegon, Michigan 49443
Phone: (616)722-3751
Fax: (616)728-7251

SCORE Office (Petoskey)
401 E. Mitchell St.
Petoskey, Michigan 49770
Phone: (616)347-4150

SCORE Office (Pontiac)
Oakland County Economic
Development Group
Executive Office Bldg.
1200 N. Telegraph Rd.
Pontiac, Michigan 48341
Phone: (810)975-9555

SCORE Office (Pontiac)
Pontiac Chamber of Commerce
PO Box 430025
Pontiac, Michigan 48343
Phone: (810)335-9600

SCORE Office (Port Huron)
920 Pinegrove Ave.
Port Huron, Michigan 48060
Phone: (810)985-7101

SCORE Office (Rochester)
Rochester Chamber of Commerce
71 Walnut Ste. 110
Rochester, Michigan 48307
Phone: (810)651-6700
Fax: (810)651-5270

SCORE Office (Saginaw)
901 S. Washington Ave.
Saginaw, Michigan 48601
Phone: (517)752-7161
Fax: (517)752-9055

SCORE Office (Upper Peninsula)
c/o Chamber of Commerce
2581 I-75 Business Spur
Sault Ste. Marie, Michigan 49783
Phone: (906)632-3301

SCORE Office (Southfield)
21000 W. 10 Mile Rd.
Southfield, Michigan 48075
Phone: (810)204-3050
Fax: (810)204-3099

SCORE Office (Traverse City)
202 E. Grandview Pkwy.
PO Box 387
Traverse City, Michigan 49685

Phone: (616)947-5075
Fax: (616)946-2565

SCORE Office (Warren)
Warren Chamber of Commerce
30500 Van Dyke, Ste. 118
Warren, Michigan 48093
Phone: (810)751-3939

Minnesota

SCORE Office (Aitkin)
c/o Donald F. Gode
Aitkin, Minnesota 56431
Phone: (218)741-3906

SCORE Office (Albert Lea)
Albert Lea Chamber of Commerce
202 N. Broadway Ave.
Albert Lea, Minnesota 56007
Phone: (507)373-7487

SCORE Office (Austin)
PO Box 864
Austin, Minnesota 55912
Phone: (507)437-4561
Fax: (507)437-4869

SCORE Office (South Metro)
101 W. Burnsville Pkwy., No. 150
Burnsville, Minnesota 55337
Phone: (612)898-5645
Fax: (612)435-6972

SCORE Office (Fairmont)
c/o Fairmont Chamber of Commerce
PO Box 826
Fairmont, Minnesota 56031
Phone: (507)235-5547
Fax: (507)235-8411

SCORE Office (Duluth)
4879 Adrian Ln.
Hermantown, Minnesota 55811
Phone: (218)723-2701
Fax: (218)723-2712

SCORE Office (Southwest
Minnesota)
112 Riverfront St.
Box 999
Mankato, Minnesota 56001
Phone: (507)345-4519
Fax: (507)345-4451

SCORE Office (Minneapolis)
North Plaza Bldg., Ste. 51
5217 Wayzata Blvd.

Minneapolis, Minnesota 55416
Phone: (612)591-0539
Fax: (612)544-0436

SCORE Office (Owatonna)
PO Box 331
Owatonna, Minnesota 55060
Phone: (507)451-7970
Fax: (507)451-7972

SCORE Office (Red Wing)
2000 W. Main St., Ste. 324
Red Wing, Minnesota 55066
Phone: (612)388-4079

SCORE Office (Southeastern
Minnesota)
Rochester Chamber of Commerce
220 S. Broadway, Ste. 100
Rochester, Minnesota 55901
Phone: (507)288-1122
Fax: (507)282-8960

SCORE Office (Brainerd)
Brainerd Chamber of Commerce
St. Cloud, Minnesota 56301

SCORE Office (Central Area)
1527 Northway Dr.
St. Cloud, Minnesota 56301
Phone: (320)240-1332
Fax: (320)255-9050

SCORE Office (St. Paul)
350 St. Peter St., No. 295
Lowry Professional Bldg.
St. Paul, Minnesota 55102
Phone: (651)223-5010
Fax: (651)223-5048

SCORE Office (Winona)
Box 870
Winona, Minnesota 55987
Phone: (507)452-2272
Fax: (507)454-8814

SCORE Office (Worthington)
Worthington Chamber of Commerce
1121 3rd Ave.
Worthington, Minnesota 56187
Phone: (507)372-2919
Fax: (507)372-2827

Mississippi

SCORE Office (Delta)
Greenville Chamber of Commerce
915 Washington Ave.

PO Box 933
Greenville, Mississippi 38701
Phone: (601)378-3141

SCORE Office (Gulfcoast)
One Government Plaza
2909 13th St., Ste. 203
Gulfport, Mississippi 39501
Phone: (601)863-4449

SCORE Office (Jackson)
1st Jackson Center, Ste. 400
101 W. Capitol St.
Jackson, Mississippi 39201
Phone: (601)965-5533

SCORE Office (Meridian)
5220 16th Ave.
Meridian, Mississippi 39305
Phone: (601)482-4412

Missouri

SCORE Office (Lake of the Ozark)
University Extension
113 Kansas St.
PO Box 1405
Camdenton, Missouri 65020
Phone: (573)346-2644
Fax: (573)346-2694

Chamber of Commerce (Cape
Girardeau)
C/o Chamber of Commerce
PO Box 98
Cape Girardeau, Missouri 63702-
0098
Phone: (314)335-3312

SCORE Office (Mid-Missouri)
1705 Halstead Ct.
Columbia, Missouri 65203
Phone: (573)874-1132

SCORE Office (Ozark-Gateway)
1486 Glassy Rd.
Cuba, Missouri 65453-1640
Phone: (573)885-4954

SCORE Office (Kansas City)
323 W. 8th St., Ste. 104
Kansas City, Missouri 64105
Phone: (816)374-6675
Fax: (816)374-6692

SCORE Office (Sedalia)
c/o State Fair Community College
Lucas Place

323 W. 8th St., Ste.104
Kansas City, Missouri 64105
Phone: (816)374-6675

SCORE Office (Tri-Lakes)
c/o Dwayne Shoemaker
PO Box 1148
Kimberling, Missouri 65686
Phone: (417)739-3041

SCORE Office (Tri-Lakes)
HCRI Box 85
Lampe, Missouri 65681
Phone: (417)858-6798

SCORE Office (Mexico)
Mexico Chamber of Commerce
111 N. Washington St.
Mexico, Missouri 65265
Phone: (314)581-2765

SCORE Office (Southeast Missouri)
Rte. 1, Box 280
Neelyville, Missouri 63954
Phone: (573)989-3577

SCORE Office (Poplar Bluff Area)
c/o James W. Carson
806 Emma St.
Poplar Bluff, Missouri 63901
Phone: (573)686-8892

SCORE Office (St. Joseph)
Chamber of Commerce
3003 Frederick Ave.
St. Joseph, Missouri 64506
Phone: (816)232-4461

SCORE Office (St. Louis)
815 Olive St., Rm. 242
St. Louis, Missouri 63101-1569
Phone: (314)539-6970
Fax: (314)539-3785

SCORE Office (Lewis & Clark)
E-mail: score01@mail.win.org
425 Spencer Rd.
St. Peters, Missouri 63376
Phone: (314)928-2900
Fax: (314)928-2900

SCORE Office (Springfield)
620 S. Glenstone, Ste. 110
Springfield, Missouri 65802-3200
Phone: (417)864-7670
Fax: (417)864-4108

SCORE Office (Southeast Kansas)
1206 W. First St.
Webb City, Missouri 64870
Phone: (417)673-3984

Montana

SCORE Office (Billings)
815 S. 27th St.
Billings, Montana 59101
Phone: (406)245-4111

SCORE Office (Bozeman)
1205 E. Main St.
Bozeman, Montana 59715
Phone: (406)586-5421

SCORE Office (Butte)
1000 George St.
Butte, Montana 59701
Phone: (406)723-3177

SCORE Office (Great Falls)
710 First Ave. N
PO Box 2127
Great Falls, Montana 59401
Phone: (406)761-4434

SCORE Office (Havre, Montana)
518 First St.
Havre, Montana 59501
Phone: (406)265-4383

SCORE Office (Helena)
Federal Bldg.
301 S. Park
Helena, Montana 59626-0054
Phone: (406)441-1081

SCORE Office (Kalispell)
2 Main St.
Kalispell, Montana 59901
Phone: (406)756-5271
Fax: (406)752-6665

SCORE Office (Missoula)
E-mail: score@safeshop.com
802 Normans Ln.
PO Box 632
Missoula, Montana 59806
Phone: (406)327-8806

Nebraska

SCORE Office (Columbus)
Columbus, Nebraska 68601
Phone: (402)564-2769

SCORE Office (North Platte)
414 E. 16th St.
Cozad, Nebraska 69130
Phone: (308)784-2590

SCORE Office (Fremont)
PO Box 325
Chamber of Commerce
92 W. 5th St.
Fremont, Nebraska 68025
Phone: (402)721-2641

SCORE Office (Hastings)
Hastings, Nebraska 68901
Phone: (402)463-3447

SCORE Office (Hastings)
Box 42
Kearney, Nebraska 68848
Phone: (308)234-9647

SCORE Office (Lincoln)
8800 O St.
Lincoln, Nebraska 68520
Phone: (402)437-2409

SCORE Office (Panhandle)
150549 CR 30
Minatare, Nebraska 69356
Phone: (308)632-2133

SCORE Office (Norfolk)
3209 S. 48th Ave.
Norfolk, Nebraska 68106
Phone: (402)564-2769

SCORE Office (North Platte)
3301 W. 2nd St.
North Platte, Nebraska 69101
Phone: (308)784-2590

SCORE Office (Omaha)
11145 Mill Valley Rd.
Omaha, Nebraska 68154
Phone: (402)221-3606
Fax: (402)221-3680

SCORE Office (Panhandle)
11145 Mill Valley Rd.
Omaha, Nebraska 68154
Phone: (402)221-3604

Nevada

SCORE Office (Incline Village)
c/o Incline Village Chamber of
Commerce
969 Tahoe Blvd.

Incline Village, Nevada 89451
Phone: (702)831-7327
Fax: (702)832-1605

SCORE Office (Carson City)
301 E. Stewart
PO Box 7527
Las Vegas, Nevada 89125
Phone: (702)388-6104

SCORE Office (Las Vegas)
300 Las Vegas Blvd. S, Ste. 1100
Las Vegas, Nevada 89101
Phone: (702)388-6104

SCORE Office (Northern Nevada)
SBDC, College of Business
Administration
Univ. of Nevada
Reno, Nevada 89557-0100
Phone: (702)784-4436
Fax: (702)784-4337

New Hampshire

SCORE Office (North Country)
PO Box 34
Berlin, New Hampshire 03570
Phone: (603)752-1090

SCORE Office (Concord)
143 N. Main St., Rm. 202A
PO Box 1258
Concord, New Hampshire 03301
Phone: (603)225-1400
Fax: (603)225-1409

SCORE Office (Dover)
299 Central Ave.
Dover, New Hampshire 03820
Phone: (603)742-2218
Fax: (603)749-6317

SCORE Office (Monadnock)
34 Mechanic St.
Keene, New Hampshire 03431-3421
Phone: (603)352-0320

SCORE Office (Lakes Region)
67 Water St., Ste. 105
Laconia, New Hampshire 03246
Phone: (603)524-9168

SCORE Office (Upper Valley)
Citizens Bank Bldg., Rm. 310
20 W. Park St.
Lebanon, New Hampshire 03766
Phone: (603)448-3491

SCORE Office (Merrimack Valley)
275 Chestnut St., Rm. 618
Manchester, New Hampshire 03103
Phone: (603)666-7561
Fax: (603)666-7925

SCORE Office (Mt. Washington Vly)
PO Box 1066
North Conway, New Hampshire
03818
Phone: (603)383-0800

SCORE Office (Seacoast)
195 Commerce Way, Unit-A
Portsmouth, New Hampshire 03801-
3251
Phone: (603)433-0575

New Jersey

SCORE Office (Chester)
c/o John C. Apelian, Chair
5 Old Mill Rd.
Chester, New Jersey 07930
Phone: (908)879-7080

SCORE Office (Greater Princeton)
4 A George Washington Dr.
Cranbury, New Jersey 08512
Phone: (609)520-1776

SCORE Office (Freehold)
Western Monmouth Chamber of
Commerce
36 W. Main St.
Freehold, New Jersey 07728
Phone: (908)462-3030
Fax: (908)462-2123

SCORE Office (North West)
Hamburg, New Jersey 07419
Phone: (973)209-8525
Fax: (973)209-7252

SCORE Office (Monmouth)
Brookdale Community College
Career Services
765 Newman Springs Rd.
Lincroft, New Jersey 07738
Phone: (908)224-2573

SCORE Office (Manalapan)
Monmough Library
125 Symmes Dr.
Manalapan, New Jersey 07726
Phone: (908)431-7220

SCORE Office (Jersey City)
2 Gateway Ctr., 4th Fl.
Newark, New Jersey 07102
Phone: (973)645-3982
Fax: (973)645-2375

SCORE Office (Newark)
2 Gateway Center, 4th Fl.
Newark, New Jersey 07102-5553
Phone: (973)645-3982
Fax: (973)645-2375

SCORE Office (Bergen County)
327 E. Ridgewood Ave.
Paramus, New Jersey 07652
Phone: (201)599-6090

SCORE Office (Pennsauken)
United Jersey Bank
4900 Rte. 70
Pennsauken, New Jersey 08109
Phone: (609)486-3421

SCORE Office (Southern New
Jersey)
c/o United Jersey Bank
4900 Rte. 70
Pennsauken, New Jersey 08109
Phone: (609)486-3421

SCORE Office (Greater Princeton)
216 Rockingham Row
Princeton Forrestal Village
Princeton, New Jersey 08540
Phone: (609)520-1776
Fax: (609)520-9107

SCORE Office (Shrewsbury)
Monmouth County Library
Hwy. 35
Shrewsbury, New Jersey 07702
Phone: (908)842-5995
Fax: (908)219-6140

SCORE Office (Somerset)
Paritan Valley Community College
PO Box 3300
Somerville, New Jersey 08876
Phone: (908)218-8874

SCORE Office (Ocean County)
33 Washington St.
Toms River, New Jersey 08754
Phone: (732)505-6033

SCORE Office (Wall)
Wall Library
2700 Allaire Rd.

Wall, New Jersey 07719
Phone: (908)449-8877

SCORE Office (Wayne)
2055 Hamburg Tpke.
Wayne, New Jersey 07470
Phone: (201)831-7788
Fax: (201)831-9112

New Mexico

SCORE Office (Albuquerque)
c/o TVI Workforce Training Center
525 Buena Vista, SE
Albuquerque, New Mexico 87106
Phone: (505)766-1900
Fax: (505)766-1833

SCORE Office (Las Cruces)
E-mail: score.397@zianet.com
Loretto Towne Center
505 S. Main St., Ste. 125
Las Cruces, New Mexico 88001
Phone: (505)523-5627
Fax: (505)524-2101

SCORE Office (Roswell)
Federal Bldg., Rm. 237
Roswell, New Mexico 88201
Phone: (505)625-2112
Fax: (505)623-2545

SCORE Office (Santa Fe)
Montoya Federal Bldg.
120 Federal Place, Rm. 307
Santa Fe, New Mexico 87501
Phone: (505)988-6302
Fax: (505)988-6300

New York

SCORE Office (Northeast)
Albany College Chamber of
Commerce
1 Computer Dr. S
Albany, New York 12205
Phone: (518)446-1118
Fax: (518)446-1228

SCORE Office (Auburn)
c/o Chamber of Commerce
30 South St.
PO Box 675
Auburn, New York 13021
Phone: (315)252-7291

SCORE Office (South Tier
Binghamton)

Metro Center, 2nd Fl.
49 Court St.
PO Box 995
Binghamton, New York 13902
Phone: (607)772-8860

SCORE Office (Queens County City)
12055 Queens Blvd., Rm. 333
Borough Hall, New York 11424
Phone: (718)263-8961

SCORE Office (Buffalo)
Federal Bldg., Rm. 1311
111 W. Huron St.
Buffalo, New York 14202
Phone: (716)551-4301

SCORE Office (Canandaigua)
Chamber of Commerce Bldg.
113 S. Main St.
Canandaigua, New York 14424
Phone: (716)394-4400
Fax: (716)394-4546

SCORE Office (Chemung)
c/o Small Business Administration,
4th Fl.
333 E. Water St.
Elmira, New York 14901
Phone: (607)734-3358

SCORE Office (Geneva)
Chamber of Commerce Bldg.
PO Box 587
Geneva, New York 14456
Phone: (315)789-1776
Fax: (315)789-3993

SCORE Office (Glens Falls)
Adirondack Region Chamber of
Commerce
84 Broad St.
Glens Falls, New York 12801
Phone: (518)798-8463
Fax: (518)745-1433

SCORE Office (Orange County)
Orange County Chamber of
Commerce
40 Matthews St.
Goshen, New York 10924
Phone: (914)294-8080
Fax: (914)294-6121

SCORE Office (Huntington Area)
c/o Chamber of Commerce
151 W. Carver St.

Huntington, New York 11743
Phone: (516)423-6100

SCORE Office (Tompkins County)
c/o Tompkins Chamber of Commerce
904 E. Shore Dr.
Ithaca, New York 14850
Phone: (607)273-7080

SCORE Office (Long Island City)
120-55 Queens Blvd.
Jamaica, New York 11424
Phone: (718)263-8961
Fax: (718)263-9032

SCORE Office (Chatauqua)
c/o Chatauqua Chamber of
Commerce
101 W. 5th St.
Jamestown, New York 14701
Phone: (716)484-1103

SCORE Office (Westchester)
E-mail: score@locke.cc11.org
2 Caradon Ln.
Katonah, New York 10536
Phone: (914)948-3907
Fax: (914)948-4645

SCORE Office (Queens County)
Queens Borough Hall
120-55 Queens Blvd. Rm. 333
Kew Gardens, New York 11424
Phone: (718)263-8961
Fax: (718)263-9032

SCORE Office (Brookhaven)
3233 Rte. 112
Medford, New York 11763
Phone: (516)451-6563
Fax: (516)451-6925

SCORE Office (Melville)
35 Pinelawn Rd., Rm. 207-W
Melville, New York 11747
Phone: (516)454-0771

SCORE Office (Nassau County)
Dept. of Commerce & Industry
400 County Seat Dr., No. 140
Mineola, New York 11501
Phone: (516)571-3303

SCORE Office (Mt. Vernon)
c/o Mt. Vernon Chamber of
Commerce
4 N. 7th Ave.

Mt. Vernon, New York 10550
Phone: (914)667-7500

SCORE Office (New York)
E-mail: score1000@erols.com
26 Federal Plz., Rm. 3100
New York, New York 10278
Phone: (212)264-4507
Fax: (212)264-4963

SCORE Office (Newburgh)
47 Grand St.
Newburgh, New York 12550
Phone: (914)562-5100

SCORE Office (Owego)
Tioga County Chamber of Commerce
188 Front St.
Owego, New York 13827
Phone: (607)687-2020

SCORE Office (Peekskill)
c/o Peekskill Chamber of Commerce
1 S. Division St.
Peekskill, New York 10566
Phone: (914)737-3600
Fax: (914)737-0541

SCORE Office (Penn Yan)
Penn Yan Chamber of Commerce
2375 Rte. 14A
Penn Yan, New York 14527
Phone: (315)536-3111

SCORE Office (Dutchess)
c/o Chamber of Commerce
110 Main St.
Poughkeepsie, New York 12601
Phone: (914)454-1700

SCORE Office (Rochester)
601 Keating Federal Bldg., Rm. 410
100 State St.
Rochester, New York 14614
Phone: (716)263-6473
Fax: (716)263-3146

SCORE Office (Saranac Lake)
30 Main St.
Saranac Lake, New York 12983
Phone: (315)448-0415

SCORE Office (Suffolk)
286 Main St.
Setauket, New York 11733
Phone: (516)751-3886

SCORE Office (Staten Island)
c/o Chamber of Commerce
130 Bay St.
Staten Island, New York 10301
Phone: (718)727-1221

SCORE Office (Ulster)
Ulster County Community College
Clinton Bldg., Rm. 107
Stone Ridge, New York 12484
Phone: (914)687-5035
Fax: (914)687-5015

SCORE Office (Syracuse)
401 S. Salina, 5th Fl.
Syracuse, New York 13202
Phone: (315)471-9392

SCORE Office (Utica)
SUNY Institute of Technology, Rte. 12
Utica, New York 13504-3050
Phone: (315)792-7553

SCORE Office (Watertown)
518 Davidson St.
Watertown, New York 13601
Phone: (315)788-1200
Fax: (315)788-8251

SCORE Office (Westchester)
350 Main St.
White Plains, New York 10601
Phone: (914)948-3907
Fax: (914)948-4645

SCORE Office (Yonkers)
c/o Yonkers Chamber of Commerce
540 Nepperhan Ave., Ste.200
Yonkers, New York 10701
Phone: (914)963-0332

North Carolina

SCORE Office (Asheboro)
c/o Asheboro/Randolph Chamber of
Commerce
317 E. Dixie Dr.
Asheboro, North Carolina 27203
Phone: (336)626-2626
Fax: (336)626-7077

SCORE Office (Asheville)
Federal Bldg., Rm. 259
151 Patton
Asheville, North Carolina 28801-5770

Phone: (828)271-4786
Fax: (828)271-4009

SCORE Office (Chapel Hill)
c/o Chapel Hill/Carrboro Chamber of
Commerce
104 S. Estes Dr.
PO Box 2897
Chapel Hill, North Carolina 27514
Phone: (919)967-7075

SCORE Office (Coastal Plains)
PO Box 2897
Chapel Hill, North Carolina 27515
Phone: (919)967-7075
Fax: (919)968-6874

SCORE Office (Charlotte)
200 N. College St., Ste. A-2015
Charlotte, North Carolina 28202
Phone: (704)344-6576
Fax: (704)344-6769

SCORE Office (Durham)
411 W. Chapel Hill St.
Durham, North Carolina 27707
Phone: (919)541-2171

SCORE Office (Gastonia)
c/o Gastonia Chamber of Commerce
PO Box 2168
Gastonia, North Carolina 28053
Phone: (704)864-2621
Fax: (704)854-8723

SCORE Office (Greensboro)
400 W. Market St., Ste. 103
Greensboro, North Carolina 27401-
2241
Phone: (910)333-5399

SCORE Office (Henderson)
PO Box 917
Henderson, North Carolina 27536
Phone: (919)492-2061
Fax: (919)430-0460

SCORE Office (Hendersonville)
E-mail: score@circle.net
Federal Bldg., Rm. 108
W. 4th Ave. & Church St.
Hendersonville, North Carolina
28792
Phone: (828)693-8702

SCORE Office (Unifour)
c/o Catawba County Chamber of
Commerce

PO Box 1828
Hickory, North Carolina 28603
Phone: (704)328-6111

SCORE Office (High Point)
High Point Chamber of Commerce
1101 N. Main St.
High Point, North Carolina 27262
Phone: (336)882-8625
Fax: (336)889-9499

SCORE Office (Outer Banks)
c/o Outer Banks Chamber of
Commerce
Collington Rd. and Mustain
Kill Devil Hills, North Carolina
27948
Phone: (252)441-8144

SCORE Office (Down East)
312 Tyron Palace Dr.
New Bern, North Carolina 28560
Phone: (252)633-6688
Fax: (252)633-9608

SCORE Office (Kinston)
PO Box 95
New Bern, North Carolina 28561
Phone: (919)633-6688

SCORE Office (Raleigh)
Century Post Office Bldg., Ste. 306
300 Federal St. Mall
Raleigh, North Carolina 27601
Phone: (919)856-4739

SCORE Office (Sanford)
Small Business Assistance Center
1801 Nash St.
Sanford, North Carolina 27330
Phone: (919)774-6442
Fax: (919)776-8739

SCORE Office (Sandhills Area)
c/o Sand Area Chamber of Commerce
1480 Hwy. 15-501
PO Box 458
Southern Pines, North Carolina 28387
Phone: (910)692-3926

SCORE Office (Wilmington)
Alton Lennon Federal Bldg.
2 Princess St., Ste. 103
Wilmington, North Carolina 28401
Phone: (910)815-4576
Fax: (910)256-5150

North Dakota

SCORE Office (Bismarck-Mandan)
700 E. Main Ave., 2nd Fl.
PO Box 5509
Bismarck, North Dakota 58506-5509
Phone: (701)250-4303

SCORE Office (Fargo)
657 2nd Ave., Rm. 225
Fargo, North Dakota 58108-3083
Phone: (701)239-5677

SCORE Office (Upper Red River)
4275 Technology Dr., Rm. 156
Grand Forks, North Dakota 58202-
8372
Phone: (701)777-3051

SCORE Office (Minot)
100 1st St. SW
Minot, North Dakota 58701-3846
Phone: (701)852-6883
Fax: (701)852-6905

Ohio

SCORE Office (Akron)
c/o Regional Development Board
One Cascade Plz., 7th Fl.
Akron, Ohio 44308
Phone: (330)379-3163
Fax: (330)379-3164

SCORE Office (Ashland)
Ashland University
Gill Center
47 W. Main St.
Ashland, Ohio 44805
Phone: (419)281-4584

SCORE Office (Canton)
116 Cleveland Ave. NW, Ste. 601
Canton, Ohio 44702-1720
Phone: (330)453-6047

SCORE Office (Chillicothe)
165 S. Paint St.
Chillicothe, Ohio 45601
Phone: (614)772-4530

SCORE Office (Cincinnati)
Ameritrust Bldg., Rm. 850
525 Vine St.
Cincinnati, Ohio 45202
Phone: (513)684-2812
Fax: (513)684-3251

SCORE Office (Cleveland)
Eaton Center, Ste. 620
1100 Superior Ave.
Cleveland, Ohio 44114-2507
Phone: (216)522-4194
Fax: (216)522-4844

SCORE Office (Columbus)
2 Nationwide Plz., Ste. 1400
Columbus, Ohio 43215-2542
Phone: (614)469-2357
Fax: (614)469-2391

SCORE Office (Dayton)
Dayton Federal Bldg., Rm. 505
200 W. Second St.
Dayton, Ohio 45402-1430
Phone: (513)225-2887
Fax: (513)225-7667

SCORE Office (Defiance)
Defiance Chamber of Commerce
615 W. 3rd St.
PO Box 130
Defiance, Ohio 43512
Phone: (419)782-7946

SCORE Office (Findlay)
Findlay Chamber of Commerce
123 E. Main Cross St.
PO Box 923
Findlay, Ohio 45840
Phone: (419)422-3314

SCORE Office (Lima)
147 N. Main St.
Lima, Ohio 45801
Phone: (419)222-6045
Fax: (419)229-0266

SCORE Office (Mansfield)
Chamber of Commerce
55 N. Mulberry St.
Mansfield, Ohio 44902
Phone: (419)522-3211

SCORE Office (Marietta)
Marietta College
Thomas Hall
Marietta, Ohio 45750
Phone: (614)373-0268

SCORE Office (Medina)
County Administrative Bldg.
144 N. Broadway
Medina, Ohio 44256
Phone: (216)764-8650

SCORE Office (Licking County)
50 W. Locust St.
Newark, Ohio 43055
Phone: (614)345-7458

SCORE Office (Salem)
2491 State Rte. 45 S
Salem, Ohio 44460
Phone: (216)332-0361

SCORE Office (Tiffin)
Tiffin Chamber of Commerce
62 S. Washington St.
Tiffin, Ohio 44883
Phone: (419)447-4141
Fax: (419)447-5141

SCORE Office (Toledo)
1946 N. 13th St., Rm. 367
Toledo, Ohio 43624
Phone: (419)259-7598

SCORE Office (Wooster)
377 W. Liberty St.
Wooster, Ohio 44691
Phone: (330)262-5735
Fax: (330)262-5745

SCORE Office (Youngstown)
Youngstown University
306 Williamson Hall
Youngstown, Ohio 44555
Phone: (330)746-2687

Oklahoma

SCORE Office (Anadarko)
PO Box 366
Anadarko, Oklahoma 73005
Phone: (405)247-6651

SCORE Office (Ardmore)
410 W. Main
Ardmore, Oklahoma 73401
Phone: (405)223-7765

SCORE Office (Northeast Oklahoma)
210 S. Main
Grove, Oklahoma 74344
Phone: (918)786-6284
Fax: (918)786-9841

SCORE Office (Lawton)
4500 W. Lee Blvd., Bldg. 100, Ste.
107
Lawton, Oklahoma 73505
Phone: (580)353-8727
Fax: (580)250-5677

SCORE Office (Oklahoma City)
c/o SBA, Oklahoma Tower Bldg.
210 Park Ave., No. 1300
Oklahoma City, Oklahoma 73102
Phone: (405)231-5163
Fax: (405)231-4876

SCORE Office (Stillwater)
Stillwater Chamber of Commerce
439 S. Main
Stillwater, Oklahoma 74074
Phone: (405)372-5573
Fax: (405)372-4316

SCORE Office (Tulsa)
Tulsa Chamber of Commerce
616 S. Boston, Ste. 406
Tulsa, Oklahoma 74119
Phone: (918)581-7462
Fax: (918)581-6908

Oregon

SCORE Office (Bend)
c/o Bend Chamber of Commerce
63085 N. Hwy. 97
Bend, Oregon 97701
Phone: (541)330-6300
Fax: (541)330-6900

SCORE Office (Willamette)
1401 Willamette St.
PO Box 1107
Eugene, Oregon 97401-4003
Phone: (541)465-6600
Fax: (541)484-4942

SCORE Office (Florence)
c/o Lane Community College, Chuck
Temple
3149 Oak St.
Florence, Oregon 97439
Phone: (503)997-8444
Fax: (503)997-8448

SCORE Office (Southern Oregon)
E-mail: pgr134f@prodigy.com
33 N. Central Ave., Ste. 216
Medford, Oregon 97501
Phone: (541)776-4220

SCORE Office (Portland)
1515 SW 5th Ave., Ste. 1050
Portland, Oregon 97201
Phone: (503)326-3441
Fax: (503)326-2808

SCORE Office (Salem)
c/o Key Bank
416 State St. (corner of Liberty)
Salem, Oregon 97301
Phone: (503)370-2896

Pennsylvania

SCORE Office (Altoona-Blair)
c/o Altoona-Blair Chamber of
Commerce
1212 12th Ave.
Altoona, Pennsylvania 16601-3493
Phone: (814)943-8151

SCORE Office (Lehigh Valley)
Lehigh University
Rauch Bldg. 37
621 Taylor St.
Bethlehem, Pennsylvania 18015
Phone: (610)758-4496
Fax: (610)758-5205

SCORE Office (Butler County)
100 N. Main St.
PO Box 1082
Butler, Pennsylvania 16003
Phone: (412)283-2222
Fax: (412)283-0224

SCORE Office (Harrisburg)
4211 Trindle Rd.
Camp Hill, Pennsylvania 17011
Phone: (717)761-4304
Fax: (717)761-4315

SCORE Office (Cumberland Valley)
Chambersburg Chamber of
Commerce
75 S. 2nd St.
Chambersburg, Pennsylvania 17201
Phone: (717)264-2935

SCORE Office (Monroe County-
Stroudsburg)
556 Main St.
East Stroudsburg, Pennsylvania
18301
Phone: (717)421-4433

SCORE Office (Erie)
120 W. 9th St.
Erie, Pennsylvania 16501
Phone: (814)871-5650
Fax: (814)871-7530

SCORE Office (Bucks County)
c/o Bucks County Chamber of
Commerce
409 Hood Blvd.
Fairless Hills, Pennsylvania 19030
Phone: (215)943-8850
Fax: (215)943-7404

SCORE Office (Hanover)
146 Broadway
Hanover, Pennsylvania 17331
Phone: (717)637-6130
Fax: (717)637-9127

SCORE Office (Harrisburg)
100 Chestnut, Ste. 309
Harrisburg, Pennsylvania 17101
Phone: (717)782-3874

SCORE Office (East Montgomery
County)
Baederwood Shopping Center
1653 The Fairways, Ste. 204
Jenkintown, Pennsylvania 19046
Phone: (215)885-3027

SCORE Office (Kittanning)
C/o Kittanning Chamber of
Commerce
2 Butler Rd.
Kittanning, Pennsylvania 16201
Phone: (412)543-1305
Fax: (412)543-6206

SCORE Office (Lancaster)
118 W. Chestnut St.
Lancaster, Pennsylvania 17603
Phone: (717)397-3092

SCORE Office (Westmoreland
County)
St. Vincent College
300 Fraser Purchase Rd.
Latrobe, Pennsylvania 15650-2690
Phone: (412)539-7505
Fax: (412)539-1850

SCORE Office (Lebanon)
252 N. 8th St.
PO Box 899
Lebanon, Pennsylvania 17042-0899
Phone: (717)273-3727
Fax: (717)273-7940

SCORE Office (Lewistown)
Lewistown Chamber of Commerce
3 W. Monument Sq., Ste. 204
Lewistown, Pennsylvania 17044

Phone: (717)248-6713
Fax: (717)248-6714

SCORE Office (Delaware County)
Delaware County Chamber of
Commerce
602 E. Baltimore Pike
Media, Pennsylvania 19063
Phone: (610)565-3677
Fax: (610)565-1606

SCORE Office (Milton Area)
112 S. Front St.
Milton, Pennsylvania 17847
Phone: (717)742-7341
Fax: (717)792-2008

SCORE Office (Mon-Valley)
435 Donner Ave.
Monessen, Pennsylvania 15062
Phone: (412)684-4277
Fax: (412)684-7688

SCORE Office (Monroeville)
William Penn Plaza
2790 Mosside Blvd., Ste. 295
Monroeville, Pennsylvania 15146
Phone: (412)856-0622
Fax: (412)856-1030

SCORE Office (Airport Area)
Chamber of Commerce
986 Brodhead Rd.
Moon Twp, Pennsylvania 15108-
2398
Phone: (412)264-6270
Fax: (412)264-1575

SCORE Office (Northeast)
8601 E. Roosevelt Blvd.
Philadelphia, Pennsylvania 19152
Phone: (215)332-3400
Fax: (215)332-6050

SCORE Office (Philadelphia)
E-mail: score46@bellatlantic.net
1315 Walnut St., Ste. 500
Philadelphia, Pennsylvania 19107
Phone: (215)790-5050
Fax: (215)790-5057

SCORE Office (Pittsburgh)
1000 Liberty Ave., Rm. 1122
Pittsburgh, Pennsylvania 15222
Phone: (412)395-6560
Fax: (412)395-6562

SCORE Office (Tri-County)
810 N. Charlotte St.
Pottstown, Pennsylvania 19464
Phone: (610)327-2673

SCORE Office (Reading)
c/o Reading Chamber of Commerce
601 Penn St.
Reading, Pennsylvania 19601
Phone: (610)376-3497

SCORE Office (Scranton)
Oppenheim Bldg.
116 N. Washington Ave., Ste. 650
Scranton, Pennsylvania 18503
Phone: (717)347-4611
Fax: (717)347-4611

SCORE Office (Central
Pennsylvania)
200 Innovation Blvd., Ste. 242-B
State College, Pennsylvania 16803
Phone: (814)234-9415
Fax: (814)238-9686

SCORE Office (Monroe-Stroudsburg)
556 Main St.
Stroudsburg, Pennsylvania 18360
Phone: (717)421-4433

SCORE Office (Uniontown)
Federal Bldg.
Pittsburg St.
PO Box 2065 DTS
Uniontown, Pennsylvania 15401
Phone: (412)437-4222

SCORE Office (Warren County)
Warren County Chamber of
Commerce
315 2nd Ave.
Warren, Pennsylvania 16365
Phone: (814)723-9017

SCORE Office (Waynesboro)
323 E. Main St.
Waynesboro, Pennsylvania 17268
Phone: (717)762-7123
Fax: (717)962-7124

SCORE Office (Chester County)
E-mail: score@locke.ccil.org
Government Service Center, Ste. 281
601 Westtown Rd.
West Chester, Pennsylvania 19382-
4538
Phone: (610)344-6910
Fax: (610)344-6919

SCORE Office (Wilkes-Barre)
7 N. Wilkes-Barre Blvd.
Wilkes Barre, Pennsylvania 18702-
5241
Phone: (717)826-6502
Fax: (717)826-6287

SCORE Office (North Central
Pennsylvania)
E-mail: score234@mail.csrlink.net
240 W. 3rd St., Rm. 227
PO Box 725
Williamsport, Pennsylvania 17703
Phone: (717)322-3720
Fax: (717)322-1607

SCORE Office (York)
Cyber Center
1600 Pennsylvania Ave.
York, Pennsylvania 17404
Phone: (717)845-8830
Fax: (717)854-9333

Puerto Rico

SCORE Office (Puerto Rico & Virgin
Islands)
Citibank Towers Plaza, 2nd Fl.
252 Ponce de Leon Ave.
San Juan, Puerto Rico 00918-2041
Phone: (787)766-5001
Fax: (787)766-5309

Rhode Island

SCORE Office (Barrington)
Barrington Public Library
281 County Rd.
Barrington, Rhode Island 02806
Phone: (401)247-1920
Fax: (401)247-3763

SCORE Office (Woonsocket)
640 Washington Hwy.
Lincoln, Rhode Island 02865
Phone: (401)334-1000
Fax: (401)334-1009

SCORE Office (Wickford)
8045 Post Rd.
North Kingstown, Rhode Island
02852
Phone: (401)295-5566
Fax: (401)295-8987

SCORE Office (J.G.E. Knight)
380 Westminster St.

Providence, Rhode Island 02903
Phone: (401)528-4571
Fax: (401)528-4539

SCORE Office (Warwick)
3288 Post Rd.
Warwick, Rhode Island 02886
Phone: (401)732-1100
Fax: (401)732-1101

SCORE Office (Westerly)
74 Post Rd.
Westerly, Rhode Island 02891
Phone: (401)596-7761
Free: (800)732-7636
Fax: (401)596-2190

South Carolina

SCORE Office (Aiken)
Aiken Chamber of Commerce
P.O. Box 892
Aiken, South Carolina 29802
Phone: (803)641-1111
Free: (800)542-4536
Fax: (803)641-4174

SCORE Office (Anderson)
Tri-County Technical College
Anderson Mall
3130 N. Main St.
Anderson, South Carolina 29621
Phone: (864)224-0453

SCORE Office (Coastal)
284 King St.
Charleston, South Carolina 29401
Phone: (803)727-4778
Fax: (803)853-2529

SCORE Office (Midlands)
Strom Thurmond Bldg., Rm. 358
1835 Assembly St., Rm 358
Columbia, South Carolina 29201
Phone: (803)765-5131
Fax: (803)765-5962

SCORE Office (Piedmont)
Federal Bldg., Rm. B-02
300 E. Washington St.
Greenville, South Carolina 29601
Phone: (864)271-3638

SCORE Office (Greenwood)
Piedmont Technical College
PO Drawer 1467
Greenwood, South Carolina 29648
Phone: (864)223-8357

SCORE Office (Hilton Head)
Hilton Head Chamber of Commerce
PO Box 5647
Hilton Head Island, South Carolina
29938
Phone: (803)785-3673
Fax: (803)785-7110

SCORE Office (Grand Strand)
E-mail: score@pelican.net
937 Broadway
Myrtle Beach, South Carolina 29577
Phone: (803)918-1079
Fax: (803)918-1083

SCORE Office (Spartanburg)
c/o Vernon Wyant Chamber of
Commerce
P.O. Box 1636
Spartanburg, South Carolina 29304
Phone: (864)594-5000
Fax: (864)594-5055

South Dakota

SCORE Office (Rapid City)
444 Mount Rushmore Rd., No. 209
Rapid City, South Dakota 57701
Phone: (605)394-5311

SCORE Office (Sioux Falls)
First Financial Center
110 S. Phillips Ave., Ste. 200
Sioux Falls, South Dakota 57102-
1109
Phone: (605)330-4231
Fax: (605)330-4231

Tennessee

SCORE Office (Chattanooga)
Federal Bldg., Rm. 26
900 Georgia Ave.
Chattanooga, Tennessee 37402
Phone: (423)752-5190
Fax: (423)752-5335

SCORE Office (Cleveland)
P.O. Box 2275
Cleveland, Tennessee 37320
Phone: (423)472-6587
Fax: (423)472-2019

SCORE Office (Upper Cumberland
Center)
1225 S. Willow Ave.
Cookeville, Tennessee 38501

Phone: (615)432-4111
Fax: (615)432-6010

SCORE Office (Unicoi County)
c/o Chamber of Commerce
PO Box 713
Erwin, Tennessee 37650
Phone: (423)743-3000
Fax: (423)743-0942

SCORE Office (Greeneville)
115 Academy St.
Greeneville, Tennessee 37743
Phone: (423)638-4111
Fax: (423)638-5345

SCORE Office (Jackson)

c/o Jackson Chamber of Commerce
194 Auditorium St.
Jackson, Tennessee 38301
Phone: (901)423-2200

SCORE Office (Northeast Tennessee)
1st Tennessee Bank Bldg.
2710 S. Roan St., Ste. 584
Johnson City, Tennessee 37601
Phone: (423)929-7686
Fax: (423)461-8052

SCORE Office (Kingsport)
c/o Kingsport Chamber of Commerce
151 E. Main St.
Kingsport, Tennessee 37662
Phone: (423)392-8805

SCORE Office (Greater Knoxville)
Farragot Bldg., Ste. 224
530 S. Gay St.
Knoxville, Tennessee 37902
Phone: (423)545-4203

SCORE Office (Maryville)
Blount County Chamber of
Commerce
201 S. Washington St.
Maryville, Tennessee 37804-5728
Phone: (423)983-2241
Free: (800)525-6834
Fax: (423)984-1386

SCORE Office (Memphis)
Federal Bldg., Ste. 390
167 N. Main St.
Memphis, Tennessee 38103
Phone: (901)544-3588

SCORE Office (Nashville)
50 Vantage Way, Ste. 201
Nashville, Tennessee 37228-1500
Phone: (615)736-7621

Texas

SCORE Office (Abilene)
2106 Federal Post Office and Court
Bldg.
Abilene, Texas 79601
Phone: (915)677-1857

SCORE Office (Austin)
2501 S. Congress
Austin, Texas 78701
Phone: (512)442-7235
Fax: (512)442-7528

SCORE Office (Golden Triangle)
450 Boyd St.
Beaumont, Texas 77704
Phone: (409)838-6581
Fax: (409)833-6718

SCORE Office (Brownsville)
3505 Boca Chica Blvd., Ste. 305
Brownsville, Texas 78521
Phone: (210)541-4508

SCORE Office (Brazos Valley)
E-mail:
102633.2612@compuserve.com
Victoria Bank & Trust
3000 Briarcrest, Ste. 302
Bryan, Texas 77802
Phone: (409)776-8876

SCORE Office (Cleburne)
Watergarden Pl., 9th Fl., Ste. 400
Cleburne, Texas 76031
Phone: (817)871-6002

SCORE Office (Corpus Christi)
651 Upper North Broadway, Ste. 654
Corpus Christi, Texas 78477
Phone: (512)888-4322
Fax: (512)888-3418

SCORE Office (Dallas)
Comerica Bank, 2nd Fl.
6260 E. Mockingbird
Dallas, Texas 75214-2619
Phone: (214)828-2471
Fax: (214)821-8033

SCORE Office (El Paso)
c/o Business Information Center

Greater El Paso Chamber of
Commerce
10 Civic Center Plaza
El Paso, Texas 79901
Phone: (915)534-0541
Fax: (915)534-0513

SCORE Office (Bedford)
100 E. 15th St., Ste. 400
Fort Worth, Texas 76102
Phone: (817)871-6002

SCORE Office (Ft. Worth)
E-mail: fwbac@onramp.net
100 E. 15th St., No. 24
Ft. Worth, Texas 76102
Phone: (817)871-6002
Fax: (817)871-6031

SCORE Office (Garland)
2734 W. Kingsley Rd.
Garland, Texas 75041
Phone: (214)271-9224

SCORE Office (Granbury Chamber
of Commerce)
416 S. Morgan
Granbury, Texas 76048
Phone: (817)573-1622
Fax: (817)573-0805

SCORE Office (Lower Rio Grande
Valley)
222 E. Van Buren, Ste. 500
Harlingen, Texas 78550
Phone: (956)427-8533
Fax: (956)427-8537

SCORE Office (Houston)
9301 Southwest Fwy., Ste. 550
Houston, Texas 77074
Phone: (713)773-6565
Fax: (713)773-6550

SCORE Office (Irving)

c/o Irving Chamber of Commerce
3333 N. MacArthur Blvd., Ste. 100
Irving, Texas 75062
Phone: (214)252-8484
Fax: (214)252-6710

SCORE Office (Lubbock)
1205 Texas Ave., Rm. 411D
Lubbock, Texas 79401
Phone: (806)472-7462
Fax: (806)472-7487

SCORE Office (Midland)
Post Office Annex
200 E. Wall St., Rm. P121
Midland, Texas 79701
Phone: (915)687-2649

SCORE Office (Orange)
c/o Orange Chamber of Commerce
1012 Green Ave.
Orange, Texas 77630-5620
Phone: (409)883-3536
Free: (800)528-4906
Fax: (409)886-3247

SCORE Office (Plano)
c/o Plano Chamber of Commerce
1200 E. 15th St.
P.O. Drawer 940287
Plano, Texas 75094-0287
Phone: (214)424-7547
Fax: (214)422-5182

SCORE Office (Port Arthur)
c/o Port Arthur Chamber of
Commerce
4749 Twin City Hwy., Ste. 300
Port Arthur, Texas 77642
Phone: (409)963-1107
Fax: (409)963-3322

SCORE Office (Richardson)
c/o Richardson Chamber of
Commerce
411 Belle Grove
Richardson, Texas 75080
Phone: (214)234-4141
Free: (800)777-8001
Fax: (214)680-9103

SCORE Office (San Antonio)
c/o SBA, Federal Bldg., Rm. A527
727 E. Durango
San Antonio, Texas 78206
Phone: (210)472-5931
Fax: (210)472-5935

SCORE Office (Texarkana State
College)
819 State Line Ave.
Texarkana, Texas 75501
Phone: (903)792-7191
Fax: (903)793-4304

SCORE Office (East Texas)
RTDC
1530 SSW Loop 323, Ste. 100
Tyler, Texas 75701

Phone: (903)510-2975
Fax: (903)510-2978

SCORE Office (Waco)
401 Franklin Ave.
Waco, Texas 76701
Phone: (817)754-8898
Fax: (817)756-0776

SCORE Office (Wichita Falls)
Hamilton Bldg.
900 8th St.
Wichita Falls, Texas 76307
Phone: (940)723-2741
Fax: (940)723-8773

Utah

SCORE Office (Logan)
c/o Cache Valley Chamber of
Commerce
160 N. Main
Logan, Utah 84321
Phone: (435)752-2161

SCORE Office (Ogden)
1701 E. Windsor Dr.
Ogden, Utah 84604
Phone: (801)226-0881

SCORE Office (Central Utah)
Old County Court House
51 S. University Ave.
Provo, Utah 84601
Phone: (801)379-2444

SCORE Office (Southern Utah)
c/o Dixie College
225 South 700 East
St. George, Utah 84770
Phone: (801)652-7741

SCORE Office (Salt Lake)
169 E. 100 S.
Salt Lake City, Utah 84111
Phone: (801)364-1331
Fax: (801)364-1310

Vermont

SCORE Office (Champlain Valley)
Winston Prouty Federal Bldg.
11 Lincoln St., Room 106
Essex Junction, Vermont 05452
Phone: (802)951-6762

SCORE Office (Montpelier)
c/o U.S. Small Business

Administration
87 State St., Rm. 205
PO Box 605
Montpelier, Vermont 05601
Phone: (802)828-4422
Fax: (802)828-4422

SCORE Office (Marble Valley)
256 N. Main St.
Rutland, Vermont 05701-2413
Phone: (802)773-9147

SCORE Office (Northeast Kingdom)
c/o NCIC
20 Main St.
PO Box 904
St. Johnsbury, Vermont 05819
Phone: (802)748-5101

Virgin Islands

SCORE Office (St. Croix)
United Plaza Shopping Center
PO Box 4010, Christiansted
St. Croix, Virgin Islands 00822
Phone: (809)778-5380

SCORE Office (St. Thomas-St. John)
Federal Bldg., Rm. 21
Veterans Dr.
St. Thomas, Virgin Islands 00801
Phone: (809)774-8530

Virginia

SCORE Office (Arlington)
2009 N. 14th St., Ste. 111
Arlington, Virginia 22201
Phone: (703)525-2400

SCORE Office (Blacksburg)
141 Jackson St.
Blacksburg, Virginia 24060
Phone: (540)552-4061

SCORE Office (Bristol)
20 Volunteer Pkwy.
PO Box 519
Bristol, Virginia 24203
Phone: (540)989-4850

SCORE Office (Central Virginia)
1001 E. Market St., Ste. 101
Charlottesville, Virginia 22902
Phone: (804)295-6712
Fax: (804)295-7066

SCORE Office (Alleghany Satellite)
c/o Chamber of Commerce
241 W. Main St.
Covington, Virginia 24426
Phone: (540)962-2178
Fax: (540)962-2179

SCORE Office (Central Fairfax)
3975 University Dr., Ste. 350
Fairfax, Virginia 22030
Phone: (703)591-2450

SCORE Office (Falls Church)
P.O. Box 491
Falls Church, Virginia 22040
Phone: (703)532-1050
Fax: (703)237-7904

SCORE Office (Glenns)
c/o Rappahannock Community
College
Glenns Campus
Box 287
Glenns, Virginia 23149
Phone: (804)693-9650

SCORE Office (Peninsula)
c/o Peninsula Chamber of Commerce
6 Manhattan Sq.
PO Box 7269
Hampton, Virginia 23666
Phone: (757)766-2000
Fax: (757)865-0339

SCORE Office (Tri-Cities)
c/o Chamber of Commerce
108 N. Main St.
Hopewell, Virginia 23860
Phone: (804)458-5536

SCORE Office (Lynchburg)
Federal Bldg.
1100 Main St.
Lynchburg, Virginia 24504-1714
Phone: (804)846-3235

SCORE Office (Martinsvile)
115 Broad St.
Martinsville, Virginia 24112-0709
Phone: (540)632-6401
Fax: (540)632-5059

SCORE Office (Hampton Roads)
E-mail: scorehr60@juno.com
c/o Eastern Shore Chamber of
Commerce
Federal Bldg., Rm. 737

200 Grandby St.
Norfolk, Virginia 23510
Phone: (757)441-3733
Fax: (757)441-3733

SCORE Office (Norfolk)
Federal Bldg., Rm. 737
200 Granby St.
Norfolk, Virginia 23510
Phone: (757)441-3733
Fax: (757)441-3733

SCORE Office (Virginia Beach)
Virginia Beach Office of Hampton
Roads
Chamber of Commerce
200 Grandby St., Rm 737
Norfolk, Virginia 23510
Phone: (804)441-3733

SCORE Office (Greater Prince
William)
Prince William Chamber of
Commerce
4320 Ridgewood Center Dr.
Prince William, Virginia 22192
Phone: (703)590-5000

SCORE Office (Radford)
Radford Chamber of Commerce
1126 Norwood St.
Radford, Virginia 24141
Phone: (540)639-2202

SCORE Office (Richmond)
Feberal Bldg.
400 N. 8th St., Ste. 1150
PO Box 10126
Richmond, Virginia 23240-0126
Phone: (804)771-2400
Fax: (804)771-8018

SCORE Office (Roanoke)
E-mail: scorerva@juno.com
Federal Bldg., Rm. 716
250 Franklin Rd.
Roanoke, Virginia 24011
Phone: (540)857-2834
Fax: (540)857-2043

SCORE Office (Fairfax)
8391 Old Courthouse Rd., Ste. 300
Vienna, Virginia 22182
Phone: (703)749-0400

SCORE Office (Greater Vienna)
513 Maple Ave. West

Vienna, Virginia 22180
Phone: (703)281-1333
Fax: (703)242-1482

SCORE Office (Shenandoah Valley)
c/o Waynesboro Chamber of
Commerce
301 W. Main St.
Waynesboro, Virginia 22980
Phone: (540)949-8203
Fax: (540)949-7740

SCORE Office (Williamsburg)
E-mail: wacc@williamsburgcc.com
c/o Williamsburg Chamber of
Commerce
201 Penniman Rd.
Williamsburg, Virginia 23185
Phone: (757)229-6511

SCORE Office (Northern Virginia)
c/o Winchester-Frederick Chamber of
Commerce
1360 S. Pleasant Valley Rd.
Winchester, Virginia 22601
Phone: (540)662-4118

Washington

SCORE Office (Gray's Harbor)
c/o Gray's Harbor Chamber of
Commerce
506 Duffy St.
Aberdeen, Washington 98520
Phone: (360)532-1924
Fax: (360)533-7945

SCORE Office (Bellingham)
101 E. Holly St.
Bellingham, Washington 98225
Phone: (360)676-3307

SCORE Office (Everett)
Everett Public Library
2702 Hoyt Ave.
Everett, Washington 98201-3556
Phone: (206)259-8000

SCORE Office (Gig Harbor)
c/o Gig Harbor Chamber of
Commerce
3125 Judson St.
Gig Harbor, Washington 98335
Phone: (206)851-6865

SCORE Office (Kennewick)
Kennewick Chamber of Commerce

PO Box 6986
Kennewick, Washington 99336
Phone: (509)736-0510

SCORE Office (Puyallup)
Puyallup Chamber of Commerce
322 2nd St. SW
PO Box 1298
Puyallup, Washington 98371
Phone: (206)845-6755
Fax: (206)848-6164

SCORE Office (Seattle)
E-mail: score55@aol.com
1200 6th Ave., Ste. 1700
Seattle, Washington 98101
Phone: (206)553-7320
Fax: (206)553-7044

SCORE Office (Spokane)
801 W. Riverside Ave., No. 240
Spokane, Washington 99201
Phone: (509)353-2820
Fax: (509)353-2600

SCORE Office (Clover Park)
PO Box 1933
Tacoma, Washington 98401-1933
Phone: (206)627-2175

SCORE Office (Tacoma)
1101 Pacific Ave., No. 300
Tacoma, Washington 98402
Phone: (253)274-1288
Fax: (253)274-1289

SCORE Office (Fort Vancouver)
1701 Broadway, S-1
Vancouver, Washington 98663
Phone: (360)699-1079

SCORE Office (Walla Walla)
Walla Walla Small Business Cebter
500 Tausick Way
Walla Walla, Washington 99362
Phone: (509)527-4681

SCORE Office (Mid-Columbia)
1113 S. 14th Ave.
Yakima, Washington 98907
Phone: (509)574-4944
Fax: (509)574-2943

West Virginia

SCORE Office (Charleston)
E-mail: score256@juno.com
1116 Smith St.

Charleston, West Virginia 25301
Phone: (304)347-5463

SCORE Office (Virginia Street)
1116 Smith St., Ste. 302
Charleston, West Virginia 25301
Phone: (304)347-5463

SCORE Office (Marion County)
PO Box 208
Fairmont, West Virginia 26555-0208
Phone: (304)363-0486

SCORE Office (Upper Monongahela
Valley)
E-mail: score537@hotmail.com
1000 Technology Dr., Ste. 1111
Fairmont, West Virginia 26555
Phone: (304)363-0486

SCORE Office (Huntington)
1101 6th Ave., Ste. 220
Huntington, West Virginia 25701-
2309
Phone: (304)523-4092

SCORE Office (Wheeling)
1310 Market St.
Wheeling, West Virginia 26003
Phone: (304)233-2575
Fax: (304)233-1320

Wisconsin

SCORE Office (Fox Cities)
227 S. Walnut St.
Appleton, Wisconsin 54913
Phone: (920)734-7101
Fax: (920)734-7161

SCORE Office (Beloit)
136 W. Grand Ave., Ste. 100
PO Box 717
Beloit, Wisconsin 53511
Phone: (608)365-8835
Fax: (608)365-9170

SCORE Office (Eau Claire)
Federal Bldg., Rm. B11
510 S. Barstow St.
Eau Claire, Wisconsin 54701
Phone: (715)834-1573

SCORE Office (Fond Du Lac)
c/o Fond Du Lac Chamber of
Commerce
207 N. Main St.
Fond Du Lac, Wisconsin 54935

Phone: (414)921-9500
Fax: (414)921-9559

SCORE Office (Green Bay)
835 Potts Ave.
Green Bay, Wisconsin 54304
Phone: (414)496-8930
Fax: (414)496-6009

SCORE Office (Janesville)
20 S. Main St., Ste. 11
PO Box 8008
Janesville, Wisconsin 53547
Phone: (608)757-3160
Fax: (608)757-3170

SCORE Office (La Crosse)
712 Main St.
La Crosse, Wisconsin 54602-0219
Phone: (608)784-4880

SCORE Office (Manitowoc)
Manitowoc Chamber of Commerce
1515 Memorial Dr.
PO Box 903
Manitowoc, Wisconsin 54221-0903
Phone: (414)684-5575
Fax: (414)684-1915

SCORE Office (Madison)
c/o M&I Bank
7448 Hubbard Ave.
Middleton, Wisconsin 53562
Phone: (608)831-5464

SCORE Office (Milwaukee)
310 W. Wisconsin Ave., Ste. 425
Milwaukee, Wisconsin 53203
Phone: (414)297-3942
Fax: (414)297-1377

SCORE Office (Central Wisconsin)
1224 Lindbergh Ave.
Stevens Point, Wisconsin 54481
Phone: (715)344-7729

SCORE Office (Superior)
Superior Business Center Inc.
1423 N. 8th St.
Superior, Wisconsin 54880
Phone: (715)394-7388
Fax: (715)393-7414

SCORE Office (Waukesha)
c/o Waukesha Chamber of Commerce
223 Wisconsin Ave.
Waukesha, Wisconsin 53186-4926
Phone: (414)542-4249

SCORE Office (Wausau)
300 3rd St., Ste. 200
Wausau, Wisconsin 54402-6190
Phone: (715)845-6231

SCORE Office (Wisconsin Rapids)
2240 Kingston Rd.
Wisconsin Rapids, Wisconsin 54494
Phone: (715)423-1830

Wyoming

SCORE Office (Casper)
Federal Bldg., No. 2215
100 East B St.
Casper, Wyoming 82602
Phone: (307)261-6529
Fax: (307)261-6530

VENTURE CAPITAL & FINANCING COMPANIES

This section contains a listing of financing and loan companies in the United States and Canada. These listings are arranged alphabetically by country, state/territory/ province, then by city, then by organization name.

CANADA

Manitoba

Manitoba Department of Industry,
Trade and Tourism
Small Business Services
Entrepreneurial Development
Business Start Program
240 Graham Ave., Rm. 250
PO Box 2609
Winnipeg, Manitoba R3C 4B3
Phone: (204)984-0037
Free: (800)665-2019
Fax: (204)983-3852
A matching loan guarantee program
that will promote the success of new
business start-ups by ensuring that
entrepreneurs have a comprehensive
business plan, by offering business
training and counseling, and by
providing access to funding up to
$10,000 via a loan guarantee through
a number of existing financial
institutions.

Ontario

Industry Canada
Small Business Loan Administration
235 Queen St., 8th Fl., E.
Ottawa, Ontario K1A 0H5
Phone: (613)954-5540
Fax: (613)952-0290

Quebec

Societe de Developpement Industriel
du Quebec
Small Business Revival Program
1200 Route de Egliase
Bureau 500
Ste. Foy, Quebec G1V 5A3
Phone: (418)643-5172
Free: (800)461-AIDE
Fax: (418)528-2063
Allows businesses facing temporary
difficulties to obtain financial
assistance aimed at reinforcing their
financial structures.

Saskatchewan

Saskatchewan Department of
Economic and Cooperative
Development
Investment Programs Branch
Labour-Sponsored Venture Capital
Program
1919 Saskatchewan Dr.
Regina, Saskatchewan S4P 3V7
Phone: (306)787-1605
Fax: (306)787-1620
Promotes the formation of venture
capital corporations by employees of
a small business, to provide equity
capital for the expansion of existing
facilities or establishment of new
businesses. Federal and provincial tax
credits are available to the investor.

UNITED STATES

Alabama

Jefferson County Community
Development
Planning and Community
Development
805 N. 22nd St.
Birmingham, Alabama 35203

Phone: (205)325-5761
Fax: (205)325-5095
Provides loans for purchasing real
estate, construction, working capital,
or machinery and equipment.

FJC Growth Capital Corp.
200 W. Court Sq., Ste. 340
Huntsville, Alabama 35801
Phone: (205)922-2918
Fax: (205)922-2909
A minority enterprise small business
investment company. Diversified
industry preference.

Hickory Venture Capital Corp.
E-mail: info@hvc.com
200 W. Side Sq., Ste.100
Huntsville, Alabama 35801
Phone: (256)539-1931
Fax: (256)539-5130
A small business investment
corporation. Prefers to invest in later-
stage companies. Will not consider oil
and gas, or real estate investments.

Alabama Capital Corp.
16 Midtown Park E.
Mobile, Alabama 36606
Phone: (334)476-0700
Fax: (334)476-0026
David C. DeLaney, President
Preferred Investment Size: $400,000.
Investment Policies: Asset based
loans with equity. Investment Types:
Seed, early, expansion, later stages.
Industry Preferences: Diversified.
Geographic Preferences: Southeast.

First SBIC of Alabama
16 Midtown Park E.
Mobile, Alabama 36606
Phone: (334)476-0700
Fax: (334)476-0026
David C. DeLaney, President
Preferred Investment Size: $400,000.
Investment Policies: Asset based
loans with equity. Investment Types:
Seed, early, expansion, later stages.
Industry Preferences: Diversified.
Geographic Preferences: Southeast.

Southern Development Council
E-mail: sdci@sdcinc.org
4101 C Wall St.
Montgomery, Alabama 36106

Phone: (334)244-1801
Free: (800)499-3034
Fax: (334)244-1421
Statewide nonprofit financial
packaging corporation. Helps small
businesses arrange financing.

Alaska

Alaska Department of Commerce and
Economic Development
Division of Investments
E-mail:
investments@commerce.state.ak.us
3601 C St., Ste. 724
Anchorage, Alaska 99503
Phone: (907)269-8150
Fax: (907)269-8147
Offers a program that assists
purchasers to assume existing small
business loans.

Alaska Department of Commerce and
Economic Development (Anchorage)
Industrial Development and Export
Authority
Alaska Industrial Development and
Export Authority
480 W. Tudor Rd.
Anchorage, Alaska 99503-6690
Phone: (907)269-3000
Fax: (907)269-3044
Assists businesses in securing long-
term financing for capital
investments, such as the acquisition
of equipment or the construction of a
new plant, at moderate interest rates.

Calista Corp.
601 W. 5th Ave., Ste. 200
Anchorage, Alaska 99501-2226
Phone: (907)279-5516
Fax: (907)272-5060
A minority enterprise small business
investment corporation. No industry
preference.

Alaska Department of Commerce and
Economic Development (Juneau)
Division of Investments
E-mail:
investments@commerce.state.ak.us
PO Box 34159
Juneau, Alaska 99803-4159
Phone: (907)465-2510
Free: (800)478-LOAN

Fax: (907)465-2103
Offers a program that assists
purchasers to assume existing small
business loans.

Alaska Department of Natural
Resources
Division of Agriculture
Agricultural Revolving Loan Fund
1800 Glenn Hwy., Ste. 12
Palmer, Alaska 99645
Phone: (907)745-7200
Fax: (907)745-7112
Provides loans for farm development,
general farm operations, chattel, and
land clearing. Resident farmers,
homesteaders, partnerships, and
corporations are eligible.

Arizona

Sundance Venture Partners, L.P.
400 E. Van Buren, Ste. 750
Phoenix, Arizona 85004
Phone: (602)252-5373
Fax: (602)252-1450
A small business investment
company. Diversified industry
preference.

Arizona Growth Partners
E-mail: jock@valleyventures.com
6617 N. Scottsdale Rd., Ste. 104
Scottsdale, Arizona 85250
Phone: (602)661-6600
Fax: (602)661-6262
Venture capital firm. Industry
preferences include high technology,
medical, biotechnology, and
computer industries.

Arkansas

Arkansas Development Finance
Authority
PO Box 8023
Little Rock, Arkansas 72203-8023
Phone: (501)682-5900
Fax: (501)682-5859
Provides bond financing to small
borrowers, who may otherwise be
excluded from the bond market due to
high costs, by using umbrella bond
issues. Can provide interim financing
for approved projects awaiting a bond
issuance.

Small Business Investment Capital, Inc.
12103 Interstate 30
P.O. Box 3627
Little Rock, Arkansas 72203
Phone: (501)455-6599
Fax: (501)455-6556
Charles E. Toland, President
Preferred Investment Size: Up to $230,000. Investment Policies: Loans. Investment Types: Start-ups and debt consolidation. Industry Preferences: Supermarkets. Geographic Preferences: Arkansas, Oklahoma, Texas, Louisiana.

California

Calsafe Capital Corp.
245 E. Main St., Ste. 107
Alhambra, California 91801
Phone: (626)289-3400
Fax: (626)300-8025
A minority enterprise small business investment company. Diversified industry preference.

Ally Finance Corp.
9100 Wilshire Blvd., Ste. 408
Beverly Hills, California 90212
Phone: (760)241-7025
Fax: (760)241-8232
A small business investment corporation. No industry preference.

Developers Equity Capital Corp.
447 S. Robertson Blvd. Ste. 101
Beverly Hills, California 90211
Phone: (310)550-7552
Fax: (310)550-7529
A small business investment corporation. Real estate preferred.

Domain Associates
650 Town Center Dr., Ste. 1830
Costa Mesa, California 92626
Phone: (714)434-6227
Fax: (714)434-6088
Venture capital firm providing early stage financing. Areas of interest include life sciences and biotechnology companies (biopharmaceuticals, medical devices, diagnostics, and new materials).

First SBIC of California (Costa Mesa)
3029 Harbor Blvd.
Costa Mesa, California 92626
Fax: (714)668-6099
A small business investment corporation and venture capital company. No industry preference.

Oxford Ventures, Inc.
650 Town Center Dr., Ste. 810
Costa Mesa, California 92626
Phone: (714)754-5719
Fax: (714)754-6802

Westar Capital (Costa Mesa)
949 South Coast Dr., Ste. 650
Costa Mesa, California 92626
Phone: (714)481-5166
Fax: (714)481-5166
Venture capital firm providing management financing and corporate buyouts. Areas of interest include information, computer and business services, health care, food processing, and defense/aerospace.

Fulcrum Venture Capital Corp.
300 Corp. Pointe, Ste. 380
Culver City, California 90230
Phone: (310)645-1271
Fax: (310)645-1272
A minority enterprise small business investment corporation. No industry preference.

Bay Partners
10600 N. De Anza Blvd., Ste. 100
Cupertino, California 95014
Phone: (408)725-2444
Fax: (408)446-4502
Venture capital supplier. Provides start-up financing primarily to West Coast technology companies that have highly qualified management teams. Initial investments range from $100,000 to $800,000. Where large investments are required, the company will act as lead investor to bring in additional qualified venture investors.

Horn Venture Partners
20300 Stevens Creek Blvd., Ste. 330
Cupertino, California 95014
Phone: (408)725-0774
Fax: (408)725-0327

Areas of interest include information technology, life sciences, specialty retail and consumer products, restaurant, and biotechnology industries.

Novus Ventures, L.P.
20111 Stevens Creek Blvd., Ste. 130
Cupertino, California 95014
Phone: (408)252-3900
Fax: (408)252-1713
Daniel D. Tompkins, Manager
Preferred Investment Size: $400,000 to $1 Million. Investment Policies: Convertible debt, Convertible stock. Industry Preferences: Information technology. Geographic Preferences: Western U.S.

Pacific Mezzanine Fund, L.P.
2200 Powell St., Ste. 1250
Emeryville, California 94608
Phone: (510)595-9800
Fax: (510)595-9801
David C. Woodward, General Partner
Preferred Investment Size: $2 to $5 million. Investment Policies: Loans with equity features. Investment Types: Expansion, later stage. Industry Preferences: Diversified. Geographic Preferences: Western US.

BankAmerica Ventures
953 Tower Lane, Ste. 700
Foster City, California 94404
Phone: (650)378-6000
Fax: (650)378-6040

BankAmerica Ventures (Foster City)
950 Tower Ln., Ste. 700
Foster City, California 94404
Phone: (650)378-6000
Fax: (650)378-6040
Robert L. Boswell, Senior Vice President

First American Capital Funding, Inc.
10840 Warner Ave., Ste. 202
Fountain Valley, California 92708
Phone: (714)965-7190
Fax: (714)965-7193
A minority enterprise small business investment corporation. No industry preference.

Opportunity Capital Corp.
2201 Walnut Ave., Ste. 210

Fremont, California 94538-2261
Phone: (510)795-7000
Fax: (510)494-5439
A minority enterprise small business
investment corporation. No industry
preference.

Opportunity Capital Partners II, LP
2201 Walnut Ave., Ste. 210
Fremont, California 94538
Phone: (510)795-7000
Fax: (510)494-5439
A minority enterprise small business
investment company. Diversified
industry preference.

San Joaquin Business Investment
Group, Inc.
1900 Mariposa Mall, Ste. 100
Fresno, California 93721
Phone: (209)233-3580
Fax: (209)233-3709
A minority enterprise small business
investment company. Diversified
industry preference.

Magna Pacific Investments
330 N. Brand Blvd., Ste. 670
Glendale, California 91203
Phone: (818)547-0809
Fax: (818)547-9303
A minority enterprise small business
investment company. Diversified
industry preference.

Brentwood Venture Capital
1920 Main St., Ste. 820
Irvine, California 92614-7227
Phone: (949)251-1010
Fax: (949)251-1011
Prefers to invest in the electronics and
health care industries.

Crosspoint Venture Partners
E-mail:
meashburn@crosspointvc.com
18552 MacArthur, Ste. 400
Irvine, California 92612
Phone: (949)852-1611
Fax: (949)852-9804
Venture capital firm investing in
medical, software, and
telecommunications.

DSV Partners
E-mail: jbergman@packbell.net
1920 Main St., Ste. 820

Irvine, California 92614-7227
Phone: (949)475-4242
Fax: (949)475-1950
Venture capital firm. Prefers to invest
in software, medical, biotechnical,
environmental, and other high-growth
technology companies.

Ventana Growth Fund L.P. (Irvine)
18881 Von Karman Ave., Ste. 1150,
Tower 17
Irvine, California 92612
Phone: (949)476-2204
Fax: (949)752-0223

South Bay Capital Corporation
5325 E. Pacific Coast Hwy.
Long Beach, California 90804
Phone: (562)597-3285
Fax: (562)498-7167
John Wang, Manager

Aspen Ventures West II, L.P.
E-mail: twhalen@aspenventures.com
1000 Fremont Ave., Ste. V
Los Altos, California 94024
Phone: (650)917-5670
Fax: (650)917-5677
Alexander Cilento, Mgr.
David Crocket, Mgr.
Preferred Investment Size: $500,000
to $2.5 million. Investment Policies:
Equity. Investment Types: Early
stage. Industry Preferences:
Information technology. Geographic
Preferences: Western U.S.

AVI Capital, L.P.
E-mail: vc@avicapital.com
1 1st St., Ste. 2
Los Altos, California 94022
Phone: (650)949-9862
Fax: (650)949-8510
P. Wolken, Mgr.
B. Weinman, Mgr.
Preferred Investment Size:
$1,000,000. Investment Policies:
Equity Only. Investment Types: Seed,
early stage. Industry Preferences:
High technology and electronic deals
only. Geographic Preferences: West
Coast, California.

HMS Group
1 1st St., Ste. 16
Los Altos, California 94022

Phone: (650)917-0390
Fax: (650)917-0394
Prefers communications industries.

MBW Management, Inc. (Los Altos)
350 2nd St., Ste. 4
Los Altos, California 94022
Phone: (650)941-2392
Fax: (650)941-2865

Bank of America National Trust and
Savings Association
PO Box 60049
Los Angeles, California 90060-0049
Phone: (714)973-8495
Venture capital firm preferring
investments of $1 million-$3 million.
Diversified industry preference.

Best Finance Corp.
4929 W. Wilshire Blvd., Ste. 407
Los Angeles, California 90010
Phone: (213)937-1636
Fax: (213)937-6393
Vincent Lee, General Manager
Preferred Investment Size: $50,000.
Investment Policies: Loans and/or
equity. Investment Types: Purchase,
seed, expansion. Industry Preferences:
Diversified. Geographic Preferences:
California.

Brentwood Associates (Los Angeles)
11150 Santa Monica Blvd., Ste. 1200
Los Angeles, California 90025-3314
Phone: (310)477-6611
Fax: (310)477-1011
Venture capital supplier. Provides
start-up and expansion financing to
technology-based enterprises
specializing in computing and data
processing, electronics,
communications, materials, energy,
industrial automation, and
bioengineering and medical
equipment. Investments generally
range from $1 million to $3 million.

BT Corp.
300 S. Grand Ave.
Los Angeles, California 90071
Phone: (213)620-8200
Fax: (213)620-8484
A small business investment
company.

Charterway Investment Corp.
One Wilshire Bldg., No.1600
Los Angeles, California 90017-3317
Phone: (213)689-9107
Fax: (213)890-1968
A minority enterprise small business
investment corporation. No industry
preference.

Far East Capital Corp.
977 N. Broadway, Ste. 401
Los Angeles, California 90012
Phone: (213)687-1361
Fax: (213)626-7497
A minority enterprise small business
investment company. Diversified
industry preference.

Kline Hawkes California SBIC, LP
11726 San Vicente Blvd., Ste. 300
Los Angeles, California 90049
Phone: (310)442-4700
Fax: (310)442-4707
Frank R. Kline, Manager

Peregrine Ventures
PO Box 491760
Los Angeles, California 90049
Phone: (310)458-1441
Fax: (310)394-0771
Venture capital firm providing start-
up, first stage, and leveraged buyout
financing. Areas of interest include
communications and health.

Riordan Lewis & Haden
300 S. Grand Ave., 29th Fl.
Los Angeles, California 90071
Phone: (213)229-8500
Fax: (213)229-8597
Venture capital firm providing all
types of financing, including
management buyouts and turn-
arounds. Areas of interest include
food and service.

The Seideler Companies, Inc.
515 S. Figueroa St., 11th Fl.
Los Angeles, California 90071-3396
Phone: (213)624-4232
Fax: (213)623-1131

Advanced Technology Ventures
(Menlo Park)
485 Ramona St.,Ste. 200
Menlo Park, California 94028-8140

Phone: (650)321-8601
Fax: (650)321-0934

Bessemer Venture Partners (Menlo
Park)
535 Middlefield Rd., Ste. 245
Menlo Park, California 94025
Phone: (650)853-7000
Fax: (650)853-7001

Brentwood Associates (Menlo Park)
3000 Sandhill Rd., Ste. 260
Menlo Park, California 94025-7020
Phone: (650)854-7691
Fax: (650)854-9513

Canaan Partners
2884 Sand Hill Rd., Ste. 115
Menlo Park, California 94025-7022
Phone: (650)854-8092
Fax: (650)854-8127
Venture capital firm providing start-
up, second and third stage, and
buyout financing. Areas of interest
include information industry products
and services, medical technology, and
health care services.

Comdisco Venture Group (Silicon
Valley)
3000 Sand Hill Rd., Bldg. 1, Ste. 155
Menlo Park, California 94025-7141
Phone: (415)854-9484
Fax: (415)854-4026
Prefers start-up businesses in fields of
semiconductors, computer hardware
and software, computer services and
systems, telecommunications, and
medical and biotechnology.
Investments range from $500,000 to
$5 million.

El Dorado Ventures (Cupertino)
E-mail: garyk@eldoradoventures.com
2400 Sand Hill Rd., Ste. 100
Menlo Park, California 94025
Phone: (650)854-1200
Fax: (650)854-1202

Glenwood Management
3000 Sand Hill Rd., Bldg. 4, Ste. 230
Menlo Park, California 94025
Phone: (650)854-8070
Fax: (650)854-4961
Venture capital supplier. Areas of
interest include high technology and
biomedical industries.

Institutional Venture Partners
3000 Sand Hill Rd., Bldg. 2, Ste. 290
Menlo Park, California 94025
Phone: (650)854-0132
Fax: (650)854-5762
Venture capital fund. Invests in early
stage ventures with significant market
potential in the computer, information
sciences, communications, and life
sciences fields.

Interwest Partners (Menlo Park)
3000 Sand Hill Rd., Bldg. 3, Ste. 255
Menlo Park, California 94025-7112
Phone: (650)854-8585
Fax: (650)854-4706
Venture capital fund. Both high-tech
and low- or non-technology
companies are considered. No oil,
gas, real estate, or construction
projects.

Kleiner Perkins Caufield & Byers
(Menlo Park)
2750 Sand Hill Rd.
Menlo Park, California 94025
Phone: (650)233-2750
Fax: (650)233-0300
Provides seed, start-up, second and
third-round, and bridge financing to
companies on the West Coast.
Preferred industries of investment
include electronics, computers,
software, telecommunications,
biotechnology, medical devices, and
pharmaceuticals.

Matrix Partners
2500 Sand Hill Rd., Ste. 113
Menlo Park, California 94025-7016
Phone: (650)854-3131
Fax: (650)854-3296
Private venture capital partnership.
Investments range from $500,000 to
$1 million.

Mayfield Fund
2800 Sand Hill Rd., Ste. 250
Menlo Park, California 94025
Phone: (650)854-5560
Fax: (650)854-5712
Venture capital partnership. Prefers
high-technology and biomedical
industries.

McCown De Leeuw and Co. (Menlo Park)
3000 Sand Hill Rd., Bldg. 3, Ste. 290
Menlo Park, California 94025
Phone: (650)854-6000
Fax: (650)854-0853
A venture capital firm. Preferences include the mortgage servicing, building materials, printing, and office products industries.

Menlo Ventures
E-mail: info@menloventures.com
3000 Sand Hill Rd., Bldg. 4, Ste. 100
Menlo Park, California 94025
Phone: (650)854-8540
Fax: (650)854-7059
Venture capital supplier. Provides start-up and expansion financing to companies with experienced management teams, distinctive product lines, and large growing markets. Primary interest is in technology-oriented, service, consumer products, and distribution companies. Investments range from $500,000 to $3 million; also provides capital for leveraged buyouts.

Merrill Pickard Anderson & Eyre I
E-mail: smerrill@Benchmark.com
2480 Sand Hill Rd., Ste. 200
Menlo Park, California 94025
Phone: (650)854-8600
Fax: (650)854-8183
Steven Merrill, President

New Enterprise Associates (Menlo Park)
2490 Sand Hill Road
Menlo Park, California 94025
Phone: (650)854-9499
Fax: (650)854-9397
Venture capital supplier.

New Enterprise Associates (San Francisco)
2490 Sand Hill Road
Menlo Park, California 94025
Phone: (650)854-9499
Fax: (650)854-9397
Venture capital supplier. Concentrates in technology-based industries that have the potential for product innovation, rapid growth, and high profit margins.

Paragon Venture Partners
3000 Sand Hill Rd., Bldg. 1, Ste. 275
Menlo Park, California 94025
Phone: (650)854-8000
Fax: (650)854-7260
Venture capital firm. Areas of interest include high technology and life sciences with an emphasis on data communications, networking, software, medical devices, biotechnology, and health care services industries.

Pathfinder Venture Capital Funds (Menlo Park)
3000 Sand Hill Rd., Bldg. 1, Ste. 290
Menlo Park, California 94025
Phone: (650)854-0650
Fax: (650)854-9010
Venture capital supplier. Provides start-up and early-stage financing to emerging companies in the medical, computer, pharmaceuticals, and data communications industries. Emphasis is on companies with proprietary technology or market positions and with substantial potential for revenue growth.

Ritter Partners
3000 Sandhill Rd. Bldg.1, Ste. 190
Menlo Park, California 94025
Phone: (650)854-1555
Fax: (650)854-5015
William C. Edwards, President

Sequoia Capital
3000 Sand Hill Rd., Bldg. 4, Ste. 280
Menlo Park, California 94025
Phone: (415)854-3927
Fax: (415)854-2977
Private venture capital partnership with $300 million under management. Provides financing for all stages of development of well-managed companies with exceptional growth prospects in fast-growth industries. Past investments have been made in computers and peripherals, communications, health care, biotechnology, and medical instruments and devices. Investments range from $350,000 for early stage companies to $4 million for late stage accelerates.

Sierra Ventures
E-mail: info@sierraven.com
3000 Sand Hill Rd., Bldg. 4, Ste. 210
Menlo Park, California 94025
Phone: (650)854-1000
Fax: (650)854-5593
Venture capital partnership.

Sigma Partners
2884 Sand Hill Rd., Ste. 121
Menlo Park, California 94025-7022
Phone: (650)854-1300
Fax: (650)854-1323
Independent venture capital partnership. Prefers to invest in the following areas: communications, computer hardware, computer software, manufacturing, medical equipment, and semiconductor capital equipment. Avoids investing in construction, hotels, leasing, motion pictures, and natural resources. Minimum initial commitment is $500,000.

Sprout Group (Menlo Park)
Bldg. 3, Ste. 170
3000 Sand Hill Rd.
Menlo Park, California 94025-7114
Phone: (650)854-1550
Fax: (650)234-2779

Technology Venture Investors
2480 Sand Hill Rd., Ste. 101
Menlo Park, California 94025
Phone: (650)854-7472
Fax: (650)854-4187
Private venture capital partnership. Primary interest is in technology companies with minimum investment of $1 million.

Trinity Ventures Ltd.
E-mail: trinityvc@aol.com
3000 Sand Hill Rd., Bldg. 1, Ste. 240
Menlo Park, California 94025
Phone: (650)854-9500
Fax: (650)854-9501
Private venture capital firm investing in computer software, consumer products, and health care industries.

U.S. Venture Partners
2180 Sand Hill Rd., Ste. 300
Menlo Park, California 94025
Phone: (415)854-9080

Fax: (415)854-3018
Venture capital partnership. Prefers the specialty retail, consumer products, technology, and biomedical industries.

USVP-Schlein Marketing Fund
2180 Sand Hill Rd., Ste. 300
Menlo Park, California 94025
Phone: (415)854-9080
Fax: (415)854-3018
Venture capital fund. Prefers specialty retailing/consumer products companies.

Hall, Capital Management
26161 Lapaz Rd., Ste. E
Mission Viejo, California 92691
Phone: (714)707-5096
Fax: (714)707-5121
A small business investment corporation. No industry preference. Provides capital for small and medium-sized companies through participation in private placements of subordinated debt, preferred, and common stock. Offers growth-acquisition and later-stage venture capital.

ABC Capital Funding
917 Waittier Blvd.
Montebello, California 90640
Phone: (213)725-7890
Fax: (213)725-7115
A minority enterprise small business investment corporation. No industry preference.

LaiLai Capital Corp.
223 E. Garvey Ave., Ste. 228
Monterey Park, California 91754
Phone: (626)288-0704
Fax: (626)288-4101
A minority enterprise small business investment company. Diversified industry preference.

Myriad Capital, Inc.
701 S. Atlantic Blvd., Ste. 302
Monterey Park, California 91754-3242
Phone: (626)570-4548
Fax: (626)570-9570
A minority enterprise small business investment corporation. Prefers

investing in production and manufacturing industries.

Marwit Capital LLC
180 Newport Center Dr., Ste. 200
Newport Beach, California 92660
Phone: (714)640-6234
Fax: (714)720-8077
A small business investment corporation. Provides financing for leveraged buyouts, mergers, acquisitions, and expansion stages. Investments are in the $100,000 to $4 million range. Does not provide financing for start-ups or real estate ventures.

Inman and Bowman
4 Orinda Way, Bldg. D, Ste. 150
Orinda, California 94563
Phone: (510)253-1611
Fax: (510)253-9037

Accel Partners (San Francisco)
E-mail: www.accel.com
428 University Ave.
Palo Alto, California 94301
Phone: (650)614-4800
Fax: (650)614-4880
Venture capital firm providing start-up financing. Areas of interest include health care, information technology, software, and telecommunications.

Asset Management Co.
2275 E. Bayshore, Ste. 150
Palo Alto, California 94303
Phone: (650)494-7400
Fax: (650)856-1826
Venture capital firm. High-technology industries preferred.

Campbell Venture Management
375 California St.
Palo Alto, California 94308
Phone: (650)941-2068
Fax: (650)857-0303

Greylock Management (Palo Alto)
755 Page Mill Rd., Ste. A-100
Palo Alto, California 94304-1018
Phone: (650)493-5525
Fax: (650)493-5575
Venture capital firm providing all stages of financing. Areas of interest include computer software, communications, health,

biotechnology, publishing, and specialty retail.

MK Global Ventures
2471 E. Bayshore Rd., Ste. 520
Palo Alto, California 94303
Phone: (650)424-0151
Fax: (650)494-2753

Norwest Venture Capital (Menlo Park)
245 Iytton Ave., Ste. 250
Palo Alto, California 94301
Phone: (650)321-8000
Fax: (650)321-8010
A small business investment corporation. No industry preference.

Oak Investment Partners (Menlo Park)
525 University Avenue, Ste. 1300
Palo Alto, California 94301
Phone: (650)614-3700
Fax: (650)328-6345
Small business investment corporation. Areas of interest include communications, computer hardware and software, high technology, manufacturing, medical equipment and instrumentation, pharmaceuticals, and retail.

Patricof & Co. Ventures, Inc. (Palo Alto)
2100 Geng Rd., Ste. 150
Palo Alto, California 94303
Phone: (650)494-9944
Fax: (650)494-6751
Venture capital firm providing equity investments, diversified by markets and stage of company. Prefers to fund growth.

Summit Partners (Newport Beach)
499 Hamilton Ave., Ste. 200
Palo Alto, California 94301
Phone: (650)321-1166
Fax: (650)321-1188
Venture capital firm providing investments in the $2 million-$20 million range. Areas of interest include technology, health care, and financial services.

Sutter Hill Ventures
755 Page Mill Rd., Ste. A-200
Palo Alto, California 94304-1005

Phone: (650)493-5600
Fax: (650)858-1854
Venture capital partnership providing start-up financing for high technology businesses.

TA Associates (Palo Alto)
435 Tasso St.
Palo Alto, California 94301
Phone: (650)328-1210
Fax: (650)326-4933
Private venture capital firm. Prefers technology companies and leveraged buyouts. Provides from $1 to $20 million in investments.

Venrock Associates
755 Page Mill, A-230
Palo Alto, California 94304
Phone: (415)493-5577
Fax: (415)493-6443
Private venture capital supplier. Prefers high-technology start-up equity investments.

Jafco America Ventures, Inc. (San Francisco)
505 Hamilton Ste. 310
Palto Alto, California 94301
Phone: (650)463-8800
Fax: (650)463-8801
Venture capital firm. Provides middle- to later-stage investments. Avoids investments in real estate, natural resources, entertainment, motion pictures, oil and gas, construction, and non-technical industries.

BankAmerica Ventures (Pasadena)
155 N. Lake Ave., Ste. 1010
Pasadena, California 91109
Phone: (626)578-5474
Fax: (626)440-9931

First SBIC of California (Pasadena)
155 N. Lake Ave., Ste. 1010
Pasadena, California 91109
Fax: (818)440-9931
A small business investment company.

The Money Store Investment Corp.
3301 "C" St., Ste. 100 M
Sacramento, California 95816
Phone: (916)446-5000
Free: (800)639-1102

Fax: (916)443-2399
Non-bank lender providing start-up and expansion financing.

Forward Ventures
10975 Torreyana Rd., No. 230
San Diego, California 92121
Phone: (619)677-6077
Fax: (619)452-8799
Venture capital firm preferring investments of $100,000-$500,000. Areas of interest include biotechnology and health care.

Idanta Partners Ltd.
4660 La Jolla Village Dr., Ste. 850
San Diego, California 92122-4606
Phone: (619)452-9690
Fax: (619)452-2013
Venture capital partnership. No industry preferences. Minimum investment is $500,000.

Sorrento Growth Partners I, L.P.
4225 Executive Sq., Ste. 1450
San Diego, California 92137
Fax: (619)452-7607
Robert Jaffe, Manager
Preferred Investment Size: $750,000 to $2 million. Investment Policies: Equity only. Investment Types: Seed, early, expansion, later stages. Industry Preferences: Medicine, health, communications, electronics, special retail. Geographic Preferences: Southern California.

Acacia Venture Partners
E-mail: sagegiven@aol.com
101 California St., Ste. 3160
San Francisco, California 94111
Phone: (415)433-4200
Fax: (415)433-4250
Venture capital firm. Health care, software, technology-based service, and specialty retailing industries preferred.

American Realty and Construction
1489 Webster St., Ste. 218
San Francisco, California 94115-3767
Phone: (415)928-6600
Fax: (415)928-6363
A minority enterprise small business investment corporation. No industry preference.

Bentley Capital
592 Vallejo St. Ste. 2
San Francisco, California 94133
Phone: (415)362-2868
Fax: (415)398-8209
A minority enterprise small business investment company. Diversified industry preference.

Bryan and Edwards Partnership (San Francisco)
600 Montgomery St., 35th Fl.
San Francisco, California 94111-2854
Phone: (415)421-9990
Fax: (415)421-0471
A small business investment corporation. No industry preference.

Burr, Egan, Deleage, and Co. (San Francisco)
Alter Partners
1 Embarcadero Center, Ste. 4050
San Francisco, California 94111-3729
Phone: (415)362-4022
Fax: (415)362-6178
Private venture capital supplier. Invests start-up, expansion, and acquisitions capital nationwide. Principal concerns are strength of the management team; large, rapidly expanding markets; and unique products for services. Past investments have been made in the fields of biotechnology and pharmaceuticals, cable TV, chemicals/plastics, communications, software, computer systems and peripherals, distributorships, radio common carriers, electronics and electrical components, environmental control, health services, medical devices and instrumentation, and radio and cellular telecommunications. Primarily interested in medical, electronics, and media industries.

Dominion Ventures, Inc.
44 Montgomery St., Ste. 4200
San Francisco, California 94104
Phone: (415)362-4890
Fax: (415)394-9245
Venture capital firm providing seed, start-up, second and third stage, and buyout financing. Areas of interest

include biotechnology, health care, telecommunications, software, and financial services.

Eurolink International
E-mail: vallee@eurolink.com
690 Market St., Ste. 702
San Francisco, California 94104
Phone: (415)398-6352
Fax: (415)398-6355
Private venture capital supplier. Provides all stages of financing.

G C and H Partners
1 Maritime Plz., 20th Fl.
San Francisco, California 94111
Phone: (415)693-2000
Fax: (415)951-3699
A small business investment corporation. No industry preference.

Hambrecht and Quist (San Francisco)
1 Bush St.
San Francisco, California 94104
Phone: (415)439-3300
Fax: (415)439-3621
Prefers to invest in computer technology, environmental technology, and biotechnology. Investments range from $500,000 to $5,000,000.

Heller First Capital Corp.
50 Beale Ste. 1600
San Francisco, California 94105
Phone: (415)356-1300
Fax: (415)356-1301
Non-bank lender providing start-up and expansion financing.

Jupiter Partners
600 Montgomery St., 35th Fl.
San Francisco, California 94111
Phone: (415)421-9990
Fax: (415)421-0471
A small business investment company. Prefers to invest in electronic manufacturing industry.

Montgomery Securities
Nations Bank
600 Montgomery St., 21st Fl.
San Francisco, California 94111-2702
Phone: (415)627-2454
Fax: (415)249-5516
Private venture capital and investment banking firm. Diversified, but will not

invest in real estate or energy-related industries. Involved in both start-up and later-stage financing.

Morgan Stanley Venture Capital Fund L.P.
555 California St., Ste. 2200
San Francisco, California 94104
Phone: (415)576-2345
Fax: (415)576-2099
Venture capital firm providing second and third stage and buyout financing. Areas of interest include information technology and health care products/services.

Positive Enterprises, Inc.
1489 Webster St., Ste. 228
San Francisco, California 94115
Phone: (415)885-6600
Fax: (415)928-6363
A minority enterprise small business investment company. Diversified industry preference.

Quest Ventures (San Francisco)
E-mail: ruby@questventures.com
126 S. Park
San Francisco, California 94107
Phone: (415)546-7118
Fax: (415)243-8514
Independent venture capital partnership. Diversified industry preference.

Robertson-Stephens Co.
E-mail: 800emailol
555 California St., Ste. 2600
San Francisco, California 94104
Phone: (415)781-9700
Fax: (415)781-0278
Investment banking firm. Considers investments in any attractive merging-growth area, including product and service companies. Key preferences include health care, hazardous waste services and technology, biotechnology, software, and information services. Maximum investment is $5 million.

Ticonderoga Capital
555 California St., No. 4360
San Francisco, California 94104-1714
Phone: (415)296-6343
Fax: (415)296-8956

A venture capital firm. Provides early-stage financing to companies in the biomedical field and the information systems industry.

VK Capital Co.
600 California St., Ste.1700
San Francisco, California 94108
Phone: (415)391-5600
Fax: (415)397-2744
A small business investment company. Diversified industry preference.

Volpe, Welty and Co.
1 Maritime Plz., 11th Fl.
San Francisco, California 94111
Phone: (415)956-8120
Fax: (415)986-6754
Prefers investing with companies involved in entertainment, multi-media, computer-aided software engineering, gaming, software tools, biotechnology, and health care industries.

Walden Group of Venture Capital Funds
750 Battery St., Ste. 700
San Francisco, California 94111
Phone: (415)391-7225
Fax: (415)391-7262
Venture capital firm providing seed, start-up, and second and third stage financing. Areas of interest include high technology, consumer products, health-related industries, hardware, software, EDP, environmental, communications, and education.

Weiss, Peck and Greer Venture Partners L.P. (San Francisco)
555 California St., Ste. 3130
San Francisco, California 94104
Phone: (415)622-6864
Fax: (415)989-5108

Allied Business Investors, Inc.
301 W. Valley Blvd. Ste. 208
San Gabriel, California 91776
Phone: (626)289-0186
Fax: (626)289-2369
Jack Hong, President
Preferred Investment Size: $50,000.
Investment Policies: Loans only.
Investment Types: Early stage.

Industry Preferences: Diversified. Geographic Preferences: Los Angeles.

Dougery & Wilder (San Mateo)
155 Bovet Rd., Ste. 350
San Mateo, California 94402-3113
Phone: (415)566-5220
Fax: (415)358-8706
Venture capital supplier. Areas of interest include computers systems and software, communications, and medical/biotechnology industries.

Drysdale Enterprises
177 Bovet Rd., Ste. 600
San Mateo, California 94402
Phone: (650)341-6336
Fax: (650)341-1329
Venture capital firm preferring investments of $250,000-$2 million. Areas of interest include food processing, health care, and communications.

Technology Funding
2000 Alameda de las Pulgas, Ste. 250
San Mateo, California 94403
Phone: (800)223-3385
Free: (800)821-5323
Fax: (650)345-1797
Small business investment corporation. Provides primarily late first-stage and early second-stage equity financing. Also offers secured debt with equity participation to venture capital backed companies. Investments range from $500,000 to $1 million.

Phoenix Growth Capital Corp.
2401 Kerner Blvd.
San Rafael, California 94901
Phone: (800)266-2344
Free: (800)227-2626
Fax: (415)485-4663
Small business investment corporation providing start-up, second and third stage, and buyout financing. Areas of interest include secured debt for high technology, biotechnology, computers and peripherals, and service industries. (All must be equity venture capital based.)

Astar Capital Corp.
9537 E. Gidley St.
Temple City, California 91780
Phone: (818)350-1211
Fax: (818)350-0868
George Hsu, President

Spectra Enterprise Associates
PO Box 7688
Thousand Oaks, California 91359-7688
Phone: (818)865-0213
Fax: (818)865-1309
Venture capital partnership. Areas of interest include information, computer, semiconductor, software, life sciences, and wireless industries.

National Investment Management, Inc.
2601 Airport Drive., Ste.210
Torrance, California 90505
Phone: (310)784-7600
Fax: (310)784-7605
Venture capital firm providing leveraged buyout financing. Areas of interest include general manufacturing and distribution.

Round Table Capital Corp.
2175 N. California Blvd., Ste. 400
Walnut Creek, California 94596
Phone: (925)274-1700
Fax: (925)974-3978
A small business investment corporation. No industry preference.

Crosspoint Venture Partners (Los Altos)
E-mail: Partners@crosspointvc.com
2925 Woodside Rd.
Woodside, California 94062
Phone: (650)851-7600
Fax: (650)851-7661
Venture capital partnership. Seeks to invest start-up capital in unique products, services, and/or market opportunities in high-technology and biotechnology industries located in the western United States.

Colorado

Opus Capital
1113 Spruce St., Ste. 406
Boulder, Colorado 80302

Phone: (303)443-1023
Fax: (303)443-0986

Capital Health Management
2084 S. Milwaukee St.
Denver, Colorado 80210
Fax: (303)692-9656

The Centennial Funds
1428 15th St.
Denver, Colorado 80202
Phone: (303)405-7500
Fax: (303)405-7575
Venture capital fund. Prefers to invest in early stage companies in the Rocky Mountain region.

Colorado Housing and Finance Authority
1981 Blake St.
Denver, Colorado 80202-1272
Phone: (303)297-2432
Fax: (303)297-2615
Operates financing programs for small and minority businesses.

Colorado Office of Business Development
1625 Broadway, Ste. 1710
Denver, Colorado 80202
Phone: (303)892-3840
Fax: (303)892-3848
Provides loans to new and expanding businesses.

UBD Capital, Inc.
1700 Broadway
Denver, Colorado 80274
Phone: (303)863-4857
A small business investment company. Diversified industry preference.

Columbine Ventures
5460 S. Quebec St., Ste. 270
Englewood, Colorado 80111-1917
Phone: (303)694-3222
Fax: (303)694-9007
Venture capital firm interested in biotechnology, medical, computer, electronics, and advanced materials industries.

Chase Capital Partners
108 S. Frontage Road W., Ste. 307
Vail, Colorado 81657
Phone: (970)476-7700

Fax: (970)476-7900
Venture capital firm providing later stage financing. Areas of interest include health, environmental, service, distribution, manufacturing, information services, and education. Exclusions are real estate and high technology.

Connecticut

AB SBIC, Inc.
275 School House Rd.
Cheshire, Connecticut 06410
Phone: (203)272-0203
Fax: (203)250-2954
A small business investment company. Prefers to invest in grocery stores.

Marcon Capital Corp.
10 John St.
Fairfield, Connecticut 06490-1437
Fax: (203)259-9428
A small business investment corporation; secured lending preferred.

Consumer Venture Partners
3 Pickwick Plz.
Greenwich, Connecticut 06830
Phone: (203)629-8800
Fax: (203)629-2019
Prefers consumer and expansion-stage investments.

FRE Capital Partners, LP
36 Grove St.
New Canaan, Connecticut 06840
Phone: (203)966-2800
Fax: (203)966-3109
A small business investment company. Diversified industry preference.

RFE Investment Partners V, L.P.
36 Grove St.
New Canaan, Connecticut 06840
Phone: (203)966-2800
Fax: (203)966-3109
James A. Parsons, General Partner
Preferred Investment Size: $5 - $9 Million. Investment Policies: Prefer equity investments. Investment Types: Later stage, expansion, acquisitions. Industry Preferences:

Manufacturing & services.
Geographic Preferences: National, eastern U.S.

Canaan Partners
105 Rowayton Ave.
Rowayton, Connecticut 06853
Phone: (203)855-0400
Fax: (203)854-9117
Venture capital supplier.

First Connecticut Capital
1000 Bridgeport Ave.
Shelton, Connecticut 06484
Phone: (203)944-5400
Free: (800)401-3222
Fax: (203)944-5405
A small business investment corporation.

Collinson, Howe, and Lennox, LLC
1055 Washington Blvd. 5th Fl.
Stamford, Connecticut 06901
Phone: (203)324-7700
Fax: (203)324-3636

James B. Kobak and Co.
2701 Summer St., Ste. 200
Stamford, Connecticut 06905
Fax: (203)363-2218
Venture capital supplier and consultant. Provides assistance to new ventures in the communications field through conceptualization, planning, organization, raising money, and control of actual operations. Special interest is in magazine publishing.

Saugatuck Capital Co.
1 Canterbury Green
Stamford, Connecticut 06901
Phone: (203)348-6669
Fax: (203)324-6995
Private investment partnership. Seeks to invest in various industries not dependent on technology, including health care, telecommunications, insurance, financial services, manufacturing, and consumer products. Prefers leveraged buyout situations, but will consider start-up financing. Investments range from $3 to $5 million.

TSG Ventures, Inc.
177 Broad St.,12th Fl.
Stamford, Connecticut 06901

Phone: (203)406-1500
Fax: (203)406-1590
A minority enterprise small business investment company. Diversified industry preference.

J. H. Whitney and Co.
177 Broad St.
Stamford, Connecticut 06901
Phone: (203)973-1400
Fax: (203)973-1422

Xerox Venture Capital (Stamford)
E-mail: xerox.com
Headquarters
800 Long Ridge Rd.
Stamford, Connecticut 06904
Phone: (203)968-3000
Venture capital subsidiary of operating company. Prefers to invest in document processing industries.

The SBIC of Connecticut, Inc.
2 Corpoate Dr., Ste. 203
Trumbull, Connecticut 06611
Phone: (203)261-0011
Fax: (203)459-1563
A small business investment corporation. No industry preference.

Marketcorp Venture Associates
285 Riverside Ave.
Westport, Connecticut 06880
Phone: (203)222-1000
Free: (800)243-5077
Fax: (203)222-6546
Venture capital firm. Prefers to invest in consumer-market businesses, including the packaged goods, specialty retailing, communications, and consumer electronics industries.

Oak Investment Partners (Westport)
1 Gorham Island
Westport, Connecticut 06880
Phone: (203)226-8346
Fax: (203)227-0372

Oxford Bioscience Partners
315 Post Rd. W.
Westport, Connecticut 06880
Phone: (203)341-3300
Fax: (203)341-3309
Independent venture capital partnership. Areas of interest include biotechnology, medical devices/services, and health care services.

Initial investments range from $500,000 to $1.5 million; up to $3 million over several later rounds of financing.

Prince Ventures (Westport)
25 Ford Rd.
Westport, Connecticut 06880
Phone: (203)227-8332
Fax: (203)226-5302
Provides early stage financing for medical and life sciences ventures.

Delaware

Delaware Economic Development Authority
99 Kings Hwy.
Dover, Delaware 19901
Phone: (302)739-4271
Free: (800)441-8846
Fax: (302)739-5749
Provides financing to new and expanding businesses at interest rates below the prime rate by issuing industrial revenue bonds (IRBs). Manufacturing and agricultural projects are eligible.

PNC Capital Corp.
300 Delaware Ave., Ste. 304
Wilmington, Delaware 19801
Phone: (302)427-5895
Gary J. Zentner, President
Preferred Investment Size: $2 to $8 million. Investment Policies: Loans and/or equity. Investment Types: Expansion, later stage. Industry Preferences: No real estate or tax-oriented investments. Geographic Preferences: Northeast.

District of Columbia

Allied Capital Corp.
1666 K St. N.W., 9th Fl.
Washington, District of Columbia 20006
Phone: (202)331-1112
Fax: (202)659-2053
Venture capital fund managed by Allied Capital Advisers, Inc. Investments range from $500,000 to $6 million. Prefers later-stage companies that have been in business for at least one year, but gives

consideration to early-stage companies and turnaround situations. Geographical preferences include the Northeast, Mid-Atlantic, and Southeast. Areas of interest include communications, computer hardware and software, consumer products, educational products, electronics, environmental, energy, franchising, industrial products and equipment, manufacturing, media, medical/health, publishing, recreation/tourism, restaurant, retail, service, transportation, and wholesale distribution industries.

Calvert Social Investment Fund
1918 18th St. NW, Ste. 22
Washington, District of Columbia 20009
Phone: (202)986-4272
Fax: (202)986-6950
Private venture capital partnership focusing on Mid-Atlantic companies involved in socially or environmentally beneficial products or services.

Helio Capital, Inc.
666 11th St., NW, Ste. 900
Washington, District of Columbia 20001
Phone: (202)272-3617
Fax: (202)504-2247
A minority enterprise small business investment corporation. No industry preference.

MultiMedia Broadcast Investment Corp.
3101 South Street NW
Washington, District of Columbia 20007
Phone: (202)293-1166
Fax: (202)872-1669
A minority enterprise small business investment corporation. Communications industry preferred.

Florida

North American Fund, II
312 SE 17th St., Ste.300
Ft. Lauderdale, Florida 33316
Phone: (954)463-0681
Fax: (954)527-0904

A small business investment corporation. No industry preference. Prefers controlling interest investments and acquisitions of established businesses with a history of profitability.

Venture First Associates
1901 S. Harbor City Blvd., Ste. 501
Melbourne, Florida 32901
Phone: (407)952-7750
Fax: (407)952-5787
Venture capital firm providing seed, start-up and first stage financing. Areas of interest include health care, advanced chemicals, computer software and hardware, industrial equipment, electronics, and communications.

BAC Investment Corp.
6600 NW 27th Ave.
Miami, Florida 33147
Fax: (305)693-7450
A minority enterprise small business investment company. Diversified industry preference.

J and D Capital Corp.
12747 Biscayne Blvd.
North Miami, Florida 33181
Phone: (305)893-0303
Fax: (305)891-2338
A small business investment corporation. No industry preference.

PMC Investment Corp.
AmeriFirst Bank Bldg., 2nd Fl. S
18301 Biscayne Blvd.
North Miami Beach, Florida 33160
Fax: (305)933-9410

Western Financial Capital Corp.
(North Miami Beach)
AmeriFirst Bank Bldg., 2nd Fl. S
18301 Biscayne Blvd.
North Miami Beach, Florida 33160
Fax: (305)933-9410
A small business investment company.

Florida High Technology and Industry Council
Collins Bldg.
107 W. Gaines St., Rm. 315
Tallahassee, Florida 32399-2000
Phone: (850)487-3136

Fax: (850)487-3014
Provides financing for research and
development for high-tech businesses.

Florida Venture Partners
880 Riverside Plz.
100 W. Kennedy Blvd.
Tampa, Florida 33602
Phone: (813)229-2294
Fax: (813)229-2028
A small business investment
company. Diversified industry
preference.

Market Capital Corp.
1102 N. 28th St.
PO Box 31667
Tampa, Florida 33605
Fax: (813)248-9106
A small business investment
corporation. Grocery industry
preferred.

South Atlantic Venture Fund
E-mail: venture@mindspring.com
614 W. Bay St.
Tampa, Florida 33606-2704
Phone: (813)253-2500
Fax: (813)253-2360
A minority enterprise small business
investment corporation. Provides
expansion capital for privately
owned, rapidly growing companies
located in the southeastern and Texas.
Prefers to invest in communications,
computer services, consumer,
electronic components and
instrumentation, medical/health-
related services, medical products,
finance, and insurance industries.
Will not consider real estate or oil and
gas investments.

Allied Financial Services Corp. (Vero
Beach)
Executive Office Center, Ste. 300
2770 N. Indian River Blvd.
Vero Beach, Florida 32960
Phone: (561)778-5556
Fax: (561)569-9303
A minority enterprise small business
investment company.

Georgia

Advanced Technology Development
Fund
1000 Abernathy Rd., Ste. 1420
Atlanta, Georgia 30328
Phone: (770)668-2333
Fax: (770)668-2330
Venture capital firm providing start-
up, first stage, second stage
expansion, purchase or secondary
positions, and buyout or acquisition
financing. Areas of interest include
information processing, health care
and specialized mobile radio.

Arete Ventures, Inc./Utech Venture
Capital Funds
E-mail: glevert@mindsceen.com
115 Perimeter Center Pl. NE, Ste. 640
Atlanta, Georgia 30346-1282
Phone: (770)399-1660
Fax: (770)399-1664
Venture capital firm providing start-
up, first stage, second stage expansion
and late stage expansion financing.
Areas of interest include utility-
related industries.

Cordova Capital Partners, L.P.
3350 Cumberland Cir., Ste. 970
Atlanta, Georgia 30339
Phone: (770)951-1542
Fax: (770)955-7610
Paul DiBella, Manager
Ralph Wright, Manager
Preferred Investment Size: $1 to $3
million. Investment Policies: Equity
and/or debt. Investment Types: Early
stage, expansion, later stage. Industry
Preferences: Diversified. Geographic
Preferences: Southeast.

Cravey, Green & Wahlen, Inc./CGW
Southeast Partners
E-mail: cgw@cgwiii.com
12 Piedmont Center, Ste. 210
Atlanta, Georgia 30305-4805
Phone: (404)816-3255
Free: (800)249-6669
Fax: (404)816-3258
Venture capital firm providing buyout
or acquisition financing. Areas of
interest include manufacturing,
distribution, and service industries.
Does not provide start-up financing or

investments in high technology and
medical industries.

EGL Holdings, Inc.
6600 Peachtree-Dunwoody Rd.
300 Embassy Row, Ste. 630
Atlanta, Georgia 30328
Phone: (770)399-5633
Fax: (770)393-4825
Venture capital firm providing late
stage expansion, purchase or
secondary positions, and buyout or
acquisition financing. Areas of
interest include information
technology, medical/health care,
industrial automation, electronic
components and instrumentation for
venture capital deals, and all
industries for buyouts.

Equity South
1790 The Lenox Bldg.
3399 Peachtree Rd., Ste. 1790
Atlanta, Georgia 30326
Phone: (404)237-6222
Fax: (404)261-1578
Venture capital firm providing second
stage expansion, late stage expansion,
purchase or secondary positions, and
buyout or acquisition financing.

Georgia Department of Community
Affairs
Community and Economic
Development Division
60 Executive Park South NE
Atlanta, Georgia 30329-2231
Phone: (404)679-4940
Fax: (404)679-0669
Provides assistance in applying for
state and federal grants.

Georgia Department of Community
Affairs
Government Information Division
1200 Equitable Bldg.
100 Peachtree St. NW
Atlanta, Georgia 30303
Fax: (404)656-9792
Central source for information on
Georgia's people, economy, and local
governments, including information
on federal and state funding sources.

Green Capital Investors L.P.
3343 Peachtree Rd., Ste. 1420

Atlanta, Georgia 30326
Phone: (404)261-1187
Fax: (404)266-8677
Venture capital firm providing purchase or secondary positions and buyout or acquisition financing.

Noro-Moseley Partners
E-mail: nmp@mindspring.com
4200 Northside Pky., Bldg. 9
Atlanta, Georgia 30327
Phone: (404)233-1966
Fax: (404)239-9280
Venture capital partnership. Prefers to invest in private, diversified small and medium-sized growth companies located in the southeastern United States.

Premier HealthCare
E-mail: BoxBenjamin@convene.com
3414 Peachtree Rd., Ste. 238
Atlanta, Georgia 30326
Phone: (404)816-0049
Fax: (404)816-0248
Venture capital firm providing start-up, first stage, second stage expansion, late stage expansion, purchase or secondary positions, and buyout or acquisition financing. Areas of interest include health care.

Renaissance Capital Corp.
34 Peachtree St. NW, Ste. 2230
Atlanta, Georgia 30303
Phone: (404)658-9061
Fax: (404)658-9064
A minority enterprise small business investment company. Diversified industry preference.

River Capital, Inc.
1360 Peachtree St. NE, Ste. 1430
Atlanta, Georgia 30309
Phone: (404)873-2166
Fax: (404)873-2158
Venture capital firm providing second stage expansion, late stage expansion, purchase or secondary positions, and buyout or acquisition financing. Areas of interest include light manufacturing and distribution companies with annual revenues exceeding $20 million.

Seaboard Management Corp.
3400 Peachtree Rd. NE, Ste. 741
Atlanta, Georgia 30326
Phone: (404)239-6270
Fax: (404)239-6284
Venture capital firm providing first stage and second stage expansion financing. Areas of interest include manufacturing and telecommunications.

Johnson Industries, Inc. (Rockville)
105 13th St.
Columbus, Georgia 31901
Phone:)706)641-3140
Fax: (706)641-3159
Haywood Miller, Manager
Preferred Investment Size: $1,000,000. Investment Policies: Subordinated debt with warrant. Investment Types: Expansion, later stage. Industry Preferences: Diversified. Geographic Preferences: National.

First Growth Capital, Inc.
Best Western Plz.
I-75 Georgia 42N Exit 63
Forsyth, Georgia 31029
Phone: (912)994-9260
Free: (800)447-3241
Fax: (912)994-9260
A minority enterprise small business investment company. Diversified industry preference.

North Riverside Capital Corp.
E-mail: Tom.Barry.Mighty.com
50 Technology Pk./Atlanta
Norcross, Georgia 30092
Phone: (770)446-5556
Fax: (770)446-8627
A small business investment corporation. No industry preference.

Hawaii

Bancorp Hawaii SBIC
130 Merchant St.
Honolulu, Hawaii 96813
Fax: (808)537-8557
A small business investment corporation. No industry preference.

Hawaii Agriculture Department
PO Box 22159

Honolulu, Hawaii 96823-2159
Phone: (808)973-9600
Fax: (808)973-9613
Provides information and advice in such areas as marketing, production, and labeling. Administers loan programs, including the New Farmer Loan Program, the Emergency Loan Program, and the Aquaculture Loan Program.

Hawaii Department of Business, Economic Development, and Tourism
Financial Assistance Branch
1 Capital District Bldg.
250 S. Hotel St., Ste. 503
PO Box 2359
Honolulu, Hawaii 96804
Phone: (808)586-2576
Fax: (808)587-3832
Provides loans to small businesses, including the Hawaii Capital Loan Program and the Hawaii Innovation Development Loan Program.

Pacific Venture Capital Ltd.
222 S. Vineyard St., No. PH-1
Honolulu, Hawaii 96813-2445
Phone: (808)521-6502
Free: (800)455-1888
Fax: (808)521-6541
A minority enterprise small business investment corporation.

Illinois

ABN AMRO Capital (USA) Inc.
135 S. La Salle St., Ste. 725
Chicago, Illinois 60603-4402
Phone: (312)904-6445
Fax: (312)904-1028
Joseph Rizzi, Chairman

Alpha Capital Venture Partners
E-mail: acp@alphacapital.com
122 S. Michigan Ave., Ste. 1700
Chicago, Illinois 60603
Phone: (312)322-9800
Fax: (312)322-9808
A small business investment corporation providing expansion or later stage financing in the Midwest. No industry preference; however, no real estate, oil and gas, or start-up ventures are considered.

Ameritech Development Corp.
30 S. Wacker Dr., 37th Fl.
Chicago, Illinois 60606
Phone: (312)750-5193
Fax: (312)609-0244
Venture capital supplier. Prefers to invest in telecommunications and information services.

Batterson, Johnson and Wang
Venture Partners
E-mail: bvp@vcapital.com
303 W. Madison St., Ste. 1110
Chicago, Illinois 60606-3300
Phone: (312)269-0300
Fax: (312)269-0021

William Blair and Co.
222 W. Adams St.
Chicago, Illinois 60606-5312
Phone: (312)364-8250
Fax: (312)236-1042
A small business investment corporation. Areas of interest include cable, media, communications, consumer products, retail, health care services, technology and information services, and other service industries.

Brinson Partners, Inc.
209 S. LaSalle, 12th Fl.
Chicago, Illinois 60604-1295
Phone: (312)220-7100
Fax: (312)220-7199

Business Ventures, Inc.
20 N. Wacker Dr., Ste. 1741
Chicago, Illinois 60606-2904
Phone: (312)346-1580
Fax: (312)346-6693
A small business investment corporation. No industry preference; considers only ventures in the Chicago area.

Capital Health Venture Partners
20 N. Wacker Dr. Ste. 2200
Chicago, Illinois 60606
Phone: (312)782-7560
Fax: (312)726-2290
Investments limited to early stage medical, biotech, and health care related companies.

The Combined Fund, Inc.
7936 S. Cottage Grove
Chicago, Illinois 60619

Phone: (773)371-7030
Fax: (773)371-7035
A minority enterprise small business investment company. Diversified industry preference.

Continental Illinois Venture Corp.
231 S. LaSalle St.
Chicago, Illinois 60697
Phone: (312)828-8023
Fax: (312)987-0887
A small business investment corporation. Provides start-up and early stage financing to growth-oriented companies with capable management teams, proprietary products, and expanding markets.

Essex Venture Partners
E-mail: sbila@aol.com
190 S. LaSalle St., Ste. 2800
Chicago, Illinois 60603
Phone: (312)444-6040
Fax: (312)444-6034
Prefers to invest in health care companies.

First Analysis Corp.
c/o Bret Maxwell
233 S. Wacker Dr., Ste. 9500
Chicago, Illinois 60606
Phone: (312)258-1400
Free: (800)866-3272
Fax: (312)258-0334
Small business investment corporation providing first and second stage, mezzanine, and leveraged buyout financing in the $100,000 to $3 million range. Will act as deal originator or investor in deals created by others. Areas of interest include environmental, infrastructure, special chemicals/materials, repetitive revenue service, telecommunications, software, consumer/specialty retail, and health care companies.

Frontenac Co.
135 S. LaSalle St., Ste.3800
Chicago, Illinois 60603
Phone: (312)368-0044
Fax: (312)368-9520
A small business investment corporation. No industry preference.

Golder, Rauner LLC
6100 Sears Tower
Chicago, Illinois 60606
Phone: (312)382-2200
Fax: (312)382-2201
Private venture capital firm. Diversified industry preference, but does not invest in high technology or real estate industries.

IEG Venture Partners
70 West Madison, Ste. 1400
Chicago, Illinois 60602
Phone: (312)644-0890
Fax: (312)454-0369
Venture capital supplier. Provides start-up financing primarily to technology-based companies located in the Midwest.

Illinois Development Finance
Authority
Sears Tower
233 S. Wacker Dr., Ste. 5310
Chicago, Illinois 60606
Phone: (312)793-5586
Fax: (312)793-6347
Provides bond, venture capital, and direct loan programs.

Madison Dearborn Partners
3 1st National Plz., Ste. 3800
Chicago, Illinois 60602
Phone: (312)895-1000
Fax: (312)895-1001
Venture capital supplier. Invests a minimum of $1 million in early stage situations to a maximum of $25 million in mature growth or buyout situations. Emphasis is placed on a strong management team and unique market opportunity.

Mesirow Capital Partners SBIC, Ltd.
350 N. Clark St., 4th Fl.
Chicago, Illinois 60610
Phone: (312)595-6000
Fax: (312)595-6211
A small business investment corporation providing later stage growth financing and acquisition financing of non-high-technology companies. Does not provide start-up and turnaround financing.

Polestar Capital, Inc.
180 N. Michigan Ave., Ste. 1905
Chicago, Illinois 60601
Phone: (312)984-9875
Fax: (312)984-9877
Wallace Lennox, President
Preferred Investment Size: $350,000
to $700,000. Investment Policies:
Primarily equity. Investment Types:
Early to later stages.

Prince Ventures (Chicago)
10 S. Wacker Dr., Ste. 2575
Chicago, Illinois 60606-7407
Phone: (312)454-1408
Fax: (312)454-9125

Shorebank Capital Corp.
7936 S. Cottage Grove
Chicago, Illinois 60619
Phone: (773)371-7030
Fax: (773)371-7035
A minority enterprise small business
investment corporation providing
second stage, buyout, and acquisition
financing to companies in the
Midwest. Diversified industry
preference.

Wind Point Partners (Chicago)
676 N. Michigan Ave., No. 3300
Chicago, Illinois 60611
Phone: (312)649-4000
Fax: (312)255-4820

Marquette Venture Partners
520 Lake Cook Rd., Ste. 450
Deerfield, Illinois 60015
Phone: (847)940-1700
Fax: (847)940-1724

The Cerulean Fund
E-mail: walnet@aol.com
1701 E. Lake Ave., Ste. 170
Glenview, Illinois 60025
Phone: (847)657-8002
Fax: (847)657-8168
Providers of equity investment.

Tower Ventures, Inc.
Sears Tower, BSC 23-27
3333 Beverly Holtman St., Ste.
AC254A
Hoffman Estates, Illinois 60179
Fax: (847)906-0164
A minority enterprise small business

investment company. Diversified
industry preference.

Allstate Private Equity
3075 Sanders Rd., Ste. G5D
Northbrook, Illinois 60062-7127
Phone: (847)402-5681
Fax: (847)402-0880
Venture capital supplier. Investments
are not limited to particular industries
or geographical locations. Interest is
in unique products or services that
address large potential markets and
offer great economic benefits;
strength of management team is also
important. Investments range from
$500,000 to $5 million.

Caterpillar Venture Capital, Inc.
100 NE Adams St.
Peoria, Illinois 61629
Phone: (309)675-1000
Fax: (309)675-4457
Venture capital subsidiary of
operating firm.

Cilcorp Ventures, Inc.
300 Hamilton Blvd., Ste. 300
Peoria, Illinois 61602
Phone: (309)675-8850
Fax: (309)675-8800
Invests in environmental services
only.

Comdisco Venture Group (Rosemont)
6111 N. River Rd.
Rosemont, Illinois 60018-5158
Phone: (847)698-3000
Free: (800)321-1111
Fax: (847)518-5440
Venture capital subsidiary of
operating firm.

Indiana

Cambridge Ventures, LP
8440 Woodfield Crossing, No. 315
Indianapolis, Indiana 46240
Phone: (317)469-9704
Fax: (317)469-3926
A small business investment
company. Diversified industry
preference.

Circle Ventures, Inc.
26 N. Arsenal Ave.

Indianapolis, Indiana 46201-3808
Phone: (317)636-7242
Fax: (317)637-7581
A small business investment
corporation. Prefers second-stage,
leveraged buyout, and growth
financings. Geographical preference
is Indianapolis.

Indiana Business Modernization and
Technology Corp.
1 N. Capitol Ave., Ste. 925
Indianapolis, Indiana 46204
Phone: (317)635-3058
Free: (800)877-5182
Fax: (317)231-7095
Invests in and counsels applied
research ventures.

Indiana Development Finance
Authority
1 N. Capitol Ave., Ste. 320
Indianapolis, Indiana 46204
Phone: (317)233-4332
Fax: (317)232-6786
Administers the Ag Finance, Export
Finance, Loan Guarantee, and
Industrial Development Bond
Financing Programs.

First Source Capital Corp.
PO Box 1602
South Bend, Indiana 46634
Phone: (219)235-2180
Fax: (219)235-2227
A small business investment
corporation. No industry preference.

Thomas Lowe Ventures
3600 McGill St., Ste. 300
PO Box 3688
South Bend, Indiana 46628
Phone: (219)232-0300
Fax: (219)232-0500
Venture capital firm preferring to
invest in the toy industry.

Iowa

Allsop Venture Partners (Cedar
Rapids)
2750 1st Ave. NE, Ste. 210
Cedar Rapids, Iowa 52402
Phone: (319)363-8971
Fax: (319)363-9519

InvestAmerica Venture Group, Inc.
101 2nd St. SE, Ste. 800
Cedar Rapids, Iowa 52401
Phone: (319)363-8249
Fax: (319)363-9683
A small business investment
corporation. Invests in later stage
manufacturing and service businesses.

MorAmerica Capital Corp.
101 2nd St. SE, Ste. 800
Cedar Rapids, Iowa 52401
Phone: (319)363-8249
Fax: (319)363-9683
A small business investment
company. Diversified industry
preference.

Iowa Department of Economic
Development
Iowa New Jobs Training Program
Iowa Work Force Development
150 Des Moines St.
Des Moines, Iowa 50309
Phone: (515)281-9328
Fax: (515)281-9033
Reimburses new or expanding
companies for up to 50 percent of
new employees' salaries and benefits
for up to one year of on-the-job
training. Coordinated through the
state's 15 community colleges.

Iowa Department of Economic
Development
Division of Financial Assistance
Community Development Block
Grants
Bureau of Business Finance
200 E. Grand Ave.
Des Moines, Iowa 50309
Phone: (515)242-4819
Fax: (515)242-4819
Bestows grants from the U.S.
Department of Housing and Urban
Development to help finance
community improvements and job-
generating expansions. Funds are
primarily awarded on a competitive
basis.

Iowa Department of Economic
Development
International Division
Export Finance Program
200 E. Grand Ave.

Des Moines, Iowa 50309
Phone: (515)242-4700
Fax: (515)242-4918
Provides funding to qualified
exporters of Iowa-manufactured and
processed products.

Iowa Department of Economic
Development
Bureau of Business Finance
Self-Employment Loan Program
Iowa Dept. of Economic
Development
Self-Employment Loan Program
Des Moines, Iowa 50309
Phone: (515)242-4793
Fax: (515)242-4749
Provides low-interest loans for low-
income entrepreneurs who are
expanding or starting a new business.

Iowa Finance Authority
100 E. Grand Ave., Ste. 250
Des Moines, Iowa 50309
Phone: (515)242-4990
Fax: (515)242-4957
Provides loans to new and expanding
small businesses. Funds may be used
to purchase land, construction,
building improvements, or
equipment; loans cannot be used for
working capital, inventory, or
operations.

Kansas

Allsop Venture Partners (Overland
Park)
6602 W. 131st. St.
Overland Park, Kansas 66209
Phone: (913)338-0820
Fax: (913)681-5535

Kansas Venture Capital, Inc.
(Overland Park)
6700 Antioch Plz., Ste. 460
Overland Park, Kansas 66204-1200
Phone: (913)262-7117
Fax: (913)262-3509
A small business investment
corporation. Prefers to invest in
wholesale or distribution, high
technology, and service businesses.

Kansas City Equity Partners
4200 Somerset Dr., Ste. 101

Prairie Village, Kansas 66208
Fax: (913)649-2125
Paul H. Henson, Manager
Preferred Investment Size: $500,000
to $2 million. Investment Policies:
Equity. Investment Types: Seed, early
stage, expansion. Industry
Preferences: Diversified. Geographic
Preferences: Midwest.

Kansas Department of Housing and
Commerce
Division of Community Development
700 SW Harrison, Ste. 1300
Topeka, Kansas 66603
Phone: (785)296-3485
Fax: (785)296-0186
Administers Community
Development Block Grants and the
enterprise zone program, in which
businesses receive tax credits and
exemptions for locating in targeted
areas.

Kansas Development Finance
Authority
700 SW Jackson
Jayhawk Tower, Ste. 1000
Topeka, Kansas 66603
Phone: (785)296-6747
Fax: (785)296-6810
Dedicated to improving access to
capital financing to business
enterprises through the issurance of
bonds.

Kentucky

Kentucky Cabinet for Economic
Development
Financial Incentives Department
Capitol Plaza Tower
500 Mero St., 24th Fl.
Frankfort, Kentucky 40601
Phone: (502)564-4554
Fax: (502)564-7697
Provides loans to supplement private
financing. Offers two major
programs: issuance of industrial
revenue bonds; and second mortgage
loans to private firms in participation
with other lenders. Also has a Crafts
Guaranteed Loan Program providing
loans up to $20,000 to qualified
craftspersons, and a Commonwealth

Venture Capital Program, encouraging the establishment or expansion of small business and industry.

Mountain Ventures, Inc.
362 Old Whitley Rd.
PO Box 1738
London, Kentucky 40743-1738
Phone: (606)864-5175
Fax: (606)864-5194
A small business investment corporation. No industry preference; geographic area limited to southeast Kentucky.

Equal Opportunity Finance, Inc.
420 S. Hurstbourne Pky., Ste. 201
Louisville, Kentucky 40222-8002
Phone: (502)423-1943
Fax: (502)423-1945
A minority enterprise small business investment corporation. No industry preference; geographic areas limited to Indiana, Kentucky, Ohio, and West Virginia.

Louisiana

Bank One Equity Investors, Inc.
451 Florida St.
Baton Rouge, Louisiana 70801
Phone: (504)332-4421
Fax: (504)332-7377
A small business investment corporation. No industry preference.

Louisiana Department of Economic Development
E-mail:
marketing@mail.lded.state.la.us
PO Box 94185
Baton Rouge, Louisiana 70804-9185
Phone: (504)342-3000
Fax: (504)342-5389

S.C.D.F. Investment Corp., Inc.
PO Box 3885
Lafayette, Louisiana 70502
Phone: (318)232-7672
Fax: (318)232-5094
A minority enterprise small business investment corporation. No industry preference.

First Commerce Capital, Inc.
201 St. Charles Ave., 16th Fl.
PO Box 60279
New Orleans, Louisiana 70170
Phone: (504)623-1600
Fax: (504)623-1779
William Harper, Manager
Preferred Investment Size: $1 to $2 million. Investment Policies: Loans, equity. Investment Types: Later stage, acquisition, buyouts. Industry Preferences: Manufacturing healthcare, retail, wholesale/distribution. Geographic Preferences: Gulf South region.

Maine

Finance Authority of Maine
E-mail: info@samemaine.com
83 Western Ave.
PO Box 949
Augusta, Maine 04332-0949
Phone: (207)623-3263
Fax: (800)623-0095
Assists business development and job creation through direct loans, loan guarantee programs, and project grants.

Maine Capital Corp.
E-mail: info@norhtatlantacapital.com
70 Center St.
Portland, Maine 04101
Phone: (207)772-1001
Fax: (207)772-3257
A small business investment corporation. No industry preference.

Maryland

ABS Ventures Limited Partnerships (Baltimore)
1 South St., Ste. 2150
Baltimore, Maryland 21202
Phone: (410)895-3895
Free: (800)638-2596
Fax: (410)895-3899
Invests in the computer software, health care, and biotechnology industries.

American Security Capital Corp., Inc.
100 S. Charles St., 8th Fl.
Baltimore, Maryland 21201
Fax: (410)547-4990

A small business investment company. Diversified industry preference.

Anthem Capital, L.P.
16 S. Calvert St., Ste. 800
Baltimore, Maryland 21202
Phone: (410)625-1510
Fax: (410)625-1735
William M. Gust II, Manager

Maryland Department of Business and Economic Development
Financing Programs Division
217 E. Redwood St.,10th Fl.
Baltimore, Maryland 21202-3316
Phone: (410)767-0095
Free: (800)333-6995
Fax: (410)333-1836
Provides short-term financing for government contracts and long-term financing for equipment and working capital. Also operates a surety bond guarantee program for small businesses and an equity participation investment program for potential minority franchises.

Maryland Department of Economic and Employment Development
Financing Programs Division
Industrial Development Financing Authority
217 E. Redwood St.
Baltimore, Maryland 21202-3316
Phone: (410)767-6300
Fax: (410)333-6911
Insures up to 80 percent of loans or obligations. Also provides tax-exempt revenue bonds for the financing of fixed assets.

New Enterprise Associates (Baltimore)
1119 St. Paul St.
Baltimore, Maryland 21202
Phone: (410)244-0115
Fax: (410)752-7721
Private free-standing venture capital partnership providing seed and start-up financing. Prefers information technology and medical and life science industries.

T. Rowe Price Associates, Inc.
100 E. Pratt St.

Baltimore, Maryland 21202
Phone: (410)345-2000
Free: (800)638-7890
Fax: (410)345-2394
Venture capital supplier. Offers specialized investment services to meet the needs of companies in various stages of growth.

Triad Investor's Corp.
300 E. Joppa, Ste. 1111
Baltimore, Maryland 21286
Phone: (410)828-6497
Fax: (410)337-7312
Venture capital firm providing seed and early stage financing. Areas of interest include communications, computer-related, medical/health-related, genetic engineering, and electronic components and instrumentation industries.

Security Financial and Investment Corp.
7720 Wisconsin Ave., Ste. 207
Bethesda, Maryland 20814
Phone: (301)951-4288
Fax: (301)951-9282
A minority enterprise small business investment corporation. No industry preference.

Syncom Capital Corp.
8401 Coalville Rd.-Ste. 300
Silver Spring, Maryland 20910
Phone: (301)608-3203
Fax: (301)608-3307
A minority enterprise small business investment corporation. Areas of interest include telecommunications and media.

Grotech Capital Group
9690 Deereco Rd.,Ste. 800
Timonium, Maryland 21093
Phone: (410)560-2000
Fax: (410)560-1910

Massachusetts

Advent International Corp.
101 Federal St.
Boston, Massachusetts 02110
Phone: (617)951-9400
Fax: (617)951-0566
Venture capital firm. Invests in all

stages, from start-up technology-based companies to well-established companies in rapid growth or mature industries; no retail clothing or real estate.

American Research and Development
30 Federal St., 3rd Fl.
Boston, Massachusetts 02110
Phone: (617)423-7500
Fax: (617)423-9655
Independent private venture capital partnership. All stages of financing; no minimum or maximum investment.

Aspen Ventures (Boston)
1 Post Office Square, Ste. 3320
Boston, Massachusetts 02109
Fax: (617)426-2181
Venture capital supplier. Provides start-up and early stage financing to companies in high-growth industries such as biotechnology, communications, electronics, and health care.

Atlas Venture
E-mail: boston@atlasventure.com
222 Berkeley St.
Boston, Massachusetts 02116
Phone: (617)859-9290
Fax: (617)859-9292

Bain Capital Fund (Boston)
2 Copley Pl.
Boston, Massachusetts 02116
Phone: (617)572-3000
Fax: (617)572-3274
Private venture capital firm. No industry preference, but avoids investing in high-tech industries. Minimum investment is $500,000.

BancBoston Ventures, Inc.
175 Federal St., 10th Fl.
Boston, Massachusetts 02110
Phone: (617)434-2442
Fax: (617)434-1153
A small business investment corporation. Minimum investment is $1 million.

Boston Capital Ventures
E-mail: info@bcv.com
Old City Hall
45 School St.

Boston, Massachusetts 02108
Phone: (617)227-6550
Fax: (617)227-3847
Venture capital firm.

Burr, Egan, Deleage, and Co. (Boston)
1 Post Office Sq., Ste. 3800
Boston, Massachusetts 02109
Phone: (617)482-8020
Free: (800)756-2877
Fax: (617)482-1944
Private venture capital supplier. Invests start-up, expansion, and acquisitions capital nationwide. Principal concerns are strength of the management team; large, rapidly expanding markets; and unique products or services. Past investments have been made in the fields of electronics, health, and communications. Investments range from $750,000 to $5 million.

Chestnut Street Partners, Inc.
75 State St., Ste. 2500
Boston, Massachusetts 02109
Phone: (617)345-7220
Fax: (617)345-7201
A small business investment company. Diversified industry preference.

Claflin Capital Management, Inc.
E-mail: ccmbost@001.com
77 Franklin St.
Boston, Massachusetts 02110
Phone: (617)426-6505
Fax: (617)482-0016
Private venture capital firm investing its own capital. No industry preference but prefers early stage companies.

Commonwealth Enterprise Fund, Inc.
10 Post Office Sq., Ste. 1090
Boston, Massachusetts 02109
Phone: (617)482-1881
Fax: (617)482-7129
A minority enterprise small business investment corporation. No industry preference, but clients must be located in Massachusetts.

Copley Venture Partners
600 Atlantic Ave., 13th Fl.

Boston, Massachusetts 02210
Phone: (617)722-6030
Fax: (617)523-7739

Eastech Management Co.
30 Federal St.
Boston, Massachusetts 02110
Phone: (617)423-1096
Fax: (617)695-2699
Private venture capital supplier.
Provides start-up and first- and
second-stage financing to companies
in the following industries:
communications, computer-related
electronic components and
instrumentation, and industrial
products and equipment. Will not
consider real estate, agriculture,
forestry, fishing, finance and
insurance, transportation, oil and gas,
publishing, entertainment, natural
resources, or retail.

Fidelity Venture Associates, Inc.
82 Devonshire St., Mail Zone R25C
Boston, Massachusetts 02109
Phone: (617)563-7000
Fax: (617)476-5015
Privately-held investment
management firm providing financing
to young companies at various stages
of development. Areas of interest
include financial services, publishing,
specialty retailing, health care,
transportation, computer systems and
software, and telecommunications
industries.

Greylock Management Corp.
(Boston)
1 Federal St., 26th Fl.
Boston, Massachusetts 02110
Phone: (617)423-5525
Fax: (617)482-0059
Private venture capital partnership.
Minimum investment of $250,000;
preferred investment size of over $1
million. Will function either as deal
originator or investor in deals created
by others.

Harbour Vest Partners, LLC
1 Financial Center, 44th Fl.
Boston, Massachusetts 02111
Phone: (617)348-3707
Fax: (617)350-0305

Venture capital supplier. Diversified
investments.

Harvard Management Co., Inc.
600 Atlantic Ave.
Boston, Massachusetts 02210
Phone: (617)523-4400
Free: (800)723-0044
Fax: (617)523-1283
Diversified venture capital firm.
Minimum investment is $1 million.

Highland Capital Partners
2 International Pl.
Boston, Massachusetts 02110
Fax: (617)531-1550
Industry preferences include health
care, software, and
telecommunications.

Liberty Ventures Corp.
E-mail: @1liberty.com
1 Liberty Sq.
Boston, Massachusetts 02109
Phone: (617)423-1765
Free: (800)423-1766
Fax: (617)338-4362
Venture capital partnership. Provides
start-up, early stage, and expansion
financing to companies that are
pioneering applications of proven
technology; also will consider
nontechnology-based companies with
strong management teams and plans
for expansion. Investments range
from $500,000 to $1 million, with a
$6 million maximum.

Massachusetts Business Development
Corp.
50 Milk St., 16th Fl.
Boston, Massachusetts 02109
Phone: (617)350-8877
Fax: (617)350-0052
Provides assistance to businesses and
individuals attempting to utilize
federal, state, and local loan finance
programs.

Massachusetts Community
Development Finance Corp.
10 Post Office Sq., Ste. 1090
Boston, Massachusetts 02109
Phone: (617)482-9141
Fax: (617)482-7129
Provides financing for small

businesses and for commercial,
industrial, and residential business
developments through community
development corporations (CDCs) in
depressed areas of Massachusetts.
Three investment programs are
offered: the Venture Capital
Investment Program, the Community
Development Program, and the Small
Loan Guarantee Program.

Massachusetts Industrial Finance
Agency
75 Federal St., 10th Fl.
Boston, Massachusetts 02110
Phone: (617)451-2477
Free: (800)445-8030
Fax: (617)451-3429
Promotes expansion, renovation, and
modernization of small businesses
through the use of investment
incentives.

Massachusetts Technology
Development Corp. (MTDC)
148 State St., 9th Fl.
Boston, Massachusetts 02109-2506
Phone: (617)723-4920
Fax: (617)723-5983
Makes investments in start-up or early
stage expansion technology-based
businesses within the Commonwealth
of Massachusetts only.

MC PARTNERS
75 State St.,Ste. 2500
Boston, Massachusetts 02109
Phone: (617)345-7200
Fax: (617)345-7201
Venture capital fund.
Communications industry preferred.

Medallion Financial Corp.
45 Newbury St., Rm. 207
Boston, Massachusetts 02116
Phone: (617)536-0344
Fax: (617)536-5750
A minority enterprise small business
investment corporation. Specializes in
taxicabs and taxicab medallion loans.

Media Communication Partners
75 State St., Ste. 2500
Boston, Massachusetts 02109
Phone: (617)345-7200
Fax: (617)345-7201

A small business investment company. Diversified industry preference.

Northeast Small Business Investment Corp.
130 New Market Square
Boston, Massachusetts 02118
Phone: (617)445-0101
Fax: (617)442-1013
A small business investment corporation. No industry preference.

P. R. Venture Partners, L.P.
100 Federal St., 37th Fl.
Boston, Massachusetts 02110
Phone: (617)357-9600
Fax: (617)357-9601
Venture capital firm providing early stage financing. Areas of interest include health care, information, and food.

Pioneer Ventures LP
60 State St.
Boston, Massachusetts 02109
Phone: (617)742-7825
Fax: (617)742-7315
A small business investment company. Diversified industry preference.

Private Equity Management
10 Liberty Sq., 5th Fl.
Boston, Massachusetts 02109
Phone: (617)345-9440
Fax: (617)345-9878

Summit Partners
600 Atlantic Ave., Ste. 2800
Boston, Massachusetts 02210-2227
Phone: (617)824-1000
Fax: (617)824-1100
Venture capital firm. Prefers to invest in emerging, profitable, growth companies in the electronic technology, environmental services, and health care industries. Investments range from $1 million to $4 million.

TA Associates (Boston)
E-mail: info@ta.com
High Street Tower
125 High St., Ste. 2500
Boston, Massachusetts 02110-2720
Phone: (617)574-6700

Fax: (617)574-6728
Private venture capital partnership. Technology companies, media communications companies, and leveraged buyouts preferred. Will provide from $1 million to $20 million in investments.

TVM Techno Venture Management
101 Arch St., Ste. 1950
Boston, Massachusetts 02110
Phone: (617)345-9320
Free: (800)345-2093
Fax: (617)345-9377
Venture capital firm providing early stage financing. Areas of interest include high technology such as software, communications, medical, and biotechnology industries. Preferred investment size is $1 million.

UST Capital Corp.
40 Court St.
Boston, Massachusetts 02108
Phone: (617)726-7000
Free: (800)441-8782
Fax: (617)726-7369
A small business investment company. Diversified industry preference.

Venture Capital Fund of New England II
160 Federal St., 23rd Fl.
Boston, Massachusetts 02110
Phone: (617)439-4646
Fax: (617)439-4652
Venture capital fund. Prefers New England high-technology companies that have a commercial prototype or initial product sales. Will provide up to $500,000 in first-round financing.

MDT Advisers, Inc.
125 Cambridge Park Dr.
Cambridge, Massachusetts 02140
Phone: (617)234-2200
Fax: (617)234-2210

Zero Stage Capital Co., Inc.
E-mail: bjohnson@zerostage.com
101 Main St., 17th Fl.
Cambridge, Massachusetts 02142
Phone: (617)876-5355
Fax: (617)876-1248

Venture capital firm. Industry preferences include high-technology start-up companies located in the northeastern U.S.

Zero Stage Capital Co., Inc.
E-mail: bjohnson@zerostage.com
Kendall Sq.
101 Main St., 17th Fl.
Cambridge, Massachusetts 02142
Phone: (617)876-5355
Fax: (617)876-1248
Paul Kelley, Manager
Preferred Investment Size: $50,000 to $500,000. Investment Types: Equity, debit with equity features. Industry Preferences: Biotech, computer hardware and software, energy. Geographic Preferences: Northeast.

Boston College Capital Formation Service
96 College Rd.
Rahner House
Chestnut Hill, Massachusetts 02167
Phone: (617)552-4091
Fax: (617)552-2730

Capital Formation Service
Boston College
96 College Rd., Rahner House
Chestnut Hill, Massachusetts 02167
Phone: (617)552-4091
Fax: (617)552-2730
Provides assistance to clients requiring financing from nonconventional sources, such as quasi-public financing programs; state, federal, and local programs; venture capital; and private investors.

Seacoast Capital Partners, L.P.
E-mail: scpltd.com
55 Ferncroft Rd.
Danvers, Massachusetts 01923
Phone: (978)777-3866
Fax: (978)750-1301
Eben Moulton, Manager
Preferred Investment Size: $1 to $6 million. Investment Policies: Loans and equity investments. Investment Types: Expansion, later stage. Industry Preferences: Diversified. Geographic Preferences: National.

Argonauts MESBIC Corp.
929 Worcester Rd.
Framingham, Massachusetts 01701
Phone: (617)697-0501
A minority enterprise small business investment company. Diversified industry preference.

Applied Technology
1 Cranberry Hill
Lexington, Massachusetts 02173-7397
Phone: (781)862-8622
Fax: (781)862-8367
Venture capital firm providing early stage investment. Areas of interest include hardware technologies, electronics, software, communications, and information services.

Business Achievement Corp.
1172 Beacon St.
Newton, Massachusetts 02161
Phone: (617)965-0550
Fax: (617)969-2671
A small business investment corporation. No industry preference.

Comdisco Venture Group (Newton)
1 Newton Executive Park
2221 Washington 3rd Fl.
Newton Lower Falls, Massachusetts 02162-1417
Phone: (617)244-6622
Free: (800)321-1111
Fax: (617)630-5599

New England MESBIC Inc.
530 Turnpike St.
North Andover, Massachusetts 01845-5812

Analog Devices, Inc.
1 Technology Way
PO Box 9106
Norwood, Massachusetts 02062-9106
Phone: (781)329-4700
Free: (800)262-5643
Venture capital supplier. Prefers to invest in industries involved in analog devices.

Advanced Technology Ventures (Boston)
281 Winter St., Ste. 350
Waltham, Massachusetts 02154-8713

Phone: (781)290-0707
Fax: (781)684-0045
Private venture capital firm. Prefers early stage financing in high-technology industries.

Charles River Ventures
Bay Colony Corporate Center
1000 Winter St., Ste. 3300
Waltham, Massachusetts 02154
Phone: (781)487-7060
Fax: (781)487-7065
Venture capital partnership providing early stage financing. Areas of interest include communications, software, environmental, and specialty financial service industries.

Hambro International Equity Partners (Boston)
404 Wyman, Ste. 365
Waltham, Massachusetts 02154
Fax: (617)290-0999
Private venture firm. Seeks to invest in software, electronics and instrumentation, biotechnology, retailing, direct marketing of consumer goods, and environmental industries.

Matrix Partners III
E-mail: info@matrixlp.com
1000 Winter St.,Ste.4500
Waltham, Massachusetts 02154
Phone: (781)890-2244
Fax: (781)890-2288
Private venture capital partnership. Industry preference includes high technology, communications, and software.

North Bridge Venture Partners
404 Wymin St. Ste. 365
Waltham, Massachusetts 02154
Phone: (781)290-0004
Fax: (781)290-0999

Ampersand Ventures
E-mail: bjt@ampersandventures.com
55 William St., Ste. 240
Wellesley, Massachusetts 02181
Phone: (617)239-0700
Free: (800)239-0706
Fax: (617)239-0824
Venture capital supplier. Provides start-up and early stage financing to

technology-based companies. Investments range from $500,000 to $1 million.

Battery Ventures (Boston)
20 Williams St., Ste. 200
Wellesley, Massachusetts 02181
Phone: (781)996-1000
Fax: (781)996-1001
Venture capital firm providing financing to early and emerging software and communications companies. Average investments are from $1 million to $5 million.

Geneva Middle Market Investors, L.P.
70 Walnut St.
Wellesley, Massachusetts 02181
Fax: (617)239-8064
James J. Goodman, Manager

Northwest Venture Capitol
40 William St., Ste. 305
Wellesley, Massachusetts 02181
Phone: (781)237-5870
Fax: (781)237-6270

Bessemer Venture Partners (Wellesley Hills)
83 Walnut St.
Wellesley Hills, Massachusetts 02181
Phone: (617)237-6050
Fax: (617)235-7068

Palmer Partners L.P.
200 Unicorn Park Dr.
Woburn, Massachusetts 01801
Phone: (781)933-5445
Fax: (781)933-0698
Venture capital partnership. Provides early stage, commercialization, and second and third stage financing. No industry preference, but does not invest in real estate or biotechnology industries.

Michigan

White Pines Capital Corp.
2401 Plymouth Rd., Ste. B
Ann Arbor, Michigan 48105
Phone: (313)747-9401
Fax: (313)747-9704
A small business investment company. Diversified industry preference.

Demery Seed Capital Fund
3707 W. Maple Rd.
Bloomfield Hills. Michigan 48301
Phone: (248)433-1722
Fax: (248)644-4526
Invests in start-up companies in
Michigan.

Dearborn Capital Corp.
PO Box 1729
Dearborn, Michigan 48126
Phone: (313)337-8577
Fax: (313)248-1252
A minority enterprise small business
investment corporation. Loans to
minority-owned, operated, and
controlled suppliers to Ford Motor
Company, Dearborn Capital
Corporation's parent.

Motor Enterprises, Inc.
3044 W. Grand Blvd.
Detroit, Michigan 48202
Phone: (313)556-4273
Fax: (313)974-4854
A minority enterprise small business
investment corporation. Prefers
automotive-related industries.

Metro-Detroit Investment Co.
30777 Northwestern Hwy., Ste. 300
Farmington Hills, Michigan 48334-
2549
Phone: (248)851-6300
Fax: (248)851-9551
A minority enterprise small business
investment corporation. Food store
industry preferred.

The Capital Fund
6412 Centurion Dr., Ste. 150
Lansing, Michigan 48917
Phone: (517)323-7772
Fax: (517)323-1999
A small business investment
company. Provides expansion
financing.

State Treasurer's Office
Alternative Investments Division
PO Box 15128
Lansing, Michigan 48901
Phone: (517)373-4330
Fax: (517)335-3668

Minnesota

Ceridian Corp.
8100 34th Ave. S
Bloomington, Minnesota 55425-1640
Phone: (612)853-8100

Cherry Tree Investment Co.
7601 France Ave. S., Ste 225
Edina, Minnesota 55435
Phone: (612)893-9012
Fax: (612)893-9036
Venture capital supplier. Provides
start-up and early stage financing.
Fields of interest include information/
software, retail, education, and
publishing industries located in the
Midwest. There are no minimum or
maximum investment limitations.

Affinity Capital Management
1900 Foshay Tower
821 Marquette
Minneapolis, Minnesota 55402
Phone: (612)904-2305
Fax: (612)204-0913
Venture capital firm providing seed,
research and development, start-up,
first stage, and bridge financing.
Areas of interest include medical
technology and health care service
industries.

Artesian Capital Limited Partnership
E-mail: fbbennett@artesian.com
Foshay Tower
821 Marquette Ave., Ste. 1700
Minneapolis, Minnesota 55402-2905
Phone: (612)334-5600
Fax: (612)334-5601
Venture capital firm providing seed
and start-up financing in the upper
Midwest. Areas of interest include
medical, communications, and
environmental industries.

Capital Dimensions Inc.
7831 Glenroy Rd., Ste. 480
Minneapolis, Minnesota 55439-3132
Phone: (612)831-2025
Fax: (612)831-2945
A minority enterprise small business
investment corporation. No industry
preference.

Coral Group, Inc.
60 S. 6th St., Ste. 3510
Minneapolis, Minnesota 55402
Phone: (612)335-8666
Fax: (612)335-8668
Venture capital firm providing all
types of financing. Areas of interest
include communications, computer
products, electronics, medical/health,
genetic engineering, industrial
products, transportation and
diversified.

Crawford Capital Corp.
713 Interchange Tower
600 S. Hwy. 169
Minneapolis, Minnesota 55426
Phone: (612)544-2221
Fax: (612)544-5885
Venture capital firm providing
financing for firm's own venture fund
limited partnerships. Areas of interest
include medical, software, and
technology industries.

Milestone Growth Fund, Inc.
401 2nd Ave. S., Ste. 1032
Minneapolis, Minnesota 55401
Phone: (612)338-0090
Fax: (612)338-1172
Minority enterprise small business
investment corporation providing
financing for expansion of existing
companies. Diversified industry
preference.

Norwest Equity Partners IV
2800 Piper Jaffray Tower
222 S. 9th St.
Minneapolis, Minnesota 55402-3388
Phone: (612)667-1650
Fax: (612)667-1660
Small business investment company.
Invests in all industries except real
estate.

Norwest Equity Partners V, L.P.
2800 Piper Jaffray Tower
222 S. 9th St.
Minneapolis, Minnesota 55402
Phone: (612)667-1650
Fax: (612)667-1660
John F. Whaley, Manager
Preferred Investment Size: $3 to $15
million. Investment Policies: Equity.
Investment Types: Start-up,

expansion, later stage. Industry Preferences: Diversified. Geographic Preferences: National.

Oak Investment Partners (Minneapolis)
4550 Norwest Center
90 S. 7th St., Ste. 4550
Minneapolis, Minnesota 55402
Phone: (612)339-9322
Fax: (612)337-8017
Prefers to invest in retail industries.

Pathfinder Venture Capital Funds (Minneapolis)
7300 Metro Blvd., Ste. 585
Minneapolis, Minnesota 55439
Phone: (612)835-1121
Fax: (612)835-8389
Venture capital supplier providing early stage financing. Areas of interest include medical, pharmaceutical, and health care service; and computer and computer-related industries in the Upper Midwest and West.

Piper Jaffray Ventures, Inc.
Piper Jaffray Tower
222 S. 9th St.
Minneapolis, Minnesota 55402
Phone: (612)342-6000
Fax: (612)337-8017

University Technology Center, Inc.
E-mail: utec@pro-ns.net
1313 5th St. SE
Minneapolis, Minnesota 55414
Phone: (612)379-3800
Fax: (612)379-3875
Venture capital firm providing start-up, first stage, initial expansion and acquisition financing. Areas of interest include environment, consumer products, industrial products, transportation and diversified industry.

Wellspring Corp.
4530 IDS Center
Minneapolis, Minnesota 55402
Phone: (612)338-0704
Fax: (612)338-0744
Venture capital firm providing acquisition and leveraged buyout financing. Areas of interest include marine transportation equipment and weighing and measuring equipment manufacturing.

Food Fund
5720 Smatana Dr., Ste. 300
Minnetonka, Minnesota 55343
Phone: (612)939-3944
Fax: (612)939-8106
Venture capital firm providing expansion, management buyouts, early stage and acquisition financing. Areas of interest include food products, food equipment, food packaging, and food distribution.

Medical Innovation Partners, Inc.
Opus Center, Ste. 421
9900 Bren Rd. E
Minnetonka, Minnesota 55343
Phone: (612)931-0154
Fax: (612)931-0003

Quest Venture Partners
730 E. Lake St.
Wayzata, Minnesota 55391-1769
Phone: (612)473-8367
Fax: (612)473-4702
Venture capital firm providing second stage and bridge financing. Areas of interest include communications, computer products and medical/health care.

Mississippi

Delta Foundation
E-mail: deltafdn@tednfo.com
819 Main St.
Greenville, Mississippi 38701
Phone: (601)335-5291
Fax: (601)335-5295
A minority enterprise small business investment corporation. No industry preference.

Mississippi Department of Economic and Community Development
Mississippi Business Finance Corp.
1200 Walter Sillers Bldg.
PO Box 849
Jackson, Mississippi 39205
Phone: (601)359-3552
Fax: (601)359-2832
Administers the SBA(503) Loan and the Mississippi Small Business Loan Guarantee.

Missouri

Bankers Capital Corp.
3100 Gillham Rd.
Kansas City, Missouri 64109
Phone: (816)531-1600
Fax: (816)531-1334
A small business investment corporation. No industry preference.

Capital for Business, Inc. (Kansas City)
1000 Walnut St., 18th Fl.
Kansas City, Missouri 64106-2123
Phone: (816)234-2357
Fax: (816)234-2952
A small business investment corporation. No industry preference.

CFB Venture Fund II, Inc.
1000 Walnut St., 18th Fl.
Kansas City, Missouri 64106
Phone: (816)234-2357
Fax: (816)234-2333
A small business investment company. Diversified industry preference.

InvestAmerica Venture Group, Inc. (Kansas City)
911 Main St., Ste. 2424
Kansas City, Missouri 64105
Phone: (816)842-0114
Fax: (816)471-7339
A small business investment corporation. No industry preference.

MorAmerica Capital Corp. (Kansas City)
911 Main St., Ste. 2424
Kansas City, Missouri 64105
Phone: (816)842-0114
Fax: (816)471-7339
A small business investment company.

United Missouri Capital Corp.
PO Box 419226
Kansas City, Missouri 64141
Phone: (816)860-7914
Fax: (816)860-7143
A small business investment corporation. No industry preference.

Midland Bank
740 NW Blue Pkwy.
Lees Summit, Missouri 64086-5707

Phone: (816)524-8000
Fax: (816)525-8624
A small business investment
company. Diversified industry
preference.

Allsop Venture Partners (St. Louis)
55 W. Port Plz., Ste. 575
St. Louis, Missouri 63146
Phone: (314)434-1688
Fax: (314)434-6560

Capital for Business, Inc. (St. Louis)
11 S. Meramec, Ste. 1430
St. Louis, Missouri 63105
Phone: (314)746-7427
Fax: (314)746-8739
A small business investment
corporation. Focuses primarily on
later-stage expansion and acquisition
in the manufacturing and distribution
industries.

CFB Venture Fund I, Inc.
11 S. Meramec, Ste. 1430
St. Louis, Missouri 63105
Phone: (314)746-7427
Fax: (314)746-8739
A small business investment
company. Diversified industry
preference.

Gateway Associates L.P.
8000 Maryland Ave., Ste. 1190
St. Louis, Missouri 63105
Phone: (314)721-5707
Fax: (314)721-5135

GE Capital, Small Business Corp.
635 Maryville Center Dr., Ste. 120
St. Louis, Missouri 63141
Phone: (314)205-3500
Free: (800)447-2025
Fax: (314)205-3699
Non-bank lender providing start-up
and expansion financing.

Montana

Montana Board of Investments
Office of Development Finance
PO Box 200126
555 Fuller Ave.
Helena, Montana 59620-0126
Phone: (406)444-0001
Fax: (406)449-6579

Provides investments to businesses
that will bring long-term benefits to
the Montana economy.

Montana Department of Commerce
Economic Development Division
Finance Technical Assistance
Small Business Development Center
1424 9th Ave.
Helena, Montana 59620-0501
Phone: (406)444-4780
Fax: (406)444-1872
Provides financial analysis, financial
planning, loan packaging, industrial
revenue bonding, state and private
capital sources, and business tax
incentives.

Nebraska

Nebraska Investment Finance
Authority
1230 "O" St., Ste. 200
Lincoln, Nebraska 68508
Phone: (402)434-3900
Free: (800)204-6432
Fax: (402)434-3921
Provides lower cost financing for
manufacturing facilities, certain farm
property, and health care and
residential development. Also
established a Small Industrial
Development Bond Program to help
small Nebraska-based companies
(those with fewer than 100 employees
or less than $2.5 million in gross
salaries).

Nevada

Nevada Department of Business and
Industry
Bond Division
1665 Hot Springs Rd., Ste. 100
Carson City, Nevada 89706
Phone: (702)687-4250
Fax: (702)687-4266
Issues up to $100 million in bonds to
fund venture capital projects in
Nevada; helps companies expand or
build new facilities through the use of
tax-exempt financing.

Atlanta Investment Co., Inc.
Call Box 10,001
Incline Village, Nevada 89450

Phone: (702)833-1836
Fax: (702)833-1890
L. Mark Newman, Chairman of the
Board
Preferred Investment Size:
$2,000,000. Investment Policies:
Equity. Investment Types: Expansion,
later stage. Industry Preferences:
Technology. Geographic Preferences:
National.

New Hampshire

Business Finance Authority of the
State of New Hampshire
E-mail: bfa@enterwebb.com
4 Park St., Ste. 302
Concord, New Hampshire 03301-
6313
Phone: (603)271-2391
Fax: (603)271-2396
Works to foster economic
development and promote the
creation of employment in the state of
New Hampshire. Provides guarantees
on loans to businesses made by banks
and local development organizations;
guarantees on portions of loans
guaranteed in part by the U.S. Small
Business Administration; cash
reserves on loans made by state banks
to businesses with annual revenues
less than or equal to $5,000,000; and
opportunities for local development
organizations to acquire additional
funds for the purpose of promoting
and developing business within the
state.

New Jersey

MidMark Capital, L.P.
E-mail: mfinlay@midmarkassoc.com
466 Southern Blvd.
Chatham, New Jersey 07928
Phone: (973)822-2999
Fax: (973)822-8911
Denis Newman, Manager
Preferred Investment Size:
$5,000,000. Investment Policies:
Equity. Investment Types: Expansion,
later stage. Industry Preferences:
Diversified, communication,
manufacturing, retail/service.

Geographic Preferences: East, midwest.

Transpac Capital Corp.
1037 Rte. 46 E
Clifton, New Jersey 07013
Phone: (973)470-8855
Fax: (973)470-8827
A minority enterprise small business investment company. Diversified industry preference.

Monmouth Capital Corp.
125 Wyckoff Rd.
PNC Bldg.
PO Box 335
Eatontown, New Jersey 07724
Phone: (732)542-4927
Fax: (732)542-1106
A small business investment corporation. No industry preference.

Capital Circulation Corp.
2035 Lemoine Ave., 2nd Fl.
Ft. Lee, New Jersey 07024
Phone: (201)947-8637
Fax: (201)585-1965
A minority enterprise small business investment company. Diversified industry preference.

Taroco Capital Corp.
716 Jersey Ave.
Jersey City, New Jersey 07310-1306
Phone: (201)798-5000
Fax: (201)798-4322
A minority enterprise small business investment corporation. Focuses on Chinese-Americans.

Edison Venture Fund
997 Lenox Dr., Ste. 3
Lawrenceville, New Jersey 08648
Phone: (609)896-1900
Fax: (609)896-0066
Private venture capital firm. No industry preference.

Tappan Zee Capital Corp. (New Jersey)
201 Lower Notch Rd.
PO Box 416
Little Falls, New Jersey 07424
Phone: (973)256-8280
Fax: (973)256-2841
A small business investment

company. Diversified industry preference.

CIT Group/Venture Capital, Inc.
650 CIT Dr.
Livingston, New Jersey 07039
Phone: (973)740-5429
Fax: (973)740-5555
A small business investment company. Diversified industry preference.

ESLO Capital Corp.
212 Wright St.
Newark, New Jersey 07114
Phone: (973)242-4488
Fax: (973)643-6062
Leo Katz, President
Preferred Investment Size: $100,000.
Investment Policies: Loans.
Investment Types: Start-ups, early stage. Industry Preferences: Business services, manufacturing. Geographic Preferences: Northeast.

Rutgers Minority Investment Co.
180 University Ave., 3rd Fl.
Newark, New Jersey 07102
Phone: (973)353-5627
A minority enterprise small business investment corporation. No industry preference.

Accel Partners
1 Palmer Sq.
Princeton, New Jersey 08542
Phone: (609)683-4500
Fax: (609)683-0384

Accel Partners (Princeton)
1 Palmer Sq.
Princeton, New Jersey 08542
Phone: (609)683-4500
Fax: (609)683-0384
Venture capital firm.
Telecommunications, software, and health care industries preferred.

Carnegie Hill Co.
202 Carnegie Center, Ste. 103
Princeton, New Jersey 08540
Phone: (609)520-0500
Fax: (609)520-1160

DSV Partners (Princeton)
221 Nassau St.
Princeton, New Jersey 08542

Phone: (609)924-6420
Fax: (609)683-0174
Provides financing for the growth of companies in the biotechnology/ health care, environmental, and software industries. Also provides capital to facilitate consolidation of fragmented industries.

Johnston Associates, Inc.
E-mail: jai181@aol.com
181 Cherry Valley Rd.
Princeton, New Jersey 08540
Phone: (609)924-3131
Fax: (609)683-7524
Venture capital supplier providing seed and start-up financing. Areas of interest include pharmaceutical research, biotechnology, and bioremediation of toxic waste.

BCI Advisors, Inc.
Glenpointe Center W., 2nd Fl.
Teaneck, New Jersey 07666
Phone: (201)836-3900
Fax: (201)836-6368
Venture capital firm providing mezzanine financing for growth companies with revenues of $25 million to $200 million. Diversified industry preference.

Demuth, Folger and Wetherill
300 Frank W. Burr, 5th Floor
Teaneck, New Jersey 07666
Phone: (201)836-6000
Fax: (201)836-5666
Venture capital firm with preferences for technology, services, and health care investments.

DFW Capital Partners, L.P.
Glenpointe Center E., 5th Fl.
300 Frank W. Burr Blvd.
Teaneck, New Jersey 07666
Phone: (201)836-2233
Fax: (201)836-5666
Donald F. DeMuth, Manager
Preferred Investment Size: $4,000,000. Investment Policies: Equity. Investment Types: Early through later stage. Industry Preferences: Healthcare, services, diversified. Geographic Preferences: National.

Business Plans Handbook, Volume 6

New Jersey Commission on Science and Technology
E-mail: njcst@scitech.state.nj.us
28 W. State St.
PO Box 832
Trenton, New Jersey 08625-0832
Phone: (609)984-1671
Fax: (609)292-5920
Awards bridge grants to small companies that have received seed money under the Federal State Business Innovation Research programs and works to improve the scientific and technical research capabilities within the state. Also provides management and technical assistance and other services to small, technology-oriented companies.

New Jersey Department of Agriculture
Division of Rural Resources
John Fitch Plz., CN 330
Trenton, New Jersey 08625
Phone: (609)292-5532
Fax: (609)633-7229
Fosters the agricutural economic development of rural areas of the state through financial assistance for farmers and agribusinesses.

New Jersey Economic Development Authority
PO Box 990
Trenton, New Jersey 08625-0990
Phone: (609)292-1800
Fax: (609)292-0368
Arranges low-interest, long-term financing for manufacturing facilities, land acquisition, and business equipment and machinery purchases. Also issues taxable bonds to provide financing for manufacturing, distribution, warehousing, research, commercial, office, and service uses.

Edelson Technology Partners
300 Tice Blvd
Woodcliff Lake, New Jersey 07675
Phone: (201)930-9898
Fax: (201)930-8899
Venture capital partnership interested in high technology investment, including medical, biotechnology, and computer industries.

New Mexico

Associated Southwest Investors, Inc.
1650 University N.E., Ste.200
Albuquerque, New Mexico 87102
Phone: (505)247-4050
Fax: (505)247-4050
A minority enterprise small business investment corporation. No industry preference.

Industrial Development Corp. of Lea County
E-mail: edclea@leaconet.com
PO Box 1376
Hobbs, New Mexico 88240
Phone: (505)397-2039
Free: (800)443-2236
Fax: (505)392-2300
Certified development company.

Ads Capital Corp.
142 Lincoln Ave., Ste. 500
Santa Fe, New Mexico 87501
Fax: (505)983-2887
Venture capital supplier. Prefers to invest in manufacturing or distribution companies.

New Mexico Economic Development Department
Technology Enterprise Division
1100 St. Francis Dr.
Santa Fe, New Mexico 87503
Phone: (505)827-0300
Free: (800)374-3061
Fax: (505)827-3061
Provides state funds to advanced-technology business ventures that are close to the commercial stage.

New Mexico Economic Development Department
Economic Development Division
1100 St. Francis Dr.
Santa Fe, New Mexico 87503
Phone: (505)827-0300
Free: (800)374-3061
Fax: (505)827-0328
Provides start-up or expansion loans for businesses that are established in or are new to New Mexico.

New Mexico Labor Department
Job Training Division
Aspen Plz.
1596 Pacheco St.

PO Box 4218
Santa Fe, New Mexico 87502
Phone: (505)827-6827
Fax: (505)827-6812
Provides new and expanding industries with state-sponsored funds to train a New Mexican workforce.

New York

Fleet Bank
69 St.
Albany, New York 12207
Phone: (518)447-4115
Fax: (518)447-4043
Venture capital supplier. No industry preference. Typical investment is between $500,000 and $1 million.

NYBDC Capital Corp.
41 State St.
PO Box 738
Albany, New York 12201
Phone: (518)463-2268
Fax: (518)463-0240
A small business investment corporation.

Vega Capital Corp.
80 Business Park Dr., Ste. 201
Armonk, New York 10504-1701
Phone: (914)273-1025
Fax: (914)273-1028
A small business investment corporation. Diversified industry preferences.

Triad Capital Corp. of New York
305 7th Avenue, 20th Fl.
Bronx, New York 10001
Phone: (212)243-7360
Fax: (212)243-7647
A minority enterprise small business investment corporation. No industry preference.

First New York Management Co.
1 Metrotech Center N, 11th Fl.
Brooklyn, New York 11201
Phone: (718)797-5990
Fax: (718)722-3533
A small business investment corporation. No industry preference.

M & T Capital Corporation
1 Fountain Plz., 3rd Fl.
Buffalo, New York 14203-1495

Phone: (716)848-3800
Fax: (716)848-3150
A small business investment corporation providing equity financing for small to mid-size companies for expansion activities, acquisitions, recapitalizations, and buyouts. Initial investments range from $500,000 - $2 million. Prefers businesses located in the Northeast and Midwest.

Rand Capital Corp.
2200 Rand Bldg.
Buffalo, New York 14203
Phone: (716)853-0802
Fax: (716)854-8480
A small business investment corporation. Prefers to invest in communications, computer-related, consumer, distributor, and electronic components and instrumentation industries.

Tessler and Cloherty, Inc.
155 Main St.
Cold Spring, New York 10516
Phone: (914)265-4244
Fax: (914)265-4158
A small business investment corporation. No industry preference.

Esquire Capital Corp.
69 Veterans Memorial Hwy.
Commack, New York 11725
Phone: (516)462-6946
Fax: (516)864-8152
A minority enterprise small business investment company. Diversified industry preference.

Pan Pac Capital Corp.
121 E. Industry Ct.
Deer Park, New York 11729
Fax: (516)586-7505
A minority enterprise small business investment corporation. No industry preference.

First County Capital, Inc.
135-14 Northern Blvd., 2nd Fl.
Flushing, New York 11354
Phone: (718)461-1778
Fax: (718)461-1835
A minority enterprise small business

investment company. Diversified industry preference.

Flushing Capital Corp.
39-06 Union St., Rm.202
Flushing, New York 11354
Phone: (718)886-5866
Fax: (718)939-7761
A minority enterprise small business investment company. Diversified industry preference.

Sterling/Carl Marks Capital, Inc.
175 Great Neck Rd., Ste. 408
Great Neck, New York 11021-3313
Phone: (516)482-7374
Fax: (516)487-0781
A small business investment company. Diversified industry preference.

Situation Ventures Corp.
56-20 59th St.
Maspeth, New York 11378
Phone: (718)894-2000
Fax: (718)326-4642
Sam Hollander, President
Preferred Investment Size: $100,000.
Investment Policies: Loans and/or equity. Industry Preferences: Manufacturing, service, retail. Geographic Preferences: New York metro area.

KOCO Capital Co., L.P.
111 Radio Cir.
Mt. Kisco, New York 10549
Phone: (914)242-2324
Fax: (914)241-7476
Albert Pastino, President
Preferred Investment Size: $2 to $3 million. Investment Policies: Equity and debt with warrants. Investment Types: Expansion. Industry Preferences: Healthcare, media, basic manufacturing. Geographic Preferences: Mid-Atlantic.

Tappan Zee Capital Corp. (New York)
120 N. Main St.
New City, New York 10956
A small business investment company.

Argentum Capital Partners, LP
405 Lexington Ave., 54th Fl.

New York, New York 10174
Phone: (212)949-6262
Fax: (212)949-8294
A small business investment company. Diversified industry preference.

ASEA—Harvest Partners II
767 3rd Ave.
New York, New York 10017
Phone: (212)838-7776
Fax: (212)593-0734
A small business investment corporation. No industry preference.

Asian American Capital Corp.
44 Wall St.
New York, New York 10005
Phone: (212)315-2600
Howard H. Lin, President

Bradford Ventures Ltd.
1 Rockefeller Plaza, Ste. 1722
New York, New York 10020
Phone: (212)218-6900
Fax: (212)218-6901
Venture capital firm. No industry preference.

BT Capital Corp.
130 Liberty St., M S 2255
New York, New York 10006
Phone: (212)250-8082
Fax: (212)250-7651
A small business investment corporation. No industry preference.

The Business Loan Center
645 Madison Ave., 18th Fl.
New York, New York 10022
Phone: (212)751-5626
Fax: (212)751-9345
A small business loan company.

Capital Investors and Management Corp.
212 Canal St., Ste. 611
New York, New York 10013-4155
Phone: (212)964-2480
Fax: (212)349-9160
A minority enterprise small business investment corporation. No industry preference.

CB Commercial, Inc.
560 Lexington Ave.,20th Fl.
New York, New York 10022

Phone: (212)207-6119
Fax: (212)207-6095
A small business investment company. Diversified industry preference.

CBIC Oppenheimer
425 Lexington Ave., 5th Fl.
New York, New York 10017
Phone: (212)856-4000
Fax: (212)697-1554
A small business investment company. Diversified industry preference.

Chase Capital Partners
380 Madison Ave., 12th Fl.
New York, New York 10017
Phone: (212)622-3100
Fax: (212)622-3101
A small business investment corporation. Areas of interest include health care, specialty retail, media and telecommunications, natural resources, consumer products, and environmental industries. Also invests in leveraged buy-outs and growth equity.

Citicorp Venture Capital Ltd. (New York City)
399 Park Ave., 14th Fl./Zone 4
New York, New York 10043
Phone: (212)559-1127
Fax: (212)888-2940
A small business investment corporation. Invests in the fields of information processing and telecommunications, transportation and energy, and health care; provides financing to companies in all stages of development. Also provides capital for leveraged buyout situations.

CMNY Capital II, LP
135 E. 57th St., 27th Fl.
New York, New York 10022
Phone: (212)909-8400
Fax: (212)980-2630
A small business investment company. Diversified industry preference.

Concord Partners
535 Madison Ave.
New York, New York 10022

Phone: (212)906-7100
Fax: (212)906-8690
Venture capital partnership. Diversified in terms of stage of development, industry classification, and geographic location. Areas of special interest include computer software, electronics, environmental services, biopharmaceuticals, health care, and oil and gas.

Cornerstone Equity Investors
717 5th Ave., Ste. 1100
New York, New York 10022
Phone: (212)753-0901
Fax: (212)826-6798
Venture capital fund. Specialty retailing, medical and health services, communications, and technology companies preferred. Will provide $3 to $7 million in equity financing for later-stage growth companies.

Credit Suisse First Boston
11 Madison Ave.
New York, New York 10010
Phone: (212)909-2000
Investment banker. Provides financing to the oil and gas pipeline, hydroelectric, medical technology, consumer products, electronics, aerospace, and telecommunications industries. Supplies capital for leveraged buyouts.

Creditanstalt SBIC
245 Park Ave., 27th Fl.
New York, New York 10167
Fax: (212)856-1699
Dennis O'Dowd, President

CW Group
1041 3rd Ave.
New York, New York 10021
Phone: (212)308-5266
Fax: (212)644-0354
Venture capital supplier. Interest is in the health care field, including diagnostic and therapeutic products, services, and biotechnology. Invests in companies at developing and early stages.

DAEDHIE
1261 Broadway, Rm. 405
New York, New York 10001

Fax: (212)684-6474
A minority enterprise small business investment company. Diversified industry preference.

DNC Capital Group
55 5th Ave., 15th Fl.
New York, New York 10003
Phone: (212)206-6041
Fax: (212)727-0563
Small business investment corporation interested in financing acquisitions in the real estate industry.

East Coast Venture Capital, Inc.
313 W. 53rd St., 3rd Fl.
New York, New York 10019
Phone: (212)245-6460
Fax: (212)265-2962
A minority enterprise small business investment company. Diversified industry preference.

Edwards Capital Co.
437 Madison Ave., 38th Fl.
New York, New York 10022
Phone: (212)682-3300
Fax: (212)328-2121
A small business investment corporation. Transportation industry preferred.

Elf Aquitain, Inc.
280 Park Ave., 36th Fl. W
New York, New York 10017-1216
Phone: (212)922-3000
Free: (800)922-0027
Fax: (212)922-3001

Elk Associates Funding Corp.
747 3rd Ave., 4th Fl.
New York, New York 10017
Phone: (212)421-2111
Fax: (212)759-3338
A minority enterprise small business investment corporation. Transportation industry preferred.

Elron Technologies, Inc.
666 5th Ave., 37th Fl.
New York, New York 10103
Phone: (212)541-2443
Fax: (212)541-2448
Venture capital supplier. Provides incubation and start-up financing to high-technology companies.

Empire State Capital Corp.
170 Broadway, Ste. 1200
New York, New York 10038
Phone: (212)513-1799
Fax: (212)513-1892
A minority enterprise small business investment company. Diversified industry preference.

Empire State Development Corp.
633 3rd Ave.
New York, New York 10017
Phone: (212)803-3100
Participates in a broad range of initiatives. Addresses the needs of the state in six areas, including downtown development, industrial development, minority business development, university research and development, and planning and special projects.

Eos Partners SBIC, L.P.
320 Park Ave., 22nd Fl.
New York, New York 10022
Phone: (212)832-5800
Fax: (212)832-5815
Marc H. Michel, Manager
Preferred Investment Size: $1 - $3 million. Investment Policies: Equity and equity-oriented debt. Investment Types: Expansion, later stage. Industry Preferences: Diversified, telecommunications, info-processing, data services. Geographic Preferences: National.

Euclid Partners Corp.
45 Rockefeller Plaza, Ste. 907
New York, New York 10111
Phone: (212)218-6880
Fax: (212)218-6877
Venture capital firm. Prefers early stage health care and information processing industries.

Exeter Group of Funds
10 E. 53rd St.
New York, New York 10022
Phone: (212)872-1170
Fax: (212)872-1198
Keith Fox, Manager
Preferred Investment Size: $3,000,000. Investment Policies: Loans and equity investments. Investment Types: Expansion, later stage. Industry Preferences:

Diversified. Geographic Preferences: National.

Exim Capital Corp.
241 5th Ave., 3rd Fl.
New York, New York 10016
Phone: (212)683-3375
Fax: (212)689-4118
A minority enterprise small business investment corporation. No industry preference.

Fair Capital Corp.
212 Canal St., Ste. 611
New York, New York 10013
Phone: (212)964-2480
Fax: (212)349-9160
A minority enterprise small business investment corporation. No industry preference.

First Wall Street SBIC, LP
26 Broadway, Ste. 2310
New York, New York 10004
Fax: (212)742-3776
A small business investment company. Diversified industry preference.

Franklin Holding Corp.
450 Park Ave.
New York, New York 10022
Phone: (212)486-2323
Fax: (212)755-5451
A small business investment corporation. No industry preference; no start-ups.

Fredericks Michael and Co.
2 Wall St., 4th Fl.
New York, New York 10005
Phone: (212)732-1600
Fax: (212)732-1872
Private venture capital supplier. Provides start-up and early stage financing, and supplies capital for buyouts and acquisitions.

Fresh Start Venture Capital Corp.
313 W. 53rd St., 3rd Fl.
New York, New York 10019
Phone: (212)265-2249
Fax: (212)265-2962
A minority enterprise small business investment corporation. No industry preference.

Furman Selz SBIC, L.P.
230 Park Ave.
New York, New York 10169
Phone: (212)309-8200
Fax: (212)692-9608
Brian Friedman, Manager
Preferred Investment Size: $2 to $6 million. Investment Policies: Equity. Investment Types: Expansion, later stage, no start-ups. Industry Preferences: Diversified. Geographic Preferences: National.

Hambro International Equity Partners (New York)
650 Madison Ave., 21st Floor
New York, New York 10022
Phone: (212)223-7400
Fax: (212)223-0305
Venture capital supplier. Seeks to invest in mature companies as well as in high-technology areas from start-ups to leveraged buyouts.

Hanam Capital Corp.
38 W. 32nd St., Rm. 1512
New York, New York 10001
Phone: (212)564-5225
Fax: (212)564-5307
A minority enterprise small business investment company. Diversified industry preference.

Harvest Partners, Inc. (New York)
767 3rd Ave.
New York, New York 10017
Phone: (212)838-7776
Fax: (212)593-0734
Private venture capital supplier. Prefers to invest in high-technology, growth-oriented companies with proprietary technology, large market potential, and strong management teams.

Holding Capital Group, Inc.
685 5th Ave., 14th Fl.
New York, New York 10022
Phone: (212)486-6670
Fax: (212)486-0843
A small business investment corporation. No industry preference. Prefers to purchase well-managed middle market companies with a minimum of $1 million cash flow.

IBJ Schroder Bank and Trust Co.
1 State St., 8th Fl.
New York, New York 10004
Phone: (212)858-2000
Fax: (212)425-0542
A small business investment
company. Diversified industry
preference.

InterEquity Capital Partners, L.P.
220 5th Ave., 17th Fl.
New York, New York 10001
Phone: (212)779-2022
Fax: (212)779-2103
A small business investment
company. Diversified industry
preference.

Investor International (U.S.), Inc.
320 Park Ave., 33 Fl.
New York, New York 10022
Phone: (212)508-0900
Fax: (212)508-0901

Jafco America Ventures, Inc. (New
York)
2 World Financial Center, Bldg. B,
17th Fl.
225 Liberty St.
New York, New York 10281-1196
Fax: (212)667-1004
Venture capital firm. Provides
middle- to later-stage financing to
technology-oriented companies.

Jardine Capital Corp.
105 Lafayette St., Unit 204
New York, New York 10013
Phone: (212)941-0993
Fax: (212)941-0998
Lawrence Wong, President
Preferred Investment Size: $360,000.
Investment Policies: Loans and/or
equity. Investment Types: Expansion.
Industry Preferences: Diversified.
Geographic Preferences: North/South.

Josephberg, Grosz and Co., Inc.
420 Lexington, Ste. 2635
New York, New York 10017
Fax: (212)397-5832
Venture capital firm. Invests in
companies having a minimum of $2.5
million in sales, significant growth
potential, and a strong management
base.

J.P. Morgan Investment Corp.
60 Wall St.
New York, New York 10260
Phone: (212)483-2323
A small business investment
company. Diversified industry
preference.

Kwiat Capital Corp.
579 5th Ave.
New York, New York 10017
Phone: (212)223-1111
Fax: (212)223-2796
A small business investment
corporation. No industry preference.

LandMark, Inc.
115 E. 69th Ave.
New York, New York 10021
Phone: (212)794-6060
Fax: (212)794-6169
Venture capital partnership.

Lawrence, Smith, and Horey
515 Madison Ave., 29th Fl.
New York, New York 10022
Phone: (212)826-9080
Fax: (212)759-2561
Venture capital firm. Prefers to invest
in health care, software, and
fragmented industries that grow by
acquisition.

McCown, De Leeuw and Co. (New
York)
101 E. 52nd St., 31st Fl.
New York, New York 10022-6018
Phone: (212)355-5500
Fax: (212)355-6283

Medallion Funding Corp.
437 Madison Ave., 38th Fl.
New York, New York 10022
Phone: (212)682-3300
Fax: (212)328-2121
A minority enterprise small business
investment corporation.
Transportation industry preferred.

Mercury Capital, L.P.
650 Madison Ave., Ste. 2600
New York, New York 10022
Phone: (212)838-0888
Fax: (212)838-7598
David W. Elenowitz, Manager

Morgan Stanley Venture Capital
(New York)
c/o M. Fazle Husain
1221 Avenue of the Americas, 33rd
Fl.
New York, New York 10020
Phone: (212)762-4000
Free: (800)223-2440
Fax: (212)762-8424
Venture capital firm providing later
stage financing. Areas of interest
include high technology and health
care.

NatWest USA Capital Corp.
175 Water St., 27th Fl.
New York, New York 10038
Phone: (212)602-4000
Fax: (212)602-3393
A small business investment
company. Diversified industry
preference.

Nazem and Co.
645 Madison Ave., 12th Fl.
New York, New York 10022
Phone: (212)371-7900
Fax: (212)371-2150
Venture capital fund. Electronics and
medical industries preferred. Will
provide seed and first- and second-
round financing.

Needham and Company, Inc.
445 Park Ave.
New York, New York 10022
Phone: (212)371-8300
Fax: (212)371-8418
John Michaelson, Manager
Preferred Investment Size: $500,000
to $1 million. Investment Policies:
Equity. Industry Preferences:
Technology. Geographic Preferences:
National.

Norwood Venture Corp.
E-mail: nvc@mail.idt.net
1430 Broadway, Ste. 1607
New York, New York 10017
Phone: (212)869-5075
Fax: (212)869-5331
A small business investment
company. Diversified industry
preference.

Paribas Principal, Inc.
787 7th Ave., 33rd Fl.
New York, New York 10019
Phone: (212)841-2000
Fax: (212)841-2146
A small business investment
company. Diversified industry
preference.

Patricof & Co. Ventures, Inc. (New
York)
445 Park Ave., 11th Fl.
New York, New York 10022
Phone: (212)753-6300
Fax: (212)319-6155
Venture capital firm.

Pierre Funding Corp.
805 3rd Ave., 6th Fl.
New York, New York 10022
Phone: (212)888-1515
Fax: (212)688-4252
A minority enterprise small business
investment corporation. No industry
preference.

Prospect Street NYC Discovery Fund,
L.P.
250 Park Ave., 17th Fl.
New York, New York 10177
Phone: (212)490-0480
Fax: (212)490-1566
Richard E. Omohundro, CEO

Pyramid Ventures, Inc.
130 Liberty St., 25th Fl.
New York, New York 10006
Phone: (212)250-9571
Fax: (212)250-7651
A small business investment
company. Diversified industry
preference.

R and R Financial Corp.
1370 Broadway
New York, New York 10018
Phone: (212)356-1400
Free: (800)999-4800
Fax: (212)356-0900
A small business investment
corporation. No industry preference.

Rothschild Ventures, Inc.
1251 Avenue of the Americas
New York, New York 10020
Phone: (212)403-3500
Free: (800)753-5151

Fax: (212)403-3501
Private venture capital firm. Prefers
seed and all later-stage financing.

767 Limited Partnership
767 3rd Ave., 7th Fl.
New York, New York 10017
Phone: (212)838-7776
Fax: (212)593-0734
A small business investment
corporation. No industry preference.

Sixty Wall Street SBIC Fund, L.P.
60 Wall St.
New York, New York 10260
Phone: (212)648-7778
Fax: (212)648-5032
David Cromwell
Seth Cunningham

Sprout Group (New York City)
277 Park Ave., 21st Fl.
New York, New York 10172
Phone: (212)892-3600
Fax: (212)892-3444
Venture capital supplier.

TCW Capital
200 Park Ave., Ste. 2200
New York, New York 10166
Phone: (212)297-4000
Fax: (212)297-4024
Venture capital fund. Companies with
sales of $25 to $100 million
preferred. Will provide up to $20
million in later-stage financing for
recapitalizations, restructuring
management buyouts, and general
corporate purposes.

399 Venture Partners
399 Park Ave., 14th Fl./ Zone 4
New York, New York 10043
Phone: (212)559-1127
Fax: (212)888-2940
A small business investment
company. Diversified industry
preference.

Trusty Capital, Inc.
350 5th Ave., Ste. 2026
New York, New York 10118
Phone: (212)629-3011
Fax: (212)629-3019
A minority enterprise small business
investment company. Diversified
industry preference.

UBS Partners, Inc.
299 Park Ave., 34th Fl.
New York, New York 10171
Phone: (212)821-6490
Fax: (212)821-6333
Justin S. Maccarone, President

United Capital Investment Corp.
60 E. 42nd St., Ste. 1515
New York, New York 10165
Phone: (212)682-7210
Fax: (212)573-6352
A minority enterprise small business
investment company. Diversified
industry preference.

Venture Capital Fund of America,
Inc.
509 Madison Ave., Ste. 812
New York, New York 10022
Phone: (212)838-5577
Fax: (212)838-7614

Venture Opportunities Corp.
150 E. 58th St., 16th Floor
New York, New York 10155
Phone: (212)832-3737
Fax: (212)980-6603
A minority enterprise small business
investment corporation. Areas of
interest include radio, cable,
television, telecommunications, real
estate development, medical
consumer products, and service and
manufacturing businesses. Second- or
third-stage for expansion, mergers, or
acquisitions. No start-up or seed
capital investments.

Warburg Pincus Ventures, Inc.
466 Lexington Ave., 10th Fl.
New York, New York 10017-3147
Phone: (212)878-0600
Free: (800)888-3697
Fax: (212)878-9351
Venture capital firm providing all
stages of financing. Areas of interest
include all industries, excluding
gaming, real estate, and investments
in South Africa.

Weiss, Peck and Greer Venture
Partners L.P.
1 New York Plz.
New York, New York 10004
Phone: (212)908-9500
Fax: (212)908-9652

Welsh, Carson, Anderson, & Stowe
320 Park Ave., Ste. 2500
New York, New York 10022
Phone: (212)893-9500
Fax: (212)893-9575
Venture capital partnership.

Wolfensohn Partners, L.P. (New York)
130 Liberty St.
New York, New York 10006
Phone: (212)250-6000
Fax: (212)250-6440

International Paper Capital
Formation, Inc. (Purchase)
E-mail: comm@ipaper.com
2 Manhattanville Rd.
Purchase, New York 10577-2196
Phone: (914)397-1500
Fax: (914)397-1909
A minority enterprise small business
investment company.

Ibero-American Investors Corp.
104 Scio St.
Rochester, New York 14604-2552
Phone: (716)262-3440
Fax: (716)262-3441
A minority enterprise small business
investment corporation. No industry
preference.

Northwood Ventures
485 Underhill Blvd., Ste. 205
Syosset, New York 11791
Phone: (516)364-5544
Fax: (516)364-0879
Venture capital firm providing
leveraged buyout financing, between
$500,000 - $1 million. Diversified
industry preference.

TLC Funding Corp.
660 White Plains Rd.
Tarrytown, New York 10591
Phone: (914)332-5200
Fax: (914)332-5660
A small business investment
corporation. No industry preference.

Bessemer Venture Partners
(Westbury)
1025 Old Country Rd., Ste. 205
Westbury, New York 11590
Phone: (516)997-2300
Fax: (516)997-2371

Venture capital partnership. No
industry preference.

SBP Technology
106 Corporate Park
White Plains, New York 10604
Phone: (914)694-2280
Fax: (914)694-2286

Winfield Capital Corp.
237 Mamaroneck Ave.
White Plains, New York 10605
Phone: (914)949-2600
Fax: (914)949-7195
A small business investment
corporation. No industry preference.

North Carolina

First Union Capital Partners, Inc.
1 1st Union Center, 18th Fl.
301 S. College St.
Charlotte, North Carolina 28288-0732
Phone: (704)374-6487
Fax: (704)374-6711
A small business investment
company. Diversified industry
preference.

Kitty Hawk Capital Ltd.
E-mail: Khcmaine@aol.com
2700 Coltsgate Rd., Ste. 202
Charlotte, North Carolina 28211
Phone: (704)362-3909
Fax: (704)362-2774
Venture capital firm. Geographical
preference is the southeast.
Investment policy is liberal, but does
not invest in real estate, natural
resources, and single store retail
businesses and does not provide
invention development financing.

NationsBanc Capital Corp.
100 N. Tryon St., 10th Fl.
Charlotte, North Carolina 28255
Phone: (704)386-8063
Fax: (704)386-6432
Walter W. Walker Jr., President
Preferred Investment Size: $3 to $25
million. Investment Policies: Equity,
sub debt with warrants. Investment
Types: Later stage, expansion.
Industry Preferences: Diversified.
Geographic Preferences: National.

Southeastern Publishing Ventures Inc.
528 E. Blvd.
Charlotte, North Carolina 28203
Phone: (704)373-0051
Fax: (704)343-0170
Private venture capital firm.
Diversified industry preference.

Center for Community Self-Help
North Carolina's Development Bank
PO Box 3619
301 W. Maine St.
Durham, North Carolina 27701
Phone: (919)956-4400
Free: (800)476-7428
Fax: (919)956-4600
Statewide, private-sector financial
institution providing technical
assistance and financing to small
businesses, non-profit organizations,
and low-income homebuyers in North
Carolina.

Atlantic Venture Partners (Winston
Salem)
380 Knollwood St., No. 410
Winston Salem, North Carolina
27103
Phone: (910)721-1800
Fax: (910)748-1208
Private venture capital partnership.
Prefers to invest in manufacturing,
distribution, and service industries.

North Dakota

Bank of North Dakota
Small Business Loan Program
700 E. Main Ave.
PO Box 5509
Bismarck, North Dakota 58506-5509
Phone: (701)328-5600
Free: (800)472-2166
Fax: (701)328-5632
Assists new and existing businesses in
securing competitive financing with
reasonable terms and conditions.

Dakota Certified Development Corp.
406 Main Ave., Ste. 404
Fargo, North Dakota 58103
Phone: (701)293-8892
Fax: (701)293-7819
Administers the 504 Loan Program.

Fargo Cass County Economic
Development Corp.
E-mail: info@fedc.com
406 Main Ave., Ste. 404
Fargo, North Dakota 58103
Phone: (701)237-6132
Fax: (701)293-7819
Certified development company that
lends to small and medium-sized
businesses at fixed rates.

North Dakota SBIC, L.P.
406 Main Ave., Ste. 404
Fargo, North Dakota 58103
Phone: (701)298-0003
Fax: (701)293-7819
David R. Schroeder, Manager

Ohio

River Capital Corp. (Cleveland)
2544 Chamberlain Rd.
Akron, Ohio 44333
Phone: (330)864-8836
Fax: (216)781-2821
A small business investment
corporation. No industry preference.

River Cities Capital Fund L.P.
221 E. 4th St., Ste. 2250
Cincinnati, Ohio 45202
Phone: (513)621-9700
Fax: (513)579-8939
R. Glen Mayfield, Manager
Preferred Investment Size: $750,000
TO $1.5 million. Investment Policies:
Equity investments. Investment
Types: Early stage, expansion, later
stage. Industry Preferences:
Diversified. Geographic Preferences:
Ohio, Kentucky, Indiana.

Brantley Venture Partners, L.P.
20600 Chagrin Blvd., Ste. 1150
Cleveland, Ohio 44122
Phone: (216)283-4800
Fax: (216)283-5324
Venture capital firm. Areas of interest
include computer and electronics,
medical/health care, biotechnology,
computer software,
telecommunications, traditional
manufacturing, information
processing, and environmental
industries.

Clarion Capital Corp.
Ohio Savings Plz., Ste. 510
1801 E. 9th St.
Cleveland, Ohio 44114
Phone: (216)687-1096
Fax: (216)694-3545
Small business investment
corporation. Interested in
manufacturing, computer software,
natural resources/natural gas, and
health care.

Gries Investment Co.
1801 E. 9th St.,Ste. 1600
Cleveland, Ohio 44114-3110
Phone: (216)861-1146
Fax: (216)861-0106
A small business investment
corporation. No industry preference.

Key Equity Capital Corp.
127 Public Sq., 6th. Fl.
Cleveland, Ohio 44114
Phone: (216)689-5776
Fax: (216)689-3204
Raymond Lancaster, President
Preferred Investment Size:
$2.000,000. Investment Policies:
Willing to make equity investments.
Industry Preferences: Diversified.
Geographic Preferences: National.

Morgenthaler Ventures
629 Euclid Ave.,Ste. 700
Cleveland, Ohio 44114
Phone: (216)621-3070
Fax: (216)621-2817
Private venture capital firm providing
start-up and later-stage financing to
all types of business in North
America; prefers not to invest in real
estate and oil and gas.

National City Capital Corp.
1965 E. 6th St.
Cleveland, Ohio 44114
Phone: (216)575-2491
Fax: (216)575-9965
A small business investment
corporation. Provides equity for
expansion programs,
recapitalizations, acquisitions, and
management buyouts. Seeks
investment opportunities ranging
from $1 million to $5 million.
Diversified industry preference.

Primus Venture Partners
5900 LanderBrook Dr. Ste. 200
Cleveland, Ohio 44124
Phone: (216)621-2185
Fax: (440)684-7342
Venture capital partnership. Provides
seed, early stage, and expansion
financing to companies located in
Ohio and the Midwest. Does not
engage in gas, oil, or real estate
investments.

Society Venture Capital Corp.
127 Public Sq. 6th Fl.
Cleveland, Ohio 44114
Phone: (216)689-5776
Fax: (216)689-3204
A small business investment
corporation. Prefers to invest in
manufacturing and service industries.

Tomlinson Industries
13700 Broadway Ave.
Cleveland, Ohio 44125-1992
Phone: (216)587-3400
Free: (800)526-9634
Fax: (216)587-0733
A small business investment
corporation. Miniature supermarket
industry preferred.

Banc One Capital Partners Corp.
(Columbus)
150 E. Gay St.
Columbus, Ohio 43215
Phone: (614)217-1100
Free: (800)837-5100
Fax: (614)217-0107
A small business investment
corporation. No industry preference.

Scientific Advances, Inc.
601 W. 5th Ave.
Columbus, Ohio 43201
Phone: (614)424-7005
Fax: (614)424-4874
Venture capital partnership interested
in natural gas related industries.

Interprise Ohio
8 N. Maine St.
Dayton, Ohio 45402
Phone: (937)461-6164
Fax: (937)222-7035
A minority enterprise small business
investment corporation. Diversified
industries.

Seed One
Park Pl.
10 W. Streetsboro St.
Hudson, Ohio 44236
Phone: (330)650-2338
Fax: (330)650-4946
Private venture capital firm. No
industry preference. Equity financing
only.

Fifth Third Bank of Northwestern
Ohio, N.A.
606 Madison Ave.
Toledo, Ohio 43604
Phone: (419)259-7141
Fax: (419)259-7134
A small business investment
corporation. No industry preference.

Lubrizol Performance Products Co.
29400 Lakeland Blvd.
Wickliffe, Ohio 44092
Phone: (440)943-4200
Fax: (440)943-5337
Venture capital supplier. Provides
seed capital and later-stage expansion
financing to emerging companies in
the biological, chemical, and material
sciences whose technology is
applicable to and related to the
production and marketing of specialty
and fine chemicals.

Cactus Capital Co.
6660 High St., Office 1-B
Worthington, Ohio 43085
Phone: (614)436-4060
Fax: (614)436-4060
A minority enterprise small business
investment company. Diversified
industry preference.

Oklahoma

Southwestern Oklahoma
Development Authority
PO Box 569
Burns Flat, Oklahoma 73624
Phone: (405)562-4884
Free: (800)627-4882
Fax: (405)562-4880

Langston University
Minority Business Assistance Center
Hwy. 33 E.
PO Box 667

Langston, Oklahoma 73050
Phone: (405)466-3256
Fax: (405)466-2909

BancFirst Investment Corp.
1100 N. Broadway
PO Box 26788
Oklahoma City, Oklahoma 73106-
0788
Phone: (405)270-1000
Fax: (405)270-1089
T. Kent Faison, Manager
Preferred Investment Size: Up to
$500,000. Investment Policies: Loans
and/or equity. Investment Types:
Early stage, expansion. Industry
Preferences: Diversified. Geographic
Preferences: Oklahoma.

Oklahoma Department of Commerce
Business Development Division
PO Box 26980
Oklahoma City, Oklahoma 73126-
0980
Phone: (405)815-6552
Fax: (405)815-5142
Helps companies gain access to
capital needed for growth. Provides
financial specialists to help businesses
analyze their financing needs and to
work closely with local economic
development staff to help package
proposals for their companies. Also
responsible for assisting in the
development of new loan and
investment programs.

Oklahoma Development Finance
Authority
301 NW 63rd St., Ste. 225
Oklahoma City, Oklahoma 73116-
7906
Phone: (405)848-9761
Fax: (405)848-3314
Issues tax-exempt industrial
development bonds for manufacturing
firms.

Oklahoma Industrial Finance
Authority
301 NW 63rd., Ste. 225
Oklahoma City, Oklahoma 73116-
7906
Phone: (405)842-1145
Fax: (405)848-3314
Provides financing for manufacturing

projects involving the purchase of
land, buildings, and stationary
equipment.

Oklahoma State Treasurer's Office
Agriculture/Small Business Linked
Deposit Programs
E-mail: Treas@oklaosF.state.ok.us
2300 N. Lincoln Blvd.
Oklahoma City, Oklahoma 73105
Phone: (405)521-3191
Fax: (405)521-4994
Provides reduced loan rates for
Oklahoma's farming, ranching, and
small business communities.

Rees/Source Ventures, Inc.
4045 NE 64th St. Ste. 410
Oklahoma City, Oklahoma 73116
Phone: (405)843-8049
Fax: (405)843-8048
Venture capital firm providing seed,
start-up, first-stage, and second-stage
financing. Prefers to make
investments in the $250,000 to
$500,000 range to companies within a
three-mile radius of Oklahoma City.
Areas of interest include recreation
and leisure, environmental products
and services, packaging machinery
and materials, energy-related
technologies, printing and publishing,
manufacturing and automation,
information processing and software,
and specialty chemicals industries.
Will not consider the following
industries: oil, gas, or mineral
exploration; real estate; motion
pictures; and consulting services.

Alliance Business Investment Co.
(Tulsa)
320 South Boston Ste.1000
Tulsa, Oklahoma 74103-3703
Phone: (918)584-3581
Fax: (918)582-3403
A small business investment
corporation. Provides later-stage
financing for basic industries.

Davis Venture Partners (Tulsa)
320 S. Boston Ste.,1000
Tulsa, Oklahoma 74103-3703
Phone: (918)584-7272
Fax: (918)582-3403

Venture capital firm. Provides later-stage financing for basic industries.

Oregon

Olympic Venture Partners II (Lake Oswego)
340 Oswego Pointe Dr., No. 200
Lake Oswego, Oregon 97034-3230
Phone: (503)697-8766
Fax: (503)697-8863
Invests in early stage high technology, biotechnology, and communications businesses.

Orien Ventures
300 Oswego Pointe Dr., Ste. 100
Lake Oswego, Oregon 97034
Phone: (503)699-1680
Fax: (503)699-1681
Venture capital firm interested in all types of investment.

Northern Pacific Capital Corp.
PO Box 1658
Portland, Oregon 97205
Phone: (503)241-1255
Fax: (503)299-6653
A small business investment company. Diversified industry preference.

Oregon Resource and Technology Development Fund
4370 NE Halsey
Portland, Oregon 97213
Phone: (503)282-4462
Fax: (503)282-2976
Provides investment capital for early stage business finance and applied research and development projects that leads to commercially viable products.

Shaw Venture Partners
400 SW 6th Ave., Ste. 1100
Portland, Oregon 97204-1636
Phone: (503)228-4884
Fax: (503)227-2471
Small business investment corporation interested in computers, retail, medical/biotechnology, consumer products and international trade investment.

U.S. Bancorp Capital Corp.
PO Box 8837
Portland, Oregon 97208
Phone: (503)275-6111
Fax: (503)275-7565
A small business investment company. Diversified industry preference.

Oregon Economic Development Department
Business Finance Section
Oregon Business Development Fund
775 Summer St. NE
Salem, Oregon 97310
Phone: (503)986-0160
Fax: (503)581-5115
Structures and issues loans to manufacturing, processing, and tourism-related small businesses.

Oregon Economic Development Department
Business Finance Section
SBA Loans Program
775 Summer St. NE
Salem, Oregon 97310
Phone: (503)986-0160
Free: (800)233-3306
Fax: (503)581-5115
A state-wide company providing Small Business Administration 504 and 7(A) financing to eligible small businesses; works closely with local certified development companies.

Tektronix Development Co.
PO Box 1000, Mail Sta. 63-862
Wilsonville, Oregon 97070
Phone: (503)685-4233
Fax: (503)685-3754
Venture capital firm interested in high tech, opto electronics and measurement systems investment.

Pennsylvania

Mid-Atlantic Venture Funds
125 Goodman Dr.
Bethlehem, Pennsylvania 18015
Phone: (610)865-6550
Fax: (610)865-6427
Private venture capital partnership providing seed and start-up financing.

Pennsylvania Department of Community and Economic Development
Bureau of Bonds
Revenue Bond and Mortgage Program
E-mail: abrennan@doc.state.pa.us
466 Forum Bldg.
Harrisburg, Pennsylvania 17120
Phone: (717)783-1109
Fax: (717)787-0879
Financing for projects approved through the Program are borrowed from private sources, and can be used to acquire land, buildings, machinery, and equipment. Borrowers must create a minimum number of new jobs within three years of the loan's closing.

Pennsylvania Department of Community and Economic Development
Governor's Response Team
100 Pine St., Ste. 100
Harrisburg, Pennsylvania 17101
Phone: (717)787-8199
Fax: (717)772-5419
Works with individual companies to find buildings or sites for start-up or expansion projects; contacts manufacturers to make them aware of financial and technical assistance available, to assist with difficulties, and to learn of future plans for expansions or cutbacks.

Pennsylvania Department of Community and Economic Development
Bureau of Bonds
Employee Ownership Assistance Program
E-mail: abrennan@doc.state.pa.us
Office of Program Management
466 Forum Bldg.
Harrisburg, Pennsylvania 17120
Phone: (717)783-1109
Fax: (717)787-0879
Preserves existing jobs and creates new jobs by assisting and promoting employee ownership in existing enterprises which are experiencing layoffs or would otherwise close.

Enterprise Venture Capital Corp. of
Pennsylvania
111 Market St.
Johnstown, Pennsylvania 15901
Phone: (814)535-7597
Fax: (814)535-8677
A small business investment
corporation. No industry preference.
Geographic preference is two-hour
driving radius of Johnstown,
Pennsylvania.

Foster Management Co.
1018 W. 9th Ave.
King of Prussia, Pennsylvania 19406
Phone: (610)992-7650
Fax: (610)992-3390
Private venture capital supplier. Not
restricted to specific industries or
geographic locations; diversified with
investments in the health care,
transportation, broadcasting,
communications, energy, and home
furnishings industries. Investments
range from $2 million to $15 million.

Patricof & Co. Ventures, Inc.
455 S. Gulph Rd., Ste. 410
King of Prussia, Pennsylvania 19406
Phone: (610)265-0286
Fax: (610)265-4959
Venture capital firm providing mid-
to later stage financing.

Core States Enterprise Fund
1345 Chestnut St., F.C. 1-8-12-1
Philadelphia, Pennsylvania 19107
Phone: (215)973-6519
Fax: (215)973-6900
Venture capital supplier. Invests with
any industry except real estate or
construction. Minimum investment is
$1 million.

Fidelcor Capital Corp.
Fidelity Bldg., 11th Fl.
123 S. Broad St.
Philadelphia, Pennsylvania 19109
Phone: (215)985-3722
Fax: (215)985-7282
A small business investment
company. Diversified industry
preference.

Ben Franklin Technology Center of
Southeastern Pennsylvania

University City Science Center
3624 Market St.
Philadelphia, Pennsylvania 19104
Phone: (215)382-0380
Fax: (215)387-6050
Public venture capital fund interested
in technology industries.

Keystone Venture Capital
Management Co.
1601 Market St.,Ste.2500
Philadelphia, Pennsylvania 19103
Phone: (215)241-1200
Fax: (215)241-1211
Private venture capital partnership.
Provides later-stage investments in
the telecommunications, health care,
manufacturing, media, software, and
franchise industries, primarily in the
mid-Atlantic states.

Penn Janney Fund, Inc.
1801 Market St., 8th Fl.
Philadelphia, Pennsylvania 19103
Phone: (215)665-6193
Fax: (215)665-6197
Private venture capital limited
partnership.

Philadelphia Ventures
200 S. Broad St., 8th Fl.
Philadelphia, Pennsylvania 19102
Phone: (215)732-4445
Fax: (215)732-4644
A small business investment
corporation. Provides financing to
companies offering products or
services based on technology or other
proprietary capabilities. Industries of
particular interest are information
processing equipment and services,
medical products and services, data
communications, and industrial
automation.

PNC Corporate Finance
(Philadelphia)
1600 Market St., 21st Fl.
Philadelphia, Pennsylvania 19103
Phone: (215)585-6282
Fax: (215)585-5525
Small business investment company.

Fostin Capital Corp.
681 Andersen Dr.
Pittsburgh, Pennsylvania 15220

Phone: (412)928-1400
Fax: (412)928-9635
Venture capital corporation.

Loyalhanna Venture Fund
PO Box 81927
Pittsburgh, Pennsylvania 15217
Phone: (412)687-9027
Fax: (412)681-0960
Venture capital firm. No industry
preference.

PNC Equity Management Corp.
3150 CNG Tower
625 Liberty Ave.
Pittsburgh, Pennsylvania 15222
Phone: (412)762-7035
Fax: (412)762-6233
A small business investment
corporation. Prefers to invest in later-
stage and leveraged buyout situations.
Will not consider real estate, coal, or
gas ventures.

Meridian Venture Partners (Radnor)
The Fidelity Court Bldg., Ste. 140
259 Radnor-Chester Rd.
Radnor, Pennsylvania 19087
Phone: (610)254-2999
Fax: (610)254-2996
Venture capital firm.

First Union Capital Market
600 Penn St.
Reading, Pennsylvania 19602
Phone: (610)655-1437
Fax: (610)655-1437
Small business investment
corporation.

TDH
1 Rosemont Business Campus, Ste.
301
919 Conestoga Rd.
Rosemont, Pennsylvania 19010
Phone: (610)526-9970
Fax: (610)526-9971
Private venture capital fund. No
industry preferences.

First SBIC of California
(Washington)
PO Box 512
Washington, Pennsylvania 15301
Fax: (412)223-8290
A small business investment
company.

CIP Capital, LP
435 Devon Port Dr., Bld. 200
Wayne, Pennsylvania 19087
Phone: (610)964-7860
Fax: (610)964-8136
A small business investment
company. Diversified industry
preference.

Safeguard Scientifics, Inc.
800 The Safeguard Bldg.
435 Devon Park Dr.
Wayne, Pennsylvania 19087
Phone: (888)733-1200
Fax: (610)293-0601
Private venture capital fund. Areas of
interest include biotechnology, health
care, information services, and high
technology industries.

Sandhurst Co. LP
351 E. Constoga Rd.
Wayne, Pennsylvania 19087
Phone: (610)254-8900
Fax: (610)254-8958
Private venture capital fund.

S.R. One Ltd.
565 E. Swedesford Rd., Ste. 315
Wayne, Pennsylvania 19087
Phone: (610)293-3400
Fax: (610)293-3419

Rockhill Ventures, Inc.
100 Front St., Ste. 1350
West Conshohocken, Pennsylvania
19428
Phone: (610)940-0300
Fax: (610)940-0301
Venture capital firm that invests in
early-stage medical technology
companies.

Puerto Rico

North America Investment Corp.
P.O. Box 191831
San Juan, Puerto Rico 00919-1813
Phone: (787)754-6177
Fax: (787)754-6181
A minority enterprise small business
investment corporation. Diversified
industry preference.

Rhode Island

Domestic Capital Corp.
815 Reservoir Ave.
Cranston, Rhode Island 02910
Phone: (401)946-3310
Fax: (401)943-6708
A small business investment
corporation. No industry preference.

Fairway Capital Corp.
285 Governor St.
Providence, Rhode Island 02906
Phone: (401)861-4600
Fax: (401)861-0530
A small business investment
company. Diversified industry
preference.

Fleet Equity Partners (Providence)
E-mail: fep@fleet.com
50 Kennedy Plaza, 12th Fl.
Providence, Rhode Island 02903
Phone: (401)278-6770
Fax: (401)278-6387
Venture capital firm specializing in
acquisitions and recapitalizations.

Fleet Venture Resources, Inc.
E-mail: fep@fleet.com
50 Kennedy Plaza, 12th Fl.
Providence, Rhode Island 02903
Phone: (401)278-6770
Fax: (401)278-6387
Robert M. Van Degna, President
Preferred Investment Size: $5 to $125
million. Investment Policies: Equity.
Investment Types: Leverage buyouts,
expansion. Industry Preferences:
Media/communications, healthcare,
printing, manufacturing. Geographic
Preferences: National.

Moneta Capital Corp.
285 Governor St.
Providence, Rhode Island 02906
Phone: (401)861-4600
Fax: (401)861-0530
A small business investment
corporation. No industry preference.

Rhode Island Economic Development
Corp.
Rhode Island Partnership for Science
and Technology
1 W. Exchange
Providence, Rhode Island 02903

Phone: (401)222-2601
Fax: (401)222-2102
Offers grants to businesses for applied
research with a potential for profitable
commercialization. Research must be
conducted in conjunction with
universities, colleges, or hospitals.
Also has a program which provides
consulting services and grants to
applicants of the Federal Small
Business Innovation Research
Program.

Rhode Island Economic Development
Corp.
Rhode Island Port Operations
Division
1 W. Exchange
Providence, Rhode Island 02903
Phone: (401)277-2601
Fax: (401)277-2102
Provides financing through tax-
exempt revenue bonds.

Rhode Island Economic Development
Corp.
Ocean State Business Development
Authority
1 W. Exchange
Providence, Rhode Island 02903
Phone: (401)222-2601
Fax: (401)222-2102
Private, nonprofit corporation
certified by the Small Business
Administration to administer the
SBA(504) loan program.

Rhode Island Economic Development
Corp.
Rhode Island Industrial-Recreational
Building Authority
1 W. Exchange
Providence, Rhode Island 02903
Phone: (401)222-2601
Fax: (401)222-2102
Issues mortgage insurance on
financing obtained through other
financial institutions.

Rhode Island Office of the General
Treasurer
Business Investment Fund
E-mail: treasury@treasury.state.ri.us
40 Fountain St., 8th Fl.
Providence, Rhode Island 02903-
1855

Phone: (401)222-2287
Free: (800)752-8088
Fax: (401)222-6141
Provides fixed-rate loans in cooperation with the U.S. Small Business Administration and local banks.

Richmond Square Capital Corp.
1 Richmond Sq.
Providence, Rhode Island 02906
Phone: (401)521-3000
Fax: (401)751-8997
A small business investment company. Diversified industry preference.

Wallace Capital Corp.
170 Westminster St., Ste.1200
Providence, Rhode Island 02903
Fax: (401)273-9648
A small business investment company. Diversified industry preference.

South Carolina

Charleston Capital Corp.
111 Church St.
PO Box 328
Charleston, South Carolina 29402
Phone: (843)723-6464
Fax: (843)723-1228
Small business investment corporation preferring secured loans. Assists the southeastern U.S. only.

Lowcountry Investment Corp.
4401 Piggly Wiggly Dr.
PO Box 118047
Charleston, South Carolina 29423
Phone: (803)554-9880
Fax: (803)745-2730
A small business investment corporation. Diversified industry preference.

Floco Investment Co., Inc.
PO Box 1629
Lake City, South Carolina 29560
Phone: (843)389-2731
Fax: (843)389-4199
A small business investment corporation. Invests only in grocery stores.

South Dakota

South Dakota Department of Agriculture
Office of Rural Development
Agricultural Loan Participation Program
Foss Bldg.
523 E. Capitol
Pierre, South Dakota 57501-3182
Phone: (605)773-3375
Free: (800)228-5254
Fax: (605)773-5926
Provides loans, administered and serviced through local lenders, that are intended to supplement existing credit.

South Dakota Development Corp.
SBA 504 Loan Program
711 E. Wells Ave.
Pierre, South Dakota 57501-3369
Phone: (605)773-5032
Free: (800)872-6190
Fax: (605)773-3256
Offers subordinated mortgage financing to healthy and expanding small businesses.

South Dakota Governor's Office of Economic Development
Revolving Economic Development and Initiative Fund
711 E. Wells Ave.
Pierre, South Dakota 57501-3369
Phone: (605)773-5032
Free: (800)872-6190
Fax: (605)773-3256
Provides low-interst revolving loans for the creation of primary jobs, capital investment, and the diversification of the state's economy. Costs eligible for participation include land and the associated site improvements; construction, acquistion, and renovation of buildings; fees, services and other costs associated with construction; the purchase and installation of machinery and equipment; and trade receivables, inventory, and work-in-progress inventory.

South Dakota Governor's Office of Economic Development
Economic Development Finance

Authority
711 E. Wells Ave.
Pierre, South Dakota 57501-3369
Phone: (605)773-5032
Free: (800)872-6190
Fax: (605)773-3256
Pools tax-exempt or taxable development bonds to construct any site, structure, facility, service, or utility for the storage, distribution, or manufacture of industrial, agricultural, or nonagricultural products, machinery, or equipment.

Tennessee

Valley Capital Corp.
100 W. Martin Luther King Blvd., Ste. 212
Chattanooga, Tennessee 37402
Phone: (423)265-1557
Fax: (423)265-1588
A minority enterprise small business investment corporation. Diversified industry preferences. Limited to the Southeast, preferably four-hour driving radius.

Coleman Swenson-Hoffman, Booth Inc.
237 2nd Ave. S
Franklin, Tennessee 37064
Phone: (615)791-9462
Fax: (615)791-9636
A small business investment corporation. Prefers to invest in the health care and biotechnology industries.

Chickasaw Capital Corp.
8354 Championship Dr., Ste. 203
Memphis, Tennessee 38125
Phone: (901)748-0214
Fax: (901)748-3135
A minority enterprise small business investment corporation. No industry preference.

Flemming Companies
4681 Burbank
Memphis, Tennessee 38118
Phone: (901)794-8660
Fax: (901)797-3987
A small business investment corporation.

Gulf Pacific
5100 Poplar Ave., No. 427
Memphis, Tennessee 38137-0401
Phone: (901)767-3400
Free: (800)456-1867
Fax: (901)680-7033
A minority enterprise small business
investment corporation.

International Paper Capital
Formation, Inc.
6400 Poplar Ave.
Tower 2, 4th Fl., Rm. 130
Memphis, Tennessee 38197
Phone: (901)763-6217
Fax: (901)763-6076
A minority enterprise small business
investment corporation. Diversified
industry preference. Involvement
includes expansion, refinancing, and
acquisitions, but no start-up projects.
Requires a minimum investment of
$50,000 to $300,000.

Union Platters Bank
158 Madison Ave.
Memphis, Tennessee 38103-0708
Phone: (901)524-5700
Free: (800)821-9979
Fax: (901)524-5713
A small business investment
corporation.

West Tennessee Venture Capital
Corp.
Tennessee Valley Center for Minority
Economics Dev.
5 N. 3rd St., Ste. 2000
Memphis, Tennessee 38103-2610
Phone: (901)523-1884
Fax: (901)527-6091
A minority enterprise small business
investment corporation.

L.P. Equitas
2000 Glen Echo Rd., Ste. 101
PO Box 158838
Nashville, Tennessee 37215
Phone: (615)383-8673
Fax: (615)383-8693
D. Shannon LeRoy, President

Massey Burch Investment Group
E-mail: masseyBurch.com
310 25th Ave. N, Ste. 103
Nashville, Tennessee 37203

Phone: (615)329-9448
Fax: (615)329-9237
Venture capital firm providing
investments ranging from $1 to $3
million. Areas of interest include
health care services, information
services, environmental services,
privatization, systems integration, and
telecommunications.

Sirrom Capital, LP
500 Church St., Ste. 200
Nashville, Tennessee 37219
Phone: (615)256-0701
Fax: (615)726-1208
A small business investment
company. Diversified industry
preference.

Tennessee Department of Economic
and Community Development
Grants Program Management Section
Rachel Jackson Bldg., 6th Fl.
320 6th Ave. N.
Nashville, Tennessee 37243-0405
Phone: (615)741-6201
Free: (800)342-8470
Fax: (615)741-5070
Administers grant money for the
community development block grant
program, the Appalachian Regional
Commission, and the Economic
Development Administration.

Texas

Austin Ventures L.P.
114 W. 7th St., STe. 1300
Austin, Texas 78701
Phone: (512)479-0055
Fax: (512)476-3952
Administers investments through two
funds, Austin Ventures L.P. and Rust
Ventures L.P., in the $1 million to $4
million range. Prefers to invest in
start-up/emerging growth companies
located in the southwest, and in
special situations such as buyouts,
acquisitions, and mature companies.
No geographic limitations are placed
on later-stage investments. Past
investments have been made in
media, data communications,
telecommunications, software,

environmental services, and general
manufacturing.

Huber Capital Ventures
11917 Oak Knoll, Ste. G
Austin, Texas 78759
Phone: (512)258-8668
Fax: (512)258-9091
Venture capital firm providing short-
term working capital funding for
specific projects. Areas of interest
include small capitalization
companies in manufacturing,
wholesaling, and technical services.

Texas Department of Economic
Development
Finance Office
Texas Capital Fund
PO Box 12728
Austin, Texas 78711
Phone: (512)936-0281
Fax: (512)936-0520
Administers several programs that
benefit small businesses, including
those authorized under the Industrial
Development Corporation Act of
1979 and the Rural Development Act,
as well as the state industrial revenue
bond program.

Triad Ventures Ltd.
AM Fund
E-mail: cole@amfund.com
8911 Capital of Texas Hwy., Ste.
2310
Austin, Texas 78759
Phone: (512)342-2024
Fax: (512)342-1993
Venture capital firm providing second
stage, acquisitions, mezzanine and
leveraged buyout financing. Areas of
interest include Texas-based
companies.

Alliance Enterprise Corp. (Dallas)
E-mail: mesbic@gan.net
12655 N. Central Expy., Ste 710
Dallas, Texas 75243
Phone: (972)991-1597
Fax: (972)991-1647
A minority enterprise small business
investment company. Diversified
industry preference.

Banc One Capital Corp. (Dallas)
300 Crescent Ct., Ste. 1600
Dallas, Texas 75201
Phone: (214)979-4375
Fax: (214)979-4355
A small business investment
corporation. Specializes in later-stage
investments for traditional businesses
with revenues in excess of $15
million annually. Areas of interest
include manufacturing, distribution,
and health care industries.

Capital Southwest Corp.
12900 Preston Rd., Ste. 700
Dallas, Texas 75230
Phone: (972)233-8242
Fax: (972)233-7362
Venture capital firm. Provides first
stage and expansion financing.
Diversified industry preferences.

Davis Venture Partners (Dallas)
2121 San Jacinto St., Ste. 250
Dallas, Texas 75201
Phone: (214)954-1822
Fax: (214)969-0256
Venture capital firm interested in
diversified industries, excluding oil,
gas, and real estate.

Diamond A. Ford Corp.
200 Crescent Court, Ste. 1350
Dallas, Texas 75201
Phone: (214)871-5177
Fax: (214)871-5199
A small business investment
company. Diversified industry
preference.

Erickson Capital Group, Inc.
5950 Berkshire Lane, Ste. 1100
Dallas, Texas 75225
Phone: (214)365-6060
Fax: (214)365-6001
Venture capital firm providing seed,
start-up, first and second stage, and
expansion financing. Areas of interest
include health care.

Gaekeke Landers
3710 Rawlins St., Ste. 100
Dallas, Texas 75219
Phone: (214)528-8883
Fax: (214)528-8058
Venture capital firm providing

acquisition, start-up, and leverage
equity financing. Areas of interest
include real estate.

Hook Partners
E-mail: hookpartners.com
13760 Noel Rd., Ste. 805
Dallas, Texas 75240-4360
Phone: (972)991-5457
Fax: (972)991-5458
Venture capital firm providing seed,
start-up and first stage financing.
Areas of interest include high
technology industries.

Interwest Partners (Dallas)
2 Galleria Tower
13455 Noel Rd., Ste. 1670
Dallas, Texas 75240
Phone: (972)392-7279
Fax: (972)490-6348

Kahala Investments, Inc.
8214 Westchester Dr., Ste. 715
Dallas, Texas 75225
Phone: (214)987-0077
Venture capital firm providing
financing for all stages including
expansion capital, leveraged buyouts,
and management buyouts. Area of
interest include a wide variety of
industries.

Mapleleaf Capital, Ltd.
3 Forest Plz., Ste. 935
12221 Merit Dr.
Dallas, Texas 75251-2248
Phone: (972)239-5650
Fax: (972)701-0024
A small business investment
company. Diversified industry
preference.

May Financial Corp.
8333 Douglas Ave., Ste. 400
Lock Box 82
Dallas, Texas 75225
Phone: (214)987-5200
Free: (800)767-4397
Fax: (214)987-1994
Brokerage firm working with a
venture capital firm. Prefers food, oil
and gas, and electronics industries.

Merchant Banking Group Ltd.
PO Box 763189
Dallas, Texas 75376

Phone: (214)337-5490
Fax: (214)337-5497
Venture capital firm providing
leveraged buyout financing. Areas of
interest include basic manufacturing
and distribution.

MESBIC Ventures, Inc.
E-mail: mesbic@gan.net
12655 N. Central Expy., Ste. 710
Dallas, Texas 75243
Phone: (972)991-1597
Fax: (972)991-1647
Donald R. Lawhorne, President
Preferred Investment Size: Up to
$1,000,000. Investment Policies:
Loans and/or equity. Investment
Types: early stage, expansion, later
stage. Industry Preferences:
Diversified. Geographic Preferences:
Mostly Southwest.

MSI Capital Corp.
6500 Greenville Ave., Ste. 350
Dallas, Texas 75206-1012
Phone: (214)265-1801
Fax: (214)265-1804
No industry preference.

Nations Bank Venture Capital
901 Maine St., 64th Fl.
Dallas, Texas 75202-2911
Phone: (214)508-0988
Fax: (214)508-9390
A small business investment
company. Diversified industry
preference.

NationsBank Capital Corp.
NationBank Plz., Ste. 71
901 Main St.
Dallas, Texas 75202
Phone: (214)508-6262
Fax: (214)508-1193
Venture capital firm providing second
stage, mezzanine and leveraged
buyout financing. Areas of interest
include communications, medical,
environmental, specialty retail,
transportation and energy services.

NCNB Texas Venture Group, Inc.
901 Maine, 22nd Fl.
Dallas, Texas 75202
Phone: (214)508-0900
Fax: (214)508-0985

Venture capital firm providing expansion and leveraged buyout financing. Areas of interest include medical products and services, energy service, environmental, specialty retail, transportation, general manufacturing, and communications.

North Texas MESBIC, Inc.
12770 Coit Rd., Ste.240
Dallas, Texas 75251
Phone: (972)991-8060
Fax: (972)991-8061
A minority enterprise small business investment company. Diversified industry preference.

Phillips-Smith Specialty Retail Group
E-mail: pssrg@aol.com
5080 Spectrum Dr., Ste. 700 W
Dallas, Texas 75248
Phone: (972)387-0725
Fax: (972)458-2560
Prefers specialty retail industry investments, including the restaurant industry.

PMC Capital, Inc.
Attn: Andy Rosemore
17290 Preston Rd., 3rd Fl.
Dallas, Texas 75252-5618
Phone: (972)349-3200
Free: (800)486-3223
Fax: (972)349-3265
A small business investment corporation, minority enterprise small business investment corporation, and SBA guaranteed lender. No industry preferred.

Pro-Med Investment Corp.
17290 Preston Rd., 3rd Fl.
Dallas, Texas 75252
Phone: (972)349-3200
Fax: (972)349-3265
A minority enterprise small business investment company. Diversified industry preference.

Sevin Rosen Funds
E-mail: info@Srfunds.com
13455 Noel Rd., Ste. 1670
Dallas, Texas 75240
Phone: (972)702-1100
Fax: (972)702-1103
Venture capital firm providing start-

up and first stage financing. Industry preferences include information sciences and electronic sciences.

Stratford Capital Partners, L.P.
200 Crescent Ct., Ste. 1650
Dallas, Texas 75201
Phone: (214)740-7377
Fax: (214)720-7888
Michael D. Brown, President
Preferred Investment Size: $3 to $9 million. Investment Policies: Equity, sub debt with equity. Investment Types: Expansion, later stage, acquisition. Industry Preferences: Manufacturing, distribution, diversified. Geographic Preferences: National.

Sullivan Enterprises
9130 Markville Dr.
PO Box 743803
Dallas, Texas 75374-3803
Phone: (972)414-5690
Venture capital firm providing refinancings and expansion, mezzanine, and leveraged buyouts financing. Areas of interest include manufacturing, service, retailing, wholesale and distribution.

Sunwestern Capital Corp.
12221 Merit Dr., Ste. 935
Dallas, Texas 75251-2248
Phone: (972)239-5650
Fax: (972)701-0024
Small business investment corporation providing start-up, first stage, second stage, third stage and leveraged buyout financing. Areas of interest include computer peripherals, software, information services, biotechnology and telecommunications.

Tower Ventures, Inc.
12655 N. Central Expy., Ste. 710
Dallas, Texas 75243
Fax: (972)991-1647
Donald R. Lawhorne, President
Preferred Investment Size: Up to $500,000. Investment Policies: Loans and/or equity. Investment Types: Early stage, expansion, later stage.

Western Financial Capital Corp.
17290 Preston Rd., 3rd Fl.
Dallas, Texas 75252
Phone: (972)349-3200
Fax: (972)349-3265
A small business investment company. Provides financing to the medical industry.

Wingate Partners
E-mail: wingatePartners.1@airmail.net
750 N. St. Paul St., Ste. 1200
Dallas, Texas 75201
Phone: (214)720-1313
Fax: (214)871-8799
Venture capital firm providing mature stage financing. Areas of interest include manufacturing and distribution.

HCT Capital Corp.
4916 Camp Bowie Blvd., Ste. 200
Fort Worth, Texas 76107
Phone: (817)763-8706
Fax: (817)377-8049
A small business investment company. Diversified industry preference.

SBIC Partners, L.P.
201 Main St., Ste. 2302
Fort Worth, Texas 76102
Phone: (817)339-7020
Fax: (817)729-3226
Gregory Forrest, Manager
Jeffrey Brown, Manager
Preferred Investment Size: $2 to $5 million. Investment Policies: Equity. Investment Types: Expansion, later stage. Industry Preferences: Diversified. Geographic Preferences: National.

Acorn Ventures, Inc.
3000 Richmond Ave., Ste. 360
Houston, Texas 77098
Phone: (713)807-7200
No industry preference.

Alliance Business Investment Co. (Houston)
1221 McKinney Ste.3100
Houston, Texas 77010
Phone: (713)659-3131
Fax: (713)659-8070

A small business investment corporation.

Aspen Capital Ltd.
55 Waugh, Ste. 710
Houston, Texas 77007
Phone: (713)880-4494
Fax: (713)880-5294
A small business investment corporation. No industry preference.

The Catalyst Fund, Ltd.
3 Riverway, Ste. 770
Houston, Texas 77056
Phone: (713)623-8133
Fax: (713)623-0473
A small business investment company. Diversified industry preference.

Chase Bank of Texas
PO Box 2558
Houston, Texas 77252-8032
Phone: (713)216-4553
A small business investment corporation. No industry preference.

Chen's Financial Group, Inc.
10101 Southwest Fwy., Ste. 370
Houston, Texas 77074
Phone: (713)772-8868
Fax: (713)772-2168
A minority enterprise small business investment corporation. Areas of interest include real estate, franchise restaurants, banking, and import/export industries.

Criterion Ventures
1330 Post Oak Blvd., Ste. 1525
Houston, Texas 77056
Phone: (713)627-9200
Fax: (713)627-9292
Venture capital fund. Raises venture capital. Interested in companies headquartered in the Sunbelt region. Areas of interest include telecommunications, biomedical, and specialty retail.

Cureton & Co., Inc.
1100 Louisiana, Ste. 3250
Houston, Texas 77002
Phone: (713)658-9806
Fax: (713)658-0476
Prefers oilfield service,

environmental, electronics, manufacturing, and distribution.

High Technology Associates
1775 St. James Pl., Ste. 105
Houston, Texas 77056
Phone: (713)963-9300
Fax: (713)963-8341
Venture capital firm providing second stage and expansion financing. Areas of interest include biotechnology, chemicals, food processing and food processing machinery. Particularly interested in companies willing to establish operations in the Northern Netherlands.

Houston Partners, SBIC
401 Louisiana, 8th Fl.
Houston, Texas 77002
Phone: (713)222-8600
Fax: (713)222-8932
A small business investment company. Diversified industry preference.

MESBIC Financial Corp. of Houston
9130 North Fwy., Ste. 203
Houston, Texas 77037
Fax: (281)447-4222
Atillio Galli, President
Preferred Investment Size: $100,000 to $1 million. Investment Policies: Loans and equity investments. Investment Types: Consolidated debt & preferred stock with warrants. Industry Preferences: Diversified - no real estate or gas and oil. Geographic Preferences: Houston.

Payne Webber, Inc.
700 Louisiana St., Ste.3800
Houston, Texas 77002
Fax: (713)236-3133

Penzoil
PO Box 2967
Houston, Texas 77252
Phone: (713)546-8910
Fax: (713)546-4154
A small business investment company. Diversified industry preference.

UNCO Ventures, Inc.
3000 Richmond Ave. Ste. 360
Houston, Texas 77098

Phone: (713)807-7200
A small business investment company. Diversified industry preference.

United Oriental Capital Corp.
908 Town and Country Blvd., Ste. 310
Houston, Texas 77024-2207
Phone: (713)461-3909
Fax: (713)465-7559
A minority enterprise small business investment corporation. No industry preference.

Ventex Partners, Ltd.
1001 Fannin St., Ste. 1095
Houston, Texas 77002
Phone: (713)659-7860
Fax: (713)659-7855
A small business investment partnership providing later stage financing.

First Capital Group of Texas
PO Box 15616
San Antonio, Texas 78212-8816
Phone: (210)736-4233
Fax: (210)736-5449
A small business investment corporation. No industry preference, but does not invest in oil, gas, and real estate industries.

Southwest Venture Partnerships
16414 San Pedro, Ste. 345
San Antonio, Texas 78232
Phone: (210)402-1200
Fax: (210)402-1221
Venture capital partnership. Invests in maturing companies located primarily in the southwest. Average investment is $1 million.

Norwest Bank & Trust
1 O'Connor Plz.
Victoria, Texas 77902
Phone: (512)573-5151
Fax: (512)574-5236
A small business investment company. Diversified industry preference.

Woodlands Venture Partners
2170 Buckthorne Pl., Ste. 170
The Woodlands, Texas 77380
Phone: (281)367-9999

Fax: (281)298-1295
Venture capital firm providing start-up, first stage, second stage and seed financing. Areas of interest include medical/biotechnology only.

Utah

Deseret Certified Development Corp. (Orem)
228 N. Orem Blvd.
Orem, Utah 84057-5011
Phone: (801)221-7772
Fax: (801)221-7775
Maintains an SBA(504) loan program, designed for community development and job creation, and an intermediary loan program, through Farmer's Home Administration.

Deseret Certified Development Corp. (Midvale)
E-mail: deseretcdc@aol.com
2595 East 3300 South
Salt Lake City, Utah 84109
Phone: (801)474-3232
Fax: (801)566-1532
Maintains an SBA(504) loan program, designed for community development and job creation, and an intermediary loan program, through Farmer's Home Administration.

First Security Business Investment Corp.
15 East 100 South, Ste. 100
Salt Lake City, Utah 84111
Phone: (801)246-5737
Fax: (801)246-5740
Louis D. Alder, Manager
Preferred Investment Size: $500,000 to $1 million. Investment Policies: Loans and/or equity. Investment Types: Expansion, later stage. Industry Preferences: Diversified. Geographic Preferences: West/midwest.

Utah Technology Finance Corp.
177 E., 100 S.
Salt Lake City, Utah 84111
Phone: (801)364-4346
Fax: (801)741-4249
Assists the start-up and growth of emerging technology-based businesses and products.

Utah Ventures
423 Wakara Way, Ste. 206
Salt Lake City, Utah 84108
Phone: (801)583-5922
Fax: (801)583-4105
Invests in the life sciences at an early stage.

Wasatch Venture Corp.
1 S. Main St., Ste. 1400
Salt Lake City, Utah 84133
Phone: (801)524-8939
Fax: (801)524-8941
W. David Hemingway, Manager
Preferred Investment Size: $500,000. Investment Policies: Equity and debt. Investment Types: Early stage. Industry Preferences: High technology. Geographic Preferences: West, midwest, Rocky.

Vermont

Vermont Economic Development Authority
58 E. State St.
Montpelier, Vermont 05602
Phone: (802)828-5627
Fax: (802)828-5474
Several financial programs to assist small and medium-sized manufacturing firms in the state.

Vermont Economic Development Authority
Vermont Job Start
58 E. State St.
Montpelier, Vermont 05602
Phone: (802)828-5627
Fax: (802)828-5474
A state-funded economic opportunity program aimed at increasing self-employment by low-income Vermonters.

Green Mountain Capital, L.P.
RD 1, Box 1503
Waterbury, Vermont 05676
Phone: (802)244-8981
Fax: (802)244-8990
A small business investment company. Diversified industry preference.

Virgin Islands

Tri-Island Economic Development Council, Inc.
PO Box 838
St. Thomas, Virgin Islands 00804-0838
Provides counseling, information, referrals, and management and technical assistance to help strengthen existing businesses and expand the rate of development of new businesses.

Virginia

Continental SBIC
4141 N. Henderson Rd., Ste. 8
Arlington, Virginia 22203
Phone: (703)527-5200
Fax: (703)527-3700
A minority enterprise small business investment company. Diversified industry preference.

East West United Investment Co. (Mc Lean)
1568 Spring Hill Rd., Ste. 100
Mc Lean, Virginia 22102
Phone: (703)442-0150
Fax: (703)442-0156
Dung Bui, President

East West United Investment Co.
1568 Spring Hill Rd., Ste. 100
McLean, Virginia 22102
Phone: (703)442-0150
Fax: (703)442-0156
A minority enterprise small business investment company. Diversified industry preference.

Ewing, Monroe, Bemiss and Co.
E-mail: embco@embco.com
901 E. Cary St., Ste. 1510
Richmond, Virginia 23219
Phone: (804)780-1900
Fax: (804)780-1901
A small business investment corporation. No industry preference.

Virginia Small Business Financing Authority
PO Box 446
Richmond, Virginia 23218-0446
Phone: (804)371-8254

Fax: (804)225-3384
Assists small businesses in obtaining financing for development and expansion.

Walnut Capital Corp. (Vienna)
8000 Towers Crescent Dr., Ste.1070
Vienna, Virginia 22182-2700
Phone: (703)448-3771
Fax: (703)448-7751
A small business investment corporation. No industry preference.

Washington

Cable and Howse Ventures (Bellevue)
777 108th Ave. NE, Ste. 2300
Bellevue, Washington 98004
Phone: (425)646-3035
Fax: (425)646-3041
Venture capital investor. Provides start-up and early stage financing to enterprises in the western, although a national perspective is maintained. Interests lie in proprietary or patentable technology. Investments range from $50,000 to $2 million.

Pacific Northwest Partners SBIC, L.P.
E-mail: pnwp@msn.com
305 108th Ave. NE, 2nd Fl.
Bellevue, Washington 98004
Phone: (425)455-9967
Fax: (425)455-9404
Theodore M. Wight, Manager
Preferred Investment Size: $1,000,000. Investment Policies: Private equity investments. Investment Types: Seed through later stage. Industry Preferences: Diversified, retail, healthcare, technology. Geographic Preferences: Pacific Northwest.

Materia Venture Associates, L.P.
E-mail: materiaventure@msn.com
3435 Carillon Pointe
Kirkland, Washington 98033
Phone: (425)822-4100
Fax: (425)827-4086
Prefers investing in advanced materials and related technologies.

Olympic Venture Partners (Kirkland)
E-mail: info@ovp.com

2420 Carillon Pt.
Kirkland, Washington 98033-7353
Phone: (425)889-9192
Fax: (425)889-0152
Prefers to fund early stage, technology companies in the West.

Washington Department of Community, Trade and Economic Development
Development Loan Fund
906 Columbia St. SW
PO Box 48300
Olympia, Washington 98504-8300
Phone: (360)753-7426
Fax: (360)586-3582
Provides capital for businesses in distressed areas to create new jobs, particularly for low and moderate income persons.

Washington Department of Community, Trade and Economic Development
Community Development Finance (CDF) Program
906 Columbia St. SW
PO Box 48300
Olympia, Washington 98504-8300
Phone: (360)753-7426
Fax: (360)586-3582
Helps businesses and industries secure needed financing by combining private financial loans with federal and state loans.

The Phoenix Partners
E-mail: dionnsto@interserv.com
1000 2nd Ave., Ste. 3600
Seattle, Washington 98104
Phone: (206)624-8968
Fax: (206)624-1907
Prefers to invest in companies involved in biotechnology, health care, medical devices, computer software, semiconductors, and telecommunications.

Washington Department of Community, Trade and Economic Development
Industrial Revenue Bonds
2001 6th Ave., Ste. 2600
Seattle, Washington 98121
Phone: (206)464-7143
Fax: (206)464-7222

Issued to finance the acquisition, construction, enlargement, or improvement of industrial development facilities.

West Virginia

Shenandoah Venture Capital L.P.
208 Capital St., Ste. 300
Charleston, West Virginia 25301
Phone: (304)344-1796
Fax: (304)344-1798
Thomas E. Loehr, President

West Virginia Development Office
West Virginia Economic Development Authority
Economic Development Authority
1018 Kanawha Blvd., E., Ste. 501
Charleston, West Virginia 25301-2827
Phone: (304)558-3650
Fax: (304)558-0206
Provides low-interest loans for land or building acquisition, building construction, and equipment purchases.

WestVen Ltd. Partnership
208 Capitol St., Ste. 300
Charleston, West Virginia 25301
Phone: (304)344-1794
Fax: (304)344-1798
Thomas E. Loehr, President
Preferred Investment Size: $500,000. Investment Policies: Combination of debt and equity. Investment Types: Expansion, early stage, spin-off. Industry Preferences: Wood products, computer industry, manufacturing. Geographic Preferences: West Virginia, Ohio, Pennsylvania, Virginia, Maryland.

Wisconsin

Impact Seven, Inc.
E-mail: impact@win.bright.net
651 Garfield Street
Almena, Wisconsin 54805-9900
Phone: (715)357-3334
Fax: (715)357-6233
Provides equity investment.

Madison Development Corp.
550 W. Washington Ave.
Madison, Wisconsin 53703
Phone: (608)256-2799
Fax: (608)256-1560
Provides loans of up to $150,000 to
eligible businesses in Dane County
for working capital, inventory,
equipment, leasehold improvements,
and business real estate.

Venture Investors of Wisconsin, Inc.
(Madison)
E-mail: vi@ventureinvestors.com
565 Science Dr., Ste. A
Madison, Wisconsin 53711-1071
Phone: (608)233-3070
Fax: (608)238-5120
Venture capital firm providing early-
stage financing to Wisconsin-based
companies with strong management
teams. Areas of interest include
biotechnology, software, analytical
instruments, medical products,
consumer products, and publishing
industries.

Venture Investors of Wisconsin, Inc.
(Milwaukee)
E-mail: vi@ventureinvestors.com
565 Science Dr.,Ste.A
Madison, Wisconsin 53711-1071
Phone: (414)298-3070
Fax: (608)238-5120
Providers of equity financing.

Wisconsin Business Development
Finance Corp.
E-mail: wbdfc@waun.tdsnet.com
PO Box 2717
Madison, Wisconsin 53701
Phone: (608)258-8830
Fax: (608)258-1664
Provides small business financing for
the purchase of land, buildings,
machinery, equipment, and the
construction and modernization of
facilities.

Wisconsin Department of Commerce
Wisconsin Development Fund
Bureau of Business Finance
201 W. Washington Ave.
Madison, Wisconsin 53707
Phone: (608)266-1018

Free: (800)HELP-BUS
Fax: (608)264-6151

Wisconsin Housing and Economic
Development Authority
Venture Capital Fund
Small Business Guarantee Loans
201 W. Washington Ave., Ste. 700
Madison, Wisconsin 53701
Phone: (608)266-7884
Free: (800)334-6873
Fax: (608)267-1099
Invests in new and existing businesses
that are developing new products.

Wisconsin Innovation Network
Foundation
PO Box 71
Madison, Wisconsin 53701-0071
Phone: (608)256-8348
Fax: (608)256-0333
Seeks to join people with marketing
and sales ideas to those willing to
finance them. Acts as a resource
center for financing information;
offers networking opportunities for
business professionals, entrepreneurs,
and small business owners at regular
monthly meetings.

Capital Investment, Inc.
1009 W. Glen Oaks Ln., Ste. 103
Mequon, Wisconsin 53092
Phone: (414)241-0303
Fax: (414)241-8451
James R. Sanger, President
Preferred Investment Size: $500,000
to $1 million. Investment Policies:
Subordinated debt with warrant.
Investment Types: Expansion, later
stage. Industry Preferences:
Manufacturing and value-added
distributors. Geographic Preferences:
Midwest, national.

Banc One Venture Corp. (Milwaukee)
111 E. Wisconsin Ave.
Milwaukee, Wisconsin 53202
Free: (800)947-1111
H. Wayne Foreman, President
Preferred Investment Size: $1 to $10
million. Investment Types: Later
stage, expansion, LBO, MBO.
Industry Preferences: Publishing,
distribution, manufacturing, mail-

order. Geographic Preferences:
National.

Capital Investments, Inc.
700 N. Water St., Ste. 325
Milwaukee, Wisconsin 53202
Phone: (414)278-7744
Free: (800)345-6462
Fax: (414)278-8403
A small business investment
corporation. Prefers later-stage
companies located in the Midwest,
involved in manufacturing and
specialty distribution.

Future Value Venture, Inc.
330 E. Kilbourn Ave., Ste. 711
Milwaukee, Wisconsin 53202
Phone: (414)278-0377
Fax: (414)278-7321
A minority enterprise small business
investment corporation. Diversified
industry preference. Minimum initial
investment is $100,000.

Horizon Partners, Ltd.
225 E. Mason St., Ste. 600
Milwaukee, Wisconsin 53202
Phone: (414)271-2200
Fax: (414)271-4016
Providers of equity financing for low-
to-medium technology industries.

Lubar and Co., Inc.
700 N. Water St., Ste. 1200
Milwaukee, Wisconsin 53202
Phone: (414)291-9000
Fax: (414)291-9061
Private investment and management
firm.

M & I Ventures Corp.
770 N. Water St.
Milwaukee, Wisconsin 53202
Phone: (414)765-7700
Free: (800)342-2265
Fax: (414)765-7850
A small business investment
corporation. Areas of interest include
manufacturing, technology,
electronics, health care, publishing,
and communications industries.
Average investment is from $1
million to $3 million.

Wisconsin Venture Capital Fund
700 N. Water St., Ste. 1200

Milwaukee, Wisconsin 53202
Phone: (414)291-9000
Fax: (414)291-9061

Wind Point Partners
420 3 Mile, Apt. B4
Racine, Wisconsin 53402
Phone: (414)639-3113
Fax: (414)639-3417
Venture capital firm.

Bando-McGlocklin SBIC
W239 N. 1700 Busse Rd.
Waukesha, Wisconsin 53188
Phone: (414)523-4300
Fax: (414)523-4193
George Schonath, Chief Executive
Officer
Preferred Investment Size:
$3,000,000. Investment Policies:
Loans. Investment Types: Early stage,
expansion, later stage. Industry
Preferences: Diversified. Geographic
Preferences: Midwest.

Wyoming

Frontier Certified Development Co.
PO Box 3599
Casper, Wyoming 82602
Phone: (307)234-5351
Free: (800)934-5351
Fax: (307)234-0501
Created by the Wyoming Industrial
Development Corporation to provide
expansion financing for Wyoming
business.

Wyoming Industrial Development
Corp.
PO Box 3599
Casper, Wyoming 82602
Phone: (307)234-5351
Free: (800)934-5351
Fax: (307)234-0501
Administers SBA 7(A) and SBA(502)
programs. Purchases the guaranteed
portion of U.S. Small Business
Adminstration and Farmers Home
Administration Loans to small
businesses to pool into a common
fund that enables small businesses to
obtain loans at more reasonable rates
and terms.

Wyoming Department of Commerce
Economic and Community
Development Division
New Business Retention and
Financing
Barrett Bldg.
2301 Central Ave.
Cheyenne, Wyoming 82002
Phone: (307)777-6303
Fax: (307)777-6005

Appendix C - Glossary of Small Business Terms

Glossary of Small Business Terms

Absolute liability

Liability that is incurred due to product defects or negligent actions. Manufacturers or retail establishments are held responsible, even though the defect or action may not have been intentional or negligent.

ACE

See Active Corps of Executives

Accident and health benefits

Benefits offered to employees and their families in order to offset the costs associated with accidental death, accidental injury, or sickness.

Account statement

A record of transactions, including payments, new debt, and deposits, incurred during a defined period of time.

Accounting system

System capturing the costs of all employees and/or machinery included in business expenses.

Accounts payable

See Trade credit

Accounts receivable

Unpaid accounts which arise from unsettled claims and transactions from the sale of a company's products or services to its customers.

Active Corps of Executives (ACE)

(See also Service Corps of Retired Executives)
A group of volunteers for a management assistance program of the U.S. Small Business Administration; volunteers provide one-on-one counseling and teach workshops and seminars for small firms.

ADA

See Americans with Disabilities Act

Adaptation

The process whereby an invention is modified to meet the needs of users.

Adaptive engineering

The process whereby an invention is modified to meet the manufacturing and commercial requirements of a targeted market.

Adverse selection

The tendency for higher-risk individuals to purchase health care and more comprehensive plans, resulting in increased costs.

Advertising

A marketing tool used to capture public attention and influence purchasing decisions for a product or service. Utilizes various forms of media to generate consumer response, such as flyers, magazines, newspapers, radio, and television.

Age discrimination

The denial of the rights and privileges of employment based solely on the age of an individual.

Agency costs

Costs incurred to insure that the lender or investor maintains control over assets while allowing the borrower or entrepreneur to use them. Monitoring and information costs are the two major types of agency costs.

Agribusiness

The production and sale of commodities and products from the commercial farming industry.

America Online

(See also Prodigy)
An online service which is accessible by computer modem. The service features Internet access, bulletin boards, online periodicals, electronic mail, and other services for subscribers.

Americans with Disabilities Act (ADA)

Law designed to ensure equal access and opportunity to handicapped persons.

Annual report

(See also Securities and Exchange Commission)

Yearly financial report prepared by a business that adheres to the requirements set forth by the Securities and Exchange Commission (SEC).

Antitrust immunity

(See also Collective ratemaking)

Exemption from prosecution under antitrust laws. In the transportation industry, firms with antitrust immunity are permitted—under certain conditions—to set schedules and sometimes prices for the public benefit.

Applied research

Scientific study targeted for use in a product or process.

Asians

A minority category used by the U.S. Bureau of the Census to represent a diverse group that includes Aleuts, Eskimos, American Indians, Asian Indians, Chinese, Japanese, Koreans, Vietnamese, Filipinos, Hawaiians, and other Pacific Islanders.

Assets

Anything of value owned by a company.

Audit

The verification of accounting records and business procedures conducted by an outside accounting service.

Average cost

Total production costs divided by the quantity produced.

Balance Sheet

A financial statement listing the total assets and liabilities of a company at a given time.

Bankruptcy

(See also Chapter 7 of the 1978 Bankruptcy Act; Chapter 11 of the 1978 Bankruptcy Act)

The condition in which a business cannot meet its debt obligations and petitions a federal district court either for reorganization of its debts (Chapter 11) or for liquidation of its assets (Chapter 7).

Basic research

Theoretical scientific exploration not targeted to application.

Basket clause

A provision specifying the amount of public pension funds that may be placed in investments not included on a state's legal list (see separate citation).

BBS

See Bulletin Board Service

BDC

See Business development corporation

Benefit

Various services, such health care, flextime, day care, insurance, and vacation, offered to employees as part of a hiring package. Typically subsidized in whole or in part by the business.

BIDCO

See Business and industrial development company

Billing cycle

A system designed to evenly distribute customer billing throughout the month, preventing clerical backlogs.

Birth

See Business birth

Blue chip security

A low-risk, low-yield security representing an interest in a very stable company.

Blue sky laws

A general term that denotes various states' laws regulating securities.

Bond

(See also General obligation bond; Taxable bonds; Treasury bonds)

A written instrument executed by a bidder or contractor (the principal) and a second party (the surety or sureties) to assure fulfillment of the principal's obligations to a third party (the obligee or government) identified in the bond. If the principal's obligations are not met, the bond assures payment to the extent stipulated of any loss sustained by the obligee.

Bonding requirements

Terms contained in a bond (see separate citation).

Bonus

An amount of money paid to an employee as a reward for achieving certain business goals or objectives.

Brainstorming

A group session where employees contribute their ideas for solving a problem or meeting a company objective without fear of retribution or ridicule.

Brand name

The part of a brand, trademark, or service mark that can be spoken. It can be a word, letter, or group of words or letters.

Bridge financing

A short-term loan made in expectation of intermediate-term or long-term financing. Can be used when a company plans to go public in the near future.

Broker

One who matches resources available for innovation with those who need them.

Budget

An estimate of the spending necessary to complete a project or offer a service in comparison to cash-on-hand and expected earnings for the coming year, with an emphasis on cost control.

Bulletin Board Service (BBS)

An online service enabling users to communicate with each other about specific topics.

Business birth

The formation of a new establishment or enterprise. The appearance of a new establishment or enterprise in the Small Business Data Base (see separate citation).

Business conditions

Outside factors that can affect the financial performance of a business.

Business contractions

The number of establishments that have decreased in employment during a specified time.

Business cycle

A period of economic recession and recovery. These cycles vary in duration.

Business death

The voluntary or involuntary closure of a firm or establishment. The disappearance of an establishment or enterprise from the Small Business Data Base (see separate citation).

Business development corporation (BDC)

A business financing agency, usually composed of the financial institutions in an area or state, organized to assist in financing businesses unable to obtain assistance through normal channels; the risk is spread among various members of the business development corporation, and interest rates may vary somewhat from those charged by member institutions. A venture capital firm in which shares of ownership are publicly held and to which the Investment Act of 1940 applies.

Business dissolution

For enumeration purposes, the absence of a business that was present in the prior time period from any current record.

Business entry

See Business birth

Business ethics

Moral values and principles espoused by members of the business community as a guide to fair and honest business practices.

Business exit

See Business death

Business expansions

The number of establishments that added employees during a specified time.

Business failure

Closure of a business causing a loss to at least one creditor.

Business format franchising

(See also Franchising)

The purchase of the name, trademark, and an ongoing business plan of the parent corporation or franchisor by the franchisee.

Business and industrial development company (BIDCO)

A private, for-profit financing corporation chartered by the state to provide both equity and long-term debt capital to small business owners (see separate citations for equity and debt capital).

Business license

A legal authorization issued by municipal and state governments and required for business operations.

Business name

(See also Business license; Trademark)
Enterprises must register their business names with local governments usually on a "doing business as" (DBA) form. (This name is sometimes referred to as a "fictional name.") The procedure is part of the business licensing process and prevents any other business from using that same name for a similar business in the same locality.

Business norms

See Financial ratios

Business permit

See Business license

Business plan

A document that spells out a company's expected course of action for a specified period, usually including a detailed listing and analysis of risks and uncertainties. For the small business, it should examine the proposed products, the market, the industry, the management policies, the marketing policies, production needs, and financial needs. Frequently, it is used as a prospectus for potential investors and lenders.

Business proposal

See Business plan

Business service firm

An establishment primarily engaged in rendering services to other business organizations on a fee or contract basis.

Business start

For enumeration purposes, a business with a name or similar designation that did not exist in a prior time period.

Cafeteria plan

See Flexible benefit plan

Capacity

Level of a firm's, industry's, or nation's output corresponding to full practical utilization of available resources.

Capital

Assets less liabilities, representing the ownership interest in a business. A stock of accumulated goods, especially at a specified time and in contrast to income received during a specified time period. Accumulated goods devoted to production. Accumulated possessions calculated to bring income.

Capital expenditure

Expenses incurred by a business for improvements that will depreciate over time.

Capital gain

The monetary difference between the purchase price and the selling price of capital. Capital gains are taxed at a rate of 28% by the federal government.

Capital intensity

(See also Debt capital; Equity midrisk venture capital; Informal capital; Internal capital; Owner's capital; Secondhand capital; Seed capital; Venture capital)
The relative importance of capital in the production process, usually expressed as the ratio of capital to labor but also sometimes as the ratio of capital to output.

Capital resource

The equipment, facilities and labor used to create products and services.

Caribbean Basin Initiative

An interdisciplinary program to support commerce among the businesses in the nations of the Caribbean Basin and the United States. Agencies involved include: the Agency for International Development, the U.S. Small Business Administration, the International Trade Administration of the U.S. Department of Commerce, and various private sector groups.

Catastrophic care

Medical and other services for acute and long-term illnesses that cost more than insurance coverage limits or that cost the amount most families may be expected to pay with their own resources.

CDC

See Certified development corporation

CD-ROM

Compact disc with read-only memory used to store large amounts of digitized data.

Certified development corporation (CDC)

A local area or statewide corporation or authority (for profit or nonprofit) that packages U.S. Small Business Administration (SBA), bank, state, and/or private money into financial assistance for existing business capital improvements. The SBA holds the second lien on its maximum share of 40 percent involvement. Each state has at least one certified development corporation. This program is called the SBA 504 Program.

Certified lenders
Banks that participate in the SBA guaranteed loan program (see separate citation). Such banks must have a good track record with the U.S. Small Business Administration (SBA) and must agree to certain conditions set forth by the agency. In return, the SBA agrees to process any guaranteed loan application within three business days.

Champion
An advocate for the development of an innovation.

Channel of distribution
The means used to transport merchandise from the manufacturer to the consumer.

Chapter 7 of the 1978 Bankruptcy Act
Provides for a court-appointed trustee who is responsible for liquidating a company's assets in order to settle outstanding debts.

Chapter 11 of the 1978 Bankruptcy Act
Allows the business owners to retain control of the company while working with their creditors to reorganize their finances and establish better business practices to prevent liquidation of assets.

Closely held corporation
A corporation in which the shares are held by a few persons, usually officers, employees, or others close to the management; these shares are rarely offered to the public.

Code of Federal Regulations
Codification of general and permanent rules of the federal government published in the Federal Register.

Code sharing
See Computer code sharing

Coinsurance
(See also Cost sharing)
Upon meeting the deductible payment, health insurance participants may be required to make additional health care cost-sharing payments. Coinsurance is a payment of a fixed percentage of the cost of each service; copayment is usually a fixed amount to be paid with each service.

Collateral
Securities, evidence of deposit, or other property pledged by a borrower to secure repayment of a loan.

Collective ratemaking
(See also Antitrust immunity)
The establishment of uniform charges for services by a group of businesses in the same industry.

Commercial insurance plan
See Underwriting

Commercial loans
Short-term renewable loans used to finance specific capital needs of a business.

Commercialization
The final stage of the innovation process, including production and distribution.

Common stock
The most frequently used instrument for purchasing ownership in private or public companies. Common stock generally carries the right to vote on certain corporate actions and may pay dividends, although it rarely does in venture investments. In liquidation, common stockholders are the last to share in the proceeds from the sale of a corporation's assets; bondholders and preferred shareholders have priority. Common stock is often used in first-round start-up financing.

Community development corporation
A corporation established to develop economic programs for a community and, in most cases, to provide financial support for such development.

Competitor
A business whose product or service is marketed for the same purpose/use and to the same consumer group as the product or service of another.

Computer code sharing
An arrangement whereby flights of a regional airline are identified by the two-letter code of a major carrier in the computer reservation system to help direct passengers to new regional carriers.

Consignment
A merchandising agreement, usually referring to second-hand shops, where the dealer pays the owner of an item a percentage of the profit when the item is sold.

Consortium

A coalition of organizations such as banks and corporations for ventures requiring large capital resources.

Consultant

An individual that is paid by a business to provide advice and expertise in a particular area.

Consumer price index

A measure of the fluctuation in prices between two points in time.

Consumer research

Research conducted by a business to obtain information about existing or potential consumer markets.

Continuation coverage

Health coverage offered for a specified period of time to employees who leave their jobs and to their widows, divorced spouses, or dependents.

Contractions

See Business contractions

Convertible preferred stock

A class of stock that pays a reasonable dividend and is convertible into common stock (see separate citation). Generally the convertible feature may only be exercised after being held for a stated period of time. This arrangement is usually considered second-round financing when a company needs equity to maintain its cash flow.

Convertible securities

A feature of certain bonds, debentures, or preferred stocks that allows them to be exchanged by the owner for another class of securities at a future date and in accordance with any other terms of the issue.

Copayment

See Coinsurance

Copyright

A legal form of protection available to creators and authors to safeguard their works from unlawful use or claim of ownership by others. Copyrights may be acquired for works of art, sculpture, music, and published or unpublished manuscripts. All copyrights should be registered at the Copyright Office of the Library of Congress.

Corporate financial ratios

(See also Industry financial ratios)

The relationship between key figures found in a company's financial statement expressed as a numeric value. Used to evaluate risk and company performance. Also known as Financial averages, Operating ratios, and Business ratios.

Corporation

A legal entity, chartered by a state or the federal government, recognized as a separate entity having its own rights, privileges, and liabilities distinct from those of its members.

Cost containment

Actions taken by employers and insurers to curtail rising health care costs; for example, increasing employee cost sharing (see separate citation), requiring second opinions, or preadmission screening.

Cost sharing

The requirement that health care consumers contribute to their own medical care costs through deductibles and coinsurance (see separate citations). Cost sharing does not include the amounts paid in premiums. It is used to control utilization of services; for example, requiring a fixed amount to be paid with each health care service.

Cottage industry

(See also Home-based business)

Businesses based in the home in which the family members are the labor force and family-owned equipment is used to process the goods.

Credit Rating

A letter or number calculated by an organization (such as Dun & Bradstreet) to represent the ability and disposition of a business to meet its financial obligations.

Customer service

Various techniques used to ensure the satisfaction of a customer.

Cyclical peak

The upper turning point in a business cycle.

Cyclical trough

The lower turning point in a business cycle.

DBA

See Business name

Death

See Business death

Debenture

A certificate given as acknowledgment of a debt (see separate citation) secured by the general credit of the issuing corporation. A bond, usually without security, issued by a corporation and sometimes convertible to common stock.

Debt

(See also Long-term debt; Mid-term debt; Securitized debt; Short-term debt)
Something owed by one person to another. Financing in which a company receives capital that must be repaid; no ownership is transferred.

Debt capital

Business financing that normally requires periodic interest payments and repayment of the principal within a specified time.

Debt financing

See Debt capital

Debt securities

Loans such as bonds and notes that provide a specified rate of return for a specified period of time.

Deductible

A set amount that an individual must pay before any benefits are received.

Demand shock absorbers

A term used to describe the role that some small firms play by expanding their output levels to accommodate a transient surge in demand.

Demographics

Statistics on various markets, including age, income, and education, used to target specific products or services to appropriate consumer groups.

Demonstration

Showing that a product or process has been modified sufficiently to meet the needs of users.

Deregulation

The lifting of government restrictions; for example, the lifting of government restrictions on the entry of new businesses, the expansion of services, and the setting of prices in particular industries.

Desktop Publishing

Using personal computers and specialized software to produce camera-ready copy for publications.

Disaster loans

Various types of physical and economic assistance available to individuals and businesses through the U.S. Small Business Administration (SBA). This is the only SBA loan program available for residential purposes.

Discrimination

The denial of the rights and privileges of employment based on factors such as age, race, religion, or gender.

Diseconomies of scale

The condition in which the costs of production increase faster than the volume of production.

Dissolution

See Business dissolution

Distribution

Delivering a product or process to the user.

Distributor

One who delivers merchandise to the user.

Diversified company

A company whose products and services are used by several different markets.

Doing business as (DBA)

See Business name

Dow Jones

An information services company that publishes the Wall Street Journal and other sources of financial information.

Dow Jones Industrial Average

An indicator of stock market performance.

Earned income

A tax term that refers to wages and salaries earned by the recipient, as opposed to monies earned through interest and dividends.

Economic efficiency

The use of productive resources to the fullest practical extent in the provision of the set of goods and services that is most preferred by purchasers in the economy.

Economic indicators

Statistics used to express the state of the economy. These include the length of the average work week, the rate of unemployment, and stock prices.

Economically disadvantaged
See Socially and economically disadvantaged

Economies of scale
See Scale economies

EEOC
See Equal Employment Opportunity Commission

8(a) Program
A program authorized by the Small Business Act that
directs federal contracts to small businesses owned and
operated by socially and economically disadvantaged
individuals.

Electronic mail (e-mail)
The electronic transmission of mail via phone lines.

E-mail
See Electronic mail

Employee leasing.
A contract by which employers arrange to have their
workers hired by a leasing company and then leased back
to them for a management fee. The leasing company
typically assumes the administrative burden of payroll and
provides a benefit package to the workers.

Employee tenure
The length of time an employee works for a particular
employer.

Employer identification number
The business equivalent of a social security number.
Assigned by the U.S. Internal Revenue Service.

Enterprise
An aggregation of all establishments owned by a parent
company. An enterprise may consist of a single, independent establishment or include subsidiaries and other
branches under the same ownership and control.

Enterprise zone
A designated area, usually found in inner cities and other
areas with significant unemployment, where businesses
receive tax credits and other incentives to entice them to
establish operations there.

Entrepreneur
A person who takes the risk of organizing and operating a
new business venture.

Entry
See Business entry

Equal Employment Opportunity Commission (EEOC)
A federal agency that ensures nondiscrimination in the
hiring and firing practices of a business.

Equal opportunity employer
An employer who adheres to the standards set by the
Equal Employment Opportunity Commission (see separate
citation).

Equity
(See also Common Stock; Equity midrisk venture capital)
The ownership interest. Financing in which partial or total
ownership of a company is surrendered in exchange for
capital. An investor's financial return comes from dividend payments and from growth in the net worth of the
business.

Equity capital
See Equity; Equity midrisk venture capital

Equity financing
See Equity; Equity midrisk venture capital

Equity midrisk venture capital
An unsecured investment in a company. Usually a
purchase of ownership interest in a company that occurs in
the later stages of a company's development.

Equity partnership
A limited partnership arrangement for providing start-up
and seed capital to businesses.

Equity securities
See Equity

Equity-type
Debt financing subordinated to conventional debt.

Establishment
A single-location business unit that may be independent (a
single-establishment enterprise) or owned by a parent
enterprise.

Establishment and Enterprise Microdata File
See U.S. Establishment and Enterprise Microdata File

Establishment birth
See Business birth

Establishment Longitudinal Microdata File
See U.S. Establishment Longitudinal Microdata File

Ethics
See Business ethics

Evaluation
Determining the potential success of translating an invention into a product or process.

Exit
See Business exit

Experience rating
See Underwriting

Export
A product sold outside of the country.

Export license
A general or specific license granted by the U.S. Department of Commerce required of anyone wishing to export goods. Some restricted articles need approval from the U.S. Departments of State, Defense, or Energy.

Failure
See Business failure

Fair share agreement
(See also Franchising)
An agreement reached between a franchisor and a minority business organization to extend business ownership to minorities by either reducing the amount of capital required or by setting aside certain marketing areas for minority business owners.

Feasibility study
A study to determine the likelihood that a proposed product or development will fulfill the objectives of a particular investor.

Federal Trade Commission (FTC)
Federal agency that promotes free enterprise and competition within the U.S.

Federal Trade Mark Act of 1946
See Lanham Act

Fictional name
See Business name

Fiduciary
An individual or group that hold assets in trust for a beneficiary.

Financial analysis
The techniques used to determine money needs in a business. Techniques include ratio analysis, calculation of return on investment, guides for measuring profitability, and break-even analysis to determine ultimate success.

Financial intermediary
A financial institution that acts as the intermediary between borrowers and lenders. Banks, savings and loan associations, finance companies, and venture capital companies are major financial intermediaries in the United States.

Financial ratios
See Corporate financial ratios; Industry financial ratios

Financial statement
A written record of business finances, including balance sheets and profit and loss statements.

Financing
See First-stage financing; Second-stage financing; Third-stage financing

First-stage financing
(See also Second-stage financing; Third-stage financing)
Financing provided to companies that have expended their initial capital, and require funds to start full-scale manufacturing and sales. Also known as First-round financing.

Fiscal year
Any twelve-month period used by businesses for accounting purposes.

504 Program
See Certified development corporation

Flexible benefit plan
A plan that offers a choice among cash and/or qualified benefits such as group term life insurance, accident and health insurance, group legal services, dependent care assistance, and vacations.

FOB
See Free on board

Format franchising

See Business format franchising; Franchising

401(k) plan

A financial plan where employees contribute a percentage of their earnings to a fund that is invested in stocks, bonds, or money markets for the purpose of saving money for retirement.

Four Ps

Marketing terms referring to Product, Price, Place, and Promotion.

Franchising

A form of licensing by which the owner—the franchisor—distributes or markets a product, method, or service through affiliated dealers called franchisees. The product, method, or service being marketed is identified by a brand name, and the franchisor maintains control over the marketing methods employed. The franchisee is often given exclusive access to a defined geographic area.

Free on board (FOB)

A pricing term indicating that the quoted price includes the cost of loading goods into transport vessels at a specified place.

Frictional unemployment

See Unemployment

FTC

See Federal Trade Commission

Fulfillment

The systems necessary for accurate delivery of an ordered item, including subscriptions and direct marketing.

Full-time workers

Generally, those who work a regular schedule of more than 35 hours per week.

Garment registration number

A number that must appear on every garment sold in the U.S. to indicate the manufacturer of the garment, which may or may not be the same as the label under which the garment is sold. The U.S. Federal Trade Commission assigns and regulates garment registration numbers.

Gatekeeper

A key contact point for entry into a network.

GDP

See Gross domestic product

General obligation bond

A municipal bond secured by the taxing power of the municipality. The Tax Reform Act of 1986 limits the purposes for which such bonds may be issued and establishes volume limits on the extent of their issuance.

GNP

See Gross national product

Good Housekeeping Seal

Seal appearing on products that signifies the fulfillment of the standards set by the Good Housekeeping Institute to protect consumer interests.

Goods sector

All businesses producing tangible goods, including agriculture, mining, construction, and manufacturing businesses.

GPO

See Gross product originating

Gross domestic product (GDP)

The part of the nation's gross national product (see separate citation) generated by private business using resources from within the country.

Gross national product (GNP)

The most comprehensive single measure of aggregate economic output. Represents the market value of the total output of goods and services produced by a nation's economy.

Gross product originating (GPO)

A measure of business output estimated from the income or production side using employee compensation, profit income, net interest, capital consumption, and indirect business taxes.

HAL

See Handicapped assistance loan program

Handicapped assistance loan program (HAL)

Low-interest direct loan program through the U.S. Small Business Administration (SBA) for handicapped persons. The SBA requires that these persons demonstrate that their disability is such that it is impossible for them to secure employment, thus making it necessary to go into their own business to make a living.

Health maintenance organization (HMO)
Organization of physicians and other health care professionals that provides health services to subscribers and their dependents on a prepaid basis.

Health provider
An individual or institution that gives medical care. Under Medicare, an institutional provider is a hospital, skilled nursing facility, home health agency, or provider of certain physical therapy services.

Hispanic
A person of Cuban, Mexican, Puerto Rican, Latin American (Central or South American), European Spanish, or other Spanish-speaking origin or ancestry.

HMO
See Health maintenance organization

Home-based business
(See also Cottage industry)
A business with an operating address that is also a residential address (usually the residential address of the proprietor).

Hub-and-spoke system
A system in which flights of an airline from many different cities (the spokes) converge at a single airport (the hub). After allowing passengers sufficient time to make connections, planes then depart for different cities.

Human Resources Management
A business program designed to oversee recruiting, pay, benefits, and other issues related to the company's work force, including planning to determine the optimal use of labor to increase production, thereby increasing profit.

Idea
An original concept for a new product or process.

Import
Products produced outside the country in which they are consumed.

Income
Money or its equivalent, earned or accrued, resulting from the sale of goods and services.

Income statement
A financial statement that lists the profits and losses of a company at a given time.

Incorporation
The filing of a certificate of incorporation with a state's secretary of state, thereby limiting the business owner's liability.

Incubator
A facility designed to encourage entrepreneurship and minimize obstacles to new business formation and growth, particularly for high-technology firms, by housing a number of fledgling enterprises that share an array of services, such as meeting areas, secretarial services, accounting, research library, on-site financial and management counseling, and word processing facilities.

Independent contractor
An individual considered self-employed (see separate citation) and responsible for paying Social Security taxes and income taxes on earnings.

Indirect health coverage
Health insurance obtained through another individual's health care plan; for example, a spouse's employer-sponsored plan.

Industrial development authority
The financial arm of a state or other political subdivision established for the purpose of financing economic development in an area, usually through loans to nonprofit organizations, which in turn provide facilities for manufacturing and other industrial operations.

Industry financial ratios
(See also Corporate financial ratios)
Corporate financial ratios averaged for a specified industry. These are used for comparison purposes and reveal industry trends and identify differences between the performance of a specific company and the performance of its industry. Also known as Industrial averages, Industry ratios, Financial averages, and Business or Industrial norms.

Inflation
Increases in volume of currency and credit, generally resulting in a sharp and continuing rise in price levels.

Informal capital
Financing from informal, unorganized sources; includes informal debt capital such as trade credit or loans from friends and relatives and equity capital from informal investors.

Initial public offering (IPO)
A corporation's first offering of stock to the public.

Innovation
The introduction of a new idea into the marketplace in the form of a new product or service or an improvement in organization or process.

Intellectual property
Any idea or work that can be considered proprietary in nature and is thus protected from infringement by others.

Internal capital
Debt or equity financing obtained from the owner or through retained business earnings.

Internet
A government-designed computer network that contains large amounts of information and is accessible through various vendors for a fee.

Intrapreneurship
The state of employing entrepreneurial principles to nonentrepreneurial situations.

Invention
The tangible form of a technological idea, which could include a laboratory prototype, drawings, formulas, etc.

IPO
See Initial public offering

Job description
The duties and responsibilities required in a particular position.

Job tenure
A period of time during which an individual is continuously employed in the same job.

Joint marketing agreements
Agreements between regional and major airlines, often involving the coordination of flight schedules, fares, and baggage transfer. These agreements help regional carriers operate at lower cost.

Joint venture
Venture in which two or more people combine efforts in a particular business enterprise, usually a single transaction or a limited activity, and agree to share the profits and losses jointly or in proportion to their contributions.

Keogh plan
Designed for self-employed persons and unincorporated businesses as a tax-deferred pension account.

Labor force
Civilians considered eligible for employment who are also willing and able to work.

Labor force participation rate
The civilian labor force as a percentage of the civilian population.

Labor intensity
(See also Capital intensity)
The relative importance of labor in the production process, usually measured as the capital-labor ratio; i.e., the ratio of units of capital (typically, dollars of tangible assets) to the number of employees. The higher the capital-labor ratio exhibited by a firm or industry, the lower the capital intensity of that firm or industry is said to be.

Labor surplus area
An area in which there exists a high unemployment rate. In procurement (see separate citation), extra points are given to firms in counties that are designated a labor surplus area; this information is requested on procurement bid sheets.

Labor union
An organization of similarly-skilled workers who collectively bargain with management over the conditions of employment.

Laboratory prototype
See Prototype

LAN
See Local Area Network

Lanham Act
Refers to the Federal Trade Mark Act of 1946. Protects registered trademarks, trade names, and other service marks used in commerce.

Large business-dominated industry
Industry in which a minimum of 60 percent of employment or sales is in firms with more than 500 workers.

LBO
See Leveraged buy-out

Leader pricing

A reduction in the price of a good or service in order to generate more sales of that good or service.

Legal list

A list of securities selected by a state in which certain institutions and fiduciaries (such as pension funds, insurance companies, and banks) may invest. Securities not on the list are not eligible for investment. Legal lists typically restrict investments to high quality securities meeting certain specifications. Generally, investment is limited to U.S. securities and investment-grade blue chip securities (see separate citation).

Leveraged buy-out (LBO)

The purchase of a business or a division of a corporation through a highly leveraged financing package.

Liability

An obligation or duty to perform a service or an act. Also defined as money owed.

License

(See also Business license)

A legal agreement granting to another the right to use a technological innovation.

Limited partnerships

See Venture capital limited partnerships

Liquidity

The ability to convert a security into cash promptly.

Loans

See Commercial loans; Disaster loans; SBA direct loans; SBA guaranteed loans; SBA special lending institution categories

Local Area Network (LAN)

Computer networks contained within a single building or small area; used to facilitate the sharing of information.

Local development corporation

An organization, usually made up of local citizens of a community, designed to improve the economy of the area by inducing business and industry to locate and expand there. A local development corporation establishes a capability to finance local growth.

Long-haul rates

Rates charged by a transporter in which the distance traveled is more than 800 miles.

Long-term debt

An obligation that matures in a period that exceeds five years.

Low-grade bond

A corporate bond that is rated below investment grade by the major rating agencies (Standard and Poor's, Moody's).

Macro-efficiency

(See also Economic efficiency)

Efficiency as it pertains to the operation of markets and market systems.

Managed care

A cost-effective health care program initiated by employers whereby low-cost health care is made available to the employees in return for exclusive patronage to program doctors.

Management Assistance Programs

See SBA Management Assistance Programs

Management and technical assistance

A term used by many programs to mean business (as opposed to technological) assistance.

Mandated benefits

Specific treatments, providers, or individuals required by law to be included in commercial health plans.

Market evaluation

The use of market information to determine the sales potential of a specific product or process.

Market failure

The situation in which the workings of a competitive market do not produce the best results from the point of view of the entire society.

Market information

Data of any type that can be used for market evaluation, which could include demographic data, technology forecasting, regulatory changes, etc.

Market research

A systematic collection, analysis, and reporting of data about the market and its preferences, opinions, trends, and plans; used for corporate decision-making.

Market share

In a particular market, the percentage of sales of a specific product.

Marketing
Promotion of goods or services through various media.

Master Establishment List (MEL)
A list of firms in the United States developed by the U.S. Small Business Administration; firms can be selected by industry, region, state, standard metropolitan statistical area (see separate citation), county, and zip code.

Maturity
(See also Term)
The date upon which the principal or stated value of a bond or other indebtedness becomes due and payable.

Medicaid (Title XIX)
A federally aided, state-operated and administered program that provides medical benefits for certain low-income persons in need of health and medical care who are eligible for one of the government's welfare cash payment programs, including the aged, the blind, the disabled, and members of families with dependent children where one parent is absent, incapacitated, or unemployed.

Medicare (Title XVIII)
A nationwide health insurance program for disabled and aged persons. Health insurance is available to insured persons without regard to income. Monies from payroll taxes cover hospital insurance and monies from general revenues and beneficiary premiums pay for supplementary medical insurance.

MEL
See Master Establishment List

MESBIC
See Minority enterprise small business investment corporation

MET
See Multiple employer trust

Metropolitan statistical area (MSA)
A means used by the government to define large population centers that may transverse different governmental jurisdictions. For example, the Washington, D.C. MSA includes the District of Columbia and contiguous parts of Maryland and Virginia because all of these geopolitical areas comprise one population and economic operating unit.

Mezzanine financing
See Third-stage financing

Micro-efficiency
(See also Economic efficiency)
Efficiency as it pertains to the operation of individual firms.

Microdata
Information on the characteristics of an individual business firm.

Mid-term debt
An obligation that matures within one to five years.

Midrisk venture capital
See Equity midrisk venture capital

Minimum premium plan
A combination approach to funding an insurance plan aimed primarily at premium tax savings. The employer self-funds a fixed percentage of estimated monthly claims and the insurance company insures the excess.

Minimum wage
The lowest hourly wage allowed by the federal government.

Minority Business Development Agency
Contracts with private firms throughout the nation to sponsor Minority Business Development Centers which provide minority firms with advice and technical assistance on a fee basis.

Minority Enterprise Small Business Investment Corporation (MESBIC)
A federally funded private venture capital firm licensed by the U.S. Small Business Administration to provide capital to minority-owned businesses (see separate citation).

Minority-owned business
Businesses owned by those who are socially or economically disadvantaged (see separate citation).

Mom and Pop business
A small store or enterprise having limited capital, principally employing family members.

Moonlighter
A wage-and-salary worker with a side business.

MSA
See Metropolitan statistical area

Multi-employer plan
A health plan to which more than one employer is required to contribute and that may be maintained through a collective bargaining agreement and required to meet standards prescribed by the U.S. Department of Labor.

Multi-level marketing
A system of selling in which you sign up other people to assist you and they, in turn, recruit others to help them. Some entrepreneurs have built successful companies on this concept because the main focus of their activities is their product and product sales.

Multimedia
The use of several types of media to promote a product or service. Also, refers to the use of several different types of media (sight, sound, pictures, text) in a CD-ROM (see separate citation) product.

Multiple employer trust (MET)
A self-funded benefit plan generally geared toward small employers sharing a common interest.

NAFTA
See North American Free Trade Agreement

NASDAQ
See National Association of Securities Dealers Automated Quotations

National Association of Securities Dealers Automated Quotations
Provides price quotes on over-the-counter securities as well as securities listed on the New York Stock Exchange.

National income
Aggregate earnings of labor and property arising from the production of goods and services in a nation's economy.

Net assets
See Net worth

Net income
The amount remaining from earnings and profits after all expenses and costs have been met or deducted. Also known as Net earnings.

Net profit
Money earned after production and overhead expenses (see separate citations) have been deducted.

Net worth
(See also Capital)
The difference between a company's total assets and its total liabilities.

Network
A chain of interconnected individuals or organizations sharing information and/or services.

New York Stock Exchange (NYSE)
The oldest stock exchange in the U.S. Allows for trading in stocks, bonds, warrants, options, and rights that meet listing requirements.

Niche
A career or business for which a person is well-suited. Also, a product which fulfills one need of a particular market segment, often with little or no competition.

Nodes
One workstation in a network, either local area or wide area (see separate citations).

Nonbank bank
A bank that either accepts deposits or makes loans, but not both. Used to create many new branch banks.

Noncompetitive awards
A method of contracting whereby the federal government negotiates with only one contractor to supply a product or service.

Nonmember bank
A state-regulated bank that does not belong to the federal bank system.

Nonprofit
An organization that has no shareholders, does not distribute profits, and is without federal and state tax liabilities.

Norms
See Financial ratios

North American Free Trade Agreement (NAFTA)
Passed in 1993, NAFTA eliminates trade barriers among businesses in the U.S., Canada, and Mexico.

NYSE
See New York Stock Exchange

Occupational Safety & Health Administration (OSHA)
Federal agency that regulates health and safety standards within the workplace.

Optimal firm size
The business size at which the production cost per unit of output (average cost) is, in the long run, at its minimum.

Organizational chart
A hierarchical chart tracking the chain of command within an organization.

OSHA
See Occupational Safety & Health Administration

Overhead
Expenses, such as employee benefits and building utilities, incurred by a business that are unrelated to the actual product or service sold.

Owner's capital
Debt or equity funds provided by the owner(s) of a business; sources of owner's capital are personal savings, sales of assets, or loans from financial institutions.

P & L
See Profit and loss statement

Part-time workers
Normally, those who work less than 35 hours per week. The Tax Reform Act indicated that part-time workers who work less than 17.5 hours per week may be excluded from health plans for purposes of complying with federal nondiscrimination rules.

Part-year workers
Those who work less than 50 weeks per year.

Partnership
Two or more parties who enter into a legal relationship to conduct business for profit. Defined by the U.S. Internal Revenue Code as joint ventures, syndicates, groups, pools, and other associations of two or more persons organized for profit that are not specifically classified in the IRS code as corporations or proprietorships.

Patent
A grant made by the government assuring an inventor the sole right to make, use, and sell an invention for a period of 17 years.

PC
See Professional corporation

Peak
See Cyclical peak

Pension
A series of payments made monthly, semiannually, annually, or at other specified intervals during the lifetime of the pensioner for distribution upon retirement. The term is sometimes used to denote the portion of the retirement allowance financed by the employer's contributions.

Pension fund
A fund established to provide for the payment of pension benefits; the collective contributions made by all of the parties to the pension plan.

Performance appraisal
An established set of objective criteria, based on job description and requirements, that is used to evaluate the performance of an employee in a specific job.

Permit
See Business license

Plan
See Business plan

Pooling
An arrangement for employers to achieve efficiencies and lower health costs by joining together to purchase group health insurance or self-insurance.

PPO
See Preferred provider organization

Preferred lenders program
See SBA special lending institution categories

Preferred provider organization (PPO)
A contractual arrangement with a health care services organization that agrees to discount its health care rates in return for faster payment and/or a patient base.

Premiums
The amount of money paid to an insurer for health insurance under a policy. The premium is generally paid periodically (e.g., monthly), and often is split between the employer and the employee. Unlike deductibles and coinsurance or copayments, premiums are paid for coverage whether or not benefits are actually used.

Prime-age workers
Employees 25 to 54 years of age.

Prime contract

A contract awarded directly by the U.S. Federal Government.

Private company

See Closely held corporation

Private placement

A method of raising capital by offering for sale an investment or business to a small group of investors (generally avoiding registration with the Securities and Exchange Commission or state securities registration agencies). Also known as Private financing or Private offering.

Pro forma

The use of hypothetical figures in financial statements to represent future expenditures, debts, and other potential financial expenses.

Proactive

Taking the initiative to solve problems and anticipate future events before they happen, instead of reacting to an already existing problem or waiting for a difficult situation to occur.

Procurement

(See also 8(a) Program; Small business set asides)
A contract from an agency of the federal government for goods or services from a small business.

Prodigy

(See also America Online)
An online service which is accessible by computer modem. The service features Internet access, bulletin boards, online periodicals, electronic mail, and other services for subscribers.

Product development

The stage of the innovation process where research is translated into a product or process through evaluation, adaptation, and demonstration.

Product franchising

An arrangement for a franchisee to use the name and to produce the product line of the franchisor or parent corporation.

Production

The manufacture of a product.

Production prototype

See Prototype

Productivity

A measurement of the number of goods produced during a specific amount of time.

Professional corporation (PC)

Organized by members of a profession such as medicine, dentistry, or law for the purpose of conducting their professional activities as a corporation. Liability of a member or shareholder is limited in the same manner as in a business corporation.

Profit and loss statement (P & L)

The summary of the incomes (total revenues) and costs of a company's operation during a specific period of time. Also known as Income and expense statement.

Proposal

See Business plan

Proprietorship

The most common legal form of business ownership; about 85 percent of all small businesses are proprietorships. The liability of the owner is unlimited in this form of ownership.

Prospective payment system

A cost-containment measure included in the Social Security Amendments of 1983 whereby Medicare payments to hospitals are based on established prices, rather than on cost reimbursement.

Prototype

A model that demonstrates the validity of the concept of an invention (laboratory prototype); a model that meets the needs of the manufacturing process and the user (production prototype).

Prudent investor rule or standard

A legal doctrine that requires fiduciaries to make investments using the prudence, diligence, and intelligence that would be used by a prudent person in making similar investments. Because fiduciaries make investments on behalf of third-party beneficiaries, the standard results in very conservative investments. Until recently, most state regulations required the fiduciary to apply this standard to each investment. Newer, more progressive regulations permit fiduciaries to apply this standard to the portfolio taken as a whole, thereby allowing a fiduciary to balance a portfolio with higher-yield, higher-risk investments. In states with more progressive regulations, practically every type of security is eligible for inclusion in the portfolio of investments made by a fiduciary, provided that the portfolio investments, in their totality, are those of a prudent person.

Public equity markets

Organized markets for trading in equity shares such as common stocks, preferred stocks, and warrants. Includes markets for both regularly traded and nonregularly traded securities.

Public offering

General solicitation for participation in an investment opportunity. Interstate public offerings are supervised by the U.S. Securities and Exchange Commission (see separate citation).

Quality control

The process by which a product is checked and tested to ensure consistent standards of high quality.

Rate of return

(See also Yield)
The yield obtained on a security or other investment based on its purchase price or its current market price. The total rate of return is current income plus or minus capital appreciation or depreciation.

Real property

Includes the land and all that is contained on it.

Realignment

See Resource realignment

Recession

Contraction of economic activity occurring between the peak and trough (see separate citations) of a business cycle.

Regulated market

A market in which the government controls the forces of supply and demand, such as who may enter and what price may be charged.

Regulation D

A vehicle by which small businesses make small offerings and private placements of securities with limited disclosure requirements. It was designed to ease the burdens imposed on small businesses utilizing this method of capital formation.

Regulatory Flexibility Act

An act requiring federal agencies to evaluate the impact of their regulations on small businesses before the regulations are issued and to consider less burdensome alternatives.

Research

The initial stage of the innovation process, which includes idea generation and invention.

Research and development financing

A tax-advantaged partnership set up to finance product development for start-ups as well as more mature companies.

Resource mobility

The ease with which labor and capital move from firm to firm or from industry to industry.

Resource realignment

The adjustment of productive resources to interindustry changes in demand.

Resources

The sources of support or help in the innovation process, including sources of financing, technical evaluation, market evaluation, management and business assistance, etc.

Retained business earnings

Business profits that are retained by the business rather than being distributed to the shareholders as dividends.

Revolving credit

An agreement with a lending institution for an amount of money, which cannot exceed a set maximum, over a specified period of time. Each time the borrower repays a portion of the loan, the amount of the repayment may be borrowed yet again.

Risk capital

See Venture capital

Risk management

The act of identifying potential sources of financial loss and taking action to minimize their negative impact.

Routing

The sequence of steps necessary to complete a product during production.

S corporations

See Sub chapter S corporations

SBA
See Small Business Administration

SBA direct loans
Loans made directly by the U.S. Small Business Administration (SBA); monies come from funds appropriated specifically for this purpose. In general, SBA direct loans carry interest rates slightly lower than those in the private financial markets and are available only to applicants unable to secure private financing or an SBA guaranteed loan.

SBA 504 Program
See Certified development corporation

SBA guaranteed loans
Loans made by lending institutions in which the U.S. Small Business Administration (SBA) will pay a prior agreed-upon percentage of the outstanding principal in the event the borrower of the loan defaults. The terms of the loan and the interest rate are negotiated between the borrower and the lending institution, within set parameters.

SBA loans
See Disaster loans; SBA direct loans; SBA guaranteed loans; SBA special lending institution categories

SBA Management Assistance Programs
(See also Active Corps of Executives; Service Corps of Retired Executives; Small business institutes program)
Classes, workshops, counseling, and publications offered by the U.S. Small Business Administration.

SBA special lending institution categories.
U.S. Small Business Administration (SBA) loan program in which the SBA promises certified banks a 72-hour turnaround period in giving its approval for a loan, and in which preferred lenders in a pilot program are allowed to write SBA loans without seeking prior SBA approval.

SBDB
See Small Business Data Base

SBDC
See Small business development centers

SBI
See Small business institutes program

SBIC
See Small business investment corporation

SBIR Program
See Small Business Innovation Development Act of 1982

Scale economies
The decline of the production cost per unit of output (average cost) as the volume of output increases.

Scale efficiency
The reduction in unit cost available to a firm when producing at a higher output volume.

SCORE
See Service Corps of Retired Executives

SEC
See Securities and Exchange Commission

SECA
See Self-Employment Contributions Act

Second-stage financing
(See also First-stage financing; Third-stage financing)
Working capital for the initial expansion of a company that is producing, shipping, and has growing accounts receivable and inventories. Also known as Second-round financing.

Secondary market
A market established for the purchase and sale of outstanding securities following their initial distribution.

Secondary worker
Any worker in a family other than the person who is the primary source of income for the family.

Secondhand capital
Previously used and subsequently resold capital equipment (e.g., buildings and machinery).

Securities and Exchange Commission (SEC)
Federal agency charged with regulating the trade of securities to prevent unethical practices in the investor market.

Securitized debt
A marketing technique that converts long-term loans to marketable securities.

Seed capital
Venture financing provided in the early stages of the innovation process, usually during product development.

Self-employed person

One who works for a profit or fees in his or her own business, profession, or trade, or who operates a farm.

Self-Employment Contributions Act (SECA)

Federal law that governs the self-employment tax (see separate citation).

Self-employment income

Income covered by Social Security if a business earns a net income of at least $400.00 during the year. Taxes are paid on earnings that exceed $400.00.

Self-employment retirement plan

See Keogh plan

Self-employment tax

Required tax imposed on self-employed individuals for the provision of Social Security and Medicare. The tax must be paid quarterly with estimated income tax statements.

Self-funding

A health benefit plan in which a firm uses its own funds to pay claims, rather than transferring the financial risks of paying claims to an outside insurer in exchange for premium payments.

Service Corps of Retired Executives (SCORE)

(See also Active Corps of Executives)
Volunteers for the SBA Management Assistance Program who provide one-on-one counseling and teach workshops and seminars for small firms.

Service firm

See Business service firm

Service sector

Broadly defined, all U.S. industries that produce intangibles, including the five major industry divisions of transportation, communications, and utilities; wholesale trade; retail trade; finance, insurance, and real estate; and services.

Set asides

See Small business set asides

Short-haul service

A type of transportation service in which the transporter supplies service between cities where the maximum distance is no more than 200 miles.

Short-term debt

An obligation that matures in one year.

SIC codes

See Standard Industrial Classification codes

Single-establishment enterprise

See Establishment

Small business

An enterprise that is independently owned and operated, is not dominant in its field, and employs fewer than 500 people. For SBA purposes, the U.S. Small Business Administration (SBA) considers various other factors (such as gross annual sales) in determining size of a business.

Small Business Administration (SBA)

An independent federal agency that provides assistance with loans, management, and advocating interests before other federal agencies.

Small Business Data Base

(See also U.S. Establishment and Enterprise Microdata File; U.S. Establishment Longitudinal Microdata File)
A collection of microdata (see separate citation) files on individual firms developed and maintained by the U.S. Small Business Administration.

Small business development centers (SBDC)

Centers that provide support services to small businesses, such as individual counseling, SBA advice, seminars and conferences, and other learning center activities. Most services are free of charge, or available at minimal cost.

Small business development corporation

See Certified development corporation

Small business-dominated industry

Industry in which a minimum of 60 percent of employment or sales is in firms with fewer than 500 employees.

Small Business Innovation Development Act of 1982

Federal statute requiring federal agencies with large extramural research and development budgets to allocate a certain percentage of these funds to small research and development firms. The program, called the Small Business Innovation Research (SBIR) Program, is designed to stimulate technological innovation and make greater use of small businesses in meeting national innovation needs.

Small business institutes (SBI) program
Cooperative arrangements made by U.S. Small Business Administration district offices and local colleges and universities to provide small business firms with graduate students to counsel them without charge.

Small business investment corporation (SBIC)
A privately owned company licensed and funded through the U.S. Small Business Administration and private sector sources to provide equity or debt capital to small businesses.

Small business set asides
Procurement (see separate citation) opportunities required by law to be on all contracts under $10,000 or a certain percentage of an agency's total procurement expenditure.

Smaller firms
For U.S. Department of Commerce purposes, those firms not included in the Fortune 1000.

SMSA
See Metropolitan statistical area

Socially and economically disadvantaged
Individuals who have been subjected to racial or ethnic prejudice or cultural bias without regard to their qualities as individuals, and whose abilities to compete are impaired because of diminished opportunities to obtain capital and credit.

Sole proprietorship
An unincorporated, one-owner business, farm, or professional practice.

Special lending institution categories
See SBA special lending institution categories

Standard Industrial Classification (SIC) codes
Four-digit codes established by the U.S. Federal Government to categorize businesses by type of economic activity; the first two digits correspond to major groups such as construction and manufacturing, while the last two digits correspond to subgroups such as home construction or highway construction.

Standard metropolitan statistical area (SMSA)
See Metropolitan statistical area

Start-up
A new business, at the earliest stages of development and financing.

Start-up costs
Costs incurred before a business can commence operations.

Start-up financing
Financing provided to companies that have either completed product development and initial marketing or have been in business for less than one year but have not yet sold their product commercially.

Stock
(See also Common stock; Convertible preferred stock)
A certificate of equity ownership in a business.

Stop-loss coverage
Insurance for a self-insured plan that reimburses the company for any losses it might incur in its health claims beyond a specified amount.

Strategic planning
Projected growth and development of a business to establish a guiding direction for the future. Also used to determine which market segments to explore for optimal sales of products or services.

Structural unemployment
See Unemployment

Sub chapter S corporations
Corporations that are considered noncorporate for tax purposes but legally remain corporations.

Subcontract
A contract between a prime contractor and a subcontractor, or between subcontractors, to furnish supplies or services for performance of a prime contract (see separate citation) or a subcontract.

Surety bonds
Bonds providing reimbursement to an individual, company, or the government if a firm fails to complete a contract. The U.S. Small Business Administration guarantees surety bonds in a program much like the SBA guaranteed loan program (see separate citation).

Swing loan
See Bridge financing

Target market
The clients or customers sought for a business' product or service.

Targeted Jobs Tax Credit
Federal legislation enacted in 1978 that provides a tax credit to an employer who hires structurally unemployed individuals.

Tax number
(See also Employer identification number)
A number assigned to a business by a state revenue department that enables the business to buy goods without paying sales tax.

Taxable bonds
An interest-bearing certificate of public or private indebtedness. Bonds are issued by public agencies to finance economic development.

Technical assistance
See Management and technical assistance

Technical evaluation
Assessment of technological feasibility.

Technology
The method in which a firm combines and utilizes labor and capital resources to produce goods or services; the application of science for commercial or industrial purposes.

Technology transfer
The movement of information about a technology or intellectual property from one party to another for use.

Tenure
See Employee tenure

Term
(See also Maturity)
The length of time for which a loan is made.

Terms of a note
The conditions or limits of a note; includes the interest rate per annum, the due date, and transferability and convertibility features, if any.

Third-party administrator
An outside company responsible for handling claims and performing administrative tasks associated with health insurance plan maintenance.

Third-stage financing
(See also First-stage financing; Second-stage financing)
Financing provided for the major expansion of a company whose sales volume is increasing and that is breaking even or profitable. These funds are used for further plant expansion, marketing, working capital, or development of an improved product. Also known as Third-round or Mezzanine financing.

Time deposit
A bank deposit that cannot be withdrawn before a specified future time.

Time management
Skills and scheduling techniques used to maximize productivity.

Trade credit
Credit extended by suppliers of raw materials or finished products. In an accounting statement, trade credit is referred to as "accounts payable."

Trade name
The name under which a company conducts business, or by which its business, goods, or services are identified. It may or may not be registered as a trademark.

Trade periodical
A publication with a specific focus on one or more aspects of business and industry.

Trade secret
Competitive advantage gained by a business through the use of a unique manufacturing process or formula.

Trade show
An exhibition of goods or services used in a particular industry. Typically held inexhibition centers where exhibitors rent space to display their merchandise.

Trademark
A graphic symbol, device, or slogan that identifies a business. A business has property rights to its trademark from the inception of its use, but it is still prudent to register all trademarks with the Trademark Office of the U.S. Department of Commerce.

Translation
See Product development

Treasury bills
Investment tender issued by the Federal Reserve Bank in amounts of $10,000 that mature in 91 to 182 days.

Treasury bonds

Long-term notes with maturity dates of not less than seven and not more than twenty-five years.

Treasury notes

Short-term notes maturing in less than seven years.

Trend

A statistical measurement used to track changes that occur over time.

Trough

See Cyclical trough

UCC

See Uniform Commercial Code

UL

See Underwriters Laboratories

Underwriters Laboratories (UL)

One of several private firms that tests products and processes to determine their safety. Although various firms can provide this kind of testing service, many local and insurance codes specify UL certification.

Underwriting

A process by which an insurer determines whether or not and on what basis it will accept an application for insurance. In an experience-rated plan, premiums are based on a firm's or group's past claims; factors other than prior claims are used for community-rated or manually rated plans.

Unfair competition

Refers to business practices, usually unethical, such as using unlicensed products, pirating merchandise, or misleading the public through false advertising, which give the offending business an unequitable advantage over others.

Unfunded accrued liability

The excess of total liabilities, both present and prospective, over present and prospective assets.

Unemployment

The joblessness of individuals who are willing to work, who are legally and physically able to work, and who are seeking work. Unemployment may represent the temporary joblessness of a worker between jobs (frictional unemployment) or the joblessness of a worker whose skills are not suitable for jobs available in the labor market (structural unemployment).

Uniform Commercial Code (UCC)

A code of laws governing commercial transactions across the U.S., except Louisiana. Their purpose is to bring uniformity to financial transactions.

Uniform product code (UPC symbol)

A computer-readable label comprised of ten digits and stripes that encodes what a product is and how much it costs. The first five digits are assigned by the Uniform Product Code Council, and the last five digits by the individual manufacturer.

Unit cost

See Average cost

UPC symbol

See Uniform product code

U.S. Establishment and Enterprise Microdata (USEEM) File

A cross-sectional database containing information on employment, sales, and location for individual enterprises and establishments with employees that have a Dun & Bradstreet credit rating.

U.S. Establishment Longitudinal Microdata (USELM) File

A database containing longitudinally linked sample microdata on establishments drawn from the U.S. Establishment and Enterprise Microdata file (see separate citation).

U.S. Small Business Administration 504 Program

See Certified development corporation

USEEM

See U.S. Establishment and Enterprise Microdata File

USELM

See U.S. Establishment Longitudinal Microdata File

VCN

See Venture capital network

Venture capital

(See also Equity; Equity midrisk venture capital)

Money used to support new or unusual business ventures that exhibit above-average growth rates, significant potential for market expansion, and are in need of additional financing to sustain growth or further research and development; equity or equity-type financing traditionally provided at the commercialization stage, increasingly available prior to commercialization.

Venture capital company

A company organized to provide seed capital to a business in its formation stage, or in its first or second stage of expansion. Funding is obtained through public or private pension funds, commercial banks and bank holding companies, small business investment corporations licensed by the U.S. Small Business Administration, private venture capital firms, insurance companies, investment management companies, bank trust departments, industrial companies seeking to diversify their investment, and investment bankers acting as intermediaries for other investors or directly investing on their own behalf.

Venture capital limited partnerships

Designed for business development, these partnerships are an institutional mechanism for providing capital for young, technology-oriented businesses. The investors' money is pooled and invested in money market assets until venture investments have been selected. The general partners are experienced investment managers who select and invest the equity and debt securities of firms with high growth potential and the ability to go public in the near future.

Venture capital network (VCN)

A computer database that matches investors with entrepreneurs.

WAN

See Wide Area Network

Wide Area Network (WAN)

Computer networks linking systems throughout a state or around the world in order to facilitate the sharing of information.

Withholding

Federal, state, social security, and unemployment taxes withheld by the employer from employees' wages; employers are liable for these taxes and the corporate umbrella and bankruptcy will not exonerate an employer from paying back payroll withholding. Employers should escrow these funds in a separate account and disperse them quarterly to withholding authorities.

Workers' compensation

A state-mandated form of insurance covering workers injured in job-related accidents. In some states, the state is the insurer; in other states, insurance must be acquired from commercial insurance firms. Insurance rates are based on a number of factors, including salaries, firm history, and risk of occupation.

Working capital

Refers to a firm's short-term investment of current assets, including cash, short-term securities, accounts receivable, and inventories.

Yield

(See also Rate of return)

The rate of income returned on an investment, expressed as a percentage. Income yield is obtained by dividing the current dollar income by the current market price of the security. Net yield or yield to maturity is the current income yield minus any premium above par or plus any discount from par in purchase price, with the adjustment spread over the period from the date of purchase to the date of maturity.

Appendix D - Bibliography

Bibliography

Bibliography citations are listed alphabetically by title under appropriate subject subheadings, which also appear alphabetically (in bold).

Accounting/Budgets and Budgeting

"15 franchises you can run from home" in Black Enterprise (Vol. 29, No. 2, September 1998, p. 60). By: Gerda D. Gallop.

"Account Yourself" in Business Start-Ups (Vol. 7, No. 8, August 1995, p. 79).

Accounting for Business. Woburn, MA: Butterworth-Heinemann, 1991. By: Peter Atrill, David Harvey, and Edward McLaney.

Accounting the Business Environment. Philadelphia, PA: Trans-Atlantic Publications, Inc. 1995. By: John Watts.

The Accounting Cycle. Menlo Park, CA: Crisp Publications, Inc. By: Jay Jacquet and William C. Miller, Jr.

An Accounting Primer. New York, NY: Mentor, Revised edition, 1992. By: Elwin W. Midgett.

Activity-Based Costing for Small and Mid-sized Businesses: An Implementation Guide. New York, NY: John Wiley & Sons, Inc. 1992. By: Douglas T. Hicks.

"Balancing Act" in Entrepreneur (Vol. 23, No. 3, March 1995, pp. 56, 58- 59, 61). By: Bob Weinstein.

"Beat the Clock" in Entrepreneur (Vol. 26, Issue 12, December 1998, p. 66). By: Joan Szaro.

"Before You File" in Income Opportunities (Vol. 32, No. 1, January 1997, pp. 27-30). By: Janine S. Pouliot.

"Bill Auditing" in Small Business Opportunities (Vol. 8, No. 2, March 1996, p. 20). By: Terry Schwartz.

"Bill of Wrongs" in Entrepreneur (Vol. 23, No. 5, May 1995, pp. 166, 168, 170-171). By: David R. Honodel.

Bookkeeping & Administration for the Smaller Business. Willowick, OH: Etta Publishing Company, 1998. By: Elvira Bellogoni.

Bookkeeping for a Small Business. Boston, MA: DBA Books, 6th ed. 1998. By: Diana Bellavance.

Bootstrapper's Success Secrets: 151 Tactics for Building Your Business on a Shoestring Budget. Franklin Lakes, NJ: Career Press, Inc. 1997. By: Kimberly Stansell.

Budgeting & Finance. New York, NY: The McGraw-Hill Companies, 1996. By: Generation X Staff.

"Budgets help managers set company's course of action" in Crain's Detroit Business (December 14-20, 1998, p. E16). By: Bryan Becker.

"Business 101" in Inc. (December 1998, p. 126).

Business, Accounting and Finance Problem Solver. Piscataway, NJ: Research & Education Association, Revised edition, 1994.

Business Finance for the Numerically Challenged. Franklin Lakes, NJ: Career Press, Inc. 1997. By: Career Press, Inc. Staff.

Business Owner's Guide to Accounting & Bookkeeping. Grants Pass, OR: PSI Research, 2nd ed. 1997. By: Jose F. Placenicia, Bruce Welge and Don Oliver.

"Calling to collect" in Entrepreneur (Vol. 26, No. 2, February 1998, p. 36).

"Cash Catchers" in Independent Business (Vol. 9, No. 7, November/December 1998, pp. 40-41). By: Alan Naditz.

College Accounting: A Small Business Approach. Burr Ridge, IL: Richard D. Irwin, Inc. 1994. By: Eleanor Schrader.

"Count on It" in Entrepreneur (Vol. 23, No. 8, August 1995, pp. 30, 32- 33). By: Cheryl J. Goldberg.

"Count on It" in Hispanic Business (Vol. 18, No. 6, June 1996, p. 122). By: Rick Mendosa.

"Counting On Profit" in Small Business Opportunities (Vol. 7, No. 3, May 1995, pp. 42-43, 82). By: Martin Waterman.

"Customers Can't Pay?" in Independent Business (Vol. 9, No. 4, July/August 1998, pp. 46-47). By: Carla Goodman.

"Dream Accountant" in Income Opportunities (Vol. 30, No. 1, January 1995, pp. 108, 110). By: Peg Byron.

Finance & Accounting. Dubuque, IA: Kendall Hunt Publishing Co. 1995. By: Henry Beam.

Financial Accounting: Guide. Dubuque, IA: Kendall Hunt Publishing Co. 1995. By: Mohamed Ibrahim.

Financial Accounting & Reporting. Cincinnati, OH: South-Western Publishing Co. 1995.

Financial Basics of Small Business Success. Menlo Park, CA: Crisp Publications, Inc. 1996. By: J. Gill.

Financial Essentials for Small Business Success: Accounting, Planning & Recordkeeping Techniques for a Healthy Bottom Line. Chicago, IL: Upstart Publishing Co. Inc. 1994. By: Joe Tabet.

"Firing Line" in Entrepreneur (Vol. 23, No. 12, November 1995, pp. 56, 59). By: David R. Evanson.

"For the Record" in Business Start-Ups (Vol. 7, No. 5, May 1995, pp. 78, 80-81). By: Cynthia E. Griffin.

"Going It Alone" in Newsweek (April 1996, pp. 50-51). By: Ellyn E. Spragins and Steve Rhodes.

"It Adds Up" in Income Opportunities (Vol. 31, No. 1, January 1996, pp. 32, 34, 38). By: Debra D'Agostino.

Keeping the Books: Basic Recordkeeping and Accounting for the Small Business. Chicago, IL: Upstart Publishing Co. Inc. 4th ed. 1998. By: Linda Pinson and Jerry A. Jinnett.

"Ledger-Demain" in Inc. (Vol. 18, No. 9, June 1996, pp. 87-88). By: Ellen DePasquale.

"A Leg Up" in Red Herring: Guide to Professional Services 1999 (1999, p. 32). By: Denise Geschke.

"Let's Get Fiscal" in Entrepreneur (June 1995, pp. 68, 70-71). By: Bob Weinstein.

"Let's Make A Deal" in Business Start-Ups (Vol. 11, No. 1, January 1999, p. 26). By: Robert McGarvey.

Managing by the Numbers: Financial Essentials for the Growing Business. Chicago, IL: Upstart Publishing Co. Inc. 1992. By: David H. Bangs, Jr.

McGraw-Hill Small Business Tax Advisor. New York, NY: The McGraw-Hill Companies, Second edition, 1992. By: Cliff Roberson.

Money Smart Secrets for the Self-Employed. New York, NY: Random House, Inc. 1997. By: Linda Stern.

"No Accounting for Success" in Inc. (Vol. 18, No. 8, June 1996, p. 2526). By: Norm Brodsky.

"Non-Taxing Matters" in Inc. (Vol. 19, No. 4, March 1997, pp. 90-92) in Inc. (1997). By: Ellen DePasquale.

"On the Books" in Income Opportunities (Vol. 32, No. 1, January 1997, pp. 38, 40, 42). By: Mike Hogan.

"Outsourcing the Overflow" in Red Herring: Guide to Professional Services 1999 (1999, p. 33). By: Denise Geschke.

"Postmortem estate planning for small business owners" in Journal of Accountancy (Vol. 186, No. 1, July 1998, p. 31). By: Joseph R. Oliver and Charles A. Granstaff.

Quarterlies, Journals, Payroll - Small Business Accounting: California, Oregon, & Washington Edition. Woodinville, WA: Rhapsody Press, Inc. 1996. By: James J. Pearce.

Record Keeping for Small Rural Businesses. Amherst, MA: University of Massachusetts By: Eligia Murcia.

"A sales tool for small business" in Computer Shopper (Vol. 18, No. 1, January 1998, p. 502). By: Kathy Yakal.

"Save on Taxes, Stay in the Black" in Income Opportunities (Vol. 34, Issue 1, January/February 1999, p. 46). By: Glenn R. Townes.

"Second Time Around" in Business Start-Ups (Vol. 8, No. 11, November 1996, pp. 74-75). By: Lisa Pelec Hyde.

"Seven steps to success" in Journal of Accountancy (Vol. 185, No. 6, June 1998, p. 73). By: Anita Dennis.

The Shoebox Syndrome (Record-Keeping). Hyde Park, MA: Nikmal Publishing By: Selma H. Lamkin.

Small Business Accountant. Cincinnati, OH: South-Western Publishing Co. 1994. By: Hamilton.

Small Time Operator: How to Start Your Own Small Business, Keep Your Books, Pay Your Taxes, & Stay out of Trouble!. Willits, CA: Bell Springs Publishing, 22nd ed. 1998. By: Bernard Kamoroff.

"Step 5: Plan a Realistic Budget" in Business Start-Ups (Vol. 8, No. 9, September 1996, pp. 80, 82). By: Kylo-Patrick Hart.

Step-by-Step Bookkeeping: The Complete Handbook for the Small Business. New York, NY: Sterling Publishing Co. Inc. Revised edition, 1992. By: Robert C. Ragan.

Successfully Self-Employed: How to Sell What You Do, Do What You Sell, Manage Your Cash in Between. Chicago, IL: Upstart Publishing Company, Inc. 1996. By: Gregory Brennan.

Tax Planning & Preparation Made Easy for the Self-Employed. New York, NY: John Wiley & Sons, Inc. 1995. By: Gregory L. Dent.

"To the Rescue" in Business Start-Ups (Vol. 7, No. 5, May 1995, pp. 68, 70-71). By: Sue Clayton.

"Tracking Your Mileage" in Business Start-Ups (Vol. 8, No. 12, December 1996, pp. 76, 78). By: Gloria Gibbs Marullo.

"Up for review" in Entrepreneur (Vol. 26, No. 10, October 1998, p. 72).

"Will Banking Go Virtual?" in Inc. (Vol. 18, No. 13, September 1996, pp. 49-52). By: Jill Andresky Fraser.

"Winning Numbers" in Inc. (Vol. 18, No. 13, September 1996, pp. 84-87). By: Ellen DePasquale.

Air Charter Service

AIM/FAR. Annual. By: Compiled by the TAB-AERO staff.

Fit to Fly: A Pilot's Guide to Health & Safety. 1992. By: Richard O. Reinhart.

"His Hand is Steady Running a Business" in Crain's Detroit Business (Vol. 5, No. 1, January 1997, p. 23). By: Jeffrey McCracken.

How to Become a Pilot: The Step-by-Step Guide to Flying. 1991. By: Compiled by the U.S. Federal Aviation Administration.

"How to Build a Million-Dollar Business" in Entrepreneur (September 1997, pp. 100-104,106). By: Gayle Sato Stodder.

"Jet Set" in Entrepreneur (September 1997, p. 40). By: Charlotte Mulhern.

Manufacturing & Business Excellence: Strategies General Aviation & Air Taxi Activity Survey. 1996. By: Ian Warnock.

The Pilot's Guide to Weather Reports, Forecasts, and Flight Planning. 1990. By: Terry T. Lankford.

The Pilot's Radio Communications Handbook. Revised edition, 1993. By: Paul E. Illman and Jay Pouzar.

Private Pilot Manual. Revised edition, 1993.

Severe Weather Flying. Second edition, 1991. By: Dennis Newton.

"Start-up Covets Spokes of Northwest's Hub" in Inc. (Vol. 20, No. 2, February 1998, pp. 19-20). By: Marc Ballon.

Amusement Arcade

Pinball Collectors Resource. Rancho Palos Verdes, CA: Mueting Electronics Co. 1992. By: Robert Hawkins.

Slot Machines: A Pictorial History of the First 100 Years. Reno, NV: Liberty Belle Books, Fourth edition, 1994. By: Marshall Fey.

Slot Machines and Coin-Op Games. Edison, NJ: Book Sales, Inc. 1991. By: William Kurtz.

"That's Entertainment" in Small Business Opportunities (Vol. 7, No. 5, September 1995, pp. 46-48, 98). By: Anne Hart.

Architectural Restoration

"Four Home Improvement Businesses That Are Hot Now" in Income Opportunities (March-April 1999, pp. 16-20). By: Stephen Wagner.

Art Gallery

Art Index. Bronx, NY: H. W. Wilson Co. Quarterly, with annual cumulation.

Art Marketing Sourcebook for the Fine Artist. Penn Valley, CA: ArtNetwork, 1992. By: Constance Franklin-Smith.

The Art of Selling Art Between Production & Livelihood. Seattle, WA: Ritchie's Perfect Press, 1996. By: Bill H. Ritchie Jr.

"Art and Soul" in Entrepreneur (December 1997, p. 206). By: Charlotte Mulhern.

"Artfully Inspired" in Black Enterprise (Vol. 27, No. 2, September 1996, p. 30). By: Lloyd Gite.

"Carving a Niche" in Income Opportunities (Vol. 30, No. 11, November 1995, pp. 82, 84, 86). By: Pamela Rohland.

"Entrepreneurial Woman" in Entrepreneur (August 1997, p. 51). By: Janean Chun.

"Entrepreneurs Across America" in Entrepreneur (Vol. 24, No. 4, April 1996, pp. 100-104, 106-108, 110-112, 114-116, 118, 120-123). By: Janean Chum, Debra Phillips, Cynthia E. Griffin, Heather Page, Lynn Beresford, Holly Celeste Fisk, and Charlotte Mulbern.

Forward Planning: A Handbook of Business, Corporate and Development Planning for Museums and Galleries. New York, NY: Routledge, Chapman & Hall, Inc. 1992. By: Tim Ambrose, editor.

"Fueling Your Own Success" in Working Woman (October 1996, p. 4043). By: Lyle Crowley.

The Gallery Management Manual. New York, NY: Consultant Press, Ltd. 1995. By: Zella Jackson.

"Hanging with a Prize-winning Businessman" in Hispanic Business (Vol. 19, No. 12, December 1997, p. 30).

"Simply Art" in Black Enterpriseit (Vol. 27, No. 6, January 1997, p. 30). By: Rhea Mandulo.

"Tables with Dragonfly Legs" in Forbes (Vol. 155, No. 2, January 16, 1995, pp. 101-104). By: Christie Brown.

Bakery/Doughnut Shop

Bakery Technology and Engineering. McAllen, TX: PAN-TECH International, Third edition, 1992. By: Samuel A. Matz.

"Big Dough in Pretzels" in Small Business Opportunities (Vol. 9, No. 4, July 1997, pp. 56, 58). By: Marie Sherlock.

Boulangerie. Old Tappan, NJ: Macmillan Publishing Co. Inc. 1995. By: Paul Rimbali.

"Brownie Points" in Income Opportunities (Vol. 31, No. 9, September 1996, pp. 96, 98, 100). By: Amy H. Berger.

"Business for Sale" in Inc. (Vol. 18, No. 14, October 1996, p. 112). By: Jill Andresky Fraser.

"Coming to America" in Entrepreneur (Vol. 26, Issue 12, December 1998, p. 109). By: Elaine W. Teague.

"Competition Rising for Bread-Makers" in Crain's Small Business (Vol. 5, No. 4, April 1997, p. 8). By: Jeffrey McCracken.

"Cook Up a Business in Your Kitchen" in Income Opportunities (Vol. 34, Issue 1, January/February 1999, p. 50). By: Stephen Wagner.

"The Cookie lady of Silicon Valley" in Business Week (No. 3595, September 14, 1998, p. S17). By: Gary Andrew Poole.

"Curb Customer Complaints" in Independent Business (Vol. 9, No. 4, July/August 1998, pp. 22-24). By: Janet Willen.

"Directory of Food Industry Resources" in Income Opportunities (Vol. 31, No. 8, August 1996, pp. 26-27). By: Stephanie Jeffrey.

"Entrepreneurial Superstars" in Entrepreneur (April 1997, pp. 108-139). By: Debra Phillips and others.

"Entrepreneurs Across America" in Entrepreneur (Vol. 24, No. 4, April 1996, pp. 100-104, 106-108, 110-112, 114-116, 118, 120-123). By: Janean Chum, Debra Phillips, Cynthia E. Griffin, Heather Page, Lynn Beresford, Holly Celeste Fisk, and Charlotte Mulbern.

"Fresh & Hot" in Entrepreneur (December 1996, p. 156). By: Karen Axelton.

"Frugal Baker's Biz is Finally Taking Off" in Crain's Small Business (June 1996, p. 9). By: Michelle Krebs.

"Growing on Scones Alone" in Crain's Detroit Business (Vol. 12, No. 48, Nov. 25-Dec. 1, 1996, pp. 3, 41). By: Marsha Stopa.

"Jammin'" in Income Opportunities (Vol. 30, No. 6, June 1995, pp. 64, 66). By: Stephanie Jeffrey.

"Lil' Orbits Operators Roll in the Dough" in Income Opportunities (Vol. 33, Issue 8, October 1998, p. 46).

"Make more money and gain time: go against the grain" in Bakery Production and Marketing (Vol. 33, No. 5, May 15, 1998, p. 64). By: Ed Dimmer.

The Market for Bakery Products. Commack, NY: Business Trend Analysts, Inc. 1995.

"My company is growing fast. How can I help employees cope?" in Inc. (Vol. 19, No. 14, October 1997, p. 112). By: Susan Greco.

"On the Rise" in Entrepreneur (Vol. 23, No. 5, May 1995, pp. 196, 198). By: Gayle Sato Stodder.

"Persuading the Persuader" in Crain's Small Business (December 1996, pp. 4, 6). By: Jeffrey McCracken.

"Pinning Hopes on Pastries" in Crain's Detroit Business (Vol. 12, No. 47, November 1996, pp. 3, 34). By: Marsha Stopa.

Practical Baking. New York, NY: Van Nostrand Reinhold Co. Inc. 1990. By: William J. Sultan.

Professional Baking. New York, NY: John Wiley & Sons, Inc. Second edition, 1993. By: Wayne Gisslen.

"Recipe for Success" in Business Start-Ups (Vol. 9, No. 6, June 1997, p. 59).

"Say When" in Inc. (Vol. 17, No. 2, February 1995, pp. 19-20). By: Steven L. Marks.

Secrets of a Jewish Baker: Professional Bread Baking Secrets Revealed. Freedom, CA: The Crossing Press, Inc. 1993. By: George Greenstein.

"The Service Boom" in Small Business Opportunities (Vol. 9, No. 3, May 1997, pp. 22-41).

"Sugar and Strife" in The Detroit Free Press (February 26, 1997, pp. C1, C6). By: Patty LaNoue Stearns.

"Warning Signs" in Black Enterprise (Vol. 27, No. 4, November 1996, pp. 89-94). By: Tonia L. Shakespeare.

Bar/Cocktail Lounge

"Biz Men Put Their Bucks on the Block" in Crain's Small Business (Vol. 5, No. 4, April 1997, pp. 16-17, 19). By: Jeffrey McCracken.

"Calling the shots" in Business Start-ups (Vol. 11, April 1999, pp. 61-62). By: Don Debelak.

The Complete Book of Mixed Drinks: Over One Thousand Alcoholic and Non-Alcoholic Cocktails. New York, NY: HarperCollins Publishers, Inc. 1993. By: Anthony Dias Blue.

"Could Drive You to Drink" in Crain's Small Business (December 1996, pp. 8-9). By: Jeffrey McCracken.

"Entrepreneurial Superstars" in Entrepreneur (April 1997, pp. 108-139). By: Debra Phillips and others.

How to Manage a Successful Bar. New York, NY: John Wiley & Sons, Inc. 1994. By: Christopher Egerton-Thomas.

"How a Small-Town Bar Owner Became a T-Shirt Tycoon" in Income Opportunities (Vol. 33, Vol. 9, November 1998, p. 18). By: Steven M. Brown.

How to Start & Manage a Bar & Cocktail Lounge Business: Step by Step Guide to Business Success. Interlochen, MI: Lewis & Renn Associates, 1996. By: Jerre G. Lewis.

"Missing Link Helps Them Bounce Back" in Crain's Small Business (March 1996, p. 19).

"Mo' Better Zanzibar Blue" in Black Enterprise (Vol. 27, No. 5, December 1996, pp. 106-114). By: Caroline V. Clarke.

"Multiply Profits with Multiple Businesses" in Income Opportunities (Vol. 33, Vol. 9, November 1998, pp. 16, 20, and 22.). By: Sandra Mardenfeld.

Start and Run a Money-Making Bar. New York, NY: TAB Books, Inc. Second edition, 1993. By: Bruce Fier.

"Still the King" in Independent Business (Vol. 9, No. 2, March/April 1998, p. 50). By: Karen M. Price.

"Worshiping a Dream" in Crain's Detroit Business (Vol. 12, No. 39, September 1996, p. 8). By: Matt Roush.

Bridal Shop/Bridal Consultant

"Baby Brings Change in Her Altared State" in Crain's Small Business (Vol. 5, No. 4, April 1997, p. 23). By: Jeffrey McCracken.

"The Bridal Business is Dearly Beloved" in Crain's Small Business (June 1996, p. 23). By: Jeffrey McCracken.

"Bridal Consultant" in Entrepreneur (1996, p. 18).

The Bride Guide: The Perfect Wedding Planner. New York, NY: Barricade Books, Inc. Revised edition, 1991. By: Dinah B. Griffin and Marla S. Schwartz.

The Business of Bridal Beauty. Albany, NY: Milady Publishing Co. 1998. By: Gretchen Maurer.

The Complete Wedding Planner. New York, NY: Avon Books, 1991. By: Suzanne Kresse.

The Complete Wedding Planner: Helpful Choices for the Bride and Groom. New York, NY: Random House Value Publishing, Inc. 1994. By: Edith Gilbert.

Designing Bridal Veils, Headpieces and Hats. Evergreen Park, IL: Hat Tree Studio, 1992. By: Stella V. Remiasz.

Emily Post's Wedding Planner. New York, NY: HarperCollins Publishers, Inc. Revised edition, 1991. By: Elizabeth L. Post.

"Here Comes the Bride" in Income Opportunities (Vol. 31, No. 11, November 1996, pp. 112, 110). By: Laurel Berger.

"Here Comes the Profits" in Business Start-Ups (Vol. 10, No. 9, September 1998, pp. 66, 68-69). By: Marcie Geffner.

How to Have a Big Wedding on a Small Budget. Cincinnati, OH: Writer's Digest Books, Second edition, 1992. By: Diane Warner.

"Lending to Bridal Shops" in Journal of Commercial Lending (Vol. 77, No. 6, February 1995, pp. 27-36). By: LaJuan Messer and Dev Strischek.

"Shoestring Start-Ups" in Income Opportunities (Vol. 30, No. 1, January 1995, pp. 34-44). By: Lori Schwind Murray.

"Success for Less" in Business Start-Ups (Vol. 7, No. 6, June 1995, pp. 26-28, 30, 32, 34, 36, 38, 40-42). By: Maura Hudson Pomije.

Wedded Bliss: A Victorian Bride's Handbook. New York, NY: Abbeville Press, Inc. 1991. By: Molly Dolan Blayney.

Wedding Music: An Index to Collections. Lanham, MD: Scarecrow Press, Inc. 1992. By: William D. Goodfellow.

A Wedding Planner for Brides: Questions You Need to Ask When Planning the Perfect Wedding. Los Gatos, CA: Garnet Rose Publishing, 1991. By: JoAnn K. Leonard.

"Wedding Wars" in Working Woman (Vol. 20, No. 5, May 1995, pp. 62-67, 103). By: Maggie Jones.

The Working Woman's Wedding Planner: Revised for the '90s. Paramus, NJ: Prentice Hall, 1991. By: Susan Tatsui-D'Arcy.

Your Wedding: A Planning Guide. Cincinnati, OH: Saint Anthony Messenger Press, 1991. By: Greg Friedman.

Business Growth and Statistics

"5 things you should know before starting a business" in Black Enterprise (Vol. 29, No. 2, September 1998, p. 66). By: Gerda A. Gallop and Roz Williams-Ayers.

"10 Tips for Success" in Business Start-Ups (Vol. 8, No. 8, August 1996, pp. 74-75). By: Kelli Reyes.

"24th Annual Report on Black Business" in Black Enterprise (Vol. 26 No. 11, June 1996, pp. 103-139). By: Derek T. Dingle.

"The 100 Fastest-Growing Companies: Under Control" in Hispanic Business (Vol. 17, No. 8, August 1995, p. 22). By: Maria Zate.

301 Great Ideas for Using Technology to Grow Your Business. Boston, MA: Inc. Publishing, 1998. By: Phaedra Hise.

"2001: An Entrepreneurial Odyssey" in Entrepreneur (Vol. 27, April 1999, pp. 106-113). By: Geoff Williams.

$10,000-a-Day Business Opportunities: Seminars, Newsletters, Cassettes, Software & More. Lancaster, TX: New Ventures Publishing Group, 1998. By: J. Stephen Lanning.

Action Plans for the Small Business: Growth Strategies for Businesses Wondering Where to Go Next. New York, NY: DBM Publishing, 1995. By: Shailendra Vyakarnam.

Advances in Entrepreneurship, Firm Emergence & Growth. Greenwich, CT: JAI Press, Inc. 1997. By: Jerome A. Katz.

"After the Storm" in Forbes (July 1995, pp. 65-66). By: Gary Samuels.

"The Age of the Gazelle" in Inc. (Vol. 18, No. 7, May 1996, p. 44). By: John Case.

"And Still We Rise" in Black Enterprise (Vol. 26, No. 9, April 1996, p. 18). By: Cliff Hocker.

"Are You Ready to Go Public?" in Nation's Business (Vol. 83, No. 1, January 1995, pp. 30-32). By: Roberta Maynard.

"Are You Trust Worthy?" in Inc. (Vol. 19, No. 12, September 1997, p. 113). By: Jill Andresky Fraser.

"At the Brink" in Inc. (Vol. 17, No. 16, November 1995, pp. 21- 22). By: Rick McCloskey.

"Auto Aftermarket & Business Services" in Income Opportunities (Vol. 34, Issue 1, January/February 1999, p. 32).

"Backyard entrepreneurs expand technology firm" in The Business Journal-Serving Phoenix & the Valley of the Sun (July 24, 1998, p. 26). By: Sean Robinson.

Basic Business Statistics. Paramus, NJ: Prentice Hall, 1995.

"Battling to Be the Big Cheese" in Income Opportunities (Vol. 32, No. 1, January 1997, pp. 14-17, 80). By: Constance Gustke.

"Best of the Best" in Entrepreneur (March 1997, pp. 136, 138-139).

"Better living through chemistry" in Red Herring (May 1998, p. 52). By: Alex Gove.

"The Bloodiest Edge" in Red Herring (May 1998, p. 78). By: Alex Gove.

"Brave New World" in Income Opportunities (Vol. 30, No. 4, April 1995, pp. 30-32, 34-36, 38, 40, 42, 44). By: Dale D. Buss.

"Braving the New World" in Entrepreneur (Vol. 27, No. 1, January 1999, pp. 131-137). By: Scott S. Smith.

"Breaking New Ground" in Income Opportunities (Vol. 31, No. 6, June 1996, pp. 22-25, 64). By: Ed Klimuska.

"Brighter Days" in Entrepreneur (Vol. 23, No. 7, July 1995, p. 16). By: Janean Chun.

"Bringing Up Business" in Entrepreneur (vol. 23, No. 1, January 1995, pp. 124-128). By: Erika Kotite.

"Building Companies to Last" in Inc. (Special Issue: The State of Small Business, February 1996, pp. 83-84, 87-88). By: James C. Collins.

"Business Finally Invests Some Trust in Bank Lending" in Crain's Small Business (October 1995, p. 8). By: Jeffrey McCracken.

"Business and Gravy" in The Red Herring (March 1997, pp. 50-51). By: Luc Hatlestad.

"Business Must Refocus Once It Outgrows Entrepreneur's Control" in Crain's Small Business (October 1995, p. 16). By: Jon Greenawalt.

Business Statistics. St. Louis, MO: Mosby Year Book, Inc. 1996.

Business Statistics of the United States. Lanham, MD: Bernan Press, 1995. By: Courtenay M. Slater

"California, Here We Come!" in Hispanic Business (Vol. 18, No. 5, May 1996, pp. 33-36, 38-39, 42, 44). By: Rick Mendoza.

"Capital City Vending thrives in N.C. by offering premium service" in Vending Times (April 25, 1998, p. 14). By: Emily J. Jed.

"Capital Steps" in Inc. (Vol. 18, No. 2, February 1996, pp. 42-44, 47). By: Jill Andresky Fraser.

"A Cautionary Tale" in Feminist Bookstore News (Vol. 19, No. 4, November/December 1996, pp. 21-23). By: Carol Seajay.

"Celebrating the Nature of Things: entrepreneur grows company after husband's death" in The Business Journal - Serving Milwaukee (Vol. 15, No. 35, May 22, 1998, p. 11). By: Mike Dries.

"Changing of the Guard: B.E. investment banks overview" in Black Enterprise (Vol. 28, No. 11, June 1998, p. 1990). By: Lynette Khalfani.

The Complete Demographic Reference Guide. Marina del Rey, CA: Urban Decision Systems, 1992.

"The Computer in the Dell" in Business Start-Ups (Vol. 8, No. 6, June 1996, pp. 22-27). By: Bob Weinstein.

"Crafts Course" in Entrepreneur (June 1995, pp. 178-180). By: Gayle Sato Stodder.

"Crain's Small Business Index" in Crain's Small Business (Vol. 4, No. 11, November 1996, p. 5).

"Deals on Wheels" in Business Start-Ups (Vol. 10, No. 8, August 1998, pp. 37-40). By: Julie Bawden Davis.

"Demographica" in Crain's Small Business (Vol. 4, No. 11, November 1996, p. 22).

"Dining Differences" in Small Business Opportunities (Vol. 11, No. 2, March 1999, p. 78).

"Downtown" in Inc. (Vol. 19, No. 15, December 21, 1997, p. 102).

"Economic Clout Growing in Florida" in Hispanic Business (Vol. 20, No. 8, September 1998, p. 16). By: Robert Brishetto.

"The Economics of Progress" in Hispanic Business (Vol. 18 No. 9, September 1996, pp. 28-30, 32). By: J. Antonio Villamil.

The Entrepreneurial Process: Economic Growth, Men, Women & Minorities. Westport, CT: Greenwood Publishing Group, Inc. 1997. By: Paul D. Reynolds and Sammis B. White.

"Entrepreneurs Collide: Will Zoning Take Town Downhill?" in Inc. (Vol. 19, No. 5, April 1997, p. 32). By: Joshua Macht.

The Entrepreneur's Guide to Growing Up: Taking Your Small Company to the Next Level. Bellingham, WA: Self-Counsel Press, Inc. 1993. By: Edna Sheedy.

"Entrepreneurs Need To Know How To Manage Their Growth" in Boston Business Journal (Vol. 19, February 19-25, 1999, p. 21). By: Harvy Simkovits.

Every Business Is a Growth Business: How Your Company Can Prosper Year after Year. New York, NY: Random House, Inc. 1998. By: N. Tichy and R. Charan.

"The Fast-Growing 100" in Hispanic Business (Vol. 18, No. 7/8, July/August 1996, pp. 40, 42, 44). By: Maria Zate.

"Fast Track" in Entrepreneur (February 1997, p. 22).

"The Fast Trackers" in Working Woman (March 1995, pp. 44-48, 86). By: Louise Washer.

Faster Company: Building the World's Nuttiest, Turn-on-a-Dime, Home-Grown, Billion Dollar Business. New York, NY: John Wiley & Sons, Inc. 1998. By: Patrick Kelly and John Case.

"A Field Guide to Your Local Economy" in Inc. (Special Issue: The State of Small Business, February 1996, pp. 51-54). By: Joel Garreau.

"Forging New Frontiers" in Black Enterprise (Vol. 26, No. 10, May 1996, pp. 70-72, 74, 76, 78). By: Marjorie Whigham-Desir.

"Get Rich in 1997" in Small Business Opportunities (Vol. 9, No. 1, January 1997, pp. 22-24, 26, 28, 30, 34).

"Global Economy Hinges on 10 nations" in Hispanic Business (Vol. 20, No. 11, December 1998, p. 22). By: Vaughn Hagerty.

"Growing Companies Gain from University Relationships" in Income Opportunities (Vol. 30, No. 4, April 1995, p. 3). By: Patricia Hamilton.

"Growing Pains" in Business Start-Ups (Vol. 9, No. 5, May 1997, pp. 8, 10, 12). By: Carolyn Campbell.

"Growing Pains" in Entrepreneur (November, 1996 pp. 214, 216-217). By: Charlotte Mulhern.

"Growing Pains: Small business owner learns hard lesson" in Washington Business Journal (April 17, 1998, p. 43). By: Marlon Millner.

"Growing Up" in Entrepreneur (July 1996, pp. 124-128). By: Lynn Beresford.

"A Growing Year for Small Business" in Income Opportunities (Vol. 30, No. 10, October 1995, p. 3). By: Heath F. Eiden.

"Growth Happens" in Inc. (Vol. 19, No. 3, March 1997, pp. 68-70, 72-74). By: Robert A. Mamis.

"Growth Moderates Leading into Election" in Crain's Small Business (Vol. 4, No. 11, November 1996, p. 5). By: David Sowerby.

The Growth Strategy: How to Build a New Business into a Successful Enterprise. Encino, CA: Knowledge Exchange, 1997. By: Peter Engel.

"A Guide May Be Needed to Set Up Shop On-Line" in Crain's Detroit Business (Vol. 11, No. 29, July 1995, p. 11).

Guts & Borrowed Money: Straight Talk for Starting & Growing Your Small Business. Austin, TX: Bard Press, 1997. By: Tom S. Gillis.

"Help Wanted" in Inc. (Vol. 19, No. 7, July 20, 1997, pp. 34-36, 40, 42). By: Michael Hopkins.

"Here comes the sun: Milwaukee retiree markets solar ovens to feed poor countries" in The Business Journal - Serving Milwaukee (Vol. 15, No. 32, May 1, 1998, p. 13). By: Carlise Newman.

"Hitting the Wall" in Inc. (Vol. 17, No. 10, July 1995, pp. 21-22). By: James L. Bildner.

"The Hottest Industries for New Business Opportunities" in Black Enterprise (Vol. 25, No. 8, March 1995). By: Carolyn M. Brown, Yolanda Gault, Lloyd Gite, Adrienne Harris, Eric Houston, Dasha Jones and Valencia Roner.

"How to Build an Inc. 500 Company" in Inc. (Vol. 19, No. 15, December 21, 1997, p. 26). By: Marth E. Mangelsdorf.

BIBLIOGRAPHY

"How the Census Bureau Devalues Black Businesses" in Black Enterprise (Vol. 26 No. 11, June 1996, pp. 223-228). By: Margaret C. Simms.

"In the Lead" in Entrepreneur (Vol. 27, No. 1, January 1999, p. 51). By: Christopher D. Lancette.

"In The Money" in Entrepreneur (September 1997, p. 15). By: Fanean Chun.

"The Inc. 500: 15th Annual List" in Inc. (October 1996, pp. 15-16). By: Joshua Hyatt.

"Incubation Period" in Income Opportunities (Vol. 32, No. 1, January 1997, pp. 20-24, 64). By: Dale D. Buss.

"Index" in Crain's Detroit Business (Vol. 5, No. 1, January 1997, p. 22). By: David Sowerby.

Innovation & Growth in an African American Owned Business. New York, NY: Garland Publishing, Inc. 1996. By: Gwendolyn P. Todd.

Introduction to Business Statistics. Ft. Worth, TX: Harcourt Brace College Publishers, 1996.

"Is Bigger Better?" in Working Woman (March 1995, pp. 39-40, 42, 90). By: Louise Washer.

"Is Black Business Paving the Way?" in Black Enterprise (Vol. 26 No. 11, June 1996, pp. 194-202, 206). By: Eric L. Smith.

"Jack of all trades" in The Red Herring (No. 44, July 1997, p. 37). By: Luc Hatlestad.

"John Galt Boulevard, Omaha" in Inc. (Vol. 19, No. 15, December 21, 1997, pp. 100-101). By: Mike Hofman.

"King of franchises" in Houston Business Journal (August 21, 1998, p. A16). By: Laura Elder.

"The Knockout Lesson" in Inc. (Vol. 17, No. 8, June 1995, pp. 21-22). By: Amy Miller.

"L.A. Quakes in the Shadow of Beautiful Downtown Burbank" in Inc. (Vol. 18, No. 18, December 1997, p. 28). By: Joel Kotkin.

"Lancaster County family sticks it out in the trenches" in Central Penn Business Journal (October 9, 1998, p. S11). By: Pamela Rohland.

"Looking for Customers? Pick on Someone Your Own Size" in Inc. (Vol. 19, No. 3, March 1997, p. 22). By: Jerry Useem.

"Making It" in Business Start-Ups (Vol. 10, No. 9, September 1998, pp. 76, 78-80). By: Linda Formichelli.

"Making a Move" in Hispanic Business (Vol. 18, No. 9, September 1996, pp. 42-43). By: Maria Zate.

"The many virtues of 'virtual services'" in Business Week (No. 3595, September 14, 1998, p. S18). By: Ann Zieger.

"Marketing by Mail" in Black Enterprise (Vol. 26 No. 11, June 1996, pp. 275-282). By: Robert W. Bly.

"Masters of Flexibility" in Hispanic Business (Vol. 18, No. 6, June 1996, pp. 62, 64, 66, 68, 70). By: Maria Zate.

"Masters of Improvisation" in Inc. (Vol. 21, February 1999, pp. 83-86). By: Donna Fenn.

Maximizing Small Business Growth: Developing a Bank's Game Plan. Philadelphia, PA: Robert Morris Associates, 1996. By: Charles Wendel.

"Mighty Morphing" in Entrepreneur (November, 1996 p. 16). By: Cynthia E. Griffin.

"A Million and Counting" in Hispanic Business (Vol. 18, No. 7/8, July/August 1996, p. 10). By: Rick Mendosa.

"Minority women set the pace" in Nation's Business (Vol. 86, No. 7, July 1998, p. 47). By: Sharon Nelton.

Modern Business Statistics. Belmont, CA: Wadsworth Publishing Co. 1995. By: George C. Canova.

"Monthly report-September 1998" in Small Business Economic Trends (September 1998, p. CP).

"Multiply Profits with Multiple Businesses" in Income Opportunities (Vol. 33, Vol. 9, November 1998, pp. 16, 20, and 22.). By: Sandra Mardenfeld.

Multiply Your Profits: A Common-Sense Approach for Small to Midsize Businesses. Cary, IL: Inverness Publishing, 1998. By: Richard Peelo.

"The ' Net Investor Link" in Hispanic Business (Vol. 18, No. 7/8, July/August 1996, p. 84). By: Rick Mendosa.

"Networking Works" in Business Start-Ups (Vol. 7, No. 10, October 1995, p. 10). By: Leann Anderson.

"Never Too Small to Manage" in Inc. (Vol. 19, No. 2, February 1997, pp. 56-58, 61). By: David Whitford.

"The new bottom line: the 'one minute manager'" in Entrepreneur (Vol. 26, No. 2, February 1998, p. 127). By: Ken Blanchard.

"A New Loan Option to Bank, Venture Capital" in Crain's Small Business (February 1996, pp. 9-10). By: Jeffrey McCracken.

"New marketing and PR firm targets startups" in Austin Business Journal (September 11, 1998, p. 4). By: Marla Dial.

"The Next Microsoft" in Inc. (Vol. 19, No. 15, December 21, 1997, pp. 68-69). By: Jeffrey L. Seglin.

"Niches That Need Filling" in Hispanic Business (Vol. 19, No. 1, January 1997, pp. 18, 20-22).

"Not Just for the big guys!" in Chief Executive (U.S.) (1998, p. 62). By: Peter Haapaniemi and William R. Hill.

"On Their Own" in Wall Street Journal Special Reports: Small Business (Special Edition) (May 23, 1996, p. R20). By: Jeffrey A. Tannenbaum.

"One-Hit Wonders" in Entrepreneur (Vol. 23, No. 1, January 1995, pp. 258-260, 262, 264). By: Mark Henricks.

"Out of the Ashes" in Entrepreneur (November, 1996, pp. 66, 68). By: Cynthia E. Griffin.

"Part 1: PEOs for CEOs" in Corporate Detroit (Vol. 13, No. 12, December 1995, pp. 23, 64). By: Steven R. Light.

"Partners work up from basement" in Crain's Detroit Business (December 14-20, 1998, p. E19). By: Joseph Serwach.

"Paying for Growth" in Inc. (Vol. 18, No. 14, October 1996, pp. 29-30). By: Norm Brodsky.

"Peer Review" in Entrepreneur (July 1996, p. 18). By: L.B.

"Persistence pays off for photo company" in Tampa Bay Business Journal (July 24, 1998, p. 33). By: Nanette Woitas Holt.

"The personal touch gives lender inroads into market" in Business First-Columbus (June 5, 1998, p. 32). By: Doug Buchanan.

"Power surge" in Entrepreneur (Vol. 26, No. 11, November 1998, p. 140). By: Mark Hendricks.

"Powerful Profits" in Small Business Opportunities (Vol. 11, No. 2, March 1999, p. 18). By: Carla Goodman.

"Preparing for Takeoff" in Red Herring: Going Public (1998, p. 96). By: Bill Davidow.

Profit Zone: How Strategic Business Design Will Lead You to Tomorrow's Profits. New York, NY: John Wiley & Sons, Inc. 1998. By: Adrian J. Slywotsky.

"Promotion Commotion" in Small Business Opportunities (Vol. 8, No. 5, September 1996, p. 56). By: Susan Froetschel.

"Reality check: today's entrepreneur isn't who you think she is" in Working Woman (Vol. 23, No. 7, July-August 1998, p. 32). By: Amanda Walmac.

"Right from the Start" in Small Business Opportunities (Vol. 9, No. 3, May 1997, pp. 20, 42). By: Dr. Sandy Weinberg.

"Sales Through Superior Service" in Business Start-Ups (Vol. 8, No. 8, August 1996, pp. 70-71). By: Donna Clapp.

Send 'Em One White Sock: 67 Outrageously Simple Ideas from Around the World for Building Your Business. New York, NY: The McGraw-Hill Companies, 1998. By: Stan Rapp and Thomas L. Collins.

"Shop Around" in Business Start-Ups (Vol. 10, No. 9, September 1998, pp. 26-29). By: Andrew A. Caffey.

"Shopping for an enterprise" in Black Enterprise (Vol. 29, No. 2, September 1998, p. 75). By: Joyce Jones.

"Sign of the times" in Houston Business Journal (June 12, 1998, p. 27). By: Chris Carroll.

"Sisters, Inc." in Hispanic Business (May 1998, p. 33). By: Joel Russell.

"The Six Secrets of Strategic Growth" in Working Woman (March 1995, pp. 50-51, 78). By: Rhonda M. Abrams.

"Small Biz Can Give Input, Vital Data Via Web Site" in Crain's Small Business (March 1996, p. 3). By: Jeffrey McCracken.

"Small Businesses are Thriving" in Income Opportunities (Vol. 30, No. 1, January 1995, p. 2). By: Eric Barnes.

"Small businesses seek directors" in The Business Journal - Serving Phoenix and the Valley of the Sun (Vol. 17, No. 14, January 23, 1998, p. 45). By: Stephanie Balzer.

"Small Is Beautiful! Big Is Best!" in Inc. (Special Issue: The State of Small Business, February 1996, pp. 39-44, 46, 48-49). By: George Gendron.

"Small firms meet challenges head on" in Industrial Distribution (Vol. 87, July 1998, p. 17). By: Jack Keough.

"Small Talk" in Wall Street Journal Special Reports: Small Business (Special Edition) (May 23, 1996, p. R28). By: Stephanie N. Mehta.

"Small World" in Entrepreneur (Vol. 23, No. 8, August 1995, p. 17). By: Heather Page.

"Something Borrowed" in Entrepreneur (February 1997, p. 26).

"Sounding Board" in Income Opportunities (Vol. 30, No. 6, June 1995, pp. 114, 116). By: Richard J. Maturi.

"A Sporting Chance" in Detroit Free Press (January 1997, pp. 1e-2e). By: Molly Brauer.

"Stage Right" in Entrepreneur (April 1997, pp. 71-73). By: Mark Henricks.

Start, Run & Grow a Successful Small Business. Riverwoods, IL: CCH, Inc. 2nd ed. 1998. By: Susan Jacksach; designed by Tim Kaage; contribution by Martin Bush.

"The Startling Truth About Growth Companies" in Inc. (Vol. 18, No. 7, May 1996, pp. 84-86, 88, 90-92). By: Martha E. Mangelsdorf.

The State of Small Business. New York, NY: Gordon Press Publishers, 1997.

"Stealth Capital" in Inc. (Vol. 19, No. 8, June 1997, pp. 104-105). By: Jill Andresky Fraser.

"Struggling courier firm named Arlington's top small business" in Business Press (Fort Worth, TX) (June 12, 1998, p. 6).

"Success Stories" in Hispanic Business (Vol. 20, No. 11, December 1998, pp. 38-49). By: Joel Russell.

"The Survival Factor" in Hispanic Business (Vol. 17, No. 8, August 1995, pp. 44-46). By: Rick Mendosa.

"Take it from the top" in Working Woman (Vol. 23, No. 7, July-August 1998, p. 40). By: Daniel Gross.

"Temp mentor" in The Kansas City Business Journal (October 2, 1998, p. 3). By: Heather Kirkwood.

"There Are No Simple Businesses Anymore" in Inc. (Special Issue: The State of Small Business, February 1996, pp. 66-79). By: Edward O. Welles.

"Think Small" in Entrepreneur (May 1996, p. 86). By: Jay Conrad Levinson.

"To Advance, Try a Retreat" in Crain's Small Business (January 1996, p. 17). By: Jim Brady.

"Toner firm turns in impressive performance" in Philadelphia Business Journal (June 26, 1998, p. B7). By: Bob Brooke.

"The top 500 women-owned businesses" in Working Woman (Vol. 23, No. 5, May 1998, p. 35). By: Rana Dogar.

"The Top Ten Biz for 1999" in Small Business Opportunities (Vol. 11, No. 1, January 1999, pp. 22-40).

"U.S. Business Data Worst in World—And Getting Worse" in Inc. (Vol. 18, No. 14, October 1996, p. 26). By: Jerry Useem.

Where to Make Money: A Rating Guide to Opportunities in America's Metro Areas. Amherst, NY: Prometheus Books, 1993. By: G. Scott Thomas.

"Where the Money Is" in Hispanic Business (Vol. 19, No. 2, February 1997, p. 60). By: Jonathan J. Higuera.

"Who Needs Growth?" in Inc. (Vol. 18, No. 14, October 1996, p. 90). By: Susan Greco.

"Who's On-Line?" in Inc. (Vol. 19, No. 4, March 1997, pp. 34-39). By: Dan Kennedy.

"Women Putting Themselves on Local Biz Map" in Crain's Detroit Business (Vol. 12, No. 13, March 1996, p. 9). By: Karen Eness Pope.

"Women's Firms Thrive" in Nation's Business (Vol. 86, No. 8, August 1998, p. 38). By: Sharon Nelton.

"The Wonderland Economy" in Inc. (Special Issue: The State of Small Business, February 1996, pp. 14-16, 18-20, 23-24, 26-27, 29). By: John Case.

"York County was firm's best move, chief says" in Central Penn Business Journal (October 9, 1998, p. S9). By: Pamela Rohland.

Business Plans

"3 Factors Help Make a Strategy Successful" in Crain's Detroit Business (Vol. 5, No. 1, January 1997, p. 19). By: Jim Brady.

"5 things you should know before starting a business" in Black Enterprise (Vol. 29, No. 2, September 1998, p. 66). By: Gerda A. Gallop and Roz Williams-Ayers.

Adams Streetwise Complete Business Plan: Create a Business Plan to Finance & Run a New or Existing Business. Holbrook, MA: Adams Media Corporation, 1998. By: Bob Adams.

"Before You Launch Your Biz" in Small Business Opportunities (Vol. 11, May 1999, p. 20). By: Sandy Weinberg.

"Best Laid Plans" in Business Start-Ups (Vol. 7, No. 11, November 1995, p. 7). By: Lynn Norquist.

"The Big Time" in Business Start-Ups (Vol. 10, No. 8, August 1998, pp. 26-29). By: Carla Goodman.

Bizplan Builder Workbook. Cincinnati, OH: South-Western Publishing Co. 1997. By: Jian Software Staff.

Blueprint for Business Objectives. Paramus, NJ: Prentice Hall, 1996. By: Fingar.

"Borrow Time" in Business Start-Ups (Vol. 10, No. 9, September 1998, p. 12). By: Paul Deceglie.

"Business Plan" in Business Start-Ups (Vol. 7, No. 12, December 1995, pp. 8, 10-11). By: Charles Fuller.

Business Plan Handbook. Detroit, MI: Rector Press, Ltd. 1995.

"A Business-Plan Outline" in Crain's Small Business (December 1995, p. 11). By: Jeffrey McCracken.

"Business-Plan Software Streamlines Process" in Crain's Detroit Business (Vol. 5, No. 1, January 1997, p. 17). By: Len Strazewski.

The Business Planner: A Complete Guide to Raising Finances for Your Business. Woburn, MA: Butterworth-Heinemann, 1992. By: Iain Maitland.

Business Planning: An Approach to Strategic Management. Philadelphia, PA: Trans-Atlantic Publications, Inc. 1992. By: Bill Richardson and Roy Richardson.

Business Planning in Four Steps & a Leap. Marquette, MI: Northern Economic Initiatives Corp. 1995. By: Scott Sporte.

The Business Planning Guide: Creating a Plan for Success in Your Own Business. Chicago, IL: Upstart Publishing Co. Inc. Sixth edition, 1992. By: David H. Bangs, Jr.

Business Plans to Manage Day-to-Day Operations: Real-life Results for Small Business Owners and Operators. New York, NY: John Wiley & Sons, Inc. 1993. By: Christopher R. Malburg.

Business Plans That Work for Your Small Business. Riverwoods, IL: CCH, Inc. 1998. By: Susan M. Jacksacke.

"Change of Plans" in Business Start-Ups (Vol. 7, No. 6, June 1995, p. 9). By: Erika Kotite.

"Change of Plans" in Entrepreneur (May 1996, p. 30).

"College Pals Won't Tamper with Success" in Crain's Small Business (Vol. 4, No. 11, November 1996, p. 21). By: Jeffrey McCracken.

The Complete Book of Business Plans: Simple Steps to Writing a Powerful Business Plan. Naperville, IL: Sourcebooks, Inc. 1994. By: Joseph A. Covello and Brian J. Hazelgreen.

Complete Business Management Guide for Kitchen & Bathroom Professionals: Starting & Staying in Business. Hackettstown, NJ: National Kitchen & Bath Assc. 1997. By: Hank Darlington.

Computer Applications for Business Planning: A Practical Hands-On Text. Lancaster, OH: Tangent Publishing, 1995. By: Andrew J. Batchelor.

"Cover Your Assets" in Inc. (Vol. 19, No. 8, June 1997, pp. 107-108). By: Jill Andresky Fraser.

Crafting the Successful Business Plan. Paramus, NJ: Prentice Hall, 1992. By: Erik Hyypia.

"Creating a Family Dynasty" in Hispanic Business (March 1998, p. 52). By: Frank McCoy.

"Credibility Gap" in Income Opportunities (Vol. 32, No. 4, April 1997, pp. 42, 44). By: Dorothy Elizabeth Brooks.

"Danger zone" in Entrepreneur (Vol. 26, No. 11, November 1998, p. 153). By: Brian Ruberry.

"Decide Where to Go Before Drawing a Map" in Crain's Small Business (Vol. 5, No. 4, April 1997, p. 22). By: Jim Brady.

"Do Business Plans Matter?" in Inc. (Vol. 18, No. 2, February 1996, p. 21). By: Mary Baechler.

"The Do's and Don'ts of Writing A Winning Business Plan" in Black Enterprise (Vol. 26, No. 9, April 1996, pp. 114-116, 120, 122). By: Carolyn M. Brown.

"Due Diligence" in Inc. (Vol. 20, No. 2, February 1998, pp. 25-26). By: Norm Brodsky.

Emergency Procedures for the Small Business & Shop: A Guide & Disaster Plan Framework. Springfield, OR: Ritchie Unlimited Publications, 1997. By: Ralph W. Ritchie.

"Entrepreneur Had Better Know Where All the Money's Going" in Crain's Detroit Business (Vol. 5, No. 1, January 1997, p. 15). By: Jerry Balan.

"Entrepreneurs Collide: Will Zoning Take Town Downhill?" in Inc. (Vol. 19, No. 5, April 1997, p. 32). By: Joshua Macht.

The Entrepreneur's Guide to Building a Better Business Plan: A Step-by-Step Approach. New York, NY: John Wiley & Sons, Inc. 1992. By: Harold J. McLaughlin.

The Entrepreneur's Guide to Developing a Basic Business Plan. Northbrook, IL: S. K. Brown Publishing, 1991. By: Chris Stevens.

The Entrepreneur's Guide to Preparing a Winning Business Plan and Raising Venture Capital. Paramus, NJ: Prentice Hall, 1990. By: Keith W. Schilit.

The Ernst and Young Business Plan Guide. New York, NY: John Wiley & Sons, Inc. Second edition, 1993. By: Compiled by Ernst & Young staff.

"Exit Gracefully" in Income Opportunities (Vol. 31, No. 11, November 1996, pp. 32, 34, 36). By: Dorothy Elizabeth Brooks.

Faster Company: Building the World's Nuttiest, Turn-on-a-Dime, Home-Grown, Billion Dollar Business. New York, NY: John Wiley & Sons, Inc. 1998. By: Patrick Kelly and John Case.

"Finding Your Niche" in Business Start-Ups (Vol. 9, No. 4, April 1997, pp. 72, 74). By: Carla Goodman.

"For GMD Studios, it pays to be small" in Orlando Business Journal (May 29, 1998, p. 27). By: Paul Dillion.

"FYI" in Income Opportunities (Vol. 32, No. 1, January 1997).

"Game Plan" in Entrepreneur (Vol. 23, No. 8, August 1995, pp. 38-41). By: David R. Evanson.

"Garbage In, Garbage Out" in Inc. (Vol. 18 , No. 11, August 1996, pp. 41-44). By: Brian McWilliams.

Getting Ready. Bellingham, WA: Self-Counsel Press, Inc. 1991. By: Dan Kennedy.

"How to Determine Your Debt Comfort Zone" in Crain's Small Business (Vol. 4, No. 10, October 1996, p. 21). By: Kevin Reitzloff.

"How to Get Biz Beyond the Start-Up Stage" in Crain's Small Business (June 1996, p. 8). By: Lawrence Gardner.

How to Prepare and Present a Business Plan. New York, NY: Simon & Schuster, Inc. 1992. By: Joseph R. Mancuso.

How to Prepare a Results-Driven Business Plan. New York, NY: AMACOM, 1993. By: Gregory J. Massarella, Patrick D. Zorsch, Daniel D. Jacobson, and Marc J. Rittenhouse.

How to Really Create a Successful Business Plan. Boston, MA: Inc. Publishing, Revised edition, 1994. By: David E. Gumpert.

How to Write a Business Plan 4.4. Berkeley, CA: Nolo Press, 4th ed. 1997. By: Mike McKeever edited by Peri Pakroo.

How to Write a Successful Business Plan: Step-by-Step Guide to Business Success. Interlochen, MI: Lewis & Renn Associates, Inc. 1995. By: Jerre G. Lewis.

How to Write a Winning Business Plan. Paramus, NJ: Prentice Hall, 1990. By: Joseph Mancuso.

Incorporate Your Business: The National Corporation Kit. Carbondale, IL: Nova Publishing Co. 1995. By: Daniel Sitarz.

"Instant Entrepreneurs" in Fortune (November 16, 1998, p. 188).

"It's a Plan" in Entrepreneur (June 1995, pp. 28, 30-31). By: Cheryl J. Goldberg.

"Key Ingredient in Recipe: The Right People" in Crain's Small Business (Vol. 4, No. 11, November 1996, p. 23). By: Jim Brady.

"Keys to Creativity" in Small Business Opportunties (Vol. 1, May 1999, p. 76). By: Art Michaels.

"King of franchises" in Houston Business Journal (August 21, 1998, p. A16). By: Laura Elder.

Launching New Ventures. Chicago, IL: Upstart Publishing Co. Inc. 1995.

"A lending niche helps small firms" in Nation's Business (February 1, 1998, p. 52). By: Joan Pryde.

"Line Forms Even Before Zone Capital Shop Opens" in Crain's Detroit Business (Vol. 12, No. 46, November 1996, pp. 16-17). By: Shekini Gilliam.

"Making a Good Idea Her Own" in The New York Times (September 23, 1998, p. G4). By: Mirta Ojito.

"Many Stop at Oakland's Shop for Business Info" in Crain's Detroit Business (Vol. 12, No. 46, November 1996, p. 17). By: Shekini Gilliam.

"Mapping Your Route" in Business Start-Ups (Vol. 8, No. 12, December 1996, pp. 40, 42-44). By: Lynn H. Colwell.

The Market Planning Guide: Creating a Plan to Successfully Market Your Business, Products or Service. Chicago, IL: Upstart Publishing Co. Inc. 5th ed. 1998. By: David H. Bangs.

"Masters of Improvisation" in Inc. (Vol. 21, February 1999, pp. 83-86). By: Donna Fenn.

"Millennium Meltdown" in Entrepreneur (Vol. 27, No. 1, January 1999, p. 122). By: G. David Doran.

"New marketing and PR firm targets startups" in Austin Business Journal (September 11, 1998, p. 4). By: Marla Dial.

"No More Business as Usual" in Inc. (Vol. 19, No. 16, November 1997, pp. 114,119). By: Donna Fenn.

"Obstacle Course" in Income Opportunities (Vol. 31, No. 11, November 1996, pp. 27-30, 96). By: Dale D. Buss.

The One Page Business Plan: Start with a Vision, Build a Company!. El Sobrante, CA: Rent.A.CFO, 1998. By: James T. Horan, Jr. edited by Rebecca S. Shaw, illustrated by Ruthie Petty, foreword by Tom Peters.

"Picking the Perfect PR Partner" in Black Enterprise (Vol. 29, April 1999, p. 31). By: Roz Ayres-Williams.

"Plan of Action" in Income Opportunities (Vol. 30, No. 7, July 1995, pp. 96, 98, 100). By: Toni Reinhold.

"Plan of Attack" in Inc. (Vol. 18, No. 1, January 1996, pp. 41-44). By: Martha E. Mangelsdorf.

"Plan Can Help Put the Success in Succession" in Crain's Small Business (June 1996, p. 13). By: Don Clayton.

"Plan Of Attack" in Entrepreneur (Vol. 23, No. 8, August 1995, pp. 150, 152-157). By: Excerpted from The Entrepreneur Magazine Small Business Advisor: The One-Stop Information Source for Starting, Managing, and Growing a Small Business by The Entrepreneur Magazine Group.

"Planning for Success" in Business Start-Ups (Vol. 8, No. 3, March 1996, pp. 50, 52-53). By: Lynn L. Norquist.

"Poor Planning Plagues Small Business" in Income Opportunities (Vol. 30, No. 4, April 1995, p. 2). By: Patricia Hamilton.

"Prepare for Frustration You'll Create Exhilaration" in Crain's Small Business (Vol. 4, No. 10, October 1996, p. 19). By: Jim Brady.

Preparing a Successful Business Plan: A Practical Guide for Small Business. Bellingham, WA: Self-Counsel Press, Inc. Second edition, 1993. By: Rodger Touchie.

The Process of Business Planning: A Practical Hands-on Text. Lancaster, OH: Tangent Publishing Tangent Publishing, 1994. By: Andrew J. Batchelor Sr.

"The Pros and Cons of Business Plan Software" in Income Opportunities (Vol. 33, Issue 8, October 1998, p. 53). By: Andre Hinds.

"Putting It Together" in Business Start-Ups (Vol. 8, No. 9, September 1996, pp. 12, 14). By: Ellen DePasquale.

"Right Adds Might When You Write Proposal" in Crain's Small Business (June 1996, p. 16). By: Jim Brady.

"Savvy Partners Weren't Taken to Cleaners" in Crain's Small Business (Vol. 4, No. 9, September 1996, pp. 9, 10). By: Tim Moran.

"SCORE Points to Success" in Black Enterprise (Vol. 25, No. 6, January 1995, p. 38). By: Christina F. Watts.

"The Seven Traps of Strategic Planning" in Inc. (Vol. 18, No. 16, November 1996, pp. 99, 101, 103). By: Joseph C. Picken and Gregory G. Dess.

Small Business Planning Workbook. New York, NY: Clark Boardman Callaghan, 1990. By: John C. Wisdom.

"Smart Small Businesses Versus Spendthrift Washington, D.C." in Boston Business Journal (Vol. 19, February 26-March 4, 1999, p. 29). By: Karen Kerrigan.

Solid Gold Success Strategies for Your Business. New York, NY: AMACOM, 1996. By: Don Taylor.

"Split Decisions" in Income Opportunities (Vol. 31, No. 9, September 1996, pp. 34, 36, 38). By: Diane M. Calabrese.

"Start with Strategic Fundamentals" in Crain's Small Business (September 1995, p. 9). By: Jim Brady.

The Start-up Business Plan. Paramus, NJ: Prentice Hall, 1991. By: William M. Luther.

"Stay the Course" in Inc. (Vol. 19, No. 8, June 1997, pp. 41-42). By: Jack Stack.

"Step 6: Compose a Winning Business Plan" in Business Start-Ups (Vol. 8, No. 10, October 1996, pp. 68, 70). By: Kylo-Patrick Hart.

"Steps to Success" in Crain's Detroit Business (December 14-20, 1998, p. E5). By: Jeffrey McCracken.

Strategic Planning for the New & Small Business. Chicago, IL: Upstart Publishing Co. Inc. 1995. By: Fred L. Fry.

Strategic Planning for the Small Business: Situations, Weapons, Objectives & Tactics. Holbrook, MA: Adams Publishing, 1990. By: Craig Rice.

"Strategies For Spicy Profits" in Black Enterprise (Vol. 29, February 1999, p. 40). By: Deidra-Ann Parrish.

"Street Smarts" in Inc. (Vol. 19, No. 14, October 1998). By: Norm Brodsky.

"Strike Spurs more Political Involvement" in Independent Business (Vol. 9, No. 2, March/April 1998, p. 20).

The Successful Business Plan: Secrets and Strategies. Grants Pass, OR: PSI Research, 1993. By: Rhonda M. Abrams.

Successful Manager's Guide to Business: Seven Practical Steps to Producing Your Best Ever Business Plan. New York, NY: The McGraw-Hill Companies, 1994. By: David Freemantle.

"Surviving the Holidays" in Hispanic Business (Vol. 18, No. 11, November 1996, pp. 60, 62). By: Graham Witherall.

The Total Business Plan: How to Write, Rewrite, and Revise. New York, NY: John Wiley & Sons, Inc. 1994, second edition. By: Patrick D. O'Hara.

Total Business Planning: A Step-by-Step Guide with Forms. New York, NY: John Wiley & Sons, Inc. 1991. By: E. James Burton and W. Blan McBride.

Trademark: How to Name Your Business and Product. Berkeley, CA: Nolo Press, 1992. By: Stephen Elias and Kate McGrath.

"When Your Banker Says No" in Income Opportunities (Vol. 30, No. 11, November 1995, pp. 24-28). By: Randall Kirkpatrick.

"Where's Your Plan" in Hispanic Business (Vol. 20, No. 3, March 1997, p. 46). By: Rick Mendosa.

"Working Capital Woes" in Black Enterprise (Vol. 26 No. 11, June 1996, p. 48). By: Carolyn M. Brown.

Writing Business Plans That Get Results: A Step-by-Step Guide. Lincolnwood, IL: Contemporary Books, Inc. 1991. By: Michael O'Donnell.

Writing a Convincing Business Plan. Hauppauge, NY: Barron's Educational Series, Inc. 1995. By: Art DeThomas.

"You bet your life" in Forbes (Vol. 161, No. 11, June 1, 1998, p. 142). By: Tom Post.

Your Business Plan. Eugene, OR: Oregon Small Business Development Center Network, Revised edition, 1990. By: Dennis J. Sargent.

Your First Business Plan: Learn the Critical Steps to Writing a Winning Business Plan. Naperville, IL: Sourcebooks, Inc. 1995. By: Joseph A. Covello.

Business Vision/Goals

"3 Factors Help Make a Strategy Successful" in Crain's Detroit Business (Vol. 5, No. 1, January 1997, p. 19). By: Jim Brady.

"5 things you should know before starting a business" in Black Enterprise (Vol. 29, No. 2, September 1998, p. 66). By: Gerda A. Gallop and Roz Williams-Ayers.

"2001: An Entrepreneurial Odyssey" in Entrepreneur (Vol. 27, April 1999, pp. 106-113). By: Geoff Williams.

"Above and Beyond" in Entrepreneur (February 1997, pp. 84-86). By: Robert McGarvey.

"Act of Courage" in Business Start-Ups (Vol. 8, No. 6, June 1996, pp. 14, 16). By: Carolyn Z. Lawrence.

"Added Attraction" in Entrepreneur: Buyer's Guide to Franchise and Business Opportunities (Vol. 22, No. 11, 1995, pp. 36, 38-40). By: Guen Sublette.

"The Affair" in Inc. (Vol. 18, No. 16, November 1996, pp. 35, 37). By: Ichak Adizes.

Aiming Higher: 25 Stories of How Companies Prosper by Combinig Sound Management & Social Vision. New York, NY: AMACOM, 1996. By: David Bollier.

"The Art & Smarts of the Deal" in Corporate Detroit (Vol. 13, No. 12, December 1995, p. 49). By: Charles Rothstein.

"Asking for Directions" in Business Start-Ups (Vol. 8, No. 2, December 1996, pp. 16, 18-19). By: Johanna S. Billings.

"Back To The Future" in Entrepreneur (Vol. 23, No. 1, January 1995, pp. 238-242, 245). By: Robert McGarvey.

Benchmarking for Best Practices: How to Define, Locate, and Emulate the Best in the Business. New York, NY: The McGraw-Hill Companies, 1995. By: Christopher E. Bogan and Michael M. English.

"The Best Of Times" in Entrepreneur (Vol. 24, No. 4, April 1996, pp. 139-142). By: Mark Henricks.

"Bright Ideas" in Business Start-Ups (Vol. 7, No. 8, August 1995, pp. 50, 52-54, 57). By: Bob Weinstein.

"Building Companies to Last" in Inc. (Special Issue: The State of Small Business, February 1996, pp. 83-84, 87-88). By: James C. Collins.

"Business Brainstorms" in Business Start-Ups (Vol. 9, No. 3, March 1997, pp. 8, 10). By: Carolyn Campbell.

"Business Must Refocus Once It Outgrows Entrepreneur's Control" in Crain's Small Business (October 1995, p. 16). By: Jon Greenawalt.

"Businesses Needn't Be Related to Construction" in Crain's Small Business (Vol. 5, No. 3, March 1997, p. 11). By: Jeffrey McCracken.

"By the Book" in Entrepreneur (June 1995, pp. 141-145). By: Jane Easter Bahls.

"Choose Your Vehicle" in Business Start-Ups (Vol. 8, No. 12, December 1996, pp. 24, 26-27). By: Lin Grensing-Pophal.

Corporate Internet Planning Guide: Aligning Internet Strategy with Business Goals. New York, NY: Van Nostrand Reinhold, 1997. By: Richard Gascoyne.

"Creating a Family Dynasty" in Hispanic Business (March 1998, p. 52). By: Frank McCoy.

"Creativity at the Edge of Chaos" in Working Woman (February 1997, pp. 47-51, 53). By: Joseph Marshall.

"Credit Card Capitalism" in Hispanic Business (March 1998, p. 40). By: Joel Russell.

"Destination Success" in Business Start-Ups (Vol. 8, No. 12, December 1996, p. 50). By: Carla Goodman.

"Don't Hang Up!" in Independent Business (Vol. 9, No. 3, May/June 1998, pp. 32-33, 36).

"Entrepreneurial envy" in Forbes (Vol. 162, No. 1, July 6, 1998, p. 40).

"Everything According to Plan" in INC. (Vol. 17, No. 3, March 1995, pp. 79-85). By: Jay Finegan.

"An exploration into home-based businesses" in Journal of Small Business Management (Vol. 36, No. 2, April 1998, p. 33). By: Loran Sanchez Soldressen, Susan S. Fiorito, and Yan He.

"Forging New Frontiers" in Black Enterprise (Vol. 26, No. 10, May 1996, pp. 70-72, 74, 76, 78). By: Marjorie Whigham-Desir.

"Fueling Up" in Business Start-Ups (Vol. 8, No. 12, December 1996, pp. 46, 48). By: Carla Goodman.

"Go for the Goal" in Entrepreneur (Vol. 26, Issue 12, December 1998, p. 112). By: Dennis Rodkin.

Goals and Goal Setting. Menlo Park, CA: Crisp Publications, Inc. By: Larrie Rouillard.

"Going It Alone" in Newsweek (April 1996, pp. 50-51). By: Ellyn E. Spragins and Steve Rhodes.

"Got Motivation" in Business Start-Ups (Vol. 11, No. 1, January 1999, p. 57). By: Jennifer Haupt.

"Ground Zero" in Entrepreneur (December 1996, p. 18). By: Janean Chun.

"Growing Strong" in Income Opportunities (Vol. 31, No. 6, June 1996, pp. 30, 32, 34). By: Dorothy Elizabeth Brooks.

"High-Technology Horizon" in Corporate Detroit (Vol. 14, No. 4, April 1996, pp. 27-29). By: Kevin J. Lamiman.

"Hiring The Best" in Inc. (Vol. 21, February 1999, pp. 29-30). By: Norm Brodsky.

How to Succeed in Employee Development: Moving from Visiom to Results. New York, NY: The McGraw-Hill Companies, 1996. By: Edward Moorby.

"The Inc. 500: 15th Annual List" in Inc. (October 1996, pp. 15-16). By: Joshua Hyatt.

"Independents Need a 'Big Picture' Person" in Crain's Small Business (Vol. 5, No. 2, February 1997, p. 22). By: Jim Brady.

"Journey of a Thousand Miles" in Business Start-Ups (Vol. 8, No. 12, December 1996, p. 4). By: Carolyn Z. Lawrence.

"Just a Suggestion" in Entrepreneur (December 1996, p. 40). By: Jacquelyn Lynn.

"Just Their Luck" in Entrepreneur (Vol. 23, No. 2, February 1995, pp. 120, 122-25). By: Gayle Sato Stodder.

"Laying out Firm's Vision Isn't Mission Impossible" in Crain's Small Business (Vol. 5, No. 4, April 1997, p. 11). By: Lawrence Gardner.

"Like Pulling Teeth" in Hispanic Business (Vol. 18, No. 6, June 1996, pp. 138, 140). By: Graham Witherall.

Managing Performance: Goals, Feedback, Coaching, Recognition. Brookfield, VT: Ashgate Publishing Co. 1997. By: Jenny Hill.

"Marketing on a Shoestring" in Small Business Opportunities (Vol. 8, No. 6, November 1996, pp. 22-24, 26, 28, 30, 32, 34). By: Jeanie Crane.

"Measuring Up" in Entrepreneur (November, 1996 pp. 168-173). By: Robert McGarvey.

"Motivating Statistics" in Business Start-Ups (Vol. 8, No. 8, August 1996, p. 4). By: Karin Moeller.

"A Nation of Owners" in Inc. (Special Issue: The State of Small Business, February 1996, pp. 89-91). By: William Bridges.

The New Business Landscape: Taking Your Business into the Twenty-First Century. Waterbury, VT: The Potlatch Group, Inc. 1997. By: Susan E. Mehrtens.

"The Not-Too-Distant Future" in Business Start-Ups (Vol. 9, No. 1, January 1997, pp. 36, 38, 40-42). By: Kris Neri.

"A Passion for Forecasting" in Inc. (Vol. 19, No. 16, November 1997, pp. 37-38). By: Jack Stack.

"Picking the Perfect PR Partner" in Black Enterprise (Vol. 29, April 1999, p. 31). By: Roz Ayres-Williams.

"Planning for Profits" in Income Opportunities (Vol. 33, Issue 10, December 1998, pp. 60-61). By: Louis Hohenstein.

"A Principal's Principles" in Hispanic Business (April 1998, p. 30). By: Andrea Siedsma.

"Q & A" in Performance (September 1995, pp. 12-16).

"Say When" in Inc. (Vol. 17, No. 2, February 1995, pp. 19-20). By: Steven L. Marks.

"Seize the Day" in Income Opportunities (Vol. 32, No. 1, January 1997, pp. 32, 34, 36, 66). By: Dorothy Elizabeth Brooks.

"Small Like Me" in Wall Street Journal Special Reports: Small Business (Special Edition) (May 23, 1996, p. R31). By: John Buskin.

"Small Talk" in Wall Street Journal Special Reports: Small Business (Special Edition) (May 23, 1996, p. R28). By: Stephanie N. Mehta.

"Sounding Board" in Income Opportunities (Vol. 30, No. 6, June 1995, pp. 114, 116). By: Richard J. Maturi.

"Spotlight on Small Business" in Independent Business (Vol. 9, No. 3, May/June 1998, pp. 16-17).

"Start Your Engines" in Business Start-Ups (Vol. 8, No. 12, December 1996, pp. 6, 9). By: Kylo-Patrick Hart.

"Startups: The Open-Source Business Model has VCs Baffled" in Red Herring (No. 63, February 1999, p. 56). By: Brian E. Taptich.

"Staying Alive" in Entrepreneur (Vol. 23, No. 3, March 1995, pp. 114-118). By: Robert McGarvey.

"Steps to Analyze and Control Your Cash" in Crain's Small Business (Vol. 5, No. 3, March 1997, p. 8). By: Lawrence Gardner.

"Stonyfield Farm chief named SBA's top businessperson" in New Hampshire Business Review (April 10, 1998, p. 3).

"Stress reduction and the small business" in SAM Advanced Management Journal (Vol. 63, No. 1, Winter 1998, p. 27). By: John H. Harris and Lucy A. Arendt.

"Tapping Creativity" in Exhibitor Times (Vol. 4, No. 2, February 1996, pp. 40-43). By: Lorraine Denham and Heather Ransford.

"Think About Where You Want to Go, How to Get There" in Crain's Small Business (Vol. 4, No. 9, September 1996, p. 18). By: Jim Brady.

"Time to Make '97's Business Resolutions" in Crain's Detroit Business (Vol. 5, No. 1, January 1997, p. 22). By: David Sowerby.

"Tomorrow Land" in Entrepreneur (Vol. 24, No. 2, February 1996, pp. 135-138). By: Robert McGarvey.

"Turn It On" in Entrepreneur (November 1996, pp. 154-158, 161). By: Robert McGarvey.

"Veridicom wants your fingerprints to be your password" in Red Herring (No. 62, January 1999, p. 30). By: Anna S. Semansky.

Vision: How Leaders Develop It, Share It, & Sustain It. New York, NY: The McGraw-Hill Companies, 1993. By: Joseph V. Quigley.

"What Does Business Really Want from Governments?" in Inc. (Special Issue: The State of Small Business, February 1996, pp. 92-103). By: Tom Richman.

"When Slow and Steady Wins the Race" in Inc. (Vol. 18, No. 17, November 1996, pp. 72-73, 76). By: Jeffrey Zygmont.

"With Luck, This Biz Will Go Down the Toilet" in Inc. (Vol. 19, No. 5, April 1997, p. 21). By: Phaedra Hise.

Christmas Decoration Store

"Answers toYour Small-Business Questions" in Business Start-Ups (Vol. 8, No. 7, July 1996, p. 6). By: Haidee Jezek.

Christmas Crafts. Danbury, CT: Franklin Watts, Inc. 1994. By: Judith H. Corwin. "Open Season" in Business Start-Ups (Vol. 7, No. 9, September 1995, pp. 68, 70-71). By: Carla Goodman.

"Season's Greetings" in Small Business Opportunities (Vol. 7, No. 1, January 1995, p. 60). By: Carla Goodman.

Compact Disc/Record Store

"20-Year Record Explosion Thrives as Last Small Chain in N.Y." in Billboard (Vol. 107, No. 4, January 28, 1995, p. 66). By: Karen Bruno.

CD Packaging and Graphics. 1994. By: Ken Pfeifer.

CD Review Digest Annual. 1992.

The Compact Disc Handbook. Second edition, 1992. By: Ken C. Pohlmann.

Goldmine's Price Guide to Collectible Record Albums. Third edition, 1993. By: Neal Umphred.

The Grove Press Guide to the Blues on CD. 1993. By: Frank J. Hadley.

"High Notes" in Entrepreneur (Vol. 23, No. 7, July 1995, p. 196). By: Heather Page.

Music Business Handbook and Career Guide. 1990. By: David Baskerville.

"Nowhere Men" in Inc. (Vol. 18, No. 8, June 1996, pp. 63-69). By: John Grossman.

The Official Price Guide to Compact Discs. 1994. By: Jerry Osborne.

Opera on CD: The Essential Guide to the Best CD Recordings of 100 Operas. 1995. By: Alan Blyth.

"Plane Fare" in Working Woman (Vol. 22, No. 9, September, 1997, p. 17). By: Cathleen Curran.

"Rap, Vinyl Fans Boogie to Columbus' Groove Shack" in Billboard (Vol. 107, No. 1, January 7, 1995, p. 78). By: Pat Hadler.

"Schoolhouse Rock" in Entrepreneur (Vol. 23, No. 1, January 1995, p. 291). By: Leah Ingram.

"Spin City" in Business Start-Ups (Vol. 11, No. 1, January 1999, p. 50). By: Michelle Prather.

World Beat: A Listener's Guide to Contemporary World Music on CD. 1992. By: Peter Spencer.

The World's Largest Record Catalogue: A Guide to Shopping for Compact Discs, Records and Cassettes Via Mail Order. 1992.

Concession Stand Business

"Almond Joy: Smell of Success Really Can Be Sweet" in Crain's Small Business (Vol. 5, No. 3, March 1997, p. 6). By: Dave Guilford.

"Flying High" in Entrepreneur (Vol. 23, No. 12, November 1995, p. 15). By: Cynthia E. Griffin.

"Lattes 'n Libraries" in The Bottom Line (Vol. 11, No. 3, July 1998, p. 97).

"Money Grows On Trees" in Small Business Opportunities (Vol. 7, No. 1, January 1995, pp. 68-69). By: Mary Ann Spicer Mohring.

"Open Season" in Business Start-Ups (Vol. 7, No. 9, September 1995, pp. 68, 70-71). By: Carla Goodman.

"Sold As Ice" in Business Start-Ups (Vol. 10, No. 9, September 1998, p. 98). By: Shara Lessley.

"Top 10 Businesses for 1996" in Business Start-Ups (Vol. 8, No. 1, January 1996, pp. 22-24, 26, 28, 30). By: Karin Moeller.

"Wealth and Health" in Small Business Opportunities (Vol. 7, No. 1, January 1995, p. 74). By: Norman Darden.

Consultants

"5 things you should know before starting a business" in Black Enterprise (Vol. 29, No. 2, September 1998, p. 66). By: Gerda A. Gallop and Roz Williams-Ayers.

"Adapt or Die" in Red Herring: Guide to Professional Services 1999 (1999, p. 46). By: Janet Kettlehut.

"Advice-For-Hire Not Just for Big Businesses" in Crain's Small Business (June 1996, p. 10). By: Fred Leeb and Eric Weiss.

"All for One" in Crain's Small Business (Vol. 4, No. 10, October 1996, p. 1). By: Kimberly Lifton.

Applied Strategic Planning: The Consultant's Kit. 1992. By: Timothy M. Nolan, Leonard D. Goodstein and J. William Pfeiffer.

Be Your Own Consultant: 188 Ways to Improve Your Business Operation. 1996. By: Irving Burstiner.

"Been there, done that" in Business Start-Ups (Vol. 11, No. 1, January 1999, p. 29). By: Sean M. Lyden.

Budgeting for a Small Business. 1993. By: Terry Dickey.

The Business of Consulting: The Basics & Beyond. 1998. By: Elaine Biech.

"Buyers should not just rubber-stamp a deal" in Crain's Detroit Business (December 14-20, 1998, p. E14). By: Andrew Goldberg.

"Can You Say Profits?" in Business Start-Ups (Vol. 10, No. 10, October 1998, pp. 58, 59-61). By: Joan Retsinas.

Client-Centered Consulting: A Practical Guide for Internal Advisers and Trainers. 1992. By: Peter Cockman.

The Complete Guide to Consulting Success. 3rd ed. 1997. By: Howard L. Shenson.

"Computer consultants starting 'one-stop' shop" in Business First-Louisville (August 3, 1998, p. 1). By: Rick Redding.

Confronting the Experts. 1996. By: Brian Martin.

"Consultant In A Box" in Entrepreneur (Vol. 27, April 1999, pp. 60-63). By: Cassandra Cavanah.

The Consultant's Calling: Bringing Who You Are to What You Do. 1992. By: Geoffrey M. Bellman.

The Consultant's Guide to Hidden Profits: The 101 Most Overlooked Strategies for Increased Earnings & Growth. 1992. By: Herman R. Holtz.

The Consultant's Guide to Proposal Writing: How to Satisfy Your Clients and Double Your Income. Second edition, 1990. By: Herman Holtz.

Consultant's Manual: A Complete Guide to Building a Successful Consulting Practice. 1994. By: Thomas L. Greenbaum.

The Consultant's Survival Guide. 1997. By: Marsha Lewin.

Consultation Skills for Health Care Professionals: How to Be an Effective Consultant within Your Organization. 1990. By: Francis L. Ulschak and Sharon Snowantle.

The Contract and Fee-Setting Guide for Consultants and Professionals. 1990. By: Howard L. Shenson.

"Corporate Universities For Small Companies" in Inc. (Vol. 21, February 1999, pp. 95-96). By: Donna Fenn.

"Dancing To A Different Beat" in Black Enterprise (Vol. 29, February 1999, pp. 91-98). By: Caroline V. Clarke.

"Enlisting a Coach to Boost Your Game" in Nation's Business (December 1998, p. 36). By: Dale D. Buss.

"Fast Forward, Garbage Guru" in Working Woman (January 1997, p. 18). By: Kambiz Foroohar.

"Fast Forward, Up & Comers" in Working Woman (January 1997, p. 20).

"For Sale: Management Expertise from Small Companies" in Inc. (Vol. 19, No. 2, March 1997, p. 26). By: Jerry Useem.

"Get a Clue" in Business Start-Ups (Vol. 10, No. 10, October 1998, p. 40). By: Pamela Rohland.

"Get It Together" in Business Start-Ups (Vol. 11, No. 1, January 1999, p. 16). By: G. David Doran.

"Get Rich in '95" in Small Business Opportunities (Vol. 7, No. 1, January 1995, pp. 20, 22, 24, 26, 28, 30, 32, 34, 36, 38-40, 42-45). By: Cheryl Rogers, et al.

"Getting engineers a game plan for success" in San Antonio Business Journal (July 17, 1998, p. 32). By: Tricia L. Silva.

"A Glass Act" in Entrepreneur (Vol. 27, No. 1, January 1999, p. 54). By: Laura Tiffany.

Going Solo: Developing a Home-Based Consulting Business from the Ground Up. 1997. By: William J. Bond.

"Good Advice" in Income Opportunities (Vol. 30, No. 4, April 1995, pp. 116-117). By: Richard J. Maturi.

"Got Motivation" in Business Start-Ups (Vol. 11, No. 1, January 1999, p. 57). By: Jennifer Haupt.

Guide to Small Business Consulting Engagements. 3 vols. 1998. By: Douglas R. Carmichael, Don Pallais, Cherie W. Shipp, Glenn J. Vice and Sharon Armendariz.

"Guiding Light" in Business Start-Ups (Vol. 10, No. 8, August 1998, p. 96). By: Karen Axelton.

"Here Comes the Profits" in Business Start-Ups (Vol. 10, No. 9, September 1998, pp. 66, 68-69). By: Marcie Geffner.

High Income Consulting: How to Build & Market Your Professional Practice. 2nd ed. 1997. By: Tom Lambert.

"High Tech Help" in Independent Business (Vol. 9, No. 2, March/April 1998, pp. 42-45). By: Kirk Kirksey.

"Hot Stuff" in Entrepreneur (Vol. 27, No. 1, January 1999, pp. 116-121).

How to Be a Consultant. 1991. By: Sally Garratt.

How to Become a Successful Consultant in Your Own Field. 1991, third edition. By: Hubert Bermont.

How to Get Started in Your Own Consulting Practice. 1998. By: Herman R. Holtz.

How to Make It Big as a Consultant. Second edition, 1993. By: William A. Cohen.

How to Make at Least $100,000 Every Year as a Successful Consultant in Your Own Field. 1992. By: Jeffrey Lant.

How to Select and Use Consultants: A Client's Guide. 1993. By: Milan Kubr.

How to Succeed as an Independent Consultant. 1993. By: Herman R. Holtz.

"Independent Contractor Status Still Undecided" in Independent Business (Vol. 9, No. 2, March/April 1998, p. 44).

Inside the Technical Consulting Business: Launching & Building Your Independent Practice. 3rd ed. 1997. By: Harvey Kaye.

"Just in Case" in Independent Business (Vol. 10, March-April 1999, pp. 48-49). By: Carla Goodman.

"Keep 'em Coming Back for More" in Business Start-Ups (Vol. 9, No. 1, January 1997, pp. 70, 72). By: Carla Goodman.

"Legal Aid" in Business Start-Ups (Vol. 7, No. 2, February 1995, pp. 78, 80-81). By: Sue Clayton.

Management Consulting: Theory & Tools for Small Business Interventions. 1998. By: Porth and Saltis.

Million Dollar Consulting: The Professional's Guide to Growing a Practice. 2nd ed. 1997. By: Alan Weiss.

"Never Too Small to Manage" in Inc. (Vol. 19, No. 2, February 1997, pp. 56-58, 61). By: David Whitford.

"New plans offer legal insurance" in The Business Journal - Serving Phoenix & the Valley of the Sun (January 23, 1998, p. 45). By: Angela Mull.

"No-cost (and Low-cost) Consulting" in Occupational Hazards (Vol. 57, No. 1, January 1995, pp. 59-63). By: Mark S. Kuhar.

"One Stop Capital Shop Not Quite Ready" in Crain's Detroit Business (Vol. 11, No. 24, June 12-18, 1996, p. 12). By: Michael Goodin.

"Pieces of Advice" in Inc. (Vol. 17, No. 6, May 1995, pp. 57-60, 62).

"Right from the Start" in Small Business Opportunities (Vol. 10, No. 6, November 1998, p. 10). By: Dorothy Elizabeth Brooks.

"Road Show" in Independent Business (Vol. 9, No. 3, May/June 1998, p. 23).

Selecting and Working with Consultants. By: Thomas J. Ucko.

"Shoestring Start-Ups" in Small Business Opportunities (Vol. 9, No. 6, November 1997, pp. 22-24, 26, 28, 30-32).

The Six Figure Consultant: How to Start (or Jump-Start) Your Consulting Career & Earn $100,000 a Year. 1998. By: Robert W. Bly.

Small-Business Consulting. 1994. By: Hugh Arnold.

"Southfield Company Handles Botsford Data" in Crain's Detroit Business (Vol. 13, No. 8, February/March 1997, p. 16). By: David Barkholz.

Start & Run a Successful Independent Consulting Business. 1997. By: Douglas B. Hoyt.

"Stax Research Finds Niche as Middle-level Consultants" in Boston Business Journal (Vol. 19, February 19-25, 1999, p. 7). By: Chris Mahoney.

"The CEO style" in Black Enterprise (Vol. 29, No. 1, August 1998, p. 111). By: Bevolyn Williams-Harold.

"Want to be a big-time consultant" in Black Enterprise (Vol. 28, No. 11, June 1998, p. 273). By: Hal Karp.

"What to Consider When Seeking Outside Advice" in Crain's Small Business (Vol. 4, No. 10, October 1996, pp. 12-13). By: Lawrence Gardner.

Entrepreneurship on the Web

101 One Hundred One Successful Businesses You Can Start on the Internet. New York, NY: John Wiley & Sons, Inc. 2nd ed. 1997. By: Daniel S. Janal.

121 One Hundred Twenty One Internet Businesses You Can Start from Your Home: A Guide to Starting a Business Online. Brooklyn, NY: Actium Publishing, Inc. 1997. By: Ron Gielgun.

"All in One" in Independent Business (Vol. 9, No. 7, November/December 1998, pp. 36-38). By: Pam Froman.

"Alternative Investments" in Black Enterprise (Vol. 27, No. 3, October 1996, p. 50). By: Glenn Jeffers.

"At Your Fingertips" in Business Start-Ups (Vol. 11, No. 1, January 1999, p. 24). By: Paul DeCeglie.

"Banner Days Ahead" in Red Herring: Guide to Professional Services 1999 (1999, pp. 8-10). By: Lauren Barack.

"Beached Dale" in Red Herring (Vol. 56, July 1998, p. 60). By: Alex Grove.

"Beastie Bandwidth" in Red Herring (No. 62, January 1999, pp. 56-57). By: Alex Gove.

"BellSouth's 5 Steps to Internet Business" in Income Opportunities (Vol. 33, Issue 10, December 1998, p. 16).

"Big Blue Horizons" in Hispanic Business (Vol. 18, No. 6, June 1996, p. 126). By: Rick Mendosa.

"Big Deal" in The Red Herring (September 1996, pp. 51-52, 54, 56). By: Andrew P. Madden.

"Bill Guru" in Red Herring (No. 60, November 1998, p. 76). By: Luc Hatlestad.

"The Birth of a Web Page 'Empire'" in Feminist Bookstore News (Vol. 19, No. 5, January/February 1997, pp. 25-28). By: Lee Anne Phillips.

"Boss wanted" in Forbes (Vol. 62, October 19, 1998, p. 118). By: Stephan Herrera.

"Buddies in Business" in Business Start-Ups (Vol. 11, April 1999, pp. 52-57). By: Geoff Williams.

"Building A Better Website: The Top 7 Tips For Business Owners" in Black Enterprise (Vol. 29, February 1999, p. 49-50). By: Rebecca Frances Rohan.

"Building a better website: Top mistakes of business websites" in Black Enterprise (Vol. 29, March 1999, p. 41). By: Rebecca Frances Rohan.

"Bulletin Board" in Inc. (Vol. 19, No. 9, August 17, 1997, p. 22). By: John Hagel III and Arthur G. Armstrong.

"Bull's-eye" in Entrepreneur (Vol. 27, No. 1, January 1999, p. 56). By: Melissa Campanelli.

Burn Rate: How I Survived the Gold Rush Years on the Internet. New York, NY: Simon & Schuster Trade, 1998. By: Michael Wolff.

"Call Collect" in Red Herring (No. 59, October 1998, p. 102). By: Alex Gove.

"Calling All Cybercustomers!" in Independent Business (Vol. 8, No. 1, Jan./Feb. 1997, p. 46). By: Eric J. Adams.

"Catch the Wave" in Business Start-Ups (Vol. 11, March 1999, pp. 48-51). By: G. David Doran.

"Chain Gang" in Red Herring (No. 63, February 1999, p. 24). By: Alex Gove.

"Chief Executive" in Red Herring (No. 59, October 1998, p. 144). By: Jason Pontin.

"Commerce by Design" in Red Herring (No. 63, February 1999, pp. 82-83). By: Luc Hatlestad.

"Content and its Civilization" in Red Herring (No. 63, February 1999, p. 84). By: Blaise Zerega.

"Contest Pool" in Independent Business (Vol. 9, No. 7, November/December 1998, pp. 44-45).

"Cyber Safety" in Entrepreneur (Vol. 27, April 1999, p. 40). By: Claire Tristram.

Doing Business on the Internet: How to Use the New Technology to Win a Competitive Edge. Philadelphia, PA: Trans-Atlantic Publications, Inc. 1997. By: Graham Jones.

"Don't Get Trapped" in Hispanic Business (Vol. 19, No. 1, January 1997, p. 46). By: Rick Mendosa.

"Drag and Click" in Crain's Small Business (Vol. 5, No. 2, February 1997, p. 3). By: Jeffrey McCracken.

"Drawing a Bead on Profits" in Income Opportunities (Vol. 33, Issue 10, December 1998, p. 18). By: Elizabeth Marie deMorest.

"E banking" in Independent Business (Vol. 9, No. 7, November/December 1998, pp. 28-30).

"E-legal; Educate Your Employees on the Legal Aspect of E-mail" in Entrepreneur (Vol. 26, Issue 12, December 1998, p. 90). By: Jacquelyn Lynn.

"The 'E' List" in Entrepreneur (Vol. 26, Issue 12, December 1998, p. 46). By: Melissa Campanelli.

"The E-Mail Edge" in Income Opportunities (Vol. 31, No. 9, October 1996, pp. 48, 50, 52,). By: Laura Klepacki.

"E-mail Etiquette" in Entrepreneur (September 1997, pp. 132,134-137). By: Calvin Sun.

"E-Ticket" in Entrepreneur (Vol. 27, No. 1, January 1999, p. 98). By: Jay Conrad Levinson.

"Easy E-Marketing" in Independent Business (Vol. 8, No. 1, Jan./Feb. 1997, p. 40). By: Pam Froman.

"Electronic Commerce Becoming a Taxing Issue for Small Business" in Independent Business (Vol. 9, No. 2, March/April 1998, p. 47).

"Entrepreneurial Spirit Awards" in Hispanic Business (Vol. 18, No. 12, December 1996, pp. 26, 28, 30, 34, 36, 38). By: Maria Zate.

"Free Mail Explosion" in Red Herring (No. 55, June 1998, pp. 63-65). By: Luc Hatlestad.

"Get With It!" in Entrepreneur (Vol. 26, Issue 12, December 1998, p. 10). By: Rieva Lesonsky.

"Getting Caught in the Web of On-Line Information" in Exhibitor Times (Vol. 4, No. 1, January 1996, pp. 38-39). By: Valerie A.M. Demetros.

"Getting the Most from the Web" in Crain's Small Business (July 1996, p. 8). By: Jeffrey McCracken.

"Giving Birth to a Web Business" in The New York Times (October 15, 1998, p. G5). By: Debra Nussbaum.

"Going Fat With Your Internet Connection" in Income Opportunities (Vol. 33, Issue 8, October 1998, p. 14).

"Going My Way?" in Entrepreneur (December 1997, p. 22). By: Heather Page.

"Grand Illusions" in Inc. (Vol. 19, No. 9, August 17, 1997, pp. 35-36). By: Moe Meyerson.

"Hat Trick" in Red Herring (Vol. 56, July 1998, p. 45). By: Brian E. Taptich.

"Have Modem Will Travel" in Black Enterprise (Vol. 29, April 1999, p. 40). By: Tariq K. Muhammad.

"He Wants PC Users to Face the Music" in Crain's Small Business (Vol. 5, No. 3, March 1997, p. 15). By: Jeffrey McCracken.

"Here we are; come and get it" in Forbes (Vol. 162, No. 2, July 27, 1998, p. 79).

"The High-Tech 50" in Hispanic Business (Vol. 18, No. 7/8, July/August 1996, p. 36). By: Maria Zate.

"Home Sweet Home" in Independent Business (Vol. 8, No. 1, Jan./Feb. 1997, pp. 30-32). By: Kirk Kirksey.

"Hot Opportunity of the Month" in Income Opportunities (Vol. 31, No. 5, May 1996, p. 6). By: Stephanie Jeffrey.

"How Do You Say Apple?" in Hispanic Business (Vol. 19, No. 1, January 1997, p. 47). By: Rick Mendosa.

"Idea Man" in Hits (Winter 1997, pp. 18-22). By: Alex Gove.

"In the Black" in Business Start-Ups (Vol. 10, No. 8, August 1998, p. 76). By: G. David Doran.

"Information, Please" in Entrepreneur (September 1997, p. 24). By: Robert McGarvey.

"Information Superhighway May Be a Dead End" in Crain's Small Business (June 1996, p. 12). By: Scott Segal.

"Internet Resources" in Small Business Opportunities (Vol. 9, No. 3, May 1997, pp. 54, 56). By: Lin Grensing-Pophal.

"Intranets on a shoestring" in Computerworld (Vol. 32, No. 40, October 5, 1998). By: Christopher Lindquist.

"Invisible & loving it" in Business Week (No. 3598, October 5, 1998, p. 124). By: Roger O. Crockett.

"Is the Internet feasible and profitable for small businesses" in SAM Advanced Management Journal (Vol. 63, No. 3, Summer 1998, p. 20). By: Amir M. Hormozi, William T. Harding, and Utpal Bose.

"Jockeying for Position" in Inc. (Vol. 19, No. 9, August 17, 1997, p. 21). By: Sarah Schafer.

"Judge and Journalist" in Red Herring (No. 60, November 1998, pp. 64-68). By: Alex Gove.

"Keep an Eye on Internet Taxes" in Independent Business (Vol. 9, No. 4, July/August 1998, p. 12).

"Keep it Simple" in Business Start-Ups (Vol. 10, No. 10, October 1998, p. 7). By: Donna Chambers.

Launching a Business on the Web. Indianapolis, IN: Que, 3rd ed. 1997. By: David Cook.

Launching onto the Web: A Small Business View. Natick, MA: A K Peters, Ltd. 1998. By: William J. Piniarski.

"Let Freedom Ring" in Black Enterprise (Vol. 29, February 1999, p. 54). By: Jacqueline Jones.

"Lost in Space" in Inc. (Vol. 19, No. 9, August 17, 1997, p. 26). By: Joshua Macht.

"Mail Call" in Business Start-Ups (Vol. 10, No. 10, October 1998, p. 8). By: Robert Schmidt.

"Making Music on the Internet" in Hispanic Business (Vol. 19, No. 12, December 1997, p. 38).

"The many virtues of 'virtual services'" in Business Week (No. 3595, September 14, 1998, p. S18). By: Ann Zieger.

"Marketers, Start Your N-Gens" in Business Start-Ups (Vol. 11, No. 1, January 1999, p. 82). By: Debra Phillips.

"Marketing 101" in Entrepreneur (March 1997, pp. 112-117). By: Robert McGarvey.

"The Message is the Medium" in Performance (September 1995). By: Ross Weiland.

"A moveable feast" in Red Herring: Going Public (1998, p. 60). By: Lauren Barack.

"Need for Speed" in Entrepreneur (Vol. 26, Issue 12, December 1998, p. 140). By: Scott S. Smith.

"Net Income" in Crain's Small Business (July 1996, p. 1). By: Jeffrey McCracken.

"Net Profits" in Working Woman (June 1996, pp. 44-49, 70, 72). By: Gloria Brame.

"Net Rewards" in Entrepreneur (March 1997, pp. 144, 146). By: Heather Page.

"Net Working" in Crain's Detroit Business (Vol. 13, No. 3, January 1997, p. 8). By: Art Dridgeforth Jr.

"New Service Tracks Subcontracting News" in Entrepreneur (December 1997, p. 177). By: Cynthia E. Griffin.

"The New Startup" in Red Herring (No. 59, October 1998, p. 34). By: Brian E. Taptich.

"News Bulletin" in Entrepreneur (September 1997, p. 24). By: Robert McGarvey.

"Nothing but Net" in Business Start-Ups (Vol. 11, No. 1, January 1999, p. 65). By: Chieh Chieng.

"Nothing but Net" in Inc. (Vol. 18, No. 18, December 1997, pp. 43-44).

"Now Hear This!" in Independent Business (Vol. 9, No. 2, March/April 1998, pp. 22-24). By: Alan Naditz.

"One woman's allergic reaction" in Boston Business Journal (September 25, 1998, p. 24). By: Roberta Holland.

"Online Advice" in Independent Business (Vol. 8, No. 1, Jan./Feb. 1997, p. 16). By: Maryann Hammers.

"Online Auction: A Seller's Dream" in Income Opportunities (Vol. 33, Issue 10, December 1998, pp. 50-51). By: Steven M. Brown.

"Online Shopping Comes to Latin America" in Hispanic Business (Vol. 20, No. 11, December 1998, p. 20). By: Derek Reveron.

"Open for Business" in Entrepreneur (December 1997, pp. 51-53). By: Heather Page.

"Our business is small. How can we afford top-quality accounting expertise?" in Inc. (Vol. 19, No. 8, June 1997, p. 96). By: Jill Andresky Fraser.

"Outsourcing the Overflow" in Red Herring: Guide to Professional Services 1999 (1999, p. 33). By: Denise Geschke.

"Owner's Manual: Tech Tools" in Independent Business (Vol. 9, No. 2, March/April 1998, p. 10). By: MaryAnn Hammers.

"Owner's Manual: Web Sales Smarts" in Independent Business (Vol. 9, No. 2, March/April 1998, p. 10). By: MaryAnn Hammers.

"Pencil Pusher" in Red Herring (Vol. 56, July 1998, p. 53). By: Constance Loizos.

"The Personnel Touch" in Red Herring (No. 60, November 1998, p. 86). By: Deborah Claymon.

"Plumbers' Helpers" in Red Herring (No. 60, November 1998, pp. 80-81). By: Luc Hatlestad.

"PR Firm Takes Press-Release Production Online" in Crain's Detroit Business (Vol. 12 No. 38, September 1996, p. 14). By: Arthur Bridgeforth Jr.

"Preparing for Takeoff" in Red Herring: Going Public (1998, p. 96). By: Bill Davidow.

"Q & A" in Performance (September 1995, pp. 12-16).

"Quick-Change Artists" in Business Start-Ups (Vol. 11, No. 1, January 1999, p. 50). By: Michelle Prather.

"Ranger Royce" in Red Herring (Vol. 56, July 1998, p. 49). By: Stephanie Gates.

"Real Law in a Virtual World" in Black Enterprise (Vol. 27, No. 5, December 1996, p. 44). By: Tariq K. Muhammad.

"Remote control" in Entrepreneur (Vol. 26, No. 10, October 1998, p. 146). By: Heather Page.

"Rev It Up" in Entrepreneur (March 1997, pp. 50, 52-53). By: Cheryl J. Goldberg.

"The Right Stuff" in Business Start-Ups (Vol. 10, No. 9, September 1998, p. 6). By: Donna Chambers.

"Ringleader" in Red Herring (Vol. 56, July 1998, p. 50). By: Andrew P. Madden.

"Room to Grow" in Business Start-Ups (Vol. 10, No. 10, October 1998, p. 5). By: Sean M. Lyden.

"Rumor Has It" in Business Start-Ups (Vol. 11, No. 1, January 1999, p. 6). By: Laura Tiffany.

"Safety Net" in Entrepreneur (February 1997, pp. 82-84). By: Steven C. Bahls and Jane Easter Bahls.

"SCORE Goes Cyber with New Web Site" in Entrepreneur (December 1997, p. 177). By: Cynthia E. Griffin.

"Search by Location" in Black Enterprise (Vol. 28, No. 1, August 1997, p. 42). By: Tariq K. Muhammad.

"Seek and Find" in Business Start-Ups (Vol. 10, No. 8, August 1998, p. 6). By: Donna Chambers.

"Set your sites on expansion" in Home Office Computing (Vol. 16, No. 3, March 1998, p. 47).

"Setting up shop: e-commerce is booming. Here's how you can get in the game" in Entrepreneur (Vol. 26, No. 8, August 1998, p. 43). By: Melissa Campanelli.

"Short Cut to a Job" in Hispanic Business (Vol. 19, No. 2, February 1997, p. 64). By: Claudia Armann.

"Site after Death" in Inc. (Vol. 19, No. 13, November 16, 1997, p. 21).

"Site Unseen" in Entrepreneur (Vol. 27, No. 1, January 1999, p. 105). By: Jerry Fisher .

"Sites to Surf" in Income Opportunities (Vol. 31, No. 5, May 1996, pp. 44, 46). By: Debra D'Agostino.

"Small Business Computing: Builder, Beware" in Independent Business (Vol. 9, No. 4, July/August 1998, pp. 52-53). By: Valerie J. Nelson.

Small Business Internet Connections for Dummies. Indianapolis, IN: IDG Books Worldwide, 1998. By: Greg Holden.

Small Business Internet Directory for Dummies. Indianapolis, IN: IDG Books Worldwide, 1998. By: Esau Barchini.

"Small Business on the Web, No. 1" in Independent Business (Vol. 10, March-April 1999, pp. 42-43).

Small Business Web Strategies for Dummies. Indianapolis, IN: IDG Books Worldwide, 1998. By: Janine Warner.

"Smart Ideas" in Entrepreneur (Vol. 27, No. 1, January 1999, p. 335). By: Heather Page.

"Speed Demons" in Business Start-Ups (Vol. 11, April 1999, p. 16). By: David Doran.

"Spin City" in Business Start-Ups (Vol. 11, No. 1, January 1999, p. 50). By: Michelle Prather.

"Spinning Your Web" in Small Business Opportunities (Vol. 10, No. 6, November 1998, pp. 70-71). By: Martin Waterman.

"Standards: Tim Berners-Lee on XML and the W3C" in Red Herring (Vol. 56, July 1998, p. 20). By: Deborah Claymon.

"Starting Over" in Hispanic Business (April 1998, p. 36).

"Stealth Marketing" in Red Herring (No. 55, June 1998, p. 23). By: Stephanie T. Gates.

"Stocking the small business engine" in Business Horizons (Vol. 41, No. 1, January-February 1998, p. 27). By: William M. Shanklin and John K. Rayns, Jr.

"Support Group" in Entrepreneur (December 1997, p. 24). By: Robert McGarvey.

"Surf's Up" in Small Business Opportunities (Vol. 9, No. 1, January 1997, p. 10). By: Lin Grensing-Pophal.

"Switching Tactics" in Red Herring (No. 55, June 1998, p. 29). By: Christina Stubbs.

"Take in the Sites" in Independent Business (Vol. 8, No. 1, Jan./Feb. 1997, p. 20). By: Rick Mendosa.

"Tech Talk" in Entrepreneur (December 1997, pp. 144, 146). By: Natasha Emmons and Adrienne S. Coelho.

"The Web Changes Everything" in Income Opportunities (Vol. 33, Issue 9, November 1998, p. 55). By: Andre Hinds.

"To Surf or Not?" in Small Business Opportunities (Vol. 9, No. 6, November 1997, pp. 10, 60). By: Lin Grensing-Pophal.

"To Website or Not to Website" in Feminist Bookstore News (Vol. 19, No. 5, January/February 1997, pp. 29-36). By: Carol Seajay.

"Toy Story" in Entrepreneur (February 1997, p. 38). By: Lynn Beresford.

"Tradeport an Excellent Source of Trade Information and Leads" in Hispanic Business (Vol. 18, No. 6, June 1996, p. 126). By: Rick Mendosa.

"Translating the Web" in Hits (Winter 1997, pp. 12-13). By: Nikki C. Goth.

"Two for T&E" in Red Herring (No. 55, June 1998, pp. 106, 108-109, 110, 112). By: Alex Gove.

"Virtual Celebrity Productions puts the dead to work" in Red Herring (No. 62, January 1999, p. 24). By: Alex Gove.

"Virtual classrooms, real education" in Nation's Business (May 1998, p. 41). By: Vicky Phillips.

"Way of the Web?" in Hispanic Business (Vol. 18, No. 10, October 1996, p. 88). By: Rick Mendosa.

"The Web and your Business" in PC World (January 1999, p. 161). By: Victoria Hall Smith.

Web Commerce: Building a Digital Business. New York, NY: John Wiley & Sons, Inc. 1998. By: Kate Maddox and Dana Blankenhorn.

"Web Fever!" in Independent Business (Vol. 8, No. 1, Jan./Feb. 1997, pp. 36-39). By: Eric J. Adams.

"WebMD tries to stake out spot as the Web's health-care portal" in The Wall Street Journal (Col. 4, January 14, 1999, p. B6). By: Anita Sharpe.

"Who makes what?" in Forbes (Vol. 62, October 19, 1998, p. S76). By: Michelle Jeffers and Scott Lajoie.

"The Winter of Content" in Red Herring: Going Public (1998, pp. 54-56). By: Christina Stubbs.

"Wired Kingdom" in Inc. (Vol. 19, No. 4, March 1997, p. 112).

"Work the Web" in PC/Computing (Vol. 11, No. 11, November 1998, p. 174).

"Working the Web" in Business Start-Ups (Vol. 10, No. 8, August 1998, pp. 64, 66-67). By: Don Debelak.

"You are What URL" in Business Start-Ups (Vol. 11, No. 1, January 1999, p. 11). By: Shannon Kinnard.

"Your Hassle-Free Web Site" in Independent Business (Vol. 8, No. 1, Jan./Feb. 1997, p. 18). By: Maryann Hammers.

"(Your Message Here)" in Inc. (March 16, 1999, pp. 76-80). By: Brownyn Fryer.

Hair Salon/Barber Shop

Afro Hair: A Salon Handbook. Malden, MA: Blackwell Science, Inc. 1994. By: Phillip Hatton.

Barber. Syosset, NY: National Learning Corp. 1994. By: Jack Rudman.

Barber-Osophy: Shear Success for Your Cutting Edge. San Antonio, TX: S E Publishing, 1998. By: Terry L. Sumerlin.

Business Management for the Hairdresser, Beauty & Holistic. Woburn, MA: Butterworth-Heinemann, 1997. By: Cressy.

"A Cut Above" in Entrepreneur (July 1996, p. 18). By: C.E.G.

Day Spa Operations. Albany, NY: Milady Publishing Co. 1996. By: Erica T. Miller.

Day Spa Techniques: The Beauty Wave of the Future. Albany, NY: Milady Publishing Co. 1996. By: Erica T. Miller.

The Esthetician's Guide to Business Management. Albany, NY: Milady Publishing Co. 1994. By: Henry J. Gambino.

Fun, Creative, & Profitable Salon Marketing: 67 Ways to Grow Your Salon Business. Winter Park, FL: Archer-Ellison Publishing Co. 1998. By: Allen R. Dangelo.

"Getting Under Their Skin" in Crain's Small Business (Vol. 5, No. 2, February 1997, p. 4). By: Jeffrey McCraken.

Hair and Hair Diseases. New York, NY: Springer-Verlag New York, Inc. 1990. By: C. E. Orfanos and R. Happle, editors.

Haircutting Basics: An Easy Step-by-Step Guide to Cutting Hair the Professional Way. Hialeah, FL: Good Life Products, Inc. Revised edition, 1991. By: Martha G. Fernandez.

Hairdressing: Theory, Science and Practice. Philadelphia, PA: Trans-Atlantic Publications, Inc. 1994. By: P. Cutting, R. Ross, and R. Hill.

"Hairy Situation, Profitable Business" in Black Enterprise (Vol. 25, No. 9, April 1995, p. 31). By: Tonia Shakespeare.

How to Cut, Curl and Care for Your Hair. New York, NY: Random House Value Publishing, Inc. 1990. By: Charles Booth.

How to Start & Manage a Hair Styling Salon Business: Step by Step Guide to Business Success. Interlochen, MI: Lewis & Renn Associates, 1996. By: Jere G. Lewis.

In the Bag: Selling in the Salon. Albany, NY: Milady Publishing Co. 1994. By: Carol Phillips.

Keep 'Em Coming Back: SalonOvations' Guide to Salon Promotion & Client Retention. Albany, NY: Milady Publishing Co. 1994. By: Lee Hoffman.

"Low-cost Franchise Opportunities" in Income Opportunities (Vol. 33, Issue 8, October 1998, p. 22).

Managing Your Business: Milady's Guide to the Salon. Albany, NY: Milady Publishing Co. 1994. By: Leslie H. Edgerton.

Playing It Safe: Milady's Guide to Decontamination, Sterilization, & Personal Protection. Albany, NY: Milady Publishing Co. 1994. By: Sheldon R. Chesky.

The Salon Biz: Tips for Success. Albany, NY: Milady Publishing Co. 1992. By: Geri Mataya.

The Standard Hair Coloring Workbook. Albany, NY: Milady Publishing Co. 1991.

High-Tech Business

301 Three Hundred One Great Ideas for Using Technology to Grow Your Business. Boston, MA: Inc. Publishing 1998. By: Phaedra Hise.

"A High Tech Entrepreneur's Guide To Venture Bank Financing" in Boston Business Journal (Vol. 19, February 26-March 4, 1999, p. 42). By: Osca Jazdowski.

"Ace in the Hole" in Entrepreneur (May 1997, pp. 69-71). By: David R. Evanson.

Advanced Technologies: Pros & Cons. Rockville, MD: Odelle Publications 1993. By: Candy F. Drew.

"Allied forces: communications experts team up to win contest" in Entrepreneur (Vol. 26, No. 11, November 1998, p. 20). By: Debra Phillips.

"The American dream is a ghost" in The Business Journal-Milwaukee (Vol. 15, No. 25, March 13, 1998, p. 10). By: Mike Dries.

"An Insider's View" in Hispanic Business (May 1998, p. 48). By: Rick Mendosa.

"At Your Fingertips" in Business Start-Ups (Vol. 11, No. 1, January 1999, p. 24). By: Paul DeCeglie.

"Attracting Advertisers" in Hits (Fall 1996, p. 68).

"Backyard entrepreneurs" in The Business Journal - Serving Phoenix & the Valley of the Sun (Vol. 18, No. 40, July 24, 1998, p. 26). By: Sean Robinson.

"Banner Days Ahead" in Red Herring: Guide to Professional Services 1999 (1999, pp. 8-10). By: Lauren Barack.

"Beached Dale" in Red Herring (Vol. 56, July 1998, p. 60). By: Alex Grove.

"Beastie Bandwidth" in Red Herring (No. 62, January 1999, pp. 56-57). By: Alex Gove.

"Bell South's 5 Steps to Internet Business" in Income Opportunities (Vol. 33, Issue 10, December 1998, p. 16).

"The Bloodiest Edge" in Red Herring (May 1998, p. 78). By: Alex Gove.

"Boss wanted" in Forbes (Vol. 62, October 19, 1998, p. 118). By: Stephan Herrera.

"The Bot Zone" in Inc. (Vol. 19, No. 13, November 16, 1997, p. 20). By: Joshua Macht.

"Bridging the Gap" in Red Herring (No. 55, June 1998, p. 70). By: Brian E. Taptich.

"Bridging the Gap" in Red Herring (No. 59, October 1998, p. 98). By: Kendall Riding.

"Building a Better Mouse" in Red Herring (May 1998, pp. 88-89). By: Brian E. Taptich.

"Bull's-eye" in Entrepreneur (Vol. 27, No. 1, January 1999, p. 56). By: Melissa Campanelli.

"Business 101" in Inc. (Vol. 19, No. 14, October 1998). By: Jill Andresky Fraser.

"Business and Gravy" in The Red Herring (March 1997, pp. 50-51). By: Luc Hatlestad.

"Bytes Can Bite Back" in Crain's Small Business Office Tech '96 Supplement (Vol. 4, No. 11, November 1996, p. T-19). By: Claudia Rast and Marc Bergsman.

"Call Collect" in Red Herring (No. 59, October 1998, p. 102). By: Alex Gove.

"Cashing In On the Web" in Hits (Fall 1996, p. 66).

"Chain Gang" in Red Herring (No. 63, February 1999, p. 24). By: Alex Gove.

"Changing the Future of Business" in Black Enterprise (Vol. 27, No. 8, March 1997, pp. 80-84). By: Marvin V. Greene.

"Chief Executive" in Red Herring (No. 59, October 1998, p. 144). By: Jason Pontin.

"College Pals Won't Tamper with Success" in Crain's Small Business (Vol. 4, No. 11, November 1996, p. 21). By: Jeffrey McCracken.

"Commerce by Design" in Red Herring (No. 63, February 1999, pp. 82-83). By: Luc Hatlestad.

Commercializing High Technology: East & West. Lanham, MD: Rowman & Littlefield, Publishers, Inc. 1996. By: Judith B. Sedaitis.

"Company offers site for sore Web pages" in The Business Journal (March 2, 1998, p. S6). By: Sue Oksanen.

"Computer consultants starting 'one-stop' shop" in Business First-Louisville (August 3, 1998, p. 1). By: Rick Redding.

"Computer Resale Shops Offer Buyers Alternative" in Crain's Detroit Business (Vol. 11, No. 14, April 1995, p. 11). By: Michael Maurer.

"Computer savvy at your service" in Nation's Business (Vol. 86, No. 3, March 1998, p. 60). By: Tim McCollum.

"Computing Success" in Small Business Opportunities (Vol. 11, No. 1, January 1999, pp. 90, 130). By: Marie Sherlock.

"Consultant Killers" in Red Herring (No. 57, August 1998, p. 45). By: Ilan Greenberg.

"Content and its Civilization" in Red Herring (No. 63, February 1999, p. 84). By: Blaise Zerega.

"Contest Pool" in Independent Business (Vol. 9, No. 7, November/December 1998, pp. 44-45).

"Could be Contenders" in The Red Herring (No. 52, March 1998, pp. 64-66). By: Alex Gove.

"Customize Customers" in Crain's Small Business Office Tech '96 Supplement (Vol. 4, No. 11, November 1996, pp. T-7). By: Arthur Bridgeforth, Jr.

"Digital Commerce" in The Red Herring (February 1997, pp. 46, 4850). By: Alex Gove.

"Don't Hold Your Breath" in The Red Herring (February 1997, p. 84). By: Andrew P. Madden.

"E-Male Dominates?" in Crain's Small Business Office Tech '96 Supplement (Vol. 4, No. 11, November 1996, p. T-4). By: Shekini Gilliam.

"E-Ticket" in Entrepreneur (Vol. 27, No. 1, January 1999, p. 98). By: Jay Conrad Levinson.

"An Entrepreneur Cries for Help" in Crain's Detroit Business (Vol. 5, No. 1, January 1997, p. 4). By: Jeffrey McCracken.

"Entrepreneurial Superstars" in Entrepreneur (April 1997, pp. 108-139). By: Debra Phillips and others.

"Entrepreneurs Back Curbs on State Suits" in The Wall Street Journal (Vol. IC, No. 99, May 21, 1997, p. B2). By: Stephanie N. Mehta.

"Even Old Machines Can Thrive in High-Tech World" in Crain's Small Business (June 1996, p. 6). By: Dave Guilford.

"Final Frontier" in Entrepreneur (Vol. 27, No. 1, January 1999, p. 26).

"Five Trends That Will Change Your Office" in Hispanic Business (May 1998, p. 44). By: Rick Mendosa.

"For GMD Studios, it pays to be small" in Orlando Business Journal (May 29, 1998, p. 27). By: Paul Dillion.

"Forging the Wired World" in Red Herring: Going Public (1998, pp. 54-55). By: Deborah Claymon.

"Four Home Improvement Businesses That Are Hot Now" in Income Opportunities (March-April 1999, pp. 16-20). By: Stephen Wagner.

"Free Mail Explosion" in Red Herring (No. 55, June 1998, pp. 63-65). By: Luc Hatlestad.

"Freeware" in Red Herring (No. 63, February 1999, p. 48). By: Nikki Goth Itoi.

"Friendship Begets 11-Years Partnership" in Crain's Small Business (Vol. 5, No. 4, April 1997, p. 23). By: Jeffrey McCracken.

"The Future of Your Business" in Business Start-Ups (Vol. 9, No. 4, April 1997, pp. 26-32). By: Kylo-Patrick Hart.

"General Stratton" in Red Herring (No. 57, August 1998, p. 124). By: Delia Craven.

"Get It Together" in Business Start-Ups (Vol. 11, No. 1, January 1999, p. 16). By: G. David Doran.

"Get-rich-quick schemers" in Red Herring (No. 59, October 1998, p. 152). By: Alex Gove.

"Going Public Proved a Rich Experience for Technology Entrepreneurs in '96" in Wall Street Journal (Vol. Ic, No. 22, 09/31/97, p. B1). By: Michael Selz.

"A golden nest egg" in Working Woman (Vol. 23, No. 4, April 1998, p. 13).

"Growth Squeezes Collectibles Shop" in Crain's Small Business (Vol. 4, No. 10, October 1996, p. 4). By: Jeffrey McCracken.

"A Guide May Be Needed to Set Up Shop On-Line" in Crain's Detroit Business (Vol. 11, No. 29, July 1995, p. 11).

"Hacker Attackers" in Crain's Small Business Office Tech '96 Supplement (Vol. 4, No. 11, November 1996, p. T-6). By: Arthur Bridgeforth, Jr.

"Hail, Bops" in Red Herring (No. 57, August 1998, p. 86). By: Alex Gove.

"The Hard Sell" in Red Herring (Vol. 56, July 1998, p. 96). By: Constance Loizos.

"Hat Trick" in Red Herring (Vol. 56, July 1998, p. 45). By: Brian E. Taptich.

"He Said, She Said" in Red Herring (Vol. 56, July 1998, p. 40). By: Andrew P. Madden.

"High flying with the FAA" in Black Enterprise (Vol. 28, No. 1, August 1997, p. 25). By: Eric L. Smith.

"High-Tech Firm Discovers Lease-To-Buy is Way to Go" in Crain's Small Business (Vol. 5, No. 4, April 1997, p. 10). By: Tim Moran.

High Tech, High Hope: Turning Your vision of Technology into Business Success. New York, NY: John Wiley & Sons, Inc. 1998. By: Paul Franson.

"High-Tech Hoods" in Inc. (Vol. 19, No. 4, March 1997, pp. 48-51). By: Sarah Schafer.

High Tech Start Up: The Complete How-to-Handbook for Creating Successful New High Tech Companies. Saratoga, CA: Electronics Trend Publications 1992. By: John L. Nesheim.

"High-Tech Success Starts in a Garage - Dot Com" in Income Opportunities (Vol. 33, Issue 7, September 1998, pp. 54-55). By: Steven M. Brown.

"His Customers' Plea Became New Calling" in Crain's Small Business (July 1996, p. 15). By: Jeffrey McCracken.

"How to zap those year 2000 bugs" in Business Week (No. 3595, September 14, 1998, p. S6).

"Hunters, Meet Gathers" in Red Herring (May 1998, p. 74). By: Andrew P. Madden.

"I Am Pharma, Hear Me Roar" in Red Herring (May 1998, p. 90). By: Andrew P. Madden.

"I want to give customers memorable but inexpensive gifts. Any Ideas?" in Inc. (Vol. 19, No. 16, November 1997, p. 105). By: Mike Hofman.

"Instant Ally" in Business Start-Ups (Vol. 8, No. 7, July 1996, pp. 12, 14). By: Pamela Palmer.

"Instant Gratification" in Business Start-Ups (Vol. 11, No. 1, January 1999, p. 11). By: Shannon Kinnard.

"InterSense smooths out the rough spots in virtual reality" in Red Herring (April 1999, p. 34). By: Christina Stubbs.

"Investors Bet on Cyberspace Path to Terra Firm Travel" in Wall Street Journal (Vol. Ic, No. 9, January 14, 1997, p. B2). By: Michael Selz.

"Invisible & loving it" in Business Week (No. 3598, October 5, 1998, p. 124). By: Roger O. Crockett.

"Is the Internet feasible and profitable for small businesses" in SAM Advanced Management Journal (Vol. 63, No. 3, Summer 1998, p. 20). By: Amir M. Hormozi, William T. Harding, and Utpal Bose.

"Jomei the Money" in Red Herring (Vol. 56, July 1998, p. 42). By: Deborah Claymon.

"Judge and Journalist" in Red Herring (No. 60, November 1998, pp. 64-68). By: Alex Gove.

"Keep an Eye on Internet Taxes" in Independent Business (Vol. 9, No. 4, July/August 1998, p. 12).

"Keep it Simple" in Business Start-Ups (Vol. 10, No. 10, October 1998, p. 7). By: Donna Chambers.

"Keeping Up With High Tech" in Independent Business (Vol. 9, No. 3, May/June 1998, p. 41).

"Leading the Pack" in Entrepreneur (Vol. 27, No. 1, January 1999, p. 26).

"The Liquidator" in Red Herring (No. 58, September 1998, p. 106). By: Constance Loizos.

"The Little Engine That Might" in The Red Herring (No. 45, August 1997, p. 86). By: Andrew P. Madden.

"Loser Chic" in Business Start-Ups (Vol. 11, February 1999, pp. 31-35). By: Jeffrey Shuman and David Rottenberg.

"Losing its Religion" in Red Herring (No. 55, June 1998, p. 114). By: Constance Loizos.

"Low Rollers" in The Red Herring (No. 53, April 1998, pp. 92, 94, 96, 100). By: Nikki Goth Itoi.

"Making the Grade" in Red Herring (No. 62, January 1999, p. 42-46). By: Deborah Claymon.

Managing High-Tech Start-Ups. Woburn, MA: Butterworth-Heinemann 1992. By: Duncan MacVicar.

Managing Information and Entrepreneurship in Technology-based Firms. New York, NY: John Wiley & Sons, Inc. 1994. By: Michael J. Martin.

"Marketers Discover Selling Electric Bikes Has Ups and Downs" in The Wall Street Journal (Vol. C, No. 19, July 28, 1997, pp. B1, B2).

"Marketers, Start Your N-Gens" in Business Start-Ups (Vol. 11, No. 1, January 1999, p. 82). By: Debra Phillips.

"Marketing Online" in Black Enterprise (Vol. 27, No. 2, September 1996, pp. 85-88). By: Tariq K. Muhammand.

"Meltdown '98: the day technology died" in Entrepreneur (Vol. 26, No. 11, November 1998, p. 10).

"The Millennium Bug" in Small Business Opportunities (Vol. 11, No. 2, March 1999, p. 10). By: Marie Sherlock.

"More Than a Passing Interest" in Inc. (Vol. 19, No. 15, December 21, 1997, pp. 52, 54). By: Stephan D. Solomon.

"A moveable feast" in Red Herring: Going Public (1998, p. 60). By: Lauren Barack.

"Network PBXs Come of Age" in PC Magazine (January 5, 1999, p. 201). By: Don Labriola.

"New law aids money crunch for small biz" in San Diego Business Journal (October 19, 1998, p. 1). By: Andrea Siedsma.

"The New Startup" in Red Herring (No. 59, October 1998, p. 34). By: Brian E. Taptich.

New Technology-Based Firms in the 1990s. Bristol, PA: Taylor & Francis, Inc. 1994. By: Ray Oakey.

"New York" in Hispanic Business (Vol. 17, No. 5, May 1995, p. 36). By: Yvonne Conde.

"Nick of Time" in Red Herring: Guide to Professional Services 1999 (1999, p. 47). By: Janet Kettlehut.

"No Line Online, but Use with Caution" in Crain's Small Business (Vol. 4, No. 11, November 1996, p. 10). By: Jeff Pace.

"Not Everyone's On-Line" in Crain's Detroit Business (Vol. 11, No. 29, July 1995, p. 10). By: Michael Maurer.

"Nothing but Net" in Business Start-Ups (Vol. 11, No. 1, January 1999, p. 65). By: Chieh Chieng.

"On-Line Upstarts Tap Big Media Companies for Funds" in Wall Street Journal (Vol. Ic, No. 19, February 10, 1997, p. B2). By: Stephanie N. Metha.

"Online Auction: A Seller's Dream" in Income Opportunities (Vol. 33, Issue 10, December 1998, pp. 50-51). By: Steven M. Brown.

"Online Salesperson" in Crain's Small Business Office Tech '96 Supplement (Vol. 4, No. 11, November 1996, p. T-3).

"Online Shopping Comes to Latin America" in Hispanic Business (Vol. 20, No. 11, December 1998, p. 20). By: Derek Reveron.

"Out of the box" in Forbes (Vol. 162, No. 5, September 7, 1998, p. 96). By: Om Malik.

"Outsourcing the Overflow" in Red Herring: Guide to Professional Services 1999 (1999, p. 33). By: Denise Geschke.

"Owner's Manual: Web Sales Smarts" in Independent Business (Vol. 9, No. 2, March/April 1998, p. 10). By: MaryAnn Hammers.

"Partners work up from basement" in Crain's Detroit Business (December 14-20, 1998, p. E19). By: Joseph Serwach.

"Peace, Love, and Interactive Media" in Boston Business Journal (Vol. 19, February 26-March 4, 1999, pp. 28, 46). By: Roberta Holland.

"Peanuts, Popcorn, or Power Tool?" in Inc. (Vol. 19, No. 13, November 16, 1997, p. 24).

"Pencil Pusher" in Red Herring (Vol. 56, July 1998, p. 53). By: Constance Loizos.

"The Personnel Touch" in Red Herring (No. 60, November 1998, p. 86). By: Deborah Claymon.

"Photo Vend's Picture-Perfect Vending Opportunity" in Income Opportunities (Vol. 33, Issue 10, December 1998, p. 32).

"Plumbers' Helpers" in Red Herring (No. 60, November 1998, pp. 80-81). By: Luc Hatlestad.

"Pop Culture" in Business Start-Ups (Vol. 11, No. 1, January 1999, p. 60). By: Elaine W. Teague.

"Preparing for Takeoff" in Red Herring: Going Public (1998, p. 96). By: Bill Davidow.

Product Strategy for High-Technology Companies: How to Achieve Growth, Competitive Advantage, & Increased Profits. Hinsdale, IL: Irwin Professional Publishing 1994. By: Michael E. McGrath.

"Profile" in Red Herring (No. 62, January 1999, p. 19). By: Nikki Goth Itoi.

"Protect Your Computer Files" in Independent Business (Vol. 9, No. 2, March/April 1998, p. 39).

"Q & A" in Red Herring (No. 59, October 1998, pp. 24-26).

"Quick-Change Artists" in Business Start-Ups (Vol. 11, No. 1, January 1999, p. 50). By: Michelle Prather.

"Ranger Royce" in Red Herring (Vol. 56, July 1998, p. 49). By: Stephanie Gates.

"Ray Dolby Sounds Off" in Red Herring (No. 62, January 1999, pp. 70-74). By: Alex Gove.

"Reflections" in Small Business Opportunities (Vol. 10, No. 6, November 1998, p. 108). By: Alwin Jennette.

"Rewriting History" in Entrepreneur (Vol. 27, No. 1, January 1999, p. 69). By: Jill Amadio.

"The Right Stuff" in Business Start-Ups (Vol. 10, No. 9, September 1998, p. 6). By: Donna Chambers.

"The Right Stuff" in Red Herring (No. 63, February 1999, p 79). By: Blaise Zerega.

"Ringleader" in Red Herring (Vol. 56, July 1998, p. 50). By: Andrew P. Madden.

"Robbing the Cradle" in Red Herring: Going Public (1998, pp. 33-34). By: Luc Hatlestad.

"Room to Grow" in Business Start-Ups (Vol. 10, No. 10, October 1998, p. 5). By: Sean M. Lyden.

"Rumor Has It" in Business Start-Ups (Vol. 11, No. 1, January 1999, p. 6). By: Laura Tiffany.

"Safeguarding Your Network" in Black Enterprise (Vol. 27, No. 3, October 1996, pp. 48-50). By: Joyce E. Davis.

"SBA award winner pushes technology" in The Business Journal-Milwaukee (Vol. 15, No. 30, April 17, 1998, p. 25). By: Robert Mullins.

"School of Vish" in Red Herring (Vol. 56, July 1998, p. 38). By: Christina Stubbs.

"Scratching the Surface" in Red Herring (No. 57, August 1998, p. 106). By: Andrew P. Madden.

"Seek and Find" in Business Start-Ups (Vol. 10, No. 8, August 1998, p. 6). By: Donna Chambers.

"Set your sites on expansion" in Home Office Computing (Vol. 16, No. 3, March 1998, p. 47).

"Setting up shop: e-commerce is booming. Here's how you can get in the game" in Entrepreneur (Vol. 26, No. 8, August 1998, p. 43). By: Melissa Campanelli.

"Shoot-Out in 3D" in Red Herring (No. 62, January 1999, pp. 37-40). By: Andrew P. Madden.

"Show Time!" in Independent Business (Vol. 9, No. 2, March/April 1998, pp. 27-29). By: Eric J. Adams.

Silicon Gold Rush: The Next Generation of High-Tech Stars Rewrite the Rules of Business. New York, NY: John Wiley & Sons, Inc. 1999. By: Karen Southwick.

"Silicon Valley South" in Forbes (November 16, 1998, p. 214). By: Julie Pitta.

"Site Unseen" in Entrepreneur (Vol. 27, No. 1, January 1999, p. 105). By: Jerry Fisher.

"Sky's the Limit" in Red Herring (No. 59, October 1998, pp. 69-72). By: Deborah Claymon.

"The Small Business Administration reaches out to tech companies" in Red Herring (No. 57, August 1998, pp. 23-24). By: Brian E. Taptich.

"Small Business Computing: Builder, Beware" in Independent Business (Vol. 9, No. 4, July/August 1998, pp. 52-53). By: Valerie J. Nelson.

"Small Businesses get the Edge" in Independent Business (Vol. 9, No. 2, March/April 1998, p. 25).

"Small biz goes high tech" in Black Enterprise (Vol. 28, No. 11, June 1998, p. 283). By: Tariq K. Muhammad.

"Smart Ideas" in Entrepreneur (Vol. 27, No. 1, January 1999, p. 335). By: Heather Page.

"So You Wanna be a Millionaire" in Business Start-Ups (Vol. 11, No. 1, January 1999, pp. 34-43).

"Something Ventured" in Red Herring (Vol. 56, July 1998, pp. 66-67). By: Nikki Goth Itoi.

"The Son Also Rises" in The Red Herring (No. 45, August 1997, pp. 30-34, 36, 38). By: Jonathan Burke.

"Spin City" in Business Start-Ups (Vol. 11, No. 1, January 1999, p. 50). By: Michelle Prather.

"Spinning Your Web" in Small Business Opportunities (Vol. 10, No. 6, November 1998, pp. 70-71). By: Martin Waterman.

"Standards: Tim Berners-Lee on XML and the W3C" in Red Herring (Vol. 56, July 1998, p. 20). By: Deborah Claymon.

"Start the presses" in Home Office Computing (Vol. 16, No. 10, October 1998, p. 116).

Starting a High Tech Company. Piscataway, NJ: Institute of Electrical & Electronics Engineers, Inc. 1995. By: Michael L. Baird.

"Startup city" in Forbes (Vol. 62, October 19, 1998, p. 108). By: Daniel Fisher.

"Startups: The Open-Source Business Model has VCs Baffled" in Red Herring (No. 63, February 1999, p. 56). By: Brian E. Taptich.

"Stealth Marketing" in Red Herring (No. 55, June 1998, p. 23). By: Stephanie T. Gates.

"Strategic Isolation" in Red Herring (No. 55, June 1998, p. 71). By: Luc Hatlestad.

"Surf's Up!" in Hits (Fall 1996, pp. 9, 11). By: Anthony B. Perkins.

"Surviving a Crash" in Hispanic Business (May 1998, p. 68). By: Rick Mendosa.

"Surviving the Year 2000 Bug" in Independent Business (Vol. 9, No. 3, May/June 1998, pp. 38-42). By: Barbara Stahura.

"Switching Tactics" in Red Herring (No. 55, June 1998, p. 29). By: Christina Stubbs.

"Tailoring Software to Small Business" in Computer Reseller News (No. 775, February 9, 1998, p. 17S). By: Daniel Lyons.

"Taking It to The Street" in Hits (Spring 1997, pp. 16-20). By: Anne T. Linsmayer.

"Taking it Outside" in Red Herring (No. 60, November 1998, p. 56). By: Alex Gove.

"Tech Trash" in Crain's Detroit Business (Vol. 11, No. 29, July 1995, p. 8). By: Mary Dempsey.

"Think Big" in The Wall Street Journal (Col. 1, January 14, 1999, p. R28). By: Quentin Hardy.

"Think or swim: Think you've seen the future of email? Tidal Wave says, Think again" in Red Herring (April 1999, pp. 62-66). By: Andrew P. Madden.

"To the rescue" in Entrepreneur (Vol. 26, No. 5, May 1998, p. 59). By: Heather Page.

"Top 50 Private Companies" in Red Herring (No. 58, September 1998, pp. 92-160).

"Tricks of the Trade" in Red Herring: Going Public (1998, p. 88). By: Paul Ross.

"Tunnel Visionary" in Red Herring (Vol. 56, July 1998, p. 56). By: Luc Hatlestad.

"Two for T&E" in Red Herring (No. 55, June 1998, pp. 106, 108-109, 110, 112). By: Alex Gove.

"The Tyranny of the Diploma" in Forbes (December 28, 1998, p. 104). By: Brigid McMenamin.

"Using Technology to Enhance Your Business" in Black Enterprise (Vol. 27, No. 8, March 1997, pp. 64-72).

"The Ventix System aims to make ERP Help Desks Obsolete" in Red Herring (No. 63, February 1999, p. 40). By: Brian E. Taptich.

"Ventures in Space" in Red Herring: Going Public (1998, p. 15). By: Christina Stubbs.

"Veridicom wants your fingerprints to be your password" in Red Herring (No. 62, January 1999, p. 30). By: Anna S. Semansky.

"Virtual Celebrity Productions puts the dead to work" in Red Herring (No. 62, January 1999, p. 24). By: Alex Gove.

"Virtual classrooms, real education" in Nation's Business (May 1998, p. 41). By: Vicky Phillips.

Walking the High-Tech High Wire: The Technical Entrepreneur's Guide to Running a Successful Enterprise. New York, NY: The McGraw-Hill Companies 1993. By: David Adamson.

"A Wall in the PARC" in The Red Herring (No. 44, July 1997, p. 53). By: Deborah Claymon.

"Was That Cybernet Inc. or Interweb Co.?" in Wall Street Journal (Vol. Ic, No. 5, January 8, 1997, pp. B1-B2). By: Rodney Ho.

"The Web and your Business" in PC World (January 1999, p. 161). By: Victoria Hall Smith.

"WebMD tries to stake out spot as the Web's health-care portal" in The Wall Street Journal (Col. 4, January 14, 1999, p. B6). By: Anita Sharpe.

"What the Doctor Ordered" in Crain's Detroit Business (Vol. 13, No. 15, April 1997, p. 9). By: David Barkholz.

"What's Hot, What's Not?" in Hispanic Business (May 1998, p. 54).

"What's It Worth" in Inc. (Vol. 21, February 1999, pp. 60-64). By: Jill Andresky Fraser.

"Who needs college!" in Forbes (December 28, 1998, p. 104). By: Brigid McMenamin.

"Who makes what?" in Forbes (Vol. 62, October 19, 1998, p. S76). By: Michelle Jeffers and Scott Lajoie.

"The Winter of Content" in Red Herring: Going Public (1998, pp. 54-56). By: Christina Stubbs.

"Wired for Success" in Black Enterprise (Vol. 27, No. 8, March 1997, pp. 75-80). By: Tariq K. Muhammad.

"The Wizards of Oz" in The Red Herring (No. 45, August 1997, pp. 46-48). By: Alex Gove.

"Work The Web" in PC/Computing (Vol. 11, No. 11, November 1998, p. 174).

"You are What URL" in Business Start-Ups (Vol. 11, No. 1, January 1999, p. 11). By: Shannon Kinnard.

Home-Based Business

"12-Step Program" in Business Start-Ups (Vol. 7, No. 7, July 1995, p. 20).

"15 franchises you can run from home" in Black Enterprise (Vol. 29, No. 2, September 1998, p. 60). By: Gerda D. Gallop.

101 Best Home Businesses. Franklin Lakes, NJ: Career Press, Inc. 1997. By: Dan Ramsey.

101 Best Weekend Businesses. Franklin Lakes, NJ: Career Press, Inc. 1996. By: Dan Ramsey.

101 Great Home-Based Businesses for Women: Everything You Need to Know about Getting Started on the Road to Success. Rocklin, CA: Prima Publishing & Communications, 1995. By: Priscilia Y. Huff.

203 Home-Based Businesses That Will Make You Rich. Rocklin, CA: Prima Publishing, 1998. By: Tyler G. Hicks.

1996 National Home Based Business Directory. Aitkin, MN: Marketing Solutions, Inc. 1996. By: Darleen J. Hoffman.

"Advantage: Home" in Business Start-Ups (Vol. 8, No. 6, June 1996, pp. 84, 86). By: Janie Sullivan.

"Alone Behind the Desk" in Business Start-Ups (Vol. 9, No. 4, April 1997, pp. 8, 10). By: Carolyn Campbell.

"Arty Parties" in Small Business Opportunities (Vol. 11, No. 1, January 1999, p. 110). By: Marie Sherlock.

"Attention Getters" in Entrepreneur (Vol 23, No. 1, January 1995, pp. 76, 78). By: Debra Phillips.

"Audit Medical Bills from Home" in Income Opportunities (Vol. 33, Issue 10, December 1998, p. 12).

"Beat the January Blues" in Business Start-Ups (Vol. 8, No. 1, January 1996, pp. 18-19).

Best Home-Based Franchises. New York, NY: Doubleday & Co. Inc. 1992. By: Compiled by Philip Lief Group, Inc. staff.

Best Home Businesses for the 90's. New York, NY: Jeremy P. Tarcher Inc. 1995. By: Sarah Edwards.

"The Big Sell" in Entrepreneur (December 1996, pp. 61-62). By: Cynthia E. Griffin.

"Bookmarks" in Inc. (Vol. 19, No. 17, January 18, 1998, p. 23). By: Michelle Keyo.

"Books, dogs, and country sports: a tale of independent living" in Mother Earth News (No. 169, August-September 1998, p. 50). By: M.H. "Dutch" Salmon.

"Bottled Profits" in Income Opportunities (Vol. 31, No. 6, June 1996, pp. 96, 94). By: Amy H. Berger.

"Broadcast News" in Business Start-Ups (Vol. 7, No. 6, June 1995, p. 16). By: Cynthia E. Griffin.

"Bucks in Buttons" in Small Business Opportunities (Vol. 9, No. 1, January 1997, p. 48). By: Carla Goodman.

"Building the Perfect Home Office" in Black Enterprise (Vol. 27, No. 8, March 1997, pp. 36-37). By: Rafiki Cai.

"Buying Wisely for Your Office" in Black Enterprise (Vol. 27, No. 9, April 1997, pp. 35-36). By: Tariq K. Muhammad.

Buying Your First Franchise. Menlo Park, CA: Crisp Publications, Inc. 1994. By: Rebecca Luhn.

"Call It Up" in Entrepreneur (December 1997, p. 18). By: Heather Page.

"Catering Requirements" in Black Enterprise (Vol. 27, No. 8, March 1997, p. 30). By: Sheryl E. Huggins.

"A Clothes Call" in Income Opportunities (Vol. 32, No. 4, April 1997, p. 12). By: Lana Sanderson.

"Collectibles Search" in Business Start-Ups (Vol. 8, No. 7, July 1996, p. 32). By: Guen Sublette.

"Community Centered" in Business Start-Ups (Vol. 8, No. 6, June 1996, pp. 68, 70-71). By: Deborah Richman.

The Complete Work-at-Home Companion. Rocklin, CA: Prima Publishing & Communications, 1993, second edition. By: Herman Holtz.

Computer Consulting on Your Home-Based PC. New York, NY: The McGraw-Hill Companies, 1994. By: Herman Holtz.

"Conference Call" in Entrepreneur (Vol. 23, No. 12, November 1995, pp. 48, 50). By: Cynthia E. Griffin.

"Congressman Plans Bill to Aid Home-Based Businesses" in Wall Street Journal (Vol. Ic, No. 16, January 23, 1997, pp. B2). By: Rodney Ho.

"Cook Up a Business in Your Kitchen" in Income Opportunities (Vol. 34, Issue 1, January/February 1999, p. 50). By: Stephen Wagner.

"Cost Controls" in Income Opportunities (Vol. 30, No. 5, May 1995, p. 8). By: Lana Sanderson.

"Couple to Relocate Sanit-Air for Sanity" in Crain's Small Business (Vol. 4, No. 11, November 1996, p. 21). By: Jeffrey McCracken.

"Day-Care Dollars" in Small Business Opportunities (Vol. 9, No. 3, May 1997, pp. 94-95). By: Marie Sherlock.

"A Delicate Balance" in Business Start-Ups (Vol. 8, No. 9, September 1996, pp. 8, 10). By: Ken Ohlson.

"Doing Your Home Work" in Income Opportunities (Vol. 32, No. 4, April 1997, pp. 24-27).

"Don't Get Zoned Out" in Income Opportunities (Vol. 31, No. 9, September 1996, pp. 21-23). By: Eric Barnes.

"Drawing a Bead on Profits" in Income Opportunities (Vol. 33, Issue 10, December 1998, p. 18). By: Elizabeth Marie deMorest.

"E-Education" in Business Start-Ups (Vol. 10, No. 9, September 1998, p. 14). By: Lynn H. Colwell.

"Earn money, help children" in Income Opportunities (March-April 1999, p. 40.).

"Earn your fortune in home party selling" Income Opportunities (March-April 1999, pp. 52-54). By: Denise Osburn.

Easy Financials for Your Home-Based Business: The Friendly Guide to Successful Management Systems for Busy Home Entrepreneurs. Windsor, CA: Rayve Publications, Inc. 1993. By: Norm Ray.

Easy to Start, Fun to Run, & Highly Profitable Home Businesses. Holbrook, MA: Adams Media Corp. 1998. By: Katina Z. Jones.

Eighty-Plus Great Ideas for Making Money at Home: A Guide for the First-Time Entrepreneur. New York, NY: Walker & Co. 1992. By: Erica Barkemeyer.

"Entrepreneur Hails Power of Marketing" in Crain's Small Business (June 1996, p. 23). By: Jeffrey McCracken.

Entrepreneur Magazine: Starting a Home-Based Business. New York, NY: John Wiley & Sons, Inc.

"Everything You Need to Know to Start Your Business at Home" in Business Start-Ups (Vol. 8, No. 6, June 1996, pp. 28, 30, 32, 34-36). By: Karin Moeller.

"An exploration into home-based businesses" Journal of Small Business Management (Vol. 36, No. 2, April 1998, p. 33). By: Loran Sanchez Soldressen, Susan S. Fiorito, and Yan He.

Family Businesses, Small Businesses, Home Businesses & General Business Possibilities Encyclopedia. Denver, CO: Prosperity & Profits Unlimited, Distribution Services, 1991.

"Family Friendly" in Business Start-Ups (Vol. 10, No. 10, October 1998, p. 96). By: Karen Axelton.

"Fast Forward, Up & Comers" in Working Woman (January 1997, p. 20). By: K.F.

"Fast-Growing Trends" in Business Start-Ups (Vol. 9, No. 2, February 1997, pp. 42, 44, 46). By: Carla Goodman.

"Fed Funds" in Entrepreneur (Vol. 23, No. 8, August 1995, pp. 50, 52- 53). By: Cynthia E. Griffin.

"Finding the Perfect Job" in Crain's Detroit Business (Vol. 11, No. 34, August 1995, p. 15). By: Steve Raphael.

"Finding Time for Your Home Business" in Income Opportunities (Vol. 33, Issue 10, December 1998, p. 34). By: Ted Tate.

"A Fine Mess" in Income Opportunities (Vol. 31, No. 4, April 1996, p. 10). By: Lana Sanderson.

"First Things First" in Business Start-Ups (Vol. 8, No. 8, August 1996, pp. 8, 10). By: Carolyn Campbell.

"From One Small Desk to $2 Million a Year" in Income Opportunities (Vol. 33, Issue 8, October 1998, pp. 50-52). By: Oneta Aldrich Dernelle.

"Get It Together" in Business Start-Ups (Vol. 7, No. 8, August 1995, p. 14).

"Getting Connected" in Entrepreneur (Vol. 24, No. 2, February 1996, pp. 48, 50-51). By: Cynthia E. Griffin.

"Giving Thanks" in Business Start-Ups (Vol. 8, No. 11, November 1996, pp. 8, 10). By: Julie Bawden Davis.

"Greener Pastures" in Income Opportunities (Vol. 30, No. 9, September 1995, pp. 24-27, 106). By: Meg North.

"Growing Pains" in Business Start-Ups (Vol. 9, No. 5, May 1997, pp. 8, 10, 12). By: Carolyn Campbell.

Growing Your Home-Based Business: A Complete Guide to Proven Sales and Marketing Communications Strategies. Paramus, NJ: Prentice Hall, 1992. By: Kim T. Gordon.

"Heading Home" in Income Opportunities (Vol. 32, No. 4, April 1997, pp. 46, 49-50). By: Robert L. Perry.

"Hello, World" in Income Opportunities (Vol. 30, No. 4, April 1995, p. 8). By: Lana Sanderson.

"Help Wanted" in Entrepreneur (May 1996, pp. 55-57).

"He's Right at Home in Chili and Shuttles" in Crain's Small Business (June 1996, p. 23). By: Jeffrey McCracken.

"High-Tech Know-How" in Small Business Opportunities (Vol. 8, No. 3, May 1996, pp. 62, 64, 106). By: Jeff Berner.

"Hints from the Pros: Try This At Home" in Business Start-Ups (Vol. 7, Nol. 6, June 1995, p. 16). By: Eileen Glick, president of the Home-based Business Administration, offers tips for running a home-based business.

"Holiday Helpers" in Business Start-Ups (Vol. 7, No. 11, November 1995, pp. 14, 16).

"Home Alone" in Small Business Opportunities (Vol. 9, No. 6, November 1997, pp. 18). By: Carla Goodman.

Home Based Business Occupational Handbook. Dubuque, IA: Kendall/Hunt Publishing Co. 1996. By: NAHBB Staff.

Home-Based Businesses, Over Two-Hundred-Fifty Ways to Earn Your Fortune. Ft. Worth, TX: Premier Publishers, Inc. 1995. By: J. Rue.

Home-Based Employment & Family Life. Westport, CT: Greenwood Publishing Group, Inc. 1995. By: Ramona K. Z. Heck.

The Home-Based Entrepreneur: The Complete Guide to Working at Home. Chicago, IL: Upstart Publishing Co. Inc. Second edition, 1993. By: Linda Pinson and Jerry Jinnett.

"Home-Based Riches!" in Small Business Opportunities (Vol. 8, No. 2, March 1996, pp. 22-24, 26, 28, 30, 32, 34, 82, 102, 122).

The Home Business Bible: Everything You Need to Know to Start & Run Your Successful Home-Based Business. New York, NY: John Wiley & Sons, Inc. 1994. By: David R. Eyler.

Home Business to Big Business: How to Launch Your Home Business and Make it a Success. Old Tappan, NJ: Macmillan Publishing Co. Inc. 1992. By: Mel Cook.

Home Business Happiness: Secrets on Keeping the Family Ship Afloat from Entrepreneurs Who Made It. Lancaster, PA: Starburst Publishers, 1996. By: Cheri Fuller.

Home Business Made Easy: How to Select & Start a Home Business That Fits Your Interests, Lifestyles & Pocketbook. Grants Pass, OR: Oasis Press, 1992. By: David Hanania.

Home Computer Business Guide. Yonkers, NY: Entrepreneur, Inc.

"Home Grown" in Business Start-Ups (Vol. 7, No. 3, March 1995, pp. 36-47). By: Guen Sublette.

Home Office Bible. Reading, MA: Addison Wesley Longman, 1997.

The Home Office Money and Tax Guide: Bringing Professional Business Practices Home. Burr Ridge, IL: Probus Publishing Co. Inc. 1992. By: Robert W. Wood.

The Home Office and Small Business Answer Book: Solutions to the Most Frequently Asked Questions about Starting and Running Home Offices. New York, NY: Henry Holt & Co. Inc. 1993. By: Janet Attard.

The Home Office & Small Business Success Book: How to Run Your Business More Profitably with Less Effort. New York, NY: Henry Holt & Co. 1996. By: Janet Attard.

"Home Run" in Business Start-Ups (Vol. 7, No. 10, October 1995, p. 72). By: Nancy L. Scarlato.

"Home Safe" in Income Opportunities (Vol. 32, No. 2, February 1997, pp. 38, 40, 42). By: Janine S. Pouliot.

"Home Suite Home" in Small Business Opportunities (Vol. 11, No. 2, March 1999, pp. 23-44, 118).

"Home Working: Here To Stay" in Income Opportunities (Vol. 31, No. 2, February 1996, p. 4). By: Michele Marrinan.

"Homebased 400 Business Opportunity" in Business Start-Ups (Vol. 8, No. 9, September 1996, pp. 31-61). By: Stephanie Osowski.

The Homebased Business Book. Irvine, CA: Entrepreneur, Inc. 1994.

"Homebased Business Insurance" in Business Start-Ups (Vol. 8, No. 7, July 1996, pp. 16, 18-21). By: Dennis Whittington.

"Homebased Business Opportunity 400" in Business Start-Ups (Vol. 10, No. 9, September 1998, pp. 31-53). By: Liza Potter.

Homemade Business. Colorado Springs, CO: Focus on the Family Publishing, 1992. By: Donna Partow.

"House Hunting" in Entrepreneur (Vol. 23, No. 4, April 1995, pp. 84, 86-87). By: Cynthia E. Griffin.

"House Rules" in Entrepreneur (Vol. 23, No. 7, July 1995, pp. 46, 48-49). By: Cynthia E. Griffin.

How to Build a Successful One-Person Business: A Common-Sense Guide to Starting & Growing a Company. Farmington Hills, MI: Bookhaus Publishers, 1995. By: Veltisezar B. Bautista.

"How to Earn a Living as a Freelance Writer" in Income Opportunities (Vol. 33, Issue 10, December 1998, pp. 48-49). By: Sandra Mardenfeld.

How to Make 1000 Mistakes in Business & Still Succeed: The Guide to Crucial Decisions in the Small Business, Home-Based Business. Oak Park, IL: Wright Track, 1995. By: Harold L. Wright.

How to Market Your Home Based Business. Chino Hills, CA: AAJA Publishing Co. 1994. By: Reece A. Franklin.

How to Open & Operate a Home-Based Catering Business. Old Saybrook, CT: The Globe Pequot Press, 1996.

How to Raise a Family & a Career under One Roof: A Personal Guide to Home Business for Parents. Moon Township, PA: Bookhaven Press, 1997. By: Lisa M. Roberts; edited by Marla Olson; illustrated by Wendy Simon and George Foster.

How to Run Your Own Home Business. Lincolnwood, IL: NTC Business Books, 1994. By: Coralee Smith Kern and Tammara Hoffman Wolfgram.

How to Start a Home-Based Antiques Business. Old Saybrook, CT: The Globe Pequot Press, 2nd ed. 1997. By: Jacqueline Peake.

How to Start a Home-Based Crafts Business. Old Saybrook, CT: The Globe Pequot Press, 2nd ed. 1997. By: Kenn Oberrecht.

How to Start a Home-Based Gift Basket Business: An Unabridged Guide. Old Saybrook, CT: The Globe Pequot Press, 1998. By: Shirley Frazier.

How to Start a Home-Based Interior Design Business. Old Saybrook, CT: The Globe Pequot Press, 1996. By: Suzanne DeWalt.

How to Start a Home-Based Photography Business. Old Saybrook, CT: The Globe Pequot Press, 1996. By: Kenn Oberrecht.

How to Start a Home-Based Resume Service. Old Saybrook, CT: The Globe Pequot Press, 1997. By: Jan Melnik.

How to Start a Home-Based Secretarial Business. Old Saybrook, CT: The Globe Pequot Press, 1996. By: Jan Melnik.

How to Start a Home-Based Writing Business. Old Saybrook, CT: The Globe Pequot Press, 1997. By: Lucy V. Parker.

How to Start a Home Business. New York, NY: Avon Books, 1995. By: Michael Antoniak.

How to Start & Manage a Home Based Business: A Practical Way to Start a Home Based Business. Interlochen, MI: Lewis & Renn Associates, 1996. By: Jerre G. Lewis.

How to Start a Successful Home Business. New York, NY: Warner Books, Inc. 1997. By: Karen Cheney.

"How to Succeed in 4 Easy Steps" in Inc. (Vol. 17, No. 10, July 1995, pp. 30-32, 34, 36-40, 42). By: Bo Burlingham.

"The Hype About Home Businesses" in Inc. (Vol. 18, No. 7, May 1996, p. 58). By: John Case.

"In The Cards" in Income Opportunities (Vol. 31, No. 2, February 1996, p. 10). By Lana Sanderson.

"The Incredible Upbeatness of Being" in Inc. (Vol. 19, No. 15, December 21, 1997, pp. 24-25). By: Susan Greco.

"Insurance: Easy Rider" in Business Start-Ups (Vol. 7, No. 6, June 1995, p. 18). By: Janean Huber.

"Interior Design" in Business Start-Ups (Vol. 7, No. 7, July 1995, p. 18). By: Wendy Neuman.

"Item-Of-The-Month Club" in Business Start-Ups (Vol. 8, No. 7, July 1996, p. 29). By: Guen Sublette.

The Joy of Working from Home: Making a Life While Making a Living. San Francisco, CA: Berrett-Koehler Publishers, 1994. By: Jeff Berner.

"Just a Mailbox Away" in Black Enterprise (Vol. 27, No. 3, October 1996, p. 34). By: Robyn Clarke.

"Keep in Touch" in Business Start-Ups (Vol. 8, No. 5, May 1996, pp. 8, 10). By: Carla Goodman.

"Keep Your Firm From Zoning Out" in Black Enterprise (Vol. 26, No. 8, March 1996, p. 29). By: Carolyn M. Brown.

"The Kiddie Zone" in Income Opportunities (Vol. 30, No. 10, October 1995, pp. 32, 34, 36). By: Pamela Rohland.

"Kids Underfoot" in Business Start-Ups (Vol. 8, No. 1, January 1996, p. 16). By: Johanna S. Billings.

The Kitchen Table Millionaire: Home-Based Money-Making Strategies to Build Financial Independence Today. New York, NY: The McGraw-Hill Companies, 1997. By: Patrick W. Cochrane.

"Loan Originators Needed: No Experience Required" in Income Opportunities (Vol. 34, Issue 1, January/February 1999, p. 48).

"Love Bytes" in Income Opportunities (Vol. 30, No. 7, July 1995, p. 8). By: Lana Sanderson.

"Make the Guidelines Clear When Home, Office Overlap" in Crain's Small Business (December 1996, pp. 10-11). By: Jeffrey McCracken.

"Making It Big" in Business Start-Ups (Vol. 7, No. 10, October 1995, p. 16).

Marketing for the Home-Based Business. Holbrook, MA: Adams Publishing, 1990. By: Jeffrey P. Davidson.

"Marketing Magic" in Business Start-Ups (Vol. 7, No. 9, September 1995, pp. 12, 14). By: Sue Clayton.

"Medical Transcription" in Business Start-Ups (Vol. 9, No. 1, January 1997, p. 30). By Karin Moeller.

"Meeting of the Minds" in Entrepreneur (August 1996, p. 55). By: Cynthia E. Griffin.

"Minimize Your Exposure" in Hispanic Business (Vol. 18, No. 11, November 1996, p. 58). By: Rick Mendosa.

"Mixed Signals" in Income Opportunities (Vol. 30, No. 10, October 1995, p. 10). By: Lana Sanderson.

"Moving Day" in Income Opportunities (Vol. 30, No. 11, November 1995, p. 10). By: Lana Sanderson.

"Moving Out" in Income Opportunities (Vol. 32, No. 4, April 1997, pp. 1418, 88). By: Dale D. Buss.

"Name That Business" in Business Start-Ups (Vol. 8, No. 4, April 1996, pp. 18, 20). By: Sue Clayton.

"Name Your Price" in Entrepreneur (Vol. 24, No. 4, April 1996, p. 52). By: Cynthia E. Griffin.

"Necessary Ingredients" in Entrepreneur (Vol. 23, No. 5, May 1995, pp. 62, 64-65). By: Cynthia E. Griffin.

"Networking from Home" in Business Start-Ups (Vol. 7, No. 11, November 1995, p. 14). By: Sue Clayton.

"A New Resolve" in Income Opportunities (Vol. 31, No. 1, January 1996, p. 10). By: Lana Sanderson.

"No Place Like Home" in Black Enterprise (Vol. 25, No. 8, March 1995, p. 39). By: Nadirah Z. Sabir.

"Noise Pollution" in Income Opportunities (Vol. 31, No. 6, June 1996, p. 10). By: Lana Sanderson.

"Northern Exposure" in Entrepreneur (Vol. 23, No. 2, February 1995, pp. 80, 82). By: Debra Phillips.

"Not-So-Impossible Dream" in Small Business Opportunities (Vol. 8, No. 6, November 1996, pp. 92, 110). By: Lin Grensing-Pophal.

"On Her Soapbox" in Income Opportunities (Vol. 32, No. 2, 1997, pp. 88, 90, 92). By: Laurel Berger.

"On Location" in Entrepreneur (Vol. 23, No. 3, March 1995, pp. 86, 89). By: Debra Phillips.

"On The Home Front" in Income Opportunities (Vol. 31, No. 4, April 1996, pp. 54-60, 62, 64-65, 72). By: Robert L. Perry.

On Your Own: A Guide to Working Happily, Productively & Successfully at Home. Paramus, NJ: Prentice Hall, 1994. By: Lionel L. Fisher.

One Hundred-One Home Office Success Secrets. Franklin Lakes, NJ: Career Press, Inc. 1994. By: Lisa Kanarek.

One Thousand One Businesses You Can Start from Home. New York, NY: John Wiley & Sons, Inc. 1992. By: Daryl Allen Hall.

Operating a Desktop Video Service on Your Home-Based PC. New York, NY: The McGraw-Hill Companies, 1994. By: Harvey Summers.

"Order from Chaos" in Small Business Opportunities (Vol. 9, No. 2, March 1997, pp. 12, 146). By: Marie Sherlock.

Organizing Your Home Office for Success: Expert Strategies That Can Work for You. New York, NY: NAL Dutton, 1993. By: Lisa Kanarek.

"Out of the Ashes" in Entrepreneur (November, 1996 pp. 66, 68). By: Cynthia E. Griffin.

"Outgrown Your Home?" in Hispanic Business (May 1998, p. 64). By: Joel Russell.

"Parental Advice" in Business Start-Ups (Vol. 7, No. 11, November 1995, p. 17).

Partners at Work and at Home: How Couples Can Build a Successful Business Together without Killing Each Other. Bellingham, WA: Self-Counsel Press, Inc. 1994, first edition. By: Annette O'Shea-Roche and Sieglinde Malmberg.

"Partytime Profits" in Small Business Opportunities (Vol. 10, No. 6, November 1998, pp. 92, 94). By: Kathleen Landis.

"Plan Healthy Schedule for Work at Home" in Crain's Small Business (January 1996, p. 4). By: Frank Provenzano.

"Pressing Matters" in Income Opportunities (Vol. 31, No. 9, October 1996, pp. 94, 96). By: Kendra Russell.

"Quiet, Please" in Business Start-Ups (Vol. 10, No. 8, August 1998, p. 14). By: Lynn H. Colwell.

"Reflections" in Small Business Opportunities (Vol. 10, No. 6, November 1998, p. 108). By: Alwin Jennette.

"Resume Writing" in Business Start-Ups (Vol. 8, No. 7, July 1996, p. 28). By: Guen Sublette.

"Right Moves" in Business Start-Ups (Vol. 7, No. 10, October 1995, p.14). By: Sue Clayton.

"Rule of Engagement" in Business Start-Ups (Vol. 8, No. 7, July 1996, pp. 8, 10). By: Janie Sullivan.

"Safe and Sound" in Business Start-Ups (Vol. 8, No. 10, October 1996, pp. 8, 10). By: Julie Bawden Davis.

Secrets to Running a Successful Business. Kirkland, WA. 1994. By: Jeanette L. Rosenberg.

"Self Worth" in Income Opportunities (Vol. 30, No. 9, September 1995, p. 10). By: Lana Sanderson.

"Sending Workers Home—To Work" in Independent Business (Vol. 7, No. 4, July/Aug. 1996, pp. 20-22). By: Verna Gates.

"Separation Anxiety" in Business Start-Ups (Vol. 9, No. 1, January 1997, pp. 8, 10). By: Carolyn Campbell.

"The Service Boom" in Small Business Opportunities (Vol. 9, No. 3, May 1997, pp. 22-41).

"Shoestring Start-Ups" in Income Opportunities (Vol. 30, No. 1, January 1995, pp. 34-44). By: Lori Schwind Murray.

"Shoestring Start-Ups" in Income Opportunities (Vol. 31, No. 2, February 1996, pp. 22-25, 72, 74, 80-81, 88, 90). By: Lori Schwind Murray.

"Shoestring Start-Ups" in Income Opportunities (Vol. 32, No. 4, April 1997, pp. 20-23, 76, 82, 84, 86). By: Lori Schwind Murray.

"Shoestring Start-Ups" in Small Business Opportunities (Vol. 10, No. 6, November 1998, pp. 22-34, 122).

"Silver Lining" in Entrepreneur (June 1995, pp. 52, 54-55). By: Cynthia E. Griffin.

The Small Business Reference Guide for Home-Based Business, Small Manufacturers, Self-Publishers, Entrepreneurs, Craftsmen, Retailers, Writers. Stratford, CT: Bluechip Books By: Belle M. Biebel.

"Solid Foundations" in Black Enterprise (Vol. 27, No. 7, February 1997, p. 38). By: Denolyn Carroll.

"The Stamp of Success" in Income Opportunities (Vol. 30, No. 5, May 1995, pp. 35-36, 94, 102). By: Amy H. Berger.

Start, Run and Profit from Your Own Home-Based Business. New York, NY: John Wiley & Sons, Inc. 1991. By: Gregory Kishel and Patricia Kishel.

Start and Run a Profitable Home-Based Business. Bellingham, WA: Self-Counsel Press, Inc. 1994, second edition (print); 1995 (audiocassette). By: Edna Sheedy.

"Start-Up Chasers Track New-Biz Storm" in Inc. (Vol. 19, No. 5, April 1997, p. 22). By: Jerry Useem.

Start Your Own: One Hundred One Extra Income Ideas. Paramus, NJ: Pfeiffer & Co. 1994. By: JoAnn Padgett.

Stay Home & Get Rich. Lenore, ID: Mountain Publishing Co. 1994. By: Stewart Kime.

"Staying Sane" in Business Start-Ups (Vol. 7, No. 10, October 1995, pp. 14, 16).

"Step 2: Do Your Homework" in Business Start-Ups (Vol. 8, No. 6, June 1996, pp. 8, 10). By: Kylo-Patrick Hart.

"A Stitch in Time" in Small Business Opportunities (Vol. 11, No. 2, March 1999, p. 120).

"Sun Block" in Income Opportunities (Vol. 30, No. 6, June 1995, p. 8). By: Lana Sanderson.

"Support System" in Business Start-Ups (Vol. 10, No. 8, August 1998, p. 14). By: Lynn H. Colwell.

"Taking Stock" in Income Opportunities (Vol. 31, No. 3, March 1996, p. 10). By: Lana Sanderson.

"Tax Rules to Ease Deducting the Costs of Home Offices and Health Insurance" in The Wall Street Journal (Vol. C, No. 22, July 31, 1997). By: Tom Herman and Rodney Ho.

"Tech Tools: No Mixed Signals" in Business Start-Ups (Vol. 7, No. 6, June 1995, p. 19). By: Irene Bennet.

"Technical Difficulties" in Income Opportunities (Vol. 31, No. 8, August 1996, p. 12). By: Lana Sanderson.

Telecom Made Easy: Money-Saving, Profit-Building Solutions for Home Businesses, Telecommuters & Small Organizations. Newport, RI: Aegis Publishing Group, Ltd. 3rd ed. 1998. By: June Langhoff; foreword by Terri Lonier.

The Telecommuter's Advisor: Working in the Fast Lane. Newport, RI: Aegis Publishing Group, Ltd. 1996. By: June Langhoff.

The Ten Best Opportunities for Starting a Home Business Today. Boulder, CO: Live Oak Publications, 1993. By: Reed Glenn and New Careers Center, Inc. staff.

Three Hundred One Plus Ways to Get Ahead—Business Success from Home. Branson, MO: Vanatech Systems, Inc. 1994. By: Susan Klopfer.

"Top 101 Homebased Franchises" in Entrepreneur (October 1997, pp. 164,166-167).

"Tough Calls" in Income Opportunities (Vol. 31, No. 11, November 1996, p. 12). By: Lana Sanderson.

"Two for the Moonlighter" in Income Opportunities (Vol. 33, Issue 10, December 1998, p. 12).

"United We Stand" in Business Start-Ups (Vol. 7, No. 8, August 1995, pp. 14-15).

The Work-At-Home Sourcebook: How to Find At-Home Work That's Right for You. Boulder, CO: Live Oak Publications, Fifth edition, 1994. By: Lynie Arden.

"Work, Suite Work" in Crain's Small Business Office Tech '96 Supplement (Vol. 4, No. 11, November 1996, p. T-9). By: Regina Baraban.

Working at Home: A Dream That's Becoming a Trend. Eugene, OR: Harvest House Publishers, Inc. 1990. By: Lindsey O'Connor.

Working from Home: Everything You Need to Know about Living and Working Under the Same Roof. New York, NY: Jeremy P. Tarcher Inc. Third edition, 1990. By: Paul and Sarah Edwards.

"The Year of the Home Network?" in Business Week (January 18, 1999, p. 22). By: Stephen H. Wildstrom.

"The Year of Living Dangerously" in Business Start-Ups (Vol. 7, No. 6, June 1995, pp. 74, 76-77). By: Jeannie Pearce.

Home Furnishings Store

"Coming Home" in Inc. (Vol. 19, No. 15, December 21, 1997, p. 57). By: Joseph Rosenbloom.

"Designing Woman" in Entrepreneur (Vol. 23, No. 2, February 1995, pp. 126, 128-131). By: Bob Weinstein.

"Designing woman" in Entrepreneur (Vol. 26, No. 11, November 1998, p. 44). By: Elaine W. Teague.

"The Fall of Bombay" in Inc. (Vol. 18, No. 1, January 1996, pp. 48-52, 54-55). By: Edward O. Welles.

Home Furnishings Merchandising and Store Design. New York, NY: Retail Reporting Bureau, 1990. By: Martin M. Pegler, editor.

Lifestyles Furniture: A Sole Proprietorship Merchandising Business Practice Set. New York, NY: The McGraw-Hill Companies, revised edition, 1990. By: Horace R. Brock.

"Pipe Dreams" in Small Business Opportunities (Vol. 10, No. 6, November 1998, pp. 2, 44, and 60). By: Stan Roberts.

"The Proof is in the Product" in Income Opportunities (Vol. 30, No. 5, May 1995, pp. 33-34, 104). By: Julie Monahan.

"The Stamp of Success" in Income Opportunities (Vol. 30, No. 5, May 1995, pp. 35-36, 94, 102). By: Amy H. Berger.

"Their Idea's Not All Washed Up" in Crain's Detroit Business. (Vol. 12, No. 2, January 1996, p. 3). By: Marsha Stopa.

Incubators

"Birth of a Business" in Hispanic Business (Vol. 18, No. 9, September 1996, p. 10). By: Rick Mendosa.

"The business factory" in Black Enterprise (Vol. 29, No. 3, October 1998, p. 119). By: Carolyn M. Brown.

Directory of Operating Small Business Investment Companies. Upland, PA: DIANE Publishing Co. 1998. By: John Wilmeth.

"Growing Places" in Entrepreneur (Vol. 23, No. 2, February 1995, pp. 108, 110-113). By: Cynthia E. Griffin.

"Hatching a Business" in Small Business Opportunities (Vol. 8, No. 5, September 1996, pp. 78, 80). By: Mary Ann McLaughlin.

"High-Tech Success Starts in a Garage - Dot Com" in Income Opportunities (Vol. 33, Issue 7, September 1998, pp. 54-55). By: Steven M. Brown.

"Incubator Roundup" in Entrepreneur (Vol. 23, No. 11, October 1995, p. 188). By: Cynthia E. Griffin.

"Ready For Takeoff" in Business Start-Ups (Vol. 11, February 1999, pp. 45-48). By: Julie Bawden Davis.

Regional Economic Analysis of Innovation & Incubation. Brookfield, VT: Ashgate Publishing Co. Inc. 1991. By: E.J. Davelaar.

"Room to Grow" in Business Start-Ups (Vol. 10, No. 10, October 1998, p. 5). By: Sean M. Lyden.

"Small-business incubator lands $75,000 challenge grant" in The Business Journal (October 12, 1998, p. 21). By: Peter Delevett.

Small Business Investment Company Directory & Handbook. Rockville Centre, NY: International Wealth Success, Inc. 10th ed. 1999. By: Tyler G. Hicks.

"Where Dreams Get Hope" in Crain's Detroit Business (Vol. 12, No. 16, April 1996, pp. 3, 26). By: Robert Akeny.

Insurance Agency

"After a Disaster" in Income Opportunities (Vol. 32, No. 7, July 1997, pp. 32, 34-35). By: Malinda Reinke.

"Are You Off or On?" in Journal of the American Society of CLU & ChFC (Vol. 49, No. 1, January 1995, pp. 10-14). By: Steve Church.

"Best Sellers" in Entrepreneur (August 1996, pp. 100-110). By: Robert McGarvey.

Best's Insurance Reports. Oldwick, NJ: A. M. Best Co. 1994.

"Bucking convention and winning clients" in Nation's Business (Vol. 86, No. 2, February 1998, p. 6). By: Terrance, Leon, and John Resnick.

"Developing a Simple Agency Marketing Plan" in Rough Notes (Vol. 138, No. 2, February 1995, pp. 14-16). By: Robert L. Stewart.

Dictionary of Insurance. Lanham, MD: Littlefield, Adams Quality Paperbacks, Seventh edition, 1990. By: Lewis E. Davids.

Ethics for the Property-Casualty Professional. Chicago, IL: Dearborn Financial Publishing, Inc. 1995.

Glossary of Insurance Terms. Santa Monica, CA: Merritt Co. 1994. By: Thomas E. Green.

"Image Makers" in Inc. (Vol. 19, No. 17, January 18, 1998, pp. 133-134, 137). By: David Abrahamson.

Insurance Agent (Accident & Health). Syosset, NY: National Learning Corp. 1991. By: Jack Rudman.

Insurance Agent—Insurance Broker (Fire & Casualty). Syosset, NY: National Learning Corp. 1991. By: Jack Rudman.

Insurance Law Anthology. Arlington, VA: International Library Law Book Publishers, Inc. 1991. By: Donald J. Hoyes, editor.

Insurance Manager. Syosset, NY: National Learning Corp. 1991. By: Jack Rudman.

"Reducing Risks and Costs" in Black Enterprise (Vol. 27, No. 4, November 1996, p. 28). By: Ann Brown.

"Success Insured Via Customer Service" in Crain's Small Business (October 1995, p. 23). By: Jeffrey McCracken.

"Successful Strategies of a Small Agency" in American Agent & Broker (Vol. 67, No. 1, January 1995, pp. 32-34). By: Paul Corbley.

Taxation of Insurance Business. Charlottesville, VA: MICHIE, Third edition, 1992. By: J. S. MacLeod and A.R. Levitt.

Veterans Claims Examiner. Syosset, NY: National Learning Corp. 1994. By: Jack Rudman.

Winning: Direct Marketing for Insurance Agents and Brokers. Naperville, IL: Sourcebooks, Inc. 1992. By: Donald R. Jackson and Irwin Lowen.

Jewelry Store

"5 Great Businesses for Young Entrepreneurs" in Black Enterprise (Vol. 27, No. 5, December 1996, pp. 96, 100, 102, 104). By: Tonia L. Shakespeare.

"Ask the Experts" in Income Opportunities (Vol. 32 , No. 3, March 1997, pp. 56, 58, 60).

The Buyer's Guide to Affordable Antique Jewelry: How to Find, Buy, and Care for Fabulous Antique Jewelry. Secaucus, NJ: Carol Publishing Group, 1993. By: Anna M. Miller.

Contemporary American Jewelry Design. New York, NY: Van Nostrand Reinhold Co. Inc. 1991. By: Ettagale Blauer, editor.

"Glass Menagerie" in Income Opportunities (Vol. 32 , No. 3, March 1997, pp. 90, 92). By: Amy H. Berger.

Handbook of Fine Jewelry. Atglen, PA: Schiffer Publishing, Ltd. 1991. By: Nancy N. Schiffer.

Jeweler's Almanac. Radnor, PA: Jewelers' Book Club, 1992.

Jeweler's Resource: A Reference of Gems, Metals, Formulas & Terminology. Thornton, CO: Jewelers Press, 1994. By: Bruce G. Knuth.

Jewelry and Gems: The Buying Guide, How to Buy Diamonds, Pearls, Precious and Other Popular Gems with Confidence and Knowledge. Woodstock, VT: GemStone Press, Third edition, 1993. By: Antoinette L. Matlins.

Master Keys for Making Profits in Lapidary. York, PA: Adamas Publishing, 1994. By: Gerald L. Wykoff.

The Pearl Buying Guide. Los Angeles, CA: International Jewelry Publications, Second edition, 1994. By: Renee Newman.

Professional Goldsmithing: A Contemporary Guide to Traditional Jewelry Techniques. New York, NY: Chapman & Hall, 1991. By: Alan Revere.

"Shoestring Start-Ups" in Income Opportunities (Vol. 32, No. 4, April 1997, pp. 20-23, 76, 82, 84, 86). By: Lori Schwind Murray.

Victorian Jewelry: Unexplored Treasures. New York, NY: Abbeville Press, Inc. 1991. By: Corinne Davidov and Ginny R. Dawes.

"The X-treme Files" in Business Start-Ups (Vol. 11, March 1999, pp. 45-47). By: Gayle Sato Stodder.

"You Win!" in Independent Business (Vol. 9, No. 3, May/June 1998, pp. 53-55). By: Natalie Hall.

Management Consulting Service

"Adapt or Die" in Red Herring: Guide to Professional Services 1999 (1999, p. 46). By: Janet Kettlehut.

"Architect of Change" in Corporate Detroit (Vol. 13, No. 12, December 1995, pp. 31-33, 35). By: Claire M. Hinsberg.

At the Service Quality Frontier: A Handbook for Managers, Consultants, and Other Pioneers. Milwaukee, WI: ASQC Quality Press, 1993. By: Mary M. LoSardo and Norma M. Rossi.

"BOOM!" in Inc. (Vol. 19, No. 6, May 1997, pp. 56-58). By: Dr. Steven Berglas.

Client-Centered Consulting: A Practical Guide for Internal Advisers and Trainers. New York, NY: The McGraw-Hill Companies, 1992. By: Peter Cockman.

"Conducting Employee Reviews" in Black Enterprise (Vol. 28, No. 1, August 1997, p. 34). By: Deidra-Ann Parrish.

"Consultants Make Integrity the Bottom Line" in Crain's Detroit Business (Vol. 11, No. 24, June 12-18, 1996, p. 11). By: Mary Dempsey.

The Consultant's Proposal, Fee, & Contract Problem-Solver. New York, NY: John Wiley & Sons, Inc. 1993. By: Ronald Tepper.

Consulting for Success: A Guide for Prospective Consultants. Menlo Park, CA: Crisp Publications, Inc. 1991. By: David Karlson.

"Entrepreneurial Spirit Awards" in Hispanic Business (Vol. 18, No. 12, December 1996, pp. 26, 28, 30, 34, 36, 38). By: Maria Zate.

Field Casework: Methods for Consulting to Small & Startup Businesses. Thousand Oaks, CA: Sage Publications, Inc. 1996. By: Lisa K. Gundry.

Finding Your Niche...Marketing Your Professional Service. Berkeley, CA: Community Resource Institute Press, 1992. By: Bart Brodsky and Janet Geis.

Flawless Consulting: A Guide to Getting Your Expertise Used. San Francisco, CA: Pfeiffer & Co. By: Peter Block.

"Graduate Turns Coach To Help Minorities Qualify for SBA Loans" in American Banker (Vol. 163, No. 65, April 7, 1998, p. 6). By: Paul Nadler.

"Graduation day from 8(a): here are the steps you need to follow" in Black Enterprise (Vol. 28, No. 7, Feb. 1998, p. 161). By: Joyce Jones.

Handbook of Management Consulting Services. New York, NY: The McGraw-Hill Companies, 1995. By: Sam W. Barcus and Joseph W. Wilkinson, editors.

"Help! I can't keep up with my business reading." in Inc. (Vol. 19, No. 12, September 1997, p. 109). By: Stephanie Gruner.

"Hire Power" in Entrepreneur (September 1997, p. 34). By: Jacquelyn Lynn.

"How Many Accountants Does It Take to Change an Industry" in Inc. (Vol. 19, No. 5, April 1997, pp. 63-64, 66-69). By: Jill Andresky Fraser.

How to Succeed as an Independent Consultant. New York, NY: John Wiley & Sons, Inc. 1993. By: Herman R. Holtz.

"JumpStart Your Business" in Inc. (Vol. 19, No. 6, May 1997, pp. 36-38, 40, 43-44, 47-48, 50,54). By: John Grossmann.

Management Consulting 1996. Boston, MA: Harvard Business School Press, 1995.

Management Consulting: A Guide to the Profession. Washington, DC: International Labor Office, Second edition, 1990.

Management Consulting: Theory & Tools for Small Business Interventions. Houston, TX: Dame Publications, Inc. 1998. By: Porth and Saltis.

"Management Recruiters International, Inc." in Income Opportunities (Vol. 31, No. 9, October 1996, p. 21).

"Modeling Your Company's Future" in Inc. (Vol. 19, No. 18, December 1997, pp. 33-34). By: Nancy K. Austin.

"Nick of Time" in Red Herring: Guide to Professional Services 1999 (1999, p. 47). By: Janet Kettlehut.

"Separated at work" in Entrepreneur (Vol. 26, No. 3, March 1998, p. 132). By: Brian Steinberg.

"Stage Right" in Entrepreneur (April 1997, pp. 71-73). By: Mark Henricks.

Start and Run a Profitable Consulting Business. Bellingham, WA: Self-Counsel Press, Inc. Third edition, 1990. By: Douglas A. Gray.

"Survival Skills" in Business Start-Ups (Vol. 7, No. 8, August 1995, p. 64). By: Anne Dullaghan.

"The Takeover" in Inc. (Vol. 19, No. 5, April 1997, pp. 72-75, 78, 80-82). By: Stephanie Gruner.

"That's Entertainment!" in Independent Business (Vol. 8, No. 3, May/June 1997, pp. 60-62). By: Echo Montgomery Garrett.

"Valassis Takes a Clipping" in Crain's Detroit Business (Vol. 13, No. 5, March 1997, p. 2). By: Matt Roush.

Manufacturing Businesses

21st Century Manufacturing Enterprise Strategy,Vol. I: An Industry-Led View. Upland, PA: DIANE Publishing Co. 1998. By: Roger N. Nagel and Rick Dove.

21st Century Manufacturing Enterprise Strategy,Vol. II: Infrastructure. Upland, PA: DIANE Publishing Co. 1998. By: Roger N. Nagel and Rick Dove.

"1996 Small Business Entrepreneurs of the Year" in Black Enterprise (Vol. 27, No. 4, November 1996, pp. 75-77). By: Robyn Clarke.

"Anasteel & Supply Co." in Hispanic Business (Vol. 18, No. 6, June 1996, p. 106). By: Graham Witherall.

"Anything Goes" in Business Start-Ups (Vol. 11, No. 1, January 1999, p. 45). By: Christopher D. Lancette.

"Ask the Expert" in Income Opportunities (Vol. 33, Issue 7, September 1998, p. 8).

Benchmarking Global Manufacturing: Understanding International Suppliers, Customers, and Competitors. Burr Ridge, IL: Irwin Professional Publishing By: Jeffrey G. Miller, Arnoud De Meyer and Jinichiro Nakane.

"Berry Booming Biz" in Small Business Opportunities (Vol. 11, No. 2, March 1999, pp. 46-48). By: Annette Wood.

"Beyond Latin America" in Hispanic Business (Vol. 18, No. 11, November 1996, pp. 34, 36, 38, 40-41). By: Joel Russell.

The Business of Injection Molding: What It Takes to Succeed As a Custom Molder. Denver, CO: Abby Communications, Inc. 1998. By: Clare Goldsberry.

"The Cable Guy: Entrepreneur Risked Everything to Start World Class Company" in The Business Journal - Serving Milwaukee (Vol. 15, No. 48, August 21, 1998, p. 9). By: Carlise Newman.

"Can We Reduce the Cost of Handling Customers' Complaints?" in Inc. (Vol. 19, No. 18, December 1997, p. 148). By: Stephanie Gruner.

"Chain Reaction" in Income Opportunities (Vol. 30, No. 1, January 1995, pp. 26-28, 30, 33). By: Dale D. Buss.

"Clothes Make the Man" in Business Start-Ups (Vol. 7, No. 7, July 1995, pp. 62, 64, 66). By: Pamala Rohland.

Common Sense Manufacturing: Becoming a Top Value Competitor. Burr Ridge, IL: Professional Publishing, 1991. By: James A. Gardner.

Competing in Manufacturing and How to Make Things Better. New York, NY: Gordon Press Publishers, 1992.

"Crash Course" in Inc. (Vol. 17, No. 2, February 1995, pp. 54-56, 59-63). By: Robert A. Mamis.

"Deal may mean minority supplier cash boom" in Ward's Automotive Reports (May 11, 1998, p. 3).

"Deejays' Chatter Brightens Tub Cleanser's Prospects" in Inc. (Vol. 19, No. 18, December 1997, pp. 25, 27). By: Marc Ballon.

"Doing Business in South Africa" in Black Enterprise (Vol. 25, No. 10, May 1995, pp. 58-62, 67-68). By: Frank McCoy.

"Enterprise resource planning unites all of a company's major business practices" in Inc. (Vol. 20, No. 13, September 15, 1998, p. 70). By: Jeffrey Zygmont.

"Entrepreneurial duo plans to build corporate jets" in Pacific Business News (September 28, 1998, p. 23). By: Michael Rose.

"Entrepreneurial Superstars" in Entrepreneur (April 1997, pp. 108-139). By: Debra Phillips and others.

"Entrepreneurs Across America" in Entrepreneur (Vol. 24, No. 4, April 1996, pp. 100-104, 106-108, 110-112, 114-116, 118, 120-123). By: Janean Chum, Debra Phillips, Cynthia E. Griffin, Heather Page, Lynn Beresford, Holly Celeste Fisk, and Charlotte Mulbern.

"Family Affair" in Small Business Opportunities (Vol. 11, No. 2, March 1999, p. 150).

Flexible Manufacturing Technologies and International Competitiveness. New York, NY: St. Martin's Press, Inc. 1991. By: Joe Tidd.

"Floating a novel idea" in Nation's Business (Vol. 86, No. 6, June 1998, p. 91). By: Roberta Maynard.

Fundamentals of Manufacturing Systems Design and Analysis. New York, NY: Chapman & Hall, 1991. By: B. Wu.

"Get the Skinny" in Business Start-Ups (Vol. 10, No. 9, September 1998, p. 94). By: G. David Doran.

Good Manufacturing Practice: Philosophy and Application. Buffalo Grove, IL: Interpharm Press, Inc. 1991. By: John Sharp.

"Here comes the sun: Milwaukee retiree markets solar ovens to feed poor countries" in The Business Journal - Serving Milwaukee (Vol. 15, No. 32, May 1, 1998, p. 13). By: Carlise Newman.

"Hold out or sell out?" in Crain's Detroit Business (Vol. 15, January 25-31, 1999, pp. 3, 41). By: Robert Sherefkin.

"Hot Tip" in Inc. (Vol. 19, No. 11, August 1997, p. 93). By: Stephanie Gruner.

"How can we improve efficiency?" in Inc. (Vol. 19, No. 10, July 1997, p. 105). By: Stephanie Gruner.

"How can I persuade top-notch people to join my advisory board?" in Inc. (Vol. 19, No. 18, December 1997, p. 149). By: Susan Greco.

How to Set Up a Retail Store, Service Company, and a Manufacturing Firm—Case Studies. Minneapolis, MN: American Institute of Small Business (AISB), 1991.

"Icemen Cometh" in Small Business Opportunities (Vol. 11, No. 1, January 1999, p. 44). By: Stan Roberts.

"Legends" in Small Business Opportunities (Vol. 7, No. 1, January 1995, pp. 46, 48).

"Living Large" in Entrepreneur (October 1997, pp. 156,158-159). By: Frances Huffman.

"Made-to-Order Profit" in Small Business Opportunities (Vol. 11, No. 2, March 1999, p. 62). By: Geri Anderson.

"Maker of golf clubs builds an image, namely by brand" in Crain's Detroit Business (December 14-20, 1998, pp. E4-5). By: Joseph Serwach.

Managing the Manufacturing Process: A Pattern for Excellence. New York, NY: John Wiley & Sons, Inc. 1991. By: Ralph W. Woodgate.

Manufacturing Development Applications: Guidelines for Attaining Productivity and Quality. Norcross, GA: Industrial Engineering & Management Press, 1992. By: Andre McHose.

Manufacturing Planning and Control Systems. Burr Ridge, IL: Richard D. Irwin, Inc. Third edition, 1992. By: Thomas E. Vollmann.

"Metallurgical Urge Beats Martial Plan" in Crain's Small Business (July 1996, p. 15). By: Jeffrey McCracken.

"Mixing Up a Recipe for Success - Hold the Gluten" in Income Opportunities (Vol. 33, Issue 10, December 1998, p. 66). By: Amy H. Berger.

"New York" in Hispanic Business (Vol. 17, No. 5, May 1995, p. 36). By: Yvonne Conde.

"Niche Marketing: Key to At-Home Bookmark Business" in Income Opportunities (Vol. 33, Issue 10, December 1998, pp. 52-53). By: Howard Scott.

"Outsourcery" in Inc. (Vol. 19, No. 5, April 1997, pp. 54-56, 58, 60). By: Edward O. Welles.

"Paper-Plas' plan provides personal marketing niche" in Crain's Detroit Business (December 14-20, 1998, p. E17). By: Joseph Serwach.

Partners in Learning: Manufacturers and Users. Scarsdale, NY: Work in America Institute, Inc. Updated edition, 1991. By: Rosow.

"The Perfect Combo" in Small Business Opportunities (Vol. 11, No. 2, March 1999, p. 82). By: Joanne Palmer Bollenbacher.

"Pipe Dreams" in Small Business Opportunities (Vol. 10, No. 6, November 1998, pp. 42, 44, 60). By: Stan Roberts.

"Portion Control" in Entrepreneur (Vol. 26, Issue 12, December 1998, p. 104). By: Tomima Edmark.

"A Profitable Feast" in Business Start-Ups (Vol. 8, No. 6, June 1996, pp. 60, 62-66). By: Sandra Mardenfeld.

"Prototyping Firm 'Can Hardly Keep Up' with Work" in Crain's Detroit Business (Vol. 13, No. 6, February 1997, p. 31). By: Arthur Bridgeforth Jr.

"Pumpkin Master Carves Out Big Profits" in Income Opportunities (Vol. 33, Issue 8, October 1998, p. 66). By: Amy Berger.

"Rainbow's Good Luck" in Crain's Detroit Business (Vol. 13, No. 13, March/April 1997, pp. 3, 14). By: Matt Roush.

"Running out of Time" in Inc. (Vol. 19, No. 2, February 1997, pp. 63-64, 68, 72-73). By: John Grossmann.

"Seawater into Gold" in Small Business Opportunities (Vol. 11, No. 2, March 1999, pp. 70, 162).

"Specialty Soap Makers Clean Up!" in Income Opportunities (Vol. 33, Issue 10, December 1998, p. 36). By: Tamara Jordan.

"Stamp out Bad Checks" in Black Enterprise (Vol. 27, No. 3, October 1996, p. 36). By: Ann L. Brown.

"Stamp of Success" in Small Business Opportunities (Vol. 11, No. 2, March 1999, p. 86). By: Sandra Mardenfeld.

"Success story" in Virginia Business (June 1998, p. 34). By: Bill Edwards.

"Success by the Tile" in Hispanic Business (May 1998, p. 18). By: Janet Perez.

"Summer's here. I know I should take a vacation, but..." in Inc. (Vol. 19, No. 10, July 1997, p. 104).

"Taking License" in Business Start-Ups (Vol. 10, No. 10, October 1998, pp. 74 and 77). By: Don Debelak.

"Tank commander" in Nation's Business (Vol. 86, No. 5, May 1998, p. 86). By: Sharon Nelton.

"Thing Big" in Business Start-Ups (Vol. 10, No. 10, October 1998, pp. 27-33). By: Don Debelak.

"This Big One Didn't Get Away" in Crain's Detroit Business (Vol. 12, No. 35, Aug. 26-Sept. 1, 1996, pp. 3, 26). By: Joseph Serwach.

"Toner firm turns in impressive performance" in Philadelphia Business Journal (June 26, 1998, p. B7). By: Bob Brooke.

"Tradition, Trends Combine for Profitable Cigar Business" in Income Opportunities (Vol. 33, Issue 8, October 1998, p. 55). By: Pamela Rohland.

"US and Mexico Produce Directory" in Entrepreneur (September 1997, p. 164).

Winning Manufacturing: The How-to-Book of Successful Manufacturing. New York, NY: The McGraw-Hill Companies, 1991. By: James A. Tompkins.

"Woven Together" in Crain's Detroit Business (December 7-13, 1998, pp. 1, 28). By: Tenisha Mercer.

Medical Claims Service

"Ask the Experts" in Income Opportunities (Vol. 32 , No. 3, March 1997, pp. 56, 58, 60).

"Audit Medical Bills from Home" in Income Opportunities (Vol. 33, Issue 10, December 1998, p. 12).

"Home Run" in Business Start-Ups (Vol. 7, No. 7, July 1995, pp. 28, 30, 32-34, 36-37). By: Bill Kemp.

Medicaid Claims Examiner. Syosset, NY: National Learning Corp. 1994. By: Jack Rudman.

"Recipients Move from Medicaid to Marketing" in Crain's Detroit Business (Vol. 11, No. 31, July/August 1995, p. 13). By: Steve Raphael.

Senior Medicaid Claims Examiner. Syosset, NY: National Learning Corp. 1994. By: Jack Rudman.

"The Senior Sell" in Income Opportunities (Vol. 30, No. 11, November 1995, pp. 20-23, 110, 112). By: Nancy Kennedy.

"Success for Less" in Business Start-Ups (Vol. 7, No. 6, June 1995, pp. 26-28, 30, 32, 34, 36, 38, 40-42). By: Maura Hudson Pomije.

Supervising Medicaid Claims Examiner. Syosset, NY: National Learning Corp. 1994. By: Jack Rudman.

"Three Catch Entrepreneur Spirit in Managed Care" in Crain's Detroit Business (Vol. 11, No. 31, July/August 1995, p. 11). By: Steve Raphael.

"The Top Ten Biz for 1999" in Small Business Opportunities (Vol. 11, No. 1, January 1999, pp. 22-40).

Medical and Dental Instrument Manufacturing

Biomedical Equipment: Use, Maintenance and Management. Paramus, NJ: Prentice Hall, 1991. By: Joseph J. Carr.

"The Bloodiest Edge" in Red Herring (May 1998, p. 78). By: Alex Gove.

"High Tech Exporting" in Independent Business (Vol. 8, No. 5, September/October 1997, pp. 28-30, 32-34). By: Ethan A. Blumen.

"Hope on Hold" in Crain's Small Business (January 1996, pp. 1, 19). By: Jeffrey McCracken.

Import of Medical Devices: A Workshop Manual. New York, NY: Gordon Press Publishers, 1994.

"Making it: Medicine Man" in Black Enterprise (Vol. 29, March 1999, p. 38). By: Wendy M. Beech.

Medical Diagnostic Kits and Products. Norwalk, CT: Business Communications Co. Inc. 1992.

The Pocket Guide to Clinical Laboratory Instrumentation. Philadelphia, PA: F. A. Davis Co. 1994. By: Terence C. Karselis.

"Some Firms See Wisdom in Avoiding Low-Cost Loans" in The Wall Street Journal (Vol. IC, No. 107, June 3, 1997, pp. B2). By: Michael Selz.

"Sonic Boom" in Inc. (Vol. 19, No. 15, December 21, 1997, pp. 36-40,43). By: David H. Freedman.

Stedman's Medical Equipment Words. Baltimore, MD: Williams & Wilkins, 1993.

New Age Services and Supplies

"A Business Odyssey" in Entrepreneur (December 1996, pp. 136, 138-139). By: Gayle Sato Stodder.

"Coming of Age" in Entrepreneur (July 1996, pp. 98, 100-101). By: Debra Phillips.

A Dictionary of New Thought Terms: The Words and Phrases Commonly Used in Metaphysics. Marina del Rey, CA: DeVorss & Co. 1991. By: Ernest Holmes.

Directory of New Age & Alternative Publications. Fairfield, IA: Sunstar Publishing Ltd. 1995. By: Darla Sims.

"Fast Forward, Up & Comers" in Working Woman (January 1997, p. 20). By: K.F.

Handbook of Metaphysics and Ontology. Herndon, VA: Philosophia, 1991. By: Hans Burkhardt, editor.

Karma Cards: A New Age Guide to Your Future Through Astrology. New York, NY: Viking Penguin, Inc. 1991. By: Monte Farber.

A Layman's Guide to New Age and Spiritual Terms. Nevada City, CA: Blue Dolphin Publishing, Inc. 1993. By: Elaine Murray.

New Age Encyclopedia. Farmington Hills, MI: Gale Research Inc. Second edition, 1992. By: J. Gordon Melton.

"The New Age" in Entrepreneur (May 1996, pp. 96, 98-99). By: Mark Henricks.

New Holistic Herbal. Rockport, MA: Element Books, Inc. 1991. By: Hoffman.

Perspectives on the New Age. Albany, NY: State University of New York Press, 1992. By: James R. Lewis, editor.

"Simon Says" in Business Start-Ups (Vol. 7, No. 10, October 1995, pp. 42, 44-46). By: Jane Hoback.

Subliminal Treatment Procedures: A Clinician's Guide. Sarasota, FL: Professional Resource Exchange, Inc. 1992. By: Paul G. Swingle.

Understanding the New Age. Grand Rapids, MI: Zondervan Publishing Corp. 1993. By: Russell Chandler.

"Voodoo Economics" in Business Start-Ups (Vol. 7, No. 10, October 1995, p. 6). By: Marvin M. Kaplan.

New and Used Car Dealer

The Automobile Sales Manager's Complete Success Formula: A Current Guide to Managing a Profitable Car Dealership. Mannford, OK: University Publishing House, Inc. 1994. By: Jon McCormick.

Automotive Encyclopedia. Tinley Park, IL: Goodheart-Willcox Co. Inc. Revised edition, 1995. By: William K. Toboldt.

"A Billion Dollar Mas?" in Hispanic Business (Vol. 19, No. 12, December 1997, pp. 12). By: Derek Reveron.

"Burning Down the House" in Inc. (Vol. 19, No. 11, August 1997, pp. 66-73). By: Edward O. Welles.

Car-Smart Automobile Negotiating Manual: Everything You Auto Know on the Art of Successfully Negotiating a Win-Win Conclusion. Renton, WA: Car-Smart Publishers, 1991. By: Andrew Hodge.

"Driving for Dollars" in Black Enterprise (Vol. 27, No. 8, March 1997, p. 18). By: Dackeyia Q. Simmons.

Edmund's Used Car Prices and Ratings. Jamestown, OH: Dell Publishing Co. Inc. 1995.

"Houston Big Wheel" in Black Enterprise (Vol. 26 No. 11, June 1996, pp. 149-150, 152). By: Lloyd Gite.

In the Driver's Seat: The New Car Buyer's Negotiating Bible. New York, NY: Random House, Inc. 1993. By: William J. Bragg.

"On the Road to Success" in Black Enterprise (Vol. 27, No. 9, April 1997, p. 28). By: Sheryl E. Huggins.

"One Happy CEO" in Hispanic Business (Vol. 19, No. 12, December 1997, pp. 19-20, 22). By: Rick Mendosa.

"The Top Fifty Women-Owned Businesses" in Working Woman (Vol. 22, No. 10, October 1997, pp. 34-68). By: Janet Bamford and Jennifer Pendleton.

The Used Car Book. New York, NY: HarperCollins Publishers, Inc. 1993. By: Jack Gillis.

What to Do Before the Money Runs Out: A Roadmap for America's Automobile Dealers. Pompano Beach, FL: Distinctive Publishing Corp. 1993. By: James J. Kaufman.

"You Win!" in Independent Business (Vol. 9, No. 3, May/June 1998, pp. 53-55). By: Natalie Hall.

Nontraditional Financing

"19 Sources of Capital for Your Start-Up" in Income Opportunities (Vol. 31, No. 2, February 1996, pp. 26-30). By: Terri Cullen.

"A High Tech Entrepreneur's Guide To Venture Bank Financing" in Boston Business Journal (Vol. 19, February 26-March 4, 1999, p. 42). By: Osca Jazdowski.

"Angels in Cyberspace" in Hispanic Business (Vol. 20, No. 3, March 1997, pp. 38, 40). By: Rick Mendosa.

"A Capital Idea Helps Nurture Small Firms in Wayne County" in Crain's Small Business (October 1995, p. 21). By: Pam Woodside.

"Cards May Be Ticket to Survive Cash-Flow Crunch" in Crain's Small Business (March 1996, p. 14). By: Lawrence Gardner.

Financing Your Business. Paramus, NJ: Prentice Hall, 1997. By: Iris Lorenz-Fife.

"Found Money" in Entrepreneur (Vol. 23, No. 4, April 1995, pp. 108-110, 112-115). By: David R. Evanson.

"Franchises That Offer Creative Financing" in Business Start-Ups (Vol. 8, No. 9, September 1996, pp. 62, 64, 67-68). By: Andrew A. Caffey.

"Going Public on Main Street, Not Wall Street" in Working Woman (June 1996, p. 11). By: Kerry Hannon.

"Green Days" in Business Start-Ups (Vol. 11, March 1999, p. 96). By: Michelle Prather.

Guerrilla Financing: Alternative Techniques to Finance Any Small Business. New York, NY: Houghton Mifflin Co. 1992. By: Bruce J. Blechman and Jay C. Levinson.

"Industrial Revolution" in Entrepreneur (Vol. 27, April 1999, pp. 68-71). By: David R. Evanson and Art Beroff.

"LEAF Me a Loan" in Business Start-Ups (Vol. 8, No. 1, January 1996, pp. 74-75).

"Leasing Lessons" in Business Start-Ups (Vol. 8, No. 2, February 1996, p. 72). By: Eric J. Adams.

"Money Hunting" in Hispanic Business (Vol. 19, No. 1, January 1997, pp. 28, 30). By: Joel Russell.

Money Sources for Small Business: How You Can Find Private, State, Federal & Corporate Financing. Santa Maria, CA: Puma Publishing Co. 1991. By: William M. Alarid.

"A New Loan Option to Bank, Venture Capital" in Crain's Small Business (February 1996, p. 9-10). By: Jeffrey McCracken.

"Niche Bank Targets White-Collar Market" in Inc. (Vol. 21, March 1999, pp. 23-24). By: Joshua Macht.

"Northern Exposure" in Entrepreneur (Vol. 23, No. 5, May 1995, pp. 15). By: Cynthia E. Griffin.

"Options, Discounts Are in the Cards" in Crain's Small Business (Vol. 5, No. 4, April 1997, pp. 1, 20). By: Jeffrey McCracken.

"Peer Power" in Entrepreneur (Vol. 23, No. 4, April 1995, p. 15). By: Heather Page.

"Pennies From Heaven" in Business Start-Ups (Vol. 11, February 1999, p. 23). By: Paul DeCeglie.

"Plastic Surgery" in Crain's Small Business (Vol. 5, No. 4, April 1997, pp. 1, 20-21). By: Jeffrey McCracken.

"Play Misty for Me" in Business Start-Ups (Vol. 7, No. 9, September 1995, p. 114). By: Eric J. Adams.

"Program Gives Small Businesses a Financial Boost" in Entrepreneur (Vol. 32, No. 7, July 1995, p. 17). By: Cynthia E. Griffin.

"Saving on Next-Day Delivery" in Black Enterprise (Vol. 27, No. 5, December 1996, p. 36). By: Ann Brown.

"Sendmail pits angel investors against VCs" in Red Herring (No. 60, November 1998, p. 23). By: Alex Gove.

"The Small Business Administration reaches out to tech companies" in Red Herring (No. 57, August 1998, pp. 23-24). By: Brian E. Taptich.

"Small Loans, Big Dreams" in Working Woman (Vol. 20, No. 2, February 1995, pp. 46-49, 72-73, 77). By: Elizabeth Kadetsky.

"SOS Call" in Business Start-Ups (Vol. 11, April 1999, p. 26). By: Sean M. Lyden.

"Stocking Up" in Entrepreneur (April 1997, pp. 58, 60-61). By: David R. Evanson.

"Treasure Hunt" in Business Start-Ups (Vol. 7, No. 7, July 1995, pp. 56-58, 60-61). By: Gloria Gibbs Marullo.

"Your Biz Booms!" in Small Business Opportunities (Vol. 11, No. 1, January 1999, p. 18). By: Marie Sherlock.

Periodical/Newspaper Publishing

"American Hopes to Conquer World—From Long Island" in Inc. (Vol. 18, No. 18, December 1997, p. 23). By: Jerry Useem.

"Book 'em" in Business Start-Ups (Vol. 10, No. 8, August 1998, pp. 46-50). By: Pamela L. Fry.

Bowker Annual: Library and Book Trade Almanac. Annual, May. By: Dave Bogart, Editor.

"Cyber Schmoozing" in Working Woman (Vol. 23, No. 3, March 1998, p. 20). By: Lorie Parch.

Desktop Publishing a Newspaper. New York, NY: State Mutual Book & Periodical Service, Ltd. 995. By: John Avieson.

Directory of Canadian Media.

Directory of Small Magazine—Press Editors and Publishers. Annual, September. By: Len Ulton, Editor, len@dustbooks.telis.org.

"Entrepreneurial Spirit Awards" in Hispanic Business (Vol. 18, No. 12, December 1996, pp. 26, 28, 30, 34, 36, 38). By: Maria Zate.

"Entrepreneurs Across America" in Entrepreneur (Vol. 24, No. 4, April 1996, pp. 100-104, 106-108, 110-112, 114-116, 118, 120-123). By: Janean Chum, Debra Phillips, Cynthia E. Griffin, Heather Page, Lynn Beresford, Holly Celeste Fisk, and Charlotte Mulbern.

"Fighting through the paper jam" in The Business Journal - Serving Milwaukee (Vol. 15, No. 15, January 2, 1998, p. 8). By: Alby Gallun.

Folio Magazine—Special Source Book Issue. Annual, October. By: Barbara Love, Editor.

Gale Directory of Publications and Broadcast Media. Annual, interedition update. By: Kristin Mallegg, Editor, kristin.mallegg@gale.com.

Gebbie Press All-in-One Directory. Annual, November. By: Amalia Gebbie, Editor.

GRAPHICS MASTER 5. Kihei, HI: Dean Lem Associates, Inc. By: Dean Phillip Lem.

"A Hair-Raising Success" in Black Enterprise (Vol. 27, No. 8, March 1997, p. 32). By: Ann Brown.

"Help! We're facing a cash-flow crisis" in Inc. (Vol. 19, No. 8, June 1997, p. 97). By: Christopher Caggiano.

Hispanic Magazine: A Pubishing Success Story. New York, NY: Walker & Co. 1995. By: John Garcia.

"How to raise capital funds for a magazine start-up" in Folio: the Magazine of Magazine Management (Vol. 27, No. 1, Jan. 1998, p. S199). By: Jeff Garigliano.

International Directory of Little Magazines and Small Presses. Annual, September. By: Len Fulton, Editor, len@dustbooks.telis.org.

"Judge and Journalist" in Red Herring (No. 60, November 1998, pp. 64-68). By: Alex Gove.

List of Journals.

"Lowrider Cruises Onto Main Street" in Hispanic Business (March 1998, p. 16). By: Maria Zate.

"Lowry Calls on Others to Promote" in Small Business Works in Independent Business (Vol. 9, No. 2, March/April 1998, p. 48).

The Magazine Article: How to Think It, Plan It, Write It. Bloomington, IN: Writer's Digest Books, 1991. By: Peter Jacobi.

Magazine & Bookseller—Who's Who of the Publishing & Distribution Industry Issue. Annual, December. By: Patricia H. McCarthy, Editor.

The Magazine: Everything You Need to Know to Make It in the Magazine Business. Old Saybrook, CT: The Globe Pequot Press, Third edition, 1992. By: Leonard Mogel.

Magazines Career Directory. Latest edition 1993. By: Bradley J. Morgan, Editor.

"The Master of Trades" in Black Enterprise (Vol. 26, No. 11, June 1996, pp. 244-248, 252-254). By: Carolyn M. Brown. Mississippi News Media Directory.

"Movie Madness" in Business Start-Ups (Vol. 7, No. 5, May 1995, P. 8). By: Cynthia E. Griffen.

"The Paper Chase" in Income Opportunities (Vol. 31, No. 11, November 1996, pp. 104, 106, 108). By: Marie Sherlock.

"Police Patrol" in Income Opportunities (Vol. 30, No. 11, November 1995, pp. 78, 80). By: Laurel Berger.

Publicity Blitz Media Directory-on-Disk. Updated continuously; printed on request. By: Stephen Hall, Editor.

Publishers—Periodical Directory. Annual.

Publishers' Trade List Annual. Annual, September. By: Frank McDermott, Editor.

"Publishing house finds niche in game industry: education" in San Antonio Business Journal (July 3, 1998, p. 1). By: James Aldridge.

Publishing a Newspaper. Westminster, CA: Teachers Created Materials, Inc. 1996. By: Belshaw.

Serials Directory: An International Reference Book. Annual, spring; cumulative updates. By: Jennifer O'Connell, Editor.

"Singular Sensation" in Income Opportunities (Vol. 30, No. 5, May 1995, pp. 128, 126). By: Laurel Berger.

Southeast News Media Directory.

"Spotlight on Small Business" in Independent Business (Vol. 9, No. 3, May/June 1998, pp. 16-17).

Standard Periodical Directory. Annual, December.

"Start-up Mambos to Beat of Booming Market" in Inc. (Vol. 19, No. 12, September 1997, p. 23). By: Marc Ballon.

Starting & Running a Successful Newsletter or Magazine. Berkeley, CA: Nolo Press, 2nd ed. 1998. By: Cheryl Woodard.

Strategic Newspaper Management. New York, NY: Allyn & Bacon, Inc. 1995. By: Conrad Fink.

"Sun Sets Quickly on Publisher's 'Empire'" in Inc. (Vol. 20, No. 2, February 1998, p. 23). By: Mike Hofman.

"Their Eyes Have Zine the Glory" in Folio: The Magazine for Magazine Management (Vol. 24, No. 1, January 15, 1995, p. 44). By: Steve Wilson.

Ulrich's International Periodicals Directory. Annual, updates two times per year under title. By: Judy Salk, Editor.

"Uneasy Rider" in Inc. (Vol. 19, No. 17, January 18, 1998, pp. 44-46, 48-52). By: Leigh Buchanan.

"Valassis Takes a Clipping" in Crain's Detroit Business (Vol. 13, No. 5, March 1997, p. 2). By: Matt Roush.

"What's Love Got to Do with It?" in Inc. (Vol. 18, No. 6, May 1996, pp. 77, 78, 80, 82, 85). By: Alessandra Bianchi.

"Within the Crystal Ball" in Detroit Free Press Business Monday (February 6, 1995, Section F).

Words into Type. Paramus, NJ: Prentice Hall, Fourth edition, 1992. By: Thomas L. Warren.

Writing and Selling Magazine Articles. New York, NY: Shooting Star Press, 1994. By: Eva Shaw.

Pizzeria

"48 Low-cost Food Businesses" in Business Start-Ups (Vol. 10, No. 10, October 1998, p. 35). By: Liza Potter.

"Hidden Treasures" in Entrepreneur (Vol. 26, Issue 12, December 1998, p. 16). By: Cynthia E. Griffin.

"Leasing a Piece of the Pie" in Entrepreneur (Vol. 23, No. 7, July 1995, p. 17). By: Cynthia E. Griffin.

"Local pizza chain plans expansion" in Crain's Detroit Business (Vol. 15, January 25-31, 1999, p. 10). By: Terry Kosdrosky.

"On Target" in Independent Business (Vol. 9, No. 4, July/August 1998, pp. 32-37). By: Alan Naditz.

"Top This" in Business Start-Ups (Vol. 11, No. 1, January 1999, p. 62). By: Chieh Chieng.

The U.S. Pizza Market. Commack, NY: Business Trend Analysts, Inc. 1995.

Real Estate Agency

101 Ways to Get 100 Plus Percent Financing for Real Estate & Business. Rockville Centre, NY: International Wealth Success, Inc. 1996. By: Tyler G. Hicks.

Agent's Guide to Real Estate: Power Your Career to Financial Success & Personal Happiness. McLean, VA: Realty Research Group, 1998.

"Back in the Saddle" in Entrepreneur (Vol. 27, No. 1, January 1999, p. 90). By: Patricia Schiff Estess.

Careers in Real Estate Management. Chicago, IL: Institute of Real Estate Management, 1996.

Doing the Right Thing: A Real Estate Practitioner's Guide to Ethical Decision Making. Scottsdale, AZ: Gorsuch Scarisbrick Publishers, 1995. By: Deborah H. Long.

Double Your Income in Real Estate Sales. New York, NY: John Wiley & Sons, Inc. 1993. By: Danielle Kennedy.

"Failure of Real Estate Brokerage is Elementary" in Inc. (Vol. 19, No. 18, December 1997, p. 37). By: Rick Stouffer.

Fast Start in Real Estate: A Survival Guide for New Agents. Chicago, IL: Dearborn Financial Publishing, Inc. 1992. By: Karl Breckenridge.

"From Boom to Bust, and Back Again" in Hispanic Business (Vol. 20, No. 8, September 1998, pp. 102 and 104). By: Jonathan J. Higuera.

Guide to Passing the Real Estate Exam (PSI). Chicago, IL: Dearborn Financial Publishing, Inc. Revised edition, 1994. By: Lawrence Sager.

How to List & Sell Real Estate in the 21st Century. Paramus, NJ: Prentice Hall, 1998. By: Danielle Kennedy and Warren Jamison.

How to Make Your Real-Estate Fortune in Second Mortgage. Rockville Centre, NY: International Wealth Success, Inc. 1996. By: Tyler G. Hicks.

How to Negotiate Real Estate Contracts. Naperville, IL: Sourcebooks, Inc. 3rd ed. 1998. By: Mark Warda.

How Real Estate Agents Earn Big!: The Flash Card Book of Revelations. San Francisco, CA: Mansion Press, 1997. By: Joan M. Tayler.

"Investigation of disasters leads firm to new heights" in The Business Journal - Serving Phoenix and the Valley of the Sun (Vol. 18, No. 35, June 19, 1998, p. 19). By: Mike Padgett.

Investment Analysis for Real Estate Decisions. Chicago, IL: Dearborn Financial Publishing, Inc. Third edition, 1993. By: Gaylon E. Greer and Michael D. Farrell.

The Language of Real Estate. Chicago, IL: Dearborn Financial Publishing, Inc. Fourth edition, 1993. By: John W. Reilly.

Modern Real Estate Practice. Chicago, IL: Dearborn Financial Publishing, Inc. 1994.

Power Real Estate Advertising: The Complete Guide for Professionals. Chicago, IL: Dearborn Trade, 1991. By: William Pivar and Bradley A. Pivar.

Real Estate Agent's Business Planning Guide. Chicago, IL: Dearborn Financial Publishing, Inc. 1994.

The Real Estate Pro's Internet Edge - Agent's Edition: Maximizing Your Business on the World Wide Web. Warren, NJ: Lingstar, 1999. By: Barbara Ling, illustrated by Jon Hapgood.

The St. James Encyclopedia of Mortgage & Real Estate Finance. Detroit, MI: St. James Press, 1991. By: James Newell, editor.

"Shoestring Start-Ups" in Income Opportunities (Vol. 32, No. 4, April 1997, pp. 20-23, 76, 82, 84, 86). By: Lori Schwind Murray.

Winning in Commercial Real Estate Sales: An Action Plan for Success. Chicago, IL: Dearborn Financial Publishing, Inc. 1990. By: Thomas Arthur Smith.

Real Estate Investment Service

Alternative Ideas in Real Estate Investment. Norwell, MA: Kluwer Academic Publishers, 1995. By: Arthur L. Schwartz.

"Back in the Saddle" in Entrepreneur (Vol. 27, No. 1, January 1999, p. 90). By: Patricia Schiff Estess.

"Entrepreneur Bob Scanlan explores billboard jungle" in Business Journal-Portland (Vol. 15, No. 13, May 22, 1998, p. 1). By: Robert Goldfield.

"From Boom to Bust, and Back Again" in Hispanic Business (Vol. 20, No. 8, September 1998, pp. 102 and 104). By: Jonathan J. Higuera.

Getting Started in Real Estate Investing. New York, NY: John Wiley & Sons, Inc. 1994. By: Michael C. Thomsett.

Handbook of Real Estate Portfolio Management. Burr Ridge, IL: Irwin Professional Publishing, 1995. By: Joseph L. Pagliari Jr.

How to Be a Second Mortgage Loan Broker. Rockville Centre, NY: International Wealth Success, Inc. 1996. By: Richard Brisky.

How to Build Your Real-Estate Fortune on Other People's Money. Rockville Centre, NY: International Wealth Success, Inc. 1996. By: Tyler G. Hicks.

How to Buy, Sell, or Invest in Real Estate. New York, NY: John Wiley & Sons, Inc. 1996. By: Robert Irwin.

How to Create Your Own Real-Estate Fortune Using Tax Shelters to Protect Your Profits. Rockville Centre, NY: International Wealth Success, Inc. 1996. By: Jens E. Hielsen.

How to Finance Real Estate Investments. Rockville Centre, NY: International Wealth Success, Inc. 1996. By: Roger Johnson.

How to Find Hidden Wealth in Local Real Estate. Rockville Centre, NY: International Wealth Success, Inc. 1996. By: Richard H. Jorgensen.

Invest Without Stress: What Successful Investors Know. Los Angeles, CA: Camden Press, 1996. By: Anne Farrelly.

Investing in Real Estate. New York, NY: John Wiley & Sons, Inc. 1996. By: Andrew McLean.

Investment Analysis for Real Estate Decisions. Chicago, IL: Dearborn Financial Publishing, Inc. 1996. By: Gaylon Greer.

Managing Real Estate Portfolios. Burr Ridge, IL: Irwin Professional Publishing, 1993. By: Susan Hudson-Wilson.

Real Estate Finance & Investments. Hinsdale, IL: Richard D. Irwin, 1996. By: William B. Brueggeman.

Real Estate Investments. Paramus, NJ: Professional Publications, Inc.

The Real Estate Investors Tax Guide. Chicago, IL: Dearborn Financial Publishing, Inc. 1995. By: Vernon Hoven.

"Shoestring Start-Ups" in Income Opportunities (Vol. 32, No. 4, April 1997, pp. 20-23, 76, 82, 84, 86). By: Lori Schwind Murray.

Sold!: The Professional's Guide to Real Estate Auctions. Chicago, IL: Dearborn Financial Publishing, Inc. 1991. By: Stephen Martin.

"Solid Foundations" in Black Enterprise (Vol. 27, No. 7, February 1997, p. 38). By: Denolyn Carroll.

Using Government Money to Borrow Your Way to Real Estate Riches. Rockville Centre, NY: International Wealth Success, Inc. 1996. By: Tyler G. Hicks.

Restaurant

"The $20 Question" in Hispanic Business (October 1998, p. 12). By: Joel Russell.

"48 Low-cost Food Businesses" in Business Start-Ups (Vol. 10, No. 10, October 1998, p. 35). By: Liza Potter.

"A & W Plants Roots as Growing Fast-Food Chain" in Crain's Detroit Business (Vol. 13, No. 6, February 1997, pp. 3, 32). By: Marsha Stopa.

"All Dressed Up and No IPO" in Inc. (Vol. 20, No. 2, February 1998, pp. 56-59, 61-62, 64, 68-69). By: Jerry Useem.

"Auntie Anne's Hand-Rolled Soft Pretzels" in Income Opportunities (Vol. 32, No. 9, September 1997, pp. 26).

"Best Bets" in Entrepreneur (December 1996, pp. 108-112). By: Lynn Bersford and Heather Page.

"Bit O' the Green" in Entrepreneur (March 1997, p. 156).

"Blimpie Seeks to Gain Synergies From an Acquisition" in The Wall Street Journal (Vol. IC, No. 98, May 20, 1997, p. B2). By: Jeffrey A. Tannenbaum.

"Calling the shots" in Business Start-ups (Vol. 11, April 1999, pp. 61-62). By: Don Debelak.

The Complete Guide to Food Service Success: What You Need to Know to Plan a Profitable Operation. Phoenix, AZ: RWI Publishing Group, 1992. By: Fred Schmid.

Controlling and Analyzing Costs in Food-Service Operations. Old Tappan, NJ: Macmillan Publishing Co. Inc. Third edition, 1993. PRC $70.00. By: James Keiser and Frederick DeMicco.

"Could Drive You to Drink" in Crain's Small Business (December 1996, pp. 8-9). By: Jeffrey McCracken.

"Counter Culture" in Entrepreneur (November 1996, pp. 110, 112-113). By: Gayle Sato Stodder.

"Delicious Success" in Selling Power (Vol. 16, No. 3, April 1996, pp. 65-66, 68). By: Malcolm Fleschner.

"Dining Differences" in Small Business Opportunities (Vol. 11, No. 2, March 1999, p. 78).

"Directory of Food Industry Resources" in Income Opportunities (Vol. 31, No. 8, August 1996, pp. 26-27). By: Stephanie Jeffrey.

"Double Take" in Income Opportunities (Vol. 31, No. 5, May 1996, pp. 92, 94). By: Maria Garcia.

"Dreams That Were Brought Up in a Barn" in Crain's Small Business (December 1995, p. 15). By: Jeffrey McCracken.

"Eating, Drinking Places Among Most Appetizing" in Crain's Small Business (October 1995, p. 13). By: Jeffrey McCracken.

Encyclopedia of Food Science, Food Technology and Nutrition. Orlando, FL: Academic Press, Inc. 1993. By: Robert Macrae, Richard Robinson, and Michele Sadler.

"Entrepreneurial Spirit Awards" in Hispanic Business (Vol. 18, No. 12, December 1996, pp. 26, 28, 30, 34, 36, 38). By: Maria Zate.

"Entrepreneurial Superstars" in Entrepreneur (April 1997, pp. 108-139). By: Debra Phillips and others.

The Fast Food & Multi-Unit Restaurant Business. Commack, NY: Business Trend Analysts, Inc.

"A fish tale of success" in Nation's Business (Vol. 86, No. 1, January 1998, p. 50). By: Mark Richard Moss.

"Flapjack Chain Runs Out of Dough" in Inc. (Vol. 19, No. 14, October 1997, p. 25). By: Tom Fudge.

Food and Beverage Service. New York, NY: John Wiley & Sons, Inc. Third edition, 1993. By: Dennis R. Lillicrap and John A. Cousins.

Food Businesses, Snack Shops, Specialty Food, Restaurants & Other Ideas: A Business Workbook. Denver, CO: Prosperity & Profits Unlimited, Distribution Services, Revised edition, 1992.

The Food Professional's Guide. New York, NY: John Wiley & Sons, Inc. 1990. By: Irena Chalmers.

Food ServiceFOODSERVICE Operations: Planning and Control. Melbourne, FL: Krieger Publishing Co. Inc. 1991. By: Thomas F. Powers and Jo Marie Powers.

"For Restaurateurs, Excellence Is Merely First Course" in Crain's Small Business (October 1995, p. 6). By: Dave Guilford.

"Franchise Finds" in Small Business Opportunities (Vol. 9, No. 6, November 1997, p. 134).

"Gain-sharing encourages productivity" in Nation's Business (Vol. 86, No. 1, January 1998, p. 21). By: Abby Livingston.

"Gatzaros' Projects" in Crain's Detroit Business (Vol. 11, No. 9, February 27-March 5, 1995, pp. 38-39). By: Michael Goodin.

"Go for It" in Black Enterprise (Vol. 27, No. 7, February 1997, pp. 72-73). By: Cassandra Hayes.

"Good for the Soul" in Entrepreneur (April 1997, p. 16). By: J.C. "Hold the Jalapeno" in Hispanic Business (Vol. 19, No. 12, December 1997, p. 34).

"Hot Plates" in Entrepreneur (June 1995, p. 20).

"House Special" in Entrepreneur (May 1996, p. 38).

How to Open & Run a Successful Restaurant. New York, NY: John Wiley & Sons, Inc. 1994. By: Christopher Egerton-Thomas.

How to Open Your Own Restaurant. New York, NY: Viking Penguin, Inc. 1991. By: Richard Ware and James Rudnick.

How to Start & Manage a Sandwich Shop Deli Business: Step by Step Guide Business Success.

Interlochen, MI: Lewis & Renn Associates, 1996. By: Jerre G. Lewis.

IRS Audit Protection & Survival Guide: Bars & Restaurants. New York, NY: John Wiley & Sons, Inc. 1996. By: Gerald F. Bernard.

"Jammin'" in Income Opportunities (Vol. 30, No. 6, June 1995, pp. 64, 66). By: Stephanie Jeffrey.

"King of franchises" in Houston Business Journal (August 21, 1998, p. A16). By: Laura Elder.

"Long-time Lark Street eyesore to house Italian eatery" in Capital District Business Review (July 6, 1998, p. 2). By: Deborah Moore.

"Love & Money" in Small Business Opportunities (Vol. 9, No. 4, July 1997, pp. 102, 104). By: Geri Anderson.

"Making News: How to Write Press Releases That Get Published" in Independent Business (Vol. 10, March-April 1999, pp. 45-46). By: Lisa Mortillaro.

"A Matter of Taste" in Income Opportunities (Vol. 30, No. 8, August 1995, pp. 22-24, 68-70). By: Meg North.

"Mexican-Food Joint Venture Gives Arby's Indigestion" in The Wall Street Journal (Vol. C, No. 30, August 12, 1997, pp. B1, B2). By: Jeffrey A. Tannenbaum.

"Mo' Better Zanzibar Blue" in Black Enterprise (Vol. 27, No. 5, December 1996, pp. 106-114). By: Caroline V. Clarke.

"Multiply Profits with Multiple Businesses" in Income Opportunities (Vol. 33, Vol. 9, November 1998, pp. 16, 20, and 22.). By: Sandra Mardenfeld.

"My Life as an Angel" in Inc. (Vol. 19, No. 10, July 1997, pp. 42-44, 46-48). By: Norm Brodsky and Bo Burlingham.

"Neighborhood watch" in Entrepreneur (Vol. 26, No. 3, March 1998, p. 116). By: Tom Shachtman.

"New Venture Flying High" in Black Enterprise (Vol. 27, No. 2, September 1996, p. 20). By: Paula M. White.

"No More Singing the Blues" in Black Enterprise (Vol. 27, No. 3, October 1996, p. 22). By: Erin Aubrey.

"Now Serving" in Entrepreneur (October 1997, p. 18).

Nutrition for the Foodservice Professional. New York, NY: Van Nostrand Reinhold Co. Inc. Second edition, 1993. By: Karen Eich Drummond.

Owner's Guide to Successful Restaurant & Retail Business. Overland Park, KS: Silent Communication, Inc. 1997. By: Anthony Ramsey.

"Partners with Success" in Hispanic Business (Vol. 20, No. 8, September 1998, pp. 56-76).

"A Perfect Match" in Business Start-Ups (Vol. 9, No. 7, July, 1997, pp. 44-49). By: Julie Bawden Davis.

"Plucking for Profits" in Black Enterprise (Vol. 27, No. 9, April 1997, p. 2830). By: Scott Wade.

"Putting a Face with a Name Gives Ads Personal Touch" in The Wall Street Journal (Vol. IC, No. 117, June 17, 1997, pp. B2). By: Jeffrey A. Tannenbaum.

"Raw Food Revolution" in Black Enterprise (Vol. 25, No. 6, January 1995, p. 32). By: Tonia L. Shakespeare.

"Recipe for Success" in Black Enterprise (Vol. 28, No. 1, August 1997, pp. 99-100, 102-105). By: Wendy M. Beech.

Restaurant Finance: Handbook for Successful Management and Operations. Middleville, MI: Bengal Press, Inc. By: John Ilich.

Restaurant Franchising. New York, NY: Van Nostrand Reinhold, 1996. By: Mahmood Khan.

The Restaurant Planning Guide: Starting and Managing a Successful Restaurant. Chicago, IL: Upstart Publishing Co. Inc. 1993. By: Peter Rainsford and David H. Bangs, Jr.

The Restaurant Start-Up Guide. Chicago, IL: Upstart Publishing Co. Inc. 1997. By: Peter Rainsford and David H. Bangs, Jr.

Restaurant Success. Boston, MA: Inc. Publishing.

"Reversal of Fortune" in Income Opportunities (Vol. 30, No. 2, February 1995, pp. 54-55, 58-62). By: Edmond M. Rosenthal.

"Roadkill Restaurateur" in Crain's Detroit Business (Vol. 11, No. 9, February 27-March 5, 1995, pp. 3, 26). By: Marsha Stopa.

Salad Bar Recipe Pages: Restaurant, Catering & Food Business Edition. Denver, CO: Prosperity & Profits Unlimited, Distribution Services, 1992.

"Set up Shop with a Specialty Retail Franchise" in Income Opportunities (Vol. 33, Vol. 9, November 1998, pp. 24-29).

"Spotlight on Small Business" in Independent Business (Vol. 9, No. 3, May/June 1998, pp. 16-17).

"Stand Out From the Crowd" in Independent Business (Vol. 8, No. 6, November/December 1997, pp. 16-17). By: Valerie J. Nelson.

"Standing Room Only" in Entrepreneur (July 1996, p. 17). By: L.B.

"Star Search" in Entrepreneur (Vol.23, No. 8, August 1995, pp. 12). By: Janean Chun.

Start & Run a Profitable Restaurant: A Step by Step Business Plan. Bellingham, WA: Self-Counsel Press, Inc. 1994. By: Michael M. Coltman.

"Starting Over" in Hispanic Business (April 1998, p. 36).

"Taking Inventory" in Small Business Opportunities (Vol. 9, No. 6, November 1997, pp. 70, 72).

"Turnaround Tactic" in Independent Business (Vol. 7, No. 2, March/April 1996, p. 48).

"Turning the Tables" in Entrepreneur (Vol. 23, No. 7, July 1995, pp. 18-19). By: Debra Phillips.

"Up With Food" in Entrepreneur (Vol. 27, No. 1, January 1999, p. 334).

"Warning Signs" in Black Enterprise (Vol. 27, No. 4, November 1996, pp. 89-94). By: Tonia L. Shakespeare.

"Will Diners Want a Lotta Ja Da?" in Crain's Detroit Business (Vol. 12, No. 45, November 1996, pp. 3, 22). By: Tenisha Mercer.

Winning the Chain Restaurant Game: Eight Key Strategies. New York, NY: John Wiley & Sons, Inc. 1994. By: Charles Bernstein and Ronald N. Paul.

"Worshiping a Dream" in Crain's Detroit Business (Vol. 12, No. 39, September 1996, p. 8). By: Matt Roush.

Your New Restaurant: All the Necessary Ingredients for Success. Holbrook, MA: Adams Publishing, 1990. By: Vincent Mischitelli.

Retailing

"20 Great Service Businesses To Get Into—Now!" in Small Business Opportunities (Vol. 7, No. 3, May 1995, p. 22).

"101 Service Businesses to Start Now!" in Business Start-Ups(Vol. 8, No. 2, February 1996, pp. 19-20, 22-28, 30). By: Guen Sublette and Karin Moeller.

Advances in Services Marketing & Management: Research & Practice. New York, NY: JAI Press, Inc. 1996. By: Stephen W. Brown.

"At Your Service" in Income Opportunities (Vol. 30, No. 6, June 1995, pp. 20-22, 24-25). By: Robert L. Perry.

Big Ideas for Small Service Businesses: How to Successfully Advertise, Publicize, and Maximize Your Business or Professional Practice. Buena Vista, CO: Communication Creativity, 1994. By: Marilyn Ross and Tom Ross.

"Get It in Writing" in Entrepreneur (Vol. 23, No. 11, October 1995, p. 26). By: Jacquelyn Lynn.

"Getting engineers a game plan for success" in San Antonio Business Journal (July 17, 1998, p. 32). By: Tricia L. Silva.

How to Set Up a Retail Store, Service Company, and a Manufacturing Firm—Case Studies. Minneapolis, MN: American Institute of Small Business (AISB), 1991.

"Jobs Move to Service Sector" in Crain's Small Business (September 1995, pp. E-1, E-3). By: Mike Casey.

The Lean Communications Provider: Managing Profitability in the Global Communications Market. New York, NY: The McGraw-Hill Companies, 1996. By: Keith Willets.

"The many virtues of 'virtual services'" in Business Week (No. 3595, September 14, 1998, p. S18). By: Ann Zieger.

The Marketing Services. New York, NY: The McGraw-Hill Companies, 1996. By: Ken Irons.

Marketing of Services. Ft. Worth, TX: Harcourt Brace College Publishers, 1996. By: Hoffman.

Marketing Your Service Business: Plan a Winning Strategy. Bellingham, WA: Self-Counsel Press, Inc. Second edition, 1992. By: Jean Withers.

No More Cold Calls. Cambridge, MA: JLA Publications, 1993. By: Jeffrey Lant.

Opportunities in Your Own Service Business. Lincolnwood, IL: NTC Contemporary Publishing Co. 1999. By: Robert McKay.

Quality of Service: Making It Really Work. New York, NY: The McGraw-Hill Companies, 1995. By: Bo Edvardsson, John Ouvreveit and Bertil Thomasson.

"The Quick Fix" in Income Opportunities (Vol. 30, No. 12, December 1995, pp. 46-50, 52, 54). By: Robert L. Perry.

Real People Working in Service Businesses. Lincolnwood, IL: NTC Contemporary Publishing Co. 1996. By: Blythe Camenson.

Relationship Marketing in Professional Services: A Study of Agency-Client Dynamics in the Advertising Sector. New York, NY: Routledge, Inc. 1997. By: Aino Halinen.

"Riches in niches" in Forbes (Vol. 162, No. 2, July 27, 1998, p. 78). By: Scott McCormack.

"The Service Boom" in Small Business Opportunities (Vol. 9, No. 3, May 1997, pp. 22-41).

The Service Economy: A Geographical Approach. New York, NY: John Wiley & Sons, Inc. 1996. By: Sven Illeris.

"Service Heats Up" in Small Business Opportunities (Vol. 11, May 1999, pp. 22-36, 100).

The Service Management Course: Cases and Readings. New York, NY: The Free Press, 1991. By: W. Earl Sasser, Jr.

Service Management: Strategy and Leadership in Service Business. New York, NY: John Wiley & Sons, Inc. Second edition, 1991. By: Richard Normann.

Service Profit Chain. New York, NY: The Free Press, 1997. By: Herskett.

"Service Sector is a Good Franchise Bet" in Washington Business Journal: Small Business Resource Guide (May 1996, pp. 8, 10). By: Lakhinder J.S. Vohra.

"Service with a Smile!" in Small Business Opportunities (Vol. 8, No. 3, May 1996, pp. 22-24, 26, 28, 30, 32, 34, 58-59).

Services and Metropolitan Development: International Perspectives. New York, NY: Routledge, Chapman & Hall, Inc. 1991. By: Peter W. Daniels, editor.

Services in the Transition Economies: Business Options for Trade & Investment. New York, NY: Elsevier Science, 1996. By: Michel Kostecki.

Start & Run Your Own Profitable Service Business. Paramus, NJ: Prentice Hall, 1992. By: Irving Burstiner.

"Suggestions on selling your service firm" in Nation's Business (Vol.86, No. 2, February 1998, p. 11). By: Roberta Maynard.

Sustaining Knock Your Socks Off Service. New York, NY: AMACOM, 1993. By: Ron Zemke and Thomas K. Connellan.

"Twice is Nice" in Independent Business (Vol. 7, No. 6, Nov./Dec. 1996, pp. 30-35). By: Dorothy Elizabeth Brooks.

"Working the Night Shift" in Income Opportunities (Vol. 31, No. 2, February 1996, pp. 18-21). By: Dale D. Buss.

Small Business Development

"10 Best Businesses to Start in 1996" in Income Opportunities (Vol.31, No. 1, January 1996, pp. 12-16, 72, 79-80). By: Jack Rosenberger.

"12 Biggest Mistakes Made By New Businesses" in Income Opportunities (Vol. 31, No. 4, April 1996, pp. 18-21). By: Pamela Rohland.

"1995 Small Business Tax Guide" in Income Opportunities (Vol. 30, No. 1, January 1995, pp. 48-60). By: Randall Kirkpatrick and Meg North.

"20 Associations Form Group Aiding Small Biz" in Crain's Detroit Business (Vol. 15, February 1-7, 1999, p. 17). By: Robert Ankeny.

201 Great Ideas for Your Small Business. Princeton, NJ: Bloomberg Press, 1998. By: Jane Applegate.

"A & W Plants Roots as Growing Fast-Food Chain" in Crain's Detro it Business (Vol. 13, No. 6, February 1997, pp. 3, 32). By: Marsha Stopa.

"A Checklist for Starting a Business" in Crain's Small Business (December 1995, p. 30).

"A Call of Arms for Black Business" in Black Enterprise (Vol. 27, No. 4, November 1996, pp. 79-86). By: Carolyn M. Brown and Tonia L. Shakespeare.

"A Sporting Chance" in Detroit Free Press (January 1997, pp. 1e-2e). By: Molly Brauer.

"A Perfect Fit" in Business Start-Ups (Vol. 7, No. 9, September 1995, pp. 78, 80-81). By: Jacquelyn Lynn.

ABC's of Starting a Business. Newnan, GA: Publicity Plus, 1990. By: Valerie White.

"Achieving Success Through a Smaller Market" in Washington Business Journal: Small Business Resource Guide (May 1996, p. 18). By: Bill Murray.

Advice from the Lemonade Stand: A Back to Basics Book for Business. Galveston, TX: Lafayette Publishing Co. 1998. By: Carroll Cobb; edited by Joanna Bremer.

"Age of the Gazelle" in Inc. (Vol. 18, No. 7, May 1996, p. 44). By: John Case. Alaska Business Monthly.

Arkansas Business.

"All Season Woman" in Small Business Opportunities (Vol. 9, No. 3, May 1997, pp. 58, 60, 72). By: Diane Morelli.

"An Olympic-Sized Letdown" in Inc. (Vol. 19, No. 2, February 1997, p. 21). By: Michael E. Kanell.

"Answers to Your Small-Business Questions" in Business Start-Ups (Vol. 8, No. 6, June 1996, p. 6). By: Lynn L. Norquist.

"Answers to Your Small-Business Questions" in Business Start-Ups (Vol. 8, No. 7, July 1996, p. 6). By: Haidee Jezek.

"Are You Online Yet?" in Black Enterprise (Vol. 25, No. 9, April 1995, p. 41). By: Valencia Roner and Matthew S. Scott.

"Ask the Experts" in Income Opportunities (Vol. 32, No. 7, July 1997, pp. 52, 54, 56). By: Caryne Brown.

"Ask the Experts" in Income Opportunities (Vol. 32 , No. 3, March 1997, pp. 56, 58, 60).

Atlanta Small Business Monthly.

Atlanta Business Chronicle.

Atlanta Magazine.

"Automatic Venture" in Small Business Opportunities (Vol. 9, No. 1, January 1997, pp. 50, 52).

Avoiding the Pitfalls of Starting Your Own Business. New York, NY: Shapolsky Publishers, Inc. 1990. By: Jeffrey P. Davidson.

Avoiding Mistakes in Your Small Business. Menlo Park, CA: Crisp Publications, Inc. By: David Karlson.

Baltimore Business Journal.

"Bankruptcies Rise 25%" in Crain's Detroit Business (Vol. 13, No. 6, February 1997, pp. 1, 32). By: Tenisha Mercer.

"Barden Trump Card: Experience" in Crain's Detroit Business (Vol. 13, No. 6, February 1997, pp. 1, 22). By: Robert Ankeny.

Bare-Bones Guide to Starting a Successful Small Business. Greenport, NY: Pilot Books.

Beating the Odds in Small Business. Coconut Grove, FL: Small Business Matters, Inc. 1998. By: Tom Culley.

Being an Entrepreneur in Illinois. 1991. By: Anthony Brogdon.

"Best Hometown Businesses in America" in Inc. (Vol. 19, No. 10, July 1997, pp. 56-57).

"Beyond Latin America" in Hispanic Business (Vol. 18, No. 11, November 1996, pp. 34, 36, 38, 40-41). By: Joel Russell.

Beyond Entrepreneurship: Turning Your Business into an Enduring Great Company. Paramus, NJ: Prentice Hall, 1992. By: James C. Collins and William C. Lazier.

Big Sky Business Journal.

Big Instruction Book of Small Business (New Mexico Edition). Peachtree City, GA: Gallopade Publishing Group, 1997. By: Carole Marsh.

BNH: The Business of New Hampshire.

Boston Business Journal.

"Bottling Success" in Hispanic Business (Vol. 18, No. 7/8, July/August 1996, p. 78). By: Maria Zate.

Break the Curve: The Entrepreneur's Small Business Blueprint. Florence, KY: International Thomson Publishing, 1998. By: Tim Burns.

"Bright Ideas" in Business Start-Ups (Vol. 7, No. 8, August 1995, pp. 50, 52-54, 57). By: Bob Weinstein.

"Bucks in Buttons" in Small Business Opportunities (Vol. 9, No. 1, January 1997, p. 48). By: Carla Goodman.

Building a Profitable Business: A Proven Step-by-Step Guide to Starting and Running Your Own Business. Holbrook, MA: Bob Adams, Inc. Second edition, 1994. By: Charles Chickadel and Greg Straughn.

"Building the Perfect Home Office" in Black Enterprise (Vol. 27, No. 8, March 1997, pp. 36-37). By: Rafiki Cai.

"Building a Business Framework" in Hispanic Business (Vol. 18, No. 11, November 1996, p. 24).

"Building a Better Burger" in Business Start-Ups (Vol. 8, No. 3, March 1996, pp. 21-22, 24-25). By: Bob Weinstein.

Building a Successful Business: What Every New Business Must Know Before Even Thinking about Making That Million Bucks!. Millersville, MD: CDS, Inc. 1997. By: Jack Funderburk.

Business Journal of Upper East Tennessee and Southwest Virginia.

Business Start-Up Guide: How to Create, Grow & Manage Your Own Successful Enterprise. Oceanside, CA: Tycoon Publishing, 1998. By: Tom Severance; edited by Becky Colgan.

Business First: The Greater Columbus Business Authority.

Business in Broward.

Business First: Newspaper of Birmingham.

"Business factory" in Black Enterprise (Vol. 29, No. 3, October 1998, p. 119). By: Carolyn M. Brown.

Business First of Buffalo.

Business Operations Guidebook: The How-to Guide for Start-up Entrepreneurs. Poughquag, NY: Info Devels Press, 1993. By: Robert Haiber.

Business Opportunities in the United States: The Complete Reference Guide to Practices and Procedures. Burr Ridge, IL: Irwin Professional Publishing, 1992. By: Robert F. Cushman and R. Lawrence Soares, editors.

Business Forms on File Collection. New York, NY: Facts on File, Inc. 1995.

Business First.

"Business Balloons" in Small Business Opportunities (Vol. 9, No. 1, January 1997, p. 76). By: Vicki Cromwell-Slakey.

Business Basics: A Microbusiness Start-Up Guide. Grants Pass, OR: PSI Research, 1998. By: Gerald Dodd; illustrated by Tim Sample.

Business Alabama Monthly.

Business Basics in Hawaii: Secrets of Starting Your Own Business in Our State. 1998. By: Dennis K. Kondo.

Business Bulletin.

Business Record.

California Corporation Formation Package and Minute Book. Grants Pass, OR: Oasis Press. Seventh edition, 1992. By: Kevin W. Finck.

"California Goes Pro-Business" in Hispanic Business (April 1998, pp. 24 and 28). By: Rick Mendosa.

Capital District Business Review.

"Career Moves" in Working Woman (February 1999, pp. 42-51).

"Carving a Niche" in Small Business Opportunities (Vol. 8, No. 6, November 1996, p. 50). By: Carla Goodman.

"Checking Out the Library" in Independent Business (Vol. 9, No. 3, May/June 1998, pp. 26-28). By: Pamela Palmer.

"Cleaning Up" in Small Business Opportunities (Vol. 9, No. 3, May 1997, p. 62). By: Carla Godman. Clevelander-Growth Association.

"Coffee Cola Talk" in Small Business Opportunities (Vol. 9, No. 2, March 1997, pp. 44, 100). By: Anne Hart.

Complete Idiot's Guide to Starting Your Own Business. Old Tappan, NJ: Macmillan Publishing Co. 2nd ed. 1998. By: Ed Paulson and Marcia Layton.

Complete Information Bank for Entrepreneurs & Small Business Managers. Wichita, KS: Center for Entrepreneurship & Small Business Management, 2nd ed. 1998. By: Ron Christy and Billy M. Jones.

"Consumer Report" in Entrepreneur (May 1997, pp. 125-130). By: Gayle Sato Stodder.

"Contacts for Contracts" in Hispanic Business (Vol. 18, No. 7/8, July/August 1996, p. 58). By: Claudia Armann. Corporate Report-Wisconsin.

Couple's Business Guide: How to Start & Grow a Small Business Together. New York, NY: Berkley Publishing Group, 1997. By: Amy Lyon.

"Crafting a Business" in Entrepreneur (March 1997, pp. 58, 60-61). By: Cynthia E. Griffin.

"Crafty Biz" in Small Business Opportunities (Vol. 9, No. 2, March 1997, pp. 54, 88). By: Carla Goodman.

Crain's Cleveland Business.

Crain's New York Business.

Creating the Successful 21st Century Enterpise. New York, NY: The Free Press, 1997. By: Main.

Creating Your Own Business, Vol. 1: A Guide to Success. Chicago, IL: MidAmerica Leadership Foundation, 1997. By: Harold P. Welsch and Joseph S. Roberts.

"Credibility Gap" in Income Opportunities (Vol. 32, No. 4, April 1997, pp. 42, 44). By: Dorothy Elizabeth Brooks.

"Cubs Send Minor-League Owners to the Showers" in Inc. (Vol. 19, No. 5, April 1997, p. 24). By: Phaedra Hise.

"Cycle of Success" in Small Business Opportunities (Vol. 9, No. 2, March 1997, pp. 86, 88). By: Stan Roberts. Daily Business Review.

"Dare to Be Different" in Entrepreneur (Vol. 23, No. 4, April 1995, pp. 122, 124-127). By: Gayle Sato Stodder.

Denver Business Journal.

"Developer Eyes 65-Acre Site in Sterling Heights" in Crain's Detroit Business (Vol. 13, No. 6, February 1997, p. 3). By: Tenisha Mercer.

"Eco-Preneuring" in Small Business Opportunities (Vol. 9, No. 2, March 1997, pp. 70, 72). By: Geri Anderson.

"Electronic Commerce Becoming a Taxing Issue for Small Business" in Independent Business (Vol. 9, No. 2, March/April 1998, p. 47).

Electronic Finance. Monthly. By: Peter Williams, Editor.

Entrepreneur's Guide to Growing Up: Taking Your Small Company to the Next Level. Bellingham, WA: Self-Counsel Press, Inc. 1993. By: Edna Sheedy.

Entrepreneur's Road Map to Business Success. Alexandria, VA: Saxtons River Publications, Inc. Revised edition, 1992. By: Lyle R. Maul and Dianne Craig Mayfield.

Entrepreneurial Assistance in Wisconsin: Sources of Management and Technical Support. 1990.

Entrepreneurial PC. New York, NY: TAB Books, Inc. 1991. By: Bernard J. David.

"Entrepreneurial Fables" in Entrepreneur (Vol. 23, No. 8, August 1995, pp. 120, 122-124, 127). By: Gayle Sato Stodder.

"Entrepreneurial training" in Colorado Business Magazine (Vol. 25, No. 10, October 1998, p. 30). By: Jack Sommars.

"Entrepreneurial Spirit Awards" in Hispanic Business (Vol. 18, No. 12, December 1996, pp. 26, 28, 30, 34, 36, 38). By: Maria Zate.

Entrepreneurially Yours: A Compilation of Articles about Starting and Managing a Small Business. Nashville, TN: Business of Your Own, 1990. By: Millicent G. Lownes.

Entrepreneurship & Small Business Development. Woburn, MA: Butterworth-Heinemann, 1996. By: David Kirby.

"Entrepreneurs Collide: Will Zoning Take Town Downhill?" in Inc. (Vol. 19, No. 5, April 1997, p. 32). By: Joshua Macht.

Entrepreneurship for the Nineties. Paramus, NJ: Prentice Hall, 1990. By: Gordon B. Baty.

Essence of Small Business. Paramus, NJ: Prentice Hall, 2nd ed. 1998. By: Colin Barrow.

"Essential Books for Start-ups" in Working Woman (February 1995, p. 54). By: Jane Applegate.

"Every Day's a Holiday" in Small Business Opportunities (Vol. 9, No. 1, January 1997, pp. 70, 72, 114). By: Anne Hart.

"Experience" in Business Start-Ups (Vol. 7, No. 12, December 1995, p. 20). By: Jacquelyn Lynn.

Family Businesses, Small Businesses, Home Businesses & General Business Possibilities Encyclopedia. Denver, CO: Prosperity & Profits Unlimited, Distribution Services, 1991.

"Family business is good business" in Agency Sales Magazine (Vol. 28, No. 2, February 1998, p. 58).

"Fifteen Start-Up Mistakes" in Business Start-Ups (Vol. 7, No. 12, December 1995, p. 22). By: Mel Mandell.

"Finding Your Niche" in Business Start-Ups (Vol. 9, No. 4, April 1997, pp. 72, 74). By: Carla Goodman.

Florida Trend.

"Food for Thought" in Small Business Opportunities (Vol. 9, No. 2, March 1997, pp. 78, 80). By: Cheryl Rodgers.

"Freebies" in Independent Business (Vol. 10, Jan.-Feb. 1999, pp. 20-22).

From Executive to Entrepreneur: Making the Transition. New York, NY: AMACOM, 1991. By: Gilbert G. Zoghlin.

George Washington's First Business: A Guide to Starting New Ventures. Woodmere, NY: Career Advancement Center, Inc. 1998. By: Eric Gelb.

"Get Rich in 1997" in Small Business Opportunities (Vol. 9, No. 1, January 1997, pp. 22-24, 26, 28, 30, 34).

"Get into Show Business" in Small Business Opportunities (Vol. 9, No. 1, January 1997, pp. 104, 114). By: Anne Hart.

"Get a Life! Start Your Home-Based Business Now: One Action Step at a Time. Carlsbad, CA: Small Business Development for Women, 1997. By: Sheila Robbins.

"Get on the Peace Train" in Small Business Opportunities (Vol. 9, No. 1, January 1997, p. 86). By: Carla Goodman.

Getting Started. Bellingham, WA: Self-Counsel Press, Inc. 1991. By: Dan Kennedy.

"Gift Keeps on Giving" in Small Business Opportunities (Vol. 9, No. 1, January 1997, pp. 56, 58). By: Marie Sherlock.

"Go West for Success" in Small Business Opportunities (Vol. 9, No. 2, March 1997, p. 118). By: Carla Goodman.

"Going It Alone" in Newsweek (April 1996, pp. 50-51). By: Ellyn E. Spragins and Steve Rhodes.

"Going Solo" in Income Opportunities (Vol. 30, No. 11, November 1995, pp. 30, 32, 34). By: Pamela Rohland.

Going Into Business in Wisconsin: An Entrepreneur's Guide. Second edition, 1992.

"Gotta Have It!" in Business Start-Ups (Vol. 11, March 1999, pp. 36-42). By: Eric J. Adams.

"Grounds for Success" in Small Business Opportunities (Vol. 9, No. 2, March 1997, p. 62). By: Carla Goodman.

"Grounds for Success" in Small Business Opportunities (Vol. 9, No. 1, January 1997, p. 54). By: Carla Goodman.

"Group Therapy" in Crain's Small Business (September 1995, pp. 1, 12-13). By: Kimberly Lifton.

"Group's Plan is to Make Knowledge Accessible" in Washington Business Journal: Small Business Resource Guide (May 1996, pp. 4, 13). By: Lakhinder J.S. Vohra.

"Growing a Business" in Small Business Opportunities (Vol. 9, No. 3, May 1997, pp. 48, 104, 122). By: Anne Hart.

Guide to Business Permitting and Licensing in Wyoming. By: Paul Howard.

Have You Got What It Takes? Bellingham, WA: Self-Counsel Press, Inc. 1993, third edition. By: Douglas A. Gray.

Hawaii Business.

"Help Getting Started" in Business Start-Ups (Vol. 7, No. 12, December 1995, pp. 28-29). By: Sue Clayton.

"Helping Biz Cope" in Small Business Opportunities (Vol. 9, No. 1, January 1997, p. 98). By: Annette Wood.

"High-Tech Success Starts in a Garage - Dot Com" in Income Opportunities (Vol. 33, Issue 7, September 1998, pp. 54-55). By: Steven M. Brown.

"Holograms Are Solid Success" in Small Business Opportunities (Vol. 9, No. 2, March 1997, pp. 126-127). By: Anne Hart.

Home Office and Small Business Answer Book: Solutions to the Most Frequently Asked Questions about Starting and Running Home Offices. New York, NY: Henry Holt & Co. Inc. 1993. By: Janet Attard.

"Home-Run Hitter" in Fortune (November 23, 1998, p. 293).

Honey, I Want to Start My Own Business: A Planning Guide for Couples. New York, NY: Harper Business, 1997. By: Azriela Jaffe; foreword by John Gray.

How to Set up Your Own Small Business Student Study Guide. Minneapolis, MN: American Institute of Small Business, 1997. By: Max Fellek.

How to Start A Business. Rocklin, CA: Prima Publishing By: Hicks.

How to Start a Business in Illinois. Naperville, IL: Sourcebooks, Inc. 2nd ed. 1998. By: Edwin T. Gania and Mark Warda.

How to Start a Business in Michigan. Naperville, IL: Sourcebooks, Inc. 2nd ed. 1998. By: Edward A. Haman and Mark Warda.

How to Incorporate & Start a Business in Tennessee. Holbrook, MA: Adams Media Corp. 1997. By: J. W. Dicks.

How to Incorporate & Start a Business in Oregon. Holbrook, MA: Adams Media Corp. 1997. By: J. W. Dicks.

How to Incorporate & Start a Business in Virginia. Holbrook, MA: Adams Media Corp. 1997. By: J. W. Dicks.

How to Incorporate & Start a Business in Washington. Holbrook, MA: Adams Media Corp. 1997. By: J. W. Dicks.

How to Incorporate & Start a Business in Georgia. Holbrook, MA: Adams Media Corp. 1997. By: J. W. Dicks.

How to Start & Finance a Business That Works for You. Rockville Centre, NY: International Wealth Success, Inc. 1999. By: Tyler G. Hicks; edited by S. David Hicks.

How to Start a Business in Texas. Naperville, IL: Sourcebooks, Inc. 2nd ed. 1998. By: William R. Brown and Mark Warda.

How to Incorporate & Start a Business in Colorado. Holbrook, MA: Adams Media Corp. 1998. By: J. W. Dicks.

How to Start a Business in California. Naperville, IL: Sourcebooks, Inc. 1998. By: Mark P. Eissman and Mark Warda.

How to Start a Business on a Shoestring. New York, NY: Gordon Press Publishers, 1992.

How to Start a Business without Quitting Your Job: The Moonlight Entrepreneur's Guide. Berkeley, CA: Ten Speed Press, 1992. By: Philip Holland.

How to Start a Business in Pennsylvania. Naperville, IL: Sourcebooks, Inc. 1997. By: Desiree A. Petrus and Mark Warda.

How to Start a Business in New York. Naperville, IL: Sourcebooks, Inc. 1997. By: Paul W. Barnard and Mark Warda.

How to Really Start Your Own Business. Boston, MA: Inc. Publishing.

How to Run Your Business So It Doesn't Run You. Redwood Valley, CA: Borah Press, 1998. By: Linda L. Francis.

"How to Succeed in 4 Easy Steps" in Inc. (Vol. 17, No. 10, July 1995, pp. 30-32, 34, 36-40, 42). By: Bo Burlingham.

How to Form Your Own Indiana Corporation Before the Inc. Dries!: A Step by Step Guide, With Forms. 1992. By: Phillip Williams.

How to Form Your Own Michigan Corporation Before the Inc. Dries!: A Step by Step Guide, With Forms. Second edition, 1993. By: Phillip Williams.

How to Form Your Own Missouri Corporation Before the Inc. Dries!: A Step by Step Guide, With Forms. 1992. By: Phillip Williams.

How to Form Your Own Texas Corporation. Fourth edition, 1988. By: Anthony Mancuso.

How to Form Your Own Ohio Corporation Before the Inc. Dries!: A Step by Step Guide, With Forms. Second edition, 1994. By: Phillip Williams.

How to Form Your Own Illinois Corporation Before the Inc. Dries!: A Step by Step Guide, With Forms. Fourth edition, 1994. By: Phillip Williams.

How to Form a Simple Corporation in Florida. 1991. By: Mark Warda.

How to Form Your Own Florida Corporation. Third edition, 1990. By: Anthony Mancuso.

How to Form Your Own New York Corporation. 1989. By: Anthony Mancuso.

How to Form Your Own California Corporation. Seventh edition, 1988. By: Anthony Mancuso.

How to Start Your Own Business on a Shoestring and Make up to $500,000 Per Year. Rocklin, CA: Prima Publishing, 1998. By: Tyler G. Hicks.

How to Incorporate & Start a Business in Indiana. Holbrook, MA: Adams Media Corp. 1997. By: J. W. Dicks.

How to Form Your Own Indiana Corporation Before the Inc. Dries!. Oak Park, IL: P. Gaines Co. 2nd ed. 1997. By: Phillip G. Williams.

How to Set up & Operate Your Own Small Business. Minneapolis, MN: American Institute of Small Business, 6th ed. 1999. By: Max Fallek.

How to Be in Business for Yourself. New York, NY: Gordon Press Publishers, 1992.

How to Incorporate & Start a Business in Minnesota. Holbrook, MA: Adams Media Corp. 1997. By: J. W. Dicks.

How to Start, Run, and Stay in Business. New York, NY: John Wiley & Sons, Inc. Second edition, 1993. By: Gregory F. Kishel and Patricia G. Kishel.

How to Start Your Own Business—and Succeed. New York, NY: The McGraw-Hill Companies, Second edition, 1992. By: Arthur H. Kuriloff.

How to Incorporate & Start a Business in Nevada. Holbrook, MA: Adams Media Corp. 1997. By: J. W. Dicks.

Hudson Valley Business Journal.

Idaho Business Review.

If You're Clueless about Starting Your Own Business & Want to Know More. Chicago, IL: Dearborn Financial Publishing, Inc. 1997. By: Seth Godin.

"Improving Your Luck" in Inc. (Vol. 19, No. 5, April 1997, pp. 35-36). By: Norm Brodsky.

"In the Zone" in Entrepreneur (May 1996, pp. 116, 118-121). By: Cynthia E. Griffin.

In Business for Yourself. Lanham, MD: Madison Books, 1991. By: Bruce Williams and Warren Sloat.

Inc. Yourself: How to Profit by Setting Up Your Own Corporation. New York, NY: Harper Business, 1996. By: Judith H. McQuown.

Incorporation and Business Guide for Florida. Bellingham, WA: Self-Counsel Press, Inc. 1992. By: Robert C. Waters.

Incorporation and Business Guide for Oregon. Bellingham, WA: Self-Counsel Press, Inc. Fourth edition, 1992. By: C. Thomas Davis.

Incorporation Forms. Bellingham, WA: Self-Counsel Press 1993.

Incorporation Forms For Washington. Bellingham, WA: Self-Counsel Press 1993.

Incorporation and Business Guide for Washington. Bellingham, WA: Self-Counsel Press, Inc. Sixth edition, 1993. By: Victoria Van Hof.

Ingram's.

Innovation in Iowa. By: Bryan Ziegler.

"Is it time to go out on your own?" in Fortune (Vol. 138, No. 7, October 12, 1998, p. 203). By: Anne Fisher.

Jane Applegate's Strategies for Small Business Success. New York, NY: NAL Dutton, 1995. By: Jane Applegate.

"Jimmy's Top Ten List" in Business Start-Ups (Vol. 7, No. 8, August 1995, p. 7).

Kansas City Business Journal.

"Keeping Small Businesses Healthy" in Franchising World (Vol. 27, No. 1, January/February 1995, pp. 56-57). By: Cindy Murphy.

Keys to Starting a Small Business. Hauppauge, NY: Barron's Educational Series, Inc. 1991.

"Know It All" in Entrepreneur (March 1997, p. 28).

"Knowledge" in Business Start-Ups (Vol. 7, No. 12, December 1995, p. 38). By: Carolyn Lawrence.

Last Best Hope: How to Start & Grow Your Own Business. Plattsburgh, NY: McClelland & Stewart Tundra Books, 1997. By: Rod McQueen.

Launching Your First Small Business: Make the Right Decisions During Your First 90 Days. Riverwoods, IL: CCH, Inc. 1998. By: Joel Handelsman.

"Leading the Charge" in Hispanic Business (Vol. 18, No. 5, May 1996, pp. 26-28, 30). By: Maria Zate.

"Leaving Home" in Inc. (Vol. 18, No. 18, December 1997, p. 127). By: Christopher Caggiano.

Long Island Magazine.

Long Island Business News.

"Looking for Customers? Pick on Someone Your Own Size" in Inc. (Vol. 19, No. 3, March 1997, p. 22). By: Jerry Useem.

"Lost Dollars" in Black Enterprise (Vol. 27, No. 4, November 1996, p. 34). By: Sheryl E. Huggins.

Louisiana Country.

"Magic Carpet Ride" in Small Business Opportunities (Vol. 9, No. 2, March 1997, pp. 104-105).

"Mail-Order Biz Sells 300 Products Made from Recycled Goods" in Small Business Opportunities (Vol. 9, No. 1, January 1997, p. 46). By: Geri Anderson.

Make Money with Your PC! Berkeley, CA: Ten Speed Press, 1994. By: Lynn Waldorf.

"Make Your Pitch" in Independent Business (Vol. 7, No. 4, July/Aug. 1996, pp. 14-15).

"Making a Hopp to Top Agency" in Crain's Detroit Business (Vol. 13, No. 6, February 1997, pp. 3, 26). By: Jean Halliday.

Mancuso's Small Business Basics: Start, Buy or Franchise Your Way to a Successful Business. Naperville, IL: Sourcebooks, Inc. 2nd ed. 1997. By: Joseph R. Mancuso.

"Mapping Your Route" in Business Start-Ups (Vol. 8, No. 12, December 1996, pp. 40, 42-44). By: Lynn H. Colwell.

McGraw-Hill Guide to Starting Your Own Business: A Step-by-Step Blueprint. New York, NY: The McGraw-Hill Companies, 1992. By: Stephen C. Harper. Memphis Business Journal.

Mercer Business.

Mid-Career Entrepreneur: How to Start a Business and Be Your Own Boss. Chicago, IL: Dearborn Financial Publishing, Inc. 1993. By: Joseph R. Mancuso.

"Millennium Fever" in Small Business Opportunities (Vol. 11, May 1999, pp. 46-48, 52).

"Mind Power" in Entrepreneur (Vol. 23, No. 5, May 1995, pp. 100, 102-106). By: Robert McGarvey.

"Mini Storage Maxi Profit" in Small Business Opportunities (Vol. 9, No. 1, January 1997, p. 84). By: Stan Roberts.

Minority Small Business & Capital Ownership Development Program. New York, NY: Gordon Press Publishers, 1996.

"Minority Banks Are on the Rise" in Hispanic Business (Vol. 18, No. 5, May 1996, p. 15). By: Joel Russell.

MiOSHA News. Semimonthly. By: Gregg Grubb, Editor.

Missouri Business.

"Money in Marble" in Small Business Opportunities (Vol. 9, No. 2, March 1997, pp. 48, 50). By: Geri Anderson.

Montana Magazine.

"More Power to You" in Entrepreneur (March 1997, p. 10). By: Janean Chun.

"More new businesses start in West" in The Business Journal - Serving Phoenix and the Valley of the Sun (Vol. 18, No. 12, January 9, 1998, p. 27). By: Angela Mull.

"Moving Out" in Income Opportunities (Vol. 32, No. 4, April 1997, pp. 1418, 88). By: Dale D. Buss.

"Murder, She Sold" in Small Business Opportunities (Vol. 9, No. 2, March 1997, pp. 64, 66). By: Mary Ann McLaughlin.

"My Company is Small. How Can I Attract My First Big Client?" in Inc. (Vol. 18, No. 18, December 1997, p. 120). By: Christopher Caggiano.

Nashville Business Journal.

"Never Too Small to Manage" in Inc. (Vol. 19, No. 2, February 1997, pp. 56-58, 61). By: David Whitford.

New Jersey Business.

New Hampshire Department of Resources and Economic Development—Agenda. By: Kristi Forrest.

New Hampshire Business Review.

New Small Business Survival Guide. New York, NY: W. W. Norton & Co. Inc. 1991. By: Bob Coleman.

New England Economic Review.

"New Beginnings" in Business Start-Ups (Vol. 8, No. 1, January 1996, p. 96). By Joann K. Jones.

New Jersey Monthly.

"No Biz Like Shoe Biz" in Small Business Opportunities (Vol. 9, No. 1, January 1997, pp. 80, 82). By: Dorothy Elizabeth Brooks.

Nobody Gets Rich Working for Somebody Else: An Entrepreneur's Guide. Menlo Park, CA: Crisp Publications, Inc. 1993. By: Roger Fritz.

North Idaho Business Journal.

"On Their Own" in "Wall Street Journal Special Reports: Small Business (Special Edition) (May 23, 1996, p. R20). By: Jeffrey A. Tannenbaum.

"On a Mission to Demystify" in Hispanic Business (Vol. 17, No. 5, May 1995, p. 42). By: Rick Mendosa.

"On Your Mark..." in Business Start-Ups (Vol. 7, No. 2, February 1995, pp. 37-44). By: Gustav Berle and Jacquelyn Lynn.

Open Your California Business in 24 Hours: It's Not As Hard As You Think. Berkeley, CA: Nolo Press, 1998. By: Peri H. Pakroo.

Operating a Really Small Business. Menlo Park, CA: Crisp Publications, Inc. By: Betty Bivins.

Orange County Business Journal.

Oregon Business.

"Out of the Blue" in Inc. (Vol. 17, No. 10, July 1995, pp. 68-72). By: Tom Ehrenfeld.

Out of Work? Get into Business!: Shifting Gears and Turning Job Loss into Success. Bellingham, WA: Self-Counsel Press, Inc. 1994, first edition. By: Don Doman.

Pacific Business News.

"Patents to Oregonians set a sizzling pace" in Business Journal-Portland (Vol. 15, No. 1, February 27, 1998, p. 7). By: Dan McMillan.

"Platinum 200 Two Hundred" in Income Opportunities (Vol. 32, No. 3, March 1997, pp. 13-15). By: Robert L. Perry.

"Power Play" in Entrepreneur (March 1997, pp. 104, 106-105). By: Tomima Edmark.

Prentice Hall Small Business Survival Guide: A Blueprint for Success. Paramus, NJ: Prentice Hall, 1993. By: Compiled by Prentice Hall editorial staff.

"Prepare for Frustration You'll Create Exhilaration" in Crain's Small Business (Vol. 4, No. 10, October 1996, p. 19). By: Jim Brady.

Principles of Small Business. Florence, KY: International Thomson Publishing, 1997. By: Robert Brown and Barrow.

"Profits in Ponds" in Small Business Opportunities (Vol. 8, No. 5, September 1996, pp. 60, 62, 64, 66).

"Profits by the Book" in Small Business Opportunities (Vol. 9, No. 2, March 1997, p. 114). By: Anne Hart.

Providence Business News.

Providence Journal Bulletin.

Quality Business: Quality Issues & Smaller Firms. New York, NY: Routledge, 1998. By: Julian North and Robert Blackburn.

"Quest for perfect sauce leads to small business founding" in Wichita Business Journal (KS) (May 15, 1998, p. 22). By: Lara Kohl.

"Quitting" in Business Start-Ups (Vol. 7, No. 12, December 1995, pp. 60-61). By: Sue Clayton.

"Rating the states for small firms" in Nation's Business (Vol.86, No. 10, October 1998, p. 10). By: Thomas Love.

"Replace Yourself" in Inc. (Vol. 18, No. 18, December 1997, pp. 125-126). By: Susan Greco.

"Restless Youth" in Wall Street Journal Special Reports: Small Business (Special Edition) (May 23, 1996, pp. R18-R19). By: Roger Ricklefs.

"Right from the Start" in Small Business Opportunities (Vol. 9, No. 3, May 1997, pp. 20, 42). By: Dr. Sandy Weinberg.

"Right Mix" in Hispanic Business (Vol. 18, No. 12, December 1996, pp. 22-24). By: Maria Zate.

Road to Self-Employment: A Practical Guide to Microbusiness Development. San Diego, CA: Women's Business Training Center, 1997. By: Gerri P. Norington; edited by Linda C. Pulg; illustrated by J. Bird Design staff; photographed by Doreen Clough.

Rochester Business Journal.

Rochester Business Magazine.

"Rudy Alvarado, Ceo" in Hispanic Business (Vol. 18, No. 7/ 8, July/August 1996, p. 32). By: Maria Zate.

"Running out of Time" in Inc. (Vol. 19, No. 2, February 1997, pp. 63-64, 68, 72-73). By: John Grossmann.

Sacramento Business Journal.

San Diego Business Journal.

"Sanchez: a Victory of Her Own" in Hispanic Business (Vol. 19, No. 4, April 1997, pp. 16, 18). By: Rick Mendosa.

"Say When" in Inc. (Vol. 17, No. 2, February 1995, pp. 19-20). By: Steven L. Marks.

SBA Hotline Answer Book. New York, NY: John Wiley & Sons, Inc. 1991. By: Gustav Berle.

"SCORE Points to Success" in Black Enterprise (Vol. 25, No. 6, January 1995, pp. 38). By: Christina F. Watts

"Search for Tomorrow" in Entrepreneur (May 1997, pp. 112, 144, 116, 122). By: Genion Chan.

"Seat-Of-The-Pants Strategy Won't Keep You Growing" in Crain's Small Business (Vol. 4, No. 10, October 1996, pp. 8-9). By: Tim Bannister.

Second Coming of the Wooly Mammoth: An Entrepreneur's Bible. Berkeley, CA: Ten Speed Press, 1991. By: Ted Frost.

Secrets to Running a Successful Business. Kirkland, WA: 1994. By: Jeanette L. Rosenberg.

"Senate Classifies Workers" in Income Opportunities (Vol. 31, No. 6, June 1996, p. 5). By: Michele Marrinan.

Send 'Em One White Sock: 67 Outrageously Simple Ideas from Around the World for Building Your Business. New York, NY: The McGraw-Hill Companies, 1998. By: Stan Rapp and Thomas L. Collins.

"Sending Workers Home—To Work" in Independent Business (Vol. 7, No. 4, July/Aug. 1996, pp. 20-22). By: Verna Gates.

"Service Sector is a Good Franchise Bet" in Washington Business Journal: Small Business Resource Guide (May 1996, pp. 8, 10). By: Lakhinder J.S. Vohra.

"Setting an Agenda" in Hispanic Business (Vol. 18, No. 11, November 1996, pp. 18, 22).

"Seven Traps of Strategic Planning" in Inc. (Vol. 18, No. 16, November 1996, pp. 99, 101, 103). By: Joseph C. Picken and Gregory G. Dess.

"Shoestring Start-Ups" in Small Business Opportuniti es (Vol. 10, No. 6, November 1998, pp. 22-34, 122).

Silver River Marine Institute.

"Silver Lining" in Entrepreneur (June 1995, pp. 52, 54-55). By: Cynthia E. Griffin.

"Sisters, Inc." in Hispanic Business (May 1998, p. 33). By: Joel Russell.

"Small Like Me" in Wall Street Journal Special Reports: Small Business (Special Edition) (May 23, 1996, p. R31). By: John Buskin.

"Small Business A to Z" in Business Start-Ups (Vol. 8, No. 7, July 1996, p. 4). By: Karin Moeller.

Small Business Success. By: Andrea Hine, editor.

Small Business Handbook. New York, NY: Simon & Schuster Trade, 3rd ed. 1997. By: Irving Burstiner.

Small Business Start-Up Guide: A Surefire Blueprint to Successfully Launch Your Own Business. Naperville, IL: Sourcebooks, Inc. 2nd ed. 1997. By: Hal Root and Steve Koenig.

Small Business Start-Up Guide: Practical Advice on Starting & Operating a Small Business. Great Falls, VA: Information International, 2nd ed. 1998. By: Robert A. Sullivan.

Small Business Test. Berkeley, CA: Ten Speed Press, 1990. By: Colin Ingram.

Small Time Operator: The Software. Willits, CA: Bell Springs Publishing By: Bernard Kamoroff CPA, Steve Steinke and Emil Krause.

Small Time Operator: How to Start Your Own Small Business, Keep Your Books, Pay Your Taxes, & Stay out of Trouble!. Willits, CA: Bell Springs Publishing, 22nd ed. 1998. By: Bernard Kamoroff.

Small Firms and Economic Growth. Northampton, MA: Ashgate Publishing Co. Inc. 1995. By: Zoltan J. Acs.

Small Firm Formation & Regional Economic Development. New York, NY: Routledge, Inc. 1996. By: Michael W. Danson.

Small Business Directory. New York, NY: U.S. Government Printing Office, 1992.

Small Business Kit for Dummies. Indianapolis, IN: IDG Worldwide, 1998. By: Richard D. Harroch.

Small Business for Dummies. Indianapolis, IN: 7260 Shadeland Sta. 1998. By: Eric Tyson and Jim Schell.

"Small Business Committed to Workplace Safety" in Independent Business (Vol. 8, No. 2, Mar./Apr. 1997, pp. 54).

"Small-business incubator lands $75,000 challenge grant" in The Business Journal (October 12, 1998, p. 21). By: Peter Delevett.

Smart Start your Maryland Business. Grants Pass, OR: PSI Research Revised edition, 1992. By: Michael D. Jenkins.

Smart Start your Massachusetts Business. Grants Pass, OR: PSI Research Revised edition, 1992. By: Michael D. Jenkins.

Smart Start your Michigan Business. Grants Pass, OR: PSI Research Revised edition, 1992. By: Michael D. Jenkins.

Smart Start your Missouri Business. Grants Pass, OR: PSI Research Revised edition, 1992. By: Michael D. Jenkins.

Smart Start your New Hampshire Business. Grants Pass, OR: PSI Research Revised edition, 1992. By: Michael D. Jenkins.

Smart Start your New Jersey Business. Grants Pass, OR: PSI Research Revised edition, 1992. By: Michael D. Jenkins.

Smart Start your New Mexico Business. Grants Pass, OR: PSI Research Revised edition, 1992. By: Michael D. Jenkins.

Smart Start your New York Business. Grants Pass, OR: PSI Research Revised edition, 1992. By: Michael D. Jenkins.

Smart Start Your Washington, D.C. Business. Grants Pass, OR: PSI Research, 1998.

Smart Start Your Wisconsin Business. Grants Pass, OR: PSI Research, 1998.

Smart Start your North Carolina Business. Grants Pass, OR: PSI Research Revised edition, 1992. By: Michael D. Jenkins.

Smart Start your Ohio Business. Grants Pass, OR: PSI Research Revised edition, 1992. By: Michael D. Jenkins.

Smart Start your Oregon Business. Grants Pass, OR: PSI Research Revised edition, 1992. By: Michael D. Jenkins.

Smart Start your Pennsylvania Business. Grants Pass, OR: PSI Research Revised edition, 1992. By: Michael D. Jenkins.

Smart Start your South Carolina Business. Grants Pass, OR: PSI Research Revised edition, 1992. By: Michael D. Jenkins.

Smart Start your Tennessee Business. Grants Pass, OR: PSI Research Revised edition, 1992. By: Michael D. Jenkins.

Smart Start your Texas Business Guide. Grants Pass, OR: PSI Research Revised edition, 1992. By: Michael D. Jenkins.

Smart Start your Virginia Business. Grants Pass, OR: PSI Research Revised edition, 1992. By: Michael D. Jenkins.

Smart Start your Washington Business. Grants Pass, OR: PSI Research Revised edition, 1992. By: Michael D. Jenkins.

Smart Start your Washington D.C. Business. Grants Pass, OR: PSI Research Revised edition, 1992. By: Michael D. Jenkins.

Smart Start your Wisconsin Business. Grants Pass, OR: PSI Research Revised edition, 1992. By: Michael D. Jenkins.

Smart Start Your California Business. Grants Pass, OR: PSI Research Revised edition, 1992. By: Michael D. Jenkins.

Smart Start Your South Dakota Business. Grants Pass, OR: PSI Research Revised edition, 1992. By: Michael D. Jenkins.

Smart Start Your Washington Business. Grants Pass, OR: PSI Research, 1997.

Smart Start Your Virginia Business. Grants Pass, OR: PSI Research, 1997.

Smart Start Your Utah Business. Grants Pass, OR: PSI Research Revised edition, 1992. By: Michael D. Jenkins.

Smart Start Your Vermont Business. Grants Pass, OR: PSI Research Revised edition, 1992. By: Michael D. Jenkins.

Smart Start Your West Virginia Business. Grants Pass, OR: PSI Research Revised edition, 1992. By: Michael D. Jenkins.

Smart Start Your Wyoming Business. Grants Pass, OR: PSI Research Revised edition, 1992. By: Michael D. Jenkins and Daniel J. Herron.

Smart Start your Colorado Business. Grants Pass, OR: PSI Research Revised edition, 1992. By: Michael D. Jenkins.

Smart Start your Arkansas Business. Grants Pass, OR: PSI Research Revised edition, 1992. By: Michael D. Jenkins.

Smart Start your Arizona Business. Grants Pass, OR: PSI Research Revised edition, 1992. By: Michael D. Jenkins.

Smart Start your Iowa Business. Grants Pass, OR: PSI Research Revised edition, 1992. By: Michael D. Jenkins.

Smart Start your Indiana Business. Grants Pass, OR: PSI Research Revised edition, 1992. By: Michael D. Jenkins.

Smart Start your Illinois Business. Grants Pass, OR: PSI Research Revised edition, 1992. By: Michael D. Jenkins.

Smart Start your Georgia Business. Grants Pass, OR: PSI Research Revised edition, 1992. By: Michael D. Jenkins.

Smart Start Your New York Business. Grants Pass, OR: PSI Research, 1997.

Smart Start Your New Jersey Business. Grants Pass, OR: PSI Research, 1997.

Smart Start Your Michigan Business. Grants Pass, OR: PSI Research, 1998.

Smart Start Your Maryland Business. Grants Pass, OR: PSI Research, 1997.

Smart Start Your Arizona Business. Grants Pass, OR: PSI Research, 1997.

Smart Start Your Oregon Business. Grants Pass, OR: PSI Research, 1997.

Smart Start Your California Business. Grants Pass, OR: PSI Research, 1997.

Smart Start Your Arkansas Business. Grants Pass, OR: PSI Research, 1998.

Smart Start Your Colorado Business. Grants Pass, OR: PSI Research, 1997.

Smart Start Your Connecticut Business. Grants Pass, OR: PSI Research, 1998.

Smart Start Your Pennsylvania Business. Grants Pass, OR: PSI Research, 1997.

Smart Start Your Florida Business. Grants Pass, OR: PSI Research, 1997.

Smart Start Your Tennessee Business. Grants Pass, OR: PSI Research, 1998.

Smart Start Your Georgia Business. Grants Pass, OR: PSI Research, 1997.

Smart Start Your Hawaii Business. Grants Pass, OR: PSI Research, 1998.

Smart Start Your North Carolina Business. Grants Pass, OR: PSI Research, 1997.

Smart Start Your Illinois Business. Grants Pass, OR: PSI Research, 1998.

Smart Start Your Ohio Business. Grants Pass, OR: PSI Research, 1998.

Smart Start Your Indiana Business. Grants Pass, OR: PSI Research, 1998.

Smart Start Your Kentucky Business. Grants Pass, OR: PSI Research, 1997.

Smart Start Your Massachusetts Business. Grants Pass, OR: PSI Research, 1997.

Smart Start your Connecticut Business. Grants Pass, OR: PSI Research Revised edition, 1992. By: Michael D. Jenkins.

Smart Start Your Texas Business. Grants Pass, OR: PSI Research, 1997.

Smart Start your Florida Business. Grants Pass, OR: PSI Research Revised edition, 1992. By: Carl R. Sniffen and Michael D. Jenkins.

Smart Start your Kentucky Business. Grants Pass, OR: PSI Research Revised edition, 1992. By: Michael D. Jenkins.

Smart Start your Hawaii Business. Grants Pass, OR: PSI Research Revised edition, 1992. By: Michael D. Jenkins and Franklin Forbes.

"So Long to Sarseps" in Hispanic Business (Vol. 18, No. 11, November 1996, p. 12). By: Rick Mendosa.

So You Want to Own Your Own Business: A Guide for Beginning Entrepreuners. Alexandria, VA: Star Mountain, Inc. 1997.

"Solid Foundations" in Black Enterprise (Vol. 27, No. 7, February 1997, p. 38). By: Denolyn Carroll.

"Something Borrowed" in Entrepreneur (February 1997, p. 26). St. Louis Business Journal.

Start Your Own Business in Thirty Days. New York, NY: Berkley Publishing Group, 1998. By: Gary J. Grappo.

Start Your Own Business After 50—or 60—or 70! San Leandro, CA: Bristol Publishing Enterprises, Inc. 1990. By: Lauraine Snelling.

Start Your Own Business: A Smart & Simple Guide. Irvine, CA: Entrepreneur Media, 1998.

Start Your Own Business: A Beginner's Guide. Grants Pass, OR: PSI Research, 2nd ed. 1997.

"Start with Strategic Fundamentals" in Crain's Small Business (September 1995, p. 9). By: Jim Brady.

Start-Up Guide: A One-Year Plan for Entrepreneurs. Chicago, IL: Upstart Publishing Co. Inc. 1994. By: David H. Bangs, Jr.

Start, Run & Grow a Successful Small Business. Riverwoods, IL: C C H, Inc. 2nd ed. 1998. By: Susan Jacksach; designed by Tim Kaage; contribution by Martin Bush.

Start Your New Business Now! New York, NY: Visions Communications, 1997. By: Arlene Appelbaum.

Start Your Own Business. Irving, TX: Dimension Four Enterprises, Inc. 1998. By: Caleb McAfee.

Starting and Operating a Business in Georgia: A Step-by-Step Guide. Grants Pass, OR: PSI Research Revised edition, 1992. By: Michael D. Jenkins.

Starting Your New Business: A Guide for Entrepreneurs. Menlo Park, CA: Crisp Publications, Inc. Revised edition, 1992. By: Charles L. Martin.

Starting and Operating a Business in Florida: A Step-by-Step Guide. Grants Pass, OR: PSI Research Revised edition, 1992. By: Michael D. Jenkins.

Starting Your Own Business & Making It a Success. Chicago, IL: TFS Publishing, 1998. By: John O. Alaba.

Starting and Operating a Business in District of Columbia: A Step-by-Step Guide. Grants Pass, OR: PSI Research Revised edition, 1992. By: Michael D. Jenkins.

Starting and Operating a Business in Delaware: A Step-by-Step Guide. Grants Pass, OR: PSI Research Revised edition, 1992. By: Michael D. Jenkins.

Starting and Operating a Business in Connecticut: A Step-by-Step Guide. Grants Pass, OR: PSI Research Revised edition, 1992. By: Michael D. Jenkins.

Starting and Operating a Business in Illinois: A Step-by-Step Guide. Grants Pass, OR: PSI Research Revised edition, 1992. By: Michael D. Jenkins.

Starting Your Own Business: No Money Down. New York, NY: John Wiley & Sons, Inc. 1908. By: M. John Storey.

Starting and Managing the Small Business. New York, NY: The McGraw-Hill Companies, 1992. By: Arthur H. Kuriloff and John M. Hemphill.

Starting Millionaire Success Kit. Rockville Centre, NY: International Wealth Success, Inc. Sixth edition, 1993. By: Tyler G. Hicks.

Starting and Operating a Business in Colorado: A Step-by-Step Guide. Grants Pass, OR: PSI Research Revised edition, 1992. By: Michael D. Jenkins.

Starting and Operating a Business. Grants Pass, OR: Oasis Press, 1992. By: Michael D. Jenkins.

Starting and Operating a Business in California: A Step-by-Step Guide. Grants Pass, OR: PSI Research Revised edition, 1992. By: Michael D. Jenkins.

Starting and Operating a Business in Idaho: A Step-by-Step Guide. Grants Pass, OR: PSI Research Revised edition, 1992. By: Michael D. Jenkins.

Starting and Operating a Business in Arkansas: A Step-by-Step Guide. Grants Pass, OR: PSI Research Revised edition, 1992. By: Michael D. Jenkins.

Starting and Operating a Business in Arizona: A Step-by-Step Guide. Grants Pass, OR: PSI Research Revised edition, 1992. By: Michael D. Jenkins.

Starting and Operating a Business in Alaska: A Step-by-Step Guide. Grants Pass, OR: PSI Research Revised edition, 1992. By: Michael D. Jenkins.

Starting and Operating a Business in Alabama: A Step-by-Step Guide. Grants Pass, OR: PSI Research Revised edition, 1992. By: Michael D. Jenkins.

Starting and Operating a Business in Hawaii: A Step-by-Step Guide. Grants Pass, OR: PSI Research Revised edition, 1992. By: Michael D. Jenkins.

Starting a Small Business of Your Own—With "No" Money. Milton, MA: The Empire Publishing, Inc. 1990. By: David F. Cox.

Starting a Small Business Handbook: How to Start and Operate Your Own Small Business. Plano, TX: Data-Lynn Book Co. Second edition, 1992. By: Andrew J. Lynn.

Starting on a Shoestring: Building a Business without a Bankroll. New York, NY: John Wiley & Sons, Inc. Third edition, 1995. By: Arnold S. Goldstein.

Starting a Successful Business on the West Coast. Bellingham, WA: Self-Counsel Press, Inc. Third edition, 1992. By: Douglas L. Clark.

Starting and Operating a Business in Iowa: A Step-by-Step Guide. Grants Pass, OR: PSI Research Revised edition, 1992. By: Michael D. Jenkins.

Starting a Small Business in Iowa. By: Bryan Ziegler.

"Starting Over" in Business Start-Ups (Vol. 7, No. 8, August 1995, p. 6). By: Lynn H. Colwell.

Starting Up Your Own Business: Expert Advice from the U.S. Small Business Administration. New York, NY: TAB Books, Inc. 1990. By: G. Howard Poteet.

Starting Up. Philadelphia, PA: Trans-Atlantic Publications, Inc. 1990. By: Gary Jones.

"Step 2: Do Your Homework" in Business Start-Ups (Vol. 8, No. 6, June 1996, pp. 8, 10). By: Kylo-Patrick Hart.

"Steps to Start a Business" in Washington Business Journal: Small Business Resource Guide (May 1996, p. 4).

Steps to Small Business Start-Up: Everything You Need to Know to Turn Your Idea into a Successful Business. Chicago, IL: Upstart Publishing Co. Inc. 1993. By: Linda Pinson and Jerry Hinnett.

Succeeding in Small Business: The 101 Toughest Problems and How to Solve Them. New York, NY: NAL Dutton, 1992. By: Jane Applegate.

"Success Secrets" in Small Business Opportunities (Vol. 9, No. 2, March 1997, p. 84). By: Carla Goodman.

"Success" in Black Enterprise (Vol. 27, No. 7, February 1997, p. 36). By: Ann Brown.

"Support System" in Entrepreneur (Vol. 23, No. 4, April 1995, pp. 136-142). By: Bob Weinstein.

Surviving the Start-up Years in Your Own Business. Cincinnati, OH: F & W Publishing, Inc. 1991. By: Joyce S. Marder.

"Takeover" in Inc. (Vol. 19, No. 5, April 1997, pp. 72-75, 78, 80-82). By: Stephanie Gruner.

BIBLIOGRAPHY

"Taking a Stand" in Hispanic Business (Vol. 18, No. 11, November 1996, pp. 26, 28, 30).

"Talking Business with Ron Dubren, Inventor of Tickle Me Elmo" in Income Opportunities (Vol. 32, No. 4, April 1997, pp. 28-32). By: Stephanie Jeffrey.

Tax Freedom: The Business Guide to Incorporating in Nevada. 1990. By: Barber.

Technology Resources for Business in Wisconsin. 1990.

Tennessee Economic Development Quarterly. Quarterly. By: Leigh Wieland, Editor.

The Ultimate No B.S. No Holds Barred, Kick Butt, Take No Prisoners, and Make Tons of Money Business Success Book. Bellingham, WA: Self-Counsel Press, Inc. 1993. By: Dan Kennedy.

"Three Criteria for a Successful New Business" in Inc. (Vol. 18, No. 5, April 1996, pp. 21-22). By: Norm Brodsky.

"Tips from the Experts" in Washington Business Journal: Small Business Resource Guide (May 1996, p. 5).

Toledo Business Journal.

"Truth About Start-Ups" in Inc. (Vol. 17, No. 2, February 1995, pp. 23-24). By: Paul Reynolds.

"Tune in & Start Up" in Business Start-Ups (Vol. 8, No. 7, July 1996, p. 4). By: Karin Moeller.

Unofficial Guide to Starting a Business. Old Tappan, NJ: MacMillan Publishing Co. Inc. 1998.

"Use Your Head" in Business Start-Ups (Vol. 7, No. 7, July 1995, pp. 44, 46-49). By: Bob Weinstein.

"Using Technology to Enhance Your Business" in Black Enterprise (Vol. 27, No. 8, March 1997, pp. 64-72).

Vault Reports: A Guide to Starting Your Own Business. New York, NY: Houghton Mifflin Co. 1998.

Venture Financing: Raising Capital in Wisconsin. 1990.

VentureTrac: Complete Business Development Program. Lancaster, OH: Tangent Publishing, 1997. By: Andrew J. Batchelor, Jr. and Timothy E, Nesmith.

"Video Offers a Way of Life Beyond the Minimum Wage" in Crain's Small Business (June 1996, pp. 2). By: Jeffrey McCracken.

Virginia Business.

"Virtue of Necessity" in Inc.2 (Vol. 18, No. 18, December 1997, pp. 80, 82, 85, 88, 93). By: Jerry Useem.

We Own It: Starting & Managing Cooperatives & Employee-Owned Businesses. Willits, CA: Bell Springs Publishing Co. Revised edition, 1991. By: Peter Honigsberg, Bernard Kamoroff and Jim Beatty.

Westchester County Business Journal.

"What's the Big Idea?" in Small Business Opportunities (Vol. 7, No. 5, September 1995, pp. 17). By: Carla Goodman.

"Where Dreams Get Hope" in Crain's Detroit Business (Vol. 12, No. 16, April 1996, pp. 3, 26). By: Robert Akeny.

"Who Needs Growth?" in Inc. (Vol. 18, No. 14, October 1996, p. 90). By: Susan Greco.

"Wired for Success" in Black Enterprise (Vol. 27, No. 8, March 1997, pp. 75-80). By: Tariq K. Muhammad.

Wisconsin Financing Alternatives. Reprinted October 1991.

Wisconsin Minority Business Resource Directory. Second edition.

"With Luck, This Biz Will Go Down the Toilet" in Inc. (Vol. 19, No. 5, April 1997, p. 21). By: Phaedra Hise.

"Women's Firms Thrive" in Nation's Business (Vol. 86, No. 8, August 1998, p. 38). By: Sharon Nelton.

Worcester Business Journal.

Working Knowledge: What You Need to Know Before Opening a Business. Plano, TX: Echelon Publishing, 1994. By: William A. Walls.

World Class: Thriving Locally in the Global Economy. New York, NY: Simon & Schuster, Inc. 1995. By: Rosabeth M. Kanter.

Writer's Voice. 10/year.

"Wrong Question" in INC. (Vol. 17, No. 3, March 1995, pp. 27). By: Henry Kressel and Bruce Guile.

"Year of Living Dangerously" in Business Start-Ups (Vol. 7, No. 6, June 1995, pp. 74, 76-77). By: Jeannie Pearce.

"Year One" in Business Start-Ups (Vol. 7, No. 12, December 1995, pp. 76-77). By: Jacquelyn Lynn.

Your New Business: A Personal Plan for Success. Menlo Park, CA: Crisp Publications, Inc. 1993. By: Charles Martin.

Your International Business Plan. Revised edition, 1990. By: James L. Otis.

Your Business Plan.

Your Marketing Plan — WBK ed.. Eugene, OR: Oregon Small Business Development Center Network, 1996. By: Chris Pryor.

Your Way: Starting Your Own Business in Rural South Dakota. Freeman, SD: Pine Hill Press, Inc. 1997. By: Tom Kilian.

Your Path to Success" in Hispanic Business (Vol. 19, No. 1, January 1997, p. 27).

Software Publishing

"Always a Payroll to Meet" in Inc. (Vol. 20, No. 1, January 1998, pp. 31-32). By: Jeffrey L. Seglin.

"The Antihero's Guide to the New Economy" in Inc. (Vol. 20, No. 1, January 1998, pp. 36-38, 40-42, 44-46, 48). By: Michael Hopkins.

"The Apartment" in Inc. (Vol. 19, No. 15, December 21, 1997, pp. 85). By: Michael E. Kanell.

"The Art of the Covenant" in Inc. (Vol. 19, No. 11, August 1997, pp. 99-100). By: Jill Andresky Fraser.

"Berkeley firm wants to be cash converter for software developers" in San Francisco Chronicle (CA) (September 24, 1998, p. B3).

"Beyond Ms. Pacman" in Working Woman (Vol. 22, No. 7, July/August, 1997, pp. 15-16). By: Michelle Kort.

"Bill Gates with a College Degree" in The Red Herring (No. 27, January 1996, pp. 92-96). By: Christopher J. Alden.

"Brain Power" in Entrepreneur (February 1997, p. 22).

"Bridging the Gap" in Red Herring (No. 55, June 1998, p. 70). By: Brian E. Taptich.

"Bridging the Gap" in Red Herring (No. 59, October 1998, p. 98). By: Kendall Riding.

"Chain Gang" in Red Herring (No. 63, February 1999, p. 24). By: Alex Gove.

"Chief Executive" in Red Herring (No. 59, October 1998, p. 144). By: Jason Pontin.

"Client/Server Redux" in The Red Herring (No. 47, October 1997, pp. 56, 58, 60). By: Alex Gove.

"Comeback Kid" in Entrepreneur (May 1997, pp. 56, 58-59). By: Cheryl F. Goldberg.

Computer-Aided Software Engineering: Issues and Trends for the 1990s and Beyond. Hershey, PA: Idea Group Publishing, 1993. By: Thomas Bergin, editor.

Computer Ethics. Paramus, NJ: Prentice Hall, 1994, second edition. PRC $22.60. By: Debra Johnson.

Computer Software. New York, NY: The McGraw-Hill Companies, 1990. By: Charles H. Fleer.

Computer Software Protection Law. Ann Arbor, MI: Books on Demand, 2 volumes. By: Cary H. Sherman.

Concepts in Data Structures and Software Development: A Text for the Second Course in Computer Science. St. Paul, MN: West Publishing Co. 1991. By: G. Michael Schneider and Steven Bruell.

"Consultant Killers" in Red Herring (No. 57, August 1998, p. 45). By: Ilan Greenberg.

"Content and its Civilization" in Red Herring (No. 63, February 1999, p. 84). By: Blaise Zerega.

"Das Human Capital" in Hits (No. 4, Summer 1997, pp. 34-35). By: Jonathan Burke.

"Death by Unnatural Causes" in Inc. (Vol. 19, No. 15, December 21, 1997, pp. 60-65). By: Stephanie Gruner.

"A Design for Better Designs" in Hispanic Business (Vol. 19, No. 12, December 1997, pp. 38).

"Destiny Software: narrowing its e-commerce focus for growth" in Red Herring (Vol. 56, July 1998, p. 30). By: Nikki Goth Itoi.

Developing Object-Oriented Software for the Macintosh. Reading, MA: Addison-Wesley Publishing Co. Inc. 1992. By: Neal Goldstein.

"Dream Team" in The Red Herring (No. 47, October 1997, pp. 90). By: Deborah Claymon.

"Droolware" in The Red Herring (No. 27, January 1996, pp. 19).

"Drop a Dime-and More" in Inc. (Vol. 19, No. 9, August 17, 1997, pp. 26). By: Sarah Schafer.

"E-commerce startup pushes business-to-business wares" in The Business Journal (October 12, 1998, p. 68). By: Adam Feuerstein.

"Eco-Preneuring" in Small Business Opportunities (Vol. 9, No. 2, March 1997, pp. 70, 72). By: Geri Anderson.

Engineering Quality Software: Defect Detection and Prevention. Reading, MA: Addison-Wesley Publishing Co. Inc. 1992. By: Ann K. Miller.

"Entrepreneurial Superstars" in Entrepreneur (April 1997, pp. 108-139). By: Debra Phillips and others.

"Entrepreneurs Across America" in Entrepreneur (Vol. 24, No. 4, April 1996, pp. 100-104, 106-108, 110-112, 114-116, 118, 120-123). By: Janean Chum, Debra Phillips, Cynthia E. Griffin, Heather Page, Lynn Beresford, Holly Celeste Fisk, and Charlotte Mulbern.

"Fading Away" in Hits (No. 4, Summer 1997, p. 5).

"Flaunt Your Expertise" in Independent Business (Vol. 7, No. 5, Sept./Oct. 1996, p. 46). By: Valerie J. Nelson.

"For GMD Studios, it pays to be small" in Orlando Business Journal (May 29, 1998, p. 27). By: Paul Dillion.

"Freeware" in Red Herring (No. 63, February 1999, p. 48). By: Nikki Goth Itoi.

"Games People Play" in The Red Herring (No. 43, June 1997, pp. 82-83). By: Luc Hatlestad.

"Get In the Game" in Black Enterprise (Vol. 29, February 1999, pp. 185-192). By: Gerda D. Gallop.

"Going Multi-Media" in Black Enterprise (Vol. 26, No. 8, March 1996, pp. 96-100). By: Joyce Jones.

"Hail, Bops" in Red Herring (No. 57, August 1998, p. 86). By: Alex Gove.

"He Said, She Said" in Red Herring (Vol. 56, July 1998, p. 40). By: Andrew P. Madden.

"Headhunters call our technical staff constantly. What can we do?" in Inc. (Vol. 19, No. 18, December 1997, p. 149). By: Christopher Caggiano.

"Heavy Metalithics" in The Red Herring (December 1996, p. 4043). By: Nikki C. Goth.

"High-water Mark" in The Red Herring (No. 53, April 1998, pp. 42-46). By: Brian E. Taptich.

"His Customers' Plea Became New Calling" in Crain's Small Business (July 1996, p. 15). By: Jeffrey McCracken.

"Hitting the Mark" in The Red Herring (No. 27, January 1996, pp. 75, 77-78). By: Virginie S. Pelletier.

"Hotter Tip" in Inc. (Vol. 19, No. 18, December 1997, p. 149). By: Stephanie Gruner.

"How Suite It Is!" in Independent Business (Vol. 7, No. 5, Sept./Oct. 1996, pp. 20-22). By: Eric J. Adams.

How to Write Macintosh Software: The Debugging Reference for the Macintosh. Reading, MA: Addison-Wesley Publishing Co. Inc. 1992. By: Scott Knaster.

"Hunters, Meet Gathers" in Red Herring (May 1998, p. 74). By: Andrew P. Madden.

IEEE Software Engineering Standards. Piscataway, NJ: IEEE Standards Office, 1993.

"Inner Space" in The Red Herring (No. 53, April 1998, p. 100). By: Constance Loizos.

"Instant Entrepreneurs" in Fortune (November 16, 1998, p. 188).

"Instant Gratification" in Business Start-Ups (Vol. 11, No. 1, January 1999, p. 11). By: Shannon Kinnard.

"IPO Candidates" in The Red Herring (No. 53, April 1998, p. 122). By: Anna C. Semansky.

"It's Up To You New York" in The Red Herring (No. 47, October 1997, pp. 44-46, 48). By: Andrew P. Madden.

"It's Your Life. Manage It!" in Working Woman (Vol. 22, No. 7, July/August, 1997, pp. 42-47). By: Sandy Sheehy.

"Jobs' Story" in The Red Herring (No. 27, January 1996, pp. 9, 11).

"Jomei the Money" in Red Herring (Vol. 56, July 1998, p. 42). By: Deborah Claymon.

"Latest Word" in Entrepreneur (March 1996, pp. 43-45). By: Cheryl J. Goldberg.

"The Liquidator" in Red Herring (No. 58, September 1998, p. 106). By: Constance Loizos.

"Logging on" in The Red Herring (No. 53, April 1998, pp. 26-27). By: Deborah Claymon.

"Mind Games" in Income Opportunities (Vol. 31, No. 5, May 1996, pp. 104, 102). By: Sheila Gibson.

"The Missing Link" in Inc. (Vol. 17, No. 8, June 1995, pp. 58-60, 62-66). By: Anne Murphy.

"Motherhood, Apple Pie and Stock Options" in Inc. (Vol. 20, No. 2, February 1998, pp. 84-86, 90, 93-94, 96-97). By: Edward O. Welles.

"New Technology Shelves Software Distributor" in Inc. (Vol. 19, No. 16, November 1997, p. 22). By: Jim Kling.

"A New Universe Next Door" in The Red Herring (May 1996, pp. 44-45, 47, 49). By: Jonathan Burke.

"The NexGen-eration" in Black Enterprise (Vol. 26, No. 7, February 1996, p. 30). By: Rhonda Reynolds.

"Nick of Time" in Red Herring: Guide to Professional Services 1999 (1999, p. 47). By: Janet Kettlehut.

"Not ready for prime time" in The Red Herring (No. 43, June 1997, pp. 50, 52-53). By: Alex Gove.

"Objects of Desire" in The Red Herring (No. 45, August 1997, pp. 78-83). By: Ilan Greenberg.

"On Sabbatical, Some Go Fishing for Jobs" in The Wall Street Journal (Vol. IC, No. 111, June 9, 1997, pp. B1, B2). By: Stephanie N. Mehta.

"Pencil Pusher" in Red Herring (Vol. 56, July 1998, p. 53). By: Constance Loizos.

"Phat, way kewl, da bomb" in Forbes (Vol. 162, No. 3, February 9, 1998, p. 72). By: Silvia Sansoni.

"Photonic synthesis" in The Red Herring (No. 52, March 1998, pp. 94, 96). By: Brian E. Taptich.

"Private Company Profiles" in The Red Herring (No. 53, April 1998, pp. 86-88, 90). By: Stephanie T. Gates and Anna C. Semansky.

"Proud to be an American" in The Red Herring (No. 47, October 1997, pp. 40-43). By: Brian E. Taptich.

"Publishing house finds niche in game industry: education" in San Antonio Business Journal (July 3, 1998, p. 1). By: James Aldridge.

Rapid Software Deployment. Cincinnati, OH: South-Western Publishing Co. 1996.

"The Rating Game" in Inc. (Vol. 20, No. 1, January 1998, pp. 93-94). By: Susan Greco.

"The Right Stuff" in Red Herring (No. 63, February 1999, p. 79). By: Blaise Zerega.

"Ringleader" in Red Herring (Vol. 56, July 1998, p. 50). By: Andrew P. Madden.

"Scratching the Surface" in Red Herring (No. 57, August 1998, p. 106). By: Andrew P. Madden.

"Setting the Scene" in Income Opportunities (Vol. 30, No. 7, July 1995, pp. 42-44). By: Penelope Patsuris.

"Silicon Valley South" in Forbes (November 16, 1998, p. 214). By: Julie Pitta.

Small Business Computing for Dummies. Indianapolis, IN: IDG Books Worldwide, 1998. By: Brian Underdahl.

Small Business ED, MS Office 97 for Dummies. Indianapolis, IN: IDG Books Worldwide, 1997. By: Dave Johnson.

Small Business Windows 95 for Dummies. Indianapolis, IN: IDG Books Worldwide, 1998. By: Stephen L. Nelson.

Small Business Windows 98 for Dummies. Indianapolis, IN: IDG Books Worldwide, 1998. By: Stephen L. Nelson.

"The Social Engineer" in The Red Herring (No. 43, June 1997, pp. 62-66). By: Andrew P. Madden.

Software Design Methods for Concurrent and Real-Time Systems. Reading, MA: Addison-Wesley Publishing Co. Inc. 1993. By: Hassan Gomaa.

Software Development with Z: A Practical Approach to Formal Methods in Software Engineering. Reading, MA: Addison-Wesley Publishing Co. Inc. 1992. By: J. B. Wordsworth.

Software Engineering. Reading, MA: Addison-Wesley Publishing Co. Inc. 1996. By: Ian Sommerville.

The Software Factory: Managing Software Development and Maintenance. New York, NY: John Wiley & Sons, Inc. Second edition, 1993. By: James R. Johnson.

"Software for Nongeeks" in Crain's Detroit Business (Vol. 13, No. 3, January 1997, p. 3). By: Joseph Serwach.

"Some Like It Haht" in The Red Herring (December 1996, pp. 74-76). By: Deborah Clayman.

"Something Ventured" in Red Herring (Vol. 56, July 1998, pp. 66-67). By: Nikki Goth Itoi.

"Spin Doctors" in Entrepreneur (May 1997, p. 36). By: Ernest W. Andberg.

Start Your Own Software Company: A Step-by-Step Guide to Setting up a Computer Software Business. Gaithersburg, MD: Pierpoint-Martin, 1998. By: David J. Cracas.

"Startup city" in Forbes (Vol. 62, October 19, 1998, p. 108). By: Daniel Fisher.

"Strategic Isolation" in Red Herring (No. 55, June 1998, p. 71). By: Luc Hatlestad.

"Stretching Director" in The Red Herring (September 1996, pp. 94-95, 97, 99, 101). By: Jonathan Burke.

"Supercharged Sell" in Inc. (Vol. 19, No. 9, August 17, 1997, pp. 42-45,48,50-51). By: Sarah Schafer.

"Tailoring Software to Small Business" in Computer Reseller News (No. 775, February 9, 1998, p. 17S). By: Daniel Lyons.

"Take Control" in Independent Business (Vol. 8, No. 3, May/June 1997, pp. 48-50). By: Kirk Kirksey.

"Taking it Outside" in Red Herring (No. 60, November 1998, p. 56). By: Alex Gove.

"Tech It Away" in Entrepreneur (Vol. 23, No. 3, March 1995, pp. 218, 220-221). By: Stephen Barlas.

"Techno Dream Team" in Business Start-Ups (Vol. 8, No. 1, January 1996, pp. 54-57). By: Bob Weinstein.

"That's Edutainment!" in Entrepreneur (June 1995, p. 21).

"Things We Love" in Inc. (Vol. 19, No. 17, January 18, 1998, p. 26). By: Alessandra Bianchi.

Tog on Software Design. Reading, MA: Addison-Wesley Publishing Co. Inc. 1996. By: Bruce Tognazzini.

"Top 50 Private Companies" in Red Herring (No. 58, September 1998, pp. 92-160).

"The top 500 women-owned businesses" in Working Woman (Vol. 23, No. 5, May 1998, p. 35). By: Rana Dogar.

"Tunnel Visionary" in Red Herring (Vol. 56, July 1998, p. 56). By: Luc Hatlestad.

"Turning Points" in Income Opportunities (Vol. 31, No. 4, April 1996, pp. 12-17). By: Malinda Reinke.

"Two for T&E" in Red Herring (No. 55, June 1998, pp. 106, 108-109, 110, 112). By: Alex Gove.

"The Tyranny of the Diploma" in Forbes (December 28, 1998, p. 104). By: Brigid McMenamin.

"The Ultimate Board Game" in Inc. (Vol. 19, No. 11, August 1997, pp. 97-98). By: Stephanie Gruner.

Using Microsoft Office 97: Small Business Edition. Indianapolis, IN: Que, 1997. By: Rick Winter and Patty Winter.

"The Ventix System aims to make ERP Help Desks Obsolete" in Red Herring (No. 63, February 1999, p. 40). By: Brian E. Taptich.

"Veridicom wants your fingerprints to be your password" in Red Herring (No. 62, January 1999, p. 30). By: Anna S. Semansky.

"Was That Cybernet Inc. or Interweb Co.?" in Wall Street Journal (Vol. Ic, No. 5, January 8, 1997, pp. B1-B2). By: Rodney Ho.

"Webbing the Information Economy" in The Red Herring (No. 27, January 1996, pp. 82-84). By: J. Neil Weintraut.

"What's NeXT?" in The Red Herring (No. 27, January 1996, pp. 30-31, 33-34, 37).

"Who needs college!" in Forbes (December 28, 1998, p. 104). By: Brigid McMenamin.

"Why give stock options rather than stock?" in Inc. (Vol. 19, No. 6, May 1997, p. 105). By: Jill Andresky Fraser.

Writing Localizable Software for the Macintosh. Reading, MA: Addison-Wesley Publishing Co. Inc. 1991. By: Daniel R. Carter.

"Y2K is not slowing down Silicon Valley's enterprise software start-ups" in Red Herring (April 1999, pp. 49-52). By: Alex Gove.

"Young Guns" in Business Start-Ups (Vol. 11, April 1999, pp. 28-35).

Specialty Foods/Wine Shop

"1996 Small Business Entrepreneurs of the Year" in Black Enterprise (Vol. 27, No. 4, November 1996, pp. 75-77). By: Robyn Clarke.

"All Season Woman" in Small Business Opportunities (Vol. 9, No. 3, May 1997, pp. 58, 60, 72). By: Diane Morelli.

"Almond Joy: Smell of Success Really Can Be Sweet" in Crain's Small Business (Vol. 5, No. 3, March 1997, p. 6). By: Dave Guilford.

"Answers to Your Small-Business Questions" in Business Start-Ups (Vol. 9, No. 2, February 1997, p. 5).

"Auntie Anne's Hand-Rolled Soft Pretzels" in Income Opportunities (Vol. 31, No. 9, October 1996, p. 20).

"Battling to Be the Big Cheese" in Income Opportunities (Vol. 32, No. 1, January 1997, pp. 14-17, 80). By: Constance Gustke.

"Berry Booming Biz" in Small Business Opportunities (Vol. 11, No. 2, March 1999, pp. 46-48). By: Annette Wood.

"Brand New" in Inc. (Vol. 19, No. 5, April 1997, pp. 48-50, 52-53). By: Christopher Caggiano.

"Breaking the Mold" in Business Start-Ups (Vol. 11, April 1999, pp. 42-47). By: Laura Tiffany.

"Coffee Cola Talk" in Small Business Opportunities (Vol. 9, No. 2, March 1997, pp. 44, 100). By: Anne Hart.

"Cooking Up $3 Million from Scratch" in Income Opportunities (Vol. 34, Issue 1, January/February 1999, p. 66). By: Sandra Mardenfeld.

"Cooking Up Deals" in Black Enterprise (Vol. 29, April 1999, pp. 104-110). By: Mark Anthony Moss.

"Don't Start a Business Without One" in Inc. (Vol. 20, No. 2, February 1998, pp. 50-53). By: Phaedra Hise.

"Drinking in Profits" in Black Enterprise (Vol. 27, No. 2, September 1996, p. 33). By: Caroline V. Clarke.

"Efforts to Save New York Winery Prove Fruitless" in Inc. (Vol. 19, No. 11, August 1997, p. 26). By: Mike Hofman.

"Food for Thought" in Small Business Opportunities (Vol. 9, No. 2, March 1997, pp. 78, 80). By: Cheryl Rodgers.

"Fruit of the Dunes" in Business Start-Ups (Vol. 8, No. 8, August 1996, p. 96). By: Deborah Richman.

"A Funny Thing Happened on the Way to the Vineyard" in Inc. (Vol. 19, No. 8, June 1997, p. 26). By: Hal Plotkin.

"Get the Skinny" in Business Start-Ups (Vol. 10, No. 9, September 1998, p. 94). By: G. David Doran.

"Get With the System" in Entrepreneur (Vol. 27, April 1999, pp. 141-147). By: Carla Goodman.

"Goodbye, Goobers" in Income Opportunities (Vol. 31, No. 12, December 1996, pp. 96, 94). By: Amy H. Berger.

"Grape Expectations" in Inc. (Vol. 19, No. 15, December 21, 1997, pp. 113-114). By: Ami Chen Mills.

"He's Right at Home in Chili and Shuttles" in Crain's Small Business (June 1996, p. 23). By: Jeffrey McCracken.

"Hitting it Big in the Salt Mines" in Hispanic Business (Vol. 19, No. 12, December 1997, p. 30).

"Hitting the Wall" in Inc. (Vol. 17, No. 10, July 1995, pp. 21-22). By: James L. Bildner.

"Homemade Advantage" in Entrepreneur (February 1997, pp. 20-21).

King Estate Pinot Noir Cookbook. Eugene, OR: King Estate Winery, 1996. By: Stephanie P. Kimmel.

"Long-time Lark Street eyesore to house Italian eatery" in Capital District Business Review (July 6, 1998, p. 2). By: Deborah Moore.

Morris H. Kushner on Specialty Foods. Brooklyn, NY: Cumberland Enterprises, Inc.,1996. By: Morris H. Kushner.

New American Cuisine Pinot Gris Cookbook. Eugene, OR: King Estate Winery, 1996. By: King Estate Winery Staff.

"One Man's Mission" in Small Business Opportunities (Vol. 11, No. 1, January 1999, p. 67).

"Pasta Profits" in Small Business Opportunities (Vol. 11, No. 1, January 1999, p. 114). By: Marie Sherlock.

"Popping Profits" in Small Business Opportunities (Vol. 9, No. 1, January 1997, pp. 94, 96). By: Marie Sherlock.

"A Profitable Feast" in Business Start-Ups (Vol. 8, No. 6, June 1996, pp. 60, 62-66). By: Sandra Mardenfeld.

"Pulp Nonfiction" in Entrepreneur (November, 1996 p. 24). By: Holly Celeste Fisk.

"Quest for perfect sauce leads to small business founding" in Wichita Business Journal (KS) (May 15, 1998, p. 22). By: Lara Kohl.

"Red Hot Chili Peppers" in Business Start-Ups (Vol. 7, No. 7, July 1995, p. 8). By: Kathy Steligo.

"Selling Smart" in Independent Business (Vol. 9, No. 2, March/April 1998, pp. 12-14). By: Marilyn Yung.

"Selling Wine by Mail" in Income Opportunities (Vol. 33, Issue 7, September 1998, p. 66).

"Ship It!" in Black Enterprise (Vol. 27, No. 10, May 1997, pp. 62-64, 66, 69, 72, 74). By: Marjorie Whigham-Desir.

"Shoestring Start-Ups" in Income Opportunities (Vol. 30, No. 1, January 1995, pp. 34-44). By: Lori Schwind Murray.

"Slice of Heaven" in Income Opportunities (Vol. 31, No. 9, October 1996, pp. 98,100). By: Blair Stevens.

"Small liquor-store owners toast statute" in Denver Business Journal (April 3, 1998, p. A17).

"Smart Cookies" in Entrepreneur (August 1996, pp. 20-21).

"Smart Snacks" in Small Business Opportunities (Vol. 9, No. 3, May 1997, p. 102).

"Solid Gold" in Entrepreneur (February 1997, p. 18). By: D.P.

"Step 9: Generate Start-Up Capital" in Business Start-Ups (Vol. 9, No. 2, February 1997, pp. 64, 66). By: Kylo-Patrick Hart.

"Step 11: Promote Your Business" in Business Start-Ups (Vol. 9, No. 4, April 1997, pp. 64, 66). By: Kylo-Patrick Hart.

"Step 12 Twelve: Live and Learn" in Business Start-Ups (Vol. 9, No. 5, May 1997, pp. 102, 104). By: Kylo-Patrick Hart.

"Strategies For Spicy Profits" in Black Enterprise (Vol. 29, February 1999, p. 40). By: Deidra-Ann Parrish.

"Sugar Beat" in Entrepreneur (December 1996, p. 26).

"The Kitchen Kings" in Small Business Opportunities (Vol. 11, May 1999, pp. 110-112). By: Sandra Mardenfeld.

"Toasting Success" in Small Business Opportunities (Vol. 9, No. 4, July 1997, pp. 46-47, 122). By: Anne Hart.

"Twist of Fate" in Entrepreneur (July 1996, p. 207). By: Holly Celeste Fisk.

"Up With Food" in Entrepreneur (Vol. 27, No. 1, January 1999, p. 334).

"Use Your Noddle" in Entrepreneur (July 1996, p. 17). By: L.B.

"Using Your Noodle" in Small Business Opportunities (Vol. 7, No. 3, May 1995, p. 64). By: Geri Anderson.

Vintage Wine Book. Binghamton, NY: The Haworth Press, Inc. Second edition, 1991. By: Compiled by the Sommelier Executive Council.

"Virtual Vineyards Rule?" in Inc. (Vol. 18, No. 9, June 1996, pp. 76-79). By: Fred Hapgood.

"What an Earful! Dogs Live High on Hog Ears" in Crain's Detroit Business (Vol. 11, No. 22, May 29-June 4, 1995, pp. 3, 37). By: Marsha Stopa.

"What's Up With..." in Entrepreneur (December 1996, p. 117). By: Lynn Beresford and others.

"Wine is Merely the 1st Course for Some Stores" in Crain's Detroit Business (Vol. 11, No. 48, November/December 1995, p. 29). By: Marsha Stopa.

"The World's Oldest Start-up" in Inc. (Vol. 21, March 1999, pp. 59-68). By: John Grossmann.

"Young Guns" in Business Start-Ups (Vol. 11, April 1999, pp. 28-35).

Your Specialty Store: How to Start & Run a Money-Making Store. Scottsdale, AZ: Duck Press, 1998. By: Ellen Rubenstein.

Venture Capital/Other Funding

"20 Best Mutual Funds" in Inc. (Vol. 18, No.12, September 1996, pp. 52, 54, 56, 58). By: Jill Andresky Fraser.

"Alternative Funding" in Black Enterprise (Vol. 26, No. 12, July 1996, p. 30). By: Kenneth Gay.

"Angel Networks" in Black Enterprise (Vol. 25, No. 12, July 1995, p. 38). By: Carolyn M. Brown.

"Anything Goes" in Business Start-Ups (Vol. 11, No. 1, January 1999, p. 45). By: Christopher D. Lancette.

"The Art of the Deal" in The Red Herring (May 1996, p.21). By: Alex Gove.

"Balancing Act" in Entrepreneur (Vol. 24, No. 2, February 1996, pp. 52, 54-55). By: David R. Evanson.

"Banks Open Their Wallets for Women" in Income Opportunities (Vol. 32, No. 1, January 1997, p. 10). By: Michele Marrinan.

"Better living through chemistry" in Red Herring (May 1998, p. 52). By: Alex Gove.

"Big corporations are investing more in start-ups" in The National Law Journal (Vol. 21, Issue 6, December 14, 1998, p. B12). By: Audrey M. Roth and Jeanne R. Solomon.

"A Bike Shop in Harlem: Part VIII of a Special Series" in Income Opportunities (Vol. 30, No. 5, May 1995, pp. 58, 60, 62-63, 66). By: Maureen Nevin Duffy.

"Bill Guru" in Red Herring (No. 60, November 1998, p. 76). By: Luc Hatlestad.

"The Billionaire Boys' Club" in The Red Herring Guide to Technology Finance (No. 31, Spring 1996, pp. 40-42, 44). By: Alex Gove.

"Blue-Ribbon Fair Presentations" in Inc. (Vol. 18, No. 11, August 1996, p. 95). By: Jill Andresky Fraser.

"Booming Venture-Capital Firms Tap Trainees for Major Projects" in Wall Street Journal (Vol. Ic, No. 14, January 21, 1997, pp. B2). By: Stephanie N. Metha.

Borrowing to Build Your Business: Getting Your Banker to Say "Yes." Chicago, IL: Upstart Publishing Co. Inc. 1997. By: George M. Dawson.

Borrowing for Your Business: Winning the Battle for the Banker's "Yes." Chicago, IL: Upstart Publishing Co. Inc. By: George M. Dawson.

"Boss wanted" in Forbes (Vol. 62, October 19, 1998, p. 118). By: Stephan Herrera.

"Brother, can you spare 80 grand?" in The Red Herring (No. 47, October 1997, p. 20).

Business Borrowers Complete Success Kit. Rockville Centre, NY: International Wealth Success, Inc. 10th ed. 1999. By: Tyler G. Hicks.

Business Capital Sources. Rockville Centre, NY: International Wealth Success, Inc. 1994. By: Tyler G. Hicks.

"Business Owners Dip into Capital" in Black Enterprise (Vol. 26, No. 9, April 1996, p. 29). By: Carolyn M. Brown.

The Business Planner: A Complete Guide to Raising Finances for Your Business. Woburn, MA: Butterworth-Heinemann, 1992. By: Iain Maitland.

"Calculated Risk" in Business Start-Ups (Vol. 8, No. 1, January 1996, pp. 75-76). By: Steve Marshall Cohen.

"Call Collect" in Red Herring (No. 59, October 1998, p. 102). By: Alex Gove.

"Can You Become a Public Company Without Realizing It?" in Inc. (Vol. 20, No. 2, February 1998, p. 111). By: Stephanie Gruner.

"Capital Questions" in Entrepreneur (March 1997, pp. 62, 64-65). By: David R. Evanson.

"The Card File" in Business Start-Ups (Vol. 7, No. 11, November 1995, p. 98). By: Karin Moeller.

"Cash Is King" in Entrepreneur (December 1997, pp. 62, 64-65). By: David R. Evanson.

"Chain Gang" in Red Herring (No. 63, February 1999, p. 24). By: Alex Gove.

"Charge It" in Business Start-Ups (Vol. 8, No. 1, January 1996, pp. 62-63). By: Gerri Detweiler.

"Cheap funding through bonds" in Nation's Business (Vol. 86, No. 7, July 1998, p. 50).

"Club Benefits" in Entrepreneur (May 1996, pp. 58, 60-61). By: David R. Evanson.

The Complete Book of Raising Capital. New York, NY: The McGraw-Hill Companies, 1993. By: Lawrence W. Tuller.

"Consumer Devices" in The Red Herring (No. 49, December 1997, p. 75). By: Jonathan Burke.

Corporate Venture Capital: Bridging the Equity Gap in the Small Business Sector. New York, NY: Routledge, 1997. By: Kevin McNally.

"Device Squad" in The Red Herring (No. 49, December 1997, pp. 76, 78, 80). By: Alex Gove.

"Dialing For Dollars" in Entrepreneur (Vol. 23, No. 12, November 1995, pp. 52, 54-55). By: David R. Evanson.

Directory of Venture Capital. New York, NY: John Wiley & Sons, Inc. 1996. By: Kate Lister.

"Doll-Makers Worked Around Obstacles" in Crain's Small Business (December 1995, pp. 13-14). By: Jeffrey McCracken.

"Dollars and Sense" in Entrepreneur (July 1996, pp. 62, 64-65). By: David R. Evanson.

"Don't Look Down" in Red Herring: Going Public (1998, p. 45). By: Stephanie T. Gates.

"Electronic Resources" in Database (February-March 1997, pp. 35-46). By: Leslie R. Fisher.

The Entrepreneur's Guide to Preparing a Winning Business Plan and Raising Venture Capital. Paramus, NJ: Prentice Hall, 1990. By: Keith W. Schilit.

Equity Finance: Venture Capital, Buyouts, Restructurings & Reorganizations, 1996 Supplement. New York, NY: John Wiley & Sons, Inc. 1996. By: Joseph W. Bartlett.

"Factors to Consider" in Small Business Opportunities (Vol. 7, No. 3, May 1995, pp. 20, 74). By: Robert Kassebaum.

"A Fair to Remember" in Entrepreneur (Vol. 23, No. 2, February 1995, pp. 38-39). By: Davis R. Evanson.

"Fatal Flaws" in Entrepreneur (November 1996, pp. 70, 73). By: David R. Evanson.

"Finance U" in Business Start-Ups (Vol. 11, No. 1, January 1999, p. 22). By: Paul DeCeglie.

"Financial Management 101" in Inc. (Vol. 18, No. 8, June 1996, p. 120). By: Jill Andresky Fraser.

Financial Risk Analytics: A Term Structure Model Approach for Banking, Insurance, And.... Hinsdale, IL: Irwin Professional Publishing, 1996. By: Dennis G. Uyemura.

Financing Sources for Business. New York, NY: Gordon Press Publishers, 1992.

Financing Your Business. Paramus, NJ: Prentice Hall, 1997. By: Iris Lorenz-Fife.

Financing Your Business Dreams with Other People's Money: How & Where to Find Money for Start-Up & Growing Businesses. Traverse City, MI: Rhodes & Easton, 1998. By: Harold R. Lacy.

"Financing Your Franchise" in Business Start-Ups (Vol. 8, No. 1, January 1996, pp. 68, 70-71). By: Jacquelyn Lynn.

Financing Your Small Business: Techniques for Planning, Acquiring, and Managing Debt. Grants Pass, OR: Oasis Press, 1992. By: Art DeThomas.

Fitzroy Dearborn Directory of Venture Capital Funds. Chicago, IL: Fitzroy Dearborn Publishers, Inc. 1994. By: A. David Silver.

"Five alternatives ways to finance your business" in Black Enterprise (Vol. 28, No. 8, March 1998, p. 81). By: Karen Gutloff.

"For What It's Worth" in Entrepreneur (Vol. 23, No. 5, May 1995, pp. 40-41). By: David R. Evanson.

"Foreign Power" in Entrepreneur (February 1997, pp. 68, 70-71). By: David R. Evanson.

"Forging the Wired World" in Red Herring: Going Public (1998, pp. 54-55). By: Deborah Claymon.

"Found Money" in Business Start-Ups (Vol. 8, No. 6, June 1996, pp. 18, 20). By: Carla Goodman.

"Free Mail Explosion" in Red Herring (No. 55, June 1998, pp. 63-65). By: Luc Hatlestad.

Free Money: For Small Businesses and Entrepreneurs. New York, NY: John Wiley & Sons, Inc. Third edition, 1992. By: Laurie Blum.

"Fueling Up" in Business Start-Ups (Vol. 8, No. 12, December 1996, pp. 46, 48). By: Carla Goodman.

Getting a Business Loan. New York, NY: Gordon Press Publishers, 1992.

Getting a Business Loan: Your Step-by-Step Guide. Menlo Park, CA: Crisp Publications, Inc. 1993. By: Orlando J. Antonini.

Getting the Money: How to Successfully Borrow the Cash Your Business Needs. San Antonio, TX: Jefferson Publishing, 1990. By: John Stonecipher.

"Good Luck" in Entrepreneur (March 1996, pp. 59-61). By: David R. Evanson.

"Greed kills" in Forbes (Vol. 162, No. 6, September 21, 1998, p. 74). By: Rita Koselka.

"Green Acres" in Business Start-Ups (Vol. 10, No. 10, October 1998, p. 78). By: G. David Doran.

"Green Days" in Business Start-Ups (Vol. 11, March 1999, p. 96). By: Michelle Prather.

Guerrilla Financing: Alternative Techniques to Finance Any Small Business. New York, NY: Houghton Mifflin Co. 1992. By: Bruce J. Blechman and Jay C. Levinson.

Guide to Business Credit for Women, Minorities, and Small Businesses. New York, NY: Gordon Press Publishers, 1992.

"Hail to the Chiefs" in The Red Herring (No. 49, December 1997, pp. 66-69). By: Luc Hatlestad.

"Heaven Cent" in Entrepreneur (Vol. 24, No. 2, February 1996, pp. 29). By: Cynthia E. Griffin.

BIBLIOGRAPHY

"High-Tech Success Starts in a Garage - Dot Com" in Income Opportunities (Vol. 33, Issue 7, September 1998, pp. 54-55). By: Steven M. Brown.

"A Hitchhikers Guide to Capital Resources" in Inc. (Vol. 20, No. 2, February 1998, pp. 74-75, 77-78, 81-82). By: Jill Andresky Fraser.

"Hot Tip" in Inc. (Vol. 20, No. 2, February 1998, p. 111). By: Christopher Caggiano.

How to Finance a Growing Business: An Insider's Guide to Negotiating the Capital Markets. Santa Monica, CA: Merritt Publishing, 5th ed. 1997. By: Royce Diener.

How to Get a Loan or Line of Credit for Your Business. Naperville, IL: Sourcebooks, Inc. 1993. By: Bryan E. Milling.

"How to raise capital funds for a magazine start-up" in Folio: the Magazine of Magazine Management (Vol. 27, No. 1, Jan. 1998, p. S199). By: Jeff Garigliano.

"How To Finance Anything" in Inc. (Vol. 21, March 1999, pp. 32-48). By: Jill Andresky Fraser.

"In general, are there marketing advantages in sharing equity?" in Inc. (Vol. 20, No. 2, February 1998, p. 110). By: Susan Greco.

"Inatome Made It, Now He Wants To Help Others" in Crain's Small Business (March 1996, p. 11). By: Jeffrey McCracken.

"Innovative Spark From Uncle Sam" in Nation's Business (December 1998, p. 50). By: Sharon Nelton.

Instant Money Ideas for Finding Business and Real Estate Capital Today. Rockville Centre, NY: International Wealth Success, Inc. Fifth edition, 1992. By: Tyler G. Hicks.

"Internet IPOs" in Boardwatch Magazine (Vol. 12, No. 9, September 1998, p. 86).

"Investors Bet on Cyberspace Path to Terra Firm Travel" in Wall Street Journal (Vol. Ic, No. 9, January 14, 1997, p. B2). By: Michael Selz.

"Investors Look for Businesses Likely to Hit a Home Run'" in Crain's Small Business (March 1996, p. 11). By: Jeffrey McCracken.

"Is it time to go out on your own?" in Fortune (Vol. 138, No. 7, October 12, 1998, p. 203). By: Anne Fisher.

"It's Who You Know" in Entrepreneur (Vol. 23, No. 11, October 1995, pp. 48, 51). By: David R. Evanson.

"Keep Your Eye on the Angels" in Inc. (Vol. 18, No. 7, May 1996, p. 22).

The Lender Liability Deskbook. Burr Ridge, IL: Irwin Professional Publishing, 1992. By: Peter M. Edelstein.

"Losing its Religion" in Red Herring (No. 55, June 1998, p. 114). By: Constance Loizos.

"Lotus Cofounder Mitch Kapor goes to Bat for Startups" in Red Herring (No. 63, February 1999, p. 24). By: Deborah Claymon.

"Low-Profile Money Sources" in Nation's Business (Vol. 86, No. 10, October 1998, p. 32). By: Roberta Reynes.

"Making a Statement" in Entrepreneur (Vol. 23, No. 7, July 1995, pp. 34-37). By: David R. Evanson.

"Merrill Lynch Targets California for Growth" in Black Enterprise (Vol. 27, No. 10, May 1997, p. 13). By: Eric L. Smith.

"Money" in Business Start-Ups (Vol. 7, No. 12, December 1995, pp. 50-51). By: Nancy Scarlato.

"Money Chain" in Wall Street Journal Special Reports: Small Business (Special Edition) (May 23, 1996, p. R12). By: Jeffrey A. Tannebaum.

Money for Entrepreneurs. Chino, CA: Alpha Publishing, Inc.

"Money Guide" in Crain's Small Business (Vol. 3, No. 1, January 1995, pp. 4-6). By: Dorothy Heyart and Gail Popyk.

"Money Hunting" in Hispanic Business (Vol. 19, No. 1, January 1997, pp. 28, 30). By: Joel Russell.

"A moveable feast" in Red Herring: Going Public (1998, p. 60). By: Lauren Barack.

"Name Your Price" in Business Start-Ups (Vol. 7, No. 11, November 1995, pp. 96-97). By: Steve Marshall Cohen.

"New law aids money crunch for small biz" in San Diego Business Journal (October 19, 1998, p. 1). By: Andrea Siedsma.

"New Enterprise Forum" in Crain's Small Business (December 1995, p. 31).

"A new friend for business?" in Hispanic Business (Vol. 20, No. 6, June 1998, p. 38).

"The New Startup" in Red Herring (No. 59, October 1998, p. 34). By: Brian E. Taptich.

"New venture-capital funds total $1B" in Crain's Detroit Business (Vol. 15, January 25-31, 1999, pp. 1, 58). By: Matt Roush.

New Venture Creation: Entrepreneurship in the 1990s. Burr Ridge, IL: Richard D. Irwin, Inc. Third edition, 1990. By: Jeffry A. Timmons.

"Niche Bank Targets White-Collar Market" in Inc. (Vol. 21, March 1999, pp. 23-24). By: Joshua Macht.

"Nothing Ventured" in Crain's Small Business (March 1996, pp.1, 10). By: Jeffrey McCracken.

"Nothing Ventured, Nothing Gained" in Entrepreneur (Vol. 23, No. 4, April 1995, p. 110). By: David R. Evanson.

Obtaining Venture Financing: Principles & Practices. New York, NY: The Free Press, 1991. By: James W. Henderson.

"On the Grow" in Entrepreneur (May 1997, p. 34). By: Michael Stout.

"On the Spot" in Business Start-Ups (Vol. 10, No. 10, October 1998, p. 12). By: Paul DeCeglie.

Outcome Funding—A New Approach to Public-Sector Grant Making. Rensselaerville, NY: Rensselaerville Institute, 1991. By: Harold S. William.

"Peer Review" in Entrepreneur (July 1996, p. 18). By: L.B.

Planning and Financing the New Venture. Amherst, NH: Brick House Publishing Co. Inc. 1990. By: Jeffrey A. Timmons.

"Pooling Community Dollars" in Black Enterprise (Vol. 27, No. 10, May 1997, p. 32). By: Sheryl E. Huggins.

"Preparing for Takeoff" in Red Herring: Going Public (1998, p. 96). By: Bill Davidow.

"The Price is Right" in The Red Herring (No. 45, August 1997, pp. 54, 56-57). By: Alex Gove.

Proposal Planning and Writing. Phoenix, AZ: Oryx Press, 1993. By: Lynn E. Miner and Jerry Griffith.

"Push Is On for Change in Single-Business Tax" in Crain's Detroit Business (Vol.14, No. 6, February 9-15, 1998, p. E-6). By: Amy Lane.

"Q & A" in Red Herring (No. 59, October 1998, pp. 24-26).

"Quick Fix" in Income Opportunities (Vol. 30, No. 3, March 1995, pp. 88, 90). By: Peg Byron.

The Radical New Road to Wealth: How to Raise Venture Capital for a New Business. Rockville Centre, NY: International Wealth Success, Inc. 1996. By: David A Silver.

Raising Capital: How to Write a Financing Proposal to Raise Venture Capital. Grants Pass, OR: PSI Research, 1997. By: Lawrence Flanagan.

Raising Capital for Your Business: By Using Private Placement Offerings, Direct Public Offerings. Glendale, CA: Griffin Publishing, 1998. By: Michael N. Brette.

Raising Money from Grants and Other Sources Kit. Rockville Centre, NY: International Wealth Success, Inc. 1993. By: Tyler G. Hicks.

Raising Money to Start of Expand Your Business Through a SCOR. Black Hawk, SD: Infoware, 1997. By: Eileen Savid.

"Ready to Trade" in Red Herring: Guide to Professional Services 1999 (1999, p. 66). By: Betsy Massar.

"Report Seeks to Show How State Should Venture Forth" in Crain's Small Business (March 1996, p. 13). By: Jeffrey McCracken.

"Reservations Accepted" in Entrepreneur (Vol. 23, No. 3, March 1995, pp. 46-47). By: David R. Evanson.

SBA Loans: A Step-by-Step Guide. New York, NY: John Wiley & Sons, Inc. Second edition, 1994. By: Patrick D. O'Hara.

"SBA Loans From A to Z" in Business Start-Ups (Vol. 9, No. 8, August 1997, pp. 52, 54-56). By: Karen Roy.

"SBA gives Spokane VC fund a capital boost" in Nation's Business (September 11, 1998, p. 10). By: Richard Ripley.

"Scoring Points" in Entrepreneur (June 1995, pp. 38-41). By: David R. Evanson.

"Sendmail pits angel investors against VCs" in Red Herring (No. 60, November 1998, p. 23). By: Alex Gove.

"Shaking the money tree" in Philadelphia Business Journal (October 2, 1998, p. 23). By: Carol Patton.

"Show Me the Money" in Inc. (Vol. 19, No. 3, March 1997, pp. 110, 112). By: Jill Andresky Fraser.

"Show and Tell" in Entrepreneur (March 1996, p. 28).

"Signet Bank Woos Minority Contractors" in Black Enterprise (Vol. 28, No. 1, August 1997, p. 29). By: Wendy M. Beech.

Small Business Financing: How & Where to Get It. Riverwoods, IL: CCH Inc. 1998. By: Alice H. Magos, SmallOffice Home Office Editorial Group Staff; illustrated by Tim Kaage, introduction by Martin Bush.

Small Business Guide to Borrowing Money. Willits, CA: Bell Springs Publishing By: R. Rubin and P. Goldberg.

The Small Business Money Guide: How to Get It, Use It, Keep It. New York, NY: John Wiley & Sons, Inc. 1998. By: Terri Lonier and Lisa M. Aldisert.

"Small Businesses get the Edge" in Independent Business (Vol. 9, No. 2, March/April 1998, p. 25).

"Small Offerings" in Entrepreneur (Vol. 23, No. 1, January 1995, pp. 40-41). By: David R. Evanson.

"Something Ventured" in Entrepreneur (September 1997, p. 26). By: Cynthia E. Griffin.

"Something Ventured" in Entrepreneur (Vol. 23, No. 11, October 1995, p. 24). By: David R. Evanson.

"Something Ventured" in Red Herring (Vol. 56, July 1998, pp. 66-67). By: Nikki Goth Itoi.

Starting Your Own Big Business with Venture Capital. Reno, NV: Western Book Journal Press, 1995. By: William A. Gilmartin.

"Startup city" in Forbes (Vol. 62, October 19, 1998, p. 108). By: Daniel Fisher.

"Startup Enterprise Bank said in 'good shape' to open doors on Oct. 26" in Pittsburgh Business Times (October 2, 1998, p. 8). By: Patty Tascarella.

"Startup Finance" in Red Herring (No. 62, January 1999, p. 98). By: Stephanie T. Gates.

"Startups: The Open-Source Business Model has VCs Baffled" in Red Herring (No. 63, February 1999, p. 56). By: Brian E. Taptich.

"Step 9: Generate Start-Up Capital" in Business Start-Ups (Vol. 9, No. 2, February 1997, pp. 64, 66). By: Kylo-Patrick Hart.

"Street Smarts" in Inc. (Vol. 19, No. 14, October 1998). By: Norm Brodsky.

"Swimming with Sharks" in Business Start-Ups (Vol. 11, March 1999, pp. 23-24). By: Paul DeCeglie.

"Three Sources to Finance a Small Business" in Crain's Small Business (December 1995, p. 15). By: Jeffrey McCracken.

"Tricks of the Trade" in Red Herring: Going Public (1998, p. 88). By: Paul Ross.

"Trillion-Dollar Jackpot Bypasses Small Biz, Says SBA" in Inc. (Vol. 19, No. 11, August 1997, p. 21). By: Hal Plotkin.

"The Trouble with Angels" in Inc. (Vol. 20, No. 2, February 1998, pp. 46-49). By: Stephanie Gruner.

"Under Inspection" in Entrepreneur (December 1996, p. 19). By: Karen Axelton.

Vankirk's Venture Capital Directory. Arlington, VA: Online Publishing, Inc. 1993. By: Clarke V. Simmons, editor.

"A VC-Friendly Year" in The Red Herring Guide to Technology Finance (No. 31, Spring 1996, pp. 47-48).

"VCs Face Increase Competition" in The Red Herring (No. 49, December 1997, p. 54). By: Alex Gove.

Venture Capital. Brookfield, VT: Ashgate Publishing Co. 1997. By: Mike Wright.

"Venture Capital" in Business Start-Ups (Vol. 7, No. 12, December 1995, p. 70). By: Nancy Scarlato.

Venture Capital & Junk Bond Financing. Philadelphia, PA: American Law Institute (ALI) & American Law Institute-American Bar Association (ALI-ABA), 1996. By: Frederick D. Lipman.

"Venture Capital Raised by Companies Was a Record $10.1 Billion in 1996" in Wall Street Journal (Vol. Ic, No. 25, Feb. 5, 1997, p. B2). By: Stephanie N. Mehta.

Venture Capital Sourcebook: The Definitive Guide to Finding Start-Up Funds & Growth Capital. Burr Ridge, IL: Probus Publishing Co. Inc. 1994. By: A. David Silver.

"Venture Capitalists Step Up Role in IPOs" in Wall Street Journal (Vol. Ic, No. 4, January 7, 1997, p. B2). By: Stephanie N. Mehta.

"Venture capital growing pains: should the market diet?" in Journal of Banking & Finance (Vol. 22, No. 6-8, August 1998, p. 1089). By: Paul A. Gompers.

"Ventures in Space" in Red Herring: Going Public (1998, p. 15). By: Christina Stubbs.

"Wanted: Innovative Ideas" in Black Enterprise (Vol. 27, No. 4, November 1996, p. 27). By: Glenn Jeffers.

When the Bank Says No!: Creative Financing for Closely Held Businesses. New York, NY: TAB Books, Inc. 1991. By: Lawrence W. Tuller.

Where to Find Venture Capital: A Resource Guide. Highland City, FL: Rainbow Books, Inc. 1995. By: Philip C. Paul.

Where to Get the Money & Management Help for New Business Start-Ups & Small Business Growth: East-North Central Region, IL, IN, MI, OH, WI. Wayne, PA: Special Reports, Inc. 1998. By: Richard S. Guyer and Frank J. Domeracki.

Where to Get the Money & Management Help for New Business Start-Ups & Small-Business Growth: East-South Central Region, AL, KY, MS, TN. Wayne, PA: Special Reports, Inc. 1998. By: Richard S. Guyer and Frank J. Domeracki.

Where to Get the Money & Management Help for New Business Start-Ups & Small Business Growth: Middle Atlantic Region. Wayne, PA: Special Reports, Inc. 1994. By: Richard S. Guyer.

Where to Get the Money & Management Help for New Business Start-Ups & Small Business Growth: Mountain Region, AZ, CO, ID, MT, NV, NM, UT, WY. Wayne, PA: Special Reports, Inc. 1998. By: Richard S. Guyer and Frank J. Domeracki.

Where to Get the Money & Management Help for New Business Start-Ups & Small Business Growth: Pacific Region, AK, CA, HI, OR, WA. Wayne, PA: Richard S. Guyer and Frank J. Domeracki, 1998. By: Richard S. Guyer and Frank J. Domeracki.

Where to Get the Money & Management Help for New Business Start-Ups & Small Business Growth: West-North Central Region, IA, KS, MN, MO, NE, ND, SD. Wayne, PA: Special Reports, Inc. 1998. By: Richard S. Guyer and Frank J. Domeracki.

Where to Get the Money & Management Help for New Business Start-Ups & Small Growth: West-South Central Region, AR, LA, OK, TX. Wayne, PA: Special Reports, Inc. 1998. By: Richard S. Guyer and Frank J. Domeracki.

"The Winter of Content" in Red Herring: Going Public (1998, pp. 54-56). By: Christina Stubbs.

"Would you please take my money?" in Fortune (March 16, 1998, p. 165). By: Eileen P. Gunn.

"You Can Bank on It" in Business Start-Ups (Vol. 8, No. 8, August 1996, pp. 56, 58, 60-61). By: Jacquelyn Lynn.

"You Can't Start Too Soon" in Inc. (Vol. 17, No. 6, May 1995, p. 144). By: Susan Greco.